D1615911

DEMOCRATIC JUSTICE

DEMOCRATIC JUSTICE

FELIX FRANKFURTER, THE SUPREME COURT, AND THE MAKING OF THE LIBERAL ESTABLISHMENT

Brad Snyder

W. W. NORTON & COMPANY
Independent Publishers Since 1923

For information about permission to reproduce selections from this book, write to
Permissions, W. W. Norton & Company, Inc., 500 Fifth Avenue, New York, NY 10110

For information about special discounts for bulk purchases, please contact
W. W. Norton Special Sales at specialsales@wwnorton.com or 800-233-4830

Manufacturing by Lakeside Book Company
Book design by Chris Welch Design
Production manager: Julia Druskin

ISBN 978-1-324-00487-5

W. W. Norton & Company, Inc., 500 Fifth Avenue, New York, N.Y. 10110
www.wwnorton.com

W. W. Norton & Company Ltd., 15 Carlisle Street, London W1D 3BS

1 2 3 4 5 6 7 8 9 0

To Shelby, Lily, and Max

To Harry and Linda Snyder

To Jack and Donna Hunt

CONTENTS

DEMOCRATIC JUSTICE

A Presidential Visit

A t 5:00 p.m. on July 26, 1962, the presidential motorcade left the back entrance of the White House for the nearly three-mile drive to Georgetown. Within minutes, President John F. Kennedy arrived at a three-story, white-brick house at 3018 Dumbarton Avenue for an "off the record" meeting with Justice Felix Frankfurter.

On April 5 of that year, the 79-year-old Supreme Court justice had collapsed at his desk and fallen to the floor in his chambers. He was carried into an ambulance and rushed to George Washington University Hospital. He had suffered a stroke and, five days later, another stroke that, like the first one, cleared itself. Doctors diagnosed it as a "cardiovascular insufficiency." *New York Times* columnist James Reston wrote: "His problem is not 'insufficiency' but over-sufficiency. . . . His difficulty is not a shortage of anything, except maybe size, too much blood and energy, too many ideas, interests and opinions racing too fast through too small an area."

Frankfurter had an over-sufficiency of friends, too. After his stroke, letters and telegrams poured in from cabinet members; U.S. senators; fellow justices; dozens of former Harvard law students, law clerks, and friends from around the world; and the youngest of three British children he and his wife had taken in during World War II. His closest friend, former secretary of state Dean Acheson, took charge limiting visitors and updating them on the justice's condition. The stroke had paralyzed his left arm and leg, slowed his lightning speech "to about the normal human rate," but left his mind mostly intact. His doctor said it was up to him whether he "lived or not," that he had to relearn how to use certain muscles and stop thinking about his work at the Court. By mid-May, Frankfurter announced that on his doctors' advice, he would not return to work until the Supreme Court's next term began in October. Frankfurter's friends, Kennedy's national security advisor McGeorge

Bundy and *Washington Post* publisher Phil Graham, believed that the bedridden justice would be forced to retire.

Retirement, however, was the farthest thing from Frankfurter's mind. After his release from the hospital on July 7, he summoned Bundy to his home with an urgent message: The president needed to address the nation with several speeches. During his hospitalization, Frankfurter had encountered numerous nurses, orderlies, attendants, and doctors and discussed their views on the president and his policies. He believed that political and social change should start with Kennedy and his legislative agenda and worried about what he had heard in the hospital.

In a memorandum to the president, Bundy relayed Frankfurter's concerns that the hospital staff was "all strongly in favor of you without knowing what you were for." Frankfurter had some advice for the president about the problem. Bundy warned the president about Frankfurter's " 'wary' attitude toward the Administration," described him as "a man I love," and insisted that the justice was "a man who prefers to like people, and in his combination of wit, zest for politics, and sense of style he should be a natural talking partner and friend for you."

Frankfurter's wife, Marion, Bundy wrote, was a different story. She suffered from rheumatoid arthritis and for several years had rarely left her bed—by choice. She was, according to Bundy, "a deeply neurotic and selfish woman" and "a deep trial to all the Justice's friends. But he adores her."

After an in-person briefing from Bundy, Kennedy set off for Georgetown to call on Frankfurter. The president knew the neighborhood well. As a congressmen and senator, he had lived in Georgetown not far from Frankfurter's residence. On the night of his inauguration, he had stopped by the home of a mutual friend and Frankfurter's neighbor, columnist Joseph Alsop. The president was close to another member of the Georgetown set, *Washington Post* publisher and former Frankfurter clerk Phil Graham, who had played a key intermediary role in Lyndon Johnson's decision to accept Kennedy's offer of the vice presidency.

Frankfurter's checkered history with Joe Kennedy, Sr., colored his views about the president. In 1933, Joe Sr. sought Frankfurter's advice about whether his sons, Joe Jr. and Jack, should go straight from the Choate School to Harvard College. Frankfurter suggested that they study at the London School of Economics with Harold J. Laski because the Socialist political scientist was "the greatest teacher in the world." Joe Sr. took Frankfurter's advice. The two men remained cordial for a time yet parted as friends over the looming war. A supporter of Neville Chamberlain's failed appeasement strategy, Joe Sr.

resented Frankfurter's interventionist influence on Roosevelt and blamed the justice for his ouster as U.S. ambassador to Great Britain. Frankfurter disliked Joe Sr. because of his isolationism and anti-Semitism. "Does anybody like Joe, Sr. . . . ?" Frankfurter asked, "anybody, except his family?" In the fall of 1960, Frankfurter, according to Phil Graham, was "pro-Nixon almost or anyway *dubitante* about Kennedy because of Papa." Knowing the justice's reservations about him, Joe Sr.'s second son nonetheless showed respect in July 1962 by calling on Frankfurter at home.

Frankfurter was skeptical that Kennedy's visit was "simply a courtesy call." More likely, he thought it was "an inspection for political reasons." For two weeks, the justice met daily with Acheson and obsessed about the details of the visit—where to receive the president (in the living room), whether Frankfurter should stand upon greeting the president (yes), and what refreshments to serve (tea). Acheson, who was as skeptical of Kennedy as Frankfurter, was there to serve as "Chief of Protocol."

Upon the president's arrival at Frankfurter's home on July 26, Acheson greeted Kennedy at the door and escorted him into the living room. The justice "stood up without assistance" to shake hands with the president. The three men sat in the living room and talked politics. There were no photographers, no journalists, and only a scant mention in the next day's newspapers.

The president complimented Frankfurter on his recovery and remarked that his own father, who had suffered a massive stroke in December 1961, was not as mobile as the justice and unable to speak. Kennedy mentioned that Bundy had shared some of Frankfurter's ideas, but the president wanted to discuss them in person.

Frankfurter recounted his numerous conversations with the hospital staff and said "it seemed to him that there was a lack of communication between the President as the leader of American democracy and many intelligent and well-meaning people." He believed that these people needed to be reminded and educated about what Kennedy was doing and thinking—specifically about "fundamental purposes of American democracy" and "the basic nature of our institutions." Frankfurter suggested that Harvard historian Samuel Eliot Morison could draft a speech about democracy, Harvard legal historian Mark DeWolfe Howe could draft one about the nature of our institutions "rooted in history, philosophy, and experience," and a Kennedy speechwriter could write one about the president's policies and ideas.

Kennedy agreed that communicating his ideas to the public was his "most perplexing" challenge as president. He believed that the problems facing his administration were far more complicated than when Franklin Roosevelt or Harry Truman had been president. And "many people" hostile to his administration, mostly business leaders, "were willfully trying to add to the complexity."

Frankfurter suggested "building a bridge from Pennsylvania Avenue to Wall Street," but added that any "Democratic president who was doing his job was not going to have good relations with business." Kennedy replied that he had come to the same conclusion and wondered why Frankfurter thought so. Frankfurter believed that the solutions to the country's domestic problems were "outside the experience of businessmen," and therefore they viewed socioeconomic programs "with doubt, if not suspicion." This required the president to be a "molder of American life; and a strong Democratic president was likely to mold it in ways that seemed alien, if not frightening, to businessmen."

During his illness, Frankfurter continued, he thought about how to achieve "greatness" in the institutions of the presidency and the Supreme Court. Outstanding presidents and justices, he believed, shared a common "conception of the nature of their offices." He mentioned Jefferson, Jackson, Lincoln, and Theodore and Franklin Roosevelt as examples, not for "guidance in modern problems" but for "how they had conceived of the nature of their office." Kennedy agreed.

For more than forty minutes, they discussed politics and drank tea. Kennedy charmed Matilda Williams and Ellen Smith, two beloved members of Frankfurter's household staff. He also suggested meeting Frankfurter again, perhaps sometime in August. As the president rose to leave, Frankfurter said the visit had been "a great honor" and "a great pleasure to him." The looming question of the justice's possible retirement, which had been rumored in the press, never came up.

Kennedy's visit to Frankfurter's home was reminiscent of a similarly historic meeting between a sitting president and a Supreme Court justice twenty-nine years earlier. On March 8, 1933, Frankfurter had arranged the visit of newly inaugurated President Franklin D. Roosevelt to Oliver Wendell Holmes, Jr., at the retired justice's residence at 1720 I Street on Holmes's ninety-second birthday. A year later, Roosevelt declared him "the wisest of all American liberals."

The standard story about Frankfurter is that he struggled to fill the seat once held by Holmes. Scholars have portrayed Frankfurter as a judicial failure, as a liberal lawyer turned conservative justice, and as the Warren Court's principal villain. None of these narratives rings true. Pro-government and a proponent of civil rights, Frankfurter rejected shifting labels such as liberal or conservative. A few months after his retirement, he sent a *Times* of London editorial to his former students teaching at Harvard Law School. He called their attention to the last paragraph: "Whether, when on the Supreme Court, [Frankfurter] was a Liberal or Conservative, or both, now matters little. He has always been a fighter for truth."

Frankfurter made three major contributions to twentieth century America's liberal democracy. First, he believed that the American people should seek political and socioeconomic change not from the Supreme Court but from the democratic political process. Thus, despite his wariness about the administration, he wanted to meet with Kennedy and to urge the president to address the American people about their history, system of government, and his administration's future policies and ideas. Frankfurter understood each branch of government's institutional role. Like Chief Justice John Marshall, whose opinions he venerated, Frankfurter believed that the Constitution was a broad outline that allowed the federal government and the states to regulate the economy and to help people through minimum-wage laws, maximum-hour laws, unemployment compensation laws, Social Security, health-care laws, and civil rights laws. Frankfurter understood that the Constitution primarily vested the power of the federal government in the people's representatives in Congress and the White House. He viewed those two institutions, not the Supreme Court, as the engines of social change and most responsive to the popular will. Indeed, he lived to see the next president and Congress protect the rights of African Americans and women with the Civil Rights Act of 1964 and almost lived long enough to see the passage of the Voting Rights Act of 1965. These landmark civil rights laws validated Frankfurter's overarching liberal faith in democracy.

Given his strong belief in the democratic political process, Frankfurter was extremely skeptical about judicial vetoes of state and federal legislation. The Court's repeated use of judicial review to make social and political policy undermined any incentive the people had to seek change through their elected representatives. The Court was conservative, backward looking, and not as accountable to the people as the two elected branches. On the basis of his deep knowledge of Supreme Court history, he knew that the Warren Court was a liberal aberration, cautioned his liberal colleagues against overturning too many of the Court's past decisions, and recognized that empowering the Court at the expense of the elected branches threatened American democracy. His last opinion, his dissent in the Tennessee reapportionment case *Baker v. Carr*, disagreed with the Court's willingness to inject itself into political controversies over legislative redistricting and gerrymandering. He believed that the Court was incapable of enforcing the desegregation of the nation's school systems and redrawing the nation's legislative maps at the same time. He predicted that the Court would struggle to devise a manageable standard for when a legislative district was illegally gerrymandered. Indeed, Frankfurter saw *Baker v. Carr* as the point where the Supreme Court became too powerful and too willing, in his words, to "enter this political thicket."

Second, Frankfurter adapted the philosophy of judicial restraint to address the most urgent constitutional problem of the twentieth century—to fulfill the promise of the Fourteenth Amendment by protecting the rights of African Americans. His record on race was far better than those of his judicial idols Holmes and Louis D. Brandeis. Despite his initial instinct to defer to the democratic political process, Frankfurter believed courts could help to protect civil rights and to prevent racial injustice.

As a lawyer, he joined the nascent American Civil Liberties Union, challenged the constitutionality of the arrest and deportation of radical immigrants during the Palmer raids, fought to save Italian anarchists Nicola Sacco and Bartolomeo Vanzetti from the electric chair, and served on the NAACP's National Lawyers Committee. Indeed, he recommended the NAACP hire his former student Nathan Margold to write a report recommending a strategy to dismantle the Court's racially "separate but equal" doctrine. Another former student, NAACP special counsel Charles Hamilton Houston, implemented Margold's report by challenging the exclusion of blacks from state-sponsored law and graduate schools.

As a justice, Frankfurter believed in using judicial power to protect the rights of African Americans. He drafted a prescient concurring opinion in 1944 in *Smith v. Allwright* outlawing Texas's all-white primary but withdrew it at his colleagues' request. Four years later, he hired the Court's first black law clerk, future secretary of transportation William T. Coleman, Jr. Frankfurter played a critical leadership role in achieving unanimity in the Court's landmark decision in 1954 in *Brown v. Board of Education* outlawing racially segregated schools. He understood the Court's institutional limitations in enforcing *Brown* better than many of his colleagues did, and during the Little Rock school crisis four years later, he wrote an opinion to speak to southerners who preferred to uphold the rule of law rather than to bow to racial prejudice. He consistently supported the ability of criminal defendants, black and white, to invoke their constitutional right to habeas corpus. And he wrote a majority opinion in *Gomillion v. Lightfoot* rejecting the Tuskegee, Alabama, city boundaries drawn to exclude black voters. To be sure, he did not always strike the right balance between liberty and security during World War II and the Cold War; his patriotism and pedantic personality sometimes got the better of his judgment and alienated his colleagues. Yet his record on race belies his critics' claim that he was a liberal lawyer who became a conservative justice. His caution in using the Court's power was a sign of liberal strength, not weakness.

Finally, Frankfurter played a major role in the creation of the liberal establishment. During the twentieth century, he mentored a who's who of American liberals in law and politics. Decades before conservatives created the Federalist Society, liberals had Frankfurter. He constructed a liberal legal and political network while working in government, teaching at Harvard Law School, and writing fifteen to twenty letters a day. His extroverted personality, inexhaustible opinions and ideas, and enormous gift for friendship gained him access to the corridors of political power. He knew almost every president from Theodore Roosevelt to Lyndon Johnson; he worked in and out of government to advance Theodore Roosevelt's New Nationalism, Woodrow Wilson's New Freedom, and Franklin Roosevelt's New Deal.

More than a skilled government lawyer, influential Harvard law professor, or scholarly Supreme Court justice, Frankfurter made his greatest contribution to twentieth century America's liberal democracy as a talent scout. During the 1910s, he befriended aspiring lawyers, journalists, and government officials at his Dupont Circle political salon named the House of Truth. As a Harvard law professor for twenty-five years, he preached the gospel of public service. He selected top students as law clerks for judges including Holmes, Brandeis, Benjamin Cardozo, and Learned Hand and placed scores of students in government posts. As a justice, he mentored an impressive array of law clerks who served in every presidential administration from Franklin Roosevelt to Jimmy Carter. Kennedy's administration alone included ten former Frankfurter clerks.

Indeed, Frankfurter's meeting with President Kennedy never would have happened without his role in creating the liberal establishment: the New Deal connection with Joe Kennedy, Sr.; the recommendation to send Joe Jr. and Jack to study with Harold Laski; the discussion with McGeorge Bundy, who co-authored the memoirs of Frankfurter's mentor Henry Stimson and whose father, Harvey Bundy, clerked for Holmes and lived at the House of Truth; the encouragement of Phil Graham, a Frankfurter clerk and influential member of the Georgetown set; and the assistance of Dean Acheson, another Georgetown neighbor and former student. And Marion Frankfurter, before she was an invalid who frustrated her husband's friends, charmed politicians, judges, journalists, academics, and British intellectuals with her literary taste and caustic New England wit. The Achesons, Bundys, and Grahams represented an influential part of the liberal establishment that Frankfurter helped construct and which was his most enduring legacy.

This is the story of an Austrian Jewish immigrant who at age eleven arrived in the United States speaking not a word of English, who by age twenty-six befriended former president Theodore Roosevelt, and who by age fifty was one of Franklin Roosevelt's most trusted advisers. It is the story of Frankfurter's rapid rise in early twentieth century American law and politics and of how a liberal lawyer was wrongly dismissed by critics as a conservative justice. It is a story about the timely importance of his inherently liberal ideas regarding the limited role of the judiciary in our democracy and the obligation of courts to protect minority rights. And it is a story about how an influential lawyer used his gift for friendship, eye for talent, and passion for public service to create the liberal establishment. Above all, it is a story about a justice who believed in democracy.

CHAPTER I

Miss Hogan

To hear Felix Frankfurter tell it, every president he advised from Theodore Roosevelt to Lyndon Johnson, every Harvard law student he nudged into public service, and every Supreme Court opinion he wrote would not have been possible without the help of his first teacher at Public School 25, Miss Annie E. Hogan.

The no-nonsense, 54-year-old Irish American had been teaching in the New York City school system for more than twenty-five years in September 1894 when 11-year-old Felix walked into her primary school classroom in a "daze." A month earlier, on August 9, he had arrived in New York Harbor on the steamship *Marsala* with his mother and four siblings. He could not speak a word of English and had never heard one spoken. Miss Hogan threatened the other children in Frankfurter's class with corporal punishment if they spoke to him in his native German. Her reputation for hitting disobedient students preceded her. No one uttered a word to Frankfurter in anything but English. He was grateful to Miss Hogan for the rest of his life.

Frankfurter relished telling the Miss Hogan story. He portrayed his life as beginning at age eleven in her classroom. P.S. 25 was his ticket to the American dream. Yet Frankfurter's origin story obscured the first eleven years of his life in Vienna, Austria, and how his parents, siblings, and other relatives contributed to one of the most rapid rises of any immigrant in American history.

BEFORE HE SET FOOT on American soil, Frankfurter had the good fortune to be born and raised in one of the cultural capitals of the world—Vienna, Austria. During the reign of Emperor Franz Joseph from 1848 to 1916, Jewish artists, actors, musicians, writers, and intellectuals thrived in Viennese cultural and intellectual life. Men frequented cafés, drank coffee, read newspapers from all over the world, and discussed art, literature, and music. Vienna produced the psychology of Sigmund Freud, the art of Gustav Klimt, and the music of Fritz Kreisler, Gustav Mahler, and Arnold Schoenberg. "There is hardly a city in Europe," Viennese Jewish writer Stefan Zweig wrote, "where the drive towards cultural ideals was as passionate as it was in Vienna."

Frankfurter's family was one of many lower-middle-class Jewish families who started their lives elsewhere in the Austro-Hungarian Empire; the successful ones migrated to Vienna. His mother, Emma, was born in Uhersky Ostroh, Moravia, about eighty-eight miles north of Vienna on the Moravia River, where her father and grandfather were prominent figures in the Jewish community. Frankfurter's father, Leopold, was born in Pressburg, Hungary (today Bratislava, Slovakia), nearly fifty miles east of Vienna on the Danube River. Leopold's mother, Lotte, died twenty-one days after giving birth to him. Leopold's father, Emanuel, remarried, moving his growing family in 1859 to Vienna and working for the *Israelitische Kultusgemeinde* (IKG), the city's Jewish community organization.

Frankfurter's father, Leopold, was the family's black sheep. He was rumored to have dropped out of rabbinical school but more likely had abandoned his religious and academic education at the neighborhood yeshiva. He married Frankfurter's mother, Emma, and started a family. Leopold eked out a living as a traveling salesman; Emma supplemented the family's income by working at a convenience store. Like many Jewish immigrants, the Frankfurters lived in Vienna's second district, the Leopoldstadt. Felix was born in an apartment at 20 Grosse Mohrengasse on November 15, 1882. He was the third of four brothers; Otto was born in 1879, Siegfried (Fred) in 1880, and Paul in 1884.

Frankfurter's living situation changed when his father, struggling financially, moved the family to Budapest. Felix's sister, Ella, was born there in October 1892. Felix was miserable attending public school in Budapest and speaking Hungarian. His father was no more financially successful in Budapest than in Vienna and sought opportunities elsewhere; the rest of the family returned to Vienna to live with their most successful relative.

For two years, Felix lived in Vienna's more upscale ninth district with his father's half-brother, Salomon. A librarian and linguist at the University of Vienna, Salomon Frankfurter had studied classical and German philology in Vienna and at the University of Berlin and, for a time, had enrolled in the Orthodox Rabbinical Seminary in Berlin before pursuing an academic life. In

1883, he received his doctorate from the University of Vienna for a dissertation on the collective biographies of Roman emperors, "Scriptores Historiae Augustae." He began his career at the University of Vienna library as a volunteer and by 1884 was a staff member who lectured on archaeology, education, and Judaism.

Frankfurter revered his balding, bespectacled uncle, describing him as an "oppressively learned man." Salomon once punished young Felix by putting him in the bathtub. From his uncle, Felix learned to appreciate the cultured world of an academic and "his high standard of scholarship as well as his liberal outlook on life." At age ten, Felix had finished elementary school and was eligible to study at a *Gymnasium*. The path to a university education, a *Gymnasium* required eight years of Latin and five years of Greek. Strict, hierarchical, and joyless, the schools produced a generation of promising artists, writers, musicians, and other intellectuals striving for cultural relevancy. Many of them were Jewish. From Vienna, Felix gained a lifelong affinity for artists, musicians, and actors. He followed an intellectual path blazed by his uncle. They forged a "deep" bond that survived Felix and his family's move to the United States.

LEOPOLD FRANKFURTER DREAMED OF a better life. He had failed to establish himself as a traveling salesman in Vienna or Budapest. His father, Emanuel, had died of heart failure in June 1891 at age 77. Nearly two years later, 39-year-old Leopold set sail from Liverpool, England, with five dollars to his name. His steamship, *Indiana*, landed in Philadelphia; he stayed with relatives in New York City and fell in love with America after attending the Chicago World's Fair. After his first day at the fair, he knew he was not returning to Europe. "Children are free and stand on two legs here," he wrote his family. "They are not cannon fodder."

He soon sent for his family. On July 26, 1894, Felix left Hamburg, Germany, with his mother and four siblings on the steamship *Marsala*. The Scottish-made ship, only 320 feet long and about 36 feet wide, carried 120 passengers from Russia, Germany, Hungary, and Austria. Felix and his family stayed belowdecks in steerage, the cheapest berths in the ship. A day into the journey, they sailed past the white cliffs of Dover, England. Fourteen days after they left Europe, they passed the Statue of Liberty and arrived at New York Harbor at 1:00 p.m. It was a perfect summer day—fair skies, northerly winds, and temperatures in the mid-to-upper 70s.

After being processed at Ellis Island, Felix and his family reunited with Leopold and settled into an apartment at 99 East Seventh Street in the East Village. It was a thriving German neighborhood with Italian and Chinese immigrants living nearby. A few blocks away on the Lower East Side, Yiddish-speaking Eastern European Jewish immigrants crowded into tenement houses. As German-speaking Jews, however, Frankfurter and his family were better off, sociologically and geographically, than their Russian and Eastern European Jewish counterparts. Frankfurter walked around his German-immigrant neighborhood and "breathed in the sense that this was the America one had heard about, the land of freedom, the land of opportunity."

Even with a year's head start and his family ensconced in a nice working-class neighborhood, Leopold Frankfurter had not figured out how to earn a living. He was a philosopher whose dreams of social justice did not match the realities of everyday life. City directories listed him as a peddler, drygoods salesman, agent, and merchant. At bottom, he was the same hapless sales-man he had been in Europe. Yet it was hard to tell that Leopold struggled financially. The happy-go-lucky businessman was always whistling classical music as he worked and inviting people home to dinner, sometimes as many as ten at a time. Felix inherited his father's whistling, extroverted personality, gift of friendship, and carefree attitude about money.

Felix's mother took charge of her family's finances. Emma was the one adding water to the soup or slicing the meat thinner to accommodate her husband's surprise dinner guests. She sent her two oldest children, Otto and Fred, to work to supplement the family's income. Felix was Emma's pet. He helped her pinch pennies by scouring the neighborhood for bargains. From his mother, he shared the same loyalty to friends, strong ethical impulses, and intense convictions. "Anybody whom I don't like," she said, "God should help him." Emma gave her son a strong sense of self and repeatedly told him: "Hold yourself dear!"

Of all the advice and advantages they gave him with his new life in New York City, Frankfurter insisted "the greatest debt I owe my parents is that they left me alone almost completely." He devoted much of his spare time to read-ing. He read books while brushing his teeth, combing his hair, washing his hands, and walking the streets of New York. He often stopped by the Otten-dorfer branch of the New York Public Library at 135 Second Avenue, the city's first free public library, less than two blocks from his family's apartment, to browse the newest arrivals.

He credited his love of American and British newspapers to another neigh-borhood institution, the reading room at Cooper Union. Warm, well-lit, and open to everyone, the reading room was stocked with newspapers from across the country and overseas. Four to five days a week after school, he headed to the third-floor reading room to devour the daily newspapers. He read them so fast and so thoroughly that he could tell by the typeface whether it was the *Emporia Gazette* or the *Louisville Courier*. And from eight to ten on Friday nights, he sat in one of the red leather chairs in Cooper Union's great hall and listened to speakers discuss current events as part of the evening forum series. He later described himself as a "two-fifths" graduate of the Cooper Union reading room and forum series.

Cooper Union's speaker series stimulated his love of American politics. In 1896, he was captivated by the presidential campaign of Democratic nominee William Jennings Bryan. He argued with his father, a McKinley man, about Bryan as the spokesman for midwestern farmers against Wall Street financiers. Frankfurter saw Bryan as standing up for the little guy. On September 23, Frankfurter skipped school, took the ferry to Hoboken, New Jersey, and wiggled his way close to the train platform to greet Bryan. The thirteen-year-old was beaming as he rode the ferry to Brooklyn with his first political hero.

On June 29, 1897, nearly three years after he arrived in the United States, Frankfurter graduated from the "College Class" of P.S. 25 and was the third chosen speaker. He recited a speech by John Adams. He was steeped in his new country's language, politics, and history. Miss Hogan and the public school system had turned him into an American.

The big decision in the Frankfurter household was not whether he would continue his education but where. There were no New York City public high schools in those days. He scored well on a qualifying examination for one of ten full scholarships endowed by Joseph Pulitzer to the progressive, private Horace Mann School. The school's principal met with Frankfurter and offered him a half scholarship for one year with the prospect of a full one if he made good. Horace Mann was attractive because it fed its students into Columbia and its law school. But the $100 half-tuition was too much for Frankfurter's family, even with two older brothers working full-time. Fortunately, Frankfurter was one of seven P.S. 25 students who passed the citywide examination to the combined five-year high school and college program at the City College of New York.

For New York City's immigrants, City College was a free ticket to higher education and the possibility of entering the professional class. Established in 1847 by the state legislature as a "Free Academy," it was designed to make higher education accessible to any city resident regardless of income or social standing. The city's immigrants, many of them Jewish, may have arrived in this country speaking another language but flocked to CCNY because, like Frankfurter, they spoke "the universal language of human aspiration."

In a small, ugly red Gothic building at Twenty-Third Street and Lexington Avenue, Frankfurter and other students in CCNY's five-year program chose between the classical or scientific curriculum. There were no electives. As part of the classical curriculum, Frankfurter took several years of Latin and Greek and classes on logic and philosophy. The students attended class four to five hours each day and, in a system modeled on West Point, received demerits for tardiness and other infractions.

Frankfurter's classmates, other highly intelligent strivers, broadened his intellectual horizons. A radical Russian Jewish classmate, Isador Goetz, introduced him to radical thinkers at East Side coffee houses. A heady City College student two years his senior, Morris Raphael Cohen, became a lifelong friend. A Russian Jewish immigrant whose family arrived from Minsk when he was twelve, Cohen was interested in philosophy; Frankfurter gravitated to history.

During Frankfurter's sophomore year at City College, his family moved uptown to a rented apartment at 112 East Seventy-First Street. He often studied nearby in the quiet reading room of the Lenox Library on Fifth Avenue between Seventieth and Seventy-First Streets, the future site of the Frick museum, and liked to browse the Lenox Library shelves. He could read Hebrew and had a bar mitzvah at age thirteen. A few years later, he abandoned organized religion when, feeling like a hypocrite as a nonbeliever at Yom Kippur services, he walked out of synagogue and never returned. He showed no interest in sports but liked to play craps in the street. He rode the Third Avenue Elevated train to school and bounced as he walked. He wore his hair long and parted down the middle and, in formal pictures, was partial to bow ties.

During extracurricular activities, Frankfurter revealed his gifts for debate and legal argument. As a sophomore, he joined one of the school's two literary societies, Clionia, which twice a year debated its rival literary society, Phrenocosmia. The year-end debate between the two societies was the highlight of the school year and the subject of a special issue of the school newspaper, the *College Mercury*. Many of his classmates were on hand the evening of May 3, 1901, at the Lenox Lyceum as Frankfurter, a junior, joined his Clionia teammates, both seniors, to argue the negative of a pending constitutional question about the territorial acquisitions after the Spanish-American War of 1898: "Resolved: That the Constitution should extend to territory newly acquired by the United States, as the immediate and necessary incident of the acquirement." Frankfurter opened the debate for his team. The *College Mercury* described him as "vehement; he is evidently secure in the strength of his side and thinks the audience rather stupid for requiring an explanation of obvious points; but really he need not get angry, for when the hammer sounds the audience is indulgently inclined toward his side of the question." His classmate Nathaniel Phillips never forgot "his stunning performance. He looked so boyish, his neatness was striking. He spoke such sense. It was as though no opposition could have any significance. He was extremely courteous in manner, but he pierced the arguments of his opponents with a deftness and finality that was devastating." Accounts differ whether Frankfurter's team won or lost the debate; a few weeks later, the U.S. Supreme Court agreed with his side.

Frankfurter finished near the top of his class and threw himself into extracurricular activities. As a junior, he was second in the class with no demerits. As a senior, he was vice president of the class and assistant editor of the school humor magazine, *Quips and Cranks*. At graduation, he finished third in his class. At commencement on June 19, 1902, he delivered an honorary oration on "The Perversion of the Law." He was only nineteen.

There was no question in his mind that he was going to law school. To earn money for tuition, he decided to work for a year. At first, he served unhappily as a substitute teacher. He took the civil service examination and on November 12 landed a job as a temporary clerk at the city's new Tenement House Department. For an annual salary of $1200 (reduced to $1050 in February when he became a permanent clerk), he helped enforce health and safety conditions in tenement houses. He also earned money on the side as a tutor in Latin and geometry. He was living in his family's Upper East Side apartment at Park Avenue and Eighty-First Street. His older brothers, Otto and Fred, had graduated in 1899 from Columbia's pharmacy school and supported the family by working as druggists. His younger brother, Paul, had been working for several years as a bank clerk.

In late fall, the City College board of trustees offered to make Felix an assistant tutor in the arts to teach classics. The board often tried to lure top students back to the school with junior teaching positions. On January 1, 1903, he declined the offer because he had "already entered upon the study of law."

Frankfurter's law school career included several false starts. He tried and quit the night programs at New York Law School and at New York University Law School because they were "bad law schools." He was determined to enroll as a day student at Columbia. During his walk to Morningside Heights to submit his ten-dollar deposit, however, he encountered a City College classmate who persuaded him to spend the day at Coney Island instead. Frank-furter "blew" the ten dollars at Coney Island and never enrolled at Columbia. A few weeks later, a doctor advised him not to go to law school in New York City because he would spend three years juggling classes and earning extra money tutoring. For a time, Frankfurter considered the University of Mich-igan because of its good reputation but decided it was too removed from city life.

One of his Tenement House Department colleagues, Meyer Rosensohn, suggested Harvard Law School. He disabused Frankfurter that Harvard was a law school only for rich kids and mentioned that his brother, Sam, an 1898 City College graduate, was a first-year student there. At Easter break, Sam Rosensohn persuaded Frankfurter to go to Harvard and promised to be his roommate. Tuition was $150 per year, plus another $190 to $476 for room, board, utilities, and textbooks. Frankfurter's mind was made up. He was bound for Harvard.

CHAPTER 2

A Quasi-Religious Feeling

In 1903, first-year classes at Harvard Law School began on the last Thursday and Friday of September. Frankfurter opted to miss the first few days to collect a full month's salary from the Tenement House Department. When he arrived in Cambridge, his roommate, Sam Rosensohn, picked him up to take him to their room at 1707 Cambridge Street. Frankfurter had never been to Cambridge or Boston and knew next to nothing about the law school. As they walked through the tree-lined streets of Cambridge, Rosensohn pointed to a small, unassuming man in front of them and whispered that he was the president of the *Harvard Law Review*. A member of the *Review*, Rosensohn spoke in such reverent tones it was as if he had said, "That's the Archangel Gabriel."

The next week, Frankfurter walked into Austin Hall for the first time for Samuel Williston's contracts class and suffered "one of the most intense frights of [his] life." Everyone was bigger, taller, and seemingly more confident. It did not help that he had missed the first few classes. Williston was a "virtuoso" of the Socratic method, calling on students, twisting them into knots with questions, and conducting the class on the basis of their answers. A student sitting in front of Frankfurter was so eager to participate that he frequently injected himself into the discussion. Another student, a two-time All-American football player at Harvard College, seemed to know all the answers. Frankfurter was certain he had made a terrible mistake.

In fact, Frankfurter landed at an institution revolutionizing American legal education thanks to Christopher Columbus Langdell. The dean of Harvard Law School from 1870 to 1895, Langdell began to require a bachelor's degree, extended law school from two to three years, and established a standard curriculum for first-, second-, and third-year students. Most important, Langdell introduced a new pedagogical approach, the case method. Students learned legal rules not by memorizing them or listening to a lecture but by figuring them out by reading appellate cases. Treatises laying out legal rules yielded to casebooks. With most Harvard law professors employing the Socratic method, they taught their students about the law by interrogating them about the judges' reasoning in the cases. The combination of the case method and the Socratic method helped Langdell achieve his goal of treating law like a science. By the 1890s, other professors and other law schools began to copy Langdell's case method. By 1903, Langdell had retired from the law faculty but continued to write and frequent the school. Seeing him wandering the streets of Cambridge with his long, white, unkempt beard and poor eyesight, Frankfurter dubbed him "blind white-whiskers."

Frankfurter did not seem ready for the rigors of the law school's Socratic method. Rosensohn, after learning that Frankfurter's mother had packed his clothes in his trunk, thought his new roommate was "a Mama's boy." He was not far off the mark; Frankfurter wrote his mother a short note every day. Rosensohn also thought Frankfurter was spreading himself too thin and would disgrace himself and City College come exam time. Frankfurter attended lectures, concerts, and exhibitions and visited libraries all over town. He studied German literature at the Germanic museum, frequented the Boston Museum of Fine Arts, and participated in Friday afternoon informal debates with Charles Townsend Copeland, an English professor who told him: "You go off like an alarm clock. Don't talk so fast." Frankfurter's wake-up call came in early February when he performed poorly on voluntary, practice midterm examinations, or "optionals." After that, he gave law school his undivided attention and came to love his first-year classes and professors.

In contracts, Williston was the nation's preeminent authority on the subject, the author of the students' casebook, and a master of the Socratic method. Frankfurter thought he was an "artist" and "model thinker." In civil procedure (pleading), the school's beloved dean, James Barr Ames, reformulated students' answers to lead them in the right direction and inculcated them with a sense that the law was a higher calling. More a teacher than a scholar, Ames institutionalized Langdell's case method by authoring several casebooks and made a tremendous impact on Frankfurter and generations of Harvard law students. Like the other professors, Ames did not have an office but sat at a desk in the stacks of the library. He liked to engage with students. Frankfurter left his conversations with Ames intellectually inspired. In criminal law, Joseph H. Beale was "the most versatile of the lot," rivaled Williston for employing the Socratic method, and created an "electric" classroom atmosphere. In property, Eugene Wambaugh was a "shy," whimsical teacher who was better in a seminar than in a large class. He and Frankfurter enjoyed a long friendship. In torts, retired New Hampshire Supreme Court judge Jeremiah Smith lectured more than the other professors.

Harvard Law School was the ultimate meritocracy—at least for white men (the school admitted only a few men of color and excluded women until 1950). The only thing that mattered was how a student performed on a single set of year-end examinations. During a two-week span at the end of June, Frankfurter took five make-or-break examinations: property, contracts, torts, criminal law, and civil procedure. More than 20 percent of his first-year class, including the outspoken football star, flunked out. His class started with 297 students; the next year there were 235. It did not matter what city a student was from, how much money his family had, or where he had gone to undergraduate school. "I have a quasi-religious feeling about the Harvard Law School," Frankfurter said. "I regard it as the most democratic institution I know anything about."

After his first-year exams, Frankfurter returned to New York City to live with his parents for the summer and worked at the Tenement House Department. In mid-August, the law school sent him his grades and notified him that he had been elected to the *Harvard Law Review*. In those days, students made the *Review* on the basis of grades alone. "There was never a problem whether a Jew or a Negro should get on the *Law Review*," Frankfurter said. "If they excelled academically, they would just go on automatically." Only the top twelve students from Frankfurter's class were invited to join. Frankfurter had received an 80 in contracts, 79 in civil procedure, 81 in criminal law, 90 in property, and an 85 in torts for an 83 average—a high "A" according to the law school's grading scale. His torts exam was so good that five years later Professor Smith still read passages of it aloud to his classes. At the time, however, Frankfurter had no idea where he stood among his twelve classmates who had made the *Review*.

Founded in 1886 by eight students under Ames's guidance and publishing its first issue in April 1887, the *Harvard Law Review* was the nation's first student-edited law journal and attracted articles by the Harvard law faculty and other leading legal minds. Students edited the articles and contributed unsigned notes, case summaries, and book reviews. The *Review* stimulated Frankfurter's interest in legal scholarship and introduced him to the school's most promising students. Given how much time they spent together, the *Review* editors were a tight-knit group. Many of Frankfurter's closest friends were *Review* editors: third-year students including his roommate, Rosensohn, and Edmund M. Morgan, Jr., and classmates including William Best, Francis Bird, Monte Lemann, Philip Miller, Robert Miller, Elihu Root, Jr., and transfer student Stanley King. Frankfurter astonished fellow editors with how quickly he could read books and write unsigned notes and recent case summaries for publication. He was known for his generosity in handing over half a day's research for a note to another editor who was struggling to balance his classwork and *Review* assignments. He made friendships he relied on the rest of his career.

The *Review* also introduced Frankfurter to legal scholarship. More than his beloved teacher Ames, more than Langdell and his case method, it was the ideas of a deceased faculty member that influenced Frankfurter more than those of any other scholar. Frankfurter had arrived a year and a half "too late to the School to encounter the mind I would have found most congenial to mine." He was referring to James Bradley Thayer, who had died in February 1902 of heart disease at age sixty-two.

In his 1893 *Harvard Law Review* essay, "The Origin and Scope of the American Doctrine of Constitutional Law," Thayer argued that federal judges should defer to the actions of Congress and the president and outlined a judicial "rule of administration" analogous to the standard of review of jury verdicts or the burden of proof in criminal cases—judges should declare federal legislation unconstitutional only in cases of "very clear" mistakes or "beyond a reasonable doubt." Judges, Thayer wrote, should possess the "combination of a lawyer's rigor with a statesman's breadth of view which should be found in dealing with this class of questions in constitutional law."

Thayer aimed to reduce reliance on the courts and to increase public participation. He did not simply write a guide for judges. Thayer called on the American people and legislators to take their constitutional duties more seriously—people needed to do a better job electing legislators, and legislators needed to do a better job drafting laws. In his 1901 biography of Chief Justice John Marshall, Thayer lamented that judicial invalidation of legislation was "too common" and tended "to dwarf the political capacity of the people, and to deaden its sense of moral responsibility." He applauded decisions such as *Munn v. Illinois* and the *Legal Tender Cases* of the 1870s, which upheld legislation "thought by many to be unconstitutional and many more to be ill-advised." He emphasized in those cases "the good which came to the country and its people from the vigorous thinking that had to be done in the political debates that followed . . . [and] far more than outweighed any evil which ever flowed from the refusal of the court to interfere with the work of the legislature." He concluded of judicial review: "The judiciary, to-day, in dealing with acts of their coordinate legislators, owe to the country no greater or clearer duty than that of keeping their hands off these acts wherever it is possible to do it. For that course—the true course of judicial duty always—will powerfully help to bring the people and their representatives to a sense of their own responsibility."

After he had read Thayer's essay, Frankfurter never stopped quoting it. With his immigrant's faith in American democracy, Frankfurter embraced Thayer's theory of limited judicial review and deference to elected officials in all but the most extreme circumstances. Though Thayer was no longer alive, Thayerian views were "in the air" at Harvard Law School. Professor Wambaugh, a former student of Thayer's, alerted Frankfurter to the similarities between Frankfurter's views and Thayer's. Thayer was Frankfurter's guiding light as a law student and beyond. Thayer's 1893 article, Frankfurter declared, was "the most important single essay" about American constitutional law: "Because from my point of view it's the great guide for judges and therefore, the great guide for understanding by non-judges of what the place of the judiciary is in relation to constitutional questions."

During the spring of Frankfurter's second year of law school, the Supreme Court decided a case that went to the heart of Thayer's argument about judicial overreach. Joseph Lochner, the owner of a Utica bakery, was fined $50 for violating a New York law that forbade the employment of bakers for more than sixty hours a week or ten hours a day. New York's maximum-hour law was one of many provisions designed to protect the health and safety of baking employees. Many states passed similar laws to prevent industrial workers from enduring long hours, unsafe conditions, and pitifully low wages. As the *Lochner* case demonstrated, the Supreme Court was hostile to laws benefiting organized labor. To strike down these laws, the justices invoked the Fourteenth Amendment's Due Process Clause ("nor shall any state deprive any person of life, liberty, or property, without due process of law") and emphasized the word "liberty" to create the concept of "liberty of contract." Over time, an amendment enacted after the Civil War to protect the citizenship rights of black people had morphed into a powerful tool for business interests.

Writing for a 5–4 majority in *Lochner v. New York*, Justice Rufus Peckham declared the New York maximum-hour law unconstitutional because it violated the bakers' liberty or freedom to contract to work for longer hours. Peckham rejected the state's health and safety justifications and suggested that the pro-labor legislation was passed for "other motives," a veiled reference to labor unions and Socialism. Indeed, the all-white bakers union was one of the law's supporters. The maximum-hour provision, however, applied only to employees, not to self-employed bakers, and sought to prevent the exploitation of men, women, and children usually paid to work in bakeries by the day or the week, not by the hour.

In dissent, Justice John Marshall Harlan defended the law as a reasonable exercise of the state's powers to protect the health and safety of baking employees and invoked several studies about the unhealthy lives of bakers. Harlan's dissent did not quibble with the idea of liberty of contract. Rather, he defended the law as reasonable in light of the scientific studies not addressed in Peckham's opinion. Harlan's dissent, given his dissents in several nineteenth century cases about race and the Fourteenth Amendment, was the one highlighted by newspapers and legal commentators at the time. The unsigned case summary in the *Harvard Law Review*, written by Frankfurter or one of his fellow editors, focused on Harlan's dissent rather than the one by his junior colleague, Oliver Wendell Holmes, Jr.

Holmes's dissent may have been neglected at first because it was so philosophical and obscure. Three years into his tenure on the Supreme Court, he accused his colleagues of reading their *laissez-faire* economic views into the Constitution through the idea of "liberty of contract." He exposed their skewed, pro-business reading of the Fourteenth Amendment by invoking a book by nineteenth century philosopher Herbert Spencer, who had coined the phrase "survival of the fittest" and had opposed government economic regulation. "The Fourteenth Amendment," Holmes wrote, "did not enact Mr. Herbert Spencer's Social Statics."

Like Thayer's essay, Holmes's *Lochner* dissent resonated with Frankfurter and other pro-labor progressives. They soon turned Holmes's dissent into a rallying cry against judicial power run amok and *Lochner* into an enduring symbol of the Supreme Court acting like a super-legislature. Holmes became a hero to Frankfurter and many others who believed in the democratic political process as the surest way to protect the rights of workers and unions. In time, Frankfurter emerged as the foremost champion of Thayer's and Holmes's view that it was up to legislatures, not the Court, to make social and economic policy.

A few weeks after the *Lochner* decision, Frankfurter received a revelatory lesson about the role of lawyers as social reformers. In May 1905, Louis D. Brandeis lectured at the Fogg Museum to Frankfurter and his law school classmates on "The Opportunity in the Law." A German-speaking Jew whose family arrived in the United States in 1849 from Prague, Brandeis was born in Louisville, educated for a brief time in Germany, and entered Harvard Law School without a college degree at age nineteen. He finished with one of the highest averages in the history of the school, co-authored a groundbreaking

Harvard Law Review article, "The Right to Privacy," in 1891, and became a highly successful Boston business lawyer. As a public service, he threw himself into social causes by acting as "counsel to the situation" and "the people's lawyer." Of late, he had been fighting for municipal regulation of the gas and electric utility and the Boston Elevated train. In his speech, he advised the students not to become corporate mouthpieces but to serve the public good. From Brandeis, Frankfurter learned he could be a different type of lawyer; he could oppose monopolies, defend the labor movement, and make America's growing industrial democracy more fair and just. If Thayer was his constitutional theorist and Holmes his ideal jurist, then Brandeis exemplified the lawyer as social reformer.

During his third year of law school, Frankfurter invited Morris Raphael Cohen, whom he had known since City College, to live with him at 1707 Cambridge Street. A doctoral student in Harvard's philosophy department, Cohen was studying metaphysics with William James and Josiah Royce and discussing law and jurisprudence with Frankfurter. Cohen started reading *Lochner* and the Supreme Court's other labor decisions. The poor young philosopher was on the verge of a nervous breakdown and credited his roommate with looking after him until he left school for a rest. After his recovery, Cohen finished his doctorate, named his oldest son Felix after his former roommate, and became a famous philosopher who often wrote about jurisprudence.

Frankfurter befriended another poor outcast in Emory Buckner. The product of an impoverished family from Hebron, Nebraska, he graduated from the University of Nebraska at age twenty-three. The dean of the law school there, Roscoe Pound, raised money so that Buckner could go to Harvard. Buckner worked his way through law school as a stenographer for prominent professors including William James and his literary brother, Henry. Buckner was so poor that he declined an invitation to join the *Harvard Law Review* because it would detract from his stenography business. Like Frankfurter and Cohen, Buckner lacked the money and social standing of Frankfurter's "Gold Coast" classmates Grenville Clark and Elihu Root, Jr., the son of Roosevelt's secretary of state. A year behind Frankfurter, Buckner also had designs on starting his career at a Wall Street law firm.

In those days, Frankfurter and other Harvard law students waited until Easter break of their third year to interview for jobs. He did not know where he stood in his class but knew as a member of the *Review* he was near the top. He had performed almost as well during his second year as in his first: he finished with an 82 average—an 83 in equity jurisdiction and procedure, 83 in evidence, 79 in property II, 87 in sales, and a 79 in trusts. Despite leading his class academically, he was not elected *Review* president. This may have been a prelude to the anti-Semitism he faced in finding a job with a Wall Street law firm.

During that era, most Wall Street law firms excluded Jews. Partners did not welcome Frankfurter into their offices. Rather, he "was made to feel as though [he] was some worm going around begging for a job." Before he interviewed, he had asked Dean Ames for letters of recommendation. Ames had gladly agreed and, in his tiny handwriting, had written half a dozen letters. At each firm, Frankfurter presented the partner with Ames's letter. At one interview, a partner read Ames's letter with a mixture of astonishment and disbelief. "Yes," he said loudly enough so Frankfurter could hear it, "that's his signature." A dismissive lawyer at another firm implied that doing well at Harvard Law School did not mean much because "the life of a lawyer in New York is not an intellectual life. You know that books are the easiest things to hire and generate." Only one prominent lawyer, Dwight Morrow, offered encouragement that "a good office needs a good man just as much as a good man needs a good office."

Finally, Frankfurter interviewed with his first choice—Hornblower, Byrne, Miller & Potter. A Wall Street firm popular with Harvard law graduates, Hornblower had not yet hired any Jews and offered little or no prospect of hiring one. His uncle Salomon warned him when he was a boy: "You'll encounter a great deal of anti-Semitism in your life, but don't go around sniffing anti-Semitism." Frankfurter was not looking for anti-Semitism and was slow to take offense. A junior partner in charge of hiring took a liking to Frankfurter and offered him unsolicited advice: "this is a good time to change your name. Frankfurter—you know, there's nothing the matter with it, but it's odd, funmaking." He politely thanked the junior partner yet declined to change his name. Rather than take offense, he accepted a job offer with the Hornblower firm for a $1000 annual salary.

With a job in hand, Frankfurter continued to distinguish himself in the classroom. As a third-year student, he earned an 86 in conflicts of laws, 80 in corporations, 81 in partnerships, and an 88 in property III. He finished with an overall average of 83—first in his class.

Frankfurter's property professor, John Chipman Gray, recognized his scholarly potential. A former Union army officer and founding partner of Ropes & Gray in Boston, Gray was the nation's preeminent property scholar. Tall, handsome, and with a beard he often "spoke into," Gray approached Frankfurter in the library at Austin Hall and asked if he would be available to work on volumes 5 and 6 of his property casebook. Frankfurter, now just a few weeks from his June 26, 1906, graduation, immediately agreed. In those days, he considered his specialties to be property and partnerships, and Gray's offer was "like asking a fiddler, 'How would you like to be the first fiddler under Toscanini?'" Frankfurter worked on revised editions of Gray's casebook for a month before returning to New York City. A note arrived in the mail with a $100 check. Frankfurter returned it and indicated that working with Gray was compensation enough. "Oh, you mustn't do that," Gray wrote back with the check. "No, I really mean this," Frankfurter replied and again returned the check. Finally, Gray sent him the check with a note: "Dear Frankfurter: Don't be a damn fool. Yours cordially, John C. Gray."

By midsummer, Frankfurter had started work at the Hornblower firm. A few weeks into the job, a phone call changed his life.

CHAPTER 3

The Dominant Impulses of Your Nature

Frankfurter had not been working at the Hornblower firm for long when the phone rang. Henry L. Stimson, the new U.S. attorney for the Southern District of New York, wanted to see him. Frankfurter could not imagine why he was being summoned and wondered what he could have done wrong. His mind raced as he met with the top federal prosecutor. Stimson looked like a man of importance; he had a high forehead, long thin face, dark hair parted down the middle, dark mustache, Roman nose, and narrow hazel eyes. Frankfurter, by contrast, looked like a schoolboy; he was five-foot-five with a cleft chin and hair swept to the side. Stimson asked Frankfurter some questions about himself before offering him a job as an assistant U.S. attorney.

In July 1906, Stimson had been tapped by President Theodore Roosevelt to be the chief federal prosecutor in the Southern District of New York to investigate monopolists and financial fraudsters. The son of a New York City surgeon, Stimson had a lot in common with the president. He was the product of several elite institutions—Andover, Yale College (where he belonged to the secret society Skull & Bones), and Harvard Law School. He had been active in New York Republican politics in opposing the Tammany Hall political machine. He was a big-game hunter who had spent time out West and had met Roosevelt in 1894 as a fellow member of the Boone and Crockett Club of New York City. He had served in the National Guard during the Spanish-American War, though in a noncombat role and therefore not alongside Roosevelt and his Rough Riders in Cuba. And he rode horses and lived on a Long Island estate eight miles from Roosevelt's home on Sagamore Hill.

The 38-year-old Stimson was a curious choice for U.S. attorney. A respected

corporate lawyer and name partner at Winthrop & Stimson, he had no prior litigation or government experience. His former senior partner and Roosevelt's
secretary of state, Elihu Root, Sr., had recommended Stimson for the top prosecutor post. Roosevelt might have been known for his "big stick" diplomacy,
but he also carried a big stick at home, enforcing federal laws against rapa-
cious robber barons and illegal monopolies. After a White House interview,
Stimson was Roosevelt's man. Before Stimson's arrival, the U.S. attorney and
his assistants had farmed out high-profile cases to outside counsel at great
expense to the federal government yet had collected lucrative salaries by pock-
eting a percentage of customs fees. The president and Attorney General William Henry Moody asked Stimson to transform the Southern District of New
York from a plum patronage post to an aggressive trust-busting arm where
Stimson would assemble a team of lawyers who would try their own cases and
prosecute monopolies. For years, robber barons had cornered markets and
created monopolies, or trusts, by procuring illegal railroad rebates, engaging
in customs fraud, and evading prosecution under the Sherman Antitrust Act
and other federal laws. The federal government's chief target, on the basis of
evidence in the Justice Department's possession, was the American Sugar
Refining Company, known as the Sugar Trust.

Stimson agreed with Roosevelt's mission of litigating cases and busting
trusts. Accepting the new job, he hired new assistants and deputies on the
basis of merit, not political patronage or party affiliation. His $22,000 bud-
get, however, made it difficult to lure experienced litigators out of private practice. Instead, he requested an additional $6000 to hire junior assistants with
more brains than experience. He wrote to law school deans at Harvard, Yale,
and Columbia and asked them to recommend top recent graduates. Dean
Ames identified Frankfurter as first in his class and "the most able man of
the graduates of that school within the past three or four years."

Stimson offered Frankfurter a $750 annual salary as a junior assistant.
It was an opportunity to practice law the Brandeis way—not as a corporate
mouthpiece but as a social reformer. In Frankfurter's eyes, there was no better client than the U.S. government. The salary was $250 less than he was
making at the Hornblower firm; no one could accuse him of jumping ship for
more money. He nonetheless asked Stimson for time to think it over.

Torn about leaving the Hornblower firm after a few weeks, Frankfurter
agonized about his decision with law school classmate Elihu Root, Jr., who
was also working at the firm and considering an offer from Stimson. Frankfurter and Root Jr. spent their days relegated to the firm's library as "clerks."
They discussed their dilemma at lunch and while walking the streets of New

York City at night. Frankfurter worried about the morality of leaving the firm so soon, especially after Root Jr. remarked, "it isn't adultery." Unlike Root Jr., Frankfurter had yearned to be the first Jew to get a job there and had relied on recommendation letters from Dean Ames. Frankfurter wrote an anguished note to Ames, who advised him: "I suggest you follow the dominant impulses of your nature."

Frankfurter accepted the job with Stimson; not surprisingly, Root Jr. stayed at the firm. When Frankfurter informed his colleagues, an irate partner made him feel like an ungrateful snake. A more forgiving partner, Mark W. Potter, insisted Frankfurter was making a mistake yet offered to keep his job open if he wanted to return in a year's time. Frankfurter never looked back.

Desperate for new lawyers, Stimson started Frankfurter in the U.S. attorney's office on August 7 before Attorney General Moody had approved the appointment. "His work," Stimson informed Moody three days later, "has already been conspicuously good."

Stimson threw Frankfurter into cases involving the Sugar Trust. Initially, they prosecuted the New York Central Railroad for providing illegal shipping rebates to the American Sugar Refining Company. Later that summer, Stimson instructed Frankfurter to write a memorandum on several issues in the New York Central Railroad case. Stimson, who was traveling out West, wanted the memorandum on his desk when he returned and warned Frankfurter to leave no stone unturned: "We have against us one of the ablest lawyers at the bar." He was referring to Austen G. Fox, who was not only one of the city's best trial lawyers but also one of the most pompous. He was president of the Harvard Club of New York and the self-appointed guardian of the WASP elite. Frankfurter described Fox's portrait at the Harvard Club as "a study in unbeaten brass."

In addition to Austen Fox, they faced another lion of the bar, Joseph Choate, who represented the American Sugar Refining Company in the railroad rebate and customs fraud cases. Stimson and Frankfurter knew they were in for a tough, protracted fight. They were outmanned in terms of resources and trial experience. The law and the facts, however, were on the government's side. In October 1906, Fox's motion to quash the indictment against the railroad was denied. The New York Central was found guilty and fined $108,000. "People talked about this," Frankfurter said, "as though it were storming the Bastille." Fox unsuccessfully argued that a corporation could not be found criminally liable and in December 1908 appealed to the Supreme Court (and lost 8–0). Stimson included Frankfurter's name on the Supreme Court brief because of his contributions to the draft; the assistant attorney general in the

Justice Department removed it. It was a small blow to Frankfurter's ego, but he had earned something far bigger—Stimson's trust.

As the only immigrant in the office, Frankfurter handled all the habeas corpus petitions from immigrants detained at Ellis Island or scheduled for deportation. Stimson thought Frankfurter would have a better perspective on these cases than the other lawyers. In one case, Frankfurter prevented an Italian immigrant who had lived in Pittsburgh from reentering the country because years earlier the man had been convicted of stabbing someone in Italy for slapping him in the face. Frankfurter took pride in determining whether immigrants should be allowed to enter or stay in the country.

Stimson also threw Frankfurter into his first solo jury trial. Emil Sonner posed as a Secret Service agent flashing a form letter from the president's secretary and a photograph from the wedding of Roosevelt's daughter Alice Roosevelt Longworth to finagle money from businessmen in Yorkville. He previously had been convicted of taking money from people after falsely promising to get them jobs in the police and fire departments. As he was summarizing his case before the jury, an astonished Frankfurter noticed Stimson sitting in the back of the courtroom. Sonner was convicted and sent to Leavenworth; his ashamed father, a prominent businessman, committed suicide.

As well as Frankfurter performed in the courtroom, he impressed Stimson most of all with his eye for talent. With his boss needing junior assistants, Frankfurter tapped into his network of friends who were elite young lawyers. He aided in the recruitment of fellow *Harvard Law Review* editors Francis W. Bird and Harold Deming, law school friends Emory Buckner and Wolcott Pitkin, Jr., former *Columbia Law Review* editor Goldthwaite Dorr, and Yale Law School student Thomas D. Thacher. Thacher became Frankfurter's office mate.

Another important new hire was Winfred T. Denison. An experienced Wall Street lawyer from Stetson, Jennings & Russell and a graduate of Harvard College and Harvard Law School, Denison worked with Stimson and Frankfurter in prosecuting the sugar fraud cases. Denison became one of Frankfurter's closest friends and a critical part of his expanding professional network.

These young men—Frankfurter, Bird, Buckner, Pitkin, Dorr, Thacher, and Denison—became the childless Stimson's surrogate sons. Stimson and his assistants worked long hours during the week. On weekends, he often invited them to Highhold, his Long Island estate.

Frankfurter found the perfect mentor in Stimson, like-minded colleagues, and a job he loved representing the U.S. government. The thought of returning to private practice repulsed him after watching railroad magnate E. H. Harri-

man demean his high-priced team of respected Wall Street lawyers. Harriman's mistreatment of his lawyers at trial made Frankfurter realize that he
never wanted to be a leading member of the New York bar.

By contrast, Frankfurter would have walked through walls for Stimson. As
U.S. attorney, Stimson reorganized the civil and criminal divisions and transformed the Southern District of New York into the nation's preeminent federal
prosecutor's office. He rewarded Frankfurter and other able assistants by regularly raising their salaries. The scrupulously honest Stimson did not want his
assistants to win convictions any way they could; he wanted them to win cases
the right way. That meant always getting a search warrant, sending Frankfurter or Thacher on raids to make sure the officers searched within the limit
of the warrant, and prohibiting wiretapping to gather evidence. Most of Frankfurter's ideas about criminal law came from Stimson's admonitions that following the search and seizure rules was more important than winning cases.

With Frankfurter helping him assemble a talented yet relatively inexpe-
rienced legal team, Stimson prosecuted crooked financiers and the Sugar
Trust. The financial panic of 1907 led to failed banks and the prosecution of
Charles W. Morse. A shipping magnate whose family had cornered the ice
market, Morse was vice president of the National Bank of North America and
issued dummy loans to his secretary and others to finance his acquisitions.
For months, Stimson, Frankfurter, and other assistants gathered evidence.
An impatient Theodore Roosevelt sent his personal secretary, William Loeb,
Jr., to New York to ask Stimson why there had been no indictments after the
panic. Stimson informed Loeb that there would be no grand jury indictments
until all the evidence was in, and if the president did not like it, he could
replace Stimson as U.S. attorney. Frankfurter never forgot "the excitement" of
hearing Stimson's response. After several months, the evidence came in, and
Morse was indicted. At trial, Frankfurter walked several witnesses through
the false financial entries and loans to Morse's secretary. After a three-week
trial, the jury found Morse guilty. He was sentenced to fifteen years in prison
and forced to liquidate all his assets. Frankfurter and Stimson successfully
defended the conviction on appeal. They also worked for several years prosecuting one of Morse's co-conspirators, F. A. Heinze, a copper magnate and
former president of the Mercantile National Bank.

The highlight of Frankfurter's prosecutorial career was the sugar fraud
cases. It was the reason why Roosevelt wanted Stimson to be U.S. attorney,
it made Stimson's career, and, for the first time, it thrust Frankfurter into
the media spotlight. Stimson and Frankfurter already had successfully pros-

ecuted the American Sugar Refining Company—the Sugar Trust—for illegal railroad rebates. In November 1907, a federal agent discovered that customs house and sugar company employees had conspired to reduce the weight of imported unrefined sugar to save the company millions of dollars in federal customs fees. The customs employees had drilled holes and inserted springs in the seventeen scales, which allowed them to reduce the recorded weight of imported sugar. It became "The Case of the Seventeen Holes."

The sugar fraud prosecutions took two years and outlasted Stimson's term as U.S. attorney. He left office to return to private practice in April 1909 shortly after William Howard Taft's inauguration as Roosevelt's successor. Frankfurter and Stimson agreed to serve as special prosecutors to finish the sugar fraud cases. Frankfurter joined his boss's law firm, Winthrop & Stimson, for about eight months before returning to the U.S. attorney's office. After three years, Frankfurter was an experienced prosecutor with valuable knowledge about the Sugar Trust. In December 1909, he arrived at the American Sugar Refining Company's massive Williamsburg, Brooklyn, refinery with a subpoena for import records. He was told that the records or technical statements from the period in question were missing. Instead, he seized the company's books and papers. For six months, a team of accountants and lawyers reconstructed the company's import records and discovered the exact disparities between the company's weights and those of the customs house. The civil and criminal prosecutions recovered about $3.5 million in customs fees.

The sugar fraud prosecution took several stages: First, Stimson, Denison, and Frankfurter won a civil suit against the company, which paid millions in back duties instead of the company facing a criminal trial; second, they tried and convicted low-level customs and Sugar Trust employees; finally, they charged the senior sugar company executive involved in the scheme, Charles R. Heike. The prosecution of Heike, secretary and treasurer of the company, was front-page news. Stimson, Denison, and Frankfurter led the prosecution team. Before his trial in April 1910, Heike unsuccessfully appealed to the Supreme Court that he was immune from prosecution on the basis of his testimony in other cases. During the month-long trial, Heike was convicted of conspiring to defraud the federal government and sentenced to eight months in prison. Frankfurter successfully briefed and argued the *Heike* case before the Court of Appeals for the Second Circuit. And Stimson, Denison, and Frankfurter successfully defended Heike's conviction before the Supreme Court. This time, Frankfurter's name was on the brief.

THE SUGAR FRAUD VICTORIES changed Stimson's life as well as Frankfurter's, thanks to the political machinations of Theodore Roosevelt. During the summer of 1910, the former president had been trying to talk a reluctant Stimson into running as the Republican nominee for governor of New York. In September, Roosevelt wangled the chairmanship of the state Republican Party, then ran roughshod over the nominating convention in Saratoga to secure the party's nomination for Stimson.

After a two-hour meeting in Albany with the outgoing Republican governor, Charles Evans Hughes, an exhausted Stimson arrived at 5:40 p.m. on September 29 in Grand Central Station. No crowd greeted him during the evening rush hour. Frankfurter joined a half dozen former prosecutors waiting on the platform to congratulate him. The *New York Times* described Frankfurter as "closely associated with Mr. Stimson in the prosecution of the Sugar Trust cases."

Dedicated to his former boss, Frankfurter took a leave of absence from the U.S. attorney's office to join Stimson's gubernatorial campaign. He wore many hats—point man at campaign headquarters at the Manhattan Hotel, campaign secretary, and chief aide to Stimson during speeches upstate and in the city. To the press, he contrasted Stimson's record—prosecuting illegal shipping rebates, crooked financiers, and customs fraud—with the corruption and patronage of the Tammany Hall political machine. "He has never stood for peanut politics nor peanut politicians," Frankfurter told the *New York Times* in late September. "Mr. Stimson has no love for the grafter, never had and never will. He will make a great campaign for the Governorship, and, take it from me, he will win."

The campaign brought the 27-year-old immigrant in frequent contact with the energetic former president known as Colonel Roosevelt. After nearly two terms in the White House, Roosevelt had declined to run again in 1908 even though he would have been only fifty years old on Election Day. Instead, he had groomed Taft, a former state and federal judge, as his successor by naming him secretary of war. By fall 1910, Roosevelt's anger and frustration with Taft had been building for months. The Colonel felt like his successor had become captured by big business. The Ballinger-Pinchot affair pitted Roosevelt loyalists and conservationists against Taft officials who allowed a Morgan-Guggenheim syndicate to purchase coal-field claims in Alaska. The controversy exacerbated the split between Roosevelt and his hand-picked successor. In June 1910, Roosevelt returned from Africa (where he was on safari) and Europe (where he accepted the Nobel Peace Prize for ending the Russo-Japanese War) and privately geared up to challenge Taft.

In late summer 1910, Roosevelt sounded like a presidential candidate as he took to the stump before huge crowds out West pledging to fight against corporate greed and for the rights of workers. On August 29 in Denver, Colorado, he criticized the Supreme Court's decisions in *E. C. Knight*, which excluded manufacturing from the reach of federal antitrust laws, and *Lochner*, which invalidated a New York maximum-hour law for bakers. The two decisions, Roosevelt argued, created a no-man's land where neither the federal government nor the states could regulate unfair competition and inhumane labor practices. Two days later before 30,000 people in Osawatomie, Kansas, he vowed in his famous "New Nationalism" speech to use the power of the federal government to fight special interests, regulate railroads, outlaw child labor, pass workmen's compensation laws, and do the people's bidding rather than that of big corporations. As in his Denver speech, he accused the judiciary of protecting property rights over human rights. Roosevelt's speeches resonated with the masses who resented growing inequality in a rapidly industrializing America as well as with Frankfurter and other legal elites who believed in social and economic change through the democratic political process rather than through the courts. For Frankfurter, Roosevelt was the leader who could implement James Bradley Thayer's ideas about limiting judicial review while empowering the federal government.

Nearly a month after the "New Nationalism" speech, Roosevelt orchestrated Stimson's run for governor as a referendum against the Tammany Hall political machine. The machine backed Democrat John Alden Dix and fought to keep Roosevelt's candidate out of Albany so as to tarnish Roosevelt's reputation as rumors swirled that he would run for president in 1912.

On the campaign trail, Roosevelt drew massive crowds, overshadowed Stimson's appearances, and dominated the political conversation. The plan was for the two men to split up with Roosevelt upstate when Stimson was in New York City and vice versa. All of Roosevelt's speeches, however, seemed to be about Roosevelt. At the end of the day, the former president asked Frankfurter how the speeches had gone. It was a moment of truth. An intimidating, charismatic former president was asking him, a 27-year-old assistant federal prosecutor, for his opinion. In the darkness of the car ride to Grand Central Station, Frankfurter summoned his courage. The New York *World*, he informed the Colonel, was keeping a running tally of the number of times Roosevelt used "I" in his speeches. Frankfurter's courage paid off. At his next campaign stop in Buffalo, Roosevelt spoke all about Stimson, his record as a federal prosecutor, his sugar fraud convictions, and the choice of a progressive government by Stimson or a corrupt government by Dix.

It made little difference in light of Stimson's inadequacies as a public speaker. Even Roosevelt conceded that while Stimson "would make the best Governor," he was "not the best candidate." Frankfurter accompanied Stimson to Sagamore Hill and witnessed Roosevelt's reaction to Stimson's acceptance speech. "Darn it, Harry," Roosevelt remarked, "a campaign speech is a poster, not an etching!"

During the final days of the campaign, Roosevelt and Stimson raced around New York City. On the night of October 31, Stimson spoke at the Grand Music Hall, a Yiddish variety theater located at the corner of Grand and Orchard Streets on the Lower East Side. Police cleared a path so Stimson and Frankfurter could enter the hall. Inside, an audience of 2,500 people cheered.

After the crowd quieted, the master of ceremonies told them about how as U.S. attorney Stimson had hired Frankfurter as an assistant when most Wall Street law firms had refused to do so because he was Jewish. "And if Tammany Hall tries this year to work off the oldtime tale of Republican race prejudice," the master of ceremonies continued, "you answer with the tale of the appointment of Felix Frankfurter, Jew." The crowd filled with Eastern European Jews erupted with cheers. Frankfurter had not grown up on the Lower East Side. Nor would he have been comfortable using his religion for political gain. But it was for a good cause. A few minutes later, Stimson invoked Frankfurter to appeal to the crowd of Jewish voters. "If there was one of my assistants in the District Attorney's office to whom I owe personal gratitude . . .," Stimson said, "Felix Frankfurter is that man."

Fifteen minutes after Stimson had finished his speech and left for his next campaign stop, five more cars pulled up at the Grand Music Hall. The crowd swelled so much that police were unable to clear a path to the front door. Undaunted, Theodore Roosevelt leaped onto the fire escape on the side of the building, bounded up a flight of stairs two at a time, and opened a window into the hall. Before he entered, he turned around and waved his hat at the cheering crowd below.

Introduced as "the greatest citizen in the world," Roosevelt was greeted with wave after wave of cheers. New Nationalism with Stimson as governor, Roosevelt told the crowd of garment workers and merchants, offered them "the chance to work for a reasonable wage under healthy conditions, and not for an excessive number of hours." It also offered "the chance for the small business man to conduct his business without oppression, without having to be blackmailed" and the chance to "stand against the worst alliance of crooked politics and crooked business that this State has seen, or this city has seen, since the days of Tweed."

That night, Stimson and Roosevelt spoke to nine audiences throughout New York City and only crossed paths at the last stop. "Isn't it bully?" Roosevelt exclaimed. Roosevelt was energized; Stimson was exhausted. Nine days before the election, Stimson trailed Tammany Hall candidate Dix in the polls.

Overshadowed by Roosevelt and overwhelmed by his inadequacies as a candidate and a Democratic landslide, Stimson never stood a chance. On election night, he saw the returns from upstate and conceded by 8:00 p.m. Frankfurter and other current and former assistant U.S. attorneys joined Stimson at campaign headquarters in the Manhattan Hotel for dinner and a party with the candidate. After the election, Stimson gave Frankfurter a watch as a token of appreciation for his hard work during the campaign.

Frankfurter had shown Stimson tremendous loyalty. He had recruited former *Harvard Law Review* editors for the U.S. attorney's office and Stimson's law firm. He had allowed Stimson to tell his story to Eastern European Jews on the Lower East Side. And he had fought for Stimson's best interests even when it meant telling hard truths to a beloved former president. Stimson, in essence, represented Frankfurter's ideal public servant. He had chosen his assistants on the basis of merit rather than political affiliation or patronage. He believed that adhering to the Fourth Amendment's prohibition against unreasonable searches and seizures was more important than racking up convictions. And he delighted in promoting the careers of his bright young assistants—he made sure, for example, that Frankfurter argued the *Heike* case on appeal. Frankfurter was grateful to the taciturn, patrician U.S. attorney for transforming him from an unhappy junior Wall Street lawyer into a fulfilled federal prosecutor and friend of Colonel Roosevelt.

The highlight of the campaign for Frankfurter was getting to know the Colonel. After the election, the former president encouraged him to stay in the political arena. "I feel exactly as you do, that there never was a more genuine fight for the people made than we made; and I am mighty glad to have had my hand in it," Roosevelt wrote Frankfurter in December 1910. "Let me also say that it was a genuine pleasure to have gotten to know you. I value you and believe in you."

The feeling was mutual. As much as Roosevelt believed in him, Frankfurter believed in Roosevelt. He may have been an ex-president, but the Colonel was a potent political force with lingering presidential aspirations and a larger-than-life figure.

Roosevelt's narrow conception of judicial power, emphasis on regulation of the economy to prosecute trusts and to fight for workers, and leadership of a national reform movement appealed to Frankfurter. In January 1911, he sent Roosevelt a copy of Justice Holmes's Supreme Court opinion upholding western states' bank guaranty laws and broadly interpreting state power to pass social and economic legislation. A few days later, Frankfurter complimented Roosevelt's article in *The Outlook* clarifying that New Nationalism did not mean simply aggrandizing federal power but allowing "the most efficient utilization" of federal and state power to regulate the economy. Roosevelt invited Frankfurter to lunch with him at the Harvard Club. Frankfurter, in turn, asked Roosevelt to speak to a small group of lawyers named "The Hecklers." In preparation for the talk, Frankfurter sent Roosevelt a six-page outline about the narrow use of judicial power and the adaptability of the Constitution to deal with economic and social problems. He included quotations from his Harvard law professor John Chipman Gray and concluded with a reference to the dissenting opinions in *Lochner v. New York* objecting to the invalidation of a maximum-hour law for bakers. Roosevelt's talk to Frankfurter's group gave the Colonel the opportunity to explain the ideas in his Denver and Osawatomie speeches about judicial usurpation of the democratic prerogative to regulate the economy. After the speech, Frankfurter indicated that Roosevelt may have converted a few skeptics about a limited role for the judiciary.

The Frankfurter-Roosevelt courtship was a two-way street. The Colonel went out of his way to show that Frankfurter's faith in him as a reformer was not misplaced. In late June 1911, he sent Frankfurter a copy of a letter opposing the idea of putting the word "Hebrew" on the passports of American Jews. "I believe that from the standpoint of the Christian, just as much as from the standpoint of the Jew, it is ill advised to treat what is really a religious matter as a race matter," Roosevelt wrote. He also invited Frankfurter to the weekly meeting of *Outlook* magazine editors. Frankfurter cut short his vacation in Vermont to attend.

Frankfurter implemented Roosevelt's New Nationalist ideas at the U.S. attorney's office by suing monopolies. He and his fellow prosecutors made headlines in 1911 by filing antitrust lawsuits against steamship companies, the lumber trust, the magazine trust, and steel wire and horseshoe men. The defendants in the last lawsuit were subsidiaries owned by U.S. Steel. Frankfurter, however, was not around to take the cases to trial.

Henry Stimson offered him another life-changing job; this time it was in Washington.

CHAPTER 4

The House of Truth

On May 12, 1911, President Taft named Henry Stimson secretary of war. Taft's administration was divided between conservatives and progressives, between Taft men and Roosevelt men; Stimson was viewed as a Roosevelt man. Frankfurter rejoiced over Stimson's appointment; he believed that Stimson could promote Roosevelt's New Nationalism in cabinet meetings and with the president. Congratulating his former boss, he predicted that Stimson would help restore the Republican Party as the liberal party: "There is still the chance to regain the momentum of liberalism, which was the great legacy of the Roosevelt period."

Stimson changed Frankfurter's life yet again by recruiting him to come to Washington. At first, he claimed to be finding Frankfurter a job in the Justice Department. Attorney General George W. Wickersham wrote to Frankfurter praising his work but explained that Stimson needed him more in the War Department. Before long, Stimson offered him the position of law officer in the Bureau of Insular Affairs overseeing U.S. territories, essentially as Stimson's "junior partner." "Faithful Frankfurter" accepted on July 1 and later that month set sail with his boss on a tour of the territories, including Puerto Rico and Cuba, his first time at sea since leaving Austria at age eleven.

IN SEPTEMBER 1911, Frankfurter arrived in Washington, D.C., and left behind his network of family and friends and a professional milieu dominated by Wall Street law firms. He knew few people, ate many meals by himself, and walked Washington's wide streets and avenues. There were no streetlights and few cars. The nation's capital was a small, southern town where everyone seemed to know everyone. People cared about ideas and power, not money. As Stimson's aide, he began to meet generals, cabinet members, and Supreme Court justices. Frankfurter did not care about money and did not "collect books or pictures," a friend explained, "he collects people." In Washington, the 28-year-old War Department aide began collecting new people by expanding his professional network beyond Harvard Law School and the Southern District of New York and by promoting Theodore Roosevelt's New Nationalism.

During his first few months on the job, Frankfurter wanted to make Stimson the Taft administration's leading New Nationalist voice. He seized an early opportunity, his boss's upcoming November 14 speech for the Kansas City Commercial Club. In a September 9 letter, Frankfurter proposed an ambitious agenda for the Kansas City speech: "I assume that your larger purpose is to identify the Republican Party in the public mind as the liberal party and thereby, more immediately further the interests of the administration as the exponent of liberalism." He wanted to define liberalism on the basis of Lincoln's and Roosevelt's "faith in democracy," the rejection of the "old laissez-faire philosophy," and tackling of the "problems of modern capitalism and labor and the growing need of a social program." Item one on Frankfurter's social program, the one he wanted Stimson to advocate before the Kansas City Commercial Club, was a call for new laws to supplement the Sherman Antitrust Act so the federal government could regulate large industrial corporations.

Like many Roosevelt supporters, Frankfurter doubted Taft's willingness to prosecute monopolies and deemed the president too deferential to the Supreme Court. Since the Court's 1895 E.C. Knight decision declaring that manufacturing was not commerce and making it difficult to prosecute the Sugar Trust, most progressives viewed the judiciary as the biggest obstacle to the enforcement of the antitrust laws. In May 1911, the Court had ordered the dissolution of John D. Rockefeller's Standard Oil Company and the American Tobacco Company. The decision, however, interpreted the Sherman Act's broad language banning any contracts or combinations in restraint of trade as a "rule of reason," meaning only *unreasonable* restraints of trade violated the law. Progressives worried that this gave the Court too much power to decide what mergers and monopolies were unreasonable. Instead, they preferred tougher enforcement of the Sherman Act, amendments to the law to specify illegal conduct, and new legislation creating an administrative agency to regulate unfair competition. They viewed antitrust policy as a way to strike the right balance between management and labor, producers and consumers, robber barons and small businesses.

The dilemma for Stimson was how to give this speech without undermining the president. During a western speaking tour in September, Taft had addressed the Sherman Act. But, ignoring Stimson's advice to write out his speeches in longhand, he had spoken extemporaneously. As a result, the president succeeded in muddling the debate about Sherman Act enforcement and the need to amend the law. The episode reinforced Frankfurter's preconceived notions that Taft was a lazy, undisciplined, and unhappy leader who would rather be chief justice than president. Roosevelt recruited policy experts and crafted his speeches with great care; Taft, by contrast, stuck to his pro-business prejudices and procrastinated so much that he never wrote out his speeches.

While his boss was out West on departmental business, Frankfurter sounded out influential people about antitrust policy, including the "people's lawyer," Louis Brandeis. In private practice, Brandeis often represented smaller manufacturers, and he was in Washington opposing the American Tobacco Company's proposed reorganization plan. He and Frankfurter had been corresponding about curbing monopoly power for nearly a year. Brandeis believed that large corporations, by their mere size and market power, stifled competition. During lunch with Frankfurter, Brandeis declared that it was "[p]erfectly easy to get back to effective competition" and suggested using the Bureau of Corporations, which was established to study and report on big business, to supervise monopolistic trade practices. He emphasized restoring competition rather than regulation.

No friend of the Taft administration, Brandeis had humiliated the president in 1910 while representing *Collier's Magazine* and advising U.S. Forest Service chief Gifford Pinchot and field agent Louis Glavis in their grievances against Secretary of the Interior Richard Ballinger. Pinchot was fired after accusing Ballinger of allowing J.P. Morgan and Guggenheim-backed interests to exploit coal-rich public land in Alaska. During the Ballinger-Pinchot affair, Brandeis revealed on cross-examination that Taft had exonerated Ballinger on the basis of a backdated memorandum. At lunch with Frankfurter, Brandeis was pessimistic about Taft, arguing that the president "doesn't care" and "has no abiding convictions about the things that are the vital issues of the day."

With a dark weathered face, deep-set eyes, and graying shock of hair, Brandeis reminded Frankfurter and others of Abraham Lincoln. Yet Frankfurter wished that the cold, serious, moralistic Brandeis shared Lincoln's "patience, his magnanimity, his humor." Brandeis was not an easy man to get to know. Yet, after their lunch, Frankfurter conceded that Brandeis was a "very big man" and "one of the most penetrating minds I know."

Frankfurter also discussed the Sherman Act with Solicitor General Frederick W. Lehmann. The solicitor general agreed with Frankfurter that the president lacked good advisers and failed to bring together the Republican Party on antitrust policy. Lehmann disagreed with Taft about the adequacy of the Sherman Act and asserted it needed either amendments or supplemental legislation. The issue, Lehmann said, was "how to deal with corporate organizations national in character." He preferred administrative regulation but had not thought through how to do it.

The only person's opinion that mattered to Frankfurter was Stimson's. Upon his return from the West, Stimson agreed with Frankfurter that Taft lacked a coherent antitrust policy. The president's declaration that the Sherman Act was sufficient contradicted earlier statements about the need for supplemental legislation with specific prohibitions and administrative regulation of corporations. In a September 18 speech in Detroit, Taft had praised the Standard Oil and Tobacco decisions and had revealed his reverence for the Supreme Court and lack of faith in legislative change and administration regulation. Frankfurter pleaded with Stimson to use the upcoming Kansas City speech to offer an alternative vision. After rereading Taft's speeches, Frankfurter argued that there was room for his boss to say something new without contradicting the president. The next day, Stimson conferred with Attorney General Wickersham, who suggested writing the speech and then trying to persuade the president. Stimson told Frankfurter to give it a shot.

By the end of October, Frankfurter finished a draft of Stimson's speech declaring the Sherman Act insufficient. They proposed amendments to the law, including specific criminal offenses and penalties and new legislation creating an administrative body like the Interstate Commerce Commission to provide guidance to businesses and to declare monopolistic practices anticompetitive. "I think we realize now better than ever before," the draft concluded, "how the interests of the manufacturer, the laborer and the consumer—the corporation, its employees and the public,—are alike bound up in common in its solution." Stimson and Frankfurter circulated the draft to lawyers in the Justice Department and to members of the cabinet. Charles Nagel, Taft's secretary of commerce and labor, endorsed the speech: "I am very glad that you are going to speak along these lines. It is just what Kansas City will want to hear."

Stimson met with Taft to ask permission to give the Sherman Act speech. The president quickly said yes, but Stimson insisted he read it. Apparently, Taft did so because he suggested a different topic, the soon-to-be-completed Panama Canal. The president preferred to address antitrust policy in his message to Congress. On November 3, Stimson broke the news to Frankfurter that the Sherman Act speech was "stillborn." They had eleven days to draft a new speech about the Panama Canal. Their hearts were not in it. "I'd give $1,000 to make that trust speech" Stimson told Frankfurter.

The episode over Stimson's antitrust speech soured Frankfurter on Taft as president. It "left a painful impression and a striking demonstration of Taft's lack of leadership and constructive thinking. Here he floats around the country talking on the industrial situation without having the thing at all thought out, without having formulated a definite policy after Cabinet consultation." Taft, according to Frankfurter, was "amiable and well-intentioned" but lacked "vision and decision. He is indeed the tragedy of opportunities of greatness unrealized."

To make matters worse, Taft tilted the Supreme Court in a more conservative direction by nominating four justices in 1909 and 1910—Horace H. Lurton, Charles Evans Hughes, Willis Van Devanter, Joseph R. Lamar, and elevating associate justice Edward Douglass White, Jr., to chief justice—and with a sixth nomination on the way. On October 14, 1911, Justice John Marshall Harlan died after nearly thirty-four years on the Court. Known for his lone dissents on race, he objected to the invalidation of the Civil Rights Act of 1875 and to upholding a Louisiana law racially segregating railroad cars. He also dissented from the Court's decisions limiting the scope of federal power to enforce antitrust laws and to regulate interstate commerce and from the invalidation of the state maximum-hour law for bakers in *Lochner v. New York*. One of Frankfurter's professors suggested Eugene Wambaugh, a Harvard law professor working in the Bureau of Corporations, as Harlan's replacement. Frankfurter and Emory Buckner preferred a younger faculty member, Roscoe Pound. Pound's 1909 article, "Liberty of Contract," landed him a job on the Harvard faculty and made him a prominent critic of *Lochner* and other anti-labor decisions. He would have been one of the Court's few progressives. After more than six months and with the 1912 election looming, Taft chose another conservative, Mahlon Pitney of New Jersey. The Supreme Court vacancy, like Stimson's aborted antitrust speech, revealed how little power Frankfurter had as a War Department aide and the differences between the Taft and Roosevelt presidencies.

Roosevelt's ideas about the judiciary continued to resonate with Frankfurter. What was refreshing for him was the Colonel's willingness to criticize the Supreme Court and to expose it as "a conservative and timid body of the community." The Court "failed and failed wretchedly" by not looking beyond its own "selfish interests," and, thanks to Roosevelt, was no longer "sacrosanct." Law schools, Frankfurter wrote, were beginning to explore Roosevelt's ideas about how much power the Court wielded over people's everyday lives by privileging property rights over human rights.

Disillusioned by Taft and his conservative Supreme Court, Frankfurter turned to the justice who exemplified deference to democracy, Oliver Wendell Holmes, Jr. Frankfurter's faith in Holmes began with his dissent in *Lochner v. New York* accusing the majority of reading laissez-faire economic views into the Fourteenth Amendment's Due Process Clause to invalidate New York's maximum-hour law for bakers. Holmes also dissented from the Court's other decisions striking down labor legislation, not because he sympathized with the working class but because he believed it was up to state and federal elected officials, not the Court, to make economic and social policy. Like Frankfurter, Holmes espoused Thayer's belief that the Court should not strike down a law unless it was unconstitutional beyond a reasonable doubt. "I have little doubt that the country likes it and I always say, as you know, that if my fellow citizens want to go to Hell I will help them," Holmes wrote. "It's my job."

In November 1911, Frankfurter sought advice from John Chipman Gray—his property professor whose casebook he had helped revise—about whether the Puerto Rico legislature could request advisory opinions from its Insular Supreme Court. Gray opposed the idea, but his efforts did not end there. He awarded him a life-changing prize: a letter of introduction to Gray's oldest friend, Holmes:

> *Dear Judge:*
>
> *Mr. Felix Frankfurter graduated some years ago at the Law School at the head of his class. He was one of the best men we have ever had. He has since been doing excellent work in the office of the U.S. District Attorney in New York. He is now counsel for the Bureau of Insular Affairs. They are now considering whether in the constitution, in imperial decree or pragmatic sanction for Puerto Rico, it is desirable to insert a provision authorizing the local legislature to call for opinions from the Insular Supreme Court.*
>
> *He has a great admiration for you, and is very desirous to learn your opinion and the result of your experience in this matter, and he has asked me to give him a note of introduction to you, which I do with pleasure. I am quite sure he will impress you favorably.*
>
> *Yours Sincerely,*
> *John C. Gray*

Ten days after Gray mailed the letter of introduction, Frankfurter walked up the steps of the wide, brick, three-story house at 1720 I Street for lunch with Justice and Mrs. Holmes. The seventy-year-old justice was more than 6 feet tall, with ramrod straight posture, a long, bushy white mustache, a full head of hair, and intense blue eyes. His wife, Fanny, a once attractive woman whose appearance and personality changed after a bad case of rheumatic fever, was short and quiet but with a wicked wit; her husband was her favorite target.

After lunch, Frankfurter and Holmes sat by the fire in the justice's second-floor study, which doubled as his full-time office. In those days, the justices worked out of their homes. The room was brimming with books in floor-to-ceiling bookshelves. His great-grandfather's swords from the French and Indian War hung above the mantel. A seven-drawer cherrywood desk that belonged to his maternal grandfather, a Massachusetts Supreme Judicial Court judge, dominated the center of the room. Holmes wrote all his Supreme Court opinions in longhand at his grandfather's standup desk near the window.

The justice did most of the talking. Indeed, there was no better talker in Washington. Holmes confirmed Gray's view on the Puerto Rico issue and more. Everything Frankfurter had heard and read about the justice was true; he was not worshiping at a false judicial idol. "I came away with the keen relish of having been on Olympus and finding that one's God did not have clay feet . . . ;" he wrote Gray, "his penetration, his contempt for mere words and formula, and his freshness of outlook, give lasting zest and momentum to one's groping and toiling."

Unbeknownst to Frankfurter, he had given Holmes a sense of hope for the future. For years, the justice had labored in the shadow of his famous physician-poet father of the same name. A founder of the *Atlantic Monthly*; author of verse, short stories, and novels; and coiner of the phrases "Boston Brahmin" and "the Hub," Holmes Sr. had upstaged his son at every turn. After his son had been badly wounded in the neck at Antietam, his father had written an *Atlantic Monthly* article, "My Hunt After the Captain," putting himself at the center of the narrative. His son's grueling Civil War experiences as a thrice-wounded Union army captain transformed him from an ardent abolitionist into a lifelong skeptic. Nothing Holmes accomplished in Boston after the war helped him eclipse his father's fame— a revised edition of Kent's Commentaries; a groundbreaking book, *The Common Law* ("the life of the law has not been logic; it has been experience"); a brief professorship at Harvard Law School; nearly 20 years on the Massachusetts Supreme Judicial

Court, including three as its chief judge; and a nomination in 1902 to the Supreme Court of the United States.

As of 1911, Holmes's tenure on the Supreme Court had been a bitter disappointment. He had a falling out with Roosevelt after a 1904 dissent in the *Northern Securities* case, which dissolved the Great Northern and Pacific Railroad Companies. Holmes thought the Sherman Act was "a foolish law." He shared little in common with his judicial colleagues, who often asked him to take his most literary and colorful language out of his majority opinions. He had not received the recognition he felt he deserved. Initially, Harlan's dissent in *Lochner v. New York* had garnered more public attention than Holmes's. Holmes was counting the days until December 8, 1912, when his ten years on the Court allowed him to retire with a full pension. He could not wait to leave the Court and believed he would die in relative obscurity—until he met Frankfurter.

Frankfurter gave Holmes something more than friendship and hope; he introduced the justice to other bright, young New Nationalists in and out of the Taft administration. Frankfurter and his friends flattered Holmes and in time helped him achieve fame and immortality.

═══

WITH HOLMES AND BRANDEIS part of his expanding professional network, Frankfurter introduced them to Roosevelt supporters in the Taft administration with the assistance of fellow sugar fraud prosecutor Winfred T. Denison. As one of the office's more senior lawyers, Denison had made a national name for himself working for Stimson and prosecuting the Sugar Trust. In January 1910, he was appointed assistant U.S. attorney general in charge of customs. He traveled the East Coast giving speeches declaring the sugar fraud cases would not have been possible without Stimson hiring on the basis of merit rather than political patronage. A 38-year-old bachelor from Portland, Maine, Denison was 5' 7½" with a wide nose, wireless oval pince-nez, prominent eyebrows, full lips, and streaks of gray in his brown hair. Nearly ten years older than Frankfurter, Denison shared the same intense ambition and extroverted personality. Denison was listed in the Social Register, belonged to the Metropolitan Club and Chevy Chase Country Club, and liked to throw parties. He referred to his constant social activity as "that damn charm of mine!" Denison's charms came with bouts of nervous exhaustion because of a history of depression. Frankfurter introduced Denison to Holmes and Brandeis; Denison introduced Frankfurter to journalist Ray Stannard Baker, Justice Department and other administration officials, and Denison's best friend from the Harvard College Class of 1896, Robert G. Valentine.

Valentine was Taft's commissioner of Indian affairs. After graduating from Harvard, he worked as a banker for New York financier James Stillman but longed to be a poet. For several years, he vacillated between working for one of Stillman's interests and teaching writing to MIT undergraduates while working on his poetry. The strain between banking and poetry eventually became so great that he suffered a nervous breakdown. After Valentine recovered, he decided to start a new life in Washington. A brief meeting with President Roosevelt had been a life-changing experience. He landed a job as a secretary to Roosevelt's commissioner of Indian affairs, Francis E. Leupp, and worked his way up to become the head of the agency. He believed in taking a scientific approach to the problems of Native Americans with health, education, and land ownership. However, the political pressures in the Taft administration proved to be difficult for Valentine. In May 1911, he suffered another nervous breakdown and, accompanied by Denison, spent part of the summer recuperating in Atlantic City.

During the fall of 1911, Denison introduced Frankfurter to Valentine, his wife, Sophie, and their infant daughter, Sophia, at the Valentines' narrow brick three-story house at 1727 Nineteenth Street north of Dupont Circle. Frankfurter described the commissioner of Indian affairs, youthful and handsome-looking with light eyes and short-cropped, dark hair, as the "very *realest* of men." In Valentine, Frankfurter had found someone as devoted to Roosevelt as he was. Along with Denison, they drew others into their social and political orbit.

By the end of 1911, Frankfurter's work for Stimson on water-power issues, the Panama Canal, and laws governing Puerto Rico and the Philippines put him in good standing in the Taft administration and led to another possible career opportunity. Sometime in late 1911 or early 1912, Stimson asked the 29-year-old Frankfurter whether he was interested in the open federal district judgeship in the Southern District of New York. The judgeship had been vacant since Judge George B. Adams died on October 9. The nomination process stalled because progressives and the legal establishment objected to the New York Republican Party's preferred nominee, Julius M. Mayer.

Years later, Frankfurter insisted that the judgeship was his for the taking. He may have been right. Despite being only 29 years old, he was an experienced federal prosecutor and Taft administration official with the former U.S. attorney for the Southern District of New York in his corner. As a prosecutor, he had impressed Wall Street lawyer C. C. Burlingham, the up-

and-coming Judge Learned Hand (appointed at age 37 in 1909 with less experience than Frankfurter), and the most respected Southern District judge,
Charles M. Hough. These legal luminaries, as well as progressives Florence
Kelley and Josephine Goldmark, would have supported him. Stimson asked
for Frankfurter's input on the judgeship and whether he was interested. It
probably did not get much further than that. Unlike one of Stimson's other
former assistants, Frankfurter never applied for the opening. He decided he
was too young to go on the bench. In February 1912, over the opposition of
progressives and leaders of the New York bar, Taft nominated Mayer in order
to stay in the good graces of the New York Republican Party.

It was obvious where Frankfurter stood between Taft and Roosevelt—as
a loyal Roosevelt man. All Frankfurter and his friends could talk about was
whether Roosevelt should run against Taft. "The thing is in the air; people
of intelligence and observation here 'feel' he will be nominated," Frankfurter
wrote to Emory Buckner on January 6. "Right now, however, if I had to stake
my life on it I should stake it on Taft's re-nomination—but I'm damn glad I
don't have to stake it!"

Roosevelt's supporters expected him to announce his candidacy during a
February 21 address to the Ohio Constitutional Convention in Columbus. "We
Progressives," Roosevelt began, "believe that the people have the right, the
power, and the duty to protect themselves and their own welfare; that human
rights are supreme over all other rights; that wealth should be the servant, not
the master, of the people. We believe that unless representative government
does absolutely represent the people it is not representative government at
all." Roosevelt described a war against privilege and on behalf of the common
man; he vowed "to free our government from the control of money in politics"
and to put government back "in the hands of the people" and to make their
representatives "responsible to the people's will." In his "Charter of Democracy" speech, Roosevelt appealed to Frankfurter and his friends. The Colonel
wanted to regulate monopolies and to protect working women and children
from low wages and long hours, and, most controversially, he attacked the
courts by proposing popular recall of state judicial decisions such as the one
invalidating a New York workmen's compensation law. Roosevelt was also
putting the nine justices on the Supreme Court on notice. "I may not know
much about law," he had once told Frankfurter, "but I do know one can put
the fear of God into judges." Roosevelt did not officially announce his candidacy in Columbus but offhandedly remarked to a reporter: "My hat is in the
ring." Three days later, he responded to a petition from the seven Republican

governors—a petition he had orchestrated—that, if it were offered to him, he would accept his party's presidential nomination.

With Roosevelt openly campaigning for the presidency, Frankfurter could not contain his inner turmoil: He was a Roosevelt loyalist stuck in the Taft administration. In a letter to friends, he confessed his "prepossessions against Taft" upon arriving in Washington and confirmed them when Taft nixed Stimson's Kansas City antitrust speech. Taft, Frankfurter believed, was a former judge miscast as president. He had no clear beliefs other than "textual worship of the Constitution," no passion for the presidency, and no ideas for the country. As a result, conservatives controlled Taft's political agenda, even though he was neither liberal nor conservative. Taft, Frankfurter argued, had done nothing to promote progressive social reform.

Roosevelt, by contrast, wanted to use the presidency to change the direction of the country—to enforce and to amend the Sherman Act and to lobby for new laws, to protect the rights of workers to fair wages and safe working conditions, and to warn the courts not to obstruct these democratic endeavors. Frankfurter recognized the Colonel's limitations as a thinker, as someone far more "keen to scent a wrong, far less resourceful to suggest a remedy." Roosevelt's idea about popular recall of state judicial decisions was antithetical to Frankfurter's legal training. Yet the Colonel's criticism of judges for striking down legislation on the basis of narrow interpretations of vague constitutional commands was, in Frankfurter's view, spot on. Despite Roosevelt's imperfections, Frankfurter's heart and mind were with the Colonel. Their bond had been forged two years earlier during Stimson's New York gubernatorial campaign. Frankfurter could not support Woodrow Wilson, notwithstanding the New Jersey Democrat's "moral endowment" and "more disciplined intellect," because of "his party's traditions on States' Rights," because "the Republican Party is the party of liberal construction of the Constitution," and because Roosevelt possessed the ability to transform the Republican Party into "the distinctly liberal party."

Among Republican Party loyalists, Roosevelt became a pariah. As soon as he announced his presidential bid, party officials shunned him. Knowing how alone he was, Frankfurter traveled to New York to see him. Their conversation reaffirmed Frankfurter's belief that the future of the country should be in Roosevelt's hands. "Oh," Roosevelt exclaimed as if he were about to mount a horse, "if only Taft knew the joys of leadership!"

Desperate to resign his War Department post to join the Roosevelt campaign, Frankfurter was torn between his loyalty to Roosevelt and that to Stimson. Much to Frankfurter's dismay, Stimson endorsed Taft on March 5 and declared that he had "carried out this Progressive faith of the Republican party." Though he owed his career in public life to Roosevelt, Stimson believed that the Colonel's campaign was a "great mistake" that would divide the party and prevent a Republican victory in November. Stimson also believed that Roosevelt had shown poor leadership and judgment by leaving the door open to running and allowing others to draft him into the race. During several honest conversations with his boss, Frankfurter disagreed with Stimson's endorsement of Taft and advised Stimson to refrain from making further comments about the presidential race. Stimson valued Frankfurter's loyalty and counsel; they agreed to disagree about Roosevelt.

As an ardent Roosevelt supporter, Frankfurter helped turn Valentine's house at 1727 Nineteenth Street into the Colonel's de facto campaign headquarters. A few months earlier, Valentine had clashed with Taft by ordering Catholic priests not to wear religious garb and insignia when they taught on Indian reservations. The president had reversed Valentine's order six days later. On the outs with the administration, Valentine was more loyal to Roosevelt than to the president. A family crisis allowed him to use his house to rally support for the Colonel. In March 1912, Valentine's wife had returned home to South Braintree, Massachusetts, because of the poor health of their infant daughter, Sophia. Valentine invited his two closest friends and fellow Roosevelt supporters, Frankfurter and Denison, to live with him. They asked two more friends, Loring C. Christie and Eustace Percy, to join them.

Justice Department lawyer Loring Christie had been a regular at Valentine's house. A native of Nova Scotia, Canada, and *Harvard Law Review* president, Christie had been recruited by Frankfurter to join Stimson's law firm, Winthrop & Stimson, after graduation. At the firm, Christie had worked with Denison and Frankfurter on the latter stages of the sugar fraud prosecutions before joining Denison as his assistant in the Justice Department. Christie and Frankfurter both admired Justice Holmes and considered themselves lucky to have chosen government jobs over Wall Street law firms even though their "friends think us damn fools." Christie, who bore the prim expression of his Scottish ancestors, was, Frankfurter noted, "an attractive fellow with a fine mind; still rather restless. He seems to have a deep emotional side which is not always administered to."

The fifth and final resident of the house was British embassy official Eustace Percy. Soon after his arrival at the embassy in May 1910, Percy had begun visiting Valentine's house. The seventh son of the seventh duke of Northumberland, Percy possessed the bloodlines of British nobility but none of the land or wealth. Educated at Eton College and Christ Church, Oxford, Percy, Frankfurter observed, was "much more of a dreamer and a mystic than the son of a great landowner." Though not always sympathetic to his housemates' politics, Percy shared their love of conversation and interest in social reform. Percy and his British friends brought a transatlantic perspective to their conversations and nurtured Frankfurter's budding Anglophilia.

During the spring and summer of 1912, Frankfurter and his friends transformed Valentine's house into a freewheeling political salon. They invited a who's who of law, politics, and journalism to nightly dinners and weekend brunches. Holmes and Brandeis were regulars. Other guests included British ambassador to the United States James Bryce; federal judge Julian W. Mack; and the sculptor Gutzon Borglum. "The days have been good to me down here," Frankfurter wrote to Buckner on April 20. "I should like to talk of Holmes and Bryce and Judge Mack (the real stuff) and Borglum and an Indian night at Val's etc. etc. with all that and so much more."

No one enjoyed himself at the house more than Holmes. The justice did not read newspapers or care about politics. He was no fan of Theodore Roosevelt and could not understand his young friends' passion for the Colonel. Nor did he subscribe to their reformist ideas. He was, however, willing to listen. They admired his intellectual curiosity, conversational skills, and sense of fun. Mephistopheles, as Holmes often referred to himself, admired their ambition, intelligence, and optimism about the future. A philosophical debate about the search for truth between Holmes and his young friends resulted in the house's name. Frankfurter and his friends believed in an objective truth supported by empirical facts and social scientific evidence. Ever the skeptic, Holmes thought that there was no such thing as truth, which he defined as "the system of my (intellectual) limitations" or "the majority vote of that nation that could lick all others." Someone, probably Denison, paid homage to Holmes by naming 1727 Nineteenth Street "The House of Truth."

The house became the place to be in Washington during the 1912 presidential campaign. "How or why I can't recapture," Frankfurter said, "but almost everybody who was interesting in Washington sooner or later passed through that house." Holmes sent his secretary, Francis Biddle, to the house's Sunday brunches to meet Frankfurter and his friends. A blue-blooded Philadelphian and Harvard law graduate, Biddle arrived at those brunches a conservative Republican and left "a Roosevelt man." Biddle's boss, Holmes, could not understand it. Had he not stopped voting since joining the bench, Holmes insisted that he would have voted for Taft even though the justice disagreed with the president's Sherman Act prosecutions. Holmes admired the success of the robber barons. He once told Taft that "if they could make a case for putting Rockefeller in prison I should do my part; but if they left it to me I should put up a bronze statue of him."

During the 1912 election, Roosevelt, not Holmes, was the hero of the house. Frankfurter conceded to Mrs. Holmes that his Roosevelt fixation was a passing fad, "the undisciplined exuberance of youth," an excitement about "the aspirations of the man rather than the man himself." Frankfurter reassured Mrs. Holmes that her husband's legacy would endure "long after the turmoil and noise of present-day politics."

Another regular at the house, Louis Brandeis, was as unconvinced about Roosevelt as Holmes, but for different reasons. Personally and politically, Brandeis was close to progressive Wisconsin senator Robert M. La Follette, Sr., and initially supported him for the Republican presidential nomination. Known as "Fighting Bob," La Follette criticized the judiciary for invalidating socioeconomic legislation, thwarting the prosecution of illegal monopolies, and interfering with "the movement toward democracy." Once Roosevelt entered the race, however, La Follette no longer stood a chance. Even so, Brandeis believed that Roosevelt's fight with Taft was counterproductive, for it divided progressives among La Follette, Roosevelt, and Taft. Brandeis looked elsewhere for leadership.

Frankfurter and his friends obsessively followed the three-way Republican presidential race. At first, things did not look good for the Colonel. La Follette returned to the campaign trail and, because of his popularity with western farmers, captured the March 19 North Dakota primary and the April 2 primary in his home state of Wisconsin. After Taft was awarded most of the delegates at the March 27 New York convention, Roosevelt cried foul. The Colonel threatened to run as a third-party candidate, then captured a string of Republican primaries: Illinois on April 9, Pennsylvania on April 13, and Nebraska and Oregon on April 19. Things turned ugly in Massachusetts. A desperate Taft broke his promise not to attack Roosevelt personally and accused him of preaching "class hatred." The Colonel denied that supporting pro-labor legislation to protect women and children was class hatred. On the night of the Massachusetts primary, Frankfurter made the rounds of newspaper offices to obtain the results. By 10:30 p.m., the Associated Press and Hearst Newspapers called Massachusetts for Roosevelt. Frankfurter and Valentine went to bed thinking the Colonel had won. The next morning, however, they learned that Taft had squeaked out a 50 to 48 percent victory, though Roosevelt was awarded more delegates. After Massachusetts, the Colonel reeled off five more primary victories, including Taft's home state of Ohio. Only some states, however, held presidential primaries. Everyone knew that the Republican nominee would be determined in June by the politicians and delegates at the party's national convention in Chicago.

Unable to attend the Chicago convention himself, Frankfurter received updates from housemate Loring Christie. The fix was in for Taft. A few days before the convention, party leaders awarded 235 of 254 disputed delegates to the president. Roosevelt's only option was to leave the Republican Party and to run as a third-party candidate. "I don't see anything but a bolt unless we are willing to compromise pretty far," Christie wrote to Frankfurter. Christie was unsure how Roosevelt would react to losing. With his defeat all but assured on the eve of the convention, Roosevelt delivered one of the most memorable speeches of his career. Charging "big bosses" and "great crooked financiers" with stealing the Republican nomination from him, Roosevelt argued that the "good of mankind" was at stake and vowed to run as a third-party candidate. His conclusion was unforgettable: "We fight in honorable fashion for the good of mankind; fearless of the future; unheeding of our individual fates; with unflinching hearts and undimmed eyes; we stand at Armageddon, and we battle for the Lord." As expected, Taft was nominated as the Republican Party candidate. Asked how he was doing, Roosevelt replied: "Fine! Fine! Just like a bull moose." After his defeat in Chicago, Roosevelt launched his third-party "Bull Moose" presidential campaign.

Roosevelt's "Standing at Armageddon" speech moved Frankfurter and his housemates to want to quit their jobs to join the Bull Moose campaign. They were swept up in a political and social movement that they saw as bigger than themselves. After a meeting in early July with Roosevelt, Frankfurter was eager to speak with Stimson about quitting. Brandeis advised Frankfurter to stay in the administration. The people's lawyer, however, lost some credibility with Frankfurter and his friends by joining the campaign of Democratic nominee Woodrow Wilson and advising him on antitrust policy. Through intermediaries, Roosevelt told Frankfurter not to quit his day job: "you would not do enough good to the cause to counterbalance the damage you would do by leaving your present position." For the moment, Frankfurter heeded the Colonel's advice and contented himself with the political discussions at the house: "here I am quite happy in good fun work, unhappy that I can't be out where my political heart is (tho I'm exposing it to every passerby) and serenely lucky to have the pal-ship of Valentine and Denison. We're having great times."

The calls for Frankfurter to join Roosevelt's campaign grew louder after the Progressive Party Convention August 5 through 7 in Chicago. Observers described the atmosphere surrounding Roosevelt's August 6 "Confession of Faith" speech as "more like a religious meeting than a political gathering." Valentine had lost all effectiveness in the Taft administration and informed Frankfurter that "the difference [between Taft as president and Roosevelt] was that when you left TR's presence 'you were ready to eat bricks for lunch,' and when you left Taft, you thought, 'What's the use.'" On September 10, Valentine announced that he was leaving the administration to join Roosevelt's campaign. As the second high-ranking Taft official to resign to join Roosevelt, Valentine made the *New York Times* front page with his announcement. Privately, he promised to bring Frankfurter with him.

During the last few months, Frankfurter and Valentine had become incredibly close running the house as a Bull Moose political salon. In a letter to a skeptical Sophie Valentine, Frankfurter defended Roosevelt against charges that the Colonel was a fly-by-night progressive. He knew all about Roosevelt's record. As governor of New York, Roosevelt had played ball with party bosses yet had fought for a more progressive tax system. As president, Roosevelt had come into office at "the high tide of national smugness," not to mention his imperialistic control of territories gained during the Spanish-American War and acquisition of the Panama Canal Zone. Yet Roosevelt's administration also had championed conservation efforts, civil service reform, and labor legislation. Frankfurter recognized Roosevelt's "deep blemishes, the crudities, at times even the brutalities, of a fighter" but believed in Roosevelt's "open-mindedness, his responsiveness to new insights, to new convictions—this is one of the great gifts of his usefulness—his capacity for growth." Frankfurter concluded his letter by apologizing because he had been "very much derelict in my duty as a reporter of the truth, but that is because Bob and I have been having such a riotously sober good time of it."

Valentine's resignation nearly pushed Frankfurter over the edge about quitting his job and joining the campaign. The only thing holding him back was his loyalty to Stimson. A tortured Frankfurter, on vacation in Massachusetts, wrote to Stimson out West submitting his resignation: "I find now the call for active work in the Progressive Party is too insistent, too dominant, not to be heeded if I have fairly considered all the controlling considerations." Frankfurter planned to return to Washington and vowed not to leave his post until he heard from Stimson. Upon receiving the letter in Yosemite, Stimson replied on September 19 that Frankfurter was making a mistake. There was not enough time for him to make a difference in the campaign. The "real work to be done," Stimson argued, was to unite progressive factions for the general election. Frankfurter promised to think it over and awaited Stimson's return to Washington in early October.

A less-than-thrilled Valentine ratcheted up the pressure on Frankfurter. "If you haven't heard from T.R. by the time you get this, please wire me, letting me know also when you feel you can cut loose," Valentine wrote on September 22. He dismissed the two people advising Frankfurter to stay: Brandeis and Stimson. "I return Brandeis's note to you," Valentine wrote Frankfurter. "He is making such remarkable statements in this campaign that I do not like to keep incriminating documents in my possession." Valentine, who rejected Stimson's suggestion that he regretted leaving the administration, insisted that he had never been happier. He believed that Frankfurter's "real job at the present time is with the Colonel himself" and told Frankfurter to wait for a call from the candidate. Roosevelt, Valentine said, needed Frankfurter more than Stimson: "With the Colonel you might well be a turning factor in the whole campaign."

It is unclear whether the advice from Stimson and Brandeis, the futility of leaving the administration with less than two months left in the campaign, or pragmatic career concerns changed Frankfurter's mind. Whatever the reason, he stayed in the War Department. "[A]fter much and dubious searching of heart I have decided it's my bigger job to stay and I can only hope that it won't come up to plague me in the years to come," Frankfurter wrote fellow Bull Mooser Learned Hand. "I'm clearer than ever in the *raison d'etre* of the movement and equally clear that it should be fought on the assumption of not being successful this year."

Frankfurter's loyalty to Stimson and willingness to stay in the Taft administration paid off. In August, his housemate Winfred Denison was named to a three-member commission to investigate the U.S. Board of General Appraisers, an administrative body that heard customs and tariff appeals. After one of the other members dropped out in mid-October, Taft named Frankfurter to the commission and Denison the chair. Their experiences on the sugar fraud cases made them well qualified for the job. Frankfurter and Denison were young, ambitious lawyers with too much to lose by quitting the administration to join the final weeks of a quixotic campaign.

On October 14, Roosevelt was speaking in Milwaukee when he was shot in the chest. Fortunately, the bullet hit his glasses case and a copy of his speech in his right breast pocket. He spoke for another fifty minutes with blood soiling his shirt and the bullet lodged in his rib cage. "It takes more than that," he remarked to the crowd, "to kill a Bull Moose." Roosevelt survived, but his bid for the presidency was already dead. In November, Wilson won easily with 435 electoral votes compared to eighty-eight for Roosevelt and eight for Taft. The New Jersey governor was the first Democrat to win the White House since Grover Cleveland twenty years earlier.

The outcome of the election had done nothing to temper the idealism of Frankfurter and his housemates. Eustace Percy wrote an essay proposing the adoption of a British civil service model in America. In December, Frankfurter circulated an anonymous copy to Roosevelt and let the Colonel know that all had not been lost during the campaign. He credited Roosevelt with inspiring "inquiries into the underlying cause of our social unrest, and the desire for an organized effort to understand and direct it."

After the election, Frankfurter stayed in the War Department until the end of Stimson's term and beyond. In late November and early December, he joined Stimson on a tour of the Panama Canal Zone. At Stimson's request, Frankfurter saw the completion of several water-power projects under Wilson's new secretary of war Lindley Garrison. In Frankfurter's eyes, Garrison paled in comparison to Stimson as a public servant. When Stimson left office at the end of the Taft administration, Frankfurter co-authored a 47-page review of Stimson's War Department stewardship of the Panama Canal Zone, insular territories, and peacetime reorganization of the military and published a long summary in the *Boston Evening Transcript*. Stimson was grateful for Frankfurter's loyalty and for the public recognition; Frankfurter was grateful to Stimson for bringing him to Washington. Their partnership in government was over, at least for now.

CHAPTER 5

To a Man,
We Want Frankfurter

D uring the early days of the Wilson administration, Frankfurter faced
a career crossroads. He wanted to advance Roosevelt's New Nationalist ideas of using the federal government to achieve labor reform but
was unsure of the best way to accomplish it. Each of his options emphasized
one of his talents and interests. Instead of stewing about his job prospects or
lurching from one extreme to another, he wrote a four-page memorandum
and circulated it to his friends who were pulling him in different directions.

Frankfurter could go into business with his former housemate Robert Valentine. Upon his return to Boston, Valentine had set up shop as the nation's
first "industrial counselor." He pitched himself as a disinterested expert who
could work with labor and management. Most important, he wanted Frankfurter to join him. "We have discovered—you and I—the center of the universe . . . ," he wrote his "co-trustee" Frankfurter in December 1912. "Don't
make any plans for the future—either for yourself or the Universe—until we
have stood at the center of it together and discussed things. This is a far cry
from lying on the floor of the front room at 1727."

In July 1912, they had laid on the floor of the House of Truth and had written an eight-page outline proposing solutions to conflicts between labor and
management. Inhumane conditions, low wages, and long hours had taken
their toll on America's industrial workers. The Triangle Shirtwaist fire in
March 1911 in New York City had killed 146 garment workers, mostly young
women. Locked in their workspace, some women had jumped from the burning building rather than suffocate to death. During the Lawrence, Massachusetts, textile mill strike from January to March 1912, 20,000 women had
walked off their jobs after management had reduced their pay because of a

new state law lowering the maximum workweek from fifty-eight to fifty-six hours. The radical Industrial Workers of the World (IWW) had organized the Lawrence strike and several others, stoking fears of Socialism.

In their eight-page outline titled "A Tentative Social Program," Frankfurter and Valentine addressed the effects of industrialization on workers and believed they had discovered the key to resolving labor problems—a stronger, more powerful government. "Government," they wrote, "is the readiest and best fitted administrative means through which the conception of the people as to their welfare may find realization in action and, rightly understood, becomes the most potent affirmative social agency on behalf of all the people." By tapping into the power of the federal government as well as that of the state governments, they wanted to level the playing field between labor and management. They proposed administrative regulation, revised election laws, and more progressive taxation. They believed that disinterested experts in and out of government could create an "industrial democracy." In their ideal scenario, management recognized unions as the legal representatives of all workers; unions embraced scientific management to capture efficiencies associated with industrialization; and management and labor recognized their interdependence and worked together to solve their problems. With their "social program," Valentine and Frankfurter joked that they had "worked out our general scheme of the Universe."

After the 1912 election, Frankfurter encouraged Valentine's industrial counseling business and gave serious thought to joining him. "Dear Pardner . . . ," Frankfurter wrote, "I don't know what else you've done, but you've sent coursing through my veins the rapturous champagne of your courage and imagination and humor and sanity that cannot be in vain, were it not sufficient unto itself." Frankfurter and his friends were enthusiastic about the possibilities of Valentine's new business and commented on his prospectus. In January 1913, they met Valentine in New York City for dinner and continued their discussions the next day on the drive to sculptor Gutzon Borglum's Connecticut home, Borgland. Frankfurter admired Valentine's fearlessness in "going it alone." Yet he procrastinated about making a decision to join Valentine because of a crush of War Department work. "The silence is the silence of much thinking and more longing for a union of the universe," he wired Valentine in February 1913.

In an article for *The Survey*, Frankfurter channeled his ideas with Valentine about the ability of government to improve the lives of industrialized workers with his Thayerian belief that the judiciary should not interfere with socioeconomic legislation. He criticized the American Bar Association for rejecting Roosevelt's ideas about the recall of unpopular judicial decisions without offering any solutions for judicial overreach. In an age of industrialization, he described government "as the biggest organized social effort for dealing with social problems" and proposed "social legislation" dealing with "economic and social conditions" and "the stuff of life."

During the transition from Taft's administration to Wilson's, Frankfurter found he did not have time to think beyond the issues of the day. On February 15, he and Denison concluded their investigation of the Board of General Appraisers. In an eighteen-page report, they recommended a reorganization of the board and its duties. Relying on their findings, Taft fired two board members for malfeasance and incompetence in one of his last acts in office. Frankfurter also defended Puerto Rico and other territories before the Supreme Court. In April, he argued *Tiaco v. Forbes* defending the governor-general of the Philippines' deportation of a Chinese immigrant on the basis of the U.S. government's inherent power over immigration. Holmes's unanimous opinion affirmed the deportation. Other justices privately praised Frankfurter's argument.

In Valentine's absence, Frankfurter and Denison maintained the spirit of the House of Truth by throwing frequent dinner parties. They celebrated a weekend visit from Valentine in March with a round of lunches and dinners and hosted a going-away party later that month for housemate Loring Christie, who was returning to Canada to work for Prime Minister Robert Borden. Another night, they invited Justice Horace H. Lurton. A Taft nominee and Kentucky Democrat, Lurton took his cocktails seriously. "I hope you mix drinks as well as you argue cases," he said to Frankfurter. A few minutes later, he added: "You mix drinks even better than you argue cases." The parties often lasted late into the night. "Felix keeps us alive most of the time," Denison wrote Frankfurter's mother, Emma. "The only trouble with him is that he wants to sit up all night and sleep all day. And he's terribly slow about getting dressed and washed and down to breakfast. Why in the world did you fail to teach him that black air means night and time to sleep and that white air means day and time to be awake?" Some people, including Brandeis, thought Frankfurter and Denison needed to socialize less and to work more. "You are right about Frankfurter's excessive sociability," Brandeis wrote his wife. "[Attorney General James] McReynolds criticised Denison also on that score."

Brandeis's humorlessness may have been one of many reasons why Holmes was the house's favorite guest. Holmes, his wife Fanny, and his new secretary, Stanley Clarke, attended Christie's farewell party. Fanny Holmes revealed that, contrary to her reputation as a recluse, she liked to socialize and to play practical jokes. For a children's party at the house, she sent a pie with ribbons coming out of it. When the children pulled the ribbons, they discovered presents instead of dessert. A live monkey playing a hand organ also appeared through the window. She bought the men a housewarming gift, a wren house for the backyard. "Truth may still be at the bottom of the well," Frankfurter wrote her, "but you have brought up for us—joy. A bountiful summer to you! In grateful humility. *Your* House of Truth."

During the summer of 1913, Frankfurter pondered another career opportunity, a Harvard Law School professorship. Denison broached the idea with one of the school's younger professors, Edward "Bull" Warren. After consulting the faculty, Warren reported: "To a man, we want Frankfurter." Frankfurter did not think he was worthy of joining a faculty that had included case method founder Christopher Columbus Langdell, judicial review theorist James Bradley Thayer, former dean James Barr Ames, or property scholar John Chipman Gray. Of Frankfurter's worthiness, Brandeis replied: "I would let those who have the responsibilities for selecting you decide your qualifications and not have you decide that."

Teaching at Harvard Law School, Frankfurter wrote in his memorandum, would allow him to mentor the nation's future leaders who would shape "jurisprudence to meet the social and industrial needs of the time" and to wrestle with "the great procedural problems of administration and legislation." He knew he was not a traditional legal scholar who would churn out law review articles. Yet, together with Roscoe Pound, Frankfurter believed that he could apply the social sciences to law in a way that would revolutionize the law school and the careers of its future graduates.

Frankfurter analyzed the competing options. First, there was "the Valentine thing." That path would force him to give up the law and waste his legal training and experience. Second, Frankfurter could stay in the Wilson administration. He never warmed to Wilson, whose "inscrutable secretiveness," "Southern-Democrat" atmosphere, and "party solidarity" bothered him. Frankfurter's boss, Lindley Garrison, was nice enough but a "first-class mediocrity." Third, Frankfurter could practice law in New York City and become the city's "citizen-lawyer" like Brandeis in Boston. Private practice, however, never appealed to Frankfurter. He did not like kowtowing to clients or advocating positions in which he did not believe. Finally, Harvard Law School, he concluded, was the "best five years' investment ahead." If he didn't like it, he would be young enough to change course. Rather than make a hasty decision, Frankfurter circulated his memorandum to friends and mentors.

The childless Stimson and his wife, who considered Frankfurter a surrogate son, opposed the idea. Stimson thought that Frankfurter's "greatest faculty of acquaintance, for keeping in touch with the center of things,—for knowing sympathetically men who are doing and thinking," would be lost on the professors and students. Frankfurter, Stimson argued, belonged "at the center of the great liberal movement which [is] now going on in national and industrial life." Researching criminology with Roscoe Pound would be a "side track." Nor did Stimson think that Frankfurter and Pound were compatible personalities. Stimson advised Frankfurter to return to New York, not out of a selfish desire to practice law with him but because he thought it would suit him best. Thanking Stimson for his advice, Frankfurter replied that the offer was not limited to criminology and that the divide between academia and politics was not so vast. He pointed to University of Wisconsin professors who had influenced state social reform. And he was not persuaded that Wall Street law practice would put him at the center of a liberal political movement.

The leader of the liberal movement, Theodore Roosevelt, urged Frankfurter to return to New York law practice and warned him that if he became a professor he would "have to adjust [his] wants." His future wife would have to "be content with a simple life" because his salary would remain mostly the same. Learned Hand was no more enthusiastic about Frankfurter joining the Harvard law faculty than was Stimson or Roosevelt. Hand thought Frankfurter should stay in the War Department with Garrison; Harvard Law School was not going anywhere. "What does Holmesy say?" Hand asked. "I suppose that you have writ[ten] him before now."

With Holmes visiting friends in Britain and Ireland, Frankfurter asked to delay his decision for a few weeks until he heard from the justice. In a July 4 letter, Frankfurter presented the offer as a five-year tryout. Holmes's experience in academia had been short and unfulfilling; he had bolted the Harvard law faculty after only a few months in the fall of 1882 to accept a judgeship on the Massachusetts Supreme Judicial Court. Replying on July 11, Holmes suggested that Frankfurter pursue private practice rather than teaching law and believed he would get "more nourishment from economics than from criminal law." The only advantage to teaching was that it would protect Frankfurter's health and allow him to slow down. Finally, Holmes objected that "academic life is but half-life—it is a withdrawal from the fight in order to utter smart things that cost you nothing except the thinking them from a cloister."

No more receptive to Frankfurter's offer from Harvard than the others were, Valentine responded with silence. He may have been annoyed that Frankfurter had failed to join him on the campaign or in exploring the "center of the universe" in the industrial counseling business. Frankfurter suggested that one of the side benefits of a Harvard professorship was the ability to collaborate on future projects. After several months without any word, Frankfurter was "saddened by" Valentine's "loss of warmth." He hoped that living near Boston would rekindle their friendship.

The last person Frankfurter asked for advice was a 22-year-old Smith College graduate, Marion Denman. The daughter of a minister from Springfield, Massachusetts, she graduated Phi Beta Kappa and president of her 1912 Smith College class and was unhappily employed in New York City as a secretary at the Spence School. During an Easter break visit to Washington in 1913 to see one of her classmates, she was one of many young ladies who found themselves at Frankfurter's dinner parties. She impressed him and his friends with her intellect and beauty. Her high cheekbones, open face, and wide-set hazel eyes reminded Holmes of one of Bernardino Luini's Renaissance portraits; the justice nicknamed her Luina. At 5'7", she was at least an inch or two taller than Frankfurter. He broadened his reading beyond nonfiction to suit her literary tastes and finished Edith Wharton's novel *The Reef*. She was what he was not—a tall, beautiful WASP. In June 1913, Frankfurter began corresponding with Marion and could not stop. He took her into his counsel and his social world, introducing her to Robert and Sophie Valentine and law school classmate Stanley King and his wife, Gertrude. But when he asked whether he should accept the Harvard professorship, she angrily refused to answer because she thought she was unqualified to do so.

Only one person urged Frankfurter to accept Harvard's offer—Brandeis. Seeing the possibilities for him as a Harvard law professor, Brandeis knew there was no better place for Frankfurter to employ his yen for connecting people and eye for talent. Frankfurter could teach aspiring lawyers about James Bradley Thayer's judicial philosophy that courts should not overturn laws unless they are unconstitutional beyond a reasonable doubt, about John Marshall's expansive view of federal power, and about Holmes's willingness to allow states to experiment with labor legislation. He could inspire law students to be the next generation of leaders seeking social and economic reform, not by working at Wall Street law firms but in government. He could create a professional network exponentially bigger than his concentric circles of friends from Harvard Law School, the Southern District of New York, and Washington. Each year, Frankfurter could capture the hearts and minds of *Harvard Law Review* editors, transform their career aspirations, and build the liberal establishment.

On July 30, 1913, Frankfurter wrote the law school's dean, Ezra Thayer, and indicated his willingness to accept the offer. The only remaining question was how to raise money to endow the professorship. For months, Brandeis led the fundraising efforts. He pledged $1000 a year for five years and, with assistance from financier Eugene Meyer's brother Walter and Judge Julian Mack, secured $1000 pledges from philanthropist Julius Rosenwald, financiers Felix and Paul Warburg, and a wealthy Harvard law alumnus. Holmes and Hand also pledged $500. Ultimately, the funds became a nonissue because Professor Bruce Wyman was forced to resign. Wyman had failed to disclose he was on a $10,000 retainer from the J.P. Morgan–owned New Haven Railroad monopoly while testifying on the railroad's behalf before the Interstate Commerce Commission and employing his brother to testify before trade boards and other organizations. Wyman's loss was Frankfurter's gain.

Before Frankfurter joined the Harvard law faculty, another career opportunity arose thanks to his friendship with writer Herbert Croly. The author of a 1909 book, *The Promise of American Life,* Croly had been inspired by Roosevelt's idea of using a robust federal government to pursue economic and social reform. It was Croly who coined the phrase "New Nationalism." Roosevelt was profoundly influenced by Croly's book and adopted New Nationalism as a political slogan. Frankfurter described Croly as the "philosopher" of the progressive movement and considered *The Promise* to be its mission statement. The book sold only 7500 copies in Croly's lifetime but made him a star political philosopher and portrayed Roosevelt as a big-government social reformer.

A shy, diffident man with a partially receding hairline and a dour expression, Croly failed to find success until he published *The Promise* at age forty. The son of two New York City journalists, he had been neglected by his mother and doted on by his religious father. For nearly twelve years, he had unsuccessfully pursued a philosophy degree from Harvard College and worked as an editor of an architectural magazine. After publication of *The Promise,* Harvard awarded him an honorary degree. He and his wife lived in Cornish, New Hampshire, where he befriended one of the town's summer residents, Learned Hand. Hand, in turn, introduced Croly to Frankfurter.

In January 1913, Croly rented a small apartment on Connecticut Avenue not far from Frankfurter's House of Truth. Frankfurter introduced Croly to Valentine, Denison, and the house's other residents and guests. After a single dinner, the introverted Croly took an instant liking to the extroverted Frankfurter. "It was my first chance to get anywhere near him and I liked him thoroughly," Croly wrote Hand. "He is one of the most completely alive men whom I have ever met."

In December 1913, Croly was seeking editors and writers for a new magazine as an outlet for Roosevelt's New Nationalist ideas about government and social reform. As one of his first editors, he recruited 23-year-old political prodigy and author of *A Preface to Politics*, Walter Lippmann. The son of third-generation German Jews from New York City's Upper East Side, Lippmann thrived at Harvard as a philosophy major and budding Socialist. After graduating in 1910, he worked as an assistant for muckraking journalist Lincoln Steffens and wrote for several Socialist publications. His large, wide eyes, portly frame, and penchant for silence earned him the nickname "Buddha." He was as quiet and solemn as Croly, who pitched his new magazine as "radically progressive" but "not socialistic," a "weekly review of current political and social events and a discussion of the theories they involve," intended "to represent progressive principles but . . . independent of any party, or individual in politics." Croly was annoyed that Norman Hapgood had turned *Harper's Weekly* into a platform for Woodrow Wilson and envisioned a counterweight for Roosevelt. Croly's first two proposed names for the magazine, *The Nation* and *The Republic*, were taken; he settled for the *New Republic*.

With funding from J.P. Morgan banker Willard Straight and his banking heiress wife, Dorothy, Croly assembled a first-rate team of editors: the preternaturally talented Lippmann; trained economist and author Walter Weyl; former *Chicago Evening Post* literary supplement editor and Ireland native Francis Hackett; longtime friend from Cornish and author of a "Books and Things" column Philip Littell; and Vassar graduate and former associate editor at *Harper's* Charlotte Rudyard.

There was one editor missing from Croly's stable—Frankfurter. In January 1914, Croly invited Lippmann to lunch at the Harvard Club in New York City to meet Frankfurter. Lippmann and Frankfurter hit it off. Croly believed that Frankfurter's personality, peripatetic travels, and political bent made him better suited to journalism than to law. Recalling his frustrating years at Cambridge as a failed philosophy major, Croly urged Frankfurter to decline Harvard's offer and to join the magazine's editorial board full-time. "If I only had Felix too," Croly wrote Hand, "I should look forward to the approaching campaign with confidence."

There was no turning back for Frankfurter. On January 12, 1914, the Harvard Corporation appointed him professor of law, and on February 27 the Board of Overseers consented to the appointment. A few months later, the *Harvard Alumni Bulletin* published a glowing profile of him by his mentor Henry Stimson. "[T]he great changes worked in the modern state" Stimson wrote, required increased study of industrial legislation and administrative law. Frankfurter, Stimson declared, was the perfect person for the job. Stimson reviewed the details of Frankfurter's rapid rise from his arrival in New York in 1894 through City College, the Tenement House Department, Harvard Law School, the Southern District of New York, and as law officer in the Bureau of Insular Affairs in the War Department. "His industry has been indefatigable; his power of absorption apparently unlimited," Stimson wrote. "With a profound scholarship he combines what we so often miss in the scholar, a never-failing good sense and feeling of proportion. With it all he has what amounts to a veritable genius for sympathetic acquaintance and friendship among all types of classes of men."

Since Frankfurter's professorship did not begin until the fall of 1914, Croly pulled him into the magazine's planning stages. On April 9, Frankfurter attended a dinner for the magazine's "counsellors contributors and friends" at The Players club in New York City. Croly implored him to maintain ties to the publication. Later that month, Frankfurter was named one of the magazine's three incorporators. He declined, however, to be on the editorial board. Instead, he promised to write for the magazine and allowed Croly to list him as a contributor.

During the *New Republic's* start-up phase, Frankfurter's most important contribution was his relationship with Colonel Roosevelt. Roosevelt was telling people that Frankfurter was "the ablest man of your name and age in public life in this or any other country." In May, Frankfurter introduced Lippmann to Roosevelt so they could discuss labor issues. On April 20, the Colorado National Guard had fired on 1200 striking miners and had killed between nineteen and twenty-five people, including women and children; the workers responded with violent counterattacks on the Rockefeller-owned Fuel and Iron Corporation; and the United Mine Workers led a strike that lasted all year. Frankfurter and Lippmann met again with Roosevelt to discuss labor policy, including the new Clayton Act provisions recognizing the right of labor unions to organize and the right of workers to strike. With input from Frankfurter and Walter Weyl, Lippmann drafted a labor platform for Roosevelt calling for a decent standard of living for workers and representation by organized labor.

Roosevelt and Frankfurter continued to discuss labor issues throughout the summer of 1914. Frankfurter wrote the Colonel that the issue of labor unrest was so big and complex that it must be addressed in a comprehensive way. For Frankfurter, the solution lay with the federal government: "That means education of the public on a national scale and the development of powers of government, the invention of new administrative methods, to give effect to community needs." Unsatisfied with Lippmann's platform, the Colonel replied to Frankfurter that efforts to help labor would fail without an end to lawlessness and an emphasis on "the right behavior on the part of the labor men." They agreed to meet again after the November election.

On June 6, 1914, Frankfurter resigned from the War Department. He was the last of his housemates to leave Washington. Winfred Denison had departed in December 1913 to become secretary of the interior of the Philippines. After a late May 1914 dinner party at The Players club in his honor, Eustace Percy had returned home to Britain. During his final days in the House of Truth, Frankfurter reflected on the fond memories. "Three happy years are within a few minutes of being at end," he wrote to Robert and Sophie Valentine. "And yet what is it ends? Surely nothing of that which was permanent and significant in the vitality of life."

The House of Truth survived in name and reputation because Frankfurter had invited Holmes's secretary George Harrison and other friends to live there. Much to Frankfurter's relief, he left shortly after the house hit the society pages. "Did you ever hear of the 'House of Truth?'" a *Washington Times* gossip columnist wrote on May 24. "It is a brand new one on me, but it seems that several smart young bachelors have a house together, somewhere in Nineteenth street, to which they give that name and where they have the most wonderful parties. Felix Frankfurter is one of them . . ."

Soon after Frankfurter moved to Cambridge to prepare for his first semester of teaching, he heard the news in Boston's South Station that Archduke Franz Ferdinand and his wife had been assassinated in Sarajevo. Few people understood the ramifications of the June 28 assassination of the heir to the Austro-Hungarian Empire, but Frankfurter did. The Viennese immigrant predicted to friends there would be a war. The prospect of war soon changed Frankfurter's relationship with Roosevelt, the fortunes of the *New Republic*, and the future of the world. It would not be long before Frankfurter found himself back in Washington living at the House of Truth and working in the Wilson administration. But first, Harvard Law School became the new center of Frankfurter's universe.

CHAPTER 6

Not Brandeis's Fight, but Our Fight

During the summer of 1914, Frankfurter holed up in the stacks of Harvard Law School's library in the new Langdell Hall. The neoclassical building featured a row of marble Ionic columns, large windows allowing light into the second-floor reading room of the library, and seven stories of stacks. Frankfurter's goal was to read all the treatises and law reviews from the past eight years to catch up on the law and legal scholarship since his graduation. His move to Cambridge reunited him with Robert Valentine as they made the rounds visiting with industrial leaders and friends. They met Frederick W. Taylor, the industrial efficiency expert, in Kennebunkport, Maine, to discuss Taylor's opposition to organized labor and dined with Rose Schneiderman, the Socialist leader of the International Ladies' Garment Workers' Union. On July 4, they rode in Valentine's Ford to Beverly Farms to see Justice and Mrs. Holmes at their North Shore residence for the first of several times that summer. And in August, Theodore Roosevelt summoned Frankfurter and Valentine to lunch in New York City to discuss labor policy. But mostly, Frankfurter was "all in books."

When classes began on September 28, Frankfurter was "scared stiff" to stand in the front of the classroom before eager students. In the fall, he taught penal legislation and administration to graduate and third-year students. During the fall and spring, he taught public service companies (later called public utilities) to second-year students. The first half of the course focused on the law of common carriers and the second half on the legislation and decisions involving the Interstate Commerce Act. In the spring, he taught criminal law to first-year students. He enjoyed his colleagues; Dean Thayer, his former professor Joseph H. Beale, and fellow progressive Roscoe

Pound welcomed him to a "happy family." Dean Thayer privately groused that Frankfurter's grades of his criminal law students were "wild and eccentric." Frankfurter found teaching "exhilarating."

The real payoff was getting to know "those boys." By teaching two upper-level classes, Frankfurter ingratiated himself with second- and third-year *Harvard Law Review* editors. As a 31-year-old bachelor, he socialized with them and took interest in their personal lives and career aspirations. The third-year editors were a memorable group. Note editor Julius Amberg, a Colgate graduate from Grand Rapids, Michigan, finished first; Chauncey Belknap, a Princeton graduate tied for sixth in his law school class, had been tapped to clerk for Holmes; and *Review* president Robert Patterson, a Union College graduate from Great Falls, New York, was third in the class and its undisputed leader. The second-year class was even stronger. The next *Review* president, Gerard "Gerry" Henderson, finished with the highest average, an 85, of any student between 1915 and 1925. Frankfurter regarded Henderson as "the ablest man" in the law school during that time. Note editor Calvert Magruder, an Annapolis native and St. John's College graduate, was another strong student. Two years later, Frankfurter befriended two *Review* editors from Yale College, Dean Acheson and Archibald MacLeish. Many of Frankfurter's protégés (Henderson, Acheson, MacLeish) hailed from WASP families and had attended elite preparatory schools and Ivy League universities. Others (Amberg, Patterson) did not. What mattered was not their social standing but their brains, their ideas, and their future goals. Amberg, Patterson, Henderson, Acheson, MacLeish, and Magruder followed Frankfurter into public service, often with a nudge from their professor. He regaled them with stories about the House of Truth and his time in the War Department.

Some students felt left out of Frankfurter's star system. Adolf A. Berle, Jr., a twenty-year-old Harvard College graduate with a master's degree in economics and a member of a prominent Boston family, finished tied for twelfth in Henderson's class yet failed to make the *Review*. He never forgave Frankfurter for excluding him from the inner circle of elite students.

Frankfurter's charisma and easy connection to the students benefited him in the classroom. He usually taught in one of the new classrooms in the south wing of Langdell Hall with photographs of Holmes and other judicial heroes behind him. In later years, he was known for going so deeply into the facts, procedure, law, lawyers, and judges of a single case that students referred to his class as "the Case-a-Month Club." Often, whether it was criminal law, administrative law, or public utilities, he taught his Thayerian judicial philosophy, his belief in federal regulation of monopolies and protection of organized labor, and his idolatry of Holmes. Francis T. P. Plimpton, a student from the early 1920s, captured Frankfurter's class in verse:

> You Learn No Law in Public U
> That is its fascination —
> But Felix gives a point of view,
> And pleasant conversation.

Yet in 1915, extant student notes from his criminal law and public utilities classes reveal that he taught a lot of law. In public utilities, he considered the economic, social, administrative, and constitutional problems of increased railroad regulation. Frankfurter believed in treating utilities like other monopolies to maintain the proper balance between profits and the public good. He urged the establishment of a utilities bureau so states and municipalities could share information about utility regulation and prices. *The Independent*, a weekly magazine, praised his addition to the Harvard law faculty to deal with these "live questions" and described him as "an inspiring teacher."

During Christmas break, Frankfurter began assembling a casebook of statutes and decisions involving the Interstate Commerce Act. In 1887, Congress had passed the law creating the Interstate Commerce Commission (ICC) to regulate railroads and other common carriers and utilities. In 1910, Congress had created a new federal court, the Commerce Court, to review ICC decisions; the special court lasted only three years. The Federal Trade Commission, created in September 1914, promised more regulation of railroads and other utilities. And states and municipalities also passed laws regulating their utilities.

Throughout his first year of teaching, Frankfurter somehow found time to contribute to the *New Republic*. He assisted Lippmann with editing copy and often took the train to New York City for weekly editorial meetings. He accompanied Croly and Lippmann to Sagamore Hill to see the magazine's political inspiration, with Roosevelt talking so late into the night that at 2:00 a.m. Croly fell asleep. The magazine's first issue on November 7, 1914, hit newsstands with little fanfare and only 875 subscribers.

The war in Europe raised the magazine's profile and changed its relationship with the Colonel. In its first issue, the magazine defended Roosevelt's outrage over Germany's invasion of Belgium as consistent with U.S. neutrality. A month later in the *New York Times Magazine*, Roosevelt accused Wilson of embroiling the United States in "a futile and inglorious little war with Mexico" by seizing the port of Vera Cruz in an unsuccessful attempt to intercept a shipment of German weapons. The Colonel blamed Wilson for a host of atrocities committed by warring Mexican factions. A *New Republic* editorial criticized Roosevelt for striking "blindly and unfairly" at the president. Roosevelt never spoke with the editors again and referred to them as "three anemic gentiles and three international Jews."

The sinking of the *Lusitania* changed everything. On May 7, 1915, a German submarine torpedoed the British passenger ship, killing 1198 people aboard, including 123 Americans. Germany had warned Americans not to travel on British passenger ships carrying munitions. The *New Republic* resisted Roosevelt's calls for immediate entry into the war. Instead, the magazine called for the United States to maintain its "disinterested neutrality," to sympathize with the Allies, and to prepare for a war it hoped to avoid. The war was a boon for the magazine's circulation. By September, it sold 9000 copies per week.

During the summer of 1915, Frankfurter delivered a paper at the American Bar Association (ABA) annual convention in Salt Lake City. He was struck by the lack of support for the war west of the Allegheny Mountains. He informed Roosevelt, with whom he was still on good terms, about the people he had spoken with and how depressed he was about their "indifference" about the war and foreign affairs and their "antiquated belief" in isolationism. The American people, he observed, needed to be educated about the stakes of the war and the need for military preparedness. Roosevelt blamed the lack of support for war with Germany on European immigrants and the country's lack of military preparedness on Wilson. Frankfurter agreed on the problems but not on the causes. Roosevelt's break with the *New Republic* notwithstanding, the lines of communication between the Colonel and Frankfurter remained open.

In his American Bar Association address, Frankfurter focused on his domestic socioeconomic concerns and outlined a vision for lawyers and law schools during an age of industrial regulation. The modern state had been transformed by new laws, new regulatory bodies and commissions, and the new field of administrative law. These changes, Frankfurter declared, "demand new premises to fit the accumulation of new facts, from which to formulate new legal principles." It was all too easy for the ABA to dismiss Roosevelt's ideas about the recall of unpopular judicial decisions. Instead, Frankfurter urged judges to be more like Holmes by approaching the law pragmatically and, as Pound suggested, by adjusting legal principles to changing social and economic conditions. Frankfurter called on law schools to teach their students to view law not as a closed system but as an evolving science driven by the discovery of new facts and social realities: "We must show them the law as an instrument" and "as a vital agency for human betterment." Finally, he challenged the assembled lawyers to play a leading role in the country's economic and social transformation, to "find ways to reconcile order with progress," and to bring to the task "fresh thinking, disinterested courage, and vision."

The judicial hero of Frankfurter's ABA speech was Holmes. It did not matter to Frankfurter and his friends that Holmes thought little of the industrial regulation and labor legislation he repeatedly voted to uphold. It was enough that Holmes had adopted a Thayerian approach to judicial review by allowing the federal government and the states to experiment with socioeconomic regulation.

In January 1915, Holmes had dissented from the Court's decision in *Coppage v. Kansas* striking down a Kansas law outlawing yellow-dog contracts that forbade union membership as a condition of employment. The Court declared that the Kansas law violated the employers' and employees' "liberty of contract" under the Fourteenth Amendment's Due Process Clause and nullified similar laws in thirteen states and Puerto Rico. Alluding to his prior dissent from *Adair v. United States* invalidating a similar federal law, Holmes dispatched with the majority opinion in a single paragraph. The Kansas law, he wrote, was a reasonable means of establishing "equality of position between the parties in which liberty of contact begins. Whether in the long run it is wise for the workingmen to enact legislation of this sort is not my concern, but I am strongly of opinion that there is nothing in the Constitution of the United States to prevent it . . ."

Four months after his *Coppage* dissent, Holmes raised awareness about unfair criminal trials when he dissented from the Court's decision upholding the capital murder conviction of Leo Frank. A Jewish superintendent of an Atlanta, Georgia, pencil factory, Frank was convicted of murdering a fourteen-year-old white girl, Mary Phagan, on the basis of the dubious testimony of a black janitor and with an angry white mob outside the courthouse. Officials were so worried about the mob that they barred Frank from attending his sentencing. In dissent, Holmes argued that a mob-dominated criminal trial violated the Fourteenth Amendment's Due Process Clause. He would have reversed Frank's conviction and remanded the case for a new trial. Brandeis and Frankfurter, who may have seen a draft of Holmes's dissent, urged non-Jews to speak out about the case. A *New Republic* editorial, perhaps written by Frankfurter, urged the governor of Georgia to read Holmes's dissent and to pardon Frank. From his jail cell, Frank wrote a moving letter to Holmes thanking him for the dissent. "A man who could write to him so sensitively as Frank," Holmes told Frankfurter, "couldn't have raped and murdered a girl." After the governor commuted his sentence to life in prison, Frank was pulled from his cell and lynched by some of the most prominent citizens of Marietta, Georgia.

Frankfurter's campaign to portray Holmes as the Court's jurisprudential star was in full swing. A *New Republic* editorial praised Holmes's *Coppage* dissent as the opinion of "a judge who deals with things, not words, and who realizes that a document which is to rule a great people must in its very nature allow for a wide and growing field for experimentation." The epigraph of Frankfurter's Interstate Commerce Act casebook quoted Holmes on judging: "we only occasionally can reach an absolutely final and quantitative determination, because the worth of the competing social ends . . . cannot be reduced to [a] number accurately fixed. . . . But it is the essence of improvement that we should be as accurate as we can." In the April 1916 volume of the *Harvard Law Review* dedicated to Holmes on his seventy-fifth birthday, Frankfurter described Holmes's constitutional opinions as "brilliant birds pulled from the magician's sleeve. It is the delusive ease of great effort and great art."

Frankfurter began a new crusade on January 28, 1916, when Wilson shocked the U.S. Senate by nominating Louis Brandeis to the Supreme Court. There was no denying Brandeis's ability. In December 1914, he had defended Oregon's minimum-wage law before the Supreme Court; his argument was so spellbinding that the chief justice kept giving him more time to speak. Justice Joseph R. Lamar's death on January 2, 1916, had left the Court deadlocked. Brandeis was no sure thing to replace him, having made more than his share of enemies. He had fought the New Haven Railroad merger and other monopolies as the "people's lawyer." He also would be the first Jewish justice. His nomination united conservatives and anti-Semites. The U.S. senators from Massachusetts, Henry Cabot Lodge and John W. Weeks, deemed him "temperamentally unfit."

An overjoyed Frankfurter told friends he was ready for the fight and knew Brandeis's opponents all too well. He had already fought for Brandeis in 1915 when the Cosmos Club, a private club in Washington, had denied Brandeis membership because he was a social reformer and a Jew. Though not a member himself, Frankfurter wrote the club's admissions committee and argued that Brandeis should be welcomed into a club dedicated to men "who are distinguished in a learned profession or in public service." He portrayed Brandeis not only as a leader of the bar but also as a public servant and "one of the great figures in this country during the last decade." As proof, he listed Brandeis's accomplishments: the application of scientific management to railroad rates, gas utility regulation in Boston, a dispute resolution protocol to avoid strikes in the New York garment industry, the defense of state minimum-wage and maximum-hour laws, and the revolutionary Brandeis brief in *Muller v. Oregon* employing sociological data to defend a maximum-hour law for women. In the process, Frankfurter conceded, Brandeis "has offended and alienated good men and true." Such offense was "inevitable" from someone who "believes as uncompromisingly as does Mr. Brandeis." Brandeis belonged in the Cosmos Club, Frankfurter concluded, because he had dedicated his life to what mattered in Washington and to the club—"the spirit of service." Nearly two weeks later, the leader Brandeis had influenced most, President Woodrow Wilson, wrote the club that he held Brandeis in the "highest personal esteem" and urged his membership. Brandeis was admitted to the Cosmos Club; the Supreme Court, however, was another story. The opposition was fiercer, and the stakes were higher. In those days, nominees did not testify in their own defense. Brandeis designated his law partner, Edward F. McClennen, to provide the U.S. Senate with information and to testify if needed. The nominee worked behind the scenes. It took everything in Frankfurter's and Wilson's power to get Brandeis confirmed.

On January 28, Frankfurter wrote an unpublished letter to the conservative *Boston Evening Transcript* and objected to its editorial opposing Brandeis's confirmation as partisan and ignorant. A few days later, he solicited a *Boston Post* article from one of his favorite third-year law students, Shelton Hale. A former journalist with the *Philadelphia Public Ledger*, Hale was moonlighting in law school as a *Post* reporter. In a February 2 article, he polled the Harvard law faculty about Brandeis: Nine of the eleven professors supported the nomination; one abstained because of his long absence overseas; and one, Edward H. Warren, was opposed because of a decade-old dispute with Brandeis over Boston's street railway consolidation bill.

In the next issue of the *New Republic*, Frankfurter wrote an unsigned editorial that linked Brandeis's nomination to the ongoing debate about the role of the Supreme Court—whether the Court would permit economic regulation or strike it down in the name of individualism and laissez-faire economics. "One public benefit has already accrued from the nomination of Mr. Brandeis. It has started discussion of what the Supreme Court means in American life." The editorial busted the myth that the justices decide cases on the basis of "pure reason" without factoring in "the concerns of the community." The vacancy was of "nation-wide importance" because the Court was "the final authority" on the "problems of government" and "limitations of power." And the text of the Constitution resolved few of these thorny questions. To these issues, the editorial declared, Brandeis had "given his whole life" and brought "a mind of extraordinary power and insight." Brandeis, the editorial insisted, was "no doctrinaire. . . . The very processes of his mind are deliberate and judicial" in considering all the relevant data and factors before reaching a conclusion.

The *New Republic* took the lead in pushing for Brandeis's confirmation as a result of Frankfurter lobbying editor Walter Lippmann. On February 17, Lippmann attended a Senate subcommittee hearing on the allegations against Brandeis. After the hearing, two Brandeis allies, editor Norman Hapgood and lawyer George Rublee, explained the dismal media situation. No daily newspapers had taken up Brandeis's cause, and Hapgood's *Harper's Weekly* went to press too late. It was up to the *New Republic* to take charge. Frankfurter had been telling Lippmann that "the fight [is] not Brandeis's fight, but our fight. . . . the situation is peculiarly one that belongs to the *New Republic*, for it presents in its concreteness loyalty to the ideas and forces in our national life that we care about."

Agreeing to team up, Frankfurter and Lippmann met to discuss a plan of attack. They refused to make the nomination fight about anti-Semitism. "It is terribly important that no Jews should make the slightest peep about a race issue," Frankfurter wrote Judge Julian Mack on January 31. "You know as well as I do that the Jew in Brandeis has nothing to do, (I except negligible isolated individuals,) with the grounds of opposition." Issue by issue, Frankfurter refuted the charges against Brandeis with substantial help from the nominee himself.

The confirmation battle brought Frankfurter closer to Brandeis than ever before. During strategy sessions in February and March, Brandeis let down his guard. "The other night I had the most intimate personal talk I have ever had with Brandeis," Frankfurter wrote Lippmann. "He talked with the complete depth of impersonalness, and, as he himself said, 'I have never talked this way before to a soul.' He is anxious to tell in complete detail the forces and the purposes that have made and moved his life. He wants to tell it so that his own career may be of use 'to the young fellows' who come along." Frankfurter's passion to see Brandeis confirmed and Brandeis's willingness to open up cemented their "half brother, half son" relationship.

In a March 4 editorial, Frankfurter rebutted allegations that Brandeis had acted unethically as counsel and a director of the United Shoe Machinery Company. Brandeis had resigned as a director in 1907 after the company's president had refused to stop enforcing contracts, tying arrangements that compelled purchases of the company's machines to buy a single product. Several years later, the company acquired a competitor to maintain its dominance over the market. Brandeis advised another potential competitor how to draft legislation to prevent such monopolistic practices. In doing so, he claimed that he did not rely on his knowledge as a director, offered the legislative advice pro bono, and paid his law firm $25,000 to compensate his partners for his time. The charges against Brandeis started only after the company faced federal antitrust charges and Brandeis testified in favor of new legislation. "In good truth the Shoe Machinery case is proof," Frankfurter's editorial concluded, "perhaps more than any other event in his life, that Louis D. Brandeis is . . . possessed of an ardent and calm sense of justice which to him is truth in action." Brandeis's critics charged that the Shoe Machinery case was one of many instances where he had acted unethically and pointed to his role in dividing the family estate of his former law partner Samuel Warren. Frankfurter, however, learned that the estate controversy was sour grapes from one of Warren's disgruntled siblings.

The magazine's most effective editorials attacked Brandeis's opponents. A March 11 editorial exposed the fifty-one Boston Brahmins who had signed a petition opposing Brandeis's nomination because he lacked "judicial temperament and capacity" as the product of a single verdict by insular, narrow-minded WASP elites. One of Brandeis's law partners prepared a chart showing their overlapping social clubs and business interests: "Somerset Club," "Trustee or Banker," "State Street Office," "Back Bay Resident," and "Large Corporation Connection or Corporate Activities." *New Republic* publisher Willard Straight, a J.P. Morgan banker, refused to allow Croly to run the chart. Lippmann, however, wrote a devastating editorial dismissing the petition as the product of "group psychology" and describing Old Boston as "the most homogenous, self-centered and self-complacent community in the United States." A March 18 editorial blasted former president William Howard Taft, who had signed a petition along with five other past presidents of the American Bar Association, as "the last man qualified to express a judgment" because of the way Brandeis had exposed and humiliated him during the Ballinger-Pinchot affair for relying on a backdated memorandum to affirm Pinchot's dismissal. At the close of the subcommittee hearings a week later, the magazine addressed each issue raised by Brandeis's accusers and concluded the case "had collapsed by its own weight." On April 3, the subcommittee voted, 3–2, to send the nomination to the full committee.

A March 5 call from his family's Bronx home took Frankfurter away from the confirmation fight. The next day, his father, Leopold, died at age sixty-two of respiratory and heart failure after a weeklong battle with pneumonia. Two days later, he was buried in Mount Hebron Cemetery in Queens. Leopold was a dreamer and black sheep who imagined a better life for his family in

America, but he had difficulty supporting his family, and he died with $125 to his name. He was a social charmer who conveyed his gift for connecting with all types of people to his third son. He had lived long enough to see his son befriend Theodore Roosevelt, work for Stimson in the U.S. attorney's office and the War Department, and teach at Harvard Law School. Frankfurter had always been closer to his mother than to his father. In many ways, Stimson, Holmes, and Brandeis had supplanted Leopold as Frankfurter's surrogate father. Yet Frankfurter refused, unlike some of his siblings, to label his father a failure. "Yes, the world called him a failure—but it makes me have more respect for 'failures,' it makes me less interested in external standards . . . ," he wrote Emory Buckner. "If you had known him my 'queerness' would be explicable to you and you would know the source of much that you like in me."

FRANKFURTER WAS TOO BUSY to grieve for long. He was teaching public utilities and criminal law at Harvard; he was fighting for Brandeis's confirmation; and he was taking over Brandeis's defense of Oregon's minimum-wage and maximum-hour laws.

By 1916, Frankfurter had become an expert about the constitutionality of minimum-wage and maximum-hour laws. In the *Harvard Law Review*, he published an article, "Hours of Labor and Realism in Constitutional Law," summarizing all the cases decided by federal and state courts and explaining why the Massachusetts Supreme Judicial Court had invalidated a state law limiting railroad employees to nine hours of work during a ten-hour period. Frankfurter concluded that the Massachusetts case had been "inadequately" briefed and argued and that the Supreme Judicial Court had erred in concluding that *Lochner v. New York*, the 1905 U.S. Supreme Court decision invalidating a ten-hour law for bakers, "governed" the case. *Lochner's* "common understanding" about the health of workers had been "cut from under" by industrial experts who had studied the effects of working long hours. *Lochner*, moreover, had been superseded by the Supreme Court's 1908 opinion in *Muller v. Oregon* upholding a maximum-hour law for women. In that opinion, the Court relied on the sociological studies in Brandeis's brief that Frankfurter described as "epoch making."

Frankfurter followed Brandeis's strategy of emphasizing sociological studies to argue that the Oregon laws were reasonable and therefore did not violate the Fourteenth Amendment's Due Process Clause. On April 11, he returned to Washington and waited to be called for another round of Supreme Court argument about Oregon's law limiting all mill, factory, and manufacturing workers to ten hours per day with up to three hours paid overtime. In the meantime, he enjoyed living at the House of Truth and responding to Brandeis's opponents.

The chances of Brandeis's confirmation began to worry Frankfurter. He wrote a letter to the *Boston Evening Transcript* correcting its description of Brandeis, not Frankfurter, as the counsel of record in the Oregon cases and for failing to mention Brandeis's revolutionary sociological brief in *Muller v. Oregon.* Frankfurter was incensed that Harvard president A. Lawrence Lowell and Harvard alumnus and New York lawyer Austen G. Fox led the conservative opposition. In response, Frankfurter solicited supportive letters to the Senate Judiciary Committee from Roscoe Pound, the law school's new dean, and Charles W. Eliot, Harvard's esteemed former president. The conservative opposition retaliated by holding up Arthur Dehon Hill's appointment to the law faculty and taking aim at Frankfurter and Pound. Frankfurter believed that "poor Lowell would not have had either of us if the Brandeis incident had arisen before." It would not be the last time Frankfurter and Pound tangled with Lowell and Fox. "Brandeis," he wrote, "is simply paying the price for the rest of us."

As Frankfurter's concern about Brandeis's confirmation mounted in early May, the Wilson administration instructed Frankfurter and his friends at the *New Republic* to lay low. After weeks of inaction, the president wrote to Senate Judiciary Committee chairman Charles Culberson on May 5 questioning the "character and motives" of Brandeis's opponents and declared the nominee "exceptionally qualified." Frankfurter worried no longer. Wilson made Brandeis's nomination about party loyalty, lobbying recalcitrant Democratic senators himself. On May 24, the Judiciary Committee voted, 10–8, to send Brandeis's nomination to the Senate floor. A week later, the Senate voted to confirm Brandeis, 47–22.

Frankfurter's closest friend Valentine quipped that the end of the confirmation fight meant that "Felix's judgments are at last swinging back toward normal." Yet Frankfurter knew that the battle over the role of the Supreme Court in America's democratic system had only begun. "The Brandeis case is closed," a *New Republic* editorial concluded. "The country has been spared humiliation, and the authority of the Court has been immeasurably strengthened." The editorial warned that future nominees, some of them conservative, might be afforded the same treatment that Brandeis had received: "Mr. Brandeis's enemies have done more to drag the Supreme Court into politics than the most extreme radical."

The victory for Brandeis was a victory for Frankfurter and fellow progressives who considered the Court the biggest obstacle to social reform. They could count on two solid votes for judicial restraint based on two very different approaches. Holmes was a philosopher who believed in expansive federal power and refused to question the wisdom of federal or state socioeconomic legislation even if he did not agree with it. Brandeis preferred a factual, data-driven approach to show the reasonableness of labor laws and believed in the rights of workers and states as laboratories of experimentation. Friends from Boston since the 1880s, Holmes and Brandeis became allies on the Court.

In 1916, Holmes and Brandeis each granted Frankfurter power to select a graduating Harvard law student to work for a year as the justice's secretary or law clerk. A combination of grades, character, and suitability for the justice factored into Frankfurter's selections. Holmes did not use his secretaries for anything more than balancing his checkbook, listening to his stories, and engaging in stimulating conversation. For Holmes, Frankfurter selected Shelton Hale. Holmes approved: "The lad here calls himself a pacifist as well as a socialist and exhibits a thin and stubborn rationality. I find myself very fond of him . . ." Brandeis, by contrast, relied on his secretaries for extensive legal research and trips to the Library of Congress to find data to support his arguments. He also expected secretaries to comment on drafts of his opinions. For Brandeis, Frankfurter selected Calvert Magruder, note editor for the *Harvard Law Review* and tied for sixth in his class. Brandeis found Magruder to be "very helpful." Holmes and Brandeis kept asking Frankfurter for more law clerks. Frankfurter also selected clerks for Learned Hand, Hand's cousin Augustus, Julian Mack, and for a time Cardozo. With the responsibility of selecting graduating students for as many as five or six judges, Frankfurter institutionalized judicial clerkships. He transformed clerkships into valuable prizes and as a farm system for the legal academy and public service.

Together with Roscoe Pound, Frankfurter transformed Harvard Law School into a training ground for social reformers, and they believed they discovered an important ally in British political scientist Harold J. Laski. Frankfurter had met the young Socialist instructor in history at McGill University in 1915 at the insistence of journalist Norman Hapgood. "Everything that Hapgood said about his extraordinary qualities," Frankfurter wrote, "was verified within an hour." Bespectacled, small, thin, fond of three-piece suits, and "Oxford all over and under," Laski impressed Frankfurter with his intellect, wide-ranging knowledge, and tall tales (including a whopper about defeating an American tennis champion). With assistance from Frankfurter, Laski began writing book reviews for the *New Republic*. In July 1916, Frankfurter brought Laski to Beverly Farms and introduced him to Holmes and initiated some of the most remarkable correspondence in the history of British and American letters. Frankfurter raised money for a job for Laski as a Harvard instructor. In the fall of 1916, Laski taught government and political theory to Harvard undergraduates and, with Frankfurter's assistance, enrolled as a law student. Frankfurter and Pound envisioned Laski joining them on the faculty as a legal historian. "Poor President Lowell," Frankfurter wrote, "doesn't know what a rebel we concealed in the Trojan horse when we rolled Laski in."

During the summer and fall of 1916, Frankfurter turned his attention to the election and the prospect of choosing a wartime president. The previous January, he had been hoping that the Republican Party, realizing the error of its ways four years earlier, would nominate Theodore Roosevelt. His friends were not persuaded. "I am pretty well convinced that T.R. will not do . . . ," Lippmann wrote him. "After all, you and I have been banking on a theoretical Roosevelt, a potential Roosevelt, but not the Roosevelt who at this moment is actually at work." Frankfurter was open to voting for Republican nominee Charles Evans Hughes. He admired Hughes, who had resigned from the Supreme Court to challenge the incumbent Wilson, for his legal acumen and for his record as a reformer as governor of New York.

In the end, Frankfurter's choice between Wilson and Hughes proved to be difficult. Unenthusiastic about either candidate, he wrote a 24-page memorandum that he sent to close friends. Party affiliation made no difference to him because he had joined the Progressive Party in 1912 to vote for Roosevelt and because the Democratic and Republican Parties contained both liberal and conservative wings. In terms of personality, he liked Hughes more than the moralistic Wilson. He was torn about the issues. With domestic economic regulation, Frankfurter lauded Wilson for his legislative achievements: the Federal Reserve Board, the Federal Trade Commission, and the Shipping Board. Hughes, by contrast, merely proposed higher tariffs. And in the labor sphere, Frankfurter praised Wilson for the Keating-Owen Child Labor Act prohibiting the interstate shipment of goods made by child labor and the Adamson Act's eight-hour day plus overtime for interstate railroad workers. Hughes had opposed the Adamson Act. Overall, Frankfurter believed that Wilson was more willing than Hughes to recognize the rights of workers and better equipped to avoid wartime labor problems. As an administrator, Frankfurter favored Hughes over Wilson yet praised some of Wilson's more recent appointments. In foreign policy, Frankfurter credited Wilson with showing tremendous growth since his early blunders in Mexico. Wilson understood the need for military and industrial preparedness before entering the war and for an international League to Enforce Peace after the war was over. Switching to Hughes was too risky with the prospect of war looming. "Surely," Frankfurter wrote, "this is a case where the doctrine of not swapping horses in the middle of the stream has a very real application." Republican Party loyalty was not a good enough reason to vote for Hughes, especially with the parties in flux and no clear-cut liberal party. Hughes's campaign, consisting of support for higher tariffs and criticism of Wilson, disappointed Frankfurter. He liked Hughes more as a judge than as a candidate and therefore voted for Wilson.

The 1916 election was one of the closest in American history. Wilson went to bed thinking he had lost yet refused to concede until he saw the returns from the western states. The next day, he woke up to learn he had carried California by 4000 votes and therefore won the election. In August, Hughes had unintentionally snubbed California governor Hiram Johnson at a Long Beach hotel. The mistake may have cost Hughes the White House. The decision to run for president had already cost him his Supreme Court seat.

The Saturday after Election Day, Frankfurter took the train to New York City for a late-night dinner at Delmonico's restaurant with Robert Valentine. Since reinventing himself in 1913 as America's first industrial counselor, Valentine had become one of the nation's leading labor relations experts. He chaired the Massachusetts Minimum Wage Commission, replaced Brandeis on the arbitration board of the dispute resolution protocol to avoid labor disputes in the New York garment industry, and earned the reputation among labor and management as a problem solver. Frankfurter invited his law school friends Sam Rosensohn and Emory Buckner and Harvard psychiatrist and criminologist Herman Adler to join them. Around midnight, Valentine fell ill. They took him back to his hotel and called a doctor. There was nothing the doctor could do. The 44-year-old Valentine had suffered a massive heart attack. He fell asleep and never woke up.

"Poor Valentine died of heart failure after a gallant and cheering struggle," Frankfurter wired Brandeis at 3:44 a.m. Back in Boston, he sent Valentine's wife, Sophie, red roses with a note: "With love from House of Truth to our Founder." In arranging his friend's funeral, Frankfurter lived up to the nicknames that Robert and Sophie had bestowed on him: Mr. Fix It, Mr. Fix, or simply Fix. He wired Theodore Roosevelt and others, helped Sophie choose pallbearers, and rode with her to the funeral at Boston's Trinity Church.

"You will know when I say that the closest friend of my own years is gone," Frankfurter wrote Holmes the day of the funeral. He and Valentine had laid on the floor of the House of Truth in the summer of 1912 and had written their social program about how to improve the nation's industrial situation.

Valentine implemented the social program as an industrial counselor and forgave Frankfurter for not joining his venture. Frankfurter, in turn, encouraged Valentine and sent business his way. Living near each other in Boston brought them closer than ever.

In late January 1917, Frankfurter presided over a celebration of Valentine's life before more than 250 people at Boston's Faneuil Hall. "We have come to gather wisdom and strength and joy of life by sharing our devotion to Robert Valentine," he told the crowd. He praised Valentine as someone who "asked questions and relentlessly put them to the test. He was Socrates, Socrates in action." As a banker, MIT instructor, Indian Affairs commissioner, and industrial counselor, Valentine "not only sought, he not only found, he followed truth." Frankfurter admired Valentine's daring spirit. "Surely if ever a man did," he told the crowd, Valentine "thought under fire."

In countless ways, Frankfurter kept Valentine's memory alive. He wrote notes of encouragement to Valentine's widow, Sophie. He encouraged a friend of Valentine's to join the industrial counseling firm and continued to steer business its way. He wrote articles about Valentine for the *Harvard Alumni Bulletin* and the *Dictionary of American Biography*. "Valentine was a pioneer . . . ," Frankfurter wrote. "This permanence he achieved, and the triumphant marvel is that he should have been able to achieve it in so short a time. His work will go on . . ."

Inspired by Valentine, Frankfurter emerged as one of the nation's leading labor-management relations experts. He continued to advocate for the ideas in their social program—an eight-hour workday, fair minimum wage, the recognition of organized labor as the lawful representative of workers, and the use of scientific management to improve industrial efficiency. Whereas Valentine pursued those ideas as an industrial counselor, Frankfurter advocated for them as a lawyer defending state labor laws before the Supreme Court and as a civil servant. In Washington, Frankfurter helped build the industrial democracy that he and Valentine had always dreamed of.

—————

EIGHT DAYS AFTER Valentine's memorial service, Frankfurter returned to Washington to defend the constitutionality of Oregon's minimum-wage and maximum-hour laws. Brandeis had defended the minimum-wage law in December 1914, but the Supreme Court was deadlocked, 4–4, after Justice Lamar's death. Frankfurter had taken over the two cases, one challenging the minimum-wage law and another the maximum-hour law, after Brandeis's

nomination to the Court. In April 1916, Frankfurter had defended the maximum-hour law before the Court. When Hughes resigned to run for president, the Court held both cases over for yet another term. Wilson nominated
John Hessin Clarke, a progressive federal judge from Cleveland, as Hughes's
replacement; Clarke was confirmed on July 21.

The third argument almost never happened. Notified in October 1916
about another argument, Oregon's attorney general declined to come East
and asked for the cases to be submitted on the briefs. He never bothered
consulting his co-counsel for the National Consumers' League—Frankfurter.
Attempts to change the attorney general's mind failed. Frankfurter, therefore,
sprang into action. He wired Chief Justice Edward Douglass White, Jr., about
the need to "take the liberty of calling" on him at home the next morning at
10:00 a.m. Worried about showing up at the chief justice's doorstep, Frankfurter had no cause for concern. He chatted for a few minutes with the chief
justice about southern students at Harvard Law School and the effects of the
Civil War on the South before White asked why Frankfurter had come all
this way. Once Frankfurter explained the situation, the chief justice asked
whether it would resolve the problem if the Court denied the request to submit the cases on the briefs and to order another round of argument. Frankfurter said it would. The Court scheduled reargument of both Oregon laws
for late January.

Not expecting to argue the cases so soon after Valentine's death, Frankfurter had good reasons for wanting another argument. The constitutionality
of minimum-wage laws in eleven states and the future of maximum-hour
laws hung in the balance. He feared that the justices would dismiss his brief
of nearly 1000 pages of social science as a worthless mountain of statistics.
He wanted to explain the factual evidence to make the best possible case for
the reasonableness of the laws. Harold Laski and Winfred Denison helped
him with the briefs and to prepare for the argument.

In the first case, *Stettler v. O'Hara*, Frank Stettler, the owner of a Portland
box factory, and his 22-year-old employee, Elmira Simpson, challenged the
constitutionality of Oregon's minimum-wage law. A state industrial commission established a minimum wage for women factory workers at $8.64 per
week and limited their hours to nine per day and fifty-four per week. Simpson made $8 per week; Stettler paid some of his employees as little as $6
per week.

In the second case, *Bunting v. Oregon*, Frank Bunting, the operator of a
Lakeview flour mill, had been fined $50 because his employees had worked
thirteen hours in a day without overtime pay. Oregon's law limited men work-

ing in mills, factories, or manufacturing to ten hours of work per day plus three hours of paid overtime. In *Muller v. Oregon*, Brandeis had successfully defended a prior Oregon law limiting the hours women could work in sweatshops on the basis of physiological differences between women and men. The Oregon Supreme Court held that the law for male factory workers was different only in degree. Differences in degree, Frankfurter argued in the *Harvard Law Review*, should be up to legislators, not judges.

On the afternoon of January 18, 1917, in the Old Senate Chamber, Frankfurter rose to defend Oregon's minimum-wage law for women. The justices, *The Nation* reported, listened "intently" to "a small, dark, smooth-faced lawyer, mostly head, eyes, and glasses, who looked as if he might have stepped out of the sophomore classroom of a neighboring college." He was extremely patient with the eight justices present; the ninth, Brandeis, had disqualified himself. Frankfurter followed Brandeis's strategy by sticking to the facts laid out in the sociological studies selected by Josephine Goldmark of the National Consumers' League. Frankfurter suggested that the law was reasonable because "the facts relative to work and fatigue are before this court." Not everyone was receptive. Justice William R. Day, a little, balding man with a prominent, dark mustache, "snapped": "How are they before Court?" Frankfurter needed the vote of Day, a moderate who often voted to uphold these laws, to win. Frankfurter appealed to the practical effects of a minimum wage. He argued that it would inspire innovations by employers and improve the health and effort of employees. Finally, he said that if employers did not pay a living wage, the state and its taxpayers would be forced to pick up the slack.

The next morning, Frankfurter returned to defend the Oregon ten-hour law for industrial workers and received a rude reception from the Court's nastiest justice, James C. McReynolds. A racist and anti-Semite, McReynolds was Wilson's former attorney general and first Supreme Court nominee. Born in Kentucky and educated at the University of Virginia and University of Virginia Law School, he had made a name for himself in the Roosevelt Justice Department as a trustbuster and had prosecuted the American Tobacco Company in private practice. At the urging of presidential adviser Colonel Edward M. House, Wilson bypassed Brandeis as attorney general in favor of McReynolds. As attorney general, McReynolds continued his aggressive prosecution of illegal monopolies but was an unpopular member of the cabinet. His personality made him a liability, and his reputation as a trustbuster and ties to Colonel House landed McReynolds a seat on the Supreme Court.

McReynolds and Frankfurter had clashed several times before. During a March 1913 dinner at the House of Truth, they argued about whether the new attorney general should follow his predecessor's practice of hiring on the basis of merit rather than political patronage. "What you young gentlemen say is all very fine," McReynolds responded, "but I am afraid you don't see as I do the 96 members of the U.S. Senate all standing hungrily in your outer office." Frankfurter, a longtime believer in civil service reform, held his ground. "May I suggest, Mr. Attorney General," he told McReynolds, "that you let the 96 Senators block your vision of the 96 million citizens of the United States." The disagreement ended the dinner.

The balding, beak-nosed McReynolds looked like the bald eagle that hung high above the Supreme Court bench in the Old Senate Chamber. The previous day during the minimum-wage argument, McReynolds had leaned back in his chair, had read the other side's brief, and had ignored Frankfurter altogether. Still, Frankfurter knew to expect trouble from him. As Frankfurter again attempted to defend the ten-hour law for male industrial workers, McReynolds pounced. "Ten hours! Ten hours! Ten!" he asked. "Why not four?" Frankfurter walked closer to McReynolds at the far end of the bench and replied: "Your honor, if by chance I may make such a hypothesis, if your physician should find that you're eating too much meat, it isn't necessary for him to urge you to become a vegetarian." From the other side of the bench, Holmes said loud enough for everyone to hear: "Good for you."

Other, more neutral observers were impressed with Frankfurter's argument. He contended that Oregon should be allowed to experiment with ways to protect the health and safety of its workers as long as the laws were reasonable. He compared the laws with those of other states and countries. And he reviewed the wages and working conditions of women and children and scientific studies of fatigue in mills, factories, and manufacturing. "Mr. Frankfurter's argument before the Supreme Court last week was brilliant," *The Independent* wrote. "What is better, it was convincing."

Frankfurter, who had worn his favorite blue tie to the arguments, felt good about his performance. On April 9, 1917, the Court voted 5–3 to uphold the ten-hour law for industrial workers. It relied on the Oregon Supreme Court's determination that the law was not unreasonable on the basis of the industrial practices in other countries and states. The Court was divided 4–4 on the minimum-wage law for women and therefore allowed the Oregon Supreme Court's decision to stand. Brandeis's disqualification prevented Frankfurter from achieving two outright victories and from establishing the constitutionality of minimum-wage laws for good. Nonetheless, Frankfurter built on Brandeis's strategy of presenting social scientific evidence of the reasonableness of labor laws and struck a partial blow against *Lochner v. New York* and the idea of "liberty of contract." For Frankfurter, it was an article of faith that the Court had no business questioning economic regulations in the workplace.

―――――

DURING THE COURT'S DELIBERATION in the Oregon minimum-wage and maximum-hour cases, Frankfurter turned his attention to the looming war in Europe. In early February 1917, Germany had resumed its submarine warfare against American vessels. Wilson appeared before Congress on February 3 to announce that the United States had broken off relations with Germany. Frankfurter supported Wilson's call for "peace without victory" (though he disliked the phrase), freedom of the seas, and respect for the sovereignty of other nations. He was not troubled by isolationist objections in Congress and knew that Germany would eventually force Wilson's hand. On March 1, the American people learned about the Zimmermann telegram, a British-intercepted cable from Germany to Mexico proposing an alliance between Germany, Mexico, and Japan and promising Mexico the southwestern United States. On April 2, Wilson asked Congress to declare war against Germany with the goal of "making the world safe for democracy." Frankfurter knew the decision "could not have been otherwise."

The day Wilson requested a declaration of war, Frankfurter was in Washington for a meeting of the Advisory Committee on Labor of the National Council of Defense. A few weeks earlier, Samuel Gompers, the president of the American Federation of Labor (AFL), had invited him to join the labor committee. Frankfurter had been reluctant to cancel class at Harvard to attend the first meeting; the imminent declaration of war, however, changed his mind. At the April 2 meeting, he urged the committee not to make the same mistake as Great Britain by removing all labor standards and restrictions on wages and hours. Women, children, and unskilled workers would flood the labor market and create industrial chaos. The war was an opportunity to implement fair wages and maximum-hour laws, not remove them.

The committee heard Frankfurter's message loud and clear. Upon his return to Cambridge, he received a phone call from Wilson's secretary of war, Newton D. Baker, to come back to Washington. His country needed him.

CHAPTER 7

These Days We Are All Soldiers

On April 16, 1917, Frankfurter returned to Washington for a week "to see how much of an effective nuisance" he could be in persuading federal officials not to lift all minimum-wage and maximum-hour regulations for industrial workers. An impressed Secretary of War Newton D. Baker turned the weeklong tryout into a permanent stay. On April 22, Baker wired Harvard president A. Lawrence Lowell to request that Frankfurter remain in Washington "indefinitely" to work with the National Council of Defense. By the end of May, Baker named Frankfurter one of three confidential advisers.

The war offered Frankfurter the opportunity to show that the federal government could take the lead on economic and social reform. During his wartime service in the Wilson administration, he wielded federal power to limit the hours of industrial workers, to recognize the rights of labor unions, and to protect the civil liberties of conscientious objectors, union organizers, and unpopular criminal defendants. He objected to abuse of federal power to repress wartime dissenters and radical immigrants. All in all, the war increased his faith in the federal government.

Frankfurter's job in the War Department was to manage the country's industrial situation to avoid work stoppages, violent strikes, and lockouts, which could impede the war effort. He was the department's labor relations expert. He worked on other matters as well because, from his time as Stimson's law officer in the Bureau of Insular Affairs, he knew many of the generals. General Enoch Crowder, who was in charge of implementing the Selective Service Act of 1917, was a devoted colleague. In August 1916, Crowder had enlisted Frankfurter to be a major in the reserves of the Judge Advocate General's Corps to decide issues of military justice.

Frankfurter's boss, Newton D. Baker, was an unlikely choice to run the War Department. A progressive former mayor of Cleveland, Baker had no experience in the federal government or the military. Small and thin, he had been rejected for service in the Spanish-American War because of poor eyesight. His critics accused him of being a pacifist. His biggest job was to make good on his vow to draft a million men in a year's time. Of Baker's three confidential advisers, Frankfurter focused on labor, Harvard law school classmate Stanley King on industry, and Columbia University dean Frederick Keppel on personnel.

On Frankfurter's recommendation, Baker hired a fourth confidential assistant, *New Republic* editor Walter Lippmann. Twenty-seven, newly married, and draft eligible, Lippmann had begged Frankfurter to find him a War Department job. After their joint struggle to get Brandeis confirmed and their interventionist views about the war, Lippmann and Frankfurter were closer than at any other point in their lives. Lippmann and his wife, Faye, lived in a small second-floor bedroom, likely the top-floor crow's nest, at the House of Truth. Frankfurter went out of his way to make Faye feel comfortable as the only woman in the house.

With Valentine dead and Denison desperately trying to recover his sanity after a disastrous stint as the interior secretary of the Philippines, Frankfurter was the de facto leader of the House of Truth. Stanley King was already living there. Frankfurter's former roommate Eustace Percy returned to the British Embassy and to life at 1727 Nineteenth Street. The house, Frankfurter reported, was "as of old" with regulars urging him to throw "the old fashioned parties."

Of all the people who came through the house, the most impressive was the man who had figured out how to feed the starving people of Belgium, Herbert Hoover. A mining engineer and multimillionaire, Hoover had been living in London in 1914 when he established the Commission for Relief in Belgium. Three years later when the United States entered the war, President Wilson named Hoover the head of the U.S. Food Administration and tasked him with feeding the allies amid growing food shortages. Frankfurter admired Hoover and considered him "a truly great man." The admiration was mutual. A few weeks later, Hoover wanted to hire him. "I'd rather work with him than anyone I have seen in Government," Frankfurter wrote. "He is the biggest thing here." Hoover was doing for food relief what Frankfurter wanted to do for American labor by employing experts to solve social and economic problems.

In early June 1917, Henry Morgenthau, Sr., the former U.S. ambassador to the Ottoman Empire, selected Frankfurter for a secret mission. He had chosen Frankfurter after consulting with Brandeis and lobbying Baker and President Wilson. Frankfurter was reluctant to go; Morgenthau had a reputation as a blowhard and publicity hound. Nor did Frankfurter want to leave his advisory role on labor relations. The president, however, thanked Frankfurter for agreeing to go as if the matter were settled. Frankfurter had no choice but to say yes. His Harvard law colleague Arthur Dehon Hill had volunteered for the Red Cross in France. Several star former *Harvard Law Review* editors, including Robert Patterson and Chauncey Belknap, were serving as infantrymen in Europe. The president was Frankfurter's commander in chief, too. "These days we are all soldiers," he wrote Wilson. "As such I go obedient to the duty with which you have generously charged me." On June 18, Frankfurter wrote A. Lawrence Lowell informing the Harvard president of the need to leave the country for a secret mission with no certain return. Frankfurter refused to divulge the reason for the mission because he had been sworn to secrecy. The next day, the administration revealed the mission's public purpose: to travel to Egypt to monitor the Ottoman Empire's treatment of 2000 Jews in Palestine. The secret purpose was to negotiate a separate peace with the empire. Wilson administration officials were as doubtful as Frankfurter that Morgenthau could use his contacts in the empire to deliver on his promise of peace.

Before he left on the Morgenthau mission, Frankfurter opened his heart to Marion Denman. He had been writing and visiting the Smith College graduate ever since they had met in the spring of 1913 at the House of Truth. She had left her secretarial job at the Spence School for a similar one in New Jersey before enrolling in the New York School for Social Work. The rigors of social work had caused her to have a nervous breakdown, and she was recovering at a sanitarium in Saranac Lake, New York. Frankfurter encouraged her to focus on her health. Neither Felix nor Marion believed in religion. Yet the relationship between the minister's daughter and the Viennese Jew gave their families pause. After visiting Marion in Saranac Lake, Frankfurter insisted on updating her family in Springfield, Massachusetts. Dinner was awkward; it was apparent to Denman's family that he wanted to marry her. Before he left for Europe, he gave Marion a photograph so she would remember him. She gave him a letter he did not read until he boarded the ship. He reread it throughout the mission and kept it "as a talisman."

Unwilling to pin all his hopes for a successful diplomatic mission on Morgenthau, Frankfurter brought along Max Lowenthal. A Minneapolis native, son of Lithuanian Jewish immigrants, and 1912 Harvard law graduate tied for third in his class, Lowenthal fell in with Frankfurter while clerking for Judge Julian Mack. A member of the short-lived Commerce Court, Mack often brought Lowenthal to the House of Truth's dinner parties. After his clerkship (and marrying Mack's niece), Lowenthal worked for a Wall Street law firm during the day and for Frankfurter at night and on weekends. He compiled Frankfurter's first casebook on the Interstate Commerce Act, beginning a lifelong interest in railroad regulation. By 1914, like Brandeis, Mack, and Frankfurter, Lowenthal became active in the Zionist movement. Three years later, he closed his struggling New York law practice to join Frankfurter overseas to gather facts and to serve as a buffer from Morgenthau.

Frankfurter's worst fears about Morgenthau were realized. A New York real estate magnate and German Jew, Morgenthau was the former chairman of the Democratic Finance Committee and a Wilson campaign contributor. Frankfurter discovered after a few briefings from friends in the State Department that the former ambassador knew less about the Ottoman Empire than he did. Frankfurter grew so tired of Morgenthau that he tried to avoid him aboard the ship to neutral Spain.

Morgenthau's mission quickly fell apart. The former ambassador had been telling everyone about the mission's secret purpose and boasting that, on the basis of his personal relationships with Turkish rulers, he could negotiate a separate peace. At a July 4 and 5 meeting in Gibraltar, British representative Chaim Weizmann and French representative Colonel Ernest Weyl persuaded Morgenthau to abandon the mission. Weizmann was as dismissive of Morgenthau and his lack of knowledge and planning as Frankfurter had been. Bald with a dark Van Dyke beard, Weizmann was a biochemist and leader of the Zionist movement. He believed in the British government's ability to seize Palestine from the Turks and its promises to establish a Jewish homeland there. Frankfurter, who had been drawn into Zionist affairs by Brandeis, was impressed with Weizmann. One positive from the mission was the beginning of a long and fruitful relationship with the Zionist leader.

Frankfurter's role in the mission was now clear—to keep Morgenthau from jeopardizing the Zionist movement and from embarrassing the Wilson administration. They never made it to Egypt. Administration officials panicked when they learned that Morgenthau was misrepresenting the president's views and trying to negotiate a separate peace with the Ottoman Empire on his own. In Paris, Morgenthau arranged a meeting with General John J. Pershing, the commander in chief of the American Expeditionary

Forces in Europe, to propose attacking the empire. When Pershing asked if the former ambassador had any military maps, Morgenthau bought a pocket map from Brentano's bookstore. The administration aborted the mission and declared it a "fiasco."

With Morgenthau sidelined, Frankfurter's marching orders changed. The State Department asked him to report on the situation in France. For days, Frankfurter and Lowenthal gathered information in Paris and the French countryside and wired a detailed report while aboard the steamship *Espagne*. France's morale, the report stated, had been destroyed by 2 million casualties. The U.S. entry in the war had provided a boost, but the French people viewed a League to Enforce Peace as a utopian solution. Secretary of State Robert Lansing was impressed with the details in Frankfurter's report and with Frankfurter. "This morning I had an hour's talk with Frankfurter . . . ," Lansing wrote Wilson on August 13. "I believe that you should see him and hear the story." In mid-August, Frankfurter returned to Boston to brief "the real cabinet," the president's influential outside adviser, Colonel House. For several years now, Frankfurter and his colleagues at the *New Republic* had been conferring with House and considered him the administration's leading voice on foreign policy.

With his stock in the administration rising, Frankfurter thanked Brandeis for suggesting him for the mission. Frankfurter had proven his ability to go into the field, to assess the situation, and to write a detailed report. He had gained firsthand knowledge about the war from the perspectives of Britain and France and had made important Zionist contacts. He returned to Washington with "the sense of what the war is and the peace that ought to be is in my marrow."

Upon his return to the War Department, Frankfurter wrote Baker a memorandum urging him to treat conscientious objectors "in a judicial spirit." He proposed a three-person board to determine the honest conscientious objectors from the dishonest ones, and to place the honest conscientious objectors in nonmilitary service jobs such as in hospitals. Baker adopted Frankfurter's suggestion of a conscientious objector board to hear appeals and tapped Judge Mack to serve on it.

Before he unpacked his trunk from the aborted trip to Egypt, Frankfurter prepared for another extended mission. On September 1, 1917, Baker recommended him to President Wilson and Secretary of Labor William B. Wilson to join a commission to investigate labor unrest in the western United States. Although he was eager to join the investigation, Frankfurter was opposed to the idea of a formal commission because he thought it would attract too much publicity. He wrote a memorandum to Baker proposing a more low-key investigation. He also explained the differences within the labor movement: established union leaders such as Samuel Gompers of the AFL, the Socialist labor leaders in the IWW, and other non-IWW radicals who could be trusted and practical. After consulting with Brandeis, Frankfurter incorrectly believed that he had killed off a public commission. Instead, Baker sent Frankfurter's memorandum to President Wilson, praised Frankfurter as "a very thoroughgoing and thoughtful fellow," and recommended him as the secretary and counsel of the President's Mediation Commission.

With Lowenthal by his side as assistant secretary, Frankfurter joined the commission in Arizona to mediate copper mining strikes. The U.S. entry into the war had created a huge demand for copper wire for munitions. During the summer of 1917, the anti-war IWW and other radical unions had organized Arizona's copper miners and persuaded them to strike. The War Department refused to send in federal troops. Instead, the commission arrived in early October to negotiate settlements, and Frankfurter implemented Valentine's labor mediation techniques.

Labor mediation appealed to Frankfurter. He enjoyed seeing a new part of the country. He learned how strikes tore apart local communities. And he established a good working relationship with Secretary of Labor Wilson. A Scottish-born Pennsylvania miner and former international secretary-treasurer of the United Mine Workers, Wilson was often ill and delegated labor negotiations to his counsel. Frankfurter befriended commission member John H. Walker, the president of the Illinois Mine Workers; William Scarlett, a progressive Episcopal priest at an influential Phoenix church; and a Catholic priest from Denver, Father David T. O'Dwyer. " 'The Education of Mr. Felix' is certainly what my historian will call this year," Frankfurter self-consciously wrote Lippmann.

In Globe, Arizona, Frankfurter and other members of the commission heard testimony for sixteen days at the Dominion Hotel about the grievances of 5000 miners, many of them European immigrants, working in Globe and the nearby mining town of Miami. The grievances had less to do with wages and hours, he wrote, than "the men felt that they were not treated as men" and they had "no security of employment" and no way to mediate grievances. The only way the workers could express themselves was to strike. The mining companies had succeeded in portraying themselves as patriotic in their efforts to mine as much copper as possible for the war and the striking miners as unpatriotic. Allied leaders in Washington, London, and Paris were following the settlement negotiations.

Frankfurter relied on his friends to help him settle the strikes. Before he left Washington, he had met with Samuel Lewisohn, a former *Columbia Law Review* editor whose family owned Arizona copper mines and who offered him access to mine owners. Frankfurter also contacted his British house-mate, Eustace Percy, who helped persuade one of the last holdouts, the Scottish manager of a British-owned mining operation, to settle. And he stayed in constant contact with Stanley King in the War Department. Frankfurter and the commission settled the Globe strike on October 22, then headed for the mountainous mining town of Clifton to hear five days of testimony involving 5000 striking miners, most of them Mexican. On October 31, they settled the Clifton strike.

Having settled mining strikes, Frankfurter and the commission confronted one of its most controversial tasks—investigating the Bisbee deportation. Bisbee, Arizona, was a company mining town controlled by the Phelps-Dodge Company. The company owned the town's largest mine, largest hotel, hospital, department store, library, and newspaper. The IWW had supplanted more established unions and struck fear in the hearts of the company and townspeople. The IWW's demands were reasonable: improved conditions, no employment discrimination for belonging to a union, and $6 per day for underground work and $5.50 per day for aboveground work. Yet the mine owners refused to negotiate with the IWW or any other union. On June 26, the IWW called a district-wide strike. The strike was peaceful and after a few weeks seemed to be petering out. The mine owners, however, wanted to send a message. On the morning of July 12, the sheriff deputized a posse of 2000 armed men who rounded up 1186 striking miners in the local ballpark and loaded them onto boxcars like cattle. The miners were shipped to Columbus, New Mexico, three miles north of the Mexican border, and told never to return. The people of Columbus refused to take the miners, who were unloaded nineteen miles away in Hermanas. For two days, the miners had no food, water, or shelter. Federal troops arrived, escorted the miners back to Columbus, and housed them until mid-September in makeshift refugee camps. Most of the miners were immigrants; 472 of them had registered for the draft.

It was up to Frankfurter to write the report on the Bisbee deportation. After listening to several days of testimony, his assistant Max Lowenthal was so sickened by the way the striking miners had been herded off like livestock that he was ill in bed. At night, Frankfurter often walked up and down Bisbee with Father O'Dwyer discussing everything from Catholic theology to world politics. During the day, Frankfurter was a more active questioner than he had been earlier. At the end of five days of hearings, he sparred with Sheriff Harry C. Wheeler, the man who had deputized the townspeople and led the deportation. Membership in the IWW, Frankfurter told Wheeler, "is not a crime."

Frankfurter's report, dated November 6, 1917, declared the Bisbee deportation "wholly illegal and without authority in law, state or federal." The report recommended that all the deported miners be allowed to return to Bisbee, and it called for regulatory and criminal investigations by the Interstate Commerce Commission and the attorney general as well as new criminal laws making such deportations illegal.

Frankfurter knew his Bisbee report would be a bombshell. "I don't know whether [President] Wilson will stand for it," he wrote Brandeis from Bisbee's Copper Queen Hotel and enclosed a copy of the report. "Its only defense is its colorless mildness and understanding accuracy." No supporter of the radical IWW, Frankfurter blamed its rise on "the National Gov't, various state governments, capital, and the old line trade unionism of the A.F. of L."

From Bisbee, Frankfurter and the members of the commission boarded a private railroad car for San Francisco and waded into another public controversy, the murder trial of labor leader Tom Mooney. He had been convicted of orchestrating one of the worst terrorist attacks in the city's history. On July 22, 1916, the city of San Francisco held a Preparedness Day parade. A suitcase containing a pipe bomb exploded south of Market Street, killing ten people, wounding forty-one others, and blowing a little girl's legs off. The police initially suspected the bombing had been the work of anarchists. Instead, they arrested radical labor leader Tom Mooney and several of his associates and tried them for murder; Mooney was the only one sentenced to death. After the trial, the chief eyewitness against Mooney had been discovered to be a perjurer and did not testify in the subsequent trials of Mooney's alleged co-conspirators. The trial judge could not do anything because the case was on appeal to the California Supreme Court; the California Supreme Court lacked the jurisdiction to order a new trial because the perjury allegation was not in the trial record.

Before Frankfurter and the other commission members had left for Arizona, President Wilson had spoken with them at the White House. He charged them to look into the Mooney case because it had troubled their Russian and Italian allies. The president singled out Frankfurter, the commission's counsel, to lead the investigation. Frankfurter, who had been overseas on the Morgenthau mission, claimed he had never heard of the case and did not even know how to spell Mooney's last name. He discovered how controversial the case was. While the commission was in Arizona, he contacted several San Francisco lawyers he knew to obtain a copy of the record and to write him a memorandum to get him up to speed on the case. The lawyers made excuses why they could not do it. Frankfurter finally found a lawyer in George S. Arnold, a 1906 Yale law graduate and former counsel in the Ballinger-Pinchot case, to assist him. When the commission arrived in San Francisco after several months in Arizona, Frankfurter, Lowenthal, and Arnold began investigating Mooney's trial.

The California Supreme Court had not yet ruled, but Frankfurter had attended the justices' deliberations and knew the court would declare that it lacked jurisdiction to order a new trial. In November 1917, Frankfurter interviewed numerous people associated with the case and went to San Quentin Prison to see Mooney. The most helpful interview was with Archbishop Edward J. Hanna. The archbishop knew Mooney's family as parishioners, described Mooney as "a bad man," yet insisted that Mooney had not bombed the parade.

Frankfurter's report on the Mooney case recommended that President Wilson ask the governor of California to stay any execution pending the outcome of a new trial. "[T]he feeling of disquietude aroused by the case must be heeded, for if unchecked, it impairs the faith that our democracy protects the lowliest and even the unworthy against false accusation," the report said. "War is fought with moral as well as material resources." Not wanting the case to be used as Communist propaganda with Russian and Italian allies, President Wilson acted on the report's recommendations. Instead of seeking a new trial, Governor William D. Stephens commuted Mooney's sentence to life in prison. The controversy lingered, and Frankfurter was smack in the middle of it.

In San Francisco, Frankfurter worked all day and socialized into the night. In addition to the Mooney case, the commission was charged with settling the strike of telephone workers for the Pacific Telephone and Telegraph Company. The company executives, however, refused to negotiate with the union and insisted on meeting the commission in Seattle. The commission members, who were staying in San Francisco's Palace Hotel, waited until the telephone executives came to them. Finally, the executives arrived and wanted to meet in their room at 10:00 p.m. Frankfurter, who had returned from a night out, wanted to attend the first meeting in his dinner coat; Lowenthal begged him not to because it would make a negative first impression. Frankfurter replied that he already had three strikes against him—he was a professor, a lawyer, and a Jew—and could afford a fourth. It turned out that the company's lead counsel was a Harvard law graduate who saw eye to eye with Frankfurter. On November 22, they reached a settlement that averted a government takeover of the telephone company.

From San Francisco, the commission headed to Seattle to try to settle a lumber strike. Spruce was critical to the production of warplanes. The IWW-led strike was impeding the production of weapons that could change the course of the war. The lumber strike was one of the commission's few failures. Frankfurter blamed the unhelpful interventions of Secretary of War Baker and AFL president Gompers. There were more successes, however, than failures. The mere threat of a visit from the commission ended a street-car strike in St. Paul, Minnesota. On Christmas night, Frankfurter settled a Chicago meat-packing strike. A prolonged work stoppage would have crippled worldwide meat production. On the whole, the commission's intervention in labor disputes was a success.

Officially released in January 1918, the Bisbee deportation and Mooney reports caused Frankfurter more trouble than anything he had written to date because of a clash with his political hero Theodore Roosevelt. The U.S. entry into the war had left an isolated Roosevelt outside of the political and military arena. Wilson had rejected his request to command a separate army unit in Europe. Most of Roosevelt's progressive admirers had abandoned him. Frankfurter, nonetheless, tried to stay on good terms even when it was hard. On August 30, 1917, Roosevelt's office had contacted Frankfurter asking him and other "Americans of foreign blood, especially those of other than Anglo-Saxon origin" to sign a statement "to re-affirm their faith in the working of the American crucible." The next day, Frankfurter politely declined because he did not want to interfere with his War Department work. "You know how passionately American I have always been," he wired Roosevelt, "and I am more so than ever, if that is possible, since my trip abroad."

Frankfurter knew where Roosevelt stood on the Mooney case. In November 1917, opponents of an attempt to recall District Attorney Charles M. Fickert for his use of perjured testimony in the case had elicited a pro-Fickert letter from Roosevelt. The Colonel wrote Fickert declaring "the issue between you and your opponents is that between patriotism and anarchy, but I also feel that all who directly or indirectly assail you for any such reason should be promptly deprived of citizenship." Frankfurter, who had studied the record and interviewed numerous lawyers and witnesses, had wired Emory Buckner on November 20 and instructed him to relay a telegram to Roosevelt explaining that the issue of recalling Fickert "is in nowise one between patriotism and anarchy." Roosevelt had replied on December 19 with a three-page jeremiad charging Frankfurter with adopting "an attitude which seems to me to be fundamentally of Trotsky and the other Bolsheviki leaders in Russia; an attitude which may be fraught with mischief for the country." The Colonel praised the trial judge's conduct of the Mooney trial and described the recall effort against Fickert as not attributable "to any real or general feeling as to the alleged shortcomings on his part, but to what I can only call the Bolsheviki sentiment."

Roosevelt's anger also could be attributed to Frankfurter's report on the Bisbee deportation. The chief instigator of the deportation was Arizona mine operator John C. Greenway, one of Roosevelt's Rough Riders during the Spanish-American War. The Bisbee report, though not mentioning Greenway by name, was an indictment of one of Roosevelt's oldest friends. The Colonel was not amused: "Your report is as thoroughly misleading a document as could be written on the subject." Roosevelt accused Frankfurter of ignoring the obvious fact that "the I.W.W. is a criminal organization" and of "excusing men precisely like the Bolsheviki in Russia."

Frankfurter knew a report backing the IWW over Greenway would not sit well with the Colonel. He did not like the IWW any more than Roosevelt did but believed that the rule of law and fair procedures applied to all people, regardless of their unpopular political beliefs and affiliations. He tried to persuade Roosevelt that IWW membership was not a crime. After he returned from the West, Frankfurter wrote the Colonel a letter seeking common ground. Frankfurter agreed that "the effective prosecution of the war and the uncompromising adherence to the aims for which this war is pursued by us embody the true test of all judgment and action these days." Frankfurter, however, refused to sacrifice civil liberties and fair criminal trials in the name of patriotism and addressed their points of disagreement. The Fickert recall, as he wrote, was a complex local issue having nothing to do with anarchy and patriotism; the Mooney investigation was an attempt to prevent the case from being used as Communist propaganda with their Russian allies and was conducted "in a thoroughgoing, judicial, and if I may say so, sensible way"; finally, he chided Roosevelt for relying "on Jack Greenway's say-so" on the Bisbee deportation rather than "a trained and impartial investigator" seeking the truth. "Surely," Frankfurter concluded, "you must know what a great sadness it is for me to find disagreement between us on important issues. I speak from the heart. . . . You are one of the few great sources of national leadership and inspiration for national endeavor. I do not want to see that asset made ill use of." Roosevelt sent Frankfurter a short reply falsely claiming that "I cannot agree with you in your assumption that the I.W.W. is patriotic and is devoted to the purposes of the war and its prosecution." Of course, Frankfurter said no such thing. The Colonel agreed with him about the need for new approaches to industrial relations and to giving workers a voice, but not if it meant violence.

Roosevelt's December 19 "Bolsheviki" letter dogged Frankfurter for years. In August 1918, Roosevelt's brash daughter, Alice Roosevelt Longworth, was walking into a Washington dinner party with her husband, Representative Nicholas Longworth, at 10:00 p.m. as Frankfurter was leaving. Frankfurter went back inside and argued with her about the Bisbee deportation and the IWW until 2:00 a.m.; they departed as friends. Other episodes rarely ended amicably. In June 1919, the *Boston Herald* published Roosevelt's letter in full without including Frankfurter's response. It was the first of many times newspapers reprinted Roosevelt's letter to attack Frankfurter. A few years later, Solicitor General James M. Beck criticized the Mooney report in the *New Republic*. Frankfurter responded in kind and knew the report had raised public awareness about the unfairness of Mooney's trial and had led to the governor's decision to commute Mooney's sentence to life in prison (Mooney was pardoned in January 1939). It was not the last time that Frankfurter challenged the legal establishment about a high-profile murder trial—or the last time he would be portrayed as a dangerous radical.

DURING HIS THREE-MONTH ABSENCE from Washington, the political landscape had shifted and not in Frankfurter's favor. Walter Lippmann had left the War Department to return to New York City to join Colonel House's secret organization—the Inquiry—which was planning for the postwar peace negotiations. From the West, Frankfurter had asked Lippmann to put in a good word for him so that he could work for the Inquiry overseas. Frankfurter underestimated House's anti-Semitism. Wilson's confidential adviser had opposed Brandeis as attorney general or secretary of commerce and had been conveniently out of the country when Wilson nominated Brandeis for the Supreme Court. House hired Lippmann despite his Jewish background because unlike other Jews he was "a silent one." Instead of simply rejecting Frankfurter, House damaged his reputation with President Wilson by accusing Frankfurter of leaking stories about the Inquiry to William C. Bullitt of the Philadelphia *Public Ledger*. Frankfurter was friendly with Bullitt and his wife, Ernesta. Yet, given Frankfurter's absence out West, the likely sources were House, who had been in frequent contact with Bullitt and his *Public*

Ledger colleague Lincoln Colcord, or Lippmann, who was also friends with Bullitt. Lippmann failed, at Frankfurter's behest, to clear his friend's name. After he returned from the West, Frankfurter wired House and asked for an in-person meeting. In January 1918, he insisted that he had not breathed a word of the Inquiry to Bullitt. Frankfurter never joined the organization but returned in good standing to the administration.

Back in Washington, Frankfurter urged his boss to reorganize the War Department. He knew based on Baker's unhelpful interventions in the lumber strike that the secretary of war was trying to do three jobs instead of one—running the army, managing war-related industries and munitions, and establishing labor policy. In a January 7 confidential memorandum, "Necessary Reorganization of the Functions Exercised by the Secretary of War," he urged Baker to preempt his January 28 congressional testimony and to propose the consolidation of agencies and the appointment of heads of war-related industries/munitions and labor relations while retaining control of the military. He also suggested a single Central Intelligence Office, a single Shipping Board for the transportation needs of the War and Munitions Departments, and a small war council "freed from the detail of administration and of executive responsibility." Frankfurter shared a copy of the memorandum with Colonel House, who claimed that "Baker was rather dumbfounded at the audacity of it." Yet House agreed to speak with the president after receiving a short note from Brandeis concurring with Frankfurter's assessment.

House and Baker could not have been too upset with Frankfurter because they tapped him for another overseas assignment. On January 27, 1918, Baker asked Frankfurter to study British and French mechanisms for settling labor disputes and to explore a confidential side issue with Zionist leaders. Three days later, Frankfurter boarded a train for Boston to see Colonel House, who had recommended him for the assignment. The next day, Frankfurter sailed from New York and arrived in London on February 8 to air raid sirens. During his eighteen days there, thanks to Eustace Percy and Harold Laski, he spoke with members of all three political parties, the radical right and radical left, and Prime Minister David Lloyd George. In Paris, he kept up his frenetic pace and felt "a little bit more vividly that it is liberty we are fighting for."

Frankfurter hoped that America could learn from its past labor struggles and from Europe's. On March 24, while aboard the USS *America*, he submitted a sixteen-page report to House explaining that the dissatisfaction of British and French workers was unrelated to workplace conditions. Rather, they distrusted their own governments and looked to Wilson for leadership and to chart a more democratic postwar future. "The ascendency of President

Wilson among the great masses of both England and France is all pervading," Frankfurter wrote House. Yet Frankfurter argued that the United States was not using its goodwill to its advantage and blamed diplomats to those countries. Walter Hines Page, the U.S. ambassador to Britain, wondered why the War Department had sent over "the 'hot dog of war'" and "[t]his little Jew." Not impressed with Page, Frankfurter recommended that the president station people in London and Paris who could convey the administration's policies. On March 27, Frankfurter reported in person to House. The confidential side issue, meeting with Zionists about the British commitment to a Jewish homeland in Palestine, stayed confidential.

Back home, Frankfurter facilitated the wartime employment of his longtime romantic interest, Marion Denman. During the past few years, Marion's health had improved. She had worked as a suffragist in Lyme, Connecticut, with Frankfurter's friend Katharine Ludington but did not take to the cause. The 27-year-old Marion wanted to do her part for the war effort and, if possible, come to Washington. Frankfurter found a job for Marion's sister Helen as a confidential clerk to his War Department colleague Frederick Keppel. And he found Marion a job as a special assistant to another War Department colleague, Raymond Fosdick. The chair of the Commission on Training Camp Activities, Fosdick was in charge of the health and recreation of American troops at home and abroad.

Six weeks after Felix returned home from Europe, it was Marion's turn to travel. She agreed to join Fosdick in Britain and France to study women workers in military camps. Her passport listed her as a social worker. Before she left for Europe, Felix and Marion spent their last night together in New York City taking a horse-drawn carriage ride around Central Park. He proposed; she accepted. They knew their families opposed the union and decided to keep the engagement secret. The next morning on May 7, she boarded the steamship *Espagne* on the French Line for Paris and dashed off a letter to her fiancé: "I want you to know while I'm gone that I love you with all of me, know it every day afresh, be happy in it & sure of it, and work & play hard until I arrive back—to you." She signed it "L," for Luina, Holmes and Frankfurter's nickname for her.

Shortly after Marion left for France, the U.S. Navy requested that daily newspapers stop publishing ship departures and arrivals. The *Espagne* zigzagged across the Atlantic Ocean to avoid lurking German submarines. Felix learned that Marion had arrived safely. She accompanied Fosdick to the Western Front to study the health and recreation provided by nonmilitary organizations including the Red Cross. They also traveled to Britain to study Naval

training camp activities. Marion saw the wounded and maimed soldiers that
her husband had heard about only secondhand. Frankfurter worried that he
would never see her again: "This is a hello and a wonderment if you're not
ever coming back. Not ever. It's good I have a 48 hours [a] day job."

Frankfurter had been swamped since President Wilson and Secretary
Baker acted on his suggestions and reorganized the War Department. Wilson named financier Bernard Baruch to head the War Industries Board to
supervise production. The president agreed to establish a war cabinet. And
he created the National War Labor Board, chaired by former President Taft
representing industry and Kansas City lawyer Frank Walsh representing
labor, to settle labor disputes. Frankfurter and other administration officials wanted a director general of labor to establish labor policy for wartime
workers and lobbied for the perfect person in Brandeis. Wilson, however,
refused to take Brandeis away from his judicial duties. Instead, the president
created the War Labor Policies Board and named as its chair the 35-year-
old Frankfurter.

The press praised Frankfurter's appointment. A *New York Times Magazine* headline described him as "Uniting the Labor Army on a Single War
Front." Lippmann declared that Frankfurter knew more about labor policy
than anyone except Brandeis. The *New Republic* reviewed his experience as
a federal prosecutor, law professor, and labor mediator; then added that "his
chief qualification is that he has been able to win his way into the esteem and
confidence of the men with whom he is now associated, men preeminently
representative of business, the professions and labor."

Nominally reporting to Secretary of Labor Wilson as one of his assistant
secretaries, Frankfurter aimed to prevent wartime labor shortages by coordi-
nating the labor needs of the War Department, the U.S. Navy, the Department
of Agriculture, the Shipping Board, the Railroad Administration, the War
Industries Board, the Aircraft Board, and the Council of National Defense.
Each of these departments would be represented on the War Labor Policies
Board. "Since the outbreak of the war the United States government has come
to be the greatest single employer of labor in the country," Frankfurter said in
his first public statement. "But it has had no operating policy with regard to
the plants as a whole. Each one has been operated individually as a separate
enterprise, quite apart from the others and, so far as the labor supply has been
concerned, in actual competition with the others."

The War Labor Policies Board allowed Frankfurter to use the federal administrative state to protect child labor, establish minimum wages, and limit
industrial workers to eight-hour days. Using his authority to standardize war-

time hiring practices, he implemented many of these ideas through new regulations and policies and circumvented reactionary Supreme Court decisions.

On June 3, the Court struck down the 1916 Keating-Owen Child Labor Act, which prohibited the interstate shipment of goods made by children under fourteen and by children between fourteen and sixteen who had worked more than eight hours a day, overnight, or more than six days a week. Roland Dagenhart, who worked in a Charlotte, North Carolina, cotton mill with his sons, Reuben, fourteen, and John, twelve, challenged the law on their behalf—and at the instigation of the company that owned the mill. In a 5–4 decision in *Hammer v. Dagenhart*, the Court agreed with the Dagenharts that the law exceeded Congress's power to regulate interstate commerce and infringed on the power of the states because manufacturing was a purely local activity. And, unlike federal bans on the interstate shipment of harmful goods, the goods themselves were harmless.

At Brandeis's urging, Holmes wrote a dissent on behalf of four justices and declared it impossible to distinguish between federal laws banning the interstate sale of alcohol, production of oleomargarine, and the transportation of lottery tickets—all found to be constitutional—and a federal law banning the transportation of goods made by child labor. Holmes also recognized the collective-action problem of relying on the states to regulate child labor: "The national welfare as understood by Congress may require a different attitude within its sphere from that of some self-seeking State. It seems to me entirely constitutional for Congress to enforce its understanding by all the means at its command."

Within six weeks of the Court's decision, Frankfurter and the War Labor Policies Board adopted a resolution on July 12 inserting the same prohibition of child labor in all government contracts. The child labor ban was one of many provisions the board drafted and implemented to create fair labor standards for all war industry employees. The representatives from the other agencies on the board signed off on the new contractual provisions.

To assist him on the board, Frankfurter relied on his indispensable network from Harvard Law School and the House of Truth. Max Lowenthal served as his full-time assistant. His law school roommate Sam Rosensohn drafted pro-labor contractual language. Two of Valentine's friends, former New Hampshire governor Robert Bass and Boston lawyer John Palfrey, represented the Shipping Board. Frankfurter's former research assistant, Herbert B. Ehrmann, assisted them.

During board meetings, the most interesting person Frankfurter worked with was Assistant Secretary of the Navy Franklin Roosevelt. They were born the same year—Roosevelt on January 30, 1882, in Hyde Park, New York, and Frankfurter on November 15 in Vienna, Austria. They knew each other as young lawyers entering Wall Street law practice. During several lunches or dinners at the Harvard Club in 1906 and 1907, Frankfurter thought Roosevelt was a "friendly fellow." Six years later when Frankfurter stayed in the Wilson administration to help Secretary of War Garrison with water-power legislation and Roosevelt was named assistant secretary of the navy, they worked on the same floor of the State, War, and Navy Building (the Executive Office Building) and often said hello to each other. Thus, they were already on a first-name basis when Roosevelt joined the board as the naval representative.

Tall and slender with a long, thin face, deep-set eyes, prominent chin, and full head of dark hair, Roosevelt cut a dashing figure. The 6'2" fifth cousin of Theodore and the 5'5" Frankfurter made an odd but effective pair. They respected each other's abilities and believed in using the power of federal administrative agencies to make labor policy. Roosevelt attended only three of the board's meetings but made a lasting impression. Frankfurter and Roosevelt began discussing labor policy almost daily by phone. In October 1918, after Franklin had brought Felix home for lunch, Franklin's wife, Eleanor, described Felix to her mother-in-law: "An interesting little man but very Jew."

The Roosevelts rented a mansion a few blocks from 1727 Nineteenth Street. The House of Truth was a lively source of administration gossip. Major Édouard Réquin of the French High Commission to the United States laid out maps on the dining room table and explained the fighting on the Western Front. Another prominent insider, Bernard Baruch of the War Industries Board, also dined there. Yet Roosevelt and his wife never attended one of the house's dinner parties. At the time, Roosevelt was having an affair with Eleanor's social secretary, Lucy Mercer. Eleanor learned about the affair in September 1918 after unpacking her husband's suitcase upon his return from Britain with a case of double pneumonia. She vowed to divorce him unless he ended the affair; he stopped seeing Lucy Mercer—for the time being.

Frankfurter was keeping a romantic secret of his own, his engagement to Marion Denman. On July 12, Marion left Brest, France, on the USS *Von Steuben* and arrived in New York City nine days later. Her sister Helen greeted her at the gangplank. The first words out of Marion's mouth were: "You know I am going to marry Felix." Felix and Marion did not tell another soul for a year. Eight weeks in Europe had taken its toll on Marion's physical and mental health. In 1918, an influenza pandemic swept a world at war. Marion, who had been in contact with soldiers in Europe, felt her health begin to fail. A chest X-ray revealed an old lung infection but no signs of flu or tuberculosis. She recovered at her parents' home in Springfield, Massachusetts, drinking a quart of milk a day, napping, and taking long walks.

Marion's intelligence, especially her research and writing ability, was never in doubt. She returned to Washington to finish her report on women workers at military camps. She was no mere administrative assistant to her boss, Raymond Fosdick. He valued her work and wanted her report on women workers to get "wide publicity." For the next two years, after she left Washington, she remained on the War Department payroll and wrote a history of the Commission on Training Camp Activities. It was the last meaningful employment of her life. She became completely invested in the aspirations and social world of her secret fiancé.

As chair of the War Labor Policies Board, Frankfurter fought for one policy goal above all others—the eight-hour workday. He had included it in the President's Mediation Commission report. The issue had been a rallying cry during the 1916 presidential campaign, with Wilson in favor and Hughes opposed. When the United States entered the war, Wilson issued an executive order suspending the eight-hour day for government and government-related workers in favor of a basic eight-hour day—eight hours plus time and a half for overtime pay. Different agencies and different factories, citing exceptions in prior laws, adopted different policies.

With broad powers during wartime, Frankfurter was determined to get war-related industries to adopt a basic eight-hour day. On June 28, the board adopted a resolution inserting a basic eight-hour day provision into all government contracts, vowing to enforce the provision where the law permitted, and attempting to extend its enforcement to private industry through conference and mutual agreement.

The board's basic eight-hour-day resolution ruffled the feathers of the co-chairs of the National War Labor Board charged with mediating labor disputes, former president William Howard Taft and Frank Walsh. They believed that the War Labor Policies Board was usurping their authority and rejected invitations to sit on Frankfurter's board. During one of his board's early executive sessions, Taft said: "Mr. Frankfurter is like a good Chancellor, he wants to amplify his jurisdiction and he is very anxious to be able to say that this Board is under him." Taft and Walsh rejected the notion that they were bound by Frankfurter's resolutions. Recalling Frankfurter's tortured service in his administration while supporting Roosevelt, Taft resorted to personal attacks: "My only experience with the gentleman whom we have been discussing from what I have heard is that if we just keep away he will tie himself up. There is no trouble about that."

For his part, Frankfurter was diplomatic with Taft and Walsh in his correspondence and during meetings. He tried to mollify their concerns about inserting the basic eight-hour-day provision into government Readjustment Boards. Taft was opposed to the provision because it went too far; Walsh was opposed because it did not go far enough toward a true eight-hour day (without additional hours of paid overtime). Frankfurter played them against each other. "I did a nifty job with Walsh today," he wrote, "by getting the big fat Taft boy (who is dull & honest so that Walsh usually 'plays' him but today I was around &—it was fun.) on my side." Taft and Walsh challenged Frankfurter to name a single private industry that had voluntarily adopted the basic eight-hour day.

Unbeknownst to Taft and Walsh, Frankfurter had been engaging for months with the leading private sector opponent of the basic eight-hour day, U.S. Steel chairman Elbert Gary. Even with his company earning record profits during the war, Gary opposed the basic eight-hour day because he feared it would become standard practice. At the suggestion of Gary's partner Charles M. Schwab of the U.S. Shipping Board, Frankfurter invited Gary to assemble a group of industry experts to discuss the issue. Ten days later, Gary replied that he would put a committee together but only if Frankfurter came to Gary's office in New York City. Frankfurter refused and suggested dates for Gary to come to Washington "to discuss our common problem." He kept following up with the steel magnate for months but received no response. Finally, on September 17, he wired Gary about the need for a meeting with no response. Two days later, he threatened to make their correspondence public.

The next day at 9:15 a.m., Gary and a colleague arrived at Frankfurter's office at the Slidell House across Lafayette Park from the White House. Frankfurter did not prepare any remarks. Instead, he engaged Gary in conversation. Gary declared the basic eight-hour day "a sham" because the time and a half for overtime was essentially "a wage increase under false pretences." Frankfurter countered that a basic eight-hour day was a way to transition industry to a true eight-hour day. That was impossible, Gary replied, given wartime labor shortages. Frankfurter said that it sounded like Gary had already made up his mind. The problem was that some government and government-contract employees worked eight-hour days, but others did not. He pressed Gary for a solution, but the steel magnate offered nothing but opposition. At Gary's steel mills, industrial workers toiled for ten hours a day at forty-two cents an hour. Frankfurter observed that Henry Ford had adopted a basic eight-hour day at his manufacturing plants and that the decisions of the National War Labor Board would continue the trend. As he rose to leave, Gary remarked: "Professor Frankfurter, you work more than eight hours every day." The steel magnate indicated that he worked more than eight hours in a day and that factory workers should, too. "Ah, Judge Gary," Frankfurter replied, "but think what interesting jobs you and I have."

After the meeting, Frankfurter wrote a memorandum to Secretary of Labor Wilson and Bernard Baruch summarizing the conversation as well as a conciliatory letter to Gary. Five days later, U.S. Steel announced it would adopt the basic eight-hour day on October 1. Frankfurter wired Secretary Wilson and exulted over the "really big achievement" and predicted "its immediate significance as well as in its implications for the days beyond." Frankfurter's pragmatism, which he learned from Brandeis and Valentine, carried the day. He advocated for a basic eight-hour day during the war rather than a true eight-hour day. He also did not try to enforce it across the board but only in industries where it was feasible. He knew that the basic eight-hour day was "honored more in breach than in observance." The principle, however, was what mattered. He envisioned a future economy with the eight-hour workday as standard practice.

As triumphant as Frankfurter was about U.S. Steel's adoption of a basic eight-hour day, the War Labor Policies Board failed as often as it succeeded. It took months to formulate new policies after receiving input from labor and management, and it was nearly impossible to enforce them. The board did not consider regulations for nighttime work for women until mid-September and did not adopt them for another two months. By that time, the Great War was over. On November 11, 1918, Germany and the Central powers surrendered.

During the war, Frankfurter used the federal administrative state to protect the rights of conscientious objectors, the IWW and its members, mine workers illegally deported from Bisbee, Arizona, and radical labor leader Tom Mooney convicted of murder on the basis of perjured testimony. He mediated labor disputes and fought for shorter hours, fair wages, and humane conditions for wartime workers. In the War Department, the President's Mediation Commission, and the War Labor Policies Board, he saw the possibilities of the federal government as a protector of civil liberties and leader of social and economic reform. The Wilson administration was far from perfect, with its wartime suppression of free speech and racial segregation of several government agencies, but it regulated the economy in many innovative ways.

Theodore Roosevelt had been the political leader who initially inspired Frankfurter to use federal power to protect the rights of working men, women, and children. On January 6, 1919, at Sagamore Hill, the Colonel died of a pulmonary embolism at age sixty. He had accomplished so much as president and inspired so many to enter politics. By the end of the war, he was a sad, jingoistic reactionary, a far cry from the inspiring, third-party presidential candidate of 1912. The *New Republic* quoted Roosevelt's "I'm a warrior and not a prophet" and opined: "He was a warrior on behalf of what he believed to be and usually were morally decisive causes. The most poignant tragedy of his life was that he was unable to fight sword in hand in the war which raised one of the clearest and greatest moral issues in history." The war had cost him dearly. His youngest son, Quentin, had been killed on July 14, 1918, during a bombing mission over France.

Roosevelt's vicious attacks on the Mooney and Bisbee reports had not shaken Frankfurter's faith in him. On August 27, 1918, Frankfurter had contacted the Colonel to request a meeting to discuss the impending peace talks. With the world at a crossroads, Frankfurter believed that the country needed Roosevelt's leadership. There is no record of a response. Frankfurter remained loyal to the Colonel until the end; Theodore Roosevelt was the first American president who believed in him and would not be the last.

Just as he never abandoned Roosevelt, Frankfurter never fully bought into the Wilson administration. He was "pessimistic" about the impending peace conference and warned Lippmann about "reactionary forces" dominating the American political scene. On February 8, Frankfurter resigned as assistant secretary of labor and chairman of the War Labor Policies Board. The Zionist movement needed him in Paris.

CHAPTER 8

Personalia in Paris

Most of Frankfurter's friends attended the Paris Peace Conference to help their respective governments negotiate a peace treaty and to create a new world order. Frankfurter, however, boarded the steamship *Baltic* to attend the conference as a member of the American Zionist delegation and to lobby for a Jewish homeland in Palestine. During the war, the British had seized control of Palestine from the brutal Ottoman regime. One of the objectives of the peace conference was to decide the future of Palestine and other Middle Eastern kingdoms. Frankfurter knew that anti-Semitic Harvard president A. Lawrence Lowell had suspected that his prior overseas trips were covert Zionist activities. Instead of requesting additional leave, Frankfurter informed Harvard law dean Roscoe Pound that he would return from Paris in time for the fall 1919 semester.

Before he left, Frankfurter had conferred with the de facto leader of the American Zionist movement, Justice Brandeis. A secular German Jew, Brandeis had donated little to Jewish causes until a 1910 interview with the editor of Boston's *Jewish Advocate*, Jacob de Haas. As Brandeis drove him to the train station after the interview, de Haas described Brandeis's uncle, Lewis Dembitz, a Louisville lawyer and religious scholar, as a "noble Jew." Brandeis, who had changed his middle name to Dembitz to honor his uncle, wondered what de Haas meant. De Haas launched into a discussion about the history of the Zionist movement; they returned to Brandeis's home and talked for hours. In Brandeis, de Haas believed he had discovered the successor to his mentor, Zionist founder Theodor Herzl. At the time, many prominent American Jews, secular and fully assimilated since arriving from Germany in the mid-nineteenth century, failed to see the need for a Jewish homeland and were opposed to Zionism. Brandeis converted Frankfurter and many others by appealing to their patriotism. "My approach to Zionism was through

Americanism," Brandeis explained. "Gradually it became clear to me that to be good Americans, we must be better Jews, and to be better Jews, we must become Zionists."

By 1914, Brandeis had tapped Frankfurter and Julian Mack as his chief lieutenants. It was Brandeis who had insisted on Frankfurter's participation in the ill-fated Morgenthau mission during the summer of 1917 to protect the interests of the Zionist movement and to meet its leader, Chaim Weizmann. Like Frankfurter, Weizmann opposed trying to negotiate a separate peace with the Ottoman Empire; rather, he favored a British military victory and takeover of Palestine. Weizmann's faith in the British government was well-placed. On November 2, 1917, after months of negotiations, British foreign secretary Arthur Balfour pledged his government's support for a Jewish homeland in Palestine.

The Balfour Declaration raised the stakes of Frankfurter's Zionist work. The confidential part of his February 1918 mission to Britain and France was to meet with Zionist officials. He conferred with Weizmann about the possibility of American participation at a Zionist conference in the Ottoman Empire (Frankfurter declined because the United States was neither at war with nor an ally of the Turks). He attended a Zionist committee meeting in London and reaffirmed American support for the European movement and for Weizmann's "undivided leadership."

After the armistice, Weizmann pleaded for Frankfurter's inclusion among the American Zionist representatives at the Paris Peace Conference. Brandeis was too tied up with Supreme Court business to attend; Frankfurter, therefore, was the next best thing. The plan was for Frankfurter to stay in Paris until June 1919 to influence the territorial negotiations and to make sure that the British received a mandate over Palestine. Brandeis promised to join him that summer to visit the Holy Land.

For several years, Brandeis had been funding Frankfurter's Zionist and other public interest activities. In late 1916, the Brandeises sent him a check for $250 for work on social and political causes; Frankfurter, however, refused to cash it. They insisted that he should be paid for his expenses, just as he was similarly paid by the *New Republic* and the National Consumers' League. Frankfurter cashed the check, the first of many the justice sent to his protégé. A multimillionaire from his Boston law practice and investments, Brandeis encouraged Frankfurter to take on social causes and disqualified himself from Frankfurter's cases before the Court. The financial arrangement raised ethical and personal concerns for both men. Brandeis funded Frankfurter's public interest work and scholarship as a way of furthering his own policy goals while on the bench. Indeed, Brandeis suggested numerous ideas for Frankfurter's articles in the *New Republic* and other publications. Over time, Frankfurter grew accustomed to living beyond his modest Harvard salary and became dependent on Brandeis's financial contributions. The relationship worked fine as long as Brandeis and Frankfurter agreed about policy. They overlooked any potential conflicts of interest because of their shared belief in social causes and in Zionism.

A few days before he sailed for Europe, Frankfurter had been inspired all over again as he listened to the justice's vision of a Jewish state influenced by the Jeffersonian ideal of a liberal, agrarian society, a place where labor and capital could create a laboratory for democracy. Brandeis did not believe all 12 million Jews should repatriate, only those who wanted to live there. He envisioned a Palestine where Arabs and Jews, Christians and Muslims, all enjoyed equal citizenship. "I wish you might have heard L.D.B. on the aims of my trip—you would have felt the reach of a profound mind and a truly 'deep' person," he wrote Marion. "[Y]ou would have also felt the world scope of the Zionist conception, as he & I perceive it." Brandeis urged Frankfurter to survey the situation and promised to meet him in Palestine as soon as the Court adjourned. Brandeis believed that they had found the ultimate place to experiment with new solutions to the socioeconomic problems of the United States: "we must make of Palestine a laboratory for our problems here."

The downside of Frankfurter's six months in Paris was that it meant another separation from his fiancée, Marion Denman. Before he set sail, he sent her flowers and love notes. The normally stoical Denman saw the flowers and read the notes and cried "as I haven't cried before."

After ten days on the water, Frankfurter arrived on April 26 at London's Piccadilly Hotel for a day of briefing by fellow Zionists. The next morning, he crossed the channel to Paris and arrived in a city teeming with representatives from countries all over the world. He learned that Weizmann had already addressed the Council of Five (Britain, France, Italy, United States, Japan) about the importance of a Jewish state in Palestine and declined Secretary of State Robert Lansing's offer of an opportunity to speak. By all accounts, Weizmann had done a fine job, and Frankfurter did not want to ruffle the Zionist leader's feathers. As much as Frankfurter admired him, Weizmann ruled with an obsessive zeal and placed his faith in the British government to promote the creation of a Jewish homeland. Frankfurter's goal was to serve as a peacemaker among the various Zionist factions and to use his American, British, and French contacts to make the proposed British mandate over Palestine a reality.

Soon after he arrived in Paris, Frankfurter understood that the key to the Zionist movement's success at the peace conference lay in his ability to tap into his international network of friends. "So much of it," he wrote, "is personalia." No one was better at "personalia" than Frankfurter. He knew every member of the American Zionist delegation—Mack, Rabbi Stephen S. Wise, Walter Meyer, and the promising young lawyer Benjamin V. Cohen. Everywhere Frankfurter went on the Rue de Rivoli, he ran into a former roommate or friend from the House of Truth: Eustace Percy with the British delegation; Loring Christie and Captain Harold Armstrong with the Canadian delegation; and former journalist William C. Bullitt in the State Department. Frankfurter also made important contacts during his 1917 and 1918 research trips to Britain and France. His secretary at the peace conference, Ella Winter, observed that Frankfurter "had a foothold, or at least a toe-hold, it seemed, in about every delegation."

Frankfurter's greatest diplomatic triumph was with the leader of the Arab delegation, Prince Faisal. Faisal was in Paris seeking Arab control of formerly Ottoman territories in Iraq and Syria. The Zionists viewed him as a critical ally in their quest for Palestine. On January 3, 1919, Faisal and Weizmann had signed a peace accord. Three months later, Frankfurter met with Faisal and made history. On March 3, he and Weizmann visited Faisal at the Arab delegation's headquarters at a small private hotel on the fashionable Avenue du Bois. They met the prince, members of his staff, and his influential British adviser and translator, Colonel T. E. Lawrence, a.k.a. Lawrence of Arabia. Frankfurter thought Lawrence was a "quiet dare-devil" and a "fascinating Englishman." The prince, with his long, thin face, his luminous, wide brown eyes, and his full dark beard and mustache, made a striking first impression. Frankfurter felt he and Faisal had made a connection. "The Arab prince & I had a grand time—he makes you think of the face of Jesus, except black-bearded, fine silken hair with a sparkling but remote smile—remote to me," he wrote Marion. "The Ends of the Earth met in him & me & yet I'm simple enough to think that he & I dealt & can deal as human beings who understand one another." With Lawrence interpreting, Faisal "said all the right things" about the Jewish people and the Zionist movement. Frankfurter "said exactly what I felt our attitude should be towards the Arabs, drawing upon our own sad experience in dealing with the Southern Negroes." Frankfurter suggested that they exchange letters of mutual understanding that could be the basis of a formal public announcement; Faisal agreed.

Immediately after the meeting, Frankfurter and Lawrence returned to the Zionist delegation's headquarters at the Hôtel Meurice. Lawrence drafted a letter representing the prince's comments. Later that day, Frankfurter received Faisal's letter. "We feel that the Arabs and Jews are cousins in race, having suffered similar oppressions at the hands of powers stronger than themselves, and by a happy coincidence have been able to take the first step towards the attainment of their national ideals together," Faisal wrote Frankfurter. "We Arabs, especially the educated among us, look with the deepest sympathy on the Zionist movement." Faisal welcomed the Jews in Palestine, pledging support for a British mandate and a Jewish homeland. After thanking Weizmann for his help and support, Faisal's letter emphasized the common struggle of Arabs and Jews after years of Turkish rule: "We are working together for a reformed and revised NEAR EAST, and our two movements complete one another. The Jewish movement is national and not imperialist. Our movement is national and not imperialist, and there is room in Syria for us both. Indeed, I think that neither can be a real success without the other."

Frankfurter's reply embraced the alliance between the Arab prince and the Weizmann-led Zionist movement: "We knew it could not be otherwise; we knew that the aspirations of the Arab and the Jewish peoples were parallel, that each aspired to re-establish its nationality in its own homeland, each making its own distinctive contribution to civilization, each seeking its own peaceful mode of life." Frankfurter concluded on a prophetic note: "For both the Arab and the Jewish peoples there are difficulties ahead—difficulties that challenge the united statesmanship of Arab and Jewish leaders." Overcoming future obstacles, Frankfurter wrote, required cooperation: "We each have our difficulties; but there are no substantial differences between us. These difficulties we shall work out as friends, friends who are animated by similar purposes, seeking a free and full development for the two neighboring peoples. The Arabs and Jews are neighbors in territory, we cannot but live side by side as friends."

At the end of March, Frankfurter attended a farewell lunch for Faisal. The prince wore a black, floor-length cashmere coat with "Oriental embroidery" and a gold and silver turban. Frankfurter described Faisal as "wise" but couldn't "help detecting a contempt of look and thought for all our Western civilization." And yet Frankfurter appreciated Faisal's cynicism about the peace conference. At lunch, the prince described the Council of Ten, which he had addressed to stake Arab territorial claims, as "a caravan of camels led by an ass." Frankfurter wrote: "That's the kind of customer he is."

As heartened as he was by the exchange of letters with the future leader of Syria and Iraq, Frankfurter knew that Arab-Jewish relations faced major challenges ahead. "THE ARAB QUESTION has ceased to exist as a difficulty to the realisation of our programme before the Peace Conference," he wrote Brandeis. "The locus of trouble from the Arabs is Palestine and not Paris. The Arab question is and will continue [to be] a source of friction in the actual life in Palestine and as such it is a challenge, to the wishes, the sympathetic understanding and the generosity of Jewish statesmanship."

No one knew more about life in Palestine at the peace conference than Frankfurter's Palestinian Jewish friend with a secret past, Aaron Aaronsohn. The director of the Jewish Agricultural Station south of Haifa, Aaronsohn discovered how to grow wild wheat in arid soil. He published his findings with the U.S. Department of Agriculture and raised money for the agricultural station from wealthy American Zionists. A big, ruddy-faced man fluent in multiple languages but still learning English, Aaron was a larger-than-life figure and unofficial ambassador for Jewish Palestine. During visits to America, he befriended Frankfurter and Mack and regaled them with first-hand accounts of Jewish settlers in Palestine. Aaron's brother Alex publicized Turkish atrocities against Palestinian Jews. In private, Aaron went even further. In an October 1916 "confession" to Mack and Frankfurter, he revealed his family's secret Jewish spy network, NILI. A Hebrew acronym that means "The Eternal One of Israel will not Lie," NILI relayed information about Turkish and German troop movements in Palestine to British forces stationed in Cairo. They believed that the British would liberate them from the Ottoman Empire. For aiding the British cause, Aaron paid a steep price. In late 1917, the spy network was exposed while Aaron and Alex were abroad. Aaron's sister, Sarah, the leader of NILI in Palestine, was tortured for four days before she shot herself in the face and died four days later. At first, Aaron learned from a telegram that his sister and father had died. While staying with Frankfurter in Washington, he was "beyond wonder" after receiving a second telegram that his father was alive.

Aaronsohn's admiration for Frankfurter ran deep. Over the years, Aaronsohn also had impressed Frankfurter's holy trinity: Holmes, Brandeis, and Theodore Roosevelt. Holmes referred to him as "the wonderful one"; Brandeis was inspired by his story of transforming Palestine into an agrarian state; Roosevelt had listened for nearly two hours as he told his family's story. Aaronsohn always stayed at the House of Truth during his visits to Washington. In March 1918, he had been Frankfurter's travel companion in Britain during confidential meetings with Zionist leaders. At the end of 1918, Aaronsohn served as an intermediary between Weizmann and Brandeis and was relieved by Frankfurter's inclusion on the American delegation.

In Paris, however, Aaronsohn clashed with Weizmann and other Zionist leaders because of philosophical differences over how to attain a Jewish state. Weizmann preferred diplomatic negotiations with the Allies; Aaronsohn advocated for military intervention. Aaronsohn's reputation as a spy made it difficult for people to trust him. Yet Frankfurter understood how to use Aaronsohn's vast knowledge of Palestine. He charged Aaronsohn with creating maps of proposed boundaries of a British-controlled Palestine for the Commission on Mandates. He urged Brandeis to overlook Aaronsohn's personal flaws. "He is *persona gratissima* to everybody who matters for us in the English and American delegations and instead of utilizing him as a scientist all these weeks he has been allowed to fritter away his spirit and energy in futile bickerings and disorganizations," Frankfurter wrote Brandeis. "I think I have put an end to it at least during our stay in Paris."

Working his diplomatic contacts, Frankfurter received assistance from another volatile personality, State Department official William C. Bullitt. The former journalist was so dismayed by Wilson's refusal to recognize Russia and by the terms of the peace treaty that he considered resigning. Frankfurter described Bullitt as "the enfant terrible" at the American delegation's headquarters in the Hôtel de Crillon. Yet Bullitt greatly aided the Zionist cause. In Paris, he arranged a meeting between House and Weizmann, admired Aaronsohn, and read a draft of the Zionist delegation's proposed mandate.

Frankfurter worried about British support for a Jewish state. Eustace Percy, who had introduced him to numerous members of the British delegation, was backpedaling. After a failed run for Parliament as a Zionist supporter, Percy returned to Paris as Balfour's secretary with a more ambivalent attitude. During lunch with Percy and his wife, Frankfurter was disappointed that his former housemate would not level with him. Others were blunt. Lady Nancy Astor, an anti-Semitic American ex-patriate active in the British social and political scene, asked Frankfurter and Weizmann: "Why don't you Jews give up Palestine?" She then tugged on the sleeve of Prime Minister Lloyd George: "Tell these Jews they can't have Palestine." He smiled and replied: "I can't because I promised they shall have it, & I must keep my promise." Frankfurter was not so sure. In May, Arab uprisings in Palestine weakened British resolve; the British seemed more intent on maintaining control over the region than in establishing a Jewish state.

With support for a Jewish state in jeopardy, Frankfurter took desperate measures by appealing to President Wilson. "As a passionate American I am, of course, most eager that the Jew should be a reconstructive and not a disruptive force in the new world order," he wrote Wilson. "I have reassured their leaders, with the conviction born of knowledge of your purposes." Frankfurter sought Wilson's public support for the Balfour Declaration so that Frankfurter and Weizmann could go to Palestine to reassure Jewish leaders there. Instead, Wilson simply acknowledged "how deeply I appreciate the importance and significance of the whole matter." A disappointed Frankfurter replied that the president's response had "occasioned almost despair to the Jewish representatives now assembled in Paris, who speak not only for the Jews of Europe but also for the American Jewish Congress, the democratic voice of three million American Jews." Surprised by Frankfurter's reaction, Wilson failed to allay Zionist concerns: "I never dreamed that it was necessary to give you any renewed assurance of my adhesion to the Balfour Declaration, and so far I have found no one who is seriously opposing the purpose which it embodies. . . . I see no ground for discouragement and every reason to hope that satisfactory guarantees can be secured." Frankfurter's faith in Wilson was deeply shaken.

More than Wilson, Frankfurter knew how desperately European Jews needed a homeland. On May 12, Frankfurter received an urgent letter from Henry Alsberg in Poland about the persecution and starvation of 1 million Jews and another 600,000 in Eastern Galicia near Ukraine who were "slowly also rotting to death." Alsberg predicted that if something were not done immediately, "there will be no Jews left to go to Palestine." He recommended that the Polish government be bullied into protecting its Jewish population. Frankfurter vouched for Alsberg and relayed the information to Colonel House, unaware of House's anti-Semitism and dwindling influence with Wilson.

As the peace conference wore on, Frankfurter's concerns about Wilson grew and not just about Palestine. He learned that the other Allied leaders had outmaneuvered Wilson and negotiated a treaty that severely punished Germany and made no provision to protect the rights of minority groups in Europe. Wilson had insisted on negotiating directly with the other members of the Big Four—Georges Clemenceau of France, David Lloyd George of Great Britain, and Vittorio Orlando of Italy—and kept Colonel House and Secretary of State Lansing at bay. For months, Frankfurter thought that Wilson should have invited a skilled negotiator such as Brandeis, Herbert Hoover, or Elihu Root, Sr., to assist him. The president, however, wanted only yes men. "No wonder," Frankfurter wrote of Wilson, "he is one of the saddest looking men I've ever seen."

Frankfurter's disappointment and heartbreak grew with the fate of Aaron Aaronsohn. The Zionist delegation hoped that Aaronsohn's maps of Palestine would play a critical role in the unfinished territorial negotiations as Britain, France, and Italy claimed different parts of the Middle East. Aaronsohn's behavior in Paris had not improved. Frankfurter kept Aaronsohn in line, berating him so harshly on one occasion that the big man burst into tears. They were closer than ever and looked forward to the summer when Frankfurter and Brandeis visited Palestine with Aaronsohn as their guide. He kept telling Frankfurter, "I must show you Palestine."

On the morning of May 11, Aaronsohn arrived at Frankfurter's hotel happier than he had been in weeks. He was headed to London to meet with Weizmann and British officials. He wanted to make sure the British, in light of recent Arab uprisings, were committed to the Balfour Declaration. He did not want his family's enormous sacrifices to have been in vain. Four days later, Frankfurter waited in Paris for the arrival of Aaronsohn's return flight. Aaronsohn crammed into a Royal Air Force plane filled with mail and confidential documents for the British delegation. A dense fog had settled over the English Channel; the wind howled. The plane took off once but returned to the base because of a problem with the propeller. Despite the poor weather conditions, the decorated pilot tried again. The plane, last seen over the harbor of the French city of Boulogne, got lost in the fog and plunged into the sea. The plane and the mail were recovered. The bodies were never found.

"And now Aaron is gone," Frankfurter wrote in his first letter about the tragedy to Marion Denman. She was relieved that her fiancé was alive and had not been on Aaronsohn's airplane, something not clear when she had initially heard the news. He regretted not wiring her that he was okay. He had grown so accustomed to discussing the tragedy in a "cold cable way" that it took him nearly a month to process Aaron's death. "I hear his warm, shrill voice, his pervasive frame fills in the room," he wrote her, "—in ceaseless ways." The author of a *Manchester Guardian* obituary described Aaronsohn as the "great Romantic figure in the history of the Jews." Frankfurter's friends Aaronsohn and Valentine were dreamers; he shared their dreams and treasured their friendship. Brandeis knew that his lieutenants in Paris, Frankfurter and Mack, were heartbroken. "I sorrow with you and Mac[k] over the loss of Aaron," Brandeis wired Frankfurter.

Before he left Paris for good, Frankfurter tried to keep the hopes of a Jewish state alive by demanding that the leader of the American Zionist movement go to Palestine. Brandeis had planned to leave Washington on June 9 to join Frankfurter and the Zionist delegation there. Mack and others, however, told the justice not to come because of Arab uprisings. They believed that the British mandate would be written into the treaty but that key territorial questions would not be decided until the fall. Frankfurter disagreed. Brandeis needed to gather facts on the ground, to urge British officials to take the mandate, and to emerge as the Zionist movement's public face. "I made up my mind that Brandeis can't continue to lead this movement from the securities of the eighth floor of Stoneleigh Court, overlooking the Potomac and the imperturbable Washington Monument," Frankfurter wrote. "He's got to *feel* the facts, get their subtle weight on the spot and in the perverse and misfiring and blended details." On June 6, Frankfurter wired Brandeis and pleaded with him to change his mind. After Brandeis tried to put him off, Frankfurter wired him again that day: "Your failure to come may have consequences that I contemplate with the utmost anxiety. Have consulted Mr. Balfour who fully agrees with need of your coming. Weizmann has read this cable and concurs."

At Frankfurter's insistence, Brandeis embarked on what the press described as a "vacation" to Palestine. On June 14, five days after the Court had adjourned for the summer, he boarded the steamship *Mauritania* with his daughter Susan, Jacob de Haas, and 658 other passengers bound for Southampton, England. Six days later, Frankfurter was waiting at the dock as the ship made its way through the fog.

During two nights in London, Brandeis met with Weizmann and other British officials and, according to Frankfurter, was "at the very height of his powers." Brandeis and Frankfurter then headed to Paris at the request of British foreign secretary Arthur Balfour. For nearly two hours in Balfour's apartment at the Rue Nitot, Brandeis outlined three successful conditions for a Jewish state in Palestine: (1) Palestine as the Jewish homeland and not just a homeland there; (2) territorial boundaries far enough north to control the water supply and far enough south and east; and (3) control of the land and natural resources essential for "a sound economic life." Balfour concurred yet believed the conditions conflicted with Wilson's desire for self-determination of former territories, with preexisting agreements with France about Syria, and with the Arab majority in Palestine. Brandeis responded that a Jewish homeland was not simply about Palestine but about "a world problem." Balfour agreed to wait for Brandeis's report on conditions in Palestine. Frankfurter, who memorialized the conversation, reported: "No statesman could have been more sympathetic than Mr. Balfour was with the underlying philosophy and aims of Zionism as they were stated by Mr. Justice Brandeis."

During his remaining time in Paris, Brandeis met with Herbert Hoover, Colonel House, Lincoln Steffens, and European and Russian Zionist leaders in what Frankfurter described as "their first glimpse of the real Joshua." Frankfurter was amazed at how "simply and profoundly impressive" Brandeis was with Balfour, Hoover, and the average Russian Jew. Frankfurter predicted that one day Brandeis would have to choose between life in America serving on the Supreme Court and life in Palestine leading the Zionist movement. Frankfurter hoped that Brandeis would resign from the Court and choose Palestine.

After a few days in Paris, Frankfurter put Brandeis on a train for Marseilles where the justice boarded a ship to Egypt. Frankfurter could barely hide his disappointment at not being able to see the Promised Land for himself. Someone had to stay in Paris to make sure that territorial issues were not decided in the Zionist Commission's absence. He saw the Treaty of Versailles signed and Wilson leave a beaten man and awaited Brandeis's return.

With little to do in Paris, Frankfurter threw himself into investigating the plight of Polish Jews that Alsberg had described in harrowing detail a month earlier. Alsberg phoned him about poverty and starvation in Hungary, Poland, Austria, and Czechoslovakia. Before Brandeis had left for Palestine, Frankfurter arranged a meeting with the diplomat Hugh Gibson to urge him to leave his posh Warsaw hotel to investigate the extermination of Polish Jewry. Frankfurter also unsuccessfully tried to prevent another hapless diplomat, the anti-Zionist Henry Morgenthau, Sr., from getting involved. Unfortunately, Wilson asked Morgenthau to investigate the Polish situation. Despite his disdain for Morgenthau because of their disastrous 1917 mission, Frankfurter agreed to accompany him to Poland.

Nothing prepared Frankfurter for the poverty and squalor in Poland. He was there for only a few days but knew it would take months to mediate disputes and to improve the lives of Polish Jews. He briefed the American Commission to Negotiate Peace and hoped that Wilson would send someone to do the job. More than 3 million Polish Jews, Frankfurter wrote Lippmann, face "systematic, pervasive anti-Semitism," "live in a state of terror," and are isolated from other German-speaking people. Frankfurter was outraged that "to study, to understand that most complicated problem Wilson sends that unsurpassed vapid Megalomaniac Morgenthau."

For anything to happen in Poland, Frankfurter knew he needed to wait for Brandeis. The justice spent a week in Egypt waiting to meet with British General Edmund Allenby, then headed to Palestine for two weeks. The visit was life-changing. Observers noticed that Brandeis's whole appearance changed "as if he had seen a vision." He was tan, wore his hair shorter and cropped on the sides, and looked younger. He was deeply moved by the country: "Aaronsohn was right. It is a miniature California, but a California endowed with all the interest which the history of man can contribute and the deepest emotions which can stir a people. . . . The way is long, the path difficult and uncertain; but the struggle is worthwhile. It is indeed a Holy Land." He toured twenty-three of the forty-three Jewish settlements. Above all, he was grateful to Frankfurter for shaming him into visiting Palestine: "Felix was very wise in insisting upon our coming. There was, in fact, no basis whatsoever for a different view."

Nothing changed politically when Brandeis returned to Paris. The Commission on Mandates was no closer to resolving Middle East territorial and sovereignty questions. Yet Frankfurter could see that the justice was "a different man." Out from under the watchful eye of his wife, Alice, he enjoyed good food, good wine, and fine hotels. Over lunch, he briefed Balfour and other British officials. Balfour "was thrilled" by Brandeis's report and urged Frankfurter to "talk Poland." For several weeks, Frankfurter and Brandeis made the rounds in London. Brandeis encouraged British officials to stay true to the Balfour Declaration's support for a Jewish state, and he and Frankfurter warned Weizmann and other Zionist leaders that democracy and inclusion must be hallmarks of the movement going forward.

An embittered Weizmann felt abandoned because Brandeis and Frankfurter were returning home and were unwilling to resign their posts in America and lead the Zionist movement from Palestine. "Brandeis could have been a prophet in Israel," Weizmann wrote in an unsent August 27 letter to Frankfurter. "You have in you the making of a Lassalle. Instead, you are choosing to be only a professor in Harvard and Brandeis only a judge in the Supreme Court." In a conciliatory yet firm note, Frankfurter reminded the Zionist leader that people had different methods of achieving "a common ideal." A clash between the Brandeis- and Weizmann-led Zionist factions was inevitable.

In August 1919, Frankfurter said goodbye to his British friends and joined Brandeis on the steamship *Rotterdam* to America. During nearly seven months in Paris, Frankfurter failed to achieve a Jewish homeland in Palestine as part of the Treaty of Versailles. He was grateful, however, that he had worked for the Zionist movement rather than the U.S. government in light of Wilson's failures during the treaty negotiations. Brandeis "buried his neck in his chin" and confessed to have thought the same thing.

While in Paris, Frankfurter had received several warnings from Dean Pound and others about what awaited him in Cambridge. The Red Scare, the postwar fear and persecution of suspected Communists and other radicals, had come to Harvard Law School. And Frankfurter was public enemy number one.

CHAPTER 9

A Dangerous Man

R oscoe Pound was alarmed. On March 1, 1919, he sent word to Julian Mack that Frankfurter should expect a "summons" from a conservative member of the Harvard Corporation and to contact the law dean before responding. "Very likely it will be informal," Pound warned, "but it will be a summons." A few weeks later, Pound wrote Frankfurter in Paris that the reactionary forces had escalated their attacks on Frankfurter as part of "a general crusade here against all things liberal." The Harvard Corporation had rejected three law faculty appointments as "Bolshevists," including Frankfurter's best former student, Gerry Henderson. Furthermore, the school's administration was trying to force Pound to take a yearlong leave of absence so they could wrest faculty hiring and curricular reform from his hands. The son of a member of the Harvard Corporation remarked that "if he had his way [Frankfurter] would be deported." Conservative alumni and members of the Harvard Corporation were trying to run Frankfurter and Pound out of the school. At first, Frankfurter was amused by the controversy and read Pound's letter aloud to friends in Paris. "It's a real fight," Frankfurter conceded, "and a fight that matters."

The situation at the law school became so dire that on May 24 Pound alerted Brandeis about what was happening and the dangers Frankfurter faced. Pound vowed that if forced to take a leave so that conservatives could remake the school, he would resign. Frankfurter wanted to take the first steamship to the states to see Pound himself. Instead, he asked Brandeis to meet with Pound before the justice left for Europe. At the City Club in New York City, Brandeis advised Pound: "Do nothing till Felix returns."

Upon his arrival in London, Brandeis explained the situation to Frankfurter: "Pound is very depressed. They're after him but he says they are really gunning for you. In short you are a 'dangerous man.'" Frankfurter and

Brandeis were almost giddy about the controversy. Frankfurter asked how much of it was anti-Semitism. "It's a make-weight," Brandeis replied, "that's all." Brandeis knew that Frankfurter was spoiling for a fight with his enemies in Cambridge. "Don't worry about Felix," Brandeis told Pound. "He'll be entirely happy. This will be something he'll like."

For several years, Brandeis had predicted this would happen. The same Harvard alumni who had opposed his nomination—President Lowell, New York lawyer Austen G. Fox, Boston lawyer Moorfield Storey, former Boston mayor Nathan Matthews, and others—led the fight to oust Frankfurter. "Old Boston is unregenerate and I am not sorry to have escaped a struggle there that would have been as nasty as it is unending," Brandeis wrote his wife, Alice. "F. F. is evidently considered by the elect as 'dangerous' as I was; and it looks as if some whom F. considered his friends are as unrelenting as were some who were called mine."

Frankfurter's enemies pointed to his November 1917 and January 1918 reports on the Bisbee deportation and the Mooney case and Theodore Roosevelt's characterization of them as "Bolsheviki." Above all, they charged Frankfurter and Pound with radicalizing the students. Pound and Frankfurter had attacked the Supreme Court's *Lochner* decision invalidating a maximum-hour law for bakers and had worked with the National Consumers' League to defend minimum-wage and maximum-hour laws. They corrupted the students by turning them into pro-government economic regulationists who favored organized labor, opposed "liberty of contract," and loathed the Court's conservative majority.

The face of the conservative opposition was someone Frankfurter had thought was his friend, Thomas Nelson Perkins. For nearly a year, Frankfurter had been corresponding with Perkins, a prominent Boston lawyer and member of the Harvard Corporation, about rumors of displeasure among Old Boston conservatives. He had worked with him in wartime Washington and dined with him at the House of Truth. In February, Perkins inquired about Frankfurter's role in investigating the Mooney case and drafting the report. This was the summons Pound had been warning him about. In mid-April 1919 from Paris, Frankfurter replied by detailing the history of his participation as secretary and counsel on the President's Mediation Commission, the facts of Mooney's case, and its use as propaganda with Russian and Italian allies.

With Frankfurter in Paris during the summer of 1919 and unable to defend himself, Brandeis turned to someone with unimpeachable Old Boston credentials and deep Harvard ties, Justice Holmes. Since February, Holmes had been hearing rumors that Frankfurter and Harold Laski were "dangerous men." Laski informed him that two of the justice's friends, Perkins and Richard W. Hale, were leading the effort to drive Frankfurter from the school. Hale, the founder of the law firm Hale & Dorr, had summoned the president of the *Harvard Law Review* and warned him to stay away from Frankfurter. Holmes was reluctant to write to Perkins or Hale, believing that Perkins and Frankfurter were friends. Laski also warned Holmes that Frankfurter and Pound were in trouble and there was "a great fight on as to the future of the School."

Harvard Law School's "Red Scare" hit Holmes close to home as the author of three opinions condoning the Wilson administration's crackdown on antiwar radicals and anarchists. Wilson's attorney general, A. Mitchell Palmer, enforced new criminal laws that gave the federal government breathtaking power: The Espionage Act of 1917 made it illegal for people to convey information that intended to disrupt the military or to obstruct the draft; the Sedition Act of 1918 expanded the Espionage Act to make it illegal to speak out against the government and the war effort. On March 3, 1919, Holmes published three unanimous opinions affirming the criminal convictions of Socialist Party secretary Charles Schenck, *Missouri Staats Zeitung* editor Jacob Frohwerk, and Socialist Party leader and presidential candidate Eugene V. Debs for their antiwar leaflets, newspaper editorials, and speeches. In affirming the constitutionality of the Espionage Act and rejecting their First Amendment claims, Holmes's opinions introduced "clear and present danger" and "falsely shouting fire in a theatre" into the American lexicon. Yet the decisions masked Holmes's fluid views on free speech.

Brandeis, who had joined the Espionage Act opinions, knew Holmes had written them with regret and understood how horrified Holmes would be if Frankfurter and Pound lost their jobs. Brandeis's influence on Holmes was significant. Since joining the Court, Brandeis had been encouraging Holmes to write dissents in high-profile cases, including one about the Keating-Owen Child Labor Act. He challenged Holmes to care more about facts and to spend part of his summer reading a study of the 1912 Lawrence, Massachusetts, textile mill strike. When Brandeis explained what was really happening to Frankfurter and Pound, Holmes was shocked. "He is as innocent as a sixteen year old girl as to the facts of human conduct," Brandeis told Frankfurter. "He is so tender & so sensitive [a] being that he can't conceive of conduct like Lowell's & those men. I showed him Pound's letter & he was stunned."

At Brandeis's urging, Holmes invoked his honorary title as the newly elected president of the Harvard Law School Association to vouch for his friends. In May 1919, Holmes wrote Frank Grinnell, the secretary of the law school alumni association and the Massachusetts Bar Association, to nominate Pound for an honorary L.L.D. degree from Harvard. A grateful Pound alerted Holmes that "most people hereabout seem to be chiefly concerned to push Frankfurter out of the school" and predicted that Frankfurter "would be made uncomfortable and will go." Holmes knew he had to do more. "If the school should lose Pound and Frankfurter it would lose its soul, it seems to me . . . ," he wrote Laski. "By Jove, I think I'll say that to Lowell." On June 2, he wrote President Lowell that he had "a very strong feeling that Pound and in his place Frankfurter have and impart the ferment which is more valuable than an endowment, and makes of a Law School a focus of life." Eight days later, Lowell replied that he was "very glad" about Holmes's nomination of Pound for an honorary degree and claimed that Pound was "somewhat discouraged" because of wartime conditions and overwork. That's why Lowell encouraged the dean to take a sabbatical. "What you say about his value to the school," Lowell wrote to Holmes, "I agree with entirely." Lowell's response did not mention Frankfurter. Whether it helped him or not, Frankfurter was humbled by the support from his judicial idol. "Think of Holmesy going into that fight—. . . ," Frankfurter wrote Marion. "Ain't that grand!"

The country was on fire while Frankfurter was in Paris. The "Red Summer" of 1919 earned its name from the white supremacist campaign of murder and bloodshed against African Americans in Chicago and other cities. Radicals and anarchists also resorted to violence. At 11:15 p.m. on June 2, an anarchist bombed the home of Attorney General Palmer, destroying the first floor and blowing out three stories of windows as well as the windows of nearby homes. Palmer's R Street neighbors, Assistant Secretary of the Navy Franklin Roosevelt and his wife, Eleanor, had just arrived home. Miraculously, no one was injured.

The attack fueled Palmer's crusade against radicals and anarchists. On June 12, the attorney general testified before Congress about the bombings in Washington and seven other cities and requested $500,000 (and $2 million total) for a special division within the Bureau of Investigation of the Justice Department to hunt radicals and anarchists. On August 1, Palmer designated a 24-year-old agent, John Edgar Hoover, to head the division.

That fall, Frankfurter returned to Harvard Law School determined to test the limits of academic freedom. He did not seem to care that the university was refusing to honor him with a new chair as the Byrne Professor of Administrative Law. He may have been overconfident that Julian Mack, who had been elected to Harvard's Board of Overseers, would protect him. Pound, who had been fending off reactionary attacks while Frankfurter and Mack were in Paris, knew better. "He and Mack are too guileless," Pound wrote Brandeis. "They don't appreciate the Puritan conscience that enabled these people to stick a knife into those with whom they maintain cordial relations with a serene consciousness that they are doing god's will." Pound informed Brandeis that people in Boston were bent on destroying Frankfurter: "I rejoice that Frankfurter appraises the situation so cheerfully. But he ought not to talk freely to everyone who greets him cordially and expresses delight at his return."

Frankfurter ignored the warnings. On November 11, the first anniversary of Germany's surrender celebrated as Armistice Day, he chaired a meeting at Boston's Faneuil Hall urging the Wilson administration to recognize Russia's Bolshevik regime. He knew he would be called a Bolshevist and announced he had "no patience for the Bolshevik form of government." Most of his comments consisted of quoting remarks from the Paris Peace Conference by Prime Minister Lloyd George and President Wilson rejecting the idea of intervening in Russia. U.S. recognition of the new Russian government was a mainstream idea and consistent with Wilson's belief in self-determination.

Enemies in Boston led by Thomas Nelson Perkins seized on Frankfurter's latest political stand. One of the city's leading Harvard fund-raisers, Perkins warned that his activities would hurt the law school's endowment. "Why do you rock the boat?" he asked Frankfurter over lunch and deemed him a "very unreasonable man." Frankfurter, however, refused to be silenced. "You know as well as I do that at present there is a raging form of lynch law in the North, much more ominous, because less crude, than the well-known brand of the South," he wrote Perkins. "It is led by some of the so-called most respectable, by some of the educated and the rich. I should feel like a poltroon if I suppressed my convictions."

The climate of fear at Harvard forced Frankfurter to speak out. He was angry that Pound was "being harassed to the point where they have been near to firing him"; that Gerry Henderson, "*the* best brains from the Law School in my time," was denied a faculty appointment as a falsely alleged Bolshevik; that Laski was "inquisitioned" for his support of the Boston police strike; and that "instructors are cowed and scared out of [their] lives." He explained the situation to Emory Buckner: "You see I'm free & don't give a damn. If I have to leave here I can make a living elsewhere. But 90% of teachers can't, so I wanted them to know what's what."

Upon seeing Frankfurter's correspondence with Perkins, Holmes cautioned that academic freedom was not absolute when it jeopardized the school's enrollment and endowment. The law school's endowment suffered because of overspending and a failed fund-raising campaign, not because of Frankfurter's activities. Nonetheless, Holmes warned him to be careful.

Holmes knew what it was like to take a stand for free speech. On November 10, he dissented from the Court's decision affirming the Espionage Act conviction of anarchist and antiwar activist Jacob Abrams. Abrams had been sentenced to twenty years in prison for printing 5000 leaflets in English and Yiddish criticizing American intervention in the Russian Revolution and calling for a general strike. Three of Holmes's colleagues, Day, Van Devanter, and Pitney, called on him at 1720 I Street and, along with his wife, Fanny, urged him not to dissent. They failed. Joined by Brandeis, Holmes published his dissent with pride and sent copies to his young friends. Unlike the three Espionage Act cases decided in March, Holmes wrote that Abrams's leaflets posed no "clear and present danger" to the war effort. Mere criticism of the war could not be a crime. Besides, Abrams and his co-defendants were "poor and puny anonymities" who deserved nominal punishments, not twenty years in prison. Finally, he warned about government limits on political speech by arguing that "the best test of truth" was the marketplace of ideas. He refined his clear and present danger test to protect unpopular speech except for "immediate interference" with the law or "to save the country."

Holmes's *Abrams* dissent thrilled Frankfurter. "And now I may tell you the gratitude and, may I say it, the pride I have in your dissent . . . ," he wrote Holmes, "you lift the voice of the noble human spirit." The justice's conservative friends reacted differently. Northwestern law dean John Henry Wigmore criticized his *Abrams* dissent in the *Northwestern Law Review*; Thomas Nelson Perkins and other members of Old Boston expressed their misgivings. Holmes relished that his oldest friends considered him to be "dangerous" but that Frankfurter and other young friends "said things that warmed my heart."

A week before Holmes published his *Abrams* dissent, Frankfurter had visited 1720 I Street and revealed his engagement to Marion Denman. Holmes "jumped up and shouted" for his wife. "Dickie," he said. "Dickie bird!" Fanny, who had been battling an illness for several months, shuffled into the room. "Tell her! Tell her!" Holmes said. She left the room without saying a word and returned holding something in each of her hands. She opened one revealing a piece of jade and another revealing a piece of amber. She asked which one Marion would like; Frankfurter pointed to the amber. Mrs. Holmes handed it to him, expressing her regard for Marion and the happy couple. The Holmeses reacted like "loving parents." Frankfurter worried about telling Brandeis after keeping the secret from him for so long. Brandeis, however, displayed a rare show of emotion and was "very devoted" to him.

The question of who would marry Felix and Marion took several twists and turns. Judge Learned Hand was supposed to perform the ceremony but lacked the legal authority of the state of New York. Holmes agreed to marry them but was not empowered to do so, either. On December 20, 1919, New York Court of Appeals judge Benjamin Cardozo married the couple in Hand's chambers. Felix's mother, who opposed her son marrying a gentile, did not attend the ceremony. In later years, however, she learned to accept the union. The newlyweds returned from their Southern Pines, North Carolina, honeymoon and started their new life together in Cambridge happy as "two cooing doves."

Frankfurter's marriage was tempered by tragedy. On November 5, Winfred Denison had died after throwing himself in front of an oncoming New York subway train. He had been battling mental illness for several years since returning from the Philippines. Frankfurter could not stop thinking about what he and Denison had been through—working for Stimson at the U.S. attorney's office, prosecuting the Sugar Trust, living together at the House of Truth, befriending Holmes, joining the Bull Moose campaign in spirit while working in the Taft administration, and investigating the Board of General Appraisers. Three of Frankfurter's closest friends—Valentine, Aaronsohn, and Denison—had died before he turned forty. He lived his own life with a fearless sense of purpose, taking on two of the scariest men in the country, A. Mitchell Palmer and J. Edgar Hoover.

At 9:00 p.m. on November 8, federal and state officials raided the offices of Communist Party members and other radicals, rounded up hundreds of suspected anarchists and revolutionists, and sent many of them to Ellis Island to be deported. In New York City alone, 700 officers raided 73 offices, arrested 500 suspects, and intended to charge 100 of them. The first of these Palmer raids, named after the attorney general but directed by Hoover, led to the deportations of more than 200 people, including anarchists Alexander Berkman and Emma Goldman.

With the Red Scare raging at Harvard Law School and Holmes's *Abrams* dissent a not-so-subtle rebuke of the Wilson administration, Frankfurter entered the fray and stood up for free speech. In February 1920, he joined the national committee of a new organization, the American Civil Liberties Union (ACLU). He and ACLU founder Roger Nash Baldwin had worked together during the war to protect the rights of conscientious objectors. As a member of the ACLU's national committee, Frankfurter agreed to advise

Baldwin on "tactics and policies," but not as the organization's counsel. He already served as counsel for the National Consumers' League and in a controversial case in Boston.

At the request of federal judge George W. Anderson, Frankfurter and Harvard law colleague Zechariah Chafee appeared as "friends of the court" in the April 1920 case of twenty radical immigrants rounded up in New England during the Palmer raids and scheduled for deportation for alleged membership in the Communist Party or Communist Labor Party. During fifteen days of testimony and 1600 pages of factual investigation, Frankfurter and Chafee revealed numerous flaws in the Justice Department's pre-arrest investigation of the suspected radicals. In his opinion, Judge Anderson found a pattern of unconstitutional and illegal conduct: warrantless searches and seizures, horrifying conditions of confinement, and hearings with little or no representation before Justice Department officials. He refused to deport the immigrants and released all but four of them from custody for "lack of due process." The federal government appealed only four of the cases and succeeded in reversing only a small part of Anderson's ruling that the immigrants could not be deported for Communist Party membership. Frankfurter and Chafee aided Anderson in saving sixteen immigrants from deportation, then took their findings public.

In a report by the National Popular Government League, Frankfurter, Chafee, and Pound joined a dozen prominent lawyers in detailing the attorney general's practice of warrantless searches, seizures, and arrests; no access to defense counsel in prison; the infiltration of radical organizations with Justice Department spies; and the publication of propaganda in newspapers and magazines. The Justice Department's "illegal acts," the report concluded, "have caused widespread suffering and unrest, have struck at the foundation of American free institutions, and have brought the name of our country into disrepute."

Attorney General Palmer rebuked Frankfurter and Chafee. Before the House Rules Committee on June 2, 1920, Palmer testified that he could not reconcile Frankfurter's representation of Communist Party members with upholding the Constitution. In response, Frankfurter and Chafee explained that they had appeared at Judge Anderson's request and that the Constitution protected the rights of defendants by providing for the writ of habeas corpus and due process. Palmer replied that Frankfurter and Chafee's allegations of misconduct were false and demanded a retraction. Frankfurter and Chafee informed Palmer and the House Rules Committee chairman of their willingness to substantiate their allegations under oath. Frankfurter also embarrassed the attorney general in the press. He chided Palmer for insinuating that the central issue in Judge Anderson's opinion, the Justice Department's flagrant violations of due process during the Palmer raids, had been appealed when it had not.

Palmer was the least of Frankfurter's concerns compared to the machination of the man who had engineered the raids, J. Edgar Hoover. On May 20, Hoover ordered an investigation of Frankfurter and Chafee's activities in Anderson's courtroom at the "earliest practicable date." Hoover opened a secret file on Frankfurter and monitored his travel to Europe for an international Zionist conference. A June 15 memorandum to Hoover described Frankfurter as a "confirmed radical," and "one of the most active elements in the stirring up and inciting to disturbances in [the] country, particularly among the foreigners." Hoover, who believed that Frankfurter was active in the Bolshevik movement, reputedly deemed him "the most dangerous man in the United States."

Harvard's reactionaries took aim at Frankfurter's outspoken friends. Harold Laski was a prime target because of his support for the Boston police strike. Alumni, faculty, and students excoriated the political science instructor as a Bolshevist. The Board of Overseers interrogated him at the Harvard Club yet declined to take further action. The final straw was an issue of the *Harvard Lampoon* humiliating him about his physical appearance, Jewishness, and Socialist politics. President Lowell privately defended Laski yet informed him he would never be promoted beyond instructor. Frankfurter's dreams of Laski joining him and Pound on the law faculty were dead. Laski accepted a full professorship in political science at the London School of Economics.

Frankfurter's enemies retaliated against him by withholding the Byrne professorship. Thomas Nelson Perkins led the opposition, alleging that Frankfurter had "no character" and was a "poor teacher." Pound and Mack fought for him, and Pound again asked Brandeis to reach out to a concerned Holmes. Frankfurter told Holmes not to worry about Perkins or the professorship. It did not bother him that his unfilled chair was the talk of the faculty. In October 1920, Frankfurter finally received the Byrne professorship.

During the 1920–1921 school year, the opposition pounced when Pound, who had received his honorary degree in June 1920, took a sabbatical. Aided and abetted by the Justice Department and backed by twenty Harvard alumni, New York lawyer Austen G. Fox filed formal charges with the university against Frankfurter, Chafee, and Pound. The alumni sought to oust Frankfurter and Chafee for their role in freeing radical immigrants in Boston and Frankfurter, Chafee, and Pound for criticizing the Justice Department in the

National Popular Government League report. Fox pointed to alleged factual errors in a clemency petition the professors had signed on behalf of antiwar activist Jacob Abrams as well as factual errors in a *Harvard Law Review* article Chafee had published about Abrams's trial. Only the charges about Chafee's law review article stuck.

The Board of Overseers allowed Chafee's case to go before a May 22, 1921, inquiry, the "Trial at the Harvard Club." Attending the Sunday trial, Frankfurter described Chafee as "the very epitome of naïve & complete honesty" and Fox as "the fit instrument of ignorant intolerance." Chafee's credentials were impeccable. The scion of a prominent Rhode Island family, he had finished second in his Harvard Law School class and practiced law in Rhode Island before joining the law faculty. He had criticized Holmes's opinions in *Schenck*, *Frohwerk*, and *Debs* and discussed the opinions with the justice during the summer of 1919. In 1920, he wrote a groundbreaking book on free speech. Chafee's defense counsel was none other than President Lowell. Five years earlier, Fox and Lowell had led the opposition to Brandeis's nomination. No fan of Lowell's, Frankfurter nonetheless described the Harvard president as an "avowed champion" of Chafee's and admired Lowell's cross-examination of Fox and closing argument. It was the last time Frankfurter and Lowell found themselves on the same side of any issue. A panel of state and federal judges nearly voted to dismiss Chafee from the faculty. Chafee won by a single vote, that of Judge Cardozo. An embarrassed Lowell kept the proceedings secret and pressured Chafee to publish five pages of corrections and qualifications about his *Harvard Law Review* article on the *Abrams* case. Everyone knew that the dispute was not really about Chafee. *The Nation*, praising the final decision, insisted that Chafee was "only the first target" and that the "reaction's real scheme" was to drive Frankfurter and Pound from the school.

Frankfurter had survived the conservative opposition to his Mooney and Bisbee reports, his participation in the Faneuil Hall meeting about recognizing Russia, his defense of radical immigrants in Boston about to be deported, and his exposure of the Justice Department's unconstitutional conduct during the Palmer raids. Palmer and Hoover did not scare him. The withholding of the Byrne professorship and the trial at the Harvard Club did not faze him. As much as conservative alumni and President Lowell disliked Frankfurter, the law faculty admired him, top students gravitated to him, and Holmes and Brandeis believed in him.

Harvard's dangerous man was not going anywhere.

CHAPTER 10

The Possible Gain Isn't Worth the Cost

O n February 14, 1921, the Court of Appeals of the District of Columbia courtroom was filled with Frankfurter's friends and fellow social reformers: Justice Brandeis's wife, Alice, and daughter Elizabeth, who was assistant secretary to the District of Columbia Minimum Wage Board; Elizabeth Glendower Evans of the Massachusetts Minimum Wage Commission; Senator Robert M. La Follette, Sr.'s, wife, Belle; Father John A. Ryan of Catholic University; and journalist Norman Hapgood. They were there to watch Frankfurter, representing the National Consumers' League, defend a District of Columbia minimum-wage law for women against charges that it would lead the country into "the morass of Bolshevism."

Minimum-wage laws, Frankfurter told the court, had been adopted by "such soviet countries as Australia, Canada and England; approved by such adherents of the Soviets as Lord Milner and Winston Churchill and Mr. Balfour; introduced in such Soviet states of our union as Arizona, Arkansas, California, Colorado, Kansas, Massachusetts, Minnesota, Oregon, Utah, Washington, and Wisconsin and upheld by the supreme courts of eight of those Bolshevik states."

One of the three federal appeals court judges was not mollified or amused. Justice Josiah Van Orsdel asked what the legislature would do next. During the war, Van Orsdel asserted, wages increased but efficiency decreased. "With all possible respect," Frankfurter replied, "it is a very dangerous generalization." Frankfurter encouraged him and the other two judges "to decide modern industrial cases" on the basis of knowledge of "modern industrial facts."

Frankfurter's argument was part of a multiyear national legal campaign to establish the constitutionality of minimum-wage laws. In 1917, the Supreme

Court had deadlocked, 4–4, after he defended Oregon's minimum-wage law for women. Children's Hospital and an elevator operator at the Congress Hall Hotel challenged the D.C. law after the city's Minimum Wage Board decreed that women and girls, except nurses in training, could earn no less than $16.50 in a week or 34½ cents an hour. Frankfurter knew as he argued the D.C. case that the constitutionality of all the states' minimum-wage laws hung in the balance.

Less than a month after Frankfurter's argument before the court of appeals, Warren G. Harding was sworn in as the nation's twenty-eighth president. Frankfurter mocked Harding's inauguration speech as "the end of the limit for mashed-potatoe [sic] language." He was equally unenthusiastic about Harding's Democratic opponent, fellow Ohioan James M. Cox. Despite Cox's inclusion of Assistant Secretary of the Navy Franklin D. Roosevelt on the vice-presidential ticket, Frankfurter voted for imprisoned Socialist Party leader Eugene V. Debs in protest. Voting for Harding was "out of the question." The U.S. senator never left his front porch in Marion, Ohio, allowed others to campaign for him, and won in a landslide by promising a war-weary country a return to normalcy.

A return to normalcy meant a return to a more conservative Supreme Court hostile to organized labor. In January 1921, the Court enjoined the machinists' union from urging other workers to boycott a printing press manufacturer, the Duplex Printing Company. The company was the only one of four U.S. printing press manufacturers that refused to recognize the union, to agree to an eight-hour day, and to a minimum wage and other fair labor standards. As a result, the union declared a strike and urged other sympathetic workers to boycott the company. The union argued that secondary boycotts were protected by the Clayton Act, which Congress had passed in 1914 to shield unions from antitrust lawsuits and labor injunctions. The Court, however, ignored the law's purpose and instead relied on its poorly drafted language to enjoin the union's secondary boycott. Brandeis, joined by Holmes and John Hessin Clarke, dissented. He accused the majority of failing to recognize the law as the culmination of a twenty-year fight against labor injunctions. In an unsigned *New Republic* editorial, Frankfurter blamed the Court for twisting the Clayton Act's language prohibiting labor injunctions so as to make it meaningless. He blamed Samuel Gompers and the American Federation of Labor for not hiring competent counsel to draft the law. And he urged union officials and intellectuals to stop portraying the labor movement as a class struggle instead of emphasizing "its broad appeal to the liberal forces of the country." Privately, Frankfurter conceded the law was poorly written yet criticized the Court for eviscerating labor's Magna Carta and protecting the "established order."

In the pages of the *New Republic*, the *Harvard Law Review*, and elsewhere, Frankfurter emerged as the Supreme Court's leading critic. He was privy to the Court's inner workings thanks to his relationships with Holmes and Brandeis. He attacked the Court by praising Holmes's and Brandeis's dissents and portraying them as liberal judicial heroes. He defended minimum-wage laws, made his case for and against judicial review, and railed against his bête noire—the Due Process Clause. The clause's broad prohibition against depriving "any person of life, liberty, or property without due process of law," he argued, gave the justices too much power to enforce their economic and social prejudices and to act like a super-legislature.

In unsigned *New Republic* editorials, Frankfurter criticized members of the Court for not invoking due process to protect freedom of speech and fair criminal trials. He ridiculed McReynolds, Day, and Pitney for dissenting from the Court's decision declaring that Judge Kenesaw Mountain Landis, who had made anti-German comments, was too biased to preside over the Espionage Act trial of Representative Victor Berger, the first Socialist elected to Congress. At least Day and Pitney conceded that Landis's comments had been intemperate. "Not so Mr. Justice McReynolds! . . ." Frankfurter wrote. "We leave Mr. Justice McReynolds to his pitiable isolation and to the judgment of his associates." A month later, Frankfurter praised Holmes's and Brandeis's dissents from a decision upholding Postmaster General Albert Burleson's revocation of second-class mailing privileges for Berger's Socialist newspaper, the *Milwaukee Leader*, during the war. "Mr. Justice Holmes," Frankfurter wrote, "with a few strokes of his pen brought down the house of cards of the majority opinion."

The most disturbing case was Holmes's 5–4 opinion narrowly upholding a temporary Washington, D.C., housing law. The law responded to a postwar housing shortage by allowing tenants to stay in their homes after their leases had expired. Four justices dissented, arguing that the law, though temporary, violated the Fifth and Fourteenth Amendments because it deprived landlords of their property. They rejected the majority's contention that D.C. housing was a business affected with a public interest. For Frankfurter, the case illustrated the dangers of the Due Process Clause. He worried about the justices using it to privilege property and contract rights over basic human rights, to veto laws passed to help people who needed it most—like the D.C. minimum-wage law.

To Learned Hand, Frankfurter worried about what a more conservative

Supreme Court could do in the name of liberty and property and questioned the need for judicial review. He believed "the price we pay for this judicial service is too great, the advantages too slim for the Cost." The Due Process Clauses, Frankfurter argued, were so indefinite as to "leave too much play to policy, without the conscious recognition that it *is* policy." He was so worked up about the Due Process Clause that he vowed to spend his summer in Hadlyme, Connecticut, writing a book about it. Events overtook his research project.

On June 6, a divided Court of Appeals of the District of Columbia upheld the minimum-wage law for women. Only the skeptical Justice Van Orsdel dissented. That same day, Jesse Adkins, the chair of the D.C. Minimum Wage Board, wrote Frankfurter to congratulate him; however, he spoke too soon. Behind the scenes, an unusual situation developed. The case was initially heard by two appellate justices and a trial judge filling in for Justice Charles Henry Robb, who had been ill. Robb, however, had recovered and injected himself into the case. Thus, the court's summer recess left Frankfurter in the dark about his evanescent victory.

But then, on June 30, Frankfurter's judicial nightmare came true.

———

ON MAY 21, Chief Justice Edward Douglass White, Jr., had died, a little more than ten years after then-President Taft had named him to the court's center chair. On June 30, Harding announced White's replacement: William Howard Taft. That summer, Frankfurter and Hand debated Taft's merits and demerits. Hand argued that Taft had been a "professionally tip top" federal judge during nearly eight years on the Court of Appeals for the Sixth Circuit and pointed to his groundbreaking *Addyston Pipe* opinion, which held that not all restraints of trade, only unreasonable ones, violated the Sherman Antitrust Act. Frankfurter claimed the credit lay not with Taft but with the lawyer who had briefed and argued the case and with Taft's able Sixth Circuit colleagues. Frankfurter could not overlook the lazy, indifferent president and jealous, naïve co-chair of the National War Labor Board who had allowed his pro-labor co-chair to steamroll him. It mattered little that the chief justiceship was Taft's dream job, which was why as president he had named the aging White chief in the first place. He had been biding his time teaching at Yale Law School. Frankfurter ridiculed Taft's reactionary views about constitutional law. The previous October, he had written an unsigned *New Republic* editorial belittling Taft for a *Yale Review* article criticizing Brandeis and

Clarke for their supposedly "new school of constitutional construction" and for stoking fears of "Socialist raids upon property rights." In Frankfurter's mind, Taft was no more fit to teach constitutional law at Yale than he was to be president, much less chief justice.

An unsigned *New Republic* editorial likely written by Frankfurter excoriated liberals who abhorred Taft as president yet applauded his appointment as chief justice. He reminded them about Taft's laziness as president and "submissiveness" on the National War Labor Board. He criticized Taft for failing to speak out against the unconstitutional Palmer raids as former justice Charles Evans Hughes and Senator Albert J. Beveridge had. Though he conceded that Taft was "a good judge," he warned progressives not to conflate Taft's "judicial competence" with "judicial greatness." Unlike judges such as Benjamin Cardozo and Learned Hand, Taft had "contributed practically nothing to legal thought."

The stakes of Taft's appointment as chief justice were high. As illustrated by the *Duplex Printing* case, the Court was not merely interpreting the law but making social and economic policy. He predicted that Taft as chief justice would be as thin-skinned about criticism as he had been as president. Yet Frankfurter emphasized that "the only safeguard against the terrible powers vested in the Supreme Court lies in continuous, informed and responsible criticism of the work of the Court." Whether in the *New Republic, Harvard Law Review*, or D.C. minimum-wage case, Frankfurter continued to lead the way.

In September while in Hadlyme, Connecticut, Frankfurter learned about the drama at the Court of Appeals of the District of Columbia. At first, the two justices in the majority, which included the trial judge sitting by designation for Justice Robb, denied the petition for rehearing. Robb then invoked his right to vote on the petition and along with the dissenting justice voted to grant it. A month later, Frankfurter reargued the case with Robb replacing the trial judge on the three-judge panel. Frankfurter objected at argument to the reversal of the motion for rehearing, removal of the trial judge sitting by designation, and the substitution of Robb as a most unusual and unfair procedure. One of the justices, presumably Robb or Van Orsdel, was so offended that he briefly left the bench, then demanded an apology from Frankfurter. The offended justice then equated minimum-wage legislation with Bolshevism. An unbowed Frankfurter observed that the word Bolshevism had not been invented when the law had been passed; the justice, however, insisted that there was no difference between the American reform movement of the past twenty to thirty years and Bolshevism. With two justices against him, the outcome was never in doubt. The court of appeals, however, delayed its decision for more than a year.

It did not take Taft long to show his true colors. In 1916, the Cooks' and Waiters' Union had declared a strike and had begun picketing the English Kitchen restaurant in the copper mining town of Bisbee, Arizona. The restaurant's owner and one of the town's most powerful men, William Truax, Sr., had cut his workers' pay and increased their hours. Truax sought a court order to stop the picketing because it interfered with his business. An Arizona law, however, prohibited "labor injunctions." The Arizona Supreme Court upheld the law's constitutionality. In December 1921, Taft wrote the U.S. Supreme Court's 5–4 decision in *Truax v. Corrigan* invalidating the Arizona law for violating the Due Process Clause and depriving Truax of his right to property. Taft also declared the law violated the Equal Protection Clause by favoring employees over employers.

In an unsigned editorial, "The Same Mr. Taft," Frankfurter began by quoting his prior editorial warning liberals about how the new chief justice would invoke the Fourteenth Amendment to make social and economic policy and about the need for "informed and responsible criticism." He then laced into Taft for declaring "it does not seem possible to escape the conclusion" that the law was unconstitutional when four of Taft's fellow justices had dissented. Frankfurter feared the decision's expansion of the Court's power to overrule laws by invoking the Due Process Clause was "fraught with more evil than any which it has rendered in a generation." The Fourteenth Amendment, he warned, was "not the arbiter of policy." He praised Holmes's dissent for criticizing the " 'delusiveness exactness' " of Taft's application of the Fourteenth Amendment and for falsely equating a business with real property such as land. Finally, he accused the chief justice of purporting to interpret the Constitution yet smuggling in personal prejudices about labor and capital "in the most sensitive field of social policy and legal control."

The ill-will between Taft and Frankfurter was mutual. Taft had not forgotten that Frankfurter had been a Roosevelt supporter in his administration or their clashes when Frankfurter had been chair of the War Labor Policies Board. "I never liked Frankfurter," the chief justice wrote Elihu Root, Sr., in 1922, "and have continued to dislike him more the more I have known him." He accused Frankfurter and Pound of leading a campaign "in favor of breaking down the Constitution, or making it a mere scrap of paper."

Frankfurter persisted with his vigilant criticism of Taft's opinions. He explained the ramifications for organized labor of Taft's unanimous decision that the United Mine Workers could be sued under the antitrust laws in future cases. Near the end of the 1921 term, the Court nixed Congress's second attempt to regulate child labor. In 1918 in *Hammer v. Dagenhart*, which had invalidated the Keating-Owen Child Labor Act, the Court had ruled, over Holmes's dissent, that Congress had exceeded its power to regulate interstate commerce because manufacturing was a purely local activity. In the second decision, *Bailey v. Drexel Furniture*, the Court declared in an 8–1 decision joined by Holmes and Brandeis that Congress could not simply repass the law as a 10 percent tax on net profits for any mill or mine that hired children less than fourteen years old. The most principled objections were that the tax was pretextual and interfered with state regulations over child labor. "We must pay a price," Frankfurter wrote in a bylined article, "for Federalism." In *Truax v. Corrigan*, however, the chief justice and his colleagues had been unwilling to pay the same price when they invalidated the Arizona law against labor injunctions.

That summer, a national debate ensued about the Supreme Court's perceived excesses. At the American Federation of Labor convention in the chief justice's hometown of Cincinnati, Senator Robert M. La Follette, Sr., declared the Taft Court "the actual ruler of the American people." He called for a constitutional amendment preventing lower federal courts from invalidating a federal law and granting Congress the power to nullify a Supreme Court decision by reenacting the law. Florence Kelley of the National Consumers' League called for a constitutional amendment outlawing child labor. Frankfurter was sympathetic with their ends but not their means. The amendment process, requiring a two-thirds vote of each house and three-quarters of the states, was long and difficult. And amendments, even if passed and ratified, could be misinterpreted and underenforced. Instead, he called for citizens, led by newly enfranchised women, to mobilize their state governments to pass child welfare laws.

Like many progressives, Frankfurter believed in political and social change not by empowering judges to interpret open-ended constitutional amendments but through new legislation guided by expert-led scientific studies. For months, he and Roscoe Pound had been directing a study of the criminal justice system in Cleveland, Ohio, known as the Cleveland crime survey. Frankfurter enlisted several friends to contribute chapters: former research assistant Herbert B. Ehrmann on the criminal courts, Raymond Fosdick on the police, and psychiatrist Herman Adler on medical science and criminal justice. In October 1921, he and Pound released the first few installments of their book, *Criminal Justice in Cleveland*, which they hoped would aid state and local efforts at criminal justice reform.

In an ideal world, Frankfurter would have written the Due Process Clauses out of the Constitution altogether (which also would have required amendments). Yet, as Brandeis explained to him, if there had been no Fourteenth Amendment, the conservative justices would have found another clause in the Constitution to strike down state laws in the name of individual freedom. Instead, Frankfurter preferred Holmes's more democratic approach, the view that the Court should not invoke the Due Process Clause "beyond the absolute compulsion of its words to prevent the making of social experiments."

During Taft's four years as president, he had nominated five justices and had elevated another to chief justice, altering two-thirds of the Court's membership. In fall 1922, as chief justice, he remade the Court again when three vacancies fell into Harding's lap. Frankfurter knew from Brandeis that the chief justice heavily influenced the president's selections by lobbying for like-minded colleagues.

Taft's second effort to pack the Court with conservatives began in September when Wilson's last nominee, John Hessin Clarke, resigned. Miserable on the Court, Clarke clashed with the racist McReynolds and disagreed with Brandeis about liberal principles. A staunch defender of the Wilson administration, Clarke wrote majority opinions upholding the Espionage Act conviction of Jacob Abrams and the suspension of the *Milwaukee Leader's* mailing privileges. Yet he was a reliable vote to uphold federal child labor laws and state minimum-wage laws. In Clarke's place, Harding/Taft chose a former U.S. senator from Utah, George Sutherland. To Frankfurter, Brandeis described Sutherland as "a mediocre Taft."

Two months later, William R. Day resigned because of chronically poor health. A moderate vote for upholding state minimum-wage laws, Day was replaced by Minnesota railroad lawyer Pierce Butler. Liberals and organized labor opposed Butler's nomination because of his efforts to oust radical University of Minnesota professors when he served as a member of the board of regents and his career representing railroad interests. (The Ku Klux Klan opposed the nomination because of his Catholicism.) The *New Republic* described him as "a reactionary of the most pronounced type." Frankfurter squelched a false rumor that he planned to testify against Butler.

On December 31, Justice Mahlon Pitney retired after suffering a stroke. One of four dissenters in *Truax v. Corrigan*, Pitney was another vote Frankfurter needed to uphold minimum-wage laws. In Pitney's place, Harding/Taft selected a Tennessee district judge, Edward Terry Sanford. Several New York judges mentioned as possible choices, including Learned Hand, Benjamin Cardozo, and Charles M. Hough, never had a chance. Taft vetoed anyone who could be a potential Brandeis ally. In place of a pro-labor Democrat and two swing votes, the chief justice had persuaded Harding to nominate three conservatives.

The prospect of Taft and Harding replacing Holmes, the Court's oldest justice, worried Frankfurter. During the summer of 1921, the 81-year-old had undergone prostate surgery. He struggled to return to the Court. For the first month, he lived at the Powhatan Hotel while an elevator was installed in his home. One of his opinions, a 8–1 decision favoring a large coal company, invoked the Due Process Clause to invalidate a Pennsylvania law banning mining beneath people's homes. Brandeis, who dissented and sided with the homeowners who had purchased only surface rights to the land, blamed it on Holmes's post-surgery fatigue and the conservative tendencies of his secretary. Frankfurter responded to the opinion with conspicuous silence.

Holmes's liberal friends let him know how much they needed him on the Court. In December, the *New Republic* celebrated Holmes's twentieth anniversary on the Court and fortieth on the bench. Frankfurter wrote an unsigned editorial quoting Holmes's phrase, "'We live by symbols,'" and proclaiming Holmes's opinions "the symbol at once of the promise and the fulfillment of the American judiciary." He praised Holmes's 1918 *Hammer v. Dagenhart* dissent in the first child labor case and his 1921 *Truax v. Corrigan* dissent about the Arizona anti-injunction law. "Behind the sceptic is invincible faith . . . ," Frankfurter concluded. "And ours still the glory of his labor, still ours the music of his dream." A "deeply moved" Holmes identified Frankfurter as the author and confessed fears that he was not pulling his weight on the Court; Taft and Brandeis insisted he was. By the beginning of 1923, Holmes's health improved, and he was mentally sharper. Retirement was the furthest thing from his mind.

At least Holmes would be on the bench when Frankfurter argued the D.C. minimum-wage case. In November 1922, the Court of Appeals of the District Columbia finally released its decision, 2–1 with the previously ill Robb now participating, striking down the D.C. minimum-wage law for women. It had been sixteen months since the court of appeals initially had decided the case the other way; by that time, the composition of the Supreme Court had completely changed.

Holmes looked like Frankfurter's only reliable vote. Moderates Clarke, Day, and Pitney had been replaced by Sutherland, Butler, and Sanford. To make matters worse, Brandeis disqualified himself. He had defended similar laws for years for the National Consumers' League; his daughter worked as assistant secretary of the D.C. Minimum Wage Board; and he had recently paid Frankfurter $1000 for his public interest work. With no Brandeis and a remade Taft Court, Frankfurter faced a difficult task in persuading five justices to reverse the court of appeals decision and to save state minimum-wage laws from constitutional extinction.

In preparation for the argument, Frankfurter left no stone unturned. His brief, at 1138 pages including an appendix and published in two volumes, was the Brandeis brief in *Muller v. Oregon* times ten. Frankfurter enlisted Dean Acheson, an associate at Covington & Burling after two years as Brandeis's secretary, to critique the brief's legal arguments. George Rublee, Acheson's mentor at Covington, commented as well. Frankfurter premised his legal argument on a single Supreme Court case—Chief Justice John Marshall's opinion in *McCulloch v. Maryland* declaring broad federal power to create a national bank and describing the Constitution as a "great" outline. Frankfurter argued that the case was "an application of Marshall's canon of constitutional construction to the concrete facts of modern industrial life." He quoted Marshall's famous passage, " 'Let the end be legitimate, let it be within the scope of the constitution, and all means which are appropriate, which are plainly adapted to that end, which are not prohibited, but consist with the letter and spirit of the constitution, are constitutional.' " The federal government, Frankfurter contended, possessed legitimate ends and appropriate means to pass a D.C. minimum-wage law for women on the basis of industrial conditions in the nation's capital. Point by point in sixty-five pages, he argued that the law was within the scope of the federal government's power and not so arbitrary as to violate the Due Process Clause.

Frankfurter's legal argument preceded more than 1000 pages of data compiled by Molly Dewson of the National Consumers' League about the success of minimum-wage laws in the District of Columbia, Arkansas, California, Colorado, Kansas, Massachusetts, Minnesota, North Dakota, Oregon, Texas, Washington, Wisconsin, Great Britain, Australia, and Canada; statistical studies about the effects of minimum-wage laws in those jurisdictions; all the existing minimum-wage law provisions; and studies about depressed wages for women in the District of Columbia showing the need for such legislation.

The day before oral argument, Frankfurter and Holmes "had one of the best talks we have ever had." At the end of the visit, Holmes "took me with both his hands, his eyes all afire." The next day, Frankfurter entered the Old Senate Chamber with a sound strategy—to win the vote of Chief Justice Taft. The odds were stacked against him. Yet if he could persuade the chief justice, other reluctant justices might follow.

The Taft-centered strategy fell short. On April 9, less than a month after the argument, Sutherland announced an opinion for five justices in *Adkins v. Children's Hospital* invalidating the D.C. minimum-wage law for women as violating the Due Process Clause's liberty of contract. The 1905 *Lochner* decision and the idea of "liberty of contract," which Brandeis and Frankfurter had spent nearly twenty years trying to destroy, returned with a vengeance. Laws are usually presumed to be constitutional unless the Court can be persuaded otherwise. Sutherland's *Adkins* opinion, however, took the opposite approach by making "freedom of contract" "the general rule and restraint the exception." In Frankfurter's view, it "struck the death knell not only of this legislation, but of kindred social legislation because it laid down as a constitutional principle that any kind of change by statute has to justify itself, not the other way around."

The chief justice, joined by the newest justice, Sanford, dissented. Taft argued that *Lochner* and "liberty of contract" had been implicitly overruled by the Court's decision three years later in *Muller v. Oregon* upholding a maximum-hour law for women, a case won by Brandeis, and by its 1917 decision in *Bunting v. Oregon* upholding a maximum-hour law for industrial workers, a case won by Frankfurter. Taft disliked dissenting but disliked departing from the Court's precedents even more. He worried about criticism of the Court and calls for reform.

Holmes wrote the last dissent. He objected to reading the word "contract," as well as the justices' economic preferences, into the liberty provision of the Due Process Clause. "The criterion of constitutionality is not whether we believe the law to be for the public good," he wrote. Every law, he observed, interferes with economic liberty, including Sunday laws and usury laws. He could not understand why maximum-hour laws were constitutional, but minimum-wage laws were not. Holmes confessed his doubts about the efficacy of the minimum-wage law yet insisted that the law's costs and benefits were "not for me to decide." Privately, Holmes consoled Frankfurter that "no one could have brought about a different decision."

Time was not on Frankfurter's side. One wonders, if the Court of Appeals of the District of Columbia had not voted to rehear the case through use of dubious procedural grounds and delayed its decision for more than year, whether he would have won the case in the fall of 1921 or spring of 1922 with a less conservative Court. To be sure, two of the dissenting justices, Taft and Sanford, would not have been there. Yet Clarke and Day probably would have sided with Frankfurter, unlike their successors Sutherland and Butler. And Pitney, like Clarke, had dissented in *Truax v. Corrigan* and was another likely vote. White probably represented the deciding vote and may have been willing to follow *Muller, Bunting,* and Holmes's 5–4 decision in the D.C. housing case. It would have been close, 5–3, or possibly a 4–4 split with Brandeis disqualified. A 4–4 split would have allowed the court of appeals's initial decision to stand and not jeopardized other state minimum-wage laws.

———

AFTER THE ARGUMENT, Frankfurter rekindled his discussion with Learned Hand about the role of the Supreme Court in American life: "[T]he possible gain isn't worth the cost of having five men without any reasonable probability that they are qualified for the task, determine the course of social policy for the states and the nation." He suggested that the usual guides for ordinary questions of law, such as precedent, have no "reasonable relevance to the kind of issues involved in determining whether a minimum wage law is included within 'the vague contours' of the due process clause." He suggested eliminating due process review from questions about "social policy," except for federal encroachment on state power. He opposed Senator La Follette's and Senator William Borah's suggestion of requiring a 7–2 or 6–3 vote to overturn a federal law because a constitutional amendment had little chance of passage and "at the rate at which the Sutherlands and the Butlers are being appointed to the Court, it wouldn't do any good if it did."

Frankfurter was opposed to invoking the Due Process Clause no matter how horrible or objectionable the law. In *Meyer v. Nebraska,* for example, McReynolds wrote for seven justices invalidating a Nebraska law that forbade the teaching of any foreign language in grade school. The law was the product of anti-German sentiment during the war; a teacher was convicted of teaching German in a Lutheran school. McReynolds declared the law violated the "liberty" of the teacher to teach and the liberty of parents to hire him to educate their children, expanding the definition of the "liberty" provision of the Due Process Clause beyond "freedom from bodily restraint." Frankfurter insisted he would have voted with the Court's dissenter, Holmes. "Of course, I regard such know-nothing legislation as uncivilized, but for the life of me I can't see how it meets the condemnation of want of 'due process' unless we frankly recognize that the Supreme Court of the United States is the revisory legislative body," Frankfurter wrote Hand. As James Bradley Thayer's article taught him, Frankfurter believed that allowing the Supreme Court to invoke the Due Process Clause to strike down abhorrent state laws robbed legislators and voters of any incentive to invest in the democratic political process. "The more I think about this 'due process' business," he wrote Hand, "the less I think of lodging that power in those nine gents at Washington."

Reflecting on the Supreme Court decisions of the era, Frankfurter developed a prescient theory of limited judicial review. The Court, he conceded, played a critical role in establishing boundaries between the power of the federal government and that of the states. The Fourteenth Amendment, moreover, was necessary to protect free speech from abusive state laws. Yet, aside from dissents by Holmes and Brandeis, during free speech cases in the late 1910s and 1920s the Court "behaved like the mob." Frankfurter understood the need to protect free speech, fair criminal trials, and racial and religious minorities. He suggested restricting the Fourteenth Amendment "to 'unreasonable' racial and religious discriminations & withdrawing from those Nine Holies the reviewing power over purely intra-state 'social legislation.'"

Holmes showed Frankfurter and other liberals how the Fourteenth Amendment could be invoked to protect racial minorities. In February 1923, Holmes wrote a majority opinion for six justices in *Moore v. Dempsey* remanding the case of Frank Moore and four black sharecroppers on death row for the murder of a white railroad agent after the Elaine massacre in rural Philips County, Arkansas. During the "Red Summer" of 1919, an attempt to break up a sharecroppers' union meeting led to gunfire, the railroad agent's death, and days of racial violence; five whites and more than a hundred blacks had been killed and more than a hundred blacks had been arrested. Moore and his co-defendants were sentenced to death in mob-dominated sham trials. A lynch mob outside the courthouse ensured that the defendants would be convicted and executed. Other defendants were beaten and tortured into testifying against them. Court-appointed defense counsel was not permitted to meet with their clients before trial, did not call any witnesses, and did not request a delay or change of venue. The trial lasted forty-five minutes; the all-white jury deliberated for five. "[N]o juryman," Holmes wrote, "could have voted for an acquittal and continued to live in Phillips County and if any prisoner by any chance had been acquitted by a jury he could not have escaped the mob." Holmes distinguished Moore's case from that of Leo Frank, the Jewish pencil factory superintendent, who for his own safety had not been allowed to attend his sentencing after being convicted of murdering fourteen-year-old Mary Phagan. If the criminal trial of Moore and his co-defendants had been so mob-dominated as to be a sham, Holmes argued, nothing could "prevent this Court from securing to the petitioners their constitutional rights." As a result of Holmes's opinion, the governor of Arkansas commuted the death sentences of Moore and his co-defendants to twelve years in prison. By 1925, the last of the men was released.

By promoting Holmes as a judicial icon, Frankfurter critiqued the Court. In June 1923, he published a *Harvard Law Review* article, "Twenty Years of Mr. Justice Holmes' Constitutional Opinions." He had been delaying its publication until after the Court decided *Adkins*. The Court, Frankfurter argued, invoked the vagueness of due process and equal protection to decide cases on the basis of the justices' personal preferences. "Should such power, affecting the intimate life of Nation and States, be entrusted, ultimately, to five men?" he asked. In lieu of repealing the Due Process Clause, he urged a more vigilant process of selecting justices de-emphasizing whether they were liberal or conservative in favor of life experiences. Holmes, he argued, was the "great exception," a philosopher who viewed the Constitution not as a revered document but a practical guide for governing the country. The other justices, he insisted, had a lot to learn from Holmes's opinions from the past twenty years: "The Supreme Court, like all human institutions, must earn reverence through the test of truth. He has built himself into the structure of our national life. He has written himself into the slender volume of the literature of all times." *Time* magazine, a new publication that employed Frankfurter's former student Archibald MacLeish, highlighted the law review article as "Honor to Justice Holmes"; the *New Republic* recommended that it be "read not only by lawyers, who would presumably be technically interested in its contents, but by laymen to whom the traditional American system of law and government is a cherished inheritance."

For his part, Frankfurter believed that the solution to the nation's labor problems lay not with curbing the Court's power through a constitutional amendment but with the state political process. At a minimum-wage conference on April 20, 1923, he argued for the continued enforcement of state and D.C. minimum-wage laws for children because they had not been challenged in *Adkins*. He suggested amending existing state minimum-wage laws from mandatory enforcement to enforcement by publicity like in Massachusetts. His goal was to establish a livable minimum wage without incurring the Court's wrath: "We have got to be practical and fight inch by inch, while we do the larger thing."

Frankfurter's larger mission was to educate the public by commissioning studies to make the necessity and efficacy of minimum-wage laws incontrovertible and to prevent justices such as Sutherland from relying on their political, economic, and social prejudices. "The heart of the difficulty was that the Supreme Court assumed certain things to be facts which are not facts," he told the people at the conference. He blamed the justices for having outdated pictures in their heads: "I am sure if you could get an intellectual X-ray of Sutherland and Pierce Butler's minds and [Mc]Reynolds, you would find an [antiquated] notion of American society."

After *Adkins*, Frankfurter never argued another Supreme Court case. He threw himself into politics and challenged the establishment at every turn—starting with the president of Harvard.

CHAPTER II

The True Function
of a "Liberal"

During the Harding-Coolidge years, Frankfurter challenged A. Lawrence Lowell and other establishment figures who trafficked in bigotry, trampled on academic freedom, or abridged civil liberties. He and other liberals found both major political parties unsatisfying. Instead, he carved out a space for liberalism by championing unpopular social and political causes, even if it meant offending friends or making enemies.

The fight with President Lowell started in the spring of 1922 when word leaked that he planned to institute a 15 percent quota on Harvard's Jewish undergraduates. Anti-Semitism seemed to be everywhere. Henry Ford promoted Jewish conspiracy theories in his magazine, the *Dearborn Independent*; he also published thousands of copies of translations of *The Protocols of the Elders of Zion*, the forged anti-Semitic Russian tract about Jews taking over the world. In June, Frankfurter's friend, journalist Norman Hapgood, began exposing Ford's anti-Semitism in a series of articles for *Hearst's International*, "The Inside Story of Henry Ford's Jew Mania." As Hapgood took on Ford, Frankfurter confronted Lowell.

There was no love lost between Frankfurter and Lowell. In 1916, Frankfurter and Lippmann had humiliated Lowell and other leaders of Old Boston who opposed Brandeis's Supreme Court nomination, mocking their insularity in a *New Republic* editorial and garnering a Brandeis endorsement from Lowell's beloved predecessor, Charles W. Eliot. Lowell resented Frankfurter's public service in the War Department, the President's Mediation Commission, and the War Labor Policies Board and suspected it was cover for Zionist activity. The Mooney and Bisbee reports, defense of radical immigrants rounded up during the Palmer raids, and public criticism of Attorney General

Palmer angered Harvard alumni and irritated Lowell because of its "unfortunate effect upon the School." Now that the war was over, Lowell advised Frankfurter to cease his outside public activities and to pay "his whole attention for a time to his work in the Law School." Frankfurter, who continued to defend the District of Columbia minimum-wage law and to take on unpopular causes, ignored Lowell's warnings.

The animus between Lowell and Frankfurter came to a head in June 1922 when the Harvard president left him, the law school's first Jewish faculty member, off the committee to consider the Jewish quota issue. At first, Frankfurter sought answers about the snub by using Judge Mack, the first Jewish member of the school's Board of Overseers, as an intermediary. Lowell informed Mack that Frankfurter was not on the committee because he lacked "the quality of solid judgment." When Frankfurter heard rumors that Lowell considered his views on the quota issue "violent" and "extreme," he confronted the president. Lowell defended his decision and denied Frankfurter's allegation that he had stacked the committee of thirteen faculty members with three "safe Jews." Frankfurter refused to let it go.

To take on Lowell, Frankfurter reached out to a prominent Jewish Harvard alumnus, Walter Lippmann. Lippmann's star was on the rise. He had left the *New Republic* for the New York *World* editorial page. His 1922 book, *Public Opinion*, about how people make political decisions on the basis of the uninformed "pictures inside their heads" rather than through facts and evidence, had transformed him into a public intellectual. Frankfurter had praised the book and had invoked its ideas in analyzing the Supreme Court's decision in the D.C. minimum-wage case. Lippmann, however, was more comfortable with praise than conflict. He was reluctant to acknowledge his privileged Upper East Side Jewish background or to support Jewish causes; he blamed rising anti-Semitism on "rich and vulgar" Jews. Frankfurter pleaded with Lippmann, as an influential Harvard graduate, to stand up for the school's "most liberal traditions" against its president "who all his life has hated Jews." He added: "Don't dismiss this as my hysteria. I am not wont to ask you to go on crusades." A flurry of follow-up letters failed to change Lippmann's mind. Privately, Lippmann informed a faculty member of his support for a Jewish quota and argued that the state should set up a Jewish-led university for immigrants seeking admission to Harvard. Lippmann's reluctance to join Frankfurter in his fight against Lowell was the first of several instances in which they found themselves on opposite sides—with Frankfurter challenging the conservative establishment and Lippmann defending it.

In April 1923, the committee ostensibly rejected Lowell's quota on Jews as contrary to the school's "policy of equal opportunity for all regardless of race and religion." It was a Pyrrhic victory. In the interim, the school had begun asking admissions questions about an applicant's race and color, where the applicant's father was born, and whether the father had changed his name. The committee recommended emphasis on geographic diversity, which privileged applicants from the South and West over ones from cities in the Northeast (i.e., Jews). Frankfurter insisted he would have been fired from the law school if he had behaved as underhandedly as Lowell had and described the president as "an arrogant autocrat driven by a passion on this subject which he will not avow." Lowell's leadership, Frankfurter wrote Lippmann, "sickens my soul."

Not content to take on Lowell over the Jewish quota, Frankfurter attacked the board of trustees of Amherst College in June 1923 for dismissing its innovative and beloved president, Alexander Meiklejohn. Amherst alumni did not take kindly to Meiklejohn's curriculum changes and faculty hires or to his comment that he would hire a Bolshevik if the person "were a good teacher." The trustees forced him to resign for alleged mismanagement of the school's resources and messy personal finances. At graduation, thirteen students protested by declining to accept their diplomas; Meiklejohn's valedictory address about the country's need to think in democratic terms instead of about privilege and social standing made national headlines. Frankfurter declared Meiklejohn's impact on Amherst "the most significant educational achievement in our times."

Frankfurter's attempt to interest Lippmann in Meiklejohn's ouster resulted in another clash of personalities and viewpoints. After a two-day visit to Amherst's campus, Lippmann wrote a New York *World* op-ed blaming Meiklejohn for privileging new faculty hires over old ones, refusing to consider campus politics like most college presidents, and losing the support of a majority of the faculty. Frankfurter criticized Lippmann for doing a "a reporter's job" that was based on insufficient research rather than analyzing the situation like an opinion columnist. The thin-skinned Lippmann resented Frankfurter's criticism and relentless stream of letters about Meiklejohn and cut off their discussion. Three months passed before Lippmann tried to put his irritation with Frankfurter behind him.

Lippmann's former employer, the *New Republic*, also disappointed Frankfurter with its coverage of the Meiklejohn affair and its refusal to take an editorial stance. He challenged the magazine to live up to its reputation as "a journal committed to the espousal of the liberal faith" and to examine "the factors that brought about such a tragedy in American liberalism [that] would seem to be nothing less than a primary duty." At a meeting with *New Repub-*

lic editors, Frankfurter urged them to seek an explanation for Meiklejohn's firing from the ringleader of the Amherst trustees, lawyer and J.P. Morgan banker Dwight Morrow. Frankfurter had known and liked Morrow since the spring of 1906 when Morrow had been the only Wall Street lawyer who had encouraged him during his job search. Nonetheless, Frankfurter viewed Morrow as the villain in the Meiklejohn affair. The magazine, owned by fellow J.P. Morgan banker Willard Straight, was reluctant to attack Morrow. A few weeks later, however, editor Alvin Johnson drafted an "Open Letter to Dwight Morrow" urging him to explain Meiklejohn's dismissal. When Morrow failed to respond for several months, Frankfurter wrote a letter to the editor charging Morrow with believing either he had no "responsibility to the public" or "that if he and his fellow-trustees will only lie low for a little while, the storm raised by the Meiklejohn affair will blow over."

The issue, for Frankfurter, was bigger than Alexander Meiklejohn; it was about the role of liberalism in higher education and in American politics. He believed that higher education was threatened not by Meiklejohn and other liberals but by "the corrosive influence of business aims and processes in the world of the spirit." His anti-Meiklejohn friends left "wholly out of account the true function of a 'liberal.'" Frankfurter described a liberal as "a ferment and a fighter" who was "apt to be a bit of a nuisance simply because he is tilting against entrenched complacency, he is seeking to dislodge injustice and to arouse indifference."

———

DURING THE PRESIDENTIAL ELECTION of 1924, Frankfurter's liberalism was on full display as he challenged the establishment and championed an unlikely presidential candidate. Harding had died on August 2, 1923, thrusting vice president Calvin Coolidge—famous for crushing the Boston police strike as governor of Massachusetts—into the presidency. Frankfurter saw little difference between the two men. "Having survived Harding," he wrote Lippmann, "I don't fear anything in particular will happen through Coolidge."

Coolidge's chances of winning the 1924 election depended on his ability to distance himself from the corruption of the Harding administration. The Teapot Dome scandal revealed that oil companies had bribed Secretary of the Interior Albert B. Fall for access to government-owned western oil reserves. And Congress was investigating corruption in the Justice Department, which led to criminal charges against Attorney General Harry M. Daugherty.

Frankfurter led the charge to eliminate Coolidge's most viable challenger in the Democratic Party, Wall Street lawyer John W. Davis. Davis's
credentials were impeccable—a former West Virginia congressman, first-rate
Supreme Court advocate as Wilson's solicitor general from 1913 to 1918, and
U.S. ambassador to Great Britain from 1918 to 1921. In 1922, he had declined
a Supreme Court seat to make money as a Wall Street lawyer. Davis's greed
and Wall Street ties troubled Frankfurter. For three years, Frankfurter had
taken on unpopular causes, preventing the mass deportation of Boston immigrants, challenging the constitutionality of A. Mitchell Palmer's raids, and
signing Jacob Abrams's clemency petition. Other prominent lawyers also had
spoken out. Yet Davis, the president of the American Bar Association from
1922 to 1923, had stayed silent. He was too busy lining his pockets at Stetson,
Jennings & Russell by working for J.P. Morgan & Company.

Two months before the Democratic convention, Frankfurter wrote an
unsigned *New Republic* editorial, "Why Mr. Davis Shouldn't Run," arguing
that Davis epitomized the corporate greed of the 1920s. The candidate, Frankfurter charged, was "under retainer by the House of Morgan" and ignored the
advice of friends to sever his ties with J.P. Morgan. Wall Street, Frankfurter
argued, changed the former West Virginia congressman: "He has become
the close associate of the most powerful banking house in the world. He has
ceased to be merely a distinguished advocate." Brandeis hoped Frankfurter's
editorial would discourage Davis from seeking the Democratic nomination;
Davis, however, stayed in the race.

The Democratic Party convention at New York's Madison Square Garden was the longest in history. It took thirteen days, fifteen candidates, and
a record 103 ballots to nominate a candidate at the convention nicknamed
the "Klanbake." The Ku Klux Klan backed the Georgia-born and Tennessee-
raised William Gibbs McAdoo, Jr. Woodrow Wilson's secretary of the treasury
and son-in-law, McAdoo was the "dry" candidate for Prohibition. Northern
Democrats favored New York governor Al Smith, a "wet" candidate against
Prohibition and a Catholic opposed by the Klan and southern and western
Democrats. With the party split between McAdoo and Smith, Davis emerged
as the compromise candidate and won the nomination. After attending the
convention, Frankfurter was angry at newspaper columnists for dramatiz-
ing and mocking the events rather than illuminating the importance of the
fight over the Klan, Prohibition, and whether Davis was fit to be the Democratic nominee.

Davis's nomination created another rift between Frankfurter and Lippmann. At first, they seemed to be on the same side. They had opposed

McAdoo because he had taken $20,000 from Edward Doheny, who had been implicated in the Teapot Dome scandal, and for being a mouthpiece for big business. When Lippmann and the *World* suddenly supported Davis as the Democratic nominee, Frankfurter was perplexed. He reminded Lippmann of Davis's "disqualifying silences" as ABA president about "cardinal issues of liberalism concerning freedom of speech and constitutional observances of law and order—what makes you regard him as a liberal? Do you know his views on economic and social issues, or do you know people who know his views intimately?"

For his part, Lippmann was shocked when Frankfurter declared his support for Progressive Party candidate Robert M. La Follette, Sr. Many believed that La Follette, not Theodore Roosevelt, would have been the Progressive Party's candidate in 1912 if La Follette had not given an intemperate speech to newspaper publishers and had not suffered from nervous exhaustion. Unlike Roosevelt, no one could question La Follette's progressive bona fides. As a Wisconsin governor and U.S. senator, he helped make his state a leader in socioeconomic legislation. La Follette also had been a longtime critic of the Supreme Court. In 1912, he had accused the Court of being "the most powerful institution in our government" and of making "one law for the rich and another for the poor." Twelve years later as a third-party presidential candidate, he proposed a constitutional amendment to allow Congress to override Supreme Court decisions invalidating federal laws.

Frankfurter tried to explain to an incredulous Lippmann why he supported La Follette when a third-party candidate had little chance of winning: "You see, I'm incorrigibly academic, and, therefore, the immediate results of the 1924 election do not appear very important. The directions which we further or retard for 1944 are tremendously important. Coolidge and Davis have nothing to offer for 1944; they have no dreams, no 'pictures in their heads' (which *Public Opinion* has taught me is the all-important thing) except things substantially as is. The forces that are struggling and groping behind La Follette are, at least, struggling and groping for a dream, for a different look of things in 1944."

Lippmann responded in print. In a *World* editorial, "The Superpurists," he criticized Frankfurter and others for dismissing Davis "before he has had a chance to open his mouth." He questioned why his former employer, the *New Republic*, co-founded by a J.P. Morgan banker, assumed "that any man who has ever touched money made in the vicinity of Wall Street is forever after a lost soul." He predicted that "[t]he violent prejudging of Mr. Davis will injure him far less than it will injure the credit of liberalism." A furious Frankfurter

wrote a four-page letter to the editor reminding the *World* of its April 2 editorial criticizing Davis for not severing his ties with J.P. Morgan before running
for president. Frankfurter received no answer to several follow-up requests
to publish the letter. Finally, Lippmann replied that he would print the letter but only if Frankfurter cut it to 300 words. Rather than simply publish
Frankfurter's truncated letter, Lippmann replied with an editor's note denying that Davis had worked for J.P. Morgan or was on retainer to the bank and
defending his decision to maintain ties with Wall Street. Lippmann, moreover, refused to publish Frankfurter's 250-word reply and considered "the
matter definitely closed." Privately, Lippmann conceded the newspaper had
changed its view. "Really, Walter, I had no desire for a debate," Frankfurter
replied. "I simply wanted The World to say publicly what you now write me in
your letter—instead of red-herringing an absurd bit of misinformation about
Mr. Davis's law practice."

In the *New Republic*, Frankfurter explained why the magazine opposed
Davis and why all liberals should. He exposed Davis as a conservative who
embraced his role as a Wall Street lawyer and corporate defender, opposed
some Supreme Court decisions as "too liberal for him," and supported
"things as they are." In another *New Republic* editorial, "Abstemious Liberalism," Frankfurter responded to Lippmann's misinformation campaign in
the *World* and its misguided suggestion that Davis was a liberal. Frankfurter
reviewed the bill of particulars against Davis: silence as ABA president during
the Red Scare and about the Palmer raids; refusal to leave his Wall Street law
firm before running for president; and defense of "the constitutional sanctity of property rights" and criticism of Supreme Court decisions upholding
socioeconomic legislation. Frankfurter reminded the *New Republic*'s readers
of the stakes: future Supreme Court nominees and laws protecting working
men, women, and children. After reviewing Davis's career from West Virginia congressman to Wall Street lawyer, Frankfurter concluded: "If, after
such a record on such basic issues of liberalism, Mr. Davis can be claimed as
a 'liberal,' 'liberalism' has lost all meaning."

During the fall of 1924, Frankfurter campaigned for La Follette, tried to
persuade skeptical friends to vote for him, and wrote editorials supporting
him. He believed that of the three candidates, La Follette represented the
future of the country, the Supreme Court, and American liberalism.

Frankfurter excelled at critiquing the candidates' views on the Supreme
Court. In an unsigned *New Republic* editorial, "The Red Terror of Judicial
Reform," he attacked Coolidge's claim that the Court protected the rights of
the minority and Davis's argument that citizens needed a venue for protect-

THE TRUE FUNCTION OF A "LIBERAL"

ing "sacred rights." Frankfurter exposed both candidates for not saying what those rights were. He declared that Coolidge, the author of *The Reds in Our Colleges*, "knows no better" and disparaged Davis, one of the Court's leading practitioners, for conveying "a mutilated, and, therefore, untrue picture." Frankfurter conceded the need for "an independent Supreme Court" yet condemned its 1918 decision invalidating the first child labor law as exceeding Congress's power to regulate interstate commerce. He agreed with Holmes that the world would not come to an end if the Court lost the power to overrule federal laws. Coolidge and Davis defended the Court by focusing on only the Bill of Rights; Frankfurter, however, argued that the Court had failed miserably to protect the free speech of Jacob Abrams and other unpopular radicals. He challenged Coolidge and Davis to defend the Court's invocation of the Fourteenth Amendment's Due Process and Equal Protection Clauses, not to defend blacks from discrimination but to invalidate pro-labor legislation. Coolidge's belief in " 'protecting the freedom of the individual, of guarding his earnings, his home, his life' " was in reality a defense of liberty of contract used to invalidate workmen's compensation laws, a maximum-hour law for bakers, laws protecting the right to join a union, and a minimum-wage law for women. Or, as Frankfurter described liberty of contract, "this doctrine which the Supreme Court has used as a sword with which to slay most important social legislation and to deny the means of freedom to those least free." Frankfurter attacked Davis for criticizing opponents of liberty of contract including Hughes, Holmes, Brandeis, and "occasionally" Taft. Davis defended liberty of contract in his speeches yet said nothing about its use in decisions from *Lochner* to *Adkins*. "Mr. Davis is silent about such decisions," Frankfurter wrote, "but he cannot be ignorant of them."

In the same editorial, Frankfurter defended La Follette's attacks on the Court not because he agreed with the candidate's precise remedies but because of the impact of the criticism on public opinion and judicial behavior. In 1912, Frankfurter had disagreed with Theodore Roosevelt's proposed popular recall of judicial decisions yet liked how Roosevelt " 'put the fear of God into judges.' " He credited Roosevelt's Bull Moose campaign with producing "a temporary period of liberalism." In 1924, Frankfurter was not enamored with La Follette's proposed constitutional amendment giving Congress veto power over certain Supreme Court decisions. Yet he understood La Follette's potential impact on federal and state judges and the justices who had invalidated the minimum-wage law for women in *Adkins*. Frankfurter favored removing the Due Process Clauses from the Constitution because they gave the justices too much power over socioeconomic legislation, power they should think twice about using in the future. "The 'fear of God,'" he wrote, "very much needs to make itself felt in 1924."

During the final days of the campaign, Frankfurter wrote numerous editorials and letters to the editor endorsing La Follette and trying to persuade friends to vote for the third-party candidate. A vote for La Follette was a litmus test for liberalism.

In the *New Republic*, Frankfurter and Herbert Croly endorsed La Follette; Lippmann endorsed Davis. In "Why I Shall Vote for La Follette," Frankfurter explained that the "'great inequality of property' is the most significant characteristic of our social-economic life," and the solutions lay neither with the "stand-pat" Republican Party nor with what he described as "the greatest immoral factor of American politics"—the Democratic Party controlled by the "solid South." The 1924 presidential campaign, Frankfurter argued, was a transitional election freighted with political significance. Industrialization, the Great Migration of southern blacks, and immigration promised a realignment of the political parties. And amidst great political and social upheaval, La Follette was the only candidate "educating public opinion" about "the claims and needs of labor and agriculture." He praised La Follette's reliance on experts during his forty years in Wisconsin politics to tackle "economic and social questions." He urged people to eschew party loyalty and to vote for La Follette to prove that "all the talk of 'throwing one's vote away' is the cowardly philosophy of the bandwagon."

Frankfurter did not regret his crusade against Davis or his support for La Follette. He did not care, as Lippmann correctly predicted, that a vote for La Follette was a vote for Coolidge. He was willing to lose the 1924 presidential election to make the country better by 1944. Aided by La Follette's third-party candidacy, Coolidge captured 15.7 million popular votes and 382 electoral votes. La Follette won only his home state of Wisconsin but outpolled Davis in twelve states. His 4.8 million votes made La Follette one of the twentieth century's most successful third-party candidates. In the end, however, it was four more years of Coolidge.

———

FOR FRANKFURTER, La Follette's candidacy was a rejection of the roaring 1920s ethos of moneymaking and greed represented by Davis and J.P. Morgan; it was also an effort to change the worldviews and career aspirations of Harvard law students. During the early 1920s, the law school was flush with talented students. Frankfurter, however, was horrified that "a pretty crass materialism is their dominating ambition." The students strove to make money as lawyers on Wall Street or in Chicago. Frankfurter's mission was to show them how unfulfilling the life of a Wall Street lawyer was and how they could change the future of the country through academia and public service. To be sure, the Harvard law professor sent many top students to law firms in New York, Washington, and Boston. Emory Buckner poached several of Frankfurter's best graduates for Root, Clark in New York City. Dean Acheson, after two years as Brandeis's secretary, was the first of several top Frankfurter students who worked at Covington & Burling in Washington.

Yet for high-achieving students, Frankfurter put them on a different track — a clerkship with Holmes or Brandeis and a postgraduate fellowship at the law school where they could receive a doctorate and lessons in legal scholarship by co-authoring articles and books with their professor. He recruited *Harvard Law Review* editors regardless of background, social standing, or race.

In 1922, Frankfurter encouraged Charles Hamilton Houston, the first black editor of the *Harvard Law Review* and one of the school's few black students, to pursue his doctorate. He supervised Houston's doctoral thesis and taught him public utilities and administrative law. He then recommended Houston for a postgraduate Sheldon Traveling Fellowship in Spain and to teach at Howard Law School. Seven years later, Frankfurter played a similar role with William Hastie, the second black member of the *Review*, supervising Hastie's doctoral thesis. Second cousins who grew up in Washington, D.C.'s, black middle class and who excelled at Amherst College, Houston and Hastie practiced law with Houston's father, transformed Howard University into a first-rate law school, and orchestrated the NAACP's legal challenges to racial segregation and discrimination. As he did with other star students, Frankfurter promoted Houston's and Hastie's careers in academia and public service.

During the mid-1920s, three exceptional students enrolled in the law school and found themselves on Frankfurter's fast track: James Landis, Thomas Corcoran, and Henry Friendly.

The first student, James McCauley Landis, was the most driven. One of five children of a Presbyterian missionary and minister father, he had grown up in Tokyo until age 13, finished first in his class at Princeton, and received a scholarship to Harvard Law School. Before he set foot in the law school, he had published a *Michigan Law Review* article, "The Commerce Clause as a Restriction on State Taxation." Thin and wiry with a receding hairline, prominent forehead, furrowed brow, and sunken gray eyes, Landis was reticent and shy with his law school classmates and struggled socially. He lost the election to be president of the *Harvard Law Review*, supposedly because

Frankfurter had urged the other editors to break the tie in favor of Landis's opponent. During his third year, Landis took Frankfurter's public utilities class to see what all the fuss was about. He was dazzled by Frankfurter's Socratic style, and Frankfurter was impressed by Landis's intellect and drive. Landis twice won the Sears Prize for having the highest grades in his class and led his class at graduation with an 81 average. Frankfurter encouraged him to stay at the law school for a fourth year to earn a doctorate as part of a graduate research program and to collaborate with Frankfurter on law review articles.

In the spring of 1924, Frankfurter adopted Landis as his constant companion during his wife's prolonged absences. Marion had suffered another nervous breakdown in December 1923 after attempting to go to medical school. She tried to recuperate in Florida and on a trip to California to see her parents. She moved to New York City to seek daily treatment from Dr. Thomas W. Salmon, a Columbia University psychiatry professor. Frankfurter reluctantly asked for and received $1500 from Brandeis for Marion's treatment. During the summer of 1925, she stayed in Darien, Connecticut, where she continued seeing Dr. Salmon and learned to play golf and to drive a car. The latter skill came in handy as her husband never learned to drive. Felix and Marion corresponded almost daily and remained as devoted and in love with each other as ever. She called him Fixi, short for the Mr. Fix moniker Robert and Sophie Valentine had bestowed on him years earlier. "Oh Fixi," she wrote him, "I could bite you, eat you up, swallow you whole!"

Others gossiped about the Frankfurters' childless marriage. The wife of a former student speculated that Frankfurter was "not interested in sex"; her husband remarked that the idea of Felix "going to bed with Marion was like a bird alighting on a tree." Yet Marion was not shy about discussing the sex lives of other couples. A biographer speculated that Frankfurter was "a deeply repressed homosexual" on the basis of his closeted gay male friends. It is true that Frankfurter had many friends who happened to be closeted gay men. He also mentored young male law students and treated them like surrogate sons. And in small, private gatherings, Marion could be caustic and at times cruel to her adoring husband. During periods of separation, however, their correspondence revealed a loving, intimate relationship. Their childless marriage may have been a conscious choice or because of infertility; no one seemed to know for sure.

During the summers of 1924 and 1925, Frankfurter taught at Cornell Law School and churned out law review articles with his ambitious young roommate Landis. He regaled Landis with stories about T.R. and Wilson, Newton Baker, and working as a federal prosecutor for Stimson. "F. F. is the whole thing," Landis wrote during the summer of 1925. Life with Frankfurter in Ithaca was one of constant talk. "He never tires and amuses himself as well as me by playing eternally with his mind," Landis wrote. "It's a marvelous gift. I satisfy myself with an idea; he's hungry for its expression in the ultimate fineness of words." Frankfurter and Landis made a great team. In June 1924, they published a *Harvard Law Review* article, "The Power of Congress over Procedure in Criminal Contempts in Inferior Federal Courts." In May 1925, they published a *Yale Law Journal* article, "The Compact Clause of the Constitution—A Study in Interstate Adjustments," on how states could enter compacts to solve their common problems. A month later, they began a groundbreaking historical study of the federal courts. The Judiciary Act of 1925 granted the Court substantial discretion over which appeals to hear. In June, Frankfurter and Landis published the first of eight installments of "The Business of the Supreme Court of the United States." Some of the *Harvard Law Review* articles did not include Landis's name while he served as Brandeis's secretary. In his spare time, he continued to crank out the "Business of the Supreme Court" series.

The second student, Thomas Gardiner Corcoran, was the most charming. With a large head, prominent chin, and sparkling eyes, Corcoran liked to entertain people by playing the piano and breaking into Irish songs. The eldest son of a Pawtucket, Rhode Island, lawyer and politician, he graduated valedictorian of his class at Brown University and earned a master's degree there. In law school, he won the Sears Prize his second year, was named note editor of the *Harvard Law Review*, and finished fourth in his class with a 77 average. As a graduate student, Corcoran co-authored a *Harvard Law Review* article with Frankfurter, "Petty Federal Offenses and Constitutional Guaranty of Trial by Jury," about plea bargaining and bench trials in Prohibition cases. Corcoran credited the article with landing him a clerkship with Holmes. At the time Corcoran was so devoted to Frankfurter "that if he'd told me to clerk for the Lord of Lappland [sic] I might have said 'Yes sir and may I ask you to recommend a haberdasher who deals in muck-lucks?"

The third student, Henry J. Friendly, was the most gifted. The only child of an Elmira, New York, wholesale boot and shoe businessman and his wife, Friendly was quiet, introverted, and bookish. He graduated as valedictorian from Elmira Free Academy at age sixteen and enrolled at Harvard College intent on attending the law school. During his senior year, a British history class with legal historian Charles H. McIlwain piqued Friendly's interest in British historian F. W. Maitland and in getting a PhD in history. Friendly's paper for McIlwain's class, "Church and State in England under William The Conqueror," won the $250 Bowdoin Prize for the best essay in the English language. Harvard awarded Friendly a year-long postgraduate fellowship to study medieval legal history in Oxford and Paris.

Friendly's parents, second-generation German Jews, were horrified that their brilliant son was reconsidering law school to be a historian. They contacted Judge Mack, who encouraged their son to meet Frankfurter. During lunch at the Brattle Inn, Frankfurter dazzled Friendly with tales of the intellectual life at the law school. He encouraged Friendly to study medieval history on his fellowship then give the law school a one-year tryout. If Friendly did not like law school, he could enroll in graduate school in the history department. In October 1925, Friendly arrived at the law school; Frankfurter made sure he liked it. In Friendly's first class, Torts professor Manley Hudson asked him whether the judicial opinion the class was reading was the original text. Friendly said it was not. When Hudson revealed the old text, Friendly identified it as Norman or Old French and translated it for the class. He later learned that Frankfurter had orchestrated the questions to boost Friendly's confidence and reputation. Friendly did not love law school except for his frequent contacts with Frankfurter. Nonetheless, he was elected president of the *Harvard Law Review*, won two Sears Prizes, and finished first in his class with an 86 average, one point higher than Gerry Henderson's more than ten years earlier and reputedly the highest since Brandeis's.

For three weeks in July 1926, Frankfurter was teaching constitutional law with Thomas Reed Powell at Columbia Law School and set up his three prized students—Landis, Corcoran, and Friendly—in a New York City apartment. The idea was to introduce them to the city's greatest legal minds. They dined with Emory Buckner, Benjamin Cardozo, Learned Hand, Julian Mack, and Powell in nightly bull sessions. During the day, they were supposed to help Frankfurter with legal research. The plan, however, quickly changed. Buckner, now the U.S. attorney for the Southern District of New York, was preparing to try Harding's attorney general Harry M. Daugherty on federal corruption charges and needed legal research assistance. Frankfurter deputized Friendly and Corcoran to work for Buckner, who paid them out of his own pocket. Landis kept researching and writing "Business of the Supreme Court" installments with Frankfurter.

Upon finishing his clerkship with Brandeis, Landis returned to the law school in the fall of 1926 as an assistant professor. He joined Calvert Magruder, another Frankfurter student and Brandeis clerk, on the faculty. Many former Frankfurter students and clerks followed. "Given another twenty years of such activity," Brandeis predicted to Harold Laski, "and he will have profoundly affected American life."

After Corcoran received his doctorate in June 1926, Frankfurter tapped him to clerk for Holmes. The justice's first Irish Catholic secretary, Corcoran endeared himself to Holmes and his wife, Fanny. Corcoran could match Holmes's penchant for tall tales and liked to argue. Holmes invited him to spend the early part of the summer of 1927 at Beverly Farms. Corcoran was growing "restless and dissatisfied with the law as law." A few months earlier, he had declined to be considered for a law faculty position. Instead, he agreed to work for Frankfurter's friend Joseph P. Cotton at the Wall Street law firm of Cotton & Franklin. Frankfurter was not too disappointed, knowing that Corcoran's future lay in government.

According to Frankfurter's grand plan, Friendly was supposed to follow Landis and Corcoran into the graduate program to receive his doctorate, then, after clerking for Brandeis, return immediately to the law school to teach. Friendly's parents, however, wanted their son to go directly to Brandeis then join a New York law firm. Brandeis counseled them to let their son "make up his own mind." In a rare pre-clerkship meeting, Friendly met with the justice to seek his advice. That fall, Friendly declined the graduate research fellowship and began working for Brandeis immediately after graduation. A tough task master and critic, Brandeis had never seen anyone work so hard. The justice adopted Friendly's suggestions about revising and restructuring his famous dissent in *Olmstead v. United States* against wiretapping and in favor of a constitutional right to privacy. Inspired by Brandeis and Frankfurter, Friendly published a *Harvard Law Review* article about the history of federal jurisdiction based on diversity of citizenship (citizens or businesses from two different states) and nearly called for its abolition.

Determined not to let Friendly get away, Frankfurter saw someone with the intellectual ability to be the next Thayer or Ames on the Harvard law faculty. Friendly and his parents, however, had other ideas. After his summer working as Emory Buckner's research assistant before the Daugherty trial, he agreed to work at Buckner's New York law firm, Root, Clark. Frankfurter was annoyed with Buckner for diverting Friendly from the graduate fellowship and from law teaching. Friendly promised he would reconsider teaching after three years. With Friendly, Frankfurter played a long game.

THE OTHER PLACE Frankfurter played a long game was with the Supreme Court of the United States. He did not always guess right about the legal and political leanings of the Court's newest justices. In March 1925, Coolidge replaced the retired Justice Joseph McKenna by nominating his attorney general and Amherst College classmate, Harlan Fiske Stone. Frankfurter had known Stone for years as dean of Columbia Law School and attorney general. In April 1924, Stone had taken over a Justice Department in disrepute from the Palmer raids and scandal under his predecessor, Daugherty. Frankfurter had written Stone a letter advising him on personnel. For the most part, Stone agreed with Frankfurter's advice with one exception—Stone made J. Edgar Hoover the new head of the Bureau of Investigation, ignoring Frankfurter's warning that Hoover might not pursue "'liberal ideas'" under a different attorney general.

Frankfurter and Learned Hand debated whether Stone was a liberal or conservative. Hand correctly saw Stone as a potential ally for Holmes and Brandeis; Frankfurter vehemently disagreed. On the plus side, Stone had urged Coolidge to promote Hand from district judge to the Court of Appeals for the Second Circuit. As much as he applauded Hand's promotion, Frankfurter could not forgive Stone for the disingenuous way he discussed the Court and some of its decisions in pro-Coolidge speeches during the 1924 presidential campaign. "If Stone is a liberal, so is Sutherland, so is Pierce Butler," Frankfurter wrote Hand. "If you call Stone a liberal, I wonder what degree of wildness attaches to Brandeis and Holmes." Once Stone joined the Court, Frankfurter revised his description of Stone as a liberal motivated more by ambition than inspiration. He predicted that Stone would vote with Holmes and Brandeis, but not always.

On the role of the Court, Frankfurter thrived as its most trenchant critic. His feelings about two decisions in June 1925 revealed his contrasting views. On the one hand, he supported judicial intervention to protect free speech and fair criminal trials and to prevent racial discrimination. On the other, he objected when the Court invoked the Fourteenth Amendment to overturn state laws and socioeconomic regulation no matter how illiberal.

On June 8, 1925, the Court affirmed the criminal conviction of radical Socialist Benjamin Gitlow. Arrested on the second day of the Palmer raids, Gitlow was convicted under a New York criminal anarchy law for publishing a 34-page manifesto predicting that increasingly violent strikes would lead to "a 'revolutionary dictatorship of the proletariat.'" He was sentenced to five to ten years of hard labor and had already served three. After two rounds of oral argument, Justice Edward Terry Sanford's majority opinion argued that states can criminalize speech advocating the overthrow of the government and characterized Gitlow's manifesto as a "single revolutionary spark." The decision was not a total loss. For the first time, the Court recognized that the First Amendment's protection of free speech applied not only to the federal government but also to the states. The Court protected the abridgement of free speech by the states through the liberty provision of the Fourteenth Amendment's Due Process Clause.

Holmes and Brandeis agreed that the states should not abridge a fundamental liberty such as free speech but disagreed with the rest of the opinion. Holmes, joined by Brandeis, charged the majority with misapplying the "clear and present danger" test. Holmes found "no present danger of an attempt to overthrow the government by force on the part of the admittedly small minority who shared the defendant's views." Gitlow's manifesto was not an "incitement" to lawless action because "[e]very idea is an incitement." Holmes, no supporter of Communism, believed in the marketplace of ideas. If the majority of the American people agreed with Gitlow's proletarian ideas, they "should be given their chance and have their way."

In another case decided a week earlier, the Court invoked the Fourteenth Amendment's Due Process Clause to invalidate an Oregon law requiring all children between ages eight and sixteen who had not finished the eighth grade to attend public schools. The Oregon compulsory education law, backed by the Ku Klux Klan and due to go into effect in 1926, sought to put the state's Catholic schools out of business. In *Pierce v. Society of Sisters*, the Court invalidated the law by relying on its past decisions voiding state laws banning the teaching of German and other foreign languages and by expanding its interpretation of the liberty provision of the Due Process Clause. The Oregon public education law, Justice McReynolds wrote for the unanimous Court, violated "the liberty of parents and guardians to direct the upbringing and education of children under their control."

As much as he admired Holmes's *Gitlow* dissent and abhorred Oregon's public education law, Frankfurter cautioned liberals not to look to the Court to solve all their problems. In an unsigned *New Republic* editorial "Can the Supreme Court Guarantee Toleration?" he highlighted the dangers of broadly interpreting liberty and property in the Due Process Clause to protect individual rights because it put social welfare experiments at risk. McReynolds's decision expanding the liberty provision to ban the Oregon law gave Frankfurter pause. He conceded that the outcome "gives just cause for rejoicing" and "did immediate service on behalf of the essential spirit of liberalism." Yet he worried that an expansive interpretation of liberty would be used to wipe out state laws establishing maximum hours, minimum wages, and the rights of unions. As he knew all too well, five justices in *Adkins* invalidated the D.C. minimum-wage law for women by expanding the word *liberty* to mean liberty of contract. The "vague words" of the Due Process Clause gave the Court too much power. "These words mean what the shifting personnel of the United States Supreme Court from time to time makes them mean," he wrote. "The inclination of a single Justice, the tip of his mind—or his fears—determines the opportunity of a much-needed social experiment to survive, or frustrates, at least for a long time, intelligent attempt to deal with a social evil."

Liberals, Frankfurter argued, should invest in the political process and in elections. At the national level, things looked grim. La Follette had died in June 1925, and there were at least three more years of Coolidge. Frankfurter urged liberals to elect state legislators and governors willing to solve their socioeconomic problems. He refused to worship at the altar of the judiciary and "to make constitutionality synonymous with propriety.... Such an attitude is a great enemy of liberalism. Particularly in legislation affecting freedom of thought and freedom of speech much that is highly illiberal would be clearly constitutional." Frankfurter praised Holmes's dissent in the Nebraska foreign language case that not all illiberal legislation was unconstitutional. He predicted that McReynolds's opinion in *Pierce* would allow states to pass laws requiring teachers and students to exhibit " 'good moral character' and 'patriotic disposition.' " He warned that "the real battles of liberalism are not won in the Supreme Court."

To promote his limited conception of judicial review as the right path for liberals, Frankfurter celebrated Holmes on his eighty-fifth birthday, working behind the scenes to get Holmes the recognition he deserved. On his birthday, Holmes graced the cover of *Time* magazine, was the subject of a *New York Times* editorial, and made national newsreels. "Wherever law is known," Frankfurter wrote in an unsigned *New Republic* editorial, "he is known."

A few weeks later, Frankfurter attacked two new Supreme Court decisions in an unsigned *New Republic* editorial, "The Supreme Court as Legislator." He reviewed the history of the Court's "veto power" over state socioeconomic legislation and declared "the costs of the due process clause outweigh its gains." As proof, he criticized the majority for invoking the Due Process Clause to void a Wisconsin estate tax law and a Pennsylvania law banning the use of shoddy in bedding for health reasons. Six justices, he argued, enforced their "own judgment of what was fair legislation and what was unfair." And he concluded: "How dubious these 'guaranties,' how ambiguous the Delphic oracles of the Constitution, which a majority of the Court are able to hear so unequivocally, is demonstrated by two crushing dissenting opinions by Mr. Justice Holmes."

At other times, he defended the Court—when, for example, it declared it lacked federal jurisdiction to hear the case of Charlotte "Anita" Whitney. A member of the radical IWW and the Communist Labor Party, she was convicted under a California syndicalism law punishing radical speech for her talk on November 28, 1919, about "The Negro Problem in the United States." For her Communist Labor Party membership, she faced up to fourteen years in San Quentin Prison. The Wellesley-educated daughter from a prominent San Francisco family (her uncle was Justice Stephen J. Field), Whitney attracted substantial media attention. Yet, as Frankfurter learned from Landis, who was then working for Brandeis, her lawyers had failed to raise a federal constitutional claim before the California Court of Appeals and therefore deprived the Supreme Court of jurisdiction. In the *New Republic* and *The Nation*, Frankfurter made no secret of his distaste for laws such as California's that punished radicals because they belonged to the IWW or the Communist Party. Rather than criticize the U.S. Supreme Court for failing to take the case, he urged people to write the governor of California to pardon Whitney. Eventually, Whitney raised a constitutional claim, and the Court heard the case, prompting Brandeis's concurrence about free speech as critical to a robust democracy.

Frankfurter was not afraid to champion an unpopular cause, whether it was that of Alexander Meiklejohn, Anita Whitney, or two radical Italian immigrants convicted of robbery and murder.

CHAPTER 12

Let Mr. Lowell Resign

A round 3:00 p.m. on April 15, 1920, two men shot and killed a paymaster and a security guard who were carrying two boxes containing the $15,778.51 of the Slater & Morrill Shoe Company payroll across Pearl Street in South Braintree, Massachusetts. The robbers grabbed the boxes, jumped into an open touring car carrying three more men, and fled the scene.

Twenty days later, the police arrested two Italian anarchists, a shoe factory worker named Nicola Sacco and a fish peddler named Bartolomeo Vanzetti. At the time of their arrest, Sacco was armed with a fully loaded Colt automatic .32 caliber pistol and 22 extra bullets, and Vanzetti was armed with a fully loaded .38 caliber pistol. During their interrogation, they lied about their whereabouts on the day of the murders. It turned out both men had alibi witnesses willing to testify on their behalf. The Palmer raids, however, had targeted radical immigrants for arrest and deportation and had created a climate of fear. Sacco had been planning to return to Italy; Vanzetti had been trying to secure the release of Andrea Salsedo, who had been arrested during the Palmer raids and, after two days in federal custody, had been found dead on a New York City sidewalk. Massachusetts state prosecutors charged Sacco and Vanzetti with the South Braintree murders and Vanzetti with a similar robbery attempt in Bridgewater, Massachusetts.

Inspired by Frankfurter's defense of radical Boston immigrants after the Palmer raids, his friend Elizabeth Glendower Evans joined the Sacco-Vanzetti Defense Committee and helped finance the legal team. At Brandeis's urging, she had reinvented herself after her husband's death as a political and social activist. She inspired Marion Frankfurter and Alice Brandeis, both of whom suffered from chronic depression yet admired her dedication to social causes. Her friends called her Bess; Brandeis's children, unable to say her name, changed it to Auntie Bee.

From May 14 to July 14, 1921, Evans attended every day of Sacco and Vanzetti's trial at the behest of their lawyer Fred H. Moore, a Socialist from California. As she sat in the courtroom taking notes, she became convinced the two men were innocent and would be acquitted. Then she noticed the jurors would not look the accused men in the eye and would barely glance at the exhibits. After the jury returned a guilty verdict, Evans vowed not to rest until Sacco and Vanzetti were free.

After the trial, Evans and Marion Frankfurter kept pestering Felix for his opinion about the case. He insisted that he had not followed the trial and had not read the newspaper accounts. During the trial, he had been preparing a chapter on newspaper coverage for *Criminal Justice in Cleveland*, the published account of the Cleveland crime survey. He knew from his experience as a federal prosecutor with Henry Stimson and from the crime survey that newspaper accounts of criminal trials were often sensationalistic and ill-informed. Despite Evans's persistent requests, he refused to opine about the Sacco-Vanzetti trial or murder convictions without having read the record.

In November 1923, Frankfurter reconsidered when William G. Thompson, a prominent member of the Boston bar, filed a motion for a new trial relying on an affidavit from the prosecution's ballistics expert, Captain William Proctor. Before the trial, Proctor, the head of the Massachusetts State Police for thirty years, indicated that he would not testify that the .32 caliber pistol found on Sacco at the time of his arrest was the same one used in the South Braintree murders. Instead, according to a pretrial agreement with the prosecution, Proctor testified: "My opinion is that it is consistent with being fired by that pistol." What Proctor meant was that the fatal bullets could have been fired from any .32 caliber Colt automatic pistol, not necessarily Sacco's. The jury, however, had missed this fine distinction. In response to Thompson's motion, the prosecution replied that Proctor had not told them "repeatedly" that he would not testify that the fatal bullets had come from Sacco's gun. "When I read about that motion something happened to my insides," Frankfurter said. He thought about what Stimson had taught him about prosecuting cases fairly and honestly. At the time, prosecutors were not required to turn over potentially exculpatory evidence by law, only by their good consciences. Frankfurter considered the prosecution's efforts to get Proctor to swear to something he would not testify to "reprehensible beyond words" and "undermined any confidence in the conduct of the case." He knew what he had to do.

Read the record.

DURING HIS INVOLVEMENT in the Sacco-Vanzetti case, Frankfurter operated on two levels. For the most part, he worked behind the scenes and encouraged others to take the lead. He did not want to be the public face of the opposition. He refused to join the Sacco-Vanzetti Defense Committee or the pair's legal team. Instead, he advised the ACLU; recruited a new defense team; and coordinated legal strategy, press coverage, and fund-raising. At a few critical points, however, he played a public role in educating the American people about the unfairness of the trial. His experience as a former federal prosecutor, Harvard law professor, defender of Boston immigrants, co-chair of the Cleveland crime survey, and *New Republic* contributor made him the ideal person to explain why an injustice may have been done.

Frankfurter's private and public roles to save Sacco and Vanzetti made his legal reputation in liberal circles yet cost him dearly in others. He tapped into his liberal network at Harvard Law School, the legal establishment, and the media. His public role pitted him against President Lowell and Old Boston and made him a pariah. His behind-the-scenes activities during the final stages of the case raised the suspicions of the Massachusetts State Police and led them to wiretap his phones. His involvement nearly cost him his job on the Harvard law faculty and reinforced his mistaken reputation as a dangerous radical. In truth, the Sacco-Vanzetti case revealed as much as any other episode about Frankfurter's judicial philosophy of seeking change through the political process rather than the courts.

Before he tried to influence public opinion, Frankfurter hoped to get Sacco and Vanzetti a new trial by finding them a prominent Boston lawyer to take the case on appeal. During the fall of 1924, he succeeded in wresting the case from the volatile, Socialist trial counsel Fred H. Moore and persuaded William G. Thompson to assume complete control. In 1923, Thompson had agreed to file and argue a few new trial motions, including the one about the ballistics expert. He requested $25,000 to appeal all the motions to the Supreme Judicial Court of Massachusetts. Frankfurter, who advised the ACLU to hire Thompson full-time because of his esteemed reputation in the state, served as the organization's intermediary with the prominent Boston lawyer. Frankfurter raised money for Thompson's legal fees and found him a talented co-counsel. In his contract to represent Sacco and Vanzetti on appeal, Thompson specifically requested the opportunity to consult with Frankfurter on legal strategy.

It took more than a year for the new trial motions to be ruled on by the trial judge and heard on appeal. From January 11 to 13, 1926, Frankfurter watched in the courtroom as Thompson argued before the Massachusetts

Supreme Judicial Court. "I wish you had been present and heard the whole argument . . . ," Frankfurter wrote Harold Laski. "The poor Judge is himself the victim of forces and of emotional and intellectual limitations he has not a glimmer of. I am very pessimistic of the outcome. I cannot believe that the Governor will ever allow them to be hung, but I fear they will not get a new trial, confident as I am that a new trial would acquit them." On May 12, 1926, the Supreme Judicial Court affirmed that the trial judge had not abused his discretion in denying the new trial motions. After the decision, Frankfurter knew he had to do something to change the public's view of the case and to get Sacco and Vanzetti clemency or a new trial.

Fortunately for Frankfurter, he had the assistance of an exceptional young Oxford graduate named Sylvester Gates. An aspiring British barrister who had received two firsts at Oxford, Gates applied for a Commonwealth Fund fellowship to study in the United States and specifically requested to work with Frankfurter at Harvard. By now a notorious Anglophile, Frankfurter welcomed Gates as a graduate student and co-author. Felix and Marion were completely charmed by him. Frankfurter was so impressed with Gates that he asked the Oxford graduate, despite not having an American law degree, to become Holmes's secretary. Gates declined to clerk for Holmes yet proved to be essential in helping Frankfurter write about the Sacco-Vanzetti case.

Gates drafted an unsigned *New Republic* article; Frankfurter edited, revised, and supervised its final publication. Frankfurter had read the 2000-page trial record, the prosecution's and defense's objections, the trial judge's order denying the new trial motions, and appellate briefs; attended the three days of argument before the Massachusetts Supreme Judicial Court; and dissected its decision. His refusal to put his name on the article was part of his strategy of staying behind the scenes.

In three full pages of the *New Republic* on June 9, 1926, Frankfurter and Gates argued that Sacco and Vanzetti had been railroaded. The prosecution convicted the men on the basis of dubious eyewitness testimony: two women who claimed to have seen the getaway car from a second-floor window sixty feet away and did not come forward for more than a year; a man working in a nearby shoe factory who claimed to have seen them through an open window; another woman who had said she saw nothing at the time yet testified against them because the police were "bothering the life out of me"; another man, who unbeknownst to the jury was facing a larceny charge, claimed he saw them from a pool hall thirty feet away yet had told people at the time of the shooting he was too scared to look at their faces. Frankfurter and Gates explained how difficult it was for eyewitnesses to identify people of different ethnicities and nationalities such as Italian immigrants. To make matters worse, some witnesses never saw a lineup, only the two defendants. "Under such conditions," Frankfurter and Gates wrote, "identification of foreigners is a farce."

Rather than rest its case on shaky eyewitness testimony, the article argued, the prosecution relied on a theory of "consciousness of guilt" following the lies the scared defendants had told after their arrests. "The prosecution harped on 'consciousness of guilt,'" Frankfurter and Gates wrote. "But was this consciousness of being a murderer or consciousness of being a Red at a time when, beneath the generous impulse of patriotism and the distorting energy of fear, the government was hunting Reds like wild beasts?" They invoked Holmes's comment in the Leo Frank case that "'any Judge who has sat with juries knows that in spite of forms they are extremely likely to be impregnated by the environing atmosphere.'"

Sacco and Vanzetti never stood a chance of receiving a fair trial, the article contended, because of their anarchist beliefs. Armed guards marched them handcuffed through the streets of Dedham to the courthouse each day. The defendants sat in the courtroom in a steel cage. District Attorney Frederick Katzmann questioned them about dodging the draft and their anarchist beliefs and concluded his closing with "stand together, you men of Norfolk County!" Judge Webster Thayer made numerous prejudicial rulings and charged the jury that "you, like the true soldier, responded to that call in the spirit of supreme American loyalty."

Frankfurter and Gates's article criticized the Supreme Judicial Court for refusing to find that Judge Thayer had abused his discretion in denying several meritorious new trial motions. Jury foreman Walter Ripley, a former Quincy, Massachusetts, police chief, had brought in his own bullets for the jury to examine as it weighed the ballistics testimony. And in response to a comment before trial that the defendants were innocent, he had replied: "Damn them, they ought to hang them, anyway." Eyewitness Roy Gould, who believed that a man who had fired a gun at him from the getaway car did not look like Sacco or Vanzetti, had not been called by the prosecution or disclosed to the defense. And Captain Proctor had refused to testify that the fatal bullets had come from Sacco's gun, yet the prosecution had left the jury with that mistaken impression. On the basis of the trial record and Thompson's persuasive argument before the Supreme Judicial Court, the article concluded: "The 2,000 pages of the record reveal the presence of other passions than that for justice, other tempers than the 'calmness of a cool mind.'"

New information cast doubt on the verdict and fairness of the trial. Twenty-three-year-old Celestino F. Medeiros, convicted of killing a bank cashier and awaiting execution, passed a message to Sacco confessing to being one of the men who had ridden in the getaway car with members of the Providence-based Morelli gang after the South Braintree murders. He told his story under oath and insisted that Sacco and Vanzetti had not been involved.

Medeiros's confession and Morelli gang story gained credence thanks to the investigative work by Sacco-Vanzetti defense lawyer Herbert "Brute" Ehrmann. The fall after his Harvard Law School graduation in 1914, Ehrmann had decided not to practice law in his hometown of Louisville. Frankfurter, the school's newest professor, helped him find a job. Ehrmann went to work for the Boston Legal Aid Society. He and his wife, Sara, became close friends with the Frankfurters. Frankfurter tapped the 24-year-old Ehrmann to be the new chair of the Massachusetts Minimum Wage Commission. Three years later, Ehrmann served as the U.S. Shipping Board's representative on the Frankfurter-chaired War Labor Policies Board. After the war, Ehrmann joined the Boston law firm of Hale & Dorr and, on Frankfurter's recommendation, co-authored part of the Cleveland crime survey of the city's criminal courts. In May 1926, Frankfurter asked Ehrmann to join Thompson on the Sacco-Vanzetti defense team and to investigate the Medeiros confession.

Initially, Ehrmann was skeptical that Medeiros's confession and story about the Morelli gang were the lies of a condemned man. The more he investigated the facts of the Bridgewater and South Braintree shoe factory robberies, however, the more the evidence suggested the Morelli gang had committed them. He employed techniques he had learned researching the Cleveland criminal courts to investigate the gang, which had been responsible for a string of train robberies of shoes and textiles, including shoes from the South Braintree factory. As a result of Ehrmann's investigation, he and Thompson made the Medeiros confession the basis of another new trial motion. In May, Frankfurter had been paying Thompson's and Ehrmann's expenses of $1500 out of Elizabeth Glendower Evans's personal funds. Around the same time, Frankfurter advised Evans to ask the ACLU-controlled Garland Fund for $5000 to pay Thompson and Ehrmann to litigate the Medeiros confession because it was like a whole new case.

With the Medeiros new trial motion pending before Judge Thayer, Frankfurter tried to generate interest with friends at New York and Boston newspapers starting with Walter Lippmann. For several months, Frankfurter had been urging the circumspect Lippmann to come to Boston to learn about the case. Finally, Lippmann sent the New York *World*'s Pulitzer Prize–winning labor and economics reporter, John J. Leary, to cover the hearings on the motion for a new trial. Leary wrote an article revealing that the Department of Justice may have secretly aided District Attorney Katzmann in prosecuting Sacco and Vanzetti. Some credited Leary's reporting with changing the tone of the press's coverage. During a four-day hearing in mid-September 1926, Judge Thayer refused to allow Medeiros to testify in person and instead relied on his prior sworn statements. Frankfurter, who attended the first day of the hearing, knew what the outcome would be. On October 23, Thayer denied the motion.

Through press coverage, Frankfurter hoped to change the minds of influential people in Old Boston and their political allies. For starters, he did not want them to be able to dismiss it as a Communist cause. As a result, he warned ACLU director Roger Baldwin to stifle calls for a new trial from two left-wing radicals, publicist Mary C. Crawford and novelist John Dos Passos. Frankfurter knew that help was coming from a more respected source, the *Boston Herald*. The *Herald*'s publisher, Robert O'Brien, had kept the newspaper neutral but was having second thoughts about the pair's guilt. Given O'Brien's doubts, Frankfurter pressed the *Herald* to change its editorial stance. Three days after Thayer denied the Medeiros motion, *Herald* editorial page editor F. Lauriston Bullard wrote "We Submit," confessing the newspaper had changed its mind. Thayer's biased opinions, the Justice Department's secret involvement, Medeiros's confession that was not heard in open court, and Captain Proctor's ballistics testimony gave Bullard pause. The editorial called for a new trial, won Bullard a Pulitzer Prize, but changed few minds in Boston. Frankfurter, therefore, decided to take a more public role.

Not content with his unsigned contribution with Gates in the *New Republic*, Frankfurter began working with his graduate student on a longer article distilling the most relevant parts of the 2000-page trial record and allowing the layperson to draw a conclusion about the fairness of the proceedings. The trial record was proving "very difficult" to summarize, and what Frankfurter once envisioned as a small "pamphlet" grew longer. During his second time reviewing the record and the objections in the bill of exceptions, he concluded "the more flimsy the case against the men appears, the more obviously biased Thayer's conduct is revealed." He deemed Sacco and Vanzetti's trial counsel Fred H. Moore "an incredibly poor lawyer" and the Captain Proctor motion "absolutely conclusive."

Initially, Frankfurter had promised the *New Republic* his article about how the Massachusetts criminal justice system had failed. The magazine, however, had seen better days. It had declared bankruptcy in October 1924; its circulation had plummeted; its founder, Herbert Croly, was more interested in a "quasi-Oriental cult" he had joined than in editing the magazine. Despite resigning as one of its trustees in 1924, Frankfurter remained loyal to Croly and was a regular contributor.

In late December 1926, Frankfurter's publication plans changed when Ellery Sedgwick, the owner and editor of the *Atlantic Monthly*, heard about the article. A Harvard College classmate of Winfred Denison, Sedgwick had been a regular visitor and overnight guest at the House of Truth. A native of Stockbridge, Massachusetts, he married into a prominent Old Boston family and purchased the magazine founded in 1857 by Ralph Waldo Emerson, Henry Wadsworth Longfellow, and Oliver Wendell Holmes, Sr., for $50,000. Sedgwick was torn between his desires to be respected by proper Bostonians and to support liberal causes "if it didn't cost him too much with what he regarded as the 'right people.' " Sedgwick first realized the worldwide interest in the case during a trip to South America where he was shocked to see people in the town square of Montevideo, Uruguay, stirred up about it. A few years later in London, everyone wanted to talk about the case. In early January 1927, Sedgwick offered to publish Frankfurter's article in the *Atlantic Monthly* in two months. Frankfurter decided to break his commitment to Croly because the *Atlantic Monthly*'s circulation dwarfed the *New Republic*'s by more than five times. The Boston-based magazine also would have a greater impact on influential Massachusetts judges, politicians, and lawyers. The *New Republic* already had two editors, Bruce Bliven and Robert Morss Lovett, writing about the case. And to his fellow editors, Croly did not seem interested in Sacco-Vanzetti. Croly agreed to release Frankfurter from publishing the article in the *New Republic* without a hint of bitterness.

In the *Atlantic Monthly*'s March 1927 issue, Frankfurter published "The Portentous Case of Sacco and Vanzetti: A Comprehensive Analysis of a Trial of Grave Importance." The article was twenty-three pages and signed by Frankfurter. A month later, the Boston-based Little, Brown and Company published a revised version with new information and footnotes as a short book, *The Case of Sacco and Vanzetti: A Critical Analysis for Lawyers and Laymen*. Frankfurter donated the proceeds from the article and the book to the Sacco-Vanzetti Defense Committee. He paid his privately acknowledged co-author, Sylvester Gates, $125, half of the magazine fee for the article.

Writing in real time to influence public opinion, Frankfurter wanted the people of Massachusetts to right a wrong and to make up their minds before it was too late. "The Sacco-Vanzetti case has been before the courts and the public for more than six years. It has divided opinion at home and been the cause of demonstration abroad, and the end is not yet," he wrote in the prefatory note to the book dated February 15, 1927. "This is no ordinary case of robbery and murder. More issues are involved in it than the lives of two men. Had that been all, its history could never have been so prolonged. Other factors, little known and less understood, explain its extraordinary vitality. What they are, these pages seek to make clear, for the first time so far as the general public is concerned."

An initial complaint about the publication of Frankfurter's article and book was the timing—with the new trial motion about the Medeiros confession pending before the Massachusetts Supreme Judicial Court. On January 27 and 28, Thompson had argued the motion. He and Frankfurter had agreed to delay publication until March because they figured the court would decide by then. On February 10, Thompson urged Frankfurter to wait to publish until after the court's decision. The next day by phone, Frankfurter offered to defer to Thompson's judgment yet insisted that Judge Thayer was not above reproach and the public had a right to know about his conduct during the trial. He also observed that Thayer's hometown Worcester County Bar Association had passed a formal resolution approving the trial judge's conduct; Frankfurter's "scientific discussion" would prevent the debate from being one-sided. After their conversation, Thompson agreed to the March publication date.

The blowback was immediate. Frankfurter's longtime antagonist at the U.S. Supreme Court, Justice McReynolds, wrote Sedgwick questioning the magazine's decision to publish the article and attacking Frankfurter's character: "The purpose of the writer seems plain enough and harmonizes with what he has done in other times." Sedgwick conceded that Frankfurter could be "hot-headed" yet described him as "upright, courageous, and able" and defended the article. McReynolds replied that Sedgwick's "estimate of the writer of the article is very much too high & that this misleads you. Other performances by him indicate what lies in the back of his head." The justice was furious about "unsympathetic assaults upon the courts by men with crooked minds," defended the Massachusetts courts, and insisted his "faith in them cannot be shaken by ill-natured flings from an exotic mind."

The people of Old Boston were more polite yet as anti-Semitic as McReynolds. They reacted to Frankfurter's article and book by shunning him. People whom Frankfurter considered old friends refused to be seen with him. His *Atlantic Monthly* editor Ellery Sedgwick asked him to lunch not at the Somerset Club, Tavern Club, Union Club, or some other place where he might run into prominent people of Old Boston, but in the far corner of a dining room at an inconspicuous hotel. Frankfurter was amused by such group-think behavior and was not surprised given Old Boston's opposition to Brandeis's nomination. He put his name on the article and the book not because he wanted limelight, money, or publicity, but because he believed that public pressure on the governor was the surest way to save Sacco and Vanzetti.

On April 5, the Supreme Judicial Court denied Thompson's new trial motion about Medeiros's confession. The court merely said that Judge Thayer had not abused his discretion. In other states but not in Massachusetts, appellate judges inquired into the evidentiary basis for a criminal conviction. Judge Thayer, however, was the only judge who had reviewed the facts of this case.

Four days later at 10:00 a.m., Frankfurter sat in the jury box with members of the press in Judge Thayer's crowded Dedham courtroom. Sheriff's deputies armed with shotguns stood inside and outside. Handcuffed together, Sacco and Vanzetti were marched in and sat in a steel cage in the center of the room. The clerk asked the two men if they wanted to say anything before their sentencing. In halting, broken English, Sacco professed his innocence: "As I said before, Judge Thayer know all my life, and he know that I am never been guilty, never—not yesterday nor today nor forever." Vanzetti, mustachioed and more fluent in English than Sacco, launched into a forty-minute soliloquy. He proclaimed his innocence in the Bridgewater and South Braintree robberies, reviewed the Medeiros confession, and accused Judge Thayer and District Attorney Katzmann of highlighting the defendants' radical views to prejudice the jury. In a stirring conclusion, he declared: "I am suffering because I am a radical and indeed I am radical; I have suffered because I was an Italian, and indeed I am an Italian; I have suffered more for my family and for my beloved than for myself; but I am so convinced to be right that if you could execute me two times, and if I could be reborn two other times, I would live again to do what I have done already."

An emotionless Judge Thayer began to sentence both men. Sacco cried out again proclaiming their innocence. The judge kept going and declared that Sacco and Vanzetti would be killed "by the passage of a current of electricity through your body" during the week of July 10. After the sentencing, Evans and other Sacco and Vanzetti supporters rushed to the cage to whisper words of encouragement.

———

DEEPLY "MOVED" by Vanzetti's speech, Frankfurter redoubled his behind-the-scenes efforts to save the two men. He advised the legal team and Sacco-Vanzetti Defense Committee, orchestrated press coverage from the *World* and other newspapers, and coordinated petitions to the governor.

Frankfurter's enemies in Old Boston were not fooled. Moorfield Storey, a founding member of the NAACP and a leading opponent of Brandeis's Supreme Court nomination, accused Frankfurter of serving as pro bono defense counsel while writing the book (which Frankfurter and Thompson denied). Storey falsely charged Frankfurter with initially writing a report declaring Tom Mooney guilty then withdrawing it because of political pressure. Finally, Storey vowed to have nothing to do with the law school as long as Frankfurter was on the faculty. Others claimed that prominent law graduates refused to contribute to the school's endowment fund because of Frankfurter's activities. The arch-conservative *Boston Evening Transcript* reprinted Theodore Roosevelt's 1917 letter attacking Frankfurter's Mooney and Bisbee reports as "Bolsheviki"; a few days later, the newspaper was shamed into reprinting Frankfurter's reply to Roosevelt.

Frankfurter's biggest disappointment was the "timidity," "fear," and lies from his dean, Roscoe Pound. An apologetic Pound privately informed the justices of the Supreme Judicial Court that he had advised Frankfurter to delay publication until after its decision. In private conversations with Frankfurter, Pound had initially disagreed with Frankfurter's decision to publish. Two days later, however, he changed his mind and praised Frankfurter for publishing when he did. Pound privately defended Frankfurter against charges that the book was "one-sided" yet never publicly defended him. Frankfurter chose not to confront Pound until after the case was over. Their relationship never recovered. Both men held grudges about the other's conduct during the case.

The most sustained attack on Frankfurter came from one of the most respected members of the legal academy, John Henry Wigmore. The dean of Northwestern University Law School and the nation's leading expert on the rules of evidence, Wigmore had turned into a superpatriot during his wartime service in the Judge Advocate General's Corps and opposed anyone who protected the civil liberties of antiwar radicals. He had disagreed with Frankfurter's 1917 recommendation of a committee to hear the claims of conscientious objectors. He undoubtedly blanched at Frankfurter's Mooney and Bisbee reports and attacks on the constitutionality of the Palmer raids and privately began referring to Frankfurter as "the most dangerous person in the U.S."

As soon as Frankfurter's *Atlantic Monthly* article appeared, Wigmore began promising colleagues that he planned to write a reply. He considered Sacco and Vanzetti "dangerous enemies to society" and intended to reveal "the character of the men, the influences behind them" in an effort to help the public understand how dangerous they were. When a colleague suggested that Wigmore might be "playing directly into Frankfurter's hands" by arguing that they were convicted because of their radical beliefs, Wigmore insisted "the facts are not as Frankfurter says they are" and vowed to get the real story from Judge Thayer. Thayer boasted to the *New York Times* "I have nothing and nobody to fear" and predicted that the article by "Professor Frankenstein [sic]" would be "answered by one of the best authorities in the United States at the proper time."

With information from Thayer and possibly from J. Edgar Hoover of the Bureau of Investigation, Wigmore published an April 25 response in the *Boston Evening Transcript*. He never used Frankfurter's name and repeatedly referred to him as "the plausible pundit." Wigmore accused him of making "errors and misstatements" and committing "libel on Massachusetts justice." He alleged that the defense had never objected to the composition of the jury pool; Judge Thayer had never said that the Supreme Judicial Court had "approved" the verdict; and the court had reviewed the facts of the case.

Around 3:00 p.m. on April 25, Frankfurter received a phone call alerting him to Wigmore's article. He and his secretary rushed to Harvard Square to buy a copy of the newspaper and brought a typewriter with them to the Frankfurters' home at 192 Brattle Street. Marion saw the front-page article while riding a streetcar and rushed home by taxi to tell her husband. By the time she arrived, Frankfurter, who did not type, was already writing a response. *Boston Herald* editor Frank Buxton was holding the presses to include the response on the next morning's front page. Taking to his bed, an anxious Sedgwick phoned Frankfurter and told him to "be temperate, be cool" in the rejoinder. Given his replies about the Mooney and Bisbee reports to Theodore Roosevelt and Solicitor General Beck, Frankfurter knew to stick to the facts. He also knew that Wigmore had not read the trial record and instead relied on Judge Thayer's word. Frankfurter, on the other hand, had read the record twice and had relied on the bill of exceptions, the prosecution's and defense's objections at trial and on appeal. Long on facts and short on invective, Frankfurter quoted from the record and bill of exceptions to show that the defense had objected to the composition of the jury pool and that Judge Thayer had claimed the Supreme Judicial Court had "approved" the verdict. He also schooled Wigmore on the limited appellate review of criminal cases in Massachusetts. "I say without fear of contradiction that Dean Wigmore could not have read the record, could not have read with care the opinion of Judge Thayer, on which his article is largely based, could not even have examined my little book," Frankfurter wrote.

Two weeks later, Wigmore returned to the *Evening Transcript* with more half-truths and name calling, referring to Frankfurter only as "the plausible pundit" and "the contra-canonical critic." He accused Frankfurter of violating the American Bar Association canon of ethics by commenting on a pending case, though the case was on appeal and not before a jury. He continued to defend Judge Thayer's honor. "I shall continue to leave vituperation to Dean Wigmore, while I stick to facts," Frankfurter replied, then reviewed, point by point, the "serious charges" in Wigmore's April 25 article and how each of "his original charges have evaporated." Frankfurter again denied allegations that he was Sacco and Vanzetti's co-counsel; Thompson published a letter insisting Frankfurter had never been part of the defense team.

Frankfurter's triumph over Wigmore was so complete that enemies in Old Boston took notice. Emory Buckner considered Wigmore's attacks "very fortunate" because they "brought for the first time portions of the 'conservative' element into the controversy on the side of the defendants, or at least on the side of urging a board of review." Even Frankfurter's nemesis President Lowell declared him the winner. "Wigmore is a fool! Wigmore is a fool!" Lowell said. "He should have known that Frankfurter would be shrewd enough to be accurate." Frankfurter's "shrewdness" continued to rankle Lowell and Old Boston, who became the real adversaries in the fight to get Sacco and Vanzetti a new trial.

Frankfurter's replies to Wigmore were his last public pronouncements during the case; all he cared about was saving Sacco and Vanzetti from the electric chair. He and Thompson shifted the campaign from the Massachusetts Supreme Judicial Court to Governor Alvan T. Fuller. At 2:00 p.m. on April 7, Thompson met with a group of concerned citizens about the next steps in the case. He declared that Sacco and Vanzetti were innocent and had not received a fair trial, blaming District Attorney Katzmann for suppressing evidence and secretly collaborating with Attorney General Palmer and Judge Thayer for his prejudicial rulings. Thompson and Frankfurter were pessimistic that an appeal to the Supreme Court of the United States would be successful and believed that all legal remedies had been exhausted. Backed by Frankfurter, Thompson proposed a committee of three distinguished citizens who would investigate the allegations against Katzmann and Thayer in an effort to persuade the governor to commute the sentences. The governor's clemency power, Thompson and Frankfurter told the group, was their best shot. Only Vanzetti signed the clemency petition; Sacco had given up hope.

The clemency petition, Thompson revealed to the concerned citizens, contained new information about the depths of Judge Thayer's prejudices.

Thayer had commented on the pending case at the University Club, where he had stayed during the trial, to members of the press, and to his friends at a Worcester country club. The defense submitted sworn affidavits from upstanding citizens that Thayer had referred to the defendants as "those bastards down there" and their lawyers as "those damn fools." "Just wait until you hear my charge," he boasted and referred to the defense's trial counsel, Fred H. Moore, as "that long-haired anarchist." After denying Sacco and Vanzetti a new trial a few years later, Thayer told a Dartmouth College professor: "Did you see what I did with those anarchistic bastards the other day? I guess that will hold them for a while. Let them go to the Supreme Court now and see what they can get out of them."

The charges against Judge Thayer gave new life to Frankfurter's campaign to persuade Governor Fuller to intervene. He coordinated petitions to the governor, one led by Robert Morss Lovett of the *New Republic* and another by Professor Karl Llewellyn of Columbia Law School, asking for the appointment of a review board. Frankfurter declined to sign any of the petitions out of an abundance of caution. At the same time, he pleaded with Lippmann and the *World* to take the lead on national media coverage. The conservative *New York Herald Tribune* attacked Frankfurter's book for "partisan distortions" and accused him of "fanning anarchistic flames." The *New York Times* refused to publish an article about the case by H. G. Wells even after having Frankfurter review it for factual accuracy because the newspaper feared a libel suit. And Boston newspapers, despite the *Herald*'s prize-winning editorial in 1926, remained silent. Only the *Springfield Republican* called for a new trial or clemency. For a time, Lippmann and the *World* stepped up with an editorial, "The Prejudices of Judge Thayer," and Rollin Kirby's cartoon depicting a wave of protest breaking over Thayer's outstretched arm. "One courageous paper" was all Frankfurter needed to change public opinion. Time and again, however, Lippmann refused to come to Boston, wrote equivocating editorials about the case, and let Frankfurter down.

On June 1, Governor Fuller acceded to requests for a three-member review board to reconsider the case; the governor, however, stacked the deck against Sacco and Vanzetti with the people he chose to review it. The chair of the committee was Frankfurter's nemesis and a leader of Old Boston, A. Lawrence Lowell. Joining Lowell was another reactionary member of Old Boston, Judge Robert Grant. A retired Suffolk County probate judge and novelist, Grant had been expressing "hostility" to Sacco and Vanzetti before Fuller's appointment. The third member, MIT president Samuel Wesley Stratton, was a mathematician, not a lawyer like Lowell and Grant, and "unquestionably conservative" and "not very bright." Of the three members, Frankfurter placed his faith in Lowell and described the Harvard president as Sacco and Vanzetti's "only hope."

With the executions stayed until August 10, the Frankfurters escaped the tense atmosphere in Boston by renting a summer home thirty-five miles away on the South Shore in Duxbury. The small white house with light green blinds and blue plant pots was next to the Bay Farm, where they bought fresh milk, eggs, and chickens, and a short walk to an inlet on Kingston Bay. Duxbury was close enough for him to take the train from Kingston to Boston, yet far enough to keep the press and members of the Sacco-Vanzetti Defense Committee at bay. The Frankfurters tried to relax there, kept tabs on the Lowell committee's investigation, and awaited the governor's decision.

From Duxbury, Frankfurter began to hear unsettling things about the Lowell committee's review process. Over the defense's objection, the committee conducted its investigation and heard from witnesses in secret with no opportunity for cross-examination. The committee refused to allow Thompson to watch its two-hour interview of Judge Thayer and the prosecutors. Lowell reacted to Thompson's argument with alarming "instances of impatiences" and "lack of understanding and indifference" about the facts of the case. On July 14, Lowell threatened Sacco's two alibi witnesses with perjury when Lowell was the one who had been confused about the facts. Despite all these disturbing events, Frankfurter remained optimistic and believed Lowell could not overlook Judge Thayer's prejudices throughout the case. "I still have hope in him," Frankfurter wrote, "because it is simply inconceivable to me how, upon the facts, they can dare send Sacco and Vanzetti to the electric chair."

New information from the defense team dampened Frankfurter's bleak hopes. Elizabeth Glendower Evans confided that the "situation is pretty grim." Thompson and Ehrmann had no "hope of the men's freedom"; only Ehrmann believed there was a "chance" of life imprisonment. Evans tried to boost Thompson's spirits by telling him "that his children and children's children would live to be proud" of his efforts. Frankfurter tried to invigorate Thompson's younger co-counsel. "Thompson is fearfully frayed out," he wrote Ehrmann and urged him to pick up the slack. "After all, no fight is lost until it is lost. And you cannot possibly know either what is in Lowell's mind or what the Governor may finally decide upon. I know the outlook is very gloomy indeed."

On the evening of August 3, Frankfurter waited in "shirt-sleeves" at the Sacco-Vanzetti Defense Committee headquarters in Boston for news about the governor's decision. The first word came from the radio; a few minutes later, they received the official word from the state house: Governor Fuller announced that he would not grant clemency because Sacco and Vanzetti had received a fair trial. He based the decision on his own investigation as well as on the Lowell report. The Lowell committee, which had presented its findings to the governor on July 27, unanimously agreed. A few days after the governor's decision, the Lowell committee released its report. Frankfurter knew the report's conclusion that the South Braintree murders were an amateur job, as opposed to a professional hit, was unsupported by the evidence. And he wired Lippmann that the governor's decision was "monstrous."

During Frankfurter's final efforts to save Sacco and Vanzetti, the Massachusetts State Police was listening to his every move. On August 1, the state attorney general authorized the tapping of Frankfurter's telephone and telegraph wires in Duxbury and hired people to transcribe almost every word. Frankfurter knew he was a marked man. Old Boston considered him a "hardheaded lawyer" and "'officious damned radical jew' who has meddled with this case." A friend tipped him off that Governor Fuller had ordered the wiretaps and had been spreading lies that he had received $100,000 in "Moscow Gold" for the *Atlantic Monthly* article and book rather than the $250 magazine fee he split with Sylvester Gates and $413.73 in book royalties he donated to the Sacco-Vanzetti Defense Committee. Frankfurter knew better than to turn it into a fight between him and Lowell or him and Fuller. Instead, he found other people to take the lead.

Frankfurter's first order of business was recruiting new defense counsel. After the governor's decision, Thompson and Ehrmann withdrew from the case. They denounced the Lowell committee for interviewing witnesses in secret, disputed the report's conclusions, and declared their clients innocent. For three years, Thompson had represented the men at enormous financial and emotional cost. At the end, he was exhausted to the point of mumbling to himself in his office and went to New Hampshire to rest. Frankfurter knew the perfect person to take over for Thompson—Arthur Dehon Hill.

The Paris-born son of a Harvard English professor, Hill had founded one of the city's most respected law firms, Hill, Barlow & Homans, and in 1909 had served as the Suffolk County district attorney. Boyish-looking and quick-witted, Hill had been ostracized from Old Boston's political establishment for supporting Theodore Roosevelt's Bull Moose campaign in 1912 and Brandeis's Supreme Court nomination four years later. Moorfield Storey had retaliated by trying to block Hill's permanent appointment to the Harvard law faculty. Frankfurter, however, intervened by soliciting a letter of endorsement from Hill's old family friend, Justice Holmes. A member of the Harvard law faculty from 1915 to 1919, Hill taught evidence and criminal law. During the war, he served in the Judge Advocate General's Corps and worked for the Red Cross in France. Resigning from the faculty after the war, Hill returned to his Boston law practice and later served as the city's corporation counsel. Hill and Frankfurter shared a lot in common—Bull Moose political pasts and a love of Holmes, liberal politics, and public service; Ehrmann described them as "brothers under the skin."

On August 1, Frankfurter phoned Hill and asked to him to consider taking over as Sacco-Vanzetti's defense counsel. Hill was intimately familiar with the case. In 1923, he had assisted Thompson with some new trial motions. Hill mulled over Frankfurter's offer for two days then suggested that they meet for lunch at the Somerset Club. After lunch and a walk to the frog pond in Boston Common, Hill agreed to exhaust Sacco and Vanzetti's appeals for $5000 or "whatever was reasonable." Hill refused to collect any fees for his time and asked only that the Sacco-Vanzetti Defense Committee cover the fees and expenses of his two associates. Hill accepted the job not because he believed the men to be innocent but out of a sense of duty.

With Hill leading the defense team, Frankfurter outlined what he viewed as the strongest constitutional argument, a due process claim about Judge Thayer's prejudicial evidentiary rulings during the trial, comments about the defendants and their lawyers outside the courtroom, and rulings on the new trial motions: "The point is this as I see it: An accused is not entitled to a wise judge, or a learned judge, or a wholly calm judge. But, surely, the essence of an Anglo-American trial, particularly in a capital case, implied a *judge*." This was especially true in Massachusetts where the trial judge's evidentiary rulings and factual determinations were unreviewable by the Supreme Judicial Court. Frankfurter emphasized Judge Thayer's "rooted prejudice against the men" as the key to winning a stay of execution, new trial, or executive clemency on the basis of a violation of their basic due process rights. Hill agreed with Frankfurter's proposed legal strategy.

Before he sought relief in federal court, Hill exhausted Sacco and Vanzetti's appeals in state court. On August 6, he filed motions for a new trial and to revoke the death sentences. The chief justice designated Judge Thayer to hear the motions. Two days later, Thayer denied Hill's objections that he was too prejudiced to hear the case and denied the new trial motions. Hill appealed to the Supreme Judicial Court and individually to Justice George Sanderson, who refused to intervene.

On August 10, Frankfurter boarded a train from Kingston to Boston to confer with Hill at 10:00 a.m. about legal strategy before Sacco and Vanzetti's midnight executions. The immediate goal was to find someone to stay the executions so that Hill could litigate the pair's constitutional claims in federal court. After meeting with Frankfurter, Hill prepared to appeal Justice Sanderson's ruling to the Supreme Judicial Court. Shortly after noon, Hill arrived at the statehouse to ask the governor and his parole board–like executive council to delay the executions to allow him to exhaust Sacco and Vanzetti's appeals in state and federal court. Around 1:30 p.m., he realized that the governor and the council had no intention of seeing him. Hill, Thompson, and two other lawyers sped off in two cars twenty-nine miles north of the city to Beverly Farms to seek relief from Justice Holmes.

Frankfurter, who returned to Duxbury that afternoon, had no intention of joining the defense team at Beverly Farms. He agreed that Holmes was the ideal judge to hear the due process claims. In 1915, Holmes had dissented in Leo Frank's case, arguing that Frank's due process rights had been violated by a criminal trial so mob-dominated that for his own safety he had been barred from attending his sentencing. The lynch mob, Holmes contended, had made it impossible for the jury to acquit Frank, the Jewish superintendent of an Atlanta, Georgia, pencil factory. Eight years later, Holmes wrote the Court's majority opinion in *Moore v. Dempsey* declaring that mob-dominated criminal trials violated the Due Process Clause. The decision had saved the lives of black sharecroppers who had been subjected to sham trials and sentenced to death after Arkansas's Elaine massacre. *Moore v. Dempsey*, Frankfurter and the defense team agreed, was Sacco and Vanzetti's best hope. Hill and Thompson asked Holmes to grant them a writ of habeas corpus declaring that Sacco and Vanzetti's conviction violated their constitutional rights. In a more likely alternative, they requested a stay of execution so the entire U.S. Supreme Court could hear the case in October.

Frankfurter waited by the phone as Hill and Thompson arrived at the justice's large Victorian house near Manchester Bay at 2:50 p.m. They argued their case in the first-floor parlor. Holmes knew this day was coming. In April, he had read Frankfurter's book, privately praised Frankfurter for writing it, and heard how the case had divided Old Boston. He knew that Frankfurter was behind the plea. In Holmes's parlor, Hill and Thompson argued that a trial before a prejudiced judge was like having no judge at all and violated due process as much as the sham trials of the Arkansas sharecroppers with an angry mob outside. Mentally sharp, the 86-year-old Holmes distinguished between an angry lynch mob and a prejudiced judge. Hill and Thompson saw no difference "whether the motive was fear or the prejudices alleged in this case." Holmes countered "most differences are differences of degree" and distinguished between "external force" and "prejudice—which could be alleged in any case." After two and a half hours, the justice denied the writ or stay in a one paragraph decision, said goodbye to Hill and Thompson, and went straight to bed. "I know of no human power at this time that can save them," Hill told a reporter. Nonetheless, he and Thompson returned to Boston to seek relief from Judge George W. Anderson. The liberal federal judge who had invited Frankfurter and Chafee to defend the rights of Boston immigrants after the Palmer raids, Anderson learned about Holmes's decision and refused to intervene.

The Frankfurters canceled their plans that night to see the Jitney Players, a traveling theatrical troupe, to wait for a phone call from the defense team. Felix told Marion to go to the theater, but as invested in the case as her husband, she stayed home, too. At 8:00 p.m., he learned that Holmes had denied any relief and the governor had not granted a stay of execution. Frankfurter rejected a request to come to Boston that night to assist defense counsel but offered one final piece of advice:

"You know where the other Justice is?" Frankfurter asked.

"No."

"In Chatham. Phone 330."

"330?"

"Yes. You will be kind enough not to talk about this talk between us. Laymen cannot sometimes appreciate."

The eleventh-hour effort, however, would be made not with the justice in Chatham, but at the statehouse.

BACK IN BOSTON, the Sacco-Vanzetti Defense Committee was losing hope. At 9:00 p.m., three hours before the men were supposed to die at Charlestown State Prison, Sacco's wife had collapsed in distress. Eight hundred police officers armed with high-pressure hoses and machine guns guarded the prison; thirty-nine protesters, including writers John Dos Passos and Dorothy Parker, were arrested for illegally picketing the statehouse. Hill arrived at the statehouse after his visits with Holmes and Anderson and could not find anyone to grant a stay. The governor and his executive council were furious that Hill had circumvented their authority by seeking relief in federal court. Later that night, they agreed to hear Hill's final plea for a stay to exhaust the appeals process. Governor Fuller favored granting the stay; his executive council did not. Finally, at 11:27 p.m., thirty-three minutes before their executions, the governor's executive council granted Sacco and Vanzetti a stay until August 22.

With another twelve days to save Sacco and Vanzetti from the electric chair, Frankfurter stifled every impulse to speak out about their innocence, the unfairness of their trial, and the erroneous conclusions in the Lowell report. He resisted entreaties from Thompson and others to answer the report and explained "for me publicly now to intervene in this matter would hurt the cause of the men and not help them." He knew that people in Old Boston despised him and tried to discredit his book. "To a considerable extent I was on trial and the Lowell report is in part a report against me, although not a single fact in my book is controverted by that report," he wrote Thompson. "Therefore, much as it goes against the grain, my role for the present is silence."

Silence did not mean inaction. Frankfurter was determined to create a groundswell of public support for a stay of execution and a new trial and believed the best way to influence Governor Fuller and President Lowell was through the press. He started with the New York *World*. Still unwilling to come to Boston, Lippmann sent a reporter to Duxbury. For many hours, Frankfurter showed the reporter new evidence he had not seen before. Not willing to take the reporter's word that he would show the evidence to Lippmann and knowing how ambivalent Lippmann had been throughout the case, Frankfurter took matters into his own hands. He boarded the train for New York City and grabbed a notable reinforcement in C. C. Burlingham. A leading New York admiralty lawyer who had represented the White Star Line after the sinking of the *Titanic*, Burlingham joined Frankfurter in an August 18 session with Lippmann lasting many hours. They "did a job" on him. The next day, under the headline "Doubt that Will Not Down," Lippmann devoted the *World*'s entire editorial page to reviewing the evidence, refuting the Lowell committee's report, and calling for a new trial in front of a new judge. "They thought Lowell was Lowell," Felix told Marion, "but when doubts appeared they began to go the other way."

With Lippmann and the *World* on his side, Frankfurter searched for other ways to reach Lowell's conscience. He asked Julian Mack for names of influential Harvard alumni who could speak with him. Mack, Thompson, Calvert Magruder, and other lawyers wrote the president questioning the report's conclusions. The *New Republic* published a full-page advertisement in the *New York Times* reviewing the evidence and challenging Lowell to reconsider his report. Meanwhile, Frankfurter holed up at Burlingham's Connecticut summer home drafting a letter to the editor at the request of the *New York*

Times. The August 20 letter, "The Advisory Report: A Review of Some of the Findings of the Lowell Committee; With Indication of Errors," picked apart Lowell's report through references to the record. It was signed only by Burlingham.

In addition to co-authoring Burlingham's letter, Frankfurter helped the Sacco-Vanzetti Defense Committee assemble a group of distinguished professionals to sign a final petition to Governor Fuller asking him to commute Sacco and Vanzetti's death sentences or stay their executions. A who's who of American liberals—Jane Addams of Hull House, historian Charles Beard, *New Republic* editor Bruce Bliven, Burlingham, *Springfield Republican* editor Waldo Cook, Columbia philosopher John Dewey, University of Chicago law professor Ernst Freund, Harvard Medical School professor Alice Hamilton, journalist Norman Hapgood, *The Survey* editor Paul Kellogg, and Columbia economics professor Henry Seager—signed the petition, but not Frankfurter. A meeting with Governor Fuller went haywire when he interrupted them and accused them with great "hostility" of doing Frankfurter's bidding.

Frankfurter was busy trying to keep the Sacco-Vanzetti Defense Committee from meddling with the legal strategy of Arthur Dehon Hill. Gardner Jackson, the publicity manager for the committee, was the prime offender. A former *Boston Globe* reporter, Jackson left the newspaper in 1926 to enroll in Harvard history classes and befriended historian Arthur Schlesinger, Sr. After a few months and with Schlesinger's encouragement, Jackson stopped attending class and joined the defense committee full-time. Frankfurter reminded Jackson that Hill, who had taken on the representation for only $5000, had cost himself financially and socially by taking the case. "He is an outcast—," Frankfurter told Jackson, "he is worse than Thompson, because he took up the fight when Thompson said nothing could be done—there was an end to the matter." On August 19, the state Supreme Judicial Court rejected Hill's latest appeal; a federal trial judge also refused to intervene in the case. Frankfurter knew the men were going to die but also knew that Hill was not giving up.

On August 20, two days before Sacco and Vanzetti's execution, Hill returned to Beverly Farms to see Justice Holmes. A few weeks earlier, Holmes had granted a stay in the case of two black Kentucky men, Nathan Bard and Bunyan Fleming, who had been sentenced to death for the rape of a white woman. Bard and Fleming had not received pretrial access to defense counsel; their wives were prevented from testifying as alibi witnesses; and an all-white jury convicted the men in ten and eight minutes, respectively. During their second trip to Beverly Farms, Hill and two attorneys raised the Bard and Fleming case in their briefs and argued that Sacco and Vanzetti deserved a similar opportunity for the full U.S. Supreme Court to consider their petition seeking a writ of habeas corpus in October. After two hours of argument, Holmes denied the request for a stay. In a three-page opinion, he distinguished Sacco and Vanzetti's case from *Moore v. Dempsey* because the trial of the Italian anarchists had not been "invaded by an infuriated mob ready to lynch prisoner, counsel and jury if there is not a prompt conviction." He said their case might be "voidable" by the state Supreme Judicial Court, but not by him. He explained that federal judges were reluctant to interfere with state criminal trials except in extreme circumstances. And, in an allusion to the case of Bard and Fleming, he wrote: "Far stronger cases than this have arisen with regard to the blacks when the Supreme Court has denied its power." Privately, Holmes critiqued Frankfurter and his liberal friends' obsession with the case of two Italian anarchists by suggesting that they cared "more for red than for black." In his opinion, Holmes permitted Hill to approach other judges.

At 7:40 p.m. on August 20, Frankfurter learned that Holmes had turned them down and knew where Hill was headed next—to Chatham to seek a stay from Louis Brandeis. Gardner Jackson pleaded with Frankfurter not to discourage Hill and to accompany him to see the justice. Frankfurter knew things that Jackson did not—Brandeis's wife had contributed $50 to the Sacco-Vanzetti Defense Committee; Brandeis family friend Elizabeth Glendower Evans had allowed Sacco's family to stay at Brandeis's Dedham home during the trial; Evans and Frankfurter had been discussing the case with the justice for years; and Brandeis paid Frankfurter $3500 in 1926 and $4500 in 1927 for public interest work on Sacco-Vanzetti and other matters. On August 5, Brandeis had written Frankfurter lamenting that the case delayed Frankfurter's annual trip to Chatham and remarked: "You & Auntie B. have played noble parts." Fifteen days later, Frankfurter conferred with Hill, who was staying overnight at the Chatham Bars Inn and who understood that Brandeis "may feel himself disqualified from sitting for reasons you can divine." At 1:00 a.m., former New York attorney general W. S. Jackson phoned Frankfurter and asked him to reconsider going to see Brandeis. Frankfurter reminded him what Holmes had said in his August 10 opinion that "a statement of prejudice, no matter however strong," was not enough to intervene in the case. "I read it and I don't agree with it," W. S. Jackson replied. Frankfurter tried to manage his expectations: "I haven't the slightest idea what will happen tomorrow—what Brandeis will do with it. I would not be a bit surprised if he disqualified [himself] from sitting and nothing more could cinch it than for me to go down to Chatham. I can't say anything more."

The next morning while Hill was having breakfast, Frankfurter phoned him before he set off to see the justice and, at the committee's request, reminded Hill of a few prejudicial statements by District Attorney Katzmann in the record. Less than an hour later, Hill and his fellow lawyers arrived at Brandeis's summer home in Chatham. Dressed in knickers and a cap and having just finished breakfast, Brandeis was waiting for them on the porch. He would not let them in the front door. "I know what you are here for," Brandeis said, "and I can't take any action at all." After a three-minute conversation, Hill began to leave and informed a *Boston Herald* reporter that Brandeis disqualified himself because of "personal relations with some of the people interested in the case."

Hill refused to give up. He and Frankfurter had already determined where to go next—to a remote island off the coast of Maine to find Justice Harlan Fiske Stone. Hill left Chatham in a hurry. At noon, his co-counsel phoned from Plymouth and confirmed the plan. Frankfurter advised them to "skillfully weave in" New York and British cases from Frankfurter's book and to remind Stone that the evidence of Judge Thayer's prejudice had not been available for seven years. Flattery was also important because Stone was "a vain man." From Chatham, Hill drove through Boston, the North Shore, New Hampshire, and southern Maine late into the night. At 2:00 a.m., he arrived in Rockland, Maine. After staying overnight, he took the ferry from Rockland to Stonington on Deer Isle, then chartered a fishing boat to Isle au Haut. At 9:00 a.m., he arrived at Stone's summer home and spoke with the justice for an hour and fifteen minutes. Stone, however, also denied relief. An exhausted Hill returned to Searsport, Maine, and told his office: "Nothing else could be done." He spent the night in Portland, Maine.

With hours before the executions, new lawyers injected themselves into the case and tried things Frankfurter and Hill had dismissed as foolish. One lawyer wired Chief Justice Taft in Port au Pic, Quebec, and President Coolidge in South Dakota and offered to fly a plane to see them. At 9:00 p.m., another lawyer visited Justice Holmes hoping the third time would be the charm. The answers, however, were the same.

Exhausted from months of rallying members of his liberal network to persuade Governor Fuller to commute the sentences, Frankfurter defended the behavior of Holmes and the other judges. He agreed with Holmes's distinction between a sham trial dominated by a mob and a trial and appeals process of six years before a prejudicial judge. He could not take any more of Gardner Jackson's criticism of Holmes for refusing to intervene. Jackson, echoing other nonlawyers on the Sacco-Vanzetti Defense Committee, complained that "it is a most awful situation where your legal system will not insure moral demands; that is what leads to revolution." Frankfurter, who believed in procedural fairness yet in the independence of state courts, was having none of it: "Now don't talk to me about that because I have had to listen to my wife all day. I can shut you up but not her."

The morning before the executions, the Frankfurters boarded an 11:00 a.m. train from Duxbury to Boston. Felix agreed to advise the defense committee but refused to take any legal action. That night, Felix and Marion walked the streets of Beacon Hill with a sympathetic friend. At 12:19 a.m., they heard the news on the radio: "Sacco gone, Vanzetti going!" Marion did not, as reports suggested, collapse and nearly hit the pavement. For many weeks, however, she was deeply depressed. It did not help matters that her psychiatrist, Dr. Salmon, had died on August 13 in a boating accident. Felix arranged for her to co-edit Sacco and Vanzetti's jailhouse letters for publication. She made "very sensitive judgments" about editing and arranging the letters and wrote the introduction. The project brought her back to life. For once, her indefatigable husband was badly in need of a rest. "To the end, you have done all that was possible for you," Brandeis wrote him. "And that all was more than would have [been] possible for any other person I know. But the end of S.V. is only the beginning. 'They know not what they do.' "

THE PURITANICAL REACTIONARIES of Old Boston knew exactly what they were doing. Angry with Frankfurter over the Sacco-Vanzetti affair, they tried to drive him from the law school. They claimed that he had stalled the school's $5 million endowment campaign. In fact, only a few people pulled pledges totaling $2000 to $3000. Philanthropist Julius Rosenwald responded with a $10,000 pledge for a Frankfurter-directed publication fund. Old Boston also spread lies that Frankfurter had been secretly on the Sacco-Vanzetti Defense Committee payroll. Frankfurter refuted the allegations by writing a history of his involvement in the case yet neglecting to mention the payments from Brandeis. Judge Mack defended Frankfurter at a September 27 meeting before the Harvard Board of Overseers, joined by an unlikely ally—President Lowell. In the name of academic freedom, Lowell absolved Frankfurter of any wrongdoing. After the meeting, Mack reassured the law school's intimidated and fearful dean, Roscoe Pound, that "nothing further will be done."

Frustrated with the tepid support from Pound, Frankfurter went on the offensive against Lowell. He thought Lowell's performance was disgraceful:

the secret investigation and interviews, the dismissive attitude toward Thompson's argument, and the report's factually unsupported conclusions. As lawyer John Moors said of his former Harvard College classmate, "Lawrence Lowell was incapable of seeing that two wops could be right and the Yankee judiciary could be wrong." Frankfurter believed that if his book had been as sloppy with the evidence as Lowell's report, he would have been driven from the legal academy. An unrepentant Frankfurter made it clear to Pound that he would not resign because of pressure from Lowell or anyone else: "When people ask me, 'Do you plan to resign?' I say to them, 'Why should I? Let Mr. Lowell resign.'"

Not able to get Frankfurter to leave on his own accord, Lowell blocked as many of Frankfurter's law faculty hires as he could, especially if the applicant was Jewish. Lowell's first victim was Nathan Margold, a former student whose life story was eerily similar to Frankfurter's. A Jewish immigrant from Romania who arrived in America at age two and graduated from City College, Margold had finished fifth in his Harvard Law School class and clerked for Learned Hand. He joined Emory Buckner in the U.S. attorney's office before leaving for a one-year tryout at the law school as an instructor. Margold received high marks as a teacher of criminal law and insurance and co-edited Joseph H. Beale's casebook on criminal law. In February 1928, the law faculty voted to make Margold an assistant professor. Lowell, however, vetoed the appointment before it could go to the Harvard Corporation. Pound, who had not voted for Margold as an instructor because his appointment would prevent the school from hiring other Jews, refused to confront Lowell. The president's conduct outraged Frankfurter and other faculty members; a committee of professors appealed to Lowell to reconsider to no avail; Frankfurter knew the real reason why Lowell had rejected the Margold appointment—"simply because he was a Jew."

A few months after the Margold affair, Lowell attempted to deny James Landis's promotion to full professor by offering the professorship to someone else. Few could match Landis's academic or scholarly record. In late 1927, Harvard University Press had published Frankfurter and Landis's series of law review articles as a book, *The Business of the Supreme Court*. At the end of the 1928 and 1929 Supreme Court terms, they published new installments. Frankfurter and Thomas Reed Powell successfully fended off Lowell's efforts to deny Landis a professorship. For nearly twenty-five years, however, Frankfurter was the law school's only tenured Jewish professor, partly by accident but mostly by Lowell's design.

Frankfurter's criticism of Lowell continued. On October 4, 1927, the *New*

Republic hosted a dinner in New York City to keep the cause of Sacco and Vanzetti alive and to honor those who had worked so hard on their behalf. Defense counsel spoke; Thompson moved the crowd with his impassioned faith in the pair's innocence; Hill explained he was simply doing his duty and was "revolted" by continued criticism of Lowell and the report. Frankfurter buoyed the spirits of the literary crowd including Dorothy Parker, Heywood Broun, and Edmund Wilson by rebuking Hill for defending Lowell. Frankfurter attacked Lowell's report as "an obstruction to a free inquiry into this case," and urged that the obstruction be "removed" by continuing to critique the report.

In his final appeal to public opinion, Frankfurter made his most enduring contribution to the Sacco-Vanzetti case by spearheading the publication of all six volumes of the record. He and Thompson discovered that much of the Lowell committee's investigation, particularly Thompson and Ehrmann's closing argument, was conveniently not recorded or transcribed. Frankfurter relied on Bernard Flexner, C. C. Burlingham, Emory Buckner, and Raymond Fosdick to recruit prominent members of the bar including Newton Baker, John W. Davis, Charles Nagel, and Elihu Root, Sr., to serve as the volume's editors and to solicit contributions from philanthropists John D. Rockefeller, Jr., and Julius Rosenwald to cover much of the $30,000 publication costs. Frankfurter kept his name out of it.

Ultimately, Frankfurter hoped the six published volumes of the Sacco-Vanzetti record would persuade people, as he had believed, that the two men were innocent or at the very least could not have been convicted on the basis of the evidence presented at trial. He refused to rest until copies of the record were "in every library in the world." He educated the nativist sculptor Gutzon Borglum about Sacco and Vanzetti and inspired him to create a bas-relief of the two men. One day, Frankfurter hoped to write the definitive history of the case and kept annotating his 1927 book and updating his files. Aside from defending his motives for writing the book or correcting the historical record, he never participated in another rally or public meeting or wrote about the case. He believed his book and the trial record spoke for themselves. Frankfurter's book, as well as a subsequent account co-authored by his Harvard law colleague Edmund M. Morgan, concluded that Sacco and Vanzetti had not received a fair trial. Historians continue to debate Sacco and Vanzetti's guilt or innocence, with some claiming that Sacco was guilty but not Vanzetti.

Everything about Frankfurter's involvement in the Sacco-Vanzetti case epitomized his philosophy about the role of courts in a democratic society. He believed that everyone was entitled to fair procedures, not fair results;

he believed in a government of laws, not of men. He blamed District Attorney Katzmann and Judge Thayer for rigging the trial. He defended Holmes and Brandeis for not staying the executions and was disturbed upon learning about a nighttime guard at Holmes's summer residence and that Brandeis was receiving abusive letters. He regarded both justices as heroes. Like Holmes and Brandeis, Frankfurter believed in a limited role for the Court in all but the most egregious state criminal cases. He meant what he said in criticizing the Taft Court that there was a price to be paid for federalism.

An opponent of capital punishment, Frankfurter believed that the best way to stop an execution was through political pressure on the governor to pardon the two men or commute their sentences rather than relying on an inherently conservative Supreme Court. He had been vindicated in the past. His Mooney report had led to the commutation of Mooney's death sentence to life in prison and eventually a pardon. He had signed the pardon petition of Jacob Abrams (Harding had pardoned Abrams and his co-defendants contingent on their deportation to Russia); he had praised New York governor Al Smith for pardoning Benjamin Gitlow in December 1925; and he had called for a pardon of Anita Whitney in the *New Republic* (the governor of California had pardoned her in June 1927). The pardon for Sacco and Vanzetti never came. All along, Frankfurter expected Governor Fuller to stop the executions and at the very least to commute their death sentences to life in prison. The governor listened to the wrong people and could not overcome his biases that "two wops" could be right and President Lowell could be wrong. The outcome was a product of Old Boston's puritanical self-righteousness, insular prejudice against two Italian immigrants, and peculiar animosity toward Frankfurter himself.

As emotionally scarring as the Sacco-Vanzetti episode was for Frankfurter, he emerged from it with an unshaken belief in fair procedures and the democratic political process as the best ways to achieve social justice. Elections and electoral politics, he learned time and again, mattered most.

CHAPTER 13

The Most Useful Lawyer in the United States

A frequent radio listener, Frankfurter likely tuned into the 1928 Democratic National Convention in Houston on the evening of June 28 to hear his friend from the War Department and War Labor Policies Board, Franklin D. Roosevelt. They had not been in touch in years. Roosevelt had congratulated Frankfurter on his marriage to Marion in December 1919; Frankfurter had written Roosevelt in January 1921 after Roosevelt's failed vice-presidential bid and again after a bout with polio eight months later permanently paralyzed Roosevelt from the waist down. At the 1924 Democratic National Convention in New York, Roosevelt had returned to the national stage to nominate New York governor Al Smith for the presidency. Four years later, in a stirring speech written for the national radio audience, he again nominated Smith for the presidency and proclaimed him "the Happy Warrior." For twenty-five minutes after Roosevelt finished, Democrats in Sam Houston Hall waved their signs and roared with approval. Smith captured the Democratic presidential nomination on his third try; Roosevelt began his return to public life.

During the spring and summer of 1928, Frankfurter worked tirelessly to elect Smith to the White House and reentered the orbit of Franklin Roosevelt. Sooner than most people, he recognized Smith and Roosevelt as the present and future of the Democratic Party and the Democratic Party as the future of America's liberal democracy.

Frankfurter viewed the Republican nominee, Herbert Hoover, as a continuation of the materialism, greed, and corruption of the Harding and Coolidge administrations. During the Great War, however, there was no one Frankfurter had admired more than Hoover, the head of the U.S. Food Administration who had fed the starving people of Belgium and all of Europe. After Wilson's failure in Paris, Frankfurter looked to Hoover as the country's next great leader. Instead, Hoover joined the Harding and Coolidge administrations as secretary of commerce and, in Frankfurter's view, failed to speak out about the Teapot Dome scandal and the corruption in the Harding Justice Department. Frankfurter also believed that Hoover's technocratic calls for increased efficiency of production ignored the detrimental effects of industrialization on American workers. "It is highly revealing that in the field of his greatest competence he has seen merely the technological and not the social significances," Frankfurter wrote Lippmann in June 1928. Frankfurter faulted Hoover's 1922 book, *American Individualism*, for relying on abstract concepts of "capitalism" and "individualism" rather than addressing the role of the government in regulating the economy and creating an industrial democracy. "I think the vapidity and ineptitude and errors (demonstrable errors of fact) in that book are a good index to his social philosophy because I think they really point the direction of his mind," Frankfurter wrote Lippmann.

Returning to Duxbury with Marion in early July, Frankfurter pressed Lippmann not to absolve Hoover of the corruption in the Harding administration. He also urged Lippmann to hold Hoover accountable for the Coolidge administration's water-power policy that allowed big business to exploit public resources. Lippmann agreed and predicted, as Brandeis had, that a dip in the stock market presaged a major crash. The justice told Frankfurter that Smith "should be able to beat" Hoover.

During the 1928 campaign, Frankfurter and Lippmann joined forces for one of the last times behind Smith's candidacy. Four years earlier, they had clashed when Frankfurter supported La Follette and Lippmann endorsed John W. Davis. The 1928 election united them behind the idea of a pro-worker and pro-farmer Democratic Party. They tried to persuade progressives in both political parties to vote for Smith.

Smith's humble origins, extolled by Roosevelt in his nominating speech in Houston, presented some political challenges. The four-time governor had grown up on the Lower East Side and risen through the ranks of the Tammany Hall political machine. He was a "wet candidate" who opposed Prohibition. And, as the son of an Irish mother and German Italian father, he was trying to become the nation's first Catholic president.

Prohibition was Smith's Achilles' heel. Soon after his nomination, he had caused an uproar by sending a telegram to the convention calling for Prohibition to be enforced by the states rather than the federal government. Dry Democratic voters were outraged. Roosevelt, who blamed Lippmann for encouraging Smith to send the telegram, believed that the columnist had done "more harm to Al Smith's candidacy than all the Republican newspapers in the United States put together."

The Tammany Hall issue was the easiest to confront. Frankfurter encouraged Lippmann and the *World* to investigate the Smith administration's record: "If Tammany left no trace or trail in Albany during Al's governorships, the argument becomes a false bogey." He suggested the newspaper compare the lack of corruption in Smith's administration with "the Harding saturnalia and Coolidge-Hoover indifference." Thanks to Frankfurter, Lippmann and the *World* were not the problem.

Some of Frankfurter's politically astute friends opposed Smith's candidacy. William Allen White of the *Emporia Gazette* wrote that as a young state legislator, Smith had voted in favor of gambling, saloons, and prostitution. White retracted the prostitution allegation yet continued to write about Smith's twenty-year-old legislative record on liquor and gambling. Frankfurter encouraged his progressive friend to view Smith not as a young legislator but as a fully formed politician. He reminded White that Albert Beveridge's biography of Abraham Lincoln revealed the sixteenth president had been as much of a party politician in the Illinois legislature as Smith had been in the New York legislature. Lincoln, Frankfurter reminded White, "rose above this early record, and achieved moral distinction." Instead of emphasizing Smith's similar moral arc, White chose to traffic in stereotypes about corrupt big-city politicians. Frankfurter chided White for joining "the blind forces of Pharisaism so rampant in America today." Given White's past support for liberal causes, Frankfurter could not explain his opposition to Smith except for "the deeply imbedded, unconscious root of anti-Catholic prejudice."

The religion issue for Frankfurter was personal. The prejudice he had experienced during the Sacco-Vanzetti case reemerged in Boston during the Massachusetts primary as Republicans appealed to the city's "snobs and bigots" while trying not to offend its "fair-minded" residents. He implored friends and colleagues in Cambridge not to fall prey to religious intolerance. "The people of New York have learned to realize that Smith the human being is more significant than Smith the Catholic," he wrote his Harvard law colleague Samuel Williston. "It would be a great thing for the people of this country to gain such an experience in humanity and reason."

Much to Frankfurter's annoyance, the Hoover campaign seized on Prohibition to stir up religious bias. Mabel Walker Willebrandt, a Harding and Coolidge Justice Department lawyer charged with enforcing Prohibition, traveled the country appealing to Methodist and Presbyterian ministers to work for Hoover and to preach to their parishioners to vote against Smith. Frankfurter praised a *World* editorial holding Hoover responsible for Wille-brandt's attacks.

The religious bigots and Prohibitionists did not disturb Frankfurter as much as former progressives who failed to recognize the Democratic Party as the liberal party. The progressivism of Theodore Roosevelt, Robert La Follette, and most Republicans was dead and gone; the Republican Party catered to big business, and its leaders cared little about the welfare of industrial workers and farmers. Frankfurter believed the advisers running Smith's campaign, Joseph Proskauer and Belle and Henry Moskowitz, were not courting former progressives hard enough. "On his record, the Governor deserves the progressive vote—the great bulk of liberal independents who supported T.R. in '12 and La Follette in '24," Frankfurter wrote Belle Moskowitz in August. "As yet, the vote is torpid—certainly it has not yet moved towards Al. Don't be sore at the progressives. Win them."

To assist the campaign, Frankfurter entered the public debate and enlisted the help of sympathetic Harvard law colleagues. Calvert Magruder wrote a memorandum advising Smith on immigration issues in an increasingly iso-lationist country and in nativist cities such as Boston. Frankfurter and Landis wrote a memorandum on water power because Hoover opposed building a dam on the Tennessee River to create a government-owned electric power facility in Muscle Shoals, Alabama. In the *New Republic*, Frankfurter critiqued Hoover's water-power policy and exposed him as a tool of "the power interests."

A week before the election, Frankfurter published "Why I Am for Smith," which *New Republic* editor Herbert Croly considered "the most comprehensive and at the same time succinct statement of the salient reasons for voting for Smith that I have seen anywhere." The editorial offered numerous reasons to vote for Smith: the rejection of religious bigotry and social class distinctions; the reality that Prohibition was a failed experiment in need of reform; the recognition of politics as a "process of popular education" and Smith as a "master of politics." Frankfurter emphasized Smith's common touch and embrace of professional experts as "indispensable for the adjustment through government of the conflicting economic interests among different sections and different classes in the country." He urged Americans to vote for Smith to "give decided momentum to the liberalizing tendencies in American social economy" and because as governor of New York he had "achieved great things for liberal causes." He rejected Hoover as the continuation of the Harding and Coolidge years and wanted to send the corrupt Republican Party "into the wilderness."

Smith was not Frankfurter's only candidate. On October 2, New York Democrats nominated Roosevelt to succeed Smith as governor. Ten days later, Frankfurter sat at the head table with other professors as Roosevelt spoke to 700 students during a luncheon at the Harvard Union. Roosevelt's Republican opponent, the state's undistinguished attorney general Albert Ottinger, was Jewish. Frankfurter congratulated Roosevelt on his nomination as an "occasion for national rejoicing" and blanched at appeals to vote for Ottinger because of religious pride (Roosevelt's running mate for lieutenant governor, Herbert Lehman, was also Jewish). "As a Jew I am particularly happy that your nomination prevented the New York contest from degenerating into an unworthy competition for the 'Jewish vote,'" he wrote Roosevelt. "Now all good and wise citizens ought to be drawn to your standard."

Unlike the final days of the efforts to save Sacco and Vanzetti, Frankfurter was front and center in the Smith campaign. In late October, he met the candidate when at least 750,000 people saw Smith speak on Boston Common and parade through the city's streets. He signed a statement along with forty Harvard professors in support of Smith and wrote editorials responding to Smith's critics. Two days before the election, Frankfurter presided over a rally of 3500 people at Boston's Symphony Hall. The crowd stood on its feet and cheered as Frankfurter, paraphrasing a line of Franklin Roosevelt's, declared victory for Smith for making "the people of the United States think" about the past seven years of Republican rule when people were encouraged not to think or to think only about themselves. "Governor Smith," Frankfurter told the crowd, "has vitalized politics and lifted them to their rightful plane of discussion, debate, controversy, exchange of opinion, full and frank, about the pressing problems of society."

On Election Day, Frankfurter held out hope that Smith might win. Smith, however, struggled in the West and the normally solid South, where he could not overcome being Catholic, a wet, and a former Tammany Hall politician. Perhaps no one stood a chance against Hoover, who captured 444 electoral votes and forty states compared to eighty-seven electoral votes and eight states for Smith. In the Northeast, Smith won only Massachusetts and Rhode Island.

The day after the election, Frankfurter walked the streets of Boston in a daze. It reminded him of January 10, 1928, when his mother, Emma, had died at age seventy-four after a monthlong battle with stomach cancer. Frankfurter and his mother were "great friends"; he had gotten his "passionate intensity" and strong feelings about right and wrong from her; she had lived for the past ten years in Cambridge to be near her daughter Ella and son Felix. After the election, "[t]here was something unreal about my surroundings, something precious had gone out of life," he wrote to Smith aide Belle Moskowitz, "but the people about me seemed to be unaware of it."

Nonetheless, Frankfurter was optimistic about the future of the Democratic Party as the liberal party. For the time being, he envisioned Smith as the leader of an opposition movement. "Certainly there is no one in sight who can begin to assume such a function," Frankfurter wrote Lippmann, who was pessimistic about the party's future, "and there will be no one unless and until Roosevelt emerges to such leadership in four years."

Frankfurter recognized Roosevelt's political promise before most people. While Smith had failed to carry his home state, Roosevelt had squeaked out his governor's race by 25,000 votes, less than 1 percent of ballots cast. Roosevelt's victory gave Frankfurter "consolation and hope" for the future. A few days after the election, he congratulated Roosevelt and praised him for having a similar "conception of government" as Smith "that the processes of government are essentially educational processes."

As much as Roosevelt represented the future, Frankfurter remained loyal to the current leader of the Democratic Party, Al Smith. In January 1929, Smith called for people to help eliminate the Democratic National Committee's $1.5 million debt. Frankfurter sent a small contribution and wired Smith: "It's refreshing to have a leader who leads." On May 8, Frankfurter arranged a private dinner in Smith's honor at the Union Club in Boston. Frankfurter sat on Smith's left at a large round table of the forty Harvard professors who had endorsed him. After Frankfurter briefly introduced him, Smith spoke for two hours on "The Business of Government" and praised Roosevelt's willingness to take on the "power trusts" over water power and public utilities.

As a new governor tackling reform of public utilities, judicial selection, and criminal justice, Roosevelt knew he needed Frankfurter's help. They began exchanging the first of many "Dear Felix" and "Dear Frank" letters. Roosevelt understood what so many others had discovered. Between Frankfurter's work on the Smith campaign and his ability to contribute to public debates about everything from criminal law and labor law to public utilities, the role of the Supreme Court, and Zionism, he was, as Brandeis wrote Harold Laski, "clearly the most useful lawyer in the United States."

DURING THE HOOVER ADMINISTRATION, Frankfurter worked behind the scenes to influence the Wickersham Commission's recommendations for reforming federal criminal law and enforcement of Prohibition. His Harvard law classmate Monte M. Lemann of New Orleans was one of the eleven commissioners. His former investigator Max Lowenthal was the commission's executive secretary. Working with Lemann and Lowenthal, Frankfurter made sure the commission tackled the right issues and hired the right experts. Frankfurter's friends Zechariah Chafee, Goldthwaite Dorr, Reuben Oppenheimer, and Frank Tannenbaum contributed chapters to the commission's report.

Frankfurter's biggest contribution during the Hoover years may have been about the evils of labor injunctions. Unions struggled to gain a foothold in the early twentieth century because management often went to court to prevent peaceful strikes, picketing, and boycotts. The Supreme Court repeatedly struck down federal and state laws eliminating labor injunctions. The Clayton Antitrust Act of 1914 attempted to limit injunctions against unions only in cases of violent strikes leading to property damage. Frankfurter often found himself advising the ACLU and other lawyers about how to prevent judges from issuing labor injunctions. He turned to scholarship as another way of influencing public policy. In April and June 1928, Frankfurter and New York labor lawyer Nathan Greene had published the first two installments on the history of labor injunctions in the British *Law Quarterly Review*. The following year, they published a third installment followed by two more in the *Harvard Law Review* and *Yale Law Journal*. Finally, in January 1930, they published the five installments as a book, *The Labor Injunction*.

As an expert on labor injunctions, Frankfurter assisted Senator George W. Norris of Nebraska in outlawing them. Beginning in May 1928, he had worked with fellow labor law experts—Chicago lawyer Donald Richberg, Herman Oliphant of Columbia University, and Edwin E. Witte of Wisconsin—in drafting new legislation. The Norris-La Guardia Act, which became law in March 1932, banned yellow-dog contracts and labor injunctions and marked the beginning of the federal government's support for organized labor. The law circumvented twenty-five years of anti-union Supreme Court decisions.

Frankfurter continued to encourage the country's "best men" to enter public service. In a series of lectures at Yale in the spring of 1930 later published as a book, he invoked Abraham Lincoln and Theodore Roosevelt as examples of why career politicians should be cultivated rather than scorned, described "politics" as "a process of popular education," and declared that "expertise is indispensable."

Nowhere was Frankfurter more concerned about getting the best people in government than on the Supreme Court. In early 1930, Chief Justice Taft announced his retirement because of chronic health problems. Predictably, his decision set off a battle over Hoover's selection of the next chief justice. Fortunately for Frankfurter, he had several influential friends who had the president's ear. His mentor Henry Stimson was Hoover's secretary of state. Stimson, in turn, continued to rely on Frankfurter to help him choose his assistants and hired Frankfurter's choice for under secretary, New York lawyer Joseph P. Cotton. Frankfurter also cultivated a relationship with Justice Harlan Fiske Stone, a member of Hoover's "medicine ball cabinet" that exercised on the White House lawn. Stimson, Cotton, and Stone were Frankfurter's backchannel to the president.

Frankfurter's ideal first choice for chief justice was New York Court of Appeals chief judge Benjamin N. Cardozo. As much as Frankfurter wanted Cardozo to be chief, he supported Stone, who often voted with Holmes and Brandeis, for the Court's center chair and for Cardozo to be nominated to Stone's seat. Cotton was lobbying for Stone as chief justice and for Learned Hand to replace Stone. Two of the Court's conservative justices, Van Devanter and Butler, went to New York to sound out their preferred candidate, former justice Charles Evans Hughes. During a dinner with Hand and Lippmann at Hand's apartment, Frankfurter was convinced that Stone's nomination as chief justice would be scuttled by "'the boys' . . . because he has shown himself to be unreliable, from their point of view, on social-economic questions."

Frankfurter insisted that his plan of persuading Hoover to name Stone chief justice nearly came to pass. Cotton told Frankfurter that Hoover was prepared to nominate Stone but decided to offer the chief justiceship to Hughes as a matter of courtesy. Since leaving the Court in 1916, Hughes had been Harding's secretary of state and established himself as a prominent Wall Street lawyer. No one, least of all Cotton, expected Hughes to take the job. His son, Charles Evans Hughes, Jr., was solicitor general and, if Hughes joined the Court, would have to resign. Hughes, according to Cotton, shocked them by accepting the offer; Hoover and several historians have discredited Cotton's story.

Hughes's nomination as chief justice infuriated Frankfurter. He was angry with Hoover for caving to the conservative wing of the Republican Party. He knew that Hoover thought highly enough of Stone to want him as secretary of state and attorney general; the president, however, may have been talked out of making him chief justice, "if I am right, because of the hostility which Stone has aroused for having decently liberal views on constitutional issues." Frankfurter did not consider Hughes to be staunchly conservative yet, as the second New Yorker besides Stone, a Hughes appointment made it difficult for Cardozo or Hand to join the Court.

What really troubled Frankfurter was that Hoover had "yielded to influences that are reactionary" and would tilt the Court in an even more conservative direction with his next nominee. He was determined to challenge the conventional wisdom about the nomination. When a *World* editorial suggested that Hughes's nomination had been met with "universal approval," Frankfurter persuaded Lippmann to write another one about the importance of the future direction of the Court. Lippmann's editorial warned Hoover about rising anger with a judiciary out of step with the American people as "no petty revolt." Frankfurter heard that the editorial landed on Hoover's desk and was assured that the president read it. Unmoved, Hoover agreed with the conservative *New York Herald Tribune* that the objections to Hughes were "mere sniping." Senate opposition, however, echoed Frankfurter's views. Several senators attacked Hughes for leaving the Court to run for president, his complicity in the Harding and Coolidge administrations, and his Supreme Court advocacy on behalf of railroads and other corporate interests. After three days of intense debate, Hughes was confirmed, 52–26. Frankfurter was not entirely disappointed. He regarded the debate as "one of the healthiest things that has happened in this country for many a year," though he wished that the Senate had rejected "Charles the Baptist" and sent the conservative Court a message.

Less than a month later, on March 8, 1930, Justice Edward Terry Sanford collapsed in the dentist's chair after a tooth extraction and died later that day at age sixty-four. With his next nominee, Hoover underestimated the liberal opposition. He was determined to replace the Tennessee-born Sanford with another southerner to help Republicans make inroads in the solidly Democratic South. The president chose a 44-year-old Republican federal appeals court judge from North Carolina, John J. Parker. The *New York Times* declared: "Senate Approval Likely."

The Parker nomination, which was based on geographic and electoral considerations rather than judicial acumen, appalled Frankfurter. He read all Parker's opinions from his five years on the federal bench and objected to their mediocrity compared to Cardozo's opinions. Employing Holmes's ranking system of lawyers according to their sharpness as stings, razors, or kitchen knives, Frankfurter declared Parker "just a kitchen knife." "I think he is one of these extreme 'conservatives' because of the limited nature of his mind . . . ," he wrote Lippmann. "Why is that not the best of all reasons for not having him on the Supreme Court—particularly for not having him for the next forty years!"

Two powerful interest groups with Frankfurter connections, the American

Federation of Labor (AFL) and the National Association for the Advancement of Colored People (NAACP), led the fight. On April 5, William Green of the AFL testified against Parker's nomination. He singled out a 1927 opinion in which Parker rejected a challenge to a yellow-dog contract forbidding union membership as a condition of employment. Green concluded that Parker would hurt unions and "strengthen the reactionary side of the Supreme Court, by adding another to that powerful influence."

Frankfurter's ties to the NAACP were stronger. In November 1929, the NAACP had invited him to join its National Legal Committee and executive board. Frankfurter joined the legal advisory group but not the executive board because the latter would require him to miss too many classes to attend board meetings in New York City.

With Frankfurter's encouragement, the NAACP opposed a Supreme Court nominee for the first time in its history. The organization discovered a 1920 *Greensboro Daily News* article during Parker's campaign for governor in which he had praised a 1900 state constitutional amendment instituting poll taxes, literacy tests, and grandfather clauses to prevent blacks from voting. Parker had said "the participation of the negro in politics is a source of evil and danger to both races and is not desired by the wise men in either race or by the Republican Party of North Carolina." The NAACP wired Parker asking him if he still held those views; it received no response. The day after he testified that Parker was unfit for the Court, the NAACP's Walter White sent Frankfurter a copy of the testimony and sought advice. Frankfurter requested copies of the *Greensboro Daily News* article and the organization's latest letter to Hoover and complimented the tone of its grassroots campaign. "I know how distressing the whole controversy raised by the Parker nomination is to you," Frankfurter wrote White, "but I think you ought to have the satisfaction of feeling that you have conducted your fight with serenity, dignity and impersonal relevance."

Not content to let the AFL and NAACP do all the work, Frankfurter worked with Lippmann and Charles Merz of the New York *World* on anti-Parker editorials. The newspaper opposed Parker's confirmation as making the Court more conservative when "the times call for the nomination of a liberal." Before the Senate vote, Frankfurter urged the *World* to reiterate that Parker's nomination "threatens us for the next thirty years with mediocrity and blindness in the most sensitive phase of government for no other reason in the world than temporary exigencies of Southern and Republican politics." The *World* adopted Frankfurter's language nearly word for word. On May 7, the Senate rejected Parker's nomination, 41–39. Fourteen years after he and Lippmann had defended Brandeis's nomination in the *New Republic,* Frankfurter credited the *World*'s editorials with helping to defeat the nomination of Parker.

Hoover's second choice, Owen J. Roberts, thrilled Frankfurter. A prominent Philadelphia lawyer, Roberts had made his name prosecuting Harding administration officials implicated in the Teapot Dome scandal. "In every way," Frankfurter wrote Brandeis, "Roberts is superior to Parker." Frankfurter wrote Roberts after he was quickly confirmed: "Who says Senate rows do no good!" Frankfurter's high hopes turned out to be somewhat misplaced. In ensuing years, Roberts was not the reliable vote to uphold federal and state economic legislation that Frankfurter had hoped.

Regardless, the Parker fight was a good thing, Frankfurter argued, because the American people held the Supreme Court accountable. In his Yale lectures, several magazine articles, and a national radio address for the League of Women Voters, he urged people to scrutinize Supreme Court nominees and sought to educate them about the Court's conservative turn. Since 1921, he wrote, the Court had been invalidating federal and state socioeconomic legislation on the basis of the justices' personal predilections and unconscious biases. He portrayed the Court as usurping the authority of Congress, the Executive, and the states and employing the Due Process and Equal Protection Clauses to exercise a judicial veto. "In theory, judges wield the people's power" he wrote. "Through the effective exertion of public opinion, the people should determine to whom the power is entrusted."

———

AS A MODEL for how judges should decide cases, Frankfurter continued to point to Holmes's jurisprudence broadly interpreting the Constitution and upholding new laws, yet he worried how much longer the 89-year-old justice could serve on the Court. The justice had not been the same since the February 1929 death of his wife, Fanny. Learned Hand believed that Holmes's opinions were not as good as they once were. Frankfurter was concerned that Holmes had tired himself out as acting chief justice after Taft's death. He was counting on Holmes's new secretary, a 25-year-old Harvard law graduate from Baltimore, Alger Hiss, to be the justice's constant companion. Hiss broke the justice's unwritten rule against married secretaries. He also instituted the practice of reading to Holmes in the afternoons and evenings as Fanny had, worried about how depressed his boss was in the spring of 1930, and kept Frankfurter apprised of the justice's condition.

At the end of the term, Holmes showed he could still write stinging dissents about his colleagues' expansive interpretation of the Due Process Clause to strike down state laws. Three times, he dissented from decisions invalidating state taxes. In the last one about a Missouri estate tax, he referred to his 1905 *Lochner* dissent and accused the majority for reading their economic views into the Constitution. The Fourteenth Amendment, he wrote, was not "intended to give us *carte blanche* to embody our economic or moral beliefs in its prohibitions." An incensed McReynolds announced his majority opinion from the bench and suggested it "ought to be clear to an unclouded mind," a comment that amused Holmes and Brandeis on their ride home. Frankfurter declared *Baldwin v. Missouri* one of the finest opinions of Holmes's career and which justified "everything that was said and done in the Hughes and Parker debates."

Upon Holmes's return to Beverly Farms for the summer, the Frankfurters kept him company. During his stopover in Boston, Marion accompanied him to see his portrait by Charles Hopkinson at Harvard Law School. Another day, the Frankfurters lunched at Beverly Farms and were amazed at how energetic he was. After Harvard's commencement in June, Frankfurter, Hand, and Lippmann drove up to see him. In early August, Frankfurter brought with him New York Court of Appeals chief judge Benjamin Cardozo. A longtime admirer of Holmes's, Cardozo referred to him as "the master." Holmes was "enchanted" by their long talk and described Cardozo as "a beautiful spirit." Frankfurter encouraged Holmes to stay on the Court and "write on!"

Holmes's ninetieth birthday on March 8, 1931, thanks to Frankfurter, became a national celebration. Frankfurter published a *Harvard Law Review* article about Holmes's early opinions on the Massachusetts Supreme Judicial Court. He edited a volume of essays about Holmes by him, Cardozo, Lippmann, John Dewey, Morris Cohen, and John Henry Wigmore. George W. Wickersham asserted in a review that the "writers of all the essays in this volume represent a school of thought to which, in general, the majority of the Supreme Court has been consistently opposed." Frankfurter responded that if he and his Sacco-Vanzetti antagonist Wigmore belonged "to the same 'school of thought,' then I should think the 'school' is sufficiently comprehensive for Mr. Wickersham also to find himself at home in it." Frankfurter defended Holmes's reputation against all comers, especially in the hostile atmosphere of Old Boston where "a Holmes is an exotic and a Coolidge its natural symbol and glory." On the evening of March 8, a CBS radio program celebrating his birthday concluded with Holmes addressing the nation in an aristocratic New England accent that sounded oddly British. Frankfurter threw a small listening party at his home. One of the guests, historian Arthur Schlesinger, Sr., repeated physician Richard Cabot's criticism of Holmes's excessive "vanity." Frankfurter exploded about the insular attitudes of Cabot and other Boston Brahmins and later apologized to Schlesinger. There was no question the connection between the Frankfurters and Holmes was deeply personal. "Holmes is a bond between us," Felix wrote Marion the day before the ninetieth birthday celebration, "as he is with no other pair."

As much as he loved and admired Holmes, Frankfurter understood that Brandeis was the real liberal leader of the Court. For a *Harvard Law Review* symposium on Brandeis's seventy-fifth birthday, Frankfurter wrote about Brandeis's constitutional opinions and included the article in an edited volume of essays celebrating Brandeis's career. Frankfurter's article declared Brandeis "a moral teacher." He admired Brandeis's empirical approach to resolving complex questions and his Jeffersonian belief in states as laboratories of experimentation. Unlike the short, epigrammatic opinions of Holmes, Brandeis wrote long, practical opinions driven by facts and sociological studies. The two justices, despite their different styles, often arrived at similar outcomes. Brandeis wrote prescient dissents about the president's authority to remove executive branch officials and about the constitutional evils of wiretapping and its invasion of a right to privacy. He often sought to limit the Supreme Court's power by avoiding constitutional questions. Brandeis's constitutional avoidance, by declining to hear a case or declaring a lack of jurisdiction, made a lasting impression on Frankfurter. " 'It is usually more important that a rule of law be settled,' " he quoted Brandeis, " 'than that it be settled right.' "

Frankfurter often followed Brandeis's political lead, especially when it came to Zionism. In 1929, Arab uprisings and the British decision to disarm Palestinian Jews led to concerns about the Balfour Declaration's commitment to a Jewish state. There was only so much that Brandeis could do as a sitting justice. The public pronouncements often fell to Frankfurter. He replied to an *Atlantic Monthly* article by William Ernest Hocking correcting its misinterpretation of Frankfurter's 1919 agreement with Prince Faisal by reprinting the letters and explaining the context of their pledge of "Arab-Jewish cooperation." In a speech at a Zionist rally at Madison Square Garden and articles in the *New York Herald Tribune* and *Foreign Affairs,* he attacked a British white paper by Lord Passfield proposing to limit Jewish immigration to Palestine as contrary to the Balfour Declaration and the promises the British made in receiving a mandate over the region. Frankfurter proved to be incredibly useful to Brandeis in what they referred to as "all things Zionistic."

THE FUTURE OF Frankfurter's political activity lay with Franklin Roosevelt. During the summer and fall of 1930, he ran interference for Roosevelt with Walter Lippmann. He reacted to Lippmann's June 1930 article in *Harper's* about Hoover's weaknesses by arguing that they were "more far-reaching." That fall, as Roosevelt ran for another two-year term as governor, Frankfurter tried to counter Lippmann's misperception of Roosevelt as a pleasant but unremarkable politician. Frankfurter explained to Lippmann why people should vote for Roosevelt: "I know his limitations. Most of them derive, I believe, from lack of incisive intellect and a kind of optimism that sometimes makes him timid, as well as an ambition that leads to compromises with which we are familiar in Theodore Roosevelt and Wilson. But on the whole he has been a very good governor . . ." Make no mistake: Frankfurter was a Franklin Roosevelt man. He was so confident in his relationship with the governor that he showed Roosevelt the letter to Lippmann. In November 1930, Roosevelt won reelection by 750,000 votes compared to the 25,000 in his first race. No one was happier than Frankfurter.

Roosevelt, in turn, admired Frankfurter. In June 1931, Frankfurter accepted the governor's offer to serve on a state commission on criminal justice reform, then reneged less than a week later. He and Marion were spending the summer in Southern California so he could work on another crime survey, and he was too busy with his classes in the fall to attend regular meetings in Albany. Other politicians might have written off Frankfurter as disloyal, but the friendship between Frank and Felix was solid. As Frankfurter wrote in *The Public and Its Government*, Frankfurter was Roosevelt's expert "'on tap, but not on top.'" In advising him on public utilities, criminal justice, or media relations with Lippmann and other establishment figures, Frankfurter was a valuable jack-of-all-trades and looked forward to assisting Roosevelt during the coming presidential election. In inscribing a copy of his book *Mr. Justice Holmes*, Frankfurter emphasized "not the least tie between us is the meaning that Mr. Justice Holmes has for us."

In January 1932, Frankfurter found himself "unprepared" for the inevitable—Justice Holmes's retirement. He had known for several months that Holmes's return to the Court in the fall of 1931 was not going well. The justice was feeling foggy and tired at conferences and oral argument; his doctor urged him to resign. On January 10, Chief Justice Hughes arrived at 1720 I Street and informed Holmes that it was time. Two days later, after Holmes delivered his final opinion, the news became public. Frankfurter kept a previously scheduled visit with the justice, accompanied him to Arlington Cemetery to visit his wife's grave, and described him as "the gallantest creature that ever lived." Holmes's retirement initiated a monthlong battle over his successor.

Desperate for a nominee worthy of Holmes's seat, Frankfurter pulled out all the stops to persuade Hoover to nominate Cardozo. A gentle, kind, and soft-spoken man from a Sephardic Jewish family, Cardozo was a lifelong bachelor who lived with his two older sisters. He was mourning the death of his oldest sister, Nellie, who raised him. Their father, Albert, was a New York trial judge who had resigned in disgrace for doing favors for Tammany Hall kingpin Boss Tweed. His only son graduated from Columbia at nineteen and from Columbia Law School and forged a judicial career above reproach. Cardozo's book *The Nature of the Judicial Process* made him a jurisprudential star; he revolutionized the law of accidents with his opinions on causation and products liability; and his literary style earned comparisons to Holmes's. In many ways, however, Cardozo's nomination was a tough sell. The Court already had two New Yorkers (Hughes and Stone), four easterners (Hughes, Stone, Brandeis, and Roberts), and one Jew (Brandeis).

Working with fellow Zionists Judge Mack and Rabbi Stephen Wise, Frankfurter gained an important ally in Senator William Borah of Idaho. A liberal Republican who had supported Hoover during the election yet voted against Hughes and Parker, Borah assured the president that Cardozo would receive universal acclaim and would be quickly confirmed.

Several sitting justices weighed in. Stone, who continued to join Hoover's medicine ball games on the White House's South Lawn, went so far as to offer his resignation if it meant nominating Cardozo. The four conservative justices Butler, McReynolds, Sutherland, and Van Devanter made their first choice known—Hoover's respected attorney general, William D. Mitchell.

Reluctant to part with his attorney general and with his reelection bid looming, Hoover was swayed more by geographic considerations and looked to the West and South. Hoover's first choice was Orie Phillips, a federal court of appeals judge Frankfurter derided as "another Parker from somewhere in New Mexico." Stone gave the president two critiques of Phillips's opinions, one from a *St. Louis Post-Dispatch* reporter and another that Frankfurter had received from Brandeis's former law firm. The law office memorandum, Frankfurter wrote Stone, "proves to the hilt what was to be expected from a young man of our generation who got his law in a correspondence school, and whose strong allegiances are with the Elks."

Hoover's second choice, Senator Joseph T. Robinson of Arkansas, was another attempt to win over the South. Unlike Parker, Robinson would be swiftly confirmed by his fellow senators. A progressive Democrat, Robinson had attacked anti-Catholic bigotry and the Ku Klux Klan in a 1928 speech and was Al Smith's vice-presidential running mate. As much as he admired Robinson's political stands, Frankfurter considered Robinson a "dreadful" Supreme Court nominee and "nothing short of a calamity." He described Robinson as an "an old-fashioned Democrat in his constitutional outlook" when what the Court needed was "strengthening not on its stand-pat side but on its imaginative side."

Rather than keep these thoughts to himself, Frankfurter revealed them to Hoover's secretary of state, Henry Stimson. No one respected Frankfurter's abilities as a talent scout more than Stimson; he had taken Frankfurter's advice on hiring Joseph Cotton as under secretary and after Cotton's death had consulted him on hiring two assistant secretaries, Harvey Bundy and Herbert Feis. During a meeting in Washington shortly after Holmes's resignation, Stimson asked what Frankfurter thought about the Supreme Court vacancy. Frankfurter took advantage of the opening to lobby for Cardozo as "*the* only appointment which would be received with national enthusiasm." Frankfurter argued that Cardozo's nomination, more than Robinson's, would win Hoover the most votes. He insisted that "the geographic argument" about another New Yorker on the Court "would evaporate like snowflakes in the face of the national acclaim." And he rejected the idea that there was a Jewish seat occupied by Brandeis. Cardozo's replacement of Holmes, Frankfurter argued, would send the message that "what counts is not geography, race or religion or party, but unqualified fitness for the functions exercised by the Supreme Court."

For several weeks, Stimson had been discussing the Supreme Court vacancy with Hoover. The secretary of state suggested Cardozo or Learned Hand as "good candidates" and declared Cardozo the "safest bet." By mid-February, Stimson informed Frankfurter that Cardozo was Hoover's "first choice." Stimson had passed along Frankfurter's objections to the idea that Cardozo could only replace Brandeis as the Court's Jewish justice. Stimson also believed that Borah had not influenced Hoover but the other way around; the president had secured Borah's pledge to fight for Cardozo's confirmation.

On February 15, 1932, Hoover nominated Cardozo; nine days later, the Senate unanimously confirmed him. Frankfurter wrote the president that "never in the history of the Court has an appointment been made to it more fitting to the needs of the Court at the particular period than is true of your appointment of Chief Judge Cardozo." In an unsigned *New Republic* editorial,

Frankfurter explained that Hoover "appointed Cardozo not because he came from the East or the West, not because he was Catholic, Jew or Protestant; he appointed him because he was Cardozo."

Cardozo's nomination exemplified Frankfurter's belief in encouraging the best minds to go into government. Frankfurter's influence extended far beyond Supreme Court justices and Henry Stimson's State Department assistants. The Harvard law professor was grooming his top students to enter the revolving door of academia and public service—first with graduate research fellowships at the law school; then by sending them to clerk for Holmes, Brandeis, or Learned Hand; and finally by recommending them for plum jobs in the Hoover administration.

A prime opportunity arose in January 1932 with the creation of the Reconstruction Finance Corporation (RFC) to aid railroads, banks, and other financial institutions and with Wall Street financier Eugene Meyer as its first chair. A friend from wartime Washington, Meyer had hired Frankfurter's stellar former student Gerry Henderson to serve as general counsel on the U.S. Shipping Board after meeting him at the House of Truth. As the new head of the RFC, Meyer asked Frankfurter for the name of other budding legal stars. Frankfurter's first choice was the law school's finest student since Henderson, Henry Friendly.

A lawyer at the Root, Clark firm, Friendly had promised to reconsider academia after three years. Frankfurter begged Friendly to accept the law school's offer of an assistant professorship and promised a full professorship within three years. In May 1931, however, Friendly elected to continue practicing law. Frankfurter refused to give up on his once-in-a-generation student. At Frankfurter's and Brandeis's urging, Friendly met with Meyer and was poised to accept the RFC job. He turned it down, erroneously concluding the RFC under Hoover was "a sinking ship."

In Friendly's stead, Frankfurter vouched for another star student, Tom Corcoran. The ebullient former Holmes clerk had been working at the Wall Street law firm of Cotton & Franklin but yearned to return to Washington. Soon after Corcoran accepted Meyer's offer, Congress expanded the RFC's responsibilities to include aid to agriculture and financing for state and local public works projects. In an independent agency with broad powers to help the country recover from the Great Depression, Corcoran began to master how to get things done.

At Harvard Law School, Frankfurter groomed the next generation of Landises, Corcorans, and Friendlys in Henry Hart and Paul Freund. A native of Butte, Montana, and summa cum laude graduate of Harvard College, Hart won the Sears Prize twice for the top grades in his law school class and was elected president of the *Harvard Law Review*. He went on to complete his doctorate during a graduate research fellowship with Frankfurter and to co-author three installments of Frankfurter's "Business of the Supreme Court" series. After the fellowship, Frankfurter sent Hart to work as Brandeis's secretary. In January 1932, Hart earned high praise from Brandeis and accepted an offer to return to the law school as an assistant professor.

Hart's successor as the *Review* president, Paul Freund, also showed great promise. A Jewish St. Louis native, he impressed the faculty with his modesty and preternatural maturity. He was an elegant writer and interested in legal history. In January 1932, Freund was finishing his doctorate, doing "interesting work" for Frankfurter, and preparing to clerk for Brandeis. Bound for academia and public service, Freund became one of Frankfurter's closest confidantes.

As much as Frankfurter relished the opportunity to work with promising students such as Hart and Freund, he faced a career crisis. In 1932 and early 1933, he was forced to choose between staying in academia, going on the bench, or working for Roosevelt.

CHAPTER 14

From the Outside

In early 1932, Frankfurter saw what many people could not—that Roosevelt was the right person to lead the Democratic Party and to challenge Herbert Hoover in the November election. Since the 1929 stock market crash, the country had been mired in the Great Depression. The American people were desperate for leadership; many of them were out of work, living in shanty towns, dubbed Hoovervilles, and waiting in breadlines for food. Frankfurter recognized that Roosevelt was a new leader for a new day and took on all comers who tried to derail his presidential hopes.

Roosevelt's influential journalistic antagonist was the new–*New York Herald Tribune* columnist Walter Lippmann. In a January 8 column, Lippmann described Roosevelt as "a highly impressionable person, without a firm grasp of public affairs and without very strong convictions," "too eager to please," and "an excessively cautious politician." He criticized Roosevelt's water-power policy and accused him of being forced into investigating Tammany Hall corruption. He warned readers that Roosevelt "is no tribune of the people. He is no enemy of entrenched privilege. He is a pleasant man who, without any important qualifications for the office, would very much like to be President." In attacking Roosevelt, Lippmann attempted to clear the way for his preferred candidate, Newton D. Baker.

To counter Lippmann's efforts, Frankfurter wrote a memorandum opposing Baker for president and circulated it to friends. Frankfurter knew Baker as well as anyone, having worked with him in defending minimum-wage and maximum-hour laws for the National Consumers' League and for him on labor issues in the War Department. He confessed a "deep personal attachment" to Baker and described their relations as "sweet and candid." He had no problem supporting Baker for a Supreme Court vacancy but not for the presidency. Frankfurter objected to Baker for the same reasons he had opposed

John W. Davis in 1924 as the Democratic nominee. During twelve years in private practice, Baker had been captured by big business. As president of the Cleveland Chamber of Commerce, he had supported the open shop, an anti-union position that led to his resignation as president of the National Consumers' League. As a founding partner of the Cleveland law firm that became Baker Hostetler, he established himself as one of "the most sought-after lawyers in big corporate litigation." He represented monopolists who wanted to merge Bethlehem Steel and Youngstown Steel and to consolidate eastern railroads. And, on behalf of his corporate clients, he attacked the constitutionality of the Federal Power Act, which established a commission to coordinate hydroelectric power projects.

What's more, Frankfurter wrote, Baker failed to use his position as a leader of the bar to stand up for civil liberties. As secretary of war, he had protected the rights of conscientious objectors. Yet the only time he defended free speech as a lawyer was on behalf of the Scripps-Howard newspaper chain. As a member of the Wickersham Commission on criminal law, he supported eliminating jury trials in Prohibition cases and endorsed the suppression of a report about the eyewitnesses who had committed perjury in the case of jailed labor leader Tom Mooney. "Baker, I am afraid, is fast getting to be a myth . . . ," Frankfurter wrote. "I am afraid Baker's liberalism has largely evaporated."

What angered Frankfurter most about Lippmann's support for Baker were the differences between what Lippmann said in their private conversations and the columnist's public pronouncements in which he tended to "pontificate like Sir Oracle." The previous November, Lippmann had conceded to Frankfurter that Baker "lacks blood and iron" and had credited Roosevelt's work with legislation on unemployment and taxation. Yet, in his January 8 column about Roosevelt, Lippmann did not mention a word about unemployment or taxation. To Frankfurter's amazement, Lippmann was "apoplectic" about Roosevelt's "lack of courage" yet supported someone as soft as Baker.

A bigger threat to Roosevelt's nomination loomed in another presidential run by Al Smith. Relations between Smith and Roosevelt had been frosty since November 1928; Smith harbored a grudge because his successor had not asked him for advice about governing New York. Smith's advisers went so far as to enter him in the 1932 Massachusetts primary yet kept denying that he was a candidate. Frankfurter was furious with them. "Out of a great public figure you fellows are making a small office seeker," he wired Smith aide Joseph Proskauer.

In his February 12 column, Lippmann played up the tensions between the Roosevelt and Smith camps to predict that Baker would go from "the logical candidate" to "the inevitable candidate." Frankfurter, by contrast, blamed Smith aides for jeopardizing the Democrats' best chance of defeating Hoover. He conceded Roosevelt's "limitations" yet insisted his "general socio-economic directions" were better than those of Baker.

In March, Roosevelt defeated Smith in the New Hampshire primary yet lost to Smith a month later in Massachusetts by a three-to-one margin. And Roosevelt lost the California primary, a three-way race, to Speaker of the House John Nance Garner. Roosevelt's struggles made Baker a viable dark-horse candidate.

Before the Democratic Convention in Chicago in late June, Frankfurter fretted that Roosevelt had not done enough to win the nomination. In fact, at the convention, Roosevelt failed to capture the nomination after the first three ballots and remained a hundred votes short of the two-thirds requirement. The delegates began considering a shift to Baker. Before the fourth and final ballot, however, Roosevelt offered Garner the vice-presidential slot on the ticket in exchange for his delegates. At the urging of William Gibbs McAdoo, Jr., and William Randolph Hearst, who preferred Roosevelt over the internationalist Baker, Garner accepted the deal. Roosevelt then decided to break with tradition and to accept the nomination on July 2 in person.

BEFORE THE CONVENTION, Frankfurter had a nomination of his own to consider. Governor Joseph B. Ely named him to the Massachusetts Supreme Judicial Court. Since January 1932, newspapers had reported that Ely was considering Frankfurter for the state's highest court. The judgeship was the idea of Sacco-Vanzetti defense lawyers William G. Thompson and Herbert Ehrmann, who saw the nomination as a way to restore the court's prestige. Ely, a Harvard law graduate two years after Frankfurter, was receptive to the idea but worried that Frankfurter, a pariah in Old Boston because of the Sacco-Vanzetti case, might not be confirmed by his executive council. Once he was confident that a majority of the council would vote to confirm, Ely wanted to go ahead. On June 20, several friends alerted Frankfurter that Ely might nominate him; Frankfurter refused to respond to a hypothetical. Rather than give him the opportunity to decline, Ely submitted the nomination to his executive council the next day and notified the press. Marion heard about it from a newspaper reporter who had come to 192 Brattle Street for an interview. She phoned her husband at the faculty club to tell him the news.

The outcry against Frankfurter's nomination from his antagonists in the Sacco-Vanzetti case was swift. Former governor Alvan Fuller, who had refused to commute the pair's death sentences to life imprisonment, insisted he "would cut off my right hand" before voting to confirm Frankfurter and predicted that with Frankfurter on the bench "I see no reason why murder should not flourish here in Massachusetts." Ely countered that Brandeis, Holmes, Cardozo, and "the greatest Democrat of all Democrats," Al Smith, endorsed Frankfurter. The Massachusetts governor received hundreds of pro-Frankfurter letters and telegrams, including from Judge George W. Anderson, Newton Baker, sixteen members of the Harvard law faculty, and many others. The conservative *Boston Evening Transcript* asserted that Frankfurter lacked "the judicial temperament," the same charge Old Boston had leveled against Brandeis during his 1916 Supreme Court nomination fight.

Receiving hundreds of congratulatory letters and telegrams, Frankfurter revealed to a few intimates that he was torn. He had been discussing the possible vacancy for six months with Brandeis and, at the justice's urging, decided to decline. Frankfurter agreed with Brandeis that he was more valuable teaching at Harvard Law School; expanding the minds and ambitions of *Harvard Law Review* editors; and recruiting them for judicial clerkships, professorships, and public service. He was convinced that he could have a greater impact on the law by teaching and grooming the next generation of students. The only question in his mind was how to tell the governor. For several days, Thompson, Ehrmann, and others urged him to ignore Brandeis's advice and to accept the offer. On June 28, Frankfurter wrote a letter thanking the governor for "[y]our confidence in me" but declining because "the long-term effects of legal education make their claim." The next day, he instructed his secretary to hand-deliver the letter to Ely's aide at the statehouse. The governor, however, was at the Democratic National Convention and asked to delay making the letter public until he could speak with Frankfurter in person.

Roosevelt learned about Frankfurter's nomination while flying to Chicago. In a July 2 phone call, Roosevelt congratulated Frankfurter, adding that he wished it were the Supreme Court of the United States because "that's where you belong." Frankfurter explained it was the state's highest court where Holmes and Lemuel Shaw had sat. He thanked Roosevelt for the call but could not be entirely candid and reveal his true intentions.

Instead, Frankfurter shifted the conversation, urging Roosevelt to reach out to Governor Ely, a Smith supporter. Roosevelt was reluctant to do so in light of negative comments Ely had made during the primary campaign. That night, Roosevelt accepted the nomination with a rousing speech. Before a packed crowd at Chicago Stadium, Roosevelt promised a radical departure from the Republican policies of the past twelve years, which had led to the Great Depression: "I pledge you—I pledge myself—to a new deal for the American people."

After the Democratic National Convention, Frankfurter met with Governor Ely about the judgeship. During a conversation at the governor's Copley Square apartment on July 6, Ely asked him to reconsider. Only Frankfurter, he said, could restore the state's highest court to its former glory. He argued that Frankfurter could make a bigger impact on the law as a Supreme Judicial Court justice than by teaching law students. They reached a stalemate until the governor asked whether Frankfurter had consulted Holmes. Frankfurter replied he did not want to bother the retired justice because he was old and frail. Ely volunteered to hold Frankfurter's declination letter a few more days. In the interim, Frankfurter contacted Holmes's secretary, Chapman Rose. He shared documents indicating his reasons for declining Ely's nomination, which Rose summarized for Holmes. Rose then informed Frankfurter that Holmes had reconsidered his prior inclination, communicated to others, that Frankfurter had no choice but to take the job. During a July 12 meeting with the governor, Frankfurter confessed that he "never made a more heartbreaking decision in my life" yet held his ground. That same day, Governor Ely released Frankfurter's letter choosing a Harvard law professorship over a judgeship on the Massachusetts Supreme Judicial Court.

Frankfurter's students, colleagues, and friends at other law schools were overjoyed. William O. Douglas, a young Yale law professor, declared Frankfurter's letter to Governor Ely "the greatest tribute to the law teaching profession ever made." For Frankfurter, the scholarly books and articles he wrote with graduate research fellows, the selection of law clerks for prominent judges, and the advice and campaigning for Roosevelt could continue unabated.

ON JULY 22, Frankfurter alerted Roosevelt that he had declined the Supreme Judicial Court judgeship because he could be "much more useful both to the law and to the country" off the bench, and "one of the things I am free to do now is to do my small share to turn out Hoover and help elect you." He had already gotten to work. Earlier that month, he had spoken with Roosevelt's son James about the political situation in Massachusetts and how the state could be won in November. He had pressed Roosevelt aide Sam Rosenman and two old friends from the National Consumers' League, Molly Dewson and Frances Perkins, for information about Roosevelt's record as governor in nine different policy areas. "You see one of the gains from not having gone on the Massachusetts Court," he wrote Dewson, "is that I can be alive during the campaign."

In Frankfurter, Roosevelt already knew he had a secret weapon for the general election campaign and was anxious to speak with him. He invited Felix and Marion to Albany on July 30 for dinner and to spend the night in the executive mansion. Marion was impressed with Roosevelt's "astounding vitality" as he talked with Frankfurter until 12:45 a.m. Felix confessed to treating him like he was "one of my students" and supplied him with potential experts on a range of subjects; Roosevelt did not seem to mind. "You stimulate me enormously," he wrote Frankfurter. "Repeat the dose again."

During his overnight stay, Frankfurter helped Roosevelt figure out how to navigate his toughest political test. Before the convention, the governor's critics had charged him with being soft on Tammany Hall and its corrupt New York City mayor, James J. Walker. In July, a report by Samuel Seabury charging Walker with rampant corruption had left those critics wondering what Roosevelt would do before the election. Frankfurter read the report and discussed it with the governor, concluding that, if true, "the facts ineluctably compel removal of the Mayor." The state constitution granted Roosevelt the power to remove Mayor Walker. Backed by Frankfurter, Roosevelt elected to conduct his own informal trial of Walker at the executive mansion. Upon learning the news, Frankfurter phoned the governor on his private line; they knew this was a make-or-break presidential moment. Roosevelt proved himself up to the challenge. For several days, the governor cross-examined Walker in such devastating fashion that the mayor resigned. "Warm congratulations," Frankfurter wired Roosevelt on September 2. "Resignation is concession and complete vindication of your firmness, skill and fairness as chief executive."

Two months before the election, Frankfurter pointed to Roosevelt's conduct of the Walker trial as proof of his fitness for the presidency. He was not shy about responding to the governor's critics, such as a state trial judge who defended Walker and argued Roosevelt had abused his power. In a letter to the New York Times, Frankfurter defended the fairness of the proceedings and concluded: "No one who has disinterestedly followed in detail the Walker hearings in Albany can have failed to be impressed with the Governor's mastery of a series of complicated transactions and with his skill and patience in exploring them."

The Walker hearings did not mollify all of Roosevelt's critics. Walter Lippmann considered the hearings a "very severe test" and endorsed him. But Rabbi Stephen Wise, an influential Democratic reformer, was disgusted that

Roosevelt confronted Tammany Hall only when it was politically expedient. Wise contended that "there is no basic stuff in the man" and saw no difference between Roosevelt and the past twelve years of Republican rule.

Frankfurter, who had worked with Wise on Zionist and other political causes, sought to change his mind. Asserting his political independence by confessing he had voted for a Democratic presidential candidate only twice, Frankfurter accused Wise of losing sight of the need to oust Hoover. In August, a bank collapse sent a spiraling economy into further chaos. A Roosevelt presidency, Frankfurter argued, promised something more than Hoover's exit. He pitched Roosevelt as a big upgrade over Hoover and claimed to be voting for Roosevelt "with an easy conscience. . . . I know his limitations and inadequacies, but I also know his qualities, and I know you do them very much less than justice." He reviewed his experiences with Roosevelt on the War Labor Policies Board; Roosevelt's "courageous" policies as governor on public utilities, water power, and public health; and his decision to raise income taxes by 50 percent to pay for unemployment relief and to keep the state solvent. Finally, Frankfurter reminded Wise that politics was "a choice of the second best." He conceded that Roosevelt did not have "an original or a powerful mind" but was "intelligent and moves in the right direction" and had "a real respect and regard for men and women generally."

Seeking to sway undecided voters, Frankfurter went public with his support of Roosevelt. He signed a National Popular Government League report endorsing Roosevelt's record on government-sponsored water-power projects compared to Hoover's. He joined the nonpartisan National Progressive League headed by Republican senator George W. Norris in endorsing Roosevelt.

During the final two months of the campaign, Frankfurter was consumed by politics and looking for ways to help the candidate. The "bonus army" was one such opportunity. By late July, 45,000 war veterans had descended on Washington, D.C., in a peaceful protest of the federal government's refusal to pass a law accelerating the payment of their bonuses that were not due until 1945. General Douglas MacArthur forcibly removed the bedraggled veterans by using tear gas and bayonets and burning their camps in the Anacostia Flats section of Washington, D.C. Hoover took the blame. Frankfurter suggested to Sam Rosenman how Roosevelt could avoid repeating Hoover's mistakes. He recommended not endorsing the bonus bill yet expressing compassion for the marchers. He advised Roosevelt on the bonus bill, the federal courts, and the economy.

A month before the election, Frankfurter sought to persuade Al Smith to make a public appearance on Roosevelt's behalf in Massachusetts, where

Smith was wildly popular with Irish Catholics. Smith and Roosevelt had already appeared together on October 4 at the Democratic state convention in Albany where they shook hands and exchanged warm greetings. Frankfurter, however, knew that Roosevelt desperately needed Smith's help in the Bay State. The day after the Albany handshake, he proposed a Boston speech to journalist Herbert Bayard Swope, a Smith confidant who agreed with Frankfurter's idea. During lunch with Swope and financier Bernard Baruch, they persuaded Smith to do it.

They scheduled Smith's speech for October 30. In the days leading up to the speech, Frankfurter took to newspapers and the stump for Roosevelt in Massachusetts. Massachusetts was an Al Smith state; he had trounced Roosevelt in the primary; Governor Ely was also a Smith supporter. Frankfurter, however, believed that Roosevelt could win there. In a *Harvard Crimson* article, he endorsed Roosevelt and attacked Hoover for ignoring "storm signals" about the economy in 1928 and 1929 and for the president's response to the October 1929 stock market crash. He compared Roosevelt's fiscal policies in New York with Hoover's. "The best hope of the country," he concluded, "as well as the working of our party system requires the rejection of President Hoover and his party." On October 23, before more than 200 members and guests of the Young People's Society at the Mt. Vernon Church in Boston, Frankfurter attacked Hoover's economic policies of "extreme individualism" and the president's comment that Congress should "be put out of business." He rejected stereotypes about Roosevelt as "a little boy scoutish" or "smiles too much" and urged people to judge him on his record as governor.

Frankfurter's crowning achievement during the campaign was Al Smith's swing through New England on Roosevelt's behalf. Frankfurter had been laying the groundwork and advising Smith's aides about Massachusetts politics for several weeks. At 2:53 p.m. on October 30, Frankfurter waited in the pouring rain for Smith's train to arrive in Providence, Rhode Island. Along with Governor Ely and other Massachusetts officials, he boarded Smith's special car headed to Boston. Smith arrived in Back Bay Station to massive crowds. That night, before a packed audience at the Boston Arena and with thousands more outside and listening on the radio, Smith asked the people of Massachusetts to give their "unqualified" support to Roosevelt. He concluded that "the salvation of the country in this crisis" requires Roosevelt's election. Smith, Frankfurter declared, was "at his very best." In Providence and in Boston, Frankfurter marveled at the "the outpouring of affection and devotion . . . such as I have never seen given to any American political figure."

Refusing to let Smith do all the work in Massachusetts, Frankfurter succeeded in getting Roosevelt to come to New England and shared the stage with the candidate. After Roosevelt spoke on October 30 to students and teachers at his alma mater the Groton School, Frankfurter introduced him to members of the nonpartisan National Progressive League. In a brief introduction, Frankfurter criticized Hoover's lack of faith in government to alleviate "unparalleled economic and social dislocation." He highlighted Roosevelt's hiring of Frances Perkins in New York as proof of his willingness to rely on experts to tackle labor problems and his effectiveness in working with the Republican state legislature. "As progressives bound to no party," Frankfurter concluded, "we look forward with high hopes to your presidency." He then introduced the governor to his Republican and Independent friends. One of them, Sacco-Vanzetti crusader Elizabeth Glendower Evans, was voting for Socialist Party candidate Norman Thomas. "Governor Roosevelt," Evans said, "I would rather see you in the White House than anyone since Abraham Lincoln and Norman Thomas, Oh, oh, I beg your pardon, I mean Woodrow Wilson." Everyone laughed. Frankfurter, however, was determined to persuade Bostonians who supported Thomas or Hoover or who planned to sit out the race entirely to vote for Roosevelt.

After stops in Massachusetts mill towns, Portland, Maine, and Portsmouth, New Hampshire, Roosevelt headed to a major event in Boston. The election was a week away. Before the speech, Frankfurter waited in Roosevelt's hotel room listening to a radio broadcast of Hoover's speech at Madison Square Garden questioning the governor's Americanism. Frankfurter and Roosevelt's son James wasted no time. They prepared attack lines to insert in Roosevelt's speech. The governor took the notes and headed out the door. With the band playing "Happy Days Are Here Again" and 15,000 people cheering, Roosevelt entered Boston Arena at 10:30 p.m. He attacked Hoover's response to the Great Depression, promised to use federal funds to feed starving people and to find them employment on public works projects, and urged them not to give in to fear.

At Roosevelt's request, Frankfurter kept up attacks on Hoover's economic policy. During a November 5 speech on Boston's WBJ radio station, he faulted Hoover for lacking "any awareness that we are living in a new economic world." After reviewing Roosevelt's record as governor on taxation, power regulation, and unemployment relief, Frankfurter urged Massachusetts to vote for Roosevelt. Roosevelt's election, he predicted, could "well be the augur of happier days."

A new day and a new deal were at hand. On the day before the election, Frankfurter wired Roosevelt: "Your campaign has educated the hopes of the nation and invigorated its faith. As a result, not since Wilson's campaign in 1912 has the public temper been more ripe to support the progressive leadership which you have espoused." On Election Day, Frankfurter's efforts paid off: Roosevelt carried Massachusetts along with forty-one other states, trouncing Hoover in the electoral college, 432–59. "The end crowns all," Frankfurter wrote the president-elect, "and a glorious end it is—a very great beginning."

Indeed, the end of the campaign was only the beginning of Frankfurter's involvement in one of the most transformative government interventions in the U.S. economy. The announcement that he had accepted the Eastman professorship at Oxford University for the 1933–1934 academic year did not dispel the buzz that he could be the next attorney general or solicitor general.

With the president not sworn in until March 4, Frankfurter was more concerned about helping Roosevelt through a difficult transition period with an embittered Hoover and a country in economic distress. People were desperate. During an impromptu presidential stop at Miami's Bayfront Park on February 15, Italian anarchist Giuseppe Zangara fired at Roosevelt's car, killing Chicago mayor Anton Cermak and wounding several others. Roosevelt, who had slid from the top of the car into his seat, was unharmed.

Relieved that Roosevelt was unhurt, Frankfurter assisted him with the transition and praised his cabinet selections including Senator Thomas J. Walsh of Montana for attorney general and Frances Perkins for secretary of labor. "You have got the essentials under way," he wrote Roosevelt on February 23. "Now I look forward to having your Inaugural modify greatly the defeatist attitude so sedulously cultivated recently." Frankfurter wished Roosevelt "godspeed" a few days before the inauguration.

March 4, 1933, was a cloudy and chilly day with rays of sunshine breaking through the clouds. Shortly after 1:00 p.m., more than 100,000 people solemnly stood on the east front of the Capitol to watch Roosevelt take the oath of office from Chief Justice Charles Evans Hughes. In his inaugural address, Roosevelt gave hope to a worried nation that in times of suffering "the only thing we have to fear is fear itself." He also promised quick legislative and executive action to meet the nation's economic crisis. On March 7, the thirty-second president thanked Frankfurter for helping him reach this point and wrote: "I shall see you soon."

Two days before the inauguration and soon after getting married, Senator Thomas J. Walsh, Roosevelt's attorney general pick, had mysteriously died on a train. The rumors of Frankfurter's appointment as solicitor general resurfaced. Walsh had objected to Frankfurter as solicitor general because he was afraid the Harvard law professor would "lose cases in the grand manner."

The president's eventual choice for attorney general, Homer Cummings, was more amenable to Frankfurter's appointment.

On the afternoon of March 8, Frankfurter found himself in Washington for a joyful occasion, a lunch invitation from Justice Holmes on his ninety-second birthday. At 1720 I Street, Frankfurter joined Holmes's current secretary, Alger Hiss's brother Donald, and former secretary and RFC counsel Tom Corcoran. During the lunchtime celebration, Frankfurter received a phone call. He declined it and instructed Hiss to hold all calls for him. The phone rang several times before they were interrupted again. At 3:00 p.m., the presidential appointments secretary, Colonel Marvin McIntyre, called to ask where Frankfurter was and said he had been expected at the White House since 1:30 p.m. "I am at a better place," Frankfurter replied, "I am at Mr. Justice Holmes's." Roosevelt's aides had neglected to tell Frankfurter about the meeting. The retired justice was amused that the president's "nose [was] out of joint" and asked what Frankfurter would tell him. Frankfurter replied that he could not drink champagne during a luncheon at the White House. The justice, who had consumed three or four glasses of his beloved "fizz water," shot back: "Young fellow, I don't want you to misunderstand things: I do not deal with bootleggers but I am open to corruption." Frankfurter and Hiss had lied to the justice that the Prohibition-era champagne had come from an ambassador.

With some reluctance, Frankfurter departed 1720 I Street, arrived at the White House at 3:30 p.m., and, within minutes, found himself in the president's office. He immediately apologized for continuing to refer to him as "Frank." Roosevelt said to keep calling him Frank except with other people present. Frankfurter remarked how much he had loved Theodore Roosevelt, had worked hard for the success of Woodrow Wilson, yet "care[d] even more about the success of your administration." The president said he knew this and offered Frankfurter the solicitor general post. Frankfurter claimed to have been shocked. During all their talks about the cabinet, Roosevelt never discussed a position for him in the administration.

Before Frankfurter could say anything, Roosevelt explained that he had wanted to make Frankfurter solicitor general since November. He needed Frankfurter in Washington "for all sorts of things, and in all sorts of ways" including utility regulation, reorganization of various commissions, and amendments to the Sherman Act. The president wanted to use Frankfurter, as he had in the past, as an all-purpose confidential adviser.

The solicitor general's responsibility of defending the U.S. government before the Supreme Court, Frankfurter explained to the president, was a full-time job. He needed to decide whether he could devote himself entirely to it. The president replied that he could delegate the responsibilities to others and free himself to work on administration matters. Frankfurter interrupted him to explain that he knew better than the president that the solicitor generalship was a sixteen-hour-a-day job and nothing less. He told the president how he really felt: "It is my general conviction—I am sure it is so—that I can do much more to be of use to you by staying in Cambridge than by becoming Solicitor General." As solicitor general, he would have no time to help the president on other matters; "it just can't be done." He mentioned his Oxford fellowship in the fall and how he could advise him on foreign policy while abroad and could be "of more use to you than as Solicitor General."

After listening to Frankfurter's reasoning, Roosevelt replied: "I am going to talk Dutch to you." He spoke as a friend or uncle would in advising Frankfurter about his career. He said Frankfurter belonged on the Supreme Court, and Roosevelt wanted to put him there. As he smiled, he ticked off the objections to naming to the Court a professor who had not practiced law, had refused to be a judge, had defended Sacco and Vanzetti, and was a Jew. "I can't put you on the Supreme Court from the Harvard Law School," he said. "But once you are Solicitor General, these various objections will be forgotten or disappear."

Grateful for Roosevelt's concern for his career, Frankfurter nonetheless refused to take "a job I don't want because it may lead to another. . . . All that must be left to the future." Roosevelt insisted there was no hurry about the solicitor generalship and urged Frankfurter to consult with Brandeis. But he also warned Frankfurter "to think a little bit selfishly" about his future. The president kept waving away interruptions until he and Frankfurter had finished their thirty-minute discussion. The conversation ended with Roosevelt's remark that he would see Frankfurter later that day.

Frankfurter had arranged the ultimate birthday surprise for Holmes—a visit from the president. At 5:30 p.m., Frankfurter returned to 1720 I Street and saw the president's black convertible Packard pull up. He accompanied the president, his wife, Eleanor, and his son James inside. The justice, who initially did not believe his young secretary that the president was there, quickly changed from his alpaca coat into his swallowtail coat. They talked in Holmes's study about things big and small. A crowd had gathered outside and waited for the president. After the visit, Frankfurter rode with Roosevelt to the White House to discuss a matter at the Treasury Department (the president had suspended banking operations for a week to prevent more collapses).

Roosevelt asked Frankfurter where he was staying. Frankfurter, who told him not to read anything into it, replied that he was staying with Solicitor General Thomas D. Thacher, his office mate during their days as federal prosecutors for Henry Stimson.

That night, Frankfurter told Brandeis and Thacher about his conversation with the president. Brandeis adamantly believed that taking the solicitor generalship would be "absurd." Frankfurter conferred with other mentors. Holmes agreed that it was "unwise" for him to accept. Cardozo lamented that the Court would not have the benefit of Frankfurter's arguments on socioeconomic matters. Frankfurter chose not to tell Holmes and Cardozo that Roosevelt wanted to name him to the Court. Newspapers continued to speculate about Frankfurter as solicitor general.

Upon his return to Cambridge, Frankfurter discussed the solicitor generalship with the person who mattered most and whose health was more precarious than ever, his wife, Marion. In July 1932, she had retreated to Ogunquit, Maine, to rest and to take a painting class after suffering another nervous breakdown. She insisted that her loving husband, despite her worries that politics had consumed his life, was not to blame. After all, he had helped her land a plum wartime post with Raymond Fosdick and edit Sacco and Vanzetti's letters for publication. "I would never have made my mark if I hadn't been married to a comet," she confided to him from Maine, "and no wonder being married to a comet makes me at times uncomfortable. I am slow, plodding, patient, hidden." She liked being hidden in Maine. In late September 1932, her health deteriorated so much that she had to be hospitalized. By February, her "hard times" had not abated. Frankfurter conceded he was "a hectic man" and "a nervous man" who makes "others nervous"; all he wanted was to be with his beloved wife and for her to be happy. The coming school year in Oxford offered them a chance to experience a new way of life and a respite from the insular social scene in Cambridge. The political hothouse of Washington was the last thing Marion needed.

On March 14, Frankfurter wrote the president about "how deeply I was moved" by their talk and reiterated how he cared more about Franklin Roosevelt's administration than he had cared about the administrations of Theodore Roosevelt and Woodrow Wilson. After reflecting and discussing the job with Brandeis and Holmes, they agreed with his conclusion that "I can be of more use to the public and you by not becoming Solicitor General." He also had done his homework about the job and explained to Roosevelt that the solicitor general had prepared briefs in 323 cases the previous term. He stuck to his decision yet let the president know where his heart was: "I should nevertheless like to feel that I am part of your Administration even outside of office."

Frankfurter's rejection of the solicitor generalship may have cost him the opportunity to be Roosevelt's first Supreme Court nominee and a few years on the bench. It may have made his eventual confirmation hearings more difficult. Yet, it certainly made him a free man and free to aid the administration. And it did not hurt his relationship with the president in the slightest. "You are an independent pig," Roosevelt joked on April 4, "and that is one reason why I cannot blame you!"

Frankfurter advised Roosevelt during a frenetic first hundred days as president. And he did it all from the outside.

CHAPTER 15

The Happy Hot Dogs

O n April 5, 1933, Frankfurter received an urgent phone message from presidential adviser Raymond Moley. The new securities bill was in trouble. Could Frankfurter come to Washington? Frankfurter and Moley had clashed while working together in the early 1920s on the Cleveland crime survey. They had since made amends and reunited in 1933 to advise Roosevelt before the inauguration and during the administration's first hundred days. Moley, along with his Columbia University colleagues Adolf A. Berle, Jr., and Rex Tugwell, formed Roosevelt's "Brain Trust." The Brain Trust advocated big-government solutions to the nation's economic problems. In contrast, they viewed Frankfurter, rightly and wrongly, as a Brandeis disciple who believed in "the curse of bigness," that anything big, whether big government or big corporations, was bad. For his part, Frankfurter rejected the Brandeis label. Describing himself as a "stark empiricist" rather than an ideologue, Frankfurter claimed that he and Brandeis did not always see "eye to eye" on socioeconomic policy. The truth is, Frankfurter was willing to do whatever worked to revive the economy and to help Roosevelt and support the administration's federal regulatory efforts big and small. Frankfurter's disgruntled former student Berle, as well as Tugwell, resented Frankfurter's easy access to the president and frequent interventions in policy and personnel matters; Moley, however, admired Frankfurter's "bubbling energy and quick intelligence" and did not feel threatened by him. With the securities bill in trouble, Moley knew that Frankfurter was the right person to call.

In a March 29 message to Congress, Roosevelt had called for a new federal securities law to restore people's confidence in the stock market. Unfortunately, the draft of the bill submitted to the House and Senate proved to be unworkable and needed to be completely rewritten. After their April 5 phone call, Frankfurter wired Moley requesting the most recent copy of the bill and asking him to reserve rooms for three people at the Carlton Hotel. The next night, Frankfurter boarded the Federal Express overnight train to Washington and brought along two protégés: James Landis and Benjamin V. Cohen.

The brilliant yet tormented Landis joined Frankfurter on the train in Boston. In 1928, when Lowell and Pound had attempted to withhold the young scholar's professorship in legislation, Frankfurter had fought for him. An expert in administrative law, Landis had researched state blue sky laws protecting the public from securities fraud. In March, Frankfurter had written him about the need for a federal securities law premised on disclosure along the lines of the English Companies Act of 1929. Landis had never worked as a Wall Street lawyer, but he had brains and grit. Few could match the work ethic of the 34-year-old Landis; at times, however, he was too intense and abrasive.

The shy, moody Cohen boarded the train in New York City. A Muncie, Indiana, native, he had graduated with one of the highest grade-point averages in the history of the University of Chicago Law School and had met Frankfurter in the fall of 1916 during a doctoral fellowship at Harvard Law School. After the fellowship, Frankfurter tapped Cohen to clerk for Judge Julian Mack and helped him land a wartime job with the U.S. Shipping Board. Like Frankfurter and Mack, Cohen became one of Brandeis's Zionist converts. In 1919, he joined Frankfurter at the Paris Peace Conference as a representative of the American Zionist delegation and stayed in Europe for nearly two years to monitor Zionist affairs. Returning to the states, he worked as a Wall Street lawyer with Max Lowenthal, lost money during the stock market crash, and knew the ins and outs of the English Companies Act. He also earned the reputation as an expert draftsman. In the 1920s and early 1930s, he wrote state minimum-wage bills for the National Consumers' League. Despite his skill as a draftsman, Cohen could be needy and difficult when things did not go his way.

Early in the morning on Friday, April 7, Frankfurter and "two thin, solemn young men" arrived at the Carlton Hotel and ate breakfast in Moley's room. An enthusiastic Frankfurter vouched for Cohen and Landis's ability to redraft the bill over the weekend and agreed to supervise them. After breakfast, Frankfurter and Moley left Cohen and Landis to do their work and walked a few blocks to the White House to brief the president. In the afternoon, Frankfurter conferred with legendary Texas congressman Sam Rayburn, the chair of the House Committee on Interstate Commerce, and assured him that Landis and Cohen were up to the task. That weekend Landis and Cohen holed themselves up in the Carlton Hotel. Late Saturday night, they finished a draft of a bill requiring full disclosure of the security being offered and including civil liability for misrepresentations.

Frankfurter, meanwhile, was everywhere. His friends in the cabinet wanted to speak with him about policy problems and personnel needs. On Sunday at 6:30 p.m., he met privately with Roosevelt for an hour before attending a small, informal White House supper. The whirlwind trip confirmed Frankfurter's decision to decline the solicitor generalship. "Everyone has been after me, as tho I can move mountains," he wrote Marion. He liked the "hopeful atmosphere" Roosevelt had created yet abhorred the feverish pace of those first hundred days. All in all, he wrote Marion, "I'm so glad we're not in office. It would be awful & distracting beyond measure & truly not satisfying." As he suspected, he could accomplish more from the outside.

On Sunday evening, Frankfurter reviewed Landis and Cohen's draft in preparation for an important congressional hearing. At 10:00 a.m., he testified masterfully before an executive session of Rayburn's committee about the revised bill. He instructed his two protégés to stay in Washington to make the bill "watertight" and to see it through the legislative process. That night, Frankfurter returned to Cambridge, promised to cover Landis's classes and other responsibilities, and managed the situation by phone, wire, and letters. On April 12, he wired Moley: "Be assured that I am watching the work closely."

One of Frankfurter's responsibilities was to keep Landis and Cohen from killing each other. He worried that Cohen was likely to react to Landis's outbursts by leaving. As a result, he brought in another prized former student, Reconstruction Finance Corporation counsel Tom Corcoran, to act as a peacemaker. Frankfurter also asked Moley to monitor the situation and to reassure Cohen about his indispensability.

The substance of the bill was foremost on Frankfurter's mind. On April 14, he wired Roosevelt and Rayburn from Cambridge. The bill, he argued, must specify the information required for securities registration and financial disclosure. He wanted to ensure the law's constitutionality and to prevent corporations from subverting the registration and disclosure requirements. Rayburn, who had spent five hours with the drafters over the weekend, assured him that "we are going to get out a good workable bill." Frankfurter, in turn, dispatched Corcoran to draft a proposed committee report. He also urged friends in the Senate to delay the old version of the bill to wait for the Landis-Cohen bill in the House. Frankfurter cautioned them that the Senate bill was "partly innocuous and partly unconstitutional." On May 1, he wrote Rayburn advising him about how to avoid unconstitutional provisions in the House bill. He reminded Moley about the importance of careful draftsmanship; he relied on RFC chair Eugene Meyer to prevent the bill from being mischaracterized as including government bonds; and he encouraged Roosevelt to put the administration's support behind the House bill. Upon introducing the bill on the House floor on May 4, Rayburn thanked Frankfurter, Landis, and Cohen for shepherding it through the committee process. Privately, Rayburn told Cohen that the bill passed the House "so readily because it was so damned good or so damned incomprehensible."

Frankfurter's participation did not come without political cost in Cambridge. On May 10, Harvard president A. Lawrence Lowell summoned him to his office to admonish Frankfurter for unexcused absences from class. "You are giving the Corporation some concern," Lowell began and repeatedly professed to be worried only about future absences. Frankfurter, who had been tipped off about the summons, explained that he was familiar with the university policy and had wired Pound several days before missing class on Monday, April 10, to appear before the executive session of Rayburn's committee. Upon his return, he also informed Pound, the likely source of the misinformation, that he would teach a legislation seminar and conduct several doctoral examinations to cover for Landis's prolonged absence.

Rather than get mired in faculty politics, Frankfurter warned of the dangers the Supreme Court posed to the securities bill and other pending legislation. In a *Yale Review* article, he described the Constitution as "flexible enough to respond to the demands of modern society" by permitting the federal government to pass securities laws and other economic regulation and the states to pass unemployment laws, minimum-wage laws, and taxes. He exposed the justices as "arbiters of social policy" and warned them against invoking the vague phrases of liberty and property in the Due Process Clause to invalidate laws simply because they disagreed with them. He conceded the Court's role in preventing the federal government from encroaching on the power of state governments. Ultimately, however, he preferred legislative solutions. He invoked Holmes's belief in legislatures as the "ultimate guardians" of liberty and concluded with Brandeis's dissent describing states as laboratories of experimentation. Senator George W. Norris, a progressive from Nebraska, included Frankfurter's article in the *Congressional Record*. In May, Frankfurter incorporated the ideas from his article in a national radio address with Learned Hand, "How Far Is a Judge Free in Rendering a Decision?"

By May 27, the securities bill had survived the House and Senate and a conference committee. All it needed was the president's signature. That morning, Frankfurter and several others met with Roosevelt at the White House; Frankfurter prepared the president's statement about the law. At noon, Roosevelt signed the Securities Act of 1933 and praised it for putting "some elementary standards of right and wrong into law." Known as the "truth in Securities" law and premised on disclosure, the Securities Act of 1933 required public corporations to register and submit a prospectus and audited financial statements before issuing securities. The underwriter, officers, and directors who signed the registration documents could be found strictly liable for inaccurate statements. To securities lawyer Bernard Flexner, Frankfurter described it as "a really important piece of legislation, carefully drawn, however inevitably imperfect." To Roosevelt, he credited the new securities law to the president's leadership.

With the Securities Act of 1933 on the books, Wall Street stepped up its attacks on the law and its most prominent author. Sullivan & Cromwell lawyer Eustace Seligman wondered how Frankfurter slept at night (just fine, he replied); Frankfurter's mentor Henry Stimson questioned the willingness of his clients to risk liability by signing disclosure forms. Responding in *Fortune* magazine, Frankfurter defended the Securities Act as based "on the principle that when a corporation seeks funds from the public it becomes in every true sense a public corporation." A corporation "honestly conceived and competently administered has nothing to fear and much to gain." To those fiduciaries who worried about the liability risk of signing financial disclosure forms, Frankfurter called for corporate leaders with more integrity "to take the place of those who shrink from responsibilities incident to the business of managing other people's money."

Three days after Roosevelt signed the Securities Act of 1933, Frankfurter opined on the administration's biggest intervention in the economy—the National Industrial Recovery Act (NIRA). In a May 17 message to Congress, Roosevelt had encouraged legislators to pass the law to "put people to work" by setting industry codes establishing prices and outputs and ending the downward spiral of price wars, overproduction, and underemployment. Unlike Brandeis, who opposed the big-government program from the outset, Frankfurter conceded "this is no time for undue theorizing" and tried to help the administration make the law work. In a May 30 memorandum, he emphasized the importance not only of controlling supply and prices but also of increasing consumer demand for goods and services and adjusting wages and hours on an industry-by-industry basis so that working people have regular employment. He assisted former student Charles E. Wyzanski, Jr., in revising the labor provisions in the bill. On June 16, Roosevelt signed the NIRA into law and named as its administrator General Hugh S. Johnson. Frankfurter declined Johnson's offer to be general counsel and succeeded in persuading him to hire Chicago lawyer Donald Richberg.

As his work on the Securities Act and the NIRA demonstrated, Frankfurter was not wedded to any theory of economic regulation other than recruiting able lawyers to draft and implement it. His eye for talent was second to none. He had been recommending lawyers for public service ever since he worked as an assistant federal prosecutor for Henry Stimson, during the Taft and Wilson administrations, and for nearly twenty years on the Harvard law faculty. He tapped *Harvard Law Review* editors for judicial clerkships and graduate research fellowships and preached the gospel of public service. Many recent graduates started at Wall Street law firms yet were miserable there; others wanted to go straight into government. Frankfurter's relationship with Roosevelt and administration insiders sent his "one-man recruiting agency" into overdrive. Administration officials could not stop asking him to recommend young lawyers; Frankfurter thought it was "the most natural thing in the world. If you want to get good groceries in Washington you go to Magruder's, or in New York to Park and Tilford, or in Boston to S.S. Pierce. If you wanted to get a lot of first-class lawyers, you go to Harvard Law School."

Frankfurter's former students seemed to be everywhere: Dean Acheson as under secretary of the treasury, Wyzanski as solicitor to Secretary of Labor Frances Perkins, Nathan Margold as solicitor to Secretary of the Interior Harold Ickes, William Hastie as assistant solicitor to Ickes, Corcoran at the RFC, and Cohen and Landis in administrative posts after they wrote the securities law. Frankfurter often recommended people to Moley and Roosevelt and passed on the recommendations of others. At Brandeis's and Stone's request, he wrote Roosevelt about retaining former *Harvard Law Review* editors Erwin Griswold and Paul D. Miller in the solicitor general's office. He also praised the hiring of former students David Lilienthal on the board of directors of the Tennessee Valley Authority and John Dickinson as assistant secretary of commerce. More often than not, Frankfurter's connection to former students found its way into the newspapers. After Wyzanski's hiring in April, the *New York Daily News* correctly attributed it to Frankfurter and warned: "Politicians take note."

Frankfurter's hires were the talk of the business community. On June 24, 1933, *Kiplinger Washington Letter* noted that two of the nation's most prominent Jews, Brandeis and Frankfurter, "have tremendous intellectual influence, exercised through intellectual protégés in strategic positions throughout government service." A week later, the publication remarked that "[m]ore Jews occupy influential positions in relation to [the] Roosevelt administration than in any previous administration" and attributed many of them to Frankfurter, "whose ideas influence a score of aggressive young lawyers here-and-there in government service,—some Jews, some not." After a few weeks of criticism,

Kiplinger defended itself that it "dealt factually with" a "whispered question" and remarked that Jews "are doing exceedingly good jobs." By early 1934, however, people began referring to the New Deal as the "Jew Deal" and to Frankfurter's former students as "Happy Hot Dogs." A playful take on Frankfurter's first and last names by *New York Herald Tribune* columnist Mark Sullivan, the Happy Hot Dogs label took on a derogatory and anti-Semitic cast.

THE ANTI-SEMITISM directed at Frankfurter paled in comparison to reports of violence against Jews by Adolf Hitler's Nazi Party in Germany. On March 28, 1933, Frankfurter received an unsigned telegram at his office from Bratislava, Czechoslovakia, by way of Vienna, Austria. The writer described "unbelievable widespread brutalities" in Germany and predicted a "whitewash" because of "fear of threatened reprisals" and government censorship. The writer warned of similar violence against Jews and Communists in Austria and asked Frankfurter not to make direct contact "unless urgent necessity and then most guardedly use my name only in greatest confidence because of Viennese friends."

The anonymous author of the telegram was Ruth Mack Brunswick, the only child of Judge Julian Mack and a psychiatrist living in Vienna and collaborating with Sigmund Freud. She used to be married to a close friend of the Frankfurters, Boston cardiologist Herrman Blumgart, and in Vienna she had married American composer Mark Brunswick. The Brunswicks were important contacts for Frankfurter, who was worried about his uncle Salomon in Vienna and Jewish academics who had lost their jobs at German universities.

Named the country's chancellor in January, Hitler blamed the country's economic depression on Jews and Communists and promoted the superiority of the Aryan race. He had preaching hatred of Jews for years and found a receptive audience, leading to widespread violence, discrimination, and economic reprisals. Hitler's Nazi Party blamed a February 27 fire at the Reichstag, the German parliament, on the rival Communist Party. Using the fire as a pretext, Hitler persuaded President Paul von Hindenburg to invoke an emergency provision in the Weimar Constitution and to issue a decree abridging civil liberties. The Nazis won more seats in March elections and passed a law enabling Hitler to govern by decree and to begin his reign of terror against the Jews. On March 22, he established the Dachau concentration camp for political opponents. On April 1, the German government authorized a one-day boycott of Jewish store owners. Six days later, the National Socialist (or Nazi) regime passed the Law for the Restoration of the Professional Civil Service expelling all Jews and dissidents, or "non-Aryans," from teaching, academia, and judicial or government posts. At the behest of President Hindenburg, an exception was made for people who had served in the German military during the Great War. Many German academics, Jewish and non-Jewish, lost their jobs and sought asylum in the United States. Legal and political obstacles stood in their way. In particular, the Immigration Act of 1924 established quotas by country and prevented European Jews from arriving in large numbers. The State Department, staffed with anti-Semitic officers unsympathetic to the plight of Jews in Germany, refused to relax the quotas or to facilitate visas.

On April 9, Frankfurter engaged Roosevelt in a "full discussion" about the situation of the Jews in Germany and was encouraged that the meeting had "started the train for action." Working with longtime Zionist allies Brandeis, Julian Mack, and Rabbi Stephen Wise, Frankfurter urged the president to relax immigration quotas for German refugees and to make a strong public statement against the Nazi regime's treatment of Jews. A week later, on April 16, he wired Roosevelt about Wise's unhappiness that the administration had not issued a public statement. Meanwhile, Frankfurter and Brandeis assured Wise that the president was "alert to the meaning of events in Germany" and that "at the right moment would give evidence of his concern." Wise, however, could not wait any longer after hearing about the plight of German refugees. "Time is of the essence," Wise warned and pleaded for "some word by the president."

The president seemed willing to act. On April 24, Frankfurter showed Moley a memorandum he had sent to Secretary of Labor Perkins, who oversaw the immigration process, expressing "the President's thought in regard to the admission of political refugees." He informed Moley that "there isn't the slightest danger of mass immigration" because "the most terrible aspect of the situation in Germany is that they are not letting people out—to that extent the present situation is worse than the Inquisition." He encouraged Moley to support an executive order calling for admission of political refugees as consistent with the "traditional domestic policy of the United States" and with "the high and wise purposes of the President." Perkins assured Frankfurter that there was no need for an executive order because the asylum laws would be construed liberally.

With no public statement or executive order forthcoming from Roosevelt, Frankfurter found other ways to help German refugees. He agreed to serve on an advisory committee to the University in Exile, a new department for

German scholars established by the New School for Social Research and its director, Alvin Johnson. A former *New Republic* editor and the associate editor of the *Encyclopedia for the Social Sciences,* Johnson turned to Frankfurter for help raising money and succeeded in bringing fourteen German scholars to the program by October 1. Frankfurter asked Moley, an assistant secretary in the State Department, for help obtaining visas for German scientists and to raise the issue of German refugees with the president. He was among the prominent signers of an ACLU petition urging Roosevelt to issue an executive order to relax immigration restrictions for refugees. In a follow-up letter to Moley, he quoted retired Justice Holmes, who joined the University in Exile committee, about Germany's "challenge to civilization."

Roosevelt did not respond to Frankfurter's pleas for relaxing immigration restrictions directly. On May 6, Secretary of State Cordell Hull wrote Frankfurter acknowledging the April 16 telegram to the president and assuring him that the administration had the situation in hand. He also informed Frankfurter that German-born applicants should have no problems obtaining visas because the quota on immigrants from Germany had not been filled.

The next evening, Frankfurter met with Roosevelt in the White House for twenty-five minutes. He reviewed a draft of the president's fireside chat that night and encouraged him to include something about the international disarmament conference. That evening, Roosevelt outlined his New Deal programs for the nation. At the end of the chat, he stressed the interrelatedness of the domestic and international situations and the importance of the upcoming international economic and disarmament conferences. He said nothing, however, about the Nazi reign of terror on Jews. The situation was deteriorating. On May 10, university students burned more than 25,000 "un-German" books in Berlin's Opera Square.

It is unclear whether Frankfurter's efforts to promote Jewish immigration ever included confronting Roosevelt. He may have known that arguing with the president was not the best way to achieve his policy objectives. Instead, he adopted a multi-prong approach and relied on his connections to high-level officials in the administration. Through Moley, he arranged for a private meeting between Secretary of State Hull and Brandeis at the justice's apartment. Hull tried to explain that the administration had privately disapproved of German treatment of Jews. Brandeis was having none of it and replied that he "felt more ashamed of my country than pained by Jewish suffering" because of the weak U.S. response compared to those of Britain and Holland. First and foremost, Brandeis advised the president to make a bold public statement like one that Woodrow Wilson would have made and to relax all immigration quotas in favor of refugees.

As a follow-up to Brandeis's meeting, Frankfurter wrote the secretary of state a blunt memorandum expressing his dissatisfaction with the State Department's diplomatic response. He argued that the United States should stay true to its first principles in speaking out about Germany's treatment of the Jewish people and its history of providing asylum to victims of political and religious persecution. "To withhold such public action out of deference to the sensibilities of the Hitler regime," Frankfurter wrote on May 23, "is in effect to give support to the baleful aspects of Hitlerism." He pointed to the liberal immigration policies of the British, Dutch, and Scandinavian governments as proof that the United States could aid refugees. He ended "on a personal note. For once in my life I wish that for a brief period I were not a Jew." Because then he would not look "sectarian" in speaking out against the challenges Nazi Germany posed to "civilization." He reiterated that he felt "attached to the welfare of the Administration of Franklin D. Roosevelt more than I have been to that of any other President."

Frankfurter blamed the inaction of Roosevelt and his administration on prominent American Jews associated with the anti-Zionist American Jewish Committee. Mostly Jews of German origin and wealthy members of the establishment, they looked down on recent Eastern European Jewish immigrants, feared that speaking out would contribute to rising anti-Semitism, and preferred that the administration do nothing. In contrast, Frankfurter, Wise, Brandeis, and Mack belonged to the pro-Zionist American Jewish Congress, which wanted the administration to take a stand. As a result, Roosevelt, Moley, and other sympathetic administration officials perceived the American Jewish community as divided. Roosevelt, according to a story relayed to Frankfurter by Rabbi Wise, said: "There are two kinds of Jews—those who want me to spread-eagle and those who want me to be silent."

Frankfurter cut off friends because of their cowardly responses to what was happening in Germany. One of them was Walter Lippmann. A week after writing about German book burning, Lippmann described Hitler as "the authentic voice of a genuinely civilized people." After reading that May 19 *New York Herald Tribune* column, Frankfurter did not speak with or write to Lippmann, a frequent Roosevelt critic, for three years.

Roosevelt's inaction on the issue of German refugees did not deter Frankfurter. He remained steadfastly loyal to the president and defended him to Wise and other critics. Frankfurter understood the anti-Semitism among high-level State Department officials and the isolationism of the country as a whole. He also was privy to conversations with Roosevelt that others were not. Finally, he may have sensed the president's unwillingness to confront recalcitrant cabinet members. Frankfurter later asserted that in March 1933 the president had "promptly and passionately responded against Hitlerism" and "if he had had his way he would have sent" Frankfurter to be ambassador of Germany. Roosevelt, however, said or did nothing publicly at the time; historians continue to debate whether the president could have done more to facilitate Jewish immigration.

AT THE END OF SEPTEMBER, Frankfurter prepared to head overseas, not as an official U.S. ambassador but as the George Eastman Visiting Professor at Oxford University. Before he left, he saw Roosevelt twice. On September 6, the president invited him to attend an 8:30 p.m. meeting of mine owners and workers about the new National Recovery Administration (NRA) code for the coal industry. Eight days later, he returned to the White House for another coal code meeting and as an overnight guest. The president wrote U.S. ambassadors to Great Britain, Switzerland, and Italy introducing Frankfurter and granting him permission to send mail via diplomatic pouch. The press reported that Roosevelt expected Frankfurter to keep tabs on the international political and economic situation.

After leaving the White House at 10:30 a.m. on September 15, Frankfurter walked across Pennsylvania Avenue just west of Lafayette Park to the Brookings Institution for a lunchtime talk organized by Corcoran. His audience included approximately sixty friends and former students working in all the major departments: State, Treasury, Justice, Agriculture, Interior, Labor, Federal Trade Commission, Interstate Commerce Commission, National Recovery Administration, Agricultural Adjustment Administration, Public Works Administration, and Tennessee Valley Authority. The parade of young administration officials into Brookings caught the watchful eye of the press, which reported on the "secret luncheon meeting of the best legal brains in town." Deeply "moved" to see so many former students in the administration, Frankfurter encouraged them to supplant the system of political patronage appointments with an expert-run civil service and tried to boost their spirits as big business fought the alphabet soup of new agencies and resisted new economic regulation. As a matter of legal strategy, he counseled delaying any constitutional defenses of New Deal programs, especially the NRA's fair competition codes setting wages and hours and establishing production quotas, for as long as possible and at least a year.

One of the bright young lawyers in the audience was Labor Department solicitor Charles E. Wyzanski, Jr. The son of a well-to-do Jewish real estate developer in Boston, he was more independent-minded than some of Frankfurter's other protégés. For example, after graduating from Harvard Law School in 1930, practicing law in Boston, and clerking for Augustus Hand and his cousin Learned on the Court of Appeals for the Second Circuit, Wyzanski had declined the opportunity to clerk for Brandeis. Frankfurter, however, refused to give up on Wyzanski, promoting him for the labor post and fighting for his Senate confirmation. It did not take long for Wyzanski to make good in the Labor Department; his boss, Frances Perkins, described him as "like having a really stout walking stick to lean on."

Before he left Washington, Frankfurter made sure that his three young stars associated with the Securities Act of 1933—Landis, Cohen, and Corcoran—were in good hands. He reminded Roosevelt about the "unique" ability of Landis, who was named a federal trade commissioner charged with enforcing the new securities law. He kept tabs on Cohen, who was in the Public Works Administration while awaiting his next major drafting assignment. Corcoran was temporarily assigned to the Treasury Department to work with Dean Acheson and invited Paul Freund, fresh off his Brandeis clerkship, to work with him. Frankfurter deputized Corcoran to be his placement agent and jack-of-all-trades while he was in Oxford, referring to Corcoran as "Centurion" after the ancient Roman commanders of a century of soldiers. Before he left for Britain, Frankfurter wrote Corcoran a letter of introduction to Roosevelt's personal secretary and confidant, Marguerite "Missy" LeHand, and urged her to see Corcoran from time to time. A frequent White House visitor, Corcoran became Frankfurter's eyes and ears in Washington.

By sending the best legal minds to work in the administration, Frankfurter supplied the growing federal administrative state with experts and problem solvers rather than political patronage appointees. With Landis, Cohen, and Corcoran taking the lead in reshaping the nation's financial regulations and Wyzanski and other bright young lawyers in key positions, Frankfurter stayed engaged in the Roosevelt administration's affairs from an ocean's remove at Oxford.

CHAPTER 16

Charming Exile

O n the afternoon of September 24, 1933, friends and former students congregated at Boston's Commonwealth Pier to say bon voyage to Felix and Marion Frankfurter. They smiled for the waiting photographers on the pleasant, 62-degree day and at 2:00 p.m. boarded the White Star Line's steamship *Britannic* bound for Galway, Queenstown, and Liverpool.

The seas were calm, but not Frankfurter. He could not stop thinking about his former students in the Roosevelt administration. He wired the president about Landis's usefulness, then wrote Corcoran at length about keeping tabs on Landis, urging him to see Brandeis, and managing pet projects. He had not yet thought about what lay ahead. For the next nine months, he was to be the George Eastman Visiting Professor at Oxford, a fellowship established in 1929 by the Eastman-Kodak founder, administered by the American Association of Rhodes Scholars, and associated with Oxford's Balliol College.

On Monday, October 2, the Frankfurters arrived at Oxford station and were greeted by Colonel Basil G. Duke, a Scottish veteran of the Boer War and the bursar of Balliol College. He took them to the Eastman House at 18 Norham Gardens, a charming brick home less than a mile north of the center of campus. The house came with a full-time staff, a husband-wife team who prepared their meals and teas, polished their shoes, and pressed their clothes, as well as a lovely rear garden ideal for afternoon teas. At their first tea, the master of Balliol, Alexander "Sandie" Lindsay, introduced himself and informed Frankfurter that he was to give three public lectures. Other than that, he could do whatever he wanted. For all this lack of responsibility, he received a $10,000 stipend. Their nine months in Oxford was the happiest time of the Frankfurters' lives.

Initially, Frankfurter worried too much about abiding by Oxford's unwritten rules. Invited to a formal dinner by the school's vice chancellor, he arrived in white tie and tails only to find all the men wearing Oxford gowns. He was mortified until he had learned that he had dressed appropriately after all; only people who had received degrees from Oxford could wear academic gowns. On October 17, he received an honorary master's degree because it was required for him to lecture; thereafter, he, too, wore an academic gown to formal dinners. By then, however, he had stopped worrying about Oxford's baffling social norms and vowed to be himself. He knew only one person at Oxford, jurisprudence scholar Arthur Goodhart, but quickly found his way.

Early on, he and Marion fell in with a group of young scholars thanks to Sylvester Gates, his former British graduate student who had worked on the Sacco-Vanzetti book. Gates was living in London and working as a junior solicitor but maintained close ties to Oxford. He introduced the Frankfurters to several up-and-coming faculty members: philosopher Isaiah Berlin, philosopher A. J. "Freddie" Ayer, and classics scholar Maurice Bowra. Berlin was twenty-two, Ayer twenty-three, and Bowra the ripe old age of thirty-five; they were ambitious, charming, and, for the Frankfurters, loads of fun. At one of their first teas, Gates and Ayer argued and bet whether the Austrian philosopher Ludwig Wittgenstein had used the phrase "Whereof one cannot speak, thereof one must be silent" once or twice. Gates said twice, including once in the preface. Ayer, who promptly biked home to grab his bedside copy of Wittgenstein's *Tractatus Logico-Philosophicus*, insisted only once and that the preface did not count. They asked Frankfurter to be the judge; Ayer lost.

As much as these young men loved Frankfurter's exuberance and admired his intellectual enthusiasm, they were instantly attracted to his quietly perceptive, bitingly caustic, well-read wife, Marion—especially young Isaiah Berlin. Born in Riga, Latvia, to a Jewish timber merchant, he moved with his family to St. Petersburg during the Great War and briefly returned to Latvia during the Russian Revolution before settling in London when he was ten. As a Russian-speaking Jewish immigrant, he learned English quickly and won an entrance scholarship in classics to Oxford's Corpus Christi College. At Oxford, he earned a first in classics and won the John Locke Prize in philosophy. After the *Manchester Guardian* refused to hire him, he returned to Oxford for graduate work in philosophy, politics, and economics. In October 1932, he was named a tutor at New College and a month later became the first Jew to earn a fellowship at All Souls. His friends called him Shaya. The cherubic-looking Berlin was pudgy with thinning dark hair, dark round glasses, and a left arm damaged at birth. Though almost nineteen years her junior, he was as taken with Marion as she was with him. They went on long walks together, liked to gossip, and corresponded intimately for years. Mrs. Frankfurter, Berlin wrote Ayer, was "a++."

In addition to establishing a lifelong friendship with Berlin, Felix and Marion grew close to classics scholar Maurice Bowra. The dean of Wadham College told them about serving in the Great War as a teenager, getting trapped in a caved-in trench, and calmly answering the telephone: "Bowra speaking." Short and stout, he had a rich, deep voice and was as intense as he was witty. He was a great source of gossip and a closeted homosexual who wrote bawdy poems about the sex lives and foibles of friends; he described the Frankfurters as "entirely happy together."

Nothing could dampen Marion's spirits, not even another round of health problems. In November, she was having trouble walking and thought it was sciatica. After various tests, a London doctor determined that she had a virus and an abscess on her hip. Chronic health problems aside, Marion had never been happier than at Oxford and described it as "like nothing I ever did before, or shall ever do again, and while it lasts I have the feeling I am in a play. Ah well, not everybody likes to be in a play and those will never understand."

Marion also saw a different side of her husband. An Anglophile and long-time reader of British newspapers, Frankfurter thrived in Oxford's lifestyle of talking and socializing, drinking and dining. He ran a weekly seminar about federalism, the relationship between the federal government and the states, for young dons. Initially, however, he was unable to find a copy of the U.S. Constitution. The only one in Oxford was in the Rare Books and Manuscripts at the Bodleian Library. Eventually, Blackwell's, the town's famous bookstore, located a copy in a book for people trying to become American citizens. With that problem solved, the seminar was a big success. Frankfurter's only scholarly failure was trying to bring together the university's historians and economists for regular discussions; despite his best efforts, they kept talking past one another.

During a ten-day visit to London in early January 1934, Marion remarked that her husband was "wholly carefree for the first time in fourteen years." They saw Mae West perform, the animated film *Three Little Pigs*, the opera, the ballet, debates at the House of Lords, and numerous old friends. Just over an hour from Oxford, London was their playground. Frankfurter accepted social invitations from a who's who of Britain: he was economist John Maynard Keynes's guest at Founders' Day at King's College, pioneering nuclear physicist Ernest Rutherford's guest at the High Table at Trinity College, and conservative politician and barrister Sir Leslie Scott's guest at Grand Day of Inner Temple.

For the most part, the Frankfurters were on a nine-month holiday. Felix belonged to two Oxford social clubs, a radical one and a respectable one. In May 1934, when it was his turn to host the respectable club, he arranged for an outing to watch the Derby at Epsom Downs Racecourse, a little more than an hour from Oxford in Surrey. They left after breakfast, brought cold chicken salad and champagne, and won money when tipped off to bet a pound on the winning horse, Windsor Lad, at ten to one odds. The outing made Frankfurter's reputation. "Well at last," they said, "we've got an American scholar."

Even at his most carefree, though, Frankfurter was promoting the Roosevelt administration and the New Deal. In January 1934, he published an unsigned article for *The Economist*, drafted by Ben Cohen, on the 1933 Securities Act. He met with *Times* of London editor Geoffrey Dawson about improving the leading British newspaper's coverage of the New Deal. A few days later, he spoke on BBC radio for half an hour to explain misconceptions between the British and American people and called on the press to alleviate them. On March 9 at the University of Manchester, he lectured on "The Roosevelt Administration and Its Background" and met philosopher Samuel Alexander.

Frankfurter's finest moment on the lecture circuit came during a February 1 discussion about the U.S. Constitution when he ended up debating 78-year-old Irish playwright and polemicist George Bernard Shaw. With Eustace Percy presiding at the Royal Institute of International Affairs at Chatham House, Frankfurter spoke for an hour about the constitutionality of Roosevelt's New Deal programs. He described the Constitution as "not a lawyers' document" but "a scheme for the development of a nation" which was meant to be "dynamic." He invoked John Marshall's line in *McCulloch v. Maryland* that "it is *a constitution* we are expounding" as the best statement on the subject. He cautioned the nine justices on the Supreme Court against reading their "fixed notions" into vague clauses when deciding the constitutionality of New Deal programs such as the National Industrial Recovery Act, and he quoted Holmes several times for support. After Frankfurter fielded questions from several people, Shaw jumped in and insisted the framers of the Constitution would "drop down dead again" if they saw Roosevelt's New Deal programs. Frankfurter, who knew Shaw "could make mincemeat of me on any other subject," turned to Percy and whispered: "The Lord hath delivered him into my hands." Treating him like a confused law student, Frankfurter calmly and gently refuted Shaw's arguments and concluded that "if the founders came to earth again they would drop dead because they would so admire the imaginative handling of the Constitution they had framed." Shaw, who knew that he had been bested, removed his name from the meeting minutes and instead was referred to as "a member." A less-than-neutral observer, Harold J. Laski declared Frankfurter's performance "as masterly a job as I have ever heard."

Balancing his social and intellectual life in London and Oxford and his legal and political life at home, Frankfurter showed no "visible signs of strain." The Frankfurters' residence at Eastman House was filled with American newspapers and magazines; letters from Corcoran, Cohen, Landis, and other protégés in the administration; letters from Brandeis on yellow paper; and copies of the latest Supreme Court opinions.

Corcoran and other New Deal protégés kept Frankfurter apprised of what was happening in Washington. During the fall of 1933, the Treasury Department was in turmoil over the legality of government purchases of gold in an effort to inflate prices. Through the summer of 1933, Dean Acheson, under secretary of the treasury, had been running the department because Secretary William H. Woodin was ineffective and chronically ill. In the fall, Acheson repeatedly clashed with Roosevelt and the administration over the legality of the gold purchases. Acheson refused to comply with the purchases without a legal memorandum from the Justice Department. The press caught wind of the dispute. The president requested his resignation, and Acheson submitted it without comment, resigning in November. Harvard economist Oliver Sprague also resigned; Acheson's aides, Corcoran and Paul Freund, decamped to the Reconstruction Finance Corporation. Roosevelt did not send Acheson a letter of appreciation but later concluded that he had resigned like a gentleman. Frankfurter, who suspected that Acheson had badmouthed the president "to the wrong people," wrote him sympathetic letters.

Relying on secure diplomatic pouches, Frankfurter provided Roosevelt with a British perspective on the New Deal. In November 1933, he sent the president a letter from Oxford economists who suggested increasing the production of consumer goods by lowering interest rates; they were less enamored of the administration's monetary policy of buying gold to inflate prices—in short, they advocated increased government spending to end the Great Depression. A few weeks later, Frankfurter sent the president an advance copy of "An Open Letter to President Roosevelt" to be published in the *New York Times* from economist John Maynard Keynes. After the Great War, Frankfurter had helped Keynes publish a *New Republic* article criticizing Wilson's performance at the Paris Peace Conference. Keynes's open letter to Roosevelt revealed British concern about the failure of the National Industrial Recovery Act to revive the economy and the administration's inability to increase spending and to put more people to work. "Your letters continue to delight and stimulate me," Roosevelt replied to Frankfurter. The president had read the Oxford economists' letter to a private gathering of his advisers and had implemented some of the suggestions; he told Frankfurter to inform Keynes that public works spending was doubling in the next fiscal year but there was "a practical limit to what the Government can borrow."

More than an overseas New Deal cheerleader, Frankfurter informed Roosevelt about the rising threat of Nazi Germany. On October 17, 1933, he had relayed British press accounts about what was happening in Germany and concluded "the significance of Hitlerism far transcends ferocious anti-Semitism and fanatical racism." He described the mood in Britain: "The air here is charged, albeit in a sober kind of way, with the kind of feeling that preceded 1914." He perceived British opinion to be united against Hitler and heard from German exiles who predicted that "the forces of violence and chauvinism of the Hitler regime will be accelerated and intensified." He suggested that Roosevelt address the people of Germany in their native tongue because "its people live in darkness." A month later, he enclosed a letter from James G. McDonald, the League of Nations high commissioner for German refugees, about Nazi decrees proclaiming Jews second-class citizens; McDonald feared a mass exodus of refugees. In February 1934, Frankfurter wired Roosevelt about the Nazi threat to Austria's Jews and described the country of his birth as "the football between the rivalries of Hitler and Mussolini." In March, he congratulated Roosevelt on naming George S. Messersmith ambassador to Austria. And in an April *World Today* article, "Persecution of Jews in Germany," Frankfurter documented the Nazis' exclusion of Jews from the civil service, academia, the bar, and the press and the 60,000 refugees who had already fled. "Palestine is undoubtedly the most promising place for settlement by the German Jews . . . ," he concluded. "For there is no doubt that the Jew in Germany is doomed."

Palestine was again on Frankfurter's mind. Thanks to a $2000 gift from Brandeis, he and Marion visited Palestine for eleven days in April and were "overwhelmed" by the region's beauty and promise. The "Palestine experience," Marion declared, "pales all else." He marveled at everything that the Jewish settlers had accomplished since his failed effort to establish a Jewish homeland at the 1919 Paris Peace Conference. He saw many people who reminded him of a young Aaron Aaronsohn, the Palestinian Jewish agronomist who died in plane crash in 1919, and left with a "transcendent" feeling of the possibilities there: "Jewish Palestine is an established civilization. . . . The organism is so powerful that while the pace of its growth may be accelerated or retarded by Government, it cannot be stopped." In light of the dismal situation in Europe, he predicted that Palestine's "sizable growth in Jewish population and power [was] inevitable."

From Oxford, Frankfurter kept tabs on his proteges as they drafted the Securities Exchange Act of 1934. On February 9, Roosevelt had called on Congress to pass a new law to oversee the sale of securities and the stock exchanges, to prevent fraud and insider trading, and to establish the Securities and Exchange Commission (SEC) to regulate the securities industry. Ben Cohen and Tom Corcoran took the lead in drafting the law, with input from Jim Landis at the Federal Trade Commission (FTC). The introverted Cohen and extroverted Corcoran showed how opposites attract: Cohen drafted the bill; Corcoran testified about it before Congress. Frankfurter declared the 1934 act, with its creation of the SEC as an independent regulatory agency, an "extraordinary achievement."

Opponents of the 1934 act took aim at Frankfurter and his "hot dog boys": Cohen, Corcoran, Landis, and Max Lowenthal (who had contributed on the basis of his work for the Pecora Commission investigating Wall Street). The March publication of *The New Dealers*, a book by "the Unofficial Observer," declared that Frankfurter had sent 75 to 100 liberal lawyers to Washington and had "succeeded in giving an accidentally Semitic cast to the New Deal." The "Jew Deal" label and charges of Communism cropped up with increasing frequency. On April 20, Representative Frederick A. Britten, an Illinois Republican, claimed that Corcoran, Cohen, and their friends lived in "a little red house in Georgetown" and held nightly meetings of "10 to 18 young men of radical minds." At these meetings, Britten claimed, they wrote "the communistic legislation we all talk about in the cloakrooms." Inspired by Frankfurter's tales of the House of Truth, Corcoran, Cohen, and their friends lived together in a rented Italianate mansion at 3238 R Street and threw dinner parties; "the little red house" name, much to their delight, stuck.

Between serious letters and telegrams about opposition to the 1934 act, Frankfurter and Corcoran joked about their Red-baiting and anti-Semitic critics. "Dear Horns and Tail," Corcoran began an April 22 letter assuring him that not "everything had gone to pot." He asked Frankfurter to return to the States as soon as possible and to "remind the Skipper [Roosevelt] that every fundamental change, like the Stock Exchange Bill, needs electioneering like a congressional campaign." "Dear Little Boys," Frankfurter wrote Cohen and Corcoran after learning they had gone to the White House and Corcoran had played the piano and sung Irish songs for the delighted president. In a letter brimming with avuncular good spirit, Frankfurter warned them about the perils of too much publicity. His admiration for Corcoran's leadership and

Cohen's draftsmanship ran deep. He began referring to Corcoran as the "general" and praised his fortitude during a tough legislative fight. He attributed "the talk against the Jews in the government" to "the powerful financial and business interests" threatened by the new securities laws. He reminded Roosevelt that the 1934 act regulating the stock exchanges and creating the SEC was the only way "to keep Wall Street in its place."

During his nine months in Oxford, Frankfurter radiated optimism about the New Deal while Brandeis, an opponent of the National Recovery Administration (NRA) and other federal regulatory programs fixing prices and outputs, exuded pessimism. Brandeis kept telling Frankfurter, either directly or through former students, that the administration was in trouble and that Frankfurter needed to return home. Enjoying a carefree and joyous time with his wife, Frankfurter was in no hurry. He had planned to stay in Europe until late July to tour England and Scotland and to gather information about Jewish immigration to Palestine. There was no imminent reason to rush back. On June 8, Roosevelt signed the Securities Exchange Act of 1934 and left on July 1 for a vacation cruise to Hawaii. Harvard Law School was not back in session until September. Instead of extending his and Marion's stay, however, Frankfurter heeded Brandeis's advice, left Oxford on June 30, and lamented the end of their "charming exile."

Shortly before 8:00 a.m. on July 8, 1934, the Frankfurters returned to Boston's Commonwealth Pier aboard the steamship *Georgic*. They were greeted by their friends Reverend Vivian Pomeroy and his wife, as well as reporters and photographers. Frankfurter raved about his stay at Oxford, his trip to Palestine, and what the Roosevelt administration meant to the rest of the world. "The New Deal in this country has excited great interest abroad," he told the press, "and there is no doubt President Roosevelt has become the symbol of encouragement and hope everywhere. All who believe in the future of liberal civilization must be profoundly thankful to the President for the spirit he has put into Democracy."

Scheduled to return to Washington at the end of the month, Roosevelt requested to see Frankfurter immediately. The New Deal was in trouble; the economy had not improved; and the National Industrial Recovery Act and other new federal regulatory programs faced stiff constitutional challenges in the Supreme Court.

CHAPTER 17

The Most Influential Single Individual in the United States

S oon after they were married in December 1919, Marion saw her husband slow down for one of the first times. "What's the matter," she said, "the wind-mill has died down." She was distressed because she "had come to depend on the wind-mill's going round and round." Before they left for Oxford, the windmill had died down again before Felix told her "there is a little breeze." Upon their return the following summer, the windmill began spinning faster than ever.

On the afternoon of August 29, 1934, the Frankfurters arrived at Hyde Park for an overnight visit with the president. Roosevelt and Frankfurter had not seen each other in nearly a year. In that time, the economy had not fully recovered from the Great Depression; unemployment was still more than 20 percent. The New Deal, moreover, faced serious political and legal challenges. The National Industrial Recovery Act (NIRA), which authorized the National Recovery Administration (NRA) to create fair competition codes in cooperation with industry, was particularly vulnerable. Big business objected to the law's interference with free market capitalism and questioned its constitutionality. Government lawyers in the NRA, some of them former Frankfurter students, had been advising administrators as they negotiated fair competition codes with more than 200 industries. Depending on the industry, the codes set wages, hours, and prices; established production quotas; and recognized labor's right to organize and collectively bargain. Industry cooperation was voluntary; the government, however, appealed to people's patriotism through the "Blue Eagle" campaign in which the symbol appeared in newspapers and in store windows of participating businesses. During his talk at the Brookings Institution in September 1933, Frankfurter had warned his former students to stall any legal challenges to the NIRA's fair competition codes for as long as possible. Others in the administration, however, disagreed with Frankfurter's strategy of delay.

In Frankfurter's view, the Supreme Court had not changed much since 1923 when it had revived *Lochner v. New York* and had declared that the District of Columbia's minimum-wage law for women violated the liberty of contract. The NIRA could be attacked on several constitutional grounds, including a broad interpretation of liberty in the Due Process Clause, a narrow interpretation of Congress's power to regulate interstate commerce, or as an unconstitutional delegation of legislative power to the executive branch. The Court had made some accommodations for state laws designed to help people during the Great Depression. In January 1934, the Court had upheld a Minnesota law temporarily postponing foreclosures. A few months later in another 5–4 decision, the Court upheld a New York law fixing milk prices because it was a regulation of private property "in the public interest." The Court gave the states latitude to prevent people from losing their homes and to save the dairy market from collapsing. The scope of federal power to regulate the economy, however, was a different story.

During their visit with Roosevelt, Marion was struck by how experienced and confident he sounded in discussing big business's antipathy toward the New Deal. A week earlier, a group of wealthy private businessmen and prominent politicians had formed the American Liberty League to rally the New Deal's opponents. Brandeis, Frankfurter told the president, had described the clash between big business and the federal government as an "irrepressible conflict." In the face of a powerful and well-financed opposition, the administration needed to defend the New Deal in the press, at the ballot box, and, ultimately, before the Supreme Court. As a prominent presidential adviser with many former students in the administration, Frankfurter became a lightning rod for Roosevelt's critics.

At Hyde Park, Roosevelt and Frankfurter talked until 1:00 a.m. and again the next morning about the most pressing policy issues: the failure of the federal housing program; how to finance an expanded public works program to employ more people; scaling back the National Industrial Recovery Act to only set minimum wages and maximum hours, mandate collective bargaining, and outlaw child labor; and working with state governments to pass federal unemployment relief.

Of course, they also discussed Frankfurter's biggest contribution to the administration—personnel. He countered Democratic National Committee chairman James Farley's efforts to fill key posts with patronage appointments by urging the president to promote the best available lawyers. For example, Farley had mentioned putting Senate Majority Leader Joseph Robinson of Arkansas on the Supreme Court, an idea Frankfurter abhorred. If a vacancy arose, Frankfurter suggested Judge Joseph C. Hutcheson, Jr., of Texas as a southern alternative. Roosevelt needed no convincing about the value of Frankfurter's surrogates Tom Corcoran and Ben Cohen. He praised their loyalty to the administration, promised to find a new post for Cohen, and described Corcoran as the "best man" at the RFC. The president increasingly relied on Corcoran and Cohen for their legislative acumen and legal advice.

For weeks before his Hyde Park stay, Frankfurter had been gathering information and offering advice to friends and former students in the administration. He treaded lightly with Raymond Moley, who had left the State Department to edit *Today* magazine and had become more conservative. He persuaded Corcoran to decline a job as an assistant in the solicitor general's office because he was more valuable as Roosevelt's jack-of-all-trades at RFC. He soothed the hurt feelings of Cohen, who had declined to be general counsel of the new Securities and Exchange Commission (SEC) after being passed over as one of the commissioners. He encouraged James Landis to extend his leave from Harvard Law School to be one of the new SEC commissioners. He spoke with SEC chairman Joseph Kennedy, Sr., who complained about the weaknesses in the 1934 act; the two men were on good terms, especially since Frankfurter had recommended that Joe Kennedy, Jr., study political science with Harold Laski at the London School of Economics. From young lawyers in the administration including Charles Wyzanski, Nathan Margold, and Melvin Siegel, he learned about what was happening at Labor, Interior, and the Tennessee Valley Authority. He spoke with Wyzanski about "the whole Jewish problem" in the administration and "put to him hard constitutional and other difficulties" about an unemployment compensation bill and the challenges to the New Deal coming to the Supreme Court.

In September, Frankfurter sat for a portrait sketch by City College classmate S. J. Woolf and consented to an accompanying *New York Times Magazine* profile. In the article, Frankfurter expounded on his familiar theme of the disinterested expert as essential to a well-functioning democracy. He argued that complex economic and social problems required expertise and critical-thinking skills. Disclaiming "a government of experts" and playing on the line about the "expert should be on tap but not on top," he suggested that the government was so afraid to have experts on top that it neglected to have them on tap. He called on politicians to educate the public about the need for technical solutions to the country's social and economic problems and on institutions of higher education to train students for public service. This was precisely what Frankfurter had been doing by sending *Harvard Law Review* editors into government for more than two decades and, of late, into the Roosevelt administration.

Harvard Law School was not a happy place during the final years of Roscoe Pound's deanship. On September 17, 1934, at Langdell Hall, Pound accepted an honorary degree from the University of Berlin. During a visit to Austria and Germany a few months earlier, Pound had praised the German government after Hitler had carried out "blood purges" against people perceived to be disloyal. Pound had met not only with academics but also with Nazi leaders and had agreed to accept an honorary degree from a university that had expelled Jewish scholars. On September 17, he accepted the University of Berlin's honorary doctor of laws from the German ambassador to the United States while Harvard president James Conant watched in the wings and then attended a post-ceremony lunch. Frankfurter refused to "attend any function in honor of a representative of a government which Mr. Justice Holmes has accurately characterized as 'a challenge to civilization.'" Pound accused Frankfurter, whose 1934 *World Today* article documented Nazi persecution of Jews, of not knowing the facts. The honorary degree from the University of Berlin was the beginning of the end of Pound's deanship and the end of his friendship with Frankfurter. Pound's timidity and lies during the Sacco-Vanzetti case, particularly his false statements to Massachusetts Supreme Judicial Court justices about the timing of Frankfurter's book, had irreparably damaged their relationship. His unwillingness to confront President Lowell after the faculty voted to hire Nathan Margold allowed anti-Semitism into the law school. His refusal to hire exiled Jewish scholars exacerbated the feeling. His acceptance of an honorary degree from the Nazi regime confirmed Frankfurter's worst fears.

Despite Pound's Nazi sympathies, Harvard Law School was the best place for Frankfurter to mold yet another generation of legal minds. He fought for a graduate research fellowship for future Harvard sociologist David Riesman and tapped him to clerk for Brandeis. There were more future academics and public servants on the way. One of the most promising third-year students was future legal historian Willard Hurst. After finishing first in his class, Hurst worked as Frankfurter's graduate research assistant and may have written the first draft of Frankfurter's book about the history of the Commerce Clause. Frankfurter selected Hurst to succeed Riesman as Brandeis's secretary and one of Hurst's fellow *Harvard Law Review* editors, Joseph L. Rauh, Jr., to clerk for Cardozo.

During the fall of 1934, Frankfurter focused on teaching and mentoring promising students and limited his White House visits to a single lunch in October with Roosevelt and businessman Samuel Zemurray. Democratic victories in the November midterm elections gave Roosevelt a boost. He asked Frankfurter to visit again before Christmas. On December 16, Frankfurter stayed overnight at the White House and discussed ideas for the State of the Union address on January 4, 1935.

In the State of the Union address, which Frankfurter missed because he was teaching, the president called for an enlarged public works program and unemployment compensation and old-age insurance legislation. He addressed the rise of fascism in Europe by pledging to seek international peace and opposing armed conflict. Most of all, he reminded the American people what the administration had already accomplished with its New Deal programs and explained how new legislation could accelerate the country's economic recovery.

THE SUPREME COURT posed the biggest threat to the New Deal. Three days after the State of the Union, the Court declared the petroleum code of the National Industrial Recovery Act an unconstitutional delegation of congressional power. An oil refiner and several producers sued to enjoin the code's prohibition of the sale of "hot oil" in excess of state quotas. In an 8–1 decision, the Court ruled that Congress did not provide any guidelines to the executive branch to set quotas on the sale or interstate shipment of oil. It also held that the National Recovery Administration violated due process by failing to produce any factual findings. Frankfurter blamed the defeat on the embarrassing oral argument by Assistant Attorney General Harold M. Stephens. At oral argument, Stephens admitted that in a related case the government had indicted four Texas oil producers under a section of the code that had been deleted during revisions. Brandeis forced Stephens to concede that the petroleum code provisions had not been published anywhere and were available only at the State Department and, according to Frankfurter, "really cross-examined & pulverized the stupid" Stephens. Frankfurter could have blamed Brandeis, who declined Chief Justice Hughes's offer to write the majority opinion yet had "a good deal to do" with the nearly unanimous final product. Only Cardozo dissented. Frankfurter believed that the Court had exceeded its authority in making administrative hearings and factual findings a constitutional requirement.

The administration was worried about pending Supreme Court decisions in the "gold clause" cases. In an effort to combat deflation and to discourage debtors from declaring bankruptcy, Roosevelt had engineered a joint resolution rendering the gold clauses in federal bonds and private contracts unenforceable, which therefore made the instruments no longer redeemable in gold. Frankfurter considered former student Paul Freund's brief for the government a "truly A-1" job. At the January 15 oral argument, Freund's former boss Brandeis was "so completely out of sympathy" with the administration's policy and so determined it was unconstitutional that he decided not to ask a single question. Somehow, Brandeis joined the decisions narrowly upholding the abrogation of the gold clauses. In the case of government bonds, the Court held there was a right to be paid in gold but no remedy to collect. The president was concerned enough about the outcome that he had prepared a fireside chat explaining why he refused to comply with the Court's decisions. He read it to Secretary of the Treasury Henry Morgenthau, Jr., and SEC chairman Joseph Kennedy, Sr., but apparently not to Frankfurter. The decisions mooted Roosevelt's willingness to disobey the Court yet revealed the antagonism between the president and the conservative justices.

"The Constitution is gone," Justice James C. McReynolds declared before reading from the prepared text of his dissent on behalf of four justices. He minced no words about the president's actions: "This is Nero at his worst." The previous August, McReynolds had spoken with reporters upon returning from Europe and had mocked the New Deal. McReynolds and fellow conservatives Pierce Butler, George Sutherland, and Willis Van Devanter were staunchly opposed to the New Deal's constitutionality; the press nicknamed them the "Four Horsemen," a reference to the Four Horsemen of the Apocalypse; Learned Hand referred to them as the Mastiffs or the Battalion of Death. The conservative justices were not the only ones out of sympathy with the administration. Speaking privately with Frankfurter, Brandeis described McReynolds's remarks as "really impressive; better than anything I have ever heard from him." McReynolds's public pronouncements and Brandeis's private comments revealed that other New Deal programs were in trouble. During an early 1935 meeting with Frankfurter, Brandeis reiterated his opposition to the National Industrial Recovery Act and his willingness to join a decision to strike it down.

One justice would have been extremely reluctant to overturn Roosevelt's New Deal programs—93-year-old Oliver Wendell Holmes, Jr. With his belief in John Marshall's broad, flexible Constitution and his Thayerian unwilling-ness to invalidate federal laws unless they were unconstitutional beyond a rea-sonable doubt, Holmes was Frankfurter's ideal jurist. In the fall of 1934, the retired Holmes was older, feebler, and more stooped. He was ably attended by a secretary Frankfurter selected annually from the law school's graduating class, during the 1933 term by future legal historian Mark DeWolfe Howe followed by future Roosevelt aide James Rowe. They each served as the jus-tice's constant social companion and read to him for hours. In October 1934, Felix and Marion had seen their old friend at Beverly Farms looking "in sur-prisingly pink condition" shortly before he left for Washington by train with his secretary in tow. As Holmes's ninety-fourth birthday approached, Frank-furter planned one final surprise—another March 8 visit from President Roo-sevelt. It never came to pass.

In late February 1935, Holmes caught a cold during one of his regu-lar automobile rides and was diagnosed with pneumonia. A few days later, Frankfurter was told to come to Washington immediately. He saw the justice hooked up to an oxygen tent, "ebbing away" yet in good spirits. The justice thumbed his nose at Jim Rowe after his young secretary said, "Every soldier to his tent, Captain Holmes." The justice's housekeeper Mary Donnellan was constantly at his bedside and calmly whispered, "Everybody loves you"; the justice replied, "Oh hell." Rowe stayed on call in the bedroom; former secretary Mark DeWolfe Howe handled the secretarial duties; and several doctors attended to the justice. In between visits to Holmes and planning funeral arrangements, Frankfurter saw the president twice and dined twice with Cardozo and once with Henry Stimson. After a few days, Holmes lapsed into a coma. Frankfurter joined secretaries Rowe, Howe, and Corcoran and members of the household staff at the justice's bedside and witnessed his last breath. At 2:00 a.m. on March 6, two days before his ninety-fourth birthday, Oliver Wendell Holmes, Jr., was pronounced dead.

At the president's request, Felix and Marion stayed at the White House. They arrived in time for an unforgettable dinner with the Roosevelts and Holmes's successor, Benjamin Cardozo. They also visited Brandeis, who was "too stricken with grief" to attend his closest colleague's funeral. Marion, who had arrived from Boston the day before the funeral, was a great comfort to her husband. She shared his grief and had known Holmes almost as long and intimately as he did. The justice had confided in her over the years; he and his wife, Fanny, had blessed their marriage in December 1919 in ways their own parents, upset about an interfaith union, could not.

The next morning, Holmes's body lay in state at 1720 I Street; Marion never forgot the sight of the justice dressed in robes in his bed. At 11:45 a.m., Felix, wearing a black top hat and dark overcoat, rode with Marion and Eleanor Roosevelt and walked up the stairs of All Soul's Unitarian Church for a brief funeral service. They drove with the funeral procession to Arlington National Cemetery for the burial. At the cemetery, rain and sleet began to fall. With his head bowed and his hat off, Felix stood under the canopy next to the bugler who played "Taps" as six military men held an American flag over Holmes's grave. Eleanor stood next to Marion; the president, assisted by aides Major General Edwin "Pa" Watson and Marvin McIntyre, walked slowly from the car to the gravesite and stood with his head uncovered. Frankfurter was forever grateful for the president's companionship and hospitality during Holmes's final days. "And I shall always associate his meaning for me *with you*," he wrote Roosevelt, "at the most poignant and triumphant hours of life."

Authorized as Holmes's judicial biographer, Frankfurter never completed the task. In 1938, he published three Harvard lectures on Holmes as a book, *Mr. Justice Holmes and the Supreme Court*, and was proudest of his 1943 *Dictionary of American Biography* entry on the justice. He later designated Holmes's secretary Mark DeWolfe Howe as the justice's official biographer. History, as Frankfurter liked to say, had its claims. In the June 1935 *Harvard Law Review*, he argued that Holmes, through his scholarship and judicial opinions, was "the most influential law teacher in the land" and that "[f]or decades throughout the English-speaking world major legal issues have been discussed . . . in the perspective of Holmes's formulation." What Frankfurter experienced, during their conversations at the House of Truth and 1720 I Street dating back to 1911, was Holmes's "passionate and poetic temperament," "charm and gayety and wit," and "his sparkling talk." He reminisced about those conversations and could see the justice's blue "eyes blaze." He admired Holmes the jurist, the conversationalist, and the intellectual mentor and friend. Only Roosevelt rivaled Holmes for Frankfurter's devotion and affection. His relationship with Brandeis was more complicated, especially given their differences about the New Deal.

———

AS WINTER GAVE WAY to spring 1935, Frankfurter tried to save the NIRA from the Supreme Court. He had been advising the president to delay any constitutional challenges for as long as possible. The law was due to expire on June 16, and Frankfurter wanted to run out the clock. He knew, based on a private conversation with Brandeis, that the Court was poised to strike it down.

THE MOST INFLUENTIAL SINGLE INDIVIDUAL IN THE UNITED STATES 247

The Justice Department, which had been prosecuting companies for violating their industry's fair competition codes, had been declining to appeal adverse decisions for fear of landing in the Supreme Court. Pressure, however, was mounting on the department to test the law's constitutionality in the case of William E. Belcher, an Alabama lumber mill owner charged with violating the wages and hours provisions of the lumber code. A federal judge had dismissed Belcher's indictment and had declared the NIRA unconstitutional for exceeding Congress's power to regulate interstate commerce, depriving Belcher of his property without due process of law, and unlawfully delegating Congress's power to the executive branch. Frankfurter urged the administration to dismiss the *Belcher* appeal to the Supreme Court; Donald Richberg, the National Recovery Administration's director and former general counsel, took the opposite view. In late March, the administration agreed with Frankfurter and dismissed the appeal. Determined to settle the matter before the Court, however, Richberg urged Attorney General Cummings to appeal the case of Brooklyn butchers from the Schechter Poultry Corporation convicted of violating the fair competition code regulating wages, hours, working conditions, slaughtering, and sale of live poultry. On April 4, Corcoran wired the president about Frankfurter's prediction of defeat and opposition to defending the *Schechter Poultry* case. Roosevelt's message to Cummings to delay the appeal never reached the attorney general. Richberg, eager for a showdown at the Supreme Court, got his wish.

Part of the problem was the weakness of Roosevelt's Justice Department. Initially, Cummings had filled it with patronage appointees. Frankfurter tried to mitigate the damage by recommending former students to Justice Department officials. Abe Feller joined Harold Stephens in the antitrust division. Harry Shulman, a former Brandeis clerk teaching at Yale Law School, assisted Stephens in briefing and arguing the Railroad Retirement Act case.

Things began to change in late March 1935 when Reconstruction Finance Corporation (RFC) general counsel Stanley F. Reed replaced J. Crawford Biggs as solicitor general. A balding, hard-working Kentuckian who had argued and won the gold clause cases, Reed agreed with Frankfurter about dismissing the *Belcher* case and delaying any NIRA appeals as long as possible. He relied on Frankfurter for legal advice and recommendations for young lawyers to work in his office. He brought with him Paul Freund, the former Brandeis clerk who had worked with him at RFC on the gold clause briefs. Other former Frankfurter students soon followed.

Liberals and progressives were becoming increasingly frustrated with the New Deal. The NIRA had failed to improve labor standards, and new legislation was stalled in Congress. The purge of left-wingers from the Agricultural Adjustment Administration, including general counsel Jerome Frank, Gardner Jackson, and former Frankfurter student Lee Pressman, cast further doubt on the administration's liberal bona fides. On April 22, Frankfurter relayed a letter from David Niles, the director of Boston's Ford Hall Forum lecture series, about the need to rally liberals and progressive politicians behind pending legislation including the Social Security bill, the National Labor Relations bill, and the Public Utility Holding Company bill. Thanks to Frankfurter and Niles's intervention, the president agreed to host a small, bipartisan group of progressives. From 8:45 p.m. to 12:15 a.m. on May 14, he met with Frankfurter, Niles, Secretary of Agriculture Henry Wallace, Secretary of the Interior Harold Ickes, and Senators Edward P. Costigan of Colorado, Robert M. La Follette, Jr., of Wisconsin, Hiram Johnson of California, George Norris of Nebraska, and Burton K. Wheeler of Montana. Led by La Follette and Wheeler, they called for the president "to assert the leadership that the country is demanding" and to answer the New Deal's opponents—the U.S. Chamber of Commerce, populist Louisiana U.S. senator Huey Long, and anti-Semitic radio preacher Father Charles E. Coughlin—by pushing the labor bill and other reform legislation through Congress. The meeting was a big success and strengthened the administration's ties to La Follette and Wheeler; Niles became an assistant to Harry Hopkins at the new Works Progress Administration and later to Roosevelt. After the meeting broke up, Frankfurter stayed behind as the president's overnight guest. He warned Roosevelt to expect bad news from the Supreme Court in the *Schechter Poultry* case; he blamed the appeal on "bad advice."

At least this time the administration was well represented before the Supreme Court. Freund wrote the *Schechter Poultry* brief while Stanley Reed and Donald Richberg argued the case. Frankfurter predicted to Reed that the "stumbling block" would be whether Congress had delegated its powers to the National Recovery Administration (NRA) with specific enough guidelines. During the May 2 and 3 oral argument, conservatives Sutherland, McReynolds, and Butler pounced on the issue; Reed later confided to Frankfurter that they had "made my life miserable." The Court gave the administration no quarter, with more than the four conservatives jumping into the fray. The already grim outlook became grimmer a few days later when the Court invalidated another piece of legislation. In a 5–4 decision by Owen J. Roberts, the Court struck down the Railroad Retirement Act's pension system because it deprived the railroads of their property without due process. Chief Justice Hughes dissented on behalf of Brandeis, Stone, and Cardozo. Frankfurter was shocked and saddened by the Court's willingness to invoke the Due Process Clause to abridge Congress's power to regulate interstate commerce and by the opinion from the supposedly moderate Roberts. Venting to Brandeis, he reminded him that Joseph Cotton had deemed Roberts "an ingrained conservative" and had predicted that "we'd be fooled by him."

The worst was yet to come. On May 27, 1935, a day known as Black Monday, the Court handed the Roosevelt administration three devastating defeats. First, a unanimous Court ruled in *Schechter Poultry* that the NIRA's live poultry code was "without precedent" as a delegation of congressional power by failing to provide proper guidance to the executive branch. Equally if not more important, the Court declared that Congress had exceeded its power to regulate interstate commerce and had infringed on the power of the states. The Court reasoned that the chickens slaughtered by Brooklyn butchers never left New York and the live poultry code covered only the New York metropolitan area; the effect on interstate commerce, therefore, was only indirect. A concurring opinion by Cardozo and Stone characterized the code as a delegation of congressional power "running riot" and as obliterating "the distinction between what is national and what is local" in purporting to regulate interstate commerce. That same day, the justices handed the administration two other unanimous defeats. In an opinion by Brandeis, the Court invalidated the Frazier-Lemke Farm Bankruptcy Act, which sought to aid debt-ridden farmers by scaling down their mortgages to prevent them from losing their farms. The Court held that the law deprived a Louisville bank of private property without just compensation. And in a decision vindicating Brandeis's dissent ten years earlier about the power of the president to remove administrative officials, Sutherland wrote for the unanimous Court that Roosevelt's firing of FTC commissioner William E. Humphrey violated separation of powers among the three federal branches of government because the commission's functions were "quasi-judicial and quasi-legislative."

After the Court announced its decisions around 2:00 p.m., a "visibly excited and deeply agitated" Brandeis summoned Corcoran and Cohen, who had been sitting in the courtroom in the Old Senate Chamber, to the ante room of the clerk's office. "You have heard our three decisions," he warned. "They change everything. The Court was unanimous." His message to them was specific and direct: "You must phone Felix and have him down in the morning to talk to the President. You must see that Felix understands the situation and explains it to the President. You must also explain it to the men Felix brought into the Government. They must understand that these three decisions change everything. The President has been living in a fool's paradise." Corcoran tried to interrupt about the implications of the Court's limits on Congress's power to regulate interstate commerce on the pending Public Utility Holding Company bill. Brandeis curtly replied he had not read it and insisted all pending legislation would need to be redrafted to comply with the Court's decisions. He cared about only one thing: "Make sure that Felix is here in the morning to advise the President."

———

AFTER WIRING ROOSEVELT, Frankfurter boarded the next day's Federal Express train and arrived at 6:30 p.m. on May 28 for the first of three nights at the White House. He sought to temper Roosevelt's anger with the nine justices and warned him not to turn it into "the Supreme Court vs. The President." He also advised Roosevelt not to listen to liberal legislators who wanted to propose a constitutional amendment to clarify the meaning of the Commerce Clause. Rather, with the public and politicians equally frustrated with the Court, the president should press for pending legislation including the Social Security bill, Public Utility Holding Company bill, National Labor Relations bill, and Guffey Coal bill and dare the Court to strike them down. In the future, he urged Roosevelt and Attorney General Cummings to make sure that the laws were more carefully drafted, the legal battles more carefully chosen, and the Supreme Court briefs and arguments more skillfully done.

In the short run, he prioritized the administration's legislative agenda: legislation inserting fair labor clauses into all government contracts; the continuation of the NRA's administrative operations until the law was revised; the passage of the National Labor Relations bill; and a meeting with state governors to pass laws supplementing the Social Security bill and a revised NRA. Overall, he wanted the president to remove the "false equation" of the NIRA as the New Deal and to make the Social Security bill, the National Labor Relations bill, the Public Utility Holding Company bill, and new tax laws the centerpiece of economic regulation—in short, to embrace what historians have referred to as the Second New Deal.

As much as he valued Frankfurter's legislative advice, Roosevelt could not resist criticizing the Supreme Court. At 11:00 a.m. on May 31, the president held a press conference venting about *Schechter Poultry* and allowed the press to quote him comparing the decision to *Dred Scott* in its ramifications for the country and criticizing the Court's "horse-and-buggy definition of interstate commerce" as thwarting any meaningful federal economic regulation.

Roosevelt's comments about the Court caught Frankfurter completely off guard—at least that's what he told Brandeis.

During the president's press conference, Felix and Marion (who joined him for the third night at the White House) were on their way to Brandeis's California Street apartment for lunch. He assured Brandeis that he did not know that the president's broadside against the Court was coming. And yet, Black Monday revealed ideological differences between the two men. Brandeis was an ideologue and "a Jeffersonian" preaching against bigness (big corporations and big federal programs)—he was not drawn to Roosevelt and did not admire his leadership. Frankfurter, on the other hand, staffed the New Deal with as many talented lawyers as possible and vowed to do whatever worked to aid the nation's economic recovery and his friend in the White House. As much as he admired the justice's carefully crafted opinions, he privately confided to the president he was "heartbroken" over Brandeis's turn against the administration. Frankfurter viewed the Supreme Court as an obstacle to be overcome through better drafting and better advocacy. He valued Roosevelt's legislative acumen and criticized the Court's railroad pension and *Schechter Poultry* decisions because they limited Congress's power to regulate interstate commerce. Unlike Brandeis, Frankfurter looked to Congress for political and economic change and saw the proliferation of expert-run federal agencies and programs as a blessing rather than a curse.

During the summer of 1935, Frankfurter was determined to make pending New Deal legislation a reality. He had no teaching responsibilities and visited the White House with more frequency than at any other time during Roosevelt's presidency. From June 1 to September 1, incomplete White House logs show that he spent at least nineteen nights and visited every week, sometimes twice. He joined Roosevelt's inner circle—breakfast in his study, social outings with his secretaries/confidants Missy LeHand and Grace Tully, and informal dinners with Eleanor when she was in town. Frankfurter also dined with many former students and friends. The main purpose was business, not personal. The stakes, for the New Deal and for Roosevelt's presidency, were high.

For Marion, the windmill was spinning too fast. Felix was so wrapped up in New Deal politics, she wrote Isaiah Berlin, she felt "almost as out of it as if he had fallen in love with another woman." She was disappointed that they had to postpone a summer trip to Oxford to see Berlin, Maurice Bowra, and other British friends. With Felix so preoccupied, she opted for a cross-country train ride to see her mother, father, and brother in Northern California, Portland, and Seattle. "Well," she wrote her husband, "next year in Jerusalem."

During his weekly White House visits, Frankfurter preferred to keep under the press's radar. His enemies were not fooled. The *Washington Herald* reported on Frankfurter's overnight stays, described him as "conferring nightly" with the president, and as having supplanted Moley and Richberg as Roosevelt's key adviser. Critics began to blame Frankfurter for the New Deal's failure to end the Great Depression.

All summer long, Frankfurter returned to the White House to help the president get his legislation through Congress. In early June, he met with Cummings and Reed about how to draft and defend a revised NIRA and worked with Treasury Department officials in drafting new tax laws. He believed Roosevelt was "showing obstinate courage" in standing behind the Public Utility Holding Company bill. Drafted by Cohen and Corcoran, the bill allowed the Federal Power Commission and the SEC to regulate public utilities, to make them more geographically compact by breaking them up, and to force holding companies to divest themselves of public utilities within five years in what became known as the "death sentence" provision. As with its opposition to the securities bills, big business pulled out all the stops. Representative Owen Brewster of Maine accused Corcoran of threatening to withhold a dam project in his district if he did not vote for the death sentence provision; Frankfurter was so incensed about the accusation he wanted to testify about Brewster's bad moral character; Corcoran denied the charges and cleared his name. Brewster's accusations backfired. Corcoran became an integral member of Roosevelt's inner circle, and Cohen was regarded as the administration's most accomplished draftsman. The president nicknamed Corcoran "Tommy the Cork"; the press referred to Corcoran and Cohen as "the Gold Dust Twins." Frankfurter's admiration for them ran deep; he made sure that the president told them why he was not nominating them for administrative posts, such as the open SEC commissionership for Cohen; they were more valuable working for Roosevelt. Corcoran, Cohen, and Wyzanski reinforced Frankfurter's belief in the need for first-rate lawyers in the federal government. Frankfurter marveled at Corcoran's legislative "stratagems and devices" as they engaged in "real fighting here" to maintain the death sentence provision in the Public Utility Holding Company bill.

In August, Frankfurter and his young charges guided the legislation through its final stages. Frankfurter learned how lawmaking worked in ways he never had in the Theodore Roosevelt, Taft, or Wilson administrations. The president began referring to him as "John" for John W. Davis because he repeatedly urged a "'conservative' compromise" to make the legislation constitutional. The public utility bill's lead sponsor in the House, Sam Rayburn, nicknamed him "Cardinal" after Vice President Garner remarked that Frankfurter reminded him of Cardinal Gibbons and French prime minister René Viviani because they were "alive all the time & don't miss a thing of what's goin' on around them." Frankfurter worked closely with Rayburn, Garner, and Senate Majority Leader Joseph Robinson. All their hard work paid off; Congress passed one piece of legislation after another. Roosevelt signed the National Labor Relations Act on July 5, the Social Security Act on August 14, the Banking Act of 1935 on August 23, the Public Utility Holding Company Act on August 25, and the Guffey Coal Act on August 30. The president, Felix wrote Marion, "got almost everything that he asked for."

Before he left the White House on September 1 after nearly three months of work, Roosevelt firmly clasped his hand and looked him in the eyes and said: "I'll see you soon in Hyde Park."

———————

WITH HIS WIFE visiting family on the West Coast on Labor Day weekend, Frankfurter took a train from Washington, D.C., to Providence where he was picked up by Joseph Kennedy's chauffeur and taken to the family's oceanfront compound in Hyannis Port on Cape Cod. He greeted Joe Sr., who was stepping down as SEC chair in favor of James Landis; Kennedy's wife, Rose; and seven of their eight children. Frankfurter enjoyed seeing 21-year-old Joe Jr., who asked about Marion, having met them in Oxford while Joe Jr. studied with Harold Laski at the London School of Economics. He met 18-year-old Jack, who was off to study with Laski "on the theory that he is something that cleans the teeth; parts the hair in the middle, etc., etc." Rose was worried about keeping Jack, whom Frankfurter described as "a sceptical spirit," "inside the church!!" Frankfurter was amused to be considered the Kennedy family's "great educational director" by recommending that Joe Jr. and Jack study with Laski; he marveled at how well the children had turned out given the enormous ego of their father and their dizzying array of trivial activities including sailing, tennis, football, driving fancy cars, and watching preview copies of the latest Hollywood movies.

There was a stark contrast between the Kennedy compound with its whirl of social activities and Frankfurter's next destination on Cape Cod, the austere Chatham cottage of Justice Brandeis, a place Frankfurter described as "almost squalid." During his two days there, he ate the notoriously awful food of the justice's wife, Alice, and visited with the justice's grown daughters, Susan and Elizabeth, and Elizabeth's son Walter. At his cottage, Brandeis was more relaxed than he had been when he had corralled Corcoran and Cohen in the ante room of the clerk's office after Black Monday. According to Elizabeth, her father had "resigned himself to his dissatisfaction with the way the world is going & consciously decided not to wear himself out" and had vowed to stop haranguing people. It remained to be seen whether, in deciding cases, Brandeis would be more charitable toward the New Deal.

After a brief stop in Cambridge, Frankfurter returned to Hyde Park. He was there to finish work he had started at the end of the summer, drafting speeches with Raymond Moley for the president's upcoming trip to western states. At Roosevelt's urging, Frankfurter preemptively attacked opponents of the new legislation and Wall Street lawyers most likely to challenge its constitutionality. In "The Liberty League Supreme Court," an unsigned editorial for the September issue of Moley's *Today* magazine, he denounced leaders of the bar retained by big business to oppose the legislation—former solicitors general James M. Beck and John W. Davis, former Massachusetts governor Joseph Ely who had nominated Frankfurter in 1932 to the state Supreme Judicial Court, former Al Smith aide Joseph M. Proskauer, Stimson's law partner George Roberts, and former attorney general George W. Wickersham. He mocked them for declaring the National Labor Relations Act unconstitutional and predicted that "the heavily financed lawyers of one side of a law suit will be laughed out of the ultimate court of America, the court of public opinion."

Frankfurter's political rivals scapegoated him for the administration's past legal failures. After the *Schechter Poultry* defeat in May, Donald Richberg informed *New York Times* columnist Arthur Krock that Frankfurter had advocated dismissing the lumber case in favor of the poultry one. In fact, however, Frankfurter, backed by Reed, had advised the administration not to press either case and counseled a strategy of delay until the law expired. Richberg was not the only one blaming Frankfurter for NIRA's demise.

Former NRA director Hugh S. Johnson seized on the "Happy Hot Dogs" theme and portrayed Frankfurter in the *Saturday Evening Post* as the man behind the throne: "The professor himself has refused every official connection. His comings and goings are almost surreptitious. Yet he is *the most influential single individual in the United States*." It was not a compliment. Nor was the Happy Hot Dogs a harmless play on his first and last name. In Johnson's view, Frankfurter's "'boys' have been insinuated into obscure but key positions in every vital department—wardens of the marches, inconspicuous but powerful." He argued that they promulgated their anti-business views in almost every agency and blamed "the Hot Dog Pressure Group" for the administration's response to Black Monday, which "diverted the New Deal, weakened party organization and conceived the Horse and Buggy comment after the Schechter case." He called for a return to the failed economic policies of "the original New Deal," including "sound money and [a] balanced budget." The article contained anti-Semitic undertones in describing Frankfurter's protégés as "infest[ing]" departments and agencies and by comparing them to a battalion that needed to be recalled for "delousing."

Frankfurter's friends wondered what he had done to alienate General Johnson. He explained that in 1933 he had advised Johnson during the passage of the NIRA and had declined his offer to be the agency's general counsel. An erratic, heavy drinker and autocrat, he had gone from *Time* magazine's "man of the year" in January 1934 to getting fired by Roosevelt nine months later and had revealed private conversations with Brandeis about administration policy. Frankfurter was somewhat shocked by Johnson's ill will. After the *Schechter Poultry* decision, they had talked pleasantly at the White House, and Johnson had apologized for his comments about Brandeis. At a meeting that same day with the president, Johnson proposed quickly drafting a new NIRA law; Frankfurter preferred a longer-term approach run by the Justice Department but agreed to review Johnson's draft. Frankfurter denied to his friends, as he had to Brandeis, any knowledge of Roosevelt's intent to hold a post-*Schechter* press conference attacking the Court and had recommended the opposite strategy. In light of the president's comments that suggestions for a new NIRA law would be handled by the attorney general and solicitor general, Frankfurter had advised Johnson during a May 31 phone call that a bill drafted by the agency's former director would be unwise. They never spoke again. Johnson's anger, though misdirected, was not surprising. He had turned against the New Deal and resented Frankfurter and his protégés. It was not the last time one of the New Deal's fallen stars used Frankfurter as a scapegoat.

Several months later, Frankfurter responded to Johnson and others with assistance from former student Archibald MacLeish. A close friend of Dean Acheson's from Yale College and Harvard Law School, MacLeish graduated in 1919 after wartime military service and finished tied for first in his law school class. Bored by Boston law practice and having declined an offer to join the Harvard law faculty, he moved his family to Paris in 1923 to write poetry. In Paris, he befriended American expatriates Ernest Hemingway, John Dos Passos, F. Scott Fitzgerald, and Gertrude Stein. In 1928, MacLeish returned to America to work for *Fortune* magazine, joined anti-Fascist political causes, and continued to write poetry. He won the Pulitzer Prize five years later for his long poem *Conquistador* yet made a living editing and writing for *Fortune*.

As a *Fortune* editor, he facilitated the publication of Frankfurter's defense of his network of young lawyers.

Published in *Fortune*'s January 1936 issue, "The Young Men Go to Washington" reviewed the charges against Frankfurter as "the most influential single individual in the United States," "this silent man," and "the IAGO of this Administration." "The actual facts of the matter," Frankfurter and MacLeish asserted in the unsigned article, "are in no way mysterious." Since he joined Stimson in the U.S. attorney's office in 1906, Frankfurter had been recruiting talented lawyers for the federal government. And, since he joined the Harvard law faculty in 1914, he had been recommending students for jobs at leading New York, Boston, and Washington firms; in the federal government; and as clerks for Holmes, Brandeis, and other federal judges. The article acknowledged that Frankfurter's friends and former students had become prominent New Dealers and that Frankfurter assisted with the Securities Acts of 1933 and 1934 and the Public Utility Holding Company Act. Yet it rejected Johnson's charges of undue influence: "No one knows, perhaps not even the President himself and certainly not General Johnson, whether Mr. Frankfurter has more influence with Mr. Roosevelt than Mr. Roosevelt's other advisers." It mocked Johnson's boast that Frankfurter had nothing to do with the NIRA, observing that the law had been the New Deal's biggest failure. And it concluded by responding to Johnson's charge that Frankfurter had "packed the Administration with his 'boys'" by explaining he "has done little more to place intelligent lawyers in contemporary Washington than he has been doing for the past twenty-five years."

Wall Street critics responded to the article by charging that MacLeish had "whitewashed" Frankfurter and ignored the "well known fact" that he had been spending two nights a week at the White House. A panicky MacLeish requested the real story from Frankfurter. By phone, Frankfurter was not candid with his former student: two or three White House and Hyde Park visits before Oxford; a Hyde Park visit in August 1934 and two or three in the summer of 1935; "a few weeks stay" at the White House during the summer, and a single two-and-a-half-hour visit since September 1935. Frankfurter underplayed his weekly visits during the summer of 1935 to push through the Public Utility Holding Company Act and other pending legislation. Not surprisingly, he refused to allow MacLeish to quote him.

The negative publicity from Johnson's article, lingering questions about "The Young Men Go to Washington," and teaching duties at Harvard Law School kept Frankfurter's White House visits to a minimum. If he did go, he rarely showed up in visitor logs. Instead, he mostly contributed to the administration from afar. In the summer of 1935, Roosevelt had acknowledged that his administration needed reorganization. Frankfurter responded by recruiting the best lawyers and placing them in the federal government.

=====

WITH MORE SUPREME COURT CHALLENGES looming, Frankfurter recommended several former students to join Stanley Reed in the solicitor general's office: Alger Hiss, a former counsel in the Department of Agriculture, joined the office in July 1935 to aid the defense of the Agricultural Adjustment Act (AAA); Charles Horsky, the 1934 *Harvard Law Review* president, was hired after his clerkship with Augustus Hand; Charles Wyzanski, the Department of Labor solicitor, came aboard in December after months of lobbying by Frankfurter. With Freund, Hiss, Horsky, Wyzanski, and Columbia law graduate Warner Gardner in the office, Solicitor General Reed relied on a strong cohort of young stars to counter the older, patronage appointees. After Black Monday, the solicitor general needed all the help he could get.

More than a source of personnel, Frankfurter provided Reed with much-needed advice and a critical eye on Supreme Court briefs and arguments. Frankfurter read Hiss's brief in *United States v. Butler,* a defense of the Agricultural Adjustment Act's taxes on cotton and other commodities so the government could pay farmers to reduce their acreage in an effort to prevent the market from collapsing. Frankfurter declared Hiss's brief "a superb performance" and advised Reed to stick to Marshall's and Holmes's broad conception of federal power and not to get too creative at oral argument. "The Court seems to me to be in one of those grips of belief in its saviourship of the nation which wrought such havoc . . . in the Dred Scott case and later in the Income Tax Cases." On December 9 and 10, Reed defended the AAA and Congress's power to levy taxes to regulate the cotton market. The solicitor general was so exhausted from overwork that, while arguing a subsequent case, he fainted. The arguments took place in the Court's new building across the street from the U.S. Capitol in a cavernous courtroom with notoriously poor acoustics. What mattered more was that the nine justices were the same as on Black Monday. On January 6, 1936, the Court, in a 6–3 decision in *Butler,* invalidated the AAA. In his majority opinion, Owen J. Roberts acknowledged Congress's broad taxing and spending powers yet concluded the tax was merely incidental to regulating agricultural production, a "purely local activity" reserved to the power of the states. Stone dissented, joined by Brandeis and Cardozo, that Congress had not exceeded its taxing and spending powers and that the "wisdom" of such legislation was up to the elected branches, not the Court. Four days after the decision, Frankfurter tried to buoy Reed's spirits by recalling what Holmes had told him after he lost the 1923 District of Columbia minimum-wage case in *Adkins v. Children's Hospital*—"that Jesus Christ, John Marshall and Daniel Webster could not have changed the result."

Once again, the Court had proven itself in *Butler* to be the biggest obstacle to the New Deal. Frankfurter's Harvard law colleagues Thomas Reed Powell and Henry Hart were furious with the Court and with Roberts in particular. Frankfurter, however, held his tongue, at least publicly. At the president's request, Frankfurter arrived at the White House at 4:30 p.m. on Sunday, January 12, and for two and a half hours discussed how to respond. Five days later, Frankfurter enclosed a draft message to Congress proposing new agricultural legislation conforming to the Court's decisions. It was not all bad news. On February 17, the Court upheld the constitutionality of the Tennessee Valley Authority. Brandeis wrote an influential concurring opinion in *Ashwander v. Tennessee Valley Authority* arguing that the petitioner had not suffered any injury, there was no real dispute between the parties, and therefore the Court should never have heard the case in the first instance. He invoked numerous cases to remind his colleagues about the Court's "series of rules" for avoiding unnecessary constitutional questions.

Brandeis privately warned Frankfurter that the Court had no intention of following its rules about avoiding constitutional questions. In late April, Frankfurter spent the afternoon with Brandeis, Stone, and Cardozo, who alerted him to more trouble. The Court, Brandeis said, "has lost its head & has allowed the Liberty League to drag us into politics." They blamed Chief Justice Hughes. Brandeis said his "judgment [had been] warped by fear of criticism & . . . about threats to property"; Stone had "no respect for Hughes' intellect & not much for his moral character." Cardozo repeated Brandeis's initial warning: "The Court has lost its head" and privately told him something even more disturbing. "I wish I were back in Albany—" the former New York Court of Appeals chief judge said. "We here have really ceased to be a Court."

After it upheld the Tennessee Valley Authority, the Court resumed striking down New Deal programs, this time the Bituminous Coal Conservation Act of 1935. The Guffey Coal Act, as the law was known, replaced the NIRA with a new fair competition code for the coal industry, regulating prices, minimum wages, maximum hours, and the right to unionize. Coal companies were induced to comply by receiving a nearly total refund of a 15 percent tax on all coal produced. The president and shareholder of a Virginia and West Virginia coal company did not want to join the program and challenged the law's constitutionality. In a 6–3 decision on May 18 in *Carter v. Carter Coal*, Sutherland declared that the law exceeded Congress's power to regulate interstate commerce because manufacturing or production, such as coal mining, was a "purely local activity." Cardozo's dissent, which Stone and Brandeis joined, argued that the commerce power was broad enough to permit Congress to regulate the coal industry.

Two days after the decision, Frankfurter returned to Washington. He spent hours with a "very fit" Brandeis, spoke with Secretary of the Interior Ickes, ate lunch with Senator Wheeler, and attended a senatorial reception and a late-night legislative strategy session at the White House with Senators Wagner, Norris, Wheeler, La Follette, Jr., Lewis B. Schwellenbach of Washington, Henrik Shipstead of Minnesota, and Sherman Minton of Indiana.

The Court was not finished. In a 5–4 decision on June 1 in *Morehead v. Tipaldo*, it declared a New York minimum-wage law violated the liberty provision of the Due Process Clause. After arguing and losing *Adkins v. Children's Hospital* about the D.C. minimum-wage law for women, Frankfurter had drafted, with Benjamin Cohen's assistance, a model minimum-wage bill. Rather than fix a minimum wage for women across all industries like in the D.C. law, the model bill established an industrial commission to set minimum wages for women after an investigation of the industry in question. The New York minimum-wage law, with an industrial commission establishing different minimum wages for women in each industry, was based on Frankfurter and Cohen's model bill. Hughes's dissent differentiated between the two laws. Stone's dissent went even further: He argued that *Adkins* had been overruled by the Court's 1934 decision in *Nebbia v. New York* establishing minimum milk prices, and he accused the majority of invoking "freedom of contract" to make economic policy. In a sense, *Morehead v. Tipaldo* was a double defeat for Frankfurter; it not only invalidated the New York law but also revived *Adkins* and freedom of contract. Three days after the Court's decision, Frankfurter returned to the White House to join Roosevelt for a two-and-a-half-hour private lunch. It was time for the president to respond to the Court the best way he knew how—by appealing directly to the American people during his 1936 reelection campaign.

———

DISSATISFIED WITH the Democratic Party platform written by Senator Wagner and his aide Simon Rifkind, Frankfurter drafted his own. He wanted a "call to arms," an outline of Roosevelt's political philosophy, and criticism of the Court's latest decisions without making it the centerpiece of the campaign. Roosevelt carefully read and marked up Frankfurter's draft. At the end, Frankfurter committed the Democratic Party to "principles of constitutional government under our Federal System." He rejected the idea, as suggested by *Carter Coal* and *Morehead v. Tipaldo*, that there could be a regulatory "No Man's Land where no government," federal or state, "can safeguard either liberty or property or protect the weak against exploitation and legitimate businesses against unfair competition." He concluded by quoting Lincoln's 1860 Republican Party platform about *Dred Scott* and rejecting " 'the new dogma' " that the Constitution forbids the federal government and the states from dealing with the nation's economic problems as "a dangerous political heresy." Despite the lofty rhetoric, he did not want the campaign to be Roosevelt versus the Supreme Court, a showdown that could wait until after the election.

In July 1936, Roosevelt accepted the Democratic Party's nomination in Philadelphia. "This generation of Americans has a rendezvous with destiny," he said in his acceptance speech, using a phrase coined by Corcoran. Frankfurter read about the speech in the British press. He and Marion were at last taking their long-delayed trip to London and Oxford.

That fall, the election arrived at the Frankfurters' front door at Harvard. On September 18, they braved rainy weather and sat in the Sanders Theatre to hear Roosevelt's Harvard Tercentenary address. It was the culmination of a months-long battle with Frankfurter's arch-nemesis, retired Harvard president A. Lawrence Lowell. Charged with arranging the school's Tercentenary celebration, Lowell asked Roosevelt to speak but only under certain conditions: The president was required to choose "something connected to Harvard," avoid anything resembling a political speech, and limit himself to ten minutes. Roosevelt showed Lowell's letter to Frankfurter along with a proposed reply that questioned whether he had been invited to speak as a Harvard graduate or as the president of the United States. If it were the latter, he could not limit himself to a subject matter or specific time.

Given his past history with Lowell, Frankfurter was outraged. Since 1916, he had fought Lowell over Brandeis's nomination, a proposed 15 percent quota on Jewish undergraduates, the one-sided report to the Massachusetts governor on the Sacco-Vanzetti case, and the veto of Nathan Margold and other appointments to the Harvard law faculty. Aside from a few defenses of academic freedom, Lowell had encouraged anti-Semitism and intolerance at Harvard. Even in retirement, he was carrying water for Old Boston. On February 26, Frankfurter had wired Roosevelt requesting to see the whole file including President James Conant's initial invitation to "Mr. Roosevelt." He thought Roosevelt should teach Lowell "a lesson in manners," yet vowed to "try to get cool" before making a "calm judgment" about a response. After reviewing the file, Frankfurter drafted a brief reply from Roosevelt to Lowell ignoring "the impertinent inquiries and implied rebuke" and accepting the invitation not as an alumnus but as president of the United States. Roosevelt sent the letter as Frankfurter suggested. In his reply, Lowell agreed that he was invited as president of the United States and again tried to limit him to ten to fifteen minutes. About to lose his "temper completely," Roosevelt asked Frankfurter what to do. Acting on Frankfurter's advice, Roosevelt curtly replied that he would speak about the significance of Harvard and ignored the time limit. Frankfurter was already disappointed with Harvard's decision to send a representative to the University of Heidelberg's 550th anniversary celebration despite the school's Nazi-led purge of Jewish scholars. He drafted a preliminary Tercentenary address about the president's love of Harvard, free academic inquiry, and America.

Before Roosevelt could deliver his speech, Frankfurter's ex-friend Walter Lippmann struck first. Lippmann had revealed his true colors in his quiet support for Lowell's 15 percent quota on Jewish undergraduates, tepid editorials about Sacco and Vanzetti, and anti-Roosevelt and Nazi-appeasing columns. For his loyalty to Lowell, Conant, and the conservative establishment, he had been elected in 1933 to Harvard's Board of Overseers. In preparation for the Tercentenary celebration, Lippmann wrote an article in June 1936 arguing that "members of university faculties have a particular obligation not to tie themselves to, nor involve themselves in, the ambitions and purposes of the politicians, the parties and the movements which are contending for power." Learned Hand showed the article to Frankfurter and was certain that the Harvard law professor and Roosevelt adviser was Lippmann's intended target. Frankfurter no longer took seriously the columnist he mocked as "Sir Oracle"; others abandoned Lippmann after he had an affair with and married the wife of his close friend, *Foreign Affairs* editor Hamilton Fish Armstrong.

At the Tercentenary celebration, Roosevelt kept his speech short, thanked everyone except Lowell, and twitted the Boston Brahmins and their staid Republicanism. He reminded them how on Harvard's 200th anniversary its alumni fretted over the presidency of Andrew Jackson, on its 250th anniversary they wrung their hands over the election of Grover Cleveland. "Now, on the three hundredth anniversary," Roosevelt remarked, "I am President." Felix, Marion, and Harvard alumnus C. C. Burlingham "celebrated" the president's "wise sauciness"; Frankfurter told the president it was a "great triumph."

Roosevelt radiated confidence about his reelection bid even though some polls showed him losing. On September 26, the president delivered his first major campaign speech against the Republican nominee, Governor Alf Landon of Kansas, and traveled the country speaking to massive crowds. Frankfurter believed that Landon was the same "tool of the interests" as Taft, Harding, Coolidge, and Hoover. Inside information from *Emporia Gazette* editor William Allen White confirmed his suspicions. "The most powerful forces behind him," Frankfurter wrote Roosevelt, "are those of laissez-faire, of xenophobia, of spiritual standpatism." With the president's permission, Frankfurter praised *New York Times* publisher Arthur Hays Sulzberger for the newspaper's editorial endorsing Roosevelt's reelection—not as a Democrat or a Republican but as "an old-fashioned mugwump" wedded to neither party. The election, Frankfurter wrote Sulzberger, was "the conflict between democracy and authoritarianism." At the end of the campaign, he wrote the president: "you have fought your fight—and ours—and the Nation will crown it with victory." On Election Day, Roosevelt crushed Landon, winning 523 electoral votes to eight, forty-six states to two, and nearly 61 percent of the popular vote.

With an overwhelming electoral mandate and majorities in both houses of Congress, Roosevelt and his advisers turned to the Supreme Court and its reactionary, anti–New Deal decisions. Solicitor General Stanley Reed instructed Ben Cohen to attempt to draft possible constitutional amendments. On December 10, 1936, Cohen spent the day with Frankfurter at Harvard Law School "canvassing the possibilities, and the problems they raise, should there be the need for constitutional reform." In Frankfurter's view, there was nothing wrong with the Constitution; there was no need for a constitutional amendment; there was something wrong with the Court, specifically the justices imposing their personal political views on the nation. Frankfurter pointed out possible loopholes in Cohen's draft amendments about Congress's taxing and spending power, Congress's power to regulate interstate commerce, and the scope of the Due Process Clauses. On January 6, 1937, Cohen informed Frankfurter that the draft amendments had been put on hold until after the president's annual message to Congress. Roosevelt, unbeknownst to them, had already decided on another course of action.

Before Christmas, Frankfurter sent Roosevelt a copy of his forthcoming book, *The Commerce Clause Under Marshall, Taney, and Waite,* lectures the professor had given in April 1936 at the University of North Carolina and published after "indispensable collaboration" with graduate student Willard Hurst. Frankfurter pointed Roosevelt to the quotation of James Bradley Thayer about the dangers of "petty judicial interpretations" to the country. He inscribed the president's copy of the book: "To F.D.R., who is a better friend of the Supreme Court than its present majority. FF. Christmas 1936."

Roosevelt's next move triggered one of the biggest constitutional crises in the nation's history. This time, he tried to shield Frankfurter from the wind.

CHAPTER 18

An Awful Shock

On a cold and rainy morning on January 20, 1937, Felix and Marion Frankfurter gathered with other dignitaries at the White House before Roosevelt's second inauguration. Shivering and "drenched inside," Felix was not dressed appropriately for the pouring rain and near-freezing temperatures. The president's valet, Irvin "Mac" McDuffie, heard about his predicament, summoned Frankfurter upstairs to the living quarters, and found him some warm clothes in Roosevelt's closet. Frankfurter questioned whether they were overstepping their bounds; McDuffie insisted that the president "will be tickled when he hears what I've done." Wearing the president's clothes, Felix joined his wife at the U.S. Capitol to see Chief Justice Charles Evans Hughes swear in Roosevelt for a second term and to listen to the president's speech.

In his second inaugural address, Roosevelt reviewed the country's history as a democracy, reminded people that it was the 150th anniversary of the U.S. Constitution, and reflected on his past four years in office: "The essential democracy of our nation and the safety of our people depend not upon the absence of power, but upon lodging it with those whom the people can change or continue at stated intervals through an honest and free system of elections. The Constitution of 1787 did not make our democracy impotent." He reminded the nation how far it had come since March 1933 and how far it had to go with "one-third of a nation ill-housed, ill-clad, ill-nourished." He vowed to use the constitutional power of the federal government to make people's lives better yet gave them no clue about how he planned to do it.

Six days before the inauguration, Roosevelt had warned Frankfurter: "Very confidentially, I may give you an awful shock in about two weeks. Even if you do not agree, suspend final judgment, and I will tell you the story." A few days later, Frankfurter replied: "Are you trying to find out how well I can sit on top of a Vesuvius by giving me notice that 'an awful shock' is in store for me 'in about two weeks'? Well, I shall try to hold my patience and fortify my capacity to withstand 'an awful shock,' but you certainly tease my curiosity when you threaten me with something with which I may not agree. That, certainly, would be a great surprise."

The president's February 5 announcement did, indeed, come as "an awful shock" and "a great surprise" to Frankfurter and many administration insiders. Without consulting legislators from his own party, his legal team of Corcoran and Cohen, or Frankfurter himself, the president proposed a bill that would increase the number of Supreme Court justices from nine to fifteen. Since shortly after the election, Attorney General Cummings, Solicitor General Reed, and a few Justice Department officials had been working on the proposal. In late January, former NRA director Donald Richberg and speechwriter Sam Rosenman had helped to polish it. Roosevelt delighted in revealing the bill like a magician pulling a rabbit out of a hat, first to the cabinet and select members of Congress, then to the press. The brainchild of the attorney general, the bill was based on the disingenuous claim that federal judges at all levels—trial courts, courts of appeals, and the Supreme Court—were behind on their work. The Judicial Procedures Reform Bill of 1937 proposed to add a new federal judge for every one older than seventy years, six months. From the outset, however, the administration's chief target was the Supreme Court. With six members (including four conservatives) over seventy years old, the bill proposed to increase the number of the justices from nine up to a maximum of fifteen (depending on how many justices over seventy years old chose to retire). As a result, the press began referring to it as the president's "court-packing plan."

After several days of outcry from the press and members of Congress and after gathering information from Corcoran and Cohen in Washington, Frankfurter wrote the president. The first paragraph he dashed off in minutes: "And now you have blown me off the top of Vesuvius where you sat me some weeks ago. Yes, you 'shocked' me by the deftness of the general scheme for dealing with the mandate for national action which you received three times, in '32 and '34 and '36, and each time with increasing emphasis. You 'shocked' me no less by the dramatic, untarnished secrecy with which you kept your scheme until you took the whole nation into your confidence. Dramatically and artistically you did 'shock' me." Yet Frankfurter was not shocked about the need for judicial reform. For several years, he recognized "that means had to be found to save the Constitution from the Court, and the Court from itself." The second paragraph about the merits of the court-packing plan took Frankfurter more than an hour to write. He acknowledged that "it was clear some major operation was necessary" and any proposal of judicial reform involved "some shock." And he reiterated his "deep faith in your instinct to make the wise choice."

The letter, however, stopped short of endorsing the plan—for good reason. For several years, Frankfurter had been opposed to court packing. "There is no magic in the number nine," he wrote in a 1934 entry on the Supreme Court in the *Encyclopedia of the Social Sciences*, "but there are limits to effective judicial action. . . . Experience is conclusive that to enlarge the size of the Supreme Court would be self-defeating." After the Court's decisions on Black Monday in 1935, Frankfurter rejected calls for court packing by philosopher Morris Raphael Cohen and others.

Sensing Frankfurter's reluctance to endorse the proposal, Roosevelt appreciated the diplomatic yet loyal response: "I am awfully glad to have your Sunday letter and to know that although shocked you have survived; but most important of all that you understand the causes and the motives." The president explained his "process of elimination." A constitutional amendment, he predicted, would have no greater than a 50 percent chance of receiving a two-thirds vote in the House and Senate in 1937 and even less in 1938 when the Democrats inevitably lost seats in midterm congressional elections. It also required ratification by three-fourths of the states, a process he estimated would take until after the 1940 election. "It is my honest belief," he wrote Frankfurter, "that the Nation cannot wait until 1941 or 1942 to obtain effective social and economic national legislation . . ." He ruled out other proposals, a mandatory retirement age or a 7–2 vote for overruling federal laws, as "unconstitutional per se." Roosevelt concluded his letter with a plea: "Do you want to help me?" He needed assistance selling the proposal to the American people and asked for a memorandum to assist him with a fireside chat. Despite his personal opposition to court packing, Frankfurter believed that the chat presented an opportunity to tackle the "very difficult problem in public education" about how the Court had abused its power. He promised, after a few days of reflection and a discussion with Corcoran, a memorandum outlining a bill of particulars against the Court.

During a follow-up phone call with the president, Roosevelt reiterated to Frankfurter that he wanted to put him on the Supreme Court one day, understood his opposition to court packing, yet advised him not to speak out. He asked Frankfurter for public silence and private assistance—an "oath of silence and public neutrality." Out of loyalty to Roosevelt and disgust with the

Court's decisions, Frankfurter agreed. He declined all public comment and worked behind the scenes to help the president.

His vow of public silence did not mean he was a recluse. Friends flocked to his home to hear his views. His wife, Marion, was in California helping with her ailing father, leaving her husband free to discuss court packing day and night. Raymond B. Stevens, the chairman of the Federal Tariff Commission, visited from New Hampshire; his Harvard law colleague Henry Hart and former student and RFC attorney Harold Rosenwald came to lunch. All three initially opposed the proposal yet after discussing the underlying issues agreed with Frankfurter that the Court had brought this on itself and that something had to be done. Another night, Frankfurter, Harvard law colleague Thomas Reed Powell, and *Boston Globe* editor Larry Winship debated former Sacco-Vanzetti lawyer Arthur Dehon Hill and Choate, Hall lawyer Robert Proctor at the home of Filene's chairman, Louis Kirstein. "Damn this Court business—," he wrote Marion, "it leaves me no peace."

Several friends pressed him to speak out against the court bill and balked at his reasons for not doing so. Grenville Clark and C. C. Burlingham, two leading members of the New York bar and longtime friends of the president, were opposed to the plan on principle and outraged by Frankfurter's silence. He claimed that any public statement involved strongly criticizing the Court and individual justices and would have no impact on the debate about the president's preferred remedy. He objected to Clark's insinuation that speaking out would "strengthen" his " 'influence in the future.' " He deemed such political considerations irrelevant since his rejection of Roosevelt's offer to be solicitor general. Finally, he reminded Clark that he had made no public statements about any pending piece of New Deal legislation because anything he said became fodder for the administration's enemies: "I have become a myth, a symbol and promoter not of reason but of passion. I am the symbol of the Jew, the 'red,' the 'alien.' . . . Instead of bringing light and calm and reason, what I would be compelled to say about the work of the Court—and it is the only subject in this debate on which I can speak with a scholar's authority—would only fan the flames of ignorance, of misrepresentation, and of passion." He respected the Court too much as an institution to go on a speaking tour about the majority's "lawless, arbitrary, unconstitutional, non-impartial, non-independent behavior" in 1935 and 1936. And he saw no need for constitutional amendments if the Court "lived up to the Marshall-Thayer-Holmes conception of the Constitution." His explanations to Clark and Burlingham and a private, off-the-record conversation with a group of New York lawyers did not satisfy his friends' insistence that he take a stand.

Frankfurter's friends had an ally in his wife, Marion. She was opposed to the "cheap and dishonest" bill and to her husband's vow of silence. "I know all the arguments against your making a public statement," Marion wrote, "but why must you martyrize yourself . . . ?" He assured her, however, that he was at perfect peace. There was no subject he knew more about than the Supreme Court's invalidation of economic legislation by invoking the Due Process Clause or an unduly narrow reading of Congress's power to regulate commerce, tax, and spend. He explained that Holmes had been railing against the practice for thirty years, and for the past fifteen years the justices "have been more & more inaccessible to Reason. And so it could be as justly said that this was a [way] of unpacking the Court as packing it." He confided to Marion what he undoubtedly made clear on the phone to Roosevelt: "I should have advised strongly against the proposal." Yet he defended it and blamed the justices: "My bottom feeling is resentment against Roberts & Hughes & some of the others that they should so needlessly have brought this on." He relished the opportunity to educate the public about how the justices purported to interpret the Constitution yet in reality allowed their personal prejudices against Roosevelt and the New Deal to guide their decisions. He kept thinking about Cardozo's comment in the spring of 1936 that "We here have really ceased to be a Court." FDR's court-packing plan reminded him of TR's proposal twenty-five years earlier of popular recall of state judicial decisions in an effort to put the "fear of God" in the justices. He did not expect anything to come of the latest gambit other than to get the Court in line with the two elected branches and public opinion. He certainly did not expect the plan to yield six more justices.

His conscience clear about staying silent while helping the president defend the court bill, Frankfurter wrote Roosevelt on February 18 enclosing a memorandum detailing two decades of judicial overreach. He believed that the president needed to educate the American people about "the real function of the Supreme Court" and quoted Theodore Roosevelt about how judges had become legislators. In his memorandum, Frankfurter charged the Court "has distorted the power of judicial review into a revision of legislative policy" and usurped the power of Congress and the states. He quoted numerous opinions, beginning with Taft's 1923 dissent in *Adkins v. Children's Hospital* invalidating the District of Columbia minimum-wage law, objecting to the Court imposing its own economic views and acting like a super-legislature. In recent years, he argued, the problem had become more acute; the Court had repeatedly rejected the Roosevelt administration's efforts to extricate the country from the Great Depression by narrowly interpreting Congress's power to regulate interstate commerce. And he identified the "climax," the Court's 1936 decision invalidating New York's minimum-wage law in *Morehead v. Tipaldo,* in which "personal economic views were attributed to the impersonal Constitution." He quoted Stone's 1936 dissent in *United States v. Butler* that the president and the Congress had as much right "to protect and defend the Constitution" as the Court. He concluded by invoking John Marshall's opinion upholding the national bank in *McCulloch v. Maryland* that the Constitution was meant to "endure for ages to come" and "to be adapted to the various *crises* of human affairs" and Holmes's 1905 dissent in *Lochner v. New York* that the Constitution does not "embody a particular economy theory." Marshall's opinion in *McCulloch* and Holmes's dissent in *Lochner* were Frankfurter's judicial lodestars; he urged the president to protect the idea of an adaptable Constitution from the Court and the Court from itself.

That same day, Roosevelt sent Frankfurter a lengthy, unpublished letter to the *New York Times* by New Deal economic adviser Stuart Chase that defended the court bill in light of the Court's decisions in 1935 and 1936 and Roosevelt's 1936 electoral mandate. Frankfurter encouraged the president, along the lines of Chase's letter, to go on the radio to "take the country to school" about "the long course of judicial abuse in preventing not only national but also state action" and to explain the options the administration had considered to deal with "this major problem of democracy."

To friends, Frankfurter maintained his neutrality about court packing yet insisted the four conservatives plus Roberts "have ceased to exercise their judicial functions in the most vital problems coming before the Court." As he remarked to court bill opponent Learned Hand: "My formula to people like Charlie Burlingham is, 'tell the truth about the Court for a good stretch of time and then I don't care what remedy you propose or oppose.'" Explaining the perils of judicial usurpation of legislative power was in his wheelhouse as an expert on constitutional law; the remedy was up to the persuasive powers of the president.

During Roosevelt's nationally broadcast speech on March 4 at the Democratic Party Victory Dinner at the Mayflower Hotel, Frankfurter was lecturing a private academic audience about the misdeeds of the Supreme Court since 1906, the year he graduated from law school. In the next morning's newspaper, he read Roosevelt's speech arguing that after winning three consecutive elections in 1932, 1934, and 1936, the only obstacle to economic reform was the Supreme Court. He wrote the president praising the "most effective speech" and arguing "[t]he country needs deep and thorough education into the world of the Court—such understanding is basic to the working of our democracy." For use in future speeches, he included a quotation from Justice Brewer that the Court was not above criticism.

During a March 9 fireside chat, Roosevelt explained the bill was necessary to counter the threat the Court posed to ending the Great Depression. He compared the three branches of the federal government to three plough horses: "Two of the horses are pulling in unison today; the third is not." He accused the Court of "acting not as a judicial body but as a policy-making body." He invoked Hughes's dissent in the Railroad Retirement Act case and Stone's in the AAA and New York minimum-wage cases as proof that a majority of the Court "has improperly set itself up as a third house of the Congress—a super-legislature." And, echoing Frankfurter, he argued that "we must take action to save the Constitution from the Court and the Court from itself." What he wanted, he told the nation, was "an appeal from the Supreme Court to the Constitution itself" and to create a truly "independent judiciary." He defended his proposal of adding new judges for those who did not retire on a full salary after reaching age seventy as the need for "new and younger blood" to make the federal system work faster and more efficiently and to bring a fresh perspective to legal problems. He rejected the idea that he was trying to "pack" the Court with political hacks and merely wanted "Justices who will act as Justices and not as legislators." The amendment process, he insisted, with its requirement of ratification by three-quarters of the states, was too long and cumbersome. Only legislation could be accomplished this year and restore the Court to its proper place in the constitutional system.

After the president's fireside chat, Frankfurter let others defend the court-packing plan. On March 10, he attended a "radio party" with Harvard law colleagues Thomas Reed Powell, Calvert Magruder, Henry Hart, their wives, and former AAA general counsel Jerome Frank to listen to Senator Burton K. Wheeler debate James Landis. Landis, who had recently been named the dean of Harvard Law School, was better about exposing the problem than defending the chosen remedy but at least was willing to puncture the Court's "false sanctity"; Wheeler, however, bested Landis on the radio with a more "relaxed" style.

The leader of the opposition to the court-packing plan, Wheeler was a formidable adversary. An independent Montana Democrat, he had investigated the corruption of the Harding administration and for his troubles had been indicted on bogus corruption charges by Coolidge's attorney general, Harlan Fiske Stone (leading Frankfurter to join Wheeler's defense committee); he had run on the Frankfurter-endorsed Progressive Party presidential ticket in 1924 as Robert M. La Follette, Sr.'s, running mate; and he had employed

Frankfurter's protégé Max Lowenthal as his longtime counsel. Wheeler's opposition to the court-packing bill hurt the president. He had been the first Democratic official to endorse Roosevelt for president in 1930 and a valuable legislative ally during his first term, especially in defending the Public Utility Holding Company Act. Everyone—Democrats, Republicans, Independents— respected his legislative skill and feared his fighting reputation. Tall and red-headed, he was not someone to be trifled with. Frankfurter was disappointed that Wheeler, rather than opposing the court-packing bill on principle, had chosen to demonize the president and his advisers. Wheeler did something far worse—he forced Frankfurter to choose between his loyalty to Roosevelt and his loyalty to Brandeis.

Shortly before Roosevelt announced the court-packing bill on February 5, Tom Corcoran had learned about it and had advised the president that some-one had to warn Brandeis and explain that it was not intended as a slight against the eighty-year-old justice. The president did not want to phone Brandeis and get into an argument with him. Corcoran hailed a taxicab in front of the Treasury Department and arrived at the Court shortly before the justices were about to take the bench. He "crashed" the justices' robing room. Brandeis briefly stayed behind in the hallway as the other justices entered the courtroom. His response, after glancing at Corcoran's copy of the bill, was harsh: "Tell your President he has made a great mistake. All he had to do was wait a little while. I'm sorry for him." Brandeis then walked through the velvet curtains into the courtroom. Corcoran conveyed the words of "Old Isaiah," as the president referred to him, to Roosevelt. "I'm sorry," the president replied, "I thought 'Old Isaiah' was my friend." Corcoran also relayed the message to Frankfurter, who shared it with Marion.

Brandeis reached out to Frankfurter that same day. "Whom did F.D. rely on for his Judicial Message & bill?" he wrote on February 5. "Has he consulted you on any matters of late?" The tone of Brandeis's questions revealed his ani-mosity toward the administration. He learned from other sources that Frank-furter had not worked on the plan. Frankfurter either did not reply or later destroyed his response. Since Black Monday, he blamed the Court, and by implication Brandeis, for pushing the president into an extreme reaction. Far from being torn between his loyalty to Roosevelt and his loyalty to Brandeis, Frankfurter sided with the president, especially after Brandeis's next move.

Brandeis's wife, Alice, aided Wheeler's attack on the bill. A friend of the Wheelers, she remarked during a visit with their daughter to see her newborn son that Brandeis opposed the bill. Wheeler took the hint. He visited Brandeis on March 20 and asked about the Roosevelt administration's claim that the

justices were behind on their work. Brandeis referred him to the chief justice;
Wheeler, however, replied he did not know the chief justice. "Well," Brandeis
insisted, "he knows you." On Brandeis's advice, Hughes declined to testify in
person against the bill. Instead, the chief justice wrote Wheeler a letter about
the Court's workload and showed it to Van Devanter and Brandeis but not to
any of the other justices. "The baby," Hughes told Wheeler, "is born."

Hughes's letter was Wheeler's secret weapon. After the administration's
witnesses testified before the Senate Judiciary Committee, Wheeler led off
the opposition. At 10:30 a.m. on March 22, he demolished the dubious rationale for adding more justices. He read his March 21 letter from Chief Justice
Hughes attesting that the Court was "fully abreast" of its work. Hughes's
letter explained that the justices enjoyed more discretion about which cases
to hear since the Judiciary Act of 1925, that 60 percent of the petitions for
certiorari were baseless, and that adding justices would create inefficiency.
Finally, Hughes claimed that he had not been able to contact all the other
justices but that Brandeis and Van Devanter "approved" the letter. As Hughes
had confided to Wheeler upon handing him the letter, no other justices' views
were necessary than those of Brandeis and Van Devanter because "they are
the court."

Unaware of Brandeis's role in orchestrating Hughes's letter, Frankfurter
drafted an angry four-page letter to the justice. Frankfurter did not dispute
Hughes's facts that the Court was abreast of its work and conceded that
someone had supplied the president with "phony arguments." Both the president and the chief justice, he insisted, had been disingenuous. He objected
to "a characteristic Hughes performance" of pretending to withdraw from
the political debate while entering it, to Hughes's "ridiculous" claim that
he did not have time to consult the other justices, and to the chief justice's
"putting you in the front line even with your approval." He accused the Court
of abusing its power and disrupting the constitutional system while hiding
behind the notion that the justices were above politics. The Court, he wrote,
cannot have it both ways. He wanted "the fear of God" put into Hughes,
Roberts, and the four conservative justices. The public, he wrote, ought to be
disabused of the myth that the Court was above politics. Frankfurter never
sent the letter; he chose to wait to confront Brandeis about his role in the
controversy. Another opportunity soon arose.

A week after Wheeler's testimony, the Court reversed itself on the constitutionality of state minimum-wage laws. In a 5–4 opinion in *West Coast Hotel
v. Parrish*, Hughes upheld Washington's state minimum-wage law for women
and children and overruled the Court's 1923 decision in *Adkins v. Children's*

Hospital, in which the Court held that such laws violated the Due Process Clause's protection of "freedom of contract." Hughes's opinion claimed that the question of overruling *Adkins* had not been put squarely to the Court nine months earlier when it had invalidated the New York minimum-wage law in *Morehead v. Tipaldo.* The chief justice's opinion was the only justification for Owen J. Roberts's decision to switch his vote, which the press named "the switch in time that saved nine."

A SINGLE SENTENCE in a note Brandeis sent a week after *West Coast Hotel v. Parrish*—"Overruling Adkins' Case must give you some satisfaction"—set Frankfurter off. In the note's only other line, the justice remembered arguing *Stettler v. O'Hara,* an Oregon minimum-wage case, in December 1914. The note was meant to be a fence-mending gesture and to remind Frankfurter of their past battles together. After all, Frankfurter had argued and lost *Adkins.* It culminated seven years of litigation for the National Consumers' League that he had assumed after Brandeis joined the Court.

Frankfurter could no longer hold his tongue. In a more caustic letter than the unsent one, he thanked the justice for thinking of the personal connection yet insisted it was "one of life's bitter-sweets and the bitter far outweighs the sweet." He was happy that the Court had decided to allow states to pass minimum-wage laws to prevent the exploitation of working women but sad it had taken twenty-three years since Brandeis had taken up the cause. Yet he could not condone the political machinations of the current Court. The "manner and circumstances of the over-ruling," he wrote, was "one of the few, real black days of my life." Since his Harvard law student days, Frankfurter had revered the Supreme Court and had portrayed Holmes and Brandeis as its brightest lights. Hughes's decision in *West Coast Hotel v. Parrish,* coming nine months after *Morehead v. Tipaldo* and less than two months after Roosevelt's message to Congress proposing the court bill, shook Frankfurter's "confidence in the integrity of the Court's process." He deemed it a "terrible performance" and "a terrible sequence of events" and blamed several justices: Butler for misrepresenting the issues before the Court in *Morehead v. Tipaldo* and ignoring the differences between the New York law and the D.C. law in *Adkins;* Hughes for playing along by claiming that the Court had not been asked to overrule *Adkins* in *Tipaldo;* Sutherland in his *Parrish* dissent for claiming all the relevant issues had been addressed in *Adkins* and *Tipaldo;* and, most of all, Roberts's switch, which Frankfurter deemed "a shameless, political response to the present row." He questioned Roberts's integrity for failing to write a short concurrence explaining his change of heart.

More than anything, Frankfurter prided himself on being "a teacher of the young" and worried the decision would breed "cynicism" in his students: "Let Hughes or Roberts come up here and defend their performance when the case will come under scrutiny, as soon it will, before my Fed. Jur. Seminar." He feared the Court had done "enduring" damage to its reputation. Ultimately, he excoriated Hughes for his letter to Wheeler "intervening in a political fight by pretending not to" and for "his disingenuous claims" he lacked time to consult the whole Court. He asked Brandeis what he should tell his students: "Not even in a Chief Justice can the end justify the means. I am very sorry to write thus, but I am very, very sad."

The day before he revealed his true feelings to Brandeis, Frankfurter had written a similar letter to the president deploring that "with the shift by Roberts, even a blind man ought to see that the Court is in politics." He also observed how Roberts, Butler, and other justices had declined to rehear *Morehead v. Tipaldo* on October 12. The nadir, however, was Hughes's letter to Wheeler, its "pretended withdrawal from considerations of policy," and worst of all Brandeis's involvement. "That Brandeis should have been persuaded to allow the Chief to use his name," he wrote Roosevelt, "is a source of sadness to me that I need hardly dwell on to you."

Brandeis waited five days to respond to Frankfurter's letter: "I reserve comments on what you say until there is chance for a talk, saying now only that you are laboring under some misapprehensions." The true story of Brandeis's role in orchestrating Hughes's letter was even worse than Frankfurter realized. Brandeis's political machinations against the court bill and Frankfurter's silent loyalty to the president fractured their "half brother, half son" relationship. For a time, they agreed not to discuss court packing.

But as Brandeis alluded to, there was a lot that Frankfurter did not know about the Court's deliberations in *West Coast Hotel v. Parrish* and about the supposed switch in time. Frankfurter came to regret his attacks on Roberts (and Hughes for that matter). He learned years later after befriending him on the Court that Roberts had wanted to reconsider *Adkins* in *Morehead v. Tipaldo* but that counsel in the briefs and at argument had tried to distinguish the New York law from the D.C. one; the issue of overruling *Adkins* first arose in the Washington State minimum-wage case, *West Coast Hotel v. Parrish*; and that Roberts had voted at the justices' private conference to uphold the minimum-wage law and overrule *Adkins* on December 19, 1936, nearly two months before Roosevelt introduced his court bill (the case was held over because Stone's prolonged illness prevented the Court from vot-ing). There had been no switch by Roberts in response to the court-packing plan—at least in the minimum-wage cases. But that hardly explained the next major decision.

The Court signaled its willingness to stop obstructing the New Deal on April 12 by upholding the National Labor Relations Act. In *NLRB v. Jones & Laughlin Steel*, another 5–4 decision, Hughes upheld the law granting unions the right to organize and to collectively bargain with management and the NLRB the power to investigate and adjudicate unfair labor practices. Hughes's opinion recognized that Congress's broad power to regulate inter-state commerce included intrastate activities that had a "close and intimate relation to interstate commerce" such as production and manufacturing. And he deemed the Court's recent decisions in *Schechter* and *Carter Coal* "not con-trolling here."

Frankfurter's reaction to *Jones & Laughlin Steel* was as strong as his response to *West Coast Hotel v. Parrish* less than two weeks earlier. He had spent a lifetime defending the power of states and the federal government to protect the rights of labor unions. He was pleased with the outcome. Yet his faith in the Supreme Court and its decisions had been shattered. He viewed Hughes's change of heart from *Schechter* and *Carter Coal* to *Jones & Laughlin Steel*, like the letter to Senator Wheeler, as another political ploy to defeat the court bill. "After today," he wired Roosevelt, "I feel like finding some honest profession to enter."

A week earlier, Roosevelt had invited Frankfurter to the White House. He appreciated Frankfurter's vow of silence on the court bill and willingness to answer Wheeler and the opposition: "You are dead right in keeping—for the moment—wholly out of the hearings." At 5:00 p.m. on April 20, Frankfurter arrived at the White House for the first time since the announcement of the court bill. He and the president talked alone for five hours except for dinner with the first lady and her secretary. The evening boosted Frankfurter's low spirits. The next day, he wrote the president that he "flew out" of the White House after "my long happy exhilarating hours with you." As unhappy as he was with the Court, he knew *Jones & Laughlin Steel* was a major victory for the president. "I have no idea about the outcome of the Court bill," he wrote Burlingham, "but whatever the outcome the President will win because he has already won."

Events made the chances of passing the court bill more remote. On May 18, 78-year-old Willis Van Devanter, the longest serving of the conservative justices, announced his retirement at the end of the term. He wrote the fewest opinions of any of the justices but, as Brandeis revealed to Frankfurter, played an instrumental role in the Court's deliberations. A 1932 law halved the salaries of retired justices as an austerity measure during the Great Depression; the full salaries of retired justices were not restored until March 1937. The diminished pensions had discouraged Van Devanter and other aging justices from retiring. Nearly five years into office, Roosevelt received his first opportunity to nominate a new justice. Four days after Van Devanter's announcement, a national poll of leading lawyers revealed their first choice for the vacancy. Frankfurter finished ahead of John W. Davis, Newton D. Baker, Senator Robert F. Wagner, Roscoe Pound, Judge Learned Hand, Senator Joseph Robinson, George Wharton Pepper, John P. Devaney, and James M. Landis. In a companion poll, only 46 percent of the American people supported the court bill. There seemed to be no need for it.

The president soon triumphed in another major case. On May 24, in a 5–4 decision in *Steward Machine Company v. Davis*, Cardozo upheld the Social Security Act as within Congress's taxing and spending powers and as not coercing the states. The Four Horsemen, including the retiring Van Devanter, dissented. Frankfurter was happy for his protégé Charles Wyzanski, who had argued the case along with another rising star, Assistant Attorney General Robert H. Jackson. He was happy for the president and about the preservation of the linchpin of the Second New Deal and social safety net. Yet he harbored a "pretty low" opinion of the Court's work the past few years, resented "the political somersaults" of Hughes and Roberts, and singled out Stone's opinions for praise. He knew the liberal trio of Stone, Cardozo, and Brandeis needed reinforcements.

With Van Devanter's retirement and two 5–4 decisions in the administration's favor, the court bill lost more steam in the Senate. On May 18, the Senate Judiciary Committee had voted, 10–8, to report the bill unfavorably. Nearly a month later, the majority issued a brutal report decrying the bill as "a needless, futile, and utterly dangerous abandonment of constitutional principle." A month earlier, Roosevelt could have attained a compromise bill adding two justices to the Court; he was determined, however, to push a more sweeping bill through the Senate and believed that Senate Majority Leader Joseph Robinson could cobble together a Democratic majority. As an inducement, he promised Robinson the first Supreme Court vacancy (which made liberals reluctant to accept the two-justice compromise because one of the seats would go to the more conservative Robinson). The senate majority leader worked himself to the bone twisting arms and counting votes as he tried to push through a revised version of the bill. On July 14, he was found dead of a heart attack at his Capitol Hill apartment. Max Lowenthal reported to Frankfurter on a last-ditch effort to broker a compromise with Wheeler. Any chance of increasing the size of the Supreme Court, however, died with Robinson.

FRANKFURTER, who in the past had opposed Robinson for the Court, mourned his death. He had revised his opinion of the Arkansas senator after meeting him a few times during the legislative battles in the summer of 1935 and in reading the *Congressional Record*. He admired Robinson's loyalty and let one person know it—Brandeis. "In the Court fight he showed more character and candor and restraint than, I am sorry to say, Burt Wheeler—not to speak of the cheap [Senator Edward R.] Burke—is showing," he wrote Brandeis on July 15. "Wheeler's canonization of Hughes is positively indecent, considering the views I heard him express about the Court two years ago, and I deeply resent his persistent effort to identify you with the Court, and to use you as a screen for hiding its grave abuses in the past." Frankfurter knew that sending the letter to Brandeis was "unwise." Yet he wanted more "candor in our relationship" and revealed what was on his mind before visiting the justice in Chatham in late August. Frankfurter understood that Brandeis, in collaboration with Wheeler, was partly responsible for the defeat of the court bill and wanted Brandeis to know that his loyalties lay with the president.

From a vacation home in Cohasset, Massachusetts, Frankfurter wrote the president on August 9 to console him about Robinson's death and to urge him to address the country about the importance of the court fight: "It will clarify the Supreme Court fight—it will dramatize why it was undertaken & how greatly, for the present at least, you attained the concrete areas that moved you." Frankfurter drafted ideas for a fireside chat for Roosevelt; the president passed along the letter and draft to Corcoran. On the 150th anniversary of the ratification of the U.S. Constitution, Roosevelt would have his say.

In an ideal world, Frankfurter would have been Roosevelt's first choice for the Supreme Court. The situation in August 1937, however, was far from ideal. The court bill, despite resulting in an expansion of the lower federal courts, had been a colossal failure and had alienated members of the president's own party, particularly in the U.S. Senate. The president wanted a nominee who was easily confirmable and from a part of the country not geographically represented on the Court. On August 9, Attorney General Cummings pared down a long list of candidates, excluding Frankfurter, and sent the president brief biographies of eleven federal judges and U.S. senators.

Two days later, Roosevelt conferred with Cummings and ruled out all the judges on the list and discussed four New Deal allies: Senator Hugo Black of Alabama, Solicitor General Stanley Reed of Kentucky, Senator Sherman Minton of Indiana, and former New Deal official Lloyd Garrison. The two finalists were Black and Reed.

Sometime in August, Corcoran traveled to Cohasset to elicit Frankfurter's views. Frankfurter's first choice was Reed because he believed that the solicitor general was a hard worker and a proceduralist who understood federal jurisdiction; Attorney General Cummings also preferred Reed. The president agreed that the solicitor general was the more qualified lawyer but decided to nominate Black because the Deep South was not represented on the Court. Cummings cautioned him that Black "will certainly stir up the dry bones and will also arouse a good many other questions in all probability."

As was his wont, Roosevelt kept his choice secret from almost everyone except the attorney general. On August 12, he submitted the name of the 51-year-old senator from Alabama, Hugo Lafayette Black. Sitting in his Senate seat when his nomination was announced, Black wore a white linen suit and looked like a bird with his slicked-back hair, high forehead, angular face, thin nose, and wide eyes. His rise to the Court was in many ways as improbable as Frankfurter's. The son of an Ashland, Alabama, storekeeper, he graduated from the University of Alabama Law School in 1906 at age twenty. During the next fifteen years, he made a name for himself as a Birmingham labor and personal injury lawyer and by serving for a year as a police court judge and four years as Jefferson County prosecuting attorney. In 1921, he married Josephine Foster, the eldest daughter of a well-to-do Birmingham family; she was fourteen years his junior. Three years later, he was elected to the U.S. Senate at age forty and earned a reputation as a crusader. In 1934, he brutally cross-examined witnesses in exposing corruption in federal air-mail contracts. A Roosevelt man, he voted for all twenty-four major pieces of New Deal legislation. He railed against the $5 million lobbying campaign against the Public Utility Holding Company bill, introduced the federal wages and hours bill that became the Fair Labor Standards Act, and supported the president's court bill.

As a sitting senator, Black was expected to receive an immediate floor vote on his nomination. The Senate, however, offered no such courtesy and referred the nomination to the Judiciary Committee. After a stormy closed-door debate on August 16, his nomination was voted out of committee, 13–4. The next day, he was confirmed, 63–16, amid rumors of a dark past denied by his Senate supporters—membership in the Ku Klux Klan. The newest justice left for a European vacation only to find himself embroiled in scandal. In mid-September, the *Pittsburgh Post-Gazette* revealed that Black had been sworn into Birmingham's Robert E. Lee Klan No. 1 in 1923, captured the Democratic Party's senatorial nomination as the Klan's candidate, and had resigned from the organization the following year. The senator, however, had spoken at a Klan meeting in 1926 and had received a "grand passport" as a lifetime member. With pressure mounting for him to resign without hearing a single case, Black defended himself in a national radio address. He admitted he had been a member of the Klan before working in the Senate and denied that he was still a member or had anything to do with the organization.

Throughout Black's stormy confirmation and post-confirmation process, Frankfurter defended him to friends and to the president. He had read the entire debate in the *Congressional Record* and knew Senator William Borah, a respected Idaho independent, had attested to Black's "character and ability." Frankfurter liked it that Black was not a "'yes' man." As for the Klan revelations, he suspected that the Alabama senator long ago had outgrown the organization yet could not tell the truth about the extent of his past affiliation. He despised Paul Block, the owner of the *Pittsburgh Post-Gazette*, because of his business ties to reactionary newspaper baron William Randolph Hearst, and distrusted the newspaper's motives in investigating the Klan rumors. And to the lawyers who preferred federal appeals court judge Joseph C. Hutcheson, Jr., of Texas as a southern nominee, Frankfurter predicted that Black would overshadow him in short order. In a more candid moment, Frankfurter conceded he was not entirely happy with Black's nomination but urged friends to wait and see. He reminded them that as a senator, Black had shown "more courage and devotion to the right things than I could find in most of the leaders of my profession."

In Frankfurter's eyes, the Constitution granted power to the people and their elected officials, not to the Supreme Court or any individual justice. On August 10, he sent Roosevelt a draft speech defending the administration's effort to pass the court bill. The Court in 1935 and 1936, he wrote, had been "acting as a super-legislature." After the president's massive electoral victory in 1936, "[s]omething had to be done" and "[s]omething was done" because the Court "reversed itself." He called on the Court to maintain its current course: "The President has merely asked that the Constitution be viewed as Marshall and Holmes viewed it, so that it would be possible for the Constitution to survive periods of economic strain and political stress." True to his belief in the democratic political process, Frankfurter praised the Court's current majority for "realiz[ing] that the function of legislation belongs to the Congress and not to the Court." The president agreed about the need to address the country; he seized the next opportunity, his September 17 Constitution Day address.

During a late August overnight visit to Hyde Park, Frankfurter was inspired by Roosevelt's optimism and sense of accomplishment in winning his battle with the Court. After the visit, he poured his earlier ideas into the heart of a presidential speech to be given on the 150th anniversary of the U.S. Constitution. Corcoran wrote the first seven pages of the president's speech; Frankfurter wrote the last seventeen. Frankfurter's section began with a history lesson about everything lawyers had thought was unconstitutional: the Constitution itself replacing the Articles of Confederation; Washington's and Hamilton's protective tariff; the regulation of slavery in the territories; the financing of the Civil War; the federal income tax; the Interstate Commerce Commission; and, most recently, the National Labor Relations Act and state minimum-wage laws. He described this history as a "constant struggle between the great mass of the plain people of the United States who want national unity and justice against the lawyers who professionally complicate things in the service of those who want neither unity nor justice" and as a clash between people and lawyers and between Congress and the Court in which the people and their elected representatives "ultimately triumphed." He urged the American people to reread the Constitution and reminded them that nothing in it prevented Congress from creating a railway pension system, regulating the coal industry, outlawing public utility holding companies, or establishing the Tennessee Valley Authority. He reminded the people that "a Constitution is a great instrument of government—not a conveyance, not a contract, not even a statute" and quoted John Marshall in *McCulloch v. Maryland*: "it is *a constitution* we are expounding." He described Holmes as "the modern Marshall" and quoted several of his opinions including one about how constitutional provisions cannot be reduced to "mathematical formulas." Frankfurter added: "Whether the Constitution is treated primarily as a text for interpretation or as an instrument of government makes all the difference in the world." He described lawyers representing corporate interests as interpreting it to thwart twenty-five years of state and federal economic regulation. He acknowledged that the Bill of Rights, passed two years after the Constitution, was essential to protecting minority rights. Yet the Constitution itself created a strong central government able "to find solutions" to large-scale problems of democracy. In a contest between competing interpretations by the people and "the partisan lawyer," Frankfurter predicted the people's Constitution as an instrument for government, "as Marshall viewed it, as Holmes viewed it," would prevail.

From Cambridge, Frankfurter listened on the radio as Roosevelt spoke at 10:30 p.m. on September 17 from Washington's Sylvan Theatre. Eight pages into his speech, he declared: "The Constitution of the United States was a layman's document, not a lawyer's contract." Building on Frankfurter's theme of the Constitution as a "great layman's document" and "a charter of general principles," he described "an unending struggle between those who would preserve this original broad concept of the Constitution as a layman's instrument of government and those who would shrivel the Constitution into a lawyer's contract." He then launched into Frankfurter's history lesson about everything the lawyers had thought was unconstitutional and how the people ultimately prevailed.

Roosevelt's Constitution Day address was the best exposition of Frankfurter's view of the Constitution as an instrument for government, as a broad outline rather than exhaustive contract. It provided a window into his theory of judicial review, especially when it came to economic legislation. And it showed how much influence he had on Roosevelt's thinking about the lessons of the fight over the court bill. They transcended how many justices sat on the Supreme Court or who those justices were. The people, through their elected representatives, had the last word.

The court fight had taken a physical and emotional toll on Frankfurter and his allies. For most of the summer, he lay on his back because of bad posture and misaligned vertebrae. His two protégés Corcoran and Cohen paid a steep price by lobbying for a bill they did not draft or know about in advance. Wheeler falsely accused them of peddling a similar bill the previous year. For a time, Corcoran refused to see Brandeis after the court fight. He believed the justice "did not shoot straight with us"—his stern words in the robing room on February 5, his endorsement of Hughes's letter, and his undue influence on Frankfurter. According to Cohen, Corcoran "feels that you are tied too much emotionally with LDB. He thinks it was LDB's hold on you which stayed your hand in the court fight. And he is particularly bitter that LDB should not even consider resigning under circumstances which might ensure your appointment."

With an eye toward Frankfurter's future Supreme Court nomination, Corcoran's attempt to put distance between Frankfurter and Roosevelt's court-packing plan backfired. Beneath an unfortunate headline "Felix Frankfurter versus Franklin Roosevelt," an October 3 story in the *St. Louis Post-Dispatch* suggested that the court bill had created a rift between the two men. Frankfurter was not upset with Corcoran; his only concern was the article's impact on Roosevelt: "I am rather distressed to have him think that in any way in which I could avoid it I could become even the unwitting instrument of criticism of him." He relied on Corcoran to convey the message.

A second vacancy came and went without Frankfurter's nomination. On January 5, 1938, Justice George Sutherland announced his retirement. Ten days later, the president nominated his solicitor general, Stanley F. Reed. Frankfurter, who blanched at the idea of federal appeals court judges Harold M. Stephens, William Denman, or Samuel Bratton joining the Court, was thrilled with Reed's nomination. He sent Reed a published volume of Holmes's speeches, selected a graduating Harvard law student to be Reed's first law clerk, and gained another inside source of information.

Roosevelt's not-so-secret wish was to name Frankfurter to the Court to replace Brandeis. On January 26, the president tried to mend fences after the court fight by inviting Justice and Mrs. Brandeis to a late afternoon tea. Old Isaiah was not retiring on the president's timetable. At the end of the previous term, Brandeis had asked Hughes whether he was still up to the work of the Court; the chief justice had urged him not to resign. There was no way that Brandeis was going to retire to make way for Frankfurter.

The court fight damaged yet did not destroy Frankfurter's relationship with Brandeis. Judge Julian Mack, according to his biographer, "found himself in the painful position of having to act as mediator between Frankfurter and Brandeis to keep them from parting as associates." Frankfurter and Brandeis agreed on too much—protesting Nazi Germany's persecution of Jews, increasing Jewish immigration to the United States and Palestine, preserving Palestine (which the British were threatening to partition) as a future Jewish state, and promoting a more limited role for the Supreme Court—to part ways. Brandeis continued to fund Frankfurter's public interest work, sending him $2000 in January 1938. Along with Stone, Cardozo, and Reed, Brandeis also continued to serve as an inside source of information about the Court.

The court-packing fight changed the president's standing with the Senate, Frankfurter's relationship with Brandeis, and the Court's role in making economic and social policy. The political fallout from the court bill made it difficult for Roosevelt to nominate Frankfurter to the Court—even when the death of a Jewish justice created another vacancy.

CHAPTER 19

Sorta Tough Ain't It!

At 2:00 p.m. on July 11, 1938, two hundred people crammed into the cream stucco home of New York Court of Appeals judge Irving Lehman in Port Chester, New York, for the funeral of Justice Benjamin Nathan Cardozo. Two days earlier, Cardozo had died at age sixty-eight after a series of heart attacks and a stroke had left him incapacitated. A tall candle burned next to the coffin, which was covered with red, yellow, and white roses. Floral arrangements from President and Mrs. Roosevelt, the Supreme Court, and the New York Court of Appeals surrounded the base. First Lady Eleanor Roosevelt and Secretary of the Treasury Henry Morgenthau, Jr., and his wife and Supreme Court justices Pierce Butler, Owen J. Roberts, and Stanley F. Reed sat with Cardozo's relatives near the coffin in front of the fireplace in the library. Frankfurter, along with other mourners, sat in the adjacent reception room and sun parlor.

The funeral lasted twenty minutes. A rabbi from Congregation Shearith Israel read the Twenty-Third Psalm and quotations from the Book of Proverbs, entirely in Hebrew, consistent with the justice's Orthodox Sephardic Jewish tradition. At Cardozo's request, there was no eulogy. Frankfurter considered Cardozo "a most beautiful spirit" and thought the funeral was "really terrible" and "quite out of keeping with his own simple and rational way of living."

At Cypress Hills Cemetery in Queens, the rabbi held a short service in the red brick chapel. Fifteen people, including the justice's law clerk, Joseph L. Rauh, Jr., stood under the canopy to watch the casket lowered into the ground at the Cardozo family burial plot. A light rain fell. The other mourners stayed in the chapel where the rabbi conducted another short service, like the others, entirely in Hebrew. The service concluded with the traditional Mourner's Kaddish. In Washington, D.C., black silk cloth hung from Cardozo's high-backed chair and in front of his spot on the Supreme Court bench.

Cardozo's death set off a six-month battle within the Roosevelt administration about his replacement, an internal political struggle about the future of the Court. In a way, Roosevelt may have won the court-packing fight because, in a series of 5–4 decisions, the Court had begun upholding his New Deal programs. And the retirements of conservatives Van Devanter and Sutherland allowed him to remake the Court by replacing them with Black and Reed. But in the process the president had lost the support of the Democratic leadership in the Senate and fractured the New Deal political coalition. Liberal northerners, conservative southerners, and moderate and progressive westerners no longer united behind his legislative agenda. He worried about his political standing during the midterm elections in 1938 and beyond. As a result, Roosevelt did not intend to name Cardozo's replacement until Congress reconvened in January 1939.

The president's waiting game regarding Cardozo's successor pitted his advisers against each other. During the next six months, two camps emerged. The administration's old guard—party politicians led by Attorney General Homer Cummings and Postmaster General James Farley—wanted Roosevelt to nominate a westerner. Roosevelt's first two Supreme Court nominees, Black and Reed, were southerners who had replaced westerners, Van Devanter and Sutherland. The new guard—idealistic New Dealers led by Tom Corcoran, Ben Cohen, Works Progress Administration administrator Harry Hopkins, Secretary of the Interior Harold Ickes, and Solicitor General Robert H. Jackson—wanted Frankfurter.

Roosevelt revealed his desire to put Frankfurter on the Court. In February and May 1937, Frankfurter had finished first in two Gallup polls of 175,000 American lawyers as their top choice. During a late-night conversation aboard the cutter *Potomac* in May 1937, Roosevelt had asked Secretary Morgenthau to choose between Frankfurter or his former student, then–SEC chairman James M. Landis, if Brandeis resigned. No friend of Frankfurter's, Morgenthau answered Landis "by all means." Roosevelt replied that "Frankfurter would rate a more popular opinion." Morgenthau countered that "the public would have more confidence in Landis." Roosevelt conceded that Frankfurter's nomination would be difficult: "Well, I think I would have a terrible time getting Frankfurter confirmed" and "I do not know if it is worthwhile" and "One of the troubles with Frankfurter is that he is over-brilliant." Morgenthau, however, knew his boss preferred Frankfurter.

Two conventional narratives have developed about Frankfurter's nomination: first, it did not come as a surprise to Frankfurter; second, the young New Dealers pulled a fast one on Roosevelt. Neither narrative rings true. As was his custom, the president seemed to leave the last person he talked to thinking they were in agreement, regardless of the person's point of view. Roosevelt, as others have pointed out, was a sphinx. He kept everyone, including his closest advisers, guessing. The only time he lowered his guard was in an important yet overlooked letter to Kansas newspaper editor William Allen White. In October 1938, Roosevelt confided to White what in hindsight seems obvious—the inside struggle about Cardozo's replacement was about the president's failed court-packing plan.

Before Cardozo's death, both sides had been touting their preferred candidates. On July 6, Cummings had met with the president and had discussed the possibility that Cardozo might not return and that Roosevelt should replace him with a progressive judge from the West. The attorney general's first choice was a southerner, not a westerner—Judge John J. Parker, a federal court of appeals judge from North Carolina whose 1930 Supreme Court nomination had been defeated in the Senate by organized labor, the NAACP, and Frankfurter and other liberals. Roosevelt expressed "a willingness" to nominate Parker if McReynolds, Butler, or Hughes retired. But Cummings believed that the next nominee had to be a federal court of appeals judge from one of the western states and could not jeopardize the Court's "narrow liberal majority." Roosevelt had been telling people before Cardozo's death that the "next appointment would be from the Far West if he could find a good progressive there who was 'up to it.'" After Cardozo's death, Cummings was certain that Roosevelt would choose a judge from the western Ninth Circuit or Tenth Circuit Court of Appeals, and that as attorney general Cummings would have input on the nominee.

Corcoran, the leader of the Frankfurter forces, knew that a westerner was the most likely option. He had visited FDR at 9:15 a.m. on July 5, the day before Cummings discussed other candidates. Corcoran told Ickes that if Michigan governor Frank Murphy lost his 1938 reelection bid, then Murphy, as a Catholic from the Midwest, would get the nomination. Corcoran and Cohen were working behind the scenes on Murphy's reelection campaign. If Murphy got reelected, Corcoran predicted that the nomination would go to another Catholic midwesterner, John P. Devaney, the chief justice of the Minnesota Supreme Court who had resigned to fight for the court-packing plan. "Otherwise, the chances are good for Frankfurter," Ickes wrote on July 16. "I would like to see Frankfurter appointed. He would be in the fine liberal tradition of Holmes and Cardozo. He would also be an excellent influence on the Court, both spiritually and intellectually."

Corcoran and Ickes were furious that Brandeis had not resigned to make way for Frankfurter. The court-packing fight had soured their relations with the 81-year-old justice. They had not visited him since. British political scientist Harold Laski was not afraid to tell Brandeis what every liberal New Dealer was thinking—retire so Frankfurter could replace him. Brandeis, however, "replied that he was not sure that Frankfurter could not do more good by teaching the younger generation."

Brandeis's refusal to retire and the conventional political wisdom about the need for a westerner on the Court did not deter Corcoran and Cohen. They revered Frankfurter and felt that they owed him so much. At Frankfurter's behest, they had worked with Landis in drafting the 1933 Securities Act. The extroverted Corcoran and introverted Cohen also had drafted the 1934 Securities Exchange Act and the 1935 Public Utility Holding Company Act, lived together at the "little red house," and became Roosevelt insiders.

The national media highlighted Corcoran and Cohen's power within the administration just as that power was beginning to ebb. Though they had nothing to do with the genesis of the court-packing plan, they had defended it throughout the summer of 1937, and their reputations took a hit after its spectacular failure. During the summer and fall of 1938, Corcoran led a "purge" of conservative congressional Democrats who had opposed the plan by aiding their opponents in the upcoming November elections. In September 1938, Corcoran and Cohen were on the cover of *Time* magazine over the headline: "They call themselves catalysts."

Corcoran and Cohen certainly catalyzed Frankfurter's nomination. On May 12, 1938, Frankfurter and his wife arrived in Washington, D.C., for an overnight stay at the White House. The next day, Frankfurter attended a luncheon in his honor in the private fifth-floor dining room of Secretary Ickes. Organized by Cohen, the lunch was a who's who of the New Deal crowd— Corcoran, Cohen, Ickes, Jackson, new SEC chairman William O. Douglas, and SEC commissioner Jerome Frank; they wanted Frankfurter on the Court and, led by Corcoran, employed their political influence to make it happen.

A week after Cardozo's death, influential columnists sympathetic to the Corcoran-Cohen forces weighed in led by Joseph Alsop. A Groton- and Harvard-educated relative of Theodore Roosevelt and a charter member of the Georgetown set, Alsop moved to Georgetown in 1935 and lived not far from Corcoran and Cohen's little red house and Frankfurter's former student Dean Acheson. He had co-authored a 1938 book about the court-packing fight, *The 168 Days,* and was working on a sequel about Roosevelt's New Deal advisers. In the summer and fall of 1938, he interviewed, corresponded with, and sent Frankfurter drafts of a series of *Saturday Evening Post* articles that became

Men Around the President. Alsop and Robert Kintner's July 18 syndicated column began by telling the supposed story of Cardozo's nomination. Hoover had wanted to appoint a westerner, but Senator William Borah of Idaho told him: "Mr. President, it doesn't matter what state Justice Cardozo comes from. He is Idaho's candidate, and I venture to say that he is the candidate of the United States." Alsop and Kintner argued that, with Cardozo's replacement, legal talent once again should trump geographic considerations because "few would deny that Felix Frankfurter is both a national figure and a great scholar of the law. . . . If others do not, Holmes and Cardozo at least thought him their fit successor." They explained how Frankfurter fought the early New Deal fights, served as a "one-man Government employment agency," and had many friends with access to the corridors of power. "If the President himself is not Felix Frankfurter's best advocate," they wrote, "Frankfurter's name will be urged at the White House by many of the President's closest advisers." Alsop and Kintner also handicapped Frankfurter's competitors. They predicted that Cummings would lobby for D.C. federal court of appeals judge Harold Stephens of Utah, and that Senator Lewis Schwellenbach of Washington, Governor Murphy, and Senator Robert Wagner of New York would be in the mix. "But, at the moment," Alsop and Kintner concluded, "Frankfurter has the edge."

The first western voice to endorse Frankfurter was another influential columnist, Irving Dilliard of the *St. Louis Post-Dispatch.* "If there is anyone more thoroughly steeped in the history of the Supreme Court and a knowledge of the evolution of our constitutional law of the last two generations," Dilliard wrote in his July 27 column, "his name does not come to mind." Dilliard reminded his readers that before Frankfurter had declined a position on the Massachusetts Supreme Judicial Court, the Harvard law professor had been endorsed in 1932 by Holmes, Brandeis, and Cardozo. Dilliard concluded that "if the President sends the name of Mr. Frankfurter to the Senate as the successor to Cardozo and Holmes, he will make a distinguished use of the appointing power."

Frankfurter's Borah-Cardozo moment came a few weeks later in a white cottage with a large front screened-in porch on Rainbow Lake in Waupaca, Wisconsin. The house had no doorbell and no telephone. Senator George W. Norris of Nebraska returned to his northern Wisconsin retreat every spring and summer to relax and to spend time with family and friends. He chopped wood, rowed, and swam almost every day. He also worked on legislative matters and dictated to his stenographer.

On August 7, Norris dictated a statement that hit the national wire services, datelined Waupaca, Wisconsin, and found its way into many of the nation's newspapers. Frankfurter and Norris went back to Frankfurter's early days in Washington at the House of Truth. In 1916, Norris had been one of three Republicans to vote to confirm Brandeis to the Supreme Court. Frankfurter and the liberal senator shared a passion for protecting the rights of working men, women, and children and those of organized labor. In 1932, Frankfurter had been one of the principal drafters of the Norris–La Guardia Act that outlawed injunctions against labor unions. After Roosevelt took office, Frankfurter and Norris joined forces again to fight for public works projects including the Tennessee Valley Authority and Rural Electrification Administration. In 1936, Norris left the Republican Party and won reelection as an Independent. Like many progressives, he opposed the Roosevelt administration's court-packing bill.

From his summer home, Norris shored up Frankfurter's western support as Cardozo's replacement. The senator argued that Roosevelt had "an opportunity to perform one of the greatest services ever performed for the American people—an opportunity that seldom comes more than once in a lifetime." Frankfurter, Norris wrote, was Holmes and Cardozo's rightful heir and shared the same judicial philosophy: "There is no man in the public eye who so fully and truly represents the philosophy of government of Justice Holmes and his successor, Justice Cardozo, as does Frankfurter." He explained that Frankfurter had been "the confidential friend and adviser" to Holmes and Cardozo and that the American people belatedly recognized the genius of Holmes and "recently mingled their tears at the bier of Justice Cardozo." Norris predicted that favorable public opinion of Holmes and Cardozo would increase over time. "Felix Frankfurter is the most outstanding personality to continue and carry out the judicial philosophy of these great statesmen," Norris concluded. "The common people of America have faith in President Roosevelt. He will perpetuate that faith if he places Mr. Frankfurter on the Supreme bench."

Norris was his own man, but the letter may have been inspired by the leader of the Frankfurter forces, Tom Corcoran. On August 6, Corcoran sent Norris two copies of a draft statement about Frankfurter, including one triple-spaced so that the senator could edit it. Corcoran's cover letter indicated that he and Norris had seen each other recently and were working together on the Frankfurter nomination. Corcoran was a gifted presidential speechwriter. This draft speech began "Dear Mr. President" and argued that Frankfurter was a worthy successor to Holmes and Cardozo and embodied "their great liberal tradition." It pointed to Frankfurter's high standing in the legal profession according to the two 1937 Gallup polls, Frankfurter's close friendship with

Holmes, and Holmes's 1932 recommendation of Frankfurter to the Supreme Judicial Court of Massachusetts. Corcoran also touted Frankfurter's personal relationships with the liberal members of the current Court (Black, Reed, and Stone) as well as with the moderates (Roberts and Hughes). "He can do much more than be one liberal vote on the Court," Corcoran wrote, "he can make the now separate members of the liberal wing a united force." Corcoran also argued that the president should ignore the clamor for a westerner, put "the best possible man on the Court no matter from where he comes," and follow the example of Hoover's choice of Cardozo. Finally, Corcoran alluded to the rising threat of Nazi Germany and urged the president "to repudiate their principles of intolerance."

Corcoran's draft had arrived in Wisconsin too late. A pink note in Norris's files, dated August 1938 from Waupaca, indicates that his "letter was already written." Ultimately it did not matter who wrote what when. Norris's statement lit up the national newswires and changed the conversation about Cardozo's successor. Not even the New York Times's delay in running the statement worried Corcoran and his allies. "The whole Times bunch has been fatuously cautious," he wrote Archibald MacLeish. "But things are booming along very nicely."

The next day, Norris's fellow Nebraska senator, Edward R. Burke, endorsed Judge Samuel Bratton of the Court of Appeals for the Tenth Circuit in New Mexico. A vocal opponent of the court bill, Burke conceded that "he would have no objection" to Frankfurter. A one-term senator, Burke had graduated from Harvard Law School a few years before Frankfurter had begun teaching there. Burke said Frankfurter's only handicap with the administration was the professor's opposition to the court-packing plan.

Norris's statement alarmed Frankfurter's most outspoken antagonist, former National Recovery Administration director General Hugh S. Johnson. "This Norris demand—for it is scarcely less—is significant," Johnson wrote in his syndicated column. "The President wears the radical Nebraska Senator on his breast as a symbol of 'liberalism.'" Johnson described Norris as "an object of adoration to all the radical extremists in the third New Deal" and Frankfurter as "an idol of the extremists. He is more than that. He is their tie-in with both the Executive Departments and the Courts."

As the leader of the "extremists," Corcoran had his fingerprints on the Norris letter and everywhere else. Corcoran's friends Alsop and Kintner revealed in an August 15 column that Holmes's 1932 letter recommending Frankfurter for a vacancy on the Supreme Judicial Court of Massachusetts was about to arrive on the president's desk. Corcoran had sent the same letter to Senator Norris. Few people could match Corcoran's access to the president. On August 17, he met with Roosevelt at the White House between presidential visits from Justice Black and Senator Sherman Minton of Indiana. After his meeting, Minton declared his support for Frankfurter.

The August 15 Alsop and Kintner column declared that "Frankfurter's adherents have gained great strength." After reprinting the Holmes letter in full and discussing a similar 1932 letter from Frankfurter's former boss Newton D. Baker, the column pointed to the importance of Norris's endorsement—not only because the Nebraska senator was a westerner but also because he was "the man in politics most highly respected by the President." The columnists disingenuously described "the movement to put Frankfurter on the high bench" as "quite spontaneous" and "actually unauthorized by him." They insisted that the president would not be afraid to nominate a second Jew to join Brandeis on the Court and that Frankfurter's supporters included "many Roman Catholics" (a sly allusion to Corcoran) even though the Catholic Church had been pressuring Roosevelt to nominate a second Catholic member (an allusion to Governor Murphy, former Minnesota chief justice Devaney, and Judge Stephens). The columnists predicted that the president would not decide until Congress reconvened in January, but that if he did not choose Frankfurter "it will be the first time he has not heeded the publicly spoken advice of George Norris."

Another New Deal insider and syndicated columnist, Raymond Clapper, went farther than Alsop and Kintner and proclaimed that Frankfurter was "as good as appointed." Clapper described Frankfurter's "former students and devoted disciples" as leading the fight and observed that Roosevelt was "favorably disposed" yet had two objections, "geographical" and "racial." Frankfurter's friends "were not concerned over the racial objection," Clapper wrote, because "they do not regard Roosevelt as a man to be intimidated by a few crackpot Jew-baiters." The geographic objection and clamor for a westerner, Clapper wrote, "has some merit." Frankfurter's friends, however, had worked hard to blunt that argument by soliciting Senator Norris's letter and by launching a "campaign of newspaper editorials and Washington columns in behalf of Frankfurter." He also noted that although Senators Burke of Nebraska and Joseph C. O'Mahoney of Wyoming preferred a western nominee, they had conceded that Frankfurter would be a good choice. Finally, Clapper invoked the two 1937 Gallup polls favoring Frankfurter and Frankfurter's eulogy of Cardozo in the August 1938 issue of the *American Bar Association Journal* and concluded: "There's been a surprising general acceptance of Frankfurter for the supreme court."

Other columnists who preferred more liberal candidates conceded that Norris's letter had made a major impact. Even Drew Pearson, a Frankfurter antagonist and co-author of *The Nine Old Men*, fell somewhat into line. On July 31, Pearson and Robert Allen's syndicated column quoted "White House insiders" that Frankfurter did not have "a ghost of a chance to be appointed." Five days later, the columnists reported that, at the annual American Bar Association convention, Frankfurter was one of three names mentioned for the Court along with Senator Wagner and Judge Hutcheson of Texas. By the end of August, Pearson and Allen conceded that Frankfurter had the "inside track" on the nomination yet suggested his "liberal background might fade like that of the one-time crusader, Justice McReynolds." They put Frankfurter's odds of landing the nomination at 10 to 1.

Most of the summer, thanks to Norris's letter and Corcoran's campaign, had belonged to Frankfurter.

───

THE LATE SUMMER and fall were a different story. Old school Democratic Party politicians Farley and Cummings led the fight against Frankfurter and in favor of a western nominee. On August 25, Farley discussed the Cardozo vacancy during nearly seven hours of wide-ranging conversation with the president at Hyde Park. Roosevelt ruled out Senator Wagner unless another New Yorker, Hughes or Stone, resigned. The president "satisfied" Farley, the postmaster general and Democratic Party chairman, that "he will name a westerner." Roosevelt observed that there were no justices from west of the Mississippi, not even Butler from St. Paul. Farley asked Roosevelt to consider another Catholic "because of the criticisms that followed" Black's nomination; namely, Black's admission that as an Alabama politician he had been a member of the anti-Catholic Ku Klux Klan. Farley's western Catholic choice was Judge Harold Stephens from Utah. Roosevelt mentioned Ninth Circuit judge Bert Haney of Oregon, but Haney was not a Catholic. Farley believed that he and the president were on the same page on timing (after the November election) and geography. On the basis of their conversation, Farley did not consider Frankfurter a viable replacement for Cardozo: "The President told me frankly that he would like to appoint Frankfurter to the Court, as he felt that his appointment would meet with more favor than anyone else he might name, but he thought it would not be possible because of his coming from the east." Roosevelt promised to "get word" to Brandeis "that if, and when Brandeis should leave the Court, that Frankfurter would be named as his successor."

Cummings fought against Frankfurter's nomination with "astonishing fervor" and made it "a personal issue." During a September 8 conference at Hyde Park, he asked Roosevelt if he had "made any progress" in selecting Cardozo's successor. The president appeared to agree with his attorney general that the nomination should "go to the West." Cummings assumed, based on their prior conversations, that Roosevelt would not choose Judge Bratton of New Mexico. Nor was Cummings familiar with Roosevelt's suggestion of Judge William Healy of the Court of Appeals for the Ninth Circuit in Idaho. Cummings raised three remaining western candidates: Judge William Denman, a 1935 Roosevelt nominee to the Ninth Circuit in San Francisco; Maurice E. Harrison, a lawyer, state Democratic Party leader, and former dean of Hastings Law School in San Francisco; and Cummings's preferred candidate and a 1935 Roosevelt nominee to the Court of Appeals for the District of Columbia, 52-year-old Judge Stephens of Utah. Roosevelt said the 65-year-old Denman, in light of the court-packing plan's purported concern about aging Supreme Court justices, was "too old." The president was not familiar with Harrison and "doubted the advisability" of nominating Stephens. "I took occasion to say that Judge Stephens had much to commend him;" Cummings wrote. "— he came from the right state; had the proper scholastic background; already held a high judicial office and his age was just about right. I did not think the President seemed particularly impressed but I cannot consider the incident closed."

Harold Montelle Stephens was driven by ambition and had made an unlikely ascendance from western outsider to Washington insider. Born in Nebraska and raised in Utah, he graduated from Harvard Law School in 1913 and joined his father's law practice in Salt Lake City. Active in Utah Democratic Party politics, he served two years as an assistant state prosecutor and four years as an elected state trial judge. After he lost an election for a seat on the Utah Supreme Court, he returned to private practice in Salt Lake City until 1928 when he moved to Los Angeles. Stephens's entry into a new legal market lasted only four months; he suffered a nervous breakdown. After a three-year recovery, he decided to enter legal academia. In 1932, he completed his doctorate in law at Harvard and was a student in Frankfurter's administrative law seminar. Frankfurter, Powell, and others on the faculty considered Stephens a "C-man." Roscoe Pound, not Frankfurter, mentored Stephens. Thanks to a chance interview with Attorney General Cummings, Stephens landed a job in the Roosevelt administration from 1933 to 1935 as an assistant attorney general in charge of antitrust matters. In December 1934, Stephens had been humiliated by Brandeis during oral argument and lost *Panama*

Refining Company v. Ryan, which invalidated the National Industrial Recovery Act's petroleum code. Nonetheless, Cummings urged the president to name Stephens to the Court of Appeals for the District of Columbia. During this early New Deal period, Frankfurter and Stephens maintained a polite correspondence, and Frankfurter offered to select Stephens's law clerks (Stephens decided to allow Erwin Griswold to choose them instead). Stephens resented Frankfurter and, by extension, Corcoran and other young New Dealers. The disdain between Frankfurter and Stephens was mutual. Frankfurter deemed Stephens "a toady and a third-rater" who was unfit for the Court compared to other leading candidates.

Since February 1938, Stephens's surrogates had been writing western senators, congressmen, governors, lawyers, and prominent law professors to lobby Roosevelt to nominate him to the Supreme Court. Stephens's strongest supporters, like Frankfurter's, had regular access to the White House. No one tended to influence the selection of a Supreme Court nominee more than the president's attorney general. Cummings, like Farley, wanted a westerner, loathed Frankfurter, and lobbied the president to select Stephens. Stephens was not only a westerner but also a Catholic, satisfying two political constituencies.

That fall, Cummings and Farley battled the Corcoran-Cohen-Ickes-Jackson forces. On September 26, Farley phoned the president and raised the remote possibility of appointing Cardozo's closest friend and former colleague, New York Court of Appeals judge Irving Lehman. Roosevelt replied that "nothing would give him any greater pleasure" than to appoint Lehman, but Lehman was sixty-four or sixty-five years old (he was actually sixty-two). That was too old given the criticism of aging justices during the court-packing fight. Furthermore, Roosevelt said, "the appointment would have to go West, as there is no appointment on the bench west of the Mississippi River."

All signs pointed to a westerner because of in-group religious prejudice, geographic considerations, and the looming November congressional elections. It did not matter that Frankfurter led Judge Bratton of New Mexico in a September 18 Gallup poll of American lawyers about the next nominee. Eight days later, the conservative *Chicago Tribune* reported that Frankfurter was "definitely out." Several western candidates saw Roosevelt at the White House—Senator Schwellenbach of Washington, one of the favorites according to the *Tribune*, and Judge Albert Lee Stephens, a Roosevelt appointee to the Court of Appeals for the Ninth Circuit in Los Angeles.

Frankfurter's most dangerous opposition came from outside the administration—wealthy German American Jews alerted the White House to fears that the nomination of another Jewish justice would trigger Nazi-style anti-Semitism in the United States. On September 21, Alsop and Kintner, presumably acting on a tip from Corcoran, wrote that "wealthy and well-known Jews of New York have pressed the President to pass Felix Frankfurter over." Members of this Jewish privileged class urged Roosevelt to wait until Brandeis retired to nominate another Jew.

One of the leading Jewish opponents of Frankfurter's nomination was *New York Times* publisher Arthur Hays Sulzberger. Sulzberger's role was unsurprising given the timidity of his newspaper. The *Times* had been "burying" news stories about Nazi atrocities against European Jews on its inside pages. Frankfurter and Sulzberger were on friendly enough terms in May 1937 to bet a dinner on whether Roosevelt would have more Supreme Court appointments before the end of his term; Sulzberger won. To Philadelphia Jewish leader Jacob Billikopf, Sulzberger confessed his opposition to Frankfurter's nomination for two reasons: first, he rejected the idea of a Jew replacing a Jew; and second, he felt that Frankfurter was too closely associated with Roosevelt's New Deal legislation. The publisher, however, regretted saying anything to his go-between, financier Henry Morgenthau, Sr.

Morgenthau Sr., like Sulzberger, was a member of "our crowd"—wealthy German Jews who downplayed their Jewishness and failed to support Zionism and other Jewish social causes. Morgenthau Sr., Billikopf believed, conveyed Sulzberger's doubts to Corcoran. Morgenthau Sr. may have told his son, secretary of the treasury and Roosevelt confidant Henry Morgenthau, Jr. Or Sulzberger may have told the president directly. Either way, Corcoran heard the story and directed Archibald MacLeish to draft a letter to the president signed by prominent American Jews objecting to the idea that Frankfurter's nomination "would be injurious to American Jews as tending to excite anti-Semitic feeling."

Of the Sulzberger–Morgenthau Sr. operation, Frankfurter and Brandeis harbored no doubts. Frankfurter wrote Billikopf that "the rumors about Sulzberger are now confirmed by him, except that part which made him communicate his views directly to the President."

Morgenthau Sr. and Morgenthau Jr., both of whom disliked Frankfurter, were the most likely candidates. Frankfurter informed Billikopf that Sulzberger "got someone who is even more influential perhaps than he is to do it for him." The Sulzberger–Morgenthau Sr. opposition, Brandeis told Frankfurter, was "one of many instances of the rich Jews' folly." Brandeis informed Ickes that "there was a certain type of rich Jew who was a coward"; the justice "spoke" of these "German Jews" with "contempt."

THE RISE OF Nazi Germany had turned Frankfurter into anything but a coward. Since May 1933, he had been lobbying Roosevelt, Secretary of Labor Frances Perkins, and Secretary of State Cordell Hull to relax immigration restrictions on European Jewish refugees. He had helped numerous Jewish academics fired from German universities find positions in American universities and at the New School's University in Exile. He had published an article while at Oxford attacking Nazi propaganda about Jews controlling Germany's economic and cultural life. He sought Roosevelt's assistance in preventing the British from partitioning Palestine into Arab and Jewish sections and lobbied for increased Jewish immigration there. "Never in my life have I been under such pressure as now," Frankfurter confessed at year's end, "— largely due to refugee problems . . ."

As Frankfurter suspected, Nazi atrocities reached his native Austria. On March 11, 1938, Germany launched the Anschluss, the annexation of Austria and the terrorization of the country's Jewish population. The Nazis looted Jewish shops, burned synagogues, and arrested prominent Austrian Jewish leaders. They came for Frankfurter's 82-year-old uncle, retired University of Vienna librarian and philologist Salomon Frankfurter.

One of the city's leading academics and a member of the Austrian government's cultural advisory council since 1934, Salomon Frankfurter was an easy target. Around 1:00 a.m. on March 12, storm troopers "dragged" him "from his bed" and threw him in the "Liesl," Vienna's police prison for political dissidents. He was wearing a collarless shirt, thin jacket, pants without a belt or suspenders, and loafers. He was not given time to grab his overcoat. After two days in the freezing cell, he caught a cold. Fellow prisoners huddled next to him to keep him warm at night, lent him their coats, and put a clean handkerchief under his head. During the day, he stood around with other political prisoners and sobbed.

The morning after his uncle's arrest, Frankfurter received a phone call from a friend in Vienna and knew he had to do something. As a child, he had lived with his uncle for two years while his father was trying to make a fresh start in the United States. His uncle inspired him to pursue a scholarly life. He had not seen his uncle since 1920 but kept tabs on him through Josef Redlich, a University of Vienna constitutional historian who taught at Harvard Law School, until Redlich's death in 1936. The extant correspondence between Frankfurter and his uncle is sparse. In an October 1931 letter written in German, Salomon asked his nephew to contact philanthropist Julius Rosenwald to donate money for Vienna's Jewish Theological Seminary and Jewish Museum. No matter how much time had passed between their last meeting or letter, the bond between Frankfurter and his uncle was unbreakable.

To hear Frankfurter tell it, he wired the one person he knew with Nazi Party contacts—Lady Nancy Astor. An American-born member of Parliament and leader of the British Cliveden set, she had known Frankfurter since the 1919 Paris Peace Conference and had seen him again during his year in Oxford. He had not forgotten her casual anti-Semitism and Nazi sympathies. At Frankfurter's urging, she contacted Joachim von Ribbentrop, the German ambassador to Britain, who "promised to do what he could." Three days later, she contacted the ambassador again and threatened him "that unless I received good news of Herr Frankfurter, I should go myself to Vienna!"

Salomon was released from prison, but not necessarily because of Lady Astor. The press reported that the request came from the U.S. consulate in Austria. Frankfurter had contacted Herbert Feis, one of the State Department's few Jews and few advocates for Jewish refugees, and one of Feis's sympathetic colleagues, former U.S. ambassador to Austria George S. Messersmith. Rather than Lady Astor, Messersmith in Washington and John Cooper Wiley at the U.S. consulate in Austria secured Salomon's freedom.

According to State Department documents, Messersmith contacted Wiley on March 13 at Frankfurter's request. Five days later, Wiley learned about Salomon's imprisonment but his whereabouts were "unknown." On March 22, Wiley reported that Salomon had been moved to a hospital suffering from "nervous shock"; Wiley also raised Salomon's case with German officials. Two days later, he reported that Salomon had been released and his condition was "good." Frankfurter's uncle returned to his apartment where he remained under house arrest.

The Lady Astor story became Frankfurter's cover because the last thing he wanted was to be seen as trading on his friendship with the president. Several years later, he informed an astounded Roosevelt that Astor, not the State Department, had secured his uncle's freedom because Frankfurter did not want to seek favors from friends in the administration.

During the Sulzberger–Morgenthau Sr. intervention against Frankfurter's nomination that fall, appeasement of Nazi Germany was a popular strategy. On September 5, Britain and France negotiated the infamous Munich Agreement that permitted Germany to annex the Sudetenland, the German-speaking part of Czechoslovakia. Isolationists, ascendant in Europe and the United States, lauded the agreement as the end of German aggression and the key to averting another world war. As he informed Roosevelt, Frankfurter was so distressed about British prime minister Neville Chamberlain's appeasement policy that he phoned London correspondent Ferdinand Kuhn of the *New York Times*. On October 12, Frankfurter spoke by phone with Roosevelt about encouraging Chamberlain to allow Jewish refugees to emigrate to British-controlled Palestine. The next day, Frankfurter dictated to Ben Cohen a draft wire to Chamberlain. Frankfurter wrote Roosevelt fawning letters praising his speeches and pillorying the remarks of isolationist Joseph Kennedy, Sr., who had been appointed U.S. ambassador to Great Britain. And at the end of 1938, Frankfurter was one of several Americans who sponsored the publication of a book, *The German Reich and Americans of German Origin*, reprinting Nazi laws, decrees, and speeches to educate and possibly to change the minds of isolationist Americans.

THE SYMBOLISM OF a possible Frankfurter nomination was not lost on his supporters. Alsop and Kintner observed that "the President is not the man to yield to the vulgar brutalities of race hatred or sectarian pettiness. But, presented by the leaders of the Jewish race itself, the racial argument against Frankfurter could not fail to have been more impressive." *The Nation* saw the Jewish opposition as making Frankfurter's nomination more likely: "Mr. Roosevelt is presented with a double opportunity. By naming Mr. Frankfurter he can further increase the clarity and boldness of the court, and at the same time demonstrate his faith in the survival of democratic tolerance." Liberal columnist Heywood Broun decried the Jewish fears of anti-Semitism as "extraneous. But it also happens to be one of the vital problems which America must solve out in the open if we are to stand as a citadel against the tide of Fascism."

The whisper campaign by Sulzberger, Morgenthau Sr., and other rich Jews outraged two of Frankfurter's longtime friends in the press, Paul Kellogg and William Allen White. The editor of *The Survey* and *Survey Graphic*, Kellogg had known Frankfurter since a 1916 National Consumers' League meeting in which Frankfurter led the organization's legal defense of state minimum-wage and maximum-hour laws. In 1927, Kellogg was one of Frankfurter's staunchest supporters in the fight for new trials for Italian anarchists Sacco and Vanzetti. Frankfurter, in turn, was a member of *The Survey*'s board of directors. Kellogg was angry about Jewish opposition to Frankfurter's nomination and contacted one of the first Jewish federal judges and a longtime Frankfurter ally, Julian W. Mack. On October 5, Mack wrote the president about the Sulzberger–Morgenthau Sr. opposition "to express my complete dissent from that position." Five days later, Kellogg wrote Roosevelt detailing the editor's professional regard for Frankfurter and arguing that bowing to Jewish fears would "give anti-Semitism a taste of blood." Frankfurter, Kellogg argued, would "only reinforce the Court on its liberal side."

Kellogg sent copies of his and Mack's letters to William Allen White. The seventy-year-old editor of the *Emporia Gazette* in Kansas, White had known every American president from TR to FDR, had written a biography of Calvin Coolidge, and sat on the Pulitzer Prize board. In short, White was one of the most influential journalists in the western United States. He had known Frankfurter since 1914 when he "was a young attorney who even then was known as a liberal," had seen him in Paris in 1919, and had been corresponding with him about politics ever since. A liberal Republican, White had lobbied U.S. senators in 1916 to support Brandeis's nomination, had encouraged Hoover to nominate Cardozo in 1932, and was determined to do the same for Frankfurter six years later. Kellogg encouraged White to write the president on Frankfurter's behalf because "the Supreme Court is in a class by itself. And so is Felix." After Frankfurter spoke at *The Survey*'s twenty-fifth anniversary dinner in New York in 1937, White remarked: "Isaiah [Brandeis], at his best, could not have surpassed Frankfurter." Mrs. White chimed in: "It was worth while coming from Emporia just to hear Frankfurter's extraordinary address."

Shortly after Cardozo's death in July, White had drafted a letter to Roosevelt endorsing Frankfurter but decided not to send it. Kellogg's correspondence and "the big rich reactionaries, both Jew and Gentile" who had made Frankfurter "their head devil" caused White to reconsider. Earlier that year, Roosevelt had sought White's insight about Kansas politics. In October, he wrote the president urging him to ignore the critics and fears of anti-Semitism and to nominate Frankfurter. White's letter, his status as one of the nation's preeminent western journalists, his faraway outpost in Emporia, Kansas, and the president's high regard for his political acumen triggered what few of Roosevelt's closest advisers had been able to muster in person—real insight about how the court-packing fight had affected the president's thinking about the next nominee.

Before he wrote to White, however, the president revealed his intentions to Frankfurter.

MONDAY, OCTOBER 3, 1938, marked the beginning of the new Supreme Court term with only eight justices. Five days later, Felix and Marion rode from the New Milford, Connecticut, home of their friend Dr. Alfred E. Cohn and arrived at Hyde Park at 5:15 p.m. for their annual overnight stay at the Roosevelt estate. They had the president all to themselves; Eleanor had returned that afternoon to Washington. Marion, however, noticed that something was amiss. "There's something constrained about the President," she told her husband. "There's evidently something on his mind. He isn't natural."

The next day after lunch, Frankfurter learned what was troubling the president. Roosevelt took him into a small study in his mother's house at Hyde Park and said: "I want to tell you why I can't appoint you to succeed Cardozo." Frankfurter insisted that no explanation was necessary. The president, however, explained that he had given "very definite promises to" Democratic senators and party leaders that the next nominee would be a westerner. Frankfurter suggested Fifth Circuit judge Hutcheson of Texas; Roosevelt frowned, perhaps because Hutcheson was close to Vice President John Nance Garner, who was on the outs with Roosevelt after opposing court packing. The president asked Frankfurter's opinion of western judges and lawyers that he and Cummings had been discussing: District of Columbia Circuit judge Harold M. Stephens of Utah; Ninth Circuit judges Albert Lee Stephens in Los Angeles, Denman in San Francisco, and Healy in Idaho; and Senator Schwellenbach. Frankfurter replied that he knew Ninth Circuit judges Albert Lee Stephens and Healy only by name and offered to read their judicial opinions and write a memorandum for the president. Roosevelt gratefully accepted the offer of assistance.

After the talk in Roosevelt's study, the Frankfurters joined the president for a ride through the countryside. With the Supreme Court nomination business off his chest, Marion thought the president was "his old self again." Roosevelt warned the press not to read too much into Frankfurter's visit or it would find itself "out on a limb." The visit, however, fueled more speculation. The conservative *Chicago Tribune* predicted that Frankfurter had the "inside track" over a westerner or a Catholic; the *New York Herald Tribune* came to the opposite conclusion citing "circles close to the summer White House." In truth, Frankfurter's chances of succeeding Cardozo were at their lowest ebb.

Five days after Frankfurter's visit to Hyde Park, Roosevelt revealed to William Allen White the real source of the trouble: the president's arguments for increasing the number of justices from nine to fifteen included making the Court more "representative" on the basis of age, outlook, and geography. In an

October 13 letter addressed "Dear Bill" and marked "private and confidential," the president explained his pledge to make the Court more geographically diverse as "a problem not so much of politics but of principle." He reminded White that eight of the nine justices, including Pierce Butler from St. Paul, Minnesota, had been born east of the Mississippi River and left two-thirds of the country unrepresented. The president vowed not to nominate another justice from the same judicial circuit. With Hughes and Stone from New York and Brandeis from Massachusetts, Frankfurter's nomination exacerbated the geographic imbalance. Roosevelt concluded: "Sorta tough ain't it!"

Another liberal western candidate entered the mix after Election Day— Michigan Governor Frank Murphy. Murphy was criticized for not ordering the removal of United Auto Workers engaged in a sit-down strike in early 1937 at a General Motors plant in Flint, Michigan. Despite Corcoran and Cohen's efforts, Murphy lost his reelection bid. The lame-duck governor was considered the "best western Catholic" for the Cardozo vacancy. On Election Day on November 8, New Deal Democrats had fared badly. Corcoran's attempted "purge" of disloyal Democrats resulted in the defeat of only a single legislator, Rep. John J. O'Connor of New York. Five days after the election, the New York Herald Tribune indicated that Corcoran was pushing for Murphy and that it was a two-man race between Murphy and Senator Schwellenbach; Frankfurter was running third. The Washington Evening Star predicted fierce Senate opposition to Murphy's nomination as "too radical" and because of his pro-labor sympathies during the sit-down strike. The Washington Post reported that "left wing New Dealers" preferred Murphy, and the "dark horse" candidate was Judge Harold Stephens.

With Murphy's name resurfacing, Cummings sought to press Stephens's candidacy. During a private lunch with the president on November 18, the attorney general once again reviewed the candidates. He said Judge Healy was too young and inexperienced and Judge Albert Lee Stephens could not be chosen over his Ninth Circuit colleague Judge Denman. Roosevelt asked if there were any deans of West Coast law schools; Cummings replied that they were all too old. The choice came down to Denman or Harold Stephens, and Denman was too old. The president "did not seem to be particularly enthused" about them or San Francisco lawyer Maurice Harrison.

Cummings made another pitch for Harold Stephens: he "could be credited to Utah" and was "the right age, had fine educational equipment, great industry, fine character, and was widely respected." Roosevelt said "the country would not be very much stirred" by a Stephens nomination. Cummings, with an obvious allusion to Frankfurter, responded: "I know why you are not enthused about Harold, he is not colorful enough for you, but it has been my experience that it is a rare thing to find a man who is both colorful and safe, and that most of the colorful people get into trouble at one time or another." Roosevelt was amused, and, according to Cummings, somewhat impressed by the argument. In the attorney general's mind, the choice was between Denman or Harold Stephens.

Roosevelt eliminated some western candidates thanks to help from Frankfurter. The day before Cummings's meeting with the president, Frankfurter had sent Roosevelt memoranda about two Ninth Circuit judges, Albert Lee Stephens of Los Angeles and William Healy of Idaho. Roosevelt also had asked about a Montana judge, but Frankfurter could not figure out which one "for I can hardly believe that you have either Judge [James Harris] Baldwin or Judge [Charles Nelson] Pray in mind." Frankfurter's views of the two Ninth Circuit judges were not much higher. Albert Lee Stephens wrote opinions that were "well conceived and lucidly expressed, but devoid of distinction" and showed no "evidence of learning." Healy had been on the court only a year and a half. His opinions, Frankfurter wrote Roosevelt, were "lucid" and free of "legal jargon," yet revealed "no real distinction of utterance and no manifestation of learning in the service of wisdom."

The Supreme Court vacancy was not on Frankfurter's mind because of tragic events in Germany and his native Austria. A November 9 pogrom, triggered by the assassination of a German diplomat by a Polish Jewish refugee, lasted for two days and littered the streets with so much glass from Jewish-owned stores it became known as Kristallnacht, the night of broken glass. Nazi storm troopers burned and looted more than 7000 Jewish-owned shops, 200 synagogues, and 29 department stores. They sent 20,000 Jewish men to concentration camps and executed those who resisted. The violence stopped only because Hermann Göring preferred to expropriate Jewish property and assets rather than destroy them. Not even the Sulzberger-owned *New York Times* could ignore or downplay the death and destruction; the story ran on page one.

"Even if I would want to, I couldn't keep the German situation out of my mind," Frankfurter wrote Harold Ickes. "It's being kept there to the exclusion of almost all else by the uninterrupted impact of letters and visitors concerned with the awful situation." He lauded Ickes for resisting pressure from the State Department and refusing to sell helium, which was needed to power grounded German airships carrying passengers but potentially munitions, to the Nazi regime. A regular White House visitor, Ickes remained confident that Frankfurter was "in the lead" for the Cardozo vacancy. Ickes also heard

rumors that two justices, Brandeis and possibly Butler, might resign. If Butler resigned, Ickes speculated that Roosevelt would nominate Murphy "since
both Butler and Murphy are Catholics and come from the Middle West." The
source of the rumor about the justices resigning likely was the person pushing hardest for Frankfurter's nomination, Corcoran.

In October, Corcoran again circulated the story that Frankfurter had
opposed the court-packing plan. "We who were fighting the bill took pains
to find this out," a source told the *New York Times*. "There is not the slightest
doubt about it." The truth about Frankfurter's feelings, judging by his public
silence and private assistance to Roosevelt, was more complicated. Years later,
Corcoran characterized Frankfurter as having been involved "up to his neck."

Corcoran and his allies continued to leak that Brandeis would resign so
that Frankfurter could replace him. The rumors became so persistent that
columnist Raymond Clapper wrote about the "pressure" on Brandeis to
retire to "make way" for Frankfurter and described Brandeis's friends as
"incensed." The pressure, Clapper wrote, came from "the Corcoran-Cohen
group . . . protégés of Mr. Frankfurter who long have dreamed that their idol
would reach the Supreme Court." Alsop and Kintner denied that the clamor
for Brandeis's retirement came from "the New Deal left wing," reiterated that
they, "like the members of New Deal left wing, have a deep and reverent admiration" for Brandeis, and "merely sought to record a choice offered to him by
the plight of his race, to alleviate which would be the only reason for his leaving the court." Brandeis, who had advised Roosevelt in October and November
about Palestine and Jewish refugee issues and corresponded with Frankfurter
about possible western candidates for the Cardozo vacancy, revealed no intention to retire. Roosevelt "will eventually remake the Court," Frankfurter predicted to Harold Laski. "No—L.D.B., I'm confident will *not* resign!"

At 11:00 a.m. on November 26, friends and admirers gathered in the
Supreme Court courtroom for a memorial service for Benjamin Cardozo.
Solicitor General Robert Jackson, the chairman of the proceedings, opened
the meeting by reviewing Cardozo's career. New York lawyer John Lord
O'Brian presided over the meeting. Former attorney general William Mitchell, Judge Irving Lehman, lawyer George Wharton Pepper, and Frankfurter's friends Dean Acheson and Monte Lemann of New Orleans paid tribute
to Cardozo. On doctor's orders, Frankfurter stayed home because of chronic
back trouble. Back in Cambridge, he drafted the Supreme Court bar's memorial resolution to Cardozo. That same month, his book, *Mr. Justice Holmes
and the Supreme Court*, came out. As Frankfurter paid tribute to Cardozo and
Holmes, the battle for their seat on the Court continued.

St. Louis Times-Star editorial page editor Irving N. Brant promoted his preferred western candidate, University of Iowa law dean Wiley Blount Rutledge. A native Iowan who had worked for several of the state's newspapers before moving to St. Louis, Brant wrote a 1936 book, *Storm over the Constitution*, about the New Deal constitutional crisis. The book, which Roosevelt had read while on a battleship in South America, may have informed his decision to propose the court-packing plan. Since 1935, Brant had been corresponding with Frankfurter and Roosevelt about the Supreme Court; both men held Brant's editorials in the highest regard. And in late 1937, Brant moved to Washington to write a multivolume biography of James Madison, worked one day a week for the *Star-Times*, and moonlighted as a consultant to Ickes and speechwriter for Roosevelt. Thus, Brant's recommendation carried great weight.

Back in 1936, Brant had encouraged Roosevelt to nominate Rutledge to the Court when a vacancy arose, and the president had responded by asking Brant to prepare a dossier. During the next few years, Brant read Rutledge's speeches and writings about constitutional law and corresponded with Rutledge. After Cardozo's death, however, Brant did not push for Rutledge "because the tumult over the court-packing plan" and the Iowa law dean's public support for it "made his nomination impossible." Roosevelt revealed the "pressure was heavy" to nominate a westerner. Brant counseled the president to "disregard the western factor" and nominate Frankfurter. Yet he lobbied for Rutledge as a second option and sent his Rutledge dossier to the president. Brant knew that one of Roosevelt's "closest advisers" was backing Rutledge as a liberal western alternative to Frankfurter and that "the western senators who are crying for a western appointment are mostly men who want a conservative named. I think they are trying to block the appointment of Frankfurter . . ." Brant, who kept Rutledge apprised of the political fight, believed that "Cummings and Farley talked geography, but there is just a faint touch of anti-Semitism in both of them."

Roosevelt was intrigued by Rutledge even as Cummings and Farley continued to advocate for a western candidate, preferably Judge Harold Stephens. On December 9, the *Baltimore Sun* reported that Stephens "appeared" to be in the lead. Gossip columnist Walter Winchell predicted that Frankfurter would not get nominated until Brandeis retired and that the Cardozo vacancy would go to Stephens.

At 9:00 p.m. on December 15, the entire cabinet assembled at the White House for the annual diplomatic reception. Roosevelt led the cabinet from the main dining room to the outer hall. The band played "Hail to the Chief." More than 1000 people proceeded through the receiving line. Farley was not there, but Cummings was. After the reception ended at 10:10 p.m., Cummings and Roosevelt discussed the Supreme Court vacancy. Roosevelt began the conversation by conceding that if Brandeis retired, "the matter would be simplified" because he could nominate Frankfurter. Cummings agreed, but with Brandeis on the bench, the Court did not need a second justice from Massachusetts or another from the East Coast. "I thought he ought to go West of the Mississippi," Cummings said. Roosevelt concurred but could not find the right person. "How did you get along with the man I mentioned to you?" Roosevelt asked. Cummings assumed the president was referring to Brant's suggestion of Rutledge. Cummings's assessment was blunt: "I told him he was a fine man and a Progressive, that I did not honestly believe he rated appointment to the Supreme Court." Roosevelt also raised Senator Schwellenbach "as a possibility." Cummings and Roosevelt agreed that Judge Denman, who had turned sixty-six, was too old.

The attorney general again made his pitch for Harold Stephens as a Catholic from the far West, with two degrees from Harvard Law School, judicial experience on the federal Court of Appeals of the District of Columbia, and respect from the bench and bar. The president, Cummings contended, "need not worry a minute about his attitude toward large questions. I said he has been through fire with us and knows what it is all about." Cummings was referring to Stephens's disastrous 1934 Supreme Court oral argument in the hot oil case. Roosevelt appeared to agree with his attorney general. "Yes," he told Cummings, "that is so, perhaps on the whole that may be the best we can do." Cummings, however, was downplaying Stephens's conservative views on constitutional and administrative law. Joseph L. Rauh, Jr., working as Corcoran and Cohen's assistant, read Stephens's judicial opinions and discovered that they tended to side with holding companies rather than the Securities and Exchange Commission. The young New Dealers had reason to worry that Frankfurter's chance depended on Brandeis's retirement and that the Court would become more conservative with Stephens.

The day after Roosevelt appeared to agree with Cummings on Stephens, Rosenman, Hopkins, Corcoran, and Cohen returned to the White House for a nearly three-hour lunch. Alsop and Kintner reported on December 26 that Frankfurter's "friends . . . are as hopeful as ever the President will name him, and not so long ago they received heartening, if not absolutely reliable assurance from the White House." The New York Herald Tribune countered that Frankfurter was "no longer considered a likely candidate" and that Stephens had "the inside track." The New Republic claimed that Senator Schwellenbach had already been offered the job. Drew Pearson falsely reported that Frankfurter had withdrawn from consideration "[l]argely because of the Jewish situation." Alsop and Kintner cautioned that "pretended inside stories about other nominees are as thick in Washington as horseflies in August."

Farley sensed victory over the New Dealers and Frankfurter. After a December 21 lunch with the president, Farley wrote: "We discussed the Jewish situation and I think he has a full realization of the existant [sic] feeling. This is one reason he will not appoint a Jew on the District Court of Appeals." A week later during a private dinner with Farley, Roosevelt said he was "having a difficult time" with the Cardozo vacancy. The president revealed that he had told Frankfurter at Hyde Park that the law professor would not be appointed: "In the first place, the appointment had to go west. In the second place, he told Frankfurter, that in view of the anti-Semitic feeling, he could not appoint him, but if Judge Brandeis should resign or die, he would appoint Frankfurter that day to that vacancy without any hesitation." Farley again encouraged Roosevelt to name a westerner such as Judge Bratton of New Mexico, Judge Haney of Oregon, or Judge Devaney of Minnesota. Roosevelt said Bratton "belonged to a judicial school of thought and should not be represented on the bench," Haney was "not up to it," and Devaney was from the same home state as Butler. Roosevelt countered with Senator Schwellenbach of Washington or Dean Rutledge of Iowa and rejected Farley's suggestions of two leading opponents of the court bill, Senator Joseph O'Mahoney of Wyoming and Senator Burton K. Wheeler of Montana. Farley believed that the president was "very much exercised with the difficulty he is having in getting someone from the west." Lastly, Farley raised Harold Stephens. Roosevelt "had given considerable thought to him" yet concluded "it just did not look like a proper appointment." Farley believed the president had "made up his mind not to appoint" Stephens.

To make matters worse for Stephens, his chief backer, Attorney General Cummings, was resigning at the end of the calendar year because of his wife's ill-health. The timing could not have been better for liberal New Dealers. It was only a few days before the Senate reconvened in early January and before Roosevelt made his final decision.

Few people knew that Roosevelt was leaning toward Brant's preferred candidate, Wiley Rutledge. The Iowa law dean and former professor at Washington University in St. Louis was both a liberal and a westerner. The president was so serious that he asked Frankfurter his opinion of Rutledge as a scholar and potential Supreme Court nominee. Frankfurter had already provided Roosevelt with unenthusiastic appraisals of Ninth Circuit judges Healy and Albert Lee Stephens. He did not have time to read all Rutledge's writings and speeches on constitutional law. Instead, he phoned one of his closest colleagues, Thomas Reed Powell, to inquire with University of Wisconsin law dean Lloyd Garrison and other professors at the annual meeting of the American Association of Law Schools about Rutledge. Powell, who understood the seriousness of the request, replied with a positive report. On December 27 or 28, Frankfurter informed the president that Rutledge "was qualified for the Court and would be a properly appointed man." Rutledge, to his credit, knew that Brant and others were promoting his candidacy yet thought that Roosevelt should nominate Frankfurter.

Liberal New Dealers, fearing Stephens's nomination and hearing rumors about Rutledge, made a final push for Frankfurter. At 2:00 p.m. on December 29, Ickes met with Roosevelt and argued that Frankfurter "was a legal statesman who stood head and shoulder above every other possible appointee." The president promised to nominate Frankfurter when Brandeis resigned. "But will Brandeis resign?" Ickes asked. The secretary of the interior was not as sure as the president that Brandeis's retirement was imminent; Ickes feared a lost opportunity to remake the Court. "If you appoint Frankfurter," he told Roosevelt, "his ability and learning are such that he will dominate the Supreme Court for fifteen or twenty years to come. The result will be that, probably after you are dead, it will still be your Supreme Court." Ickes's prophecy about Frankfurter did not sway Roosevelt, who insisted on appointing a westerner yet conceded that none "really ranked." Ickes dismissed newspaper reports touting Stephens as "another leak" by Farley but was convinced that Roosevelt's insistence on choosing a westerner would lead to Stephens.

The next day, Ickes blasted Stephens as "stupid" and not worthy of the Supreme Court to Roosevelt's secretary, confidant, and longtime travel companion, Missy LeHand. Especially fond of Frankfurter, LeHand agreed and asked if Ickes wanted to speak to the president again. Ickes declined because he knew how busy Roosevelt was with the budget. She wondered if she should say something to the president; Ickes "told her to use her own judgment." The next day, she repeated Ickes's arguments about Frankfurter to the president. Previously, the president had told her "the whole thing was settled." This time, he did not say that—which made her feel as if Frankfurter had a chance.

Those chances depended on the capable hands of a very worried Corcoran. Corcoran had begun the campaign for Frankfurter with the August letter from Senator Norris, kept the mailboxes of senators and Harvard law alumni full of pro-Frankfurter material, and throughout December and early January updated his former law professor during nightly phone calls. Yet for all the work that Corcoran had done, he confessed to Ickes that the nomination would go to Stephens. Corcoran was "so disgusted that he said that if this appointment were made he would probably retire from the Government altogether." Harry Hopkins, the newly appointed secretary of commerce and longtime presidential adviser, was extremely worried, for he had met with the president for nearly three hours on December 29 with Corcoran, Cohen, and Rosenman. Hopkins believed that Roosevelt was considering Senator Schwellenbach and Rutledge and was dead set on a westerner. But Stephens still had "a chance."

On Saturday December 31 at 1:00 p.m., Roosevelt invited Hopkins and Robert Jackson to lunch in the president's upstairs study and informed Jackson that he would not be named attorney general. As with the Cardozo vacancy, Roosevelt wanted a westerner as attorney general and therefore chose former Michigan governor Frank Murphy. The president promised Jackson that the appointment would be temporary because Murphy wanted to be secretary of war and that Jackson could remain as solicitor general until he was named attorney general. Roosevelt then raised the Supreme Court vacancy and revealed that Cummings "was on his knees to get Harold Stephens." The president, however, was still considering Schwellenbach, Rutledge, and Frankfurter.

Despite his disappointment about being passed over as attorney general, Jackson believed that the Cardozo vacancy was more important than the attorney generalship and made a final pitch for Frankfurter. A frequent companion of Roosevelt's, Jackson told the president "that all I would ask of him for myself was to leave me as Solicitor General, but give me Felix Frankfurter on the bench." Jackson insisted that he knew the Court better than the attorney general. Cummings's "notion of geography was wholly political." Jackson pleaded that "the President's greatest contribution in the light of history would be the change of Supreme Court interpretation of the Constitution." Only Frankfurter, Jackson argued, could stand up at the justices' private conference to Chief Justice Hughes, who "looked like God and talked like God." Jackson told Roosevelt to act as if this were the president's final Supreme Court nomination because "the future is uncertain" about who will be president in 1940. The Court's "importance is far-reaching," he told Roosevelt, so "leave me at the Bar of the Supreme Court and give me Felix as the new Judge." The president "said it sounded pretty good and that he, too, felt that the best thing for the future was Felix." Hopkins "joined enthusiastically" with Jackson's comments. As they left the president at 2:45 p.m., Jackson and Hopkins "agreed that Felix was in, and I had the feeling that it was accomplished." After Hopkins informed Ickes what had happened at lunch, Ickes wrote: "This appointment is probably the most important that the President has been called upon to make. I think that he will be committing a grave error if he does not appoint Frankfurter."

The New Deal liberals were not content to rely on Roosevelt's assurances. At noon on January 2, 1939, forty-four guests gathered in Roosevelt's second-floor study for Murphy's swearing-in ceremony. Roosevelt read Murphy's commission; Justice Stanley F. Reed administered the oath of office; and the guests signed Murphy's Bible that he had received as a high-school graduation present. The president's decision to choose Murphy over Jackson as attorney general infuriated the liberals. They worried that Roosevelt would disappoint them again in selecting Cardozo's successor. "The Frankfurter appointment," Jackson wrote three days after his New Year's Eve lunch with the president, "was still uncertain."

One of the guests in Roosevelt's study was Murphy's predecessor and Harold Stephens's biggest booster, former attorney general Cummings. Jackson wrote that Cummings "lingered and, as the President put it, hung on his neck for the appointment of Stephens. It had come to be the matter on which hung his own prestige and he hated Frankfurter with a cordial hate. Frankfurter had no hate, but had a genial contempt for Cummings."

A worried Jackson sought out the most important person at Murphy's swearing-in besides the president, Senator Norris. Norris's August 8 statement from Waupaca, Wisconsin, had started the movement for Frankfurter. The Nebraska senator possessed the gravitas, liberal bona fides, and rapport with Roosevelt to close the deal. At 2:30 p.m. on the day of Murphy's swearing-in, Jackson, Corcoran, and Cohen went to see Norris. Norris, who had written the president urging him to name Jackson attorney general and was angry about Murphy's appointment, greeted them that "his influence seemed to have little weight at the White House." They insisted otherwise. Corcoran asked him to go to the White House, talk to Roosevelt about the Frankfurter nomination, and "urge it as a westerner." They emphasized the importance of the appointment to the future of the New Deal. Norris phoned the White House; Roosevelt "told him to come over immediately."

At 4:30 p.m., Norris met alone with the president and "strongly urged" him to nominate Frankfurter. Norris was not the last person to meet with Roosevelt, but the senator was certainly the most influential. Roosevelt considered Norris one of the country's great liberal statesmen and respected Norris's judgment. The president, however, denied to the press that he had decided on Frankfurter and was "mildly ruffled" by reports that he had indicated as much to Norris.

Immediately after he saw Norris, Roosevelt had tea in his study with Justice Stone. At the president's request, journalist Irving Brant had arranged the meeting. Stone had played a pivotal role in 1932 in persuading Hoover to ignore geographic considerations and nominate Cardozo. That evening with Roosevelt, Stone swayed the decision about Cardozo's successor. Stone argued that selecting a judge from every circuit made it impossible to "get a distinguished Supreme Court that way because you cannot find a distinguished judge or lawyer in every circuit." In his mind, there were only a few distinguished Supreme Court candidates in the whole country. Stone also revealed the inner workings of the current Court and his contempt for Chief Justice Hughes. He said that if two liberal justices disagreed at the conference table, the chief justice "will get his big toe in and widen the cleavage." Stone emphasized the importance of appointing "a man like Frankfurter who is capable of meeting the Chief Justice in the fields both of law and social policy."

The next morning at 11:00 a.m., Ickes went to see the president and was bent on making a final pitch for Frankfurter until he heard Stone's arguments and noticed their effect on the president. When Ickes left the White House, he "felt perfectly confident that [Roosevelt] would appoint Frankfurter." At 12:30 p.m., Murphy met with the president. Ickes learned from Corcoran and Hopkins that the new attorney general "would go down the line for Frankfurter." Irving Brant believed that Murphy helped nullify Farley's influence on the president and that among the four or five factors in Frankfurter's favor "the most important was the shift from Cummings to Murphy in the cabinet and the work Murphy did immediately afterward."

Unaware of the importance of Roosevelt's meetings with Norris, Stone, and Murphy, the media consensus had swung to Stephens. The *Chicago Tribune* insisted that the liberal Murphy's nomination as attorney general had made the more conservative Stephens's nomination to the Supreme Court a done deal. The conservative newspaper considered Stephens "a compromise" compared to the "radical" Senator Schwellenbach. "Stephens Expected to Go on Supreme Bench," the paper declared. Alsop and Kintner explained the internal power struggle between New Dealers led by Corcoran and "the orthodox Democrats" led by Cummings and Farley. The columnists declared Cummings the winner and insisted that the liberal New Dealers had lost the attorney generalship and the Cardozo vacancy. Frankfurter, they wrote, "is out." The orthodox Democrats favored Stephens; the New Dealers countered with Judge Hutcheson of Texas or Dean Rutledge of Iowa. The Associated Press claimed that Stephens had "the inside track." The *New York Herald Tribune* reported that Frankfurter's stock was rising but that Stephens's friends remained "confident" and Schwellenbach was "still in the running." Despite Stephens's lead the past two weeks, the *Washington Post* declared that Frankfurter had moved "to the fore again."

On the morning of January 4, Cummings lobbied his successor Murphy that the president should choose a westerner and that Stephens was the most "eminently qualified." Cummings believed, incorrectly, that Murphy agreed with him. Upon hearing from a newspaperman that Frankfurter would be nominated the next day, Cummings replied: "If I were you, I wouldn't bet a nickel on that." Yet privately he was not so sure. "There are rumors, apparently well founded, that the President's thoughts are turning again toward Frankfurter," Cummings wrote. "I am sorry that this is so. I think Frankfurter is eminently qualified but I do not believe that the great West should be overlooked." Cummings did not bother the president that day. At 12:45 p.m., Roosevelt left the White House for the U.S. Capitol to deliver his annual message to Congress. He returned to the White House at 2:00 p.m., held a 4:15 p.m. press conference, and two hours later left the office for his private residence.

At 7:00 p.m., the doorbell rang at the Frankfurter home at 192 Brattle Street in Cambridge. Their friend, University of Chicago professor Robert Morss Lovett, had arrived for dinner. Marion Frankfurter was dressed and ready and annoyed that her perennially late husband was still in his BVD underwear. "Please hurry," she said. At that moment, the phone rang. Frankfurter picked it up in the study across from his bedroom. It was President Roosevelt. After they exchanged pleasant greetings, Roosevelt said: "I told you I can't appoint you to the Supreme Court." "Yes," Frankfurter replied. "You told me that." Roosevelt repeated the message. "Yes, you've told me that," Frankfurter replied again. "You've made that perfectly clear. I understand that." After all, Frankfurter had written memoranda critical of the opinions of judges Albert Lee Stephens and Healy and a week earlier had responded positively to Roosevelt's queries about Rutledge. "But wherever I turn," he told Frankfurter, "wherever I turn," he repeated, people told him to nominate the Harvard law professor. Unless Frankfurter raised an "insurmountable objection," Roosevelt was going to send his name to the Senate tomorrow at noon. The voluble Harvard law professor was "moved to mumbling silence." Somehow, Frankfurter waited until his dinner guest Lovett left at midnight. As soon as the front door closed, he said: "Marion, let me tell you what your fate and mine is."

Roosevelt kept all his closest advisers—liberals Corcoran, Hopkins, Ickes, Jackson, and Murphy and conservatives Cummings and Farley—in the dark.

As he had done with Black's nomination, Roosevelt filled out the blank nomination form in longhand. Not even the president's executive secretaries Rudolph Forster or Marvin H. McIntyre knew about it. Roosevelt sent the nomination to the Senate Judiciary Committee shortly before noon on January 5. Just before the news of the nomination flashed across the Associated Press wire in Emporia, Kansas, William Allen White received a telegram from the president: "I have done it."

ROOSEVELT'S ADVISERS LEARNED about the nomination over the newswires. Cummings and Farley were shocked. Stephens blamed Corcoran. The liberal New Dealers broke into celebration. At 2:00 p.m., Corcoran interrupted a lunch at the Interior Department between Ickes and Murphy. Corcoran was carrying two magnums of champagne. Hopkins, Jackson, SEC chairman Douglas, Hopkins aide David Niles, Missy LeHand, and Corcoran's secretary Peggy Dowd joined the party. They viewed Frankfurter's nomination as the culmination of the court-packing fight. "We were all very happy and I noted that Bob Jackson was particularly joyous," Ickes wrote. "He told us that now there would be a man on the Supreme Court before whom he could argue a case in the knowledge that his argument was being listened to with sympathy and understanding. All of us regard this as the most significant and worthwhile thing that the President has done. He has solidified his Supreme Court victory, and, regardless of who may be President during the next few years, there will be on the bench of the Supreme Court a group of liberals under aggressive, forthright and intelligent leadership."

Another New Deal insider, columnist Raymond Clapper, saw challenges ahead. He understood the importance of Frankfurter's role as Roosevelt's unofficial policy adviser and as a talent scout placing friends and former students throughout the administration. In his column, he predicted that it would be difficult for the law professor-turned-justice to sever those ties: "Even though Frankfurter will be busy with his Supreme Court duties, it is not unlikely that Roosevelt will call frequently upon him for private counsel, even more so than in the past because Frankfurter will now be conveniently at hand. . . . Frankfurter's ripened judgment and balanced liberalism are much needed by Roosevelt in this period when the tide is running against him and when he seems to be groping for bearings. In fact he is as much needed at the White House as on the Supreme Court, perhaps more so at the moment."

The 56-year-old Frankfurter faced a daunting set of expectations. First, he was billed as the Court's liberal savior. The New Dealers expected him to go toe-to-toe with Chief Justice Hughes and to lead the Court's liberal wing for decades. They underestimated how riven with conflict the Court was, how the issues had changed since the court-packing fight, and how contentious those new issues would be. Second, he continued to advise the president and friends and former students in government. He liked being an administration insider. In many ways, he brought this role upon himself and even cultivated it. The dual burdens of liberal leader and policy adviser were too much for any new justice. Frankfurter's "balanced liberalism" was no match for the awaiting political maelstrom. It took all of Frankfurter's facility and skill, as well as assistance from members of his liberal political network, just to survive his unprecedented Senate confirmation hearings.

CHAPTER 20

The Oddest Collection
of People

The day after Roosevelt submitted his name to the Senate, Frankfurter wired the president: "Says Marion: 'I hope that you'll be on the stand for days so that I can learn something about you.'" Marion expected her husband to have to testify; she could not have expected that his Senate appearance would change the Supreme Court nomination process forever.

Frankfurter's confirmation hearings were a public spectacle unlike any the country had ever seen and revealed rising anti-Communism, anti-Semitism, and anti–New Deal sentiment in late 1930s America. Opponents of Frankfurter's nomination charged him with being a Communist and disloyal alien who had infiltrated the highest reaches of the United States government. The previous year, Congress had established the Special Committee to Investigate Un-American Activities. Referred to as the Dies Committee after its chairman, Representative Martin Dies, Jr., of Texas, it was officially named the House Un-American Activities Committee (HUAC). On December 8, 1938, a retired army colonel had testified before the Dies Committee about the radical activities of the American Civil Liberties Union (ACLU), Frankfurter's participation on the organization's national committee since its inception in 1920, and his opposition that same year to the roundup and deportation of radical immigrants during the Palmer raids.

Amid rising fears of Communism, Frankfurter's Senate confirmation hearings resembled a three-day HUAC trial replete with unreliable witnesses and unsubstantiated testimony. Not even Brandeis, who had waited 117 days for a committee vote in 1916 and had been represented before a subcommittee by his law partner, had endured such a humiliating ordeal. In many ways, Frankfurter experienced the first modern Supreme Court confirmation hearing. People publicly testified against him and made wild accusations. He was the second Supreme Court nominee to testify in person—and not by choice. He experienced the first confirmation process as an open public debate not only over his fitness to serve on the Court but also over his loyalty to the country.

On January 7, 1939, a Senate judiciary subcommittee convened to review letters and telegrams about Frankfurter's nomination. Several people requested the opportunity to testify against him. Senator William H. King, an anti–New Deal Democrat from Utah, suggested public hearings. Despite his doubts whether the hearings would reveal any new information about the nominee, King argued that "this is supposed to be a democratic form of government" and described an associate justiceship as "an office of great importance." If people wanted to be heard, King said, it was the committee's "duty to hear them." The other members unanimously agreed.

That afternoon, the subcommittee chairman, Senator Matthew Neely, a pro–New Deal West Virginia Democrat, wired Frankfurter offering him the opportunity to appear "in person or by counsel." No Supreme Court nominee had testified on his own behalf except for Harlan Fiske Stone in 1925 to explain why, as Coolidge's attorney general, he had continued the unsuccessful prosecution of the Harding administration's chief antagonist, Senator Burton K. Wheeler. Stone, however, was the attorney general and had testified about a single prosecution; Frankfurter was a private citizen who did not want to set a bad precedent for future nominees or to expose himself to wide-ranging questions. He sought advice from longtime friends about how to respond. First, he phoned Neely and indicated that he preferred to continue to teach his Harvard law classes. Later that night, he wired his willingness to testify if needed and preferred to be represented by his counsel, Dean Acheson.

Tall and handsome, raised on a Middletown, Connecticut, farm, and educated at Groton and Yale College, Dean Gooderham Acheson was expected to join the establishment. What was decidedly unexpected was the son of an Episcopal bishop's lifelong bond with an immigrant Jewish law professor. Frankfurter tapped Acheson, a *Harvard Law Review* editor and fifth in his class, to serve as Brandeis's secretary after graduation. After working two terms for Brandeis from 1919 to 1921, he joined the Washington law firm of Covington, Burling & Rublee as its fourth attorney and first associate. Frankfurter encouraged Acheson's passion for public service and unsuccessfully lobbied for him to be Roosevelt's solicitor general. In May 1933, Roosevelt named Acheson under secretary of the treasury. After five months of infighting, Acheson resigned over his disagreement with the president's gold-purchasing policy. He quietly returned to his partnership at Covington with his government career in shambles—until he found himself back in the public eye because of Frankfurter's nomination.

At 10:00 a.m. on January 10, a few hours before Frankfurter taught his public utilities class at Harvard, Acheson represented him before the Senate subcommittee. In Room 237 of the Old Senate Office Building, the Covington lawyer cut quite a figure with his dark double-breasted suit, white pocket square, and carefully cultivated mustache. He sat in his chair, took notes, and listened as each witness testified for half an hour on a first-come, first-serve basis. He chose not to cross-examine any of the witnesses he later described as "the oddest collection of people I have ever seen. All were fanatical and some were very definitely mental cases."

The first witness, Collis O. Redd, the self-described national director of the Constitutional Crusaders, purported to speak for everyone in America except for the largest labor unions and in reality represented only himself. Bald, bespectacled, and dressed in a three-piece suit, Redd asked why Roosevelt did not appoint "an American from Revolution times instead of a Jew from Austria just naturalized." Senator Norris observed that a justice from the Revolutionary War era would be "too old." Senator Borah, an Idaho Republican and another Frankfurter champion, asked: "Are you opposing Mr. Frankfurter on the ground that he is a Jew?" After Redd denied the accusation, Borah asked: "Then why drag these things into the record?" Redd insisted that he was opposed to Frankfurter as the author of the National Industrial Recovery Act even though it was pointed out that others had drafted the law. Redd contended that his "interest in this fight is against the liberalism, as now called modern liberalism, as laid down by Frankfurter, Rosenman, Baruch, and President Roosevelt." He argued that Frankfurter "corresponds more to the theories of Russian Communism, instead of upholding the liberal ideals of the founders of this country."

The next witness, a respectable-looking Washington lawyer named George E. Sullivan, wrote about Communist activity for Catholic publications. During the mid-1930s, he had served on a federation of citizens' associations trying to force District of Columbia public school teachers to sign loyalty oaths to receive their pay. In late 1938, he had represented accusatory witnesses before the Dies Committee. He turned his Red-hunting sights on Frankfurter. As he gripped the sides of the conference table, Sullivan argued that "Mr. Frankfurter's alien-minded affiliations do not inspire confidence in him as fit to be an American official of any kind, much less a member of our highest judicial tribunal." Sullivan excoriated Frankfurter for joining the national committee of the ACLU, an organization filled with "a number of notorious Reds" including Communist Party chairman William Z. Foster. Sullivan also read Theodore Roosevelt's 1917 letter accusing Frankfurter of "Bolsheviki" activity in investigating the Bisbee deportation and the Mooney case for the Wilson administration. Senator Neely observed that Sullivan had neglected to quote Frankfurter's reply to Roosevelt and included it in the record. Neely also asked Sullivan whether his objections were "based upon the ground that he is a Jew?"

The day's third and final witness, Colonel Wade H. Cooper, tried to use Frankfurter's hearings to relitigate a frivolous lawsuit. A former stockholder of a defunct District of Columbia bank, Cooper had failed to persuade the Supreme Court to hear his case seeking $500,000 in damages because the government had forced his bank to close. Senator Norris asked whether it would be "proper" to ask Frankfurter his opinion about whether the Court should have taken the case. "I think you should get his opinion," Cooper replied. "It is not only me, but the whole country." Acheson sat a few feet away from Cooper with a look of exasperation and disbelief. Several senators "lost interest" and "walked out." The press was not amused; the conservative *Chicago Tribune* described Cooper and Redd as "cranks"; columnist Raymond Clapper concluded: "This pitiful showing was an unintended compliment to Frankfurter."

The real show began with the next morning's star witness, Elizabeth Dilling. A suburban Chicago housewife and devout Catholic, Dilling had studied the harp at the University of Chicago and married a lawyer and chief engineer with the Chicago Sanitary District. A 1931 summer trip to Russia transformed her into an anti-Communist crusader. For the next seven years, she devoted her time and energy to stamping out Communism in America. In 1934, she self-published a book, *The Red Network*, of facts, innuendos, and associations to smear prominent people. Frankfurter earned an entry in the "Who's Who" section. Her 1936 book, *The Roosevelt Red Record and Its Background*, described Frankfurter as "one of that clique of foreign-born Jewish revolutionaries so strongly behind Roosevelt and so powerful in his Administration."

Before the Senate subcommittee, Dilling announced her appearance "as an American citizen who devotes her time to noncommunistic activities at my own expense." She wore a blue and gold dress with three embroidered flowers on each side and a large gold locket around her neck. Her red, curly hair peeked out beneath a dark pillbox hat with three small white ribbons on the front and a white lace veil on the back. The press described her as "comely" and "fast talking" with "a high voice." With papers piled in front of her, Dil-

ling began to read seventeen pages of testimony and relied on newspaper articles to support her primary assertions: "that Felix Frankfurter has long been
one of the principal aids to the 'red' revolutionary movement in the United
States" and that he "worked in conjunction with and in behalf of leading 'red'
revolutionaries, and published propaganda for them, working directly with
the Communist Party."

Exhibit A of Communist propaganda, according to Dilling, was Frankfurter's 1927 book arguing for a new trial for Italian anarchists Sacco and Vanzetti.
She invoked John Henry Wigmore's criticism as proof of Frankfurter's "prejudice in favor of radicals" and "that he is unqualified not only for the Supreme
Court bench but as a lawyer." She quoted at length from Wigmore's articles in
the *Boston Evening Transcript* and *Boston Herald* attacking Frankfurter's book.
She referred to the ACLU's participation in the case and described the fight
for a new trial for Sacco and Vanzetti as "a communist agitation."

Dilling also attacked him on the basis of Marion's co-editing of Sacco's and
Vanzetti's jailhouse letters with Gardner Jackson ("Communist supporter")
and Frankfurter's associations with New Deal official Donald Richberg
("socialistic activities"), professor Max Lerner (Communist Party lecturer),
ACLU director Roger Baldwin ("'red' revolutionary"), and labor organizer and
former student Albert Weisbord. Then there was Frankfurter's longtime position on the ACLU's national committee. "The history of the American Civil
Liberties Union," she asserted, "is the history of the entire Communist and
'red' revolutionary movement."

Senators Neely and Norris took turns rebutting Dilling's accusations.
Neely questioned whether she could attribute Baldwin's ACLU writings to the
nominee because the latter was a member of the organization's national committee and argued that it would be like attributing whatever someone in the
Democratic or Republican Party wrote to one of its members. Norris clarified
that Frankfurter's book had not defended the actions of Sacco and Vanzetti,
only that they had not received a fair trial. "Frankfurter was a member of
that organization," Dilling insisted, referring to the ACLU, "and he defended
those men, and he knew they were guilty of every kind of crime done by 'reds,'
and they were against our form of government."

Dilling's testimony unraveled during questioning about *The Red Network*'s
accusations of radicalism against many prominent public officials including
Norris himself. "You classify as 'reds' practically this entire committee," Norris said. Neely reminded her that *The Red Network* had tagged as radicals
Hughes, Brandeis, Cardozo, Roberts, and Stone. "I didn't know Hughes was
in it," she replied. "I knew the rest of them were. I don't keep all these radi-

cals in my mind." Dilling insisted that Brandeis was "one of the most radical individuals in the United States." She argued that "Brandeis is the father of the policies and social philosophies of Frankfurter" and "in that respect they are father and son." She also deemed as radicals Senators Shipstead, Borah, Norris, La Follette, and Frazier, Republican senate candidate Glenn Frank of Wisconsin, as well as President and Mrs. Roosevelt. Neely was incredulous about Dilling's willingness to smear the president and first lady. "Do you want the evidence on them. I have got it here," Dilling said in a high-pitched voice. "Give me 15 minutes, and I will give it to you. If what I said about Roosevelt is not so, I ought to be in jail." Despite skepticism from several members of the committee, Dilling remained steadfast in her belief that Frankfurter was "one of the brilliant minds in connection with the 'red' movement. It will be a terrible thing in every community in this country when he is put on the Supreme Court Bench."

Life magazine's "picture of the week" featured an image of Dilling leaning forward, teeth clenched, and in mid-sentence. The magazine declared the "restless suburban Chicago matron . . . easily the star performer." Her testimony overshadowed the rest of the day's witnesses, most of whom veered from paranoid to prejudiced. They opposed Frankfurter's nomination because he was "imbued with collectivist ideas of government," "specialized in turning out international lawyers . . . because these international people are mostly Jews," was an "alien," and an ACLU member whose organization favored federal laws that "communized" Native Americans.

One witness matched Dilling's anti-Communism, anti-Semitism, and right-wing extremism—Allen A. Zoll. A Harvard Law School dropout, sales consultant, and ally of anti-Semitic radio preacher Father Coughlin, Zoll testified as executive vice president of the American Federation Against Communism. He was involved in the Coughlin-inspired Christian Front and founded his own far-right organization, American Patriots. On October 30, 1938, Zoll had led a 2000-person "Pro-American Rally" in New York City. Dilling, one of the rally's speakers, criticized Mayor Fiorello La Guardia and Eleanor Roosevelt as radicals. A movie shown at the rally featured a swastika and images of Hitler and Mussolini. On December 18, Zoll organized picketing of New York City radio station WMCA for its refusal to broadcast Coughlin's anti-Semitic speeches. Margaret Hopper, a housewife and one of the picketers that day, testified at Frankfurter's Senate hearing that people chanted "Down with Frankfurter" and "Keep him off the Supreme Court." The reason, she said, was that "Frankfurter is a 'red.'"

After a lunchtime recess on January 11, the 43-year-old Zoll confirmed that he was testifying against Frankfurter's nomination "because he is a Jew." Borah interjected: "You are raising the same question that is drenching Europe in blood. . . . In this country we do not deny any man privileges because of his religion or race." Zoll claimed that his opposition stemmed not from anti-Semitism but because the nomination "would stir up more anti-Semitism in this country." Senator King said he had heard from two Jewish friends along the same lines, though he disagreed with the position. "Some of the leading Jews feel the same way," Zoll said, alluding to the Sulzberger–Morgenthau Sr. opposition. Borah tried to strike the "offensive" testimony from the record, but his colleagues disagreed. After the overruled objections from Borah, Zoll said: "This appointment, in my opinion, would do more than any occurrence for years to intensify this spreading anti-Jewish feeling, which, if allowed to grow, will prove disastrous to Christian and Jew alike, in fact to all America." Nazi Germany's official news agency seized on Zoll's and Dilling's testimony as proof of rising anti-Semitism in the United States and proclaimed that Frankfurter's nomination had "caused considerable consternation and excitement in the committee."

Zoll's testimony took an even more sinister turn when he argued that Frankfurter "has not only constantly been on the side of these un-American groups for 20 years, but that he has been one of the guiding lights in these un-American forces." He rehashed old evidence about Frankfurter's position on the "communistic" ACLU national committee, Theodore Roosevelt's criticism of Frankfurter's reports about the Bisbee deportation and the Mooney case, and Wigmore's criticism of the book about the Sacco-Vanzetti case.

Near the end of Zoll's testimony, Acheson offered to produce proof of Frankfurter's father's citizenship. With assistance from Judge Learned Hand and Judge Sam Rosenman, Acheson had been tracking down this information because the New York City customs house had burned down. They apparently obtained a copy of the immigration and naturalization papers from the Treasury Department. They were trying to rebut a prior witness's charges that Frankfurter was an alien and to silence false rumors that his father had "obtained his citizenship through fraud."

Acheson had been consulting with Neely throughout the day's proceedings. Frankfurter's counsel did not cross-examine a single witness, not even Dilling or Zoll, because Senators Neely, Borah, and Norris were doing it for him. A *Washington Post* editorial praised these subcommittee members for challenging "unsubstantiated charges" from "witnesses who see 'red' wherever they look" and contrasted it with the unfair conduct of Dies Committee hearings.

One subcommittee member, however, also saw red—Senator Pat McCarran. The Nevada Democrat was one of the Senate's leading isolationists and most rabid anti-Communists. He quickly turned against the New Deal, opposed the court-packing plan, and had been one of the unsuccessful targets of Roosevelt's attempt to "purge" legislative opponents during the 1938 midterm elections. His reelection, after Roosevelt had backed his primary challenger, made McCarran more powerful and more vigilant in his inquiry about the loyalty of the president's Supreme Court nominee. With his nativism and anti-Communism, Pat McCarran was Joe McCarthy before Joe McCarthy. And Frankfurter was McCarran's prey.

During the January 11 hearings, McCarran encouraged the testimony of Red hunters Dilling and Zoll. The Nevada senator questioned Dilling about Frankfurter's ties to the ACLU and whether the organization "is controlled at the present time by a Communist group." After Dilling produced documents that showed Frankfurter's name on ACLU letterhead as a member of its national committee, McCarran said: "I just want to say at this time, Mr. Chairman, that I believe this situation should be explored by this committee, and I believe that we should go to the bottom of it and find what it means." McCarran repeatedly asked Zoll and other witnesses about the ACLU's link to Communism. He also defended Zoll's right to oppose Frankfurter on religious grounds. McCarran had been the reason why Acheson sought to produce Frankfurter's father's immigration and naturalization papers.

At 4:05 p.m. on January 11, the Senate judiciary subcommittee adjourned and went into executive session. With Acheson present, McCarran demanded that Frankfurter testify before the subcommittee to respond to the accusations about his Communist and other radical ties. Acheson laid a few ground rules: First, no questions about issues that could come before the Court. Second, no questions about the nominee's views on the court-packing plan in light of Frankfurter's public silence about the issue. Finally, the subcommittee must formally request Frankfurter to appear. The last point proved to be the stickiest. "A long wrangle ensued; I did not budge," Acheson wrote. "Frankfurter would not appear as a seeker after office, but would comply with a request by the Committee to appear." The subcommittee agreed to make a formal request. After Frankfurter talked with Acheson by phone, the law professor quickly packed his things, declined to comment to the press waiting for him at the train station, and boarded the overnight Federal Express from Boston to Washington, D.C. The next morning's newspapers led with word of his appearance. McCarran wanted a showdown; Frankfurter would give it to him.

ARRIVING IN WASHINGTON the next morning, Frankfurter bought a newspaper before heading to Acheson's house in Georgetown. The nominee thought that his testimony would be held in the smaller Judiciary Committee room like the first two days of testimony. Instead, he found himself at 10:42 a.m. in a room he compared to Madison Square Garden. With its high ornate ceilings and six white marble Corinthian columns on each side, the Senate Caucus Room had been the scene of some of the most sensational congressional hearings: the 1912 sinking of the *Titanic*, the 1924 Teapot Dome scandal, the 1929 stock market crash, and the 1937 court-packing plan.

On that morning of January 12, people crowded the hallway outside the caucus room. A sign met them at the door—"S.R.O."—standing room only. Capitol Police had never seen so many people inside. Police officers cleared a path so that Acheson and Frankfurter could make their way to the witness table. The 6-foot-tall Acheson entered first and made the 5-foot-5-inch Frankfurter look even shorter as the nominee trailed behind him. Spectators, journalists, photographers, and cameramen from several newsreel companies filled the room to capacity. They stood in the aisles and against the walls. Frankfurter's postgraduate fellow, Edward F. Prichard, Jr., conspicuous with his mop of curly hair and rotund frame, stood in front of one of the Corinthian columns. As the nominee entered the room, people applauded. A few hissed.

Dressed in a dark double-breasted suit and dark check tie and wearing pince-nez glasses, Frankfurter arrived at the front of the room and shook hands with Chairman Neely and the other subcommittee members. The senators sat across from Frankfurter behind two long mahogany tables: Neely directly across from the nominee; anti–New Deal Democrats McCarran and King; two additional Democrats, Tom Connally of Texas and James H. Hughes of Delaware; three Republicans, Borah of Idaho, Warren R. Austin of Vermont, and John A. Danaher of Connecticut; and one independent, Norris of Nebraska. Other senators sat behind them and on the sides.

As soon as Frankfurter took his seat, photographers began snapping pictures of him and asked him to assume different poses. "I suppose that's constitutional," he said. Large microphones were arrayed before him on the table. He opened a light brown briefcase containing a copy of his book, *Mr. Justice Holmes and the Supreme Court*, and pulled out his prepared statement. Acheson sat behind him and to his right. This was one Senate hearing where counsel felt almost powerless to control his client. The show was Frankfurter's and Frankfurter's alone. Acheson "just sat there."

Neely opened the proceeding and indicated that the subcommittee had invited Frankfurter to testify so that it "may become acquainted with" him. King then invited Frankfurter to read his prepared remarks. Frankfurter acknowledged that he was only the second Supreme Court nominee to testify before the Senate, preferred not to do so, and believed it was not in "the best interests of the Supreme Court." He said it would be improper for him to testify about issues that might come before the Court, but that his "attitude and outlook on relevant matters" could be gleaned from his writings and spoke for themselves. "That is all I have to say."

Senator Borah, the subcommittee's senior member and one of Frankfurter's staunchest allies, asked him a series of questions about the genesis and nature of his involvement with the ACLU. Frankfurter reviewed his background as a Manhattan federal prosecutor under Henry Stimson, who instilled in him "a very high and fastidious sense of obedience to the Constitution and laws of this country." He explained that his connection to the ACLU stemmed from his investigations of the abridgement of civil liberties during and after the Great War; his representation of twenty immigrants arrested during the Palmer raids; and his decision to sign the National Popular Government League report criticizing the Justice Department's unconstitutional conduct during those raids.

Frankfurter could not recall how or when Roger Baldwin had invited him in January 1920 to become a founding member of the ACLU's national committee. Nor could he recall many of his specific duties with the organization. Newspapermen and observers reported that he looked nervous. Given his experience as a prosecutor, he emphasized "the great importance of having a group of people whose special job it should be to be watchful that the Bill of Rights should be defended in case it is invoked." He supported the ACLU's defense of the right of the Ku Klux Klan to march in Boston and concluded the same thing about American supporters of the Nazi Party. "Of course," he had advised the ACLU, "civil liberty means liberty for those whom we do not like or even detest." As an example, he testified that he had advised the ACLU in 1938 when it had protested the censorship of radio broadcasts by none other than Elizabeth Dilling, his chief antagonist at the previous day's hearing. Borah then asked him about the ACLU's relationship to Communism, and the nominee insisted that there was none—except that the ACLU would defend a Communist's right to speak the same way it had defended Dilling's. Borah asked him if he had ever written about Communism. Frankfurter replied that he had not but there was a chapter in his 1930 book, *The Public and Its Government*, that addressed "the nature of democracy."

Finally, Borah asked him about his November 1917 and January 1918 reports for the President's Mediation Commission about the Bisbee deportation and the Tom Mooney case (the labor leader had just been pardoned on January 7, 1939, after twenty-two years in prison). Frankfurter read from the reports and explained that he had drafted them for Secretary of Labor William B. Wilson and at the request of President Wilson. Prior to his investigation in California, Frankfurter had been completely unfamiliar with Mooney's case. Nor had he anything to do with the Mooney case or the Bisbee deportation after drafting the reports. He explained the source of his disagreements about the reports with Theodore Roosevelt. One of Roosevelt's friends had brought him into the fight against the recall of Mooney prosecutor Charles M. Fickert. And another friend of Roosevelt's, John C. Greenway, had been implicated in the Bisbee deportation of Arizona copper miners.

Through his questions, Borah attempted to inoculate Frankfurter against charges he was a Communist or a radical. Other senior members of the committee, Norris, King, and Connally, declined to question him. Then Chairman Neely turned to McCarran. "I should like to ask the doctor a few questions," McCarran replied. Frankfurter, who was not a doctor because he lacked a PhD, thought McCarran repeatedly invoked the word "doctor" like it was "a contagious disease" and Harvard like it was "a plague sport."

Seizing on Frankfurter's involvement with the ACLU, McCarran tried to associate him with Communism. He asked about a former member of the ACLU's national committee, William Z. Foster, who was the Communist Party USA's chairman and perennial presidential candidate. Frankfurter could not remember if Foster was still on the national committee (he wasn't). McCarran asked about the role of the national committee, which Frankfurter characterized as advisory and distinguished from the organization's policy-making executive committee. The senator asked about the legislative committees that had investigated the ACLU. Frankfurter confessed not to have read the reports of the Dies, Fish, or Lusk Committees. Nor had he read the American Legion's report about the ACLU. "There are only 24 hours in a day," the nominee said. McCarran chided him for not knowing more about "his associates." Frankfurter rejected McCarran's insinuations about the link between Communism and the ACLU: "The record of its activities and my relation to them is not what somebody else may have said about those activities."

Changing tactics, McCarran pursued rumors that Frankfurter's father had illegally obtained citizenship. He asked Frankfurter where he was born and when he came to the country. Frankfurter explained he was born in Vienna, Austria, and had come to America in 1894 with his mother, three brothers, and sister. His father, Leopold, had arrived in America a year earlier and had become a citizen in June 1898. He referred to his father's naturalization papers, which Acheson had provided to the subcommittee the previous day and which McCarran had received that morning. The senator replied that he had "what purports to be the certificate to which you refer."

The real entertainment began when McCarran asked about British political scientist Harold J. Laski. Frankfurter explained that he knew Laski "very well," having met him at McGill University and helping him land a job in 1916 as a Harvard instructor until he left a few years later for the London School of Economics. At the time of the hearings, Laski was a visiting professor at the University of Washington and in frequent contact with his New Deal friends. What Frankfurter neglected to mention was that Laski was a well-known Socialist who, at the height of the 1919 Red Scare, had been run out of Harvard for supporting the Boston police strike. McCarran was more interested in Laski's writings. "Do you agree with his doctrine?" McCarran asked. Frankfurter insisted he had read some of Laski's books but not all of them. The Red-hunting senator was primarily interested in Laski's book *Communism*. After Frankfurter admitted he had read it, McCarran asked: "Do you subscribe to his doctrine as expressed in that volume?" The law professor, after years of employing the Socratic method to question students, turned those skills on his interrogator. This time, the joke was on Senator McCarran.

"Have you read the book?" Frankfurter asked. The senator conceded that he had "just casually glanced at it." The audience laughed.

"What would you say is its doctrine?" Frankfurter asked.

"The doctrine is the advocacy of communism," McCarran replied.

"You see," Frankfurter retorted, "we could debate all day on whether that is in fact the doctrine of that book."

"Do you believe in the doctrine set forth in this book?" McCarran asked.

By this point, Frankfurter was enjoying himself: "I cannot answer, because I do not know what you regard as the doctrine. You have never read it." He was having "the time of my life with Senator Pat McCarran."

"If it advocates the doctrine of Marxism," McCarran restated the question, "would you agree with it?"

Frankfurter refused to give McCarran a yes or no answer: "Senator, I do not believe you have ever taken an oath to support the Constitution of the United States with fewer reservations than I have or would now, nor do I believe you are more attached to the theories and practices of Americanism than I am. I rest my answer on that statement." The packed caucus room, despite prior warnings from the chairman about showings of approval or disapproval, "broke into applause that lasted more than two minutes."

"Is that all the answer you want to make?" McCarran asked. "Do you prefer to let your answer to the question I propounded rest in that form?" Frankfurter said he did. Senator King, the other anti–New Deal Democrat on the subcommittee, was not satisfied with the answer. He asked if the nominee believed in "the ideology of Marx or Trotsky?" Again, Frankfurter refused to answer in a straightforward way because of issues that a Supreme Court justice might have to decide. "If I were before this committee for any political office," he responded, "nothing would give me more pleasure than to pursue the line of inquiry of Senator McCarran and Senator King." He preferred to rest on his prior statement to Senator McCarran. "You will have to decide," he told the subcommittee, "in the light of my whole life, what devotion I have to the American system of government."

A more fraught question arose about court packing. Senator Austin, an isolationist Vermont Republican, asked him about his 1934 entry on the Supreme Court in the *Encyclopedia of the Social Sciences* in which he discussed historical changes in the number of justices. "There is no magic in the number 9," Frankfurter wrote, "but there are limitations to effective judicial action." In light of history and experience, he wrote, efforts "to enlarge the size of the Supreme Court would be self-defeating." Austin asked him to comment on the article and, by implication, Roosevelt's court-packing plan. Frankfurter, however, insisted the article touched on issues pending before the Court and chose to let what he had written stand for itself. He decided not to read a prepared statement about the court-packing fight that he had "refrained" from public comment and had told people privately that "the Court proposals were matters on which men equally patriotic could reasonably differ." His testimony and unused statement elided his behind-the-scenes advice to the president.

Frankfurter's supporters on the subcommittee were worried about the nominee's responses to McCarran's questions about Communism. They encouraged him to go further. Borah requested that Frankfurter's answer be read back, then asked if his belief in the "theories and practices" of Americanism also included "principles." Frankfurter agreed: "I mean the doctrines that led to the formation of the Union, that body of principles that the greater founders from Washington down represented in their lives, their messages, and their activities."

Chairman Neely, who had supported Frankfurter throughout the proceedings, refused to end them there. He was worried about Frankfurter's evasive answers to some of McCarran's questions and motioned to Acheson to tell him so. Acheson agreed and urged his client to be more forthcoming.

McCarran sensed another opening. He asked whether Frankfurter believed in the Constitution. After Frankfurter readily agreed, McCarran remarked: "I am very glad to get that positive answer from you." Frankfurter retorted: "I infer that your question does not imply that you had any doubt about it." Neely interjected and expressed concern that several witnesses had "in a very hazy, indefinite way, attempted to create the impression that you are a Communist." Neely refused to let that impression stand and asked: "Are you a Communist, or have you ever been one?"

"I have never been," Frankfurter replied, "and I am not now."

McCarran was not satisfied: "By that do you mean that you have never been enrolled as a member of the Communist Party?"

"I mean much more than that," Frankfurter replied. "I mean that I have never been enrolled, and have never been qualified to be enrolled, because that does not represent my view of life, nor my view of government."

The crowd roared with delight. Some people stood on chairs to cheer, clap, and wave. Neely banged his gavel to restore order. The chairman thanked Frankfurter for his testimony. Frankfurter thanked the chairman. The hearing was adjourned. The crowd rushed toward Frankfurter and nearly engulfed him. Police officers created a space around him. The newsreels had missed the climactic scene, so he and Neely reenacted it several times. The photographers once again began snapping pictures. Frankfurter shook hands with Neely as well as with many other senators. Dilling, dressed in the same blue and gold dress as the day before, rushed to the front of the room and whispered something to McCarran. She also lurked behind Frankfurter while he shook hands with Senator Alexander Wiley of Wisconsin.

Frankfurter's testimony lasted an hour and a half, but it took a while to clear the crowded caucus room. At noon, the subcommittee went into executive session to vote on the nominee. McCarran, however, was nowhere to be found. Senate pages could not find him. Finally, someone tracked him down in the Senate restaurant. McCarran refused to interrupt his lunch to vote. In a humorous effort to force him to vote for or against the nominee, his colleagues sent a clerk with a ballot for McCarran to fill out; he refused. The clerk returned with the empty ballot. The subcommittee voted unanimously to move Frankfurter's nomination to the full committee. McCarran insisted to reporters that he had been "called away on business" and later voted with the majority. "I think at times past Frankfurter has perhaps inadvertently found himself in bad company, but there is no evidence that has come to my attention that he ever followed the leadership or dictates of that company," he told the *Washington Post*. "Had I discovered anything in the record indicating he was inclined to follow or give sanction to thoughts of Harold Laski I would have voted against confirmation."

In celebration, Frankfurter and Acheson went to lunch with Neely and Judiciary Committee chairman Henry Ashurst. A tall, dashing Arizona Democrat who quietly had opposed the court-packing plan, Ashurst did not drink alcohol but arranged for a chilled bottle of brandy for the witness. Frankfurter wanted to discuss his interlocutor. "Tell me about McCarran," he said to Ashurst. "He seems like a hardheaded, shrewd sort of man, but obsessed with communism. Explain it. Are there Communists in Nevada?" Ashurst replied that McCarran had never seen a Communist. Everyone, the chairman said, was obsessed about something. Ashurst admitted that he was obsessed with the legendary nineteenth century senator Roscoe Conkling of New York. Frankfurter confessed that he was obsessed with Kate Chase, the daughter of Chief Justice Salmon Chase and Conkling's lover. Acheson had heard of Conkling, but not Kate Chase. Ashurst began reciting Conkling's speeches. The lunch lasted well into the afternoon. Acheson thought the Arizona senator and Supreme Court nominee were as "crazy as loons." Ashurst promised the pair that the full Judiciary Committee would vote on his nomination on Monday, January 16, and expected it to go smoothly.

After their long lunch, Frankfurter proposed to Acheson that they tell the McCarran story to Roosevelt. Acheson, who had not seen the president since his resignation as under secretary of the treasury six years earlier, suggested that Frankfurter go alone. Nonsense. They took a taxi to the north gate of the White House, and the officer let them in because Frankfurter was such a frequent guest (so frequent that they were not included on the White House visitors' logs). Missy LeHand greeted them and heard part of the McCarran story. Though the president was an hour behind schedule, she promised them fifteen minutes. "The story poured noisily out of FF—the McCarran inquisition, the crisis, the triumph, the lunches," Acheson wrote. "The President roared with delighted laughter." He laughed harder after Acheson told him the Roscoe Conkling story. After half an hour, Missy came in to break up the storytelling because people could hear the laughter emanating from the Oval Office. The president asked for five more minutes. Ten minutes later, Missy came in again, ushered Acheson and Frankfurter out the north entrance, and sent them home in a White House car.

The meeting with Roosevelt had a dual purpose—to share the confirmation hearing anecdotes and to thaw relations between Acheson and the president. On February 5, Roosevelt phoned Acheson and offered him a federal appeals court judgeship in the District of Columbia. The next day, Acheson met with the president and officially declined the position as too "sedentary." Roosevelt then offered him a position as assistant attorney general in charge of the newly created civil rights unit. Acheson again declined to return to public life full-time but agreed to serve on the Attorney General's Committee on Administrative Procedure. Thanks in part to his advice and counsel to Frankfurter at a time of rising anti-Semitism and anti-Communism, Acheson returned to the president's good graces and discovered his "road back" to public life.

A prelude to rising anti-Communism at home, the HUAC-style hearings had no impact on Frankfurter's confirmation. Nor did his hidden advisory role during the court-packing fight. Senator Wheeler, the leader of the court bill opposition, endorsed Frankfurter and urged a quick vote. As Senator Ashurst had promised, on Monday, January 16, the Senate Judiciary Committee unanimously voted to send the nomination to the full Senate. The next day on the Senate floor, Neely moved that Frankfurter be confirmed. Senator Key Pittman (D-NV), the president pro tempore, announced: "The question is: Will the Senate advise and consent to this nomination?" No roll call vote was taken. No dissenting votes were recorded. The Republican senators had decided in advance not to oppose him. Anti–New Dealers McCarran and King answered the quorum call and did not oppose him, either.

At 12:30 p.m., Harvard law professor Thomas Reed Powell interrupted Frankfurter's noon class in Langdell Hall and handed him a note. Frankfurter, who was sitting in the third row while graduate student Seymour J. Rubin presented the 1911 *Standard Oil* antitrust case, read the note and put it in his pocket. The student's presentation continued. A minute before class ended at 1:00 p.m., Frankfurter announced: "Pardon me, gentlemen. This is the last time I shall speak to you in this class-room. I should like you to know that it is not an easy thing for me to go to Washington. While there, I shall think of you often. I wish you well in June and a very full life thereafter!" His students greeted him with "a storm of applause." After his last class ever, he bounded up the aisle to attend a *Harvard Law Review* luncheon.

―――――

ON JANUARY 18, Felix and Marion arrived at Back Bay station seven minutes before the 9:05 p.m. Federal Express was scheduled to depart. Marion, who remarked about how cold it was, wore a dark green coat with a mink collar and a corsage of orchids. Her husband headed to the newsstand and purchased all the Boston newspapers, several from New York, and the *Manchester Guardian.* Reporters and friends bid them farewell. They arrived the next morning to photographers at Union Station. A White House car took them to their destination—the executive mansion. Along with Judge Sam Rosenman and his wife Dorothy, Martha Gellhorn and other journalists, and former Roosevelt aide Molly Dewson, the Frankfurters stayed at the White House as guests of the president. That night, Roosevelt held a state dinner for ninety-four people in honor of the chief justice and associate justices. It was the justices' first time at the White House since the court-packing fight; McReynolds and the ailing Brandeis were absent. The Frankfurters sat with the other unofficial guests because he had not been sworn in as an associate justice. During dinner and the musical event afterward, they were "the centers of attention."

During their two-day visit to Washington, the Frankfurters rented a furnished house at 3624 Prospect Avenue in Georgetown. They had loaned their Cambridge home to the family of journalist Irving Dilliard, who was coming to Harvard for a Nieman Fellowship. On January 28, they returned to Washington for good. As a surprise farewell gift, his friends arranged for the purchase of his new robe, which cost $100, matched the chief justice's, and was reserved for special occasions.

On January 30, the 56-year-old Frankfurter wore his new robe as Chief Justice Charles Evans Hughes swore him in during a private ceremony in the justices' conference room. At noon, Frankfurter marched in last behind the other justices for the public swearing-in ceremony inside the crowded Supreme Court courtroom. The press described it as "one of the largest throngs" in the courtroom, which necessitated overflow chairs in the aisles. Marion sat in a special first row to the left of the high bench. Her husband's former professor Joseph H. Beale and his wife, Elizabeth; Missy LeHand; Cohen; Corcoran; Dr. Alfred Cohn; and Dean Acheson's wife, Alice, sat next to Marion. The justice's sisters Estelle ("Stella") and Ella and his brothers Otto, Fred, and Paul and their wives sat on the other side of the aisle. Other friends and administration officials, including Frances Perkins and Harry Hopkins, filled the courtroom. Attorney General Murphy and Solicitor General Jackson were ushered in at the last minute. Frankfurter's friend and mentor, 82-year-old Justice Brandeis, suffering from the flu, was absent. Another mentor, Henry Stimson, was also recovering from the flu and "too wobbly" to brave the winter weather. The clerk of the court, Charles Elmore Cropley, recited the oath again. Frankfurter repeated it ending with "so help me God." The marshal, Thomas E. Waggaman, escorted him to his seat on the far left next to Justice Black, who bowed and shook Frankfurter's hand. Frankfurter listened as the Court announced an opinion dismissing a lawsuit challenging the constitutionality of the Tennessee Valley Authority. He asked a few questions during a criminal case.

At 5:45 p.m. that afternoon, Justice and Mrs. Frankfurter arrived at the White House for a visit with the president. It was Roosevelt's fifty-seventh birthday. Earlier that day, Frankfurter had written his first letter on Supreme Court stationery to the president. "In the mysterious ways of Fate, the Dutchess County American and the Viennese American have for decades pursued the same directions of devotion to our beloved country," he wrote in one of his favorite letters. "And now, on your blessed birthday I am given the gift of opportunity for service to the Nation which, in circumstances would be owing, but which I would rather have had at your hands than at those of any other President barring Lincoln."

Germany's Nazi government saw "the appointment of a Jew as one of the supreme guardians of law of the United States" as proof that Roosevelt had decided "to make the United States a plantation of Jewish interests in domestic and foreign policy." A German newspaper published a cartoon of Roosevelt dressed in Roman armor with a bridle in his mouth and a small Jew on his back holding a whip with Jewish stars on the end. The caption read: "America's president debases himself to become a handy man for world Jewry, to secure Jewish help for a third term election."

In the face of anti-Semitism at home and abroad, Frankfurter's nomination represented a public rebuke to the Nazis. The same day as Frankfurter's swearing-in and Roosevelt's birthday, Adolf Hitler delivered his 1939 Reichstag speech commemorating the sixth anniversary of Nazi rule over Germany. Large Nazi flags hung from each side of the crowded German parliament. Legislators stood and hailed Hitler with stiff-armed Nazi salutes, and they cheered as the Fuhrer vowed: "The peoples [of the earth] will soon realize that Germany under National Socialism does not desire the enmity of other peoples. . . . I want once again to be a prophet. If the international Finance-Jewry inside and outside of Europe should succeed in plunging the peoples of the earth once again into a world war, the result will be not the Bolshevization of earth, and thus a Jewish victory, but the annihilation of the Jewish race in Europe."

In the eyes of American liberals, Roosevelt's nomination of an Austrian Jewish immigrant to the Supreme Court was the perfect response to Hitler's hatred of the Jews. Rabbi Stephen Wise wired the president that it was "a double barreled reply to Hitlerism." *The Nation* editor Oswald Garrison Villard wrote that it "makes me proud of being an American to have our President honor so notable a Jewish-American when even in our own country the abominable tide of antisemitism is rising." Secretary of the Interior Ickes wrote that Frankfurter "feels he is a symbol and that his appointment means much to the liberal cause." Senator Borah replied to an anti-Semitic constituent: "If we should then reject this man because he is a Jew, we would have repudiated the most vital principles of free government."

No one was happier than Frankfurter's 82-year-old uncle Salomon. He heard about the nomination on the radio while under house arrest in Vienna after being released from a Nazi prison. He "rejoiced" when he learned the Senate had confirmed his nephew.

Frankfurter's public life took on a new dimension with his return to Washington. He refused to retreat into a Supreme Court justice's monastic existence. Instead, he continued to enter the White House without being recorded on the daily logs and to advise the president. He continued to socialize with senators and other government officials he had known for years. Most important, he continued to place his mentors, friends, and former students, with names such as Acheson, Hiss, McCloy, Patterson, and Stimson, in the executive branch. And as another European war loomed, Frankfurter never stopped advising them on policy matters. He began his career as a justice with a hand in all three branches of government and with friends and former students just a phone call or a few Georgetown houses away. His yen for federal policy making, willingness to cross ethical lines in advising friends in government, intense Americanism, reputation as a civil libertarian, and vast liberal network all contributed to the challenges and complications that faced him as a new justice. On top of all that, he faced the inevitable comparisons to Holmes and Brandeis and tried to adapt their judicial restraint to a new world order.

CHAPTER 21

The Brandeis Way

On February 5, six days after he had been sworn in as an associate justice, Frankfurter learned what no one else in official Washington knew but what insiders had been speculating about for months—Louis Brandeis was retiring. Frankfurter heard the news at Brandeis's fifth-floor apartment. Like many of the older justices, Brandeis had refused to move into the Court's new building when "the marble palace" opened in October 1935. He worked out of his Kalorama apartment, not far from Dupont Circle, and owned a smaller unit a few floors down that served as an office for his law clerk.

For the past month, the 82-year-old Brandeis had battled the flu and may have suffered a mild heart attack. He insisted to Frankfurter and others, however, that he was not resigning because of old age or ill health. Nor did he lack mental acuity and "judgment." At the end of the past several terms, he had asked Chief Justice Hughes whether he was still up to the job and had received reassuring responses. He had approached Hughes again on February 4; the chief justice's answer was the same. In fact, a year earlier, Brandeis had written one of his most enduring and controversial opinions, *Erie Railroad v. Tompkins*, about applying state law in federal cases involving litigants from different states. Yet on February 5 he confided to Frankfurter that he was "quantitatively not able to do as much" and "opinion writing demands an intensity & I find it gets to be hard."

The next day, Brandeis returned to the bench fully recovered from his illness and sat for a week with his new colleague. That Friday evening, he hosted a pre-conference meeting at his apartment, where Frankfurter joined him, Stone, and Roberts to review the week's cases. It was the last time he would host the meeting. On Monday, February 13, Brandeis sent a one-sentence letter to the president announcing his retirement on "this day." Roosevelt, though in bed with the flu, dictated a gracious, three-paragraph reply: "The country had needed you through all these years, and I hope you will realize as all your old friends do, how unanimous the nation has been in its gratitude to you."

Frankfurter's relationship with Brandeis had not been the same since the court-packing fight. Brandeis thought less of Frankfurter for not coming out publicly against the bill and for quietly supporting the president. Frankfurter, for his part, was unhappy that Brandeis had orchestrated and signed Hughes's letter to Senator Wheeler that showed the justices were not behind on their work and which undercut the plan. Yet Frankfurter and Brandeis had been through too much together—debating the 1912 election at the House of Truth, defending Brandeis in the *New Republic* during his Supreme Court confirmation battle, fighting for a Jewish state at the 1919 Paris Peace Conference and beyond, transforming Harvard Law School into a petri dish for public servants, and financing Frankfurter's public interest work on behalf of labor and civil liberties throughout the 1920s and 1930s—to be anything but "half brother, half son."

Sitting for only a week with the justice he admired most besides Holmes, Frankfurter was deeply moved by the "poignant aspect" of Brandeis's resignation. "The work is done," he wrote Brandeis, "in so far as one man can do it, and others must carry on where you leave off, inspired by your example and energized by the driving force of your vast achievement." Brandeis, Alsop and Kintner observed, "has always done at least three jobs, and, in retiring from the court, he has relinquished only one of them." The retired justice continued to pursue the other two—Zionist activities on behalf of the Jewish people and mentoring young men in government. He no longer had to husband his physical and mental energy for the Court's work. Aside from his Sunday afternoon teas, he almost never socialized in official Washington, never talked on the telephone, and always refused dinner invitations. Now he had more time for visitors and more energy.

Frankfurter took Brandeis's example of trying to do multiple jobs at once to the extreme. The rise of European dictatorships and Hitler's threat to the Jewish people led him to spend too much time engaged in policy making and recruitment on behalf of the Roosevelt administration and not enough time on his primary job. He was an extrovert, with a vast network of friends and former students in the administration. The growing threat of war had already been a constant distraction, one that was not going away simply because he donned a judicial robe.

The issues before the Court were also very different than the ones that

Brandeis had faced. In deciding whether to uphold Roosevelt's New Deal programs, Brandeis had been confronted with balancing his belief in judicial
restraint and avoiding constitutional questions with his distrust of federal
power and faith in states as laboratories of experimentation. Since the court-
packing fight and Roosevelt's opportunities to appoint new justices, however,
the New Deal no longer hung in the balance. The issues, with a war looming
in Europe, were beginning to change. The Court was forced to decide when
it should defer to elected officials and when it should protect minority rights.
Brandeis, despite his celebrated free speech dissents and concurrences, had
shown little interest in defending the rights of racial minorities; Frankfurter,
on the other hand, had spent the past two decades advising the ACLU and
NAACP. As a justice, the question was whether Frankfurter could adapt his
steadfast belief in deferring to democracy to protect minority rights. Extrajudicial federal policy making and adaption of judicial restraint were tall orders
for a new justice who had been on the job for only two weeks and whose last
surviving judicial idol had retired.

Fortunately for Frankfurter, he recruited an able and experienced first law
clerk in Joseph L. Rauh, Jr. A Reform Jew from Cincinnati, graduate of Harvard College, and *Harvard Law Review* editor, Rauh had planned to join a
leading Jewish law firm in Cincinnati after graduation until a chance hallway encounter during the winter of his third year. "What are you going to
do next year?" Frankfurter called out to the tall, jug-eared student. Rauh told
him about the Cincinnati firm. "Well," Frankfurter replied, "tell them you're
not coming." He wanted Rauh to clerk for Cardozo, but since there was no
immediate opening, he found his federal jurisdiction student a job in the
Roosevelt administration. Nominally assigned to the Securities and Exchange
Commission, Rauh worked day and night from the fall of 1935 to the spring of
1936 assisting Corcoran and Cohen in defending the constitutionality of the
Public Utility Holding Company Act. He marveled at the boisterous Corcoran
in action and loved and admired the unassuming Cohen. After they defeated
the legal challenges to the act, Rauh became Cardozo's last law clerk. He
reluctantly agreed when Cardozo asked him in the spring of 1937 to stay a
second year and frequently corresponded with Frankfurter about Cardozo's
deteriorating health. During the spring of 1938, Rauh, his wife, Olie, and
their two-year-old son, Michael, moved into the Westchester County home of
Judge Lehman in order to care for Cardozo during the justice's final weeks.
Rauh was devoted to Cardozo, Frankfurter wrote, like a son. After Cardozo's
funeral, Rauh returned to Washington at the behest of Cohen and Frankfurter to work for Calvert Magruder, the general counsel of the Labor Depart-

ment's Wage and Hour Division. Rauh relished enforcing the new Fair Labor Standards Act on behalf of working men and women. He spent many nights working with Corcoran and Cohen on their lobbying campaign to persuade Roosevelt to nominate Frankfurter. After his former professor was confirmed by the Senate, Rauh volunteered to serve as his first law clerk for the remainder of the 1939 term. Frankfurter gladly accepted, telling Rauh: "You've got more experience on the Supreme Court than I do."

Frankfurter's chambers in the new Supreme Court building were nothing like what Rauh had experienced working in an office in Cardozo's quiet apartment. Cardozo had marshaled every ounce of remaining energy to write his assigned opinions in longhand. He had memorized the cases in the New York and U.S. reports and used Rauh only to supplement his legal citations with other state cases and occasional legal research. Frankfurter's office in the Supreme Court building, by contrast, was buzzing with people and activity. Catherine Hiss, the wife of former student Donald Hiss, helped with typing before the justice hired his first official secretary. Rauh quickly began to read the latest petitions for certiorari (requests for the Court to hear cases) while Frankfurter entertained a parade of journalists, lawyers, longtime friends and former students, and other well-wishers. People described his chambers as "Felix's barbershop."

After a few weeks, Frankfurter allowed Rauh to return to the Labor Department's Wage and Hour Division. A relieved Rauh knew that the justice was in good hands because Adrian Fisher, Brandeis's law clerk, was taking over. In fact, when Brandeis had summoned Frankfurter on February 5 to discuss his retirement plans, his main concern was Fisher's future employment. The son of a Tennessee congressman and a Princeton football player who had switched to rugby in law school, "Butch" Fisher had been a *Harvard Law Review* editor and Frankfurter's postgraduate research fellow. Fisher knew the fellowship was a tryout for Brandeis and after a few months was offered the clerkship. For the remainder of the 1937–1938 school year, Fisher helped research and write Frankfurter's lectures and 1938 book, *Mr. Justice Holmes and the Supreme Court.* As Frankfurter's law clerk, Fisher discovered how different his new boss was from his old one. Unlike Brandeis, who labored over numerous drafts and invited his law clerks' criticism, Frankfurter dictated his opinions while Fisher typed. Because Frankfurter disliked interruptions, Fisher typed slower when he wanted to make a suggestion.

Frankfurter embraced the Washington social scene that Brandeis and Cardozo had shunned. With help from Rauh's wife, Olie, the Frankfurters rented a small house in Georgetown with views of the Potomac River and the Key

Bridge. On February 4, they threw a dinner party for Secretary of the Interior Ickes and his young wife, Jane, Jane's sister, Ann Dahlman, Attorney General Murphy, and Roosevelt aide Missy LeHand. "Felix is a very vivacious person," Ickes wrote, "and Mrs. Frankfurter had difficulty in getting responses to her signals from across the table to proceed with the business of the table so as not to make dinner an unduly long affair."

The following evening, the Frankfurters attended a White House dinner, but it was the justice's pre-dinner celebration that made news. Around 4:00 p.m., he went to see Vice President John Nance Garner. Roosevelt warned Frankfurter that the vice president liked to drink whiskey. Frankfurter boasted he could match the Texan's capacity for alcohol. Three hours later, the fast-talking Frankfurter returned to the White House slightly "worse for wear" and enunciating every word. The president mimicked his deliberate diction. Frankfurter, however, had won the bet. Garner had to be "helped home, where Mrs. Garner put him on the carpet and made him promise not to do it again." Pearson and Allen's syndicated column, headlined "Garner vs. Frankfurter," reported that the justice had drunk the vice president "under the table."

The Frankfurters also continued the Brandeis tradition of afternoon teas and had the *Emporia Gazette*'s William Allen White as one of their first guests. On the morning of April 5, he invited Tennessee Valley Authority commissioner David Lilienthal for breakfast and complained that there weren't "enough hours" and about being hemmed "in a routine" because of the Court's schedule. Gossip columnist Leonard Lyons dished that Frankfurter "is dining in public places and will not seclude himself—the first Supreme Court Justice to do this since John Marshall."

On April 15, he and several other justices attended the Gridiron Club's spring dinner at the Willard Hotel with Roosevelt, Postmaster General Farley, Secretary of State Cordell Hull, and Secretary of Commerce Hopkins. Nearly a month later, Frankfurter attended a birthday party for lawyer Ned Burling and watched with delight as Judge Learned Hand sang and Corcoran accompanied him on the accordion. "He and Tom Corcoran could easily turn into a professional duet on the vaudeville stage," Frankfurter wrote Judge Mack. "To hear B [Billings Learned Hand] sing his favorite Gilbert and Sullivan ditties to Tom's accompaniment is far better than I have seen on the light comedy stage."

If his busy social schedule were not enough, Frankfurter took on a public role for the administration. On February 12, he had agreed to serve on the President's Committee on Civil Service Improvement. Nominally chaired by Justice Stanley Reed, the committee was Frankfurter's idea about how to apply Roosevelt's executive order expanding civil service reform to lawyers. An admirer of the British civil service, Frankfurter had been championing the hiring of government lawyers on the basis of merit rather than patronage, Alsop and Kintner wrote, since he had debated the issue at the House of Truth in 1913 with then–Attorney General McReynolds. An administrative law expert, he had spent his entire professional life recruiting talented lawyers into government. Two former students and Roosevelt aides, James Rowe and Tom Corcoran, helped him make the civil service committee a reality.

Influential former students aside, he maintained a direct line to Roosevelt for matters big and small. In a March 8 letter that began "Dear C-i-C" as in commander-in-chief, Frankfurter submitted his resignation as a major in the army's Judge Advocate General's Corps reserve. He had held the rank and position since General Enoch Crowder had enlisted him during the Great War. Six days after receiving Frankfurter's letter, Roosevelt responded that the resignation "has been rejected." The president, who enclosed a memorandum from the War Department chief of staff suggesting that Frankfurter could be an associate justice and retain his military rank, indicated that it was "impossible" to promote Frankfurter to lieutenant colonel, but that the justice should reapply in two years. In a jocular reply, Frankfurter wrote: "I recognize a military order when issued."

The lighthearted correspondence belied grim news from Europe and the failure of British appeasement. On March 15 and 16, Hitler, not content with the Sudetenland as part of the Munch Agreement, seized all of Czechoslovakia. A few weeks later, General Francisco Franco triumphed over left-leaning loyalists in the Spanish Civil War. That same month, the British issued the first draft of a white paper revoking the Balfour Declaration's pledge of support for a Jewish homeland in Palestine. In May, the House of Commons approved the white paper and voted to limit Jewish immigration to British-controlled Palestine to 75,000 people during the next five years. With Hitler on the march and appeasement in shambles, the Jews of Europe had no place to go.

Few Americans were more interested in the plight of the Jewish people and in helping the Roosevelt administration prepare for the war in Europe than Frankfurter. On March 25, the Frankfurters dined with British journalist Sir Arthur Willert, Solicitor General Jackson and his wife, Irene, and Harry Hopkins at the White House. The justice praised Roosevelt's April 15 appeal to Hitler and Mussolini for ten years of peace and not to attack thirty-one nations as "not words but acts—the most potent of acts, the mobilization of the moral forces of the world."

On issues of personnel, Frankfurter aided Roosevelt in the recruitment of Archibald MacLeish. On May 3, the president inquired whether MacLeish would be a good choice for the Librarian of Congress. MacLeish was many things—a lawyer, Pulitzer Prize–winning poet, and magazine writer, but he was not a librarian. What mattered to Frankfurter was the different skills that MacLeish had exhibited as a law student and throughout his life. In his reply to Roosevelt, Frankfurter emphasized that "Archie" had been "one of the leaders of his class" in law school and had been invited to join the faculty. Frankfurter also highlighted MacLeish's organizational skill since he had left *Fortune* in 1938 to become the curator of Harvard's Nieman Fellowship for journalists: "He unites in himself qualities seldom found in combination— those of the hard-headed lawyer with the sympathetic imagination of the poet, the independent thinker and the charming 'mixer.' He would bring to the Librarianship intellectual distinction, cultural recognition the world over, a persuasive personality and a delicacy of touch in dealing with others, and creative energy in making the Library of Congress the great center of the cultural resources of the Nation in the technological setting of our time."

At first, MacLeish was prepared to decline the job so that he would have time to write poetry. Frankfurter, however, advised him to see the president. Before his May 23 lunch with Roosevelt, MacLeish ate breakfast with Frankfurter and Corcoran at the justice's Georgetown home. They emphasized MacLeish's duty to "the Republic and the obligation to serve it." Five days after his White House meeting, he declined the post. Corcoran called and arranged another lunch with the president, who employed all of his charm and persuasive powers. After the second presidential pitch, MacLeish changed his mind and accepted. The Senate, however, balked because of rumors that MacLeish was a "Red." His 1935 poem *Panic* was a critique of capitalism. Like his former law professor, he had supported his share of radical causes. Nonetheless, he was easily confirmed by the Senate and on October 2 took office. MacLeish developed into more than the Librarian of Congress; he was the head of Facts and Figures, the administration's wartime propaganda arm, and a presidential speechwriter and adviser.

Between his social schedule and recruiting for the Roosevelt administration, Frankfurter announced his first two majority opinions. The first invalidated a Florida law requiring an inspection fee for imported cement as interfering with interstate commerce; the second rejected a federal agency's request for immunity from a lawsuit. Consistent with the tradition for new justices, the opinions were short, noncontroversial, and unanimous. Frankfurter was amused by his first two assignments. "Ain't it funny that in the first opinion it fell to me to deliver, I declared a statute unconstitutional, and that in the next one I was agin the government!" he wrote former colleague Thomas Reed Powell.

The media's and legal profession's reaction to Frankfurter's initial opinions was not favorable. The press began to notice Frankfurter's unusual choice of language. Some of the words and phrases—"seductive cliché," "touchstone," and "linchpin" and "trivialize"—seem commonplace today. Others, such as "alembic," are more obscure.

The bar blanched not only at Frankfurter's unfamiliar words in published opinions but also at his incessant, professorial questioning at oral argument. Back at Harvard, Powell mocked Frankfurter's writing style in one of his famous limericks and sent copies to friends including his former colleague (Frankfurter did not respond). Powell relayed the Boston bar's criticism of his opinions and questions at oral argument to New York lawyer C. C. Burlingham, who alerted an already-concerned Justice Stone. "Felix is luxuriating in the new job," Stone wrote Burlingham. "He doesn't yet realize how he is going to be tied to it, or how heavy the chains will be, but I expect that he will make an important contribution to the Court."

Stone must have been alarmed by Frankfurter's budding friendship with Chief Justice Hughes, the very man Frankfurter was supposed to oppose. At his first conference with the other justices, Frankfurter arrived in an alpaca coat instead of a suit as all the other justices wore. At lunchtime, Frankfurter was able to change clothes only to find Hughes in an alpaca coat to make Frankfurter feel comfortable. Hughes, Frankfurter quickly discovered, was masterful in the "taut" way he conducted the justices' conferences as well as oral argument between opposing counsel. "To see him preside" at oral argument, Frankfurter wrote, "was like witnessing Toscanini lead an orchestra."

Like Hughes, Frankfurter was an institutionalist. They believed in preserving the Court's legitimacy and in deferring to the other federal branches and the states. Rather than stand up to Hughes as Stone and Jackson had predicted, Frankfurter began to receive plum opinion assignments from the chief justice—for better or worse. One of the few cases where Hughes and Frankfurter differed that first term was *Coleman v. Miller*. Frankfurter wrote an opinion for four justices declaring that whether the Kansas legislature had ratified the 1924 Child Labor Amendment was not within the Court's jurisdiction because it involved "political issues" more appropriate for state or federal elected officials, rather than the courts, to decide. Neither Hughes nor Stone joined Frankfurter's opinion dismissing the case on these grounds. Frankfurter's failure to receive a fifth vote for the "political question" doctrine assumed great importance in his subsequent attempts to limit the Court's institutional role.

By spring 1939, the back row of the Supreme Court's official photograph looked completely different since Holmes and Brandeis had sat with Hughes nearly a decade earlier. Since the court-packing fight, Roosevelt had appointed four justices: Black for Van Devanter, Reed for Sutherland, Frankfurter for Cardozo, and Brandeis's replacement as of April 17—SEC chairman William O. Douglas. Roosevelt had chosen the forty-year-old Douglas over Senator Schwellenbach, Judge Harold Stephens, and Iowa law dean Wiley Rutledge. Raised in Yakima, Washington, and a graduate of Whitman College in his home state, Douglas nominally satisfied the clamor for a westerner even though he had spent his entire legal career on the East Coast. He had studied law at Columbia, worked at a Wall Street law firm for two years, taught corporate and securities law at Columbia and Yale, and succeeded Joseph Kennedy, Sr., as SEC chairman. In Washington, he became a poker-playing pal of the president's. The same liberal New Dealers who had fought for Frankfurter's nomination had fought for Douglas's. Harold Laski, who was teaching at Indiana University, wrote Roosevelt rejoicing over the nomination of Douglas as "second only to Felix."

As liberal New Dealers who traveled in similar circles, Douglas and Frankfurter were supposed to be allies for years to come. Instead, they battled over Brandeis's legacy. Douglas believed that the legacy lay with protecting civil liberties and found an ally in Black. Frankfurter, on the other hand, believed that Brandeis's legacy lay in protecting the Court's limited institutional role, especially after the court-packing fight, by avoiding constitutional questions and deferring to the democratic political process. Personal and ideological conflict was unavoidable among such strong personalities as Black, Douglas, and Frankfurter. For the time being, however, they were on the same side. Douglas and Black had joined Frankfurter's opinion in *Coleman v. Miller*. The next term, they joined another Frankfurter opinion they later came to regret. The fight over Brandeis's legacy, viewed through the prism of the looming war in Europe, had only just begun.

CHAPTER 22

Preaching the True Democratic Faith

On a clear, 74-degree day on June 14, 1939, Felix and Marion Frankfurter arrived at Pier 88 on West Forty-Eighth Street and the Hudson River at 2:00 p.m. and boarded the French steamship *Normandie*. They were bound for Britain for more than a month so Felix could accept an honorary degree from Oxford and to see their friends from his 1933–1934 year as the Eastman professor at Balliol College. Instead of a carefree vacation, the trip was a grim reminder about the looming war in Europe and fueled Frankfurter's efforts at wartime policy making. At home, isolationists in Congress dominated the political discourse about the war and clamored for American neutrality. Frankfurter, however, was determined to move the Roosevelt administration and the nation in a more interventionist direction— not only to help British friends and Jewish refugees but also to help save the world from a brutal dictatorship. The threat of Nazi Germany was personal and political.

Fortunately for Frankfurter, he enjoyed unparalleled access to the president. During the spring and summer of 1939, he claimed to have written Roosevelt "nearly three hundred" notes on Supreme Court memoranda pads. In recent weeks, he had sent Roosevelt three memoranda about how to respond to Nazi aggression. On June 6, the president agreed that "Felix was at least headed down the right road." Six days later during a West Point commencement address, Roosevelt emphasized the goal of "peace by honorable and pacific conduct of our international relations; but that desire for peace must never be mistaken for weakness." Frankfurter wanted stronger, more affirmative language. On June 13, the night before he left for Oxford, he spoke with the president by phone about the plight of Jewish refugees and the Senate's refusal to revise or repeal the neutrality laws. The Neutrality Acts forbade the United States from sending arms, munitions, or airplanes to England, France, and other Allied nations opposing Nazi Germany. The president and his administration, while speaking the language of peace and isolation, were preparing for war.

At Oxford, the Frankfurters stayed with classics scholar Maurice Bowra and saw philosopher Isaiah Berlin. Marion's spirits soared during her reunion with Berlin. "There is no one I'd rather spend hours with, walking, talking, listening, eating; whatever it is," she wrote him. The Frankfurters visited American-born jurisprudence scholar Arthur Goodhart, who had nominated Felix for the honorary degree. On June 21, the justice received a doctorate in civil laws from Oxford along with British ambassador to the United States Lord Lothian, High Commissioner Vincent Massey of Canada, and novelist P. G. Wodehouse. The public orator introduced Frankfurter by making a Latin pun on Felix from Virgil's *Georgics*: "Happy the man who understood the causes of suitors." The Frankfurters had suitors of all political stripes. At commencement, he was photographed in full regalia talking animatedly with Lady Astor. Newspapers ran an Associated Press photograph and caption "Don't Point" wondering why she was stabbing her finger at Frankfurter's chest—perhaps because he was not shy about confronting her about her isolationist views.

From Oxford, the Frankfurters returned to London to catch up with friends. They saw Harold Laski, who had returned to the London School of Economics and was keeping Roosevelt informed about British politics and the "grim" mood in Europe. They spent many hours, in Oxford and London, with Felix's former graduate student Sylvester Gates, his collaborator on the 1927 Sacco-Vanzetti book, and met Gates's wife, Pauline, and their three children.

Between discussions about the Nazis and Jewish refugees, the rest of the trip was "not joyous" and was dominated by a "war atmosphere." He spoke at a June 29 dinner at the Dorchester Hotel to raise money to send Jewish refugee scholars and scientists to Hebrew University in Jerusalem. He promised that he would return home and inform Americans that "in the menacing grimness that faced all who believed in and hoped for civilization," he had met people willing "to defy those who believed that force and matter would ultimately dominate society." By the fall, the number of refugees who had appealed to Frankfurter for help ran "into the hundreds"; he asked numerous friends, including the president, to help them.

In London, he met Prime Minister Chamberlain and other members of the cabinet even though Frankfurter opposed the Chamberlain government's strategy of appeasement and the Munich agreement. Winston Churchill, an outspoken opponent of appeasement and private citizen, impressed him as "the one man who gave me a sense of power." One of the wisest people he met was Ambassador Quo Tai-chi of China. The ambassador alerted him to the danger to America after it abrogated a treaty with the militarist regime in Japan, a warning that Frankfurter shared with Roosevelt.

Despite their political differences, the Frankfurters ate lunch with Ambassador Joseph Kennedy, Sr. American Zionist leaders criticized Kennedy for not advocating on behalf of Jewish refugees and for a Jewish homeland in Palestine. The previous October, he had allayed the concerns of Frankfurter and Brandeis during a meeting with Ben Cohen. He had done little, however, to advance their cause. In May 1939, the British had limited Jewish immigration to Palestine. Kennedy was also an ardent isolationist: He had supported Chamberlain's appeasement, had fallen in with Lady Astor's antiwar Cliveden set, and had lost the confidence of the Roosevelt administration. The American press called for Kennedy to "come home." On July 13, Kennedy and his wife, Rose, graciously entertained the Frankfurters. By this time, Joe Jr. and Jack had studied with Harold Laski at the London School of Economics. Joe Jr., who had taken a year off in Europe, was set to enroll in Harvard Law School in the fall and lamented that Frankfurter was no longer teaching there. Jack, a rising Harvard senior who aborted his time with Laski after only a few months, was also thinking about law school, possibly at Yale. Frankfurter did not see Kennedy's eldest sons, who were traveling in Europe that summer. Unlike Joe Jr., Jack had rejected his father's isolationist views.

Thanks to Kennedy's introduction, Frankfurter saw Prime Minister Chamberlain three times and numerous other British officials. Yet the justice refused to let social niceties prevent him from speaking his mind about foreign policy and complained to Kennedy about Chamberlain's ineffective leadership. Kennedy asked what Frankfurter would do in Chamberlain's place, and Frankfurter replied that he would put Churchill in the cabinet. "Aw, nuts," Kennedy replied, "Winston is nothing but a drunk." For the time being, they agreed to disagree. "Trying days are ahead," Frankfurter wrote the American ambassador on July 13 on the ship home. "But you and I agree that a real man wants to be tested by great events."

Even on the journey home on the American steamer *Manhattan*, the justice could not escape news of the impending war. One of the passengers was Gregor Ziemer, a Buffalo native and former headmaster of the American School in Berlin. Ziemer quit the school after the Jewish ghetto or segregation law had gone into effect and the Gestapo had removed all the Jewish students. Ziemer discussed the horrors of Nazi Germany with Frankfurter and informed the press that the Germans had captured the Polish port of Danzig and would soon control all of Poland. Frankfurter knew what was coming: "How ghastly it all is—the whole world directly or indirectly at the mercy of one man's will." From his time in London, he knew "all the public & private arrangements are being made for war."

On July 20, the Frankfurters arrived in New York City and vacated their Cambridge home at 192 Brattle Street for good. They lived for a month in the Connecticut home of their friend Dr. Alfred Cohn and, after Labor Day, they vacationed for two weeks in Heath, Massachusetts, with theologian Reinhold Niebuhr and other longtime friends. Felix interrupted the vacation for two days in Washington. It was the world's final moments of peace.

On August 23, Hitler and Stalin announced the Nazi-Soviet nonaggression pact. "You at least are doing all that any mortal can do," Frankfurter wired the president. A week later, he reminded Roosevelt's secretary Missy LeHand that he had heard in London the war would begin on September 21. The Frankfurters were "glued to the radio during the day and for a good part of the night" for news from Europe. "I reflect not only on those enduring values of man we call civilization and the fate of friends and relatives in Vienna and Paris and London," he wrote Roosevelt, "but also think of what burdens these anxious days are casting on you." On September 1, the Nazis invaded Poland. Two days later at 4:30 a.m., Roosevelt was awakened by Prime Minister Chamberlain informing him that Britain and France had declared war on Germany. Near the end of his fireside chat that night, Roosevelt pledged to a national radio audience that America "will remain a neutral nation, but I cannot ask that every American remain neutral in thought as well." He could have been speaking directly to Frankfurter.

In early September, Frankfurter cut his Massachusetts vacation short to assist Roosevelt in amending the Neutrality Acts. He relayed information from *Boston Herald* editor Frank Buxton that many of the nation's major newspapers were against the law. He also drafted language for the president about why the acts should be amended: "A so-called Neutrality law which in practical operation favors the forces of oppression must be fundamentally wrong in conception. It runs counter to American traditions and ideals and is in conflict with international law." Roosevelt copied Frankfurter's statement in longhand and attached it to notes for a major speech. On September 21, the president called Congress back for a joint special session and asked for the repeal of embargo provisions in the Neutrality Acts preventing the sale of arms and war materials to Allied countries fighting the Nazis.

The next day, Frankfurter made front-page news by attacking neutrality. Before a crowd of 700 people, the Ford Hall Forum awarded him the gold medal for public service. In his acceptance speech, he blasted neutrality as "one of those slogans and catch words that cover up thought." As he had written to Roosevelt, he argued that "we can agree to be a non-combatant. But it is our right and duty to have thoughts on issues involving human destiny. No man who thinks really is neutral." He referenced a recent speech by Hitler criticizing the democratic tradition of free speech and free press: "How can we be neutral on an issue like that unless we close our minds to the cardinal, basic doctrines of our civilization?"

The war had been on the Frankfurters' minds since their return to America two months earlier. "You know how deeply our visit touched us—for we never escaped the conviction that war was inevitable," Frankfurter wrote Arthur Goodhart. "The leopard couldn't change his spots—and John Bull, once the issue was clear, was John Bull." Marion wrote Isaiah Berlin, "You would think we were in it up to the neck." She described housewives hoarding sugar, congressmen pontificating during long radio addresses, and Senator Borah vowing to fight the repeal of the Neutrality Acts—"everybody in Washington is working day and night."

———

WORKING SINCE JUNE on Frankfurter's day job was his precocious former student and new law clerk, Edward Fretwell Prichard, Jr. Everyone called him Prich. He was young, brash, and fat. At more than 250 pounds and with a large shock of hair, he had been impossible to miss in the back of the crowded Senate Caucus Room at Frankfurter's confirmation hearings or at the swearing-in ceremony. A native of Paris, Kentucky, Prich had enrolled at Princeton at age sixteen and had graduated summa cum laude and class orator. Frankfurter had met Prichard in April 1935 while giving a series of Princeton lectures about federalism and was miffed when the young man had not come to see him upon arriving in Cambridge. He asked whether Prich expected a "Tiffany engraved invitation" and informally invited him to the house for tea. Prich quickly became a regular at the Frankfurters' Sunday afternoon teas, made the *Harvard Law Review*, and aspired to succeed Rauh as Cardozo's law clerk. Instead, he became Frankfurter's last graduate research assistant, working on *Mr. Justice Holmes and the Supreme Court*; a memorial tribute to Cardozo; and several articles with Henry Hart including an installment of "The Business of the Supreme Court." He interacted with professors, particularly Frankfurter and Thomas Reed Powell, more like a colleague than a student. After he heard about Frankfurter's nomination, he wired him: "When do we leave?" Frankfurter, who wanted Prichard to finish his fellowship, wired back: "I leave on confirmation, you leave at the end of the term." Prich was irreverent, gossipy, and destined for greatness. The Louisville *Courier-Journal* story about his Frankfurter clerkship described him as "the 'future governor of Kentucky.'"

During the summer of 1939, Frankfurter had asked the Clerk of the Court to send copies of petitions for certiorari to Kentucky so that Prichard could read them. While the Frankfurters were living at the New Milford, Connecticut, home of Dr. Alfred Cohn, Prichard joined them for about ten days. During the day, he and Frankfurter reviewed certiorari petitions and prepared for the coming term; at night they listened to the radio for news about the war in Europe.

In October, the Frankfurters moved back to Washington, D.C., renting a home at 1511 Thirtieth Street in Georgetown where they lived for the next two years. Prichard and several friends moved into a Dupont Circle house at 1915 S Street, but it was too small. They rented an old mansion named Hockley, which overlooked the Potomac River on the other side of the Key Bridge in Virginia. The next iteration of Corcoran and Cohen's little red house, Hockley was House of Truth 3.0. A group of young men, mostly lawyers, lived at Hockley. Prich's housemates were his friends from Princeton and Harvard Law School: Covington associate William DuBose Sheldon; former Frankfurter clerk and Covington associate Adrian Fisher; and *Washington Post* reporter John Oakes. They threw noisy dinner parties where they debated ideas with Frankfurter, Acheson, Learned Hand, and other special guests. They also invited interesting young women, including the *Washington Post* publisher's daughter, Katharine Meyer.

A young reporter at her father's newspaper, Meyer gravitated to one of the most charismatic Hockley boys besides Prich himself—a tall, skinny, former *Harvard Law Review* president named Phil Graham. They had met at the S Street house, where he continued to live with two other former *Review* presidents, former Brandeis clerk Graham Claytor and Ed Huddleson. The son of a struggling Florida dairy farmer and former state senator, Graham had attended the University of Florida (where he had roomed with future U.S. senator George Smathers) and had thrived at Harvard Law School. After he made the *Review*, he became fast friends with Prich, who was a year ahead of him. It was Prich who had helped Graham become the compromise candidate for *Review* president and who had introduced Graham to Frankfurter. As he did with Prich, Frankfurter grew close to Graham. In those days, justices hired only one clerk. Frankfurter was forced to choose: he hired Prich for the coming term, sent Graham to clerk for Stanley Reed, and promised Graham that he would succeed his friend in Frankfurter's chambers.

The 24-year-old Prichard was riding high after co-editing a book of Frankfurter's articles, essays, and lectures, *Law and Politics*. Yet his work in chambers got off to a rocky start. In writing opinions, Frankfurter would dictate, and Prichard would type. They would discuss the issues in each opinion, then they would revise two or three times. In an opinion released in December 1939, Frankfurter relied on an Oklahoma Supreme Court decision that Prichard had neglected to Shepardize; that is, check by looking in *Shepard's*, a series of books that would have revealed the case had been overruled. As soon as a petition for rehearing pointed out the error, Prich left town. Frankfurter asked Rauh and Graham where he was. "Prich," Graham quipped to Claytor, "has an acute case of Sheparditis." Frankfurter, who withdrew and revised the opinion, informed Rauh all was forgiven; a chastened Prichard returned to chambers and begged Frankfurter for forgiveness.

On November 16, 1939, Justice Pierce Butler died. With Van Devanter and Sutherland's retirements and Butler's death, James C. McReynolds was the last of the conservative Four Horsemen; the other three had been replaced by Roosevelt. To succeed Butler, Roosevelt nominated another Catholic midwesterner, Attorney General Frank Murphy. Murphy hired Ed Huddleson, Graham's housemate and predecessor as *Harvard Law Review* president, as his first clerk. Frankfurter tried to take Murphy under his wing as he vied with Black and Douglas for the Court's leadership.

Black was emerging as a leading liberal voice. In February 1940, he authored the majority opinion in *Chambers v. Florida* reversing the murder convictions of four black men because their confessions had been coerced. The opinion was a major rebuke to law enforcement officials accustomed to beating and torturing blacks into confessing to crimes. Like Black, Frankfurter believed that the Fourteenth Amendment's Due Process Clause could be used to outlaw egregious criminal procedure violations as a way of eradicating the two-tiered system of racial justice in the South. The following term, Frankfurter stayed the execution of Joe Vernon, a black Alabama man who had been beaten until he confessed to murdering a white gas station attendant, five minutes before Vernon was supposed to die. The Court agreed to hear the case and summarily reversed Vernon's conviction on the basis of *Chambers v. Florida*. Frankfurter sent Black's groundbreaking opinion on coerced confessions to Roosevelt and several others, admired how hard Black was working on the Court, and predicted that "when the history of the Supreme Court was written, Black would stand out as one of the great justices."

A December 1939 decision revealed fissures between Frankfurter and Douglas. Frankfurter wrote a majority opinion affirming that the state of Kansas had improperly collected taxes from the Pottawatomie tribe but that the tribe had been improperly awarded interest under federal law. Black added a concurring opinion that the interest payment had been forbidden by state law. In the robing room before the justices announced the decision, Douglas, who had joined Frankfurter's opinion with words of hearty praise, informed Frankfurter that he was joining Black's not because he was persuaded by its reasoning but because he did not want his colleague to be concurring alone. Douglas's decision to switch his vote to curry favor with a colleague rubbed Frankfurter the wrong way and portended future conflicts.

———

ON NEW YEAR'S DAY 1940, Frankfurter greeted Roosevelt with an impassioned and patriotic letter: "Not even you can quite feel what this country means to a man like me, who was brought here as an eager sensitive lad of twelve—for America has been in your blood, as it were, for generation upon generation. My father—who was a small businessman—came here, in 1893, on a business trip, and fell in love with the country, and particularly with the spirit of freedom that was in the air. And so he persuaded my mother to uproot the family, and from the moment we landed on Manhattan I knew, with the sure instinct of a child, that this was my native spiritual home. I began to read English avidly, and very soon Lincoln became my hero." He explained he had read all the great works on Lincoln and understood the physical and psychological burden of the presidency, especially during the Civil War, on the sixteenth president. He also grasped that the war in Europe presented "difficulties not less grave and heavy than those that weighed on Lincoln's soul" and how Roosevelt "carries them as gallantly as he did and with the inevitable solitude of Lincoln's compassion and wise private humor." He wished Roosevelt, "as a man and friend . . . personal solace and happiness and strength . . . to continue to live with fortitude and gayety and wisdom." Roosevelt thanked Frankfurter for the "extraordinarily touching note. . . . It is things of this kind and there are not too many—which have helped lighten the task of this office." The New Year's Day letter, biographer Max Freedman remarked, was "the frankest and most emotional avowal of Frankfurter's devotion to Roosevelt."

During the first half of 1940, Frankfurter's patriotism and the war in Europe dominated his political and legal outlook. He sought to assist Roosevelt in preparing America for war by editing speeches, making policy suggestions, and recruiting mentors and friends into the highest reaches of government. He also wrote a judicial opinion in the *Gobitis* flag salute case that destroyed his reputation in liberal circles and prompted charges that he was a conservative. The opinion, though frequently attributed to his pride in his adopted country, was as much a product of his obsession over the war and his second job as an informal executive branch adviser.

Visitors from abroad frequently sought Frankfurter's counsel because he was a leading interventionist with access to the president. In late 1939, German lawyer and former Oxford student Adam von Trott had arrived in the United States for a conference and with the not-so-secret agenda of persuading Frankfurter and other American officials to help him overthrow Hitler. A former Rhodes scholar at Balliol College, Trott had befriended Isaiah Berlin and Maurice Bowra. Through a letter of introduction from Berlin, the Frankfurters had seen Trott for four days in Cambridge in June 1937 and had been favorably impressed, though Felix had "thought his mind confused." In early 1939, Trott had begun making the rounds in Britain and met with Prime Minister Chamberlain about a plot to kill Hitler. Bowra and Berlin, however, did not trust the tall, handsome German. In a letter to Frankfurter intercepted by British postal censors, Bowra questioned Trott's character and what Trott's new regime would do once in power. In July, Churchill met with Frankfurter and relayed Bowra's warnings. Frankfurter's friend Reinhold Niebuhr tried to vouch for Trott. An official with the Institute of Pacific Relations, Edward C. Carter, phoned Frankfurter and asked him to see Trott. Trott's meeting with Frankfurter went so badly—it ended after Trott insulted Churchill—that the justice relayed his concerns to George S. Messersmith in the State Department. Due in part to the intercepted letter from Bowra to Frankfurter, the FBI believed that Trott was a Nazi spy and monitored his every move. Trott never saw the president. Frankfurter never said a word to Roosevelt about it until Trott's departure when they joked about J. Edgar Hoover's surveillance. In 1940, Trott joined the Nazi Party and worked its ministry of information as a cover while waiting for the opportunity to overthrow Hitler. Four years later, he was hanged after a bomb exploded near the Führer but did not kill him. Some have blamed Frankfurter for FDR's failure to see Trott. Yet, as Trott biographer Christopher Sykes observed, many people misjudged Trott's motives.

In February 1940, Frankfurter threw a "stag dinner" for British ambassador Lord Lothian, who informed Robert Jackson, Herbert Feis, Francis Biddle, and Harold Ickes how outgunned the British and French were in the air compared to the Germans. After dinner they engaged into a heated debate about whether Hitler spoke for the youth of Germany. Biddle, Jackson, and Ickes thought he did. An "almost angry" Frankfurter retorted it was like saying that gangster Al "Capone had given leadership to the youth of Chicago" and that "leadership that leads to oppression and war and tyrannies of all sorts is not leadership."

During the spring of 1940, Hitler's army marched across Europe. On April 9, Germany occupied Denmark and invaded Norway. The British government, meanwhile, changed hands with Chamberlain resigning as prime minister in favor of Churchill. For the past month, Churchill had been in charge of British military operations. On May 10, the same day that Churchill became prime minister, Germany invaded Belgium, Luxembourg, the Netherlands, and France.

On April 25, the Court heard the case that tested Frankfurter's liberal reputation and pitted him against some of his closest friends. William and Lillian Gobitas (misspelled by the Court as Gobitis), two children of Jehovah's Witnesses, had been expelled from their Minersville, Pennsylvania, elementary school for refusing to salute the flag. Jehovah's Witnesses believed that the flag salute violated the teachings of the Bible. Their father sued the school district, which responded that the flag salute was essential to teaching respect for the flag and national loyalty. A federal trial judge barred the school district from expelling the two students, and the Court of Appeals for the Third Circuit affirmed the trial judge.

Frankfurter's law school classmates Grenville Clark and Monte Lemann rallied leading members of the bar behind the Gobitas children's claims of religious freedom. A Republican and name partner at the Root, Clark law firm, Clark had criticized Frankfurter for his public silence about Roosevelt's court-packing plan. As Clark began defending the Court and the Constitution in articles and public speeches, Frankfurter pressed him to think about the Court's and the bar's role in safeguarding civil liberties. As a result, Clark agreed to chair the American Bar Association's Special Committee on the Bill of Rights. The special committee was a who's who of the bar and included Lemann, a New Orleanian who had finished fourth in Frankfurter's class and whom Frankfurter had recommended for a judgeship on the Court of Appeals for the Fifth Circuit; Zechariah Chafee, Frankfurter's former Harvard law colleague and a First Amendment scholar; and Lloyd Garrison, Frankfurter's former student and dean of the University of Wisconsin Law School.

Frankfurter was pleased the American Bar Association (ABA), under Clark's direction, was taking a stand in favor of the Bill of Rights because the organization had done nothing during the first postwar Red Scare. Before becoming a justice, Frankfurter had encouraged Clark to file a friend of the court brief with the Supreme Court in a 1939 case challenging Jersey City mayor Frank Hague's refusal to provide a permit for the Committee for Industrial Organization (CIO) meeting because of the organization's alleged Communist ties. Frankfurter declared at the time the "whole country" was praising the ABA special committee's brief in that case. A divided Court, with Frankfurter recused, held that Hague's refusal to supply a permit violated the First Amendment right of free assembly.

As early as January 8, 1939, the special committee had begun discussing whether to file a similar brief in the *Gobitis* case. A month later, Clark inquired about Lemann's desire to get involved and sent him a memorandum from Harvard law professor George K. Gardner about the issues. After he read the memorandum, Lemann was opposed to getting involved. Something, perhaps a face-to-face meeting with Clark, changed his mind. On March 4, 1940, the Supreme Court agreed to hear the case. Clark, Lemann, and other special committee members therefore decided to prepare a friend of the court brief in time for the April 25 oral argument.

Fortunately for Clark, he tapped the ideal Root, Clark associate to draft the ABA special committee's brief about the compulsory flag salute—Louis Lusky. A Columbia law graduate, Lusky had clerked for Harlan Fiske Stone during the 1937 term and had helped draft one of the most famous footnotes in constitutional history. In the April 1938 *Carolene Products* decision, the Court upheld a federal law banning the sale of milk infused with coconut oil. The law, backed by bogus health and safety claims, was the dairy industry's attempt to eliminate non-dairy competitors. It was a case in which the Court went to an extreme to uphold economic legislation in the wake of the New Deal constitutional crisis. In Footnote Four of the opinion, however, the Court detailed in three paragraphs instances in which it might take a harder look at legislation that infringed on specific guarantees in the Bill of the Rights (paragraph one); restricted the political process such as voting rights (paragraph two); and discriminated against "discrete and insular minorities" (paragraph three). Stone and Lusky took great pride in their joint authorship of the footnote. Footnote Four, however, was not yet Footnote Four. Not a single scholar had written about it. It had made hardly a ripple in the nation's constitutional discourse. Lusky wanted to see if the Court would live up to the promise of Footnote Four and take a harder look at the compulsory flag salute.

Lusky's *Gobitis* brief went through many drafts and revisions by Lemann and the other lawyers. The day before the oral argument, the special committee filed a brief arguing that the compulsory flag salute violated the children's free exercise of religion and individual liberty. The brief concluded with powerful language contrasting America's belief in constitutional rights with those of totalitarian regimes spreading across Europe: "The philosophy of free institutions is now being subjected to the most severe test it has ever undergone. Advocates of totalitarian government point to the speed and efficiency with which such systems are administered, and assert that democracy can offer nothing to outweigh these advantages. The answer is to be found in the value of certain basic individual rights and the assurance afforded by free institutions that these shall not be required to yield to majority pressure no matter how overwhelming. . . . We believe that the letter and spirit of our Constitution demand vindication of the individual liberties which are abridged by the challenged regulation."

The ABA brief's arguments and stirring conclusion, coupled with the powerful names of Clark, Lemann, Chafee, Garrison, and other distinguished members of the bar who signed it, dwarfed anything that happened at oral argument. The *New York Herald Tribune* published an editorial about the special committee's brief and concluded: "To compel school children to salute the flag is a step in the 'Heil Hitler' direction."

The members of the Bill of Rights committee knew that their brief might face resistance from their patriotic immigrant friend. During oral argument, Frankfurter passed a note to the newest justice, Frank Murphy: "Is it at all probable that the framers of the Bill of Rights would have thought that a requirement to salute the flag violates the protection of 'the free exercise of religion.'" Frankfurter aimed to persuade Murphy and his colleagues of the constitutionality of the compulsory flag salute in the *Gobitis* case.

Two days later at conference, Chief Justice Hughes did most of Frankfurter's work for him. A master of the Saturday conference, he discussed the issues so thoroughly and in a such a persuasive way that it was extremely difficult for any justice, much less one new to the Court, to disagree with his assessment. The justices proceeded around the table in order of seniority and explained their views, if any. Then, in reverse order, they voted on the case. Hughes, if he was in the majority, would assign the opinion either to himself or another justice in the majority.

In *Gobitis*, Hughes discussed the issues as if this were an easy case and there was no choice but to reverse the lower courts and to uphold the flag salute. "As I see it the state can insist on inculcation of loyalty," he said. "It would be extraordinary if in this country the state could not provide for respect for the flag of our land." Many state laws, he pointed out, offend people. The religious freedom issue, however, made Hughes nervous: "I come up to this case like a skittish horse to a brass band." He explained his "profound belief" in "religious freedom." Indeed, in 1938 Hughes had suggested the inclusion of the first paragraph of *Carolene Products*'s Footnote Four that suggested the Court would take a harder look at laws infringing on specific guarantees of the Bill of Rights. Yet he did not believe that the compulsory flag salute violated the First Amendment's Free Exercise Clause given the justifications of teaching loyalty to the country and respect for the flag. "I don't want to be dogmatic about this," he concluded, "but I simply cannot believe that the state has not the power to inculcate this social objective." Six justices agreed with Hughes and voted to reverse the lower courts. Only Black and Stone passed without voting.

Hughes was deeply moved by what Frankfurter said at conference, so much so that he assigned the opinion to him. Frankfurter's remarks have been lost to history, but, as he wrote in his New Year's Day letter to Roosevelt, he likely told the story of his arrival in America not knowing a word of English; how Miss Hogan at P.S. 25 had forced his classmates to speak to him in English and not his native German; how public school had taught him the nation's history and traditions; and how the states should have the latitude to teach their students loyalty to the country and respect for the flag. Both Frankfurter and Roberts approached Hughes and encouraged the chief justice to assume the responsibility of writing the *Gobitis* opinion himself. Hughes stuck to his assignment "because of Frankfurter's moving statement at conference on the role of the public school in instilling love of country in our pluralist society."

It must not have been lost on Hughes to assign a highly charged case, a compulsory flag salute that infringed on religious freedom and prompted references to Nazi Germany, to the only Jewish justice. Frankfurter practiced only one religion—Americanism. It is too simplistic, however, to chalk up his views merely to the psychological factors that lay behind his love of his adopted country. His opposition to American neutrality and isolationism in the face of a cataclysmic European war and Hitler's threat to exterminate Europe's Jews was a more overriding concern. He also was preoccupied with his wartime policy making and recruitment efforts on behalf of the Roosevelt administration. Many factors, legal and nonlegal, played a role. The psychological ones, however, have been overemphasized and have crowded out equally persuasive legal explanations.

The philosophy of judicial restraint, a constitutional theory he learned by reading James Bradley Thayer's famous essay and Holmes's and Brandeis's opinions, spearheaded his thinking about the *Gobitis* case. According to Frankfurter, his personal views about a law were irrelevant. His decision to uphold the flag salute was consistent with his long-standing opposition to invoking the liberty provision of the Due Process Clause to invalidate state and local laws. Since 1905 when the Court declared in *Lochner v. New York* that a maximum-hour law for bakers violated "liberty of contract," he had repeatedly invoked Holmes's *Lochner* dissent that the justices should not use the Due Process Clause to read their economic views into the Constitution. In 1916, Frankfurter had taken over for Brandeis in defending state minimum-wage and maximum-hour laws for the National Consumers' League. After initial success defending Oregon's laws, he lost in 1923 when the Court invalidated a District of Columbia minimum-wage law for women in *Adkins v. Children's Hospital. Adkins* reinforced his belief that the Due Process Clause should be written out of the Constitution because it gave the justices too much power. Unlike other liberals, he insisted there was no such thing as "good" and "bad" reasons to invoke the liberty provision—especially when it came to state and local public education laws. He disagreed with the Court's decisions, written by McReynolds, expanding the concept of liberty to invalidate a Nebraska law banning the teaching of foreign languages in grade schools as well as an Oregon law requiring children to attend public schools in an effort to shut down private Catholic schools. It did not matter to Frankfurter that the Nebraska law was motivated by post–World War I prejudice against Germans or that the Oregon law was motivated by the Ku Klux Klan's prejudice against Catholics. Nor did it matter that he personally disagreed with both laws. He refused to invoke the Due Process Clause in any context except to overturn criminal convictions for procedural reasons such as police, prosecutorial, or judicial misconduct.

The briefs on behalf of the Gobitas children relied on the Due Process Clause's liberty provision because at the time the Court had never applied the Free Exercise Clause to the states. For nearly 150 years, the First Amendment forbade the federal government but not state and local governments from abridging free speech, exercise of religion, and assembly. In 1925, the Court "incorporated" the Free Speech Clause into the Fourteenth Amendment's Due Process Clause and therefore applied it to the states. In early 1940, however, the Free Exercise Clause remained unincorporated, and the state and local governments remained free to infringe upon religious liberty.

Nearly a month before oral argument in the *Gobitis* case, the Court had heard oral argument in another case involving Jehovah's Witnesses. Newton Cantwell and his two sons had been convicted under a Connecticut anti-solicitation law for knocking on doors on a New Haven residential street and passing out religious literature. In *Cantwell v. Connecticut*, a unanimous Court agreed to apply the Free Exercise Clause to the states. *Cantwell*, however, was not decided until May 20—nearly a month after the *Gobitis* oral argument. Frankfurter and his colleagues already knew what the outcome would be in *Cantwell*. As Frankfurter was drafting his opinion in *Gobitis*, however, the Court had never struck down a state law on the basis of a claim of religious freedom.

Finally, there was the issue of precedent. In three prior cases, the Court had upheld school-mandated flag salutes. Frankfurter was reluctant to overturn those decisions. He believed that the nation's public schools had relied on them and that the Court should depart from precedent only in extreme circumstances. In his majority opinion, however, he refused to rely on precedent. He worried about the Supreme Court acting like a super-legislature and invading the power of the states to set their own educational agendas. He believed that the Court should give state and local laws wide latitude—whether they were state minimum-wage laws or local school boards compelling schoolchildren to salute the flag.

All these concerns came into play in his majority opinion that he circulated in early May and published on June 4. He began by acknowledging the "grave responsibility" that came with "conflicting claims of liberty and authority," particularly liberty claims about freedom of religion or conscience. He also praised the friend of the court briefs from the ABA's Bill of Rights committee and the ACLU because they "helped us to our conclusion." And he acknowledged that *Cantwell* had expanded the reach of the First Amendment and prevented state and local governments from interfering with organized religious activities. And when religious faith conflicts with laws of general applicability, "every possible leeway should be given to the claims of religious faith."

Yet, unlike state laws that suppressed free speech or press, Frankfurter recognized an equally important state interest "inferior to none in the hierarchy of values. National unity is the basis of national security. To deny the legislature the right to select appropriate means for its attainment presents a totally different order of problem from that of the propriety of subordinating the possible ugliness of littered streets to the free expression of opinion through distribution of handbills." He quoted Lincoln on the balance between promoting individual liberty and having a strong state. And he insisted that "it is not the personal notion of judges of what wise adjustment requires which must prevail." National unity and national security, however, were foremost

on Frankfurter's mind. "The ultimate foundation of a free society is the binding tie of cohesive sentiment," he wrote and emphasized the symbolic importance of respect for the flag. "The flag is the symbol of our national unity,
transcending all internal differences, however large, within the framework of
the Constitution."

Frankfurter saw no role for judges in telling the nation's public schools
how they should teach respect for the flag, especially during "the formative
period in the development of citizenship." In his mind, Mr. Gobitas had made
a choice to send his children to public school rather than private school. Public
education, the Court held in *Pierce v. Society of Sisters*, was not constitutionally
required. But once Mr. Gobitas had made the choice not to send his children
to private school, Frankfurter believed it was "a very different thing for this
Court to exercise censorship over the conviction of legislatures that a particular program or exercise will best promote in the minds of children who attend
the common schools an attachment to the institutions of their country." The
school had a right, contrary to the parent, to teach respect for the flag.

If parents did not like what the school was doing, Frankfurter argued, the
solution was not judicial intervention but resort to the democratic political
process. He acknowledged Footnote Four's call for more judicial scrutiny to
protect the Bill of Rights and to prevent obstruction of the political process.
Unless "the transgression of constitutional liberty is too plain for argument"
and as long as "the remedial channels of the democratic process remain open
and unobstructed," he argued, the courts should defer to the legislature. For
he believed that "to the legislature no less than to courts is committed the
guardianship of deeply-cherished liberties." The lesson for Frankfurter from
the New Deal constitutional crisis and court-packing fight was less judicial
intervention, not more. He concluded: "To fight out the wise use of legislative
authority in the forum of public opinion and before legislative assemblies
rather than to transfer such a contest to the judicial arena, serves to vindicate
the self-confidence of a free people."

Not everyone was persuaded by Frankfurter's paean to national unity,
national security, the civic education function of public schools, and judicial restraint—least of all Harlan Fiske Stone. The author of Footnote Four
had passed when the justices voted at their conference about *Gobitis*. Stone
responded to Frankfurter's majority opinion with a dissent in the Holmes-
Brandeis tradition of protecting free speech. He argued that the flag salute
violated both freedom of speech and free exercise of religion: "For by this
law the state seeks to coerce these children to express a sentiment which, as
they interpret it, they do not entertain, and which violates their deepest reli-

gious convictions." Stone recognized the government's power in wartime—to "make war and raise armies" and to require "military service." Indeed, he and Frankfurter had fought for a rigorous independent screening of conscientious objectors during World War I and had sought to provide them with noncombat service to their country. And, in this case, he believed that "where the performance of governmental functions is brought into conflict with specific constitutional restrictions," the government must make a "reasonable accommodation." Stone argued that "there are other ways to teach loyalty and patriotism which are the sources of national unity" than by compelling students with sincere religious objections to salute the flag.

Stone referred to Footnote Four of his *Carolene Products* opinion as another reason the judiciary should not be so deferential in this case. In an allusion to the footnote's third paragraph, he decried the abridgement of civil liberties of "politically helpless minorities." And in a reference to the footnote's first paragraph, he argued that "[t]he very terms of the Bill of Rights," the Free Speech and Free Exercise Clauses, "preclude" a compulsory flag salute. He rejected Frankfurter's assertion that courts should defer to the legislature if the political processes are "open and unobstructed," a reference to the footnote's second paragraph. Instead, Stone argued that the flag salute should "be subject to the same judicial scrutiny as legislation which we have recently held to infringe the constitutional liberty of religious and racial minorities." He concluded that the problems of making reasonable accommodations for religious minorities were not "so momentous or pressing as to outweigh the freedom from compulsory violation of religious faith which has been thought worthy of constitutional protection."

During his early years on the Court, Frankfurter corresponded with Stone more than any other justice. He had questioned Stone's liberalism during the 1920s, thought Stone could be pompous and vain and wanted too much to be Holmes's and Brandeis's successor, but never doubted Stone's intellect. He had warmed to Stone during the 1930s and during the New Deal constitutional crisis had sympathized with Stone's frustration with Hughes and the conservative majority. As colleagues, he wanted them, despite their differences in *Gobitis*, to maintain their mutual admiration and friendship.

In a May 27 letter, he confessed that Stone's dissent "stirred me to an anxious re-examination of my own views." He also claimed that "all my bias and predisposition are in favor of giving the fullest elbow room to every variety of religious, political, and economic view." Yet he remained steadfast in his belief that "[w]e are not exercising an independent judgment; we are sitting in judgment upon the judgment of the legislature." He praised Stone's explanation of Footnote Four of *Carolene Products.* "I agree with that distinction;" he wrote to Stone, "I regard it as basic." Yet in his opinion and in his letter to Stone, Frankfurter emphasized only the second paragraph's focus on unobstructed political processes. He was determined not to repeat the mistakes of nineteenth century justices who used the Fourteenth Amendment to protect property rights by using it to protect liberty rights. He also understood that "time and circumstances," including the need for "national security," affected the outcome. This was one reason he did not rely on the Court's past decisions and treated it as "a new question." He intimated, on the basis of his conversations with Holmes, that the war had influenced Holmes's decisions affirming the Espionage Act convictions in *Schenck, Frohwerk,* and *Debs* and that the postwar Red hysteria had moved him to dissent in a similar case in *Abrams.*

Above all, he wrote Stone, his *Gobitis* opinion was an essay about the proper role of the Court. *Adkins v. Children's Hospital* symbolized the so-called *Lochner* era and the Court's willingness to invalidate state and federal economic legislation. He wanted his *Gobitis* opinion to be "a vehicle for preaching the true democratic faith of not relying on the Court for the impossible task of assuring a vigorous, mature, self-protecting and tolerant democracy by bringing the responsibility for a combination of firmness and toleration directly home where it belongs—to the people and their representatives themselves." He thought the school board's refusal to make an exception for Jehovah's Witnesses was "foolish." Of course, he deemed his personal views irrelevant and preferred "to let the legislative judgment stand and put the responsibility for its exercise where it belongs."

Frankfurter shared a copy of his May 27 letter to Stone with the Court's newest justice and the one most troubled by the case, Frank Murphy. In fact, Murphy had drafted his own dissent but elected not to publish it. He was so new to the Court that he lacked the intellectual confidence to take a civil libertarian stand. On June 3, he reluctantly joined Frankfurter's opinion. "This has been a gethsemane for me," the deeply religious Murphy wrote. "But after all the constitution presupposes a government that will nourish and protect itself and therefore I join your beautifully expressed opinion."

A justice with more intellectual confidence than Murphy, Hugo Black harbored his own doubts about Frankfurter's opinion. One of two justices who had passed at conference, Black had already joined Frankfurter's opinion. At 10:00 a.m. on Saturday, June 1, he had stopped by Frankfurter's chambers and said, "like you, I don't like this kind of law & wish we could stop it, but I don't see that there is anything in the Due Process Clause that possibly can enable us to hold this unconstitutional." Frankfurter also noted that "Hugo, in oral discussion, made me take out a detailed argument as to [the] 'polyglot' racial composition of [the] Minersville school population."

Other justices praised Frankfurter's opinion. Douglas joined it and wrote: "This is a powerful moving document of incalculable contemporary and (I believe) historic value. I congratulate you on a truly statesmanlike job." On a subsequent draft, Douglas added that Frankfurter had "done a magnificent job." Hughes thanked him: "You have accomplished most admirably a very difficult and highly important task—The Court is indebted to you." Owen J. Roberts, who grew close with Frankfurter, wrote: "I have no suggestion of any kind. I am enthusiastically for this opinion. It is among the best ever prepared by a judge of this court." Even Stone, who was surprised that not a single colleague had joined his dissent, praised Frankfurter's work and described him as "a great addition to the Court." Frankfurter reported that Brandeis, after reading the draft, was shocked that the entire Court had not joined the *Gobitis* opinion.

Several people close to Frankfurter were horrified by his opinion, notably his law clerk, Prich. Prich and Phil Graham had been arguing with him about the case. One evening, Prich broke the Court's rules about confidentiality and removed the draft *Gobitis* opinion from chambers. He took it to the home of Frankfurter's first clerk, Joseph Rauh, who at age twenty-nine had become an older brother/father confessor to Prich and Graham. Rauh never forgot the sight of Prich, at more than 250 pounds, huffing and puffing up the hill to the Rauh family home across Connecticut Avenue near the National Zoo. Prich "plunged" into their biggest chair, "pulled out of his pocket the printed drafts of Frankfurter's opinion," and in between deep breaths explained what was troubling him. "This is the end of our Justice's role on the Court," Prich told Rauh. "Phil and I have tried every argument we know to get him to change his mind but it doesn't do any good. *You* have to do something." Prich wanted Rauh to persuade Frankfurter to withdraw his opinion and to switch sides. They knew, however, the task was hopeless. Rauh could not even raise the issue with Frankfurter because the question would arise how Rauh had seen the opinion in the first place. Rauh read it anyway and agreed with Prich that Frankfurter was ruining himself and sacrificing any chance of leading the Court.

Two days after the justices had announced their opinions in *Gobitis* on June 3, the arguments about the case between Frankfurter and his clerks continued during a lunchtime discussion in Mount Kisco, New York, before Graham's wedding to Katharine Meyer. Frankfurter's first few law clerks argued so hard with him about cases that Marion referred to them as "the barbarians." That day, the arguments between Frankfurter and Prich grew so heated and so personal that "great large tears rolled down Prich's reddened, rotund cheeks." The other guests, including photographer Edward Steichen, joined the debate. With the minister waiting an hour for the wedding to start and Graham's best man Prich inconsolable, Frankfurter took the bride by the arm: "Come along, Kay. We will go for a walk in the woods and calm down." At 5:00 p.m., Kay Meyer, wearing an ivory silk Bergdorf Goodman dress, was escorted down the aisle by her father, Eugene, photographed by Steichen, and married Phil Graham. Graham had asked for Frankfurter's permission to marry because of an unwritten rule against married law clerks. That June, Graham succeeded his best man Prich as Frankfurter's clerk with the justice's liberal reputation in tatters.

Many of Frankfurter's liberal friends did not have the heart to tell him how disappointed they were. "I want to tell you how right I think you are in that Educational case from Pennsylvania and, to my deep regret, how wrong I think Felix is," Harold Laski wrote Stone. Ben Cohen, the architect along with Corcoran in getting Frankfurter nominated, praised Stone: "when a liberal judge holds out alone against his liberal brethren I think he ought to know when he has spoken not for himself alone, but has superbly articulated the thoughts and feelings of a great many of his contemporaries who believe with him in an effective but tolerant democracy." Finally, New York lawyer C. C. Burlingham confided to Stone: "Felix is puzzling us very much. . . . I certainly thought he would be with you in the Jehovah [sic] Witnesses case. It is not easy for a judge to be a successful policy maker or defender. J. Marshall had a pretty good background of political experience, did he not?"

Liberal newspapers, magazines, and organizations with which Frankfurter had long been associated praised Stone's dissent. "Since we have for many years admired the abilities and character of Mr. Justice Frankfurter," the New Republic editorial said, "and have usually agreed with his views whether on legal problems or others, it is with particular regret that we are forced to say we think Mr. Justice Stone is right and Mr. Justice Frankfurter and the seven other justices who concurred are wrong." The Nation echoed those sentiments: "We don't like disagreeing with Felix Frankfurter, whose social wisdom has been tempered and tested in many honorable battles." In his St. Louis Post-Dispatch editorial, Irving Dilliard declared Frankfurter's opinion "dead wrong," "a violation of American principle," and "a surrender to popular hysteria." He praised the ABA Bill of Rights committee's brief and honored Stone. Louis Lusky, Stone's co-author of Footnote Four in Carolene Products and drafter of the ABA Bill of Rights committee's brief, praised his former boss's opinion as "one of the most inspiring documents I have ever read" and in the tradition of Holmes's and Brandeis's free speech dissents. Stone had made good on his promises about protecting the specific guarantees of the Bill of Rights and "discrete and insular minorities" in Footnote Four.

Most of Frankfurter's former Harvard law colleagues and elite lawyers disagreed with his opinion. During extensive correspondence with the retired Harvard medical professor and social activist Alice Hamilton, Frankfurter reminded her that the Court was not making an independent decision about the merits of a compulsory flag salute but was "sitting in judgment on the power of the Legislature to make adjustments between ultimate interests in society."

His *Gobitis* opinion reflected Frankfurter's belief in a limited policy-making role for the judiciary as much as his wartime concerns with national unity and national security. He had known war was inevitable since his trip the previous summer to Britain and his meetings with British leaders. The German Army had invaded France and Belgium and was heading for the English Channel. On May 27, the trapped British Army began its evacuation at Dunkirk while the German Army inexplicably halted for three days. On June 3, the same day Frankfurter announced his *Gobitis* opinion, German planes began bombing Paris. The next day, the British Army completed its evacuation at Dunkirk and saved 330,000 Allied troops. On June 10, Italy declared war on Britain and France. Four days later, the German Army entered Paris. A law clerk for Hugo Black referred to *Gobitis* as "Felix's Fall-of-France Opinion." France had not fallen, at least not yet. For his part, Frankfurter rejected the "Battle of France hypothesis" and pointed to the case's "Due Process issues" and "what the function of the Supreme Court is in relation to state decisions." He observed that the case was argued a month before the fighting on April 25 and discussed at conference two days later: "The guns weren't booming until May."

At the time, however, Frankfurter alienated his liberal friends with his "angry vehemence" about the war. At a stag dinner at Archibald MacLeish's on June 1, Frankfurter became "very emotional" discussing the war and insisted that the United States should enter on the side of the Allies. He and Attorney General Robert Jackson argued late into the night about whether the United States should intervene. At one point, Jackson blurted out: "But you have no son." The remark hurt Frankfurter, who, of course, had lots of "sons," including his former graduate student Sylvester Gates at risk in London and former students and law clerks who eventually fought overseas. Even people at the dinner who agreed with Frankfurter, such as Solicitor General Francis Biddle, thought he was too pro-British and anti-German. Of the Jackson-Frankfurter debate, Harold Ickes concluded: "The latter is really not rational these days on the European situation."

DURING THE FINAL MONTHS of the Supreme Court term, Frankfurter was consumed by the events in Europe and how he could help the Roosevelt administration prepare for war. As he had done in the past, he recruited people and placed them in the highest levels of the administration—starting with his mentor Henry Stimson. The 72-year-old Stimson exemplified Frankfurter's ideal public servant. He had been Frankfurter's boss as the U.S. attorney for the Southern District of New York and in Taft's War Department, then had served as Hoover's secretary of state. Unlike other Republicans, Stimson was not an anti-Roosevelt isolationist; he was the same interventionist he had been during the Taft and Wilson administrations.

The night of May 2, Stimson dined with the Frankfurters at their home and heard their "ardently pro-Ally" views and their concerns about influential people in the U.S. government willing to stand pat. He heard about tension between the State Department and the British Foreign Office and about fears of a Republican isolationist presidential platform in the coming election. The next day, Stimson met with State Department officials and tried to impress upon them the importance of good relations with the British. Frankfurter then picked him up for a 1:00 p.m. White House lunch with Roosevelt. It was the first meeting between Roosevelt and Stimson since 1934. Roosevelt revealed his covert efforts to keep Mussolini from joining forces with Hitler. He also confided his concern with the "disappointingly low" number of planes that American manufacturers had produced for the Allies. Frankfurter thanked Roosevelt for seeing Stimson: "He is a fine old Roman . . . and wants to feel he is still of use to the Republic. . . . You made Stimson feel he *is* of use—and gave him fresh impulse to go on. Many thanks for taking me out of my marble prison."

Unwilling to stay in his "marble prison," the justice made it his mission to bring Stimson into the Roosevelt cabinet. On the morning of May 25, Frankfurter met with the president in the White House for nearly an hour and discussed how to transform the cabinet into a war cabinet, specifically who should lead the War Department. Roosevelt had clashed with Secretary of War Harry Woodring over airplane production and military preparedness. A few days later, Frankfurter conferred with former classmate Grenville Clark about making Stimson secretary of war and checked on Stimson's health. On June 3, after he announced his *Gobitis* opinion, Frankfurter and his wife, preparing to leave Washington for the summer, visited with Roosevelt for a "goodbye cocktail" at the White House. During this "very happy party," Frankfurter raised the possibility of making Stimson secretary of war and Second Circuit Court of Appeals judge Robert Patterson assistant secretary. Roosevelt did not say anything at the time, but Frankfurter knew that he had "struck fire."

After a night of "hard thinking," Frankfurter wrote Roosevelt "the more I think the more sense Stimson and Patterson make." He reviewed Stimson's career and emphasized not only his experience but also his lack of ambition for higher office and deep loyalty. He also described Patterson's career after serving as *Harvard Law Review* president the year that Frankfurter had begun teaching at the school. "He has, I believe, four children and no means," Frankfurter wrote of Patterson, "but I know of no man whose devotion to country is greater." He recounted a recent afternoon with Patterson after which Marion remarked: " 'Why isn't he the man to be Secretary of War?' " Patterson, Frankfurter argued, had "all the brains and productive capacity that are needed for the job, but in addition he has that very rare quality of leading." The next day, Frankfurter pressed his case with the president: "Ideas are like men. . . . The more I have lived with the idea of the Stimson-Patterson combination, the more right it seems." Frankfurter believed that to prepare the country for war, Roosevelt needed a bipartisan or coalition cabinet that included interventionist Republicans such as Stimson and Patterson in key defense positions. Since 1915, Stimson had been associated with the Plattsburg movement, a summer training camp in Plattsburg, New York, where businessmen and professionals learned to be soldiers and military officers and prepared for war. Patterson, who was awarded a Distinguished Service Cross and a Silver Cross as an infantryman in France during World War I, was a longtime friend of Stimson's and a Plattsburg graduate. After the Graham-Meyer wedding and with the Frankfurters staying for a month with friends in Cambridge, he informed Roosevelt on June 13 that Stimson and Patterson were "available" and "regard themselves as soldiers" willing to lead the War Department and to serve under Roosevelt.

As he wrote the president about Stimson, Frankfurter knew the situation in Europe was dire. On June 19, the same day that Hitler offered the British a final opportunity to surrender, Roosevelt phoned Stimson and offered to make him secretary of war. A few hours later, Stimson accepted after learning Colonel Frank Knox, the 1936 Republican vice-presidential candidate and *Chicago Daily News* publisher, had agreed to be secretary of the navy. And

Stimson concurred that Judge Patterson would make a fine assistant secretary of war. The next day, Roosevelt shocked official Washington by naming Stimson and Knox to head the War and Navy Departments; Republican isolationists seethed. Frankfurter rejoiced. "Simply Grand," he wired the president. "You have again shown how to summon the country's service and place the nation's need on the level where it belongs. Let me express my gratitude of this new manifestation of leadership for a free people." To Stimson, Frankfurter wired: "You are where the country needs you." On June 22, two days after Roosevelt remade his cabinet into a war cabinet, France surrendered to Germany. The next day, Hitler triumphantly marched through the streets of Paris. On July 11, Frankfurter cut his New England vacation short to swear in Knox in the Oval Office. The small ceremony resulted in one of the few photographs of Roosevelt and Frankfurter. Two weeks later, Patterson resigned as a federal court of appeals judge and replaced Louis Johnson as Stimson's assistant secretary. "I never had a doubt you would get Bob. P—but I'm glad it's done," Frankfurter wrote Stimson. "He ought very quickly to relieve you of multitudinous details, and keep you free for the major lines of policy. I'd give a deal to be by your side these days."

With Stimson and Patterson leading the War Department, Frankfurter advised them in August on what he considered their most pressing issue— the destroyer deal. The question was whether the executive branch, without seeking new legislation, could transfer old navy destroyers to the British. After the Dunkirk evacuation, the British desperately needed ships; Ambassador Kennedy reported that without the American destroyers, the British would be forced to surrender. Opponents argued that transferring the old warships violated federal neutrality laws. And there was no way to amend the laws because isolationists in Congress vowed to filibuster. Dean Acheson and Ben Cohen collaborated on a memorandum arguing that no federal laws would be violated by exchanging old destroyers, as opposed to new ones built for the express purpose of sending them to a belligerent country. They published a *New York Times* letter to the editor signed by Acheson and leaders of the bar C. C. Burlingham, George Rublee, and Thomas D. Thacher. Stimson wrote Frankfurter asking for the justice's opinion. After thinking about the problem for two or three days, Frankfurter phoned Stimson on August 15 and agreed with Burlingham's opinion that the destroyer deal was within the president's power but "thought the line was a narrow one." A relieved Stimson immediately phoned the president, who was "greatly pleased and said he felt very much encouraged." On September 2, the United States agreed to exchange fifty warships for 99-year leases of British bases on Newfoundland, Bermuda, and the British West Indies.

No one said anything about the propriety of a sitting justice interpreting federal law and opining on executive power for the president who had nominated him. Frankfurter may have felt emboldened by the common practice of justices advising presidents: William Moody with Theodore Roosevelt, Brandeis with Woodrow Wilson, Taft with Harding, and Stone with Hoover. Yet, in advising Roosevelt and Stimson on issues that might come before the Court, Frankfurter was crossing dangerous ethical lines because, rightly or wrongly, he believed that when it came to winning the war, the ends justified the means.

Frankfurter's role in remaking Roosevelt's cabinet for war was as consequential and, in his mind, as important as his flag salute opinion in *Gobitis*. He did not care whether he was sufficiently "liberal" for his friends in government, the media, or the legal academy. He ignored the obvious conflicts of interest and violations of separation of powers about advising the president and the new secretary of war. Nor was he concerned whether he would be the future intellectual leader of the Court. He remained steadfast in his belief that liberals should rely on the political process rather than the judiciary for political and social change. He contributed to the most consequential political events of his life by serving the Roosevelt administration as a wartime recruiter and policy maker while sitting on the Supreme Court as an associate justice. The war dominated his work life. And it soon transformed his home life.

CHAPTER 23

Uncle Felix and Aunt Marion

T he day that France surrendered to Germany on June 22, 1940, Frankfurter knew that the Nazis would bomb Britain next. He thought
about what would happen to the three children of his British former
graduate student Sylvester Gates. The Frankfurters had seen the entire family
in London the previous summer and delighted in meeting Ann, 12, Venetia,
10, and Oliver, 3.

At 11:51 that morning, Frankfurter wired Gates: "Marion and I hope Pauline and you will entrust your children to our ca[re]." Sylvester and Pauline
cried when they received the telegram. They had been hiding with the children in Dorset in southern England but realized there was nowhere safe in
the country. They could not immediately respond to the Frankfurters' offer
because it was difficult to send transatlantic cables in wartime London. Three
days later, Gates was able to wire: "There is no one in world to whom we
would as happily in trust [sic] the children as you and Marion and we can
find no words for our gratitude but the decision torments us." They asked
for twenty-four hours to ponder the gut-wrenching decision of sending away
their children. Their main hesitation was that other parents lacked the same
opportunity. Frankfurter responded that they should take their time, asked
them to send a nurse with Oliver, and cautioned that the children might have
to be placed in different households.

Sylvester Gates was one of Frankfurter's best former graduate students.
He co-authored Frankfurter's book, *The Case of Sacco and Vanzetti*, but, for
political reasons, received only an inside acknowledgment, a personal inscription acknowledging his labor, as well as half the fee for the magazine article.
Frankfurter was so impressed with Gates, an Oxford-educated barrister who

was studying private international law at Harvard, that he had offered him the opportunity to succeed Tom Corcoran as Holmes's secretary. Gates, however, declined the Holmes clerkship to begin his legal career in London. In 1933, when the Frankfurters lived in Oxford, Gates introduced them to leading intellectuals including Maurice Bowra and Isaiah Berlin. Three years later, Gates married Pauline Murray. It was the second marriage for both of them. From her previous marriage, Pauline had two children, Ann and Venetia. Pauline and Sylvester had Oliver.

On July 4, Sylvester and Pauline Gates "gratefully" accepted the Frankfurters' offer to safeguard their children in America. Six days later, the Battle of Britain—the German Luftwaffe's air raids over the country in an attempt to bomb it into submission—began. The Royal Air Force defended the country from the onslaught. Germany also initiated a blockade of British commercial vessels, but the British maintained an advantage at sea. The Gateses wasted no time getting their children out of the country. On July 17, they obtained immediate passage for the children and their nurse to Montreal, Canada. Frankfurter indicated that he had wired Ambassador Kennedy at the American embassy as a condition of obtaining the proper visas and on July 18 wired Gates: "Delighted at their coming."

After twelve years as a barrister, Sylvester became a banker and during the war worked for Alfred Duff Cooper in the British Ministry of Information. He thus knew his children were in danger. On July 20, he and Pauline watched in Liverpool as their three children, accompanied by their nurse, Bertha "Nana" Hector, boarded the steamship *Duchess of Atholl* on a 10-day voyage to Quebec. "All we can do," Sylvester Gates wrote Frankfurter, "is to thank you from the bottom of our hearts for what you are doing for them."

Surprised by the suddenness of the children's arrival in Canada, Frankfurter turned to his contact for helping European Jews gain entry into the United States, Jacob Billikopf. The director of the Federation of Jewish Charities in Philadelphia, Billikopf dedicated himself to helping European Jews escape the Nazi regime and developed numerous contacts in the United States and Canada. He phoned Cyril James, the principal and vice chancellor of McGill University. A member of the Refugee Section of the American Friends Committee, James agreed to meet the children and their nurse in Montreal and put them in a sleeper car on a 9:00 p.m. train bound for Baltimore. In Baltimore, they were met by Edwin C. Zavitz, the headmaster of the Friends School, who agreed to take the children for the summer. The Gateses received a telegram from the nurse that the children had made it safely across the Atlantic Ocean rife with German submarines and were happy with the

Zavitz family. The Frankfurters, whose Washington home was closed for the summer, telephoned the Zavitz household at 7:45 p.m. on the Gates children's first night in Baltimore to find Oliver sleeping and Ann and Venetia playing with the Zavitz children.

The arrival of three British refugees and their nanny made the newspapers. The *Baltimore Sun* reported that Ann wondered why the cars were on the wrong side of the road and did not need drivers because they were sitting in what the British consider to be the passenger seats. Ann and Venetia delighted in playing with the automatic doors at the drugstore. The newspaper failed to connect them to Felix and Marion Frankfurter, who declined all media requests. "It is a joy to us to have the children under our wing," Marion wrote Pauline. "Incidentally I detect signs of morbid curiosity and amazement in certain of our friends who have children. But I think we won't do so badly as parents, though F[elix] and I will often disagree—I can see that."

The children escaped London just in time. On September 6, Germany began the Blitz—days of continuous nighttime bombings that lasted until May the following year. Sylvester slept many nights at his office in the Ministry of Information; Pauline vacated their sixth-floor apartment and slept in a crowded bunker with other tenants. Their children were unquestionably better off in America.

On September 24, the Frankfurters drove to Baltimore to pick up Ann and Venetia Murray and Oliver Gates and his nurse Nana and moved them into their home at 1511 Thirtieth Street. The two girls occupied one of two large adjoining rooms on the top floor; Oliver and Nana occupied the other. School was all arranged. In August, Kay Graham had made inquiries at Washington area private schools for Ann and Venetia on the Frankfurters' behalf and had helped the girls land full scholarships from her alma mater, the Potomac School. For the time being, three-year-old Oliver would stay behind with nurse Nana. Almost immediately, he became the star of the household. Every morning, after finishing his own breakfast, Oliver sat quietly next to Felix watching him eat. The children called them Uncle Felix and Aunt Marion.

For 50-year-old Marion and 57-year-old Felix, the presence of three British children in their home changed their lives. It exposed the childless couple to the joys of parenthood and emphasized the perilous times in which they and the children's parents lived. "The children never ask about the war, have not heard the radio since they came, and I doubt if they see a paper," Marion wrote Pauline Gates. Felix was astonished at how easily the children adjusted to life in America.

The war, with or without the children, was always on Frankfurter's mind.

"Never in my life have I so unremittingly kept my mind sealed on the calendar," he wrote Monte Lemann. "Every day that passes means a day for civilization & freedom." On the night of October 1, he entertained British ambassador Lord Lothian, whom he had known since World War I, and Sir Walter Layton, a Liberal Party politician working in the Ministry of Supply. Soon after advising Stimson about the destroyer deal, Frankfurter confided to a colleague that it was hard to concentrate on the job he had been confirmed to do. "Do the <u>certs.</u> seem as dreary to you as they do to me—less interesting than the stream of the last two Terms?" he wrote Stone. "Or it is merely that my thoughts are largely elsewhere—'over there,' with all that the Battle of Britain means to them and to us."

An Anglophile to his core, Frankfurter knew more about what was happening in London than just about anyone in Washington thanks to his many British friends and visitors, foremost among them Isaiah Berlin. On July 9, nine days before the Murray and Gates children embarked on a similar voyage, Berlin had left Oxford for Quebec on a Cunard Line steamship with hundreds of British children aboard. Born in Riga, Latvia, and fluent in Russian, he came to the United States on a fool's errand—to obtain a visa so that he could become a press attaché to the British ministry in Moscow. The idea was for Berlin to bring British propaganda to the Russians, who were bound by their nonaggression pact with Germany. The British government, however, had no intention of sending Berlin to Moscow. During a long, miserable summer waiting for a nonexistent visa, Berlin bided his time in New York City and Washington, D.C. The Frankfurters introduced him to their friends—theologian Reinhold Niebuhr, historian Arthur Schlesinger, Jr., Librarian of Congress Archie MacLeish, and Frankfurter's law clerks Edward Prichard and Phil Graham. The 31-year-old Oxford philosopher befriended Prich, Graham, and Graham's wife, Kay. He was young enough to relate to them and old and wise enough to be right at home with the Frankfurters and their Washington friends. Together with Prich, the Grahams, Joseph Alsop, and Dean Acheson, he became a charter member of the wartime Georgetown set. Berlin's network of influential American contacts and lively summaries of Associated Press dispatches for the British Ministry of Information made him invaluable in the States.

In wartime Washington, Berlin found himself less entranced by Marion. The woman he had met at Oxford in 1933 and as late as 1936 had deemed "a++" because of her quiet discernment and intellectualism had lost some of her allure in the United States. "Mrs. Frankfurter here seems much simpler and much more directly the outcome of surroundings," Berlin wrote in July

1940. "Not needing to work hard to comprehend our complex system she relaxes and obeys reflexes. One can only admire the extraordinary acuteness of her perceptions in Oxford when one realizes the lack of effort with which she—& everyone else—lives here." He continued to write Marion long letters revealing how depressed he was during the frustrating summer of 1940 yet confided to others that she "loses half her mystery here."

As a bachelor who married later in life, Berlin failed to notice Marion's transformation into a mother preoccupied with the health and happiness of her three British children. The girls had adjusted seamlessly to the Potomac School and impressed Marion with their intellect and maturity. Marion took them to see Osa Johnson's movie *I Married Adventure*, which did not end until midnight. She reported how "beautiful" Ann and Venetia looked in their velvet dresses at a dinner at the home of Gifford and Cornelia Pinchot. Then there was Oliver—the apple of Marion's eye, the "amazingly 'bright' child" who charmed his way into everyone's heart. Felix told the story of a morning when Oliver accompanied his sisters on the car ride to school. At breakfast, Felix asked: "Well, Oliver, did you take your sisters to school." "No," Oliver replied. "Louis [the Frankfurters' driver] took them. I went with them." The justice liked to tell another story about Oliver: After a photograph of his mother arrived from overseas, the boy declared: "I don't like it. Mummy's much nicer looking."

The Frankfurters weren't the only ones intrigued by Oliver. In mid-December, *New Yorker* writer Alexander Woollcott visited the Frankfurters' Georgetown home for an early evening drink and had the "high honor" of meeting Oliver. As he wrote Sylvester and Pauline Gates on White House stationery (he was staying there as a guest of the president), Woollcott considered Oliver a "great gentleman" and destined for greatness: "If I should live to a ripe old age, one of the compensations will come some day in the form of a chance to say, in a casual manner that will madden everybody and fool nobody: 'This Oliver Gates?' Oh yes, I used to know him rather well. Why once in Washington long ago, he let me help him off with his overcoat."

After a brief report in the Jewish press about the children, the Frankfurters declined all media inquiries and photograph requests. That did not stop them from showing off the children to their friends. The Frankfurters' holiday card featured a summertime picture of the children and a handwritten note from the justice: "Our three English children—Ann, Venetia, and Oliver—join us in affectionate good wishes." On New Year's Eve, they took them to an afternoon party at the White House. Oliver, unaware the president was paralyzed from the waist down, was unimpressed because Roosevelt did not know how to hop.

———

DURING THE SUMMER and fall of 1940, Frankfurter encouraged Roosevelt's bid for an unprecedented third term as the only way to save civilization from Nazi rule. He continued to disregard concerns about the ethics of advising the president or the possibility of issues coming before the Court, writing Roosevelt memoranda and contributing to campaign speeches. In July, he and speechwriter Sam Rosenman collaborated on Roosevelt's acceptance speech for the Democratic National Convention in Chicago. Despite an attempt by James Farley and John Nance Garner to block his renomination, Roosevelt won it easily and chose Agriculture Secretary Henry Wallace as his running mate. After listening to Roosevelt's acceptance speech on the radio, Frankfurter wired the president: "You have enduringly expressed the liberty-loving aspirations of mankind. Marion called it noble and her three children will soon echo her sentiments." For Frankfurter, Roosevelt's bid for a third term was an act of patriotism by the greatest wartime president since Abraham Lincoln. On November 5, Roosevelt defeated Indiana Republican Wendell Willkie, winning 449 electoral votes and 54 percent of the popular vote. Frankfurter, who believed that Roosevelt accepted a third term out of a sense of duty to the country rather than personal ambition, wrote the president: "Terrible days are ahead—and the world is fortunate to have you where you have been."

After the election, Roosevelt recalled Joseph P. Kennedy as ambassador to Great Britain. An isolationist and proponent of Chamberlain's failed appeasement, Kennedy "never forgave" Roosevelt for dismissing him and blamed Frankfurter. The justice sent the president Kennedy's parting shots in the *Boston Globe*; Kennedy predicted that democracy in Britain was doomed; he also vowed to fight to keep America out of war. The newspaper, Frankfurter wrote, "watered down some of the things Joe said. They were so raw the *Globe* did not want to print them." Kennedy, for his part, encouraged an anti-Semitic campaign against Frankfurter, which portrayed him as a Rasputin-like foreign policy maker behind the throne.

Kennedy was right about Frankfurter's active role in foreign policy. During the fall and winter of 1940, Frankfurter advised Stimson about how to assist the Allies, to prepare the country for war, and to recruit former Harvard law students for Stimson's staff. Stimson was unsympathetic with the White House's request for a black civilian aide in the War Department or for equal rights for black soldiers and pilots. With Frankfurter's encouragement, Stimson hired William Hastie, the second black editor on the *Harvard Law Review*, assistant solicitor in the Department of the Interior, the first black federal judge in 1937 in the Virgin Islands, and as of 1939 the dean of Howard University Law School. Hastie had no idea how skeptical his new boss was about racial equality. "The negroes are taking advantage of this period just before [the] election to try to get everything they can in the way of recognition from the Army," Stimson wrote in his diary.

Another former Frankfurter student entered Stimson's inner circle—John J. McCloy. Like Hastie, McCloy had attended Amherst College and Harvard Law School yet had finished in the middle of his law school class. Frankfurter had paid no attention to him in class in contrast to Acheson, MacLeish, and other high-achieving students who usually sat in the front row. The short, balding McCloy, however, made a name for himself as a Wall Street lawyer and managing partner at Cravath. For nine years, he had investigated the case of a massive explosion at the Black Tom railroad terminus that had destroyed ammunition headed for the Allies during World War I. He discovered new evidence that pointed to German saboteurs and forced an arbitration commission to reopen the case, which in 1939 resulted in a $50 million ruling against the German government. During the Black Tom case, McCoy traveled to Germany, met Nazi leaders Hess and Göring, and became an expert about German espionage. In the summer of 1940, one of Stimson's law partners vouched for McCloy's "first class ability." Like Frankfurter, McCloy idolized Stimson and aspired to emulate the elder statesman's career in public service. In September, he began working part-time in the War Department and by year's end became one of Stimson's most trusted full-time assistants.

Another Wall Street player, French political economist and diplomat Jean Monnet, relied on Frankfurter to enter the corridors of power. The lone French member of the British Purchasing Mission, Monnet arrived in the United States in August 1940 and became more influential than his British counterparts in persuading American officials to sell supplies to the Allies. On December 2, he and Frankfurter met with Stimson in what the secretary of war deemed "one of the most interesting luncheon conferences I have ever had" as Monnet explained the political situation in France and how the United States could help. McCloy, who knew Monnet from their Wall Street days, observed to Frankfurter that the French diplomat "has the advantage of knowing both the British and the Americans well, but he contributes his own method of thinking which neither the British nor the Americans seem to be able to duplicate for its effect."

Monnet's ideas found their way into presidential speeches thanks to Frankfurter's frequent contact with Roosevelt. On December 19, Frankfurter relayed a memorandum from Monnet arguing that Roosevelt needed to challenge Hitler's "New Order" in Europe. Frankfurter's cover letter described Monnet as "a 'free' Frenchman of proved sagacity, extraordinarily well-informed about French currents of opinion" and "a man in whose understanding and discretion I have complete confidence." During a late December lunch with Frankfurter, Monnet described America's decision to provide weapons and supplies to Britain as the "Arsenal of Democracy." Frankfurter made Monnet promise never to use the phrase again and passed it along to the president for use in his December 29 fireside chat—his "Arsenal of Democracy" speech.

"The Arsenal of Democracy" speech introduced one of Roosevelt's most important wartime policies—the 1941 Lend-Lease Bill. The idea of Lend-Lease grew out of the destroyer deal: allow the financially strapped British to acquire American weapons and supplies without having to pay money for them. The challenge was to get the bill through Congress, a challenge addressed by Frankfurter. According to Frankfurter biographer Max Freedman, Frankfurter and Roosevelt worked more closely on Lend-Lease than "they ever did on any large matter of public policy." Frankfurter suggested that the House bill be named H.R. 1776 and declared the threat of Nazi rule "a crime against civilization." On January 26, 1941, Frankfurter and McCloy helped prepare Stimson for Senate testimony. A month later, Frankfurter wrote a memorandum to the president about the need for increased American weapons production to help Britain defeat Germany. On March 11, Congress passed the Lend-Lease Bill, Roosevelt signed it into law, and the United States began shipping weapons and supplies to the Allies. Frankfurter sent a copy of the law to CBS's London-based chief correspondent, Edward R. Murrow.

Frankfurter's involvement with wartime policy making grew more conspicuous. During the justices' annual White House visit on December 17, 1940, he had conferred with Stimson about the reorganization of the president's Advisory Defense Commission and spoke with labor leader Sidney Hillman about the proposed changes and their fairness to workers. Around Christmas, he and Harry Hopkins met with Roosevelt about sending Hopkins to meet with Churchill about the strategic importance of Ireland. Before Inauguration Day, he worked during breakfast with Sam Rosenman on the president's third inaugural address and discussed it "at length" with Roosevelt in his bedroom. In February 1941, he continued to advise Stimson on the administration of the pending Lend-Lease Bill. That spring, he and Harold Ickes discussed how to get the president to prepare an isolationist country for war.

Frankfurter's extrajudicial activity did not go unnoticed by his political enemies. In February, Senator Wheeler continued his isolationist crusade by accusing a "Supreme Court justice" of running the War Department and U.S. embassy in London. Syndicated columnist Drew Pearson outed Frankfurter and deemed him responsible for the appointments of Stimson and John Gilbert Winant, Joseph Kennedy's replacement as ambassador to Great Britain. At the Gridiron Club's spring dinner, the press put on a skit about Frankfurter's chambers, "Ten Minutes in the Routine Life of the Justice." During the skit, Frankfurter made calls to Secretary Knox, Secretary Hull, General George C. Marshall, and Chief Justice Hughes. For each call, Frankfurter's character wore a different costume, including an "army tunic" during the call with General Marshall and in suggesting a Roosevelt appointment a cap labeled "U.S. Employment Service." *Baltimore Sun* syndicated columnist Frank R. Kent went for the jugular in observing that Frankfurter's political activity would have distressed the nonpolitical Holmes.

—————

THE LAST OF THE conservative Four Horsemen and certainly the most bigoted finally left the Court. In late January 1941, James C. McReynolds announced that he was retiring as of February 1. As a possible replacement, Roosevelt asked Frankfurter about John J. Parker, chief judge of the Court of Appeals for the Fourth Circuit. A decade after playing an instrumental role in the Senate's rejection of Parker's Supreme Court nomination, Frankfurter replied with a lukewarm evaluation of Parker's judicial opinions. Roosevelt looked elsewhere for a southerner. Months before the official announcement, Frankfurter correctly predicted Senator James F. Byrnes of South Carolina would be nominated and would "add to the wisdom of the Court."

Washington *Evening Star* cartoonist Clifford K. Berryman latched on to McReynolds's fall and Frankfurter's rise. A notoriously racist and anti-Semitic justice, McReynolds had been rude to Frankfurter and black advocates during oral argument, had shunned Brandeis and Cardozo as colleagues, and had spearheaded the conservative opposition to the New Deal. Frankfurter, on the other hand, was expected to lead Roosevelt's five Supreme Court nominees. On the *Evening Star*'s February 5 front page, Berryman depicted a triumphant Frankfurter lifting the Supreme Court building upside down in one hand and a dismayed McReynolds remarking, "I Told You He'd Do It!"

Perception was different from reality as Frankfurter's leadership of the liberal wing of the Court began slipping away. In the spring of 1941, he wrote a majority opinion upholding the contempt conviction of Australian-born labor leader Harry Bridges. The leader of the International Longshoremen's Association, Bridges had wired Secretary of Labor Frances Perkins threatening to go on strike if the Los Angeles Superior Court did not rule in the union's favor. The *Los Angeles Times* wrote three editorials criticizing the union while the case was pending; the trial judge held Bridges and the *Times* in contempt of court. The California Supreme Court upheld the convictions. At conference, the justices of the U.S. Supreme Court voted 5–3 to affirm. Frankfurter researched and wrote the majority opinion himself because his law clerk, Phil Graham, disagreed so strongly that he refused to work on it. After Frankfurter circulated the draft, however, he lost his majority. Murphy, who increasingly joined Black and Douglas on free speeches issues, switched his vote from the majority to the dissent, leaving a 4–4 tie (without the retired McReynolds) and forcing the case to be reargued the next term. Frankfurter showed his draft opinion to the retired Brandeis, who replied: "You're going to get a unanimous court on this?" "Unanimous?" Frankfurter replied. "I'll be lucky if I get a Court. Black is thundering against it, and he certainly has at least two others and he may well have a fourth." To which Brandeis replied, "Black and Company have gone mad on free speech."

The politics of the Court, with Black, Douglas, and Murphy on the left, had changed since Brandeis's day. So did the Court's leadership. On July 1, Chief Justice Charles Evans Hughes retired. Frankfurter felt "a deep wrench" and considered the chief justice "among the very few really sizeable figures of my lifetime." In the eyes of Frankfurter and many others, Hughes was one of the nation's great chief justices. Hughes's retirement presented Roosevelt with an opportunity to put his stamp on the leadership of the Court. During a June 5 lunch with the president, Hughes recommended Stone as his replacement and suggested that the president speak to Frankfurter because he "knew more of the history of the Court and its needs than anyone else." Four days later, Frankfurter was summoned to the White House. The serious expression on the president's face revealed it was a business lunch. As an initial matter, Roosevelt asked if he could delay naming a new chief justice until the fall. Frankfurter said no, it would not be fair to Harlan Fiske Stone, who would be serving as acting chief justice, or to someone else. Roosevelt then asked Frankfurter to choose between Stone or Attorney General Robert H. Jackson. "I wish you had not asked me that question," Frankfurter replied. On the basis of personal friendship and ideological affinity, he favored Jackson. But for the good of the country, he preferred Stone because he was a Republican on a Court dominated by New Deal Democrats. Given America's inevitable entry in the war, Frankfurter wanted Roosevelt to be "the Nation's President, and not a partisan President." He could accomplish this by naming Stone as chief justice. The president agreed and on July 12 announced Stone as chief and Jackson as associate justice. Frankfurter confessed to a disappointed Jackson why he was not chief justice and believed that his "candor— only deepened the friendship between Bob and me." Initially "delighted" with the choice of Stone as chief justice, Frankfurter later regretted his endorsement of Stone for the Court's center chair.

At the end of the term, Frankfurter hired a new law clerk to replace Phil Graham. The justice designated his former student and co-author, Harvard law professor Henry Hart, to select his clerks sight unseen. After recommending several good candidates, however, Hart could not decide. Frankfurter was one of the first justices to prefer clerks with a year of experience with a federal court of appeals judge, usually Learned Hand on the Second Circuit or Calvert Magruder on the First Circuit. In the spring of 1941, Frankfurter chose between Hand's clerk Louis Henkin and Magruder's former clerk Phil Elman. On the basis of Hart's and Hand's recommendations, Frankfurter selected Henkin—the son of an Orthodox Jewish rabbi, a Yiddish-speaking immigrant from Belarus, and former president of the *Harvard Law Review*. After Henkin was drafted and postponed his clerkship, Frankfurter offered the job to Elman. The child of Polish Jewish immigrants, CCNY graduate, and *Review* editor, Elman had been working for Frankfurter's former clerk Joseph Rauh at the Federal Communications Commission. Unlike Prich and Graham, Elman was "not a brilliant raconteur"; he was a workhorse at a time when Frankfurter desperately needed one with his attention preoccupied by the war.

All spring and summer of 1941, German submarines sank American merchant ships crossing the Atlantic Ocean loaded with supplies for the Allies. The cautious State Department and interventionist War Department differed on the best way to respond. In May, Stimson frequently consulted with Frankfurter and showed him a May 23 letter he had sent to Roosevelt in preparation for a major presidential speech on the war. Frankfurter commended Stimson's letter to the president and encouraged Roosevelt to incorporate Stimson's ideas. Speaking to the Pan American Union on May 27 while sitting in the East Room of the White House, Roosevelt vowed to send American destroyers to protect merchant ships and declared an unlimited state of emergency. "I have not known greater unanimity in our lifetime," Frankfurter wrote Roosevelt. He sent Roosevelt a *Baltimore Sun* cartoon about the speech titled "For All the World to See" and depicting Lady Liberty's torch and the words "Freedom" billowing from the smoke.

Before he left Washington for the summer, Frankfurter saw Roosevelt at the White House one last time. After a June 14 lunch, he sent the president a memorandum advocating for an American base in Iceland as an "ideal first move" toward intervention and emphasized the country's strategic importance.

During a June 18 commencement address at Radcliffe College, Frankfurter went public with his interventionist ideas, attacking the isolationist line that "war never settles anything" and countering that America must enter the war in Europe to save civilization. "The Civil War settled slavery," he told 214 Radcliffe graduates. "This war will settle the quality of your lives and the lives of your children and your children's children. It simply is not true that war never settles anything." He rejected the isolationist argument that "a country at war" was "already under dictatorship." He observed that American democracy had "expanded despite four wars." And Britain had been at war since September 1939 and had been "more democratic today than she ever has been." He urged people to read the debates in the House of Commons about how best to protect their country.

Frankfurter's Radcliffe speech was informed by thoughts of his three British children and news from their parents. In mid-May, Sylvester and Pauline Gates were nearly killed when a bomb destroyed their London flat. They had just left their bedroom where the bomb hit. They emerged "covered with soot and glass but quite unscathed." Pauline was no safer at their country home in Cornwall, where an airplane machine gunner killed two people. They decided not to tell their children. In May, Frankfurter sent photographs of Ann, Venetia, and Oliver to Roosevelt, who was so "delighted" that he asked to see them at the White House before they left Washington for the summer. On June 10, Marion and the children visited the president for thirty minutes. "Uncle Felix and Aunt Marion are now the centre of their lives," their grandmother Beatrice Gates wrote Marion, "and I feel, securely in their hearts."

In mid-June, the Frankfurters sent the children to live with a friend of their grandparents, actress Ruth Draper. The theatrical star owned a large house in the village of Dark Harbor on Isleboro, an island off the coast of Maine. Ann, Venetia, and Oliver, along with another group of British children and their nanny, enjoyed the outdoors and cooler climate. Oliver, who celebrated his fourth birthday on July 21, offered to share his bed with Felix "as there's lots of room." Draper took Oliver sailing. He loved the toy boats the

Frankfurters sent him as a birthday present, said he missed Washington, and painted Uncle Felix and Aunt Marion a picture. In mid-July, Felix visited the children after speaking at Eleanor Roosevelt's student leadership conference four hours north at Eastport and at Campobello Island. Marion missed Oliver terribly. She wrote his parents that Treasury Secretary Henry Morgenthau, Jr., no friend of the justice's, could not get enough of Oliver. Neither could Marion. "I might as well break down at once and confess that I don't think there was ever anyone like him," she wrote his grandmother Beatrice Gates. "Just to hear his voice in the house is a joy, it is such a lovely voice, and everything he says and does shows such an interesting, strong character."

Frankfurter's Radcliffe commencement address made national news. He sent a copy to Roosevelt, who took a hard line against the Nazis in his June 20 message to Congress. Two days later, Germany invaded Russia. Frankfurter was buoyed by the lack of opposition to the July 7 announcement of a U.S. base in Iceland, correctly believed the Russians would put up a hard fight against Germany, and predicted to Roosevelt that "we have entered a new phase of the struggle."

The isolationists fought back. On July 19, Senator Wheeler charged that Roosevelt based his foreign policy on the advice of "a motley crew" including Knox, Stimson, Ickes, Hopkins, and Frankfurter. Roosevelt jokingly wrote Frankfurter: "If somebody kidnaps Wheeler and shanghais him on board an outgoing steamer for the Congo, can a habeas corpus follow him thither? You need not answer, if you don't want to because it would never get as far as the Supreme Court. Wheeler or I would be dead, first!" Antiwar sentiment in America continued to run high as Lend-Lease was extended to Russia. On August 12, Congress reauthorized the Selective Service Act by a single vote in the House. Two days later, after a secret meeting off the coast of Newfoundland, Roosevelt and Churchill announced the Atlantic Charter, a jointly issued policy statement pledging international security including no territorial gains by either country, territorial adjustments in accord with the wishes of the people, the right to self-determination, freedom of the seas, and the disarmament of aggressor nations. The charter signaled U.S.-British resolve against Germany. Frankfurter informed Roosevelt that "truth compels me to say that somewhere in the Atlantic you *did* make history for the world."

Frankfurter wrote the president adulatory letters comparing his actions to those of Jefferson and Lincoln; Roosevelt knew the justice would outlive him. On September 26, Roosevelt asked Frankfurter to come to the White House at 3:30 p.m. after the funeral of Eleanor's youngest brother, G. Hall Roosevelt. While getting his hair cut in his office, the president explained to Frankfurter

that the only memorial he wanted was a plain tablet that said "In memory of
_____" on the triangle of grass in front of the National Archives. Frankfurter
vowed to carry out the president's wishes.

Frankfurter continued to help Roosevelt by recruiting former students into
the administration. In January 1941, Julius Amberg left his law practice in
Grand Rapids, Michigan, and, at Frankfurter's and Patterson's urging, joined
Stimson as a special assistant. Four months later, Frankfurter arranged for
a New York meeting between Stimson and Harvey Bundy, the first Holmes
clerk to live at the House of Truth in 1914; Bundy also joined the War Department as one of Stimson's special assistants. McCloy was promoted to assistant
secretary of war, Robert A. Lovett to assistant secretary for war and air, and
Patterson to under secretary. Together with Bundy, McCloy and Lovett became
Stimson's tennis partners, frequent dinner companions, and key advisers.
Frankfurter often joined them for dinner and policy talk. Frankfurter's clos-
est friend in Washington, Dean Acheson, also returned to the administration.
His support for the destroyer deal and interventionist speeches made him a
good fit to work on foreign policy. On February 2, Acheson joined the State
Department as an assistant secretary. His boss was the cautious Secretary of
State Cordell Hull; his role model was the interventionist Stimson. Assistant
Secretary of State Adolf A. Berle, Jr., believed, based on information from J.
Edgar Hoover, that Frankfurter was angling to replace Hull with Acheson.
Still harboring grudges about being excluded from Frankfurter's elite group
of Harvard law students, Berle referred to Acheson and State Department col-
league Herbert Feis as "the Frankfurter boys."

With Acheson, Bundy, Lovett, and McCloy in ascendancy, two other Frankfurter protégés and Roosevelt administration insiders were on the outs—Tom
Corcoran and Ben Cohen. In late January 1941, Corcoran quit the administration in a huff. He had taken the brunt of the blame for defending the
court-packing plan and leading the failed purge of Roosevelt political opponents a year later. He was a Harvard-educated lawyer and former Holmes
clerk who wanted to be considered a great legal mind rather than a political operative. He felt underappreciated after placing friends on the Supreme
Court and in the Justice Department. "For a combination of reasons Tom
lacks mental health just now," Frankfurter had advised Roosevelt on January
8 and suggested making Corcoran special assistant to then–Attorney General
Robert Jackson. Roosevelt wrote Corcoran, apologized "how much your front-
line fighting has put you 'on the spot,'" and offered him the special assistant
post. A few months later, Corcoran was offered assistant secretary of the navy,
also at Frankfurter's urging, but Secretary Knox urged Corcoran not to take

it. Instead, Corcoran, a new father, decided to make a clean break with the administration. He could not shake his reputation as a fixer. In May, rumors surfaced that he had helped his clients illegally procure defense contracts. At the end of the year, he testified before the Senate to try to clear his name.

Several incidents destroyed the Corcoran-Frankfurter relationship. Corcoran claimed the Frankfurters and Roosevelt had advised him in 1940 not to marry his secretary of seven years, Margaret "Peggy" Dowd, but he married her anyway. Corcoran was deeply hurt when the president refused to see him and his bride. The Frankfurters chafed at Corcoran's half-hearted attempts to end Irish neutrality; Marion could no longer stand to hear him play Irish songs on his accordion with three British children in her home. Corcoran was angry at Frankfurter for not fighting harder for Corcoran's housemate Stuart Guthrie to be named the administrative officer of the U.S. Courts. Frankfurter tried to assuage his protégé's hurt feelings, to no avail. The final straw came in 1941 when Frankfurter refused to support Corcoran for solicitor general. Corcoran received endorsements from four other justices he had helped put on the Court (Black, Reed, Douglas, and Murphy), but not from his mentor and former professor. Frankfurter met with Roosevelt's assistant, former Holmes clerk James Rowe, and explained his opposition: Corcoran could not refrain from politics as solicitor general, and the hard confirmation fight would hurt the Court as well as the administration. Rowe, who eventually became Corcoran's law partner, agreed with Frankfurter. A few months later, Corcoran took his case public as syndicated columnist Drew Pearson and others reported on the controversy and on Frankfurter's opposition. A furious Corcoran confronted Frankfurter, a shouting match ensued, and Corcoran "stormed" out of the justice's chambers and supposedly yelled: "I put you there; now produce." They never spoke again.

Frankfurter's relationship with Cohen was never the same, either. As Frankfurter predicted to the president, Cohen was loyal to his hurt friend, stopped advising Roosevelt on domestic policy, and that spring joined Ambassador Winant in London. Cohen resented Frankfurter treating him like a lackey and secretly wanted to be solicitor general. In October 1941, Cohen threatened to resign from the government altogether and sulked so much that Marion quickly tired of "his self-indulgence in melancholy." Brandeis regretted Cohen's departure from the domestic political scene but wrote Frankfurter that Roosevelt's refusal to make Corcoran solicitor general was "most heartening."

For the past two years, Frankfurter and Brandeis had often discussed the war. Each week after the fighting began, Brandeis asked: "Are the English ready to die?" Then, after the British evacuation at Dunkirk, he said to Frankfurter: "I believe the English *are* ready to die, and because they are ready to die, they will live."

Many of Frankfurter's oldest friends had died of natural causes during the past two years: his law school roommate Sam Rosensohn in May 1939; child labor expert Grace Abbott in June 1939; Lord Lothian, the British ambassador to the United States, in December 1940; his law school pal and fellow federal prosecutor Emory Buckner in March 1941; and his House of Truth roommate and Canadian ambassador to the United States, Loring Christie, in April 1941.

Frankfurter's biggest worry was the plight of his uncle Salomon. The former University of Vienna librarian had been living under house arrest for more than three years since Frankfurter used State Department contacts to extricate him from a Nazi prison. In the meantime, the director of the National Library of Austria had tipped off the Nazis to Salomon's extensive book collection. In October 1940, the Gestapo seized his private library and expropriated it for the National Library of Austria. Salomon's requests for its return were denied. After several years of caring for her father, Salomon's daughter Lisa joined her brother in the United States; Salomon stayed in his Vienna apartment.

Unable to get his uncle out of Vienna and with no word from him since May 1941, Frankfurter discovered the State Department could no longer get information about him or other Viennese Jews. On August 21, the justice asked his Jewish refugee expert, Jacob Billikopf, to inquire of his Quaker contacts in Europe and explained: "He is particularly dear to me—I was partly brought up in his household as a boy." A few weeks later, Frankfurter learned that his uncle was "well & surprisingly fit for his years" but "in need of food," especially coffee, tea, chocolate, oil, and butter. The justice vowed to cover any costs. Billikopf's German Quaker contacts promised to do what they could. On September 24, 1941, Salomon Frankfurter died of bronchitis at age 84. He was buried in Vienna by the city's Jewish community. During the two years Felix had lived with him as a boy, his uncle gave him a window into the culturally rich world of an academic and a role model for scholarly excellence. Frankfurter considered him "the true scholar" who "set standards before me that went deep."

As heartbreaking as the loss of his uncle was, Frankfurter had a "strange premonition" the end was near for another father figure, Louis Brandeis. On September 30, Frankfurter visited him and thought Brandeis's mind was as sharp as ever. But afterward, he stopped at the nearby home of Chief

Justice Stone to update him on Brandeis's condition and predicted that "he was not likely to be with us for many more days." The next day, Brandeis suffered a heart attack, his second, after a drive through Rock Creek Park. Three days later, he lapsed into a coma and died on October 5 at age 84. "The morning that Holmes died, L.D.B. greeted me with 'And so the great man is gone,'" Frankfurter wrote Harold Laski. "And now it's Brandeis himself—he went beautifully."

"Half brother, half son," Brandeis was Frankfurter's father protector, financial benefactor, and frequent co-conspirator. They defended the constitutionality of minimum-wage and maximum-hour laws for the National Consumers' League, fought for a Jewish homeland in Palestine, turned Harvard Law School into a breeding ground for public servants, and clashed over the New Deal's expansion of federal power and Roosevelt's court-packing plan. Through it all, no one played a greater role in advising Frankfurter about his career—from joining the Harvard law faculty to declining positions on the Massachusetts Supreme Judicial Court and as solicitor general. He also prevented Frankfurter from joining the U.S. Supreme Court sooner by refusing to retire.

Most of all, Brandeis practiced his own version of judicial restraint. He believed in avoiding unnecessary constitutional questions and preferred a limited a role for the judiciary, particularly when it came to interfering with the role of states in solving socioeconomic problems. As a justice, Frankfurter built on Brandeis's ideas about constitutional avoidance and deference to state regulation. In February 1941, he wrote a majority opinion affirming an Illinois court's injunction against the milk wagon drivers' union. Instead of simply picketing, the union and its members had resorted to more than fifty instances of violence against dairies and stores that were using a non-unionized milk delivery system. Frankfurter distinguished First Amendment decisions upholding the right to picket and to publicize labor disputes. And at the end of the opinion, Frankfurter explained that the Court should intervene against the states to protect the constitutional rights of criminal defendants from coerced confessions and erroneous state court decisions. But free speech and press cannot prevent states from protecting people from "extensive violence." "If the people of Illinois desire to withdraw the use of the injunction in labor controversies" Frankfurter wrote, "the democratic process for legislative reform is at their disposal." Nathan Greene, Frankfurter's co-author on *The Labor Injunction* book, questioned his *Milk Wagon Drivers* opinion and asked him when the Court should intervene against the states in labor disputes. "When Brandeis inveighed against the Court becoming a 'super legislature,' " Frankfurter replied, "we applauded, I assumed, not with the thought that it should become a 'super legislature' for 'our crowd' but not for the other crowd."

On October 7, Frankfurter was one of two speakers and fifty mourners at Brandeis's California Street apartment during the secular funeral service. Fighting back tears and describing it as one of the hardest things he had ever done, he described Brandeis as a combination of the Hellenic and the Hebraic. "His pursuit of reason and his love of beauty were Hellenic," Frankfurter said, and, unlike Socrates, Brandeis "found it impossible to be at ease in Zion. The moral law was a goad. That was his Hebraic gift. It gave him ceaseless striving for perfection, it also gave him inner harmony." Frankfurter concluded by reciting several paragraphs from one of Brandeis's favorite poems, John Bunyan's *Pilgrim's Progress*, about the death of "Mr. Valiant-for-truth." "*My Sword* I give to him that shall succeed me in my Pilgrimage," Frankfurter read, "and my *Courage* and *Skill* to him that can get it."

THOUGH NOT Brandeis's literal successor, Frankfurter was his spiritual one. The burden of living up to the legacies of Holmes and Brandeis would have weighed on any Supreme Court justice, especially one publicly accused of betraying liberalism.

In October 1941, *Harper's* magazine featured an article, "Felix Frankfurter, Conservative." The author was a Yale law professor and erstwhile Frankfurter protégé, Fred Rodell. In a matter of months, he turned on his former professor who had found him his first job out of law school. During the spring of 1930 at Yale Law School, Rodell had taken a seminar of Frankfurter's and was "one of the bright boys." In December of that year, Rodell wrote Frankfurter about the possibility of clerking for Judge Learned Hand. Frankfurter explained that Hand preferred Harvard law graduates but invited Rodell to come to Harvard for a postgraduate fellowship under Frankfurter's direction, a known tryout for the Hand clerkship and others. Rodell declined. Rather than take offense, Frankfurter found the Philadelphia-born Rodell a job as a speechwriter and special assistant for Pennsylvania governor Gifford Pinchot. After Rodell joined the Yale law faculty in 1933, he and Frankfurter continued to correspond. In the preface to his 1939 book, *Woe Under You, Lawyers!*, Rodell thanked Frankfurter as one of ten professors who were the book's "intellectual godfathers." Frankfurter did not hold back in criticizing the book's simplistic message about the law. Yet Rodell continued to praise

Frankfurter's opinions. On February 3, 1941, he complimented Frankfurter's "stiletto work" in a tax case. Eight days later, after responding to Frankfurter's criticism of his book, Rodell replied: "I *still* think you've been turning out some perfectly grand opinions." Finally, on February 18, he asked if he and his wife Katherine could visit Frankfurter in chambers.

Rodell's changed attitude baffled Frankfurter. It could not have been *Gobitis*, which had been decided in June 1940. The *Harper's* article alluded to a beef that spring with Yale law colleague and former Frankfurter student Harry Shulman. In March 1941, Rodell claimed (and Shulman denied) that Shulman had persuaded the *Yale Law Journal* to reject a Rodell book review that praised Black and Douglas and criticized Frankfurter. Rodell later claimed that he had found Frankfurter's conduct on the Court "shocking."

Rodell's instigator may have been his more senior Yale law colleague, Walton Hamilton. An economist without a law degree, Hamilton had been mentioned for Frankfurter's eventual seat on the Court and had been critical of him in the *Yale Law Journal*. In June 1941, Hamilton wrote Rodell a two-page memorandum with gossip and critiques of Frankfurter and his first few years on the bench. Some derogatory comments in Hamilton's letter found their way directly into Rodell's article and detracted from the incisive argument.

In *Harper's*, Rodell contended that Frankfurter was not a liberal lawyer who had turned into a conservative justice; rather, Frankfurter had always been conservative. Liberals should not have been "surprised and shocked" about his *Gobitis* decision forcing two children of Jehovah's Witnesses to salute the flag, his *Milk Wagon Drivers* decision upholding a labor injunction against a union, or other anti-labor decisions. He pointed to the prediction of a Boston Brahmin that Frankfurter would not be a radical justice and to Frankfurter's support in polls of the conservative American Bar Association. "'Felix hasn't changed his views one iota,'" Rodell quoted someone, perhaps Hamilton. "'Take a close look at his life and judge for yourself.'" Frankfurter, Rodell concluded, was "a tragic figure" who had lost his position as the Court's decisive vote and predicted that "as the Court moves past him," Frankfurter would stick to his judicial philosophy and become "as great a dissenter as were his two heroes, Justices Holmes and Brandeis, in days gone by."

In private correspondence and magazine profiles, Rodell praised his new heroes on the Court—Black and Douglas. The Yale law professor spent the remainder of his career burnishing their reputations and engaging in a one-man holy war against Frankfurter, Harvard Law School, and its graduates. This was not only a Yale-Harvard rivalry, though Rodell tried to make it seem that way. Several of Frankfurter's protégés joined the Yale law faculty. And at least one Harvard faculty member, Thomas Reed Powell, excelled at Rodell's clever, put-down style. Frankfurter's friends knew how to twist the knife, too. In January 1942, Jacob Billikopf chastised Rodell about the *Harper's* article's nasty tone. Rodell responded by attacking Billikopf's "blind prejudice in favor of all respectable Jews, simply because they are Jews. . . . It is just the sort of 'party line', to use your own phrase, that breeds anti-Semitism." Billikopf described the response as "pathetic" and "expressed by one who claims not to be a Jew, or who does not want to be known as such! (For which statement a fond relative of yours is my authority)." Another Frankfurter ally, Frederick Bernays Wiener, raised questions of Rodell's anti-Semitism in a 1956 book review and revealed that at Haverford College, Rodell's last name had been Roedelheim.

The stakes were much higher than Yale v. Harvard or Rodell v. Frankfurter. Rodell applauded Black's and Douglas's increasing use of judicial power to promote liberal causes. Frankfurter envisioned a more limited role for an inherently conservative judiciary and believed that liberalism's success or failure depended on the democratic political process. The challenges, for Frankfurter, were how to advocate Holmes and Brandeis's belief in a limited judicial role while protecting the rights of African Americans and other racial minorities as well as how to balance his full-time job as a Supreme Court justice with his behind-the-scenes role in helping the Roosevelt administration prepare for war.

Throughout the fall of 1941, Frankfurter and Acheson walked each morning from their Georgetown homes to Acheson's office at the State Department (a car took Frankfurter the rest of the way to the Court). They spent many hours discussing the administration's preparations for war. On the basis of numerous conversations with Stimson and McCloy, Frankfurter knew about the Victory Program, the administration's secret plans for war against the Nazis, and that the United States and Germany were headed for war. On December 1, Frankfurter called Stimson after visiting Harry Hopkins in the hospital and was "extremely anxious that Knox and I should not let what they call the Appeasers pull the president back." The next day, an Army Air Corps captain leaked the nation's top-secret war plans to Senator Wheeler, who gave them to *Chicago Tribune* reporter Ches Manly and to the *Washington Times-Herald*. A December 5 *Tribune* headline declared "F.D.R.'S WAR PLANS!" and described the U.S. plan to declare war against Germany in July 1943. For two days, McCloy and other War Department officials discussed the leak and sought advice from Frankfurter. In the end, the administration decided to do nothing and to say nothing to the press. In many ways, the Victory Program leak moved the country closer to war with Germany.

At home, the Frankfurters continued to care for their British children Ann, Venetia, and Oliver. That fall, Ann and Venetia returned happily to the Potomac School; Ann had grown four inches and gained twenty pounds in two years; Venetia had survived a flu that required a brief hospitalization; Oliver made an aborted attempt to start nursery school but could not bear to part with his nurse, Nana. For Marion, the experience of watching Oliver come home crying every day was painful. She planned to try again in December when some of his friends in the neighborhood started nursery school. The brunt of the child-rearing decisions fell on her. "Since I see very little of them," Felix wrote Monte Lemann, "I get nothing but pleasure out of them. All the chores fall on Marion." Marion, Isaiah Berlin wrote his parents, "wears dresses of white silk & sails about like [a] neurotic & distinguished Vestal." She may have been a neurotic mother, but the children brought out her love, tenderness, and warmth. "I do not think Felix and I are particularly gifted with children. Not having any of our own, we have grown up without them and are now practiced in one way rather than another," Marion wrote. "But I do not think they or Nana could ever have been in any doubt that we loved them and their happiness and well-being were our first concern always—and that is surely the most important thing. We loved them just for their parents' sake, and then, very soon, for themselves."

Events off the West Coast soon made the Frankfurters question whether their three British children were safe in the United States.

CHAPTER 24

F. F.'s Soliloquy

At 11:30 a.m. on December 7, 1941, Frankfurter phoned John McCloy to discuss Raoul Desvernine. A former general counsel of U.S. Steel and lawyer for the anti–New Deal American Liberty League, Desvernine represented the interests of the Japanese government and its special envoy Saburo Kurusu. Frankfurter was one of the few people in Washington who knew why Kurusu, after two years as the Japanese ambassador to Germany, had come to the United States. On November 17, Frankfurter had written the president that Kurusu was in Washington "to find out if we mean business in case Japan moves. The rest of Kurusu's mission is all window dressing." Frankfurter's letter shocked Roosevelt because few people knew about Japan's true intentions. Roosevelt phoned and asked how he knew about the diplomatic smokescreen. Frankfurter promised to tell Roosevelt his source in person at the White House. The justice's information could have come from Stimson or McCloy in the War Department, Acheson or Fcis in the State Department, French diplomat Jean Monnet, or British and Chinese diplomats.

At 2:05 p.m. on December 7, Kurusu and Japanese ambassador Kichisaburo Nomura sat in the diplomatic waiting room preparing to meet Secretary of State Cordell Hull and intending to break off peace negotiations and to reject American demands about withdrawing its troops from China and severing its ties with Germany and Italy. Hull already knew this from intercepted cables. Fifteen minutes later, he called the two diplomats into his office, read their charges against the United States, accused them of deceptions and falsehoods, and threw them out the door. By that time, he heard the unconfirmed report from the president that an hour earlier the Japanese had attacked Pearl Harbor.

The president called Secretary of War Stimson and asked him to come to the White House because the Japanese had attacked. Stimson, who knew that the Japanese fleet had moved south toward Indo-China and was worried about the breakdown of peace negotiations, asked if it was Malaya or Siam. "Hell no," Roosevelt replied, "it is Pearl Harbor." Stimson told the story to Frankfurter, who wired the White House that if the attorney general or solicitor general could not be reached for legal advice, the president should call Dean Acheson. Frankfurter gave Roosevelt Acheson's home phone number and the number of Acheson's housekeeper. Acheson heard the news at his farm in Sandy Spring, Maryland, and immediately drove to the office.

At 8:30 p.m., Roosevelt convened what he described as the most important cabinet meeting since the spring of 1861. The president then proceeded to tell his cabinet much of the recent history that he and Frankfurter knew. For about two weeks, the U.S. government had known that Germany was "pressing" Japan for military action in Asia; Japan's State Department peace negotiations were a ruse; and Japan was "headed for war." U.S. officials thought the target was the Allies' supply lines in Siam, Thailand, and Burma. The previous day, Roosevelt had sent the Japanese emperor a note to see if his country was still interested in peace. The president also informed his cabinet about the Japanese diplomats' meeting with Secretary Hull after the attack. The casualties, Roosevelt informed the cabinet, had been "extremely heavy," three or four battleships had been sunk, others had been damaged, and many aircraft had been destroyed. The Japanese, moreover, had captured Guam and attacked the Philippines and other islands. The entire U.S. fleet in the Pacific had been caught off guard. The War and Navy Departments had failed to connect the available intelligence and cryptography and did not know about the attack in advance. Stimson was so impressed with Roosevelt's poise during the cabinet meeting that he told Frankfurter: "*There* is my leader." The Roosevelt-Stimson team made Frankfurter feel safe. On the afternoon of December 7, Frankfurter wrote the president: "the whole American people are behind you."

Shortly before 12:30 p.m. the next day, Frankfurter and seven other justices wore their black robes and walked across the street to the U.S. Capitol. As they walked, Stanley Reed predicted that in ten minutes the United States would be at war with Japan and Germany. "I said not with Germany," Frankfurter said. "This man will not go to war. Germany has to declare war. He will then say a state of war exists." Frankfurter and the other justices watched from the front left of the packed chamber as Roosevelt addressed both houses of Congress. Marion was watching from the gallery where Eleanor Roosevelt sat. As the president entered, Democrats and Republicans, interventionists and isolationists, stood and clapped until Speaker of the House Sam Rayburn banged his gavel. Roosevelt began by declaring that December 7, 1941, was "a date which will live in infamy." He briefly reviewed the details of the "unprovoked and dastardly attack" at Pearl Harbor, then asked Congress to declare that a state of war existed with Japan. He said nothing about Germany. Thirty-three minutes after the speech, members of both houses of Congress, with a single exception, voted to declare war against Japan. Britain and many other Allied nations followed suit. At 10:00 p.m. on December 9, Felix and Marion listened to Roosevelt's national radio address at their home with the Polish ambassador and his wife, former Federal Reserve governor Adolph Miller and his wife, and friend Elizabeth Ellis. Felix wrote the president that the fireside chat brought "calm and confidence to our people."

On December 8, as Frankfurter was getting ready to attend Roosevelt's joint message to Congress, he informed his law clerk Phil Elman "about how dependent he was going to be on me from here on. He said he was going to need me as no justice had ever needed a law clerk before. He was going to have to devote his full energies to helping in the war effort, to helping FDR. That would be his overwhelming priority, to which everything else had to yield."

Indeed, Pearl Harbor had changed everything for the nation and for Frankfurter. The U.S. entry into the war had cast everything in a new light—his home life, his activity on behalf of the administration, his work on the Court, and the types of cases he had to decide. The war made Frankfurter more confident, often overconfident, that the democratic political process, the federal administrative state, and the Roosevelt administration could solve the gravest and most delicate of the world's problems.

Marion's first thought was about the safety of her three British children. "Your cable came yesterday and it is easy to imagine how you have been thinking given Sunday's news," she wrote Pauline and Sylvester Gates on December 10. "I have been thinking ever since, what I can do to ensure the children's safety in case steps have to be taken. F. says it's premature, but who knows what's premature." The children, Marion wrote, "seem unconcerned." On Saturday December 20, the three children attended a "toy matinee" at the Uptown Theater in which children from embassies donated wrapped toys for American families who could not afford Christmas presents. The Washington *Evening Star* published a photograph of Oliver and his four-year-old British friends donating toys.

The war made Frankfurter's judicial duties seem insignificant. When he heard the news about Pearl Harbor, he had been preparing for an upcoming oral argument about whether greens fees at the Winchester Country Club counted as "dues or membership fees" for tax purposes. The day before the December 12 argument, Germany and Italy had declared war against the United States.

Instead of dwelling on an insignificant tax case, Frankfurter helped the Roosevelt administration wage war. On December 9, he met with the general counsel of the Lend-Lease Administration, Oscar Cox. The next morning, he and McCloy discussed the formation of a Joint Allied War Council similar to the one during World War I. On December 16, McCloy visited Frankfurter to discuss the possibility of Justice Owen J. Roberts serving as the chair of a committee to investigate what had gone wrong at Pearl Harbor. Shortly before noon, Frankfurter phoned McCloy that Roberts had accepted. On December 17, Frankfurter sent Roosevelt a memorandum summarizing discussions since September 1939 with "some of the best brains" about the mistakes the British and French had made during the war and how the United States could avoid them. Before he sent the memorandum, he showed it to his newest colleague James F. Byrnes, who was itching to join the administration and who "entirely agrees with it." On December 30, he hosted a dinner with McCloy, Monnet, Cox, Byrnes, and British shipping mission chief Arthur Salter about the "best means" to revamp the prewar Office of Production Management into a wartime agency. Byrnes wanted to leave the Court to take on the task himself.

As of December 1941, Frankfurter's closest colleagues on the Court were its more conservative members Roberts, Byrnes, Jackson, and to some extent Reed. Frankfurter's estrangement from the Court's liberals Black, Douglas, and Murphy had begun. No case illustrated their differences more than *Bridges v. California*. The Court had heard reargument in October about the contempt of court convictions of labor leader Harry Bridges and the *Los Angeles Times*, this time with Stone as chief justice and Jackson and Byrnes as the newest associate justices and potential tiebreakers. Frankfurter, who had lost his majority the previous term, expected the Court's newest members to read the briefs and listen to the arguments and decide for themselves. But Black found a fifth vote by privately circulating his draft dissent from the previous term to Jackson while Frankfurter had refrained from lobbying him. Black also persuaded Jackson not to write a concurring opinion so that the majority could project a "united front." Frankfurter blamed Black, not Jackson, who was hearing the case during his first week on the Court.

Bridges was a battle for the legacy of Holmes and Brandeis. This was the case in which Brandeis, after reading the draft opinions after the first argument, remarked to Frankfurter that "Black and Company have gone mad on free speech." For Black, the contempt convictions violated freedom of speech and press. He invoked Holmes's "clear and present danger" test from *Schenck* and Brandeis's concurrence in *Whitney v. California* to argue that the evil must be substantial and imminent. Black contended that Bridges's telegram threatening a strike and the *Times* editorials did not interfere with the criminal justice system or pose a clear and present danger. Therefore, his majority opinion reversed the contempt convictions.

Frankfurter's *Bridges* dissent, joined by Stone, Roberts, and Byrnes, sided with Brandeis's deference to state courts and sought to preserve "trial by courts rather than trial by newspapers." The contempt power of state judges, he argued, was "essential for the effective exercise of the judicial process" and to "the right of California to keep its courts free from coercion." Frankfurter's dissent was part of an ongoing debate with Black about the extent to which the First Amendment and other provisions in the Bill of Rights applied to the states through the liberty provision of the Fourteenth Amendment's Due Process Clause. He also disagreed with Black's argument that the First Amendment right to free speech trumped other Bill of Rights safeguards. Invoking Lincoln's message to Congress in 1861, Frankfurter wrote: "Free speech is not so absolute or irrational a conception as to imply paralysis of the means for effective protection of all the freedoms secured by the Bill of Rights." He argued that free speech must be balanced against other rights including a right to fair trial by an "impartial judiciary," citing Holmes's opinion in *Moore v. Dempsey* outlawing mob-dominated criminal trials and Black's opinion in *Chambers v. Florida* outlawing coerced confessions. In his *Bridges* dissent, he insisted that the Constitution was not "a doctrinaire document," and the Bill of Rights was not "a collection of popular slogans." After discussing the history of the power of judges to prevent interference with pending cases, he argued that "the Bill of Rights is not self-destructive. Freedom of expression can hardly carry implications that nullify the guarantees of impartial trials." For Frankfurter, *Bridges* exemplified the Supreme Court invoking free speech to substitute its judgment for those of state courts. Ultimately, he argued for a constitutional flexibility that balanced freedom of speech against the right to a fair trial before an impartial judge and jury. The Court in *Bridges*, he argued, had overprotected free speech at the expense of a fair criminal trial.

On December 8, Frankfurter read a summary of his dissent from the bench. He could not believe that Jackson had joined Black's opinion. Years later, Jackson could not recall "why he went with Black." Frankfurter was so proud of his *Bridges* dissent that he was "ready to be judged on judgment day by my dissent in that case." But one wonders what he would have said if he had been held in contempt by the Massachusetts Supreme Judicial Court for publishing his *Atlantic Monthly* article about Sacco and Vanzetti while their appeals were pending. The ACLU's Osmond Fraenkel, Frankfurter's ally in the Sacco-Vanzetti case, had argued the *Bridges* case before the Supreme Court. And Fraenkel argued the next major civil liberties case that pitted Frankfurter against Black, Douglas, and Murphy.

———

FRANKFURTER KNEW his flag salute opinion in *Gobitis* was still fresh in the minds of the three liberal justices who had joined it. Many liberal newspapers and magazines had praised Stone's dissent and had criticized Frankfurter's majority opinion. During the summer and fall after the *Gobitis* decision, newspapers reported brutal acts of violence against Jehovah's Witnesses across the country. At the beginning of the 1940 term, Douglas, who saw Frankfurter for the first time since the summer, remarked: "Hugo tells me that now he wouldn't go with you in the *Gobitis* case." Frankfurter replied: "Has Hugo been re-reading the Constitution during the summer?" "No," Douglas said, "he has been reading the papers."

On February 5, 1942, Jehovah's Witnesses, represented by Osmond Fraenkel, returned to the Court to challenge an ordinance of the city of Opelika, Alabama, requiring a license and a fee for selling books and pamphlets door to door. On April 30, they again appeared before the Court to challenge several similar city ordinances requiring licenses. They argued that the licenses violated free speech and the free exercise of religion. Overruling *Gobitis* was not raised in the briefs, at oral argument, or at conference. Stanley Reed, the senior justice in the majority, assigned the case to himself and wrote a majority opinion rejecting the free speech and religion challenges. Stone, in a dissent joined by Black, Douglas, and Murphy, declared that the ordinances violated the First Amendment. On May 30, however, Black, Douglas, and Murphy circulated a joint opinion, drafted by Douglas, contending that *Gobitis* had been "wrongly decided" and concluded: "The First Amendment does not put the right freely to exercise religion in a subordinate position. We fear, however, that the opinions in these and in the *Gobitis* case do exactly that." Frankfurter was blindsided. He confirmed with Reed and Roberts that *Gobitis* was not raised at oral argument and "never discussed or alluded to" at conference. As in the *Bridges* case, Black and now Douglas had employed sneaky tactics to win votes and to avoid a direct confrontation with Frankfurter. On June 10, the Court announced its decision in *Jones v. Opelika*.

The Black-Douglas-Murphy joint dissent was applauded in the press as well as by Frankfurter's enemies. "For years Mr. Frankfurter was himself a zealous evangelist for social reform, a watchful critic of government," estranged former Roosevelt administration official Raymond Moley wrote in *Newsweek.* "He feared power then. He evidently does not fear it now. Government is in the hands of friends."

Moley was wrong—Frankfurter only feared the power of the judiciary. It did not matter whether it was in the hands of conservatives from 1911 to 1936 and in the hands of liberals for the past five years. He especially feared justices who refused to follow precedent, refused to debate legal issues, and preferred to invalidate legislation, state or federal, on the basis of shifting political winds rather than on constitutional principle and argument.

After *Jones v. Opelika*, Frankfurter was at loggerheads with Black, Douglas, and Murphy. He demonized them and unduly personalized their philosophical differences and what he regarded as their political approach to judging. He and others on the Court privately began referring to Black, Douglas, and Murphy as "the Axis." Douglas, Frankfurter's chief antagonist, made sure that Frankfurter's humiliation was more public. Douglas and Corcoran gossiped to a Frankfurter foe, syndicated columnist Drew Pearson.

On the last day of the Supreme Court term, Pearson and Robert Allen devoted their June 1 column to exposing Frankfurter's extrajudicial activity. "Justice Frankfurter," they asserted, "has more to do with guiding our destinies of war than anyone in Washington." They began the column by claiming that Frankfurter had recommended a member of the Australian government take a position in the British cabinet, outraging the British and Australian governments. They observed that Frankfurter was on "intimate terms" with British ambassador Lord Halifax and Chinese foreign minister T. V. Soong and with former student Dean Acheson in the State Department. "Almost no move of major importance is made these days without Frankfurter having his finger in it," Pearson and Allen wrote. They pointed to Frankfurter participating in discussions about sending a mission to India, his recommendation of Owen J. Roberts to chair the Pearl Harbor investigation, and his successful lobbying for Charles E. Wyzanski, Jr., to receive a federal judgeship in Boston.

The columnists argued that Frankfurter's background as a Jewish immigrant from Vienna, his uncle's imprisonment by the Nazis, and "the persecution of his race" had "long before Pearl Harbor made Frankfurter one of the most energetic and effective promoters of intervention." They rightly chided Frankfurter for spending time in the British embassy and the War Department and ignoring warnings from friends that justices should not engage in political activities. They alluded to criticism of Van Devanter and Sutherland for involving themselves in their home state politics in Wyoming and Utah but wrote that Frankfurter "considers himself in a different category."

Three cabinet members, Stimson, Knox, and Attorney General Francis Biddle, according to Pearson and Allen, owed their jobs to Frankfurter. The columnists accused Frankfurter of trying to replace Secretary of State Hull with Acheson. And they claimed that Biddle, a former Frankfurter protégé, had "cooled toward him" because Frankfurter was "too indiscreet to be trusted." They observed that Frankfurter's "greatest influence" was in the War Department because of his close relationships with Stimson and McCloy. The one significant thing the article left out was Frankfurter's frequent contacts with the president.

Though couched in sinister and salacious terms, Pearson and Allen's column mischaracterized Frankfurter's extrajudicial activity. Frankfurter's interventionism was not a product of his Jewish background but of his 1912 support for Theodore Roosevelt, his experience in the Taft and Wilson War Departments, and his understanding of the German threat to the world. It was not unusual for justices to engage in presidential policy making, as Brandeis did with Wilson, Taft with Harding, and Stone with Hoover. Nor was Frankfurter the only current justice advising Roosevelt. Douglas, Murphy, Jackson, and Byrnes counseled him and aspired to succeed him as president. Frankfurter's refusal to refrain from political activity stemmed not from any desire for personal or professional gain but to help the United States win the war and to save civilization from Hitler and the Nazi regime.

Frankfurter's friendship with Stimson helped him in a rare time of personal need. The "sheer joys" in his life, the three British children living in his home, were thriving in Washington. In January 1942, Oliver had started nursery school, and Ann and Venetia had done extremely well at the Potomac School. By June, however, Pauline Gates could not bear to live without her children.

On June 30, Felix and Marion accompanied the children to New York City to see them off on a Pan American B-314, a flying boat called the Clipper, bound for Southampton, England. The seas, patrolled by German U-boats, were too dangerous. The children, however, were bumped from the flight to make room for munitions. A panicked Frankfurter phoned War Department aide Harvey Bundy, who in turn informed Stimson. Stimson, who had heard from the Frankfurters about their plans to send the British children home, called the officers in charge. It turned out that General Dwight D. Eisenhower had personally requested Signal Corps munitions. Stimson explained this to

Judge Learned Hand and Marion Frankfurter, who along with her husband was staying with the Hands. After several days of delay, the children and their nanny boarded a midnight flight. A Pan American executive insisted to McCloy that they had received no special favors. After the flight took off, Felix wrote Sylvester Gates that the children were "as good samples of civilization as I know." He and Marion left the airport with heavy hearts: "We hate to have them go—and rejoice that they are going to Pauline and you." At 2:00 a.m. on July 8, the Frankfurters received a message that "relieved our anxiety"—the Gates children had arrived safely in Ireland, and their parents "found the children unchanged." Frankfurter thought that for "the children—especially little Oliver—to cross the Atlantic must be an experience that will remain with him for a lifetime."

The biggest void for the Frankfurters was the absence of four-year-old Oliver. Marion believed that he "seems to me to have every gift a child could have." In the taxi on the way to the airport, Felix remarked that some of his friends were traveling on the same plane. "I hope not," Oliver replied. He repeated the remark thinking Oliver had not heard him correctly. Again, Oliver said "I hope not." Felix asked why: "Oliver leaned over and patted his cheek very gently and said: 'I like you very much, Uncle Felix, and I don't want any of your friends to go away when I'm leaving you because I don't want you to be lonely.'"

THE NIGHT BEFORE taking the children to New York, Frankfurter had advised Stimson about an issue bound to come before the Court—the trial of Nazi saboteurs. On June 27, the FBI announced the capture of eight German spies who had landed on the Atlantic Seaboard with large amounts of explosives. They had arrived in mid-June via German submarines, four on Long Island and four near Jacksonville, Florida. Their mission: to blow up American war industries and transportation lines. The FBI started a manhunt after the four Long Island spies were spotted by a member of the U.S. Coast Guard. One saboteur turned himself in, confessed, and helped the FBI apprehend the others.

On June 29, members of the War and Justice Departments suggested that the Nazi saboteurs should not be tried in federal court or by court martial but before a special military commission. Attorney General Biddle wanted Stimson to chair the commission. Stimson suggested Under Secretary of War Patterson, a former Second Circuit judge. Patterson, however, thought the commission should consist of only military officers. During dinner with Stimson, Frankfurter agreed with Patterson that the commission "should be entirely composed of soldiers." On July 2, the president announced that the Nazi saboteurs would be tried by seven generals, led by Major General Frank R. McCoy, in a special military commission. The commission's verdict was reviewable only by the president. The procedures were highly irregular (a minimum two-thirds vote to convict instead of unanimity, no review by the judge advocate general) and did not follow federal military regulations, the Articles of War.

A few days later, Frankfurter asked about the trial, and Stimson revealed his clashes with publicity-hungry Attorney General Biddle. Stimson was annoyed that the FBI had publicized facts about the case, that Biddle had insisted on appearing as one of the prosecutors at the trial, and that Biddle had gone behind Stimson's back to lobby the president for three media observers. Frankfurter, who had known the attorney general since 1912 when the Holmes clerk had dined at the House of Truth, informed Stimson that he was "not an admirer of Biddle and his admiration was not kindled by what he heard from me."

As a justice likely to hear the Nazi saboteurs' case, Frankfurter never should have offered advice about the composition of the military commission, asked about the trial, or revealed his views about Attorney General Biddle. Before the trial began, military lawyers for the saboteurs asked Stimson and Roosevelt whether they could file a writ of habeas corpus, a petition challenging the spies' confinement and the lawfulness of the special military commission. Stimson and Roosevelt declined to see the defense lawyers. The saboteurs faced death sentences for violating the laws of war by wearing civilian clothes, by attempting to commit acts of sabotage, and for acting as spies. Soon after the trial had begun in secret on July 10 at the Justice Department, defense counsel sought relief from members of the Supreme Court. After the first recess, the saboteurs' defense attorneys, opposed by Attorney General Biddle, flew to Philadelphia and motored to the nearby Chester Springs, Pennsylvania, farm of Owen J. Roberts. They asked Black, who was visiting Roberts, to urge Chief Justice Stone to reconvene the Court to hear the case. Black referred them to Stone in New Hampshire. Stone, who had anticipated that the case would come before the Court, phoned the individual justices for their views. On July 27, the chief justice announced that the Court would hold an unprecedented special term to hear the saboteurs' constitutional challenge to the special military commission.

The night before the special term, Frankfurter dined with Stimson and informed him that numerous military officers had requested to see the oral argument. On Frankfurter's advice, Stimson banned officers from attending except those assisting the government's case. Douglas, who was returning from Oregon, was unable to make it in time. Murphy, who invoked his inactive status in the army reserve to spend the summer as a lieutenant colonel at Ft. Dilworth, North Carolina, arrived at the justices' private conference in his military uniform. At Frankfurter's urging, Murphy disqualified himself. "It was not the most congenial thing in the world to express the views I did . . . ," Frankfurter wrote to Murphy. "But had the roles been reversed I should have expected the same from you." Yet Frankfurter did not think of disqualifying himself on the basis of his advice to Stimson. Nor was he the only justice with a conflict of interest. Stone's son, Lauson, was a member of the defense team (both sides agreed Stone should not recuse himself). Earlier that year, Byrnes had been advising Attorney General Biddle and other administration officials in drafting the Second War Powers Act. What other justices considered a conflict of interest was irrelevant. On two occasions with Stimson, Frankfurter had opined about the Nazi saboteurs' case. He also was a major on inactive status in the army's Judge Advocate General's Corps reserve. Frankfurter should have recognized the appearance of a conflict of interest and disqualified himself.

In the Nazi saboteurs' case, the Court wrestled with numerous jurisdictional hurdles and with real limits on its own power. First, one of the defendants had been denied habeas corpus by a federal trial judge but had not appealed the judge's decision to the federal court of appeals. Second, *Ex Parte Milligan*, a Supreme Court decision about the use of a military tribunal at the end of the Civil War, held that when the federal courts are open and the trial is not on a battlefield, spies must be tried in federal court, not by a military commission. Third, the president departed from the procedures established in the Articles of War in organizing a special military commission. Finally, the president asserted that his power as commander in chief during wartime trumped the other two branches, particularly when spies violated the laws of war by sneaking onto U.S. soil in civilian clothes and arriving armed with explosives to blow up American factories and infrastructure.

During the first day of oral argument on July 29, Frankfurter "immediately began" questioning defense counsel Colonel Kenneth C. Royall about why he had not gone to the federal court of appeals before petitioning the Supreme Court. A former student whom Frankfurter had encouraged to join Robert Patterson in the War Department, Royall agreed to file the appropriate paperwork with the court of appeals. Frankfurter, along with Jackson, asked

numerous questions about the defense's contentions that the saboteurs had
been trying to escape Nazi Germany rather than harm war industries and
infrastructure in the United States. Frankfurter and Jackson also questioned
Attorney General Biddle, who argued that the eight enemy spies had no
right to petition for habeas corpus, even though two were American citizens.
Frankfurter thought Biddle never should have participated as a prosecutor
in the military proceeding. Frankfurter's enemies pounced on his persistent
questioning. Columnist Drew Pearson wrote that another justice passed
Frankfurter a note on the bench: "For heaven's sake, Felix, try to restrain
yourself." No such note has been found. And the justice most likely to gossip
to Corcoran or Pearson, the late-arriving Douglas, was absent from the Court
that day. There was no doubt, however, that Frankfurter's rapid-fire questioning annoyed many of his colleagues.

Douglas finally made it back from Oregon in time for the second day of
oral argument, which lasted another three hours and forty-five minutes (most
arguments in those days were one hour per side). On the second day, Biddle appealed to the Court to "sustain to the limit the power of the President
in war time." He argued that the president's power as commander in chief
trumped the power of Congress or the Court. In response to a question from
his predecessor Jackson, Biddle intimated that the president was not bound
by federal law and, even if the Court found him in violation of the law, the
president's power as commander in chief was the "final authority." Privately,
Roosevelt was more explicit about refusing to obey a decision in the prisoners'
favor. "I won't give them up . . . ," he told Biddle. "I won't hand them over to
any United States marshal armed with a writ of habeas corpus. Understand?"
Biddle had alerted the justices that the "president will order [the] men shot
despite [the] proceedings of this Court." Roosevelt's disregard for the rule of
law revealed how tenuous the Court's position was. More than the lives of the
eight Nazi saboteurs was at stake; the Court's power and legitimacy were, too.

In a short, unsigned opinion, the Court announced on July 31 that the
president was authorized to order a military commission, the commission
was "lawfully constituted," and the saboteurs were in lawful custody and
therefore not entitled to a writ of habeas corpus. The government had won;
the saboteurs had lost; the Court had deferred to the executive branch. After
the Court's decision, the trial resumed in secret. On August 2, Stone wrote
Frankfurter that he was "a bit uncomfortable" about the opinion's lack of references to the Articles of War. He wished he had not deleted a paragraph
assuming the articles applied to the president because it would have helped
the president defend his decision to have a military commission and "would

have saved us from the possible embarrassment" of writing about the issue "for the first time after some of the prisoners have been executed." The next day, Frankfurter praised the chief justice's conduct of the case and relayed a conversation with Black who, like Frankfurter, agreed that the Court should speak through only one opinion and as succinctly as possible.

On August 8, the president announced that he had approved the commissioners' decision that all eight saboteurs were guilty and that six of them had been executed. The two spies who had assisted the government had been sentenced to a lifetime of hard labor and thirty years' hard labor, respectively, even though the FBI had promised them pardons after two-year prison terms. The trial records were sealed until the end of the war.

With six men executed, two imprisoned, and no access to the trial record, Stone spent the rest of the summer recess trying to write the Court's opinion on the basis of briefs he described as written to create "legal chaos." As he wrote, he worried about the omissions of the Articles of War from the Court's initial opinion as creating a no-win situation. If the Court again failed to address them, then the surviving spies sentenced to prison could raise them in a new petition. If the Court were to interpret the Articles of War, then it would in essence be offering an "advisory opinion" because the defendants did not raise them in their briefs or at oral argument. Nor had the president or the military commission opined on them. And it was unclear whether they had been raised at trial because there was no available record. "It seems almost brutal," Stone wrote Frankfurter, "to announce this ground of decision for the first time after six of the petitioners have been executed." Frankfurter suggested that Stone circulate a draft opinion to the other justices as a memorandum rather than an opinion to emphasize its "fluid form" and to deter other justices from writing separate opinions. He tried to calm Stone's unease by relaying his own experience in the War Department of the Wilson administration when General Enoch Crowder had revised the Articles of War and had debated how to implement them during World War I. Stone's law clerk, Bennett Boskey, drafted a memorandum about the legislative history of the Articles of War. The memorandum provided some arguments, which Stone described as "make weights which together have some persuasive force," that the Articles of War supported the president's decision to deviate from standard military procedure. He was so unsure of himself that he proposed two alternatives. On September 25, Stone circulated two opinions, both of which involved "some embarrassment": Memorandum A omitting any discussion of the Articles of War and Memorandum B arguing the Articles of War supported the government. He invited his fellow justices to choose which one to publish. Five days later, Frankfurter circulated a memorandum endorsing Memorandum B because it rested on the inapplicability of the Articles of War and the belief that the president did not violate them by acting as the final review of the military commission. Frankfurter hoped that the decision based on Memorandum B would be unanimous. To Stone, he wrote that he was "very happy over the whole outcome of this business."

Before the justices returned to work in early October to discuss Stone's memoranda, Frankfurter attacked isolationism and exuded Americanism in another public address that made national news. This time he spoke at his alma mater, City College of New York (CCNY). "We did not go to war. War came to us," he reminded the audience. He observed that isolationists could foster "spiritual unity" by recanting their prior position as America fought "a war to save civilization." He urged colleges and universities not to lower their standards and to continue to train leaders to meet the world's postwar problems: "The difference between leaders as true servants of a community and as self-designated overseers of peons is the difference between a free society and a concentration camp." He described colleges and universities as "the special guardians of the free pursuit of truth" and pointed to Hitler's rise as marked by book burnings and seizure of universities. He blamed "self-destructive isolationism" on "faulty education," sacrificing "security and decency" in the name of "money-making." In a stirring conclusion that reflected his immigrant roots, rapid rise after graduating from CCNY at age 19, and devotion to his adopted country, he reminded the students and faculty what made American democracy different than Nazi totalitarianism and what the United States was fighting for: "The ideal that holds us together is our sincere respect for the common man whatever his race or religion."

After the CCNY speech, Frankfurter returned to Washington determined that the Court project a similar unity in the Nazi saboteurs' case. Stone's September 25 circulation of Memorandum A and Memorandum B had failed to unify the Court. Roberts raised several concerns with Memorandum B. On October 14, Frankfurter suggested compromise language, and Stone made revisions. Six days later, Roberts proposed more changes. Jackson also found Memorandum B unsatisfying. For nearly a month, he had been drafting a memorandum and concurring opinion that he circulated to his colleagues. Jackson argued that the Court should not address any issues other than that the saboteurs were not entitled to protection under the Articles of War or the Constitution because they were "unlawful belligerents" who were "properly in military custody." "The magnitude and urgency of the menace" left it up to "the Commander in Chief to decide" how to try the spies. Though it was not necessary to decide the case, Jackson contended that the president was not bound by the procedures outlined in the Articles of War and "had a right to do" it his way. On October 19, Frankfurter read Jackson's memorandum, agreed with its conclusion, but asked him not to publish it: "And the fact that it's done in 30 instead of in 3 pages does not seem to me a strong enough reason for writing a separate piece in this case!"

Frankfurter was perplexed by the conference discussion between Stone and Jackson and the lack of discernible differences between their views. Stone, Jackson, Black, Frankfurter, and every other justice on the Court agreed that they should avoid the thorny constitutional question about the scope of the president's commander-in-chief power. On October 23, in an effort to clarify the issues and unify the Court, Frankfurter circulated a hypothetical question and answer discussion between himself and the saboteurs titled "F. F.'s Soliloquy." His references to the defendants as "damned scoundrels" and "low-down, ordinary, enemy spies" who could have been shot on sight may have been a lame attempt at gallows humor and obscured his legal reasoning and institutional concerns. He argued that the president was within his commander-in-chief power and therefore the "procedural safeguards" of the Articles of War did not apply. Frankfurter refused, however, to define the scope of the president's power: "You've done enough mischief already without leaving the seeds of a bitter conflict involving the President, the courts and Congress after your bodies will be rotting in lime." He dismissed the request for an interpretation of the Articles of War, which he deemed inapplicable to the situation, as a "foolish fancy."

After the question and answer section, Frankfurter explained the concerns that lay behind his dismissal of the saboteurs' constitutional claims: "Some of the very best lawyers I know are now in the Solomon Islands battle, some are seeing service in Australia, some are sub-chasers in the Atlantic, and some are on the various air fronts." He wondered what these men, former students he knew "very, very intimately," would think if the Court declined to speak in a unanimous opinion and revealed "internecine conflict about the manner of stating that result." The men, Frankfurter wrote, would say: "'What in the hell do you fellows think you are doing? Haven't we got enough of a job to lick the Japs and the Nazis without having you fellows on the Supreme Court dissipate the thoughts and feelings and energies of the people at home . . . ?'"

On the afternoon of October 23, after he circulated his "soliloquy," Frankfurter sat on the bench exchanging notes with Roberts and Jackson to cajole them into joining Stone's opinion. Jackson wrote Frankfurter: "How can you treat so unimportantly something that is causing others such prayerful consideration. You don't know the half of it! If I win the bet on the writings alone I expect my cocktail." Jackson evidently suspected Roberts would not join Stone's opinion and believed that Frankfurter's rhetoric was an attempt at gallows humor (not everyone, including Murphy, was amused). In another note, Jackson wrote Frankfurter: "Your Anatole France opinion is like a loud laugh at a funeral—over here. The only one who enjoys it is the corpse—I." Meanwhile, Roberts wrote a note to Frankfurter disagreeing with some of Jackson's conclusions about presidential power and doubting that Jackson would join Stone's lengthier Memorandum B without publishing a concurrence. Roberts, who agreed with Black's suggestion of a shorter-form opinion without addressing any collateral constitutional issues, concluded: "Have I said even part of an earful, O, King?" Frankfurter's reply reassured Roberts that he had written Jackson praising his concurrence as the "fullest illumination of what we already knew" yet expressing the "deepest hope" that there would be only one opinion. In a final note, Jackson confirmed that he would not write separately but expected more revisions and negotiations to come: "A new strategy of avoiding the issue—which you say isn't there—is in the making. The chief will be asked to back down."

Stone made revisions to satisfy Jackson and Roberts and on October 29 released the Court's unanimous opinion in the saboteurs' case. The opinion argued that the bar for interfering with the president's power "in time of war and of grave public danger" was high—such power was "not to be set aside by the courts without the clear conviction that they are in conflict with the Constitution or laws of Congress constitutionally enacted." The 1866 case of *Ex Parte Milligan* did not apply because Milligan was not part of "the armed forces of the enemy" and therefore was "not subject to the law of war." And the president did not violate the Articles of War, the opinion argued, by creating a special military commission that relied on a different set of procedures. The opinion acknowledged that some of the justices believed that Congress did not intend for the Articles of War to limit the president's power to try "admitted enemy invaders" by a military commission; "others" believed that the Articles of War did not "foreclose" the special commission's unusual procedure of final review only by the president and no review by the Judge Advocate General.

To friends and colleagues, Frankfurter revealed that he was not satisfied that the Court had gotten it right. On October 29, he wrote Black confessing "an incurable faith in reason and in exchanging views as a means of attaining reason." He thought that he and Black had agreed about the "applicability" of the Articles of War to the case, but was not sure. So "now the shooting

is all over in the *Saboteur* cases," he sent Black a copy of the memorandum
he had sent to Stone after the chief justice's circulation of Memorandum B.
"Someday when you feel like it and have time," Frankfurter wrote, "tell me
wherein you disagree in what I said in that memorandum." He also asked
former student Frederick Bernays Wiener, author of the leading treatise on
military law, for his views on the Court's decision. On November 5, Wiener
replied that "the opinion reflects a good deal of confusion as to the proper
scope of the Articles of War as they related to military commissions" because
the president's military commission "disregarded almost every precedent in
the books." He also concluded that "the president's power to prescribe rules of
procedure" did not allow him to prevent review by the judge advocate general
or the attorney general. Nor was the commander-in-chief power "sufficient
to justify" what in Wiener's view "was palpably illegal." The Court, however,
did the right thing in denying the request for writ of habeas corpus—in part
because the saboteurs "were lawfully in custody" and because they failed to
raise the issue of the lack of review by the judge advocate general. And even
with the proper procedures and review, Wiener argued the outcome would
have been the same.

From the beginning, Frankfurter had been uncomfortable with the Court's
rush to judgment in the Nazi saboteurs' case, *Ex Parte Quirin*—its review
before the trial had been completed, before the federal court of appeals had
ruled on the denial of habeas corpus, and without access to the trial record.
Most important, he knew the Court had blundered in issuing a short opinion that allowed the trial to continue, then a longer decision months after
six of the eight spies had been executed. Eleven years later, the Court made
the same rush to judgment and delayed writing a full opinion in another
high-profile capital case fraught with national security implications, the allegations of atomic spying by Julius and Ethel Rosenberg. The *Rosenberg* case
prompted Frankfurter to remark that the experience in *Quirin* was "not a
happy precedent."

IN 1942, Frankfurter got his wish in the Nazi saboteurs' case, with help from
his "soliloquy" and months of working with his colleagues—a unanimous
opinion. The case, however, also revealed how much the Court had changed.
Stone lacked Hughes's ability to command the justices' conferences. The
Court's newer justices were too smart, too opinionated, and too independent
for any chief justice to control. *Quirin* also revealed that, notwithstanding

Gobitis, Bridges, and *Jones v. Opelika,* Frankfurter had not lost his ability to build coalitions on the Court given his close relationships with Stone, Roberts, and Jackson, as well as his intellectual respect for Black. The overly simplistic narrative that Frankfurter was a judicial failure who had alienated all his colleagues achieved its power by fast-forwarding from *Gobitis* to the next flag salute case and eliding his intervening accomplishments. Yet his conflicts of interest; closeness to Roosevelt, Stimson, and other executive branch officials; and overheated patriotism created problems for Frankfurter going forward.

Nothing was the same for Frankfurter after Pearl Harbor. His patriotism was in overdrive, his loyalty to the Roosevelt administration compromised his judgment, and the sacrifices of young people groomed for public service deeply moved him. "F. F.'s Soliloquy" in *Quirin* alluded to former students fighting for their country. After Pearl Harbor, many former clerks and students enlisted. The day after the attack, Rauh and Graham were laughed out of the Army Air Corps recruitment office: one was married with children; the other wore glasses. Frankfurter assisted an impatient Rauh in leaving the Lend-Lease Administration in April 1942 to join General MacArthur's staff in the South Pacific. Fisher relinquished his State Department post to become a lieutenant in the Army Air Forces. Graham resigned from the Lend-Lease Administration in July 1942 to join the Army Air Forces and became an army intelligence officer. The nearly 300-pound Prich was drafted into the army ("They have scraped the bottom of the manpower barrel," he quipped, "—now they've taken the barrel"), received a medical discharge after a few months, and returned to his White House job in the Office of Economic Stabilization.

On Thanksgiving Day 1942, Frankfurter hosted "a houseful of young lads," including former student and Hockley House resident William DuBose Sheldon. The son of a rear admiral who was assistant surgeon general, Sheldon published his Princeton thesis as a book about southern populism and was a year ahead of his friend Prichard in college and law school. Before the war, he was one of "the most beloved" Hockley residents and worked at Covington & Burling. At the firm, he was the custodian of the justice's life insurance policies. In the navy, Sheldon was a lieutenant flying planes in the Solomon Islands. One of his letters was so moving that Frankfurter sent it to Roosevelt and asked the president to speak to the troops on December 8, 1942, the day after the silence observed during the first anniversary of Pearl Harbor. On March 10, 1943, Bill Sheldon died at age twenty-nine. Felix and Marion attended his funeral at Arlington National Cemetery. In a tribute published by the *Washington Post* and the *Evening Star,* Frankfurter described him as "a leader of men" who earned the nickname "Uncle Bill" for his quiet, moral

authority. Frankfurter wrote that Sheldon had "died . . . from illness at Gua-
dalcanal and at other South Pacific engagements." In reality, however, Sheldon, suffering from shell shock and deemed unfit to fly, had shot and killed
himself at a naval base in El Cerrito, California. His former professor apologized for anything "exaggerated or false" in the tribute and asked "Bill's pardon": "There is no swifter way to bury the dead. And Bill is some one to think
back upon, to measure one's self by, to cherish in death as in life."

CHAPTER 25

A Great Enemy
of Liberalism

During the fall and winter of 1942, Frankfurter made a final attempt to prevent Black, Douglas, and Murphy from dominating the Court. Against his own self-interest, he had encouraged his "most congenial pal," Jimmy Byrnes, to leave the Court as he decided to join Roosevelt's wartime administration. Byrnes resigned from the Court on October 3 after only fifteen months to serve as the director of the Office of Economic Stabilization and in effect as Roosevelt's "assistant president." Frankfurter wrote Roosevelt that Byrnes's departure marked "the first time in my life something very good for my country is very bad for me!"

Desperate for a colleague who would not join the Black-Douglas-Murphy bloc, Frankfurter lobbied Roosevelt to nominate the best judge not on the Supreme Court—Learned Hand. Appointed by President Taft to a judgeship on the Southern District of New York in Manhattan in 1909, Billings Learned Hand had been serving on the federal bench longer than any judge except one. During the 1912 presidential election, he supported Theodore Roosevelt's third-party candidacy, joined Frankfurter and his pro-TR crowd at the House of Truth, and two years later helped Herbert Croly found the *New Republic*. In 1914, Hand stayed on the federal district bench while running as the failed Progressive Party candidate for a seat on the New York Court of Appeals. His groundbreaking free speech opinion in the 1917 *Masses* case held that the postmaster general had violated the First Amendment by revoking the second-class mailing privileges of an antiwar publication. Though the federal court of appeals reversed it, his *Masses* opinion put him on the vanguard of wartime protection of civil liberties. He debated the judiciary's role in protecting free speech with Holmes during a chance 1919 meeting on a train, and they continued their exchange by mail. During Wilson's second term, Hand was repeatedly passed over for vacancies on the Court of Appeals for the Second Circuit. At the insistence of then–Attorney General Harlan Fiske Stone, Coolidge finally promoted him to the Second Circuit in 1924. As a federal court of appeals judge, Hand rivaled Holmes and Cardozo as the nation's finest judicial stylist. With Frankfurter, he shared a deep admiration for Holmes, a belief in limited judicial intervention, and a lively correspondence.

After Holmes's retirement in 1932, Frankfurter initially promoted Hand for the Supreme Court. Stimson, who was Hoover's secretary of state, asked for Frankfurter's views on Holmes's successor. Frankfurter suggested Cardozo and Hand. "Not L. Hand," Stimson replied, probably because of Hand's Progressive Party past. With Stimson as his primary conduit to Hoover, Frankfurter successfully lobbied for Cardozo, not Hand, to succeed Holmes.

Ten years later, Frankfurter desperately needed Hand on the Court as an intellectual ally. The Court was stacked with senators (Black), administration officials (Reed, Douglas, Murphy, Jackson), law professors (Stone, Frankfurter, Douglas), and private lawyers (Jackson, Roberts, Stone), but no federal judges. Frankfurter, as well as Reed, believed the Court lacked "legal learning and experience, more particularly in the domain of federal law" and that Hand was the "outstanding judicial figure in the country off the Supreme Court—and in my judgment a more distinguished mind than any man on the Court." This time, Frankfurter directly lobbied the president. During the next three months, he spoke with Roosevelt about Hand five or six times in person or by phone and wrote numerous letters. It turned out to be Roosevelt's eighth and final Supreme Court nomination.

Initially, Frankfurter argued that Hand's presence on the Court dominated by New Deal Democrats would add another Republican and would win Roosevelt more bipartisan support. On September 30, he wrote Roosevelt about "a chance to do something for Court and Country comparable to what you did when you made Stone the Chief Justice." More than a month later, Frankfurter continued to promote Hand as the best choice "on the score of politics." He argued that Hand was "the only lad who will create no headaches for you—or, if you will, break no eggs." Frankfurter predicted that Hand was "*the* one choice who will arouse universal acclaim in the press" and would not lead to questions about why he had been chosen. "Every other person," he predicted, "would divide feeling and opinion."

The political fallout from the court-packing fight dominated Roosevelt's thinking about Supreme Court nominees. In introducing the plan, Roosevelt had proposed adding a justice for every one over seventy years old on the basis of the disingenuous argument that the justices were too old to keep up with their work. Hand was seventy years old. Age, Frankfurter knew, was a sticking point, but he believed that it could be overcome the way Roosevelt had dismissed geographic concerns in nominating Frankfurter. In a postscript to a November 3 letter, Frankfurter observed that Roosevelt's decision to serve a third term, his appointment of 79-year-old Admiral William D. Leahy as chief of staff to the commander in chief on July 24, and the departure of Byrnes from the Court after only fifteen months were "all more extraordinary than the Hand business."

During one of several early November meetings, Frankfurter learned that Roosevelt had a young federal court of appeals judge in mind—48-year-old Wiley Blount Rutledge. Thanks to the efforts of *St. Louis Star-Times* editorial writer and administration insider Irving Brant, Rutledge had emerged as Roosevelt's first choice from the Midwest in 1939 when the president had nominated Frankfurter to replace Cardozo. Ten days before his own nomination and at Roosevelt's request, Frankfurter had conveyed that the University of Iowa law dean was highly regarded by legal luminaries including Lloyd Garrison and Thomas Reed Powell. Indeed, if Roosevelt had not chosen Frankfurter in January 1939, he would have nominated Rutledge. A few months later, Rutledge was again the runner-up, this time for Brandeis's seat filled by Douglas. As a consolation prize, Roosevelt nominated Rutledge for a seat on the Court of Appeals for the District of Columbia. By fall 1942, based on his small body of work as a judge, Rutledge was another sure liberal vote for Black, Douglas, and Murphy to overturn Frankfurter's flag salute opinion. In a lengthy dissent, Rutledge had argued that the convictions of Jehovah's Witnesses for failing to pay a license tax for selling literature on the street violated their freedom of religion and press. He lamented that during the war "Jehovah's Witnesses have had to choose between their consciences and public education for their children." The stakes for Frankfurter and the future of the Court could not have been higher. Yet, as a result of his endorsement of Rutledge in 1939, Frankfurter could not criticize him or compare him to Hand.

Fortunately for Frankfurter, eminent New York admiralty lawyer C. C. Burlingham joined the Hand campaign. A frequent correspondent with the president and chief justice, the 84-year-old Burlingham informed them that Hand's nomination would be universally acclaimed like Cardozo's. Frankfurter believed that Stone secretly preferred Rutledge as another vote to reverse the flag salute decision. Attorney General Biddle told the president that Stone favored Rutledge. As the months wore on, Biddle noticed that Roosevelt had cooled on Hand. "The longer F.D. delays the less chance," Burlingham wrote Frankfurter on November 20. After the cabinet meeting that day, Roosevelt discussed the Supreme Court vacancy with Biddle for half an hour and asked him "to prepare the papers" for Rutledge. "He still spoke of the possibility of Hand's appointment," Biddle wrote in his diary, "but agreed that he was too old."

Refusing to give up, Frankfurter took a final shot at persuading Roosevelt to nominate Hand on the basis of the "best man" argument he had made about Cardozo. Holmes, Brandeis, and Cardozo, Frankfurter wrote the president on December 3, were the "only truly great judges here since the Civil War." And Hand was "the only man worthy to rank with Holmes, Brandeis, and Cardozo. Were you to name Learned Hand, five minutes after the news flashed to the country all considerations of age, geography and the like will be seen to have had no relevance. If only for a few years, Hand could not but bring distinction to the Court and new lustre to the President who made it possible." Frankfurter enclosed a three-paragraph announcement of Hand as Roosevelt's nominee. In a December 4 letter labeled "private," Roosevelt replied: "Sometimes a fellow gets estopped by his own words and his own deeds—and it is no fun for the fellow himself when that happens."

While sitting on the bench on January 11, 1943, Frankfurter learned from Frank Murphy that Roosevelt had submitted Rutledge's name to the Senate. Hand, ever gracious, thanked Frankfurter: "I shall never forget the warmth and persistence with which you pressed me for the place, long after it was in the least probable that I could be appointed." Hand suspected he would have been unhappy on the Court: "Except for you and Roberts—and possibly in the end Jackson—I doubt if I should have formed any real ties, etc., etc." Frankfurter responded that "your regret at your not coming here is probably considerably less than mine." He confessed that "one of the real ambitions of my own public concerns for now 25 years has been the yearning to see you on this Court" and knew that he would miss "the pure joy" of having Hand as a colleague. To former clerk Louis Henkin, Hand confided: "Felix raised Heaven and Earth to try to get F.D.R. to put me in Byrnes's place, but F.D.R. had too much sense to do it, and while I should have been ass enough to accept, I am really greatly his debtor that he didn't. It would not be a pleasant place now with all the discords going on and I a man of peace."

To Burlingham, Hand revealed complicated feelings about Frankfurter: "I don't believe a word of what F. F. says about what F.D.R would have done; he wants to believe it. He doesn't like Biddle much now, and he is getting a little out with the New Hampshire Farmer [Stone]. I am sorry; he has great possibilities where he is, and he is somewhat—indeed a good deal—injuring them by talking too much, and misbehaving on the bench. I wish he wouldn't; especially, as the New Dealers are now running out on him, and he will never be quite 'kosher' with the other group. I am too fond of him to want him to fall between two shoals; besides, as I said, he is really the best."

Frankfurter's enemies claimed that he had "pressured" Roosevelt and therefore had cost Hand a Supreme Court seat. It seems odd that Roosevelt resented Frankfurter and Burlingham's efforts in 1942 but not the intense campaigns for Frankfurter in 1938 and 1939, Douglas in early 1939, or Charles Wyzanski in 1941 for his federal judgeship in Boston. What doomed Hand's nomination was the same thing that had nearly scuttled Frankfurter's—Roosevelt's bogus rationale for the court-packing plan. Frankfurter considered the emphasis on aging justices "the most foolish part of the whole Court fight" because "the most liberal judges on the Court had been Holmes, although ninety, and Brandeis, although past eighty." Frankfurter acknowledged that Roosevelt, if he had nominated Hand, would have been subjected to criticism and the press "might have poked a little fun at him," but "the acclaim that would have greeted Learned Hand's appointment would have drowned the fun-poking. In any event, to have a man of Learned Hand's stature on the Court would have been worth the price of a little fun."

In early 1943, Roosevelt lacked a sense of urgency to remake the Court. His New Deal programs had never been more constitutionally secure. A few months earlier, the Court had unanimously upheld the Agricultural Adjustment Act's limits on an Ohio farmer's production of wheat in one of the broadest interpretations of Congress's power to regulate interstate commerce. From the president's perspective, the legal stakes of choosing between Hand and Rutledge seemed low; from Frankfurter's perspective, however, they were quite high.

―――――

HAND REPRESENTED Frankfurter's last best hope for another justice who believed in limiting judicial power. Without him, Frankfurter knew that he would be on the losing end of conference discussions with Jackson, Roberts, and Reed on one side, Black, Douglas, Murphy, and Rutledge on the other, and Chief Justice Stone stuck in the middle. The Court, in many ways, was destined for trouble. Stone's Saturday conferences dragged on for more than eight hours as he often interrupted other justices if he disagreed with them. During these "contentious" discussions, Frankfurter and the Black-led contingent were at each other's throats. There was a reason why Frankfurter referred to them as "the Axis." Douglas and Murphy refused to join an opinion without checking with Black. As Byrnes remarked to Frankfurter, in the U.S. Senate Black had only one vote out of ninety-six. On the Supreme Court, however, he had three votes out of nine "in all important matters." And with Rutledge soon joining the Court, Black would have a fourth.

The primary target for Frankfurter's ire was Douglas. He was angry that Douglas was using the Court as "a jumping-off place" for a presidential bid. During a January 11 conversation on the bench, he asked Murphy "how many plugged nickels would you give Bill Douglas' chance of becoming President?" Murphy predicted that Douglas would get the Democratic nomination. Frankfurter asked if Murphy was bothered by a presidential candidate sitting on the Court. "Well, I don't like it," Murphy replied. "Well, it's much more than a matter of not liking," Frankfurter told Murphy. "When a priest enters a monastery, he must leave—or ought to leave—all sorts of worldly desires behind him. And this Court has no excuse for being unless it's a monastery. . . . We are all poor human creatures and it's difficult enough to be wholly intellectually and morally disinterested when one has no other motive except that of being a judge according to one's full conscience."

Proof for Frankfurter was Douglas's response to the federal tax evasion conviction of Atlantic City political boss Enoch "Nucky" Johnson. The issue was whether the trial judge had committed error by allowing the prosecutor to comment on Johnson's claim of a partial privilege against self-incrimination on his 1938 tax returns out of fear of future prosecution (he was only on trial for his returns from 1935 to 1937). At trial, Johnson's counsel had withdrawn his objection to the comments. At conference three days after the January 15 oral argument, Frankfurter derided some of his colleagues' "quest for error" and suggestions that the conviction should be reversed. The majority opinion was assigned to Douglas. He was troubled by the case, but, after discussing it on February 2 with Frankfurter, agreed that the error was too "fine" a point to warrant reversal. The next day, Black suggested that Douglas wanted the case reassigned because he was troubled about writing an opinion affirming the conviction of a Republican Party boss (Johnson) after writing one on January 4 reversing the contempt conviction of a Democratic Party boss (Tom Pendergast of Kansas City). Frankfurter was outraged that outside considerations and political party affiliations had entered into the Court's decision making—in this case how it would affect Douglas's political prospects. After Black and Douglas backed off about reassigning the case, Douglas insisted on writing in the opinion that the error had been waived. Frankfurter wrote a concurrence that the judge had conducted the trial "with conspicuous fairness," had shown Johnson leniency by allowing him to testify and to claim a partial self-incrimination privilege, and that Johnson's lawyer had withdrawn any objections. Other justices, Roberts and Stone (on behalf of Black and Douglas), asked him to withdraw the concurrence; Frankfurter refused. On February 15, the Court affirmed Johnson's conviction with Frankfurter's concurrence intact. That same day, Rutledge took his seat on the Court.

Ignoring his hypocrisy, Frankfurter somehow distinguished his extrajudicial activities from Douglas's presidential aspirations. In Frankfurter's mind, the difference was that Douglas's potential candidacy affected his votes on cases and how he wrote opinions. Frankfurter's activities affected him in other ways. His diary from the first half of 1943 offers a snapshot of the administration officials, foreign dignitaries, journalists, and former students who stopped by his chambers to discuss some government agency, wartime policy, or problem overseas. After work, he dined nightly with foreign and domestic political players including French diplomat Jean Monnet, Secretary of War Stimson, Assistant Secretary McCloy, Assistant Secretary of State Dean Acheson, and Librarian of Congress Archibald MacLeish. Presidential speechwriters Sam Rosenman and Robert Sherwood often showed up at his house at 10:00 p.m., and they talked into the night. Frankfurter was a social animal who liked to see his friends in the administration and foreign governments and never saw this as a conflict of interest or as limiting his effectiveness as a justice.

Yet Frankfurter's active social life and yen for policy making forced him to sacrifice judicial craftsmanship and prevented him from emulating his heroes Holmes and Brandeis in writing opinions. During his early years on the Court, he dictated his opinions as Prichard and other law clerks typed and challenged him about various points. Frankfurter continued this practice but also delegated some of the drafting to his workhorse of a law clerk, Phil Elman. Yet Elman was often busy entertaining people waiting to see Frankfurter in chambers. It was no wonder that Frankfurter was behind on his assigned opinions. The issue, however, was bigger than that. Frankfurter failed to follow the example of Holmes, who quickly wrote his opinions in longhand and rarely revised. Douglas adopted this model during his entire career. Nor did Frankfurter follow the example of Brandeis, who wrote his own drafts and then revised many times after sending them to the printer. Jackson, one of the Court's finest writers, adopted Brandeis's model. Instead, Frankfurter dictated a rough outline to his secretary, instructed Elman to draft the opinion, then edited Elman's draft (often only a single time). Or, if he dictated the entire opinion to Elman, the justice often preferred not to read it again. Thus, Frankfurter's opinions were often only as good as his law clerk's editing skills.

Fortunately for Frankfurter, Elman was a strong editor and their collaboration produced some fine opinions. In *Chenery I*, a 1943 decision involving the Securities and Exchange Commission, the Court held, over dissents by Black, Reed, and Murphy, that an administrative agency's ruling can be affirmed only on the grounds in the original agency decision. *Chenery* was a groundbreaking opinion because it wrote a clear-statement rule into administrative law and limited judicial review of administrative agency decisions. But with important war-related issues before the Court that term—a citizenship case, curfew for Japanese Americans on the West Coast, and another Jehovah's Witnesses' flag salute case—Frankfurter's reluctance to revise his opinions hurt his final work product and damaged his legacy.

The nightly dinner parties and dual roles as Supreme Court justice and wartime adviser took a physical toll. Before a February 21 White House luncheon, Roosevelt ushered the Frankfurters into his study and began joking with Marion that her husband could no longer button the bottom of his vest. Tennessee Valley Authority commissioner David Lilienthal remarked how Frankfurter looked "quite gray" with a bald spot. The justice, though grayer and heavier, remained indefatigable. Isaiah Berlin described Marion as "thinner & whiter than ever" and Felix as "a cricket chirping along, talking sense & nonsense, but with brio & spirit & optimism." Marion remarked to one of his law clerks: "do you know what it's like to be married to a man who is never tired?"

Private threats and public criticism could not dampen Frankfurter's zest for life. On February 16, his secretary Lee Watters received a phone call from an FBI agent with a message from J. Edgar Hoover. Given the hostility between Hoover and Frankfurter since Frankfurter's constitutional challenges in 1920 to the Palmer raids (directed by Hoover) and Hoover's secret files on Frankfurter and others who had signed the National Popular Government League report, it was not a social call. A man named George Rukert had tried to enlist an FBI informant in a plot to assassinate Frankfurter. The justice revealed that he had been receiving threatening postcards from Los Angeles and had been ripping them up. The FBI official encouraged him to save any future hate mail. Frankfurter thanked Hoover for the warning yet took no "stock in these threats."

Isolationist critics blamed him and Harry Hopkins for the administration's war policy. On March 15, Senator Robert Taft, a leading Republican isolationist, charged New Dealers with "running the war" and pointed to Frankfurter's influence on key War Department positions. On April 1, Congressman Fred Bradley of Michigan took to the House floor and charged presidential adviser Dave Niles as part of a "radical clique" including Frankfurter, Harold Laski, and James Landis pushing for a Socialist state and a fourth Roosevelt term. The instigator of the congressional rant, Niles learned from Senator Wheeler, was Joseph Kennedy, Sr. Embittered about his dismissal as the U.S. ambassador to Great Britain, Kennedy blamed Frankfurter and Hopkins for his exclusion from the war effort. After Niles came to see him, Frankfurter wrote in his diary: "I don't suppose it ever enters the head of a Joe Kennedy that one who was so hostile to the whole war effort as he was" and "so outspoken in his foul-mouthed hostility to the President himself, barred his own way . . ."

The Court's internecine disputes dampened the spirits of Frankfurter's closest colleagues. "Do you also feel as depressed as I do after these Saturday Conferences?" a "none too happy" Jackson asked Frankfurter. Frankfurter agreed and blamed Black: "every time we have that which should be merely an intellectual difference gets into a championship by Black of justice and right and decency and everything and those who take the other view are impliedly always made out to be the oppressors of the people and the supporters of some exploiting interest." Rutledge's participation at conference added to their dismay. After conference on March 6, Reed worried about Rutledge's justice-seeking state of mind and lack of consideration for the consequences of his votes. Frankfurter "expected" that from him: "Rutledge evidently is one of these evangelical lads who confuses his personal desire to do good in the world with the limits within which a wise and humble judge must move."

On May 14, Learned Hand visited Frankfurter's chambers for lunch. "We talked about everything under the sun," Frankfurter wrote in his diary. "He was at his best, perceptive, full of disinterestedness, curiosity, witty, and speculative." Hand believed that the trouble with Stone's opinions of late was that the chief justice no longer had "the guidance" of Holmes, Brandeis, or Cardozo. Frankfurter did not say anything but believed "the matter is much more complicated than he is aware of."

Disillusioned and dispirited, Jackson questioned his future on the Court. Like Douglas, Jackson harbored political ambitions—he had flirted with a bid for the Democratic nomination for governor of New York in 1938 because Roosevelt believed that Jackson could succeed him as president. The Jamestown lawyer had distinguished himself as a first-rate legal mind and Supreme Court advocate during more than five years in the Justice Department capped off as solicitor general and attorney general. By contrast, his two years on the Court were frustrating and demoralizing. Like Frankfurter, Jackson believed that on the Black-led Court, personal politics trumped legal principles. "I have a rather long expectancy of life and I don't know whether I want to spend it in this atmosphere," he told Frankfurter on March 12. "It is an awful thing at this time of the Court's and country's history, with the very difficult and important questions coming before this Court to have one man, Black, practically control three others, for I am afraid Rutledge will join the Axis. But on the other hand, I say to myself it would be rather cowardly to leave the field to them. But I can tell you that it is very sad business for me and it isn't any fun to be writing opinions to show up some of their performances." Frankfurter tried to calm Jackson down and urged him not "to decide this afternoon what you are going to do with your life."

Roberts was similarly downcast. After a long conference on April 17, he told Frankfurter that he went home "tired and dispirited" and after another long conference three days later went home "tired and dispirited again" about "the way we tear up law with indifference to the precedents or the consequences." Roberts was upset by Black and described him as having two additional votes in Douglas and Murphy, possibly a fourth in Rutledge or Jackson and with another vacancy would "have the majority in his pocket." The Court's longest active member, Roberts blamed Stone for not being as "strong at the helm" as Hughes.

Rather than submit to his colleagues' despair, Frankfurter explained his judicial philosophy in a major national address—a speech at the Library of Congress on the 200th anniversary of the April 13 birthday of Thomas Jefferson. On March 20, Frankfurter holed up in a vault at the Library of Congress to read the original 236 folio volumes of Jefferson's Papers. He marveled at the "beautifully mounted" volumes which were "meticulously indexed both chronologically and alphabetically." For months, he immersed himself in Jefferson's political and legal thought.

Before a national radio audience on April 13, Frankfurter delivered his speech, "The Permanence of Jefferson," at the Library of Congress on the same day that Roosevelt dedicated the Jefferson Memorial. Frankfurter's speech praised Jefferson's "democratic faith" and defended him as "no simple-minded believer in the popular will. The popular will can steer a proper course only when sufficiently enlightened to know what is the proper course to steer. . . . Jefferson had faith but it was not founded on naiveté. . . . For he knew that freedom and democracy are unremitting endeavors, not achievements." "The Permanence of Jefferson" captured the enduring ideas in Frankfurter's jurisprudence. Frankfurter advocated Hamilton's belief in a strong federal government but Jefferson's belief in democracy. Neither a lifelong Democrat nor a Republican, Frankfurter was a small "d" democrat. He believed that the democratic political process and enlightened public opinion advanced societal interests and protected individual liberties. By contrast, he distrusted courts as historically reactionary institutions that thwarted the popular will and social change. He shared Jefferson's democratic faith.

Frankfurter's democratic faith knew no bounds given that America was fighting a war to save civilization from the totalitarian regimes of Germany, Japan, and Italy. From January 14 to 24, Roosevelt and Churchill had met at the Anfa Hotel in Casablanca, Morocco, to plan the Allies' strategy for the coming year (Stalin could not attend because of the Russian military campaign against the Germans on the Eastern Front). They tried to get the leaders of the two rival French governments, General de Gaulle and General Giraud, to cooperate. And they agreed not to accept anything from Germany and other Axis powers except unconditional surrender.

At noon on May 19, Frankfurter and other members of the Court walked across the street to hear Churchill address the U.S. Congress. A week later at a White House dinner for the president of Liberia, Roosevelt and Frankfurter discussed the president's conversations with Churchill in Casablanca. Roosevelt sensed a change in Churchill, who "no longer says what he used to say, that all he wants is a big victory and he'll quit." Frankfurter said that Churchill seemed like an old man. Roosevelt, perhaps providing a window into his own health but also into Churchill's youthfulness, replied, "I have a feeling when I am with Winston that I am twenty years older than he is." The next day, Frankfurter met with Zionist leader Chaim Weizmann and Assistant Secretary of State Sumner Welles about the obstacles—anti-Semites in the State Department, the timidity of the British government, and Arab resistance—to creating a Jewish state in Palestine.

In late June or early July, Frankfurter heard firsthand about the Nazi extermination of Polish Jews. As a Polish diplomat and reserve army officer, Jan Karski had been tortured by the Gestapo, had entered the Warsaw ghetto twice in October 1942, and, disguised in an Estonian army uniform, had visited a death camp. Keeping a promise to a member of Poland's Jewish underground, Karski informed leaders throughout Europe and the United States about the horrors he had seen. In Washington, Karski, accompanied by Polish ambassador Jan Ciechanowski, briefed Frankfurter. The justice's reaction, according to Karski's vivid account years later, was disbelief. "I do not believe you," Frankfurter said according to Karski. Ciechanowski interrupted: "Felix, what are you talking about?" Frankfurter, according to Karski, replied: "Mr. Ambassador, I did not say that he is lying; I said that I don't believe him. These are different things. My mind and my heart are made in such a way that I cannot accept it. No. No. No." The justice did not want to believe that the Nazis were capable of slaughtering Jews like cattle. Karski's account, however, would not have come as a complete shock. After World War I, Frankfurter had journeyed to Poland, had seen the persecution and starvation of Polish Jews, and had urged the Wilson administration to intervene. Since 1933, he had been helping European Jewish academics escape to American universities. In March 1938, he had engineered his uncle's release from a Vienna prison. Six months later, he had read a British white paper about vicious Nazi beatings of Jewish prisoners. In late October 1939, the press had reported on the concentration camps and that 1.5 million Polish Jews faced extinction. And in December 1942, the Polish Ministry of Foreign Affairs published a report, "The Mass Extermination of Jews in German Occupied Poland." What Karski told Frankfurter six to seven months later about the Nazi death camps would have been horrifying yet consistent with the Polish ministry's report. After he saw Frankfurter, Karski met with Roosevelt on July 28 for an hour and twenty minutes and concluded by informing him about the extermination of Polish Jews. To Karski's amazement, Roosevelt did not ask a single question. "When I left, the President was still smiling and fresh," Karski said. "I felt fatigued."

In August 1943, the Washington *Evening Star* identified Frankfurter as a member of Roosevelt's inner circle and referred to him as the president's "idea man." He often wrote Roosevelt and socialized with him, usually over cocktails during late afternoon sessions not recorded on White House logs. After an October 19 tea for the justices and other Court personnel in the Red Room of the White House, Frankfurter wrote Roosevelt about the justices' "unanimous decision—on the grand form you were in yesterday. A very good time was had by all—even on tea!"

Frankfurter's foreign policy efforts continued. On November 6, he hosted a Sunday dinner for French diplomat Jean Monnet to celebrate his return from North Africa. Monnet told the guests—Stimson, Under Secretary of State Edward R. Stettinius, Rosenman, Dean Acheson, and McCloy (who joined them after dinner)—"what France needed." Stimson replied the administration needed "brains," not "the New Deal youngsters that the President was appointing on many of these things." Frankfurter served as a conduit between Roosevelt and the young New Dealers and Stimson, McCloy, and other members of the War Department. The justice often phoned McCloy or met him for breakfast or lunch. He usually saw Stimson in the evenings, cheering him up on the second anniversary of Pearl Harbor and providing a healthy dose of optimism about the war to his stoic yet tense former boss.

FRANKFURTER'S RELATIONSHIPS with Roosevelt, Stimson, and McCloy compromised his legal judgment, intensified his patriotism, and consumed much of his attention. He failed to recognize that his friends in the War Department—Stimson, Patterson, and McCloy—were capable of violating the constitutional rights of Japanese Americans on the West Coast. On February 19, 1942, three months after Pearl Harbor, President Roosevelt had signed Executive Order 9066 authorizing military officials to exclude people of Japanese ancestry from the West Coast. The next day, Stimson and McCloy worked on the draft of directions for General John L. DeWitt about "the steps which we think might be taken." With assistance from McCloy, DeWitt established exclusion areas in the western part of California, Oregon, and Washington; evacuated about 120,000 Japanese Americans from their homes; and imprisoned them in internment camps. In passing along to McCloy criticism of the exclusion order, Frankfurter encouraged the department's efforts. Several Japanese Americans challenged the military order before the Supreme Court.

The case of University of Washington student Gordon K. Hirabayashi reached the Court first. Choosing to stay with Quakers on campus, he was convicted of violating the curfew and relocation order. On May 10 and 11, 1943, the Court heard argument about whether the president had the power to issue the orders and whether they discriminated against Japanese Americans. Hirabayashi's lawyers argued that Roosevelt had unlawfully delegated power to the military with not enough specificity. "Then the issue of citizenship is not important," Frankfurter said. "Not so far as to this phase of the case is concerned," counsel Harold Evans replied, "but the discrimination against American citizens of Japanese ancestry will be seen when we discuss the proclamations themselves." Evans did not disagree with Jackson's contention that the president, as commander in chief, could anticipate possible attacks, but that "military control over civilians" required congressional legislation spelling out definite standards. Frankfurter conceded that much of the Court's decision in *Ex Parte Milligan* about military tribunals "will not stand scrutiny in 1943."

At conference on May 15, the justices agreed with Stone that the order was within the president's war powers and with Black and Frankfurter that the opinion should narrowly focus on the curfew measures. The consensus nearly unraveled because of Douglas's political instincts and Murphy's uncertainty. Douglas circulated a concurrence that took no legal issue with the majority opinion but held out hope that Hirabayashi might be afforded administrative remedies. Murphy declared it "[t]he most shocking thing that has ever been written by a member of this Court" and "a regular soap-box speech." Yet Murphy was no more comfortable with the broad conception of the president's war powers in Stone's majority opinion and described it as aimed at the American Legion. "Well," Frankfurter replied, "if the Chief's was addressed to the American Legion, Bill's was addressed to the mob." During a two-hour talk with Frankfurter, Black argued military matters were unreviewable by the Court and feared that Douglas's concurrence would lead to "a thousand" habeas corpus petitions. Jackson described Douglas's opinion as a "hoax" because "it promised something that could not be fulfilled." Roberts and Frankfurter wanted the Court to speak in one voice as it did in the Nazi saboteurs' case. The next day, Frankfurter learned from Stone that Douglas had made "impossible" demands for changes to the majority opinion in order to join it and withdraw his concurrence.

At conference on June 5, Frankfurter passed notes to Murphy trying to talk him out of publishing a dissent in *Hirabayashi* objecting to the military order as discrimination on the basis of "ancestry." He asked whether Murphy was writing his two Indian law cases "on the assumption that rights depend on 'ancestry'? If so—I cannot give my imprimatur to such racial discrimination!" Murphy answered: "I would protect rights on the basis of ancestry— But I would never deny them." Frankfurter replied: "That's not good enough for me. I don't want any of my fellow-citizens to be treated as objects of favor i.e. as inferiors!" A few days later, Frankfurter encouraged Murphy to ask Stone to make changes to the majority opinion rather than jeopardize "the great reputation of the Court." Much to Frankfurter's relief, Murphy published his dissent as a concurrence. Murphy's opinion raised important concerns that this was "the first time" the personal liberty of citizens had been abridged "based upon the accident of race or ancestry," compared it to the treatment of Jews in Germany and the rest of Europe, and warned that the government had created "two classes of citizens . . . on the basis of ancestry." Frankfurter had no such qualms. "For the life of me," he wrote to Stone in joining his opinion, "I cannot see why this should not satisfy every one. It will—all who are guided by reason."

Frankfurter's intense patriotism and the Court's internal discord collided in a case involving the secretary of the California Communist Party, William Schneiderman. A Russian immigrant who had arrived in this country at age two, Schneiderman joined the party at age sixteen and became a naturalized U.S. citizen five years later. He ran for governor of Minnesota at age twenty-four on the Communist Party ticket, visited Russia in 1935, and was a follower of Stalin. A federal judge revoked Schneiderman's citizenship as fraudulently obtained because he had lied about his political affiliation with the Communist Party—which advocated the overthrow of the U.S. government in direct contrast to his oath as a naturalized citizen to uphold the Constitution. The trial judge's decision was affirmed on appeal.

At the request of Schneiderman's counsel, the Court delayed the case during the spring of 1942 because the United States and Russia had become allies against Germany and the case might jeopardize the war effort. The case was originally argued on November 9, 1942, before a seven-member Court (Byrnes had resigned and Jackson had recused himself as a former attorney general) and with 1940 Republican presidential nominee Wendell Willkie representing Schneiderman.

At conference on December 5, 1942, Frankfurter launched into an impassioned speech, the kind that annoyed his colleagues to no end. As the only naturalized citizen on the Court, he acknowledged that "this case arouses in me feelings that could not be entertained by anyone else around this table. It is well known that a convert is more serious than one born to the faith. None of you has had the experience that I have had with reference to American citizenship." He remembered his joy in college when his father became naturalized and his experience as an assistant U.S. attorney in naturalization proceedings. He acknowledged his overriding patriotism: "As one who has no ties with any formal religion, perhaps the feelings that underlie religious forms for me run into intensification of my feelings about American citizenship." After reading a letter by another naturalized citizen, Italian historian Gaetano Salvemini, Frankfurter argued that "American citizenship implies entering upon a fellowship which binds people together by devotion to certain feelings and ideas and ideals summarized as a requirement that they be attached to the principles of the Constitution." The only question about the case was whether there was enough evidence to overturn the findings of a federal judge that Schneiderman was not "attached to the principles of the Constitution" as required by law. He did not argue that every Communist Party member was not attached to the Constitution. But, in this case, he saw no grounds for reversal. Frankfurter's speech did not win any votes. Two of the justices who had spoken before him, Stone and Roberts, voted to affirm. But Black, Reed, Douglas, and Murphy voted to reverse. The Court, however, was unwilling to reverse on only four votes. A week later, they agreed to reargue the case later in the term so the new justice could join them.

Few newspapers covered the March 23, 1943, reargument, and the ones that did wrote only about Willkie's performance and new justice Rutledge's

frequent questions. They missed a verbal showdown, captured in Frankfurter's diary, between Frankfurter and Black. "Is there anything more than his
agreement to general political talk?" Black asked Solicitor General Charles
Fahy. "Is it suggested that the Communist Party has no principles?" Frankfurter interrupted. Black, "with blazing eyes and ferocity in voice," shot back:
"The Hearst Press will love that question." Frankfurter, who was still smart-
ing about Douglas's comment in the fall of 1940 that Black had changed his
mind about the flag salute case after reading the newspapers, responded: "I
don't give a damn whether the Hearst press or any other press likes or dislikes
any question that seems to me relevant to the argument. I am a judge and not
a politician." To which, Black replied: "Of course, you, unlike the rest of us,
live in the stratosphere."

At conference, Black had the upper hand. If Learned Hand had been nominated, the Court likely would have been divided 4–4 and the lower court
opinion would have been allowed to stand. Instead, with Rutledge joining
Douglas, Murphy, and Reed, Black had five votes to stop the revocation of
Schneiderman's citizenship and assigned the majority opinion to a former
attorney general and the justice most on the fence, Murphy. Stone agreed to
write on behalf of the three dissenters.

In Frankfurter's mind, Murphy and Douglas were to blame for the outcome and bad feelings. On May 31, Frankfurter wrote in his diary that Murphy's majority opinion "reflects cunning and disregard of legal principles to
which Hugo Black gave expression from time to time in connection with this
case. It is one of those extraordinarily shortsighted opinions which, to accomplish an immediate end, is quite oblivious of its implication for the future."
Roberts was "deeply disheartened" by it. The next day, Murphy confessed that
his own opinion "skates on the thinnest possible ice—awfully thin"; Roberts
suspected that Black may have written most of it. On June 15, Douglas circulated a concurrence just before he left for the West, leaving Murphy little
time to adjust his majority opinion before the end of the term. Murphy was
"shocked by such behavior" and "skullduggery." Frankfurter and Murphy
believed that Douglas's concurrence was motivated by his desire to restore
Schneiderman's citizenship yet maintain his anti-Communist bona fides so
that he could run for president in 1944. The next day, Frankfurter tried to
persuade Murphy to abandon his majority opinion and create a 4–4 tie—
which would have preserved the lower court opinions revoking Schneiderman's citizenship. Murphy, however, said "it was too late." On June 20, the
Court announced Murphy's majority opinion restoring Schneiderman's citizenship. Frankfurter contributed ideas to Stone's dissent and concluded: "If

Law were only half-Reason in this case, the majority opinion could not survive your dissent."

The biggest case of the term for Frankfurter—and the one that epitomized his democratic faith—was the second Jehovah's Witnesses flag salute case. It was only a matter of time before his majority opinion in *Gobitis* was reversed. With Rutledge on their side, the Black-led liberals had shown little regard for precedent in Jehovah's Witnesses cases earlier in the term. Rutledge provided a fifth vote for invalidating license taxes for selling literature door to door, reversing the Court's decision the previous term in *Jones v. Opelika*. Stone confided that he was "very sorry" to join and "ashamed" of Douglas's "inexcusable" majority opinions because they "did not properly formulate or discuss the issues." In dissent, Frankfurter argued that a tax cannot be invalidated "merely because it falls upon persons engaged in activities of a religious nature" and that exempting religious organizations from taxes of general applicability jeopardized the separation between church and state. He also dissented from another 5–4 decision overturning a city ordinance outlawing door-to-door knocking and proselytizing.

The growing opposition to *Gobitis* was unsurprising. The 1940 decision had sparked violence against Jehovah's Witnesses all over the country. Less than a week after the decision, a mob in Kennebunk, Maine, had burned the Witnesses' place of worship to the ground. Inspired by *Gobitis*, many states had passed laws about teaching schoolchildren about American citizenship and respect for the flag. A West Virginia law commanded its schools to provide classes in history, civics, and the U.S. Constitution "for the purposes of teaching, fostering and perpetuating the ideals, principles and spirit of Americanism." On January 9, 1942, the state board of education adopted a resolution that required a stiff-armed flag salute and pledge of allegiance as part of each school day. Unlike in *Gobitis*, where the flag salute in Minersville, Pennsylvania, was merely a local custom, this one was backed by state law and the state board of education.

Walter Barnett (incorrectly spelled "Barnette" by the district court clerk), a pipefitter for the DuPont chemical company and devout Jehovah's Witness, sued the school board on behalf of his two daughters, Marie, eight, and Gathie, nine, both of whom were sent home from school every day for refusing to salute the flag. Each morning, Marie and Gathie returned to school only to be sent home to prevent their father from being arrested because of his daughters' truancy. As Jehovah's Witnesses, the Barnetts believed that saluting the flag was worshipping a false idol. Along with several other families, the Barnetts challenged the state's compulsory flag salute law in federal court.

A three-judge panel heard the Barnetts' case, led by federal court of appeals judge John J. Parker. Parker's Supreme Court nomination had been rejected by the Senate in 1930 and another potential nomination scuttled in 1941 by Frankfurter's unenthusiastic evaluation of his opinions. In writing the lower court's opinion, Parker ordered the board of education to stop enforcing its compulsory flag salute against the plaintiffs and to permit the return of the Barnett daughters to school. The flag salute, Parker wrote, violated their "religious liberty." In a bold move for a lower court judge, Parker declared Frankfurter's majority opinion in Gobitis had been "impaired as an authority" because of the opposition of Stone and three additional dissenting justices in Jones v. Opelika in 1942. For his prediction to come true, Parker needed a fifth vote to reverse Gobitis from one of the Court's newest members, Jackson or Rutledge.

The state of West Virginia appealed Parker's decision directly to the Supreme Court. The ACLU and the ABA Special Committee on the Bill of Rights filed friend of the court briefs in support of the plaintiffs and advocated overruling Gobitis. Four days after the March 11, 1943, oral argument, six justices (Stone, Black, Douglas, Murphy, Jackson, and Rutledge) voted to do just that. The lone dissenter in the 1940 case, Stone could have written the opinion himself but decided to assign it to someone who could retain the most votes. He and his senior law clerk Bennett Boskey ruled out the newest justice, Rutledge, who would have written such a bold opinion that others in the majority may have declined to join it. Instead, Stone assigned the opinion to the Court's second-newest justice and Frankfurter's closest colleague, Jackson.

Having concurred and dissented with Frankfurter in other Jehovah's Witness cases that term, Jackson drew the line at a compulsory flag salute. He believed that the Court should intervene to protect free speech and had made his opposition to Gobitis known. He was the ideal justice to write the majority opinion overruling Gobitis because he was a former attorney general and longtime Justice Department lawyer who could not be charged with disloyalty to his country. And he was an elegant writer who crafted eloquent essays rather than opinions filled with citations and legal jargon.

In Barnette, Jackson described the compulsory flag salute as a violation of free speech, not religion. The First Amendment, he wrote, protected "the individual's right to speak his own mind" and forbade "public authorities to compel him to utter what is not in his mind." He characterized Frankfurter's view in Gobitis that liberty of the individual to speak his mind cannot trump the ability of government to function as an "oversimplification." And he rejected Frankfurter's argument that the policies of public schools should be left to the states and to the democratic political process. "The very purpose of a Bill of Rights," Jackson argued, "was to withdraw certain subjects from the vicissitudes of political controversy, to place them beyond the reach of majorities and officials and to establish them as legal principles to be applied by the courts." Freedom of speech and religion, he continued, "may not be submitted to vote; they depend on the outcome of no elections." Jackson concluded by celebrating the country's "rich cultural diversities" and making speech, thought, and religion free from governmental coercion: "If there is any fixed star in our constitutional constellation, it is that no official, high or petty, can prescribe what shall be orthodox in politics, nationalism, religion, or other matters of opinion or force citizens to confess by word or act their faith therein."

Frankfurter refused to allow his law clerk Phil Elman to prepare a draft dissent and procrastinated so much that Chief Justice Stone started to become anxious about completing the term. On June 2 and 3, Frankfurter worked all day on his *Barnette* dissent. He dictated thoughts to secretary Lee Watters and put them in a drawer. On June 4, Frankfurter apologized to Jackson for the delay in writing "the expression of my credo regarding the function of this Court in invalidating legislation." He stayed home from the office on June 10 to work on it. That night, he invited Elman to dinner. At 9:00 p.m., fortified by food and wine, they retreated to the justice's second-floor study to write the dissent. Frankfurter pulled out his folder of papers and began dictating the opinion to Elman, who sat at the typewriter and made suggestions along the way. They worked until 2:00 a.m. Elman did not go to bed. He took home the "huge stack of pages," edited and "rearranged" it, and the next morning gave the draft to the secretary so that it could be sent to the printer. On June 11, Frankfurter spent the entire day reading and editing the printed version. The next morning, he circulated it to his colleagues.

During their late-night drafting session, Elman and Frankfurter had disagreed about including the dissent's personal opening paragraph: "One who belongs to the most vilified and persecuted minority in history is not likely to be insensible to the freedoms guaranteed by our Constitution. Were my purely personal attitude relevant I should wholeheartedly associate myself with the general libertarian views in the Court's opinion, representing as they do the thought and action of a lifetime. But as judges we are neither Jew nor Gentile, neither Catholic nor agnostic. We owe equal attachment to the Constitution and are equally bound by our judicial obligations whether we derive our citizenship from the earliest or the latest immigrants to these

shores." Elman argued that the reference to Frankfurter's Jewishness undermined his argument about judicial "disinterestedness." But their disagreement ended that night when Frankfurter said: "Phil, I've heard enough. This
is my opinion, not yours." Frankfurter's colleagues agreed with Elman. At
the final conference on June 13, Frankfurter explained to Roberts that he had
been inundated with letters after *Gobitis* telling him that "as a Jew" he "ought
to protect minorities, etc." After Parker's lower court opinion, he received letters insisting that it was Frankfurter's "duty" to rule in favor of the Jehovah's
Witnesses as "a Jew and an immigrant." Frankfurter was determined "to go
on record that in relation to our work on this Court, all considerations of race,
religion, or antecedents of citizenships are wholly irrelevant." Roberts said he
was satisfied by Frankfurter's explanation, but few others were. Frankfurter
believed that Black had put Roberts up to it because of Black's policy of "not
mentioning such things." Yet Frankfurter believed that "to keep all reference
to anti-Semitism or anti-Catholicism hidden is the best kind of cover under
which evil can operate." Just before they announced the *Barnette* opinions
the next day from the bench, Murphy approached Frankfurter "as a friend"
and "for your benefit" and argued that the opening sentences were "too personal." C. C. Burlingham also caught wind of it and advised him to remove
the opening sentences. Frankfurter, however, had been thinking about the
opening lines of his dissent "for months" and wanted to underscore "what I
conceive to be basic to the function of this Court and the duty of the Justices
of this Court."

THE LASTING IMPORT of Frankfurter's dissent in *Barnette* was its deep skepticism about judicial power. His takeaway was that, except in extreme circumstances, the Court should not overrule state or federal laws. Judges, moreover,
should not read their personal views into the Constitution by invoking the
liberty provision of the Fourteenth Amendment's Due Process Clause. Nor
did the underlying free speech issues provide the justices with more right to
intervene than if some other provision of the Bill of Rights were at stake. The
question, for Frankfurter, was not whether he agreed with the West Virginia
law but whether "reasonable legislators" could have enacted a flag salute law
with the goal of promoting "good citizenship." He believed that "judicial self-
restraint" meant that the Court's function was not "comparable to that of a
legislature," and the justices were not "free to act as though we were a super-
legislature." He invoked a Holmes opinion that " 'it must be remembered that

legislatures are ultimate guardians of the liberties and welfare of the people in quite as great a degree as the courts.'" *Barnette* went to the heart of Frankfurter's faith that "responsibility for legislation lies with legislatures, answerable as they are directly to the people, and this Court's only and very narrow function is to determine whether within the broad grant of authority vested in legislatures they have exercised a judgment for which reasonable justification can be offered."

The Court's precedents, Frankfurter argued, also pointed to a different result. Walter Barnett had a choice—send his children to public school to participate in flag salutes and other forms of civic education or enroll his children in a private religious school. Frankfurter invoked *Pierce v. Society of Sisters*, which invalidated an Oregon law requiring children to attend public schools. He also argued that Jackson's opinion had failed to distinguish Cardozo's concurring opinion in *Hamilton v. Regents of the University of California*, which rejected a student's religious objections to a public university's required military science class. Finally, he argued that the Court had considered the flag salute issue on five prior occasions: three times dismissing it as raising no federal question, once dismissing it in a summary opinion, and once in Frankfurter's 8–1 *Gobitis* opinion. He listed the "outstanding judicial leaders" who had joined those opinions including Hughes, Brandeis, and Cardozo, "to mention only those no longer on the Court."

At lunch on Monday, June 14, Stone confessed to Frankfurter that the references to these prior cases and judicial heroes had made the chief justice "writhe" because Stone had not spoken up before *Gobitis*. Stone, however, claimed that Cardozo had voiced concerns during one of the earlier cases. And Black claimed that he had suppressed his negative vote. A few days earlier, Stone's law clerk Boskey had suggested to Elman that the chief justice would request that the references to those past decisions "be changed" because Stone and Cardozo had expressed doubts at prior conferences—contrary to what Stone had confided to Frankfurter at lunch. Roberts remembered "no such protest" by Cardozo or anyone else and that Brandeis had suggested affirming the case "without an opinion." The justices' private docket books reveal that Stone and Brandeis, but not Cardozo, voted to hear one or two of the early cases on the merits.

The outcome also should not have been different in *Barnette*, Frankfurter argued, merely because of the additions of Jackson and Rutledge. The Court, he insisted, should resist the "pressures of the day" and should "take a view of longer range than the period of responsibility entrusted to Congress and legislatures." He observed how the Court looked like a legislature in *Barnette* because "[t]hat which three years ago had seemed to five successive Courts to lie within permissible areas of legislation is now outlawed by the deciding shift of opinion of two Justices."

In a stirring conclusion about the dangers of unchecked judicial power, Frankfurter observed that Jefferson's opposition to judicial review may have been rejected but not his and Lincoln's "admonition against confusion between judicial and political functions." Frankfurter refused to equate "judicial humility" with "an abdication of the judicial function." He reminded his colleagues that *Barnette* was not a case requiring judicial intervention about the division of power between the federal government and the states or the separation of powers among the federal government's legislative, executive, and judicial branches: "We are not discharging the basic function of this Court as the mediator of powers within the federal system. To strike down a law like this is to deny a power to all government." He quoted at length from James Bradley Thayer's essay about Chief Justice John Marshall warning about the judiciary's ability " 'to dwarf the political capacity of the people, and to deaden its sense of moral responsibility.' " And he concluded by distinguishing his personal views about the West Virginia law from his role as a judge: "Of course patriotism can not be enforced by the flag salute. But neither can the liberal spirit be enforced by judicial invalidation of illiberal legislation." He warned against confusing the wisdom of legislation with its constitutionality as "a great enemy of liberalism. Particularly in legislation affecting freedom of thought and freedom of speech much which should offend a free-spirited society is constitutional. Reliance for the most precious interests of civilization, therefore, must be found outside of their vindication in courts of law."

The justices announced their opinions in *Barnette* on June 14, Flag Day. Neither of his dissenting colleagues, Roberts and Reed, joined his dissent because it was so personal—though Reed privately praised the opinion as "perfect" and "its teaching is the real basis of our judicial authority." Liberal publications and commentators pilloried Frankfurter's dissent. His friend and former Harvard law colleague Thomas Reed Powell attacked his dissent in the *New Republic* as "point[ing] strongly in the direction of legislative absolutism." Powell, who apologized for accusing Frankfurter of misstating facts, groused to C. C. Burlingham, "I can't help feeling that many of his votes are determined by the fact that Black votes the other way."

Only a few people's opinions mattered to Frankfurter. On June 15, he sent his *Barnette* dissent to retired Chief Justice Hughes even though he knew that Hughes had received all the circulated opinions. He wrote Hughes that the *Gobitis* assignment three years earlier was "one of the most cherished memories of all my years—all too short—under your leadership." Hughes broke his rule of not commenting on his former colleagues' opinions. He praised Jackson's opinion for stating his side "as cogently as was possible" but believed that Frankfurter had "knocked one of the main props of the decision" by pointing out that *Pierce v. Society of Sisters* outlawed compulsory public education. Once the parents decided to send their children to public schools, Hughes wrote, the state had the "authority" to use its public schools "to provide for instruction and training and to promote good citizenship," including "appreciation of our institutions of which the Flag is a symbol." Hughes rejected the argument that the compulsory flag salute was arbitrary and capricious and therefore violated the Due Process Clause. He surmised that Cardozo, based on his opinion about public universities in *Hamilton v. Regents*; Brandeis, based on his concurrence in prior flag salute decisions; and Holmes, "unless he departed from principles he so stoutly maintained," would have joined Frankfurter's dissent. Hughes's letter and references to Cardozo, Brandeis, and Holmes reaffirmed that Frankfurter had made the right decision and had not changed his constitutional principles one iota.

On June 27, the president hosted the Frankfurters for their annual late afternoon visit before they left Washington for the summer. The previous month Frankfurter had sent Roosevelt some of the term's earlier Jehovah's Witnesses opinions for his presidential library. "They ought to furnish to the future historian food for thought on the scope and meaning of some of the Four Freedoms—their use and their misuse," he wrote the president. During the Frankfurters' 1940 visit to Hyde Park a few months after the *Gobitis* decision, Eleanor had remarked that "there seemed to be something wrong with an opinion that forced little children to salute a flag" contrary to their religious beliefs and "had feared the decision would generate intolerance, especially in a period of rising hysteria." The president had sided with Frankfurter that the law was "'stupid, unnecessary, and offensive' but it fell within the proper limits of their legal power."

A few days after his June 27 White House visit, Frankfurter praised the president for commuting the death sentence of a pro-Nazi Detroit restauranteur, Max Stephan, to life imprisonment. The Court had declined to hear Stephan's case on April 3 and rejected a final appeal on June 1. After reading the record, Frankfurter voted not to hear the case because it raised no constitutional issues. For harboring and arranging transportation for an escaped German prisoner, Stephan had been convicted under the Espionage Act and sentenced to death by hanging. Frankfurter praised the president's "profoundly wise" decision differentiating between "evil deeds that do require the ultimate punishment and those that do not."

Frankfurter's *Barnette* dissent cannot be divorced from his obsession with the war to save civilization, his belief that Roosevelt was the greatest wartime president since Lincoln, and his extensive involvement with wartime policy making. His flag salute opinions revealed his skepticism about judicial power and his boundless democratic faith. It was not hard for Frankfurter to believe that the political process, not the Court, led to more liberal outcomes—especially with Roosevelt in the White House for the past eleven years. Some of the Roosevelt administration's war policies clashed with its commitment to liberalism. And at the state level, the political process failed to stop racial injustice. As a result, Frankfurter began to adapt judicial restraint to protect minority rights.

CHAPTER 26

Race, Redemption, and Roosevelt

A fter a summer in which liberals lambasted his dissent in *West Virginia v. Barnette*, Frankfurter received the perfect opportunity to explain the role of the Supreme Court in American democracy, when the Court should depart from prior decisions, and how the Fourteenth Amendment should be interpreted to protect the rights of African Americans. *Smith v. Allwright* could have transformed his reputation in the eyes of his liberal critics and charted a new course for the Court with regard to race.

Shortly before 4:00 p.m. on November 10, 1943, Thurgood Marshall, the NAACP's special counsel, stood before the justices on behalf of Dr. Lonnie E. Smith, a black Houston dentist who had been denied the right to vote in the Texas Democratic Party's congressional primary because of his race.

The NAACP and its Texas chapters had been fighting the state's exclusion of black voters for years. In 1927, Justice Holmes wrote a unanimous opinion in *Nixon v. Herndon* that Texas had violated the Fourteenth Amendment rights of black El Paso physician L. A. Nixon by excluding him from the state's Democratic primary because of his race and that Nixon had a claim for damages. Texas responded by passing a law that delegated the primary process to the state executive committee of the Democratic Party. Five years later, Nixon returned to the Court because he had again been denied the right to vote in the Democratic primary. In a 5–4 decision in *Nixon v. Condon*, the Court ruled that the state's delegation of power still constituted "state action" in violation of the Equal Protection Clause. In response, the Texas Democratic Party, a private organization, passed its own resolution banning blacks from voting in its primary elections. R. R. Grovey, a black voter denied an absentee ballot by the county clerk, sued for damages. In a unanimous opinion in

Grovey in 1935, Justice Roberts agreed with the Texas courts that the state's Democratic Party primary elections were paid for and run by private officials and not by state officers, and therefore there was no equal protection violation. As a result, southern states dominated by the Democratic Party turned their primary systems over to private organizations and effectively excluded black voters from the political process. The stakes, nine years later in *Smith v. Allwright*, were enormous. "This is conceivably the most important case affecting the Negro which has come before the Supreme Court," NAACP executive secretary Walter White said while waiting for the oral argument to begin.

The NAACP's legal team looked much different than the one that Frankfurter had advised during the 1930s. In 1938, Charles Hamilton Houston, a former student and the first black member of the *Harvard Law Review*, had returned to private practice while continuing to advise the organization. Houston's protégé Marshall had become the NAACP's special counsel and William Hastie, another former student and the second black member of the *Harvard Law Review*, had replaced Houston as chair of the NAACP's National Legal Committee. On January 31, 1943, Hastie had resigned as a civilian aide in the War Department to protest the Army Air Forces' decision to establish a separate training facility for black soldiers. That fall, Hastie resumed his deanship of Howard University Law School and made his first Supreme Court appearance as Marshall's co-counsel.

Marshall and Hastie faced a much different Court in 1943 than their predecessors had eight years earlier. Only two justices, Roberts and Stone, remained from *Grovey v. Townsend*; Roosevelt had named seven new justices and Stone as chief justice. With Stone presiding, Marshall argued that *Grovey* should be overruled in light of the Court's 1941 decision in *United States v. Classic*. In *Classic*, the Court upheld the indictments of Louisiana officials for miscounting and tampering with ballots in the Democratic Party's congressional primary election. In his majority opinion, Stone refused to be bound by the argument that the framers of Article I, Section 2, did not have primary elections in mind. Instead, he insisted that congressional power over elections extended to primaries because they had become an integral part of the electoral process. Stone's opinion in *Classic* did not address the validity of *Grovey v. Townsend*. Nor did the U.S. government ask the Court to overrule *Grovey* in the *Classic* briefs or at argument. Frankfurter, however, had wanted to be explicit about *Classic*'s racial implications and had suggested that Stone add a paragraph: "The Fourteenth Amendment by its prohibition of racial discrimination meant to put all citizens of the United States on a political equality. If interference with a Negro's right to participate in a primary is interference with a right secured by the Constitution, the same interference against citizens who are not Negroes must equally be an interference with the right secured to all citizens by the Constitution." Instead, Stone ducked the Fourteenth Amendment question out of fear of losing his five-vote majority. Douglas, joined by Black and Murphy, had dissented in *Classic* because they believed that the federal criminal law in question only addressed general elections, not primaries. Frankfurter's Fourteenth Amendment paragraph would have put the dissenters in a tough position—which was just what he wanted. "There are some things that one wishes one had never seen," Frankfurter wrote Stone. "The Classic dissent is for all one of these."

During his oral argument in *Smith v. Allwright*, Marshall observed that Texas primary elections were no different than Louisiana's and urged the Court to follow its reasoning in *Classic*. Hastie added that the record in *Smith* "destroys the factual basis for the decision in *Grovey*"—that the state played no role in the primary process or in denying blacks voting rights. The other justices turned to a "redden[ed]" Roberts, *Grovey*'s author, and expected a response. Neither Roberts nor his colleagues asked any questions. On November 13, all the justices except Roberts, who passed, voted to overrule *Grovey*. But they were concerned because the state of Texas had not filed a brief or appeared in the case (on the theory that the primary had been run by a private organization). On December 6, they granted a motion from Texas officials to file a brief and to appear at a second oral argument.

On January 10, 1944, Marshall and Hastie once again represented Lonnie Smith, this time opposed by Texas's assistant attorney general George W. Barcus. Barcus claimed that the Democratic Party was merely a private club, not a state entity capable of violating the Fourteenth Amendment. And in response to Hastie's assertion that there were 571,000 black residents of voting age in Texas, Barcus suggested that they should form their own political party and "could whip us any time." Marshall countered that "Texas was run by Democrats" and if blacks wanted to participate in their government in a meaningful way, "they must go with the Democratic party."

At conference, the justices, except for the dissenting Roberts, again voted to overrule *Grovey v. Townsend*. Stone wanted to rely on his opinion in *United States v. Classic*. Frankfurter, however, emphasized that the Court should overrule *Grovey* "without any pussyfooting and in the most candid possible way we should state that the Court has changed its vie[w]s not on any new facts or any new factors but solely on different notions of policy." The Court in *Classic* had explicitly declined to reconsider *Grovey*. Frankfurter did not want to rest the Court's opinion on the importance of the primary process.

Instead, he wanted to concede that the Court had changed its interpretation of the Fourteenth Amendment and its requirement of state action to include the exclusion of blacks from primary elections. The Court should admit that *Grovey* had been a wrong turn. The problem was the exclusion from primaries on the basis of "irrelevant discrimination."

Two days later, Stone assigned the majority opinion in *Smith v. Allwright* to Frankfurter. That afternoon, Jackson stopped by Frankfurter's chambers and argued that he was the wrong choice to write the opinion from the perspective of the South for three reasons: "You are a New Englander, you are a Jew and you are not a Democrat—at least not recognized as such." Frankfurter conceded that Jackson's "accusations are true." Jackson believed that Stone should reassign the opinion and that it should be written either by the chief justice or by one of the Court's southerners, Black or Reed. "Of course, I am primarily interested in this matter for the Court's sake, but I am also concerned about you," Jackson told Frankfurter. "A lot of people are bent on exploiting Anti-Semitism, as you well know, and I do not think that they ought to be given needless materials." Frankfurter was not offended by Jackson's suggestion and gave him permission to write Stone. Jackson's letter to Stone described his discussion with Frankfurter and warned him that "the Court's decision, bound to arouse bitter resentment, will be much less apt to stir ugly reactions if the news that the white primary has been outlawed is broken to it, if possible, by a Southerner who has been a Democrat and is not a member of one of the minorities which stir prejudices kindred to those against the Negro."

That night, Stone phoned Frankfurter and asked to see him the next day in chambers. With a pained and burdened look on his face, Stone began to recount his conversation with Jackson. Frankfurter cut him off, insisted "we were all on the same team," and it would be fine if Stone reassigned the case. Stone then asked Frankfurter for suggestions, mentioning Black and Reed but confessing he "did not know what Black would do to it." Stone discounted Douglas, who hoped to be on the presidential ticket in November 1944, as "political." The comments reflected Frankfurter's mistrust of Black and Douglas as much as they did Stone's.

———

IN JANUARY AND FEBRUARY 1944, Frankfurter's clashes with Black, Douglas, and Murphy made national headlines. Black and Murphy accused him on January 3 of interpreting patent law on the basis of his "personal views on 'morals' and 'ethics' " and in a utility rate-making case charged him with making "what is patently a wholly gratuitous assertion as to constitutional law." In a January 31 maritime case, Frankfurter joined Roberts's dissent objecting to Stone's majority opinion's "tendency to disregard precedents" and invoking the Court's flip-flopping in the flag salute and literature distribution cases involving Jehovah's Witnesses. In response to Douglas's February 7 bankruptcy decision, Frankfurter argued that "a wholly novel doctrine of constitutional law should not be resorted to gratuitously" when the case could be decided on other grounds.

The national media blamed Frankfurter for the feud. "Frankfurter Views Cause Court Rift," the *Los Angeles Times* proclaimed. "Frankfurter Adds to Court Conflict," the *New York Times* declared. Two *Washington Post* editorials rehashed the internal conflicts; a *New York Times* editorial dubbed it "An Unstable Court." A *St. Louis Star-Times* editorial criticized Frankfurter's dissent from the dismissal of a Louisiana community tax case as "his third reprimand of the majority of his fellow justices in less than two months" and sided with Black that Frankfurter was reading his "personal views" into the law.

Frankfurter's allies defended him. Elman, a former clerk who was working in the solicitor general's office, wrote *PM* editorial writer Max Lerner and challenged his claim that "the Frankfurter group" wanted the Court to have the last word on economic regulation but that "the Black group" believed it should be left to the legislature. In March, Elman published a letter to the editor in *PM* rebutting a comment that Frankfurter's dissent in a community property tax case marked the first time one of Stone's opinions had been criticized and provided a long list of cases. Dean Acheson wrote a note to *Washington Post* editorial page editor Herbert Elliston challenging the paper's factual assertions about the justices' votes in the flag salute and literature distribution cases. Isaiah Berlin, who was working at the British embassy, wrote columnist Joseph Alsop: "The Justice's enormous knives are magnificent. . . . I suppose it is the Justice's indestructible innocence which makes him so impregnable. I wish I had a similar capacity for ignoring dangers." Learned Hand wrote Frankfurter and applauded him for joining Roberts's dissent in *Mahnich,* the maritime case "written and assented to by men who did not understand what they were talking about. It is discouraging; they are sowing the wind, those reforming colleagues of yours. As soon as they convince the people that they can do what they want, the people will demand of them that they do what the people want. I wonder whether in times of bland reaction— they are coming—Hillbilly Hugo [Black], Good Old Bill [Douglas] and Jesus lover of my Soul [Murphy] will like that."

Experienced Court watchers knew that many strong personalities were to blame. In an anonymous letter to the *New York Herald Tribune* from a "member of the bar of the Supreme Court," C. C. Burlingham chided Frankfurter and his colleagues about their "growing tendency to disagree." The letter to the editor prompted a flurry of correspondence between Burlingham and Frankfurter. Frankfurter observed that "the history of dissents is part of the history of this Court." Burlingham agreed about "the importance of dissents," but only on "vital matters." An admiralty lawyer, Burlingham praised Frankfurter for joining Roberts's dissent in *Mahnich* but opposed Frankfurter's frequent concurring opinions: "I have a notion that there are mighty few concurring opinions *ante adventum F. F.*" Concurring opinions, Frankfurter replied, were "as old as the hills." Burlingham, who deplored Black and Douglas and admired Frankfurter and Jackson, passed along criticism of Frankfurter from members of the New York bar: "They are all disgusted with Black and Douglas, but they think that you brought it on yourself in part by your schoolmaster's ways in open court and, they suspect, still more in conference." Frankfurter, who had heard similar criticisms from Hand, replied that "it is a true kindness of friendship to tell me of things that are within the remedial possibilities of my temperament."

Another longtime friend, Benjamin V. Cohen, was concerned about Frankfurter's concurring and dissenting opinions. "Is there anything we can do to save Felix from himself," Cohen wrote Burlingham. "He feels so very strongly he is writing for history. He may be right and I may be all wrong, but I am afraid that he has become so emotionally involved that his work on the Court and his opinions will be historically judged far different from what he now fervently believes." Cohen, who worked for James F. Byrnes in the Office of War Mobilization, had maintained a polite distance from Frankfurter since the justice's break with Corcoran over the solicitor generalship. With great reluctance, Cohen wrote Frankfurter about the multiplicity of Supreme Court opinions and suggested that each case warranted a majority opinion and a single dissent. In response, Frankfurter wondered why Cohen's letter was "addressed to me. Munich is not the only place where peace can be bought if only you give to men who know exactly what they are after that which they are not entitled to and what is not yours to give away and ought not to be taken. 'Dearie you don't know the half of it' . . ." Frankfurter's friends did not understand the depths of the friction between him, Roberts, Jackson, and sometimes Reed on one side and Black, Douglas, Murphy, and Rutledge on the other and with Stone stuck in the middle.

THE HANDLING OF *Smith v. Allwright* reinforced Frankfurter's belief that Stone was a "'fundamentally flabby creature'" who had lost control of the Court and paled in comparison to his predecessor Hughes. As chief justice, Hughes had stayed after conference until he had assigned all the opinions; Stone's assignments, as in *Smith v. Allwright*, arrived a few days later. And whereas Hughes ran a tight ship at conference, Stone had lost control of the discussions. Frankfurter, moreover, was bitter that Stone's dissent in *Gobitis* and the Court's majority opinion in *Barnette* had contradicted Stone's votes in four prior flag salute cases. Stone's refusal to assign himself the majority opinion in *Smith v. Allwright* reinforced Frankfurter's view that he was not the leader that Hughes was. "I did not tell him what seemed to me the obvious thing," Frankfurter wrote of Stone, "that the Chief Justice should write an opinion like this, particularly when he was helping to overrule an opinion in which he had joined only a few years ago." Instead, he suggested that *Smith* required "delicacy of treatment and absence of a raucous voice" and therefore the chief should reassign the case to Reed, whom Frankfurter described as "a soldier." Stone agreed and swapped one of Reed's cases with Frankfurter's all-white primary case.

After the reassignment, Frankfurter spoke with Reed "at length" to reiterate "the importance of the most aggressive candor in dealing with *Grovey v. Townsend* and the duty of resting the overruling on a change of opinion and our duty in the case of constitutional questions to follow our convictions even though a prior decision has to be overruled." Reed and Frankfurter seemed to be on the same page. At conference, Reed had said that *Classic* had not overruled *Grovey*, but "now we should do it clearly."

On March 10, when Reed sent him and Stone a draft of the majority opinion, Frankfurter was flabbergasted. Reed had done exactly what Frankfurter "had begged him not to do." Reed's opinion portrayed overruling *Grovey* as dictated by the Court's decision in *Classic*. The draft did not acknowledge that the justices had reconsidered their policy views about the enforcement of the Fourteenth Amendment and the importance of primary elections to southern black participation in the political process. After failing to persuade Reed to change the opinion in a face-to-face meeting on March 14, Frankfurter wrote him the next day to explain their differences: "You are of the opinion that the South can be gently eased into acceptance of our decision in *Allwright* if only we are not too explicit. My own prophecy is precisely the opposite—that no matter with what tissue paper covering the blow is administered, it will be felt, and by appearing to screen it an added grievance will be aroused." He was particularly dismayed how Reed's draft attempted to portray *Smith v.*

Allwright as a new factual situation from *Grovey* rather than "a square unmitigated overruling." Instead of "disingenuousness," Frankfurter insisted that the Court should overrule *Grovey* by explaining that "our inescapable responsibility is to the command of the Constitution and not to the command of any one decision." *Grovey*, he contended, was "a deviation" not only from the Constitution but also from the principles behind the Court's prior decisions in *Nixon v. Herndon* and *Nixon v. Condon*. He also wanted the Court to acknowledge that it reacted to changing times. "For myself," he wrote, "the more explicitly and clearly we accept the view about 'the realities of political life' which Cardozo put to one side in *Nixon v. Condon* . . . as the basis of the present decision the nearer we are to truth and the farther away we are from treacherous speculation about insinuating truth by indirection into Southern sensitivities." If Reed could not find a way to change the opinion, Frankfurter wrote that he would be forced to concur in the result; Reed, however, "would not budge." Frankfurter also discussed the issue with the dissenting Roberts, who agreed that "the only thing to do was to deal with the matter in the way in which I proposed."

Frankfurter's team-player moment was over. Two days after he wrote Reed, he described Reed's draft opinion to Stone as "appeasement." To the chief justice, Frankfurter attached a draft concurring opinion forthrightly explaining why the Court overruled *Grovey v. Townsend*: "We are now pronouncing a decision precisely the opposite of that rendered less than ten years ago, shared in by judges not less sensitive than ourselves to claims of citizenship free from racial discrimination. Such a change of view cannot be justified by any assumption on our part of knowledge and wisdom denied to our predecessors. And no decision of this Court since *Grovey v. Townsend* has qualified its explicitness." He described the Constitution "as a dynamic scheme of government for a democratic society," which dictated "a different conclusion from that reached in *Grovey v. Townsend*." In the draft concurrence's second paragraph, he reiterated his respect for the Court's past decisions yet refused to be shackled by them when they conflicted with "the great principles that are enshrined in the Fourteenth and Fifteenth Amendments to assure equality of participation in the political processes by which the Nation is governed." In the third and final paragraph, he concluded that "if in fact free access to the electoral process by which the States and the Nation are governed is denied to a person on account of race or color that which the post-war Amendments sought to achieve is frustrated. We cannot escape the duty of construing those Amendments in the light of their purposes. We cannot escape this duty because one prior decision had taken a different turn. And our duty ends with such construction." In his cover letter to Stone, Frankfurter wrote: "Something like this I feel should be said. Of course, it would be best of all if you said it. If you do, I shall eagerly suppress this."

The chief justice had other ideas. The day before, he had joined Reed's opinion and suggested a few minor changes. Stone urged Frankfurter to wait for Reed's revised draft "before putting out anything else." He claimed to agree with Frankfurter that "something more should be said along the lines which you have written." After all, Stone had caused the problem by not addressing *Grovey* in his majority opinion in *Classic*. "We should not now draw an inference against *Grovey* which in *Classic* we were careful to withhold," Frankfurter wrote Stone. Yet the chief justice was irritated that Frankfurter had joined Roberts's dissent from Stone's majority opinion in *Mahnich*, the maritime case that prompted Roberts to warn of "[t]he evil resulting from overruling earlier considered decisions." Frankfurter, sensing Stone's refusal to write, also circulated his draft concurrence to Reed. "I wrote the Chief that I feel that some such thing as this should be said and by him, & that then I'll eagerly suppress this." The Chief, as Frankfurter guessed, was not willing to write anything. And Reed's revised *Smith v. All-wright* opinion continued to rely on *Classic*. Frankfurter, therefore, refused to join it. "I congratulate you on taking over the Chief's defense—" he wrote Reed on March 28, "minus *Mahnich*!!"

Only one justice was capable of talking Frankfurter out of publishing his draft concurrence, Robert H. Jackson. During his first few years on the Court, Jackson "had a difficult time getting along with Justice Frankfurter until they had an open fight." Jackson realized that Frankfurter's outbursts were merely a product of how "seriously" he cared about the Court, its decisions, and how the justices interpreted the Constitution. Frankfurter, in turn, had dissuaded Jackson, who, like Douglas, harbored frustrated presidential ambitions, from leaving the Court in late 1943 and joining the New York law firm of Simpson, Thacher as its new lead name partner. By the time of the *Smith v. Allwright* episode, the Frankfurter-Jackson friendship was unshakeable.

A few days before the Court released its opinions in *Smith v. Allwright*, Jackson tried to talk a "furious" Frankfurter out of publishing the concurrence. "I think it would be a great mistake," Jackson said, "for the same reasons that led me to think it would be a mistake [for Frankfurter] to write the Court's opinion." Frankfurter said he respected Jackson's judgment but "could not swallow the pussyfooting and pettifogging of Reed's opinion and especially the uncandid use he was making of the *Classic* case." Frankfurter asked if he could simply concur in the judgment. Jackson said he could. In light of Jackson's counsel and the criticism earlier that year for publishing too many concurring and dissenting opinions, Frankfurter pulled his three-paragraph concurrence. His unpublished draft contains a handwritten notation: "circulated but suppressed for reasons set forth in my memorandum of April 10, [19]44 herewith." The *United States Reports* state that "Mr. Justice Frankfurter concurs in the result." It was one of the few times that term that he decided not to publish.

After the Court announced its decision in *Smith v. Allwright* on April 3, Roberts told Frankfurter that the chief justice should have assigned the case to himself because Stone had joined *Grovey* and written *Classic*. And Roberts's dissent would have been much harder to write if the majority opinion had been more candid along the lines of Frankfurter's unpublished concurrence. All Roberts could have said was "my Brethren act on their consciences and I on mine."

Frankfurter's unpublished draft concurrence is historically significant for several reasons. First, it reflected frustration with his colleagues about overruling his flag salute opinion in *Gobitis* three years later in *Barnette*. In *Barnette*, the Court changed its legal rationale from free exercise of religion to compelled speech, contradicted four decisions prior to *Gobitis* rejecting challenges to flag salutes, and benefited from a change in the Court's personnel. If the justices had changed their minds about the meaning of the Free Exercise Clause and its application to state and local laws and suddenly found the free speech claim more compelling because of violence at home against Jehovah's Witnesses or the Nazi reign of terror against the Jews, then, in Frankfurter's view, his colleagues should have said so.

Second, Frankfurter's unpublished concurrence could have provided direction to the Court about how to overrule its notorious 1896 decision in *Plessy v. Ferguson*. By upholding a Louisiana law about racially "separate but equal" railroad cars, *Plessy* had encouraged southern states to pass Jim Crow laws that racially segregated all aspects of life. In 1927, the Court had reaffirmed *Plessy* by rejecting a challenge to Mississippi's racially segregated schools. Implementing a report by former Frankfurter student Nathan Margold, the NAACP began demanding the "equal" part of the "separate but equal" doctrine. Houston and Marshall sued Maryland and Missouri for operating state-sponsored law schools for whites but none for blacks. In 1936, the Maryland Court of Appeals ordered the University of Maryland to admit Donald Murray to its law school. Two years later, the Supreme Court ruled that Missouri's failure to operate a law school for black students and its refusal to admit Lloyd Gaines to all-white University of Missouri Law School violated the Fourteenth Amendment's Equal Protection Clause. In 1941, Frankfurter joined the Court's unanimous opinion in *Mitchell v. United States* reversing the Interstate Commerce Commission's decision denying black congressman Arthur Mitchell's claim of racial discrimination on interstate railroad cars. By 1944, Frankfurter knew that the Court would be confronted with overruling its decisions permitting state-sponsored racial segregation. *Smith v. Allwright* began to give southern blacks the ability to vote, enlarged the concept of state responsibility for racial discrimination, and culminated a sixteen-year legal battle against all-white primaries. The victory, moreover, gave the NAACP the momentum it needed to attack *Plessy*. Looking back on all his Supreme Court victories, Thurgood Marshall deemed *Smith v. Allwright* "the greatest one."

Frankfurter's *Smith v. Allwright* concurrence could have helped Marshall persuade the Court to overrule *Plessy*. The concurrence contrasted "slavish adherence to precedent" with the Fourteenth Amendment's guarantee of "citizenship free from racial discrimination," the Fourteenth and Fifteenth Amendment's principle of "equality of participation in the political process," and the Constitution "as a dynamic scheme of government for a democratic society." He urged his colleagues to be more forthright about why they overruled past decisions—to prevent the grand principles of the "post-war Amendments" from being "frustrated" and because of the Court's "duty of construing these Amendments in light of their purposes."

Finally, although he may have suppressed his draft concurrence because of critics who claimed he published too many concurring and dissenting opinions, he picked the wrong case to censor his views. It is unfortunate that the *United States Reports* do not contain his *Smith v. Allwright* concurrence. Indeed, he had forgotten about the unpublished opinion until oral historian Harlan B. Phillips brought it to his attention in August 1957. The next time the opportunity arose, Frankfurter would not hold his fire—especially when it came to issues of racial segregation and the Fourteenth Amendment.

━━━

MAY 21, 1944, was the fourth annual "I Am an American Day." Millions of people attended rallies across the country, including 1.4 million in Central Park, to honor the 400,000 people who had achieved voting age or had become naturalized citizens during the past year. Hollywood stars Bob Hope, Dinah Shore, and Bing Crosby spoke to crowds in Los Angeles and San Francisco. Before his speech at the base of the Washington Monument, Frankfurter presented naturalization certificates to nine men and women including Angiolina Cieri from Italy and U.S. Army private Mok Kim from China. The only naturalized citizen on the Supreme Court then explained American democracy to a crowd of 10,000 people. Frankfurter described democracy as "the bold experiment of freedom" and "the most difficult collaborative effort." "Freedom and democracy," he said, "are unremitting endeavors, not achievements." Frankfurter's faith in America's democratic experiment flowed from the country's "moral cohesion" and its status as "the most significant racial admixture in history."

Four days after his "I Am an American Day" speech, Frankfurter paid tribute to NAACP executive director Walter White on his twenty-fifth anniversary with the organization. As a member of the NAACP's National Legal Committee, Frankfurter had advised White throughout the 1930s and during the organization's successful opposition to John J. Parker's Supreme Court nomination. White, Frankfurter wrote, had "dedicated himself" to fighting for "the moral worth of the common man, whatever his race or religion." And in the foreword to an edited volume about Zionist leader Chaim Weizmann, Frankfurter described Adolf Hitler's anti-Semitism as "a challenge to the whole blend of forces that constitute the process of modern civilization."

The end of the war was in sight. On November 28, 1943, Roosevelt had met with Churchill and Stalin in Tehran to discuss the timing of the invasion of France. The Soviet Union had been bearing the brunt of the casualties on the Eastern Front and needed its Allies to open up the Western Front. On December 20, Frankfurter wrote Roosevelt: "Just a word to tell you how relieved and happy Marion and I are that you are again on *terra Americana*." Three days later, the president replied: "I realized on the trip what a dreadful lack of civilization is shown in the countries I visited—but on returning I am not wholly certain of the degree of civilization in *terra Americana*." During a January 11, 1944, radio address, the president bemoaned "selfish agitation" and warned that "overconfidence" and "complacency" could prolong the war. Sending 300 copies of these words to friends, Frankfurter wrote: "Don't let the Commander-in-Chief's words apply to you!"

On January 30, Frankfurter wrote Roosevelt wishing him a happy sixty-second birthday. Six weeks later, he ate lunch with the president in "a long, joyous, old-fashioned visit." They talked for so long that both men were "in the doghouse" with the president's schedulers, secretary Grace Tully and aide Edwin "Pa" Watson. For the first time, the president complained about his health—that he had not enjoyed a day "without pain because of this damned sinus since the first of the year." During the visit, Roosevelt confided to Frankfurter that he saw no way of avoiding a fourth presidential bid with the war in doubt, particularly in the Pacific theater. The European invasion was imminent. On June 6, American troops launched Operation Overlord, the D-Day invasion at Normandy, France. Three weeks later, they liberated Cherbourg. On July 11, Roosevelt announced he would seek a fourth term: "All that is within me cries out to go back to my home on the Hudson River. . . ." Frankfurter never forgot these words and, privy to the state of Roosevelt's health and having heard the fatigue in his voice, knew that the president meant it.

Frankfurter was delighted not to be in Washington and avoided phone calls from Harry Hopkins about the plot to make his least favorite colleague, William O. Douglas, vice president. After Roosevelt dumped Vice President Henry Wallace from the ticket, Frankfurter watched as his ex-protégé Tom Corcoran pushed Douglas's candidacy "with subterranean skill." Roosevelt wrote a letter to Democratic Party chairman Robert Hannegan proposing two possible running mates, U.S. senator Harry Truman of Missouri and Douglas. Presidential secretary Grace Tully claimed that Hannegan had asked her to retype the letter and to reverse the order of the names to put Truman's first so that the convention would choose the Missouri senator. Roosevelt's real first choice may have been James F. Byrnes, who left the Court to become "assistant president" yet did not make the list. As he drank old-fashioneds with Byrnes in August, Frankfurter learned that Roosevelt "finally wanted" Douglas "but the leaders & rank & file would have none of him." From Jackson, another person Roosevelt had considered to be his running mate, Frankfurter learned that Wallace blamed Ickes and other New Deal liberals for ousting him to make a play for Douglas. "And instead of getting Bill," Frankfurter wrote Marion, "they, the Harold Ickeses, are now sore to have got Truman!"

The summer of 1944 had been a difficult one for the Frankfurters. In August, Marion had undergone a "major" and "very serious" operation, probably a hysterectomy, in Boston. As she recuperated at the New Milford, Connecticut, home of their friend Dr. Alfred Cohn, Felix arranged for them to move into their new Georgetown home at 3018 Dumbarton Avenue, where they lived for the next eighteen years. During a few weeks in mid-September as a Washington bachelor, he socialized with Byrnes, Jackson, Stimson, and members of the Georgetown set and heard the gossip about how Truman had landed the vice-presidential slot.

Because of Roosevelt's poor health in the fall of 1944, Frankfurter knew they may have been electing Truman the next president. The justices were shocked at Roosevelt's wan, gray appearance when they visited the White House on October 16 for tea in the Red Room. So was Roosevelt's former ambassador to Great Britain, Joseph Kennedy, Sr. With the election between Roosevelt and New York governor Thomas Dewey very much in doubt, the president invited Kennedy for a private discussion on October 26 at the White House. Kennedy was a bitter man: he had been dismissed as a Nazi appeaser; his son Joe Jr. had been killed in August 1944 when his military plane had exploded in mid-air; and his son Jack was hospitalized with a back injury after nearly being killed in the Pacific. A "sore and indignant" Joe Sr. blamed the Rosenman-Hopkins-Frankfurter cabal with ousting him as ambassador and ruining his reputation. He was not shy about informing Roosevelt that his administration was "Jew controlled": "I was with the group who felt that the Hopkins, Rosenmans, and Frankfurters, and the rest of the incompetents would rob Roosevelt of the place in history that he hoped." The president protested to Kennedy: "Why, I don't see Frankfurter twice a year." To which Kennedy replied, "You see him twenty times a day but you don't know it because he works through all these other groups of people without your knowing it."

Frankfurter was privy to America's most closely held secret that had been kept even from Roosevelt's running mate, something Stimson referred to in his diary as S-1—the Manhattan Project to build an atomic bomb. Frankfurter was one of a handful of American public officials who knew about it thanks to his friendship with "some distinguished American scientists, because of past academic associations."

The justice likely learned about the bomb from disgruntled New York University physicist Irving S. Lowen. Working at the Chicago Metallurgical Laboratory, Lowen complained about unnecessary delays in the project. In late July 1943, he had informed Eleanor Roosevelt and, at her urging, had obtained a White House meeting on July 28 with the president. Eleanor continued to meet and correspond with Lowen and arranged for him to see press secretary Steve Early, speechwriter Sam Rosenman, adviser Bernard Baruch, and presumably Frankfurter. Lowen kept the president and first lady apprised of unnecessary delays. Two of the project's leaders, James Conant and Vannevar Bush, dismissed Lowen's concerns. They were more worried about the widening circle of people, including Frankfurter, who knew about S-1.

Frankfurter's knowledge of S-1 may have come from Lowen, but his influence on the country's emerging atomic energy policy resulted from his friendship with the pioneer of nuclear fission, Danish physicist Niels Bohr. They had met in Oxford during Frankfurter's 1933–1934 Eastman professorship. In April 1939, they had seen each other again at the Danish embassy, and the shy scientist and extroverted justice had "hit it off" while discussing their mutual concern about the appeasement of Hitler. In October 1943, Bohr escaped from Denmark to Sweden just before the Nazis began rounding up Danish Jews. During a tea in the scientist's honor two months later at the Danish embassy in Washington, Bohr and Frankfurter resumed their friendship. A few days later at Frankfurter's home, they discussed problems of "cultural co-operation." Finally, during a private lunch in his Supreme Court chambers in February 1944, Frankfurter "made a very oblique reference" to S-1 or X, claimed that he knew about it from American scientists, and figured that Bohr had come to America to help. Without revealing any classified information, Bohr explained that X "might be one of the greatest boons to mankind or might become the greatest disaster." The disaster, in Bohr's view, was an arms race between the Soviet Union and the United States culminating in nuclear war. From his discussions with Soviet scientists, he knew the country's nuclear capability was only a matter of time. Bohr believed that scientific knowledge should be shared with the Soviets in the spirit of international cooperation and world peace. "He was a man weighed down with a conscience," Frankfurter wrote a year later in a memorandum for British ambassador Lord Halifax, "and with an almost overwhelming solicitude for the dangers to our people."

During lunch at the White House on March 13, 1944, Frankfurter shared Bohr's concerns with the president that "it might be disastrous if Russia should learn on her own about X" and about "the possibility of an effective international arrangement." Project X, Roosevelt confided to Frankfurter, "'worried him to death.'" There is a difference of opinion about the president's real reaction. According to atomic energy adviser Vannevar Bush, Roosevelt distrusted Bohr and was "disturbed" that Frankfurter had learned about S-1. According to Frankfurter, Roosevelt was eager to meet Bohr and open to the scientist's ideas. In a hint that he may not have been entirely aboard, the president suggested to Frankfurter that Bohr should broach the topic with the British. Frankfurter helped Bohr draft "a formula" in an April 12 letter to the scientist's British government contact, Sir John Anderson. Bohr's mid-May meeting with Winston Churchill, who was preoccupied with the impending Normandy invasion, was disastrous. Churchill distrusted Bohr and was determined to maintain a secret Anglo-American alliance on atomic weapons. Bohr knew it had not gone well, and a May 22 follow-up letter did not ameliorate the situation. Roosevelt, Bohr hoped, was another story. In July, Frankfurter passed along a memorandum from Bohr and urged the president to see the scientist again. Roosevelt met with Bohr on August 26 and instructed him to use Frankfurter as a go-between for future messages. Indeed, Frankfurter made sure that Roosevelt received a September 8 follow-up letter from "my Danish friend" before the president left for the second Quebec Conference with Churchill. Roosevelt was not as receptive to Bohr's ideas as he seemed to Frankfurter and Bohr. During a September 18 meeting with Churchill at Hyde Park, Roosevelt consented to a secret agreement with the British, to exclude the Soviet Union, and to initiate a leaks investigation of Bohr. Frankfurter continued to press Bohr's ideas; the justice's involvement with S-1 and the war effort were far from over.

With the European invasion in full swing, Frankfurter remained in constant contact with Stimson and McCloy about the war. On June 14, he listened as Stimson spoke with the president by phone about the lack of British support for French leader Charles de Gaulle and about de Gaulle's increasing support among the French people. On August 25, Allied troops liberated Paris. A few weeks later, Stimson invited Frankfurter to dinner to build opposition to Secretary of the Treasury Henry Morgenthau, Jr.'s, harsh plans for postwar Germany. Frankfurter "snorted with astonishment and disdain" at the idea of summarily executing Nazi leaders rather than subjecting them to war crimes trials. He also agreed with Stimson and McCloy that dismantling the heavily industrialized Ruhr Valley would repeat the mistakes after World War I and destroy the best chance for the economic reconstruction of Europe. Frankfurter enlisted foreign policy expert Hamilton Fish Armstrong to explain the problems with Morgenthau's plan to the president. Stimson informed Frankfurter about the progress of the Second Quebec Conference and Roosevelt-Churchill discussions about the Morgenthau plan and the Allies' occupation of Germany. Above all, Frankfurter was relieved about the impending German defeat. "And generally—thank God!" he wrote McCloy on August 26. "I was brought up not to respect the 'efficiency' of these Germans and certainly to know that they are not 'invincible.' What a lot of blind and even craven folk there were on both sides of the Atlantic—and really took stock in that Napoleonic Charlie Chaplin & his 'new wave of the future.'"

⸻

GIVEN HOW CLOSE HE WAS to Stimson and McCloy and how often he participated in their policy discussions, Frankfurter struggled to overcome his biases in deciding the constitutional challenges of Fred Toyosaburo Korematsu and Mitsuye Endo to the internment of Japanese Americans.

On May 30, 1942, Korematsu was arrested on the streets of San Leandro, California, for violating General John L. DeWitt's exclusion order. Korematsu's draft card said his name was Clyde Sarah, he claimed to be of Spanish origin, and he had even undergone botched plastic surgery on his eyelids and nose to try to look less Japanese. He had already tried and failed to join the U.S. Army in July 1941 because of stomach ulcers, and he had lost his job as a welder after Pearl Harbor. He had changed his name and undergone the cosmetic surgery to stay in Oakland and make some money before evacuating with his white girlfriend. After his arrest, he was tried and convicted of violating the relocation order and joined his family in the Central Utah Relocation Center in Topaz, Utah. At the internment camp, he made $12 per month as an unskilled laborer. Represented at trial and on appeal by the ACLU, Korematsu decided to take his case to the Supreme Court.

Unlike Korematsu, Endo complied with the evacuation order and voluntarily reported to the Tanforan Assembly Center, a makeshift camp at a horse-racing track in San Bruno, California. Lawyers for Japanese Americans held at Tanforan selected Endo, a 22-year-old clerical worker at the California Department of Motor Vehicles in Sacramento, as a test case. She did not speak Japanese, had never visited Japan, had been raised a Methodist, and had a brother serving in the U.S. Army. They believed that Endo and other Japanese American citizens at Tanforan had a right to challenge the constitutionality of their confinement in federal court by filing writs of habeas corpus. The government moved Endo from Tanforan to an internment camp in Topaz, Utah, to try to moot her case. It did not work; the Supreme Court agreed to hear Korematsu's and Endo's cases during two consecutive days of argument.

Less than two weeks before the argument of Korematsu's and Endo's cases, an intense debate raged within the Roosevelt administration. Two courageous members of the Justice Department's Alien Enemy Control Unit, Edward J. Ennis and John L. Burling, wanted to alert the Court to serious concerns about the factual accuracy of General DeWitt's final report about the military necessity for evacuating and interning Japanese Americans. The report had been produced by members of the War Relocation Authority at the direction of DeWitt, who testified that "a Jap's a Jap" and whose report described Japanese Americans as the "enemy race." The report's concerns about Japanese radio signaling and transmissions to ships offshore had been contradicted by FBI and Federal Communications Commission investigations. The government's draft brief, therefore, initially contained a footnote that the Justice Department was in possession of information that undermined the DeWitt report's reasons for the evacuation and pointed to the lack of radio signaling as an example. To Ennis and Burling's displeasure, Solicitor General Charles Fahy watered down the footnote, but not enough to suit McCloy and the War Department. On the morning of September 30, 1944, McCloy sent his new deputy, former Frankfurter clerk and Army Air Forces captain Adrian Fisher, to scuttle the footnote altogether. After Ennis informed Fisher that the brief had gone to the printer, McCloy phoned Fahy, who stopped the final printing and again revised the footnote. In a blistering memorandum, Ennis insisted that the original footnote should be restored because the Justice Department had an obligation not to deceive the Court. He and Burling felt so strongly that they considered not signing the government's brief. Fisher countered that the Justice Department could refrain from relying on the report without calling the Court's attention to specific factual inaccuracies. On October 2, Herbert Wechsler, a former Stone clerk and assistant attorney general in the Justice Department, revised the footnote even further. He watered down the language about the government's reliance on the facts in DeWitt's final report and omitted the sentences regarding contradictory evidence about offshore radio transmission and signaling. Fisher indicated that the War Department would have preferred no footnote at all, but that the revised footnote was preferable to the original version. In the end, Wechsler's footnote made it into the final brief.

Earlier that spring, Burling had considered including a paragraph in the government's brief designed to appeal to Frankfurter as an immigrant and a Jew. The paragraph, which may have been sent to Frankfurter, suggested that the military had the power to use "protective custody" to shield minorities from "mob violence." The ploy was unnecessary in light of Frankfurter's views about the president's broad war powers. During the Court's internal debate about the *Hirabayashi* case in 1942 and 1943, he had been adamant that the Roosevelt administration was within its war powers in establishing a curfew for Japanese Americans. The justices unanimously upheld the curfew. At Frankfurter's urging, Murphy changed his dissent to a concurrence. Others suppressed their concerns about the curfew's constitutionality. This time, with Korematsu challenging the evacuation and detention of about 120,000 Japanese Americans, the justices were much more fractured.

During oral argument on October 11 and 12, Frankfurter and other justices questioned Fahy about General DeWitt's final report justifying the internment of Japanese Americans; they were more concerned about whether the Court could question the president's military orders during wartime and on what basis. Korematsu's counsel Wayne Collins contended that General DeWitt lacked "military necessity" to order his client's evacuation. In response, Frankfurter asked: "Does your argument come to this: That there is no rational basis for [the] exclusion order? Do you think we can say that there were no other facts that General Dewitt knew, which we do not? Did he say that he had no other facts?" At another point, he asked whether military necessity was even "a tryable issue." Jackson echoed Frankfurter's concerns about the Court's ability to second-guess the military's intelligence reports. Korematsu's co-counsel Charles Horsky, having been tipped off by Burling about the falsehoods in DeWitt's report, alerted the Court to the government's watered-down yet "extraordinary footnote" that disclaimed reliance on the report. Frankfurter asked Fahy whether a 24-hour curfew would be constitutional. After Fahy said no, Frankfurter asked what the difference was between a 24-hour curfew and the detention of Japanese Americans "in their homes and elsewhere." Fahy's strategy was to urge the Court to decide only the constitutionality of the exclusion of Japanese Americans, rather than their "temporary" yet indefinite detention. The *Endo* case was even more difficult to defend, as the government did not contest her loyalty to the United States. Roberts pressed Fahy about how long the government could hold Endo and whether twenty-five years would be unconstitutional; the solicitor general refused to specify a time limit.

Given the ongoing war with Japan, Frankfurter was reluctant to second-guess military orders. At conference on October 16, he agreed with Stone that the curfew upheld in *Hirabayashi* in 1943 as an exercise of the president's war power was indistinguishable from the evacuation and detention orders in *Korematsu*. He also agreed with Stone that Congress had ratified the military orders by funding the War Relocation Authority and internment camps. Nor was he willing to declare that there was an "absence of security" concerns. Only three justices joined Stone and Frankfurter: Black, Reed, and tentatively Rutledge. The liberal Rutledge believed that he had no choice given his vote to uphold the curfew in *Hirabayashi*. Besides Douglas and Murphy, the dissenters included two of Frankfurter's usual allies, Roberts and Jackson. Jackson drew the line at *Hirabayashi* and was uncomfortable with exclusion and detention orders that were based solely on "Japanese ancestry." He refused to accept a military order "without any inquiry into reasonableness." In an effort to maintain a five-justice majority, Stone assigned the majority opinion in *Korematsu* to Black.

The day after Black circulated his draft *Korematsu* opinion on November 8, Frankfurter replied with a minor suggestion yet insisted he was "ready to join in your opinion without the change of a word." After he read Roberts's dissent, however, Frankfurter changed his mind and drafted a short concurrence. On December 1, he circulated a paragraph arguing that the exclusion order was no different than the curfew in *Hirabayashi* and it was within Congress's powers to allow for the enforcement of the military orders by establishing criminal offenses. The next day, Frankfurter circulated a revised concurrence that read more like a dissent. First, he characterized the military orders as part of the war powers of Congress and of the president. Second, he referred to *Hirabayashi*'s quotation of Charles Evans Hughes that "the power to wage war is the power to wage war successfully." As a result, Frankfurter argued that military orders that invoked "the war power must be judged wholly in the context of war." And what is constitutional in wartime might not be constitutional in peacetime. Later that day, Frankfurter added the most important part of his concurrence, contrasting his concerns with those in Jackson's draft dissent. Jackson argued that the justices, unlike national security experts with access to classified information, lacked the knowledge and expertise to judge the reasonableness of General DeWitt's report and military orders. Frankfurter was more concerned with not limiting Congress's and the president's exercise of their war powers. Along these lines, he added a sentence to distance himself from affirming the supposed factual bases for interning Japanese Americans: "To find that the Constitution does not forbid the military measures now complained of does not carry with it approval of that which Congress and the Executive did. That is their business, not ours."

The Court's unanimous opinion in *Endo*, written by Douglas, found that she had a right to request a writ of habeas corpus and granted her release, given the lack of evidence of disloyalty to her country. As strongly as he felt about the president's power to wage war and Congress's power to declare that violations of DeWitt's military orders were criminal offenses, Frankfurter felt the same way about the safeguards provided by access to the writ of habeas corpus. He apparently had been talking to Jackson about both cases. In a letter to Jackson, Frankfurter included several references to the long history of habeas corpus in British and American law and argued that Endo must have access to the writ of habeas corpus or else there would be no "constitutional restriction" on Congress's power to authorize and criminalize DeWitt's military orders.

The Court's decision in *Endo*, also announced on December 18, has been overshadowed by its decision in *Korematsu*. Roberts's dissent referred to the imprisonment of Korematsu and other Japanese Americans in "concentration camps" on the basis of their ancestry. Roberts's reference to German-style concentration camps prompted an angry rejoinder in Black's majority opinion about the phrase's "ugly connotation." Murphy's dissent excoriated his colleagues for "this legalization of racism."

The Roberts, Murphy, and Jackson dissents have been vindicated by history, and *Korematsu* is regarded as one of the worst Supreme Court decisions of the twentieth century. At the time, however, General DeWitt's report had been questioned yet had not been publicly discredited. Few people knew that the perceived threat of a Japanese American–led attack on the West Coast was based on racism and bogus intelligence. More important, the Court's Fourteenth Amendment jurisprudence was impoverished compared to today. The justices had not articulated what the Fourteenth Amendment protected and, as of 1944, had not struck down racially "separate but equal" laws. Earlier that year, Frankfurter had withdrawn his *Smith v. Allwright* concurrence arguing that the purpose of the Fourteenth Amendment was to protect "citizenship free from racial discrimination." Indeed, Black's majority opinion in *Korematsu* marked the first time the Court declared that "all legal restrictions which curtail the civil rights of a single racial group" were "immediately suspect" and would be subject "to the most rigid scrutiny." The Court in *Korematsu* was operating in a constitutional void.

Yet, even with these factual and legal obstacles, *Korematsu* was an institutional failure driven by strong personalities and weak leadership. As in *Smith v. Allwright*, Stone should have authored the Court's majority opinion in *Korematsu*. Perhaps he remembered his unhappy experiences in 1942 drafting the majority opinion in the Nazi saboteurs' case. Perhaps he believed that Black could hold together a five-justice majority and prevent the liberal Rutledge from joining the four dissenters. Either way, Stone had lost control of the Court—conference discussions that went on for hours, the multiplicity of concurring and dissenting opinions, and personal attacks from the bench and in written opinions. In many ways, the personalities were too strong for any chief justice to control—a former United States senator in Black; four former attorneys general in Stone, Reed, Murphy, and Jackson; aspiring presidential candidates in Douglas and Jackson; an ornery Republican in Roberts; and Roosevelt administration insiders in Frankfurter, Douglas, Jackson, and Murphy. These men, backed by a lifetime of public service on and off the bench, held profoundly different views about the role of the Supreme Court in American life. Frankfurter believed that the powers of Congress and the president trumped those of the Supreme Court.

Frankfurter's concurrence in *Korematsu*, particularly the line disclaiming any agreement with the decisions of the legislative and executive branches, was as close as he could come to dissenting from the awful decision to remove Japanese Americans from their homes, to take their private property and their jobs, and to imprison them in internment camps. Unlike Jackson, Murphy, and Roberts, Frankfurter stopped short of denouncing the military orders as unlawful racial discrimination rather than a reaction to legitimate national security threats. He was too invested in the American war effort. And he was too close to Stimson, McCloy, and especially Roosevelt.

One of Roosevelt's fiercest critics, Red-baiting syndicated columnist Westbrook Pegler, observed that Frankfurter was "an immigrant from an enemy country" (Austria) and argued that "it would have been more to the interest of the United States to snatch Frankfurter from the bench and lock him up, than to intern a thousand Korematsus in the Arizona desert." Pegler compared Frankfurter's *Korematsu* concurrence with his November 1917 report about the lawlessness of the Bisbee deportation in which immigrant workers in Arizona were rounded up and left for dead. "Now finally," the columnist concluded, "we find Frankfurter joining in the condemnation of an innocent man legally qualified to be president of the United States, an office to which he can't even aspire."

ON NOVEMBER 7, 1944, the Frankfurters waited for the results on election night with the Achesons and the MacLeishes, drinking champagne left over from the weddings of two Acheson daughters. Around midnight, they learned that Roosevelt had defeated Governor Dewey by 3 million votes.

Two months later on January 20, 1945, the Frankfurters looked on as Roosevelt took the oath of office, administered by Chief Justice Stone, for the fourth time. After the ceremony, Marion remarked to her husband about their friend the president: "He has the look of a doomed man. He looks like a man a good deal of whom is no longer here." Roosevelt must have sensed that he was in bad health. Before he left for the Yalta Conference two days after the inauguration, Roosevelt instructed Secretary of State Edward R. Stettinius how to run the cabinet in case he became incapacitated and Secretary of War Stimson to do it in case Stettinius could not. At Yalta, a haggard-looking president was wearing a black overcoat and sitting between Churchill and Stalin with what Churchill described as "a faraway look" in his eyes. The three Allied leaders prepared for the German surrender and the beginning of the new world order in Europe. One of the young State Department aides on the trip was Frankfurter's former student and Holmes's former secretary, Alger Hiss. On the voyage home, Roosevelt's senior aide and Frankfurter's friend Edwin "Pa" Watson died on February 20 of a cerebral hemorrhage. At Watson's funeral eight days later at Arlington National Cemetery, Frankfurter was one of a handful of mourners selected to stand near the coffin. The justice had spent countless hours at the Watson home in Charlottesville and maintained a lifelong friendship with Watson's wife, Frances. A completely exhausted Roosevelt, who had arrived home a few hours earlier, sat in his limousine a few yards from the burial site to avoid the sleet and rain. His face looked "grave and immobile." Frankfurter arrived home from the funeral and reported to Marion that Roosevelt was "a 'ghastly' sight." "Life," Frankfurter wrote the president after Watson's death and the Yalta triumph, "seems to be thus—bitter-sweet at the core."

His friendship with Roosevelt and influence within the administration made Frankfurter an inviting target for right-wing critics. Two journalists and FBI informants, William Hutchinson of the International News Service and Walter Trohan of the *Chicago Tribune*, joined forces to compile a dossier on Frankfurter in an effort to get him impeached. A *Tribune* story claimed that the Senate was making inquiries about Frankfurter's oldest brother Otto, who had left an $8000 a year job in the Treasury Department buying alcohol and chemicals for Lend-Lease to become the export director of Heyden Chemical Corporation selling pharmaceuticals in Latin America. Nothing, however, came of the investigation. A few years later, the *Tribune* revealed that Otto had been convicted in 1905 for passing a bad $100 check.

The *Tribune*'s anti–New Deal bureau chief and a longtime FBI informant, Trohan crusaded against Frankfurter. In February 1945, he placed the justice at the center of " 'palace guard' intrigue" and a "grand conspiracy" to shake up domestic and international politics. Relying on unnamed sources, he claimed that Frankfurter was angling for Roosevelt to name him chief justice of the new postwar International Court of Justice at The Hague. In addition to his own purported ambitions, Frankfurter, Trohan asserted, aimed to secure jobs for friends in the administration: the solicitor generalship for presidential speechwriter Sam Rosenman, general counsel of the State Department for Oscar Cox, chairmanship of the Reconstruction Finance Corporation for steel magnate Henry Kaiser, and a federal court of appeals judgeship for Solicitor General Charles Fahy. Fahy was being "held in reserve" for the next Supreme Court vacancy, Trohan insisted, with Frankfurter and others trying to persuade Frank Murphy to return to his old job as governor-general of the Philippines.

Trohan's article about "the Frankfurter scheme" incited calls for impeachment and nativist and anti-Semitic rants by members of Congress. The day after the article's publication, Representative Dan R. McGehee of Mississippi described Frankfurter as one of "the Rasputins of this administration," called for the House Un-American Activities Committee run by Martin Dies to investigate the justice, and urged the committee to draft articles of impeachment. The goal, McGehee insisted, was to send Frankfurter "back to private life and, if possible, send him back to the land from whence he came and let him teach his un-American doctrines there rather than try to contaminate a patriotic American citizenship." A few days later, Representative Clare Hoffman of Michigan, a notorious anti-Semite and isolationist, reprinted a June 1942 Drew Pearson column about Frankfurter's influence on the War Department and referred to the justice's friendship with Stimson. Hoffman wondered whether "the acceptance of the Communists as [U.S. military] officers who can send our sons to death on foreign soil is due to Frankfurter's influence?" McGehee and Hoffman quoted Theodore Roosevelt's 1917 comments describing Frankfurter's Bisbee deportation report as "Bolsheviki." On March 14, Representative Matthew Neely, the former West Virginia U.S. senator and governor, invoked Christian Brotherhood Week and rose to Frankfurter's defense. The chair of the senate judiciary subcommittee on Frankfurter's nomination, Neely had witnessed the anti-Semitic and anti-Communist attacks on him. An indignant Hoffman denied that he was a "Jew baiter" or that he "criticized Justice Frankfurter because he was a Jew." Hoffman refused to apologize for referring to Frankfurter as foreign born and reiterated that he objected to a Supreme Court justice involving himself in politics and the war effort: "If Justice Frankfurter wants to take the position—and we hear and see in the press almost every day where he has something to do with the policies of the administration—if he wishes to do that, that is a matter for his conscience."

Unsuccessful in their attacks on him, Frankfurter's enemies in Congress and the administration blocked the advancement of his former students. Senator McCarran, Frankfurter's Red-baiting antagonist during his Supreme Court nomination hearings, sought revenge against his star-crossed protégé Nathan Margold. After Roscoe Pound and A. Lawrence Lowell conspired to deny him a Harvard law professorship, Margold had thrived in private practice in New York, serving as special counsel to the New York Transit Commission, advising the NAACP on how to challenge racially "separate but equal" education laws, and working on Indian affairs issues. When Roosevelt took office in 1933, Margold joined the Interior Department as its solicitor. He earned the reputation as talented yet difficult and "high-strung." Since 1940, Corcoran, Cohen, and Ickes had been promoting Margold for a federal judgeship. In 1942, Margold was appointed to the newly reorganized municipal court of the District of Columbia. The campaign for a federal judgeship continued. Finally, at the suggestion of Attorney General Biddle, Roosevelt nominated Margold on January 21, 1945, to the federal district court in Washington, D.C. The chairman of the Senate Judiciary Committee, McCarran established a subcommittee (which he chaired) to hold hearings on Margold's nomination. In a highly unusual effort to blunt McCarran's opposition, Biddle, Fahy, and Ickes testified on Margold's behalf. After three days of hearings beginning in late February and early March 1945, McCarran countered with a parade of Washington lawyers who attacked Margold's credibility and accused him of charging to perform marriages. The chair stretched the hearings into the summer until the Senate adjourned on August 1. No vote was ever taken on his nomination. He was not renominated and, after two more years on the D.C. municipal bench, Nathan Margold died in December 1947 of a heart attack.

Frankfurter was deeply loyal to and invested in the careers of his former students—whether Alger Hiss at the State Department, Margold at the Interior Department or on the bench, or his closest friend in Washington, assistant secretary of state Dean Acheson. Frankfurter worried that after the war Acheson's partners at Covington & Burling were going to pull him back into private practice. As much as he admired Charles Fahy's work as solicitor general, he believed that Acheson would be a worthy successor. After he had declined Roosevelt's offer to be solicitor general in 1933, Frankfurter had suggested Acheson for the job, but Attorney General Cummings had nixed the idea. Twelve years later, Frankfurter renewed the recommendation. On March 17, he wrote Roosevelt proposing Acheson as solicitor general. Three days later, the president wrote Attorney General Biddle: "What would you think of Dean for Solicitor General? He would have the definite liking of the Court." Biddle, who preferred Assistant Solicitor General Hugh Cox, must have been opposed because three days later the Washington Post reported Acheson as a possible candidate. Columnist Drew Pearson predicted, undoubtedly to embarrass the justice, that Frankfurter would pick the next solicitor general. Pearson's column did not prevent the president from working on the problem with Biddle and Secretary of State Stettinius. Before he left for Warm Springs, Roosevelt assured Acheson that he would be the next solicitor general. It was the last suggestion Frankfurter ever made to the president.

On the afternoon of April 12, Frankfurter went for a long walk in Rock Creek Park with British ambassador Lord Halifax. Halifax had to return to the embassy by 4:30 p.m. so they stopped at the old Peirce Mill to pick up the ambassador's car. During the ride back to Frankfurter's home, Halifax asked about Roosevelt's physical condition. Frankfurter "fear[ed] the worst." He described how the president had looked like a "doomed man" at his inauguration, how "ghastly" Roosevelt had looked at Pa Watson's funeral nearly two months ago, and even worse at Frankfurter's last glimpse of the president.

Four hours before Roosevelt left for Warm Springs on March 29, Frankfurter had accompanied British minister of production Oliver Lyttelton and minister of food John J. Llewellin to meet the president at the White House. Frankfurter had been "simply shocked" at the change in the president's appearance. Two hours after Halifax and Frankfurter parted ways on April 12, Frankfurter heard the news that Roosevelt had died of a cerebral hemorrhage at age sixty-three. Despite being prepared for the president's death on an intellectual level, Frankfurter was stunned: "One cannot take in for a long time that such a vital force is spent." He was only glad that, unlike Wilson, whose stroke in the fall of 1919 had left him incapacitated, Roosevelt died with all his faculties. Two and a half hours after Roosevelt's death and with the cabinet present, Chief Justice Stone swore in Harry Truman as the next president.

The next night, the Frankfurters stopped by the home of Secretary of War Stimson. The Stimsons had finished dinner with Ellen McCloy, whose husband John was in France to plan the future of postwar Germany. They had a "very pleasant and cheering chat" about what Roosevelt had done for his country and for the free world. Stimson liked Roosevelt, admired his judgment on foreign policy and the war, but thought he had run a "disorderly" White House. Truman had urged the entire cabinet, especially Stimson and other officials crucial to the war effort, to stay.

The next morning at 9:55 a.m., Frankfurter watched with the other justices, the cabinet, President Truman, and Roosevelt family members and close friends as Roosevelt's funeral train pulled into Union Station. An estimated 500,000 people lined the streets as six white horses pulled the president's flag-draped casket on a caisson escorted by 2800 troops, 1000 police officers, and 400 firefighters and followed by cars carrying public officials to the northwest gate of the White House.

At 3:55 p.m. in the East Room of the White House, Felix and Marion Frankfurter sat in the second row with the other justices and their wives waiting for the start of Roosevelt's official state funeral. A few minutes later, they forgot to stand when President and Mrs. Truman entered. After twelve plus years of Roosevelt, they were unaccustomed to the idea of anyone else as president. The Truman family sat in the first row in front of the justices. Shortly before 4:00 p.m., everyone stood as Eleanor Roosevelt and her family walked in and took their seats in the first row on the other side of the aisle. It was a humid April day and hot and stuffy with 150 people packed into the East Room and another 50 in the adjacent Blue Room. Frankfurter thought Reverend Angus Dun performed the half-hour funeral service "beautifully."

That night around 9:30 p.m., the Frankfurters arrived early at Union Station to board a 17-car special train bound for Hyde Park, New York. "The Secret Service took extraordinary precautions . . . ," the *New York Times* reported. "Probably never before had such an assemblage of leaders of the United States Government traveled on one train." Members of the Roosevelt family, President Truman and his family, most of the cabinet, all nine justices, and other dignitaries spent the night talking in somber tones. The Frankfurters sat next to their friend Frances Watson, who was in mourning over her husband Pa's death.

The next morning at the burial service, Frankfurter and his fellow justices stood in the west side of the rose garden. Under a bright sunshine and a deep blue sky, eight West Point cadets escorted the caisson up the hill. An old rector recited a few prayers followed by a benediction as the casket was lowered into the ground. West Point cadets fired a 21-gun salute. A bugler at the foot of the grave played taps. "I wish you had been at Hyde Park when we took leave of him," Frankfurter wrote C. C. Burlingham. "It was a perfect day and a flawless ceremony. The sky was swept clean, the Gods smiled on him at the last and there was a tang in the air that sharpened the pain."

"Franklin Roosevelt cannot escape becoming a national saga," Frankfurter wrote in a memorial essay for the *Harvard Alumni Bulletin*. He reminisced about Roosevelt's "friendliness," "optimism," and "resoluteness" in the face of the Great Depression; his calmness after Pearl Harbor, which prompted Stimson to remark after that first cabinet meeting, "*There* is my leader"; and Roosevelt's recognition that "the utter defeat of Nazism was essential to the survival of our institutions."

The day before Roosevelt's death, the U.S. Army had liberated the concentration camp at Buchenwald; a few days later, the British liberated Bergen-Belsen. Delegates from around the world convened in San Francisco for two months to establish the United Nations. The Axis powers were crumbling. On April 28, Mussolini was hanged. Two days later, Hitler committed suicide in his bunker. Frankfurter knew that the defeat of the Axis powers would define Roosevelt's presidency more than the New Deal, his fireside chats, and his failed court-packing plan. "Roosevelt will claim an even larger share of history as long as the civilization endures that he helped to save," he wrote. "Fluctuations of historic judgment are the common lot of great men and Roosevelt will not escape it. What history will ultimately say, it is for history to say. Only one thing is certain: he will remain among the few Americans who embody its traditions and aspirations."

ON THE TRAIN home from Roosevelt's funeral, many cabinet members and politicians stopped mourning Roosevelt; they schemed about their political futures in the Truman administration, and some even met with Truman himself. Frankfurter was not among them. Unlike others on the train home from Hyde Park, he professed no interest in who would stay or who would go.

In the days after Roosevelt's death, newspaper reporters and columnists speculated that Frankfurter's influence in the Truman administration would be "dimmed" and that the justice would "spend more time on" his "official duties." The conventional wisdom was that the "palace guard" of Frankfurter, Hopkins, and Rosenman could not possibly have the same personal relationship with Truman that they had with Roosevelt. "Justice Felix Frankfurter no longer will slip in the back door of the White House o'nights to use the political lobe of his judicial brain to jockey for Frankfurter-endorsed appointments in key Administration posts," syndicated columnist John O'Donnell wrote, "—and so the Frankfurter boys are packing up." The last part of the prediction turned out to be wrong. Many of Frankfurter's friends, former students, and law clerks—Stimson, Patterson, and McCloy in the War Department; Acheson, new assistant secretary MacLeish, Ben Cohen, and Hiss in the State Department; Prichard in the Office of War Mobilization and Reconversion; and many people in the solicitor general's office and elsewhere in the Justice Department—stayed in the administration. Frankfurter insisted to Stimson that the secretary of war "may have more influence with Truman than he did" with Roosevelt because the late president "was so much more self-sufficient." Frankfurter was optimistic about Truman because "he is an educable man and it all depends who will do the educating." With Stimson, Acheson, and Frankfurter's other allies in the administration, they would be Truman's teachers. Apropos of Joe Kennedy's remark to Roosevelt in October 1944, Truman would see Frankfurter "twenty times a day."

CHAPTER 27

The Real Architect
of the Victory

A few weeks after Roosevelt's death, Henry Stimson received word that Frankfurter wanted to see him "on some important matter" and invited the justice to a May 3 lunch at the Pentagon. Frankfurter usually visited the secretary of war at his Woodley estate for dinner or after-dinner conversation. This meeting, however, was top secret.

At 1:00 p.m., the justice arrived at the Pentagon with a memorandum in hand and some startling information. Stimson was surprised to learn that Frankfurter knew "quite a good deal" about S-1 and had discussed the project with Danish physicist Niels Bohr as well as with the late president. Over lunch, Frankfurter recounted his conversations with Bohr and Roosevelt and left Stimson the original copy of a memorandum reviewing the entire history. The memorandum detailed Bohr and Frankfurter's preoccupation for more than a year—the necessity of sharing atomic secrets with the Soviet Union in an effort to build trust between the two countries and to avert a nuclear war.

The new president, not Stimson, worried Frankfurter. On issues of atomic energy, Truman was green. He had no knowledge of S-1 until Roosevelt's death. As a U.S senator, he had chaired the Senate Special Committee to Investigate the National Defense Program, or Truman Committee, and had asked Stimson about a large appropriation for a new weapon at plants in Washington State and Tennessee. The secretary of war had declined to answer for reasons of national security. On April 15, 1945, three days after Roosevelt's death, Stimson briefed Truman for the first time about S-1. The new president understood why Stimson had refused to discuss the project with the Senate oversight committee. On April 25, Stimson presented Truman with a memorandum: "Within four months we shall in all probability have completed the most terrible weapon ever known in human history, one bomb of which could destroy a whole city." He explained that many scientists in many countries knew about the technology and that controlling access to these weapons required international cooperation and inspections. He also raised the issue of sharing the technology with others and with "a certain moral responsibility upon us which we cannot shirk without very serious responsibility for any disaster to civilization . . ."

During his May 3 meeting with Frankfurter, Stimson explained that he had constituted an Interim Committee to address these issues and had asked Frankfurter's former colleague James F. Byrnes to be a member. Frankfurter, according to Stimson, "was much relieved to find how well we had the affair in hand."

Four days after Stimson's meeting with Frankfurter, Germany officially surrendered. May 8 was celebrated as Victory in Europe (V-E) Day. "The road ahead is steep and rocky—but at least we have been saved from the abyss," Frankfurter wrote Stimson. "And we can stop long enough to give thanks to the handful of men who apart from the anonymous millions in the services are the real architects of the victory. That you are of that very small company there is not a shadow of a doubt. I shudder to think what would have happened to us if you [had] not been at the head of the War Department."

No one was more responsible for Stimson's position as secretary of war than Frankfurter. To prepare the country for the looming war in Europe in 1940, the justice and law school classmate Grenville Clark had persuaded Roosevelt to name Stimson secretary of war and Judge Robert Patterson assistant secretary. For Frankfurter and many others, Stimson was the paragon of public service. He had hired Frankfurter to work in the U.S. attorney's office in Manhattan and in Taft's War Department. A lifelong Republican, Stimson had been Hoover's governor-general of the Philippines and secretary of state. His service to his country had inspired generations of elite young men. Many of them, like Stimson, had gone to Yale College, had been tapped for the secret society Skull and Bones, and had attended Harvard Law School. Before and after he joined the Harvard law faculty in 1914, Frankfurter was Stimson's talent scout. Many of Frankfurter's best men found their way onto Stimson's War Department staff. In 1945, Stimson's assistants included former Holmes secretaries George Harrison and Harvey Bundy and former student John J. McCloy.

The atomic bomb tested Stimson's abilities and problem-solving skills and those of Harrison, Bundy, and McCloy. Two issues confronted them: (1) The decision about whether to drop the atomic bomb on Japan to hasten the end of the war in the Pacific; and (2) the question of sharing atomic secrets with the Soviet Union. Frankfurter left the first question up to the military and political experts. The second one, however, he refused to let die. He employed all his persuasive powers and administration contacts to influence Truman's decision about sharing atomic secrets with the Soviets and ensuring a lasting peace.

The president knew what Frankfurter was thinking because of gossipy phone calls—wiretapped, transcribed, and sent to the White House—with former student and law clerk Edward F. "Prich" Prichard, Jr. A trusted aide to fellow Kentuckian Fred M. Vinson in the Office of War Mobilization and Reconversion, Prich worked in the East Wing and was not shy about sharing White House gossip. He socialized with Frankfurter, Isaiah Berlin, Phil and Katharine Graham, and other members of the Georgetown set. Yet he aroused the suspicions of Truman and FBI director J. Edgar Hoover as a Roosevelt loyalist, ardent New Dealer, and leaker to columnist Drew Pearson and other journalists. In an effort to curry favor with the new president, Hoover tapped Prich's White House phone. The wiretaps caught Prich and Frankfurter dishing about the new administration. On the evening of May 8, Prich bragged to Frankfurter about writing a speech for Truman and compared himself to ventriloquist Edgar Bergen and the president to Bergen's wooden dummy Charlie McCarthy. He also aroused Frankfurter's concern about the new administration's Soviet policy and claimed that the United Nations conference in San Francisco had been "mismanaged." The justice argued that the new president "seems to be coming around" and "the Russians are determined to play ball."

Five days after V-E Day, Frankfurter met with Roosevelt's former ambassador to the Soviet Union, Joseph Davies. The friendship between Frankfurter and Davies dated to the Wilson administration, when Frankfurter had worked in the War and Labor Departments and Davies, a Wisconsin Democrat, had served as head of the Bureau of Corporations, the first chair of the Federal Trade Commission, and an economic adviser during the Paris Peace Conference. In 1936, Roosevelt named Davies to succeed William C. Bullitt as the ambassador to the Soviet Union. Ambassador Davies and his wife, General Foods heiress Marjorie Merriweather Post, bought valuable Russian art at bargain prices from the Stalin-led government. Davies's subordinates in the embassy viewed him as a "Pollyanna" who accepted what the Soviets told him at face value. "He took the Soviet line on everything," Russia expert Chip Bohlen wrote, "except issues between the two governments." After two years in the Soviet Union, Davies served as ambassador to Belgium and minister to Luxembourg. His 1941 best-selling book, *Mission to Moscow*, portrayed the Soviet Union and Stalin in a positive light and became a major motion picture viewed by experts as Soviet propaganda. He never shook the label of Soviet sympathizer and never wavered from his belief that American-Soviet cooperation was critical to the future of the world. At the end of April, Truman invited him to the White House for advice about how to negotiate with Soviet officials. A week earlier, Truman had taken a hard line with Soviet foreign minister Vyacheslav Molotov yet had begun to question his "get tough policy."

On Sunday, May 13, Davies visited Frankfurter at home. The justice, Davies wrote in his diary, "was worried over Russia" and "feared that there was dynamite 'in the situation.'" Frankfurter did not reveal his knowledge of S-1 and, at that point, Davies knew nothing about the project. Instead, the justice told the story of Truman's April 23 meeting with Stimson, Secretary of State Edward Stettinius, and Secretary of the Navy James Forrestal. During the meeting, they had reacted to an "insulting" note from Stalin to Roosevelt with "much 'banging of fists' on the table" and had insisted it was "'high time' to take a 'tough line'" with the Soviets. Truman vowed to give them "a 'one-two blow, straight to the jaw.'" Stimson, who was not the source of Frankfurter's story, reserved judgment. The justice opened a copy of John Quincy Adams's memoirs, described him as Davies's "great predecessor in Russia," and read a passage from Adams's "The Mission to Russia," which reflected the deteriorating U.S.-Soviet relationship since Roosevelt's death. Frankfurter encouraged Davies to see Stimson and others "to avert the possible impending 'disaster.'"

Davies, whose health did not permit him to accept a major diplomatic assignment, informed Frankfurter what had transpired between Truman and Molotov and that he had been corresponding with the Soviet foreign minister. He showed the justice his correspondence with Molotov as well as a four-page draft letter to Truman expressing dismay over "the rapid and serious deterioration" of relations between the Soviets and their Anglo-American allies. Davies's letter argued that the danger was the isolation of the Soviet Union, that Truman was "in the best position to avert it for our country and for the world," and that the situation required a practical approach rather than trying to "out-tough" the other side. Isolating the Soviets, Davies argued, "might prolong the war against Japan." Frankfurter read it and thought it was "a great letter" and urged Davies to phone Truman and arrange an appointment for that afternoon.

At 4:00 p.m., Davies called Truman and within half an hour was reading the letter to a "greatly worried" president in his study at the White House. He also read Truman his recent correspondence with Molotov, briefed the president on the country's history with the Soviets, and offered his views on the recent situation. Davies and Truman talked until after midnight and ended with a glass of scotch.

In Davies, Frankfurter had found an inside man with the president. During a May 18 lunch at the Supreme Court, Davies told a "heartened" Frankfurter about the former ambassador's conversation with Truman. They discussed British views of the Soviet Union, and Frankfurter encouraged Davies to write to Winston Churchill. Two days later in the garden behind the justice's home, they reviewed and discussed the draft of Davies's letter to Churchill, but it was never sent. At Truman's request, Davies headed to London to meet with Churchill in person. The machinations for improved U.S.-Soviet relations and, at least from Frankfurter's perspective, about sharing the secrets of S-1 were far from over.

───────

S-1 CONSUMED STIMSON. "The reputation of the United States for fair play and humanitarianism is the world's biggest asset for peace in the coming decades," he wrote Truman on May 16. "I believe the same rule of sparing the civilian population should be applied as far as possible to the use of any new weapons." Stimson tried to balance his humanitarian concerns with his desire to use the atomic bomb on Japan. During a May 31 meeting with the Interim Committee and a team of physicists, Stimson predicted that the "new weapon" would be either "a Frankenstein which would eat us up" or "a project 'by which the peace of the world would be helped in becoming secure.'" On June 1, the committee, after only a brief discussion of alternatives the previous day, recommended the use of the new weapon on Japan. Stimson was told that the Army Air Forces could not limit itself to "precision bombing" because, unlike in Germany, the Japanese people lived near industrial and military areas. General George C. Marshall, though he preferred "straight military objectives" such as a "large naval installation," suggested identifying "a number of large manufacturing areas from which the people would be warned to leave" before using the bomb. During a June 6 meeting with Truman, Stimson tried to update him on the Interim Committee, but Byrnes had already briefed the president. Stimson and Truman agreed "[t]hat there should be no revelation to Russia or anyone else of our work in S-1 until the first bomb had been successfully laid on Japan." Stimson, nearly three months after the U.S. firebombed Tokyo, claimed that he was trying to minimize civilian casualties but that Japanese manufacturing was too scattered. Stimson was worried that "the United States [would] get the reputation of outdoing Hitler in atrocities" and that Japan would be so "bombed out that the new weapon would not have a fair background to show its strength." Truman "laughed and said he understood."

Frankfurter sought another opportunity to try to change Stimson's mind about sharing atomic information with the Soviets. At 10:30 a.m. on June 12, he arrived at the Pentagon and explained Bohr's ideas—the Soviets were well on their way to building an atomic bomb, the sharing of information with them could be coupled with international control and inspections, and the lack of secrecy between the two countries could prevent an arms race. Though Stimson knew about most of Bohr's views, the secretary conceded that the physicist "made through Frankfurter some good suggestions too on which I called in Bundy and got them injected into our plans in S-1."

With Frankfurter departing Washington for the summer, he relied on friends in and out of government to advocate his ideas. On June 19, Davies met with Stimson to discuss U.S.-Soviet relations. During their "long talk," Stimson was as concerned as Davies about the "recent pinpricks and little explosions" between the two countries. The president invited Stimson and Davies to attend a meeting in July with Allied leaders in Potsdam. Frankfurter was thrilled that Davies had gone to London to speak to Churchill and to Germany to assist Truman: "the services you rendered your country and the forces of Peace in recent days loom bigger and bigger." Before he left for Potsdam, Davies had tried to phone Frankfurter in New Milford, Connecticut, and instead had written him a letter thanking him for his "judgment and inspiration." After his London meeting, the former ambassador had become more optimistic: "The situation is infinitely better than in those dark days last spring, when we counselled together. I have firm faith and high hope that all will be well, with a reasonable prospect for 'peace on earth.'"

In late June and early July, Stimson and his assistants drafted an ultimatum in an attempt "to try to warn Japan into surrender." On July 2, he showed Truman the warning and a memorandum about the attack on Japan. The next day, Stimson and Truman discussed what to say to Stalin about the atomic bomb. If Stalin brought it up at Potsdam, Stimson advised the president not to reveal any details but to say that we were "working like the dickens and we knew he was busy with this thing" and that the United States was "pretty nearly ready" and "intended to use it" to end the war. On June 4, American and British officials had consented to use the weapon against Japan. The final decision, however, was not made until they arrived at Potsdam.

In Potsdam, Germany, Stimson received word on the evening of July 16 that the first atomic test in New Mexico had been successful and conveyed the news to the new secretary of state James F. Byrnes and Truman. Five days later, they received a more detailed and encouraging report about the bomb's destructive power and expedited availability. Truman was so "pepped up" by the news that Churchill noticed at once that the president was "'a changed man.'" The big disagreement was between Stimson and Byrnes—Stimson wanted to include in the warning to the Japanese that they could keep their emperor as a figurehead; Byrnes, however, refused to include the provision and insisted on an unconditional surrender. The new secretary of state argued that the message had already been given to the Chinese to give to Japan and the issue of the emperor could be worked out in post-surrender negotiations. Truman backed Byrnes about deleting the emperor provision; the president, however, agreed with Stimson's other request: to remove from the list of possible nuclear targets the city of Kyoto. During a visit to Japan as Hoover's governor-general of the Philippines, Stimson had admired the ancient imperial capital's Buddhist temples and Shinto shrines and had learned about the city's cultural significance to the Japanese people. On July 24, Davies updated Frankfurter on Stimson's role at Potsdam: "This is being dictated under considerable strain. It is primarily to tell you that I have just returned from a conference with that greatest of American elder statesmen, your friend, the Secretary of War. He is looking well and going strong. The other evening, after dinner, the President spoke warmly of the Secretary's contribution over here. He said that he had relieved his mind of a great load." In truth, Truman and Byrnes marginalized Stimson at Potsdam and made the key decision to delete the emperor provision in the warning letter.

The warning to Japan failed as Stimson had predicted because it gave no indication that the country could retain its emperor. On August 6, the United States dropped the first atomic bomb, "Little Boy," which destroyed the Japanese city of Hiroshima and killed 140,000 people. Frankfurter wrote Stimson after hearing the news: "Reading between the lines the bits that came out of Potsdam and especially the ultimatum to Japan, it was not too difficult for me to infer the vital part you played at the Potsdam Conference. And now comes the news of the atomic bomb's successful application—one of those few decisive events that change the course of man's destiny. It's too vast and awful in its implications to encompass in one's thoughts, at least in mine. But that this calls for re-orientation of our thinking, calls for a new and deeper reconsideration of public morals, of international ethics, I have not the slightest doubt." He urged Stimson to lead the debate about the country's "new obligation the atomic bomb entails." In a letter to Davies that same day,

Frankfurter believed in "full publicity" about dropping the atomic bomb as "the first step" and praised "the prompt and ample disclosure by the President as a great act of statesmanship. The bearing of it all on our friendly relations with Russia is obvious."

Three days after Hiroshima, the United States dropped another atomic bomb, "Fat Man," on the city of Nagasaki and killed 70,000 people. The next day, the Japanese indicated that they wanted to surrender provided they could keep their emperor. Stimson blamed Truman and Byrnes for striking the emperor provision from the warning letter. He believed most people's knowledge of the emperor's symbolic importance to Japan came from Gilbert and Sullivan's *The Mikado*. The secretary of war was shocked that people he admired in the administration, including Harry Hopkins and assistant secretaries of state Acheson and MacLeish, were "anti-emperor" and insisted on an unconditional surrender. Even his right-hand man McCloy could not understand "the Emperor business." Stimson and Byrnes continued to debate the issue on the basis of past presidential statements about an unconditional surrender. On August 14, the Japanese officially surrendered and were allowed to keep the emperor, something that the Truman administration could have achieved without the use of nuclear weapons on civilians.

"Everything seems insignificant compared to the implications of the atomic bomb," Frankfurter wrote *Boston Herald* editor Frank Buxton. "I think it will begin a new calendar—this year 1, A.A.B.—Anno Atomic Bomb." Frankfurter viewed the secretary of war as the best hope of bringing sanity to the country's atomic energy policy vis-à-vis the Soviets. The justice suggested to McCloy that, if Stimson retired, the former secretary of war could lead a committee to develop the country's atomic energy policy. In an August 16 letter, Frankfurter praised Stimson for helping the United States end the war: "The long hard journey is over and humanity may again breathe freely the air of freedom. You began to lead the journey in 1931 and History will undoubtedly confirm the feeling of so many of your countrymen that it was almost providential to have had your decisive share in freeing mankind from the very serious threat of subjugation by a barbarous tyranny. Awful new tasks lie immediately and grimly ahead. But you have earned every right to let others have the burden of realizing the opportunities you so largely have made possible."

Stimson had completely come around to Frankfurter and Bohr's point of view about cooperating with the Soviets regarding the atomic bomb. Secretary of State Byrnes, however, opposed the idea and wanted to keep the nation's atomic energy secrets "in his pocket" during upcoming diplomatic negotiations. On September 11, Stimson wrote Truman and enclosed a memorandum about how to control the atomic bomb through cooperation rather than exclusion: "I consider the problem of our satisfactory relations with Russia as not merely connected with but as virtually dominated by the problem of the atomic bomb." Truman, Acheson, and leading scientists Conant and Bush agreed with him. In his final days as secretary of war, Stimson persuaded his successor, Robert Patterson, that "the safest way is not to try to keep the secret." On his last day of work on September 17, Stimson addressed the cabinet that "we should approach Russia at once with an opportunity to share on a proper quid pro quo the bomb." He worried that the desire of Byrnes and others to keep atomic secrets "rather ostentatiously on our hip" would increase Russian fears and suspicions of American motives.

After he addressed the cabinet, Stimson returned to the Pentagon at 3:00 p.m. to pick up his wife and an aide. An hour later, he arrived at nearby National Airport to find his generals as well as his civilian aides in two long lines on the tarmac to say goodbye. As Stimson and his wife reached the generals, they were greeted with a 19-gun salute. A band played "Happy Birthday" (he turned 78 in four days) and "Auld Lang Syne." He waved goodbye to the waiting crowd, shook hands with General George C. Marshall and other top generals, and boarded the airplane.

At 11:55 a.m. on the secretary's last day in office, Frankfurter wired Stimson: "Marion and I affectionately salute you. History will note this day in grateful acknowledgment of the great debt the nation owes you." Stimson's record during World War II was mixed. Pearl Harbor happened on his watch, but he had advocated moving the Pacific fleet to the Atlantic. He carried out the internment of Japanese Americans. The racist policy was driven by California officials and General DeWitt and approved by Roosevelt himself, but neither Stimson nor McCloy offered any resistance or alternatives. Stimson also never considered in any great depth alternatives to dropping the atomic bomb on Japan, though the killing of innocent civilians may have been avoided if Truman and Byrnes had not deleted the emperor provision in the warning letter. Stimson, however, persuaded Truman to spare the city of Kyoto.

In response to criticism about the destruction of Hiroshima and Nagasaki, Stimson published a 1947 article in *Harper's*, "The Decision to Drop the Atomic Bomb." The article contained two glaring flaws: (1) it contended for the first time that dropping the bombs avoided a ground invasion and saved "over a million" American casualties; (2) it omitted the controversy about deleting the emperor provision. The article's author was young McGeorge Bundy, whose father, Harvey, had worked with Stimson on the issue and had suggested the article as a response to critics. In late 1946, Stimson harbored doubts about publishing the article, but Frankfurter read it several times and encouraged him. For Frankfurter, Stimson could do no wrong during his "five epic years of your own service to country and to mankind." Indeed, the secretary of war brought much-needed discipline, efficiency, and experience to Roosevelt's wartime administration. During forty years of public service, he inspired generations of Harvard law graduates. And he came around to the Frankfurter-Bohr idea of sharing atomic secrets with the Soviets to establish a new pattern of trust and cooperation between the two nations and to avert a future nuclear war.

After Stimson retired and McCloy, Harvey Bundy, and George Harrison resigned from the War Department, Frankfurter continued to dabble in domestic and foreign policy. His friends determined the future of the nation's atomic weapons. He walked to work every day with Acheson; befriended Manhattan Project director J. Robert Oppenheimer; and another former student, David Lilienthal, chaired the Atomic Energy Commission. Unlike the Roosevelt years, however, Frankfurter lacked a direct line to the president. And thanks to the FBI wiretaps on Prichard, Truman knew about the justice's intervention in administration affairs.

The key, for Frankfurter, was Davies. The former ambassador agreed to stay "on the job" as Truman and Byrnes's unofficial Soviet adviser. After they spoke on the phone in late August, Frankfurter sent Davies an August 11 *Times* of London article by Niels Bohr about sharing atomic research and international cooperation. Bohr, Frankfurter wrote, agreed with Davies's "views of what are the essentials if we are to have Peace & not merely a short interlude between wars." Frankfurter believed the United States held the balance of power and "its statesmen have the greatest opportunities for the world good." He and Davies saw "eye to eye" that "we must conduct our affairs on the assumption that Russia agrees with us in desiring a peaceful, non-aggressive, prosperous world" and in a foreign policy based on cooperation. Davies thanked Frankfurter for the Bohr article and predicted that the exclusion of the Soviets "because of hostility or lack of trust" would have an "explosive psychological effect." The former ambassador wished that Frankfurter could play a larger role in the Truman administration: "It irks me to see your great qualities and powers confined to the judiciary, at this critical time. You are rendering inestimable service there; but in these times I feel it nothing short of tragic that they are not more directly applied. Your vision, steady judgment, your wisdom and mental vigor, ought to be also more directly employed in this other field."

Frankfurter turned his attention to the Court, where relations among the justices were so bad that they could not even agree to sign a single congratulatory letter.

CHAPTER 28

Frankfurter against Black

On June 30, 1945, Justice Owen J. Roberts submitted his resignation letter to President Truman. One of Frankfurter's closest friends on the Court, Roberts had served for fifteen years and recently turned seventy and therefore satisfied the legal requirements to retire yet collect his full salary. He had been counting the days. Indeed, he had made up his mind the previous October when he had designated Frankfurter his "judicial executor."

Despite a yearlong effort to talk him out of retirement, Frankfurter was stunned by the news. He was indirectly responsible for Roberts's place on the Court, having joined the NAACP's and organized labor's opposition to Hoover's first choice, federal court of appeals judge John J. Parker. After the Senate rejected Parker, Hoover nominated Roberts. In time, Parker matured into a leading court of appeals judge; Frankfurter's high hopes for Roberts, however, never materialized. As a law professor, Frankfurter had criticized Roberts for joining the conservative justices in 1935 and 1936 in striking down New Deal programs and state minimum-wage laws and had incorrectly believed that Roberts's 1937 "switch in time" had stemmed from the announcement of Roosevelt's court-packing plan (Roberts's vote, it turned out, had already been cast). Once on the Court, however, Frankfurter grew close to Roberts partly out of ideological affinity but mostly out of personal friendship. He knew that Roberts was neither a deep thinker nor a great justice. Yet Roberts was a reliable ally who had made Frankfurter's life on the Court more enjoyable.

In a July 11 letter to Frankfurter, Roberts explained that he had enjoyed his time on the Court with Charles Evans Hughes as chief justice but not under Hughes's successor, Harlan Fiske Stone. Stone's inability to control the conference discussions and refusal to write many of the Court's controversial decisions left a power vacuum often filled by Hugo Black. With his tremendous intellect and the reliable votes of Douglas, Murphy, Rutledge, and sometimes Reed, Black dominated the Court and made Roberts's life miserable. Roberts could not stand Black and Douglas (the feeling was mutual) and blamed Stone for enabling them. It was an easy decision to retire at age seventy with full pay. The only reason he could think of for staying was his "rare relationship with" Frankfurter.

Two of the main reasons for the Court's dysfunction—Stone's lack of leadership and Black's stubbornness—played out with the Court's customary letter congratulating Roberts on his retirement. In the third week of July, Stone drafted the letter and sent it to Black and several other justices scattered across the country and overseas. He expected them to sign it without incident. The three-paragraph letter was cordial but not over the top. After a few weeks, however, Black indicated that he would not sign the letter unless Stone deleted two complimentary passages. At the end of the first sentence expressing a "profound sense of regret," Black removed the phrase "that our association with you in the daily work of the Court must now come to an end." At the end of the second paragraph, he eliminated: "You have made fidelity to principle your guide to decision." For the sake of unanimity, Stone agreed to the changes and asked Black to circulate the letter to the other justices—but not before informing Frankfurter and Jackson about Black's objections.

In his reply to Stone, Frankfurter encouraged the chief justice to hold his ground. Frankfurter did not mind the removal of the first clause but objected to Black's deletion of the second sentence about "fidelity to principle." Frankfurter argued that this was Roberts's "outstanding characteristic" and that Brandeis had admired this quality of Roberts's. Removing this sentence, Frankfurter argued, was a "gross injustice to Truth, let alone injustice to Roberts." In a postscript, he acknowledged that Stone's letter as originally drafted was "the minimum of what you could write and say anything that wasn't ungracious." Black, however, had deleted a sentence that merely recognized Roberts's "devotion to duty." Five days later, Frankfurter asked Stone to include the original letter in the circulation to the other justices, and Stone agreed.

Frankfurter refused to let Black coerce the Court into accepting his changes and disrespect a departing colleague and dear friend. In an August 31 letter mailed to the other justices, Frankfurter explained why he refused to sign Black's draft without the "fidelity to principle" sentence, reminded his colleagues that Brandeis held Roberts "in the highest esteem," and suggested they put past battles behind them: "My numerous and serious disagreements with Roberts are, of course, beside the point." Stone was none too pleased about the ruckus that Frankfurter had started and tried to portray Black's changes as innocuous—to no avail. "To such derogatory excision," Frankfurter replied, "I could not be a party."

To his closest colleague, Robert H. Jackson, Frankfurter groused about "Black's latest performance—and the Chief's acquiescence." Since late May 1945, Jackson had been in Europe serving as the chief U.S. prosecutor of Nazi war criminals. During a brief return home to McLean, Virginia, in early September, Jackson wrote the chief justice: "I am surprised that any issue could arise over the proposed letter to Roberts. It seemed a formal and not too cordial letter originally. To strike from it all that it contained of tribute seems to me to leave it reading like a left-handed condemnation." Jackson urged Stone to stand behind the initial draft to the second-longest-serving justice and appealed to Stone's vanity as someone on the right side of the New Deal constitutional crisis: "You often differed with him and time has vindicated you in most of these differences. Certainly you are in a position to be not only just but generous and I know it is your temperament to be such. I hope you will not allow yourself to be compromised in this respect."

"You may have written better letters than yours to the C.J. on the Roberts business," Frankfurter wrote Jackson, "but it is hard for me to believe that you could have." With Jackson's return to Europe, Frankfurter continued the fight on his own. On September 18, Stone updated Frankfurter on where the letter stood. Black had withdrawn his draft but refused to sign Stone's. Reed had not responded. Frankfurter refused to sign Black's and would sign only Stone's. Douglas would sign only Black's. Murphy preferred Stone's but would sign Black's. Jackson preferred Stone's. Rutledge had not responded. Stone preferred his own "or something better."

Before Frankfurter returned to the Court in mid-September from New Milton, Connecticut, he stopped at the Chester Springs, Pennsylvania, farm of Owen Roberts. It is unlikely that Frankfurter breathed a word about the controversy over the letter. Designating him as his judicial executor, Roberts indicated that he wanted no letter upon his retirement. Nor was Roberts under any illusions about how his former colleagues felt about him. He enjoyed the letters he received from Frankfurter and Jackson and joked about the emotionally over-the-top letters from "the Saint" (Murphy) and the "silly" ones from Stone, Reed, and "John Marshall" (Rutledge). He was glad that Black and Douglas had not bothered to write him because it would have been "hypocritical."

In late September, Stone stopped by Frankfurter's chambers. The chief justice explained that five justices had agreed to sign Black's letter, with only

Frankfurter and Jackson holding out for Stone's original draft. For the sake of "unanimity" and because he preferred "not 'washing our dirty linen in public,'" Stone also agreed to sign Black's letter. It was now six to two. Frankfurter was so angry that he did not say a word. Stone asked him "to think it over." The next day, Stone returned to see if Frankfurter had changed his mind and argued that the line about "fidelity to principle," though true, was inconsequential. Frankfurter replied that "intellectual differences were one thing and implied attacks on a man's character quite another and that I would not be a party to this performance." A "helpless" Stone confessed that he did not know what to do and that Jackson had taken the same position as Frankfurter.

Before the Court officially opened its 1945 term on Monday, October 1, eight justices gathered in their conference room so that the newest justice could be sworn in by Stone. Frankfurter (and everyone else) thought that Judge John J. Parker, whose nomination had been rejected by the Senate in 1930, was a shoo-in for the seat he had nearly assumed fifteen years earlier. To the surprise of many, Truman nominated a former Senate colleague, Harold Burton of Ohio. A Republican and former mayor of Cleveland, Burton had been a "low-C man" at Harvard Law School. Yet he quickly impressed the justices and law clerks with his fairness, integrity, and ability to stay out of petty disputes. He would not be a reliable vote for Black or for Frankfurter.

At noon after Burton was sworn in, eight justices, sans Jackson, shook hands and took their seats on the bench. After he welcomed Burton, Stone read a tribute to the retired Roberts. "I could hardly believe my ears," Frankfurter wrote, as Stone began "reading word for word" from Black's letter. Frankfurter had told Stone "at least a dozen times" and in a memorandum to the other justices why he refused to sign Black's letter, then the chief justice read as if he spoke for the entire Court. Stone revealed his "guilty conscience" at a reception in Burton's chambers. The Frankfurters made their way through the receiving line, shaking hands first with the Burtons then with the Stones. As Felix reached Stone, the chief justice said "in a low voice": "I am glad you are still shaking hands with me." Frankfurter "mumbled nothing in particular" and moved on to Mrs. Stone.

The showdown came the next day at the justices' first conference. The chief justice asked Burton to wait in his chambers until the other justices discussed a private matter—the valedictory letter to Roberts. Stone began by reciting the history of the letter and explained he had read Black's version yesterday in Court because he believed that "everybody acquiesced." Frankfurter did not interrupt because he wanted to see if others spoke first. Stone also justified his public statement as a way to continue the tradition of congratulating a retired justice. He said he was unsure about what to do if disagreement about the letter developed, but argued that the justices should "let the matter stand in his public statement in Court on Monday."

After Stone finished, he asked the justices to speak in order of seniority which meant Black went first. Black bluntly stated his position: "I will do nothing more." Reed agreed that Stone's public remarks had been sufficient. Frankfurter spoke next. He explained that, if Stone had not solicited their views, he would not have said anything. He then proceeded to unload on the chief justice for assuming that, since no one protested, Frankfurter had "acquiesced." He wondered if Stone had expected him to read a dissent—which would have been impossible since Frankfurter had no idea that Stone would read Black's letter. Frankfurter insisted that Stone had spoken only for himself, not the other justices, and definitely not for Frankfurter.

At that point, Reed interrupted him: "Why, Felix, you are surely wrong. What the Chief said was said on behalf of the Court and therefore took care of the tradition of an expression by the members of the Court." Frankfurter insisted that Stone could not have spoken for him without consulting him and because he had repeatedly refused to sign Black's letter. When Reed tried to interject again, Frankfurter warned him: "Stanley I suggest you do not push me, or I might act in this matter in ways that none of you would like." This seemed like a veiled threat to issue a dissent from Stone's public remarks. As tempers flared, Stone quickly sided with Frankfurter: "Reed, Frankfurter is right about Roberts, what I said, I said solely on my own behalf—less than I would have wanted to say about Roberts, and only at the end I wished him well on behalf of all of us." Frankfurter reiterated that he objected to Black's letter because it questioned Roberts's "rudimentary honesty" as a judge. Stone asked Frankfurter what they should do. Frankfurter replied that he would never sign Black's letter. Murphy explained that he was "satisfied" with Stone's letter, but would sign Black's. Black had the last word. He refused to sign any letter, and, "with eyes blazing," explained that he did not realize that the other justices had seen Stone's original draft. Finally, he argued that the tradition of a letter to retiring justices should end, the openly racist and anti-Semitic McReynolds was right to decline one upon his retirement in 1941, and Black would make the same request. Stone chimed in that he would do the same. "And then," Frankfurter concluded his memorandum, "the music stopped."

The justices never sent a valedictory letter to Roberts. The controversy stayed private for thirteen years until Stone's biographer revealed a skewed account, from Frankfurter's perspective, of the episode. The next time Black attacked one of Frankfurter's friends on the Court, Stone was not around to blame.

―――――

AT 11:30 A.M. on April 22, 1946, Frankfurter introduced Lord Wright, a British judge headed to Japan to chair the United Nations War Crimes Commission, to Stone. As happy as Frankfurter had seen him in a long time, the chief justice discussed the Folger Shakespeare Library outside the window from his chambers. At noon, the justices entered the courtroom to announce their decisions. Stone repeated himself several times in announcing his dissent in a naturalization case. As the Court approached its lunchtime recess around 1:45 p.m., he was staring at a typewritten stack of papers as he prepared to announce three of his majority opinions and began mumbling to himself. The other justices turned to look at him; one of them said, "something is wrong." The chief justice looked pale. A gray lock of hair uncharacteristically fell over his forehead. He began to announce one of the Court's decisions in a lower voice than normal: "The case should be stayed . . . and investigation." The Court quickly recessed. The justices on each side of Stone, Black and Reed, led him from the bench. Stone laid down in the robing room, and several doctors attended to him. The initial diagnosis of indigestion turned out to be incorrect. He was taken home in an ambulance. At 6:45 p.m., with his family at his bedside, the chief justice died at age seventy-three after suffering a cerebral hemorrhage.

"Almost from the time that Stone became Chief Justice the burden of the job was like a millstone around his neck," Frankfurter wrote a mutual friend. "To such an extent was this so that one felt, most of the time, that the burden was transferred to one's own neck." Nearly five years earlier, Frankfurter had advised Roosevelt to name the Republican Stone, not the New Deal Democrat Robert Jackson, chief justice. By the end of Stone's chief justiceship, Frankfurter thought Stone was not a great lawyer, indecisive, vain, and petty. "He would always talk <u>big</u>," Frankfurter privately noted, "and too often act small." Frankfurter omitted most of these criticisms from a memorial essay for the *American Philosophical Society Year Book*.

Stone's death triggered a behind-the-scenes fight—an ugly episode that exposed the Court's internal disputes—over the identity of the next chief justice. The initial favorite was Frankfurter's closest friend on the Court, Robert Jackson. Roosevelt had promised Jackson the next opening as chief justice;

Truman had picked Jackson to be the chief U.S. prosecutor at the Nazi war crimes tribunal. Jackson was the Court's best writer and an eloquent spokesman, based on his experiences during the 1937 New Deal constitutional crisis, for limited judicial intervention. He often joined Frankfurter in dissent from Black-led majorities.

Black and Douglas made their objections to Jackson as chief justice known through their emissaries—Senator Lister Hill of Alabama, ex-Frankfurter protégé Tom Corcoran, and columnist Drew Pearson. On his April 28 radio program, Pearson reported that "two liberal members of the Court," known to be Black and Douglas, would resign if Jackson were named chief. On April 30, Hill met with Truman and presumably conveyed Black's threat to resign. Corcoran discussed the conflict on wiretapped telephone calls with Pearson and Office of Strategic Services liaison officer Ernest Cuneo. They wanted Black to be chief justice and if not Black, then Douglas. Black and Douglas, Cuneo told Corcoran, "seem to be taking a very strong position against Jackson."

"Well Jackson is Frankfurter," Corcoran replied.

"Yeah I know it," Cuneo replied.

"It's the old, old struggle, the guy can't keep out of it," Corcoran concluded, "It's Frankfurter against Black. That's what it is."

If the fight over the new chief justice was Frankfurter against Black, then Frankfurter was at a disadvantage because he lacked direct access to the president. He could not enter through the back door of the White House and have an unofficial chat with Truman as he used to do with Roosevelt. And fewer Truman insiders were Frankfurter's friends or former students.

Truman's closest adviser and fellow Missourian, Postmaster General and Democratic Party chairman Robert Hannegan, visited the president during a weeklong cruise on the USS *Williamsburg* and added to the chorus of anti-Jackson voices. Hannegan was angry that Jackson had refused to name an unqualified St. Louis lawyer to the Nazi war crimes prosecution team. After Hannegan's talk with the president, Corcoran was more confident that Jackson would not be chief justice.

Yet in late April, Corcoran worried that Frankfurter's allies had changed the president's mind. On the afternoon of April 29, retired chief justice Charles Evans Hughes met with the president. Later that night, Corcoran feared that Hughes had persuaded Truman to pick Jackson and described the retired chief justice as "Frankfurter's man." Corcoran speculated that Hughes had recommended another longtime friend of Frankfurter's, New York Court of Appeals judge Thomas D. Thacher; Corcoran began insisting to people that Thacher was "Frankfurter's present choice." In fact, Hughes later insisted that he had recommended Jackson. Retired justice Roberts twice had come to the White House at Truman's request and had recommended Jackson, too.

One of Frankfurter's remaining allies in the Truman White House, speechwriter Sam Rosenman, weighed in. Corcoran was convinced that, through Rosenman, Frankfurter would persuade Truman to choose Jackson. Corcoran informed Pearson that Truman wanted to name Douglas chief justice, and "then Felix threw in behind Jackson hard, as hard as he could throw." Rosenman, Corcoran informed Pearson, "went to bat" for Frankfurter's candidate. To Pearson and the wife of Justice Stanley Reed, whose husband supported Douglas, Corcoran claimed that "the thing was settled for Jackson two days ago."

On his May 5 radio program, Pearson repeated Corcoran's gossip and described the fight over the vacant chief justiceship as the "greatest tug-of-war in court history." Revealing that Truman was aware of Black's threat to resign, Pearson predicted that the president would pick an outsider "who could harmonize the two bitter factions." Another columnist, however, beat Pearson to print and laid bare the Court's internal strife. On May 16, below the headline "Supreme Court Feud," Doris Fleeson wrote about Black's threat to resign if Jackson were named chief justice and pointed to a dispute the previous term between Black and Jackson about "the portal-to-portal" coal mining case, *Jewell Ridge*. She accused Frankfurter, who had joined Jackson's opinions in *Jewell Ridge*, as "surreptitiously booming him for Chief Justice." Jackson knew that the story could have come from only one place—"from inside the Court."

In prosecuting Nazi war criminals, Jackson had been criticized for temporarily leaving the Court to engage in what many prominent lawyers and judges, including Stone and Learned Hand, considered vengeful show trials. Stone had been unhappy about Jackson's absence during the 1945 term. By January, newspapers had begun to blame Jackson for the number of cases held over for another term because the justices were divided 4–4. Jackson's opening statement at Nuremberg and his detailed documentation of what is now referred to as the Holocaust were widely praised. His cross-examination of Nazi leader Hermann Göring was thwarted by the tribunal's judges who refused to limit Göring to yes or no answers and enabled him to evade questions with long speeches. As he continued to prosecute Nazis for war crimes, Jackson learned from friends that Black, by threatening to resign, had blocked his nomination as chief justice. Black and Douglas's emissaries continued to poison the well at a time when Jackson could not defend himself. Fleeson's column was the *coup de grace*. On June 6, Truman named his treasury secretary, Fred M. Vinson, chief justice.

Initially, Frankfurter had "high expectations" for Vinson. The 56-year-old chief justice, who looked like a basset hound with his long face and sad-looking eyes, had worked in all three branches of the federal government. He had represented Kentucky during two separate stints in Congress, where he had befriended then-Senator Truman. In December 1937, Roosevelt had named Vinson to the Court of Appeals for the District of Columbia. Nearly six years later, he left the bench to be Roosevelt's director of the Office of Economic Stabilization before becoming Truman's treasury secretary. Yet Edward "Prich" Prichard, who had enjoyed working for his fellow Kentuckian in the executive branch, warned Frankfurter that Vinson was miscast as chief justice and no match for the intellects and personalities in the Supreme Court's snake pit.

Isolated at Nuremberg and without consulting anyone after the Vinson announcement, Jackson made a major error in judgment—by writing a letter to the president, which laid bare private details of his dispute with Black about the 1945 *Jewell Ridge* case. The case involved whether, under the definition of a "work week" under the Fair Labor Standards Act, coal miners were entitled to be paid for their time traveling to and from the surface of the mine ("portal to portal"). A few years earlier in a case involving iron miners, the plaintiffs' counsel had insisted in his briefs that the provision did not apply to coal miners. In *Jewell Ridge*, he contradicted that position. The counsel for the United Mine Workers in both cases was Black's former law partner and Senate investigations counsel, Crampton Harris. The ties between Harris and Black ran deep. Harris was a Birmingham Ku Klux Klan leader who had used the organization to finance Black's first Senate campaign and had helped Black draft his national radio address in 1937 explaining the justice's Klan past. And as a Birmingham lawyer Black had represented the United Mine Workers before handing off the client to his former partner Harris. Jackson, however, did not know the extent of the Black-Harris connection in March 1945 when the Court heard argument in the *Jewell Ridge* case.

After the oral argument in *Jewell Ridge*, the justices initially voted 5–4 against the coal miners. Reed, however, changed his vote, giving Black a five-justice majority with Stone, Roberts, Frankfurter, and Jackson in dissent. As the senior justice in the majority, Black assigned the case to the justice Frankfurter derided as Black's "Stooge," Frank Murphy. Jackson's letter to Truman revealed that Black had tried to force Murphy to announce the decision before the majority and dissenting opinions had been completed in an effort to influence negotiations in an ongoing United Mine Workers strike. Murphy refused; the strike was settled without the benefit of the Court's decision.

In his dissent, Jackson observed that Harris had contradicted his argument in the iron mining case, and, in a footnote, published Senator Black's comments in the *Congressional Record* introducing the Fair Labor Standards Act and assuring his colleagues that the law would not interfere with collective bargaining agreements. The coal miners had not collectively bargained for "portal to portal" pay. *Jewell Ridge* resulted in a 5–4 decision in the coal miners' favor, but the case was not over.

On May 31, 1945, the coal company petitioned the Court for a rehearing on the basis of Black's failure to disqualify himself from a case argued by his former law partner Harris. At the Supreme Court, each justice decides whether to disqualify himself. Jackson, Murphy, and Stone had disqualified themselves from many cases involving the Department of Justice. Stone had disqualified himself from a case in which his former law partner had represented one of the parties. Black's supporters argued that, even if the case had ended in a 4–4 tie, the federal appeals court's decision in favor of the coal miners would have been allowed to stand. In denying the rehearing petition, Stone proposed an unsigned, single-paragraph opinion explaining that disqualification was up to the individual justice, not the entire Court. Black objected and demanded that the justices who agreed with Stone's opinion should sign it. Jackson countered with a multi-paragraph draft opinion explaining that only Black could decide whether he should have disqualified himself. At conference, Black threatened that if Jackson published his opinion it would be a "declaration of war." Jackson replied that he "would not stand for any more of his bullying." Frankfurter was the only justice who joined Jackson's opinion and explained why he could not remain silent. A year later, Jackson, in his June 7, 1946, letter to Truman, revealed Black's bullying at conference and argued that Black had "made good" on his declaration of war by threatening the president with his resignation. Black was also a likely source of information for Fleeson's column.

Jackson's letter to Truman, which the justice also sent to the House and Senate Judiciary Committees, made front-page news on June 11, 1946, for all the wrong reasons. The publicly silent Black became the victim. The press, politicians, members of the Court, and Truman (at least privately) speculated that Jackson would be forced to resign. Drew Pearson relied on information from an anonymous justice—presumably Black, Douglas, or Murphy—to blame the whole episode on Frankfurter as "the quiet spearhead of the anti-Black faction" and who was "at personal odds" with Black, Douglas, and Murphy. In fact, in their overseas correspondence, Frankfurter had not written to Jackson about the vacant chief justiceship. "The trouble with poor Bob was his difficulty in telling the real story—the deep elements of the situation of which he felt propelled to expose one surface outcropping," Frankfurter wrote Learned Hand. "I wouldn't have done it, and I would, had he consulted me, have doubtless advised against it, but—I so completely understand what made him do it . . ."

Frankfurter was as unhappy about the state of the Court as Jackson was. "Never before in the history of the Court were so many of its members influenced in decision by considerations extraneous to the legal issues that supposedly control decisions," he wrote Murphy on June 10. "Never before have members of the Court so often acted contrary to their convictions on the governing legal issues in decision. Never before has so large a proportion of the opinions fallen short of requisite professional standards."

Frankfurter's allies were dwindling. The previous June, Roberts had resigned as soon as he was eligible for a full pension. Now, Frankfurter was worried he might lose Jackson, too. In a June 12 letter, he tried to reassure his friend under fire that everything in the letter to Truman was accurate and did not require his resignation. He relayed his conversations with Marion, after Vinson had been named chief justice, about Jackson. Felix remarked that "this is the first time in American history that a man failed of the Chief Justiceship because he showed character when character needed to be shown." Marion expressed "hope that Bob doesn't resign." Felix replied: "I can't imagine he will."

The letter, Jackson wrote, "gave me comfort." He assured Frankfurter that he would not resign, but could not return to the Court if he "had not taken this audacious and desperate step" of informing the nation about Black's behavior. Like Frankfurter, Jackson knew that the fight with Black had begun long before Stone's death: Black and Douglas's political maneuvering in numerous cases since 1941, whether they involved civil liberties or portal-to-portal pay for miners; Roberts's resignation and the petty dispute over the Court's customary letter; and Black and Douglas's veiled threats to resign. In his June 19 letter to Frankfurter, Jackson summed up the situation: "Black is now rid of the Chief, whose reputation as a liberal made his opposition particularly effective and irritating. Black, as you and I know, has driven Roberts off the Bench and pursued him after his retirement. Now if he can have it understood that he has a veto over the promotion of any Associate, he would have things about where he wants them."

After Jackson's letter to Truman, Black and Jackson returned to the Court for the 1946 term and publicly resumed cordial relations as if nothing had happened. The ideological fight between Black and Frankfurter, however, had only just begun.

———

WHILE SITTING ON THE bench during the announcement of the Court's decisions on January 6, 1947, Frank Murphy quietly accused Frankfurter of a serious impropriety. *Fortune* magazine had just published an article by historian Arthur Schlesinger, Jr., about the justices' personal and jurisprudential conflicts. Acting on a rumor from one of their colleagues, Murphy accused Frankfurter of having reviewed Schlesinger Jr.'s article prior to publication. Frankfurter began scribbling a note on the bench. Instead of handing it to Murphy, he had the note typed and circulated it to the entire Court.

Denying the accusation as an "unmitigated untruth," Frankfurter explained in the note that he had known "Young Arthur" since Schlesinger Jr. was a boy. In 1924, he had befriended Arthur Schlesinger, Sr., when the historian had joined the Harvard faculty. Three years later, Schlesinger Sr. had supported Frankfurter's fight for a new trial for Sacco and Vanzetti. Since his freshman year at Harvard College in the mid-1930s, Schlesinger Jr. had been corresponding with Frankfurter about history, politics, and journalism. During the war, he had worked for the Office of War Information and the Office of Strategic Services and had fallen in with the Georgetown set, including former Frankfurter clerks Rauh, Graham, and Prichard; journalist Joseph Alsop; and philosopher Isaiah Berlin. In May 1946, 28-year-old Schlesinger Jr. won the Pulitzer Prize for his book *The Age of Jackson.* He was living in Chevy Chase, Maryland, and dabbling in journalism for *Fortune* magazine before joining his father on the Harvard faculty.

On the morning of October 20, 1946, Schlesinger Jr. had arrived at Frankfurter's chambers for an interview about the Court. Frankfurter interrogated him and learned that the historian had read all the right things and talked to all the right people—Judge Learned Hand; Harvard law professors Paul Freund, Henry Hart, and Thomas Reed Powell; Douglas's friends and promoters Corcoran, Yale law professor Fred Rodell, and journalist Eliot Janeway; and all the justices except Vinson. Black, Schlesinger Jr. indicated, had been the most tight-lipped and wanted to discuss only *The Age of Jackson.* Frankfurter refused to discuss Black, Douglas, Murphy, or anyone else by name. Yet Frankfurter addressed why the Court should not be a "super-legislature," warned against "judicial lawmaking," and supplied Schlesinger Jr. with a quote from

Justice Morrison R. Waite about why justices should not have political ambitions. "The unspoken application," Schlesinger Jr. later acknowledged, "was to Bill Douglas."

In his January 6, 1947, reply to Murphy, Frankfurter only partially revealed the substance of his conversation with Schlesinger Jr. Frankfurter claimed that he had refused to discuss the Court's "work or . . . any of its members" and had referred Schlesinger Jr. to people (Hand, Hart, Freund) to whom the historian had already spoken. Upon leaving Frankfurter's chambers, Schlesinger Jr. told him that "only one member of the Court was as tight-mouthed with him as I was." But their discussion about super-legislatures, judicial lawmaking, and quotes about justices harboring political ambitions suggested otherwise. Somewhat more plausibly, Frankfurter insisted that he had not spoken to Schlesinger Jr. about the article again until after its publication.

Schlesinger Jr.'s *Fortune* article pitted Frankfurter and Jackson against Black and Douglas, crystallized their disputes about the role of the Supreme Court in American democracy as restraint versus activism, and coined the phrase "judicial activism." Schlesinger Jr. used judicial activism to describe the Black-Douglas-Murphy approach to judging as results-oriented—reasoning backward from a desired result on the basis of the parties and interests at stake rather than examining the legal issues. He accused the activist wing of politicizing the Court's decision making in favor of labor and civil liberties and "promoting the social welfare" in the same way that the conservative "Four Horsemen" had struck down New Deal programs in 1936 on the basis of their preference for big business and their opposition to the Roosevelt administration's policies. He portrayed Frankfurter as promoting the Holmesian tradition of "judicial self-restraint" and in trying to separate his personal views from legal outcomes. And he concluded Frankfurter and Jackson were "surely right" that "[t]he larger interests of democracy in the U.S. require that the Court contract rather than expand its power . . ."

What rankled Black and Douglas's supporters, as well as Murphy and other members of the Court, were Schlesinger Jr.'s unflattering descriptions of the justices' personalities: Black ("bullying"); Douglas ("highly ambitious," "fond of intrigue," presidential hopeful); Murphy ("strange, complicated, self-dedicated," and "messianic"); Jackson ("cocky," "ulterior ambitions"); Reed ("slow and affable"); Frankfurter ("warm and impetuous," "satirical," "self-righteous"). These descriptions, particularly the ones about Murphy, seemed like they came from Frankfurter and other members of the Court.

The Black-Douglas partisans viewed the article through the lens of Harvard versus Yale and dismissed it as a pro-Frankfurter, pro-Harvard hit piece. Indeed, Schlesinger Jr. attributed the inspiration for Black and Douglas's activist and results-oriented views to the legal realism practiced at Yale Law School by Frankfurter antagonists Walton Hamilton and Fred Rodell. The realists, Schlesinger Jr. wrote, viewed Frankfurter's judicial restraint as merely "a cover for conservativism." Rodell and Janeway did not appreciate being exposed as Douglas's public relations team. Rodell's Yale law colleague Judge Jerome Frank wrote a six-page letter pointing out the article's shortcomings and objected to the "Yale thesis." The Yale versus Harvard characterization, as Frank alleged, may have been overdrawn. Black thought the article was "naïve" and its criticism of Douglas "unfair." Schlesinger Jr. saw Frankfurter at a dinner party at Phil and Kay Graham's home shortly after the article's publication; Frankfurter, however, withheld comment for several months. He finally wrote Schlesinger Jr. that the Harvard historian "could not be wronger" in characterizing Brandeis as a proto-activist, described journalism as "the profession of shallowness," and argued that the young Pulitzer Prize winner was "really too good for it." The justice insisted that he did not "think 'ill' of the article—I think 'ill' of the procedure, the intellectual procedure which lies behind it & things of yours which I have read!" All was soon forgiven. In May 1947, Frankfurter published his attack on judicial lawmaking, a New York City bar lecture, "Some Reflections on the Reading of Statutes." He sent a copy to Schlesinger Jr. with a note: "For A.M.S. Jr.—who is equipped to write about the judicial process as few lawyers I have known . . ."

Despite complaints from the Black and Frankfurter camps, Schlesinger Jr.'s article captured some fundamental truths. The activism-restraint paradigm described the way the Court operated in 1946–1947 and, indeed, for more than fifty years after the 1937 New Deal constitutional crisis. The Court circa 1947 was dominated by Black and Frankfurter, two men, Schlesinger Jr. wrote, "of unusual intellectual ability and personal force." The stakes for the Black and Frankfurter positions were high: whether an increasingly powerful Supreme Court was consistent with its role in America's liberal democracy.

During the 1946 Supreme Court term, the major dispute between Black and Frankfurter was about "incorporation"—the extent to which the Bill of Rights, particularly the first eight amendments to the Constitution, restrained state and local governments. The Court's 1833 decision *Barron v. Baltimore* held these amendments applied only to the federal government. The Civil War and its aftermath changed the constitutional landscape. In 1868, Senator Jacob Howard, the floor manager for what became the Fourteenth Amendment, argued that one of the purposes of the amendment's

Privileges or Immunities Clause was to apply the Bill of Rights to the states. During Reconstruction, however, the Court's 1873 decision in the *Slaughter-House Cases* rejected this interpretation and defined privileges or immunities of national citizenship so narrowly as to make the provision useless. During the early twentieth century, the justices employed the Fourteenth Amendment's Due Process Clause to apply a few of the Bill of Rights' most fundamental provisions, including the First Amendment's freedom of speech and free exercise of religion, to the states. Black believed that all the first eight amendments should be incorporated. Frankfurter preferred to follow Cardozo's 1937 opinion in *Palko v. Connecticut*, which refused to incorporate the Double Jeopardy Clause or any other provision unless it was "implicit in the concept of ordered liberty" and to do otherwise violated " 'fundamental principles of liberty and justice.' "

The fate of Willie Francis, a seventeen-year-old African American sentenced to death, depended on the scope of the Court's incorporation doctrine. On May 3, 1946, the state of Louisiana had attempted to electrocute him. After his executioners flipped the switch, Francis groaned as his lips swelled and his body seized. He yelled for them to remove his hood: "Take it off. Let me breath[e]." The electric chair had malfunctioned. Two years earlier, Francis had confessed to the murder of his employer, a white Cajun drug store owner in St. Martinville, Louisiana. His confession contained a cryptic line suggesting a sexual relationship: "it was a secret about me and him." The gun was never found. At his trial, his inept court-appointed lawyers did not request a change of venue, tried to withdraw his not-guilty plea, called no witnesses, and filed no appeals. After the botched execution, a St. Martinville lawyer, Bertrand De Blanc, and a Washington lawyer and New Orleans native, J. Skelly Wright, appealed Francis's case to the Supreme Court. In their petition for certiorari to the Court, they argued that attempting to execute Francis a second time violated the Fifth Amendment's prohibition against double jeopardy and the Eighth Amendment's prohibition against cruel and unusual punishment. In the past, the Court had not applied these provisions to the states.

For Frankfurter, the Willie Francis case must have triggered painful memories of the summer of 1927 when he had failed to save the lives of Italian anarchists Sacco and Vanzetti. Four justices, including Holmes and Brandeis, had refused to stay their executions. Appeals to the governor of Massachusetts for clemency had failed. Frankfurter was personally opposed to capital punishment. From Sacco-Vanzetti, he knew how inadequate defense lawyers and how prejudiced a trial judge could be. And he knew how the system was unfair to outsiders and the less fortunate. Although the odds were long, he wanted the Court to hear the Francis case. On June 4, 1946, Hugo Black, acting as chief justice, granted Francis a temporary stay of execution so that the Court could consider the case. At 11:00 a.m. that day, the justices discussed Francis's petition for certiorari. Frankfurter voted with Murphy and Rutledge to grant it; Black and Douglas voted with Burton and Reed to deny it. It usually takes four votes to hear a case. By June 1946, Stone had died, and Jackson was in Nuremberg. With only seven justices present, they agreed to hear the case during their fall calendar on the basis of three votes. An error by the clerk's office, which was quickly corrected, listed Francis's petition as denied when, in fact, it had been granted. Four days before his scheduled second execution, Willie Francis learned that he would live for a few more months while the Court considered his case.

During oral argument on November 19, 1946, Wright contended that the Double Jeopardy Clause meant someone could not be tried twice and could not be punished twice for the same offense. A second attempt at electrocuting Francis, Wright argued, was also cruel and unusual punishment. The state of Louisiana, contrary to several eyewitnesses, claimed that no electrical current had reached Francis's body the first time. Wright also argued that the incompetent lawyers at Francis's trial, consistent with the Court's decision in *Powell v. Alabama* about the trial of the Scottsboro Boys, had been like having no lawyers at all. With no trial transcript, however, Wright described the trial as shrouded in "abysmal darkness." The focus of Wright's argument was not on the fairness of the trial but on the unconstitutionality of attempting to electrocute Francis a second time. Frankfurter asked whether it would be cruel and unusual punishment if the execution had been postponed after Francis had been taken from his cell to the death chamber. Frankfurter also debated with Jackson whether, if the Court found the second execution unconstitutional, the case could be remanded for a different punishment.

At conference four days later, the justices voted 6–3 to affirm Francis's conviction and to lift his stay of execution. Only Murphy, Rutledge, and Burton voted to dissent. Chief Justice Vinson, Black, Reed, Frankfurter, Douglas, and Jackson voted to affirm. Black and Douglas said nothing at conference. The majority opinion was assigned to Reed, but the Court was as fractured as in other recent cases. Black drafted a separate concurrence but shelved it and ended up joining Reed's majority opinion. Rutledge and Murphy drafted dissents but did not publish them and joined Burton's dissent. Douglas switched sides and joined Burton's dissent, but only after it was clear that Francis would be executed.

As Frankfurter said at conference, he thought this was "not [an] easy case." He was reluctant to use the Fourteenth Amendment's Due Process Clause to second-guess state courts. The "technicalities" of Francis's double jeopardy argument did not bother him. The cruel and unusual punishment argument, however, was a different story because of its "progressive nature, shocking the feelings of the time—here, though it is hardly [a] defensible thing for [the] state to do, it is not so offensive as to make [me] puke—does not shock [the] conscience." Frankfurter invoked Holmes's puke test for whether to reverse a criminal conviction on due process grounds, a "shocks the conscience" test that Frankfurter later wrote into law. In the Francis case, however, he was not content simply to vote to affirm. He asked for time to write.

For the rest of his career, Frankfurter admired that Burton had dissented in the Willie Francis case after initially voting not to hear it as epitomizing Burton's honesty and fairness. On December 13, Frankfurter wrote Burton that he had read the dissent "with sympathy" but could not join it because of his long-standing refusal to invoke the Due Process Clause to interfere with state power. He again referenced Holmes's test whether the state law "made him 'puke'" as well as the Court's 1945 decision in *Malinski v. New York* about its "extremely limited" review of state criminal convictions. "I cannot say," Frankfurter wrote of a second electrocution, "it so shocks the accepted, prevailing standard of fairness and justice . . ." He reminded Burton that he had pushed the Court to take the case and had been "struggling with myself." He read Burton's dissent with "satisfaction" and praised Burton's contributions to the case as "one of the most cheering experiences since I have been on this Court." On December 26, Burton invited him to take another look at the dissent. Five days later, he dismissed Burton's considerations as based on state law and insisted the decision to execute Francis was up to the state of Louisiana, not the Court. "I am sorry I cannot go with you," he concluded, "but I am weeping no tears that you are expressing a dissent."

On January 11, 1947, Frankfurter informed his fellow justices that he could not join Reed's majority opinion, either. Reed's opinion assumed that the Fifth Amendment's prohibition against double jeopardy applied to a state criminal conviction such as Francis's and was "contrary to the whole tenor" of *Palko v. Connecticut*. *Palko* had refused to apply the Double Jeopardy Clause to the states.

Instead of joining the majority or dissenting opinions released on January 13, Frankfurter wrote a concurring opinion explaining why the Court should not invoke the Due Process Clause to interfere with Francis's conviction. He reminded his colleagues that the Court's 1873 *Slaughter-House* decision prevented the Privileges or Immunities Clause from applying the first eight amendments to the states. Nor, he argued, did the Due Process Clause confine the states to an eighteenth century criminal code: "The Fourteenth Amendment did not mean to imprison the States into the limited experience of the eighteenth century. It did mean to withdraw from the States the right to act in ways that are offensive to a decent respect for the dignity of man, and heedless of his freedom." In an effort to define the "very broad terms by which to accommodate freedom and authority," he reviewed the Court's due process decisions and concluded: "it involves the application of standards of fairness and justice very broadly conceived." Fairness and justice, he argued, did not depend on his personal opinion. Rather, they involved "great tolerance toward a State's conduct." He explained that his own views about capital punishment were irrelevant: "this Court must abstain from interference with State action no matter how strong one's personal feeling of revulsion against a State's insistence on its pound of flesh." He declined to enforce "my private view rather than that consensus of society's opinion." Because Louisiana's actions were not " 'repugnant to the conscience of mankind,' " he concluded, "I cannot say that the Constitution withholds it."

Any hope for Willie Francis, Frankfurter knew from the Sacco-Vanzetti case, was up to executive clemency. Under the Louisiana Constitution at the time, the governor could not pardon or commute a sentence without the consent of the lieutenant governor, attorney general, and trial judge (or any two of the three). In late May 1946, this three-member Pardon Board already had denied clemency. Frankfurter received numerous letters about his opinion. A January 19, 1947, letter from Mrs. Harold Evans of New York City asked how Louisiana could execute a child and whether the justice could contact state officials. Two days later, he replied: "You will permit me to say that I quite appreciate your compassionate feeling on the Willie Francis case. I share it. But a judge of this Court isn't God—he is not even the Governor of the State, in whom is vested the power of executive clemency."

Reprising his role in the Sacco-Vanzetti case, Frankfurter tried to influence the clemency process. This time, he wrote his law school classmate, New Orleans native, and leading member of the Louisiana bar, Monte Lemann. In yet another example of crossing ethical lines, Frankfurter asked Lemann to intervene with state officials: "I have little doubt that if Louisiana allows Francis to go to his death, it will needlessly cast a cloud on Louisiana for many years to come, and, what is more important, probably leave many of its citizens with disquietude." Frankfurter noted Francis's case weighed "heavily on my conscience" and asked whether Louisiana officials could show "humaneness" and "compassion." Lemann, in turn, wrote the trial judge in Francis's case, James Simon, who happened to be one of Lemann's former Tulane law students, and copied the lieutenant governor and state attorney general. In his letter to Judge Simon, Lemann wrote: "I realize that the eyes of the world are in a sense upon us in this case" and alluded to his discussions with lawyers "of high standing." In a veiled reference to Frankfurter, Lemann indicated that one prominent lawyer "wrote me recently that he felt it would be a serious blot upon our State if Francis was permitted to be executed." Frankfurter circulated Lemann's letter to Simon to the entire Court. On April 22, 1947, the Pardon Board again denied Francis's clemency petition. Francis's attorneys frantically asked the Supreme Court to rehear the case on the basis of new information that his executioners had been drunk the first time they had tried to execute him; his attorneys also made last-ditch appeals to state officials. The rehearing petition and appeals were denied. On May 9, 1947, Willie Francis was strapped into the electric chair for a second time. This time, the chair worked. At 12:10 p.m., he was dead.

Frankfurter's concurrence in the Willie Francis case reflected a lifelong reluctance to invoke the Fourteenth Amendment's Due Process Clause to interfere with the state political process. He shared Holmes's skepticism about judicial intervention in political disputes, a skepticism reinforced by the 1937 New Deal constitutional crisis. Like Holmes, he also tried to separate his personal views from the outcome in a given case. Yet he lacked Holmes's intellectual and political detachment. As his letters to Mrs. Harold Evans and Monte Lemann indicated, the Francis case was gut-wrenching. Frankfurter's friends knew this. Learned Hand, who had disagreed with him in 1927 about the Sacco-Vanzetti case, applauded Frankfurter's concurring opinion in the Willie Francis case as "most admirable; but you know what I feel about the whole business of judges as final arbiters on such matters. Our Constitution in this aspect has debauched our courts, diminished our collective responsibilities, and falsified the whole basis of civilized society. The nearer I come to my end, the more certain I am that a Bill of Rights, administered by a bench, is what William James called Santayana's philosophy: 'The perfection of rottenness.'" Frankfurter responded by reasserting his belief since 1923 that the Fourteenth Amendment would be better off without a Due Process Clause because it gave judges too much power. He observed that a proposed Irish Home Rule Bill before World War I did not include such a clause and neither did the Australian Constitution. During the mid-1930s, he had discussed his opposition to the Due Process Clause in correspondence with Cardozo. In 1947, he tried to persuade Indian jurist B. N. Rau not to include the clause in India's new constitution. "One of the strangest things about our people," he wrote Hand, "is the way in which they blow hot and cold regarding the judiciary—nothing is easier than to gain applause for attacks upon lawyers and judges, often with good reason, and nothing is more habitual than to leave the most delicate problems of statesmanship for determination by judges."

Frankfurter's debate with Black over incorporation reflected different approaches about how to limit judicial power and climaxed in the 1947 case of another black man sentenced to death for murder, Admiral Dewey Adamson. During the trial, the state prosecutor, consistent with California law, remarked to the jury that Adamson had failed to testify in his own defense (Adamson refused to take the stand to avoid discussing several prior convictions). In federal court, the prosecutor's comments would have violated Adamson's Fifth Amendment privilege against self-incrimination. In a 1908 case, *Twining v. New Jersey*, the Court held the self-incrimination privilege did not apply to the states; Cardozo's 1937 opinion in *Palko v. Connecticut* reaffirmed *Twining*. Adamson's lawyer, in an effort to save the San Quentin prisoner from the gas chamber, appealed to the Supreme Court.

After oral argument on January 15 and 16, 1947, the justices voted 5–3 to affirm Adamson's conviction. Only Black voted to pass. He was not sure that Adamson had been forced to incriminate himself in the case. Yet Black was certain, based on the first Justice Harlan's dissent in *Twining v. New Jersey*, that the self-incrimination clause applied to the states. Frankfurter, when his turn came to speak, defended *Twining*. "Twining," Frankfurter responded, "is 'cloudless'—It is right and has lots of authority." As a result, Frankfurter and Black wrote concurring and dissenting opinions that overshadowed Reed's majority opinion in *Adamson* and that dominated the constitutional debate over incorporation.

Frankfurter wanted to limit the expansiveness of the Due Process Clause by following precedent. He revered Justices William Henry Moody and Benjamin Cardozo and believed that their reasoning in *Twining* and *Palko*, respectively, was unassailable. He described *Twining* as "the judicial process at its best" and "one of the outstanding opinions in the history of the Court" and observed that *Palko* had been joined by Hughes, McReynolds, Brandeis, Sutherland, Stone, and Black himself. In the seventy years since the passage of the Fourteenth Amendment until the current Court, forty-three justices had considered the issue of incorporation and only one "eccentric exception" (Harlan) had embraced the idea that the first eight amendments applied to the states. He listed deceased justices including Holmes, Brandeis, Stone, and

Cardozo who had considered the issue and described them as "alert in safe-guarding and promoting the interests of liberty and human dignity through law" yet "mindful of the relation of our federal system to a progressively democratic society and therefore duly regardful of the scope of authority that was left to the States even after the Civil War." Basically, he argued, if Black were right about incorporation, then all these dead judicial luminaries would have been wrong.

After discussing Supreme Court precedent, Frankfurter turned to the text and history of the Fourteenth Amendment. He argued that the language of the first section must be read "in a 'sense most obvious to the common understanding at the time of its adoption.'" Considering the ordinary meaning of the words "the political and legal history" of due process, the relationship between the federal government and the states, and the provisions in the Bill of Rights, Frankfurter argued that no one would "recognize the Fourteenth Amendment as a cover for the various explicit provisions of the first eight Amendments." He rejected Black's emphasis on the congressional speeches of Representative John Bingham, Senator Jacob Howard, and others who tried to persuade their colleagues to vote for the Fourteenth Amendment: "Remarks of a particular proponent of the Amendment, no matter how influential, are not to be deemed part of the Amendment. What was submitted for ratification was his proposal, not his speech." Nowhere in the text of the Fourteenth Amendment, Frankfurter argued, did it suggest the states were giving up their different approaches to grand juries and other forms of criminal procedure. The states would not have ratified the amendment, he insisted, if they knew it "uprooted their established methods for prosecuting crime and fastened upon themselves a new prosecutorial system."

Rather than an approach to incorporation driven by a justice's individual personal preferences for a particular Bill of Rights provision, Frankfurter understood *Palko* as articulating a basic conception of due process rooted in "certain minimum standards which are 'of the very essence of a scheme of ordered liberty.'" Frankfurter interpreted the Due Process Clause as requiring the states to observe "basic liberties." In analyzing a criminal conviction such as Adamson's, he focused on whether the process violated "those canons of decency and fairness." Frankfurter's "standards of justice" approach, though general, required "an alert deference to the judgment of the State court under review." The total incorporation of the Bill of Rights, he contended, would have eliminated any judicial deference to the states. His insistence on basic due process—the same approach he took in the Willie Francis case—emphasized procedural fairness and limited judicial intervention. He refused to use the Due Process Clause to transform the Supreme Court into a nine-member super-legislature.

In his dissent, Black rejected *Twining*'s focus on "civilized decency" and "fundamental liberty and justice" as a "natural law–due process formula" that gave judges too much discretion. He preferred bright-line rules and argued, based on congressional debates over the Fourteenth Amendment, which he summarized in an appendix, that all eight amendments applied to the states. Black's dissent was a tour de force and announced his transformation into a major constitutional thinker. His aims, in many ways, mirrored Frankfurter's: how to control judges. "I fear to see the consequences of the Court's practice of substituting its own concepts of decency and fundamental justice for the language of the Bill of Rights as its point of departure in interpreting and enforcing the Bill of Rights . . . ," Black wrote. "To hold that this Court can determine what, if any, provisions of the Bill of Rights will be enforced, and if so to what degree, is to frustrate the great design of a written Constitution."

Adamson v. California revealed Frankfurter's and Black's different approaches to achieving similar goals. Frankfurter sought to limit judicial power by narrowly interpreting the Fourteenth Amendment's Due Process Clause on the basis of its text and the Court's past decisions. Black wanted to cabin judicial discretion through the wholesale application of the Bill of Rights to the states on the basis of the Fourteenth Amendment's legislative history. Frankfurter and Black came from different parts of the country and took very different paths to becoming powerful constitutional thinkers. Frankfurter made his reputation as a Harvard law professor and Court critic who had befriended Holmes, Brandeis, and Cardozo; Black taught himself constitutional law after he had joined the Court in 1937 and after many years as an Alabama trial lawyer and U.S. senator. Their clashes during the 1945 and 1946 terms obscured important similarities—their opposition to using the Due Process Clause to invalidate state laws and their willingness to invoke the Fourteenth Amendment to achieve racial equality.

And somehow, amidst his jurisprudential battles with Hugo Black, Frankfurter found time to work behind the scenes for a Jewish state in Palestine.

CHAPTER 29

My Eyes Hath Seen
the Glory of the
Coming of the Lord

More than 1500 people had crowded into the large ballroom of the Waldorf-Astoria Hotel on November 27, 1945, to celebrate the seventy-first birthday of Zionist leader Chaim Weizmann. They filled the balconies and the side halls of the grand New York City hotel. They sat and listened to Frankfurter, by telephone from Washington, D.C., explain Weizmann's vision of a Jewish homeland in Palestine: "A Jewish Palestine for Dr. Weizmann means creation—the creation of new moral and cultural values." Frankfurter described Weizmann as "a dreamer—the dreamer of one of those dreams which becomes a reality when men have the vision and the will to make it so. May it be given to him and to us to witness the fulfillment of his hopes and labors those many years. For the building of a Jewish Homeland in Palestine, large enough to admit and absorb all those who need it so urgently, without hurt and with help to those now dwelling there, is a task laid upon statesmen by the conscience of the world."

Frankfurter's postwar efforts to secure a Jewish homeland in Palestine revealed his continued ability to influence world affairs. He intervened in the country's atomic energy policy because of the issue's importance to the future of the world. His investment in the fight for a Jewish homeland was more personal. His commitment to Zionism had begun in 1914 when Brandeis, the de facto leader of the American Zionist movement, had enlisted him and Judge Julian Mack as lieutenants. They had rejoiced in 1917 over the Balfour Declaration's commitment to a Jewish homeland in Palestine. They had failed two years later at the Paris Peace Conference—despite Frankfurter's correspondence with Prince Faisal pledging Arab-Jewish cooperation and insistence that Brandeis visit Palestine—to persuade the Allies to create a Jewish state as part of the Treaty of Versailles. During the 1920s and 1930s, the British government had controlled the region yet sided with Arab interests over Jewish ones. With Brandeis's encouragement, Frankfurter had published a 1931 article in *Foreign Affairs* blasting British limits on Jewish immigration to Palestine. Hitler's rise to power made the British policy even more tragic. A 1939 British white paper limited Jewish immigration to Palestine to 75,000 people over the next five years, conditioned additional Jewish immigration on Arab consent, and restricted Jewish land acquisition. The Zionist efforts of Brandeis and Mack ended in despair; Brandeis died in November 1941 and Mack in September 1943. Six million Jews perished during the Holocaust; 200,000 to 250,000 Jewish refugees had survived the war but languished in displaced-persons camps. With Brandeis and Mack gone, Frankfurter was the elder statesman lobbying for a Jewish homeland in Palestine.

AS A SUPREME COURT JUSTICE, Frankfurter insisted he played no public role in Zionist affairs. Like Brandeis, he declined invitations to appear at Zionist events. In truth, he intentionally underplayed his work behind the scenes. Frankfurter was a facilitator. "There isn't a single important figure in the leadership of the country," Rabbi Stephen Wise informed Eliahu Elath (né Epstein) of the Jewish Agency of Palestine, "whom Frankfurter does not know." Wise, however, warned Elath that Frankfurter "can only open doors." To advance the Zionist cause, Frankfurter tapped his network of liberal friends in the State Department, the Truman administration, foreign governments, and the press. He also served as an important back channel between Weizmann and government officials. Most of all, he relied on several protégés with close ties to the president, led by David K. Niles.

Niles's friendship with Frankfurter began in Boston. The son of Jewish immigrants from Russia-controlled Poland, he had changed his last name after high school from Neyhus to Niles. As the associate director and later director of the Ford Hall Forum, a public lecture series in Boston, he traveled in Frankfurter's circle of liberal social reformers including Brandeis, Harold Laski, and Elizabeth Glendower Evans. Like Evans and Frankfurter, Niles had fought for a new trial for Sacco and Vanzetti. And like Frankfurter, Niles had endorsed third-party presidential candidate Robert M. La Follette, Sr., in 1924 and Democratic nominee Al Smith four years later. In 1932, Niles had organized independent voters for Roosevelt.

Like many of Frankfurter's protégés, Niles ended up in the Roosevelt administration. For several years, he served as chair of the Massachusetts Adjustment Board for the National Recovery Administration. In August 1935, Niles helped Frankfurter to rally progressives' support for the New Deal. The following year, Niles began to work in Washington full-time—first with Harry Hopkins in the Works Progress Administration and Commerce Department, then as head consultant in the Office of Production Management, and in July 1942 as a special assistant to the president. Enemies of Roosevelt and the New Deal identified Niles as part of the Frankfurter- and Hopkins-led "palace guard." On the floor of the House of Representatives in 1943, Congressman Fred Bradley of Michigan railed against "this Harvard Frankfurter-Laski-Niles radical clique." Bradley emphasized Niles's Russianimmigrant parents named Neyhus, placed him at the center of efforts to create a Socialist state, and accused him of being a Communist. Niles survived Bradley's accusations and, after Roosevelt's death, was one of the few administrative aides who stayed to work for Truman. Niles worked unobtrusively out of the Old Executive Office Building as a liaison on issues about racial and religious minorities. He lived in the Carlton Hotel in Washington, returned to Boston every weekend, and avoided the Washington cocktail party scene. The balding, bespectacled Niles earned the reputation as having "a passion for anonymity"—with good reason. He was dogged by rumors of homosexuality and Communist ties. Through it all, he was a committed Zionist.

Niles helped Truman overcome opposition from the State Department and the British government and insist on increased immigration of Jewish refugees to Palestine. After Roosevelt's death, Truman learned that in February 1945 after Yalta, his predecessor had assured King Ibn Saud of Saudi Arabia that the United States would consult with him about Palestine and would not take any action "hostile to the Arab people." State Department officials warned Truman about pressure from Zionist leaders and advised him not to do anything to alienate Arab interests in the region. The new president refused to ignore the evidence of Nazi atrocities and the suffering of Jewish refugees. He dispatched Earl G. Harrison, the American representative on the Intergovernmental Committee on Refugees, to Europe to investigate the issue of displaced persons. Harrison's report described Jews living and dying in filthy conditions behind barbed-wire fences, including in former concentration camps. On August 31, Truman asked the British government to lift restrictions on Jewish immigration to Palestine. The Attlee government responded by proposing a joint study of the problem.

On November 13, 1945, Truman announced the creation of the Anglo-American Committee of Inquiry on Palestine consisting of six American and six British members. Truman, special counsel to the president Sam Rosenman, and Secretary of State James F. Byrnes independently made lists of prospective American members. Niles rebuffed the State Department's attempt to stack the committee with pro-Arab Americans and succeeded in lobbying for two Zionists—an outspoken Catholic and San Francisco lawyer, Bartley C. Crum, and the League of Nations high commissioner for refugees, James G. McDonald. Rosenman, an ally of Niles's and Frankfurter's, also included Crum and McDonald on his list. For a third pro-Zionist member of the committee, Niles received an assist from Frankfurter.

A week after his phoned-in tribute to Weizmann, Frankfurter lobbied for an inside man on the committee—*Boston Herald* editor Frank Buxton. A Vermont native and 1900 Harvard College graduate, Buxton had joined the *Herald* four years after graduation, had risen to the position of managing editor, and had won a Pulitzer Prize for a 1923 editorial, "Who Made Coolidge?" In 1927, Buxton, like Niles, had forged a lifelong friendship with Frankfurter on the basis of their interest in the Sacco-Vanzetti case. It was Buxton who had stopped the *Herald*'s presses so that Frankfurter could respond to Northwestern law school dean John Henry Wigmore's attack on Frankfurter's *Atlantic Monthly* article and book. Buxton was horrified that sympathetic Bostonians refused to be seen in public with Frankfurter and that hostile Harvard alumni called for Frankfurter's ouster from the law faculty. Two years later in 1929, Buxton was named the editor of the *Herald*, where he worked until his retirement in 1946. He served as a trustee of civic organizations and belonged to several exclusive social clubs.

As a member of Boston's WASP establishment, Buxton was the perfect Trojan horse for Frankfurter's Zionist views. Frankfurter had contacts at the highest levels of the State Department. He was close to his former judicial colleague, Secretary of State Byrnes. Byrnes's counselor, Ben Cohen, had accompanied Frankfurter and other American Zionists to Paris in 1919 and, though not as close in 1945 to the justice as he once had been, remained a committed Zionist and friend. It was no surprise, therefore, that Buxton ended up on Byrnes's list. As soon as Byrnes called to ask him to be one of the American representatives, Buxton knew the source. "I presume, as they say in Windham County, Vermont, that Jimmy Byrnes has told you that he has asked me to serve on an Anglo-American Palestine Committee," Buxton wrote Frankfurter on December 4. "Item: dear Mr. Justice, I assume it's not a presumptuous presumption that one F. F. made the suggestion to one J.F.B."

For Frankfurter, Buxton was the best hope of preventing a pro-Arab committee report. He sent Buxton reading material: the phoned-in tribute to Weizmann, British documents and letters about Palestine, and Balfour's speeches on Zionism. Buxton kept him informed about the committee's activities. In mid-December, the newspaper editor arrived in Washington for the committee's first four sessions and meetings with Truman and General Dwight D. Eisenhower. After the meetings were over, Buxton and Frankfurter discussed the committee's prospects. Frankfurter began to despair as he reviewed the names of the other American and British members. "At the end of the farewell," Buxton wrote, "he broke down, bowed his head into his hands and sobbed."

Buxton buoyed the justice's spirits with vivid accounts of the committee's work in Europe and the Middle East. On February 15, 1946, from the Hotel Savoy in Berlin, Buxton wrote that when he and two British members visited the Warsaw ghetto he became "so sickened" he had to return to the car. "I am afraid that I shall always carry a vivid picture of the horrible things done to the ghetto here . . . ," he wrote Frankfurter. "Our journey was like a trip through an endless chamber of unspeakable horrors—devastation, burial pits, earth flecked with human ashes, bits of skull, and fragments of the signs of old civilization." The next day, they visited Frankfurter's birthplace in Vienna. Buxton insisted to his British counterparts that the United States would not budge on Jewish immigration to Palestine: "I hope when we get to Palestine and Jerusalem, the Jewish champions will not fail to hammer hard on the absorptive capacity of the country and the feasibility and financial possibility of widespread development . . ."

In Vienna, the committee heard from numerous witnesses and saw four demonstrations with banners such as "Free Palestine" and "Destroy the White Paper." "Only Palestine is in the minds and hearts of those poor, harried Jews . . . ," Buxton wrote. "My English colleagues here have been inclined to think that the preference for Palestine is the result of Zionist propaganda, but the evidence to the contrary has become so strong that it is absolutely conclusive." He informed Frankfurter about the American and British members and the group's tentative conclusions: "We can't escape the conviction that there is little place in any part of Europe or anywhere else in the world just now for the Jews—except Palestine." At the end of the letter, he asked for Frankfurter's opinion if a "declaration for the admittance of X thousands into Palestine were accompanied by passages adverse to the principles of Zionism?"

"Not in many a moon have such epistolary meteorites fallen into our house as your two letters," Frankfurter replied on March 13 after he and Marion had "devoured them." They enjoyed Buxton's descriptions of postwar Europe and of his role as the "vulgar American" compared to his British counterparts. But the main purpose of Frankfurter's letter was to answer Buxton's question by challenging its premise that there was such an abstract concept as "the principles of Zionism." He urged Buxton to make the committee's report more concrete and to defend three "propositions": (1) The "need and incontestable desire" of European Jews for a "permanent" home in Palestine; (2) "Due regard for the absorptive capacity of Palestine for such Jewish settlement, remembering however that absorptive capacity 'does not grow on a tree'"; and (3) "Safeguarding of equal civil rights of all inhabitants without regard, of course, to race, religion or political opinion." Frankfurter insisted that the committee should pursue these goals rather than abstract Zionist principles. He invoked his two favorite philosophers, Jefferson that "no statesman can plan for more than a generation ahead" and Holmes that "the first duty of man is to remember that he is not God."

In early April, Buxton reported on his trip to Palestine: "Now that I have seen Palestine and spent hours at the various redeemed places I share your enthusiasm and Marion's. How my Vermont father, who used to glory in the land cleared by him and his brothers, would have been amazed at the greater deeds of the Palestinian Jews! They have put into the land something which they were not known to possess and have taken out of it products which once seemed alien to it."

Buxton's major contribution to the committee was coaxing a pro-Zionist stance out of its American chairman, Judge Joseph C. Hutcheson, Jr. During the summer and fall of 1938 as Roosevelt searched for a Supreme Court nominee from the South or West, Frankfurter had suggested Hutcheson, a Texas federal judge since 1918 and member of the Court of Appeals for the Fifth Circuit since 1931, as a possible replacement for Cardozo. Roosevelt had dismissed the suggestion with a shake of his head and eventually named Frankfurter. Six years later, Hutcheson was Truman and Byrnes's choice as the American chairman of the committee and, among the American members, its most anti-Zionist. He did not support a Jewish state or an Arab one. Yet, after lobbying by Buxton, Crum, and McDonald, Hutcheson supported the immediate immigration of 100,000 Jewish refugees into Palestine. "The miraculous or semi-miraculous has happened," Buxton wrote Frankfurter. "Judge Hutcheson has seen the light."

With Hutcheson aboard, the American members won over their British counterparts. Buxton estimated that they had nine or ten votes (out of twelve) for the immigration of 100,000 Jewish refugees "and the rest of the program." In fact, the report was unanimous. In addition to recommending the immediate immigration of 100,000 refugees to Palestine, the committee refused to condition immigration on the consent of Arab countries or disarmament of the Zionist paramilitary organization, the Haganah. Buxton concluded by asking Frankfurter to convey the contents of the report to their friends in Washington—Byrnes and Cohen in the State Department and Niles in the White House.

At midnight on April 30, 1946, Niles spoke with Frankfurter about the Anglo-American committee's final report and the next day wrote a memorandum intended for the president. Niles described Frankfurter as "perhaps the most prominent supporter of Palestine in public life today among the Jews" and as Brandeis's longtime friend and fellow Zionist. "I have only one regret," Frankfurter told Niles, whose "heart sank a little bit" until the justice finished his thought. "My regret is that Justice Brandeis did not live to see this report. He would have called it a miracle." Frankfurter then "launched into a tirade" against Rabbi Abba Silver and other American Zionist leaders who "prefer a Jewish State on paper rather than doing something real for human beings." Niles said he planned on using Frankfurter's private comments to assuage Zionist concerns that the report repudiated the Balfour Declaration's goal of a Jewish state. Earlier that night in a public statement, Truman had praised the report's recommendations of immediately admitting 100,000 Jewish refugees to Palestine and its renunciation of the restrictions on Jewish immigration and land acquisition in the 1939 British white paper as a return to "the further development of a Jewish National Home."

After he relayed Frankfurter's support for Truman's policies, Niles fought internal battles within the administration. State Department officials, who were staunchly pro-Arab and resisted the report's recommendations, reminded Truman of Roosevelt's promises to King Saud. Truman forwarded Niles copies of Roosevelt's letter to Saud and a memorandum of their conversation. Niles advised the president that the immigration of 100,000 Jews to Palestine was not a policy change and, based on Roosevelt's pledge to consult with Arab nations, required nothing more than a telegram to the Saudi king. In a May 27 memorandum to the president, Niles dismissed the warnings of Myron Taylor, the president's representative at the Vatican, that concentrating Jewish refugees in Palestine would alienate Arab countries and lead to another war. "May I again respectfully point out that you are concerning yourself now only with the transference of 100,000 Jews," Niles wrote Truman. "The other parts of the report you, yourself have publicly said that you would take under consideration for future study." Niles drafted replies to Taylor as well as to concerned Zionist leaders emphasizing the president's commitment to the immediate immigration of 100,000 Jewish refugees.

The bigger obstacle than the State Department was the British government's refusal to implement the report and resistance to sending 100,000 Jewish immigrants to Palestine. Prime Minister Clement Attlee demanded financial and military assistance from the United States. Foreign Secretary Ernest Bevin blamed the "agitation" for immigration to Palestine on the United States "because they did not want too many of them in New York." To top it off, the Royal Navy prevented ships carrying Jewish refugees from entering Palestine. For an Anglophile such as Frankfurter, the British government's stance on Jewish immigration was crushing. "I think I can honestly say," he wrote Buxton, "that I am more grieved by what Gt. Britain or rather the Attlee Gov't has done from the point of view of Anglo-American & therefore world-relations than I am pained by the suffering of Jews."

Not content to wait for the British government to find its conscience or to let Buxton and Niles do his bidding, Frankfurter worked on influential members of his Georgetown social circle. A lot had changed for the Frankfurters and their friends since the end of the war. Phil and Kay Graham purchased a Georgetown mansion at 2920 R Street from former Office of Strategic Services director William "Wild Bill" Donovan. Phil was working for his father-in-law Eugene Meyer's newspaper, the *Washington Post*, and within the year replaced Meyer as publisher. Graham's co-clerk and best friend, Edward "Prich" Prichard, returned to his native Kentucky to practice law, got married, and worried his friends by embroiling himself in state politics. Alice Roosevelt Longworth, the reactionary 62-year-old daughter of Theodore Roosevelt and nicknamed "Mrs. L," grew close to the Frankfurters; some thought too close given the boorish way she spoke to the justice. Philosopher Isaiah Berlin left the British embassy in late March 1946 to return to Oxford. Marion missed Berlin for his insight into other people and intellectual conversation; Felix missed Berlin as a friend and a Zionist ally inside the British government.

Frankfurter leaned hardest on the de facto leader of the Georgetown set, syndicated columnist Joseph Alsop. Alsop reported to Berlin that Frankfurter was "in a positive passion against your government because of Palestine."

The Frankfurters invited Alsop to dinner and excoriated him for a series of columns he had written about Palestine while overseas. The justice, Alsop informed Berlin, "spoke with fury, eloquence and interminable repetition for a full hour and a quarter, halting not one instant, going over the whole story from the Balfour declaration onward, and coming close to apoplexy every time he had occasion to mention the very names of Attlee and Bevin. They have made a Tory of him, forever and a day." After seventy-five minutes without getting in a word, an irritated Alsop tried to mount a "mild defense." Marion, however, insisted that he had "no heart." He was "denounced" for unkind references to Niles in one of the articles. Unbowed, Alsop held his ground. All was soon forgotten. A few days later, Frankfurter complimented one of his brother Stewart's columns. Alsop sent Marion flowers, and she replied with a thank-you note that Alsop admired because of its "true 'elegance of spirit.' That, I must say, M[arion] does possess in a marked degree. Life, as you can see, resumes."

In contrast to Alsop, Frankfurter treaded more lightly with his closest friend in Washington, Under Secretary of State Dean Acheson. During their morning walks to work, one topic was off limits to preserve their friendship— Palestine. Acheson "revered" his former boss Brandeis and described his former professor as an "intimate friend." He claimed that he "learned to understand, but not to share, the mystical emotion of the Jews to return to Palestine and end the Diaspora." He faulted Brandeis and Frankfurter for allowing "their emotion to obscure the totality of American interests."

After the publication of the Anglo-American committee report and negative British reaction, Acheson refused to take a stance on behalf of the State Department but soon found himself mired in the debate. In mid-June, Truman sent a new American delegation headed by State Department representative Henry F. Grady to discuss the problem with British officials on the Anglo-American Cabinet Committee. The Grady report recommended partitioning Palestine into Arab, Jewish, and central government districts; leaving the region entirely under British military control; and delaying the immigration of 100,000 Jews. On July 31, 1946, Truman recalled the American members of the Grady-led committee to Washington to meet with the American members of the Hutcheson-led committee. Acheson was charged with mediating between the two groups. Buxton assured Frankfurter that the Grady report did not stand a chance with Truman. Hutcheson described the counterproposal of partitioning without sovereignty as a "ghetto in attenuated form." The most outspoken, San Francisco lawyer Bartley Crum, blamed mid-level State Department officials and called for the resignation of the director of Near East and African affairs, Loy Henderson. Acheson publicly rebuked Crum and defended Henderson and other members of the State Department. Privately, Acheson believed the Hutcheson-led committee's recommendation of immediate immigration of 100,000 Jews "had gone too far" and the Grady report "had in it the makings of a compromise."

Though Palestine was off-limits on their morning walks, Frankfurter knew where Acheson stood and tried to change his mind. "You spent many weeks on a petty court of claims case," he wired Acheson at the State Department on July 30, "do you think that the problem of Palestine with all its ramifications lends itself to a wise solution in drastic break with the past by so short a process anyhow affectionately yours." On August 7, Frankfurter read a *New York Times* account of miserable conditions on a ship of Jewish refugees stranded outside the port of Haifa in Palestine. The next day, he sent Acheson a copy of a cable to the British ambassador, Lord Inverchapel. "My dear Archie . . . ," Frankfurter wrote, "I cannot resist expressing to you the hope that [His Majesty's Government] may allow the landing of these fellow human beings solely as a humane act, stripped of all implications of policy such a response to an appeal to elementary pity and forbearance surely accords with British tradition." A few months later, Frankfurter sent Acheson a copy of his 1931 *Foreign Affairs* article on Palestine with the note: "You will believe me when I say that I'm not sending this in any wrangling or controversial mood. For the rest, it will have to speak for itself."

During the summer of 1946, Frankfurter watched and waited for action as Jewish refugees suffered in displaced-persons camps and on ships that were prevented from entering Palestine. He refused to allow Palestine to "be entirely left to God—or even to Truman!" On July 2, Truman had met with Rabbi Wise and several other members of the executive committee of the Jewish Agency and in a public statement reaffirmed his support for the immediate immigration of 100,000 Jewish refugees. With encouragement from Niles, Truman ignored the recommendations of the State and War Departments and opposed the Grady report. On August 12, Truman officially notified the British government. Frankfurter believed that Truman "means well and is determined" but did not share the president's optimism. Privately, Truman believed that the Palestine issue was "insoluble." The British government continued to refuse to admit Jewish refugees to Palestine and held a Palestine conference in London, which Jewish leaders boycotted. "Not in months," Frankfurter wrote Buxton in September, "have I had anything but heart-break over Palestine."

Niles, not the State Department, continued to dominate Truman's think-

ing about Palestine. In mid-September, Truman initially agreed with the
State Department's recommendation not to endorse a new partition proposal
backed by Zionist leaders. The president, fed up with the British and Zionists, elected not to say anything. Yet the day before Yom Kippur on October
4, 1946, he endorsed the Zionist proposal—the creation of a Jewish state in
part of Palestine and the immediate immigration of 100,000 Jewish refugees. The press, based on leaks from the State and War Departments, blamed
Truman's change of heart on Niles. Columnist Drew Pearson claimed that
a week before Truman's press release, Niles had learned that the presump-
tive Republican presidential nominee, New York governor Thomas Dewey,
was preparing to speak to the United Jewish Appeal about the need for Jewish immigration to Palestine. The White House, Pearson wrote, did not like
the State Department's initial draft and forced Acheson to spend most of the
night strengthening it. *Time* magazine attributed the president's statement to
"one of the few shrewd politicos left in Washington from Roosevelt days"—
the "short, quiet" Niles.

As the State Department gunned for Niles in the press, Frankfurter
attempted to court his friends in the department in private. In January 1947,
the Frankfurters threw a farewell dinner for outgoing Secretary of State
Byrnes and his wife. Byrnes's successor, General George C. Marshall, was
another longtime friend of Frankfurter's. "Marshall has candor, courage,
and clarity of mind," Frankfurter wrote Buxton and insisted that Marshall
would tackle "the problem on its merits." The conventional wisdom was that
Marshall, given his battlefield experience, would be more sympathetic to
the Jews in displaced-persons camps. What Frankfurter did not know was
that Marshall was as cool to Zionism as Acheson and other members of the
department. On January 7, Chaim Weizmann wrote Frankfurter bemoaning
the tactics of more radical American Zionists and urged the justice to advise
them: "I hope you will exercise your great influence in the direction of moder-
ation and sanity. Don't let them hope, above all, to use the American Government to press the British beyond a certain point."

The British government was ready to give up. A Palestine conference that
had begun on September 27, 1946, and resumed on January 27, 1947, went
nowhere. On February 18, Bevin announced that the British would submit
the problem of Palestine to the United Nations. A few weeks later during a
debate in the British Parliament, the foreign minister blamed Truman for the
region's problems and attributed his support for 100,000 Jewish immigrants
to Palestine to partisan politics. Without mentioning Bevin by name, Truman
immediately responded that America's interest in Palestine was "of long and

Felix, age twelve in 1895, a year after arriving in America.

Emma Frankfurter always told her son Felix: "Hold yourself dear!"

Felix's father, Leopold (sitting second from right), visiting his family in Hungary in 1914.

Frankfurter, standing third row center, with members of his CCNY literary society, Clionia.

Frankfurter sitting in his off-campus boarding house room at 1707 Cambridge Street in Cambridge circa 1903 to 1906.

Frankfurter (standing, third from left) with his fellow assistant federal prosecutors of the Southern District of New York, including Winfred T. Denison (seated, first on left) and U.S. attorney Henry Stimson (seated, third from left).

The original residents at the House of Truth. From left: Winfred T. Denison, Robert G. Valentine (top), Frankfurter (right), and Loring C. Christie (bottom).

Justice Oliver Wendell Holmes, Jr., was a regular at the House of Truth in 1913 and the one who inspired its name.

The "people's lawyer," Louis Brandeis, in 1914. Two years later, Frankfurter and Lippmann fought for his Supreme Court confirmation.

Marion Denman in 1918 before heading to the Western Front to study the health and recreation of Allied soldiers for the Commission on Training Camp Activities.

Frankfurter (standing) challenging his third-year and graduate students during a seminar.

Frankfurter (sitting front row, second from left) and Roscoe Pound (sitting front row, third from left) in 1926 with their graduate students, including Tom Corcoran (standing center), in front of Harvard Law School's Langdell Hall.

Nicola Sacco (right) and Bartolomeo Vanzetti (left) handcuffed in 1923 in Dedham, Massachusetts.

Frankfurter and 1928 Democratic presidential nominee Al Smith (right) at a May 1929 private dinner arranged by Frankfurter in Smith's honor at the Union Club in Boston.

Frankfurter and Brandeis (right) outside of Brandeis's Chatham home on Cape Cod.

At Brandeis's instigation, Chief Justice Charles Evans Hughes sent a letter to Senator Burton K. Wheeler (far right) destroying the court-packing plan's bogus rationale that the justices were behind on their work.

Tom Corcoran (right), leaving the White House with Harold Ickes after a December 1938 meeting with Roosevelt, led the campaign for Frankfurter to fill Cardozo's seat.

Robert H. Jackson (left) and Benjamin V. Cohen, at the back door of the White House after meeting with Roosevelt in 1938, lobbied the president to nominate Frankfurter.

To the Committee on
the Judiciary.

The White House,
January 5 1939

To the
Senate of the United States.

I nominate Felix Frankfurter
of Massachusetts
to be an Associate Justice of the Supreme Court of the
United States, vice Benjamin N. Cardozo, deceased.

Franklin D Roosevelt

Committee on
the Judiciary.

Roosevelt kept his Supreme Court nominee a secret from his closest advisers until he submitted this handwritten form to the U.S. Senate on January 5, 1939.

Felix and Marion circa 1942.

Dean Acheson (left) and Frankfurter in the Senate Caucus Room on January 12, 1939, before Frankfurter testified before the Senate judiciary subcommittee about his Supreme Court nomination.

This Nazi newspaper cartoon caption reads: "America's president debases himself to become a handyman for world Jewry, to secure Jewish help for a third-term election."

Frankfurter assumed all the expectations of taking the seat held by two of his judicial idols, Oliver Wendell Holmes, Jr. (top) and Benjamin N. Cardozo (middle).

IN A GREAT SUCCESSION.

Jan 6 '39

In March 1938, Frankfurter relied on State Department contacts to help secure the release of his uncle Salomon, a librarian and philologist at the University of Vienna, from a Nazi prison.

Frankfurter and Lady Nancy Astor (right) talk animatedly on June 21, 1939, at Oxford's commencement, where he received an honorary degree. Frankfurter credited her, not the State Department, with securing his uncle's release.

Justices William O. Douglas (left), Frankfurter, and Owen J. Roberts at an October 2, 1939, call on President Franklin D. Roosevelt at the White House.

On July 11, 1940, Frankfurter cut his summer vacation short to swear in Secretary of the Navy Frank Knox in the Oval Office. This is the only known photo of Frankfurter and President Roosevelt.

Oliver Gates warmed the hearts of Uncle Felix and Aunt Marion from September 1940 to July 1942 when he and his sisters, Ann and Venetia, lived with the Frankfurters to escape the bombing of Britain. In July 1941, Felix visited Oliver in Dark Harbor, Maine, before Oliver's fourth birthday.

When Justice James C. McReynolds retired on February 1, 1941, Washington *Evening Star* cartoonist Clifford K. Berryman proclaimed that the Court was Frankfurter's.

(Left to right) Chief Justice Harlan Fiske Stone, Attorney General Francis Biddle, Frankfurter, Solicitor General Charles Fahy (over Frankfurter's shoulder), and Justice Owen J. Roberts on April 24, 1943, at the National Press Club Canteen for Servicemen in Washington, D.C.

SUPREME COURT OF THE UNITED STATES.

No. 51.—OCTOBER TERM, 1943.

Lonnie E. Smith, Petitioner, *vs.* S. E. Allwright, Election Judge, and James E. Liuzza, Associate Election Judge, 48th Precinct of Harris County, Texas.	On Writ of Certiorari to the United States Circuit Court of Appeals for the Fifth Circuit.

[ ]

Mr. Justice FRANKFURTER, concurring.

When, in defining the constitutional basis of the admiralty jurisdiction, this Court in *The Genesee Chief*, 12 How. 443, 446, had to overrule the prior decision of Chief Justice Marshall's unanimous Court in *The Thomas Jefferson*, 10 Wheat. 428, Chief Justice Taney said, "We are sensible of the great weight to which it is entitled." The same feeling of deference is stirred by *Grovey v. Townsend*, 295 U. S. 45. We are now pronouncing a decision precisely the opposite of that rendered less than ten years ago, shared in by judges not less sensitive than ourselves to claims of citizenship free from racial discrimination. Such a change of view cannot be justified by any assumption on our part of knowledge and wisdom denied to our predecessors. And no decision of this Court since *Grovey v. Townsend* has qualified its explicitness.

No mere individual preference but only a compelling regard for the Constitution as a dynamic scheme of government for a democratic society can justify a different conclusion from that reached in *Grovey v. Townsend*. "*Stare decisis* is ordinarily a wise rule of action. But it is not a universal, inexorable command." Brandeis, J. in *Washington v. Dawson & Co.*, 264 U. S. 219 at 238. We cannot forego our responsibility for judgment of constitutional issues because other judges discharged theirs. We must exercise that judgment not by slavish adherence to precedent but by summoning the utmost disinterestedness as trustees of the great principles that are enshrined in the Fourteenth and

51

2   *Smith vs. Allwright et al.*   2

Fifteenth Amendments to assure equality of participation in the political processes by which the Nation is governed.

Howsoever attenuated the relation of the machinery of the State to the political mechanism whereby the result is achieved, if in fact free access to the electoral process by which the States and the Nation are governed is denied to persons on account of race or color that which the post-war Amendments sought to achieve is frustrated. We cannot escape the duty of construing those Amendments in the light of their purposes. We cannot escape this duty because one prior decision had taken a different turn. And our duty ends with such construction.

On April 10, 1944, Frankfurter decided not to publish his draft *Smith v. Allwright* concurrence.

Frankfurter on April 15, 1945, at Franklin D. Roosevelt's funeral at Hyde Park, New York.

Frankfurter shaking hands with retired chief justice Charles Evans Hughes at Harlan Fiske Stone's funeral at Washington National Cathedral on April 25, 1946. Stanley Reed (left) and Hugo Black (right) stand behind them.

William T. Coleman, Jr. (left) and Elliot Richardson, law school friends and co-clerks during the 1948 term, outside of Frankfurter's office door.

Frankfurter and Dean Acheson (right) regularly walked to work together from their Georgetown homes. The *New York Times* captured them on January 17, 1948.

Frankfurter's notes to Robert H. Jackson during the steel seizure oral argument in May 1952 about Chief Justice Fred Vinson's questions to attorney John W. Davis (the greyhound) and Vinson's running commentary to Hugo Black.

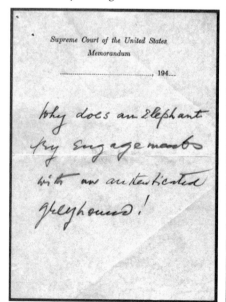

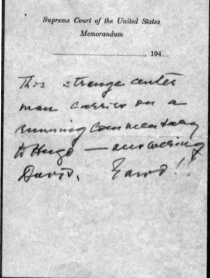

Hugo Black (left), Robert H. Jackson (center), and Frankfurter at Chief Justice Fred Vinson's funeral on September 11, 1953, in Louisa, Kentucky.

The justices on a special train car to the Army-Navy football game in Philadelphia on November 27, 1954. From left to right: William O. Douglas, Hugo Black, Earl Warren, Stanley Reed, Tom C. Clark, Sherman Minton, Harold H. Burton, and Frankfurter in front.

Frankfurter and Chief Justice Earl Warren, in their honeymoon period after *Brown v. Board of Education*, at a September 1955 conference on "government under law" at Harvard Law School.

At a memorial service on May 30, 1956, at Roosevelt's grave at Hyde Park, New York, Frankfurter predicted that the former president "cannot escape becoming a national saga." From left: Frankfurter, Franklin Roosevelt, Jr., Eleanor Roosevelt, and Everetta Kilmer.

For the Harvard Law School for its collection of judicial photographs

N.Y. Times April 10 '59

Felix Frankfurter

At a celebration of Learned Hand's fiftieth anniversary on the federal bench in the lower Manhattan federal courthouse on April 10, 1959, Frankfurter remarked that Hand was "lucky not to get on the Nine." From left: Earl Warren, Learned Hand, Frankfurter, and John Marshall Harlan II.

Frankfurter's famous iron grip.

Frankfurter consulting in 1959–1960 with his devoted secretary, Elsie Douglas, who had previously worked for Frankfurter's closest friend on the Court, Robert H. Jackson.

Frankfurter's messenger Thomas Beasley, pictured during the 1959 term, played an integral role in his life on and off the bench.

Frankfurter spoke incoherently at the swearing-in of D.C. Circuit judge Carl McGowan on April 23, 1963, with Attorney General Robert Kennedy and many longtime friends present. Former clerk Joseph Rauh advised against any future public speeches. From left: Josephine McGowan, Frankfurter, Carl McGowan, and Robert Kennedy.

Frankfurter visited President
Kennedy at the Oval Office
on June 17, 1963. From left:
Kennedy, Frankfurter, and
Frankfurter's longtime friend
Wilmarth Lewis.

Frankfurter spoke with a
Washington *Evening Star* reporter
on August 18, 1963, while being
taken for a stroll at Hains Point
accompanied by messenger
Thomas Beasley and nurse
Margaret MacKay.

President Lyndon B. Johnson
leaving Frankfurter's
Massachusetts Avenue
apartment after the justice's
memorial service on
February 25, 1965. Dean
Acheson, who arranged the
service, is behind him on the
steps.

Frankfurter's portrait
taken by John F.
Costelloe, law clerk
to Justice Robert H.
Jackson, in October 1943.

continuing standing" and was "shared by our people without regard to political affiliation."

The United Nations Special Committee on Palestine convened on April 28, 1947, in Lake Success, New York. From his home in Rehovot, Palestine, Weizmann updated Frankfurter on the political situation: "I have tried not to worry you all these days, but you were almost constantly in my thoughts, and I am quite certain that you were thinking of us here." Weizmann argued that the only solution was to partition Palestine into Arab and Jewish sovereign states. A partition plan, Weizmann wrote, had the support of Acheson and the State Department, "but this support must not be merely platonic; they must take some responsibility." Weizmann asked Frankfurter, "in the name of our life-long association, and of all the energy, devotion and love which we have all expended in order to build up the present Palestine," to rally the support of his moderate Zionist friends and political insiders—Henry Morgenthau, Jr., Ben Cohen, State Department official David Ginsburg, Rabbi Wise, and others— for partition. Frankfurter lamented the political bickering among American and British leaders and infighting among moderate and militant Zionists. Yet he responded to Weizmann with a letter that gave the Zionist leader "joy and strength" as terrorism in Palestine was "in full swing."

The tension between militant Zionists and the British government came to a head in July 1947, during the *Exodus* crisis. The Haganah, a Zionist paramilitary organization, purchased a decommissioned American ship, loaded it with more than 4500 Jewish refugees from France, and tried to enter Palestine. British naval officers boarded the ship twenty miles off the coast of Haifa, faced armed resistance from passengers and Haganah members, and killed three people. The British loaded the remaining passengers onto three ships and tried to deport them to France. The passengers refused to return to France and were interned in the British-controlled section of Hamburg, Germany. The image of Holocaust survivors being held in German camps was the beginning of the end of British rule over Palestine.

Frankfurter wisely refused to lobby Truman directly; the president was peeved when Henry Morgenthau, Jr., asked him to intervene in the *Exodus* crisis. "The Jews have no sense of proportion nor do they have any judgment on world affairs," Truman scrawled in his diary. He criticized Morgenthau for bringing 1000 Jewish refugees to New York on a temporary basis, then they ended up staying in the country. "The Jews, I find are very, very selfish," Truman wrote to himself. "They care not how many Estonians, Latvians, Finns, Poles, Yugoslavs or Greeks get murdered or mistreated as [displaced persons] as long as the Jews get special treatment." Publicly, Truman issued a Niles-drafted statement on June 5 urging Americans not to say anything to exacerbate the tense situation in Palestine or to sabotage the work at the United Nations.

As much as Truman liked to blow off steam about the lobbying of American Jews, he never lost confidence in Frankfurter's inside man, Niles. In a July 29 memorandum to the president, Niles observed that the United States was represented before the United Nations special committee by two of the most pro-Arab advocates in the State Department, Loy Henderson and George Wadsworth. Niles suggested the addition of Major General John Hilldring, who had been working as a special assistant in the department on behalf of displaced persons in Europe. Hilldring's presence, Niles argued, would silence more radical and outspoken Zionists; Truman added Hilldring. Niles knew where he stood with Truman. In September, the president awarded him the medal of merit.

ON SEPTEMBER 1, the United Nations special committee's majority report recommended the division of Palestine into Arab and Jewish states and the admission of 150,000 Jewish refugees. The British government announced on September 26 that it would withdraw the mandate and all troops from Palestine on May 15, 1948. Frankfurter knew whom to thank for doing the hard work. "Mazel tov!" he wrote Niles, who was a baseball fan unlike the justice. "All's well that ends well. And while we have not reached the end—Even I now know the game isn't won till the end of the ninth inning—we have reached the beginning of the end. And I know how much is due to your devotion, will & skill."

With a vote looming before the United Nations General Assembly, Frankfurter and other American Zionists began to tap their diplomatic contacts to line up votes in favor of the partition plan. He and Justice Murphy were accused by anti-Zionist Loy Henderson of lobbying the ambassador of the Philippines. Frankfurter denied the accusation as an "untruth" and claimed: "I never sent a message by any mode of communication, direct or indirect, to the Philippine Delegate of the Assembly or to any other Delegate." The denial may have been too specific. Frankfurter's correspondence with Weizmann reveals several attempts to influence foreign delegations. In mid-November 1947, Frankfurter introduced Weizmann to Sir B. N. Rau, whom the justice had advised on the drafting of the Indian Constitution, as "a far-sighted statesman." Weizmann, in turn, asked Frankfurter to reach out to French

ambassador Henri Bonnet and to the justice's contacts in the Indian delegation. From Weizmann, Frankfurter learned that France might abstain, and
India was probably going to vote no. Frankfurter spoke with Rau about relations between India and a future Jewish state; the justice also forwarded a letter from Bonnet and congratulated Weizmann on his efforts with the French
ambassador.

The justice had ample opportunity to influence foreign affairs given how
active he and Marion were on the diplomatic party circuit. On October 4, he
had attended a stag lunch at Blair House in honor of the French foreign minister. Three days later, he and Marion went to Constitution Hall to see the Philadelphia Orchestra; the Philippine ambassador was there, too. On November
14, they went to a buffet supper hosted by the Indian ambassador, and three
days later they attended a dinner in honor of the Luxembourg prime minister.

At these diplomatic events, Frankfurter frequently ran into two of the
staunchest opponents of partition within the Truman administration, Secretary of War James Forrestal and Under Secretary of State Robert A. Lovett.
Both Forrestal and Lovett worried that Arab opposition to partition would
jeopardize U.S.-Arab relations and access to Arab oil and increase Soviet
influence in the region. They tried to promote a modified partition plan that
denied the Jews the southern part of the Negev. In mid-November, Weizmann
took the train to Washington for a meeting with the president. Frankfurter
greeted Weizmann at Union Station, accompanied him to the Shoreham
Hotel, and strategized and reminisced over dinner. "The memory of the evening will remain with us for a long time," Weizmann wrote Frankfurter a few
days later. "It went in a flash and I am only sorry that it can't be repeated—but
perhaps such things should not be repeated. It would be somewhat like a second Seder night."

At a November 19, 1947, White House meeting with Truman, Weizmann
explained that denying the Jewish state the southern part of the Negev would
cut off access to the Gulf of Aqaba (or Gulf of Eilat). Truman instructed the
State Department and other American officials at the United Nations not to
give away the Jewish right to the southern part of the Negev. In the days leading up to the United Nations vote, Frankfurter and Weizmann remained in
close contact. Their diplomatic efforts succeeded with United Nations member countries. On November 29, the United Nations General Assembly voted
33–13 for the partition plan and kept the southern Negev in Jewish hands.
Before Weizmann left the United States on December 17 on the steamship
Mauretania, a relieved Frankfurter wired him at the pier: "You came heavy
laden and do not leave with a light heart but you go back with new solid hopes

which could not have been realized without your long years of vision and devoted statesmanship. . . . I have some notion of what is ahead but contemplate it with confidence largely because by virtue of your intrinsic authority you will express the benign purposes of the new State."

Partition's opponents, Forrestal and Lovett, blamed Frankfurter and other Zionists for meddling in American foreign policy. Forrestal claimed in his diary that Lovett "was importuned" about Palestine by Frankfurter at the Gridiron Club dinner on December 18 and that Frankfurter got "annoyed" when Lovett refused to discuss the issue. Frankfurter denied the incident took place as the secretary of war described. On the morning of the United Nations General Assembly vote on partition, Frankfurter had wired Lovett about the "wisdom and balance" of a *New York Herald Tribune* editorial and argued, based on thirty years of experience with the Palestine problem, that "[t]he alternative to acceptance of our policies today is chaos and its consequences which I hardly dare contemplate." At the Gridiron dinner, Frankfurter asked why Lovett, who had replaced Acheson as under secretary of state, failed to respond. Lovett insisted that he knew as much about Palestine as Frankfurter did. Frankfurter, citing his thirty years of experience, replied he knew "a little more about the attitude" of men in the State Department than Lovett.

Given the opposition to partition in the State Department, Zionists needed the full support of Truman. The 1948 presidential election was a looming concern. Truman sought the Democratic nomination for the first time, faced the prospect of an experienced Republican nominee in New York governor Thomas Dewey, and needed the support of northeastern Democrats and Jews. Yet partition's opponents in the State and War Departments argued that domestic politics should be irrelevant. In March 1948, forty-one congressional Democrats protested to Secretary of State Marshall that the president had not been supportive enough of partition. Zionist pressure alienated the State Department. On March 15, Marshall rebuffed Frankfurter's efforts to arrange a meeting with Weizmann. Frankfurter also helped draft a letter requesting a meeting for Weizmann with the president. Niles, who was hospitalized in late February and early March with strep throat, was not around to help. After a plea from his old Kansas City friend and business partner Eddie Jacobson, Truman met on March 18 with Weizmann for forty-five minutes and pledged his support for partition. The next day, Weizmann and Truman received a shock: U.S. ambassador Warren Austin asked the United Nations Security Council to reconsider partition in favor of a trusteeship because of the impending British withdrawal from the region and increasing violence between Jews and Arabs. The president was furious with Marshall and the "strip[]ed pants conspirators" in the State Department for making him look like "a liar and a double crosser." In the face of public criticism, Truman declared the administration's policy had not changed and the trusteeship would be temporary. Frankfurter praised Weizmann's measured response to the administration's "pathetic" pro-Arab turn: "Tragedy is man's lot. And so what matters is not tragedy but how we meet it. . . . I am not whistling in the dark when I say that the new turn of events gives the cause of the Jewish State new opportunities—provided we draw resources from the strength of our moral position."

Another longtime Frankfurter protégé, Max Lowenthal, helped stiffen Truman's resolve. A committed Zionist, Lowenthal had accompanied Frankfurter in July 1917 on the ill-fated Morgenthau mission to try to make peace with the Ottoman Empire. On that trip, he and Frankfurter had met Weizmann for the first time in Gibraltar and, after the mission failed, had reported on wartime conditions in Europe. Back home, Lowenthal had worked as Frankfurter's assistant on the Presidential Mediation Commission and on the War Labor Policies Board. After the war, he started a lucrative New York law practice and made frequent returns to public service. In 1929, he was executive secretary of the Wickersham Commission on criminal justice reform and worked with Frankfurter in staffing the commission with experts. On Frankfurter's recommendation, Lowenthal returned to Washington in 1933 as research director for Ferdinand Pecora's Senate investigation of the causes of the 1929 stock market crash. He helped draft the Securities Exchange Act of 1934 but, unlike Corcoran and Cohen, shied from the limelight. The low-key Lowenthal quietly became a Senate insider, working for Senator Burton Wheeler in 1935 as chief counsel of the Interstate Commerce Committee and advising the Banking Committee on railroad reorganization and other financial issues. At the Interstate Commerce Committee, Lowenthal was impressed by the junior senator from Missouri, Harry Truman. He worked with Truman in 1937 on the Committee to Investigate Railroad Finance and introduced Truman to Brandeis. "You know," Truman said to Lowenthal, "I'm not used to meeting men like that." Truman and Lowenthal shared Brandeis's belief in regulating monopolies, opposition to wiretapping, and support for organized labor. Lowenthal became a trusted outside political adviser to Truman. He helped Truman land the vice-presidential spot on the Democratic ticket in 1944 and after Truman became president frequently worked at the White House as a troubleshooter and adviser on Palestine.

Together with Niles and the president's special counsel Clark Clifford,

Lowenthal countered State Department opposition to a Jewish state. After the backlash from Austin's trusteeship proposal, they advised the president to make several changes in a memorandum titled "Actions": (1) to remove pro-Arab State Department official Loy Henderson as head of Near East Affairs; (2) to replace anti-Semitic and pro-Arab State Department official George Wadsworth as ambassador to Iraq; and (3) to lift the arms embargo on Palestine so that outnumbered Jewish forces could defend themselves and protect their territory. Although he did not act on Wadsworth or the arms embargo, Truman reduced Henderson's influence by appointing a pro-Zionist, General Hilldring, as special assistant to the secretary of state for Palestine affairs. Clifford drafted the president's March 25 press statement that the trusteeship proposal was a temporary measure in light of the British departure from the region and was consistent with the president's steadfast commitment to a Jewish state. It was issued over Niles's objections that it would be "shot full of holes."

An optimistic Frankfurter wired Weizmann on April 6, 1948, at the Waldorf-Astoria Hotel and urged him to stay in the United States for at least another week to influence public officials and to "see more clearly the situation here and there." He also sent Weizmann an April 14 Herblock cartoon from the *Washington Post*, which depicted the United States standing on its head before the United Nations Special Committee on Palestine below the headline: "We want to make our position perfectly clear—." In his cover note, Frankfurter wrote that "it seems like 2000 years since those heydays of Balfour." A few days later, Frankfurter urged Weizmann: "Keep of good cheer and of stout heart" and promised that Niles would update the Zionist leader on the latest developments.

By early May, Lowenthal, Niles, and Clifford battled the State Department with one goal in mind: U.S. recognition of a Jewish state. During a six-day period, Lowenthal wrote Clifford five or six memoranda to prepare the special counsel for a White House debate with Marshall, Lovett, and other State Department officials. Niles showed Truman polling data that the American people supported his policy on a Jewish state. On the morning of May 12, Niles, Lowenthal, and Clifford conferred with the president. At 4:00 p.m., Truman listened to Clifford (and Niles) and Marshall (and Lovett) debate the issue for an hour and a half. The discussion between Clifford and State Department officials continued the next day. Marshall and Lovett tried to scare the president that the new Jewish state might be Communist; Truman was not scared. He told Niles that Marshall and Lovett meant well but listened too much to their State Department subordinates. Niles reminded the president that the

United States should recognize the Jewish state before the Soviets or Soviet bloc countries did; Truman agreed.

By the end of the day on May 13 and after receiving a letter from Weizmann urging him to be the first country to recognize the Jewish state, the president had made up his mind. Marshall agreed neither to support nor to oppose him. Clifford and Lovett began drafting a recognition statement. Both Niles and Lowenthal were traveling and unavailable, so the statement was revised by another former Frankfurter student, David Ginsburg, who was counsel to the Jewish Agency. At 6:11 p.m., eleven minutes after the British Mandate for Palestine expired, Truman officially recognized, on a de facto basis, the provisional government of the State of Israel. Lowenthal heard the news after leaving the New York subway. Truman phoned Niles in Boston. "Dave," he said, "I want you to know that I've just announced recognition. You're the first person I called, because I knew how much it would mean to you." The president sounded "jubilant that now at last he was being allowed to do what he wanted to do in this—meaning, of course, that State was agreeing to do it and he does not want to overrule Marshall on things." Frankfurter gave credit where it was due—to Niles: "It's been a long and steep and stony road—and a steep, stony and long road it will remain in my time, perhaps even in yours. But a high plateau has been reached, gracing a commanding position for a promising continuance of the great journey."

"There have been many travelers on this sad-glad journey," Frankfurter continued in his tribute to Niles. "Some, alas! no longer here to rejoice over the plateau that has been won—especially do you and I think of L.D.B. and Judge Julian Mack. Of those who have brought us to this inspiring stage, history is bound to accord you an honorable place for your ceaseless and wise endeavors, your antiseptic humor, your unflagging and creative faith."

The day after the mandate expired, five Arab countries—Egypt, Syria, Jordan, Lebanon, and Iraq—attacked Israel. The British government was supplying the Arab countries with arms; an arms embargo prevented the United States from doing the same for Israel. As much as Niles and Lowenthal immediately wanted to lift the embargo, they sought to strengthen U.S.-Israeli ties by arranging a White House meeting between Truman and the new president of the provisional government, Chaim Weizmann. They pleaded with an ailing Weizmann to delay his return to Israel for an official meeting with Truman. Niles arranged for Weizmann and his family to stay at Blair House and to fly the Israeli flag above the house. Just in case the navy could not make an Israeli flag in time, Niles arranged for Weizmann's secretary to bring one from the Waldorf-Astoria Hotel. The State Department opposed the Blair

House visit because the United States had recognized Israel only on a de facto, not de jure, basis.

Weizmann had been in Frankfurter's thoughts since Israeli independence day: "'My eyes hath seen the coming of the glory of the Lord.' Happily you can now say that—and can say what Moses could not. I salute you with a full heart . . ." The night before Weizmann's May 25 meeting with Truman, Frankfurter saw the first president of Israel at Blair House. The 73-year-old Weizmann stayed quiet to preserve his strength for the next morning.

At 11:30 a.m. in the Rose Garden, Weizmann presented Truman with a gift—a Torah. "I always wanted one," Truman claimed as he received the Jewish holy scroll covered in blue velvet and embroidered with a Star of David. Niles smiled and suppressed a laugh. Weizmann did not just come bearing gifts. He asked Truman to lift the arms embargo as soon as possible, to allow 15,000 Jews from Germany to enter Palestine each month, and for a $90 million to $100 million loan. After the half-hour meeting, Weizmann returned to the Blair House garden and spoke with reporters. The Israeli president's hands shook as he talked in a low voice; his nurse was never far from his side. Frankfurter stayed away from the horde of media and politicians. "At last it's all spelled out," he wrote Weizmann five days after their late-night meeting. "It was a great refreshment for me to see you—even if you had to keep quiet."

During the next year, Frankfurter continued to counsel his protégés as they overcame State Department opposition and assisted the new Jewish state. On June 4, Frankfurter suggested that Lowenthal and Simon Rifkind write a *New York Times* or *Herald Tribune* editorial critical of the British refusal to allow Jewish immigration from Cyprus to Palestine. Five days later, Lowenthal lunched with Frankfurter at the Court about possible replacements for an ailing General Hilldring with respect to Palestine affairs. They rejected the State Department's pro-Arab candidate and installed a Zionist and non-Jew, former Anglo-American committee member James G. McDonald, as the first U.S. representative to Israel. They fought for de jure recognition. The justice advised Lowenthal that Israel's boundaries did not need to be fixed for de jure recognition and referred to Czechoslovakia after World War II. On January 31, 1949, six days after the country held popular elections, the United States recognized Israel on a de jure basis.

Frankfurter praised Weizmann's February 15, 1949, address before the United Nations. On March 4, the United Nations Security Council voted 9–1 in favor of Israeli membership. On May 11, the United Nations General Assembly voted by a two-thirds majority to seat Israel. "It has been a glorious journey—but a hazardous and painful one—from November 29, 1947 to May

11, 1949, when the world formally authenticated the unique event in history of the reestablishment of a nation after two thousand years," Frankfurter wrote Niles. "The important, if not indispensable share that you had in bringing about this furtherance of justice and reason in a strife-torn world, is made the more significant by the modesty and selflessness by which you pursued the faith of duty and of devotion to your chief, whose policy you were vindicating."

Frankfurter and Weizmann never saw each other after 1948. Weizmann lasted only a few years as the first president of Israel because of poor health. In November 1949, the justice wished Weizmann a happy seventy-fifth birthday. In early 1952, Weizmann was well enough to greet Eleanor Roosevelt on her visit to Israel. On November 9, he died at age seventy-eight of respiratory inflammation.

Niles was also in ill-health. When he retired from the Truman administration in 1951, the president called him a "tower of strength." Few people knew Niles was battling stomach cancer. On September 28, 1952, he died in his native Boston at age sixty-three. In his official statement, Truman remarked that "the underprivileged people of the world have lost a great and steadfast friend" and noted that his trusted aide never realized his dream of visiting the Jewish state. Along with Lowenthal and Clifford, Niles was chiefly responsible for Truman's support for Israel—with behind the scenes assistance and encouragement from Frankfurter.

Since 1947, Marion had been telling her friends that she was counting the days until her husband's retirement from the Court. Her prediction may have been the product of her increasing health problems. She also may have been referring to a justice's ability to retire after ten years with a full pension. But Frankfurter's most important work lay ahead of him. He was on the verge of making history by adapting the theory of judicial restraint to fulfill the Fourteenth Amendment's promise of equal citizenship. And he was to play a leading role in dismantling the Court-sanctioned system of racial segregation, beginning in his own chambers.

CHAPTER 30

I Don't Care What
Color a Man Has

On December 20, 1947, Chief Justice Vinson raised a budding controversy at conference. The law clerks proposed hosting a Christmas
party and, in contrast to the previous year's affair run by the secretaries, wanted to include the Court's messengers. The messengers, who worked
for individual justices and in the clerk's and the marshal's offices, were black.
The law clerks insisted there should be no "color line" at the Court's Christmas party. The secretaries claimed they refused to include the messengers,
not because they were black but because they were servants. "The upshot of
the matter," Frankfurter wrote in his diary, "was that the secretaries withdrew
from the proposed party and the law clerks decided to go on their own as
hosts and invite the Justices' messengers and a few other colored employees."
The clerks ran into an obstacle. The Court's marshal, Thomas Waggaman,
denied them use of a room in the Court building absent permission from
the chief justice. In his second year on the job, Vinson believed that the law
clerks should be permitted to use a room for their party yet brought the matter before the other justices. Douglas whispered something to the chief and
left (Murphy was also absent). The Court's two southerners besides the chief
justice, Black and Reed, agreed with Vinson without comment. Frankfurter,
who spoke next in order of seniority, concurred but believed the issue had
nothing to do with allowing black messengers to attend the clerks' party. The
Court, he argued, had a general policy of allowing its personnel to hold social
functions in the building without submitting a guest list. Neither the marshal nor the justices should exercise the "power of censorship" over certain
guests. Frankfurter's closest colleague, Robert Jackson, disagreed. He saw
the issue as "an explosive one" given the Court's role as "the umpire of great

social conflicts in the country" and its need "to keep out of such conflicts." In Jackson's view, the Court should forbid anyone from hosting a party in a room in the courthouse; the justices, however, could continue to hold informal parties in their own chambers. Frankfurter agreed that "there was a great deal to be said not to mix up social problems with essentially Court problems by permitting social functions" in the building. The justices, except for Jackson and Frankfurter, voted against Jackson's proposal. Vinson and Reed feared that it "might leak" and would look bad if the rule applied to the law clerks' Christmas party. The Kentucky-born Reed then volunteered that "of course" he would refuse to attend any integrated affair. "I asked him," Frankfurter wrote in his diary, "whether he realized the terrible position in which he was placing himself to abstain from going to a party where there are colored people." He warned Reed that it would get out and would contradict the Court's "noble utterances . . . against racial discrimination." An unmoved Reed said "this is purely a private matter and he can do what he pleased in regard to private parties." Frankfurter responded that "the very fact that we have been sitting here for nearly an hour discussing the right to hold the party makes it difficult to regard it as purely private. The Court is entangled no matter what way you look at it." No party was held that year. Indeed, there was no official Supreme Court Christmas party, much less an integrated one, until 1959.

What Frankfurter did not share with his colleagues was his correspondence that week with Harvard law professor Paul Freund. On December 16, Freund wrote Frankfurter and enclosed a clerkship recommendation for a University of Pennsylvania graduate, ex-lieutenant in the Army, *Harvard Law Review* editor, and law clerk to federal appeals court judge Herbert Goodrich—William Thaddeus Coleman, Jr. Like Frankfurter, Coleman had finished first in his law school class. Like Frankfurter, Coleman had encountered difficulty finding a job with a law firm. Unlike Frankfurter, Coleman was black.

Coleman's bid for a clerkship with Frankfurter faced a few obstacles. Unaware that the selection process was entirely up to Harvard law professor Henry Hart, Coleman had broken protocol by inquiring directly with the justice. Hart did not know Coleman because the professor had been absent from the law school during Coleman's third year. The impetus to hire Coleman came from Freund. Frankfurter held no former student in higher esteem than Freund—a former Brandeis clerk, assistant in the solicitor general's office, and rising academic star whom Frankfurter thought should have succeeded James Landis in 1946 as the dean of Harvard Law School (the job went to Erwin Griswold). Freund thought highly of Coleman, who had received the Beale Prize for the highest grade in Freund's conflict of laws class. "From my observation of him in that course and in Federal Jurisdiction, I should say that his outstanding ability is in his power of analysis and accurate knowledge of many fields of the law; his distinction does not depend on a literary gift, which indeed I should say he scarcely possesses," Freund wrote in his clerkship recommendation to Judge Goodrich. "I should be prepared to recommend him for almost any kind of legal work, but particularly, in view of the qualities I have indicated, for the work of a law clerk to an appellate judge." Unsure whether Frankfurter was hiring a second law clerk, Freund let the justice know that Coleman and Judge Goodrich had hit it off and had co-authored a *University of Pennsylvania Law Review* article and that Coleman "would welcome a chance to graduate to the varsity team." Two days after he received Freund's letter, Frankfurter replied that he had heard a lot about Coleman at the sixtieth anniversary dinner of the *Harvard Law Review* but that Hart had complete "power of attorney" over the selection of Frankfurter's law clerks. "I don't have to tell you that I don't care what color a man has," he wrote Freund, "any more than I care what religion he professes or doesn't."

Hart was reluctant to designate a student he didn't know. Nor was Coleman clerking for one of the federal appellate judges, Learned and Augustus Hand or Calvert Magruder, from whom Frankfurter preferred to hire law clerks. On the other hand, Coleman had finished first in his class and had completed a postgraduate Langdell teaching fellowship at the law school; Frankfurter had begun the practice of hiring two clerks in 1947, had agreed to hire Coleman's best friend from law school, Elliot Richardson, as one of his clerks for the 1948 term, but still needed a second one. Richardson, the Boston Brahmin son of a Harvard medical professor, knew about Coleman's trouble finding a job with a law firm and, along with another classmate, tried to help. After Richardson's efforts with Boston firms failed, Coleman informed Freund that Lloyd Garrison, a partner at the New York firm of Weiss & Wharton (now Paul, Weiss), had expressed interest in hiring Coleman and that a job might be available if Coleman clerked for another year. On January 22, 1948, Hart inquired whether Coleman would be "willing" to delay law practice for a year and to have his name sent to the justice. By the middle of February, Frankfurter had heard nothing about Coleman's decision and had begun to grow impatient. There was some confusion on Coleman's part whether he had been offered the job. On February 27, Hart informed Frankfurter that Coleman had accepted.

"For the first time in the Supreme Court's 158-year history, one of its justices will have a Negro law clerk," the press reported on April 27. The *Washington Post* ran the story on the front page. Frankfurter received letters from former

students, congressmen, federal appeals court judges, and citizen groups congratulating him. He insisted that the decision was not deserving of praise.
In response to similar comments from his black messenger Thomas Beasley, he replied: "Tom, I've heard others say that, but I never thought I'd hear
that from you. Don't you know I selected Mr. Coleman because on the basis
of brains and character he deserves it?" Frankfurter never forgot Beasley's
rejoinder: "Mr. Justice, in this world do you think our people get what they
deserve?" In Frankfurter's eyes, Coleman fit the same profile as his other law
clerks—a *Harvard Law Review* editor who had finished at the top of his class
and had clerked on the federal court of appeals. The 26-year-old Coleman was
married with a 1-year-old child. He was a year younger than another black
Army veteran who the previous April had made his debut with the Brooklyn
Dodgers and broken Major League Baseball's color barrier—Jackie Robinson.
Whether Frankfurter liked it or not, Bill Coleman would be the Jackie Robinson of Supreme Court law clerks.

IN THE MONTHS BEFORE Coleman joined Frankfurter's chambers, race had
been a hot topic at the Court. As in his unpublished concurrence in *Smith v.
Allwright*, Frankfurter never wavered from his belief in using the Fourteenth
Amendment to promote racial equality. Yet, as several opinions decided in
the first six months of 1948 indicated, he often approached issues of race in a
cautious, incremental way.

In *Lee v. Mississippi*, Frankfurter initially refused to join Murphy's majority opinion about a seventeen-year-old black teenager who had confessed to
assaulting and attempting to rape a white woman after receiving the "third
degree"—two detectives had beaten and threatened him to extract a confession. The Court unanimously agreed that the Mississippi courts could
not prevent Lee from arguing that his confession had been coerced simply
because there was contradictory eyewitness testimony. Frankfurter, however, balked at inflammatory language in Murphy's majority opinion. "Murphy made a characteristic harangue, full of sophomoric rhetoric, tasting like
rancid butter" Frankfurter wrote in his diary. "Stanley Reed agreed that it
was 'awful.'" On January 3, 1948, Frankfurter informed Murphy of his decision to join Reed's concurring opinion, which Burton also joined, because it
was "mild." On the basis of his experiences working on racial issues in the
War Department during World War I and as a member of the National Legal
Committee of the NAACP, he wrote Murphy, Frankfurter believed that the

Court "should deal with these ugly practices of racial discrimination with fearless decency, [but] it does not help toward harmonious race relations to stir our colored fellow citizens to resentment, however unwittingly, by needless detail . . ." Nor, he wrote, did inflammatory language persuade northern and southern whites to abandon their prejudicial behavior. He offered Murphy a model way of handling a "third degree case" involving race, a Brandeis opinion unanimously reversing the conviction of a Chinese national held incommunicado and questioned for ten days without sleep. Murphy redrafted his opinion. Frankfurter marked up the revised draft and noted: "This satisfies me, but I have some minor edits for your consideration . . ." Murphy incorporated Frankfurter's edits as well as the last paragraph of Reed's draft concurrence (which was not published). Murphy's unanimous but more muted opinion ordering the Mississippi Supreme Court to consider whether Lee's confession had been coerced masked divisions among the justices about how to approach issues of race.

Another case decided in early February 1948 revealed fissures about racial issues with Frankfurter once again at the center of things. Sarah Elizabeth Ray, a black Detroit secretary taking classes to join the city ordinance department, joined her white classmates for a trip to an amusement park on Bois Blanc Island (known by locals as Boblo Island). Ray, however, was denied passage on the boat because of her race. The Bob-Lo Excursion Company was tried and convicted under a Michigan civil rights law passed in response to the Court's decision in the Civil Rights Cases of 1883, which invalidated the Civil Rights Act of 1875 because the Fourteenth Amendment did not apply to private discrimination. In appealing its $25 fine under the Michigan law, the company argued that, because the island was in Ontario, Canada, the state conviction violated the Constitution's Commerce Clause by interfering with federal regulation of foreign commerce. At conference, seven justices rejected the company's argument. Frankfurter urged his colleagues to decide the case narrowly because of "the very unique situation" of Boblo as Detroit's Coney Island. Vinson and Jackson dissented because they believed that the law interfered with the federal government's regulation of foreign commerce. Black, the senior justice in the majority, assigned the majority opinion to Wiley Rutledge.

After reading Rutledge's draft opinion in Bob-Lo Excursion Company v. Michigan, Frankfurter urged him to eliminate the description of how the company mistreated and discriminated against Ray as irrelevant to the legal issues and unnecessarily inflammatory. In a January 2 cover memo and in a heavily marked-up draft, he argued that his experiences advising the NAACP and his time on the Court "led me to the conclusion that the ugly practices of racial discrimination should be dealt with by the eloquence of action, but with the austerity of speech. . . . By all means let us decide with fearless decency, but express our decisions with reserve and austerity." He worried about increasing resentment among blacks and racist whites and concluded: "Forgive this little sermon." Rutledge was glad to have Frankfurter's "little sermon," made most of his changes, yet refused to trim the facts. Rutledge referred to their dissents in *Fisher v. United States* containing offensive language about a 1946 murder case. In that case, Frankfurter replied, the language had been relevant to the defendant's mental state at issue on appeal, but the details about how Ray was discriminated against were not relevant to the regulation of foreign commerce: "My point is that it does not make the slightest difference to our decision whether Miss Ray was asked to leave the ship with Chesterfieldian courtesy or with barroom roughness." He insisted that "this Court should avoid exacerbating the very feelings we seek to allay." Rutledge reconsidered the issue and satisfied Frankfurter. "Felix is now in," Rutledge wrote on January 5. Frankfurter was one of six justices who joined Rutledge's majority opinion that the Michigan law did not "impose any undue burden" on foreign commerce.

In the case of aspiring black Oklahoma law student Ada Lois Sipuel, Frankfurter also argued for an incremental approach. Sipuel had been denied admission to the University of Oklahoma College of Law because of her race. State law prohibited blacks and whites from attending class together; Oklahoma, however, lacked a state-run law school for black students. Thurgood Marshall, continuing his strategy of chipping away at *Plessy v. Ferguson*'s racially "separate but equal" doctrine by challenging the exclusion of blacks from state-run law schools, appealed Sipuel's case to the Supreme Court. The law was on Sipuel's side. Ten years earlier, the Court had ruled in favor of a black student, Lloyd Gaines, who had been denied admission to the University of Missouri Law School because of his race and had rejected the state's offer to pay for him to attend law school in another state.

After oral argument on January 7 and 8, most of the justices agreed that Oklahoma had violated Sipuel's right to attend a state-run law school but disagreed on the remedy. Frankfurter suggested that the state had four possible options regarding Sipuel's admission: the makeshift law school at Langston University for black students; the University of Oklahoma Law School on a provisional basis until a segregated school could be opened; a temporary law school; or the University of Oklahoma on a permanent basis. The southerner Reed passed and mentioned he was "not in sympathy with [the] court's treatment of the problems that come here of this kind." Other justices, including Douglas and Murphy, wanted the Court to order Sipuel's admission to the University of Oklahoma. Several others, including Vinson, Jackson, and Burton, preferred a short unsigned opinion following the *Gaines* case but leaving the remedy up to the state courts. The Court opted for a narrow approach and, in a unanimous unsigned opinion, ordered the state, per *Gaines*, to provide Sipuel with "legal education afforded by a state institution" and to do so "in conformity with the equal protection clause of the Fourteenth Amendment and provide it as soon as it does for applicants of any other group."

Oklahoma responded to the Court's decision by offering Sipuel admission to a makeshift law school for black students in Oklahoma City as a branch of Langston University. Sipuel refused to attend the school, which enrolled only one student, and continued to seek admission to the University of Oklahoma. Marshall returned to the Supreme Court and filed a petition for a writ of mandamus, an extraordinary remedy ordering the state court to admit her. The Court voted to reject Sipuel's mandamus petition in an unsigned opinion that Frankfurter counseled "should avoid every possibility of serving as a target for contention." He believed that the Court merely decided that, by refusing to admit Sipuel to the University of Oklahoma and with no state law school for black students, Oklahoma had violated the Court's decision in the *Gaines* case. He did not want to address an issue not briefed and argued before the Court, whether a separate law school for black students violated the Fourteenth Amendment's Equal Protection Clause. He did not want to decide whether the makeshift law school was equal to the University of Oklahoma's. He preferred, as the Court's unsigned opinion suggested, that those issues should be addressed as an initial matter by the Oklahoma courts. The Court's two most liberal justices disagreed: Murphy wanted the Court to hear oral argument; Rutledge dissented because the makeshift law school could not be equal to the University of Oklahoma's. Instead, the Court followed Frankfurter's approach of not tackling every conceivable issue. It would not be long before Marshall returned to the Court and forced it to confront whether separate law schools for black and white students could be equal.

As he counseled caution in the *Lee*, *Bob-Lo*, and *Sipuel* cases, Frankfurter knew that the Court intended to expand the reach of the Fourteenth Amendment to prevent the enforcement of racially restrictive housing covenants. Historically, the Court had invalidated only a few restrictive covenants because most were based on private contracts, not action by state and local governments subject to the Fourteenth Amendment. In a case brought by a black St. Louis home buyer, *Shelley v. Kraemer*, the Court expanded the concept of "state action" to include the enforcement of racially restrictive covenants by state and local judges. In a companion case, *Hurd v. Hodge*, the Court ruled that the enforcement of racially restrictive convents in Washington, D.C., by federal judges violated the Fifth Amendment's Due Process Clause. In a one-paragraph concurrence in *Hurd v. Hodge*, Frankfurter emphasized that a federal judge should be forbidden from enjoining a white homeowner from selling a house to a black person when a similar order by a state judge violated the Fourteenth Amendment "not for any narrow technical reason, but for considerations that touch rights so basic to our society that, after the Civil War, their protection against invasion by the States was safeguarded by the Constitution. This is to me a sufficient and conclusive ground for reaching the Court's result."

His aversion to the Due Process Clause as a tool for empowering judges in no way prevented Frankfurter's invocation of the Fifth and Fourteenth Amendments to promote racial equality. He was proud of former student Charles Hamilton Houston, the NAACP's chief architect who had litigated *Hurd v. Hodge* and of former clerk Phil Elman, who had played an integral, behind-the-scenes role in drafting the federal government's brief in *Shelley v. Kraemer*. Frankfurter's incremental approach in *Lee, Bob-Lo, Sipuel*, and the restrictive covenant cases reflected his understanding that the Court could not reverse a long line of precedents undermining the Fourteenth Amendment's promise of equal citizenship in one fell swoop. The Court lacked a way to enforce its decisions absent support from the American people and their elected officials. On July 26, 1948, President Truman ordered the desegregation of the armed forces, and on December 5 he established a presidential commission on civil rights. Unlike the president's executive orders, Frankfurter believed that the Court could not make bold pronouncements about race because of its institutional limitations. His reluctance to take giant steps was consistent with his support for racial equality as well as his belief in a more limited role for the judiciary.

———

COLEMAN STARTED IN Frankfurter's chambers on September 1, 1948, three months behind his co-clerk and best friend, Elliot Richardson. During his World War II army service as an infantryman storming Utah Beach on the coast of France, Richardson had carried with him an edited volume of Justice Holmes's speeches, *The Mind and Faith of Justice Holmes*, and had been moved by Holmes's 1884 Memorial Day address. Frankfurter had been charmed by the handsome, aristocratic Richardson since meeting him in January 1947 at a lunch in Boston. Richardson had been president of the *Harvard Law Review* and had clerked for Frankfurter's longtime friend, Learned Hand. It was no surprise that Richardson, not Coleman, had been Hart's first choice to clerk for Frankfurter.

During his head start in Frankfurter's chambers, Richardson had read and summarized all of Frankfurter's opinions to date. In July, Richardson had prepared a survey of the fifty states and of foreign countries and identified which ones followed the "exclusionary rule"—the exclusion from criminal trials of evidence that was the product of an illegal search or seizure. Richardson's research became an appendix to Frankfurter's majority opinion in *Wolf v. Colorado*, which held that the Fourteenth Amendment's Due Process Clause did not forbid the use of illegally obtained evidence in state criminal trials. The states, the opinion said, were free to experiment with other remedies including disciplining offending police officers. Richardson worked with Frankfurter on the opinion, which followed the Court's decision the previous term in *Adamson* that the Due Process Clause only applied to the states the provisions of the Bill of Rights that were "implicit in the concept of ordered liberty." Rutledge, Murphy, and Douglas dissented. Black, despite his disagreement with *Adamson*, concurred in the result because he considered the exclusionary rule a judicially created doctrine rather than a textual command of the Fourth Amendment's prohibition against unreasonable searches and seizures. For Frankfurter, *Wolf* reinforced his belief in limiting the scope of the Due Process Clause.

Frankfurter's chambers was arranged differently than those of other justices. Frankfurter, the two law clerks, and the secretary all worked together in the center office. The other justices usually occupied the office at the end of the chambers, which had a fireplace and a bathroom. The bullpen-like atmosphere produced constant collaboration on opinions and easy banter about history, literature, and current events. The office environment was informal and carefree. The justice was interested in his clerks' personal and professional lives. When Coleman's parents visited Frankfurter's chambers, the justice discussed history and world affairs with Coleman's mother. When Coleman's three-year-old son Billy visited, the justice got on the floor and played with Billy's red toy car.

The friendship between Coleman and Richardson was free of any jealousy or hostility. They worked six days a week and looked forward to Saturday afternoons when the justice discussed what had happened at conference. Before the justice arrived each day, the two clerks read Shakespeare or Romantic poets for an hour. They often played badminton together on the roof of the Court. Upon the birth of Coleman's second child, Lovida Jr., in May 1949, Richardson was named her godfather. As he did in law school, the tall, handsome, bespectacled Richardson had the back of the short, portly Coleman. And Coleman knew it.

Coleman's status as the first black Supreme Court clerk did not shield him from the realities of life in racially segregated Washington. During a holiday in which the Supreme Court cafeteria was closed, the clerks decided to have lunch at the Mayflower Hotel. As the noon hour approached, Richardson claimed to have too much work and asked Coleman to eat with him at Union Station. Richardson confessed he had called ahead to the Mayflower and had discovered that the hotel did not serve blacks in its dining room. Union Station was one of the few places in the city where blacks and whites could eat lunch together. The whole incident left Frankfurter shaken. After lunch, Coleman saw him talking with Richardson and "noticed the justice had tears in his eyes."

As helpful as Richardson's appendix in *Wolf v. Colorado* may have been, Coleman made a more enduring contribution to Frankfurter and the Court's work. At Frankfurter's request, Coleman spent the last few months of his clerkship writing a memorandum about the graduate school segregation cases making their way to the Court. In 1946, Heman Marion Sweatt, a black Houston former schoolteacher, had been denied admission to the University of Texas Law School because of his race. Instead, the state began a law school for black students. By the time the Court had agreed to hear Sweatt's case, twenty-three black students had enrolled in the segregated law school; Sweatt, however, demanded admission to the University of Texas. Another black student, George W. McLaurin, had been admitted to the University of Oklahoma's doctoral program in education but was forced to sit apart from white students in an anteroom during class, was assigned a special table in the library, and was not permitted to eat with his classmates. In his 24-page memorandum, Coleman focused on the factual and procedural issues with Sweatt's case. As a factual matter, the two schools were not equal: the black law school had twenty-three students in one leased floor of a building; the University of Texas had 850 in a building designed to be a law school; the black school had 16,000 books in its law library; the University of Texas had 65,000; the black school was unaccredited; the University of Texas was accredited. "No one would seriously controvert," Coleman wrote, "that nothing short of equality of facilities would satisfy the Equal Protection Clause of the Fourteenth Amendment." Coleman also observed that intangible factors including "the advantages of an established alumni, a law review, and other forms of training," were "an important part of a legal education" and prevented the two schools from being equal. In that vein, he quoted Holmes's Harvard Law School address about education and highlighted the importance in graduate and professional school of "the exchange of ideas and participation with a large number of students and professors expert in the field." As a result, Coleman urged the Court to hold that "the only way States can satisfy the requirement of the Fourteenth Amendment is that the petitioner be admitted to the long-established and existing university maintained for all other citizens." Moreover, to prevent the University of Oklahoma's racial isolation of George McLaurin, the facilities "must be tendered on a non-discriminatory, non-segregated basis to all that are otherwise qualified."

In a note to Frankfurter, Coleman worried that his bold approach clashed with the justice's cautious instincts, yet the two cases called for decisive action. If the Court permitted the University of Oklahoma's racial segregation of McLaurin, it would be forced to reaffirm the "separate but equal" doctrine of *Plessy v. Ferguson*. And if the Court was prepared to hold that racially separate graduate and professional schools could not be equal, it should act quickly in Sweatt's case because Texas had appropriated money to build a new building for black law students. The Court's decision in *Sipuel*, Coleman noted, had already persuaded four southern states to begin admitting black graduate students. If the Court refused to address the issue in the Texas case, he argued, that momentum would be lost. Coleman quoted Frankfurter's concurrence in *Hurd v. Hodge* that the graduate school cases implicated "rights so basic to our society that, after the Civil War, their protection against invasion by the States was safeguarded by the Constitution."

Coleman concluded by urging Frankfurter and his fellow justices to confront the looming issue in the graduate school cases: "When faced with the question whether segregation is constitutional, the Court will have to overrule *Plessy v. Ferguson* . . ." He argued that the Court would have to follow the restrictive covenant cases that "classifications based upon race are illegal." He rejected *Plessy*'s assertion that "segregation does not bring about the inferiority of the race" as unsupported "by history or the study of psychologists and sociologists." He quoted a *Vanderbilt Law Review* note declaring that "in the South the inferior position of the Negro has been recognized and accepted by both races alike." And, referring to numerous decisions from southern states, he concluded: "Segregation is always a humiliating experience, but even clearer evidence that to designate, on the basis of race, is a sign of inferiority of a minority group is contained in the adjudications of almost every Southern State."

Coleman's memorandum about the graduate school cases was a power-ful and prescient document. The next term, the Court heard oral argument in *Sweatt* and *McLaurin*. Frankfurter's notes about *Sweatt* recited Coleman's facts about the physical facilities, number of books, and accreditation. They also emphasized the "imponderable inequalities"—such as the inability of black schools with few students to attract high-quality professors and there-fore engage in high-level discussion. "Restriction based on race," Frankfurter wrote, "necessarily restricts opportunities to get instructions from [the] ablest teachers [the] state can demand."

Another document in Frankfurter's *Sweatt* and *McLaurin* file was a complete copy of a 1948 report, *Segregation in Washington*. Frankfurter understood—based on Coleman's aborted attempt to eat at the Mayflower Hotel with the other clerks, the advocacy of former students Houston and Hastie, and many years of living in Washington—that life in the nation's cap-ital was racially segregated. Blacks could not eat in the same restaurants, stay in the same hotels, sit in the same sections of movie theaters, or try on clothes in most department stores.

During the late 1940s, Frankfurter was more sensitive to issues of race than gender. In *Goesaert v. Cleary*, Frankfurter dictated the first draft of his major-ity opinion upholding a Michigan law that forbade a woman from becoming a licensed bartender unless she was the wife or daughter of the owner. Frank-furter's opinion rejected an equal protection challenge and upheld the law's distinction between the wives and daughters of owners and non-owners of bars. Frankfurter asserted that the state could forbid all women from tend-ing bar: "This is so despite the vast changes in the social and legal position of women. The fact that women may now have achieved the virtues that men have long claimed as their prerogatives and now indulge in vices that men have long practiced, does not preclude the States from drawing a sharp line between the sexes, certainly in such matters as the regulation of the liquor traffic." Black joined the majority opinion after Frankfurter agreed to include cases and references to the Twenty-First Amendment, which repealed pro-hibition yet left the regulation of alcohol up to the states. Rutledge wrote a short dissent, which Douglas and Murphy joined. Several women wrote Frankfurter protesting the decision. "By your reasoning it would be utterly fair for the state to bar a negro or a Jew or a person of any race or even of any religion from holding certain jobs," wrote Dr. Alice E. Palmer of Detroit. "Your enmity toward women counts more against you than your friendship toward Negroes counts in your favor," wrote Alma Booker of Pittsburgh. As a dismissive *Detroit Free Press* columnist observed, the law had nothing to do with regulating alcohol but was the product of the all-male Bartenders Union capturing the Michigan legislature. Frankfurter's opinion in *Goesaert* is indefensible on many levels: It was the product of an all-male Court, an all-male group of law clerks, and a male-dominated workforce. Nor would it be the last time that Frankfurter's gender bias resulted in a serious error in professional judgment.

The Court considering *Sweatt* and *McLaurin* looked different after the death of its two most liberal members. In July 1949, Frank Murphy died in his sleep of a heart attack at age fifty-nine. On September 10, two weeks after suffering a stroke, Wiley Rutledge died at age fifty-five. Truman replaced Murphy with Attorney General Tom C. Clark and Rutledge with Senator Sherman Minton of Indiana. Together with his appointments of Burton and Vinson, Truman had remade the Court in a more pedestrian, moderate direction. It was also more southern with the Texan Clark, Kentuckians Vinson and Reed, and Alabaman Black.

At conference about *Sweatt* and *McLaurin* on April 8, 1950, Reed was the most vocal defender of segregation: "it is hard for me to say something that has been constitutional for years to be suddenly bad." Reed also argued that the Fourteenth Amendment had not intended to abolish racial segregation and pleaded with his colleagues not to attack *Plessy*: "We have made great progress. It would be unfortunate at this time for us to say segregation [is] unconstitutional."

Frankfurter responded that no one knew what the framers of the Fourteenth Amendment intended, but he must have allayed Reed's fears of drastic change: "This is no Dred Scott case. Here is the slow growth of insight and understanding." He argued that the Court "should not go beyond what is necessary" and therefore should base its decision only on the unreasonableness of segregation in graduate education. Echoing Coleman's memorandum, he read from Holmes's speech on education and argued that the strength of a law school was its student body and faculty. "To have two schools," he argued, "is not equality. It can't be made so."

Frankfurter's incremental approach to constitutional change carried over to two other cases that term about race. In *Cassell v. Texas*, he wrote a concurring opinion that condemned the exclusion of blacks from grand and petit juries but emphasized that the discrimination must be intentional as it was in that case. In an unpublished memorandum in a companion case to *Sweatt* and *McLaurin*, *Henderson v. United States*, he urged the Court to rule in favor of a black man discriminated against during interstate railroad travel on federal statutory grounds rather than emphasize the "symbolic" factors of racially separate railroad cars and take on segregation per se. He distinguished the intangible factors in the graduate school cases: "A totally different situation is presented by segregation in graduate schools. . . . Colored students who are restricted to segregated instruction cannot possibly have the same educational opportunities given in State institutions to white graduate students."

Following Frankfurter's incremental approach, the Court's unanimous opinions in *Sweatt* and *McLaurin* emphasized the "intangible factors" of graduate school education including reputation, alumni networks, and job prospects that made Texas's efforts to establish a separate black law school unequal. During the 1949 term, the Court stopped short of reconsidering *Plessy*'s "separate but equal" doctrine. But once it considered the intangible factors in evaluating inequality, the overruling of *Plessy*'s "separate but equal" doctrine was only a matter of time. Coleman's memorandum had provided the blueprint.

Coleman described his clerkship with Frankfurter as "the most rewarding of my life thus far." He enjoyed the back-and-forth with the justice about legal and historical issues. He stood up to Frankfurter for asserting that Roger Taney was a great justice despite Taney's notorious opinion in *Dred Scott v. Sandford* declaring that blacks were not citizens entitled to constitutional protection. In later years, he defended Frankfurter's liberal bona fides and argued that the justice's commitment to racial equality was "absolute."

The admiration between Frankfurter and Coleman was mutual. The justice quoted Coleman with pride that "without strict adherence *to reason* and refraining from permitting personal biases to enter adjudication, judges become covert little Hitlers." He admired Coleman's "judicial temperament" and hoped that he would seize any opportunity to become a federal judge: "I have never known anyone more equipped, better suited for judging than you." He reminded Coleman that "too many so-called liberals . . . are seduced by what Justice Brandeis rightly called the 'odious doctrine that the end justified the means.'" Frankfurter described it as "a joy to have worked with you for the year, and I shall watch you with great hopes." A year later, he wrote Coleman: "What I can say of you with great confidence is what was Justice Holmes's ultimate praise of a man: 'I bet on him.' I bet on you, whatever choice you may make and whatever the Fates may have in store for you."

Coleman's memorandum about *Sweatt* and *McLaurin* made a lasting impact on his boss. The justice placed several copies in his files and soon showed the memorandum to one of his most talented law clerks, Alexander M. Bickel. In the early 1950s while in private practice, Coleman joined Thurgood Marshall's legal team at the NAACP attacking racially segregated public primary and secondary schools. It was up to Frankfurter and the Court to figure out how to overrule *Plessy*'s "separate but equal" doctrine and how to enforce the dismantling of state-sponsored racial segregation. The most powerful argument against racial segregation, whether in law schools or grade schools, was the story of Bill Coleman himself.

The Frankfurter Cult
on Trial

About 12:15 p.m. on Friday, December 17, 1948, the phone rang in Frankfurter's chambers. The justice's secretary, Katherine Watters, answered it. The man on the other end of the line asked if it was Frankfurter's office. He identified himself as Westbrook Pegler, and the Red-baiting syndicated columnist was talking so fast and so unclearly that Watters could barely understand him. Pegler "wanted to know if the Justice would see him—he said that it was in regard to the Alger Hiss affair. He went on to tell me that Alger Hiss mentioned the Justice in his testimony, and he wanted to know if the Justice would have something to say about it and would I find out." Watters explained that the justice did not give interviews; Pegler interrupted her and asked to make an exception and whether she knew that Alger Hiss had been indicted. "In fact," Pegler told Watters, "it is even possible that the Justice might give testimony." After Watters held firm and hung up the phone, she wrote a memorandum that Frankfurter circulated the next day to his colleagues along with a note: "Since Westbrook Pegler evidently intends to bring his poisonous pen into action against me in connection with the Alger Hiss affair, and since he will thereby inevitably involve the Court, I should like my colleagues to see the attached memorandum by way of background."

By the late 1940s, Cold War hysteria about Communists infiltrating the federal government was in full swing. In 1945, Soviet spy Elizabeth Bentley had renounced the Communist Party and had provided the FBI with a list of alleged spies in the federal government. J. Edgar Hoover initiated a massive investigation and encouraged federal prosecutions; the House Un-American Activities Committee (HUAC) initiated hearings about Communist spies in government and in Hollywood. During his HUAC testimony on August 3,

1948, former *Time* magazine editor Whittaker Chambers accused Alger Hiss of belonging to an underground Communist cell in the mid-1930s; Hiss wired the committee denying the allegations or that he knew Chambers. Since the story broke, Pegler had been writing numerous columns about Frankfurter's ties to Hiss and how the justice had used his radical protégés to create an "invisible government."

The Hiss case tested the strength of Frankfurter's liberal network. It not only hurt the justice's reputation but also those of his protégés. In their refusal to abandon Hiss, Frankfurter, Acheson, and others revealed the depth of their loyalty to their friend and their disbelief that he could be a Communist.

Since his days as a first-year Harvard law student, Hiss could do no wrong in Frankfurter's eyes. A Johns Hopkins graduate, Hiss grew up in a "shabby genteel" middle-class Baltimore family. William Marbury, a former Frankfurter student and Baltimore neighbor, had provided Hiss with a letter of introduction to the Harvard law professor. They were soon on a first-name basis. Hiss became a regular at Frankfurter's Sunday afternoon teas at 192 Brattle Street, made the *Harvard Law Review* after his first year, and as a third-year student took Frankfurter's seminars on administrative law and federal courts. Frankfurter was impressed by the tall, thin Hiss's cultural sophistication and charm. It was no shock, therefore, when Frankfurter selected Hiss to be Justice Holmes's secretary.

It was during the postgraduate year with Holmes that Frankfurter began to overlook Hiss's small deceptions. Three months into his job, Hiss broke Holmes's unwritten rule about no married secretaries—informing the justice the day before his wedding and Frankfurter two days later and claiming to have been unaware of the rule. Hiss also engaged in a "benign conspiracy" to cajole Holmes, whose wife, Fanny, had died the previous winter, into permitting him to read to the justice in the late afternoons. Finally, in April 1930 Frankfurter urged John Lord O'Brian, assistant attorney general in charge of the Justice Department's Antitrust Division, to hire Hiss. Frankfurter described Hiss as "one of the very best men we have in many a day," "a man of unusual cultivation, charm, and prematurely solid judgment," a far better writer than most Harvard law graduates, and "a Godsend." O'Brian interviewed Hiss, offered him a job, and thought the young man had accepted. Instead, Hiss joined the white-shoe Boston law firm of Choate, Hall & Stewart without bothering to inform O'Brian. Hiss and his wife became regulars in the Frankfurters' Cambridge social set. Frankfurter selected Hiss's younger brother Donald, also a Harvard law student, to be Holmes's secretary for the 1931 term.

During the early Roosevelt years, Frankfurter guided Alger Hiss's career and acted as his father-protector. In March 1933, he helped Hiss, then working at Cotton & Franklin in New York City, land a job with the Agricultural Adjustment Administration (AAA) working for general counsel Jerome Frank. Hiss's reputation grew as a counsel to the Nye Committee investigating the munitions industry. In December 1934, he had met Whittaker Chambers, who was using the alias Carl, during meetings of an underground Communist cell named the Ware Group. During the spring of 1935, Hiss somehow managed to escape the "purge" of Frank and other radicals from the AAA. Hiss sought counsel from Frankfurter, who instructed Gardner Jackson and other purge victims who blamed Hiss for keeping his job to back off.

With Frankfurter's assistance, Hiss rose through the ranks of the Roosevelt administration. In August 1935, he left the AAA to work as a special assistant to then–Solicitor General Stanley Reed to defend the Agricultural Adjustment Act's constitutionality before the Supreme Court. A year later, Hiss joined the State Department as an aide to one of Frankfurter's Harvard law colleagues, Assistant Secretary of State Francis B. Sayre, to implement trade agreements. In September 1939, Chambers, having broken with the Communist Party, informed Assistant Secretary of State Adolf A. Berle, Jr., that the Hiss brothers were Communists. At the State Department, however, Hiss was a rising star; the rumors were ignored. From 1941 to 1944, he worked in the Far East Division on China and in August 1944 helped organize the Dumbarton Oaks Conference about the future of international law and the creation of the United Nations. In February 1945, he was a junior member of the U.S. delegation at Yalta and adviser to Secretary of State Edward Stettinius. Two months later, the forty-year-old Hiss was named the director of the Office of Special Political Affairs and served as the secretary-general at the San Francisco Conference, which drafted the United Nations charter. In 1946, Secretary of State Byrnes informed Hiss that several members of Congress, based on information from the FBI, had accused him of being a Communist. At Byrnes's suggestion, Hiss voluntarily submitted to an FBI interview. In December 1946, he was named president of the Carnegie Endowment for International Peace and left the State Department.

After Chambers testified before HUAC on August 3, 1948, Frankfurter and his protégés rallied around Hiss—led by Max Lowenthal. Truman's influential outside adviser had known Hiss since his days as Holmes's secretary. In the days before and after Israel's independence, Lowenthal had relied on Hiss's knowledge of the State Department, United Nations, and international affairs. By early August, Lowenthal turned his attention to Truman's presidential campaign and the spy hearings before HUAC, which Lowenthal feared could jeopardize the president's reelection. On August 7, Lowenthal phoned Hiss and asked if he could see him in person for two minutes. Upon arriving at Hiss's apartment, Lowenthal discovered that Hiss was not eating or sleeping and all alone. He took Hiss to his Central Park West apartment, gave him a shot of whiskey to help him sleep, and made him breakfast the next morning. Lowenthal owned a farm in Connecticut, sent Hiss there to rest, and instructed him that his number one job was to take care of himself. He asked Hiss where his lawyer William Marbury was; Hiss said in England (it was actually Geneva). Lowenthal urged Hiss to hire someone full time.

Hiss's sworn testimony on August 16 and his insistent denials that he had never met Chambers had not helped his cause. Nor had the surprise confrontation with Chambers—orchestrated by the ambitious freshman California congressman Richard Nixon—the next day at the Commodore Hotel in New York City. During a cross-examination by Nixon, Hiss said he may have known someone who looked like Chambers as journalist George Crosley and threatened to sue Chambers for defamation if Chambers publicly repeated the allegations about Hiss belonging to an underground Communist group. During televised HUAC hearings on August 25, Hiss and Chambers again testified under oath about their conflicting recollections of the past. After Chambers repeated his charges two days later on *Meet the Press*, Hiss sued him for slander and by November had begun depositions.

Lowenthal knew that Hiss was in trouble and sought Frankfurter's advice. On November 4, Lowenthal spoke with the justice about advising Hiss's lawyer to delay the lawsuit until they could learn more about Chambers and his allegations. Frankfurter agreed and added that Marbury should not be leading the legal team. Marbury, Frankfurter argued, was a perfectly fine Supreme Court advocate but not a trial lawyer. The justice instructed Lowenthal to reach out to Charles Horsky, a partner of Acheson's at Covington & Burling. A former colleague of Hiss's in the solicitor general's office, Horsky was unafraid to take on controversial cases. In 1944, he had argued Fred Korematsu's Supreme Court case challenging the internment of Japanese Americans. Lowenthal ran into several roadblocks: Horsky was out of town, and Hiss lawyer Harold Rosenwald disagreed with Lowenthal's go-slow strategy. After the talk with Frankfurter, Lowenthal invited Hiss to his Connecticut farm and relayed Frankfurter's message about getting a real trial lawyer, not a Supreme Court advocate, to represent him full time. "You are going through a painful period," he told Hiss, "you will be vindicated when the whole truth has been unearthed, in the meantime you must have fortitude and take the pain as it comes."

Hiss's depositions for his slander suit backfired when his counsel requested that Chambers turn over any relevant documents. On November 17, Chambers produced State Department documents from 1938, which he said Hiss had given him to relay to the Soviets. Chambers testified that the documents had been typed on the Hiss family typewriter. It was the first time that Chambers had accused Hiss of espionage. Chambers also produced five rolls of microfilm allegedly containing documents from Hiss, known as the "Pumpkin Papers" because he hid them in a hollowed-out pumpkin at his Westminster, Maryland, farm before revealing them to HUAC investigators. On December 15, Hiss testified before a federal grand jury that he had not given Chambers any documents and had not known him after 1937 and only as journalist George Crosley. After Hiss and Chambers testified, Richard Nixon appeared twice before the grand jury to urge them to indict Hiss, but not Chambers, for perjury (the three-year statute of limitations on espionage had expired). The grand jury indicted Hiss on two counts of perjury.

On December 17, Lowenthal received the phone call he dreaded most: a request to testify before HUAC about his conversations with Hiss. Lowenthal agonized about what to do. He believed that Hiss was "an honorable man." Yet Lowenthal worried that his past clashes with Hoover and the FBI over wiretapping had caught up with him. He hired former U.S. senator Burton K. Wheeler as his lawyer, recounted recent efforts to advise Hiss, and confessed: "Either I am a skunk who runs out and tries to protect solely his own hide, or an honest man, and if being honest and decent makes me suspect, I can't help it." Either way, Lowenthal's ability to serve as Frankfurter's go-between with the Hiss legal team was over. As Pegler predicted that day to Katherine Watters on the phone, the justice soon found himself embroiled in the Hiss affair. And Frankfurter was not the only one.

====

ON JANUARY 7, 1949, Dean Acheson was nominated as Truman's new secretary of state. Acheson's nomination reflected a lifetime of Frankfurter's efforts to cultivate a liberal network and to send Harvard Law School's best men into public service. The justice wrote that Acheson, who had resigned as under secretary of state in July 1947 to return to private practice, was nominated because of his "intrinsic" worth and not because of any personal or political considerations. No former student was closer to Frankfurter than Acheson.

Nearly ten years earlier to the day, Acheson had appeared at Frankfurter's Senate confirmation hearings and heard a parade of witnesses falsely accuse Frankfurter of being a Communist. Before the Senate Foreign Relations Committee on January 13, Acheson faced accusations of disloyalty because of his ties to Alger and Donald Hiss.

The allegations stemmed from HUAC testimony by Columbia law professor and longtime New Dealer Adolf A. Berle, Jr. In September 1939, Berle had learned from Chambers that the Hiss brothers may have been Communists. Nine years later before HUAC, Berle insisted that he had informed Acheson at the time and in 1941 when Acheson became assistant secretary of state. According to Berle, Acheson vouched for the Hiss brothers and said that Frankfurter would, too. Berle falsely alleged that Alger Hiss had been Acheson's "executive assistant" and that Hiss and Acheson had been soft on the Soviets during the fall of 1944 whereas Berle had been a hardliner. This dispute, Berle claimed, led to his exit from the State Department for an ambassadorship to Brazil. He conceded he had "a biased view."

Berle's biases included a lifelong vendetta against Frankfurter and his inner circle. As a Harvard law student, he had resented his exclusion from Frankfurter's preferred group of high-achieving students. During the early New Deal, Berle was a member of Roosevelt's "Brain Trust" and had viewed Frankfurter and his protégés as influential rivals. For his part, Frankfurter placed Berle on par with Yale law professor Fred Rodell in his "pathological hate of me" and described Berle the law student as "a boring, humorless creature." Others, including C. C. Burlingham, regarded Berle as a typical State Department anti-Semite. As the years went by, Berle became extremely jealous of Acheson, Frankfurter's protégé who overshadowed Berle in the Treasury and State Departments. In 1942, Berle attempted to block what he regarded as a Frankfurter-inspired plot to make Acheson secretary of state. Berle may have exaggerated his HUAC testimony about Alger and Donald Hiss to settle old scores with Frankfurter and Acheson.

At the outset of his January 13 testimony before the Senate Foreign Relations Committee, Acheson vouched for Alger and Donald Hiss. He insisted that Donald had "served the country with complete fidelity and loyalty," describing them as "intimate friends" and law partners. He also considered Alger a friend. Acheson told the committee that "my friendship is not easily given, and it is not easily withdrawn." He refuted almost all of the allegations and insisted Berle's memory had "gone badly astray." First, Alger Hiss had never been Acheson's "executive assistant" in the State Department or worked for him in any capacity except for a few months when Acheson had been acting secretary of state. Donald Hiss had been his assistant when Acheson was assistant secretary of state and, according to Acheson, had served with distinction. Second, Acheson and Alger Hiss had never clashed with Berle over U.S.-Soviet policy in 1944; Acheson and Berle had not worked in the same part of the world at the time. Finally, Berle's warnings had not been as specific as he claimed in his HUAC testimony. In February or March 1941, Berle had come to Acheson with information that one of the Hiss brothers had "associations" that could be "embarrassing to me and to the Department." Berle, who learned that Donald was Acheson's assistant, could not tell Acheson which brother. Nor would Berle reveal the source of the information. Acheson asked Donald Hiss to reflect on whether he had any "associations which would embarrass me." Donald said he did not, and Acheson reiterated his "complete confidence in him" and considered the matter "closed." Berle, perhaps recognizing the problems with his HUAC testimony, wired the Senate Foreign Relations Committee that Acheson should be confirmed.

Acheson's January 13 testimony vouching for Donald and Alger Hiss and rebutting Berle's HUAC testimony satisfied the Senate Foreign Relations Committee. Senator Arthur Vandenberg defended him on the Senate floor and, with Acheson's permission, summarized the testimony: "An assertion of personal friendship for the Hiss brothers; a staunch defense of Donald Hiss; a purpose to leave Alger Hiss to the courts. Total and aggressive hostility to subversion in the State Department." By an 83–6 vote, the Senate confirmed Acheson as secretary of state. On January 21 in the Oval Office, Frankfurter watched as Chief Justice Vinson swore in Acheson as the smiling Truman looked on. That day, Frankfurter presented Acheson with a photograph of one of the justice's most admired secretaries of state, John Quincy Adams. "Dear Dean," Frankfurter wrote beneath the photograph, "Even old John Quincy Adams has a contented look as he sees you sitting at his memorable desk!" Frankfurter and Acheson continued their tradition of walking part of the way together from their Georgetown homes to work. The looming perjury trial of Alger Hiss tested their loyalty to one of Harvard law school's best men. Columnist Westbrook Pegler insisted that during the Hiss case "the whole Frankfurter cult and the Roosevelt myth are on trial."

The most damaging blow to Hiss's credibility were the State Department documents that Chambers produced and claimed were typed on the Hiss family typewriter. In April 1949, after months of searching Washington, D.C., junkyards and secondhand dealers and working with the sons of former Hiss family maid Claudia Catlett, Hiss's defense lawyers located the typewriter—a Woodstock Model 5, #230099. FBI and defense experts agreed, based on comparisons to documents typed by Alger's wife, Priscilla, during the 1930s, that the State Department documents produced by Chambers had been typed on the same machine. Fortunately for Hiss, he had taken the advice of Frankfurter and Lowenthal and hired one of the nation's best trial lawyers, Lloyd Paul Stryker of New York City. Stryker knew that the typewriter was a huge blow and therefore made the trial about whether the jury believed Hiss or Chambers.

With the defense's emphasis on Hiss's credibility compared to Chambers's, Stryker lined up numerous character witnesses and on June 22, 1949, announced: "Call Mr. Justice Felix Frankfurter." The justice wore an "ordinary brown suit" into the Foley Square Courthouse in lower Manhattan. During direct examination by Stryker, Frankfurter recalled meeting Hiss as a second-year student at Harvard Law School (it probably was a year earlier) and how he had chosen Hiss over other third-year *Harvard Law Review* editors to be Holmes's secretary on the basis of personality, character, and other "indispensable characteristics." Stryker ended his direct examination by asking Frankfurter about "the reputation of Mr. Alger Hiss for loyalty to his government, integrity and veracity" and whether it was "good or bad." Frankfurter responded: "I never heard it called into question" and "I would say it is excellent."

Frankfurter's cross-examination made headlines because he sparred with Assistant U.S. Attorney Thomas F. Murphy. Murphy began by asking whether Hiss's reputation "wasn't too good" in 1944 on the basis of Jerome Frank's feelings about him. Frankfurter, correctly assuming Murphy meant 1934 and the AAA purge the following year, replied that Frank's "differences" with Hiss "did not bear on loyalty or integrity." "It didn't, Judge?" Murphy retorted. Frankfurter insisted that he did not want to "fence" with the prosecutor, who blamed the justice for starting it. Frankfurter could not recall what Frank had told him in 1933 or 1934 but emphasized that he "thought highly" of the former AAA general counsel and Second Circuit judge. Murphy then asked Frankfurter whether he had recommended Lee Pressman, another member of the Ware Group who later admitted to being a Communist, to AAA. Stryker objected. Judge Samuel Kaufman agreed and struck it from the record. Frankfurter said it was "highly unlikely." Murphy asked if Pressman was a member of the *Harvard Law Review*. An irritated Frankfurter replied: "Yes, I believe he was." Again, Kaufman sustained Stryker's objection on relevance grounds and struck the testimony from the record. At the end of the cross-examination, Frankfurter admitted that it was the first time he had ever been called as a witness. His colleague Stanley Reed, who had been

Hiss's boss in the solicitor general's office, followed him to the stand and was less effusive about Hiss than Frankfurter was.

After Frankfurter and Reed testified, a bill was introduced to Congress to bar the ability to subpoena a Supreme Court justice. Reed had been subpoenaed; Frankfurter, however, had appeared at defense counsel's informal request. To an Associated Press reporter, Frankfurter corrected the record and emphasized the constitutional right of the accused to produce relevant evidence. He knew he would have been disqualified from hearing Hiss's case whether he testified or not. He considered himself under a "duty" to testify. A few years later, Frankfurter equivocated when asked whether he "appeared 'voluntarily' in the Hiss trial. Even in law one cannot always answer 'yes' or 'no.'"

Legal historian G. Edward White has argued that Frankfurter's testimony was not "particularly effective" and "had not done [Hiss] much good." As White acknowledged, however, the mere fact that Frankfurter and Reed took the stand boosted Hiss's credibility. And in other respects, Frankfurter had given Hiss the best piece of advice—to hire a first-rate trial lawyer. The decision to make the case about the character of Hiss versus Chambers and not about the typewriter was spot on. On July 7, 1949, the jury deadlocked, 8–4, about Hiss's guilt.

Red baiters blamed Frankfurter for the jury's failure to convict Hiss. An infuriated Westbrook Pegler attacked Judge Kaufman for protecting Frankfurter on cross-examination and preventing the justice from answering tough questions about Pressman and himself. "I don't know whether or not Frankfurter is a Communist," Pegler wrote. "I would have liked to hear it put to him." Nixon, who doggedly pursued Hiss and pleaded with the grand jury to indict him, described Frankfurter's testimony as "unprecedented and inexcusable." Not privy to the sealed grand jury testimony, Frankfurter mistakenly believed that Nixon had "introduced decency" into the HUAC hearings and "his conduct as to Hiss was not, so far as I know, subject to criticism."

The justice received numerous letters from the American people, most of whom opposed his decision to testify. One critic wrote Chief Justice Vinson that by testifying on Hiss's behalf, Frankfurter and Reed had violated judicial ethics. Frankfurter replied to Vinson that "the past relations which led to my being called as a witness in the Hiss trial of course disqualified me from sitting in any case involving his liberty. . . . If the circumstances were the same I would do the same, for I would feel like a craven not to." Frankfurter was not cowed by the criticism. "As for Alger, you know all I feel," Frankfurter wrote Harold Laski a few weeks after the first trial. "But even you'd be surprised at the flood of vituperation the matter has let loose—a reminder of S[acco]-V[an-zetti] days."

A critic of Frankfurter's testimony in the Hiss case inquired why he did not testify as a character witness for another former student in trouble with the law. In July 1945, Edward F. Prichard, Jr., had returned to his native Kentucky and aspired to run for governor. His friends worried about his involvement in rough-and-tumble state politics. He and his law partner were charged with federal election fraud for forging signatures of Bourbon County election officials on 254 ballots in 1948 for U.S. Senate candidate Virgil Chapman. Prich had confessed to a state judge who was the father of another of his law partners. Over the defense's objections, the judge was permitted to testify against him at trial. A week after Hiss received a hung jury, the 34-year-old Prichard, but not his law partner, was found guilty and sentenced to two years in federal prison. Prichard's conviction was affirmed on appeal despite the best efforts of former Frankfurter clerk Joseph Rauh and former assistant solicitor general Hugh Cox to persuade the Court of Appeals for the Sixth Circuit that the judge's testimony should have been excluded at trial. Prichard's conviction shook the Frankfurters and other members of the Georgetown set. "I take the line I was for Dreyfus and I am for Prich," Prichard's former roommate Isaiah Berlin wrote. "But what with Hiss and Prich . . . the foundations of F. F.'s universe are tottering." Berlin reported that Frankfurter was "for once, very unamused."

Frankfurter was worried about Hiss's second trial when he heard CBS television commentator Edward R. Murrow predict, with the trial already under way, that no jury would convict because it would be unable to determine whether Hiss or Chambers was lying. Frankfurter pleaded with Dr. Alfred Cohn to intercede with their mutual friend Murrow and to set him straight. First, the justice was troubled that Murrow had opined about Hiss's case during the trial. Second, Frankfurter argued that if the jury believed Chambers was lying it could not convict Hiss of perjury beyond a reasonable doubt. Rather than misstate the jury's charge, Frankfurter preferred that Murrow "keep his mouth shut."

Frankfurter knew better than Murrow that Hiss faced an uphill battle during his second trial. Stryker had withdrawn as lead counsel and been replaced by Claude B. Cross of Boston. The defense called many character witnesses, but not Frankfurter or Reed. Hiss claimed it was to spare them "risk of embarrassment" and specifically referred to the negative columns by Pegler; it also may have been because two pro-prosecution jurors from the first trial felt "antagonized" by the justices' testimony. The prosecution wised up and focused on the Woodstock typewriter and the unrebutted evidence that someone had typed the State Department documents on that machine. On January 21, 1950, the jury convicted Hiss of both counts of perjury—that he did not know Chambers after 1937 and had not given Chambers documents. Four days later, Hiss was sentenced to five years in federal prison and was released on $10,000 bail pending appeal. At his sentencing, he claimed to have been a victim of "forgery by typewriter."

The Hiss case divided members of the Georgetown set. The Frankfurters vowed to stop seeing Alice Roosevelt Longworth, a regular attendee at Hiss's second trial and a firm believer in his guilt. Marion Frankfurter thought Mrs. L was a "dreadful woman" but didn't hold it against pen pal Isiah Berlin for his belief that Hiss was "a little guilty and a little innocent."

Hiss's conviction would have been the perfect time for his friends in high places to abandon him. Instead, they took a more courageous course. After Hiss was sentenced on January 25, Acheson agonized over what to tell the press. He was prepared not to answer any questions about the case or to say anything newsworthy. The secretary of state, however, refused to hide his true feelings when he told the press: "I do not intend to turn my back on Alger Hiss." Acheson's defiant comments, culminating with references to Christian principles and the Bible, exposed him to intense criticism and calls for his resignation. Outraged members of the Senate Appropriations Committee interrogated him on February 28 about his relationship with Hiss. Acheson answered their questions and read a lengthy statement insisting he could support Hiss as a friend without condoning perjury or disloyalty in the State Department.

Acheson's loyalty to Hiss won him eternal admiration from Felix and Marion Frankfurter. The justice urged C. C. Burlingham, Grenville Clark, and Henry Stimson to write a letter to the editor of the *New York Times* in support of Acheson. "To me," he wrote Burlingham, "it manifested not so much courage as moral clarity." Nothing made Frankfurter happier than in June when Harvard conferred an honorary degree on Acheson. "The timid silence of those who should have spoken all these months in regard to Acheson," he wrote Burlingham, "is one of the least edifying experiences of my life." He thanked Learned Hand for writing Acheson a private note and remarked: "This is a cruel town."

Frankfurter still believed in Hiss's innocence and solicited others to help with his appeal. Six days after the guilty verdict, Frankfurter's former Harvard law colleague Edmund M. Morgan wrote to the justice: "I know him and his family so well and have such faith in him that I would not believe him guilty even if he confessed." Frankfurter encouraged Morgan, an expert on evidence, to help with the appeal, "wholly apart from all the implications of it for our unshaken faith in Alger."

———

THE RED-BAITING ATTACKS on Frankfurter for his faith in Hiss and admiration for Acheson must be taken into account as he approached several cases involving the government's pursuit of Communists. Frankfurter's opinions belie the notion that he turned his back on civil liberties or switched from a liberal lawyer to a conservative justice. They articulate his belief in a limited role for the judiciary compared to the elected branches in protecting civil liberties. His opinions sought to protect the rights of suspected Communists through fair procedures while recognizing Congress's broad powers to defend the nation from security threats.

For Frankfurter, the question in most of these cases was when the power of Congress yielded to freedom of speech and thought. In May 1950, he wrote a concurring opinion in *American Communications Association v. Douds* about the constitutionality of a provision in the Taft-Hartley Act requiring union leaders to swear that they were not Communist Party members. Congress could enact such a provision, he argued, as part of its long-standing power to encourage industrial peace. Frankfurter's concurrence read more like a dissent. He argued that the provision as written was "much more extensive" and required union leaders to disavow not only membership but also belief in any organization that advocates overthrow of the government. The provision, he agreed with Jackson, went too far because "probing into men's thoughts trenches on those aspects of individual freedom which we rightly regard as the most cherished aspects of Western civilization." As a result, he would have invalidated the overbroad provision and allowed the rest of the legislation to stand.

Frankfurter was no more lenient on the executive branch in its use of the Loyalty Review Board to expel suspected Communists from the federal government. On October 11, 1950, the Court heard argument in *Joint Anti-Fascist Refugee Committee v. McGrath* about whether the federal government could designate organizations as Communist on a list for the Loyalty Review Board without giving the organizations fair notice and a hearing. The next day, he was outraged by the government's insistence that the Loyalty Review Board could use confidential informants to expel suspected Communists from the federal government. He heard about "the tragic story of Dorothy Bailey," a labor relations expert who had been drummed out of the U.S. Employment Service after seventeen years. The Loyalty Review Board, relying on a confidential FBI informant, concluded that she was a Communist and dismissed her. At oral argument, Frankfurter got into a shouting match with Solicitor General Philip B. Perlman over whether the government had enough evidence to fire Bailey. "The most important fact of this case is that the secret, untested finding by the Attorney General is not subject to review by anybody but those with the power to chop off heads," Frankfurter told Perlman. The solicitor general blew his cool after Frankfurter suggested that the report of a confidential FBI informant was insufficient evidence. "That isn't so, and Justice Frankfurter should not say it is so," Perlman shouted. Jackson, a former attorney general, responded that FBI reports were not evidence because most of the information had not been verified. Bailey's lawyers, former New Dealers Paul Porter and Thurman Arnold, argued that she was not able to confront her accuser. Neither she, her lawyers, nor the judges knew the person's identity. Porter argued that Bailey should be reinstated and was a "victim of the hysteria of our times."

At conference two days later, Frankfurter passed during the discussion of the subversive organizations in *Joint Anti-Fascist Refugee Committee* and preferred to wait for the case of Dorothy Bailey. He railed against the dangers of giving the executive branch unlimited power. The fired employee could not confront her accusers, and the Loyalty Review Board could not confirm the truth of the allegations. As a result, the employee "becomes a pariah." The procedures in Bailey's case, he argued, offended any notion of due process. "This hearing," he concluded, "is worse than none." He voted to reverse in both cases.

Six weeks after the conference discussion, Frankfurter circulated a memorandum attacking Burton's draft majority opinion in the *Bailey* case for avoiding the obvious constitutional issues. In his memorandum, Frankfurter insisted that the Court had the power to review the Loyalty Review Board's procedures and concluded that the procedures in Bailey's case had been unfair. She had the right to reinstatement and to confront any future evidence used against her. Frankfurter's best efforts failed. With Clark disqualified as Truman's former attorney general, the justices were divided 4–4. Thus the lower court decision affirming Bailey's dismissal was allowed to stand.

Unable to obtain a fair hearing for Bailey, Frankfurter joined five justices in *Joint Anti-Fascist Refugee Committee v. McGrath* to prevent the attorney general from designating organizations as subversive without notice and a fair hearing. He argued in a concurring opinion that these organizations had standing to sue the attorney general and were entitled to fair procedures under the Fifth Amendment's Due Process Clause. "The requirement of 'due process' is not a fair-weather or timid assurance," he wrote. "It must be respected in periods of calm and in times of trouble; it protects aliens as well as citizens." The right to notice and a fair hearing went to the heart of Frankfurter's conception of a democracy: "a democratic government must therefore practice fairness; and fairness can rarely be obtained by secret, one-sided determination of facts decisive of rights."

As willing as Frankfurter seemed in *Douds, Bailey,* and *Joint Anti-Fascist Refugee Committee* to curb the excesses of Congress and the executive branch, his opinions in those cases are often overshadowed by the Supreme Court's review of the criminal convictions of general secretary Eugene Dennis and ten other Communist Party USA leaders. After a contentious nine-month trial, a jury found them guilty of conspiring under the Smith Act "to organize or help to organize any society, group, or assembly of persons who teach, advocate, or encourage the overthrow or destruction of any such government by force or violence."

The Court of Appeals for the Second Circuit affirmed their convictions on the basis of a majority opinion written by Frankfurter's fellow believer in judicial restraint, Learned Hand. Hand's free speech credentials were second to none. His groundbreaking *Masses* opinion in 1917 had protected the right to criticize the government absent direct "incitement" to illegal action but had been reversed on appeal. He had criticized Holmes's "clear and present danger" test in 1919 and had influenced Holmes's evolution on free speech. In his majority opinion for the Second Circuit in the *Dennis* case, Hand reinterpreted "clear and present danger" as "whether the mischief of the repression is greater than the gravity of the evil, discounted by its improbability." Hand wrote that this was not the speech of "an unhappy, bitter outcast" as in the Court's World War I cases but members of the Communist Party USA, "a highly articulated, well contrived, far spread organization, numbering thousands of adherents, rigidly and ruthlessly disciplined." In *Dennis,* Hand found a clear and present danger of a conspiracy to overthrow the U.S. government. He observed that at the time of the indictment in the summer of 1948, the Soviet Union had violated the Yalta agreement by refusing to hold free elections and by installing Communist governments in Eastern Europe; it also had blockaded Berlin in June 1948, which required U.S. and British airlifts of food and supplies for nearly a year to West Berlin. The same type of aggressive action could happen here. "We do not understand how one could ask for a more probable danger," Hand wrote, "unless we must wait till the actual eve of hostilities."

After the publication of his opinion in August 1950, Hand asked Frankfurter for "a compassionate lenity" because the case had caused Hand "much travail" and "now the rest lies in the laps of the nine Gods. . . . I can only say of myself what Thayer used to say in exegesis of a particularly obscure decision: 'It is, as it is: and whatever it is, this is it.'" Hand wrote that without his "Peerless Paragon" of a law clerk, Hugh Calkins, "this Old Grab Bag of Antiques would have completely crumpled." A former *Harvard Crimson* and *Harvard Law Review* president, Calkins joined Frankfurter's chambers the following year and worked extensively on the *Dennis* case.

The nearly four hours of oral argument in the *Dennis* case on December 4, 1950, featured "fewer than usual questions" with Frankfurter, Black, and Douglas asking about the clear and present danger test. Five days later at conference, Frankfurter argued that the case raised four important questions: (1) the status of the clear and present danger test since the 1925 decision in *Gitlow v. New York*; (2) how imminent the danger must be; (3) the difficult question of whether clear and present danger was a question of fact that should have been reserved for the jury; and (4) whether the justices can take judicial notice of facts outside the record of a clear and present danger. The discussion was also brief. Four justices (Vinson, Reed, Burton, and Minton) voted to affirm; one (Black) voted to reverse; Jackson passed; Douglas "didn't know" until he read the record. Frankfurter did not vote, either. "The amazing thing about this conference on this important case was the brief nature of the discussion," Douglas wrote later. "Those wanting to affirm had minds closed to argument or persuasion. The conference discussion was largely *pro forma*. It was the more amazing because of the drastic revision of the 'clear and present danger' test which affirmance requires."

Contrary to the notes from his antagonist Douglas, Frankfurter rejected Chief Justice Vinson's opinion as "farrago" because it relied on the clear and present danger test and explicitly adopted Hand's reformulation of it. Frankfurter believed that clear and present danger was unhelpful language. He explicitly refused to join Vinson's opinion because he did not want it to be a binding precedent. Jackson also decided to write separately. Only Burton, Minton, and Reed joined the chief justice's opinion. During their extensive correspondence in February and March 1951, Frankfurter chided Reed for signing on to Vinson's opinion on the assumption that clear and present danger had been satisfied and faulted Reed's "argumentative windings" for starting "with an answer instead of a problem."

Frankfurter showed his correspondence with Reed to Calkins and asked his law clerk to write a memorandum about his own views of the case. Calkins offered three possibilities: (1) a "literal application" of the clear and present danger test as in Douglas's dissent; (2) a theory, endorsed by Jackson and probably Reed, based on *Gitlow v. New York* that the legislature has the power to prohibit advocacy of the overthrow of the government by force and violence; or (3) a "rule of reason" theory restating Hand's approach in the Second Circuit. Calkins wrote many memoranda about the case as well as the first draft of Frankfurter's opinion in *Dennis*; the ideas and heavily edited final product were Frankfurter's.

Aided by Calkins, Frankfurter published a concurring opinion affirming the convictions yet rejecting the clear and present danger test. He believed that clear and present danger obscured the balancing of "competing interests"— Congress's interest in protecting national security and the free speech rights of the members of the Communist Party. He quoted former student and Harvard law professor Paul Freund on the perils of relying on clear and present danger: " 'No matter how rapidly we utter the phrase 'clear and present danger,' or how closely we hyphenate the words, they are not a substitute for the weighing of values. They tend to convey a delusion of certitude when what is most certain is the complexity of the strands in the web of freedoms which the judge must disentangle.' "

One of the most important quotations in Frankfurter's extensive handwritten notes for his *Dennis* opinion was from Chief Justice John Marshall's 1819 decision in *McCulloch v. Maryland* upholding the constitutionality of the national bank and recognizing implied federal power: "we must never forget, that it is *a constitution* we are expounding." As he argued four years later in an essay commemorating the 200th anniversary of Marshall's birth, Frankfurter believed that the quotation was "the single most important utterance in the literature of constitutional law" and agreed with James Bradley Thayer that *McCulloch* was Marshall's "greatest single judicial performance." In *McCulloch*, Marshall explained that the framers of the Constitution had created a broad outline with implied powers to deal with the nation's future problems to ensure its survival.

His concurrence in *Dennis* was Frankfurter's *McCulloch* moment, his reaffirmation of the broad powers of Congress to save the country from potential destruction. He began by quoting another Marshall opinion, *Cohens v. Virginia*, that under the Constitution the "government is complete; to all these objects, it is competent." Frankfurter argued that Congress's implied and inherent powers were broad when it came to the security of the nation: "The right of a government to maintain its existence—self-preservation—is the most pervasive aspect of sovereignty."

His balancing approach to the First Amendment offered an alternative to a literal reading of "Congress shall make no law" in which free speech was absolute. Instead, he argued that "free speech in the democratic society" and "national security" are "competing interests." The balancing of the "relevant factors," he argued, must be done in the first instance not by the court but by Congress. And in an allusion to James Bradley Thayer's limited conception of judicial review, he argued that the Court should disregard the judgment of the legislature "only if there is no reasonable basis for it." Frankfurter quoted a Brandeis dissent, joined by Holmes, that "this Court's power of judicial review is not 'an exercise of the powers of a super-legislature.'" No majority opinion, he argued, suggested that a federal law can be struck down "merely because the Court would have made a different choice between the competing interests" than the legislature.

Regarding the Smith Act, he believed that "there is ample justification for a legislative judgment that the conspiracy now before us is a substantial threat to national security and order." He relied on J. Edgar Hoover's 1947 HUAC testimony that the Communist Party USA had at least 60,000 members. The threat, he emphasized by referring to British atomic spy Klaus Fuchs, was real. To Douglas's argument in dissent that the defendants had not been convicted of "a conspiracy to overthrow the Government," Frankfurter responded that "it would be equally wrong to treat it as a seminar in political theory." Congress was within its power in determining "that the danger created by advocacy of overthrow justifies the ensuing restriction on freedom of speech." Ultimately, Frankfurter believed in a more limited judicial role than his dissenting colleagues Black and Douglas: "Our duty to abstain from confounding policy with constitutionality demands perceptive humility as well as self-restraint in not declaring unconstitutional what in a judge's private judgment is deemed unwise and even dangerous."

Instead of simply pleading for judicial restraint, Frankfurter distanced himself from the merits of the Smith Act by distinguishing between the constitutionality of the law and its wisdom. He quoted at length from warnings by Sir William Haley, the director-general of the British Broadcasting Corporation, and George F. Kennan, the author of the containment strategy, about the perils of silencing the opposition in the name of fighting Communism. Frankfurter strongly hinted that his personal views differed from those of the legislators who had passed the Smith Act. He urged Americans not to look to the courts to solve all their problems but to the people themselves:

"The mark of a truly civilized man is confidence in the strength and security derived from the inquiring mind. . . . Without open minds there can be no open society. And if society be not open the spirit of man is mutilated and becomes enslaved."

Frankfurter's concurrence was so long that he circulated a summary to his colleagues on May 29 because he had not finished the opinion. A few days later, he circulated his draft in sections along with an appendix of the Court's free speech cases. On June 4, 1951, the Court announced its opinions affirming the Smith Act convictions of the eleven Communist Party members.

The *New York Times* front-page photograph of Dennis in a caged van on his way to prison infuriated Frankfurter as too sensationalistic and not worthy of "news fit to print." The negative commentary about his opinion made him more upset. He was frustrated by commentary "from people who ought to know better" because of their "misconceptions as to the Court's function." Irving Dilliard of the *St. Louis Post-Dispatch* accused the six justices who voted to affirm the convictions as "amending the Constitution without submitting their amendment to the states for ratification." Frankfurter dismissed Dilliard's editorial and those in the *New Republic* and *The Nation* because they were written before the availability of the full text of his concurrence. Privately, Dilliard conceded to Frankfurter that his concurring opinion was "very moving. How I wish I could feel I could agree." His liberal friends, First Amendment scholar Zechariah Chafee and theologian Reinhold Niebuhr, shared Dilliard's preference for the dissents. Niebuhr admired Frankfurter's "very persuasive presentation" and his "very important" distinction between constitutionality and wisdom. Learned Hand was peeved that Frankfurter had rejected a reformulation of clear and present danger. Frankfurter bristled at federal judge Charles Wyzanski's characterization of his opinion as "the voice of the dead past!"

Frankfurter's concurrence was a tour de force about his constitutional philosophy of judicial restraint during a time of great political and social unrest; it was scholarly, historical, philosophical, and nuanced. He boldly disassociated himself from Vinson's plurality opinion and rejected the clear and present danger test and Hand's reformulation of it. Frankfurter's forthright balancing of congressional power with individual rights was more realistic and practical than an absolutist view of free speech. Above all, he urged the American people to look to their elected representatives in Congress and the executive branch, not the Court, to solve the problems of the Red Scare.

Frankfurter's concurrence in *Dennis* should be read as part of a larger body of work in these early Communist cases. He fought for the due process rights of Dorothy Bailey and allegedly subversive organizations to notice, fair hearings, and the ability to confront their accusers. His measured concurrences in *Douds* and *Dennis* trimmed the sails of Congress and the Truman administration yet recognized the federal government's capacious power to defend the country from national security threats. He sought to protect civil liberties by emphasizing fair procedures. A year after *Dennis*, he refused to join Jackson's majority opinion affirming the contempt convictions of Harry Sacher and other lawyers who had clashed repeatedly with Judge Harold Medina during the nine-month trial of the eleven Communist Party leaders in the *Dennis* case. "Bitter experience," Frankfurter began his *Sacher* dissent, "has sharpened our realization that a major test of true democracy is the fair administration of justice." Yet he cautioned that the power to punish for contempt of court "does not authorize the arbitrary imposition of punishment." He voted to reverse the convictions because another judge should have ruled on the contempt charges. He was troubled by Medina acting as "accuser and judge."

THE COMMUNIST HYSTERIA of the late 1940s and early 1950s and the deaths of several close friends had taken its toll on the "grayer and sadder" Frankfurters. Harold Laski, the 56-year-old British political scientist whom Frankfurter had brought to Harvard as an instructor in 1916, died of the flu in March 1950; former student Charles Hamilton Houston, the 54-year-old architect of the NAACP's legal campaign against racial segregation, died of a heart attack a month later; Henry Stimson, the 83-year-old paragon of public service who had hired Frankfurter to work in the U.S. attorney's office in 1906 and had brought him to Washington in 1911, died of a heart ailment in October; and Thomas D. Thacher, the 69-year-old former solicitor general and federal judge who had worked with Frankfurter in the U.S. attorney's office, died of a heart attack a month later. Frankfurter believed that Laski's legacy was that of a great teacher. He tried to provide for Laski's widow, Frida, by arranging for the purchase of her husband's massive library and for the publication of the Holmes-Laski letters. He attended Stimson's private funeral with Herbert Hoover, Acheson, and other public servants; he served as an honorary pallbearer at Thacher's funeral. The past several years, Joseph Alsop observed, "have not reduced his bounce, but they have increased her tendency to melancholy and even to self-pity, and have made his optimism sound a little forced." Alsop noticed that Frankfurter "seems a bit grayer every month; and they, like me, are worried about the Fascist tendency in America. But they have forgiven Prich, are resign[ed about] A His[s], and not so combative about Dean [Acheson] as formerly."

Acheson was under fire as secretary of state because of his support for Hiss, the fall of China to the Communists, the dismissal of General Douglas MacArthur, and foreign policy decisions that embroiled the United States in the Korean War. Frankfurter's defense of Acheson, particularly when it came to Hiss, was relentless. In December 1950, Frankfurter's ex-friend Walter Lippmann had named the Hiss defense as one of the reasons why Acheson should resign. In response, Frankfurter circulated copies of Lippmann's Nazi-appeasing 1933 New York Herald Tribune column and reminded Learned Hand what Brandeis had said of Lippmann: "the trouble with Walter is that he lacks character." After an April 1951 Washington Post editorial deemed Acheson's defense of Hiss "singularly inappropriate," the justice wrote former clerk Phil Graham and urged the young newspaper publisher to "condemn the throwing of the Hiss stone" at Acheson and the editorial for "exploiting all the fears and prejudices of the mob." No member of the Georgetown set was safe. Alsop, after defending Acheson's performance as secretary of state for months, finally gave up and expected the Frankfurters "to cross me off the list when I took my stand. Oddly they did not—really I suspect because even Dean's close friends in their hearts share my views . . ." Two of Frankfurter's colleagues, Vinson and Douglas, were mentioned as Acheson's possible successor. The idea of Vinson as secretary of state made Frankfurter "shiver," and he considered the campaign for Douglas "disgraceful of the duties of the Court." As Frankfurter had predicted, Truman stood by his secretary of state.

In July 1950, Edward Prichard began to serve his two-year prison sentence after the Supreme Court, with Frankfurter, Vinson, Reed, and Clark disqualifying themselves, declined to review his case because of a lack of a quorum. A few days before Christmas in 1950, Truman commuted Prichard's sentence after five months in Ashland federal prison. Prich had befriended two fellow prisoners, blacklisted Hollywood writers Dalton Trumbo and John Howard Lawson. A Chicago Tribune editorial blasted Truman for helping "Felix Frankfurter's fat boy." A few weeks after his release, Prichard declined an invitation to a Frankfurter clerkship reunion citing his recovery from a car accident. "Please convey to all present," he wrote Phil Elman, "the high regard in which Mr. Justice Frankfurter and his juristic views are held by the criminal classes." After Elman showed the letter to Frankfurter, the justice thanked him and expressed faith in Prichard the man: "His experience & especially his wife may yet give that extraordinary creature the necessary steel in his makeup to make his great gifts appropriately fruitful."

Prich struggled to put his finances, his life, and his career in order. Truman again helped his cause by pardoning him before leaving office; Prichard also managed to regain his bar license. What Prich wanted most was forgiveness from his friends starting with the Frankfurters: "Don't think I don't know what a rotten deal it has all been for you and Mrs. F. To know that those you have loved and on whom you have showered your hopes and goodness are foolish, reckless and unworthy is no trivial matter." To his friends in the Georgetown set including former roommate Isaiah Berlin and Arthur Schlesinger, Jr., Prich was a sad, cautionary tale. It took years of personal and professional struggles for Prich, the one-time New Deal wunderkind, to find his calling as an influential adviser to Kentucky governors on education issues.

And the day that Max Lowenthal dreaded finally came. On September 16, 1950, he was summoned to appear before HUAC a few weeks after Congressman George A. Dondero of Michigan described him as a "man of mystery" and accused him of "unswerving loyalty to Soviet Russia." With former U.S. senator Burton K. Wheeler representing him before the committee, Lowenthal was not asked about his advice to the convicted Hiss. Instead, Lowenthal answered questions about his long career in government service; his legal advice to Bartley C. Crum, the San Francisco lawyer who had represented blacklisted Hollywood producers, directors, and screenwriters who refused to testify before HUAC; his membership for a few years in the National Lawyers Guild; his sponsorship of a left-leaning legal magazine, the International Juridical Association, which included Hiss and Pressman as contributors; and his connection to radical lawyer Carol Weiss King, who had worked in his law office for a few months. On the whole, Lowenthal's testimony had been innocuous.

The real reason for Lowenthal's HUAC subpoena was to humiliate him in advance of the publication of his book about the FBI. The book was highly critical of J. Edgar Hoover and the FBI's use of wiretapping and other evidence-gathering techniques. After his HUAC testimony and the publication of the FBI book, Lowenthal never worked in government again. Frankfurter, who had earned himself a secret FBI file after signing a 1920 report criticizing Hoover's unconstitutional conduct of the Palmer raids, admired Lowenthal's book. After former clerk Joseph Rauh favorably reviewed it in the *Washington Post*, Frankfurter exulted: "you sure gave it to that swine, Hoover."

Red baiters used Lowenthal's book to attack Frankfurter and his protégés. Armed with information supplied by Hoover, Senator Bourke B. Hickenlooper of Iowa denounced the book as an "utterly biased piece of propaganda" and remarked of Rauh's review: "One may well inquire whether the writing of Mr. Rauh is his own or whether it is from the pen of Lowenthal, Felix Frankfurter, or William W. Remington. . . . The Post omits stating that Mr. Rauh is a former Frankfurter law clerk, friend of the Hiss brothers, and at the present time the attorney for Remington, who stands accused of perjury in denying his Communist membership."

During the perjury trial of Commerce Department economist William Remington, Frankfurter again found himself caught in the anti-Communist cross-fire. On December 28, 1950, Remington's ex-wife testified that her former husband had sought career advice from Frankfurter and had consulted with his late Socialist friend Harold Laski. The former Mrs. Remington did not mention Frankfurter by name but described him as a former Harvard law professor and Supreme Court justice. Westbrook Pegler fumed that the *New York Times* and *Herald Tribune* had omitted Frankfurter's name from their trial coverage. Pegler noted this was "the second time that Frankfurter had been dealt into a trial with implications of treason. For Remington, like Hiss, is accused of handing over secret Government papers to a Russian agent." A few days earlier, Pegler had urged Truman to ask for Frankfurter's resignation and described the justice as "a pushful, bumptious politician" who had sponsored Hiss, Pressman, and other Harvard Law School "study-boys of the same type."

Then came the denouement in the Alger Hiss case. On March 12, 1951, the Supreme Court declined to hear his appeal. Frankfurter left the conference room when six justices voted, 4–2, not to review it. He had disqualified himself along with fellow character witness Reed and former attorney general Clark. In one of his unreliable, score-settling memoirs, Douglas wrote that the Court would have voted to hear the case and to reverse Hiss's conviction if Frankfurter or Reed had participated. Even absent his trial testimony, Frankfurter had to disqualify himself. His ties to Hiss ran too deep.

Hiss served three years and eight months in Lewisburg federal prison. Frankfurter never saw him again after the first trial. Hiss, who remained grateful to Frankfurter for testifying on his behalf, never tried to reach out to him. Frankfurter preferred to communicate through Hiss's brother Donald, who was the executor of Frankfurter's estate, and other third parties. In private, Frankfurter continued to defend Hiss. In 1963, he blasted Harvard Law School dean Erwin Griswold for objecting to Hiss as the editor of an abridged edition of the Holmes-Laski letters. After his release from prison, Hiss never found a steady job other than being Alger Hiss and trying to clear his name. The Watergate scandal disgraced Nixon and helped Hiss rehabilitate his reputation and regain his Massachusetts bar license. Max Lowenthal's son, John, served as one of Hiss's lawyers, took a year's leave of absence as a law professor to make a documentary film about the case, and continued to fight for Hiss's exoneration. Hiss died of emphysema on November 15, 1996, at age 92. The 1995 and 1996 release of the Venona project, U.S.-decrypted Soviet intelligence agency messages, settled the debate about his guilt or innocence. Most scholars believed that the code name "Ales" in the files established Hiss's role as a Soviet spy beyond a reasonable doubt; a few, however, disagreed.

In defending a former Holmes secretary's right to edit the Holmes-Laski letters, Frankfurter fought for Hiss's dignity, not his innocence. Of all people, Frankfurter had witnessed Hiss's rise and fall—from working for Holmes to lawyering in the New Deal to negotiating the United Nations Charter in the State Department to serving prison time for perjury and being labeled a Soviet spy. The Red Scare had destroyed Hiss's reputation beyond repair, and, in the process, had damaged Frankfurter's liberal network. Nothing, however, could shake Frankfurter's loyalty to his former students, whether they became secretary of state like Dean Acheson or a convicted felon like Alger Hiss. He was invested in their lives and their careers and considered them surrogate sons. He stood by them during their successes and failures. He bet on them.

CHAPTER 32

The First Solid
Piece of Evidence
There Really Is a God

On the morning of November 21, 1951, Chief Justice Fred Vinson and his wife arrived at Washington National Airport and joined the Trumans and their traveling party on the presidential airplane, *Independence*. At 10:00 a.m., the Douglas VC-118, a propeller plane that seated twenty-four people and featured a rear presidential stateroom, took off for Truman's Little White House in Key West, Florida. For the next two days in Key West, Truman tried to persuade his former secretary of the treasury, poker buddy, and closest friend in politics to run for president. When they arrived back in Washington, the 61-year-old Vinson, citing his age and health, declined.

If the idea of Vinson as secretary of state in 1950 gave Frankfurter the shivers, then the thought of the chief justice as president was laughable. Frankfurter's initial high hopes for Vinson, based on the chief justice's experience in all three branches of the federal government, had been quickly dashed. Along with Jackson, Frankfurter viewed Vinson as thin-skinned, incompetent, lazy, and uninterested in the Court's day-to-day work. Indeed, the chief justice delegated his most vital and time-consuming task, opinion writing, entirely to his law clerks. It was telling that in the most high-profile case of the 1951 term, Frankfurter and Jackson had refused to join Vinson's *Dennis* opinion and had deprived it of the fifth vote required to make it a binding precedent. They had no respect for him as a judge.

Vinson was one thing that Frankfurter would never be, an insider with President Truman. Not that Frankfurter wanted to be a Truman insider. He thought Truman was "decent and sound" but "shallow . . . in terms of convictions." No one could compare, in Frankfurter's mind, to Franklin Roosevelt. There were critical differences between Frankfurter's insider role with Roosevelt and Vinson's with Truman—Frankfurter never sought political office, never assured the administration that its actions were constitutional, and never discussed pending cases with FDR. Vinson's chummy relationship with Truman—the poker games, off-the-record White House visits, trips to Key West, and political aspirations—came back to haunt the chief justice.

"TONIGHT, our country faces a grave danger," Truman explained during a nationwide radio and television broadcast at 10:30 p.m. on April 8, 1952. "We are faced by the possibility that at midnight tonight the steel industry will be shut down. This must not happen." He explained how an impending steelworker strike threatened the production of weapons for U.S. troops fighting Chinese-led Communist forces in Korea. He blamed the strike on the steel companies' refusal to share their record profits by agreeing to a wage increase and predicted that the work stoppage also would stall the country's atomic energy program and hurt the domestic economy. "These are not normal times," he said. "These are times of crisis." As a result, Truman issued Executive Order 10340 directing Secretary of Commerce Charles Sawyer to seize control of the nation's steel mills at midnight and to keep them operating. Both the steelworkers and the steel companies would be under government control.

Truman could have invoked an emergency provision in the Taft-Hartley Act to delay for eighty days any strike that could cause a national emergency. For the president, using the Taft-Hartley Act was politically undesirable. Backed by organized labor including the Steelworkers union, he had vetoed the law five years earlier because it was anti-labor; Congress, however, had overridden his veto. To the national audience on April 8, Truman explained that the Taft-Hartley Act did "not fit the needs of the present situation" because, he claimed, the emergency provision "could not prevent a steel shutdown of at least a week or two." Instead, Truman asserted his inherent power as president to deal with an emergency and triggered a two-month constitutional crisis.

In a matter of weeks, the showdown over Truman's seizure of the steel mills found its way to the Court. An hour after Truman's announcement, the steel companies phoned the home of federal judge Walter Bastian seeking a temporary restraining order. Bastian scheduled a hearing the next day.

The case rotated, as they usually did in emergency requests, to a new judge. Judge Alexander Holtzoff, a Truman nominee and former Justice Department official, denied the motion because "the balance of the equities" favored the government. The next day, the steel companies requested a preliminary injunction against the seizure. Judge Bastian disqualified himself because he owned thirty shares of steel company stock and transferred the case to Judge David A. Pine. The Justice Department assumed that Pine would follow Holtzoff's decision. During the April 24 oral argument, however, Pine was troubled that the seizure had not been authorized by an act of Congress and was based solely on the president's own power. Pine was alarmed by Assistant Attorney General Holmes Baldridge's assertion that the administration did not need an act of Congress to seize the mills and was not bound by the federal courts. "Our position is that there is no power in the Courts to restrain the president . . . ," Baldridge said. Pine asked the assistant attorney general whether in this situation the president had "unlimited power." Baldridge replied: "He has the power to take such action as is necessary to meet the emergency." Pine observed that if the emergency was great, then the power was unlimited. "I suppose if you carry it to its logical conclusion, that is true," Baldridge replied and suggested the only limit would be another election or impeachment. Baldridge insisted the president determined the scope of the emergency, and his decision was unreviewable by the courts. The argument and briefing continued the next day. So did the Truman administration's claims of unlimited executive power: "It is our position that the President is accountable only to the country, and that the decisions of the President are conclusive." On April 30, Judge Pine granted the steel companies' request for a preliminary injunction. That same day, the Truman administration asked the Court of Appeals for the District of Columbia Circuit to stay Judge Pine's order pending an appeal. The appeals court voted, 5–4, to grant the stay provided by May 2 the government filed for certiorari with the U.S. Supreme Court. On May 2, the Truman administration asked the Court to hear the case.

At the Saturday conference, Frankfurter spoke at length against granting expedited review. He worried about bypassing the court of appeals. He argued "what will really settle this" was a collective bargaining agreement between labor and management about wage increases for steelworkers. He also lamented that Judge Pine had chosen to confront the constitutionality of the president's actions rather than simply rule on the preliminary injunction on the basis of equitable or statutory considerations. Finally, he laid out the massive constitutional difficulties—whether the president, not Congress, can

THE FIRST SOLID PIECE OF EVIDENCE THERE REALLY IS A GOD   551

make the laws. Expressing his "deepest concern against [the] eagerness of the Court to seize a big abstract issue," Frankfurter voted to deny certiorari and argued that the Court should remand the case to Judge Pine to rule on the preliminary injunction on nonconstitutional grounds. Frankfurter's argument for constitutional avoidance had few takers. Only Burton voted not to review the case and objected to skipping the court of appeals; Jackson passed. The other justices voted to hear it.

The chief justice announced five hours of oral argument to begin at noon on Monday, May 12, and to continue the next day. Frankfurter preferred to let the court of appeals hear the case during the intervening week. Two days before the argument, the justices received hundreds of pages of briefs. The stakes were high: the scope of presidential power at home during an armed conflict abroad and the willingness of the Court to declare that the president had exceeded his power or usurped the power of Congress. Frankfurter believed that "the best thing the [Supreme Court] can do these days is not to decide issues entangled in politics."

People waited in line for hours at the Supreme Court to see the oral argument in *Youngstown Sheet & Tube Company v. Sawyer*—the *Steel Seizure Case*. "Had you found yourself in the court room on Monday and Tuesday, I am sure you would probably have wondered whether you had not wandered in to the wrong place," Frankfurter wrote C. C. Burlingham, "—whether it wasn't the crowd waiting for the World Series." An hour before the noon argument, about 300 people, including senators and congressmen and several justices' wives, scored seats in the main part of the courtroom; 200 other people stood in the rear and on the sides. Several hundred more people waited in line in the hallway. Few spectators could hear because of the marble courtroom's notoriously bad acoustics. Frankfurter, who referred to the Supreme Court building as Taft's "folly" and hoped that architect Cass Gilbert "is sizzling in one of the circles of Dante's hell," wished they still heard argument in the Old Senate Chamber in the U.S. Capitol.

At noon, the justices emerged from the red velvet curtains and listened to oral argument. It was not a fair fight. John W. Davis, representing U.S. Steel, had argued nearly eighty cases and was one of the finest Supreme Court advocates in American history. The white-haired, 79-year-old Davis was a legendary former solicitor general under Wilson, had declined a seat on the Supreme Court to make money as a Wall Street lawyer, and in 1924 had been the Democratic Party's presidential nominee. In *New Republic* editorials, Frankfurter had questioned candidate Davis's ethics for choosing to line his pockets by working for J.P. Morgan and for not speaking out about the post–World War I assault on civil liberties as American Bar Association president. No one questioned Davis's skills as a constitutional lawyer.

During his ninety-minute argument, Davis answered only four questions. He spoke for the first fifty-three minutes without interruption until Frankfurter inquired about the 1915 *Midwest Oil* case. Davis had argued the case, which involved congressional acquiescence in the executive withdrawal of public land, as solicitor general. Before discussing *Midwest Oil*, Davis was allowed to continue his argument. Frankfurter raised the case again. When Vinson asked Davis three questions about *Midwest Oil*, Frankfurter passed a note to his immediate right to Jackson: "Why does an elephant try engagements with an authenticated greyhound!" As Davis continued his argument, Frankfurter wrote Jackson another note about what was happening to Frankfurter's immediate left with Black and Vinson: "This strange center man carries on a running commentary to Hugo—answering Davis. Grand!!"

With almost no questions to interrupt him, Davis reviewed the factual background and all the potentially applicable federal laws and explained why none of them authorized the president's conduct. He then detailed, clause by clause, all the powers Article II of the Constitution granted to the president. He argued that those powers were limited and subject to the Fifth Amendment's prohibition of the deprivation of property without due process of law. Before he finished, Davis reviewed Assistant Attorney General Baldridge's assertions to Judge Pine that the president's power was unlimited, unreviewable by the courts, and responsive only to the American people. Davis reminded the justices of the stakes of unbridled executive power by quoting from Jefferson's Kentucky Resolution in 1798, which questioned the constitutionality of the Adams administration's Alien and Sedition Acts: "In questions of power let no more be said of confidence in man, but bind him down from mischief by the chains of the Constitution."

Solicitor General Philip B. Perlman, representing the Truman administration and wearing the customary morning coat and striped pants, faced a more hostile audience. The former Baltimore newspaperman had argued fifty-six cases before the Court yet had not endeared himself to the justices. Frankfurter and Jackson were particularly unimpressed, challenging his assertions about the reliability of a secret FBI informant in Dorothy Bailey's Loyalty Review Board case. They were no kinder to Perlman during the *Steel Seizure Case.*

In response to a question from Frankfurter, Perlman argued that by failing to act on the president's message to Congress after he had seized the steel mills, Congress had acquiesced. Frankfurter, as well as Jackson, asked

Perlman whether "any legal significance" can be inferred from congressional inaction. Black pressed Perlman whether he was relying on an act of Congress or the Constitution. Perlman conceded that no federal law "specifically" authorized the seizure, therefore he relied on the Constitution. Frankfurter observed that the scope of presidential power had been narrowed from the Court's "tall talk" in *Myers* in its 1935 decision in *Humphrey's Executor.* When Perlman tried to raise criticisms of *Humphrey's Executor* in Jackson's 1940 book, *The Struggle for Judicial Supremacy,* Frankfurter snapped: "I point out what the Court said." Jackson added: "Justice Frankfurter did not read the book." Perlman responded by recommending the book to an unamused Frankfurter, who made it clear that the solicitor general had missed the point. Frankfurter and Jackson debated with Perlman about other presidential seizures and other actions in wartime without statutory authorization including Lincoln's during the Civil War, Wilson's during World War I, and Roosevelt's during World War II. Throughout his argument, Perlman promised to answer questions about why Truman had not invoked the procedures of the Taft-Hartley Act but never did.

Perlman fared no better during day two of his argument. He exceeded his allotted time of two and a half hours and was permitted to continue for another forty minutes because he still had not addressed the Taft-Hartley Act. He countered that the Defense Production Act authorized the president's conduct. Yet Frankfurter and Jackson observed the law was inapplicable because there had been no condemnation proceedings and no contractual relationship between the government and the steel companies. At the end of the argument, Perlman pleaded: "This is an extraordinary case and it calls for the exercise of the authority that the Chief Executive has exercised in order to avert a national catastrophe . . . we are at war. . . this is wartime." Jackson and Frankfurter were having none of it. Jackson observed that Congress had not declared war, and Congress and the president referred to the U.S. troops in Korea as a "police action." Perlman insisted that Truman was invoking his commander-in-chief power as well as war-related statutes. "But," Frankfurter replied, referring to the president, "he has said that in the most peaceful era of our country that there ever was." Frankfurter thought it was "absurd" that it had taken the solicitor general more than three hours to make his argument. Perlman had not helped the president's cause. By contrast, Frankfurter thought Davis, who had used half his allotted time, was "an artist." After Perlman's poor showing, the rest of the argument was an afterthought.

The justices devoted most of their Friday conference to discussing the *Steel Seizure Case.* Vinson made it clear from his opening remarks that he was voting to uphold the president's action. He did not believe that the president's power was unlimited or that there was no power unless Congress acted. He observed that presidents throughout history had seized property in wartime with or without congressional authorization. The Korean War and the North Atlantic Treaty Organization (NATO) made it imperative to produce steel "to supply arms around the world." He had "no doubt . . . there is war" and that the United States had the right to defend itself. He rejected the argument that this is "a defiance of Congress" because Congress had not specified that the president must invoke the Taft-Hartley Act. He emphasized "world conditions" and congressional inaction after Truman announced he was seizing the mills.

Five justices—Black, Douglas, Frankfurter, Jackson, and Burton—disagreed. Black rejected Vinson's discussion of the international situation as "irrelevant" to the constitutional questions. The president could have invoked the eighty-day provision in the Taft-Hartley Act or requested a declaration of war from Congress. Black argued that an emergency situation did not create executive power. The case, according to Black, mandated the Court's enforcement of separation of powers: "The President can not legislate." Reed, taking the Truman administration's side, preferred to avoid the constitutional questions and did not believe the president was limited by acts of Congress.

Frankfurter began by suggesting that all the justices should write opinions in the case. In contrast to Black, he believed that presidential power was not limited to express provisions in the Constitution or a specific act of Congress. For example, he did not believe that the president's war powers could be invoked only after Congress had declared war. He argued that from 1916 to 1951, sixteen congressional statutes had authorized the seizure power. He concluded by invoking Brandeis's *Myers v. United States* dissent about the importance of separation of powers.

Douglas agreed with Black that it was "a legislative function." Jackson added that the question was not whether there was an emergency but what power the president had invoked in such an emergency. The president, Jackson insisted, "can throw the Constitution overboard but we can't." Jackson, however, wanted to do as "little damage as possible." Burton read from a memorandum that the president should have invoked the Taft-Hartley Act. Clark, Truman's former attorney general, and Minton, another Truman nominee, were on the fence. Clark said the constitutional crisis could have been avoided on a statutory basis and tentatively voted against the president. Minton voted with Vinson because of the president's power to defend the nation and because the Taft-Hartley Act was not mandatory.

As the senior justice in the majority, Black assigned the majority opinion to himself. In his brief opinion, he argued that the president's power must "stem either from an act of Congress or from the Constitution itself." He found no express statutory authorization. And he recognized only express presidential power because, unlike Congress, the executive branch lacked implied or inherent power to deal with emergencies. In seizing the mills without congressional authorization, Truman had overstepped his bounds. "The Founders of this Nation," Black concluded his opinion, "entrusted the lawmaking power to the Congress alone in both good and bad times." Black's strict textural reading of Article II and rigid approach to separation of powers had its limitations because it put the presidency in a constitutional straitjacket, especially when it came to war powers. Frankfurter congratulated Black on the majority opinion, agreed to join it, yet asked him to publish a disclaimer. Frankfurter believed that Black's opinion was right as it applied to Truman's steel seizure, but separation of powers was more "complicated and flexible." As he had suggested at conference, Frankfurter and most of the justices wrote separately. The *Steel Seizure Case*, he argued, illustrated the "necessity and desirability" of concurring opinions. Frankfurter and Jackson, though they joined his opinion, rejected Black's approach to separation of powers as too "rigid."

Frankfurter's concurrence, like his *Dennis* opinion, was based on Chief Justice Marshall's idea in *McCulloch* that the Constitution was a broad outline. He twice quoted Marshall's "greatest judicial utterance" that "it is *a constitution* we are expounding" and urged the Court "to avoid putting fetters upon the future by needless pronouncements today." He recognized this as one of the rare instances in which the Court should limit executive power because Congress had not authorized Truman's seizure of the steel mills. He refused to define the president's power "comprehensively" and reminded his colleagues that "[t]he Constitution is a framework for government." To that end, he argued that executive power was not limited to the constitutional text and could be expanded based on past practice: "Deeply embedded traditional ways of conducting government cannot supplant the Constitution or legislation, but they give meaning to the words of a text or supply them. It is an inadmissibly narrow conception of American constitutional law to confine it to the words of the Constitution and to disregard the gloss which life has written upon them." He elaborated that "a systematic, unbroken, executive practice, long pursued to the knowledge of the Congress and never before questioned, engaged in by Presidents who have also sworn to uphold the Constitution" may be treated as part of the structure of government and "as a gloss on 'Executive Power.'"

No such gloss, Frankfurter insisted, was present in Truman's seizure of the steel mills. He distinguished the executive branch's withdrawal of public land in the *Midwest Oil* case as common practice. He reviewed the history of presidential seizures, most of which had been authorized by Congress before or after the fact, in the text of his opinion and in a thirteen-page chart/appendix. He quoted Brandeis's dissent in *Myers v. United States* that the framers of the Constitution established separation of powers among the legislative, executive, and judicial branches " 'not to promote efficiency' " and " 'not to avoid friction' " but to create " 'inevitable friction . . . to save the people from autocracy.' " He described it as "not a pleasant judicial duty" to find that the president had "exceeded his powers." He concluded on an optimistic note by recounting Chief Justice John Jay's refusal to allow the Supreme Court to give informal advice to President Washington. Frankfurter reiterated his faith "that the President and the Congress between them will continue to safeguard the heritage which comes to them straight from George Washington."

Frankfurter's gloss theory on executive power was a major constitutional contribution yet has been overshadowed by Jackson's landmark concurrence. Writing a personal essay more than a judicial opinion, Jackson established a tripartite framework for assertions of executive power: (1) it was "at its maximum" based on express or implied congressional authorization; (2) it was in "a zone of twilight" when Congress was silent; and (3) it was "at its lowest ebb" when it contravened the express or implied will of Congress. Given Congress's refusal to provide for seizure as part of the Taft-Hartley Act, Jackson concluded that Truman's takeover of the steel mills contravened the implied will of Congress and therefore was unconstitutional. Jackson's concurring opinion, not Black's, has guided courts and scholars for generations. As influential and rhetorically powerful as Jackson's opinion has been, Frankfurter's concurrence also offered a useful and realistic way for thinking about the role of the Court in interpreting the Constitution and in policing assertions of executive power.

The June 2 announcement of the Supreme Court's decision in *Youngstown* was a major blow for the Truman administration. Particularly painful for the president was the negative vote of his former attorney general, Tom C. Clark. As attorney general, Clark had advised Truman to seize the coal mines before a 1946 strike. Yet, in the *Steel Seizure Case*, he wrote a concurring opinion that the president lacked authorization under the Taft-Hartley Act or the Defense Production Act and had not complied with the procedures of the Universal Military Training and Service Act (the former Selective Service Act). Clark credited Frankfurter and Frankfurter's clerk with helping him see that the last law did not apply; Frankfurter praised Clark's opinion for making "an important contribution to the great tradition of an independent judiciary." Truman, not surprisingly, was upset with Clark. The president's other two nominees, Vinson and Minton, did not disappoint him.

At the June 2 Court session announcing the decision, Vinson read aloud for an hour from his lengthy dissent, which Minton joined, justifying the seizure because of external national security concerns. The opinion reviewed the international issues facing the president: the United States agreement to participate in the United Nations; U.S. troops joining United Nations forces in Korea; the Truman Doctrine's vow to assist Greece and Turkey; the Marshall Plan's economic revitalization of Western Europe; and the Senate's agreement to join NATO. Vinson argued that billions of dollars of military appropriations and the Defense Production Act made it Truman's "duty" to seize the mills. The plaintiffs, Vinson contended, failed to contest "the President's finding that *any* stoppage of steel production would immediately place the Nation in peril." He concluded that "judicial, legislative and executive precedents throughout our history demonstrate that in this case the President acted in full conformity with his duties under the Constitution." The drafter of Vinson's dissent, his law clerk Howard Trienens, believed it had nothing to do with the chief justice's "loyalty" to Truman. Vinson's experiences in the Roosevelt administration as the head of the Office of Economic Stabilization during World War II dominated his thinking about the case. "He felt so strongly about that that it wouldn't have mattered who was president," Trienens said.

Vinson's conduct suggested he may have violated separation of powers by advising the president about the seizure before, during, and after the case. Weeks before the seizure, he had met with Truman "off the record" at the White House and had seen him at numerous social functions. He also had visited the White House the day the case was submitted to the Court. Finally, he attended a 5:00 p.m. "off the record" meeting in the president's study on June 20 with Truman and special counsel Clark Clifford.

A few weeks after the decision, Frankfurter and Jackson began to hear rumors that Vinson had advised the president prior to the seizure that it was constitutional and that the Court would uphold it. "The only thing harder to believe than that the 'prior consultation' took place is to believe that it didn't," Frankfurter wrote former clerk Phil Elman. "I was taken aback some time ago when Lafayette [Black] complained to me of the evils of this intimacy. And believe me, that centre Johnnie [Vinson] made it hot for [steel seizure dissenter] Tawm [Clark]." Jackson expressed concern about the rumors. "I just do not know what to think of the prior consultation item," he wrote Frankfurter. "I wish I could rise in wrath and say it is a damn lie. I once remarked to Tom [Clark] that I had heard a rumor to that effect, and he did not seem either surprised or disposed to enter denials. The fierceness of the opposition which we have witnessed is comparable to the zeal with which former commitments are defended by the man in question. I just don't know what to think."

A WEEK AFTER the Court announced its steel seizure decision, Black entertained the president and all the justices at his Alexandria home. Truman was "a bit testy" until he drank Black's bourbon and dined on steak. Frankfurter thought the party was "excellent"—with one exception. He overheard Douglas telling Truman that the government's case had been poorly argued. Solicitor General Perlman resigned later that summer. "I have little doubt that the All-High blames S.G. for the 'inherent' defeat," Frankfurter wrote Elman. "When I see you I shall a tale unto you unfold that it will leave no doubt in your mind, if you have any left that the ace-momser [bastard] is the Yakima lad [Douglas]. He told Harry how that case was butchered! How do I know? Well—I heard it!!"

Frankfurter understood the institutional importance of the *Steel Seizure Case.* After he had received many letters from the American people, he wrote colleague Tom C. Clark: "What is the most significant thing about it is the meaning of that decision to thoughtful people who are fairly to be called 'liberal'—New Dealers & Fair Dealers. It indicated and restored their faith in 'Law.' They feared that our Court was just like Hitler's Court & Stalin's Court & Peron's Court: merely a political agency of the Government. And you more than anyone else proved the Court's independence."

In 1952, Frankfurter and Jackson were in many ways at the height of their powers because they occupied the Court's center. They often voted with Black and Douglas on important cases and could forge five-justice majorities by persuading Burton or Clark to go along with them. Frankfurter admired Burton and often dropped by his chambers to discuss cases. Before the steel seizure argument, Burton thought he might be the only justice who believed the president had exceeded his power; he ended up writing a short concurrence he thought would be a dissent. Jackson related to Clark as a former attorney general and ate lunch with him at several critical junctures during the *Steel Seizure Case.* Frankfurter helped Clark come around to the view that Congress had not authorized the seizure.

Not that Frankfurter always agreed with the Court's three other leading lights, Black, Douglas, and Jackson. In January 1952, Frankfurter wrote the Court's majority opinion in *Rochin v. California,* holding that pumping a suspected drug dealer's stomach for two morphine capsules violated the Fourteenth Amendment's Due Process Clause because it "shocks the conscience." He tried to make due process review of state criminal convictions a high bar on the basis of whether the accused's treatment violated fundamental "decencies of civilized conduct." Black, who believed total incorporation of the Bill of Rights and the Fifth Amendment's prohibition against self-incrimination resolved the case more clearly, wrote a concurrence blasting Frankfurter's "accordion-like" standard as imperiling the Bill of Rights. Douglas agreed and described Frankfurter's opinion as contributing to the "erosion of civil rights of the citizen in recent years." *Rochin,* which Learned Hand questioned as giving judges too much power, was another example of Frankfurter's flexible approach to constitutional questions compared to Black's more rigid, textual preferences.

During the summer of 1952, Frankfurter and Jackson anticipated some high-profile cases for the coming term and questioned Vinson's ability to lead the Court. "Some tough stuff seems to be shaping up for us next term & not in numbers but in issues," Jackson wrote Frankfurter on August 16. "I suppose the C.J. is studying them diligently at home ready to make the positive and careful thought out recommendation on which his leadership is based."

THE CASE OF atomic spies Julius and Ethel Rosenberg revealed Vinson's lack of leadership and Frankfurter and Jackson's enmity toward Douglas. Beginning in the fall of 1952, the case landed in the Court's lap and would not go away. To Frankfurter and Jackson, Douglas, not the Rosenbergs, "became the accused."

On March 25, 1951, a jury convicted Julius and Ethel Rosenberg of conspiring to commit espionage by passing atomic secrets to the Russians. The chief witnesses against them had been two members of the spy ring: Ethel's brother, David Greenglass, a machinist at the secret atomic energy site at Los Alamos, and his wife, Ruth Greenglass. After secret communications with Justice Department officials, federal prosecutors, and several federal judges, Judge Irving Kaufman sentenced the Rosenbergs to death. He called their crimes "worse than murder" and held them responsible for 50,000 deaths in the Korean War. The Second Circuit denied their direct appeal that Kaufman had improperly questioned witnesses, they could not be sentenced to death under the Espionage Act, and their death sentences violated the Eighth Amendment prohibition of cruel and unusual punishment.

On October 7, 1952, only three justices voted to hear the *Rosenberg* case: Frankfurter, Black, and Burton. Frankfurter argued the Court should review all cases in which federal judges impose the death penalty. This is especially true in "a case which had raised conscientious doubts in the minds of men of good will whose hostility to communism was beyond doubts. It was in the public interest to put such doubts to rest, and we alone could do it." Only Black agreed with him, wanting to determine whether this had been a peacetime prosecution for treason. In a treason case, the Constitution required two witnesses for each overt act or confession. Burton voted yes only because Frankfurter and Black had "strong feelings" about the case. Jackson, who was tough on criminals and Communists after prosecuting Nazis at Nuremberg, voted no. Douglas voted to deny review "with startling vehemence."

Less than a month later, the Rosenbergs filed a petition for rehearing with the Supreme Court. At conference on November 5, Frankfurter made another impassioned plea that the Court should hear the case because of "heightened public feeling, not the irrational passions aroused in and by the Communists, which, I said, should not influence us, but the disquietude of impartial men of good will." The vote, however, was the same. Two weeks later when the Court denied the petition for rehearing, Frankfurter wrote separately to emphasize that it was not up to the Court to reduce a death sentence. He wanted to signal to the president to use his clemency power; Truman, however, did nothing before leaving office. On February 11, 1953, newly inaugurated President Eisenhower rejected their clemency petition because the Rosenbergs "betrayed the cause of freedom for which free men are fighting and dying at this very hour." Judge Kaufman set their executions for the week of March 9.

The Court's involvement had only just begun. The Rosenbergs alleged that federal prosecutor Irving Saypol had committed misconduct by unsealing a perjury indictment of a potential witness, William Perl, during their trial. Saypol had discussed the indictment with the *New York Times* and said he expected Perl to corroborate the testimony of the Greenglasses; Perl, however, never testified. The lower courts rejected the prosecutorial misconduct claim. But in his opinion, Second Circuit Judge Thomas Swan described Saypol's statement to the press as "wholly reprehensible" and stayed the executions until March 30 so that the Rosenbergs could appeal to the Supreme Court. At conference on April 11, Black wanted to hear the case and to grant a new trial.

Frankfurter was Black's lone ally. "I charge your conscience," Frankfurter told his colleagues, "You have a duty to consider how this sentence, and this Court, will stand in the light of history if you leave the cloud of these allegations hanging over the trial." Douglas again voted to deny "in the same harsh tone."

In "a real struggle with [his] conscience" about whether to write a dissent from the Court's refusal to hear the case, Frankfurter asked his colleagues to delay the announcement of the decision. Two weeks passed. At conference on May 16, Vinson urged his colleagues to announce their decision before Frankfurter wrote his opinion. Five justices voted to give Frankfurter another week. Jackson confessed to Frankfurter that he might join an opinion focusing on Saypol's misconduct: "I cannot imagine that you can be too severe on him to suit me." Ultimately, Frankfurter chose not to write anything. In a May 20 memorandum to his colleagues, he confessed that "the Court's failure to take the case of the Rosenbergs has presented for me the most anguishing situation since I have been on the Court." He believed that the Court possessed the "moral authority," after full briefing and argument and examination of the record, to put the public controversy about the case to rest. He decided not to write anything because he worried about "feeding those flames of disquietude and passion and disunity in the country." He and Black simply noted that they adhered to their prior positions.

Before the Court announced it had declined to review the case, all hell broke loose. On May 22, Douglas wrote his colleagues that he had studied the problem further and was troubled by the allegations of prosecutorial misconduct. He wanted a sentence added to the Court's denial of review that he, too, found the prosecutor's behavior " 'wholly reprehensible' " and voted to grant certiorari. After reading Douglas's memorandum, Frankfurter wrote his colleagues asking them to reopen their discussion. Thinking he was at "the end of a long and laborious intellectual journey," Frankfurter reacted to Douglas's memorandum by promising "to sleep over it so as to bring the coolest and most responsible judgment to bear of which I am capable." Douglas's memorandum should have been a blessing, but, absent a fourth vote to review the case, made things worse. That afternoon, Frankfurter visited Burton in chambers and wrote him a lengthy memorandum urging him to grant review of the case. Frankfurter admired Burton's ability to be fair and open-minded and remembered Burton's dissent in the Willie Francis case after he had initially declined to hear it. Douglas's memorandum, Frankfurter wrote Burton, "puts the whole Court in a hole" and would cast "a cloud" on the institution. The Court would look "heedless to the pronouncement . . . by a member of the Court who has created for himself the reputation of being especially sensitive to the claims of injustice." While his memorandum to Burton was being typed, Frankfurter visited Jackson in chambers and confessed his fears and concerns. Jackson then read Frankfurter's memorandum to Burton before Frankfurter sent it. "Don't worry," Jackson told Frankfurter, "Douglas' memorandum isn't going down Monday." Jackson described Douglas's memorandum as "the dirtiest, most shameful, most cynical performance that I think I have ever heard of in matters pertaining to law."

The next day at conference, Jackson called Douglas's "bluff." Black, who was hospitalized with a severe case of shingles, was absent but still voted to grant. So did Frankfurter. Douglas, alerted to "prejudicial error" by Frankfurter's May 20 memorandum, voted to grant. Jackson provided the fourth vote to hear the case because Douglas's memorandum had put the Court "in an impossible position." It would leak that four justices at various times had voted to hear the case. "It was impossible to deny under those circumstances," Jackson said. Vinson declared the case granted and discussed the briefing and argument schedule. It was near the end of the term. As with the *Steel Seizure Case*, Vinson wanted an expedited briefing schedule. The other justices objected. Burton offered to postpone his summer vacation plans. Vinson then suggested holding argument on July 6, announcing its decision, and writing opinions later. The other justices, recalling the Court's unhappy experiences in *Ex Parte Quirin* in which the Nazi saboteurs were executed before the full opinion was written, rejected that suggestion as well. Finally, Douglas spoke and acknowledged the situation in which he put the Court. "What he had written was badly drawn, he guessed," Frankfurter recounted. "He hadn't realized it would embarrass anyone. He would just withdraw his memorandum if that would help matters." After Douglas withdrew his memorandum, Jackson withdrew his fourth vote. On May 25, the Court declined certiorari for the second time. Douglas merely noted that certiorari should have been granted. "That S.O.B.'s bluff was called," Jackson told Frankfurter. Frankfurter visited Black, who was recovering from shingles at his Alexandria home. He had been checking in on his ailing colleague ever since Black's wife, Josephine, had died in 1951 of a suspected suicide after a prolonged struggle with depression. Frankfurter was incredibly fond of Josephine as well as Black's children. The Court's intellectual adversaries had grown closer during this period and found themselves on the same side in the *Rosenberg* case. To Black, Douglas had told a completely different version of events, that the justices had voted only to hear argument about whether to review the case, not about the merits of the claims. Frankfurter insisted this was "untrue"; Jackson later described it as "wholly false. . . . We voted to grant until Douglas withdrew his memorandum."

Judge Kaufman scheduled the Rosenbergs' executions for the week of June 15; the lawyers' race to stop them was on, and it ran back to the Supreme Court. The discovery of compelling new evidence prompted civil liberties lawyer John Finerty and University of Chicago law professor Malcolm Sharp to join the defense team. On June 6, they filed a motion for a new trial and stay of execution because new evidence suggested the Greenglasses had lied and prosecutors may have committed misconduct. At trial, David and Ruth Greenglass had testified that the Soviets had given the Rosenbergs a hollowed-out wooden console table with a lamp underneath to microfilm Ethel's typed notes. The table could not be found before trial, but a reporter for the *National Guardian* later discovered it in the apartment of Ethel's illiterate mother. The table was not hollow, and there was no lamp. A Macy's official submitted an affidavit that it was the type of console table sold there in 1944 or 1945 for $21, just as the Rosenbergs had testified at trial. The console table may seem like a minor point, but it arose several times at trial and during the closing argument. Sharp later explained that the console table "was important at the trial as a vivid item of testimony which may well have caught the jury's mind in the course of the long and sometimes tedious proceeding. It became, however, more important in another respect: it served as a test of the dependability of the Greenglasses' testimony." The discovery of the table confirmed the Rosenbergs' testimony and suggested that the Greenglasses were lying. It did not prove that the prosecution knew the Greenglasses were lying, but other new evidence revealed what the government had known and when. The Rosenbergs' lawyers discovered a handwritten pretrial statement that David Greenglass had given to his lawyer about what he had told the FBI in his initial interview, a copy of which somehow wound up in France. After three hours of argument on June 8, Judge Kaufman denied the motions because the government could not be held accountable for failing to find the console table since it had been in Ethel's mother's apartment all along. The Second Circuit affirmed his decision two days later.

On June 12, the Rosenbergs' lawyers traveled to Washington to ask for a stay of execution from Jackson, the circuit justice for the Second Circuit. They argued in their brief that David Greenglass's "pre-trial story to authorities . . . was a very different tale from the trial testimony of the Greenglasses—as different as 'Hamlet' without Hamlet." After hearing argument from both sides in his chambers, Jackson thought the petition had merit and recommended that the Court hear oral argument on it on June 16. At their Saturday conference, the justices voted 5–4 not to hear argument whether to grant the stay of execution and 5–4 to deny the stay. Frankfurter, Black, and Jackson had been in the minority both times. Burton had voted to hear oral argument but to deny the stay. Douglas was willing to grant the stay but not to hear oral argument. Jackson was furious with Douglas because "every time a vote could have been had for a hearing Douglas opposed a hearing in open Court, and only when it was perfectly clear that a particular application would not be granted, did he take a position for granting it." Jackson was so eager to expose what he perceived as Douglas's hypocrisy that, after the case was over, he invited *St. Louis Post-Dispatch* columnist Marquis Childs into his chambers and showed him Douglas's June 13 conference votes.

On June 15, the last day of the Supreme Court term, Finerty filed an original writ of habeas corpus alleging that the prosecutors in the *Rosenberg* case had knowingly used perjured testimony, a claim based on the Supreme Court's decision in the 1935 case of convicted Preparedness Day bomber Tom Mooney. The tension in the justices' conference room was high. Douglas voted with the majority to deny Finerty's petition and claimed: "[You've] got to do more than use perjured testimony, [you've] got to manufacture it." Frankfurter vehemently disagreed: "Oh! no! Oh! no! [The] knowing use of perjured testimony is enough. I know a good deal about Mooney." Jackson, though he voted with the majority, agreed with Frankfurter's reading of the *Mooney* case. Only Black and Frankfurter voted to hear the Rosenbergs' case. The executions were three days away.

That same afternoon, the Rosenbergs' lawyers approached Douglas in his chambers about granting a stay of execution. Douglas agreed to see them the next morning at 10:00 a.m. but only if they had a new argument. A new argument had been found, but not by the Rosenbergs' lawyers. The next morning, two new lawyers appeared in Douglas's chambers and contended that the Rosenbergs had been tried and sentenced under the wrong federal law, the Espionage Act, when they should have been tried under the Atomic Energy Act of 1946. The Atomic Energy Act permitted a death sentence only on the basis of the recommendation of the jury; otherwise, the maximum penalty was twenty years. The government alleged that the Rosenbergs had begun stealing atomic secrets in 1944 and 1945, prior to the passage of the Atomic Energy Act, but the conspiracy had continued until 1950. Douglas commenced studying the record and concluded that, because most of the conspiracy had taken place after the passage of the Atomic Energy Act, the Rosenbergs may have been convicted and sentenced under the wrong law. Several times that afternoon, he consulted with Frankfurter about the issue. Later that evening, he discussed it with Vinson at the chief justice's apartment in the Sheraton (Wardman) Park Hotel. That night and the next morning, the chief justice tried to discourage Douglas from granting a stay of execution and, in the alternative, asked him to present the issue to the entire Court. Black thought the issue was "very substantial." Frankfurter was noncommittal: "Do, I said, what your conscience tells you, not what the Chief Justice tells you. Further, I said, I cannot advise you. Tête-à-tête conversation cannot settle this matter." Douglas wanted to talk to Jackson and Burton, but Frankfurter insisted, "this was a matter for [Douglas's] conscience."

At noon on June 17, the day before the Rosenbergs' executions, Douglas issued a stay of execution. He assumed the issue of whether the Rosenbergs had been convicted and sentenced under the wrong law would be reviewed by the lower courts, and the Supreme Court would review their decisions in October. He immediately left for the West and planned to stop at the home of journalist Irving Dilliard in Collinsville, Illinois. Frankfurter, thinking the same thing as Douglas, headed to Owen J. Roberts's farm in Pennsylvania on the way to Charlemont, Massachusetts, for the summer.

Vinson was having none of it. At 11:00 p.m. on June 16, he had met secretly with Attorney General Herbert Brownell and acting Solicitor General Robert Stern in the chief justice's apartment. Brownell asked Vinson to recall the Court and hold the third special term in its history. Brownell and Vinson met again the next afternoon in Vinson's chambers. At 2:00 p.m. the next day, the Justice Department filed a motion for a special term to vacate Douglas's stay. Vinson conferred with three justices in the building: Burton, Clark, and Jackson. He spoke by phone with several others: Black in Alexandria, Virginia; Minton in New Albany, Indiana; and Reed in Durham, North Carolina. Only Black objected to a special term.

At 6:00 p.m. on June 17, Vinson ordered a special term at noon the next day to hear three hours of oral argument about Douglas's stay. He phoned Frankfurter at Roberts's farm and asked him to return to Washington immediately. The Frankfurters had already closed their Georgetown home for the summer so they stayed with former clerk Joseph Rauh. Sitting on Rauh's porch that evening, the justice lamented every aspect of the *Rosenberg* case: Irving Kaufman, "unjudicious in both the manner and substance of the sentence," Brownell and Vinson's "haste" to execute the Rosenbergs, and Douglas's repeated refusals to hear oral argument followed by his last-minute "grandstand play."

At 11:45 a.m. on June 18, the justices met in a pre-argument conference. Black objected that the chief justice had no authority to convene a special term on his own; all the justices had voted whether to have a special term in the Nazi saboteurs' case. Vinson knew from a law clerk's memorandum that his actions were unprecedented and blamed Clerk of the Court Harold Willey. Over Black's objection, the Justices proceeded twelve minutes late to oral argument.

The oral argument was a circus. Five lawyers spoke, one for the government, two for the Rosenbergs, and two representing a third party as a "next friend." Some of the defense lawyers berated the justices. No one was prepared to address the complicated question of whether the Rosenbergs had been tried and convicted under the wrong law. Douglas suspected that Vinson had lined up five votes to vacate the stay "in advance of the argument & in advance of any exposure or explication of the point!!" Frankfurter agreed with Douglas: "The fact is that all minds were made up as soon as we left the Bench—indeed, I have no doubt from some remarks made to me, before we went on it!" At the post-argument conference, Vinson insisted the claim should have been raised earlier. Black, Frankfurter's staunchest ally, accused the Court of being in "a race for death. . . . This will be a black day for the Court. I plead that it not be decided today." Frankfurter's voice was so loud that Vinson's law clerk could hear him "screaming" from the other side of the wall. Frankfurter argued that the Court had no authority to vacate the stay and that an indictment under the wrong statute cannot be waived: "it is never too late to [dis]allow a sentence to be carried out where there is no consent in law for it." The justices voted 5–3 against maintaining the stay so the lower courts could consider the issue. They voted 5–4 against a full hearing on the merits of the issue. And they voted 6–3 to vacate the stay. Frankfurter passed on the first vote but was in the minority in the others. After nearly three hours, the conference adjourned; Burton returned to the courtroom at 6:29 p.m. and announced a recess until the following day.

Around 11:00 a.m. Friday, June 19, Vinson met in his chambers with Reed, Jackson, Burton, Clark, and Minton to discuss the majority and concurring opinions vacating Douglas's stay. Forty-five minutes later, the justices met in conference about the protocol for announcing their opinions. The Court convened at noon. Vinson, "in a low voice," read a short per curiam vacating the stay and ruling that the Atomic Energy Act did not supersede the Espionage Act. He indicated the issuance of a full majority opinion at a later date. Jackson and Clark released their concurring opinions later that day. Douglas spoke next and read from his dissent in an "emotion-filled and cracking" voice. Black, in "a high-pitched drawl," spoke next and described oral argument as "wholly unsatisfactory."

Frankfurter instructed Vinson to read a short paragraph describing the statutory issues as "complicated and novel." He was still working on his dissent when the Court announced its decision. In a dissent released three days later, he argued that the conspiracy to steal atomic secrets had lasted from 1944 to 1950 and therefore the Rosenbergs could have been charged under the Atomic Energy Act. He needed more time, however, to review the record and to interpret the statute: "I am clear that the claim had substance and that the opportunity for adequate exercise of the judicial judgment was wanting." He acknowledged the "pathetic futility" of writing about the case three days after the fact. "But history also has its claims. . . . Only by sturdy self-examination and self-criticism can the necessary habits for detached and wise judgment be established and fortified so as to become effective when the judicial process is again subjected to stress and strain. . . . Perfection may not be demanded of the law, but the capacity to counteract inevitable, though rare, frailties is the mark of a civilized legal mechanism." Frankfurter's friends and former clerks praised his opinion. Phil Elman, a former clerk working in the solicitor general's office, was so disillusioned with the way the Court had handled the *Rosenberg* case that he said he needed the last two paragraphs of Frankfurter's opinion "for the sake of my soul." Frankfurter was telling Elman and other current and former clerks: "This isn't the end, errors are inevitably made but you go on, you don't lose faith in the process of law."

The Court denied several other attempts to stay the Rosenbergs' executions on the afternoon of June 19. At 2:30 p.m., Eisenhower denied clemency for the second time. The Rosenbergs were supposed to have died on June 18, their fortieth wedding anniversary. The government did not want to execute them on the Jewish Sabbath on Friday, June 19, after sundown (8:31 p.m.). Instead of delaying the executions, they moved them up three hours. At 8:04 p.m., Julius was strapped in to Sing Sing's wooden electric chair. After three shocks of 2000 volts, he was pronounced dead at 8:06. Five minutes later, Ethel walked into the room not knowing her husband was already dead. She was strapped into the same chair. Three shocks later, her heart was still beating. After two more shocks, she was dead. Until the end, federal officials thought that the Rosenbergs might provide useful information about Soviet espionage. The Justice Department knew that it had a weak case against Ethel but was using her as "leverage" to extract a full confession from Julius. Instead, Ethel went to her grave in silence, remaining true to her husband and orphaning her two boys, ages ten and six.

THE GREENGLASSES HAD lied during the trial to save themselves. Years later, David admitted he had lied about his sister's involvement to save his wife, Ruth. Only ten days before trial, Ruth had added the critical detail that Ethel had typed her brother's notes for the Russians. The Greenglasses' grand jury testimony, which was later unsealed, contained none of the incriminating details about the console table or Ethel's role in typing notes. According to the Venona project (decrypted and declassified Soviet intelligence messages), Julius, code-named Liberal, operated a Communist spy ring and recruited the Greenglasses. Ethel knew all about the conspiracy and may have participated in it. Unlike her husband, brother, and sister-in-law, she was not an active spy.

Frankfurter described the *Rosenberg* case as "the most disturbing single experience I have had during my term of service on the Court thus far." In the weeks after the decision, he confided to friends and former clerks how upset he was about the Court's handling of the case. A few asked about rumors that he might retire. The Court's rush to judgment troubled Frankfurter. He did not believe that the Rosenbergs were innocent, as in the case of Sacco and Vanzetti. Yet he thought the Court should have heard allegations that their trial had been unfair and they had been prosecuted under the wrong law. Despite not having read the trial record, he was troubled by allegations of prosecutorial misconduct against Saypol. Frankfurter understood there was more at stake than the lives of the Rosenbergs. The Court's institutional role in defining what amounts to a constitutionally fair trial and its ability to calm public hysteria about a high-profile case warranted full briefing and argument. He believed the Court should review all death penalty cases, especially a federal espionage case during peacetime when the Soviet Union had been an ally. Above all, he wanted the Court to avoid another " 'self-inflicted wound.' "

If the Supreme Court was at its best during the *Steel Seizure Case*, it was at its worst during the *Rosenberg* case. Only Black and Frankfurter consistently voted to hear the case. Yet Black was too incapacitated by shingles and grief after his wife's death to provide leadership. And Frankfurter was not an effective coalition builder and often alienated his colleagues with long, pedantic conference remarks. Frankfurter's closest colleague, Jackson, let his sound judgment get clouded by "primitive, elemental anger—anger that the 'hero' of the hour was the cause of the basic fault." Douglas's grandstanding destroyed any hopes of a civil relationship with Jackson or Frankfurter. Seven years earlier in the Willie Francis case, Douglas had voted to deny review yet had added his name to a dissent after the case was effectively over. He pulled the same stunt in the *Rosenberg* case at least three times. He never voted to grant review when there was a meaningful chance of hearing the case on the merits. He repeatedly added his name to dissents so that he could be on the "right" side. His stay on the last day of the term may have been brave, but it was hypocritical in light of his refusal to hear oral argument about Jackson's proposed stay to review an equally meritorious claim of prosecutorial misconduct. Only Burton, who twice voted to hear the case, kept an open mind.

The bulk of blame for the *Rosenberg* case falls on Fred Vinson. The chief justice had violated judicial ethics and separation of powers, as he likely had done in the *Steel Seizure Case*, by holding secret meetings with Attorney General Brownell in an effort to vacate Douglas's stay and to keep the executions on schedule. He also flouted the Court's internal procedures by calling a special term without a vote of all the justices and by vacating a single justice's stay before sending the issue to the lower courts. He was the last justice to issue a formal opinion in the *Rosenberg* case, circulating his law clerk's draft in July and publishing it on July 16. Frankfurter derided the opinion as a law clerk's "pseudonymous prose." It was one of the last judicial acts of Vinson's life. On September 8, 1953, he died of a heart attack.

Frankfurter returned to Washington from Massachusetts for Vinson's funeral. At Union Station, Phil Elman saw his former boss and noticed that he was "in high spirits." "I'm in mourning," Frankfurter said sarcastically of Vinson's death. He grabbed Elman's arm, looked him in the eye, and said: "Phil, this is the first solid piece of evidence I've ever had that there really is a God." After lunch that day with law clerk Alexander M. Bickel in chambers, Frankfurter was getting dressed in his striped pants and kept repeating that Vinson's death was "an act of Providence, an act of Providence." It sounded harsh, and it was. Yet the justices were only a few months from hearing reargument in the most important issue that had come before the Court in Frankfurter's lifetime—the school segregation cases. Frankfurter knew that the chief justice would not have been up to the challenge.

CHAPTER 33

The Wise Use of Time

ach term the law clerks arranged a lunch with individual justices.
During the spring of 1952, the lunch with Frankfurter erupted into
what he enjoyed most—an argument. One of the clerks asked why the
Court had ducked the school segregation cases. In January, the Court had
remanded a case from Clarendon County, South Carolina, so that the lower
court could review the state's efforts to comply with an order to make the black
and white schools equal in terms of funding, facilities, and curricula. Black
and Douglas dissented because they thought the funding issues were "wholly
irrelevant." They also objected to the Court's decision to hold a case from
Topeka, Kansas, and to wait for cases from South Carolina and several other
states. The clerks wanted to know the reason for the delay. "You think we're
going decide those cases in an election year?" Frankfurter replied. Minton's
clerk Abner Mikva, Vinson's clerk Newton Minow, and several others were
shocked at the Court's naked consideration of electoral politics. Frankfurter's
clerk Abram Chayes was "embarrassed" by his boss's blunt response. The
justice explained that the school segregation cases were a political powder keg
and basically told them to "grow up." "In retrospect," Mikva said, "Frankfurter
had more judgment than the clerks did." In June 1952, the Supreme Court
agreed to hear oral argument in the South Carolina and Kansas cases—and
later added cases from Delaware, the District of Columbia, and Virginia—but
not until a month after the election.

The Court faced numerous obstacles to declaring racially segregated public schools unconstitutional. Section 1 of the Fourteenth Amendment consisted of broad generalities preventing the states from denying "privileges
or immunities of citizenship," "due process of law," and "equal protection of
the laws." The legislative history of the amendment did not suggest that the
framers intended to outlaw racial segregation. And the Court had allowed

state-sponsored segregation to flourish. In 1896, *Plessy v. Ferguson* upheld a Louisiana law about racially "separate but equal" railroad cars. In 1927, *Gong Lum v. Rice* unanimously reaffirmed the "separate but equal" doctrine in education by upholding Mississippi's power to exclude the daughter of Chinese immigrants from the state's white schools. By 1950, the Court had declared that segregated law schools could not be equal because of intangible factors associated with attending flagship state institutions. The Court, however, was careful to limit its reasoning to graduate school. It refused to interfere with the long and unbroken state tradition of racially segregating primary and secondary schools. Finally, there was the question of how the Court, even if it wanted to eliminate the "separate but equal" doctrine and to desegregate primary and secondary schools, would enforce its decision.

There was no doubt where Frankfurter stood on the issue. During the summer of 1952, he wrote a two-page memorandum about why the school segregation cases were hard cases. "Only for those who have not the responsibility of decision," he wrote in the memorandum, which he revised on September 26, "is it easy to decide these cases." It would be wrong, he insisted, for the justices to base their decision on their personal feelings about the wrongness of segregation. He also rejected any purported scientific studies that black and white people should be "kept apart" as belied by the history of race relations since World War I. He turned to the purpose of the Thirteenth, Fourteenth, and Fifteenth Amendments: "The outcome of the Civil War, as reflected in the Civil War Amendments, is that there is a single American society. Our colored citizens . . . are not to be denied opportunities to enjoy the distinctive qualities of their cultural past. But neither are they to be denied opportunities to grow up with other Americans as part of our national life." He pointed to the Fourteenth Amendment's Equal Protection Clause forbidding any state from "deny[ing] any person within its jurisdiction the equal protection of the laws." Equal protection, he argued on the basis of the Court's past decisions, was "not a fixed formula defined with finality at a particular time." It was based on the "evolution of opinion and not merely to changes due to physical alterations." He concluded by offering a working theory about how to decide the school segregation cases: "Law must respond to transformation of views as well as to that of outward circumstances. The effect of changes in men's feelings for what is right and just is equally relevant in determining whether differentiation of treatment by law is a denial of 'the equal protection of the laws.'"

Frankfurter played a central leadership role in achieving unanimity in the school segregation cases. As his conversation with the law clerks indicated, he counseled a strategy of delay at several critical junctures. He and Jackson controlled the center of the Court and wielded considerable influence over other moderate justices, particularly two southerners, Clark and Reed. Frankfurter also knew that the Justice Department under the Truman and Eisenhower administrations could play a pivotal role, and he crossed ethical lines to make it happen. Finally, Frankfurter anticipated some of the thorniest legal issues confronting the Court. In doing so, he tried to take those issues off the table so that the Court could come to a consensus in one of the most important cases in its history. And he had just the law clerk to help him do it.

IF FELIX FRANKFURTER COULD have cloned a new and improved version of himself, he would have created his law clerk Alexander Mordecai Bickel. Born in Bucharest, Romania, Bickel was the son of a prominent lawyer and Yiddish essayist. In 1939, his family arrived in America when he was fourteen. After graduating from high school in New York City, he served in the U.S. Army from 1943 to 1945 as an infantryman and light machine gunner in Italy and France. His fellow soldiers taught him to swear and to speak English like an all-American boy. In 1947, he graduated Phi Beta Kappa from City College with a degree in social sciences and enrolled at Harvard Law School. Bickel served as treasurer of the *Harvard Law Review* yet described himself as "a real bad guy" who drunkenly argued with professors at student-faculty parties. After graduation, he clerked for Judge Calvert Magruder on the Court of Appeals for the First Circuit. Most top students went directly from Magruder or Learned Hand to clerk for Frankfurter. Bickel, however, was passed over. For two years, he worked for the State Department, first in the office of the U.S. High Commissioner in Germany and then in the U.S. Observer Delegation to the European Defense Community Conference in Paris. In April 1952, after a strong push from Judge Magruder, Professor Henry Hart finally selected Bickel to clerk for Frankfurter. Bickel was close friends with his predecessor in Frankfurter's chambers, Abe Chayes, and liked his co-clerk, Donald Trautman. Bickel's friends marveled at his analytical ability, graceful writing style, and encyclopedic knowledge that ranged from Irish poetry to the middle names of baseball players. Hart praised Bickel's early attempts at legal scholarship, recognized his potential as a law professor, and promised Frankfurter: "I am sure Bickel will do well for you. I am sure also . . . that he is one of those who can profit best from you."

Shortly after his arrival in Frankfurter's chambers in mid-summer, Bickel received one of the most important assignments ever given to a law clerk. The justice wanted him to study the legislative debates that led to the Fourteenth Amendment and to write a memorandum about what members of the Thirty-Ninth Congress had intended regarding racial segregation. Frankfurter was unsatisfied with the leading account of the history of the Fourteenth Amendment. As a model, he pointed Bickel to Stanford political scientist Charles Fairman's 1950 law review article analyzing the legislative debates in the Thirty-Ninth Congress about whether they had intended the Fourteenth Amendment to apply the Bill of Rights to the states. The Court's librarians kept a cart filled with volumes of the *Congressional Globe* next to Bickel's desk. Once Bickel finished typing notes on those volumes, the library sent another cart. The cart stayed next to Bickel's desk all year long. "I am currently having a very interesting time with the volumes of the Congressional Globe . . . ," Bickel reported to a vacationing Frankfurter in early September 1952. "I can't say that I have found very much evidence bearing on our problem as of yet, but I should note that I have wasted time occasionally reading some of the heated and less than strictly relevant debates which were held pretty regularly in both the House and Senate."

Before the summer recess was over, Frankfurter was raving about Bickel to another product of CCNY, Harvard Law School, and Magruder's chambers— former clerk Phil Elman. The justice compared Bickel's abilities as a law clerk to Elman's. With some assistance from Frankfurter, Elman also played a critical role in the school segregation cases. In the spring of 1952, Elman had urged his boss, Solicitor General Philip Perlman, to file a friend of the court brief in favor of the NAACP's position. The Justice Department had filed supportive briefs in the NAACP's racially restrictive covenant and graduate school segregation cases. Perlman, however, drew the line at primary and secondary schools. Fortunately for Elman, Perlman resigned during the summer of 1952. And the acting solicitor general, Robert L. Stern, agreed with Elman. They received permission from Truman's new attorney general, James P. McGranery, to file a brief in support of the NAACP.

Elman drafted the Truman administration's brief after months of private conversations with Frankfurter about the school segregation cases. "FF was talking to me," Elman said, "not as lawyer in the SG's office, but as his law clerk for life and perhaps his closest confidant about his problems with fellow justices." According to Elman, Frankfurter believed the Court lacked five votes to overrule the "separate but equal" doctrine, feared the cases would generate nine different opinions on a fractured Court led by the hapless Vinson, and emphasized how important it was for the executive branch to weigh in on the issue. Elman did not discuss with his former boss what the government's brief should say; he wrote it with an eye to gaining a fifth vote to overrule *Plessy*'s "separate but equal" doctrine. His brief, which the government submitted a week before oral argument, proposed an alternative to immediate integration: declare segregated schools unconstitutional and remand the cases to district judges to devise programs for an "orderly and expeditious transition to a non-segregated system." Elman came up with the idea of a delayed remedy from the Court's decisions in complex antitrust cases. He did not breathe a word of it to Frankfurter, whom he feared would poke holes in delayed relief of individual constitutional rights. Elman's brief was the first one to argue for a delayed remedy. The NAACP dismissed Elman's solution as gradualism. The brief, Elman insisted, was written "the Frankfurter Way."

"Phil," Frankfurter told him after Elman had filed the brief, "I think you've done it." Frankfurter's extrajudicial conversations with a Justice Department lawyer about a pending case violated judicial ethics and separation of powers. Yet an unrepentant Elman believed the ends justified the means given the importance of the school segregation cases for the Court and the nation. Years later, he described his Justice Department brief in 1952 as "the one thing I'm proudest of in my whole career."

On the afternoon of December 9, NAACP attorney Robert L. Carter began three days and ten hours of argument in the five school segregation cases. The courtroom was packed with 300 people, about half of them black. Only fifty members of the public, waiting in line since 6:30 a.m., made it into the courtroom. Hundreds more black spectators, wearing suits and dresses, stood in the hallway hoping for the opportunity to see the historic argument. Frankfurter dominated the questioning during Carter's argument in the Kansas case. He asked Carter about the Court's unanimous opinion in *Gong Lum v. Rice* joined by justices "very sensitive and alert to questions of so-called civil liberties" including Holmes, Brandeis, and Stone. Frankfurter asked about the "long-established historical practice by the states." Carter insisted that the "separate but equal" doctrine "should be faced" and "should be overruled." Frankfurter asked about the purpose of the Fourteenth Amendment. Carter replied that it was "intended to protect Negroes in civil and political equality with whites." Burton asked Kansas assistant attorney general Paul E. Wilson whether in the seventy-five years since the passage of the Fourteenth Amendment "the social and economic conditions and the personal relations of the nation may have changed" and therefore changed the interpretation of the Constitution. For the most part, the Kansas case was merely a warm-up act. The lower court in Kansas had agreed with the NAACP, segregation in the state was up to local districts, and the state did not want to appear before the Court to defend its law.

The main event was the South Carolina case and the argument between Thurgood Marshall and John W. Davis. At 3:15 p.m., Marshall took the podium. He was outwardly calm, unemotional, and almost bland. As courageous a trial lawyer as Marshall was in risking his life to defend blacks accused of rape and murder before hostile, all-white southern juries, Elman did not think he was much of a Supreme Court advocate. Yet Marshall brought his "A" game that day. He argued that the Court's decisions in *Plessy* and *Gong Lum* were not necessarily controlling in light of numerous decisions, including the Japanese internment cases, that "distinctions on a racial basis or on a basis of ancestry are odious and invidious." Frankfurter questioned Marshall at length about whether the Court could simply say segregation was bad as a matter of natural law. The NAACP, Marshall contended, had attacked South Carolina's use of race as an "unreasonable classification," therefore the burden was on the state to defend the law's reasonableness. "I follow you when you talk that way," Frankfurter replied and suggested the issue of racial segregation in primary and secondary schools was "more complicated" than in graduate schools. "I agree that it is not only more complicated," Marshall replied. "I agree that it is a tough problem. But I think that it is a tough problem that has to be faced." On the basis of his experiences litigating cases in the South, Marshall insisted the dire predictions of violence were overblown. He said the "only thing we ask for is that state-imposed racial segregation be taken off," then leave the problem to state and local school boards. Frankfurter was shocked by Marshall's proposed solution: "I think that nothing would be worse than for this Court . . . to make an abstract declaration that segregation is bad and then have it evaded by tricks."

As calm as he may have appeared on the outside, the tall, thin, 44-year-old Marshall was scared out of his wits going up against Davis. "John W. Davis!" Marshall said. "He was the greatest solicitor general we ever had. You and I will never see a better one. He was the greatest." Davis was hired at the behest of South Carolina governor and former Supreme Court justice James F. Byrnes, who was determined to enforce "separate but equal" by raising $75 million in bonds to make the state's black and white schools equal. The 79-year-old Davis made one concession to age during the school segregation arguments: he read from notes. No one underestimated him. The previous term, Davis had defeated Truman's seizure of the steel mills and had spoken uninterrupted for fifty-three minutes. A southerner born in West Virginia and part-time resident of South Carolina, Davis was passionate about states' rights.

In a masterful argument, Davis insisted that the justices should interpret the Fourteenth Amendment in two ways: the " 'common understanding at the time of its adoption' " and by putting themselves " 'in the condition of the men who framed the instrument.' " He referred to evidence that the Thirty-Ninth Congress that had passed the amendment also had voted in 1866 to continue to segregate the District of Columbia schools. Frankfurter's colleague, Harold Burton, responded to Davis's historical arguments by asking about changed "conditions and relations between the two races" and by suggesting the Constitution was "a living document that must be interpreted in relation to the facts of the time in which it is interpreted." Davis replied that changed circumstances did not alter the meaning of the words. Frankfurter interrupted that the meaning of "commerce between the states" had changed over time, therefore the meaning of what is "equal" could have changed, too. Davis countered the meaning was fixed at the time of the adoption and ratification of the amendment. He observed that twenty-three of the thirty states that had ratified the amendment were operating racially segregated schools. These were precisely the types of questions about the Fourteenth Amendment's legislative history that Frankfurter had assigned to Bickel.

In reviewing the Court's decisions in the graduate school cases, Davis argued that nothing had changed the "separate but equal" doctrine. That question was settled. He read from Judge John J. Parker's lower court opinion in the South Carolina case that " 'if conditions have changed so that segregation is no longer wise, this is a matter for the legislatures and not for the courts. The members of the judiciary . . . have no more right to read their ideas of sociology into the Constitution than their ideas of economics.' " Davis was appealing to Frankfurter, Jackson, and other justices who had lived through the New Deal constitutional crisis and believed in judicial restraint. Davis demolished the NAACP's sociological evidence, especially social psychologist Kenneth Clark's test of sixteen black South Carolina children, which asked them to choose between black and white dolls. He referred to Clark's larger study, which showed black children were more likely to choose white dolls in northern schools; the choice had nothing to do with South Carolina's separate but equal system.

Marshall's rebuttal was every bit as strong. He argued that "Negroes are taken out of the main stream of American life in these states. There is nothing involved in this case other than race and color." He reminded the justices that "under our form of government, these individual rights of minority people are not to be left to even the most mature judgment of the majority of the people, and that the only testing ground as to whether or not individual rights are concerned is in this Court." Marshall and Frankfurter continued to debate how easy or hard it would be to devise a remedy in these cases; Marshall insisted that "the solution was not to deprive people of their constitutional rights." Stanley Reed, a Kentuckian sympathetic to state rights, jumped into the fray. He suggested that the purpose of the South Carolina law was "to avoid racial friction" and asked whether it was "a problem of legislation or of the Judiciary." Marshall responded that "the rights of minorities . . . have been protected by our Constitution, and the ultimate authority for determining that is this Court."

The Court heard two more days of oral argument about cases from Virginia, the District of Columbia, and Delaware. Jackson asked during the Virginia argument whether Congress could invoke its power to enforce the Fourteenth Amendment to outlaw racially segregated schools. Frankfurter asked during the District of Columbia argument whether, if racial classifications were forbidden, so were bans on interracial marriage. NAACP counsel George E. C. Hayes sidestepped the question by replying that "legislation based upon race is immediately suspect" but not necessarily invalid. Nothing, however, matched the Marshall-Davis South Carolina showdown.

At conference on the afternoon of December 12 and continuing the next day, it was hard to find five votes to overturn *Plessy*'s "separate but equal" doctrine. At Jackson's suggestion, no vote was taken at this conference. As a result, most of the justices' votes must be inferred from their comments. These comments can be interpreted in different ways and based on different justices' notes.

Vinson seemed afraid to overturn separate but equal. He began by reciting the history of segregation in District of Columbia schools at the time of the passage of the Fourteenth Amendment. He also noted that the first Justice Harlan had not mentioned racially segregated schools in his famous *Plessy* dissent and had written a unanimous opinion three years later refusing to interfere with segregated schools. The South Carolina case proved most troubling to Vinson because of the large numbers of black students and the prospect that the state would react to a desegregation order by simply closing its public schools. The South Carolina case, he predicted, required "courage" and "wisdom."

Black was troubled by the District of Columbia case because Congress was not bound by the "same limitations" in the Fourteenth Amendment.

The states, however, were a different story. He saw racial segregation as grounded in the belief in black inferiority and therefore a "per se" violation of the amendment. He argued it conflicted with the purpose of the Fourteenth Amendment to eradicate racial discrimination. Yet he felt Marshall was underestimating the problem of enforcing such a decision. The Alabama native warned his fellow justices that reversing *Plessy* would lead to southern racial violence and put the Court on the front lines of the conflict.

Reed took a "different view" than Black and was a solid vote to uphold separate but equal. The Kentuckian believed in the rights of states to equalize the funding and quality of black schools. By the time Frankfurter spoke, one justice was on the fence (Vinson), another wanted to abolish separate but equal schools but was troubled by the District of Columbia case (Black), and another preferred to uphold separate but equal schools (Reed).

Frankfurter went into the conference discussion with one goal in mind— delay, delay, delay. He wanted to set the cases down for reargument on specific issues. He emphasized that it was important when the Court decided and invoked Brandeis that the "most important things . . . often [are] what we do *not* do." In contrast to Black, he firmly declared that the District of Columbia's segregated schools violated the Fifth Amendment's Due Process Clause. He said it was "intolerable" for the federal government to permit segregation. He recalled the discrimination his law clerk, William Coleman, had faced a few years earlier in the nation's capital. He conceded he had never lived near black people but mentioned his experiences on the National Legal Committee of the NAACP. He proposed rearguing the District of Columbia case later in the term to give the incoming Eisenhower administration an opportunity to help the Court to shape the decrees and to propose remedies. On the cases involving the states, he questioned how Black could know the purpose of the Fourteenth Amendment. He wondered whether the framers of the Fourteenth Amendment intended to abolish segregation, the same question he had assigned to Bickel. He did not believe that the Equal Protection Clause limited equality to "physical things" such as school buildings. He wanted to ask counsel "what justifies us in saying what was equal in 1868 is not equal now." Another argument in March on the District of Columbia case and reargument of the state cases would give the Court time to figure out answers to these hard questions. There was never any doubt whether Frankfurter would vote to invalidate the "separate but equal" doctrine. He had made his position clear in his September 1952 memorandum and his willingness at conference to declare segregation in District of Columbia schools unconstitutional. Rather than being on the fence, he merely wanted more time to discern the best way to do it and to generate the most support from his colleagues.

Douglas was the least sympathetic to Frankfurter's request for reargument. He said the cases were "very simple." The states and the federal government cannot classify on the basis of race. He would outlaw racial segregation in public schools. The only case he would reargue was the District of Columbia one in March.

Frankfurter's plea for reargument was geared to his close colleague, Robert Jackson. Jackson could not find support for outlawing segregation in the words of the Fourteenth Amendment, the history of the amendment, or the Court's precedents. He was frustrated with Marshall's brief as "sociology" and not a "legal issue." As a result, he "would have to say it *is* constitutional." The lawyer from western New York confessed to not being "conscious of racial issues" until he had arrived in Washington, D.C., as a New Deal lawyer in 1934 and as attorney general in 1941 when he had ordered the all-white District Bar Association to allow black lawyers to use its library in a federal building. He refused to "be a party" to a decision ordering schools immediately desegregated and emphasized that the Court must give them time to comply. He concluded by saying he would be okay with the Court saying segregation is "bad," enlisting the support of Congress, and phasing in desegregation over a period of years. In rearguing the District of Columbia cases, he suggested obtaining briefs from the U.S. Congress charged with governing the city.

Burton favored overruling *Plessy*. He believed that the Court had "crossed the threshold" in the *Sipuel* and *Sweatt* cases that black law schools could never be equal because of intangible factors. States needed to face the modern reality that segregation violated equal protection. He referred to his experiences as mayor of Cleveland with black nurses in white hospitals and with a black housing project. He believed that the segregated schools should be given time to comply with the Court's decision.

Clark wanted the same result in all the cases. He wanted to give lower courts leeway to implement the Court's decision. He referred to the problem of Mexican American children in black schools in Texas. He came out strongly in favor of reargument and delay. He worried that the Court had "led [the] states on" by saying for more than sixty years that separate but equal was okay. He believed that lower courts should give the school districts the option of withholding immediate relief to avoid trouble.

Minton believed that the "separate but equal" doctrine had been "whittled away" by the graduate school cases and that racial classifications were "not reasonable" and "invidious" and "segregation [was] per se unconstitutional."

The justices left the conference without taking a vote but with support from several justices for Frankfurter's suggestion of reargument. Five justices seemed poised to abolish separate but equal schools: Black, Douglas, Frankfurter, Burton, and Minton. Three were noncommittal but could be persuaded to go along: Vinson, Jackson, and Clark. One was likely to dissent: Reed. Frankfurter wanted to avoid a fractured Court and many different opinions as in the *Steel Seizure Case*; he saw the best strategy as delay.

Frankfurter's push for reargument and delay gained force as other cases revealed how fractured the Vinson Court was on racial issues. On January 16, 1953, the justices heard argument in *Terry v. Adams,* which they also had delayed until after the presidential election. Black voters in East Texas challenged the all-white Jaybird primary run by the private Jaybird Democratic Association. The Jaybirds consisted of all whites in Fort Bend County, Texas, and for nearly sixty years the winner of its primary always captured both the Democratic nomination and elected office. The Court had outlawed the all-white primary in 1944 in *Smith v. Allwright.* The Fifteenth Amendment, however, forbids the abridgement of voting rights on the basis of race only by the federal government or the states, not by a private club. As a result, the district court held that the black voters in *Terry v. Adams* lacked "state action"; the decision was affirmed by the court of appeals.

The justices were divided 4–4 over *Terry v. Adams* at conference on January 17 with Frankfurter voting initially to reverse then passing. Black assigned the decision to himself; his opinion attracted only Douglas's and Burton's votes. Frankfurter wrote separately in favor of the black voters; he argued that there was state action under the Fifteenth Amendment because Texas election officials were implicated in the private primary scheme. Yet he disagreed with Black's proposed remedy as too intrusive on the state's electoral process. Jackson voted to dissent at conference and, egged on by his law clerk William Rehnquist, drafted a dissent arguing that there was no state action. Jackson, however, decided not to dissent and instead joined Clark's concurring opinion. Only Minton dissented because he found no state action. The result was a victory for black voters. The case, however, resulted in four different opinions and no controlling precedent. An outcome like that in the school segregation cases would have been an institutional disaster.

The justices projected a more united front in another race case at the end of the term. Thompson's Restaurant in Washington, D.C., denied service to 86-year-old black civil rights leader Mary Church Terrell and her activist friends; the owner of the establishment was criminally indicted under 1872 and 1873 "lost laws" requiring equal service in D.C. restaurants and other public accommodations. The laws were dropped from the D.C. code but never formally repealed. A municipal court quashed the indictments because the laws had been implicitly overruled. A divided federal court of appeals disagreed. In a unanimous opinion by Douglas (Jackson did not participate because of thyroid surgery), the Court held the laws had not been overruled by Congress, survived the changes in the structure of the District of Columbia government, and therefore were valid and enforceable. Bickel learned from Reed's clerks what their boss, who lived at the Mayflower Hotel, had said after conference discussion: "Why—why, this means that a nigra can walk right into the restaurant of the Mayflower Hotel and sit down to eat right next to Mrs. Reed!"

NO LAW CLERK PLAYED a bigger role at the end of the 1952 term in the school segregation cases than Bickel. During several conference discussions that spring, the justices agreed to Frankfurter's suggestion to hear another round of argument the following term about a series of questions. Bickel drafted five questions, with substantive input and edits from Frankfurter, for the parties to brief and argue. In a May 27, 1953, cover letter to his colleagues, Frankfurter wrote that the five questions did not "disclose our minds" and pointed "in opposite directions. Some give comfort to one side and some to the other, and that is precisely the intention."

The first three questions addressed the legislative history of the Fourteenth Amendment, which Frankfurter had assigned to Bickel. Question 1 asked for any evidence that the Thirty-Ninth Congress that drafted and voted on the amendment and the state legislatures that ratified it understood the amendment to outlaw racially segregated public schools. Question 2 asked for any evidence that the drafters of the amendment intended for Congress with its enforcement powers or the Court to be able to outlaw racially segregated public schools in the future. Question 3 asked, absent any historical evidence, whether the Court possessed the power to outlaw racially segregated public schools. The last two questions assumed that racially segregated public schools were unconstitutional and, in multiple parts, addressed possible remedies. Question 4 asked whether black students should be admitted immediately to the schools of their choice or whether desegregation should proceed gradually. Question 5, assuming a gradual remedy, asked whether the Court should issue detailed decrees, whether it should appoint special masters to carry them out, or whether it should remand the cases to the lower courts and with what instructions. As he wrote in his cover memorandum, Frankfurter

believed that the remedy questions were essential. He may have been thinking about the threat of his former colleague, South Carolina governor James
F. Byrnes, to turn the state's schools into private academies rather than desegregate them. "[F]or me," Frankfurter wrote, "the ultimate crucial factor in the
problem presented by these cases is psychological—the adjustment of men's
minds and actions to the unfamiliar and the unpleasant."

On the whole, the other justices endorsed Bickel and Frankfurter's five
questions. Vinson liked the first three about the history of the Fourteenth
Amendment but not the last two about remedies. Black and Douglas liked the
two remedy questions but not the first three about the history. Reed, Jackson,
Burton, Clark, and Minton liked all of them. After some slight redrafting
and back-and-forth between Frankfurter and his colleagues, they agreed to
reargument about the five questions. Black, who had opposed delay during
the 1951 term, had changed his tune. "It can't hurt the colored people," Frankfurter noted him as saying at conference, "& it can't hurt [the] states to put
these cases over." Frankfurter reminded Vinson that the Court's order should
include not only the five questions but also an invitation to the U.S. attorney
general to appear before the Court. He invoked Jackson's comment at conference on December 13 about how essential it was to have input from the Eisenhower administration because of its role in enforcing desegregation in the
District of Columbia and possibly elsewhere. On June 8, the day it announced
the Thompson's Restaurant decision, the Court ordered reargument in the
school segregation cases about the five questions.

With three of the five questions addressing the legislative history of the
Fourteenth Amendment, Bickel's memorandum assumed greater importance. He expected to be able to work on the memorandum all summer, but
the last-minute stays of execution and special term in the *Rosenberg* case
delayed him a few weeks. He worked closely with Frankfurter during those
frantic final days, and his other summer assignment consisted of drafting
Frankfurter's history of the *Rosenberg* case. With the Frankfurters in Charlemont, Massachusetts, for the summer, Bickel wrote and revised his Fourteenth Amendment legislative history on the basis of his notes on all the
relevant volumes of the *Congressional Globe* and the documentary and scholarly sources about Reconstruction. He "enjoyed the work hugely."

On August 22, 1953, Bickel submitted a 58-page draft memorandum preceded by a three-page, single-spaced cover letter and summary. Acknowledging that his memorandum was "nowhere near complete," Bickel began
by explaining how the political order had changed in 1866 with Congress
pushing for Reconstruction and President Andrew Johnson opposing it.

During this struggle, few people were focused on the language in Section 1 of the Fourteenth Amendment, which resulted in the Citizenship, Privileges or Immunities, Due Process, and Equal Protection Clauses. Some acknowledged that the language was broad. No one, Bickel wrote, intended for racially segregated schools to be abolished because in 1866 there were very few efforts to educate blacks. "In any event," he wrote, "it is impossible to conclude that the 39th Congress intended that segregation be abolished; impossible also to conclude that they foresaw it might be." He believed it was impossible to know what was in the mind of the amendment's principal drafter, Congressman John Bingham, a moderate Ohio Republican. The radical Republicans, Thaddeus Stevens and Charles Sumner, understood that the amendment did not provide for black suffrage. What the radicals did get was broad language and the power of Congress to enforce the amendment in the future. In the most important conclusion from his prodigious research, Bickel argued "all this only means that the legislative history is inconclusive."

Given his finding that the legislative history was "inconclusive," Bickel argued the Fourteenth Amendment's broad, flexible language empowered the Court to apply it to new or unforeseen factual circumstances. He observed that none of the legislators in 1866 had focused on the right of blacks to serve on juries, yet fourteen years later in *Strauder v. West Virginia* the Court outlawed racial discrimination in jury service. He contended the Fourteenth Amendment was consistent with one of Frankfurter's favorite ideas: John Marshall's description of the Constitution as a great outline. "I think the legislative history leaves this Court free to remember that it is a *Constitution* it is construing," Bickel wrote, paraphrasing Marshall's most famous line from *McCulloch*. "I think also that a charitable view of the sloppy draftsmanship of the Fourteenth Amendment would ascribe to them the knowledge it was a *Constitution* they were writing."

With Bickel's memorandum, Frankfurter possessed everything he needed to unite the Court in the school segregation cases. The amendment's broad language was an asset. The "inconclusive" legislative history was no longer an obstacle. Months before the reargument, Frankfurter knew the answers to the three questions, which pointed in favor of overruling *Plessy* and desegregating the public schools.

WITHOUT CONSULTING FRANKFURTER and the other justices, Vinson delayed the second round of oral argument in the school segregation cases from October to December 7. A month after ordering the delay, the chief justice was dead. The Vinson Court probably would have outlawed racially segregated schools, but with multiple opinions from the justices in the majority and at least one dissent. Frankfurter's strategy of delay and reargument proved to be a stroke of genius. Bickel's memorandum removed several stumbling blocks and inspired the Court's treatment of the legislative history as "inconclusive." The Court, thanks to Frankfurter's repeated calls for reargument and a memorandum by one of his finest law clerks, was primed to take a more unified approach under the new chief justice.

During the debates over Vinson's successor, columnists Arthur Krock and Marquis Childs proposed Frankfurter's friend Robert H. Jackson. In 1941 and 1946, Jackson had been passed over as chief justice. Politics again intervened. During the 1952 presidential election, California governor Earl Warren had campaigned for Eisenhower. A year later, Eisenhower promised to name Warren solicitor general until a Supreme Court vacancy opened. The president had assumed that the vacancy would not be the Court's center chair. Krock predicted that Warren's lack of judicial experience precluded him from being chief justice. A former prosecutor and state attorney general who had supported Japanese internment before being elected governor three times, Warren had never argued before the Supreme Court. On September 30, Eisenhower announced his intention to name Warren chief justice as a recess appointee. The president privately denied that Warren was "a 'political' appointment" and predicted that the California governor would be up to the job's administrative and leadership challenges. A week later in the Supreme Court conference room, Frankfurter and the other justices watched Hugo Black swear in Warren as chief justice. Black presided over the Court's early conferences while the new chief justice, who was initially nominated as a recess appointment on October 2, found his bearings. Another round of argument in the school segregation cases was two months away.

The Eisenhower administration was not sure how to respond to the Court's invitation for the attorney general to appear in the school segregation cases. Elman and acting Solicitor General Stern told Attorney General Herbert Brownell and Deputy Attorney General William P. Rogers that it was not an invitation but the "equivalent of a royal command." They had no choice given the Truman Justice Department's brief the previous term had declared segregation "illegal." That summer, Elman was charged with drafting the Justice Department's supplemental brief. Prior to its submission, Brownell reviewed it line by line, and Eisenhower read the brief's conclusion. On November 27, Brownell filed the Eisenhower Justice Department's 188-page brief as a supplemental brief to the Truman administration's, dutifully answering the questions about the legislative history of the Fourteenth Amendment and advocating gradual desegregation carried out by the lower courts of each jurisdiction.

On December 3, four days before the reargument, Frankfurter circulated Bickel's memorandum with a prefatory note. The justice explained that he had been troubled by "the unreliability" of the leading scholarly literature about the Fourteenth Amendment, had enlisted "one of the most dependable of the law clerks I have had," and how Bickel had "devote[d] many weeks" to reading "every word" of the *Congressional Globe* about the amendment's legislative history. He described Bickel's memorandum, which the justice edited, as "a fair, well-balanced, summary of the story." He highlighted the memorandum's main conclusion that "the legislative history of the Amendment is, in a word, inconclusive." He explained that "the 39th Congress as an enacting body neither manifested that the Amendment outlawed segregation in the public schools or authorized legislation to that end, nor that it manifested the opposite."

Frankfurter's circulation of Bickel's memorandum on the eve of the argument mooted the first three questions about the Fourteenth Amendment's legislative history. The only unanswered questions were numbers 4 and 5 about an immediate or gradual remedy and the best way to supervise desegregation. In many ways, the second round of oral argument was irrelevant. With Bickel's memorandum and another round of briefs, the justices already possessed enough information to make up their minds.

Not much of import happened during the three days of oral argument. The rematch between Davis and Marshall lacked the drama of the first round. During the combined argument of the South Carolina and Virginia cases on December 7, Frankfurter questioned Marshall and fellow NAACP attorney Spottswood Robinson about the amendment's legislative history. Frankfurter chided Marshall for attempting to rely on the Civil Rights Act of 1871 to inform what had happened from 1866 to 1868. After Marshall sat down, Davis answered only two questions. Jackson and Frankfurter asked him whether the Constitution's Necessary and Proper Clause empowered Congress to enforce the Fourteenth Amendment. Davis replied that Congress could not broaden the amendment's meaning or scope. The Virginia lawyers answered very few questions as well. At the start of Marshall's rebuttal, Frankfurter asked him to discuss possible remedies. Marshall disagreed with the Eisenhower administration's brief that some school districts should be given more than a year to desegregate. During his concluding remarks, Marshall rejected the idea of leaving the problem to Congress or the states: "The argument of judicial restraint has no application in this case. . . . The duty of enforcing the Fourteenth Amendment is placed upon this Court." Marshall charged that the only way the Court could rule in favor of the states and uphold racial segregation was "to find that for some reason Negroes are inferior to all other human beings." The states, Marshall insisted, were trying to keep former slaves in "as near" slavery "as is possible; and now is the time, we submit, that this Court should make it clear that that is not what our Constitution stands for." As stirring as Marshall's words were, the outcome was a foregone conclusion. During the three days of argument, the justices seemed more concerned with how to desegregate the schools than with which way to decide the case. It made no difference who was sitting in the Court's center chair.

Warren presided over the conference on December 12 about the school segregation cases and began by suggesting they discuss them "informally" and without taking a vote. He was persuaded that the "separate but equal doctrine rests on [the] basic premise that the Negro race is inferior—that is [the] only way to sustain *Plessy*." The argument of Marshall and his co-counsel, he argued, "proves they are not inferior." The Reconstruction Amendments, Warren contended, "were intended to make equal those who were slaves." He acknowledged that the time element in the South would be important. Black, another vote to abolish separate but equal, was absent. Reed tried to put his past prejudices aside and recognized that we had "a dynamic Constitution" and "what was correct in *Plessy* might not be correct now." Yet, in contrast to the chief justice, he argued the Equal Protection Clause could be satisfied by equal facilities. He denied the existence of an inferior race. The only way segregation could be unconstitutional was if it violated due process as an unreasonable classification. He urged his colleagues to leave the issue up to Congress.

With two votes to overturn *Plessy* and one vote to affirm, Frankfurter began by insisting that the justices should be careful in how they discuss these issues. He suggested that the Court put a time limit on when the case would be decided. He referred to the 1901 *Insular Cases* about the legal status of the U.S. territories after the Spanish-American War. "The awful thing" about those cases, he said, "was not too many opinions" or the number of pages, but that "they looked in too many directions." He wanted his colleagues to think hard about finding the right way to overturn separate but equal. He was concerned about Reed's suggestion of invoking the Due Process Clause because due process gives judges too much power. Frankfurter emphasized Bickel's conclusion that the legislative history of the Fourteenth Amendment was "inconclusive." He counseled that the Court's opinion should not be "self-righteous" and referred to labor lawyer Arthur Goldberg as "Gold Almighty" because of the high moral tone in the Steelworkers union's friend of the court brief. Time, Frankfurter insisted, would lead to change. And this case required "psychological changes" in people's attitudes.

Douglas, a definite vote to reverse Plessy, was oddly circumspect. He joined Warren on the state cases but suggested remanding the District of Columbia case to decide whether segregated schools were mandatory or permissive. Jackson, who was noncommittal after the last term, could "go along with" making "a political decision." He deemed the legislative history unhelpful and custom and precedent cut against and as a result found it hard "to justify the abolition of segregation as a judicial act." He preferred Congress to address the issue, not the Court. "If we have to decide the question," he said, "then representative government has failed." The Court, he argued, could not outlaw segregation without providing guidance to lower courts about remedies. Most important, he had signaled his willingness to overturn Plessy as a political decision rather than a legal one. Burton, another vote against separate but equal, believed that the Court had "no choice" but "to act." Clark, a Texan, predicted violence in the South if the Court mishandled the case. He favored allowing different states to take different approaches to desegregation. He made it clear that, like Jackson and Burton, he would vote to abolish segregation as long as the Court worked out a remedy. Minton pointed to the integration of the armed forces as proof that fears of violence were overstated. He believed the Fourteenth Amendment intended to wipe out racial inferiority, argued that after the Court's graduate school decisions Plessy was a "weak reed," and favored its reversal.

By the end of the conference, eight justices—Warren, Black in absentia, Douglas, Frankfurter, Jackson (though he struggled with the reasoning), Burton, Clark, and Minton—were poised to declare racially segregated schools unconstitutional. Only Reed voiced opposition. During the next few weeks, the justices discussed the school segregation cases informally. Frankfurter never attended the justices' lunches. But on the morning of December 23, he and Burton discussed the cases in Burton's chambers. The next conference discussion was less than a month away.

On January 15, 1954, in advance of the next day's conference, Frankfurter circulated a memorandum about possible remedies in the school segregation cases. "As is doubtless true of the rest of you," he wrote in his cover letter, "all sorts of considerations have arisen within me in regard to the fashioning of a decree." He assured his colleagues that his memorandum had been typed "under conditions of strictest secrecy." Frankfurter highlighted the difficulty of getting states to desegregate their schools and that a "declaration of constitutionality is not a wand by which these transformations can be accomplished." He recognized that it involved "physical and educational changes" and hoped that it would lead to "social betterment" rather than a "social deterioration." He cautioned against trying to improve the situation overnight: "Not even a court can in a day change a deplorable situation into the ideal. It does its duty if it gets effectively under way the righting of a wrong. When the wrong is a deeply rooted state policy the court does its duty if it decrees measures that reverse the direction of the unconstitutional policy so as to uproot it 'with all deliberate speed.'" This was the first time in this case that Frankfurter invoked the "all deliberate speed" language from Holmes's opinion in *Virginia v. West Virginia*. It would not be the last. He urged his colleagues to think of desegregation as "a fact-finding problem" depending on the demographics of each state. As Elman had discussed in the Truman Justice Department's brief, Frankfurter predicted that the process would take time and that "future litigation is almost certain." Rather than leave the problems to district judges, he proposed appointing special masters, either by the Supreme Court or the district court, to engage in the necessary fact-finding in each jurisdiction. Both alternatives, he concluded, "raise serious questions."

At conference, Warren suggested that the Court as an institution do "as little administration as we can" by providing guidance to the district courts. Black favored allowing individual district courts to work out remedies according to local conditions and did not support a one-size-fits-all remedy. Reed pleaded with the Court to give district judges time and not to rush southern states "to adjust." Douglas agreed that deciding on a remedy would be difficult and preferred "generosity, flexibility, [and] possible use of a master." Jackson suggested delaying the remedy problem for another argument the next term. Burton hoped to be able to normalize the schools within fifteen years. Clark agreed with Jackson's idea of another argument on remedies. Minton did not want the Court "throwing its weight around." Black concluded the discussion by suggesting that a vague remedy was not going to hurt and agreed to let the issue "simmer." He had no objection to a reargument on the remedy. The Alabama native said most liberals in his home state were "praying for delay." Above all, Black worried about a "storm over this Court." With the justices focused on remedies, the outcome was not in doubt. The justices were not enthusiastic about Frankfurter's proposal of special masters. Yet they had come around to his belief in the benefits of delay and time.

Warren and Frankfurter were in a honeymoon period. Many believed that Frankfurter treated the tall, genial chief justice like a constitutional law student and, at least initially, Warren was a willing pupil. The chief justice was receptive to Frankfurter's input on the school segregation cases. Between March 19 and May 17, Frankfurter met privately with Warren eleven times—more than any other justice. He admired the chief justice's dedication and willingness to work with others on the school segregation cases. "May I ask you to postpone our talk on *Segregation Cases* till Monday . . . ," Frankfurter wrote Warren in late March. "Why not have our discussion at my house on Monday afternoon, say at 4:30, to the stimulating accompaniment of a bourbon highball!"

Not confirmed by the Senate until March 1 and not sworn in until March 20, Warren waited until the justices took a formal vote at one of their private conferences before drafting an opinion. During a walk with Burton around the Capitol building and a discussion in his chambers on the afternoon of April 20, he revealed his preliminary thoughts. A week later, he wrote a nine-page memorandum in longhand on yellow paper. Warren's original handwritten draft contained many of the final opinion's most famous lines. He had the notes typed and on April 29 or 30 instructed his law clerk Earl Pollock to turn them into an opinion that in short, simple, and nonlegal language attempted to explain to the American people why racially segregated public schools were unconstitutional. On May 3, Pollock submitted a typewritten draft dated May 4 but suggested that the District of Columbia case be treated in a separate opinion about the Fifth Amendment's Due Process Clause (because the Fourteenth Amendment applied only to the states, not the federal government).

Frankfurter was one of the first justices, if not the first, who saw the typewritten draft. He met privately with the chief justice on May 1 during a 1:30 p.m. break from the justices' conference and again at 11:00 a.m. on May 3 before court was in session. No other justice saw Warren in chambers during this period. On May 4, the date of Warren's first printed draft, Frankfurter suggested several editorial changes and wrote Warren a short memorandum with additional "jottings." Frankfurter's comments resulted in a change to one of the opinion's most famous lines. Warren had written in his original handwritten draft that racially segregated schools "puts the mark of inferiority" on black children; Frankfurter proposed to change it to "generates a feeling of inferiority."

After incorporating Frankfurter's comments, Warren hand-delivered the drafts to his colleagues on May 7 and 8 "as a basis for discussion of the segregation cases." He emphasized they "were prepared on the theory that the opinions should be short, readable by the lay public, non-rhetorical, unemotional and, above all, non-accusatory." Burton responded enthusiastically and predicted it might be unanimous. Two justices, Jackson and Reed, posed the biggest obstacles to unanimity but for very different reasons.

On March 30, Jackson had been admitted to Doctors Hospital after suffering a heart attack. He was not expected back at the Court anytime soon. On April 20 and April 29, Frankfurter visited Jackson in the hospital. Frankfurter may not have seen what Jackson showed to Warren—a draft concurrence. Since the day before the second oral argument, Jackson had been writing a "memorandum." He may have figured there would be multiple opinions as in the *Steel Seizure* or *Rosenberg* case and thought his way through legal problems by drafting opinions. By March 15, he had completed six drafts and produced a 23-page opinion. For most of the opinion, he argued that the history of the Fourteenth Amendment, the Court's decisions, and custom supported "separate but equal" and predicted two decades of litigation. Near the end, however, he highlighted two reasons for a new interpretation: the rapid rise of African Americans since the abolition of slavery and the lack of reasonableness of race or color as a basis of classification. He showed the opinion to his lone law clerk, E. Barrett Prettyman, Jr., who was not impressed. In a memorandum, Prettyman urged Jackson to "*begin*, not with doubts and fears— not with a negative attitude, but with a clear and affirmative statement of your legal position." Prettyman was not shy about expressing his displeasure with the opinion's tone: "I say this in all frankness: if you are going to reach the decision you do, you should not write as if you were ashamed to reach it." He encouraged the justice to expand the concurrence's most important point: "dealing with the question whether there is any longer a valid basis for a classification based upon race alone." Jackson, according to Prettyman, was "about to start re-working it when he had a heart attack."

On the morning of May 8, Warren hand-delivered his draft school segregation opinion to Jackson at Doctors Hospital. Jackson liked the opinion's simplicity, straightforwardness, and great care it took in not blaming the South. Jackson showed it to Prettyman. They "agreed that it could use a little more law." Jackson asked Prettyman to type a paragraph of suggestions that he wanted to discuss with Warren. Later that afternoon, the chief justice returned to the hospital; Prettyman waited in the hallway as they reviewed the opinion and discussed Jackson's suggestions. The chief justice agreed to include one sentence of Jackson's in the final draft about the changed conditions since the Court's 1896 *Plessy* decision: "Today, in contrast, many Negroes have achieved outstanding success in the arts and sciences as well as in the business and professional world."

There was only one possible holdout—Stanley Reed. In early May, Warren

met three times with the Kentucky-born Reed about the opinion. The previous summer, Reed had revealed to his law clerks his "deep reservations"
about reversing *Plessy* but knew his colleagues had the votes to overturn it.
He thought that Vinson and possibly another justice might have joined him
in dissent the previous term. During the February 1954 recess, Reed began
to draft a dissent and showed it to his law clerk Jack Fassett. Reed's dissent
argued that equal protection required only substantially equal facilities and
that the only possible claim was based on a due process argument about the
unreasonableness of racial classifications. Fassett faulted his boss for evading
why racially separate but equal schools did not violate equal protection. Reed
believed that public policy should be made by Congress, not by the Court.
He asked his clerks if they favored a "krytocracy"—government by judiciary.
After informal lunches and closed-door meetings with Warren about the
opinions, Reed realized he could not be the lone dissenter.

On May 13, Warren circulated a revised draft and personally delivered it
to Jackson in the hospital. Frankfurter had met with Warren in Frankfurter's chambers two days earlier and must have known that Jackson and Reed
were aboard. As soon as he read Warren's revised draft, Frankfurter wrote the
chief justice that he was "very happy" to join the opinion. He praised Warren's efforts to produce a unanimous result: "When—I no longer say 'if'—you
bring this cargo of unanimity safely to port it will be a memorable day no less
in the history of the Nation than in that of the Court. You have if I may say so,
been wisely at the helm throughout the year's journey of this litigation. *Finis
coronat omnia* [the end crowns all]." Two days later at conference, the justices
formally approved the opinions and planned to announce them on Monday.
Most of the justices returned their printed copies to the chief justice to avoid
leaks. Frankfurter warned Warren to let nothing delay the announcement:
"An opinion in a touchy and explosive litigation, once it has been agreed to
by the Court, is like a soufflé—it should be served at once after it has reached
completion. And so I venture to urge that no room be left for contingencies—
one can never tell—not for the real danger of leakage, since walls are supposed to have ears. I am assuming, of course, that all are *in* and that Bob
[Jackson] can be here Monday!"

———

THE PRESS AND PUBLIC did not know what was coming on Monday, May
17, 1954. The first clue came when Jackson, accompanied by his doctor and
nurse, checked out of the hospital and arrived at the Court at 11:30 a.m. At

noon, Jackson took his seat next to Frankfurter on the bench. Thurgood Marshall and other NAACP lawyers had been attending the Court's Monday opinion announcements for several weeks. Marshall had postponed a trip to Los Angeles and had flown to Washington from Alabama to be there that day. The justices announced several minor opinions. Finally, at 12:52 p.m., Warren began reading the school segregation decisions. When he added the word "unanimously," the crowd in the courtroom gasped.

The landmark opinion is known today by the lead case from Topeka, Kansas—*Brown v. Board of Education.* In an unstated nod to Bickel's memorandum, *Brown* declared the Fourteenth Amendment's legislative history "inconclusive." In a line from Warren's handwritten outline, the opinion rejected John W. Davis's pleas to interpret the Fourteenth Amendment on the basis of its meaning in 1868: "In approaching this problem, we cannot turn the clock back to 1868 when the Amendment was adopted, or even to 1896 when *Plessy v. Ferguson* was written." *Brown's* most controversial sentence dismissed *Plessy's* psychological claims about self-imposed "badges of inferiority" with a footnote containing citations to sociological and psychological studies including Kenneth Clark's doll tests and Gunnar Myrdal's *An American Dilemma.* The opinion's most memorable line also came from Warren's handwritten outline with the slight revision from Frankfurter: "To separate [black schoolchildren] from others of similar age and qualifications solely because of their race generates a feeling of inferiority as to their status in the community that may affect their hearts and minds in a way unlikely ever to be undone." Rather than overrule *Plessy,* the opinion merely concluded that "in the field of public education the doctrine of 'separate but equal' has no place." In the final paragraph, the Court requested another argument the next term about remedies.

"*This* is a day that will live in glory," Frankfurter wrote Warren on May 17. "It is also a great day in the history of the Court, and not in the least for the course of deliberation which brought about the result. I congratulate you." The glory was all Warren's. But the strategy of delay, the Bickel memorandum about the "inconclusive" legislative history, and the Elman briefs on behalf of the Truman and Eisenhower administrations had been all Frankfurter.

As much as the school segregation cases had been a personal triumph for Warren, Frankfurter knew they had been an intense personal struggle for Stanley Reed. Three days after the announcement, he wrote Reed that if the cases had been decided after the 1952 term, there would have been multiple opinions from the justices in the majority and four dissenters—Vinson, Reed, Jackson, and Clark. Frankfurter may have been exaggerating about the number of dissenters, particularly Jackson and Clark, to make Reed feel less isolated. A fractured Court, Frankfurter wrote Reed, "would have been catastrophic. And if we had not had unanimity now inevitably there would have been more than one opinion for the majority. That would have been disastrous."

Frankfurter, Jackson, and Reed had been through the wars together. They had defended the constitutionality of Roosevelt's New Deal, had remained loyal to the president during the court-packing fight, and believed in judicial restraint as a liberal theory of constitutional interpretation. Frankfurter considered Reed's decision to go along with the majority an act of judicial statesmanship: "I am inclined to think, indeed I believe, in no single act since you have been on this Court have you done the Republic a more lasting service. I am not unaware of the hard struggle this involved in the conscience of your mind and in the mind of your conscience. I am not unaware, because all I have to do is look within. As a citizen of the Republic, even more than as a colleague, I feel deep gratitude for your share in what I believe to be a great good for our nation." That next day, Reed replied that Frankfurter's note "was appreciated by me. While there were many considerations that pointed to a dissent, they did not add up to a balance against the Court's opinion." Reed referred to cases since he had arrived on the Court in 1938 invalidating all-white primaries, racial segregation on interstate buses and trains, and exclusion from graduate schools as "the factors looking toward a fair treatment for Negroes are more important than the weight of history. While 'due process' seemed a better ground to me, there really isn't much difference. Equal protection comes close in this situation."

Frankfurter's former clerks lauded his role in achieving a unanimous decision. William Coleman, who had been working with Marshall and other NAACP lawyers on the briefs and in preparation for oral argument, found it "difficult to place in words appreciation and thanks for a courageous and forward looking decision which affects greatly things that one believes in deeply." He credited his former boss's "part in the job which I have a feeling was considerable." Elman, who knew more than almost anyone about Frankfurter's efforts, may have overstated the case in describing him as the Court's "grand strategist."

The idea that Warren single-handedly willed the Court to a unanimous opinion, however, gives him too much credit. To be sure, Warren capitalized on the honeymoon period after Vinson's death. In late April and early May 1954, the new chief justice compensated for his lack of constitutional law experience with interpersonal skill and political sense about how to achieve a unanimous opinion. Yet to give Warren all the credit is overly simplistic, ignores the major events during the 1952 term prior to his arrival, and fails to acknowledge what Frankfurter had accomplished with his persistent strategy of delay. "It is a long story how unanimity was achieved in the *Segregation* cases and not at all a dramatic one," Frankfurter wrote Learned Hand. "It could not possibly have come to pass with Vinson, which does not remotely mean that Warren drew votes out of his hat."

Frankfurter attributed the unanimous decision to multiple factors: (1) delaying the South Carolina and Kansas cases, over the objections of Black and Douglas, until after the 1952 presidential election and consolidating them with cases from other states and the District of Columbia; (2) holding a second round of oral argument during the 1953 term about Frankfurter and Bickel's five questions; and (3) Vinson's death because a Vinson-led Court would have produced multiple concurring and dissenting opinions. All the justices knew how the cases would be decided before the second round of argument. At the January 16 conference, they discussed only possible remedies. Warren was not confirmed by the Senate until March 1. By then, Frankfurter's strategy of delay had made the result a fait accompli. To his former clerk Elman, Frankfurter credited the decision to keep the case out of politics "mainly due to the clear thinking, skillful maneuvering and disinterestedness of Jackson, J., and FF. I shudder to think the disaster we would have suffered the country that is—if the 'libertarians,' the heir of Jefferson and the heir of Brandeis had had their way!" To Learned Hand, Frankfurter was even more explicit about Black and Douglas's initial rush to hear the cases in 1951: "if the 'great libertarians' had had their way we would have been in the soup." Above all, Frankfurter concluded that "the wise use of time," that is, delay and reargument, "was probably the chief factor in the ultimate decision."

Frankfurter's archenemy on the Court, William O. Douglas, tried to rewrite history by claiming that Frankfurter had been willing to affirm *Plessy*. The day that *Brown* was decided, Douglas wrote a memorandum for his files contending that in December 1952, Frankfurter had been one of five justices in favor of affirming racially separate but equal schools. Douglas's claim is unsupported by any of the five justices' extant conference notes. It is contradicted by Frankfurter's September 1952 memorandum and comments at the December 1952 conference in favor of striking down the District of Columbia's segregated schools. Douglas also contended in his 1953 conference notes that Frankfurter said that "history in Congress and in this court indicates that *Plessy* is right," a quote contradicted by Burton's notes and by Frankfurter's endorsement of Bickel's conclusion that the amendment's legislative history was "inconclusive." The obvious explanation is that Frankfurter and Douglas hated each other. This was especially true after Douglas's eleventh-hour grandstanding, preceded by his repeated unwillingness to hear oral argument, in the *Rosenberg* case. Twelve days after he wrote his self-serving memorandum about *Brown*, Douglas revealed the depths of the enmity between him and Frankfurter. In a May 29, 1954, letter that Frankfurter circulated to the entire Court, Douglas wrote: "Today at Conference I asked you a question concerning your memorandum [about two cases]. The question was not answered. An answer was refused, rather insolently. This was so far as I recall the first time one member of the Conference refused to answer another member on a matter of Court business. We all know what a great burden your long discourses are. So I am not complaining. But I do register a protest at your degradation of the Conference and its deliberations."

Relying on Douglas's unreliable accounts and other evidence, some historians have claimed that Frankfurter was willing to affirm *Plessy* or at the very least was wavering about the result. The evidence, however, suggests otherwise. Frankfurter's delay in initially hearing the cases until after the 1952 presidential election and his request for another round of argument gave the Court time to produce a unanimous opinion. His research assignment to Bickel took the legislative history of the Fourteenth Amendment off the table. His extrajudicial conversations with Elman, though ethically problematic, helped the Truman and Eisenhower Justice Departments file briefs in support of eliminating racially separate but equal schools. Finally, Frankfurter provided advice and encouragement to Warren when the new chief justice needed it most.

Above all, *Brown* was a triumph for Frankfurter because he demonstrated— as he did in his unpublished concurrence in the 1944 all-white primary case of *Smith v. Allwright*, in his September 1952 memorandum about the school segregation cases, and in his cautious yet consistent support for outlawing racial segregation—the adaption of judicial restraint to enforce the Fourteenth Amendment's promise of equal citizenship for African Americans. Frankfurter's idols, Holmes and Brandeis, had joined the Court's unanimous opinion upholding racially segregated schools in *Gong Lum v. Rice* and never squared their judicial philosophies with how the Fourteenth Amendment changed the Constitution. *Brown* was a hard case for Frankfurter and other proponents of judicial restraint. Their ability to argue for a more limited role for the Court yet protect civil rights demonstrated that judicial restraint remained a viable liberal constitutional theory. Now that *Brown* had been decided, their next goal was to avoid Black's fears of a "storm over this Court."

CHAPTER 34

All Deliberate Speed

*B*rown v. Board of Education was a triumph and a dilemma. It was a triumph because Frankfurter, by adapting judicial restraint to fulfill the Fourteenth Amendment's promise of equal citizenship, had succeeded where his judicial idols Holmes and Brandeis had failed. Yet *Brown* also posed a dilemma about how to prevent the Court from becoming too powerful. For his entire legal career, Frankfurter had railed against the vagueness of the Due Process Clause and the evils of "liberty of contract." He regretted that Holmes and Brandeis had signed on to decisions extending due process beyond purely procedural matters and faulted Holmes for introducing the unhelpful phrase "clear and present danger" into First Amendment jurisprudence. After *Brown*, Frankfurter found himself caught between two extremes. On the one hand, he criticized lawyers and judges who wanted the Court to take a leading role in making social policy and protecting civil liberties. He derided Stone's Footnote Four in *Carolene Products* suggesting that the Court intervene when the political process fails as "mischievous" and too open-ended to cabin the Court's power. On the other hand, Frankfurter defended *Brown* from critics including Judge Learned Hand who were skeptical about using the Fourteenth Amendment to eliminate racially segregated schools. To Hand, Frankfurter predicted "less trouble than you fear" and expected the "serious difficulties" would be limited to the Deep South. "I am assuming that the [Supreme Court] will continue to behave wisely," Frankfurter wrote Hand. "Shaping decrees is fundamentally a function of wisdom!"

From Charlemont, Massachusetts, where he and Marion escaped Washington's summer heat, Frankfurter had been gathering information for the decrees from his legal contacts in the South. He turned to the same law school classmate he had consulted about the Willie Francis case, Louisiana lawyer Monte M. Lemann.

Two of the top students in the class of 1906 at Harvard Law School, Frankfurter and Lemann were both Jewish yet came from different worlds. Lemann's family emigrated to Louisiana from Germany in the 1830s, and Lemann graduated at age fourteen from Tulane and at age nineteen from Harvard College. Two of the youngest law students, Frankfurter and Lemann became fast friends and often walked the streets of Cambridge speculating about their futures. After they finished first and fourth, respectively, in their class, Frankfurter and Lemann chose different career paths. Frankfurter loathed private practice during his stint with a Wall Street law firm, jumped at Henry Stimson's offer of public service, and essentially never left. Lemann returned home to New Orleans and stayed at the same influential law firm for his entire career. The firm, Monroe and Lemann, bore his name and included his two sons. Lemann did not restrict himself to private practice. He served on the U.S. Shipping Board in 1918, the Wickersham Commission on law enforcement in 1929, the Supreme Court's Advisory Committee on the Federal Rules of Civil Procedure for nearly twenty years, and the Council of the American Law Institute. As president of the Louisiana State Bar Association, he pioneered legal aid in his state and clashed with Huey Long's political machine. Despite Frankfurter's best efforts, Lemann declined Roosevelt's offer of a federal judgeship on the Court of Appeals for the Fifth Circuit because of his wife's poor health. Fifteen years later in 1953, Frankfurter urged him not to decline to be solicitor general if asked (he wasn't, on account of age). Soft-spoken and self-deprecating, Lemann put his family first and preferred to work behind the scenes.

After the *Brown* decision, Lemann reached out to sympathetic members of the southern bar to rally support for the rule of law and to implement the decision in "good faith." As a longtime member of private, black Dillard University's board of trustees, he was familiar with issues of racial injustice in education. On June 10, 1954, he sent Frankfurter a letter from a leading member of the Louisiana bar about *Brown*. The justice, in turn, sent Lemann a letter from a crackpot New Orleans lawyer who questioned whether the Supreme Court was "a constitutional body" given the justices' political pasts. The lawyer incorrectly referred to Frankfurter as a former assistant secretary of state. "I've been called many things," Frankfurter wrote Lemann, "but never before have I been made an Asst Sec of State." The bigger canard, in Frankfurter's mind, was the argument that prior judicial experience should be a prerequisite to serving on the Supreme Court. He defended Eisenhower's choice of Warren as chief justice and dismissed the bar's clamor for Arthur Vanderbilt of the New Jersey Supreme Court or John J. Parker of the Fourth

Circuit as wrongheaded. Frankfurter argued that some of the best justices lacked prior judicial experience. Lemann confessed his initial doubts about Warren's lack of judicial experience yet in no way sympathized with the lawyer's letter. "While I do not believe that there are any members of the Southern bar for whom I have respect who would sink to the level of [the lawyer] in expression," Lemann replied on June 29, "I am sure that there are many dissenting southern lawyers who resent the segregation decision and would like to circumvent it if possible."

Inspired by letters from southern lawyers and his correspondence with Lemann, Frankfurter wrote the chief justice some preliminary thoughts about how to enforce school desegregation. "I suppose that the most important problem is to fashion appropriate provisions against evasion. American experience has shown great fertility in gerrymandering devices," he wrote Warren on July 5. "One need not be cynical or too distrustful of one's fellow-countrymen to assume that there will be not a little temptation to resort to gerrymandering in devising school districts." Frankfurter suggested that the Court obtain information from northern, midwestern, and western states "that have not had racial segregation" about how they assign students to schools: "The Southern States are fever patients. Let us find out, if we can, what healthy bodies do about such things." Despite the disclaimer that he was thinking out loud, Frankfurter revealed his naïveté about de facto racial segregation in northern, midwestern, and western states; he also underestimated the extent of southern opposition.

Frankfurter's reeducation happened quickly. On July 8, he received a phone call from his former colleague and governor of South Carolina, James F. Byrnes. Before the *Brown* decision, Byrnes had threatened to close his state's schools by turning them into all-white private academies and therefore putting them beyond the reach of the Fourteenth Amendment. After the decision, he sounded more conciliatory. During his private conversation with Frankfurter, Byrnes referred to "'chaotic' conditions" in his state and his efforts to prevent state legislators from acting until the Court decided on a remedy. Byrnes, however, would be out of office before the Court issued a decree implementing the decision. Frankfurter assured Byrnes, who was concerned about the date of the oral argument, that southern state officials would have their say. In a letter to Warren, Frankfurter added that "throughout the talk Jim Byrnes could not have been more correct and more reasonable." Byrnes's reasonableness did not last long. A few months later, Warren alerted Frankfurter to Byrnes's public comments about "isolated instances in the border states and 'far more serious ones' in the deep south." Byrnes observed that the disturbances had occurred in West Virginia, Ohio, and Delaware with smaller black populations than in Clarendon County, South Carolina, where the ratio of blacks to whites was ten to one. "Jimmy saddens me," Frankfurter replied to Warren. "Two forces are evidently contending within him—the 'deep' Southerner and the believer in Law, and too often the intuitive, elemental passion prevails."

On July 17, Frankfurter received from Lemann letters from southern lawyers willing to sign a statement of goodwill about implementing the decision. Yet the justice also learned from Lemann that the Louisiana legislature had passed laws designed to circumvent it, and the Mississippi, South Carolina, and Georgia legislatures were expected to follow suit. With Lemann's permission, Frankfurter showed the letters from southern lawyers to the chief justice. "The Lemann correspondence is both thoughtful and enlightening . . . ," Warren told Frankfurter. "I feel certain that even a comparatively few men like him can do much to help the situation which I cannot believe is as bad as his friend . . . believes it to be."

Frankfurter alerted Warren to the opposition in Louisiana and other southern state legislatures and was glad that the oral argument in *Brown II* about the school desegregation remedy would not be scheduled until the justices met in the fall. That way, the argument would take place after the November elections and could not be exploited as a political issue. On September 22, the Court announced oral argument in *Brown II* on December 6.

It was impossible to keep politics out of school desegregation. On September 25, Warren spoke at the College of William & Mary in Williamsburg, Virginia, in honor of Chief Justice John Marshall. Warren's comments that "'we have never failed in our climb toward the pinnacle of true justice' was interpreted as a 'hint of race decision.'" He never mentioned *Brown* but did not have to. Virginia's governor Thomas B. Stanley, attorney general J. Lindsay Almond, U.S. senator Harry Byrd, and other state politicians declined to attend to show their disapproval of the decision. Frankfurter, who attended the event along with Clark and Burton, praised Warren's speech: "I am very glad that we went—and very glad you said what you did and the way you did it."

Jackson, who spent much of the summer recuperating from his heart attack, informed Frankfurter that he had skipped the William & Mary event because he preferred to rest before the new term began. On October 4, the Court opened for business, announced the denial of several hundred petitions for certiorari, issued summary orders in several cases, then adjourned. It was Jackson's last public appearance. That Friday around 2:00 p.m., he felt

very tired in chambers and around 3:00 p.m. laid down in his office to nap
until his drive home two hours later.

Early in the afternoon on Saturday, October 9, Jackson's law clerk E. Barrett
Prettyman, Jr., was working alone in chambers when the telephone rang. It
was Frankfurter. "He said that the justice had died. I was stricken. I couldn't
believe it," Prettyman said. "And then he said, 'And we've got a problem.' He
told me where he had died. He said, 'We have him shopping at Sears and
then at her apartment.' It was rough." Jackson was found in the apartment
of his secretary, Elsie Douglas, with whom he was rumored to be having an
affair. In 1945–1946, the pair had worked together in London and Nuremberg
while Jackson's wife stayed home in McLean, Virginia. Prettyman never forgot the day he walked in on the justice and his secretary in Jackson's office
and saw lipstick on the justice's face. And in his will Jackson left Elsie $1000
as well as all his personal and official papers. The newspapers reported that
Jackson was shopping at Sears at 4500 Wisconsin Avenue, suffered a heart
attack while driving to the Court, and stopped at 4201 Massachusetts Avenue, Douglas's apartment. At 11:45 a.m., his personal physician arrived at the
apartment and pronounced him dead of a heart attack at age sixty-two. The
Court delayed the announcement of Jackson's death for four and a half hours.
Some claim that J. Edgar Hoover leaked the untoward circumstances of where
Jackson was found because of a vendetta with the former attorney general
over wiretapping. Prettyman intimated that Frankfurter may have concocted
the story that Jackson was shopping at Sears in an effort to save Jackson's
family from embarrassment. Either way, Frankfurter's closest friend and colleague was gone.

The Court convened briefly on Monday morning, and Warren paid a brief
tribute to Jackson. The next day, Frankfurter and the justices sat in the front
row at Jackson's funeral before 1000 people at the Washington National
Cathedral. As honorary pallbearers, they stood on both sides of the coffin as
court personnel removed it from the chapel. The justices boarded an overnight train and accompanied the casket to Jamestown, New York, for a second
funeral and burial in nearby Frewsburg. "All of Jamestown turned out for Bob
Jackson's funeral," Frankfurter reported to C. C. Burlingham. "He sure was
the home town boy." Frankfurter understood how Jackson's rural upbringing
shaped his "preference for truculent independence over prudent deference
and conformity" and his congenial yet distant relationships with others: "He
liked his kind without being sentimental about it; he was gregarious but shy
about intimacies."

After the two funerals, Frankfurter fought to preserve Jackson's legacy from sniping commentators. Alistair Cooke contended in the *Manchester Guardian* that former New Dealers Jackson and Frankfurter had turned to the right. Drew Pearson claimed that Jackson was "nervous," and "not in good health" after his return from Nuremberg and "somewhat embittered" about not succeeding Roosevelt as president and being passed over twice for the chief justiceship. A mouthpiece for friends of Black and Douglas, Pearson again blamed Frankfurter for Jackson's blowup at Black despite all evidence to the contrary.

Frankfurter labored for many hours over his short *Columbia Law Review* and *Harvard Law Review* tributes to his staunchest ally. Jackson had accomplished so much in only thirteen years on the Court. He was the best writer since Marshall and Holmes and authored memorable opinions in the second flag salute case, the *Steel Seizure Case*, and many others. His epigrammatic lines and essay-like opinions have resonated with generations of lawyers and judges and reflected his personality. "Justice Jackson wrote as he felt," Frankfurter observed. "In his case the style was the man." Frankfurter argued that Jackson's "style sometimes stole attention from the substance" and was as unpretentious as the man himself: "No man who ever sat on the Supreme Court, it seems to me, mirrored the man in him in his judicial work more completely than did Justice Jackson." Yet Frankfurter also alluded to Jackson's flashes of "temper or irritation." Jackson twice considered quitting the Court, once during the war and again at Nuremberg. His ambition, as a possible successor to Roosevelt and thrice-spurned chief justice candidate, was never satisfied. His temper, especially his fury over Douglas's shenanigans in the *Rosenberg* case, sometimes got the better of his judgment. Passion often guided Jackson's pen. After *Rosenberg*, Frankfurter explained that "the key to Jackson is 'Goddamned is his major premise.'" Jackson understood that his ability to turn a phrase, Frankfurt argued, could be a double-edged sword: "Deeper insight made him aware that the best of phrases may be less than the truth and may even falsify it. He had the habit of truth-seeking and faithfully served justice." Frankfurter recognized that Jackson was at his best as an advocate—as "Solicitor General for life" in Brandeis's view and as the chief U.S. prosecutor at Nuremberg, which Jackson regarded as "the most satisfying and gratifying experience" of his life. The experience changed Jackson, Frankfurter argued, but only for the better. It "had a profound influence on his endeavor to understand the human situation" and made him aware of "how ultimately fragile the forces of reason are and how precious the safeguards of law so painstakingly built up in the course of the centuries." Frankfurter concluded his *Columbia Law Review* tribute on a personal note about his friend and the author of classic Supreme Court opinions: "His voice is stilled. His vitality persists. And not merely in the memory of his familiars. His speech breaks through the printed page. He was one of those rare men whose spoken word survives in type."

For Frankfurter, Jackson's death left a huge void on the Court both as an intellectual ally and friendly seatmate on the bench. After he read Learned Hand's critical comments about Jackson's role in the Nuremberg prosecutions, which Hand viewed as ex post facto show trials, Frankfurter revealed to Hand what he had been telling Marion in private. Without Jackson, life on the Court would never be the same; "the oasis in my desert was swept away." To Hand, Frankfurter exposed his bitter feelings about the minds and personalities of the other seven members on the Court save one or two:

BLACK: "a self-righteous, self-deluded part fanatic, part demagogue, who really disbelieves in Law, thinks it is essentially manipulation of language. Intrinsically, the best brains in the lot—but undisciplined and 'functional' in its employment, an instrument for supporting a predetermined result, not a means for responsible inquiry. Withal, he is quite devoid of play & humor."

REED: "largely vegetable—he has managed to give himself a nimbus of reasonableness but is as unjudicial-minded, as flagrantly moved, at times, by irrelevant considerations for adjudication, as any of them. He has a reasonable voice in the service of a dogmatic, worldly, timid mind."

DOUGLAS: "the most cynical, shamelessly amoral character I've ever known. With him I have no more relation than the necessities of Court work require. He is too unscrupulous for any avoidable entanglement."

BURTON: "a purity of character not excelled by Cardozo. He is the most openminded colleague—unlike Reed, is ready to change his mind & does not deem it a weakness to do so. One has an easy, an inviting access to his mind. The difficulty is with what one finds when one is welcomed to enter it. And he has no humor, no esprit . . . so far as insight and wit are concerned." Frankfurter was not looking forward to sitting next to Burton on the bench because it would not be nearly as much fun as sitting next to Jackson.

CLARK: "very friendly in the slap-on-the-back fashion, in a shallow way no fool, but of course he was without adequate equipment when he came here and no intellectual drive to make up for it now."

MINTON: "gives my risibles the most satisfaction. He has wit and shrewd-ness & he is absolutely straight. He calls them as he sees them—but his sight has very limited range. But he is very [collegial]—he ministers to what you call 'the blue-Danube' in me more than all the others, now that Bob is gone."

WARREN: "the best of the lot from the point of view of the job—not learned, of course, but a good, experienced lawyer for the main tasks of this job, without any side, eager to learn & aware that it takes time & thought to learn, easy in personal relations and up to the symbolism of his office, but not too gay or frolicsome, as Bob was. I like Warren much, respect him even more—but he isn't a playmate . . . as Bob was here."

The subtext of Frankfurter's harsh assessments of his colleagues was that none of them was as good a judge as Hand or Jackson. Nor could any of them offer the type of banter and friendship Frankfurter had with Hand and Jack-son. Frankfurter insisted that Hand "would have found Bob a delight as I did and would sorely miss him as I do."

Jackson's memory was alive in Frankfurter's chambers. Later that year, Frankfurter hired Jackson's secretary Elsie Douglas. He also took on Jackson's law clerk E. Barrett Prettyman, Jr. Prettyman was beginning the second year of his clerkship when Jackson died. That summer and early fall, Prettyman was part of a team of six clerks who researched school desegregation to aid the justices in devising a remedy. On November 17, 1954, the law clerks circulated a "Segregation Research Report" to the justices. By that time, Frankfurter had persuaded Jackson's successor to hire Prettyman "virtually sight unseen."

FROM THE OUTSET, Frankfurter knew that John Marshall Harlan II was the leading candidate for Jackson's seat. In January 1954, Attorney General Her-bert Brownell had succeeded in persuading Eisenhower to name Harlan to succeed Augustus Hand on the Second Circuit. A Princeton graduate and Rhodes scholar who studied law for three years at Oxford's Balliol College, Harlan attended New York Law School at night while working for the Root, Clark firm run by Frankfurter's longtime friend Emory Buckner. When Buckner was named U.S. attorney for the Southern District of New York in 1925, Harlan joined him as an assistant prosecutor who enforced Prohibition. Two years later, Harlan returned to the firm and worked there before and after his World War II service in the Army Air Forces. In 1951, Harlan was named chief counsel to the New York State Crime Commission before becoming a Second Circuit judge. Buckner had died in 1941 so Frankfurter turned to other friends to find out whether Harlan would be a good judge. On the basis of Harlan's advocacy skills, Learned Hand predicted that Harlan would be an "outstanding" justice; Hand's Second Circuit colleague Thomas Swan agreed. Frankfurter passed along the endorsements to Warren, the only person on the Court who could influence the Eisenhower administration. On November 8, Eisenhower followed his attorney general's advice and named Harlan to the Court.

As the grandson and namesake of the dissenter in *Plessy v. Ferguson*, John Marshall Harlan II was red meat for southern politicians spoiling for a fight about *Brown*. It did not matter that Harlan, a cautious, conservative Republican, was nothing like his radical Kentucky grandfather, or that the Court's school segregation decisions had not invoked the first Justice Harlan's *Plessy* dissent. The Georgia House of Representatives passed a resolution decrying Harlan's nomination as a "direct slur to the people of the South." Six Southern Democrats who dominated the Senate Judiciary Committee succeeded in delaying the nomination for more than four months. Senator James Eastland of Mississippi, the segregationist committee chairman, delayed for so long that Eisenhower had to renominate Harlan in the new Congress. The committee accused Harlan of harboring "Communist sympathies" and being a "one-worlder" who favored world government over the United States. The southerners on the committee compelled Harlan, like Frankfurter sixteen years earlier, to testify. Recalling his own experiences with Senator McCarran, Frankfurter wished Harlan luck and urged him to stand his ground. During his brief appearance on February 25, 1955, not a single senator asked Harlan about *Brown*. Eastland inquired whether the Court "should change established interpretations of the Constitution to accord with the economic, political, and sociological views" of the justices. Harlan removed his horned-rim glasses and replied: "To lay the inquiry bare, as I understand it, you are asking me how I would have voted on the segregation issue?" Eastland quickly backtracked: "No, sir. That has not anything to do with it." On March 16, 1955, the Senate voted, 71–11, to confirm Harlan. Nine southern senators voted no. The storm had barely begun.

Taking an instant liking to Harlan, Frankfurter described him as well mannered on the bench and at conference and predicted that he would be a much better judge than his grandfather. Frankfurter believed the first justice Harlan's "Constitution is colorblind" rhetoric in his *Plessy* dissent was inconsistent with his subsequent opinion in *Cummings* upholding racially segregated schools and as a result his reputation as an "anti-segregationist" with "the 'liberals'" was "undeserved." Harlan's grandson was a different story. "John will carry weight here—he has persuasiveness, an atmosphere of reasonableness like Reed, but unlike Reed, also a good head," Frankfurter wrote Learned Hand. Frankfurter correctly predicted that he and Harlan would be close allies. Yet, for Frankfurter, Harlan lacked Jackson's earthiness, edge, and sense of fun: "I miss Bob terribly."

With the delay over Harlan's nomination, oral argument over the enforcement of the school segregation decisions was postponed until April 11. The justices heard four days and thirteen hours of argument, most of which was inconsequential. No one on the Court supported the NAACP's request for a decree "forthwith"—immediate desegregation—or even a one-year deadline. There was no way to enforce such a decision. Publicly, President Eisenhower offered no personal opinion about *Brown* other than "to uphold" and to "obey" it out of a sense of duty; privately, he preferred a "moderate" ruling and gradual implementation. The justices favored a similar approach.

The oral argument, which included advocates for the defendant school districts and other states, reinforced the obstinacy of the southern opposition. Chief Justice Warren asked an attorney representing Clarendon County, South Carolina, whether "there would be an honest attempt to conform to this decree, if we did leave it to the district court?" The attorney replied: "Let us get the word 'honest' out of there." "No," Warren snapped, "leave it in." "No," the attorney finally answered, "because I would have to tell you that right now we would not conform; we would not send our white children to the Negro schools." An attorney representing the Prince Edward County, Virginia, school board claimed that one of the problems of desegregation was that black students had lower IQ test scores and higher rates of tuberculosis, syphilis, gonorrhea, and illegitimacy. He argued that "white parents at this time will not appropriate the money to put their children among other children with that sort of background." Thurgood Marshall, in his rebuttal for the NAACP, responded to the health argument that "it is interesting to me that the very people that argue for this side would object to sending their white children to school with Negroes, are eating food that has been prepared, served, and almost put in their mouths by the mothers of those children."

A frequent participant in the four days of questioning, Frankfurter had been working since February with his law clerks on four different desegregation decrees. On April 14, the last day of oral argument, he shared a memorandum with Warren that offered two possible alternatives: (1) "a 'bare bones' decree" enjoining the race-based exclusion of children from any public school in the defendant school districts and remanding the cases to district court judges; or (2) a more detailed order laying out "some standards" for implementing the decisions to prevent evasion yet providing district judges with enough flexibility to adapt to local conditions. The advantage of the first option was that it maximized flexibility; the disadvantage of the second one was the Court's ignorance about local conditions. He did not share with Warren a third option, which asked the Court to appoint special masters, or a fourth option, which was a detailed decree. Frankfurter understood the Court's institutional limitations: "Platitude though it be, it does become relevant to say that we do not propose to operate as a super-school board. But the Court can say that school districts must be 'geographically compact and contiguous.'" He still saw the problem as one of gerrymandering or subtle evasion, not outright defiance. In a cover note, Frankfurter explained that his views were "tentative" and advised Warren not to take a vote at the upcoming conference: "From what Brethren have said to me I am sure time will be needed for various feelings and impressions and worries to coagulate into what I deeply hope will be one expression of the Nine." Frankfurter's goal was the same as Warren's: another unanimous opinion.

At conference on April 16, Warren began by explaining what the Court "should not do": no special masters as requested by the Eisenhower Justice Department and no fixed date for desegregating schools. Instead, he believed the decree should provide guidance to lower courts. Black, whose Alabama roots gave him the most insight into the difficulties of implementing the decision in the Deep South, explained that white people in the South were taught to dislike federal officials because of the race issue. He predicted there would be massive efforts to circumvent any decree. Along those lines, Black preferred a very narrow decree declaring racially segregated schools unconstitutional, admitting only the seven named plaintiffs on a nonsegregated basis, and making no mention that the cases were class actions. "Nothing could injure the court more," he warned, "than to issue orders that cannot be enforced." Reed, like Black, wanted something short with no mention of class actions. Frankfurter insisted "by all means there should be an opinion" and emphasized that "this is a slow process and something should be said about it." He also suggested remanding the cases to three-judge panels rather than putting the onus on a single judge. Douglas agreed there should be an opinion, and the Court should set no deadline; he also had concerns about any remedy beyond the named plaintiffs. Burton disagreed that the admission of seven children would make a difference and insisted the problem was the color line; above all, he wanted a unanimous opinion. Clark agreed mostly with Frankfurter and wanted to be "careful what we say." Minton agreed that unanimity was key, doubted the necessity of an opinion, but did not want "big talk in [an] opinion and little talk in [a] decree." Harlan also agreed that it must be unanimous, believed an opinion could be helpful, and was particularly struck by Black's comments.

On April 28, Warren drafted a memorandum about what he planned to say and not to say in the opinion. He vowed that the decrees would be "as simple and as uniform as possible" and serve as "guideposts" to give three-judge district courts "maximum leeway." The opinion would not include supervision by the Supreme Court, a special master, a time limit for completion, specific instructions, mention of class actions, or any of the principles in the *Brown* opinion. The opinion would include the fact that on May 17, 1954, *Brown* held racially segregated schools to be unconstitutional and that the enforcement of those rights should take into account local conditions. The three-judge district courts should require that the defendants "in good-faith, make an immediate, reasonable start toward full compliance with our May 17, 1954 ruling."

Frankfurter suggested several changes to Warren's memorandum. First, instead of characterizing *Brown* as outlawing segregation, he inserted discrimination. Second, he suggested that the sentence about good faith and a reasonable start end with a quotation from Holmes's 1911 opinion in *Virginia v. West Virginia*—"with all deliberate speed." Holmes attributed the phrase to the English Chancery court; the only known reference was in British poet Francis Thompson's 1893 poem, "The Hound of Heaven" ("And unperturbed pace, / Deliberate Speed"). Frankfurter's campaign for the inclusion of the phrase had only just begun.

In mid-to-late May, Warren began drafting an opinion in *Brown II*. Before he circulated it to the entire Court, the chief justice showed the draft to Frankfurter. Frankfurter read it twice and on May 24 again asked Warren to change good-faith compliance "at the earliest practicable date" to "with all deliberate speed." He explained Holmes's phrase in *Virginia v. West Virginia* as emphasizing the difficulty of enforcing a judicial order against a state. Three days later, Frankfurter pressed for the inclusion of his preferred language once more: "I still strongly believe that 'with all deliberate speed' conveys more effectively the process of time for the effectuation of our decision." He emphasized the importance of a citation to *Virginia v. West Virginia* because, in trying to get West Virginia to pay its share of debts to Virginia prior to becoming a separate state, it was "the nearest experience this Court has had in trying to get obedience from a state for a decision highly unpalatable to it." He was realistic about the Court's institutional ability to force the southern states to desegregate their schools: "I think it is highly desirable to educate public opinion—the parties themselves and the general public—to an understanding that we are at the beginning of a process of enforcement and not concluding it."

Willing to accommodate Frankfurter, Warren included the "all deliberate speed" language, yet, to Frankfurter's dismay, failed to contextualize the phrase by citing *Virginia v. West Virginia*. On May 31, Warren announced the Court's unanimous opinion in *Brown II*, which reiterated *Brown*'s holding that "racial discrimination in public education is unconstitutional" and ordered district courts to use "practical flexibility" in shaping remedies and to adjust for "public and private needs." *Brown II* emphasized the "personal interest of the plaintiffs in admission to public schools as soon as practicable on a nondiscriminatory basis." Before granting any extensions of time because of local conditions, Warren's opinion reiterated that "the courts will require that the defendants make a prompt and reasonable start toward full compliance . . ." Finally, *Brown II* remanded the cases to district courts and instructed them "to take such proceedings and enter such orders and decrees consistent with this opinion as are necessary and proper to admit to public schools on a racially nondiscriminatory basis with all deliberate speed the parties to these cases." The day the Court announced *Brown II*, Frankfurter wrote the chief justice a handwritten note: "The harvest of today's planting won't be fully assessed for many a day. For me it's a safe bet that the wisest historian of the Court a half century hence will acclaim the long-headed wisdom of what your opinion said and not less so what it didn't say. In any event, I am content."

What Frankfurter could not have imagined was how "all deliberate speed" became a touchstone for southern delay and opposition to school desegregation and how his insistence on "all deliberate speed" made him the fall guy for the Court's failed gradualist approach. Ever since Phil Elman had suggested a delayed remedy in the Truman Justice Department's brief, however, the justices recognized that any compliance would have to be gradual. No one on the Court supported an opinion in *Brown II* calling for the immediate desegregation of all southern schools because such an opinion was unenforceable. Black, who knew the Deep South better than any of the other justices, said as much at conference. He tried to narrow the Court's remedial approach by removing any references to class actions and emphasizing the rights of the named plaintiffs. In Black's ideal world, *Brown II* would have ordered the token integration of seven black students into white schools. As the Court soon realized, even token integration was nearly impossible in some southern states with segregationist governors. *Brown II* could have explicitly asked Congress and the president for assistance, but such support was years away. The opinion could not have been written in any way to break down southern resistance. Frankfurter's insistence on the "all deliberate speed" language may have been too colorful. Yet, if anything, it reflected his clear-eyed recognition about how difficult it was for the Court to force a recalcitrant state to comply (which a citation to *Virginia v. West Virginia* and brief discussion of the case would have clarified). It would not be the last time he emphasized the Court's institutional limitations and was content to play the long game.

USUALLY, the Frankfurters left Washington for the summer for Connecticut or western Massachusetts and socializing with friends. In 1955, however, they installed air conditioning in their Georgetown home and hunkered down. Marion's health made her unwilling to travel. In fact, she secluded herself in her room and refused to come out, even for meals. For the past ten years, she had been suffering from weakness in her leg. The cause was an undiagnosed arthritic condition in her left hip. After several years of tests and visits to doctors, she saw a specialist at George Washington University Hospital, Dr. Thomas McPherson Brown. Dr. Brown diagnosed her with rheumatoid arthritis in her hip but not the kind that caused any pain. The problem was not Dr. Brown's diagnosis but his unusual method of treatment. He believed that arthritis was caused by bacteria, prescribed daily doses of antibiotics, and claimed to have improved the lives of thousands of patients. The theory and treatment have been widely discredited since then by the medical profession. Yet in 1955 the Frankfurters placed their faith in Dr. Brown and believed the treatment would work.

Marion chose to stay in her room. She confided to Isaiah Berlin her desire "to turn in, to be alone, to discover. . . . I don't mind a bit. I made little enough of my youth when I had it." She spent her days reading books. Her intellectual depth and inner life once made her attractive and intimidating to Berlin, other British intellectuals, and journalist Joseph Alsop but not anymore. In letters to Berlin, she criticized their friends. She wondered how Arthur Schlesinger, Jr., could be "so naïve" in relying on Harold Ickes's "doubtful" diaries for the first of three forthcoming volumes about Franklin Roosevelt's presidency, and she hoped that Phil and Katharine Graham returned from Britain with more "sensitiveness and humility." One of the few things that made her happy was Berlin's visits from Oxford.

Marion contrasted her dour state of mind with her husband's: "I see only the despondent to be sure, except Felix, whose whistle seems to my ear to get more forced all the time, but I may be wrong." Friends believed that the times had passed the Frankfurters by with the Democrats out of political power for the first time in twenty years and liberals in exile. He could no longer enter the back door of the White House to talk to FDR or get the inside scoop on the Truman administration during walks to work with Acheson or from White House aides David Niles and Max Lowenthal. Alsop described the Frankfurters as having "the feeling that they were the most privileged of spectator sportsmen—onlookers of great events with permanently reserved ringside seats—which the last 20 years gave them." The columnist admired Frankfurter "more with each passing year & I'm afraid her less. That sensibility that inner life no longer so intimidates me. And although you can say what you please about his judgment you cannot deny him courage & goodness of heart—qualities which our new Washington make more precious by the day."

The burden of Marion's illness and seclusion fell on her husband. He enjoyed people so much yet because of her health rarely traveled and curtailed most of his social outings. Every night they ate dinner together on trays in her room. He waited on her during the weekends when their household staff was away. On Sundays, he perked himself up with phone calls to friends. Occasionally, she encouraged him to travel to New York City to see a Broadway show and visit with C. C. Burlingham, to dine with the Achesons, or to attend the Gridiron dinner to gather gossip. She learned about the outside world entirely through him. To friends, he described Marion "as happy as she has ever been. I'm not suggesting euphoria. I do say that being a woman of internal resources and never having given a damn about the so-called social life of Washington, she feels that on the whole she doesn't miss anything by that part of the world which is shut out from her and derives great relish from the books that she reads and from so much of the world as I bring to her from without. And speaking for myself, I can assure you that we have nothing but a good time . . ." His adoration for his wife was undimmed. Nonetheless, the man who relished interactions with other people squeezed them into his working hours at the Court and rare nights out.

AT WORK, Frankfurter's primary concern was protecting "the Court as an institution." Yet he derided references to "lack of institutional awareness" and "the Court as a team" as phrases devoid of meaning. Earlier that year, he had written his former law clerks asking them for their ideas about the Court as an institution. He agreed with Elliot Richardson's response that it meant deferring to legislative policy judgments and avoiding unnecessary constitutional questions. Frankfurter channeled his law clerks' responses into one of his most important essays.

During the summer of 1955, he immersed himself in the constitutional opinions of Chief Justice John Marshall in preparation for an address at Harvard Law School commemorating the 200th anniversary of Marshall's birth. The September 23 lecture, "John Marshall and the Judicial Function," emphasized Marshall's "hardheaded appreciation of the complexities of government" and "deep instinct for the practical." He referred to Marshall's "ambiguously expressed" opinion in *Gibbons v. Ogden,* which deemed Congress's power to regulate interstate and foreign commerce to be plenary but not exclusive (thereby leaving room for some state regulation). This led Marshall to permit state interference with interstate commerce in *Willson v. Black Bird Creek* and to strike a "vitally important accommodation between national and local needs." Frankfurter could have added Marshall's opinion in *Marbury v. Madison* striking down a federal law for the first time while refusing to order the Jefferson administration to give William Marbury his commission as justice of the peace. Marshall also struck cautious notes in *McCulloch v. Maryland* establishing implied federal powers but not grounding the constitutionality of the national bank in the Commerce Clause or any other express congressional power.

In his Marshall lecture, Frankfurter pivoted into a discussion about the role of the judiciary in the American system of government. He acknowledged the difficulties of adjudicating claims on the basis of the Fourteenth Amendment's vague commands of due process and equal protection: "Only for those who have not the responsibility of decision can it be easy to decide the grave and complex problems they raise, especially in controversies that excite public interest." Those clauses are hard to interpret because they "are precisely defined neither by history nor in terms." He referred to the Court's conclusion in *Brown* that the history of the Fourteenth Amendment was "inconclusive" on the issue of racially segregated schools and "not for want of searching inquiry by Court and counsel." He warned that the "vagueness" of due process and equal protection could "make of the Court a third chamber with drastic veto power."

In reviewing attempts to limit judicial power, he argued that "courts have a strong tendency to abstain from constitutional controversies." He referred to Brandeis's call for constitutional avoidance in his concurrence in *Ashwander v. Tennessee Valley Authority*. He also pointed to the overruling of infamous Supreme Court decisions including the Fourteenth Amendment's rejection of *Dred Scott*'s declaration that blacks were not citizens under the Constitution, the Sixteenth Amendment's overriding the Court's decision invalidating the income tax, and the Supreme Court's 1937 decision in *West Coast Hotel v. Parrish* reversing *Adkins v. Children's Hospital*'s declaration that minimum-wage laws violated "liberty of contract."

Near the end of his lecture about "government under law," Frankfurter pleaded guilty to harboring "an old-fashioned liberal's view" of "the humane and gradualist tradition in dealing with refractory social and political problems, recognizing them to be fractious because of their complexity and not amenable to quick and propitious solutions without resort to methods which deny law as the instrument and offspring of reason." He denied that he preferred "the limited scope of judicial enforcement of laws"; rather, he advocated "the pervasiveness throughout the whole range of government of the spirit of law." He warned that courts "release contagious consequences" every time they agree to hear a case and seemed to be speaking directly to his interventionist Court colleagues Black and Douglas: "If judges want to be preachers, they should dedicate themselves to the pulpit; if judges want to be primary shapers of policy, the legislature is their place. Self-willed judges are the least defensible offenders against government under law."

Frankfurter's "John Marshall and the Judicial Function" simultaneously defended the Court's decision in *Brown v. Board of Education* and outlined a more cautious role for the Court in the post-*Brown* legal and political arena. Shortly after his address in the fall of 1955, Frankfurter displayed a Marshallian awareness of the Court's institutional limitations, the virtues of constitutional avoidance, and a belief that the judiciary cannot solve the country's social problems in one fell swoop. He tried to head off a constitutional question he saw as fraught with danger—state interracial marriage bans.

The case of Ham Say Naim began as an immigration matter. A Chinese national, Naim abandoned a British merchant vessel in favor of an American ship and in 1947 made Norfolk, Virginia, his home port. Five years later, he met Ruby Elaine Lamberth, a white woman from Saginaw, Michigan. They moved in together in Norfolk and on June 26, 1952, were married in Elizabeth City, North Carolina. They got married in another state because Virginia's Racial Integrity Act of 1924 prohibited whites from marrying non-whites. In September 1953, Ham's seamen's visa was about to expire. He sought assistance from David Carliner, a radical immigration attorney, to assist him in obtaining permanent resident status. After Ham obtained counsel, Ruby filed for divorce on the grounds of adultery (she was also allegedly committing adultery). The state trial judge annulled the Naims' marriage because it was barred by the state's Racial Integrity Act of 1924. On June 13, 1955, the Virginia Supreme Court of Appeals declared the marriage void and upheld the constitutionality of the Racial Integrity Act. The Fourteenth Amendment, the state supreme court declared, did not prevent a state "from enacting legislation to preserve the racial integrity of its citizens, or which denies the power of the State to regulate the marriage relation so that it shall not have a mongrel breed of citizens."

Naim was not the first time after *Brown* Frankfurter and his colleagues had confronted the issue of miscegenation. In November 1954, the Court had declined to hear the case of Linnie Jackson, a black Alabama woman sentenced to two years in prison for living with a white man in violation of the state's interracial cohabitation and marriage law. The Court denied Jackson's petition for certiorari without comment.

A year later, Naim's lawyer Carliner sought advice from Phil Elman, Frankfurter's former clerk who was working in the solicitor's general office. Carliner asked Elman if the Justice Department would support his appeal of the Virginia Supreme Court of Appeals's decision upholding the Racial Integrity Act to the U.S. Supreme Court. Elman told him that the timing was all wrong. It was too soon after *Brown*. Elman's liberal boss, Solicitor General Simon Sobeloff, agreed. Elman also raised the issue privately with Frankfurter, who said that bringing the case to the Court was a "big mistake." Carliner disregarded Elman's advice. Because the case was an appeal from a state court decision rejecting a federal constitutional claim, Carliner filed a notice of appeal, rather than petition for certiorari, to trigger the Court's mandatory jurisdiction. Elman preferred a discretionary certiorari petition that would have given the Court the opportunity to decline to hear the case.

At conference on November 4, Frankfurter opposed hearing the *Naim* appeal. "So far as I recall," he read to his colleagues from a short memorandum, "this is the first time since I've been here that I am confronted with the task of resolving a conflict between moral and technical legal considerations." He explained that the Court had a lot of discretion to decide whether an issue was "substantial" enough to hear on appeal. He argued that "a Court containing Holmes, Brandeis, Hughes, Stone and Cardozo" would have declined to hear the case. He reminded his colleagues of the number of state laws at stake, the "deep feeling" and "moral and psychological presuppositions," and concluded that "the issue has not reached that compelling demand for consideration which precludes refusal to consider it." Finally, he addressed the elephant in the room: his fear that the "moral considerations" raised by the miscegenation issue would interfere with "the enforcement of its decision in the segregation cases." He predicted that a decision on the constitutionality of interracial marriage would "very seriously, embarrass the carrying-out of the Court's decree of last May."

On November 4, Frankfurter and four other justices (Burton, Clark, Minton, and Harlan) voted to dismiss the case; four others (Warren, Black, Douglas, and Reed) voted to hear it. The Court held the case over for a week. Frankfurter's concerns were premised on a record free of "subsidiary or preliminary questions." At conference on November 11, Burton raised the issue that the state supreme court had jumped to the Fourteenth Amendment question rather than consider whether it was bound by the Constitution's Full Faith and Credit Clause to recognize marriage licenses from other states. Another problem, raised by Clark, was that the state was not a party to the case; *Naim v. Naim* was a private marital dispute in which one side requested an annulment. Two justices, Warren and Reed, decided to vote with the majority and to issue an order vacating and remanding the case to the Virginia Supreme Court of Appeals.

Working with Clark on the order and expecting input from Reed, Warren, and other justices, Frankfurter suggested "the shortest and least explicit formula" in an effort to keep the instructions to the Virginia Supreme Court of Appeals as vague as possible. On November 14, the Court issued an unsigned order citing the "inadequacy of the record" about the relationship of the parties at the time of their marriage in North Carolina and upon their return to Virginia and "the failure of the parties to bring here all the questions relevant to the disposition of the case," an allusion to the full faith and credit claim. These two issues prevented the Court from addressing the constitutionality of the miscegenation law "'in clean-cut and concrete form, unclouded' by such problems." After vacating the judgment, the Court instructed the Virginia Supreme Court of Appeals to remand the case to the trial court "for action not inconsistent with this opinion."

On January 18, 1956, the Virginia Supreme Court of Appeals thumbed its nose at the nation's highest court. It claimed there were no state procedures to remand the case to the trial court and considered the matter closed: "The decree of the trial court and the decree of this court affirming it have become final so far as these courts are concerned." The *Washington Post* observed: "Did the State's highest court have a chip on its shoulder because of the

Supreme Court's segregation ruling? Virginians asked. Was this open defiance?" The Richmond *Times-Dispatch* praised the state supreme court and charged that the Supreme Court of the United States "sought to interfere with a State court's handling of matters over which the Federal court has no jurisdiction." Instead of defiance, the newspaper described the Virginia Supreme Court of Appeals's opinion as having "deftly put the Federal court in its place."

On February 2, Carliner filed a motion in the U.S. Supreme Court to recall the mandate and to set the case for oral argument. A month later, the justices voted 6–3 to deny the motion but held the case over for a week. On March 9, the Court voted five (Frankfurter, Burton, Minton, Clark, and Harlan) to four (Black, Douglas, Reed, and Warren) not to reopen the case. Black initially wanted his dissent noted but changed his mind. On March 12, the Court denied the motion because the Virginia Supreme Court of Appeals's second decision "leaves the case devoid of a properly presented federal question."

There was an important reason why the justices, at Frankfurter's urging, ducked *Naim v. Naim* and the issue of interracial marriage—the Court was busy desegregating other aspects of southern life that went way beyond primary and secondary schools. On October 10, 1955, it had affirmed an injunction against the University of Alabama that prevented it from discriminating against Autherine Lucy and other black undergraduate students. The Court began issuing unsigned, one-paragraph orders about the desegregation of public accommodations without elaborating on the reasoning of *Brown*, which was limited to the importance of education. On November 7, 1955, the Court had affirmed a court of appeals decision ordering the city of Baltimore and the state of Maryland to desegregate public beaches and bathhouses. The same day, the Court reversed a lower court decision that allocated an Atlanta municipal golf course to different races on different days of the week and ordered the golf course desegregated pursuant to its decision in the Baltimore beaches case.

The cases about Baltimore's beaches and Atlanta's municipal golf courses essentially overruled *Plessy's* "separate but equal" doctrine. The same day it again declined to hear *Naim v. Naim*, the Court issued a one-paragraph decision ordering the University of Florida College of Law to admit a 48-year-old black student, Virgil Hawkins. Hawkins had been seeking admission since 1949 on the basis of the Court's decisions desegregating graduate and professional schools. Even after the Supreme Court's March 12 decision, the Florida Supreme Court refused to admit him and insisted on states' rights.

The biggest news on March 12, 1956, came not from the Supreme Court in the case of Ham Say Naim or Virgil Hawkins but from the halls of Congress.

On the floor of the U.S. Senate, Senator Walter F. George, a Georgia Democrat, read a "Declaration of Constitutional Principles." Nineteen southern senators and seventy-seven representatives signed the legal response to the school segregation cases, the "Southern Manifesto." The drafters included Senator Strom Thurmond, a South Carolina Democrat, and a trio of experienced constitutional lawyers including Senator Sam Ervin, Jr., a North Carolina Democrat. Their response to *Brown* appealed not to violence but to the Constitution. "The unwarranted decision of the Supreme Court in the public school cases," the manifesto began, "is now bearing the fruit always produced when men substitute naked power for established law." It declared that the decision circumvented the process of constitutional amendment, was "a clear abuse of judicial power," usurped the power of Congress to legislate, and "encroach[ed] upon the reserved rights of the States and the people." The manifesto then proceeded to critique *Brown* by invoking the Constitution's text and history, the Court's precedents, and custom. It argued that the text of the Constitution did not mention education. The history revealed that the same Congress that proposed the Fourteenth Amendment also agreed to segregate the District of Columbia's public schools. And at the time of the amendment's adoption, twenty-six of the thirty-seven states had some form of segregated schools. The manifesto then observed that the Court approved of segregated schools in 1849 in Boston, held in *Plessy v. Ferguson* in 1896 that the "separate but equal" doctrine did not violate the Fourteenth Amendment, and unanimously reaffirmed the constitutionality of segregated schools in 1927 in *Gong Lum v. Rice*. As a result of these decisions, the manifesto argued that racial segregation "became a part of the life of the people of many of the States and confirmed their habits, customs, traditions, and way of life." It invoked early twentieth century due process decisions to insist that "parents should not be deprived by Government of the right to direct the lives and education of their own children." The justices, the manifesto asserted, "undertook to exercise their naked judicial power and substituted their personal political and social ideas for the established law of the land." The manifesto, which George read into the Senate record and Representative Howard Smith of Virginia read into the record in the House, praised the states "which have declared the intention to resist forced integration by any lawful means."

The Southern Manifesto exposed the weaknesses of Warren's opinion in limiting the reasoning of *Brown* to education and writing it like a layman's document rather than a constitutional lawyer's brief. After George and Thurmond spoke, two Senate liberals, Wayne Morse of Oregon and Hubert Humphrey of Minnesota, offered responses that Frankfurter described as "uneducative." Frankfurter was disappointed that moderate southern senators, Lister Hill of Alabama and William Fulbright of Arkansas, had signed the document. Only three southern senators, led by Majority Leader Lyndon Johnson, refused to sign it.

Unable to respond to the Southern Manifesto from his seat on the Court, Frankfurter relied on two protégés in the legal academy, Alexander Bickel and Paul Freund. A junior scholar on a two-year contract at Harvard, Bickel had accepted a permanent offer at Yale. Frankfurter made an impassioned plea to Dean Erwin Griswold and other members of the Harvard law faculty to hire Bickel; Griswold, however, insisted that the faculty thought the young scholar needed more seasoning and "maturity." As close to Frankfurter as any former clerk, Bickel had played an integral role during the first round of argument in the school segregation cases. Frankfurter sent Bickel a copy of his memorandum to the Court about *Naim v. Naim*. Bickel replied that he assumed the memorandum "had its effect on those who don't like to 'duck.'" At the time, Frankfurter strongly encouraged Bickel to publish his history of the Fourteenth Amendment as an article in the *Harvard Law Review*. After seeking advice from Frankfurter, Bickel responded to James F. Byrnes in print after the former South Carolina governor mischaracterized the article and the Fourteenth Amendment's inconclusive history.

Given Bickel's knowledge of the history of the Fourteenth Amendment, the Southern Manifesto was in his wheelhouse. In a *New Republic* article, "Ninety-Six Congressmen versus the Nine Justices," he described the manifesto as a moderate compromise and praised its faith in the Constitution and its pledge to resist *Brown* " 'by any lawful means.' " Then he countered that the Court had provided for the only "lawful means" by allowing for gradual desegregation. As for the history of the Fourteenth Amendment, he challenged the manifesto's premises. He said an amendment specifying segregated or desegregated schools would not have received a two-thirds vote. Instead, as with other constitutional provisions, the Thirty-Ninth Congress "deliberately chose broad language capable of growth and application to matters and in circumstances not foreseeable in 1866." The intent of the framers of the amendment, therefore, was irrelevant. To the manifesto's argument that the Constitution does not mention education, he responded that it also does not mention the Air Force, minimum wages, collective bargaining, or traffic in narcotics, either. He concluded with a quote from James Bradley Thayer that the Constitution was " 'astonishingly well adapted for the purposes of a great, developing nation, shows its wisdom mainly in the shortness and generality of its provisions, in its silence, and its abstinence from petty limitations.' "

Frankfurter praised Bickel's response to the Southern Manifesto as "superb" and "deftly and devastatingly done."

Compared to Bickel, Frankfurter's relationship with former student Paul Freund was longer and deeper. In 1931, Frankfurter had marveled at Freund as president of the *Harvard Law Review* and selected him as a graduate research fellow and to clerk for Brandeis. After working in the Treasury Department, Reconstruction Finance Corporation, and in the solicitor general's office during the 1930s, Freund had joined the Harvard law faculty as a lecturer in 1939 and emerged as a leading constitutional law scholar. In 1954, he published the first edition of a constitutional law casebook that influenced thousands of students. Frankfurter made Freund the executor of Brandeis's papers and hoped that Freund would write Brandeis's biography. The justice also tapped Freund for a larger historical project, the editorship of the Holmes Devise series on the history of the Supreme Court. Funded from Holmes's estate, the Freund-led project involved working with the Library of Congress and selecting leading scholars to complete different volumes on the Court's history. A gifted stylist, Freund excelled at short essays and speeches.

In the first of two articles in the *Christian Science Monitor* defending *Brown*, Freund attacked the Southern Manifesto's argument about the Fourteenth Amendment's text and history. The textual argument that the Fourteenth Amendment does not mention education, Freund wrote, "proves much too much." The applicable language of the amendment was written broadly. The silence of the Constitution, he wrote, supports neither segregation nor desegregation. As for the historical argument that the framers of the Fourteenth Amendment did not intend to outlaw segregated education, Freund responded that this was "undoubtedly true" but only because of "the relatively minor role of public education at the time." In light of this fact, Freund agreed that the legislative history was "inconclusive." Frankfurter praised Freund's articles about the school segregation cases as "exquisitely good." Frankfurter also lauded Freund's commencement speech at Washington University in St. Louis on the rule of law as best response to "the kind of outlook that lies behind that congressional Manifesto."

During the early morning of July 14, someone burned a six-foot cross, "still smoldering," on the front lawn of the Frankfurters' home at 3018 Dumbarton Avenue. A cross also had been burned in front of the northwest Washington apartment building of Solicitor General Simon Sobeloff accompanied by a partially burned sign that said: "Sobeloff . . . Jew." Two men in a car with Virginia license plates left the scene after burning a six-foot cross in front of the Sheraton (Wardman) Park hotel where Chief Justice Earl Warren lived. Someone also burned an eight-foot cross at the home of the chairman of the Belts-ville, Maryland, branch of the NAACP. "Good God! And poor fools!" Bickel wrote Frankfurter. "Do they know whom they're trying to scare?" Frankfurter was not scared. He had battled Theodore Roosevelt over the Bisbee depor-tation and the Mooney case, A. Mitchell Palmer and J. Edgar Hoover over the Palmer raids, A. Lawrence Lowell over the proposed quota against Jew-ish undergraduates at Harvard, the Massachusetts State Police and most of Old Boston over Sacco and Vanzetti, Senator McCarran over his nomination, Westbrook Pegler and other Red baiters during the second Red Scare, and many others more powerful and frightening than a cross-burner.

Frankfurter engineered the Court's avoidance of the interracial marriage issue in *Naim v. Naim* not because he was scared or a crypto-conservative or because he was having second thoughts about the school segregation deci-sions. He was more attuned to the Court's institutional limitations than were many of his colleagues. He was troubled that the Court was initiating social change rather than taking its cue from Congress or the president. He knew that the elected branches had the power to cripple the judiciary. He saw that Black's prediction was coming true; the storm over the Court was in full swing.

CHAPTER 35

Red Monday

On a sweltering 90-degree day, Frankfurter walked in the academic processional through Harvard Yard next to Pulitzer Prize–winning historian Paul Buck, past the statue of John Harvard and the graduating seniors from the class of 1956, and to his seat on the stage. One of the graduation speakers, Senator John F. Kennedy, walked behind Frankfurter. The 39-year-old Kennedy told the audience of more than 15,000 people that the nation needed more cooperation between scholars and politicians. Politicians, Kennedy argued, "need both the technical judgment and the disinterested viewpoint of the scholar, to prevent us from becoming imprisoned by our own slogans." Both Kennedy and Frankfurter, who chatted after the ceremony, received honorary doctor of laws.

Frankfurter's honorary degree was long overdue, especially compared to that of the young senator whose intellectual gifts he questioned. The 73-year-old justice was the Court's oldest member and had served twenty-five years on the Harvard law faculty. The anti-Semitic Harvard president A. Lawrence Lowell never would have awarded him anything after their clashes over a proposed 15 percent quota on Jewish undergraduates, the Sacco-Vanzetti case, and a host of other issues. And Lowell's successor, James Conant, was equally hostile and resented Frankfurter's meddling with Roosevelt and Truman on atomic energy policy. Frankfurter's friends on the Harvard Corporation, Board of Overseers, and faculty prevailed upon the new president, Nathan Pusey, to honor the justice. At the ceremony, Pusey read Frankfurter's citation: "A brilliant and exciting teacher, he has brought to the highest court of the land the stimulus of an incisive mind." The citation, though true, missed a central point of Frankfurter's career. He had dedicated a lifetime to building bridges between the academy and government and encouraging his former students to use their legal expertise and problem-solving skills in public service. His liberal network exemplified Senator Kennedy's call for experts in government.

Frankfurter's protégés excelled during the New Deal and found an inspiring leader in Franklin Roosevelt. On Memorial Day, 1956, Frankfurter had spoken to 350 people at the president's Hyde Park gravesite about how Roosevelt "cannot escape becoming a national saga, enshrined in myths" like Lincoln. The day before the Harvard graduation ceremonies, Frankfurter had been "100 per cent of the show" at Harvard's law school and graduate school alumni day on Harkness Commons as he discussed what the law school had been like fifty years earlier under Dean James Barr Ames and how the law school had prepared its graduates for public service. He observed that the most important secretaries of war and secretaries of state had been "cultivated, intellectually disciplined lawyers."

On the night of June 14 after the main campus ceremonies, Frankfurter's friends and former students honored him in Boston with a small dinner at the Somerset Club. Former student and federal judge Charles Wyzanski presided over the affair. Two other former students, Pulitzer Prize–winning poet and former librarian of Congress Archibald MacLeish and Harvard law professor and former New Deal lawyer Paul Freund, spoke. MacLeish began by wondering why Harvard had waited twenty years to honor Frankfurter and highlighted his nonjudicial achievements: "What gives Felix the extraordinary importance he has in our time is the fact that he is himself and that, being himself, *he enhances life.*" The "poet of the occasion," Frankfurter thought, was Freund. In his closing remarks, Freund described Frankfurter as "the most self-searching, the most introspective of judges" who "asks the most profound questions." Freund observed that "it is essential, that this company gathered in his honor should include philosophers, scientists, historians, and poets." Indeed, the guests included theologian Reinhold Niebuhr, whose seventeen-year-old daughter, Elisabeth, had written a poem read at the dinner, and atomic scientist J. Robert Oppenheimer, who had befriended Frankfurter after leaving the Manhattan Project. Freund concluded of the diverse crowd: "For the questions that F. F. puts to himself and to us cannot be answered by mere judges and lawyers alone." Frankfurter's oldest friends enjoyed his after-dinner speech about his memories of life in Boston. About half a dozen people stayed until 1:00 a.m.

Two of the younger attendees, Wyzanski and Oppenheimer, informed columnist Joseph Alsop that Frankfurter's after-dinner speech was "rather awful." An unsurprised Alsop reminded them of Frankfurter's contributions to the country: "it gave me great pleasure to tell R. Oppenheimer and C.

Wyzanski, who were both rather patronizing, about his intellectual powers, that I thought he was one of the two or three most useful American citizens of his time, solely because he had outlined a new standard of public service in America, had persuaded so many others that this new standard was valid and recruited so many men who exemplified what he was talking about."

Deeply moved by the presence of his close friends and former students, Frankfurter solicited copies of Freund's and MacLeish's remarks and Elisabeth Niebuhr's poem so he could show them to Marion. His wife had left her bedroom a dozen times that summer to be wheeled on a glider into the rear garden. She spent most of her days reading novels, had made no medical progress, and was "really very low." Alsop reported to Isaiah Berlin that "the prospect of a real recovery is very slight, and the worst of it is, I'm not altogether sure she really wants to recover." The justice declined most social and professional engagements, except for the Hyde Park speech and Harvard commencement, so that he could take care of her at night and on weekends. "The Justice is somewhat dimmed . . . ," Alsop wrote Berlin, "by being so cut off from the human contacts which he so visibly adores" yet he remained "fairly cheerful."

Frankfurter's life at the Supreme Court took a new turn on September 7 when his favorite remaining colleague Sherman Minton announced his retirement because of chronic anemia. The former Indiana senator, though he served seven undistinguished years on the Court, charmed Frankfurter with his warmth, straightforwardness, and tart tongue. Minton's departure, two years after Jackson's death, left Frankfurter with one less person who was "good company." The press floated several prominent names for the vacancy including three politicians: former New York governor Thomas Dewey, Secretary of State John Foster Dulles, and Attorney General Herbert Brownell. They also mentioned three judges: 70-year-old federal court of appeals judge John J. Parker, 68-year-old New Jersey Supreme Court chief justice Arthur Vanderbilt, and former Frankfurter student and the first black federal court of appeals judge William Hastie.

The Supreme Court vacancy came nearly two months before the 1956 presidential election, a rematch between Eisenhower and Democratic nominee Adlai Stevenson. Frankfurter, who had been gossiping about the election for months, thought Eisenhower was a mediocre leader and Stevenson lacked the common touch. The clear favorite, Eisenhower had spent the last year fending off questions about his health after suffering a heart attack. He also considered dropping his vice president, Richard Nixon, from the ticket. For his part, Frankfurter understood that "the difficulty" with Nixon was he had "damn little anchorage in convictions . . . I suspect he is not without brains and powers of assimilation, but is greedily ambitious and thinks almost anything is justifiable in political long warfare." Frankfurter mistakenly believed that Nixon's treatment of Alger Hiss was a "shining contrast" to Joe McCarthy's. An independent who had not voted for president since joining the Court, Frankfurter remained neutral during the election.

In an attempt to boost his chances of reelection, Eisenhower instructed Attorney General Herbert Brownell to find a conservative Catholic Democrat to nominate to the Court. After a personal interview, Eisenhower had found his man. On September 29, he chose a former Frankfurter student virtually unknown to his professor and the rest of the liberal establishment—fifty-year-old New Jersey Supreme Court associate justice, William J. Brennan, Jr.

A few days after the Brennan announcement, Frankfurter wrote Paul Freund and Ernest Brown inquiring about their Harvard law classmate. Neither Freund, Brown, nor their Harvard law colleague and classmate Milton Katz remembered Brennan. Another Harvard law professor, Benjamin Kaplan, knew Brennan from the War Department and described him as "a blend of ability and affability." At Frankfurter's request, Freund reported on Brennan's law school grades. He was a good student—with averages (out of 90) each year of 71, 72, and 68. His grade in Frankfurter's public utilities class was a 70. Brennan, whose grades did not qualify him for the *Harvard Law Review*, was a member of the Legal Aid Society. He had not taken a class in constitutional law.

From his experiences with Warren, Black, and Burton, Frankfurter knew better than to underestimate someone on the basis of prior knowledge of constitutional law, pedigree, or grades. He liked it that Brennan had frequently dissented from "that martinet" Chief Justice Vanderbilt and often did so with Associate Justice Nathan Jacobs, a former student Frankfurter described as "a very good judge." He warned former clerk Philip B. Kurland not to "undervalue Brennan." Frankfurter quickly added that neither Brennan nor Harlan was "in Jackson's class." Yet Frankfurter was "delighted" that Brennan had chosen to emulate his method of empowering a member of the Harvard law faculty to select his Supreme Court law clerks. Frankfurter had designated Henry Hart (and later Al Sacks); Brennan chose Paul Freund. Brennan's requirements, Freund informed Frankfurter, were "very reassuring," placed no restrictions on "geography, race, creed, or color," and insisted the "best for the work is what interests him." Brennan, in turn, thanked Frankfurter for a warm welcome note and looked forward to having "a 'friend in court.'"

A month after Brennan was sworn in as a recess appointee, Frankfurter threw a black-tie dinner party at his home on Saturday, November 17, in the new justice's honor. The guest list included a who's who of Harvard law alumni: Dean Acheson, Washington lawyer John Lord O'Brian, and New Orleans lawyer Monte Lemann. Another legal luminary, Judge Learned Hand, could not make it. The cocktail-filled dinner lasted until 1:00 a.m. Brennan made a great impression on Frankfurter's friends.

Nearly thirty years later, Brennan described the party as part of a sinister "plot" or indoctrination. At dinner, Acheson told a story about his Brandeis clerkship when he had included two bad citations in an opinion and had worried about getting fired. Brennan interpreted the story as a signal from Frankfurter that Brennan needed to be meticulous. But the dinner was simply a nice way to honor a former student who had joined the Court and to allow legal luminaries to meet him. If there was any subtle message, it was that Brennan was part of something bigger than himself—a long tradition of Harvard law graduates including Brandeis, Hand, O'Brian, Lemann, Frankfurter, and Acheson who had pursued the higher calling of public service.

With Brennan's chambers next door to his, Frankfurter was a frequent visitor and made it his business to get to know Brennan's law clerks. To skeptical friends including Learned Hand, Frankfurter predicted that Brennan would be "a hard-working, conscientious, intelligent Justice" and described him as "a most agreeable colleague." Basing his high hopes for Brennan on his law school training and track record on the New Jersey Supreme Court, Frankfurter went above and beyond his usual charm offensive to assist his former student. As much as Frankfurter liked Harlan and respected him as a lawyer, he saw in the younger, warmer Brennan the chance to make a new friend. Brennan could have filled the void left by Jackson and Minton had he not been insecure and suspicious of Frankfurter's motives.

At first, it looked like Frankfurter and Brennan might be allies. In January 1957, Brennan joined Frankfurter's concurring opinion in *Fikes v. Alabama* that the police had coerced the defendant's confession. Frankfurter argued that holding the accused incommunicado for a long period, failing to arraign him, and breaking him down while supplying him with details of the crime until he confessed violated the Anglo-American standard of decency of the Due Process Clause. Brennan's willingness to join Frankfurter's opinion, which expressed caution in interfering with the state criminal cases, suggested the possibility of both friendship and jurisprudential kinship.

On February 23, 1957, Frankfurter's colleague, 73-year-old Stanley Reed, announced his retirement. Reed and Frankfurter had a complicated relationship. They were both New Dealers and the two oldest members of the

Court. As Roosevelt's solicitor general, Reed had hired former Frankfurter students including Paul Freund, Henry Hart, and Charles Wyzanski to work in the office. As judicial colleagues, Frankfurter often tried to persuade Reed to change his mind about certain cases. On the one hand, he admired Reed for putting aside his personal views on race and making *Brown v. Board of Education* unanimous. On the other hand, it irritated Frankfurter that Reed often refused to consider a new line of argument and decided complex issues on the basis of irrelevant considerations. His respect for Reed as a judge was minimal at best, and he mocked the praise for Reed's judicial temperament. "Suffice it to say," Frankfurter wrote Learned Hand, "that in my judicial resurrection I wish for myself a quiet voice, a bald head, an emotionless face, a dreary style, and I'll bet you dollars to doughnuts that I shall be deemed an exemplar of judicial temperament."

Frankfurter's concern turned to Reed's replacement. President Eisenhower, based on his disappointment with Warren as chief justice and Warren's lack of a judicial track record, was determined to nominate a federal court of appeals judge from the Midwest. This type of thinking drove Frankfurter crazy. As he privately told friends, he blanched when Eisenhower sought to nominate a Catholic Democrat. He also thought it was unwise to choose a Supreme Court justice on the basis of geography. And he deemed it unnecessary for a nominee to have prior judicial experience. For Frankfurter, religion, party affiliation, geography, and prior judicial experience were irrelevant factors.

Instead of keeping quiet, he pressed his case against prior judicial experience on March 20 at the first Owen J. Roberts memorial lecture at the University of Pennsylvania Law School. In "The Supreme Court in the Mirror of Justices," he observed that twenty-eight former justices and many of the great justices—Marshall, Story, Taney, Curtis, Campbell, Hughes, and Brandeis—lacked prior experience. "Greatness in the law," he said, "is not a standardized quality, nor are the elements that combine to attain it." A state judgeship, he argued, often did not prepare someone to serve on the Supreme Court. He contrasted the commercial and common law cases that Holmes and Cardozo faced as state court judges versus the constitutional ones that confronted them as Supreme Court justices. Of the four greatest justices of his time, Holmes, Hughes, Brandeis, and Cardozo, only two had prior judicial experience. "One is entitled to say without qualification," Frankfurter said, "that the correlation between prior judicial experience and fitness for the functions of the Supreme Court is zero." He also rejected geographic considerations, citing Idaho Senator Borah's support for another New Yorker on the Court, Cardozo, to replace Holmes; and political affiliation, contrasting Wilson's appointment of two Democrats, the conservative McReynolds and progressive Brandeis. Supreme Court nominees, Frankfurter concluded, should be selected on the basis of "functional fitness"—both for the Court to function as an institution and to maintain "the confidence of the people" and their "ultimate reliance on the Court as an institution."

Eisenhower did not heed Frankfurter's advice. Determined to nominate a midwestern federal court of appeals judge to replace Reed, the president chose a 56-year-old Eighth Circuit judge from Kansas City, Missouri, Charles Evans Whittaker. Frankfurter was appalled that two potential nominees were excluded for the wrong reasons: Sixth Circuit judge Potter Stewart of Ohio because another justice, Burton, hailed from the same state, and Walter V. Schaefer, an Illinois Supreme Court justice, because he was a Democrat. Whittaker's comment that "I read the law to understand it, and when I have its meaning I apply it, without leaning one way or another" gave Frankfurter additional cause for concern about Whittaker's fitness for the Court. Months earlier after conference on October 19, Frankfurter had pulled Brennan aside and had explained that the ideas about prior judicial experience in his upcoming "The Supreme Court in the Mirror of Justices" lecture were not directed at him. Rather, they reflected years of thinking about the history of the Court and debating the benefit of prior judicial experience with C. C. Burlingham and others. If anything, the speech was a subtle rebuke of Warren's critics who argued that the chief justice was not up to the job. And it was a plea to name the best legal minds, regardless of background or geography, to the federal bench and especially to the Supreme Court.

Where he could, Frankfurter tried to encourage the Eisenhower administration to choose judges on the basis of legal acumen rather than political patronage. In January 1957, he had urged Attorney General Brownell to name former student Henry J. Friendly as Jerome Frank's replacement on the Court of Appeals for the Second Circuit. Friendly was no ordinary former student. His 86 average at Harvard Law School was one of the highest on record. Unlike other top students, he resisted Frankfurter's entreaties to teach law or to work in the federal government. Instead, he joined the Root, Clark law firm led by Frankfurter's friend Emory Buckner and emerged as a preeminent Wall Street lawyer. Friendly's former partner John Marshall Harlan II also highly regarded him. Unfortunately, the front-runner for the Second Circuit vacancy was Irving Kaufman, the federal trial judge who had sentenced the Rosenbergs to death. Hand and Frankfurter loathed Kaufman as a publicity hound and lobbied hard for Friendly. Neither Friendly nor Kaufman received the vacancy. But with his January 1957 letter, Frankfurter initiated a two-year campaign to put Friendly on the federal appellate bench.

———

THE SELECTION OF federal judges was bound up with the two biggest legal issues facing the Court: racial desegregation and the rights of suspected Communists. The Southern Manifesto spearheaded attacks portraying *Brown* and subsequent desegregation decisions as part of a Communist plot to end Jim Crow in the South. The civil rights movement was gaining steam. On November 13, 1956, the Court's unanimous, unsigned opinion in *Gayle v. Browder* had affirmed the three-judge district court's decision that Montgomery, Alabama's, racially segregated bus system violated the Fourteenth Amendment's Equal Protection Clause. On December 20, after the Court denied the motion for rehearing, Martin Luther King, Jr., and the Montgomery Improvement Association ended their 381-day boycott of the city's bus system.

The cases of suspected Communists plunged the Court, amidst intense criticism for its desegregation decisions, into the second Red Scare. Two law graduates, Raphael Konigsberg in California and Rudolph Schware in New Mexico, had been denied admission to their state bars because of past Communist Party activity. Joined by Harlan and Clark, Frankfurter dissented from the Court's reversal in *Konigsberg* because he wanted to remand the case to clarify the legal basis of the California Supreme Court's decision. Frankfurter concurred in the reversal of the New Mexico Supreme Court's decision in *Schware* not because the Supreme Court of the United States was the ultimate overseer of state bar applications but because the decision that Schware lacked moral character was "wholly arbitrary." After all, Frankfurter argued, Schware had disclosed his teenage Communist Party affiliation and use of aliases, had served honorably in World War II, and had applied for admission to the bar at age thirty-six. Harlan, who joined Frankfurter's narrow factual opinion, deemed it "splendid."

Better than many of his colleagues, Frankfurter understood the potential harm these Communist cases could do to the Court as an institution. On June 17, 1957, the Court announced four decisions reversing the convictions of suspected Communists—prompting critics to label the day Red Monday. With some reservations, Frankfurter sided with the suspected Communists in all four cases. Five years earlier in *Dennis v. United States*, he had warned about the potential for abuse of the Smith Act to prosecute suspected Communists. These cases revealed the abuses Frankfurter feared.

Before the term began, Frankfurter had instructed his law clerk to write a memorandum about the case of Oleta Yates and thirteen members of the Communist Party of California convicted under the Smith Act for conspiring to overthrow the government. Each member had been sentenced to five years in prison and fined $10,000. At the first conference discussion, Frankfurter was "not prepared to vote." A few weeks later, he sided with the defendants on the basis of the judge's defective jury instructions and joined Harlan's majority opinion. Harlan narrowly interpreted the word "organize" to mean only the establishment of a new organization, not to carry out the organization's activities. Because the Communist Party of California had started in 1945 and the defendants were not indicted until 1951, the three-year statute of limitations had expired on the organizing charge. The Court also found fault with the trial judge's jury instructions for failing to distinguish between teaching about the overthrow of the government as an abstract principle and the Smith Act's prohibition against instigating action. The Court ordered the acquittals of five defendants and the retrial of the other nine. *Yates* clarified the Court's opinion in *Dennis* and made it more difficult for the federal government to use the Smith Act to convict Communists suspected of attempting to overthrow the government.

Frankfurter also joined Harlan's majority opinion in *Service v. Dulles* overturning the discharge of Foreign Service officer John Service because the State Department had failed to follow proper procedures and regulations. Douglas insinuated that Frankfurter should have recused himself because Service had been discharged by then–Secretary of State Dean Acheson. Douglas alleged that Frankfurter had revealed that he had discussed the case with Acheson during their walks to work. Yet Frankfurter's friendship with Acheson did not stop him from voting against the State Department.

The last two cases, about congressional and state investigations of suspected Communists, posed more difficulty for Frankfurter.

He voted with the majority to reverse the contempt conviction of union leader John T. Watkins. Before the House Un-American Activities Committee (HUAC), Watkins denied that he had been a member of the Communist Party, admitted that he had participated in Communist activities, yet refused to testify about the activities of other union officials. Frankfurter, however, was reluctant to join Warren's majority opinion. On May 27, he wrote the chief justice that *Watkins* was "not a First Amendment case." Rather, he believed that Congress had exceeded its power to punish someone for contempt because of the overly broad scope of the questioning. He proposed numerous changes designed to "save us from future embarrassment and leave unimpaired the power of congressional investigations . . ." Before he made a final decision, he promised to reconsider Warren's opinion over the weekend. Four days later, Frankfurter indicated his doubts had not dissipated and recounted past attempts to interfere with congressional investigations of corrupt Harding administration officials. In 1924, he had written a *New Republic* editorial urging people to keep their "hands off" the procedures of congressional investigations. To Warren, he observed that the history "is relevant to our duty to look ahead and not have what we say in *Watkins* make trouble for the future, when trouble may be so easily avoided."

To preserve the five-justice majority, Frankfurter joined Warren's opinion in *Watkins* out of "weakness." But in an effort to narrow the majority opinion's scope, Frankfurter wrote a separate concurrence to emphasize that the case was not about free speech but due process. He argued that Watkins could not be convicted of contempt of Congress because the scope of the committee's inquiry and relevance of the questions had not been clearly defined and the witness had lacked notice that his refusal to answer those questions could result in contempt proceedings. Harlan pleaded with Frankfurter not to publish the concurrence to avoid "rancor" on the Court; Frankfurter published it anyway. In his dissent, Tom Clark referred to his experience as Truman's attorney general, described the majority's demands on Congress as "unnecessary and unworkable," and rebuked Frankfurter by citing his 1924 *New Republic* article urging "hands off" congressional investigations.

The harder question for Frankfurter was whether to join Warren's opinion overturning the state contempt conviction of Paul Sweezy. A Harvard-trained economist and co-founder of *Monthly Review* magazine, Sweezy was a Socialist who had befriended Frankfurter's friend Harold Laski, had worked for the Office of Strategic Services during World War II, and in the early 1950s had delivered a guest lecture at the University of New Hampshire. In 1954, New Hampshire's attorney general ordered Sweezy to testify on two occasions about his lecture and political affiliations. Under oath, Sweezy denied being a member of the Communist Party or knowing there were any Communists in the Progressive Party. Yet he invoked his right to free speech when asked about his Progressive Party activities, the contents of his lecture, and the political activities of his wife. Sweezy was convicted of contempt.

There was a "wide, wide gulf," Frankfurter reminded Warren on June 3, between judicial review of congressional investigations and its review of state investigations. Nothing in the Fourteenth Amendment's Due Process Clause prevented the New Hampshire legislature from delegating all authority over investigations of suspected Communists to the state attorney general. And no one was more reluctant to invoke the Constitution's open-ended language about the denial of life, liberty, and property without due process than Frankfurter. He believed the Due Process Clause gave judges too much power. And yet, he wrote Warren, academic freedom had been a "chief concern" of his during twenty-five years on the Harvard law faculty. Indeed, Laski had been driven out of Harvard as a political science instructor in 1919 after supporting the Boston police strike; Zechariah Chafee nearly had lost his job on the law faculty over errors in a law review article about the *Abrams* case; and conservative alumni had tried and failed to run off Frankfurter and Roscoe Pound. Attaching a draft concurrence to his letter to Warren, Frankfurter emphasized the need to balance the "privacy of one's political affiliations" with "our very limited function of judicial review over state action." Two days later, Warren thanked Frankfurter for showing him the draft concurrence, incorporated many of Frankfurter's suggestions, and hoped that Frankfurter and Harlan might join the revised draft. It was not meant to be. After he read the revisions, Frankfurter declined to join Warren's *Sweezy* opinion and deprived it of the fifth vote needed for a majority opinion. Instead, Frankfurter published a separate concurrence in *Sweezy* (which Harlan joined) emphasizing the differences between judicial review of federal and state investigations. As he explained to the chief justice, Frankfurter believed that the Due Process Clause did not require the Court "to enforce greater responsibility by state legislatures in carrying on their investigations."

Friends and former clerks regarded Frankfurter's *Sweezy* concurrence as one of his best expositions of judicial restraint. In the opinion, he explained that *Watkins* was a case about federal separation of powers, *Sweezy* was not, and therefore the New Hampshire legislature and attorney general were entitled to more deference. Yet the sweeping and wide-ranging nature of the attorney general's inquiries, Frankfurter argued, threatened Sweezy's academic and political freedom. In balancing "the right of a citizen to political privacy" and "the right of a State to self-protection," Frankfurter laid bare his past struggles with the Due Process Clause and referred to his concurring opinions in the Willie Francis case and several others. He described his approach to balancing the right to political privacy and state security as "an overriding judgment founded on something much deeper and justifiable than personal preferences," as "an impersonal judgment" accomplished with "a spirt of humility."

Frankfurter's differences with Warren over *Watkins* and *Sweezy* was the beginning of the end of their collaborative relationship. To his closest friends, Frankfurter circulated copies of his *Sweezy* concurrence and criticized Warren's opinions. He could not understand why the chief justice refused to avoid constitutional questions and to decide the cases on narrower, more defensible grounds. He wrote his concurrences in *Watkins* and *Sweezy* to try to trim the sails of his liberal colleagues and to protect the Court from unnecessary harm. In contrast to the chief justice, Frankfurter preferred a more cautious approach because he could see the storm coming.

The Red Monday decisions overturning the convictions of suspected Communists served as a rallying cry for southern members of Congress upset with the Court's desegregation decisions. On June 24, several House members vowed to draft articles of impeachment against all nine justices. That same day, Senator James Eastland of Mississippi and Senator Olin D. Johnston of South Carolina proposed a constitutional amendment that Supreme Court justices be reconfirmed every four years. "The court is on the march," Eastland warned his Senate colleagues. "It is attempting to consolidate all governmental power in its own hands."

Eastland and his Senate colleagues also introduced legislation to overrule another decision at the end of the term about compelling the disclosure of intelligence agency reports. The case involved union official Clinton Jencks. In April 1950, Jencks had complied with the Taft-Hartley Act by filing an affidavit with the National Labor Relations Board swearing that he was not a member of the Communist Party. On the basis of the testimony of two former Communist Party members, Jencks was tried and convicted of two counts of perjury. On appeal, he argued that the trial judge should have ordered the FBI to disclose its reports about the two former Communist Party members. Frankfurter voted with the majority to reverse Jencks's conviction and to remand the case to the trial court. He was troubled that Jencks's lawyer had been excluded from the government's argument to the judge that the FBI reports were not material. After Brennan circulated his majority opinion on May 6, Frankfurter sent him detailed comments, suggestions, and words of encouragement. Most important, Frankfurter agreed to join the opinion. Six days later, Brennan recirculated the draft opinion. "I'm still with you," Frankfurter replied and suggested responding to concerns in Tom Clark's dissent about identifying particular reports. On May 21, Brennan circulated yet another draft. "I remain steadfast," Frankfurter replied. On June 3, the Court announced its decision reversing Jencks's conviction. In his majority opinion, Brennan argued that the two informants' testimony had been critical to convicting Jencks. As a result, the FBI reports were his only chance of rebutting the informants' testimony. The trial judge, Brennan wrote, was perfectly capable of requesting the reports, reviewing them privately in chambers, and determining if they contained any relevant evidence. In dissent, Clark predicted that if Congress did not change the rule laid out by the Court, *Jencks* would force intelligence agencies to "close up shop."

The day after the decision, Senator Eastland requested that Attorney General Brownell recommend legislation to reverse or to limit the decision. Vice President Richard Nixon urged Congress not to adjourn until it acted. FBI director J. Edgar Hoover was worried that the bureau would have to open its files. New legislation seemed certain. On September 1, Congress passed the Jencks Act. The compromise legislation permitted the defense to request a government witness's signed written statement, a stenographer's transcript of an oral statement, or a statement to a grand jury—but only after the witness had testified and only for impeachment purposes. If the subject matter of the statement was not the same, the government could request that the judge review the statement privately and determine its relevancy. The FBI's files were safe from pretrial subpoenas by suspected Communists.

The Jencks Act was mild in comparison to legislation Senator William E. Jenner of Indiana introduced on July 26 to prevent the Supreme Court from hearing any appeals from suspected Communists. Congress has the power to determine the scope of the Court's appellate jurisdiction. The Jenner bill proposed to strip the Court of the ability to hear appeals of any cases about contempt of Congress, federal security regulations, state anti-subversive laws, and state bar admission rules—basically all the types of cases decided in the spring of 1957 and on Red Monday. The Jenner bill was like a sword of Damocles hanging over the Court's head. Introducing the bill on the Senate floor, Jenner interpreted Brennan's majority opinion in *Jencks* as saying: "We can trust Communists. We can trust criminals. But we cannot trust the trial judges of our own Federal bench."

The summertime controversy over *Jencks* brought Brennan and Frankfurter closer than they would be ever again. Frankfurter blamed himself for not writing a concurrence, as he had done in *Sweezy* and *Watkins*, responding to Clark's "hot air" that the decision would cripple the intelligence agencies. "I firmly believe," he wrote Brennan, "that if I had not allowed my good colleagueship to suppress my good sense the rumpus would have been avoided." If Frankfurter had written a concurrence, he believed that Brennan also would have responded directly to Clark's arguments. And together they might have persuaded Harlan to join the majority opinion. Frankfurter brushed aside criticism of the decision and derisively referred to Attorney General Brownell and several other Justice Department officials as "the enslaved tools of Edgar Hoover." Two days later, Brennan agreed that a Frankfurter concurrence would have done the trick yet placed the blame on himself. He regretted not taking more of Frankfurter's advice: "you suggested not once but several times (once I think, even before Tom's dissent was circulated) that something be done to anticipate Tom's approach." Frankfurter was "cheered" by Brennan's humility and regret "which I interpreted to mean that you will not follow the unedifying practice of two of our brethren of paying no attention to a dissent, so long as one 'has the votes.'" Taking a clear shot at Black and Douglas, Frankfurter hoped the *Jencks* episode might make Brennan more cautious about vote counting and responding to the arguments of dissenting justices. In Brennan, Frankfurter thought, incorrectly, he had found a possible ally. A few days after the Jencks Act had become law, Frankfurter followed up with more words of encouragement: "The past is irredeemable; the future of the Court is in our keeping. And it is profoundly reassuring—not that it comes as a surprise—to know that for the long stretch of years on the Court that lies ahead of you self-searching honesty and candor will guide you."

———

ULTIMATELY, a Frankfurter-Brennan partnership was not meant to be, at least in part because of their different conceptions of the role of the Court. Frankfurter believed that enduring social and political change should start with the elected branches. He agreed with Senator Kennedy's Harvard commencement speech about the need for collaboration between disinterested scholars and state and federal officials. Frankfurter looked to Congress and the president, not the Supreme Court, to lead the fight for racial justice. During the summer of 1957, he read the entire Senate debates over the Civil Rights Bill intended to protect black voting rights. As he wrote Brennan, he was impressed with Senator Sam Ervin's knowledge of constitutional law despite the North Carolina Democrat's racial biases. Southern senators attempted to water down the bill by including a mandatory jury trial provision in all criminal contempt cases and by eliminating enforcement of school desegregation. Despite his low regard for Senator Kennedy as an intellect, Frankfurter credited him with seeking advice from Harvard law professors Paul Freund and Mark DeWolfe Howe, who advised Kennedy that the jury trial provision would not hamper the force of the act. Frankfurter understood the historical importance of passing the first federal civil rights legislation since Reconstruction. The justice may have played a small role in mobilizing liberal support for the bill. In July, he rode to Phil Graham's Virginia farm with Joseph Rauh and pleaded with him and other liberal civil rights lawyers to accept the southern senators' compromises because of the long-term importance of voting rights. Rauh believed that Frankfurter and Graham had been lobbying him on behalf of Senate Majority Leader Lyndon Johnson. On August 7, 1957, the Senate, by a vote of 72–18, approved legislation that established the Civil Rights Division of the Justice Department, permitted federal prosecutors to obtain injunctions against interferences with the right to vote, and created a Civil Rights Commission to investigate discriminatory practices and to recommend reforms. A month later, it became law. "I rejoice over the expected enactment of the Civil Rights Bill," Frankfurter wrote Brennan. "It is an important step forward."

The controversy over the desegregation of Little Rock's Central High School revealed critical differences between Brennan and Frankfurter about the limits of the Court's power.

CHAPTER 36

The Judicial Response
to Little Rock

On the morning of September 4, 1957, fifteen-year-old Elizabeth Eckford worried about what to wear on the first day of school. She chose a white blouse and new homemade skirt with a wide gingham border. Her mother fixed her hair. Her father led the family in prayer before she left to catch a city bus to Little Rock's Central High School. As she walked from the bus stop carrying a notebook, she saw the Arkansas National Guard surrounding the school and 400 people gathered outside. Each time she tried to enter the school, however, the guardsmen crossed their rifles and turned her away while allowing white students to pass. Several white women trailed behind her yelling racial epithets. With her dark sunglasses and pursed lips masking her inner terror, Eckford retreated to a nearby bus stop. The crowd surged toward her. White men taunted her and threatened her with lynching. She waited for what seemed like an eternity for a city bus. Later that morning, eight other black students, including seven accompanied by white ministers, tried to enter Central High School (Eckford had not joined the group because her family lacked a home telephone). The Arkansas National Guard rebuffed the other black students, too.

Two nights earlier, Arkansas governor Orval Faubus had announced that he was calling out the National Guard to Central High School to preserve order and prevent violence. In reality, he had instructed the National Guard and state police to bar the black students and to defy a federal judge's order to proceed with the local school board's integration plan. More than three years after the Court's decision in *Brown v. Board of Education*, the Arkansas governor started a constitutional showdown with the federal government the likes of which the country had not seen since the Civil War.

The southern resistance came as no surprise to Frankfurter. "Of course, I won't tell you that I foresaw a Governor Faubus," he wrote Learned Hand on September 8, "but I can honestly say that I expressed my strong conviction that we shall be in for a long process & probably with some ugly episodes. That's why I so strongly urged the phrase 'with all deliberate speed' from Holmes's opinion in [*Virginia v. West Virginia*]. Why the phrase wasn't quoted & the case cited—the indication of another long & drawn-out litigation—is another story." Frankfurter's comments revealed his fraying relationship with Warren and his differences with the civil libertarian wing of the Court about how to respond to massive resistance.

The Little Rock school crisis once again put the Court at the center of a national political debate. Frankfurter believed that Eisenhower was not up to Faubus's challenge and described the president as "a natural-born unleader." Eisenhower had been lukewarm in his support for the school segregation decisions. The president insisted that "you cannot legislate morality." Yet, as the nation's chief executive and commander in chief, he publicly affirmed his constitutional duty to enforce the *Brown* decision. Privately, he worried about the physical toll the Little Rock crisis was taking on his health and second term: "The demands that I 'do something' seem to grow."

On the morning of September 14, Eisenhower met with Faubus near the president's vacation home in Newport, Rhode Island. He asked the governor to instruct the National Guard to allow the nine students to attend Central High School. In exchange, the Department of Justice would drop its request that the governor appear in federal court in the NAACP's efforts to obtain an injunction. A noncommittal Faubus asked Eisenhower for patience and understanding and defended himself on national television. On September 21, a federal trial judge ordered the governor to remove the National Guard and to allow the black students to enter. Two days later, a crowd of 1000 pro-testers rioted outside of Central High School upon learning the nine black students had slipped into the building through a side entrance; outnum-bered local police quickly escorted the black students from the school for their own safety. Eisenhower described the riots as "disgraceful occurrences." On September 24, he ordered the 101st Airborne Division of the U.S. Army to Little Rock and federalized the Arkansas National Guard. The next day, federal troops escorted Elizabeth Eckford and other members of the Little Rock Nine up the steps and through the front door of Central High School. Federal troops patrolled the school for more than two months; federalized national guardsmen stayed there most of the year. Eckford and the other black students endured daily harassment from white students. The constitutional clash between the Arkansas governor and the federal government over school desegregation was far from over.

━━━━━

DURING THE 1957 TERM, Frankfurter clerk Bill Doolittle often drove his 1956 jungle green Volkswagen Beetle to 3018 Dumbarton Avenue in the morning, picked up his boss, and dropped him off at Dean Acheson's house four blocks away. The justice and former secretary of state walked 1.7 miles to Acheson's office at Covington & Burling in the Union Trust Building at Fifteenth and H Streets. From there, Doolittle drove the justice the rest of the way to the Supreme Court. On rainy days, Doolittle sometimes drove Frankfurter and Acheson to the Union Trust Building with the tall Acheson riding in the front seat and the justice sitting in the back.

Yet on the morning of November 15, 1957, Doolittle drove the justice directly to chambers. There was no time for a morning walk or ride with Acheson. It was Frankfurter's seventy-fifth birthday. Upon arriving at the office, the justice and his secretary, Elsie Douglas, opened congratulatory letters and telegrams from political figures, artists, former students, fellow scholars, scientists, Israeli leaders, judges, and Court colleagues. At 11:00 a.m., he attended the conference, which ended promptly at 5:00 p.m. because sixteen former clerks had arrived to join current clerks Doolittle and John Mansfield in chambers for a surprise birthday celebration. It was reminiscent of Holmes's eightieth birthday when his former secretaries surprised him and celebrated with Prohibition-era champagne. Frankfurter ended the night eating dinner at home with Marion recounting the Holmes-inspired affair. He told her about the "warm and generous remembrances . . . particularly by the young." To which she replied, "Well, now you are 75 and back to normalcy: business as usual."

As the oldest member of the Court, Frankfurter began to attract the type of media attention reserved in later life for his idol Holmes. Newspapers all over the country ran wire stories about him. The *Boston Globe* and *Washington Post* profiled him; a *New York Times* editorial questioned "[h]ow could this youthful jurist have reached such venerable an age," quoted his flag salute dissent, and urged him not to retire.

A week later, the birthday celebration continued with a dinner in the Continental Room at the Sheraton-Park Hotel to benefit the Felix Frankfurter Scholarship Fund at Harvard Law School; fellow Harvard law graduates Brennan and Burton joined Frankfurter at the head table. The editors of the *Yale*

Law Journal dedicated their December issue to Frankfurter and published a series of scholarly articles about his jurisprudence.

Reviewing the justice's life and career in the *New Republic*, Alexander Bickel concluded by quoting the last paragraph of Frankfurter's 1957 *Sweezy* concurrence, which proposed to balance the right to political privacy and state security not on the basis of personal preferences but by impartial judgment and judicial humility. The magazine, which Frankfurter had helped start in 1914 as an outlet for progressive ideas and which he had contributed to for several decades, excerpted his July 1930 tribute to its founding editor Herbert Croly: "In fair weather and foul he lived his faith with extraordinary fidelity. Though highly sensitive and strong-willed, he maintained his intellectual and emotional rectitude with unruffled serenity."

Of all the tributes, nothing captured Frankfurter and his jurisprudence as well as a *New York Times Magazine* profile by the newspaper's new Supreme Court correspondent, Anthony Lewis. Like Bickel, Lewis had benefited from Frankfurter's eye for talent. For years, the justice had complained to Washington bureau chief James "Scotty" Reston and to publisher Arthur Hays Sulzberger that the newspaper would never cover "the World Series as incompetently" as its reporting on the Supreme Court. A recurring problem was that the reporter assigned to the Court lacked legal training. In Lewis, a 1955 Pulitzer Prize winner for his *Washington Daily News* stories about U.S. Navy employee Abraham Chasanow's successful appeal of his dismissal as a security risk, Frankfurter found the perfect solution. As a result of his Chasanow stories, Lewis became interested in the law. He landed a job at the *Times* and a Nieman Fellowship to spend the 1956–1957 academic year at Harvard. With a phone call to Dean Erwin Griswold, Frankfurter arranged for Lewis to spend the year at "the Law School." To former students, clerks, and friends on the faculty—Abram Chayes, Paul Freund, Henry Hart, Mark DeWolfe Howe, Donald Trautman, and Al Sacks—the justice raved about the 29-year-old Lewis and urged them to mentor him. During the academic year, Lewis took first-year, second-year, and third-year classes. In two classes, Freund's on constitutional law and Hart's (with guest lectures by Herbert Wechsler) on federal courts, Lewis received exam grades "very few men attain."

In many ways, Anthony Lewis the Supreme Court correspondent was another Frankfurter-inspired creation. The justice persuaded Washington bureau chief Scotty Reston to assign Lewis to the Supreme Court full time. Before Lewis started, Frankfurter encouraged him to do "more thorough preparation" of cases, more pre-decision coverage including oral argument, and "more reflective stories" a few days after major decisions. He suggested

writing two-thirds of a story about a major case before it had been decided
and a regular column about interesting issues. He charged Lewis to educate
the public about the Supreme Court. Lewis's analysis, Frankfurter argued,
could compensate for the lack of "serious criticism" of the Court and counter
"the really wild attacks made by Eastland, Jenner, et al." in the Senate. Finally,
Frankfurter suggested story ideas on recent cases and the Court's jurisprudential debates.

In his magazine profile "An Appreciation of Justice Frankfurter," Lewis
made the justice come alive. He began by describing Frankfurter walking the
halls of the Court whistling "The Stars and Stripes Forever." He quoted the
first few paragraphs of the flag salute dissent in *West Virginia v. Barnette* to
show how Frankfurter attempted to put aside his personal views and to defer
to legislatures. He then explained the philosophical underpinnings of Frankfurter's belief in "judicial self-restraint": Overreliance on the Court to protect
civil liberties undermined the responsibilities of legislatures and the people
themselves; it gave nine justices an undemocratic veto of legislation, which
they had invoked too frequently during the 1920s and 1930s; and it imperiled
the Court's legitimacy in the eyes of the American people, as evidenced by
the 1937 New Deal constitutional crisis. Frankfurter, Lewis wrote, sought to
protect the Court's institutional standing through judicial restraint and by
avoiding unnecessary constitutional questions. In this regard, Holmes and
Brandeis were his judicial idols. Labels such as liberal or conservative held no
purchase for Frankfurter, Lewis wrote, because the justice rejected "the idea
that a judicial decision has anything whatever to do with 'liberalism' or 'con-
servatism' in a political sense."

Frankfurter's importance as an institutional player, Lewis argued,
stemmed from his ability to frame the dispositive issues and his frequent
position as the deciding fifth vote. To illustrate his point, Lewis recounted
Frankfurter's strategy of delay and reargument in *Brown v. Board of Education*
and his willingness to embrace a gradual desegregation remedy and "all deliberate speed" in *Brown II*. Lewis also observed that, based on Frankfurter's
experience as a federal prosecutor under Henry Stimson, he emphasized fair
criminal procedures and the warrant requirement in search and seizure cases
and opposed wiretapping.

On a personal and emotional level, Lewis described the justice's intellectually egalitarian relationship with his wife, Marion; his voracious reading
of mainstream and obscure newspapers; his wide circle of friends; and his
love of children. Drawing on his recent experiences in the justice's chambers,
Lewis captured Frankfurter's "electric presence" and zest for argument on

and off the bench: "No one could fail to see this in the intensity with which he will argue any subject except Supreme Court business in private conversation, his small frame darting here and there, his hand now and then gripping his listener's elbow as he makes a point."

Last and most important, Lewis explored Frankfurter's internal struggle as an "exponent of judicial restraint" and "a man of emotion." The personal references at the beginning of his flag salute dissent in *Barnette* and his frequent concurring and dissenting opinions revealed a "passionate man" striving for but not always achieving "judicial disinterestedness." And yet as the most prominent advocate of judicial restraint during a time of increasing intervention by civil libertarians Warren, Black, Douglas, and Brennan, Frankfurter loomed larger than ever in the eyes of his legal allies and admirers. As Learned Hand told Lewis: "I regard him at the moment as the most important single figure in our whole judicial system."

LEWIS HAD A ringside seat for the major jurisprudential battle of the 1957 term—whether Congress possessed the authority to take away someone's U.S. citizenship. At the end of the previous term, the Court heard the denationalization cases of Albert Trop, Mitsugi Nishikawa, and Clemente Perez. Private Trop had been court martialed during World War II for escaping the U.S. Army stockade and deserting for a day while serving in Casablanca, Morocco. Nishikawa had been denied reentry in the United States after serving in the Japanese army during World War II but claimed his service had not been voluntary. Perez was born in El Paso, Texas, lived there until he was ten or eleven, then moved to Mexico. When he tried to return to the United States as a citizen in 1947, he admitted not returning during World War II to avoid the draft and having voted in Mexican elections. Under the Nationality Act of 1940, U.S. citizenship could be revoked for military desertion during wartime, serving in the military of a foreign government, avoiding the draft, or voting in foreign elections. In May 1957, Warren was prepared to reverse all three decisions and to declare the denationalization provisions of the Nationality Act unconstitutional. At the May 3 conference, Frankfurter contended that if Congress could execute someone, it could revoke the person's citizenship. The only limit on Congress's power, he argued, was the Due Process Clause. After he read Warren's drafts, Frankfurter wrote his colleagues: "The issues at stake are too far-reaching and the subject matter calls for too extensive an investigation" for him to write a dissent before the end of the term.

The other justices must have agreed because on June 24 they announced reargument in the fall.

Tensions between Warren and Frankfurter were reaching a breaking point. As the denationalization cases demonstrated, Warren gravitated to Black's and Douglas's civil libertarian positions and away from Frankfurter's judicial restraint. Frankfurter's professorial personality grated on Warren. "Felix irritates;" one of Warren's clerks explained, "Hugo soothes." During the 1955 term, Warren became so concerned about Frankfurter's ability to "brainwash" Jerome Cohen and another Warren clerk that the chief justice forbade them from speaking with him. Before the next term, Frankfurter found himself with only one clerk, Andrew Kaufman, because the other clerk who had been selected by Henry Hart could not get himself discharged from the army's Judge Advocate General's Corps in time. At Kaufman's suggestion, Frankfurter asked Cohen to join his chambers for the following term.

In July 1957, Cohen wrote Frankfurter a memorandum about the inadequacy of Warren's draft opinion in *Perez v. Brownell*. At the justices' private conference after the second day of reargument on October 29, it was clear that Warren no longer had a majority in *Perez* to declare the Nationality Act's denationalization provisions unconstitutional. As the senior justice in the six-justice majority in *Perez*, Frankfurter assigned the case to himself. Warren assigned the *Trop* and *Nishikawa* cases to Frankfurter as well. Harlan, who had switched sides in *Perez* and *Trop*, remarked at conference: "These are tough cases." To which Frankfurter replied in a note that if an issue is "tough" and "you are in serious doubt about it, the doubt must be resolved in favor of constitutionality." He invoked James Bradley Thayer's essay, which Harlan had read the previous summer at Frankfurter's insistence. Frankfurter reminded Harlan that "this is the 100th anniversary of a decision that we do not celebrate," *Dred Scott v. Sandford*'s declaration that blacks were not citizens and that the Missouri Compromise was unconstitutional. And, alluding to the New Deal constitutional crisis during the 1930s, he concluded that "this Court gets into hot water about every twenty years, and the reason that it does so invariably is disregard of the considerations that profess to control us in constitutional adjudications."

Frankfurter may have been preaching the doctrine of judicial restraint to the wrong justice. On November 14, based on memoranda and drafts prepared by Doolittle, he circulated three denationalization opinions. His majority in *Perez*, *Trop*, and *Nishikawa* depended on the Court's two newest justices, Brennan and Charles Evans Whittaker. On November 15, Whittaker joined Frankfurter's "excellent opinion" in *Perez*. On March 5, however, he confessed

that all three cases had given him "a great deal of trouble," and he was reconsidering Warren's *Perez* dissent. That same day, Frankfurter responded that
Congress's power to take away someone's citizenship was limited only to a
due process and "a shock to the conscience" standard. The chronically indecisive Whittaker was not persuaded and ended up writing a separate opinion.

A few weeks later, Brennan joined Frankfurter in *Perez* and thus preserved
the five-justice majority. Yet Brennan agreed to join the chief justice's opinion in *Nishikawa* about the burden of proof for revoking citizenship. Frankfurter was furious. "The Chief assigned the writing of the *Nishikawa* opinion
to me," he wrote Brennan. Warren claimed their views were similar about
remanding the case to determine whether Nishikawa's Japanese army service had been voluntary. Yet instead of asking Frankfurter to make changes
to his opinion, Warren wrote a competing draft. Frankfurter refused to join
Warren's *Nishikawa* opinion not out of spite but because "the overtones and
the undertones are really the view which is explicitly spelt out by the Chief in
Perez. I wonder if it is the fact that English is not my mother tongue that I cannot read the Chief's opinion, no matter what he says in conversation about it,
as being the kind of denial of power that Black and Douglas espouse. Look at
the last page of his recirculation. I think they joined his opinion in *Nishikawa*
because the whole atmosphere, if not the very words, represent their views."
As proof, Frankfurter highlighted a sentence from the chief justice's *Nishikawa* opinion: "But every exercise of governmental power must find its source
in the Constitution. The power to denationalize is not within the letter or the
spirit of the powers with which our Government was endowed."

The debate between Frankfurter and the Warren-led civil libertarians
boiled down to different ideas about the scope of congressional power. In his
majority opinion in *Perez*, Frankfurter detailed a long history of legislative
and executive revocation of U.S. citizenship and reviewed the legislative history of the Nationality Act of 1940. He argued that Congress could condition
U.S. citizenship on not voting in foreign elections as part of its inherent sovereign power over foreign affairs. Congressional conditions, Frankfurter wrote,
need only be rationally related to protecting U.S. interests. He also contended
that the Necessary and Proper Clause gave Congress implied powers, in its
conduct of foreign affairs, to revoke citizenship for voting in foreign elections.
Like John Marshall in *McCulloch v. Maryland*, Frankfurter believed that Congress had broad implied powers. He was reluctant to encroach on Congress's
authority over foreign affairs: "The importance and extreme delicacy of the
matters here sought to be regulated demand that Congress be permitted
ample scope in selecting appropriate modes for accomplishing its purpose."

Warren, Black, and Douglas pushed back on Frankfurter's deference to Congress. Warren's dissent emphasized the first sentence of the Fourteenth Amendment ("All persons born or naturalized in the United States, and subject to the jurisdiction thereof, are citizens of the United States and of the State wherein they reside.") as an irrevocable grant of citizenship and a "basic right . . . nothing less than the right to have rights." In a separate dissent, Douglas and Black accused Frankfurter of legislative supremacy; Frankfurter, however, saw Warren, Black, and Douglas as the supremacists, judicial supremacists.

Warren embraced judicial supremacy in his landmark opinion, joined by Black, Douglas, and Whittaker, in *Trop v. Dulles*. The chief justice argued that Congress could not revoke someone's citizenship for deserting the army during wartime because it violated the Eighth Amendment's ban on "cruel and unusual punishment." Historically, the Court had invoked the Eighth Amendment only for inhumane criminal punishments. Warren's opinion, however, reinterpreted "cruel and unusual punishment" as about "the dignity of man" and transformed it into a judicial veto of legislation on the basis of "the evolving standards of decency that mark the progress of a maturing society." In time, "evolving standards of decency" came to mean whatever five justices believed it meant and epitomized the Warren Court's aggrandizement of judicial power at the expense of the legislative branches.

Frankfurter's dissent in *Trop v. Dulles* warned about the dangers of judicial overreach. "All power is . . . 'of an encroaching nature,'" he wrote, quoting James Madison in the Federalist Papers. "Judicial power is not immune against this human weakness. It also must be on guard against encroaching beyond its proper bounds, and not the less so since the only restraint upon it is self-restraint." In determining whether Congress has exceeded its power, the Court must determine whether the law is "clearly outside the constitutional grant of power." He quoted Holmes in *Blodgett v. Holden* that the Court's "judgment on the action of a co-ordinate branch" was "'the gravest and most delicate duty that this Court is called on to perform.'" Frankfurter added: "This is not a lip-serving platitude." As tired as his civil libertarian colleagues were of his references to Holmes, he reminded Warren, Black, and Douglas that they were no longer a governor, senator, or SEC chairman: "it is not the business of this Court to pronounce policy. . . . self-restraint is of the essence in the observance of the judicial oath, for the Constitution has not authorized the judges to sit in judgment on the wisdom of what Congress and the Executive Branch do." Frankfurter insisted that Congress was within its war powers to revoke a soldier's citizenship for desertion during wartime.

The starkly different constitutional visions of Frankfurter and Warren took a personal turn on March 31, 1958, as the justices announced their denationalization opinions from the bench. The press and law clerks in the courtroom noticed the discord. In a column a few days later, Anthony Lewis reported that the "remarks in the courtroom verged on the bitter, even waspish." Frankfurter objected to Lewis's "adjectival paprika" and emphasized the "'deep, unbridgeable differences in philosophy.'" The antagonism, however, was real. At one point, Warren remarked that the Court had overruled eighty-one acts of Congress. Frankfurter responded that those decisions were "nothing to boast about," and many of them had been overruled. After Frankfurter announced his majority opinion in *Perez*, Warren replied that "his opinion was directed at the printed opinion of the Court, not the oral opinion of Mr. Justice Frankfurter." Frankfurter scribbled a note to his clerk Bill Doolittle: "Does he mean my oral was more persuasive?"

The ideological battle lines between the two sides had been drawn. As Lewis wrote, Warren, Black, and Douglas espoused "a vigorous, assertive view of the Supreme Court's role," and Frankfurter, Burton, Clark, and Harlan preferred a "more restrained, deferential approach." For the time being, Brennan and Whittaker occupied the center. One thing was clear from the denationalization cases: The trust between Frankfurter and the chief justice during *Brown* and *Brown II* had eroded. Frankfurter led the opposition to Warren's outsized role for the judiciary. And he was not alone.

===

FOR THREE STRAIGHT DAYS in the packed James Barr Ames Courtroom at Harvard Law School's Austin Hall, Learned Hand blasted the Court's excesses. Many regarded Hand as the best judge never to sit on the Supreme Court—despite Frankfurter's best efforts to persuade Roosevelt in 1942 and 1943 that Hand was not too old. Stocky, broad shouldered, and beetle-browed, the 86-year-old Second Circuit judge delivered his Oliver Wendell Holmes Lectures with an aristocratic upstate New York accent reminiscent of Franklin Roosevelt's and offered an alternative, progressive vision of a more restrained judiciary. Hand's lectures were broadcast into law school classrooms and on a Boston radio station. On the first day, Hand conceded, despite the lack of textual support in the Constitution for judicial review, that it had been essential for the Court to have the final word on the Constitution to keep the states, Congress, and the president in line or else "the whole system would have collapsed." At the end of his second lecture, however, he criticized the Court for acting like "a third legislative chamber." As an example, he asserted that *Brown v. Board of Education* was based on "its own reappraisal of the relative values at stake. . . . I have never been able to understand on what basis it does or can rest except as a *coup de main*." During the third and final lecture titled "Guardians," he rejected the idea of government by judiciary and captured the anti-democratic fears of judicial review: "For myself it would be most irksome to be ruled by a bevy of Platonic Guardians, even if I knew how to choose them, which I assuredly do not. If they were in charge, I should miss the stimulus of living in a society where I have, at least theoretically, some part in the direction of public affairs."

A few days after the lectures, Frankfurter congratulated Hand and assured him that on the "central theme" about judicial review, "you cannot scare me." Yet regarding Hand's criticism of *Brown*, Frankfurter wondered "whether in the end you would have held out against the decision in the *Segregation Cases*. On the basis of some of the attitudes that he manifested during the short single term that Jimmy Byrnes was on the Court, I am bold enough to believe that even Byrnes, had he stayed on the Court, would no more have dissented than Reed and Tom Clark dissented." Frankfurter mentioned Jackson's efforts to justify *Brown* on the basis of Congress's power to enforce the Fourteenth Amendment. He also found it difficult to "square" Hand's criticism of *Brown* with their prior correspondence about state anti-miscegenation laws.

In the months before and after the lectures, Frankfurter asked how Hand would decide the constitutionality of a state anti-miscegenation law given that *Brown*'s reasoning was limited to education. Frankfurter was defending his past and present attempts to avoid the miscegenation cases. He rejected Hand's suggestion that the Fourteenth Amendment prohibited any racial classifications as inconsistent with the amendment's text and legislative history. As proof, Frankfurter provided Hand with a copy of Alexander Bickel's *Harvard Law Review* article about the history of the amendment's origins in the Thirty-Ninth Congress. On the basis of Bickel's article, Frankfurter argued that *Brown* was "justified" in concluding that the history was "inconclusive" with regard to segregated schools and that "the boys on the Hill left the scope of [the Fourteenth Amendment] for the Court's 'interpretation.'" Before the lectures, Frankfurter had pleaded with Hand "for the love of Mike don't say anything that lawyers and the cynical, unscrupulous Bill [Douglas] can quote as the clear view of 'the greatest living judge' that the Segregation decision covers miscegenation!!"

Southern segregationists and anti-Communists in Congress seized on Hand's lectures as proof that the Warren Court had overstepped its bounds.

The Jenner-Butler Bill was pending in the Senate and proposed to strip the Court's jurisdiction over appeals of convictions of suspected Communists. In May, Hand announced his opposition to the legislation, which Senate Majority Leader Lyndon Johnson succeeded in killing a few months later. Alistair Cooke correctly predicted in the *Manchester Guardian* that Hand's lectures "may well convert their 86-year-old author into the latest idol of the South."

For his part, Frankfurter declared Hand's lectures a "great triumph" and a necessary corrective. "I'm afraid some of [his] views will give many a so-called liberal a jolt," Frankfurter wrote C. C. Burlingham. "These liberals, so-called, were outraged when in the old days the Supreme Court declared unconstitutional legislation that they approved of. Now they are outraged if the Court does not declare unconstitutional legislation they disapprove of. How I disrespect this jug-handled view of the law." Indeed, after the announcement of the denationalization decisions in *Perez, Trop,* and *Nishikawa* on March 31, Frankfurter wrote Hand: "Read Monday's batch of opinions. You will not be shaken in your Holmesian outlook."

His duties at the Court and increasingly stressful home life had prevented Frankfurter from attending Hand's lectures. Hand and other friends knew that Frankfurter was reluctant to leave Marion. Joseph Alsop described her as "permanently bedridden (if, indeed, it is not her actual desire)." One morning in April, Frankfurter found her curled up on the floor covered by a blanket. The night before, she had gotten up to go to the bathroom, stumbled, and broken a little bone in her foot. Rather than cry out, she lay on the floor until her husband found her the next morning. "It upset him horribly, as you can imagine," Alsop wrote Isaiah Berlin. "The foot is better now. She's back from the hospital. But aside from his work, he spends his whole life as a male nurse. Both their servants go out over the weekend, and he even prepares meals and carries trays on Saturday and Sunday. He must have incredible reserves of vitality, for although he looks grey, he is still full of bounce." For her part, Marion was content to read books in bed and never wavered from her faith in her doctor and his misguided regimen of antibiotics for her rheumatoid arthritis.

————

AT THE COURT, Frankfurter steeled himself at the end of the term for a major decision affecting southern race relations. The state of Alabama had ordered the NAACP's local chapters to cease their activities for failing to comply with a state law requiring the registration of out-of-state corporations. As part of the lawsuit, a state judge compelled the NAACP's state affiliates to disclose registration information, officers, membership lists, dues, books, and records. The NAACP produced everything except the membership lists. As NAACP lawyer Robert L. Carter explained to the Court on January 15, 1958, the disclosure of membership lists infringed on the organization's freedom of speech and association and exposed rank-and-file members to violence, harassment, and intimidation. At the justices' conference, Frankfurter warned his colleagues: "The less we say the better." He preferred to reverse the state court's contempt conviction on the basis of procedural unfairness (the state judge increased the fine after five days from $10,000 to $100,000) and the irrelevance of membership lists to the state's interest in registering out-of-state corporations. In his draft majority opinion, Harlan sought to reverse the state court on the basis of freedom of speech. Frankfurter persuaded his colleagues to reverse on the basis of the NAACP members' implied right of a freedom of association. He extensively edited Harlan's draft and deleted a description of the Court's effort to avoid constitutional questions as "not inflexible" because it "will be quoted by Black next week or next term to mean in effect that we can pass on constitutional issues whenever we want to." A few weeks later, Frankfurter succeeded in discouraging Tom Clark from dissenting on procedural grounds that did not warrant "a break in the unanimity of the Court in what is, after all, part of the whole Segregation controversy."

Before the end of the term, the Little Rock crisis landed on the Court's doorstep and put Frankfurter at odds with the chief justice. Of the nine students, eight, including Elizabeth Eckford, survived the school year guarded by military troops and having endured relentless racial harassment by white students. One black student retaliated and was expelled. In light of these incidents, threats of violence, and continued military presence, the Little Rock School Board requested permission to postpone desegregation of Central High School. On June 20, 1958, federal district judge Harry Lemley granted a delay until January 1961. He acknowledged that black students in Little Rock had a right not to be excluded from white schools, but he claimed that "the time for the enjoyment of that right has not yet come." Judge Lemley refused to stay his decision pending appeal. NAACP lawyers Thurgood Marshall and Wiley Branton immediately appealed to the Court of Appeals for the Eighth Circuit and requested a stay of the district court's decision. Rather than wait for a ruling, they also appealed directly to the Supreme Court. The justices discussed the Little Rock appeal at lunch.

The Court refused to hear the case but not without a "stiff fight" between Frankfurter and the chief justice. In the Court's unsigned opinion, Frankfurter insisted on a paragraph instructing the court of appeals to resolve the case before the beginning of the school year. Warren feared "'we'd be out on a limb if they told us to go to hell.'" Frankfurter fought for the paragraph and received "tepid" support from Black. "Some plain talking & an ultimatum to the C.J. became necessary," Frankfurter wrote and blamed it on Warren's "professional inadequacies" and "inexperience" as a judge and "shortsighted-ness" of a former politician. In an unsigned opinion drafted by Frankfurter and announced on June 30, the Court declared in the hard-fought paragraph: "We have no doubt that the Court of Appeals will recognize the vital impor-tance of the time element in this litigation, and that it will act upon the appli-cation for a stay or the appeal in ample time to permit arrangements to be made for the next school year."

The bad blood between Frankfurter and Warren spilled into public view on the last day of the term. On May 21, the Court heard oral argument in a case brought by two California death row inmates, Bart Luis Caritativo and William Francis Rupp. California law prohibited executions of the insane, yet it gave the warden unreviewable discretion to make sanity determinations. At conference, a majority of the Court agreed to affirm the convictions; Frank-furter dissented because of the procedural unfairness of giving the warden final say. The chief justice did not assign the majority opinion to anyone. Rather, he made his own determination to affirm the death sentences with-out a written opinion. On June 30, Warren announced the decision from the bench. Frankfurter summarized his dissent, joined by Brennan and Doug-las, concluding that "it would be 'far better' to have 'minor inconveniences' to prison administration 'than that the State of California should have on its conscience a single execution that would be barbaric because the victim was in fact, though he had no opportunity to show it, mentally unfit to meet his destiny.'" Frankfurter later claimed that he "said nothing that was not in my circulated dissent." As soon as he finished speaking, however, the chief jus-tice launched into a rebuttal lasting several minutes: "Neither the judgment of this court nor that of California is quite as savage as this dissent would indi-cate." The New York Times remarked that Warren sounded more like the gov-ernor of California than the chief justice as he concluded: "I merely make this statement because I don't believe that this case is as bad as it might appear."

The latest disagreement in open court was "'the final break'" between Warren and Frankfurter. They were such different people. Warren was a good politician but a bad constitutional lawyer; Frankfurter was a bad politician but a good constitutional lawyer. Warren was warm in public but could be cold in private; Frankfurter could be cold in public but warm in private. Warren was insecure about his intellectual abilities and resented Frankfurter's professorial discourses. Frankfurter viewed Warren as nothing more than a politician in a robe.

In private, Frankfurter compared the civil libertarian bloc of Warren, Black, Douglas, and Brennan to the conservative Four Horsemen of the 1920s and 1930s. He bristled over the Court's "intellectually indefensible hog-wash" in the "Red Monday" cases *Watkins* and *Sweezy*; Warren's expansive interpretation of cruel and unusual punishment in *Trop v. Dulles*; and another justice's (probably Brennan's) assertion at a law clerk lunch that he was not bound by any cases before he joined the Court. Frankfurter's closest friend on the Court, John Harlan, realized how difficult the term had been. "I hope that no news means good news, and that you are quite yourself again," Harlan wrote on July 15. "The Term was arduous, and I know that it was otherwise not an easy one for you."

The news that Frankfurter and Harlan feared from Little Rock arrived before the end of the summer recess. On August 18, the Court of Appeals for the Eighth Circuit reversed Judge Lemley's decision delaying any desegregation of Little Rock's Central High School until January 1961. The court of appeals, however, stayed the implementation of its decision pending an appeal to the Supreme Court. Frankfurter hoped that the Court simply could decline to hear the case but concluded that it would be "wiser" to hear the lawsuit and to affirm the court of appeals's decision. During the Court's deliberations, he sent Bickel his unpublished concurrence in the all-white Texas primary case of *Smith v. Allwright*. During the final days of the Little Rock crisis, Frankfurter would have his say.

On August 25, Warren announced the first special term since the case of atomic spies Julius and Ethel Rosenberg five years earlier. Before he announced the special term, the chief justice had conferred with Brennan, Whittaker, and Clark at the American Bar Association annual meeting in Los Angeles and with other justices by telephone. The Little Rock public schools were scheduled to open on September 2. As it stood, black students were barred from Central High School.

Governor Faubus responded to the Court's special term by convening a special session of the Arkansas legislature. On August 26, the Arkansas legislature passed numerous laws giving Faubus broad powers to prevent the desegregation of the Little Rock schools, including the option to close them. Faubus waited to sign the laws until after the Court's special term.

The justices arrived in Washington, D.C., from all over the country. Warren, Brennan, Clark, and Whittaker flew in from Los Angeles; Douglas arrived from the Pacific Northwest; Harlan left his summer home in Westport, Connecticut; Burton curtailed his European vacation. Within hours of his return, the chief justice conferred with Frankfurter and Black, the only two who had stayed in Washington. The justices were united in the need to uphold the original desegregation orders yet divided over how. Frankfurter revealed to Bickel the internal discord: "The special session order also has much more than meets the eye."

The day before the August 28 oral argument, Frankfurter circulated a history of the Little Rock crisis from 1954 to the Court's refusal to hear the case in June 1957, along with a short memorandum "for my own information" that attempted to strike a conciliatory tone: "Compliance with decisions of this Court, as the constitutional organ of the supreme law of the land, has often, throughout the whole course of the Nation's history, depended on active support by state and local authorities. Indeed, it presupposes such support. To withhold it precludes the effective maintenance of our federal system."

At oral argument, NAACP counsel Thurgood Marshall charged that "here we have Negro children" who "have done nothing bad" yet "that these children must be forced to surrender their constitutional rights is unimportant in this Court today." Marshall viewed Judge Lemley's decision and the Eighth Circuit's stay as "a surrender to obstructionist and mob action and that is much more destructive of democratic government than it is of some few Negroes' rights."

To Richard Butler, the lawyer for the Little Rock School Board, Frankfurter asked whether Brown I and Brown II had made the meaning of the Fourteenth Amendment, "a national policy" of school desegregation, and its enforcement in the hands of local district judges. He emphasized to Butler that the actor obstructing the law was Governor Faubus, not the school board. The Court agreed to hear a second oral argument on September 11 after both sides had filed expedited briefs. As a show of good faith, the school board delayed the start of the school year until September 15 to give the Court time to announce a decision and to prevent Governor Faubus from denying black students the right to attend Central High School.

Frankfurter was "relieved" by the school board's decision and considered Butler's advice to the board "much wiser" than the chief justice's comments to his colleagues. Before the September 11 argument, Frankfurter had learned that Warren viewed the case as a dispute between the chief justice and governor of Arkansas. Brennan had told Frankfurter as much on the basis of Warren's comments at lunch. During the argument, Warren at times failed to distinguish between the school board's arguments and Governor Faubus's actions. "Of course Faubus has been guilty of trickery, but the trickery was as much against the School Board as against us," Frankfurter wrote Harlan on September 2. "And in any event the fight is not between the Supreme Court and Faubus, tho apparently that is the way it lay in the C.J.'s mind. I am afraid his attitude towards the kind of problems that confront us are more like that of a fighting politician than that of a judicial statesman."

Throughout the Little Rock school crisis, Frankfurter was convinced that the Court ought to avoid demonizing the South and to speak to moderate southerners who believed in upholding the rule of law. Butler, Little Rock school board president Wayne Upton, *Arkansas Gazette* editor Harry Ashmore, and *Atlanta Constitution* editor Ralph McGill fell into that category. "These are not men who can be won to desegregation on the merits," Frankfurter wrote Harlan, "but they ought to be won, and I believe will be won, to the transcending issue of the Supreme Court as the authoritative organ of what the Constitution requires. In everything we do, and how we do it, we must serve as exemplars of understanding and wisdom and magnanimity to the Butlers and Uptons of the South . . ."

Despite his waning influence with the chief justice, Frankfurter urged Warren to differentiate between Governor Faubus and the school board's lawyer Butler. In a note to the chief justice on the morning of the September 11 argument, Frankfurter referred to a *Washington Post* editorial praising the school board's conduct as " 'courageous' " and suggested that before the argument the Court acknowledge the board's decision to delay the beginning of the school year until September 15. Frankfurter argued that Faubus's failure to sign a state law postponing the school year "was as much an attempted trick against the School Board as against this Court." He praised Butler and Little Rock school superintendent Virgil Blossom for showing "a good deal of enterprise and courage to stand up against Faubus and Company." Finally, Frankfurter tried to impart his larger message to the chief justice: "My own view has long been that the ultimate hope for the peaceful solution to the basic problem largely depends on winning the support of lawyers of the South for the overriding issue of obedience to the Court's decision. Therefore I think we should encourage every manifestation of fine conduct by a lawyer like Butler."

At the outset of the September 11 argument, Warren offered a more neutral statement: "And may I say before we start that the Court appreciates the co-operation that we've had from counsel on both sides of the case in facilitating the hearing for today." Much to Frankfurter's dismay, the chief justice reacted to Butler's request to delay the implementation of the desegregation orders with a "blunt mentality" and "prosecutorial animus." Warren failed to differentiate between the legal position of Butler and the school board and the defiance of Governor Faubus. "Butler could not say it," Frankfurter wrote Bickel, "but I bet you a magnum of Churchill's Bollinger that if he were free to say it he would have said to the Court, 'I don't represent Gov. Faubus, *he* is your defendant, not the School Board, whom I represent and who have made the most honest effort of any school board in the South.'" After the argument, Butler confided to a sympathetic journalist that he did not have "a snowball's" chance of obtaining a two-and-a-half-year delay yet wanted the Court to understand the school board's practical problems of implementing immediate desegregation. Butler remarked that at least Frankfurter understood. Frankfurter had succeeded in achieving Brandeis's "aim . . . to make the defeated litigant understand why the decision went against him."

The day after the argument, the Court announced a short, unsigned decision drafted by Frankfurter and Harlan affirming the Court of Appeals for the Eighth Circuit and reinstating the prior orders to desegregate Central High School. The same day, Governor Faubus suspended the operation of all four Little Rock high schools pending a public vote to close them for the entire school year. Since the Court's first graduate school segregation decision in 1938, Frankfurter understood the inevitability of outlawing all segregated schools as contrary to the Fourteenth Amendment and "the extremely limited part the Court would have in realizing its legal promise." He considered the Court's role to be "very important" yet sought to avoid "harmful and hampering steps."

The justices revealed their philosophical differences about the role of the Court during the drafting of a more detailed opinion in *Cooper v. Aaron* about the constitutional issues at stake in Little Rock. Warren assigned the majority opinion to his new lieutenant, Brennan. Frankfurter considered offering Brennan advice about drafting the opinion yet decided against it, believing Brennan to be both cocky and overly sensitive, especially about comments from his former professor. In his first draft circulated on September 17, Brennan quoted Chief Justice John Marshall's opinion in *Marbury v. Madison* ("It is emphatically the province and duty of the judicial department to say what the law is") and derived from it "the basic principle that the federal judiciary is supreme in the exposition of the Constitution." Brennan's opinion ignored *Marbury*'s larger context that the Marshall Court went to great lengths to avoid a showdown with the Jefferson administration. Instead, Brennan seized on Marshall's ambiguous language to declare the Court the last word on the meaning of the Constitution.

Brennan's draft did not sit well with Frankfurter or Harlan. On September

19, Harlan drafted an alternative opinion omitting the reference to *Marbury*. He observed that the Constitution recognized that federal law was supreme over state law, not that the Supreme Court was supreme over the whole country. He awaited Brennan's revisions before circulating anything. Brennan's September 22 draft contained the same reference to *Marbury*. The next day, Harlan proposed inserting five pages about the Fourteenth Amendment and the Supremacy Clause in lieu of Brennan's five-page constitutional discussion. Harlan deemed Brennan's September 24 draft "a patchwork job" and Black's attempt at compromise language about the role of the Court to be "terrible." At the September 23 conference, Brennan insisted on including the reference to *Marbury*.

Frankfurter also made numerous suggestions to Brennan's drafts. After he read the September 22 draft, Frankfurter informed Brennan: "I strongly favor—after much over-night reflection and again, after your explanation for your reluctance to use it—John's closing full ¶ on pp. 24–25 of his memo." Harlan's paragraph would have supplanted Brennan's discussion of *Marbury*. Yet after reading Brennan's September 25 draft and offering a few minor comments, Frankfurter joined the opinion: "You have now made me content."

Frankfurter refused to be silenced by the Court's desire for unanimity. At the justices' four-hour conference on September 26, he announced that he was joining the majority opinion yet planned on publishing a concurrence. Douglas, who skipped the final deliberations to go on a canoe trip to Minnesota and Canada, later described the concurrence as a "bombshell." All eight justices, "with varying intensity," opposed his decision to publish. At Warren's request, Black tried to talk Frankfurter out of it. Harlan also met with him in private but was unable to change his mind. The only concession Frankfurter made was to delay publication of his concurrence for a week after the Court's opinion.

In the end, all nine justices joined Brennan's opinion and took the unusual step, based on Frankfurter's suggestion to Harlan, of each justice signing his name at the top. Only Tom Clark seriously considered dissenting. On September 29 in the Supreme Court courtroom, Warren read the entire opinion, except for case citations, for forty-five minutes. The final version contained the reference to *Marbury* and the much-criticized assertion that the Court was the final authority on the Constitution. There was no mention of Frankfurter's concurrence.

On October 3, Frankfurter circulated a draft concurrence appealing to southern lawyers who may not have agreed with the Court's decision in *Brown v. Board of Education* or *Cooper v. Aaron* but who respected the rule of law. In

654 DEMOCRATIC JUSTICE

contrast to Brennan's opinion and consistent with his earlier memorandum to his colleagues, Frankfurter outlined a more modest role for the judiciary: "'Every act of government may be challenged by an appeal to law, as finally pronounced by this Court. Even this Court has the last say only for a time. Being composed of fallible men, it may err. But revision of its errors must be by orderly process of law. The Court may be asked to reconsider its decisions, and this has been done successfully again and again throughout our history. Or, what this Court has deemed its duty to decide may be changed by legislation, as it often has been, and, on occasion, by constitutional amendment.'"

For Frankfurter, *Cooper* was not about the authority of the Supreme Court but about the states obeying federal law. It was of no import whether that law came from the legislative, executive, or judicial branch, but that the law came from the Constitution. "Particularly is this so where the declaration of what 'the supreme Law' commands on an underlying moral issue is not the dubious pronouncement of a gravely divided Court but is the unanimous conclusion of a long-matured deliberative process," he wrote. "The Constitution is not the formulation of the merely personal views of the members of this Court, nor can its authority be reduced to the claim that state officials are its controlling interpreters."

In the context of maintaining a federal system, Frankfurter believed in a little judicial supremacy. As he wrote Alexander Bickel, he believed that "Southern influences [were] to be won not on the merits of desegregation but on the overriding issue of non-nullification of final deference to the constitutional umpire." Like Thayer and Holmes, Frankfurter argued that the Court had more power to enforce the Constitution against the states than against co-equal branches of the federal government. With this added power, the Court protected the rule of law and the federal system against state defiance and mob violence.

At Brennan's behest, Warren called a special conference at 10:00 a.m. on October 6 about Frankfurter's concurrence. Warren and Black stated their objections to its publication. Black and Brennan drafted a special concurrence explaining that Frankfurter's concurrence "must not be accepted as any dilution or interpretation of the views expressed in the Court's joint opinion." They withdrew it after Harlan drafted (and Clark joined) a mock, one-paragraph concurrence/dissent from the Brennan-Black concurrence. Harlan "doubt[ed] the wisdom" of Frankfurter's concurrence yet saw no "material difference" between it and the Court's opinion and left it up to Frankfurter whether to publish.

Over the opposition of his colleagues, Frankfurter released his *Cooper v.*

Aaron concurrence after the Court convened briefly at noon on October 6. He must have remembered how he had been persuaded to suppress his *Smith v. Allwright* concurrence fourteen years earlier and refused to make the same mistake. The immediate battle—keeping Central High School open—had been lost. On September 27, the people of Little Rock had voted to close the city's high schools for the year. In his *Cooper* concurrence, Frankfurter spoke directly to southern lawyers and law professors who could persuade their fellow citizens to respect the rule of law even when they disagreed with the decisions of the Supreme Court.

The publication of Frankfurter's concurrence elicited praise from old friends, colleagues, former clerks, the nation's newspapers, and, most important, southern lawyers. Frankfurter sent the justices a letter from A. F. House, counsel to the Little Rock School Board, and an excerpted letter from New Orleans lawyer Monte Lemann. After seeing the positive public reaction to the concurrence, several justices conceded that he had been right and they had been wrong about his decision to publish. Longtime observers of the Court including Dean Acheson, Ben Cohen, Learned Hand, and Roscoe Pound lauded Frankfurter's opinion because its measured tone was what the country needed during a time of constitutional crisis. Compared to the majority's empty boasts about judicial supremacy, Frankfurter's concurrence in *Cooper v. Aaron* offered a more modest, democratic vision of the Supreme Court.

CHAPTER 37

A Health Scare

On Saturday November 22, 1958, Frankfurter attended a black-tie dinner at the Metropolitan Club in honor of his former student Archibald MacLeish. Frankfurter's former clerk Elliot Richardson drove him to the event attended by longtime friends Dean Acheson, Frances Watson, William Bundy's wife, Mary (Acheson's daughter), and journalist Max Freedman. After dinner, they went to the National Theatre for the premiere of MacLeish's *J.B.*, a play in verse about Job, which won the 1959 Pulitzer Prize for drama. The next day, Frankfurter went for a brisk walk with "an athletic friend," as he described him, struggled to keep up, yet refused to ask his younger companion to slow down. After the walk, the justice did not feel right. On Monday, he went about business as usual—sitting for a new Supreme Court photograph (because Sixth Circuit judge Potter Stewart filled the seat left by Harold Burton's resignation) and attending a brief noon court session. At 2:30 p.m., he visited his doctor and discovered he had suffered a mild heart attack.

The doctor immediately admitted the ashen-faced Frankfurter to George Washington University Hospital for an extended stay. In those days, the only treatment for a heart attack was rest. The justice told friends not to worry. He blamed it on the fast pace of the Sunday walk and neglected to tell them he had seen his doctor four times that month. "This onset was not due to Nature but to my own stupidity . . . ," he wrote Learned Hand. "The docs think this heart of mine will be better at the end of this business than the beginning."

The heart attack was more serious than Frankfurter let on. The doctors asked him to do what he was almost incapable of—slow down. He was forbidden from reading. His secretary, Elsie Douglas, took over his correspondence. On December 2, he sat up three times in half-hour intervals. A few days later, he walked across the room. The doctors vowed to keep him in the hospital for several weeks for "rest and observation."

The justice was obeying the letter but not the spirit of the doctor's orders. On December 4, he dictated a letter to Clark about two tax cases. Clark urged him to stop worrying about delaying the Court's opinions and to "take care of yourself." He also sent a cheesecake; Frankfurter ate two "generous servings" in the hospital. Old friends, former students and law clerks, and other admirers sent him get-well letters, including one from Senator John F. Kennedy. "Please acknowledge this of the maybe next President," Frankfurter scrawled to his secretary Douglas at the top of Kennedy's note. "You might employ some of your Irish warmth."

A letter from another politician offering words of advice and comfort made the biggest impression. Former Frankfurter clerk Phil Graham had informed Lyndon Johnson that the justice was a great "admirer" of the Senate majority leader, knew Johnson had recovered from a heart attack, and would appreciate a note of encouragement. On December 3, Johnson sent an arrangement of bronze chrysanthemums followed three days later by a note. "It is not often I have an opportunity to lecture a Supreme Court Justice on a subject I know a great deal more about than does he or any of his colleagues—and I don't mean civil rights!" Johnson wrote.

"I have been sitting down here on my ranch watching the Pedernales River flow past my door, and cleaning my guns for the quail and deer hunting season, I have been thinking about you lying in that hospital and staring at the ceiling and remembering that I did quite a lot of it more than three years ago."

Recalling his own heart attack, Johnson offered Frankfurter several tips. First, ignore the well-meaning advice of friends. Second, "behave yourself in the early stage of this business." Third, given the importance of good work, "keep yourself in shape at the moment so you can get back to that work." Johnson reviewed the "concessions" he had made, working sixteen hours a day instead of eighteen and altering his diet. He also warned about a future bout of "mental depression" but assured the justice that it would pass. The Senate majority leader concluded: "This 'heart' business is, however, not the only thing we have in common. I think that each of us in his own way tries to do the best he can for his Country. When you get all through you can't say much more than that about anyone."

Allowed to write back in his own hand on December 18, Frankfurter thanked Johnson for the flowers and "heart-warming" letter. While in the hospital, the justice had read a talk Johnson gave to the Washington Heart Association, appreciated the private words of wisdom, and pledged to be following "the Johnson formula." He urged Johnson to "store up refreshment and strength for the days ahead of you when the self-confident new innocents will try to teach you how to make an omelette without breaking eggs—while you try to keep a party together and govern a country wisely."

Frankfurter considered Johnson to be the future of the republic. He admired Johnson's pragmatism in settling for the voting rights provisions in the Civil Rights Act of 1957. After he read a *New Republic* editorial supporting Johnson's introduction of new civil rights legislation, Frankfurter praised the "wisdom in encouraging" the majority leader's "right direction." On issues of voting rights and school desegregation, he knew that the solutions would not come from the Court but from Johnson and other elected officials.

By mid-December, Frankfurter was beginning to feel like his old self. He had learned the names of all the doctors, nurses, and orderlies and had asked about their families. He reflected on his work at the Court. He was writing letters railing against outsiders who gave Warren too much credit and agreeing with insiders who referred to it as "the Black not the Warren Court." He was summoning his law clerks to his hospital room and instructing them to bring briefs from soon-to-be argued cases. On January 3, 1959, he was discharged after seven weeks in the hospital. He arrived home to find an automatic stair-lift, a gift from his law clerks, from the garage to the first floor. A similar device already had been installed from the first to the second floor. Absent the new ground-floor stairlift, the Frankfurters probably would have had to move from their Dumbarton Avenue home.

Nine days after leaving the hospital, he was back on the bench questioning lawyers as vigorously as ever. A *Washington Post* editorial acknowledged his return to the Court and urged him not to retire: "The Court urgently needs the ripe wisdom and extensive knowledge of its oldest member." A few weeks later, the *New York Times* editorial page celebrated his twentieth anniversary on the bench and recognized his importance to the Court: "His influence goes beyond his opinions, important as many of them have been, and beyond the role his questions from the bench and comments during the court's deliberations are said to play in shaping decisions." The *Times* lauded "his approach to the most demanding of jobs"—"his continued skepticism about pat formulas, his recognition of the fallibility of men, including judges, his reverence for history and tradition, his moral and intellectual struggle to balance the needs of the individual with those of society."

During the final two years of the Eisenhower administration, Frankfurter showed that he could use his influence in the political sphere with the March 11 nomination of his brilliant former student Henry J. Friendly to the Court of Appeals for the Second Circuit. For several years, Frankfurter and Learned Hand had been lobbying Attorney General Herbert Brownell to name

Friendly, not Irving Kaufman, the politically ambitious trial judge who had sentenced the Rosenbergs to death, to the federal appeals court. Frankfurter credited Brownell's successor, William P. Rogers, for ignoring Kaufman's political boosters and persuading Eisenhower to nominate Friendly. The *New York Times* ran a glowing profile, headlined "From Clerk to Judge," of the 55-year-old former Brandeis clerk and esteemed Wall Street lawyer. When a Kaufman supporter, Senator Thomas Dodd, delayed Friendly's confirmation, Frankfurter called on his friend Lyndon Johnson. Johnson met with Dodd and assured Frankfurter "all will be o.k." Frankfurter thanked the Senate majority leader for his "great service to the Federal Judiciary." After his confirmation, Friendly succeeded Hand as one of the nation's most influential federal appellate judges.

Upon his return to the Court, Frankfurter curtailed his outside activities and travel except for the celebration of Hand's fiftieth anniversary on the bench. On April 10, 1959, Frankfurter left on a morning train from Washington to New York City for a 3:30 p.m. Court of Appeals for the Second Circuit special session honoring Hand. In the Second Circuit courtroom at Foley Square in Manhattan, Frankfurter spoke without notes about his closest friend on the bench. Frankfurter revealed what he had often told Hand in private—that he was "lucky not to get on the Nine." He did not think Hand would have relished "the joy of battle."

THE BATTLE BETWEEN Frankfurter and his fellow justices intensified over incorporation, the application of the first eight amendments of the Constitution to the states, in the case of convicted bank robber Alfonse Bartkus. In December 1953, Bartkus had been tried in federal court and acquitted. A month later, based on evidence the FBI had turned over to state officials, he was indicted in state court, tried, convicted, and sentenced to life in prison as a habitual offender. Bartkus's lawyer argued that the conviction violated the Fifth Amendment's prohibition against double jeopardy.

As the senior justice in the majority, Frankfurter assigned the opinion to himself and rejected the argument that the Fourteenth Amendment's Due Process Clause applied all eight amendments to the states. For Frankfurter, the issue was about respect for history and precedent. He relied on political scientist Charles Fairman's conclusion that the Thirty-Ninth Congress had not intended the Fourteenth Amendment to apply the first eight amendments to the states. Frankfurter also pointed to provisions in the constitutions of ratifying states that differed from those in the federal constitution and detailed them in an appendix. He deeply respected Cardozo's 1937 opinion in *Palko v. Connecticut*, which had rejected the incorporation of the Double Jeopardy Clause, because it was not "implicit in the concept of ordered liberty." Because the Double Jeopardy Clause did not apply, the only question for Frankfurter was whether the defendant's Fourteenth Amendment right to due process had been violated. No one was more reluctant to invoke the Due Process Clause to encroach on the power of state and local governments than Frankfurter. He referred to numerous state and federal court decisions permitting a state prosecution after a federal prosecution or vice versa as reflecting "the two-sovereignty principle."

Frankfurter's intellectual adversary, Hugo Black, believed that the framers of the Fourteenth Amendment had intended to incorporate the first eight amendments as limits on the power of the states. Although Black had joined Cardozo's opinion in *Palko*, he had renounced it long ago. In his stirring dissent in *Bartkus*, Black argued that "double prosecutions for the same offense are so contrary to the spirit of our free country that they violate even the prevailing view of the Fourteenth Amendment" in *Palko*. He then explained the history of prohibitions against double jeopardy as "one of the oldest ideas found in western civilization." Finally, he rejected the two-sovereignty principle: "If double punishment is what is feared, it hurts no less for two 'Sovereigns' to inflict it than for one."

Frankfurter was more annoyed by Brennan's dissent, which only Warren and Douglas joined, than by Black's. Brennan argued that the state prosecution of Bartkus was "actually a second federal prosecution." Frankfurter, who took great pride in his ability to read a record, circulated a memorandum insisting Brennan had exaggerated and misstated the facts. Brennan responded in kind. Much to Frankfurter's regret, other justices in the majority persuaded him not to publish his rebuttal. Brennan's clerks described the episode as a "hot feud." Yet Frankfurter persuaded Brennan to narrow his majority opinion in *Abbate v. United States*, another case that term rejecting a similar double jeopardy claim.

In *Frank v. Maryland*, a 5–4 decision announced a few months later, Frankfurter rejected the application of the Fourth Amendment's prohibition against unreasonable searches and seizures to a city health inspection. He upheld the warrantless inspection of a Baltimore home for rodent infestation, which resulted in a $20 fine for violating the city health code. He differentiated a voluntary health inspection to prevent a nuisance to the community from an involuntary, warrantless search of a home as part of a criminal investigation.

In contrast, Douglas's dissent, which Black, Warren, and Brennan joined, took a more absolutist approach in prohibiting all warrantless searches of the home, regardless of the health or safety reason.

The end of the 1958 term was one of the last times that Frankfurter—voting with Clark, Harlan, Whittaker, and Stewart—could find himself on the winning side of 5–4 decisions. He assigned and joined Harlan's 5–4 majority opinion affirming the conviction of Vassar College psychology instructor Lloyd Barenblatt for refusing to answer HUAC questions about Communist Party membership. Rather than invoke his Fifth Amendment privilege against self-incrimination, Barenblatt asserted his First Amendment right to free speech. He was convicted of contempt of Congress and sentenced to thirty days in jail. For Frankfurter, the case was not about infringing on Barenblatt's free speech but about upholding Congress's broad investigatory powers.

Near the end of the term, Frankfurter made headlines for criticizing the Court for hearing a case reinstating a $7500 jury verdict in favor of a North Dakota widow. For years, he had been writing his colleagues memoranda at the beginning of each term and often counseled them against voting to hear trivial cases. In announcing the majority opinion, Warren recounted the "folksy" story about how the widow had sued the New York Life Insurance Company for double indemnity for accidental death. The insurance company had declared a suicide after her husband was found shot to death on his farm. Some of the justices took the time to inspect the shotgun. Frankfurter orally dissented: "This is a case that should never have been here. It will set no precedents. It will guide no lawyers. It will guide no courts." The lecture to his colleagues made the front pages of the *New York Times* and *New York Herald Tribune*. The *Herald Tribune* editorial page observed: "It is disheartening to think of our highest court frittering away its days on minutiae."

———

IN HIS REFUSALS to apply the Double Jeopardy Clause to the states, to expand the prohibition against unreasonable searches and seizures, to encroach on Congress's investigatory powers, and to hear trivial cases, Frankfurter continued to advocate for a more limited role for the Court. He had faith in elected state and local officials to be responsive to the needs of the people, in Congress to use its investigatory powers wisely, and in state and lower federal judges to do their jobs. He did not believe the Court should try to solve all the country's problems and should limit its own power by respecting history and following precedent. In his view, his liberal colleagues, Black, Douglas, Warren, and Brennan, failed to recognize the dangers of overruling precedent and of a government by judiciary. "They don't understand that there will come a time when there is a very different majority," Frankfurter told his law clerk Howard Kalodner. "They will be free to undo all of this. And even more."

Another view, however, was that Frankfurter was too caught up in the past; too reverential of the decisions of Holmes, Brandeis, and Cardozo; and too stuck in his old ways—particularly when it came to hiring law clerks. Harvard law professor Henry Hart and later his colleague Al Sacks selected Frankfurter's clerks. They occasionally floated names of possible candidates but almost always selected a former member of the *Harvard Law Review* with little consultation from the justice.

On November 30, 1959, Sacks proposed a candidate of a different sort— 26-year-old Columbia law graduate Ruth Ginsburg. As Sacks explained in his letter to the justice, Ginsburg had achieved a "distinguished record" as a Cornell political science major and had married her husband, Martin, after graduation. Martin enrolled at Harvard Law School and after his first year served two years in the military. Upon their return to Cambridge, Ruth enrolled at Harvard Law School as well. After her first two years, she was fourteenth in the class and a member of the *Harvard Law Review*. Sacks had read her law review contributions, deemed her short paper for his legal process class to be "most impressive," and believed she might have become an officer on the *Review* if she had stayed for her third year. After Martin graduated, however, he landed a job with a New York law firm, so Ruth finished her law degree at Columbia. She served on the *Columbia Law Review*, finished tied for first in her graduating class (Sacks incorrectly said second), and wrote the best paper in Herbert Wechsler's federal courts class. Wechsler thought she was "tops"; his colleague Gerald Gunther was "equally enthusiastic" and had helped her land a federal district court clerkship with Judge Edmund Palmieri. Sacks's recommendation was more measured than those of Wechsler and Gunther: "In terms of analytical powers alone, I think that Ruth, despite her Columbia record, is not at the very top of the Harvard group. I should put her in a class just below the top group of three or four, the difference being a small one." Sacks, however, believed that "her qualities of mind and person would make her most attractive to you as a law clerk." Sacks admired her "extraordinary self-possession. She is the kind of person who is quiet until it is time to talk but who then reflects the fruits of solid, independent thought." As an aside he remarked, "I believe that I have successfully put to one side the fact that she is a pleasantly attractive female."

Finally, Sacks raised "problems posed by her family status." The Ginsburgs hired full-time child care for their four-year-old daughter, Jane, while Ruth worked for Judge Palmieri. Martin would be able to work in his firm's Washington office. The biggest issue was his health. As a third-year law student, he had been diagnosed and treated for testicular cancer. Sacks reported that "the doctors are optimistic" and praised Martin as "a very personable fellow who made a fine record at the law school." Sacks left the final decision up to Frankfurter: "The very fact that I have taken so long in describing this girl should make it clear that I think your reactions concerning her are most relevant and significant." Sacks acknowledged that "an appraisal of her family situation" was a consideration: "As I see it, there is no issue of discrimination here . . . there is a question whether her family status may subtly and intangibly interfere with the necessary assignment of heavy work loads. While I have considered this, your appraisal will be much surer than mine."

On December 7, Frankfurter reiterated that Sacks had carte blanche power to select his law clerks yet chose not to hire Ginsburg: "Had you named Mrs. Ginsberg [sic] for the remarkable fellowship of my law clerks, I would have accepted her without demurring and welcomed her cordially. But since you deemed it appropriate to invite my wish in the matter, I choose not to have her." Unlike Holmes, Frankfurter did not care if his law clerks were married. Nor did Frankfurter require his law clerks to work nights. The reason Frankfurter gave for declining to hire Ginsburg was the preservation of his health after his December 1958 heart attack: "Mrs. Ginsberg [sic] evidently has her life so arranged that she can work as a professional. But while she may not have a young child and a potentially sick husband on her mind, I would have them on my mind. The only thing my doctors have enjoined upon me is to try to simplify my life, reduce my concerns and not add to them. Willy-nilly, to have Mrs. Ginsberg [sic] would tend to complicate it." He concluded: "I am very sorry to have reached this conclusion, because as the years go on I indulge myself in wanting more charm and more ability rather than less, and evidently I surrender both in not having Mrs. Ginsberg [sic]. But you lead me to believe that the Law School's resources will not deprive me of charm and ability even though of feminine charm."

After he sent the letter to Sacks, Frankfurter discussed the matter with his law clerks, Paul Bender and Morton Winston. "You can't believe who Al Sacks wants me to hire," Frankfurter said. "Ruth Ginsburg." Bender had known Ginsburg since they were classmates at Brooklyn's James Madison High School; Winston had known and admired her in law school. "We both said, 'Wow, that's great,'" Bender said.

"I can't do it," Frankfurter replied. "She's got a sick husband. She has a young kid." He offered his law clerks a series of implausible excuses. "I work you guys too hard" was the first. He did not work them hard; Frankfurter reviewed all the petitions for certiorari on his own; Frankfurter's clerks, according to Bender, were "the least worked of the law clerks." "Well, I curse a lot" was the second. "He didn't curse a lot," Bender insisted. "He was inventing these excuses." Bender and Winston knew that Frankfurter had already told Sacks no. "He was willing to argue about it," Bender said, "but it was not an open question with him."

Sacks, who had informed Ginsburg that she was under consideration for the Frankfurter clerkship, broke the bad news. "He said that he recommended me and John French," she remembered, "and that French had gotten the job." Ginsburg knew nothing about Frankfurter's concerns about her small child and sick husband until she read the Sacks-Frankfurter correspondence nearly sixty years later and described it as rife with "typical 1950s attitudes about women."

On some levels, it is surprising that Frankfurter refused to hire Ginsburg. Early in his career, he had worked with Florence Kelley, Josephine Goldmark, and Molly Dewson on legal briefs for the National Consumers' League. Throughout his life, he befriended numerous strong, intellectual women including suffragist Katharine Ludington, Harvard physician Alice Hamilton, activist Elizabeth Glendower Evans, Secretary of Labor Frances Perkins, writer and socialite Alice Roosevelt Longworth, and actress Ruth Gordon. He liked women and made a conscious effort to get to know the wives and daughters of his friends, former students, and law clerks. Finally, he was willing to buck convention in hiring the first African American Supreme Court clerk in William T. Coleman.

On the other hand, Harvard Law School did not admit women when he taught there. He had spent a lifetime mentoring male former students and encouraging them to enter public service. As a justice, he had revealed his blind spots about gender equality in writing the majority opinion in *Goesaert v. Cleary*, which upheld a Michigan law forbidding the licensing of most women bartenders. At the time, only one woman, University of Washington Law School graduate Lucile Lomen, had clerked on the Supreme Court, with Douglas during the 1944 term. In hindsight, not hiring Ginsburg as the second woman clerk was one of the biggest blunders of Frankfurter's judicial career.

Given his sincere concerns about his health and his shakier handwriting since his heart attack, perhaps Frankfurter should have considered retirement. Before the start of the 1959 term, syndicated columnists Robert Allen and Paul Scott floated a rumor that Frankfurter was thinking about resigning in June. The rumor was based on several false premises. They claimed that Frankfurter had indicated to friends that the work of the Court was becoming more difficult for him. The work was no harder than usual. They claimed he had returned to work only part time after his heart attack. In truth, he only limited his travel schedule and worked from home on Fridays. They claimed he had "high regard" for Eisenhower and viewed Henry Friendly as his successor. As pleased as he was about Friendly's nomination, Frankfurter thought Eisenhower was miscast as president and showed little enthusiasm for the job. He lobbied for Friendly's nomination to improve the quality of judging on the Second Circuit after Learned Hand took senior status and to block Irving Kaufman, not to name his own successor. Frankfurter also belittled Eisenhower's insistence on limiting his Supreme Court nominees to federal appeals court judges.

ON APRIL 30, 1960, the Harvard Law School Association honored Frankfurter. That afternoon, he spoke to Harvard law students about public service. He recounted a World War II–era conversation with French diplomat Jean Monnet, who had observed that " 'the most effective, the most fruitful, the most creative' " people in the government were Harvard-educated lawyers. Frankfurter replied that "the training of the lawyer is to a degree training for disinterested analysis not true in any other profession." The justice advocated that the students should sustain the law school's "ever-continuing heritage of service." He took questions and responded by sprinkling in references to some of the law school's great public servants including Henry Stimson and Joseph Cotton. That evening, the law school unveiled a bust of Frankfurter by Eleanor Platt, which still sits in the law library. The tributes included a moving message from Learned Hand, who was unable to attend for health reasons yet described Frankfurter as "the outstanding figure on any court today." Hand admired how "in the most provocative of settings he has been able to lay aside what would be his own appraisals. . . . It would have been a high achievement for one who was tepid in disposition; but his is an ardent, indeed a passionate, nature, eager to take sides and ready to realize those results that commend themselves to his judgment and his feelings." During the evening, Frankfurter concluded the proceedings with a talk to faculty and alumni reminiscing about his arrival at Harvard Law School fifty-seven years earlier as "the scaredest kid that you can imagine"; his legendary professors

Ames, Gray, Williston, and Beale; his belief that he was unworthy to join the faculty; and his reverence for the school.

At the end of May, he put his life story in print with the publication of *Felix Frankfurter Reminisces*. The book was the product of a series of tape-recorded interviews with Columbia University oral historian Harlan "Bud" Phillips. In 1948, historian Allan Nevins had started the Columbia University Oral History Research office and had sent Phillips and other trained interviewers to record the recollections of hundreds of leading figures in American life. During a fifteen-year period, Phillips had interviewed at least 182 people. In the early 1950s, Phillips had interviewed Frankfurter's closest colleague on the Court, Robert Jackson, and had become an informal part of Jackson's staff. From 1953 to 1955, Frankfurter sat for a series of interviews with Phillips and became similarly charmed by the young man. During the summer of 1957, Phillips interviewed Frankfurter another fifteen times. Early on, Phillips gained access to the justice's correspondence locked in eighty-four file cabinets in the basement of the Supreme Court. Phillips and publisher Eugene Reynal persuaded a reluctant Frankfurter to become the first person to publish an edited version of his Columbia oral history as a book.

Felix Frankfurter Reminisces, as the foreword observes, is not an autobiography but "just talk." Frankfurter answered Phillips's questions about everything from his arrival in New York City at age eleven until his Supreme Court nomination at age fifty-six. The Court years were off limits. Along the way, Frankfurter narrated his rapid rise from Ellis Island to Harvard Law School to public life with Henry Stimson and opined on presidents and personalities he knew from TR to Woodrow Wilson to FDR. He vividly recounted living with Robert Valentine at the House of Truth; founding the *New Republic* with Herbert Croly and Walter Lippmann; investigating the Bisbee deportation and the Mooney case during World War I; his admiration for Holmes and Brandeis; his involvement in the Sacco and Vanzetti case; his rejection of a seat on the Massachusetts Supreme Judicial Court and Franklin Roosevelt's offer of the solicitor generalship; and the phone call from Roosevelt informing him of his Supreme Court nomination. The book received rave reviews in the nation's major newspapers; the *Washington Post* ran thirteen excerpts. As a work of history, the book suffers from poor fact checking of names, places, and dates; Isaiah Berlin considered it "an appalling embarrassment." Nonetheless, the book offers the experience of sitting down with a gifted conversationalist. "It has long been a kind of well-authenticated rumor that Justice Frankfurter is the best talker in Washington," the Washington *Evening Star*'s reviewer wrote. "Now we have proof that he is."

A best seller for five months, the book went into six printings, sold more than 20,000 copies, and was a finalist for the 1961 National Book Award. Neither the proceeds nor the honor went to Frankfurter. He had put the copyright and authorship in Phillips's name. Just as he had donated all the royalties from *The Case of Sacco and Vanzetti*, he gave all the royalties from *Felix Frankfurter Reminisces* to Phillips because he knew the struggling academic and his family needed money. As his late friend Laski observed, Frankfurter cared little about money and preferred to collect people. Not surprisingly, he received scores of letters from old friends exulting over the book. As enjoyable as the letters were, he could have used the royalties for Marion's medical bills and his own long-term security. His carefree attitude about money was his Achilles' heel.

FOR THE PAST SEVERAL YEARS, the Frankfurters had aspired to spend part of their summer at Frances Watson's summer home in Maine. Yet, after consulting with her doctor, Marion opted to continue with physical therapy rather than venture out of the house for the first time in years. Contrary to her husband's optimistic reports, her health was not improving. Another summer in Washington made her more reclusive than ever. She would see only three people—Kay Graham, Frances Watson (Pa's widow), and Catherine Hiss (Donald's wife) in sessions described as "hellish." Phil Graham described the Frankfurters' home life, in which the justice served as his wife's nurse on weekends, as "burdensome." The justice limited his travel and rarely dined out with friends. To the outside world, Felix was carefree and, according to Graham, "maintains an activity of terrifying intensity, never manifests any concern or strain, and in my opinion is kept going strongly by the work of the Court."

During the summer and fall of 1960, Frankfurter watched with bemusement as friends and former clerks threw themselves into John F. Kennedy's presidential campaign. Phil Graham was an ardent supporter and persuaded Kennedy to put Lyndon Johnson on the ticket as vice president. Former clerk Richard Goodwin signed on as a Kennedy campaign aide and speechwriter. At their first meeting a few years earlier, Kennedy had remarked to Goodwin that the justice was "not my greatest fan." Frankfurter thought Kennedy was a lightweight. Some of this stemmed from his low opinion of Kennedy's anti-Semitic, Nazi-appeasing father Joe Sr. but also from his observation of Kennedy's time in the Senate. Frankfurter believed that his friends hated Richard

Nixon so much that they had fallen in love with Kennedy. As proof that people had lost their minds, he recounted Walter Lippmann's assertion that Kennedy was "a wiser statesman than F.D.R." In the justice's view, Kennedy could not hold a candle to Churchill or Roosevelt and urged people, as he had written about Woodrow Wilson in 1916, to " 'know what you're supporting and what you are in for.' "

The justice imparted his lukewarm attitude toward Kennedy to his favorite British schoolboy-turned-young adult, Oliver Gates. Frankfurter would have done anything for the youngest of three British children who had lived with him and Marion during the bombing of Britain. Frankfurter's best friend, Dean Acheson, knew how happy it would make him to have Oliver, a recent Oxford graduate, return to the United States. In 1960, the former secretary of state and Covington & Burling law partner helped Gates land a position in DuPont's training program. Acheson, in his three-piece suit, accompanied Gates to the job interview in Wilmington, Delaware, and waited during the required two-hour medical exam. Working for DuPont in nearby Richmond, Gates often spent weekends with the Frankfurters. One October evening, he was invited to a dinner party at Joseph Alsop's Georgetown home in Kennedy's honor. The justice thought the party for Kennedy was a waste of time. Instead, he arranged a dinner for Gates with Alexander Bickel, who was spending the year in Washington to research his history of the White Court from 1910 to 1921. Gates dined with Bickel several times that year and claimed never to regret missing the dinner with Kennedy.

After he listened to the second televised debate between Kennedy and Nixon on October 7, Frankfurter concluded that the vice president had been "betrayed by his own vanity as a crack debater" and never should have agreed to share the stage with Kennedy. Nixon, Frankfurter believed, had thrown away all his advantages—the country's economic prosperity, his support in the Bible Belt, his status as "a *de facto* incumbent" in the White House the past seven years, and Kennedy's reputation for "immaturity." The justice was not a fan of either candidate. In the end, he predicted that "more people will vote against Nixon than will vote against Kennedy."

Kennedy's narrow victory over Nixon failed to alleviate Frankfurter's skepticism about the president-elect: "I dare to believe that no one will be quicker or more ready than I to recognize greatness in our new President. But I think there was no evidence of it during the campaign . . ." Some Boston friends informed Frankfurter that the 42-year-old Kennedy's biggest flaw was "hubris" and he was in need of a "comeuppance." The justice could not understand why so many of his friends "slid from dislike or hatred of Nixon to love of Kennedy" and caused him to question "my confidence in the power of reason."

Kennedy knew he needed astute legal and policy advisers and borrowed heavily from Frankfurter's liberal network for friends, former students, and law clerks. Ten former Frankfurter clerks joined the administration, including Phil Elman as a federal trade commissioner, Abram Chayes as legal adviser to the State Department, and Richard Goodwin as a presidential aide and speechwriter. Other Frankfurter friends at Harvard, including special assistant Arthur Schlesinger, Jr., and National Security Advisor McGeorge Bundy, played prominent roles in the administration.

The one Frankfurter disciple who got away from Kennedy was Harvard law professor Paul Freund. For weeks, Freund had been rumored to be the president's top choice to be solicitor general. A leading constitutional law scholar, Freund had advised the Massachusetts senator on the Civil Rights Act of 1957 and during the presidential campaign. On December 5, Kennedy phoned Freund and officially offered him the job representing the federal government before the Supreme Court. He wanted Freund to be solicitor general "to set exemplary standards for the profession." For his part, Freund admired Kennedy making good on his 1956 Harvard graduation speech by recruiting scholars and experts for the administration.

The standard story is that Frankfurter advised Freund to decline the job because Frankfurter had passed on a similar offer from Roosevelt and ended up on the Court. The truth is that Freund was very conflicted, and his first impulse was "to stay put" at Harvard. He understood the differences between the offers from Roosevelt and Kennedy. Frankfurter had known Roosevelt for years, had been hand-picked by the president to be solicitor general, and had been recruited not only to be solicitor general but also to be an administration insider. Freund knew Kennedy very superficially, had been suggested by his Harvard colleagues to attorney general–designate Robert Kennedy and others, and was not recruited to be anything more than a solicitor general, as Bobby would be his brother's primary source of legal advice. Frankfurter and Freund also were very different personalities. Frankfurter had worked for three presidents in government service, liked the thrust and parry of politics, and never tired of meeting new people. Freund, aside from his New Deal service during the 1930s, stayed out of political controversies and was more passive and introverted. He also took his position as the editor in chief of the multivolume Holmes Devise history of the Supreme Court and his authorship of the volume on the Hughes Court very seriously.

Four days after Kennedy's offer, Freund spoke with the president-elect by phone and declined the job. "The soul-searching is over," he wrote Frank-furter, "and I am once more at peace with myself." One of the reasons Freund gave was his editing and writing responsibilities for the Holmes Devise history. To which Kennedy apparently replied, "I thought you would rather make history than write it." It was a clever line but obscured some fundamental truths about Kennedy's offer.

Freund's decision crushed his Harvard law colleagues Abram Chayes and Freund's longtime housemate Ernest Brown, who had been pushing him to take the job. They blamed Frankfurter for Freund's decision "as tho Paul were wax!" They believed that Freund could have influenced the Kennedy administration's policy agenda, a notion Frankfurter dismissed as a romantic fantasy as long as brother Bobby was attorney general. They also argued that as solicitor general, often referred to as "the tenth justice," Freund could transform the "discordant, rationally unguided body into a harmonious, reason-guided tribunal." Frankfurter considered anyone's ability to influence his colleagues to be extremely limited. He knew that Stewart's "obstinacies" and Brennan's disregard for precedent were not subject to persuasion. Nor did he think that Freund could have performed any better before the Court than Archibald Cox, another Frankfurter student and Harvard law professor who accepted the solicitor general post.

No one—not Freund, Cox, or even Frankfurter himself—could temper the perceived excesses of the Warren Court. For his part, Frankfurter gave it one last try.

CHAPTER 38

The Political Thicket

D uring his last two Supreme Court terms from 1960 to 1962, Frankfurter imparted his most enduring lessons about the role of the Court in American life. He was not always on his best behavior. He infuriated several colleagues, notably Chief Justice Warren. He did not get every case right. Yet he warned that the Warren Court's liberal trend would not last forever, that the Court would revert to its historically conservative ways, and that the American people should seek change not from the Court but from the democratic political process. For Frankfurter, two cases, *Gomillion v. Lightfoot* and *Baker v. Carr*, exemplified his philosophy of judicial review—that the Court should protect minority rights yet refrain from injecting itself into purely political disputes better left to the people and their elected representatives. Those competing goals came to a head in *Gomillion*.

At 4:00 p.m. on October 18, 1960, Fred D. Gray stood before the nine justices. The black Montgomery, Alabama, civil rights lawyer had defended Claudette Colvin and Rosa Parks and the Montgomery Improvement Association's boycott of the city's racially segregated bus system culminating in the Court's decision in *Gayle v. Browder*. He also had prevented Alabama officials from shutting down the state's NAACP chapter, and in May 1960 he had persuaded an all-white jury to acquit Martin Luther King, Jr., of tax evasion. Yet he considered his first Supreme Court appearance in *Gomillion v. Lightfoot* "the most important" case of his career.

As he uttered "May it please the Court," Gray had something behind him that "fascinated" the justices—a large-scale map. The map showed how an Alabama law had changed the Tuskegee city limits from a perfect square into a 28-sided figure that Gray described as a "sea dragon." The new boundaries retained all 1310 of the city's white registered voters yet excluded all 400 of the city's registered black voters except four or five. Under the old boundaries,

Tuskegee contained 6700 residents, including 5397 blacks. As a result of the sea dragon, only four or five black voters lived in the new city limits and therefore remained eligible to vote in municipal elections.

This seemed like an open and shut case of racial discrimination. But Frank Johnson, a liberal Republican district court judge, had dismissed the complaint for failing to state a claim. And the federal court of appeals, including a concurring opinion by liberal Republican judge John Minor Wisdom, had affirmed Johnson's decision. Johnson and Wisdom relied on the political question doctrine that judges should avoid deciding political disputes. In a 1946 Supreme Court opinion, *Colegrove v. Green*, the Court refrained from deciding a redistricting case rather than risk entering what Frankfurter described as a "political thicket."

The political question doctrine, Frankfurter believed, prevented the courts from injecting themselves into purely political controversies, including redistricting and elections, which he believed should be decided by the other branches, the states, or the people. The doctrine also prevented the Court from having to decide cases in which it could not come up with a judicially manageable standard. "We are of opinion that the appellants ask of this Court what is beyond its competence to grant," he wrote in *Colegrove*. Frankfurter's opinion in *Colegrove*, however, was not a binding precedent. It was a plurality opinion because Chief Justice Stone had died and Jackson was serving as the chief U.S prosecutor at Nuremberg. Only two justices joined Frankfurter's opinion. Rutledge concurred in the result. Black and Douglas, who dissented, sought to overrule *Colegrove*. They dissented again in a 1950 challenge to Georgia's county unit system that diluted state legislative representation of the people of Atlanta and in another Atlanta challenge eight years later.

Gray knew that Frankfurter would play a crucial role whether the Court decided to address Tuskegee's racially exclusionary city limits. Minutes into Gray's argument, Frankfurter asked where the Tuskegee Institute, the historically black college and secondary school founded by Booker T. Washington in 1881, was on the newly redrawn map. Gray pointed to the northwest corner and said: "It is no longer in the city." "That's now outside?" Frankfurter asked. "It is now outside. Yes, sir," Gray replied. Frankfurter asked Gray a few more questions about the history of the institution. At that point, Gray knew that Frankfurter would be on his side and that *Colegrove* would not be an obstacle.

The case's lead plaintiff, Charles G. Gomillion, was a Tuskegee sociology professor and dean of students. He was also the head of the Tuskegee Civic Association (TCA), which had been boycotting the city's white merchants since Alabama's 1957 decision to draw the city's boundaries to exclude blacks from voting. The state attorney general had tried and failed to enjoin the TCA from boycotting. Three years later, Gomillion had turned the tables on the state by challenging the new city limits in the Supreme Court.

After Gray discussed the facts of the case, the NAACP's Robert L. Carter argued that the new city map violated not only the Fourteenth Amendment's Equal Protection and Due Process Clauses but also the Fifteenth Amendment's prohibition against excluding blacks from voting. Carter, who had litigated the school segregation cases with Thurgood Marshall, impressed Frankfurter and other justices with his skillful argument in the Tuskegee case. Carter encouraged the Court to intervene as it had in the past. "We take the position that this is purely a case of racial discrimination," Carter said, and that it "is as gross a case of racial discrimination as any case that has come before this Court between *Yick Wo v. Hopkins* and *Cooper v. Aaron.*" And in questioning that continued the next afternoon, Carter responded to Hugo Black that they were not asking the Court to overrule *Colegrove.*

The United States government advanced Gray and Carter's racial discrimination claim thanks to a skilled argument by former Frankfurter clerk Philip Elman. More than six years after his ethically questionable *ex parte* conversations with the justice about the school segregation cases and briefs on behalf of the Truman and Eisenhower Justice Departments, Elman again put the executive branch squarely on the side of racial justice. He argued that the new Tuskegee city limits were "in substance and effect a racial discrimination" and "class legislation on the basis of race or color" as in *Brown.* But, like many "separate but equal" laws, the Alabama law about Tuskegee's city limits was facially neutral—the text said nothing about excluding black residents or black voters. Black pressed Elman for proof of discriminatory purpose. Elman insisted such proof was not required; it was obvious from the law's effect on black voters.

The Montgomery, Alabama, lawyer defending the law, James J. Carter, urged Frankfurter and his colleagues to rely on *Colegrove* and to refuse to intervene. "If the courts are to enter this thicket," he concluded, "the cure is going to be much worse than the disease if a disease really exists." In a brief rebuttal, the NAACP's Robert L. Carter responded: "The abatement of racial discrimination has always been the business of the courts and particularly, the federal courts since the Civil War."

At conference on October 21, Warren emphasized that the case could be resolved without revisiting the *Colegrove* political question issue and voted to reverse because the state was denying blacks the right to vote. Black, however, questioned the "distinction" from *Colegrove.* From his experience in Alabama, he commented that all cities in the South do this. But in this case it "was done for [the] express & exclusive purpose to preventing these negro citizens from voting in Tuskegee." He voted to reverse on the basis of either the Fourteenth Amendment's Equal Protection Clause or the Fifteenth Amendment. Frankfurter believed that this was a "simple case" that had "nothing to do" with *Colegrove* or legislative reapportionment. In *Colegrove*, the final word rested with Congress whether to seat a state's representatives. In this case, by contrast, "negroes are forced out because they are negroes." Douglas voted to reverse in a narrow opinion about the purpose of excluding blacks from voting. The other justices—Clark, Harlan, Whittaker, and Stewart—also voted to reverse with Stewart preferring a narrow opinion relying on the Fifteenth Amendment.

Warren assigned the unanimous majority opinion to the justice with the most at stake—Frankfurter. A few weeks before oral argument, Frankfurter's law clerk, John French, had drafted a bench memorandum about the case, which formed the basis of the majority opinion. Frankfurter heavily edited French's memorandum and sought to distinguish *Colegrove* and other reapportionment cases. The justice, however, knew that he needed help from someone more experienced than his law clerk.

Before he circulated the draft opinion, Frankfurter sent it to the justice most intent on overturning *Colegrove*, Hugo Black. For many years, the two men had been locked in an ideological battle over the application of the Bill of Rights to the states, free speech, and role of the Court. In private, Frankfurter railed against Black's politically motivated decision-making, especially about race cases in which he worried how they would make him look in the South. In public, Frankfurter cried at the wedding of Black's daughter, Jo-Jo, and remained close to Black and his children. After years of jurisprudential battles, they respected each other as intellectual adversaries and as people.

Frankfurter knew he needed Black's sign-off on *Gomillion*. At conference, Black had predicted that the South would be as hostile to *Gomillion* as it was to *Brown v. Board of Education*. In a November 1 cover memorandum to Black, Frankfurter indicated his hope in issuing a unanimous opinion, reflecting the justices' views at conference, and "avoiding what is avoidable. . . . No one else has seen it. I shall be grateful for your help." Black spoke with Frankfurter, who deleted some references to *Colegrove* and then circulated the opinion to the entire Court.

Frankfurter continued to tinker with the references to *Colegrove* because of concerns from Bill Douglas. Frankfurter grew increasingly tired of Douglas's "crookery" and "shamelessness" and had long ago concluded with Jackson that Douglas was "the most unqualified cynic we ever encountered." He had not forgotten Douglas's grandstanding during the Willie Francis and Rosenberg cases and his absence during the justices' final deliberations and opinion announcement in the Little Rock case in order to go on a canoe trip. Because of Douglas's performance in several cases involving Jews, Frankfurter thought Douglas was anti-Semitic and "used to say he had known only two really evil men," Douglas and Joe Kennedy, Sr. For his part, Douglas often circulated memoranda designed to needle Frankfurter and wrote private memoranda for his files portraying Frankfurter in a negative light. In *Gomillion*, Douglas threatened to publish a concurring opinion unless Frankfurter toned down his characterization of past redistricting challenges; Frankfurter made the changes.

Even though the *Gomillion* opinion satisfied Black and Douglas, Whittaker published a short concurrence that the opinion should rest on the Fourteenth Amendment rather than on the Fifteenth Amendment. But to Frankfurter and the other seven justices, this was a clear case about excluding blacks from voting in Tuskegee elections and therefore violated the Fifteenth Amendment.

On November 14, Frankfurter announced his opinion preserving the municipal voting rights of Tuskegee's black residents yet safeguarding the political question doctrine and his opinion in *Colegrove v. Green*. "The decisive facts in this case . . . are wholly different from the considerations found controlling in *Colegrove* . . . ," Frankfurter wrote for the Court. "While in form this is merely an act redefining metes and bounds . . . , the inescapable human effect of this essay in geometry and geography is to despoil colored citizens, and only colored citizens, of their theretofore enjoyed voting rights. That was not *Colegrove v. Green*."

Gomillion was a triumph for Frankfurter. It exemplified his judicial philosophy of protecting minority rights yet not deciding purely political questions left to the other branches and the states. It revealed that, when assigned a majority opinion of delicacy and significance, he could incorporate the concerns of his fellow justices and navigate sensitive subjects. It showed that his philosophy of judicial restraint was compatible with fulfilling the promise of the Reconstruction Amendments. *New York Times* reporter Anthony Lewis, an "unreconstructed sinner" who opposed *Colegrove* yet admired Frankfurter, praised the opinion.

DURING A TERM packed with high-profile cases in the spring of 1961, Frankfurter was at the center of things whether he was in the majority or in dissent.
He wrote the majority opinion upholding Congress's power to force members of the Communist Party USA to register. He also wrote an opinion for
four justices dismissing a challenge to a Connecticut law banning the use of
or medical advice about contraceptives because of the lack of a real threat of
criminal prosecution. In the contraceptive case, Frankfurter sought to follow
Brandeis's admonition to avoid constitutional questions when the case could
be decided on other grounds.

In dissent, he chafed at his colleagues' willingness to alter the balance of
power between the federal government and the states and to overturn precedent. He was the lone dissenter in *Monroe v. Pape*, an important jurisdictional decision that held that racist Chicago police officers who conducted an
unreasonable search and seizure could be liable under federal civil rights law.
Frankfurter believed the officers should be liable only under state or local law.
Prior to the justices' conference about the case on November 11, he circulated
a 53-page memorandum on the legislative history of the Ku Klux Klan Act
of 1871 and contended the case had not been adequately briefed and argued.
Frankfurter's historically narrow view of Reconstruction Era legislation failed
to persuade a single justice. Warren admitted he had not read the memorandum before he voted. Harlan, for one, was shocked that his colleagues could
reach a "firm" conclusion only two days after receiving Frankfurter's memorandum and by the chief justice's admission about not having read it.

Frankfurter's colleagues' conduct in *Monroe v. Pape* was nothing compared
to what happened in *Mapp v. Ohio*. In *Mapp*, the Court applied the Fourth
Amendment's "exclusionary rule" barring the admission of illegally seized
evidence to the states. Frankfurter joined Harlan's dissent objecting to the
majority's willingness to impose another federal rule on the state courts and
to overrule Frankfurter's 1949 majority opinion in *Wolf v. Colorado* without briefing, argument, or an initial conference discussion and vote on the
issue. At a subsequent conference, Frankfurter railed about his colleagues'
eagerness to decide unnecessary constitutional questions as "the worst tragedy since *Dred Scott*." *Mapp* left lingering bad feelings. Frankfurter, who was
angry at Clark and puzzled about why Stewart joined Clark's majority opinion, confided to Bickel: "If I told you why Clark did what he did in *Mapp* perhaps you would want to be reasonable and even have more sympathy with L.
Hand's extreme views [about judicial review]. . . . What a Term this was, from
the point of view of Reason and Rectitude."

The chief justice showed no rectitude with his reactions in the Supreme

Court courtroom to two Frankfurter oral dissents. On March 20, Frankfurter explained his dissent, which three justices joined, in a federal larceny case. Warren, who had not written an opinion in the case, chose to rebut Frankfurter's arguments. Offered the opportunity to respond, Frankfurter said "but of course I won't. I have another case." Their testy exchange, the second in the courtroom in recent years, made the *New York Times* front page. A month later, Warren responded to another of Frankfurter's oral dissents, this time from a 5–4 decision reversing Willie Lee Stewart's murder conviction after three trials because the defendant had alluded to his previous testimony. Although Warren again did not write the majority opinion, he objected to Frankfurter's "lecture" and publicly accused him of "degrading this court." Frankfurter, once again, simply said: "I'll leave it to the record." Douglas thought the chief justice's behavior was "disgraceful." At least four justices, including Black, thought Frankfurter had not departed from the text of his opinions and that Warren's rebuttal was "inexcusable." For his part, Frankfurter could not understand how someone who had been in politics all his life could be "so sensitive."

A few days before Warren's outburst, the justices had begun to reconsider *Colegrove* and the legislative apportionment issue in a Tennessee case that they had delayed until after the resolution of *Gomillion*. On April 19 and 20, they heard oral argument in *Baker v. Carr*, which challenged the Tennessee legislature's refusal to reapportion its state legislative districts since 1901. Though the failure to redistrict certainly affected urban blacks, *Baker* did not make an explicit claim about racial discrimination. The argument was that the Tennessee legislature, by refusing to reapportion for sixty years, favored rural voters over urban and suburban ones. Indeed, the case was brought by white suburbanites and the League of Women Voters. The question before the Court was whether it should hear legislative reapportionment cases, ignore the political question doctrine, and overrule Frankfurter's opinion in *Colegrove v. Green*.

Baker was a slightly different case than *Colegrove*. *Colegrove* was about state apportionment of congressional districts—if it did not like the way a state had apportioned its districts, Congress could refuse to seat the state's members. *Baker* was about state legislative districts—Congress's only constitutional remedy was to pass a law to enforce the Fourteenth Amendment. The plaintiffs argued that voters would be stuck in malapportioned districts forever—unless, the plaintiffs argued, the Court entered the political thicket.

After two days of oral argument in *Baker*, the Court was deadlocked 4–4–1. At conference on April 21, Warren, Black, Brennan, and Douglas voted to reverse *Colegrove*. If they did so, Frankfurter said, they would "rue the results." In what Brennan described to his clerks as "a brilliant tour de force," Frankfurter began pulling volumes of the *United States Reports* off the bookshelves in the conference room and quoting from the Court's past decisions. He argued at length that *Colegrove* had been correctly decided, that no state was free of legislative gerrymandering, and that the Court was not capable of coming up with an applicable standard. He voted to affirm, as did Harlan, Clark, and Whittaker, the latter two emphasizing the need to follow the Court's precedents. But the youngest and most moderate justice, Potter Stewart, could not make up his mind. A week later, the undecided Stewart deemed the case as important as the school segregation cases and asked the Court to rehear *Baker v. Carr* the following term.

Just as he had benefited from Alexander Bickel writing an influential memorandum about the origins of the Fourteenth Amendment during the first round of argument in the school segregation cases, Frankfurter benefited from the "extraordinary gifts" of another law clerk during the first round of argument in *Baker v. Carr*—Anthony G. Amsterdam. Unlike most Frankfurter clerks, Amsterdam did not come from Harvard Law School or the chambers of Learned Hand or Calvert Magruder. Nor was he chosen, like the other Frankfurter clerks of that era, by Harvard law professor Al Sacks. Amsterdam was recommended by another former Frankfurter clerk, Louis Henkin. A University of Pennsylvania law professor who had clerked for Learned Hand for a year and then for Frankfurter for two years during the early 1940s, Henkin was not just recommending the editor in chief of his school's law review but a once-in-a-generation legal talent, albeit an intellectually unsatisfied one. Law school occupied only a fraction of Amsterdam's time. He was enrolled in graduate classes in art history at Bryn Mawr and had majored at Haverford in French literature. The law could barely contain him. During his last semester of law school, he wrote a third-year paper that became a groundbreaking note on the void-for-vagueness doctrine.

As talented as Amsterdam was, Frankfurter had already hired two Harvard law students for the coming term. In November 1959, Henkin wrote Frankfurter about the possibility of a third clerk. Frankfurter suggested that Henkin write him a letter "about your Amsterdam lad" that could be passed along to the other justices. The letter must have been intriguing because Frankfurter broke his clerkship hiring protocol and interviewed Amsterdam himself. That same day, Amsterdam also interviewed with Stewart. The frenetic Frankfurter and the laconic Stewart were a complete contrast in styles. Frankfurter never stopped talking and mesmerized Amsterdam. As a result, Frankfurter offered Amsterdam a nonpaying position as a clerk, and Amsterdam accepted. Amsterdam quickly earned a reputation as a "24-hour-a-day worker" who often slept in a room in an attic at the Court.

In the spring of 1961, Amsterdam drafted Frankfurter's memorandum/ draft opinion in *Baker v. Carr*. By July, the sixty-page opinion was finished and sent to the printer. After his clerkship ended that summer, Amsterdam continued to write and to assist the justice; his memorandum in *Baker v. Carr* formed the basis of Frankfurter's last and most prophetic opinion.

———

AFTER MORE THAN fifty years of friendship and correspondence, Frankfurter received his last letter from Learned Hand. When Frankfurter received an honorary degree from Yale on June 12, Hand offered Frankfurter high praise: "You are the best of them all, and I was glad that Yale has had the sense to know it." In a barely legible scrawl, Hand regretted hearing only twenty-five or twenty-six cases during the past year and had "fallen into near idleness." Hand's back was so bad that he spent his days in a wheelchair. He lamented how infrequently he and Frankfurter saw each other, and he confessed that he talked about the justice "all the time." He pleaded with Frankfurter to visit him in Windsor, Vermont. In a postscript, he criticized the justices on "your Court," suggested it would be better to decide issues of human rights in "popular assemblies," and reinforced "the impossibility of letting a court have the last word."

Frankfurter replied by letting off steam about his colleagues. "This has been the heaviest docket since I've been here and the least edifying. How often I think with relief—for your sake—that the Fates kept you from this crowd, or the old Battalion of Death. It isn't merely of the intrinsic difficulty of making judicial determination of what so largely are—certainly under the Fourteenth Amendment—policy questions. The old Court—McReynolds & Co.—at least voted their convictions, confusing their narrow views with the Constitution. This crowd—too many of them—often enough don't do that. Chicane and log-rolling play a considerable part." He excluded from his charges only Harlan, Stewart, and Whittaker. And he reminded Hand that Owen J. Roberts had quit "because of his unwillingness to work with unscrupulous colleagues" and that Robert H. Jackson had threatened to quit until John Lord O'Brian and Frankfurter intervened. "Oh Liberty," Frankfurter concluded, "what crimes are committed in thy name."

Frankfurter found a respite from the difficult Supreme Court term with a finally realized summer vacation in Maine. Marion left the house for the first time in seven years and handled her first airplane flight with equanimity. Beginning in mid-July, the Frankfurters stayed for a month at Overcliff, the Northeast Harbor summer home of their friend Frances Watson. Not even the fogged-in harbor could dampen their happiness. The vacation turned out to be the last one of their lives.

Soon after he arrived home from Maine in mid-August, Frankfurter received word that Learned Hand had suffered two heart attacks. After the first one, the 89-year-old judge had been transported to New York City and admitted to St. Luke's Hospital. On the afternoon of August 18, Frankfurter received a telegram from Hand's wife, Frances: "B DIED PEACEFULLY THIS MORNING, NO FUNERAL SERVICE OR FLOWERS." Frankfurter issued a short statement: "A truly great man has left us, but he has left behind him an important addition to our national heritage. History will duly appraise the significance of his contribution to law and to American civilization." The *New York Times* reprinted Frankfurter's 1959 tribute in the Second Circuit court-room in which he had opined that Hand, a federal district judge from 1909 to 1924 and Second Circuit judge from 1924 to 1961, had been "lucky" never to have served on the Supreme Court because Hand's vote "would have been diluted eight-ninths and [on the Second Circuit] only two-thirds."

The truth is that Hand would have loathed deciding contentious consti-tutional questions that Frankfurter confronted on a regular basis. Hand's judicial philosophy was very different from Frankfurter's. In his 1958 Bill of Rights lectures, Hand dismissed *Brown v. Board of Education* as a *"coup de main,"* rejected the idea of being governed by "a bevy of Platonic Guardians" on the Supreme Court, and concluded that there should be no power of judicial review. Hand considered Frankfurter the Court's "saving grace." Yet he also concluded that Frankfurter was not a great justice on par with Robert Jackson, Brandeis, or "the great master" Holmes. Hand perceptively remarked that Frankfurter's opinions were "too discursive"; he had the "initial handicap" of "a very passionate nature"; and he lacked "supreme self-restraint. . . . He's learned a good deal of it. But he hasn't it." Hand's assessment of Frankfurter was spot on. But Hand's solution for the Warren Court's judicial excesses bordered on nihilism. Even in his darkest hours such as after the Court's deliberations in *Mapp v. Ohio*, Frankfurter never endorsed Hand's idea about eliminating judicial review.

Whereas Hand's Bill of Rights lectures offered only despair, Frankfurter's majority opinion in *Gomillion* offered hope. Like Hand, he believed in judicial restraint and a more limited role for the Supreme Court in American democ-racy. Unlike Hand (and Holmes and Brandeis), Frankfurter adapted judicial restraint to fulfill the promises of the Fourteenth and Fifteenth Amendments by protecting minority rights. And unlike his liberal Warren Court colleagues, Frankfurter had faith in the American people to use the democratic political process to solve their problems.

———

FRANKFURTER MADE HIS final plea for democratic political change during the Court's second round of deliberations about legislative reapportionment. The reargument of *Baker v. Carr* on October 9 revealed no new insights and proved particularly unsatisfying. The next day, he wrote his colleagues that "neither side dealt with aspects of what I deem involved and with controlling decisions other than those specifically dealing with reapportionment." Beneath his cover note, he circulated Amsterdam's sixty-page memorandum as a way of influencing Stewart and the perpetually indecisive Whittaker and attempted to set the agenda for the Court's conference.

The day after Frankfurter circulated his memorandum, Harlan wrote directly to Stewart and Whittaker to remind them that this case was the most important since the school segregation cases and perhaps in the history of the Court and that their votes would likely determine the outcome. Harlan wrote that "the independence of the Court, and its aloofness from political vicissitudes" was at stake. A Democratic presidential administration, he reminded them, was pressing for reapportionment, and people would view the Court's apportionment decisions through the lens of the political ideologies of the justices. Thus, Harlan argued, the Court should refrain from entering the political thicket. Frankfurter praised Harlan's letter.

In response to Frankfurter's memorandum, Brennan circulated an eleven-page chart prepared by his law clerk Roy Schotland analyzing the exhibits in the case and showing the state's disparate representation among counties of the exact same size. "I should think that at the very least," Brennan wrote in his cover note, "the data show a picture which Tennessee should be required to justify if it is to avoid the conclusion that the 1901 Act applied to today's facts, is simple caprice." The difference between Frankfurter's memorandum and Brennan's chart was stark—Frankfurter was concerned about whether the Court had the power to hear the case; Brennan emphasized the egregiousness of the merits.

At conference on October 13, Warren declared that the Tennessee legislature's failure to reapportion presented an equal protection violation but, as in *Brown*, the Court should delay the remedy. Black described Frankfurter's memorandum as "a good brief for a weak cause" and *Colegrove* as "a weak reed." Black had dissented in *Colegrove* and believed that legislative apportionment should be "approximately fair." There was no other remedy besides judicial intervention unless Congress passed a law to enforce the Fourteenth Amendment. This time, instead of pulling books off the conference room shelves, Frankfurter referred to the arguments in his memorandum and deferred to Harlan. Yet Frankfurter warned his colleagues that the case was "dangerous to our whole system" of government and questioned whether the Court could fashion a remedy. Douglas argued that Frankfurter's opinion in *Gomillion* required reversal on equal protection grounds, ignoring that *Gomillion* was not an equal protection case, that Douglas had withdrawn his concurring opinion along these lines, and that the plaintiffs in *Baker* had made no explicit showing of racial discrimination. Clark voted to affirm because the plaintiffs had failed to exhaust other remedies including those in Congress. He recognized that there was a racial component as to why the white power structure refused to redistrict in the South, but that was not at issue in the case. Harlan, Frankfurter's staunchest ally, argued "with most intense emotion" that there were "no constitutionally protected rights" at issue in the case. He observed that *Gomillion* was about the "denial of the right to vote" on the basis of race under the Fifteenth Amendment and warned the Court about "getting into these political contests" and that "the greatness of the Court has been in refraining from them." (Douglas jotted in his notes: "What does he think the Segregation Cases were—or the Youngstown case—or the Tuskegee case?") Brennan agreed with Warren that there was "an equal protection problem presented here" and that the burden was on the state to justify the capriciousness of its legislative districts. Whittaker was "very shaky" about the case; he had written two "diametrically opposed" memoranda and was less sure now than he had been the previous term. A week earlier, Frankfurter had attempted to allay some of Whittaker's concerns by reminding him that the Tennessee Supreme Court had ruled the state constitutional provisions on apportionment were not judicially enforceable. Whittaker tentatively voted to affirm with Frankfurter, Clark, and Harlan because it was a state constitutional issue. Whittaker's vote was irrelevant given that there was a fifth vote to overrule *Colegrove*. Stewart, though grateful for Frankfurter's memorandum, announced that there was no political question in this case. But even if the Court reached the merits, he was unsure whether there was an equal protection violation and believed there was a heavy burden on the plaintiff to show that the apportionment was arbitrary and capricious.

Judging by the tentative votes at conference, Frankfurter had lost. The battle for Stewart's vote (and others), however, had only just begun. "I assume that nothing that I said in my *Baker* v. *Carr* [memorandum] led to your conclusion in the case," Frankfurter wrote Stewart. "But feeling as deeply as I do about the evil genii to be released by the decision, I think I ought to dissipate any misapprehension that any infelicity in my phrasing may have occasioned." In his letter, Frankfurter took another crack at changing Stewart's mind: "The whole direction and details of my memorandum were in agreement with what I understood to be what you said that there is nothing in the Fourteenth Amendment that requires what Hugo called 'approximately fair' distribution or weight in votes." If that is true, Frankfurter believed that the malapportionment claim in *Baker* was not "legally enforceable." That did not mean, however, that all claims would be unenforceable. At conference, Stewart had referred to Frankfurter's memorandum as leaving open the possibility of different circumstances " 'in kind.' " Alluding to his opinion in *Gomillion*, Frankfurter wrote: "Disallowing all Christian Scientists or Jews to vote, or to reduce votes in any county that has Christian Scientists or Jews, would present circumstances different 'in kind.' "

Warren employed his power of assigning the majority opinion to make sure that he would not lose Stewart's vote. He mulled over the assignment for ten days. At first, he planned to take the traditional route of assigning it to Stewart, the most moderate justice in the majority and the one most likely to change his vote. Black and Douglas, however, advised Warren not to do that. Douglas believed that he could not sign on to Stewart's idea about the heavy burden of proof on the plaintiff. Black believed that Stewart's views were so moderate that Stewart might lose Douglas's vote and therefore the five-person majority. On Douglas's suggestion, Warren assigned the opinion to Brennan.

Though Black may have been the Warren Court's intellectual leader on issues such as applying the Bill of Rights to the states, Brennan was the justice who implemented Black's ideas. The most important rule, Brennan famously told his clerks, was the rule of five. "Five votes," he said holding up his hand and wiggling his fingers. "Five votes can do anything around here." Since joining the Court in 1956, Brennan had earned Warren's confidence and trust and was the Court's rising liberal star. Paul Freund had done a stellar job choosing Brennan's law clerks. For the 1961 term, Freund selected two top Harvard law graduates, Roy Schotland and Frank I. Michelman, who went on to distinguished academic careers. A future election law expert, Schotland took the lead in drafting Brennan's opinion in *Baker v. Carr.*

During the month of December, Brennan's law clerks worked one of three "black nights" drafting the opinion and realized that it would not be ready for some time. On January 22, 1962, Brennan showed a long draft to Stewart, who indicated that he would sign on to it. Five days later, Brennan informed Warren, Black, and Douglas of their solid fifth vote and sent them the opinion. In his cover memorandum, Brennan argued for the opinion's "full discussion of 'political question' . . . if we are effectively and finally to dispel the fog of another day produced by Felix's opinion in *Colegrove* v. *Green*." Douglas wanted several changes to the opinion, including fewer references to the political question doctrine. Black also made some suggestions. Brennan made the changes after checking with Stewart, circulated the opinion to the entire Court on January 31, and informed Black that it "looks as though we have a court agreed upon this as circulated."

The day after Brennan circulated his majority opinion, Frankfurter responded by circulating his dissent. That same day, Stewart joined Brennan's opinion. On February 3, Clark joined Frankfurter's dissent and described it as "unanswerable." Two days later, an emotional Harlan joined Frankfurter's dissent after declaring it "a remarkably fine document" and decided to write his own dissent about the lack of constitutional rights at stake. Indeed, Harlan asked Stewart to keep an open mind until he read the dissent. Harlan considered Stewart, not Whittaker, the deciding vote. Whittaker had been privy to Brennan's opinion before its circulation and had passed along a memorandum to Brennan. After "much uncertainty," Whittaker announced on February 14 that he was joining Frankfurter's dissent. Neither Whittaker nor Clark ended up on Frankfurter's final opinion. Clark had trouble writing a separate dissent about the exhaustion of remedies, reconsidered the entire case, and a month later switched sides. Whittaker suffered a nervous breakdown and at Douglas's urging entered the hospital. He never returned to the Court and did not participate in the case. In the end, only Harlan joined Frankfurter's opinion.

Whether *Baker v. Carr* was 5–4 or 6–2 made little difference to Frankfurter. The outcome had been settled for some time. Indeed, of the two dissenters, Harlan was far more upset about the outcome. Frankfurter seemed at peace and in good humor. After Douglas and Stewart wrote concurring opinions (and nearly unraveled Brennan's majority in the process), Frankfurter joked with his archenemy Douglas about a reference in one of Douglas's footnotes to Cuban leader Fidel Castro. Frankfurter wondered if they could revive the Platt Amendment and "enjoin Castro from pursuing his nonsense." Douglas responded that the Court could enjoin Castro under its original jurisdiction. It was a rare lighthearted moment between two men who hated each other.

Frankfurter was not writing for the nine justices on the Warren Court or for 1962; he was writing for the American people with a prophetic warning about the future of their democracy. Frankfurter feared a Supreme Court on judicial steroids, embroiled in electoral and other political disputes on the basis of a flimsy equal protection rationale, and forgetting about the historic purposes of the Reconstruction Amendments of protecting the rights of African Americans and other minorities. Aside from the protection of minority rights and a few notable exceptions (illegal searches and seizures, the separation of church and state), he preferred that the American people look not to the Court but to the political process to solve their problems.

On March 26, Brennan read for an hour from the bench in announcing the majority opinion in *Baker v. Carr*. Warren passed him a note that it was "a great day for the country"—the chief had crossed out the word "Irish." In his memoirs, Warren declared that *Baker*, not *Brown*, was "the most important case of my tenure on the Court." Frankfurter, by contrast, privately accused the Brennan- and Warren-led majority of "impos[ing] their will on the nation and the fifty states by exultingly overruling their distinguished predecessors" and of failing to understand the Court's role in America's democratic system.

To Frankfurter and others, Brennan's opinion in *Baker* exemplified the Warren Court's excesses and did not bode well for the future. First, Brennan's opinion eviscerated an important bulwark against judicial power run amok—the political question doctrine—by limiting it to disputes where the Constitution had granted authority to another branch of the federal government. Second, it empowered the Court to decide on a "case-by-case inquiry" when the political question doctrine applied because the Court, not the other branches or the people, was the "ultimate interpreter of the Constitution." This bold statement, reminiscent of Brennan's Little Rock opinion four years earlier, lacked any support in the text of the Constitution, the historical intent of the framers, or judicial precedent. It was a breathtaking assertion of judicial supremacy—that the Supreme Court was entitled to the last word on the Constitution. Finally, Brennan's opinion in *Baker* provided no guidance to lower courts about how to decide whether legislative districts violated the Equal Protection Clause. It declared that the Court's equal protection law was "well developed and familiar" and satisfied by discrimination that was based on "simply arbitrary and capricious action."

Frankfurter's dissent, by contrast, projected a more limited judicial role for the Court and emphasized the enforcement of the Fourteenth and Fifteenth Amendments to stop discrimination against minority groups. He understood that the historic purpose of the Reconstruction Amendments was to protect the rights of African Americans. He was more than willing to invoke the power of the judiciary to protect minorities from discrimination, especially when it came to voting rights. But *Baker* was not about the "denial of the franchise to individuals because of race, color, religion or sex." Unlike *Gomillion*, *Baker* was "not a case in which a State has, through a device however oblique and sophisticated, denied Negroes or Jews or redheaded persons a vote, or given them only a third or a sixth of a vote."

Second, after objecting to the Court's overruling of *Colegrove* and other cases that had relied on the political question doctrine, Frankfurter correctly predicted that the Court would struggle to achieve a judicially enforceable standard in reapportionment disputes. The Court could not possibly eliminate gerrymandering without redrawing the legislative maps of all fifty states. He saw the political question doctrine not only as a limit on the Court's power but also as a recognition of historical experience of the "futility of judicial intervention in the essentially political conflict of forces" in apportionment decisions.

Third, he criticized the majority for providing no practical or theoretical guidance to the lower courts about when a state legislative district violated the Fourteenth Amendment. The majority's invocation of an "arbitrary and capricious" standard reminded him of the due process cases in which the Court had invalidated a maximum-hour law for bakers in *Lochner* in 1905, the minimum-wage laws for women in *Adkins v. Children's Hospital* in 1923, and the 1936 minimum-wage case overturned a year later during the New Deal constitutional crisis. He questioned the Fourteenth Amendment's application to the legislative apportionment issue. And he exposed Brennan's failure to address or acknowledge complicated questions about democratic theory: "Talk of 'debasement' or 'dilution' is circular talk. One cannot speak of 'debasement' or 'dilution' of the value of a vote until there is first defined a standard of reference as to what a vote should be worth. What is actually asked of the Court in this case is to choose among competing bases of representation— ultimately, really, among competing theories of political philosophy—in order to establish an appropriate frame of government for the State of Tennessee and thereby for all the States of the Union." Federal judges, he predicted, would be forced to rely on "their private views of political wisdom" because the Fourteenth Amendment "provides no guide for judicial oversight of the representation problem." The *Baker* majority offered none. Two years later in *Reynolds v. Sims*, the Court adopted a "one person, one vote" standard.

Finally, Frankfurter encouraged people to turn to their elected representatives to solve their problems. His call to political action came after eight years of judicial failure to desegregate the nation's schools after *Brown v. Board of Education*; it came amidst one of the greatest mass political and social movements in American history—the civil rights movement; and it came with calls for Congress to pass landmark civil rights legislation.

Frankfurter's dissent reflected his belief, not in the rule of five or in aggrandizing the power of the judiciary, but in the power of democracy: "In a democratic society like ours, relief must come through an aroused popular conscience that sears the conscience of the people's representatives. In any event there is nothing judicially more unseemly nor more self-defeating than for this Court to make *in terrorem* pronouncements, to indulge in merely empty rhetoric, sounding a word of promise to the ear, sure to be disappointing to the hope."

IN HIS *BAKER V. CARR* DISSENT, Frankfurter invoked former clerk Alexander Bickel's 1961 *Harvard Law Review* foreword, "The Passive Virtues," in defense of the "political question doctrine" because the Court "recognized a class of controversies which do not lend themselves to judicial standards and judicial remedies." In "The Passive Virtues," Bickel argued that the Court should avoid constitutional questions and husband its resources. By rigorously enforcing its procedural and jurisdictional rules, the Court could defer to the political branches until there was enough popular support to tackle a contentious issue such as school desegregation. He argued that the Court sacrificed its legitimacy not only when it invalidated a state or federal law but also when it validated an unjust law. As an example, he referred to the Court's infamous decisions upholding racially "separate but equal" laws and encouraging more than half a century of state-sponsored racial segregation by "legitimating it." He called this *"Plessy v. Ferguson*'s Error" after the Court's 1896 decision upholding racially separate railroad cars. Thus, Bickel defended the Court's intervention in the school segregation cases and differentiated between Frankfurter's invocation of the political question doctrine in *Colegrove* and willingness to invalidate the exclusion of nearly every black voter from the Tuskegee city limits in *Gomillion*. In most instances, however, Bickel argued that the Court was better off avoiding constitutional questions than deciding them prematurely.

For several years, Bickel and other Frankfurter protégés in the legal academy had been criticizing the Warren Court and its decisions that empowered the judiciary to decide the nation's political and social issues. Known as the "legal process" school, they emphasized the belief that the solutions to most of the country's problems, including the vexing problem of race, lay with the political process. They questioned the future of judicial review after *Brown* and reacted with alarm to the Warren Court's assertions that it was the "ultimate constitutional interpreter." They emphasized the need for judicial decision-making that was based on "reasoned elaboration" rather than the justices' individual political views. They recognized the Court's limited "institutional competence" compared to the other branches and the states and studied the interrelationships among courts, legislatures, and administrative agencies. Above all, they cared about fair and democratic procedures over results.

Frankfurter's connection to leading process theorists ran deep. It is inaccurate, however, to attribute the theory to him. He is best described as "one of the [theory's] godparents." He never promulgated process theory yet encouraged his former students and law clerks leading the charge. Henry Hart was his star student and co-author; Bickel, Al Sacks, and Harry Wellington were his law clerks; and Herbert Wechsler was one of his admirers. Indeed, Hart and Wechsler dedicated the first edition of their casebook, *The Federal Courts and Federal System*, to "Felix Frankfurter who first opened our minds to these problems."

No one articulated Frankfurter's constitutional vision better than Bickel. *Brown v. Board of Education* dominated Bickel's worldview. He had clerked for Frankfurter during the first round of argument in the school segregation cases and had authored the all-important memorandum about the legislative history of the Fourteenth Amendment. Bickel believed that the Court should refrain from taking on other political or social causes in light of its thwarted efforts to enforce *Brown*. He agreed with Frankfurter that the reapportionment cases threatened the Court's institutional standing.

After he read excerpts of the *Baker v. Carr* opinions in the *New York Times*, Bickel took a more measured view of the case than his former boss. Although he thought Brennan's opinion was a " 'slick and shallow' performance" and Douglas's and Clark's were "shockingly irresponsible," Bickel believed that Tennessee's failure to reapportion for sixty years could have been addressed more narrowly and without overruling *Colegrove*. He suggested that the Court order the state to reapportion within a set number of years in order "to break the log-jam." But he completely rejected the majority's attempt to achieve "the impossible and unthinkable—namely, the laying down of constitutional rules of apportionment" and agreed with Frankfurter "that the attempt would morally damage the Court."

Frankfurter poked fun at Bickel's attempt to order Tennessee to reappor-

tion without overruling *Colegrove* and eviscerating the political question doctrine: "Am I right in assuming that your headnote for *Baker* v. *Carr* would be
'*Held*, a little judicial pregnancy is permissible.'" Frankfurter did not hesitate
in revealing his distaste for his colleagues on the Court. "I'm afraid if you had
been privy to the process by which the guardian of political morality exercised its Constitutional power 'to prod the recreant political institutions into
action,' your stomach too would have turned," he wrote Bickel. "L.D.B. was
fond of saying—or, rather, had frequent occasion for saying that too many
'liberals want to attain their desirable purposes on the cheap.'" Frankfurter
wondered if the people of Tennessee, Maryland, and Vermont challenging
their states' failure to reapportion had engaged the political process as hard
as Florence Kelley of the National Consumers' League had in establishing the
federal Children's Bureau and state minimum-wage laws for women.

In a November 1962 *Yale Law Journal* article, Bickel took his initial crack at
Baker and tried to rehabilitate *Colegrove v. Green* and the political question doctrine. He criticized the Court's arbitrary and capricious standard of reviewing
redistricting cases as circular reasoning: "Rationality—the presence of *some*
policy, the absence of 'simply arbitrary and capricious action'—sounds good,
but aside from temper tantrums, it chases its own tail." He reminded readers
of the Court's opinions—judges, lawyers, and law students—that in *Colegrove*
the Court neither rejected nor blessed the political action in that case. The real
danger of a minimum rationality standard lay in the Court's willingness to
affirm a redistricting plan because "the Supreme Court may see its function
not merely to let an apportionment be, but to legitimate it." He concluded
that this would repeat the "grave error" in *Plessy* "that legitimated segregation in 1896."

During the fall of 1962, Bickel incorporated his critique of *Baker* into
his most enduring contribution to constitutional law, *The Least Dangerous
Branch: The Supreme Court at the Bar of Politics*. With its title borrowed from
Alexander Hamilton's benign description of the judiciary in the Federalist
Papers, *The Least Dangerous Branch* became a symbol for post-*Brown* anxiety
about the outsized role of the Court as an engine for social change. Instead,
Bickel advanced the dominant theory of judicial review for a generation of
lawyers and judges. He defended *Brown*, elaborated on his theory of employing the passive virtues to avoid constitutional issues, and questioned judicial
review as a "deviant institution in American democracy." Coining the phrase
the "counter-majoritarian difficulty," Bickel emphasized the "undemocratic"
nature of judicial review. Five justices deciding political and social policy for
the nation undermined our democratic institutions and imbued the justices

with too much power. He argued that the Court could maintain its legitimacy in the face of rising public hostility only by deciding not to decide. Yet, if the justices picked their spots better and offered the lower courts better reasoning and more guidance on how to implement their decisions, he believed in the Court's ability to conduct a "'vital national seminar'" on the Constitution and to educate the people about the nation's democratic values. Bickel's section on *Baker v. Carr* quoted at length from Frankfurter's dissent in an effort to distinguish the Court's intervention in the school segregation cases from its standardless inquiry into legislative reapportionment.

In late October 1962, Bickel informed Frankfurter that his take on *Baker* "necessarily relies heavily on your dissent, but, as you said when we last discussed this, perversely comes to the conclusion that the Court became only a little pregnant and that that is not an intolerable state." By that point, the justice's health prevented him from reading the *Yale Law Journal* article, much less *The Least Dangerous Branch*. Bickel learned from Elsie Douglas that the justice's "chief occupation from now on is to amass the necessary strength to be able to read your book and not merely savor it." Yet Frankfurter could not resist a dig at the book's title: "He finally wants to know whether the other two branches are really 'dangerous.'"

Frankfurter knew it was a mistake to expect the courts to solve all the nation's problems. Courts were limited in their ability to devise and enforce remedies for complex issues such as school segregation or legislative reapportionment. Government by judiciary eroded the need for the American people to invest in the democratic political process or the need for their elected officials to compromise. From his first day in government working as an assistant U.S. attorney for Henry Stimson until his last opinion on the Supreme Court, Frankfurter never lost faith in American democracy. He sometimes took his belief in judicial restraint too far; he placed too much trust in the states and other federal branches to police themselves; and he sided too often with national security and not enough with liberty. He alienated some colleagues with his conference lectures, memoranda, and overlong opinions. But in *Gomillion v. Lightfoot* and in his final opinion in *Baker v. Carr*, he struck a balance between protecting minority rights and recognizing that some problems were not capable of judicial resolution. He firmly rejected the Warren Court's embrace of judicial supremacy. He left it to former students and law clerks to elaborate on his powerful constitutional vision and to the verdict of history to vindicate his hopes for democratic political change.

CHAPTER 39

Father to Them All

On the night of March 26, 1962, the same day he announced his *Baker* dissent in the courtroom, Frankfurter spoke at the eighty-eighth birthday celebration of poet Robert Frost. Standing in the receiving line at the black-tie dinner for 200 people, Frankfurter joked with fellow speakers Frost and poet Mark Van Doren about who would be the first to "join the angels." Other speakers included U.S. ambassador to the United Nations Adlai Stevenson, Chief Justice Warren, and poet Robert Penn Warren. The politicians and poets were no match for Frankfurter's eloquence. The justice began by recalling the first time he had met Frost forty years earlier in a Cambridge bookshop. The two men had talked for four hours, including after the shop closed, without knowing each other's name. The conversation sparked a lifelong friendship. "Robert Frost is a moralist who does not moralize but instills," Frankfurter told the audience. "He is an educator who does not teach but shares. He makes us aware of what we so often look at but do not see."

What most people could not see about Frankfurter was how his influence extended far beyond Supreme Court opinions. By encouraging generations of former students and law clerks to enter academia and public service, he had helped create the mid-century liberal establishment. It was no accident that he was asked to choose the speakers and to serve as the toastmaster at the *Harvard Law Review*'s upcoming seventh-fifth anniversary celebration on April 14. He viewed Harvard Law School as the ultimate meritocracy. Making the *Review* in 1904 on the basis of his stellar first-year grades had changed his life. He had met lifelong friends in fellow editors Emory Buckner and Monte Lemann. He had been recruited, based on the recommendation of Dean Ames, to work for Henry Stimson as an assistant U.S. attorney in the Southern District of New York. From Stimson, he had learned the ethos of public service. He had followed Stimson to Washington to work in the War

Department and had widened his circle of friends at the House of Truth. Upon joining the Harvard law faculty in 1914, he steered *Review* editors away from Wall Street law firms by selecting them for clerkships with Holmes, Brandeis, and other judges and by recommending former students for government jobs. As a professor, justice, and talent scout, he altered the aspirations of *Review* editors from financial gain to political leadership and instilled in them the higher calling of public service.

In the days leading up to the April 14 celebration, Frankfurter carefully arranged the list and order of speakers representing each generation of the *Harvard Law Review*, a who's who of his friends and disciples. He was looking forward to seeing former colleagues, students, and law clerks. He wanted to continue his conversation with Bickel and others about *Baker v. Carr.* But he never made it to Cambridge.

At 4:30 p.m. on April 5, shortly after speaking to reporter Ward Just about the *Harvard Law Review* celebration, Frankfurter fell from his desk onto the floor. His secretary, Elsie Douglas, found him mumbling to himself. His messenger, Thomas Beasley, lifted him onto the couch. Within ten minutes, his doctor arrived, gave him glycerin tablets and other treatment, and rode with him in an ambulance to George Washington University Hospital. The doctor diagnosed it a "transient episode of acute cerebrovascular insufficiency," a stroke that "cleared spontaneously and left no residual after effect." The press release indicated that the justice would remain in the hospital for "a short period of rest." Indeed, the stroke had been minor, and the justice showed few ill effects. Five days later, however, he suffered a second stroke and possibly several others. They paralyzed his left side and affected his speech. Once again, his speech improved, and he regained some use of his left leg.

Public and private reports downplayed the seriousness of his condition. An April 19 press release revealed that he had suffered another stroke but "improved rapidly and is now getting out of bed." His doctors predicted that he would be able to return to the Court "in due time." On April 30, he announced that he was staying in the hospital for "further treatment," would not return before the end of the term, but expected to be ready for the beginning of the next term. Privately, Elsie Douglas reassured his friends that the justice "continues to improve" and was "gaining strength and fussing about hospital food," which meant he was getting better. He planned on using the summer recess to prepare to rejoin the Court.

For the first few weeks in the hospital, the justice's friends, except for Dean Acheson and John Harlan, were barred from seeing him. Acheson's private reports revealed the paralysis and impaired speech and prepared close friends

for the possibility that Frankfurter would never return to the Court. Frankfurter kept writing Harlan about the Court's pending cases. Acheson knew
that the intensity of the work was the last thing the justice needed, but the
possibility of a return aided his recovery. Either way, Acheson understood that
Frankfurter would never be the same. "In short," he wrote a mutual friend,
"Felix is a very sick man."

By early May, visitors began to see the contrast between the optimistic
reports and Frankfurter's condition. Samuel Behrman, the longtime *New
Yorker* writer and playwright, planned on staying for only five minutes but
listened to the justice, with slurred speech, talk "a blue streak" for forty-five
minutes. "I was very moved," Behrman reported to Isaiah Berlin. "He was
lying flat in his bed and held my hand and clutched it practically the whole
time." His doctor informed the justice that "whether he lived or not depended
on Felix, on how much he wanted to live. That he must not think about the
Court. That he must 're-educate certain muscles.' Felix loved that phrase and
repeated it." During Behrman's visit, Frankfurter conveyed his opinion of
President Kennedy by quoting political philosopher Max Ascoli: "He is not
Napoleon the First, he is not even Napoleon the third—I'd say he is about
Napoleon the 7th." Behrman "had a good feeling about Felix when I left" and
"felt that he would survive and be all right again." Yet there was something
about the justice, usually so animated and lively, lying in bed and gripping his
hand, which left Behrman "quite shaken."

Dr. Herrman Blumgart, a Harvard Medical School professor and physician in chief at Beth Israel Hospital, left an early May visit with Frankfurter
with a similar impression. They talked for thirty-five to forty minutes about
Baker v. Carr, Harvard Law School, Harvard Medical School, Harvard president Nathan Pusey, and mutual friends in Cambridge. Blumgart described it
as "a kaleidoscopic experience as of old!" After he saw the justice, Blumgart
conferred with Frankfurter's doctor, and they agreed that "the improvement
should continue and that we have good ground for optimism."

The purpose of Blumgart's visit was to check not only on the justice but
also on Marion. Her health, despite the trip to Maine the previous summer,
had not improved. She was, however, less reclusive than in the past. On January 28, in honor of her husband's twenty-third anniversary on the Court, she
had hosted an eggnog party for his present and former clerks, had spoken for
"nearly an hour, with not a little wit and interstitial wisdom," and had dished
a few barbs at her delighted husband. With Felix in the hospital, Marion was
attended to by the couple's longtime household staff, Matilda Williams and
Ellen Smith. Felix kept a photograph of Marion on a bedside table and phoned

her every night. He told her the nurses had remarked about her beauty. Several times, she left the house in a wheelchair to visit him, cried when she saw him lying there, and found the experience so emotionally draining that she quickly returned to her bed. Blumgart visited her and eased her mind about Felix's prognosis. At home by herself, she complained that she was "terribly lonely and alone." Some of their oldest friends were not too sympathetic. Acheson urged the doctors to keep her away from Felix to aid his recovery. On the basis of reports from Behrman and Acheson, Isaiah Berlin wrote: "I adore and admire Marion, but there is something marvellously egomaniacal about her, about her whole relationship with Felix and her general view of the world. She reminds me of Virginia Woolf, whose genius lay in this direction and whose universe had wonderful content, which nobody ever succeeded in describing anything like so marvellously as she, even at her worst, but which possessed no windows of any kind."

After three months in the hospital, the justice returned home on July 7 and struggled to recover his normal speech and use of his paralyzed left side. His voice was low, his speech was slurred, and sometimes he had to start over when his thoughts got ahead of his words. His left arm was still paralyzed. His left leg had improved to the point where, once helped to his feet, he could walk ten to fifteen feet on a rail. He was learning to use a cane but was very unsteady. A hospital orderly and nurse helped him with his recovery. When he was not in physical therapy, he liked to read the newspaper each morning and sit in the rear garden on a chaise lounge. He prepared obsessively for his July 26 visit from President Kennedy.

Though charmed by the president, Frankfurter was determined not to give Kennedy another Supreme Court vacancy. In late March, Charles Whittaker had resigned after suffering a nervous breakdown. Kennedy's advisers had urged him to nominate his initial choice for solicitor general, Paul Freund. "The best and most confidential advice from Cambridge," McGeorge Bundy wrote the president, "is that Paul Freund would have voted with the majority in the Tennessee re-apportionment case, and might even have carried Frankfurter with him." Bundy described Freund as "a great scholar—but not a closet scholar; a Brandeis in conviction, but a Cardozo in temperament. He is a deeply amusing as well as a cultivated man—a genuine wit—he could become a close personal help to you, with his detachment, his high personal style, and his regard for you." Of all the people on Kennedy's shortlist, Bundy predicted that Freund was "the most likely to be a great judge."

Bobby Kennedy, whom Frankfurter thought was completely unqualified to be attorney general, consulted Earl Warren and longtime Kennedy family friend William O. Douglas. They opposed Freund and William Hastie, a federal court of appeals judge since 1949, as "just one more vote for Frankfurter." The president's decision came down to Freund and Byron White, Kennedy's Colorado campaign chairman and deputy attorney general. After a week of indecision, Kennedy chose White over Freund. The decisive factor was White's work on the campaign. According to Kennedy aide Arthur Schlesinger, Jr., the president previously had asked journalist Max Freedman, a Frankfurter confidant and biographer, if the justice was willing to resign provided he and Kennedy could agree on a successor. "I guess he decided that he was indispensable to the Court," Kennedy quipped. Bobby's opposition to Freund would have made a deal with Frankfurter a nonstarter. Frankfurter blamed White's nomination on the president's brother: "What does Bobby understand about the Supreme Court? He understands about as much about it as you understand about the undiscovered 76th star in the galaxy."

As determined as Frankfurter was to stay on the Court, his July 26 visit from the president had sapped his strength. "[T]he spirit just seemed to ooze out of him," Acheson reported. "It is heart-breaking to see that invincible vitality tamed at last." Frankfurter uncharacteristically refused to see any visitors except for Acheson. For a while, Acheson thought the justice might be able to make a token return to the Court, but no longer. He and Elsie Douglas dreaded the discussion about the coming term. Together with John Harlan, who returned to Washington in mid-August, they hoped they could persuade Frankfurter to retire.

For three difficult weeks in August, Frankfurter agonized about his decision, which to his friends was inevitable. His doctors and close friends repeatedly told him he was not capable of returning to the Court. Yet, as late as mid-August, he was working hard at physical therapy "with confident progress" and hope for a last-minute recovery. His problems were not merely physical. In his few handwritten letters, his writing was shaky, and the words did not come easily. He had no choice but to resign. Knowing he was writing for history, he labored as hard over retirement letters to his colleagues and to the president as on his toughest judicial opinions. He received editorial assistance and repeated reassurance from Acheson and Harlan. In the cover letter to his colleagues, Frankfurter attached his August 28 letter to President Kennedy announcing that he was retiring effective immediately. He explained that his doctors initially expected him to return to the Court for the start of the new term in October but subsequently advised against it. He refused to leave the Court in a state of "uncertainty" about his status or to return in a diminished or restricted capacity. "I am thus left," he wrote the president, "with no choice but to regard my period of active service on the Court as having run its course." He expressed his "reluctance with which I leave the institution whose concerns have been the absorbing interest of my life." He concluded by thanking the president for his visit and "for the solicitude you were kind enough to express."

That same day, Kennedy responded that he "shared the general hope that you would return soon to the Court's labors. From my own visit I know of your undiminished spirit and your still contagious zest for life." He recognized that Frankfurter had "been part of American public life for well over half a century. What you have learned of the meaning of our country is reflected, of course, in many hundreds of opinions, in thousands of your students, and in dozens of books and articles." He believed that Frankfurter had "a very great deal still to tell us" and urged him "not to retire, but only to turn to a new line of work, with new promise of service to the nation." Finally, the president expressed "our respectful gratitude for the character, courage, learning, and judicial dedication with which you served your country over the last twenty-three years." The next day, Frankfurter thanked the president for his "very friendly and movingly handsome response" and for understanding "the fruitful potentialities of the life that is ahead of me."

The lovefest between Frankfurter and Kennedy came to an abrupt halt with the August 29 announcement of Frankfurter's successor. The Kennedys were determined to fill the seat with another Jew despite the fact that Frankfurter abhorred the idea of a Jewish seat. At first, they considered Freund, a Jew from St. Louis and one of the nation's leading constitutional law professors. Bobby Kennedy, however, could not forgive Freund for declining the solicitor generalship and argued that Solicitor General Archibald Cox "deserved the appointment more than Paul Freund." Cox, however, was not Jewish and did not get the job. And the fact that Freund was Frankfurter's first choice meant nothing. When Frankfurter's preferred candidates, Freund, Hastie, and Judge Henry Friendly, came up, Bobby Kennedy remarked: "What have they ever done for us?"

At 4:00 p.m. in the new State Department auditorium, President Kennedy began his press conference by announcing Frankfurter's retirement and the nomination of his replacement, Secretary of Labor Arthur Goldberg. Kennedy lauded Goldberg's "wealth of experience" from thirty years of law practice and as general counsel to the Steelworkers union, "his scholarly approach to the law," and "his deep understanding of our economic and political systems."

Before the announcement, Kennedy had dispatched his aide McGeorge Bundy to 3018 Dumbarton Avenue to break the news. Bundy's friendship with

Frankfurter went back to 1947 when the young Yale graduate had assisted Henry Stimson with his autobiography. The conversation with the justice failed to soften the blow. A few weeks later, Bundy infuriated Frankfurter by comparing Goldberg to Louis Brandeis "at the same age." Frankfurter lamented that there was not a legal scholar on the Court, someone, such as his former student Freund, who knew its history and could save it from "self-inflicted wounds." "I suggest," Frankfurter wrote Bundy, "you begin to repair the justification you will have to make on Judgment Day should Paul not be on the Supreme Court at the time your tenure of power is over." He insisted that several state and federal judges, including Friendly and Charles Wyzanski, were more qualified to be on the Court than White and Goldberg. The retired justice argued that Goldberg should have stayed in the Labor Department, did not think much of his ability as a Supreme Court advocate, and was unworthy of the seat once held by Holmes and Cardozo. Privately, Frankfurter derided Goldberg as "the scholar."

FRANKFURTER'S FRIENDS who had been instrumental in persuading him to retire rescued him from financial ruin. His devil-may-care attitude about money and mounting medical bills finally caught up with him. Even with his annual salary of $36,000 continuing in retirement, he was running a monthly deficit that threatened to wipe out his meager savings and life insurance. Acheson, Phil and Kay Graham, and others intervened to move the Frankfurters out of 3018 Dumbarton Avenue and into a more accessible apartment. Persuading Marion to agree to the move, Acheson remarked, was "a minor miracle." Neither she nor her husband knew how miraculous it was. The sale of the Frankfurters' Georgetown home, which netted $56,000, was not enough to cover the $75,000 Embassy Row apartment at 2239 Massachusetts Avenue and the necessary renovations. Phil and Kay Graham loaned the justice more than $43,000 to be repaid with the eventual sale of the apartment. An audit of Frankfurter's finances by Acheson, Donald Hiss, and another Covington & Burling lawyer revealed overspending, mounting medical bills, and long-term indebtedness. Acheson began soliciting money from the justice's longtime friends and raised nearly $7000 to reduce the debt. "Justice Brandeis used to say that most people thought too much or too little about money," Acheson wrote Harvard law graduate Benjamin F. Goldstein, who donated $2600. "Felix has always belonged to the latter class, which, of course, is a part of his endearing, happy nature." With assistance from secretary Elsie Douglas, Acheson and his law partners changed the Frankfurters' health insurer and instituted cost-cutting measures. The monthly deficits, however, continued. Each year the justice lived would be a financial struggle, and Marion's long-term care was a looming problem. Their biggest benefactors, the Grahams, were miffed when Frankfurter's sister Estelle began soliciting $400,000 for a chair at Harvard Law School in her brother's name when he did not have enough money to survive. Acheson proposed that Frankfurter write another memoir, as a book or in magazine articles, "only this time getting paid himself—General Grant did."

An October 1962 visit from Isaiah Berlin briefly revived the justice's flagging spirits. The Oxford philosopher thought the new apartment was larger and brighter than their Georgetown home. Felix and Marion lay in separate beds in different rooms. During his conversation with Berlin, Felix came alive talking about British friends Maurice Bowra and Sylvester Gates. He was "cheerful and gay" and spoke without slurring but like "a man with a heavy cold at most." Marion, who was asleep during most of Berlin's visit, was a different story. Berlin heard that she was "infinitely unkind to Felix because she wishes to be the only patient and cannot bear the fact that he too is an object of sympathy." Shortly before he left, a bell rang, and Berlin was summoned to her room. She confessed she never thought her husband, so full of energy and life, could succumb to such an illness and began to cry. Once they began gossiping, the old Marion returned. She "denounced most of our friends" and singled out the Grahams for their "materialism, love of power, wicked gossip, etc." Berlin described Marion as "as delightful as ever, very sharp, very grand."

As much as the move into the apartment improved his quality of life, Frankfurter was in no condition to write anything. He barely had enough energy for social engagements. Accompanied by his doctor and in a wheelchair, he attended a State Department concert by violinist Isaac Stern that October and enjoyed himself tremendously. At 5:00 p.m. on January 5, 1963, the Vienna Boys Choir sang to him and Marion at their apartment for half an hour; he thanked them in his native German. A month later, he received a private, after-hours showing at the National Gallery of the *Mona Lisa*. Elsie Douglas, who continued to serve as the justice's secretary and amanuensis, hoped these events would aid his recovery. For the most part, however, the triweekly physical therapy sessions sapped him of strength and failed to rehabilitate his paralyzed left arm and leg. His body was failing him, and his mind was, too. Berlin described him as "gently ebbing."

As with many stroke victims, the most striking change about Frankfurter was his personality. The justice who radiated optimism was becoming bitterly negative about everyone and everything. He was not only losing physical strength but also his mental acuity and emotional self-control. The doctors prescribed sedatives to keep him from becoming too excited about trivial things. The drugs made him more erratic and led to more outbursts. His eightieth birthday party at Acheson's house was a "horror." Every week, Acheson visited him out of a sense of duty and tried to prevent him from sending a missive to his former colleagues about the Court's latest opinion. Acheson was not always around or successful.

At the April 23, 1963, swearing-in of Judge Carl McGowan to the Court of Appeals for the District of Columbia Circuit, Frankfurter requested to speak to the audience and babbled incoherently for nearly twenty minutes in the presence of Attorney General Kennedy, Anthony Lewis, and longtime friends. "I have something on my mind," he began, "and I want to say it." He argued that lawyers "know more of history than historians" and began citing cases to prove it. He refused to quit talking even after former clerk Joseph Rauh, who accompanied him to the event, urged him to stop. Finally, Frankfurter's microphone was cut off. Rauh signaled for a few of the justice's friends to start clapping. Frankfurter was completely aware of the poor impression he had made. Rauh informed Acheson that future public speaking opportunities "must be avoided."

After the disastrous public appearance, Frankfurter sent two long, rambling letters to Hugo Black. No one missed Frankfurter on the Court more than his longtime intellectual adversary. The 76-year-old Alabaman had been one of the first justices to write Frankfurter after his stroke and had looked forward to his return to the Court. Nearly a month after Frankfurter's retirement, Black had visited him and had confessed: "We miss you because we need you. I wish you had been there for the N.Y. prayer case." Black was referring to his majority opinion in *Engel v. Vitale* outlawing state-imposed prayers in public schools, which Frankfurter undoubtedly would have joined given his votes in favor of separation of church and state. The love and respect between the two legal giants was mutual. Frankfurter worried about the impropriety of writing Black about pending cases of civil rights demonstrators arrested during sit-ins. Nonetheless, he wrote Black on May 7 and 8, 1963, to say how much he admired him and to reminisce about their shared history in the school segregation cases. The letters were as incoherent as his speech at Judge McGowan's swearing-in ceremony. At 4:00 p.m. on May 8, Black phoned, told him not to worry, and assured a relieved Frankfurter that he "should not hesitate ever to write to him." Frankfurter kept writing, especially when he liked one of Black's opinions. And Black kept visiting, knowing that his former colleague's best days were behind him.

"These are not good days," Elsie Douglas informed Paul Freund. Frankfurter was becoming more and more emotional. On May 24, he asked Freund and former clerk Louis Henkin to speak at his funeral. He wanted Freund to give the eulogy and Henkin, the son of a prominent Orthodox rabbi and product of yeshiva schools, to say the Mourner's Kaddish in Hebrew. The request surprised friends who knew that Frankfurter had walked out of synagogue as a fifteen-year-old and never returned. "I came into the world a Jew," the justice explained, "and although I did not live my life entirely as a Jew, I think it is fitting that I should leave as a Jew." As Frankfurter spoke, Marion, who was lying on her back in bed, was crying. After Freund and Henkin left, she told her husband: "I'm so relieved those two boys took a ton off my mind." He was as worried about the funeral arrangements as she was, if not more. Indeed, he told several friends about his funeral plans. Frankfurter's death was not imminent. "Every one of your vital organs is intact," his doctor informed him. "You are not at all a sick man; you are merely partially invalided."

One of Frankfurter's preoccupations was the career aspirations of Sylvester Gates's son, Oliver. Thanks to the intervention of Acheson, Oliver had worked for two years in a DuPont training program in Richmond, Virginia. After several more years of working for DuPont in England, Gates was considering a switch from business to law. Ultimately, Gates, who had married and returned to London, never pursued a legal career and, like his father Sylvester, thrived as a banker. "I wish I were around ten or fifteen years from now," the justice remarked, "to see what time will do to him or he to it."

By mid-1963, Frankfurter was thinking more about the past than the present or future by assigning former students and clerks to write judicial biographies. He informed Bickel and Phil Elman that they were "best equipped" to write about his judicial career and should be given access to his papers. He also granted access to journalist Max Freedman, who planned on writing a more popular biography. As the executor of the Holmes and Brandeis papers and with access to the papers of other justices, Frankfurter had been designating former students and law clerks to write judicial biographies: Holmes to Mark DeWolfe Howe, Cardozo to Andrew Kaufman, Jackson to Philip Kurland, and Brandeis to Paul Freund. Their collective output was sparse; Kaufman was the only one who finished, and it took him thirty-five years. Before his death in 1967, Howe had annotated and published some of Holmes's correspondence and had completed two magisterial volumes on Holmes's early life, volumes that gave Frankfurter great joy. Howe's embittered wife, Mary, blamed Frankfurter for saddling her husband with the Holmes biography and charged that he was a vampire who sucked the blood out of his protégés. "While I must agree that there is some truth in this contention," Edward "Prich" Prichard wrote Arthur Schlesinger, Jr., "it is also true that he, at the same time, pumped their blood full of life, giving oxygen, so that it was Felix's giving and Felix's taking away."

Thirteen former Frankfurter clerks and countless former students joined the legal academy at Harvard, Yale, and other top law schools. Together with Frankfurter's former graduate student Willard Hurst, Howe reinvented the field of American legal history. At Yale, Bickel was one of the preeminent constitutional law scholars of his generation. He died of cancer at age forty-nine after sacrificing any chance of a Supreme Court nomination of his own by defending the right of the *New York Times* to publish the Pentagon Papers over the objections of the Nixon administration. Anthony Amsterdam, who had worked with the justice on a possible Harvard lecture during the summer of 1963, became a legendary criminal law professor, a first-rate Supreme Court advocate, and the architect of the NAACP Legal Defense Fund's attack on the death penalty. Former clerks Louis Henkin and Abram Chayes became leading experts in international law.

With more bad weeks than good ones during the summer of 1963, Frankfurter made few public appearances except for a June 17 visit to the Oval Office to see President Kennedy. The retired justice asked who the "Mr. Buttinsky" of the administration was; Kennedy pointed to historian Arthur Schlesinger, Jr. Frankfurter launched into criticism of Schlesinger's multivolume work on the New Deal (which Frankfurter believed relied too much on Harold Ickes's diaries and the unreliable recollections of Tom Corcoran). During their "extremely pleasant" conversation, Frankfurter sat in his wheelchair next to the president behind his desk. Wilmarth Lewis, a longtime friend, sat by Frankfurter's side. The visit was "a great success," and the justice thanked the president for the White House photograph of "three Yale men." Lewis was a Yale graduate and trustee; Kennedy and Frankfurter were Harvard men who had received honorary Yale degrees.

A few weeks later on July 1, Frankfurter learned Kennedy had selected him for the nation's highest civilian award, the Presidential Medal of Freedom. Sadly, Kennedy did not present the award. On November 22, 1963, he was assassinated while riding through Dallas's Dealey Plaza in an open convertible. Four days after the assassination, Frankfurter learned that the Medal of Freedom ceremonies would take place as scheduled.

After Kennedy's assassination, Frankfurter's first order of business was writing a letter of encouragement to the new president, Lyndon Johnson. "My confident wishes are that you may discharge these burdens with courage and wisdom and humaneness," Frankfurter wrote on November 29, "and I am 'confident' that you will do so because of the one intimate experience I had the good fortune to have had with you." He was referring to Johnson's 1958 letter after Frankfurter's heart attack, which had kindled a friendship between the two men and revealed Johnson's "qualities of sensitiveness of thought and feeling."

Another loss brought Frankfurter and Johnson closer together—the suicide of former Frankfurter clerk and Johnson confidant Phil Graham. In 1958, Graham had encouraged Johnson to write Frankfurter after the justice's heart attack. For the past five years, the *Washington Post* publisher had been battling mental illness. He frenetically had begun transforming the *Post* into a national newspaper and buying other media properties including *Newsweek*. During the 1960 presidential campaign, Graham's equilibrium briefly returned. He had been instrumental in brokering Johnson's spot on the Kennedy ticket. In October 1962, Kennedy named Graham chair of the thirteen-member committee to establish the Communications Satellite Corporation (COMSAT). Graham's behavior, including an affair with a correspondent in *Newsweek*'s Paris bureau and bizarre phone calls berating the president, grew so erratic that he was forced to resign. He was hospitalized and diagnosed with manic depression. On August 3, 1963, he shot and killed himself at his Virginia farm, Glen Welby. Mourning the loss of one of his closest friends, Frankfurter lamented that Johnson had been thrust into the presidency without Graham's "devoted, highly intelligent, resourceful, and effective support for all your efforts."

In Johnson, Frankfurter saw a leader with the legislative and political skill to be a transformative president. In concluding his letter, he wished Johnson "one of the most important ingredients in successful statesmanship, namely luck—that is, right breaks at the right time." A savvy politician, Johnson appealed for Frankfurter's continued advice and support. "I need your help— I need your mind," Johnson replied on December 5. "We must seek out and serve the Nation's interest. We must erase the divisions in this country. We must find a new sense of union—a return to mutual reasonableness. This is the awesome burden I face. In this, I seek your counsel and your guidance."

During a noon reception on December 6 in the White House state dining room, Johnson presented Frankfurter with the Presidential Medal of Freedom. Joined at the ceremony by Kennedy's widow, Jackie, as well as former Supreme Court colleagues, Frankfurter listened as Johnson read his citation:

"Jurist, scholar, conversationalist, he has brought to all his roles a zest and wisdom which has made him teacher to his time." With a nurse in white uniform and hat at his side, Frankfurter rose from his wheelchair, just as he had stood to greet President Kennedy at Dumbarton Avenue the previous year, to accept the medal from President Johnson. Frankfurter's moving gesture made the *New York Times* front page. Fellow honoree John McCloy remarked that the justice lived up to his billing as a gifted conversationalist by engaging the president in "a rather long exchange."

The day after the ceremony, Frankfurter replied in longhand to Johnson's request for help and guidance: "Whatever strength is left in me is at the disposal of my country and therefore at your disposal." Johnson was so moved by Frankfurter's words that he wanted them included in textbooks and proclaimed them "the best definition of what American citizenship ought to be that I have ever seen." He reiterated that he was "serious in my request for your wisdom." If Frankfurter did not want to offer advice directly, Johnson suggested that the justice should relay it through Dean Acheson. Finally, Johnson wanted to continue the Roosevelt-Holmes and Kennedy-Frankfurter tradition of visiting Frankfurter at his apartment: "The Secret Service is understandably difficult these days, but I hope sometime in the future I may be able to slip away for a few moments and visit with you. In the meantime, remember that I need your counsel."

In many ways, Frankfurter was providing Johnson with counsel through the generations of former students, law clerks, and other protégés he had encouraged to enter public service. Kennedy aide Richard Goodwin and National Security Advisor McGeorge Bundy stayed to work for Johnson. Acheson and McCloy joined the "wise men" who advised the president on foreign policy, including the increasing military intervention in Vietnam. Joseph Rauh, Frankfurter's first clerk, became an adviser to Johnson and future presidents on civil rights. As Arthur Schlesinger, Jr., remarked of Rauh, Graham, Prichard, Goodwin, and many others, Frankfurter was "father to them all."

Some of Frankfurter's star protégés flamed out after fast starts in public service. James M. Landis was one of Frankfurter's most brilliant students, his co-author, and an FTC commissioner and SEC chairman during the early New Deal. After a failed marriage, unhappy deanship at Harvard Law School, and years of womanizing and heavy drinking, Landis tried to rehabilitate himself as a special assistant in the Kennedy administration in charge of overseeing administrative agencies. His demons caught up with him. In August 1963, he was convicted of failing to file federal income tax returns for five years. A year later, he was found dead in his swimming pool. Before his death, Landis had reconciled with his old mentor (the Frankfurters had sided with his first wife, Stella, during the divorce). "I loved that guy," Landis said. "All those wasted years." Tom Corcoran, by contrast, never forgave Frankfurter for opposing him as Roosevelt's solicitor general and never shook his reputation as a political fixer. Frankfurter remained fiercely loyal to other former students who had fallen from grace. Prichard had been convicted of election fraud in 1948 but rehabilitated himself as an adviser to several Kentucky governors and a proponent of education reform in the Bluegrass State. Alger Hiss had been convicted of perjury, was accused of being a Communist spy, and fought for his exoneration until the end of his life. For every Landis, Hiss, or Prichard, there was a Calvert Magruder, William Hastie, Charles Wyzanski, and Henry Friendly in the federal judiciary and a Dean Acheson, Richard Goodwin, and John McCloy in the executive branch.

For months, Johnson had been attempting to find time to visit the 81-year-old Frankfurter. At 3:45 p.m. on April 11, 1964, Johnson left the White House with his aide Goodwin. Seven minutes later, they arrived at Frankfurter's second-floor apartment. During his 23-minute visit, Johnson charmed Felix and Marion. The justice recommended a book by diplomatic historian Herbert Feis, the Pulitzer Prize–winning *Between War and Peace: The Potsdam Conference*. At 4:15 p.m., the president shook hands with the cook and elevator operator and left to play golf at Burning Tree Country Club. A few days later, he asked the justice to "allow me to consult with you from time to time; and that you will let me know when I am going wrong."

Even with his mind failing, Frankfurter periodically wrote the president. A few weeks after their visit, he sent a handwritten note, at Marion's behest, asking about Lady Bird Johnson after lightning had struck her airplane. On June 24, Frankfurter wrote about a talk he had with Israeli prime minister Levi Eshkol and Eshkol's positive impression of the president. Johnson replied by revealing the details of his meeting with the prime minister. In July, Johnson sent Frankfurter a pen from the signing of legislation to preserve historical documents and to publish the papers of the founding fathers, an idea the justice had endorsed several months earlier. A month later, Frankfurter promoted the candidacy of Phil Elman, his former clerk and FTC commissioner, for a federal judgeship on the Court of Appeals for the District of Columbia Circuit.

The summer of 1964 was time of triumph for Johnson. He marshaled all his political prowess to orchestrate the passage of one of the most transformative pieces of legislation in our nation's history. On July 2, 1964, he signed into law the Civil Rights Act of 1964. It was the type of landmark political and social change that Frankfurter dreamed of, change that should come not from the Supreme Court but from the nation's elected branches.

In November, Johnson won reelection in a landslide over Senator Barry Goldwater. After watching the president's inaugural address on television, Frankfurter wrote his last letter to an American president. Johnson's response implicitly acknowledged Frankfurter's dedication to encouraging the best young lawyers to pursue government service, some of them in Johnson's administration. "I am sure you know how deeply I share your view that it is our people who are our greatest strength . . . ," Johnson wrote. "Now we will be setting about the business of getting the very best ones we can find to join in the work of the next four years."

Johnson and Frankfurter had a lot in common. They overcame hardscrabble beginnings—Johnson from a small town in the Texas Hill Country to a small teacher's college to a job teaching Mexican immigrant children how to speak English; Frankfurter as an Austrian Jewish immigrant who had arrived at Ellis Island at age eleven not able to speak or understand a word of English. They both worked their ways into the corridors of political power by befriending wise mentors, Sam Rayburn in Johnson's case and Henry Stimson in Frankfurter's. They both adored Franklin Roosevelt. They both strived to bring the best people into government service. And they both believed that in a democracy, from the New Deal to the Great Society, from Ellis Island to the Hill Country, anything was possible.

It was little wonder that Johnson returned to Frankfurter's apartment one last time on the afternoon of February 24, 1965.

Epilogue

Accompanied by Secret Service agents and a personal assistant on a windy, 40-degree afternoon, President Johnson left the White House at 2:53 p.m. on February 24 and arrived seven minutes later at 2239 Massachusetts Avenue wearing an overcoat, a hat, and a hangdog expression. He joined 130 of Frankfurter's family, friends, former clerks and students, fellow justices (except for Bill Douglas) and their wives in the second-floor apartment for Frankfurter's memorial service. People arrived from all over the country and overseas; Hugo Black, whose eyes welled with tears when he heard the news, drove from Florida; Sylvester and Oliver Gates flew in from Britain.

In February 1965, Frankfurter had begun to deteriorate, slept most of the time, and could barely speak in an intelligible way. He arranged one last luncheon on February 16 for Dean Acheson, John Harlan, and two others. He was wheeled from his bed to the drawing room to greet his guests and to have a "small drink." He served rich food prepared by his former cook Matilda Williams and cocktails and white wine in antique glasses he had purchased in a London shop thirty years earlier. He played a recording of one of his favorite pieces of classical music, a work of Mozart's that the composer regarded as his best and which Frankfurter referred to as *"the* Quintet." He could barely swallow and had difficulty speaking. Somehow he managed to drink a third of an old-fashioned. He held Acheson's hand practically the entire time. Before coffee was served, Frankfurter shook hands with Acheson, Harlan, and the other guests; excused himself; and was wheeled to his bedroom to take a rest. A few days later, on February 22, he suffered a heart attack, was rushed to George Washington University Hospital at 4:30 p.m., and was pronounced dead at 5:05 p.m. Just before he was stricken, the 82-year-old justice had uttered his last words to longtime messenger Thomas Beasley: "I hope I don't spoil your Washington's Birthday."

Frankfurter's funeral was exactly as he would have wanted it. He had left few instructions aside from designating the two speakers. Acheson arranged it similarly to Brandeis's. There was no casket or ashes (Frankfurter's body had been cremated earlier that day). A trio of musicians led by former student and clarinetist Max Isenbergh played another of Frankfurter's favorite classical compositions, Handel's Andante from Trio Sonata in G Minor.

In a quiet voice barely audible to people in the apartment, Paul Freund began his eulogy by quoting several stanzas of a George Santayana poem and by recalling Frankfurter's "three great loves—love of country, of friends, and of law." He described the justice as "an unabashed, an almost childlike patriot" ever since the steamship *Marsala* pulled into New York Harbor and he had begun to learn English at age eleven at P.S. 25. Freund explained Frankfurter's tremendous gift for friendship by recalling his "iron grip on the arm," "explosive laughter," and "solicitous inquiries about ourselves and our dear ones that seemed to emanate from some miraculous telepathic power." He recounted their last meeting in January 1965 in which the justice asked him to read aloud the epigraph from Edmund Wilson's *The Shock of Recognition*, a quotation from Herman Melville—"For genius, all over the world, stands hand in hand, and one shock of recognition runs the whole circle round."—and Frankfurter's characteristic remark, "Good, isn't it?" Freund described Frankfurter's regard for the law as a "sacred calling" and alluded to his legal battles for the powerless and despised: for the copper miners in Bisbee, Arizona; jailed labor leader Tom Mooney in San Francisco; and Italian anarchists Sacco and Vanzetti in Boston. "In the end," Freund remarked of those episodes, "the word for F. F. is courageous." Freund praised Frankfurter's judicial philosophy of "forbearance in the use of power" as having "meaning and relevance far beyond the stage of his office and his time."

To conclude his ten-minute eulogy, Freund recited Mr. Valiant-for-truth's speech before his death in John Bunyan's *Pilgrim's Progress*, the same lines that Frankfurter had uttered to conclude his eulogy for Brandeis:

> My *Sword* I give to him that shall succeed me in my Pilgrimage, and my *Courage* and *Skill* to him that can get it. My *marks* and *scars* I carry with me, to be a witness for me, that I have fought His battles, who now will be my Rewarder. When the day that he must go hence was come, many accompany'd him to the River-side, into which as he went, he said, *Death, where is thy Sting?* And as he went down deeper, he said, *Grave,*

> *where is thy Victory?* So he passed over, and all the Trumpets sounded for
> him on the other side.

Freund's final words moved the audience in 1965 as Frankfurter's had in 1941, words binding two justices who fought so many legal and political battles and awaited the final verdict of history. As promised, former clerk Louis Henkin recited the Mourner's Kaddish in Hebrew and translated it into English. The musical trio concluded the service with Frankfurter's favorite composition, Mozart's Adagio from Clarinet Concerto.

As soon as the service was over, a "very moved" President Johnson walked over to Marion, who was sitting in the back in a chair, and offered his condolences before he left. For days, she received condolence letters from all over the world. Soon after her husband's death, she was moved into the Washington Home for Incurables, a charitable health facility. "Poor Marion is in bad shape," Acheson wrote, "and almost deserted." Her brother Don, who had pledged to provide for her financially, died in June 1965 of cancer; her sister Helen was estranged from her; only Elsie Douglas regularly visited her. Mentions of Felix caused Marion to "burst into tears." Alone in the world, she survived another ten years in increasing physical and mental decline. Frankfurter's friends once again raised money to provide for her care.

Two days after the memorial service in the Frankfurters' apartment, several professors—former colleague Austin Scott, former student Freund, and former clerk John Mansfield—spoke at a memorial service at Harvard Law School. The law school had transformed the trajectory of Frankfurter's life. He had an almost religious feeling about the school and the people who had taught there—the case method devised by Christopher Columbus Langdell, the theory of judicial restraint espoused by James Bradley Thayer, and Harvard's emergence as a preeminent law school under dean James Barr Ames. During his twenty-five years on the faculty, Frankfurter carried on the grand tradition and improved it in fundamentally important ways.

More than 600 faculty, students, and friends from Cambridge crammed into the Ames Court Room in Austin Hall for an hour of reminisces about Frankfurter's impact on the law school, the careers of his students, and the lives of his former clerks. Dean Erwin Griswold opened and closed the proceedings. Standing two deep in the back of the courtroom, the students listened as Austin Scott described Frankfurter as a legendary student who had finished first in the class of 1906, his recruitment of Scott to work at Henry Stimson's law firm, and as a vibrant colleague who had left "a great void" at the law school, which no one could fill. As he surely knew, Frankfurter was not a great scholar. His graduate students often co-authored his law review articles and wrote the first drafts of his books. His major contribution was as a teacher who challenged his students and inspired them to pursue public service.

His former student Freund remembered how Frankfurter had dissected cases down to the geography, personal histories of the judges and lawyers, legislative history, and backgrounds of the congressmen who had drafted the law. Freund marveled at how Frankfurter had thrived on argument in class and compared Frankfurter's discovery of an intellectually engaging student to "a grand new book." After a student challenged him in his public utilities class, Frankfurter gripped Freund by the arm in the hallway and asked: "Tell me about Mr. K! Where is he from? Where did he go to college? Isn't he good! Why haven't I known him before?"

In the most moving speech, Mansfield conveyed how stimulating it was to be one of Frankfurter's law clerks—his interest in their personal lives, the steady stream of visitors in chambers, the weekend afternoons in Frankfurter's book-filled study at Dumbarton Avenue, and the lack of anything that resembled work. What Mansfield remembered most was the conversation during their springtime walks: "It always seemed to be springtime that year; I can't remember any winter at all. Shall I tell you of the talk, and talk, and more talk, on a thousand subjects?"

During the fall of 1965, Frankfurter's former students and law clerks honored him with public and private tributes. Acheson and Bickel wrote the bar's memorial resolution for the Supreme Court's October 26 session dedicated to Frankfurter. Acheson, MacLeish, and Friendly spoke at the courtroom service. On the afternoon of November 29, a dozen of Frankfurter's former students and law clerks teaching at Harvard Law School interred his ashes at Cambridge's Mount Auburn Cemetery. Mark DeWolfe Howe read passages from the Book of Job and Holmes's 1884 Memorial Day address.

Above all, Frankfurter's friends remembered how passionately he cared about the law. He believed in fair procedure, not fair results. "The history of liberty," he wrote in *McNabb v. United States*, "has largely been the history of observance of procedural safeguards." In February 1962, he had taken the train to New York City with Australian ambassador Howard Beale and his wife to see the play "A Man for All Seasons." In a famous scene from Robert Bolt's drama about Sir Thomas More, the British lord chancellor during the reign of Henry VIII, More refuses to arrest an evil man who has not broken any law. More asks what happens when they ignore the law and try to arrest you. "That's the point," Frankfurter whispered to Beale and his wife in the darkened theater, "that's it. that's it!"

In the ensuing years, Frankfurter's judicial reputation suffered as liberal scholars celebrated the legacy of the Warren Court. Meanwhile, a full-length biography of Frankfurter was never written. Two of his chosen biographers, Max Freedman and Alexander Bickel, died young. His massive correspondence, even with some diaries and documents stolen from the Library of Congress, overwhelmed many others. A 1977 exhibit at Harvard Law School, "A Passionate Intensity," highlighted important sources and contributions. Oftentimes, however, scholars approached Frankfurter's career with preconceived notions. A psychobiography portrayed him as a "neurotic personality" with an "idealized and inflated" self-image. Frankfurter's reputation took a hit in 1982 with the publication of a sensationalistic book about Brandeis's funding of Frankfurter's public interest work. A centennial celebration of Frankfurter's birth in 1982, a gathering of former students and clerks at Harvard Law School, tried to repair some of the damage. For many years, Frankfurter was on the wrong side of history. As the Court has become more interventionist, however, some scholars have begun to reassess Frankfurter's more modest, incremental, and democratic approach to judging.

In contrast to many of his Warren Court colleagues, Frankfurter insisted that the best way to protect people's rights was through the democratic political process. He understood that nothing was more damaging to our democracy than to expect the Supreme Court to solve our problems. And, like James Bradley Thayer, he knew it was an even bigger mistake for the Court to invalidate federal laws unless they were unconstitutional beyond a reasonable doubt. In his final opinion, his *Baker v. Carr* dissent, he emphasized that the Court should leave purely political questions to the elected branches and to the people themselves.

We the People needed Felix Frankfurter to steer generations of elite lawyers into public service, to shape the liberal establishment, and to oppose government-by-judiciary. He never lost faith in electoral politics and the ability of people to choose their leaders. He treasured free speech and religious freedom yet feared that overprotecting the First Amendment undermined the government's ability to meet people's basic needs. Like John Marshall, he viewed the Constitution as a "great" outline flexible enough to "adapt to the crises of human affairs" yet able to guard against political overreach. Like Holmes and Brandeis, he maintained that the Court should defer to the elected branches in initiating transformative political and social change. Like Franklin Roosevelt, he trusted an expert-run federal government to solve the

most pressing economic and social issues of our time. And like Lyndon Johnson, he understood how laws such as the Civil Rights Act of 1964 and the
Voting Rights Act of 1965 could make our country more fair, equal, and just.

There is no one on the Supreme Court today quite like Felix Frankfurter.
A lifetime of political experience. A mentor to countless public servants. A
mugwump with no political party affiliation. A skeptic about judicial power.
A willingness to oppose a state-sponsored racial caste system but an abiding faith in the American people to resolve their most pressing, hot-button
issues. He loved America, he loved Franklin Roosevelt, and he believed in
government by and for the people and not by judges. Felix Frankfurter was a
democratic justice.

ACKNOWLEDGMENTS

As an assistant professor at the University of Wisconsin Law School in 2008, I wrote an article about the Supreme Court's repeated refusal to hear the case of convicted atomic spies Julius and Ethel Rosenberg. By using the justices' papers, I reconstructed the behind-the-scenes infighting and the reasons for the Court's multiple institutional failures—dismissing viable claims of prosecutorial misconduct, rushing to hold a special term to lift a stay of execution before new claims could be heard by lower courts, ethically problematic private conversations between Chief Justice Fred Vinson and the Justice Department, and judicial opinions written after the Rosenbergs had been executed.

During my research, I was struck by Felix Frankfurter's consistent support to hear the *Rosenberg* case and by the last two paragraphs of his dissenting opinion: "To be writing an opinion in a case affecting two lives after the curtain has been rung down upon them has the appearance of pathetic futility. But history also has its claims. This case is an incident in the long and unending effort to develop and enforce justice according to law. The progress in that struggle surely depends on searching analysis of the past, though the past cannot be recalled, as illumination for the future. Only by sturdy self-examination and self-criticism can the necessary habits for detached and wise judgment be established and fortified so as to become effective when the judicial process is again subjected to stress and strain."

Former Frankfurter clerk Phil Elman, a lawyer in the solicitor general's office who was dismayed by the Court's refusal to hear the case, confided that he needed Frankfurter's concluding paragraphs "for the sake of my soul." Elman interpreted Frankfurter as saying: "This isn't the end, errors are inevitably made but you go on, you don't lose faith in the process of law."

Frankfurter's insistence that "history also has its claims" and his emphasis on procedural fairness resonated with me and inspired me to explore his philosophy of judicial restraint and his career on and off the bench.

Historians have not been kind to Justice Frankfurter. They have characterized him as a liberal lawyer turned conservative justice, as a judicial failure, and as the Warren Court's principal villain. But as the Court has become increasingly interventionist, scholars have begun to reassess the role of the Court in our democracy and Frankfurter's incremental approach to judging, respect for precedent, and invocation of the political question doctrine as a safeguard against government by judiciary.

No comprehensive biography about Frankfurter has ever been written in part because of the massive amount of source material. He wrote ten to fifteen letters a day and left huge collections at the Library of Congress, Harvard Law School, and at archives and in private collections all over the world. He had a long career in government and the legal academy before joining the Court, requiring in-depth research at the National Archives and in presidential libraries.

As a legal historian, I have enjoyed poring over letters in archives and private collections for insights into Frankfurter's life and career. So many talented people have helped me with my last book on Frankfurter and his friends at the House of Truth and on *Democratic Justice*. It has been an incredible journey. I could not have done it without assistance from talented librarians, archivists, scholars, students, and friends.

First and foremost, I am indebted to all my colleagues at Georgetown University Law Center. Getting hired there nearly five years ago transformed my personal and professional life. The law library staff, including Jennifer Krombach, Hannah Miller, Thanh Nguyen, Yelena Rodriguez, Leah Prescott, Erie Taniuchi, Tammy Tran, Austin Williams, and Michelle Wu, tracked down every book, article, and reel of microfilm at libraries near and far. Like all great librarians, they never said no. Faculty assistants and staff George E. Belton, Jennifer Lane, Ronnie Reese, Alina Schmidt, and Jana Sneed assisted me with requests big and small. Brent Futrell generously took my author photograph (he did not have much to work with).

My colleague David Vladeck is the best FOIA lawyer in America. I am extremely grateful for all the time and effort he and his talented team spent on my behalf. They fought for FBI and State Department files that yielded many new insights about Frankfurter and his protégés David Niles and Max Lowenthal. On behalf of myself and other scholars, David also successfully sued for the release of grand jury testimony in the *Rosenberg* case. Finally, he connected me with several leading Cold War–era scholars. Thanks, David.

Associate deans Greg Klass, John Mikhail, Paul Ohm, and Joshua Teitelbaum supported me throughout this project. Dean Bill Treanor was always in my corner and granted me a crucial second semester of leave when I needed it most. A talented legal historian, Bill has inspired me with his scholarship on Gouverneur Morris and has encouraged me at every turn.

Another great legal historian, Dan Ernst, has listened to me talk about Frankfurter for more hours than any person should have to endure. I have profited from his mentoring, archival knowledge and documents, editing, good cheer, and first-rate scholarship about New Deal lawyers more than he will ever know. I am lucky to have him as a colleague and a friend.

Second, I want to thank my dear friends and former colleagues, library staff led by Bonnie Shucha and Steven Barkan, associate deans, and former dean Margaret Raymond at the University of Wisconsin Law School for supporting me at the beginning of this intellectual journey. I could not have written this book without learning how to be a legal historian at the intellectual home of Willard Hurst. Part of my heart will always be in Madison—teaching in the law school, researching at the Wisconsin Historical Society, walking around the farmer's market, and sitting outside the Memorial Union on a sunny day.

My friends at the Library of Congress Manuscript Division—the repository of papers of Supreme Court justices, government officials, members of Congress, and presidents—have put up with me throughout every phase of this project. They are some of the most talented archivists, librarians, and historians in the country and even better people. Researching there is a dream. I thank members of the library staff, past and present, including the late Fred Augustyn, Connie Cartledge, Loretta Deaver, Jeff Flannery, Dave Kelly, Lia Kerwin, Patrick Kerwin, Bruce Kirby, the late Joe Jackson, Alex Lorch, Elizabeth Pugh, Ryan Reft, Edith Sandler, Lara Szypszak, Kerrie Williams, Lewis Wyman, and Daun van Ee. Special thanks to Patrick Kerwin for retrieving documents for me when I have been unable to visit the library, for cheering me on, and for being an all-around great friend. We have had a lot of fun yet miss our friend Joe.

The Historical and Special Collections Library at Harvard Law School has been my second home away from home. I have spent countless hours there in the papers of Frankfurter and those of his former law school colleagues in the great company of Jane Kelly, Ed Moloy, and Lesley Schoenfeld. Lesley, more than anyone else, made publication of many of *Democratic Justice*'s photographs, including the cover, Frankfurter's official portrait by Gardner Cox, possible. She worked countless hours with me during the pandemic. Ed Moloy helped me with permissions to publish from various manuscript collections. They have taught me so much about the history of Harvard Law School and the library's extensive manuscript collections. Frankfurter's Harvard Law School Papers have been digitized by ProQuest and are available on ProQuest Vault, which enabled me to search the collection electronically and not lose my mind when I couldn't find a document.

Matthew Hofstedt and Franz Jantzen at the Supreme Court of the United States Curator's Office provided me with access to documents and photographs and worked with me on numerous occasions. Special thanks to Paul Bender for permission to publish his photographs of Elsie Douglas and Thomas Beasley and to the family of John F. Costelloe—Kevin, Paul, and Ann Costelloe Landenberger—for permission to publish their father's 1943 photograph of Frankfurter. Clare Cushman and Jennifer Lowe at the Supreme Court Historical Society are trusted friends and allies who helped me at many stages of this project.

I am grateful to the following archivists and institutions: Anna Clutterbuck-Cook, Hannah Elder, Daniel Hinchen, Elaine Grublin, Brenda Lawson, Laura Lowell, Tracey Potter, Kate Viens, and Conrad Wright at the Massachusetts Historical Society; Kimberly Reynolds at the Boston Public Library; Christian Belena, Kirsten Strigel Carter, Patrick F. Fahy, Matthew C. Hanson, Virginia H. Lewick, and Sarah L. Navins at the FDR Library; Robert Clark at the Rockefeller Archive Center; Robert Ellis, David Langbart, Gene Morris, Richard Peuser, Eric van Slander, and Gary Stern, National Archives; Jim Armistead, Randy Sowell, and Tammy K. Williams, Harry S. Truman Library; Jennifer Cuddeback and Allen Fisher, Lyndon B. Johnson Library; Stacey Chandler and Abigail Malangone, John F. Kennedy Presidential Library; Scott S. Taylor, Lauinger Library, Special Collections, Georgetown University; Madeline Bradford, Sarah McLusky, Malgosia Myc, and Cinda Nofziger, Bentley Library, Special Collections, University of Michigan; Chloe Morse-Harding, Brandeis University Archives; Joellen El Bashir, Moorland Spingarn Research Center, Howard University; Genevieve Coyle, Bill Landis, Stephen Ross, Eric Sonnenberg, and Judith Schiff, Sterling Library, Manuscripts Division, Yale University; Dana Herman, Joe Weber, and Julianna Witt, the American Jewish Archives; Sydney Van Nort, City College of New York Archives; Scott Campbell, University of Louisville Law Library; Elizabeth E. Hilkin, Tarlton Library, University of Texas Law School; Doug Boyd, Terry L. Birdwhistell, Sarah Dorpinghaus, Judy Sackett, Jeff Suchanek, and Kopana Terry, Margaret I. King Library, University of Kentucky; Anne Causey and Penny White, Albert & Shirley Small Special Collections Library, University of Virginia; Margaret Dakin, Amherst College Archives; Carolyn Marvin, Portsmouth Athenaeum; April C. Armstrong, Amanda Ferrara, Rachael Reitano, and Rosalba Varallo Recchia, Seely Mudd Library, Princeton University; Lisa Marine, Wisconsin Historical Society; Anne Engelhart, Zoe Hill, and Sarah Hutcheon, Schlesinger Library, Harvard University; Timothy Driscoll, Pusey Library, Harvard University; Jessica Suarez, Andover-Harvard Theological Library; Leslie Martin, Chicago Historical Society; Judith Wright, University of Chicago Law School Library; Cate Kellett, Ryan Greenwood, Fred Shapiro, and Michael Widener, Yale Law School Library; Scout Noffke and Morgan Swan, Rauner Special Collections, Dartmouth College; Lisa Warwick, Martin Luther King Library; Ronald Gaczewski, University of Buffalo Law Library; Kristen McDonald, Lewis Walpole Library; Irina Kandarasheva, Columbia University Law School Special Collections; Gaby Hale, Wilson Special Collections Library, University of North Carolina; Linda S. Stahnke, University of Illinois Archives; Brenda L. Burck and James E. Cross, Clemson University Special Collections; Matthew Schaefer, Herbert Hoover Presidential Library; Gaye Morgan, Codrington Library, All Souls College; Michael Simonsen and Agata Sobczak, Leo Baeck Institute; Lior Hecht-Yacoby, Chaim Weizmann Archive; Nina Gershuni and Illanit Levy, Aaronsohn Museum; Lori Reese, Redux Pictures; Christiana Newton, Getty Images; Tricia Gesner, AP Photo.

Numerous scholars have shared their expertise and documents including Jose Anderson on Charles Hamilton Houston, Jeffrey H. Bowman on the Willie Francis case, Daniel R. Coquillette and Bruce Kimball on the history of Harvard Law School, Bruce Craig on Alger Hiss, Nelson Dawson on Brandeis and Frankfurter, Rebecca Erbelding on the War Refugee Board and displaced persons, Sam Erman on the Bureau of Insular Affairs, Tony Freyer on the Little Rock school crisis, Gerard Magliocca on the gold clause cases, Donald Ritchie on Drew Pearson and James M. Landis, the late Martin Sherwin on J. Robert Oppenheimer and the atomic bomb, Seth Stern on William J. Brennan, Richard Primus for help with Bentley Library research assistance, Todd Peppers on William T. Coleman, Kathryn Smith on Missy LeHand, and Mel Urofsky on Brandeis and all things Zionistic (as Brandeis and Frankfurter used to say), and Steve Usdin on Ethel Rosenberg.

The biggest lift for me was trying to reconstruct Frankfurter's life in Austria with no knowledge of German and a raging pandemic preventing a research trip to Vienna. Numerous scholars and genealogists lent me their time, expertise, contacts, and documents including Evelyn Adunka, Steven Beller, Peter Ebner, Banai Feldstein, Martha Keil, Christina Köstner-Pemsel at the University of Vienna Library, Marsha Rozenblit, E. Randol Schoenberg, and Marlene Singer Zakai.

I am honored to follow in the footsteps of past Frankfurter scholars: Liva Baker, Max Freedman, H. N. Hirsch, Joseph P. Lash, Michael Parrish, Harlan B. Phillips, and Melvin Urofsky. Hirsch, Joseph's son Jonathan Lash, Parrish, and Urofsky were extremely generous with their time; Parrish shared invaluable notes and interview transcripts. Special thanks to Judge Martin H. Freedman and his family for permission to quote from *Roosevelt and Frankfurter* and for sharing memories of his uncle Max Freedman and to Leslie Tuthill and her family for permission to quote from *Felix Frankfurter Reminisces* and for sharing memories of her father Harlan Phillips.

Others people generously shared documents with me: Mary A. Bundy for a photograph of her grandfather Dean Acheson's portrait of John Quincy Adams inscribed by Frankfurter; Tim Corcoran (and Philip Kopper) for permission to quote from Thomas G. Corcoran's unpublished autobiography, *Rendezvous with Democracy*; Thomas Lemann for his time and for access to his father Monte Lemann's private papers; Nicholas Lemann for archiving Monte Lemann's Papers at Tulane University; the late David Lowenthal for memories of his father Max Lowenthal; Elizabeth Leiman Kraiem for letters from Frankfurter's sister Estelle; and Dr. David Sachar for portions of his David Niles thesis.

Thanks to many people who sat for interviews with me over the years: The late David Acheson, Mary Acheson Bundy, Paul Bender, Judge Guido Calabresi, the late William T. Coleman, Jerry Cohen, Bill Doolittle, the late Mercedes Eichholz, Oliver Gates, the late Justice Ruth Bader Ginsburg, Howard Kalodner, Andrew Kaufman, Thomas Lemann, Daniel Mayers, the late Judge Abner Mikva, Sarah Hormet Milam, Newt Minow, the late Judge Vincent McKusick, the late James C. N. Paul, Walter Brandeis Raushenbush, Tom Reston, the late Daniel Rezneck, the late Elisabeth Sifton, and Howard Trienens.

Special thanks to Oliver and Sarah Gates for inviting me to stay in their lovely home in the British countryside and for giving me unfettered access to their family's private correspondence with the Frankfurters. It was a memorable experience sleeping in his father Sylvester Gates's daybed and getting to know the legendary Oliver Gates. The man more than lived up to the legend. I am forever grateful for his and Sarah's grace and kindness to a weary traveler. The Isaiah Berlin Papers, which I saw at Oxford's beautiful Bodleian Library on that same trip, were a research goldmine for me.

During my fourteen years of teaching, I have been blessed with incredibly talented student research assistants who diligently worked on this project. Many have traveled to archives near their homes and spent countless hours photographing documents and on microfilm machines.

At Georgetown: Joshua Adler, Hannah Beiderwieden, Brett Bethune, Daniel Chozick, Courtney Christensen, Cory Dodds, Lillian Gaines, Joshua Goode, Hali Kerr, Will Magatha, Cameron Miller, Eva Schlitz, Molly Thornton, and Courtney Yadoo. Special thanks to Courtney Yadoo for all her archival work in New York and Israel and to Hannah Beiderwieden for translating documents from Austria and for exploring every conceivable rabbit hole for me about Frankfurter's early life and education. Thanks also to the students in my Warren Court seminar for their insights and fine papers about this era of Frankfurter's career.

At Wisconsin: David Blinka, Steven Curry, Patrick Proctor-Brown, Debbie Sharnak, Betsy Stone, and Annie Ziesing. Debbie Sharnak, now a historian of Latin America at Rowan University, went above and beyond in helping me with archival research for *The House of Truth*. Much of her research helped me in writing *Democratic Justice*. I look forward to reading her books one day.

At other schools and institutions: Mihal Ancik, Amy Butner, Sarah Elkordy, Antonia Ferguson, Cat Foley, Timothy Garrett, Alison Kahn, Eryn Killian, Jake Lieberman, Irina Rodina, and Audrey Springer-Wilson.

In 2019, the John Simon Guggenheim Memorial Foundation named me a Guggenheim Fellow in Constitutional Studies. I thank the committee for selecting me and Dorothy Tapper Goldman and her foundation for generously funding the fellowship in constitutional studies. The fellowship enabled me to extend my sabbatical for a second semester and to complete a first draft of the manuscript.

My secret weapon during the editing of *Democratic Justice* was Betsy Kuhn. A talented children's and young adult nonfiction book author and extraordinary editor of faculty books and articles at Georgetown University Law Center, Betsy spent hundreds of hours reading and editing my longer first draft and challenged me to make it shorter, clearer, less repetitious, and flow better. Our conversations guided me throughout the editing phase. She made the book so much better than I could have on my own. I am in her debt forevermore. Thank you, Betsy.

A core four of leading scholars read every page of the manuscript and provided detailed feedback: John Barrett, Dan Ernst, Laura Kalman, and Mark Tushnet. They read it during late spring and early summer of 2021 in time for me to turn around edits prior to production. Their unsparing criticism and observations helped me revise the manuscript and hopefully improve it. It was an honor to have the dream team of Barrett-Ernst-Kalman-Tushnet take time away from their own scholarship to read and comment on mine. Thanks to you all. I hope to return the favor someday.

John Barrett, who is writing a biography of Justice Robert H. Jackson, spent hours with me at the Library of Congress and on the phone discussing primary sources about Jackson, Frankfurter, and *Brown v. Board of Education*. For more than fifteen years, John has been one of the nicest and best friends any scholar could have. He and his wife Sarah Walzer have graciously hosted me in their New York City apartment. Thanks for everything, John.

Mel Urofsky generously read a few chapters and saved me from errors of fact and interpretation about Frankfurter's financial relationship with Brandeis and their Zionist activity. My law school roommate and dear friend Ben Kerschberg proofread the entire book and served as a wonderful sounding board about grammatical and other writing questions.

John Glusman, editor in chief at Norton, believed in this book from the outset and fought for its publication in full. He read the entire manuscript over his Christmas holiday break, made insightful editorial suggestions and comments throughout, and then commented on the manuscript again. I am so lucky to have him as my editor. Thanks to John for believing in me and in my book. John's whip-smart editorial assistant, Helen Thomaides, has helped me every step of the way with permissions, photographs, and fielding my annoying questions. Thanks, Helen. Copyeditor Christopher Curioli improved the book immensely with his meticulous eye for names, dates, and places. Finally, thank you to Ingsu Liu for the art direction, Jared Oriel for the cover design, and to senior production editor Dassi Zeidel.

Flip Brophy is the literary agent every writer dreams of having. She has done everything in her power to make this book a reality and has stuck with me through thick and thin. We have known each other for so long that she is part of my extended family. I am so lucky to have her in my life. Thanks to Flip, her former assistant Nell Pierce, her colleague Jessica Friedman, and the entire team at Sterling Lord Literistic.

My family has put up with me for many years as I've traveled to distant archives or holed myself up writing and rewriting. I have not always been the easiest person to live with during particularly stressful periods of finishing the book. Thanks to my sometimes-funny brother, Ivan, his wife, Tamara, and their amazing daughters, Elana and Maya; and to my fabulous and supportive in-laws, Jack and Donna Hunt, and my sister-in-law, Beth Hunt.

My parents, Linda and Harry Snyder, continue to inspire me and amaze me and help me grow as a husband and as a father. They are two of my best friends. My mother is a talented writer, former local newspaper editor, and amateur photographer. Her voice was in my head as I wrote each chapter. She proofread the entire manuscript, consulted with me on every photograph, and suggested how the photographs could be cropped. My dad is my biggest cheerleader and, though he lacks a social media account (and knowledge about how to use one), blasts my accomplishments to anyone who will listen. Thanks for everything both of you have done for me.

I owe the biggest debt of gratitude to my immediate family. My wife, Shelby Hunt, is a hardworking lawyer and loving wife and mom who somehow kept the family together and organized during the chaos and challenges of the pandemic. She lived through all the ups and downs of this book, is a trenchant critic, and has been an amazing life partner and friend. She also nearly fainted when I told her I wanted to write another book. My children, Lily and Max, make me smile every single day and help me keep my obsessive work habits in check. Nothing is worthwhile unless Shelby, Lily, and Max are in my life. I love you more than you will ever know.

It sounds ridiculous to say after writing more than 700 pages about Felix Frankfurter but there is a lot more to write and research about his life, his relationships with his friends and family, and his work on and off the Court. New discoveries will be made if and when his papers and those of other justices at the Library of Congress and the papers of Learned Hand at Harvard Law School are digitized. Except for Frankfurter's correspondence with Holmes and Brandeis, most of Frankfurter's correspondence with Hand, Robert H. Jackson, John Marshall Harlan II, and others has not been published.

The biggest breakthrough will come if and when the stolen diaries and correspondence from Frankfurter's Papers at the Library of Congress are returned. Between August and October 1972, someone stole the most historically significant Frankfurter diaries, including his 1927 diary about the Sacco-Vanzetti case and his 1937 diary about FDR's court-packing plan, as well some of Frankfurter's correspondence and other files. Only about twenty scholars viewed the collection during the period in question. Beginning in November 1972, the FBI investigated, narrowed its list of suspects, but did not indict anyone. A public plea from syndicated columnist Jack Anderson on September 14, 1973, resulted in the return of some documents, but not the aforementioned diaries and select correspondence with Hugo Black and other justices. No one has claimed responsibility for the theft. My message to the scholar or scholars (or their families) who have Frankfurter's stolen papers in their possession is simple: Give them back. The Library of Congress Manuscript Division will accept their return with no questions asked. History, to quote Frankfurter's *Rosenberg* dissent, has its claims.

Much remains to be learned about Frankfurter's early life in Vienna and Hungary. Frankfurter's paternal grandfather worked for Vienna's Jewish organization known as the *Israelitische Kultusgemeinde* (IKG). The IKG's archives remain a possible source of material. The lives of Frankfurter's father, Leopold, and uncle Salomon are worthy of more research as are the family's temporary move to Budapest and Frankfurter's early education in Austria. Once the pandemic abates and travel to Austria reopens, I plan on visiting the Vienna apartment building where Frankfurter was born as well as several archives. As Billy Joel says in one of his most unforgettable songs, Vienna waits for me.

Brad Snyder
Washington, D.C.
June 2022

ABBREVIATIONS

AA	Aaron Aaronsohn
AAB	Adolf A. Berle, Jr.
AABD	Adolf A. Berle, Jr., Diary, FDRL
ADH	Arthur D. Hill
AGB	Alice Goldmark Brandeis
AH	Alger Hiss
AL	Anthony Lewis
ALL	A. Lawrence Lowell
ALLOP	A. Lawrence Lowell Official Papers, Harvard University
ALP	Anthony Lewis Papers, Library of Congress
ALLPP	A. Lawrence Lowell Personal Papers, Harvard University
AM	Archibald MacLeish
AMB	Alexander M. Bickel
AMBP	Alexander M. Bickel Papers, Yale University
AMP	A. Mitchell Palmer
AMS Jr.	Arthur M. Schlesinger, Jr.
AMS Sr.	Arthur M. Schlesinger, Sr.
AMSP	Arthur M. Schlesinger, Jr., Papers
AtlConst	Atlanta Constitution
AWS	Austin Wakeman Scott
BAA	Baltimore Afro-American
BaltSun	Baltimore Sun
BB	Bennett Boskey
BDE	Brooklyn Daily Eagle
BET	Boston Evening Transcript
BG	Boston Globe
BH	Boston Herald

BKW	Burton K. Wheeler
BKWP-MSU	Burton K. Wheeler Papers, Montana State University
BP	Boston Post
BvBP	Brown v. Board of Education Papers, Yale University
BVC	Benjamin V. Cohen
BVCP	Benjamin V. Cohen Papers, Library of Congress
CCB	C. C. Burlingham
CCBP	C. C. Burlingham Papers, Harvard Law School
CEH	Charles Evans Hughes
CEHP	Charles Evans Hughes Papers, Library of Congress
CEW	Charles E. Wyzanski, Jr.
CEWP-MHS	Charles E. Wyzanski, Jr., Papers, Massachusetts Historical Society
CHH	Charles Hamilton Houston
ChiDef	Chicago Defender
COH	Columbia Oral History
CSM	Christian Science Monitor
CT	Chicago Tribune
CW	Chaim Weizmann
CWP	Chaim Weizmann Papers
CZA	Central Zionist Archives
DA	Dean Acheson
DAP	Dean Acheson Papers, Yale University
DDE	Dwight D. Eisenhower
DDED	Dwight D. Eisenhower Diary
DDEL	Dwight D. Eisenhower Library
DFF	Diaries of Felix Frankfurter
DFP	Detroit Free Press
DKN	David K. Niles
DKNP	David K. Niles Papers, HSTL
EBP	E. Barrett Prettyman, Jr.
EBPP	E. Barrett Prettyman, Jr., Papers, University of Virginia Law School
ED	Elsie Douglas
EFP	Edward F. Prichard
EFP OH	Edward F. Prichard Oral History, University of Kentucky
EG	Erwin Griswold
EGE	Elizabeth Glendower Evans

EGEP	Elizabeth Glendower Evans Papers, Harvard University, Schlesinger Library
EGF	Elizabeth Gurly Flynn
EMH	Edward M. House
EMHD	Edward M. House Diary
EMHP	Edward M. House Papers, Yale University
ER	Eleanor Roosevelt
ERB	Emory R. Buckner
ES	Ellery Sedgwick
EW	Earl Warren
EWP	Earl Warren Papers, Library of Congress
FB	Francis Biddle
FBD	Francis Biddle Diary, FDRL
FBP-GU	Francis Biddle Papers, Georgetown University
FBP-FDRL	Francis Biddle Papers, FDRL
FDR	Franklin D. Roosevelt
FDRL	Franklin Delano Roosevelt Library
FF	Felix Frankfurter
FF Hearings	Nomination of Felix Frankfurter to be an Associate Justice of the Supreme Court, Hearings before a Subcomm. of the Comm. on the Judiciary, U.S. Senate, 76th Cong., 1st Sess. (1939)
FFHLS	Felix Frankfurter Papers, Harvard Law School
FFLC	Felix Frankfurter Papers, Library of Congress
FFR	Felix Frankfurter Reminisces
FH	Fanny Holmes
FLLDB	Family Letters of Louis D. Brandeis
FM	Frank Murphy
FMP	Frank Murphy Papers, University of Michigan
FMV	Fred M. Vinson
FMVP	Fred M. Vinson Papers, University of Kentucky
FR	Fred Rodell
FRP	Fred Rodell Papers, Haverford College
FWB	Frank W. Buxton
GC	Grenville Clark
GCP	Grenville Clark Papers, Dartmouth University
GJ	Gardner "Pat" Jackson
GJP-FDRL	Gardner Jackson Papers, FDRL

HarCour	Hartford Courant
HBE	Herbert B. Ehrmann
HBEP	Herbert B. Ehrmann Papers, Harvard Law School
HBHS	Half Brother, Half Son (LDB-FF Correspondence)
HC	Herbert Croly
HCrim	Harvard Crimson
H-E Letters	Holmes-Einstein Letters
HF	Herbert Feis
H-FF Corr.	Holmes-Frankfurter Correspondence
HFS	Harlan Fiske Stone
HFSP	Harlan Fiske Stone Papers, Library of Congress
HHB	Harold H. Burton
HHBD	Harold H. Burton Diary, Library of Congress
HHBP	Harold H. Burton Papers, Library of Congress
HI	Harold Ickes
HID	Harold Ickes Diary, Library of Congress
HIP	Harold Ickes Papers, Library of Congress
HJF	Henry J. Friendly
HJFP	Henry J. Friendly Papers, Harvard Law School
HJL	Harold J. Laski
HLB	Hugo Lafayette Black
HLBP	Hugo Lafayette Black Papers, Library of Congress
HLL	Holmes-Laski Letters
HLS	Henry L. Stimson
HLSD	Henry L. Stimson Diary, Yale University
HLSP	Henry L. Stimson Papers, Yale University
HLSSC	Harvard Law School Special Collections
HMH	Henry M. Hart, Jr.
HMHP	Henry M. Hart, Jr., Papers, Harvard Law School
HMS	Harold M. Stephens
HMSP	Harold M. Stephens Papers, Library of Congress
H-P Letters	Holmes-Pollock Letters
HSC	Homer S. Cummings
HSCD	Homer S. Cummings Diaries, University of Virginia
HSCP	Homer S. Cummings Papers, University of Virginia
HST	Harry S. Truman
HSTD	Harry S. Truman Diary
HSTL	Harry S. Truman Library
HSTP	Harry S. Truman Papers

IB	Isaiah Berlin
IBP	Isaiah Berlin Papers, Oxford University
INB	Irving N. Brant
INBP	Irving N. Brant Papers, Library of Congress
Int.	Interview
JA	Joseph Alsop
JAF	James A. Farley
JAFD	James A. Farley Diary, Library of Congress
JAFP	James A. Farley Papers, Library of Congress
JB	Jacob Billikopf
JBP	Jacob Billikopf Papers, American Jewish Archives
JCG	John Chipman Gray
JCM	James C. McReynolds
JFB	James F. Byrnes
JFBP	James F. Byrnes Papers, Clemson University
JFK	John F. Kennedy
JFKL	John F. Kennedy Library
JFKPOF	John F. Kennedy President's Office Files
JJM	John J. McCloy
JJMD	John J. McCloy Diary, Amherst College
JJMP	John J. McCloy Papers, Amherst College
JLO	John Lord O'Brian
JLR	Joseph L. Rauh, Jr.
JLRP	Joseph L. Rauh, Jr., Papers, Library of Congress
JMH	John Marshall Harlan II
JMHP	John Marshall Harlan II Papers, Princeton University
JML	James M. Landis
JMLP-LC	James M. Landis Papers, Library of Congress
JNF	Jerome N. Frank
JPK	Joseph P. Kennedy, Sr.
JPKP	Joseph P. Kennedy, Sr., Papers, JFKL
JSAP	Joseph & Steward Alsop Papers, Library of Congress
JTA	Jewish Telegraphic Agency
JWM	Julian W. Mack
KL	Katharine Ludington
LAT	Los Angeles Times
LBJ	Lyndon B. Johnson
LBJL	Lyndon B. Johnson Library
LC	Library of Congress

LCC	Loring C. Christie
LCJ	Louisville Courier-Journal
LC P&P	Library of Congress Prints and Photographs Division
LDB	Louis D. Brandeis
LDBP-Brandeis U	Louis D. Brandeis Papers, Brandeis University
LDBHLS	Louis D. Brandeis Papers, Harvard Law School
LDB-Louisville	Louis D. Brandeis Papers, University of Louisville, Louis D. Brandeis School of Law
LE	Lewis Einstein
LH	Learned Hand
LHP	Learned Hand Papers, Harvard Law School
LLDB	Letters of Louis D. Brandeis
MB	McGeorge Bundy
MD	Marion Denman
MDF	Marion Frankfurter
MDH	Mark DeWolfe Howe
MDHP	Mark DeWolfe Howe Papers, Harvard Law School
ML	Max Lowenthal
MLD	Max Lowenthal Diary, University of Minnesota
MLH	Missy LeHand
MLP	Max Lowenthal Papers, University of Minnesota
MML	Monte M. Lemann
MMLP	Monte M. Lemann Papers, Tulane University
MRC	Morris Raphael Cohen
MRCP	Morris Raphael Cohen Papers, University of Chicago
MSF	Master Speech File
NARA	National Archives and Records Administration
NCG	Nina Chipman Gray
NDB	Newton D. Baker
NDBP	Newton D. Baker Papers, Library of Congress
NJG	Norfolk Journal & Guide
NYDN	New York Daily News
NYH	New York Herald
NYHT	New York Herald-Tribune
NYPL	New York Public Library
NYSun	New York Sun
NYT	New York Times

NYTM	New York Times Magazine
NYTrib	New York Tribune
NYW	New York World
OH	Oral History
OJR	Owen J. Roberts
OJRP	Owen J. Roberts Papers, Library of Congress
OWH	Oliver Wendell Holmes, Jr.
OWHP	Oliver Wendell Holmes, Jr., Papers, Harvard Law School
PAF	Paul A. Freund
PAFP	Paul A. Freund Papers, Harvard Law School
PBK	Philip B. Kurland
PBKP	Philip B. Kurland Papers, University of Chicago
PC	Pittsburgh Courier
PE	Philip Elman
PEP	Philip Elman Papers, Harvard Law School
PG	Phil Graham
PGates	Pauline Gates
PhillyTrib	Philadelphia Tribune
PPWL	Public Papers of Walter Lippmann
PS	Potter Stewart
PSF	President's Secretary's File
RCM	Raymond C. Moley
RCMP	Raymond C. Moley Papers, Hoover Institution
R&FF	Roosevelt & Frankfurter: Their Correspondence, 1928–1945
RGV	Robert G. Valentine
RGVP	Robert G. Valentine Papers, Massachusetts Historical Society
RHJ	Robert H. Jackson
RHJP	Robert H. Jackson Papers, Library of Congress
RM	Robert Menzies
RNB	Roger Nash Baldwin
RP	Roscoe Pound
RPP	Roscoe Pound Papers, Harvard Law School
SFExam	San Francisco Examiner
SFR	Stanley F. Reed
SFR OH	Stanley F. Reed Oral History Project, University of Kentucky
SFRP	Stanley F. Reed Papers, University of Kentucky

SFV	Sophie French Valentine
SGates	Sylvester Gates
SIR	Samuel I. Rosenman
SIRP	Samuel I. Rosenman Papers, FDRL
SIR-TL	Samuel I. Rosenman Papers, HSTL
SK	Stanley King
SM	Sherman Minton
SMC	Small Manuscript Collection
SNB	S.N. Behrman
SSW	Stephen S. Wise
SSWP	Stephen S. Wise Papers, American Jewish Historical Society
STLPD	St. Louis Post-Dispatch
STLST	St. Louis Star-Times
SVDC	Sacco-Vanzetti Defense Committee
SVDC-BPL	Sacco-Vanzetti Defense Committee Papers, Boston Public Library
SV Trial Tr.	Sacco-Vanzetti Trial Transcripts
TCC	Tom C. Clark
TCCP	Tom C. Clark Papers, University of Texas Law School
TGC	Thomas G. Corcoran
TGCP	Thomas G. Corcoran Papers, Library of Congress
TNP	Thomas Nelson Perkins
TNR	The New Republic
TR	Theodore Roosevelt
TRP	Theodore Roosevelt Papers, Library of Congress
ToL	Times of London
WashHerald	Washington Herald
WashTimes	Washington Times
WAW	William Allen White
WAWP	William Allen White Papers, Library of Congress
WBR	Wiley B. Rutledge
WBRP	Wiley B. Rutledge Papers, Library of Congress
WBW	William B. Wilson
WDN	Washington Daily News
WES	Washington Evening Star
WGT	William G. Thompson
WHH	William H. Hastie
WHHP	William H. Hastie Papers, Harvard Law School

WHT	William Howard Taft
WHTP	William Howard Taft Papers, Library of Congress
WJB	William J. Brennan, Jr.
WJBP	William J. Brennan, Jr., Papers, Library of Congress
WL	Walter Lippmann
WLP	Walter Lippmann Papers, Yale University
WLPB	War Labor Policies Board
WOD	William O. Douglas
WODP	William O. Douglas Papers, Library of Congress
WP	Washington Post
WTC	William T. Coleman, Jr.
WTD	Winfred T. Denison
WW	Woodrow Wilson
WWP	Woodrow Wilson Papers, Library of Congress
YLS	Yale Law School
ZC	Zechariah Chafee
ZCP	Zechariah Chafee Papers, Harvard Law School

NOTES

INTRODUCTION: A PRESIDENTIAL VISIT

1 **5:00 p.m. & "off"**: JFK Daily Log, 7/26/1962, JFKPOF, JFKL.

1 **stroke:** NYT, 4/6/1962, at 1, 23.

1 **"cardiovascular":** NYT, 4/8/1962, at E8.

1 **letters:** FFLC, Box 124.

1 **"to about":** MB to JFK, 7/26/1962, at 1, JFKPOF, 088a-011, at 17, JFKL.

1 **"lived":** SNB to IB, 5/15/1962, at 1, IBP, Box 168, #229.

1 **October:** ED to PAF, 5/1/1962 & ED to PAF, 5/15/1962, FFHLS, Pt. III, Reel 38, Pages 298–99.

2 **retire:** MB to JFK, 7/26/1962, at 1.

2 **July 7:** ED to HF, 7/9/1962, Feis Papers, Box 34.

2 **summoned:** MB to JFK, 7/26/1962, at 1.

2 **"all strongly" & "'wary'" & "a man":** MB to JFK, 7/26/1962, at 1–2.

2 **"a deeply":** MB to JFK, 7/26/1962, at 2.

2 **briefing:** JFK Daily Diary, 7/26/1962, at 2.

2 **Georgetown set:** Gregg Herken, *The Georgetown Set* (2014); Robert W. Merry, *Taking on the World* (1996).

2 **vice presidency:** Robert A. Caro, *The Passage to Power*, 129–38 (2012).

3 **"Does anybody":** FF OH Pt. 1, 6/10/1964, at 3–5, JFKL.

3 **"pro-Nixon":** PG to IB, 10/9/1960, at 2, IBP, Box 161, #38.

3 **"simply":** ED to JMH, 7/24/1962, FFLC, Box 66 & FFHLS, Pt. III, Reel 1, Page 640.

3 **details & "Chief of Protocol":** DA to RM, 8/14/1962, at 1–2, *id.*, Reel 14 & *Among Friends*, 233–34 (David S. McLellan & David C. Acheson, eds. 1980).

3 **skeptical:** Walter Isaacson & Evan Thomas, *The Wise Men*, 590 (1986).

3 **"stood up":** ED to JMH, 7/30/1962, at 1, FFLC, Box 66.

3 **politics:** DA, "The President's Call on Justice Frankfurter," at 1, in FF OH Pt. II, 6/19/1964, at 66 & FFHLS, Pt. III, Reel 38, Pages 302–7.

3 **scant mention:** NYT, 7/27/1962, at 22; WES, 7/27/1962, at A-9; Victor Riesel, "Inside Labor," n.d., FFHLS, Pt. III, Reel 38, Page 301.

3 **his own father:** DA, "The President's Call on Justice Frankfurter," at 1 & FF OH Pt. 1, 6/10/1964, at 15.

3   **"it seemed" & "fundamental" & "the basic" & "rooted":** DA, "The President's Call on Justice Frankfurter," at 1–2.

3–4 **"most perplexing" & "many people":** *Id.* at 2–4.

4   **"building" & "Democratic president" & "outside" & "with doubt" & "molder":** *Id.* at 4–5.

4   **"greatness" & "conception" & "guidance" & "how they":** *Id.* at 5.

4   **Matilda Williams & Ellen Smith:** Andrew L. Kaufman, "The Justice and His Law Clerks," in *Felix Frankfurter: The Judge*, 227–28 (Wallace Mendelson, ed. 1964).

4   **household staff & "great honor":** DA, "The President's Call on Justice Frankfurter," at 5–6; FF to Bickel, 8/9/1962, at 2, FFHLS, Pt. III, Reel 32, Page 969.

4   **August:** ED to AMB, 8/3/1962, FFHLS, Pt. III, Reel 32, Page 967.

4   **the visit of newly inaugurated:** Brad Snyder, *The House of Truth*, 561–64 (2017).

4   **"the wisest":** FDR to OWH, 3/8/1934, at 2, OWHP, Reel 40, Page 3, Box 52, Folder 20.

4   **judicial failure:** Michal R. Belknap, *The Supreme Court under Earl Warren, 1953–1969*, at 98 (2005) (describing FF as "an overrated judge who left a very limited judicial legacy" and whose "long-term influence on constitutional law was minimal"); Melvin I. Urofsky, *Felix Frankfurter: Judicial Restraint and Individual Liberties*, x (1991) ("A quarter-century after his death, his opinions are all but ignored by both the courts and academia."); Mark Tushnet, "Antonin Scalia as Felix Frankfurter," Balkinization, 8/19/2004, https://balkin .blogspot.com/2004/08/antonin-scalia-as-felix-frankfurter.html ("Frankfurter['s] reputation has declined substantially—even from the time when I was a law student—to the point where he's regarded, I think, as at most a moderately interesting failure."); G. Edward White, "The Canonization of Holmes and Brandeis," 70 N.Y.U. L. Rev. 576, 576 (1995) (describing FF as having "passed from revered to ridiculed status in two recent decades"); Michael E. Parrish, "Felix Frankfurter, the Progressive Tradition, and the Warren Court," in *The Warren Court in Historical and Political Perspective*, 54 (Mark Tushnet, ed. 1993) ("There is now almost a universal consensus that Frankfurter the justice was a failure. . . . who . . . left little in the way of an enduring jurisprudential legacy"); Melvin I. Urofsky, "The Failure of Felix Frankfurter," 26 U. Rich. L. Rev. 175, 176 (1991) (arguing FF was a failure because of his "abrasive personality" and "he became a prisoner of jurisprudential views that he had developed and solidified during his tenure as professor at the Harvard Law School"); Joseph P. Lash, "A Brahmin of the Law: A Biographical Essay," in *From the Diaries of Felix Frankfurter*, 73 (Joseph P. Lash, ed. 1975) (describing FF's refusal to privilege the protection of civil liberties as having "uncoupled him from the locomotive of history").

5   **former students:** FF to PAF, 12/28/1962, FFHLS, Pt. III, Reel 38, Pages 317–18.

5   **"Whether":** ToL, 11/15/1962, at 13. *See* Louis L. Jaffe, "The Judicial Universe of Mr. Justice Frankfurter, 62 Harv. L. Rev. 357, 357–58 (1949) (rejecting liberal or conservative label).

6   **John Marshall:** FF, "John Marshall and the Judicial Function," 69 Harv. L. Rev. 217 (1955) in *Felix Frankfurter on the Supreme Court*, 533–57 (Phil Kurland, ed. 1970) & James Bradley Thayer et al., *John Marshall* (Phil Kurland, ed. 1967).

6   **broad outline:** McCulloch v. Maryland, 17 U.S. 316, 407 (4 Wheat 316) (1819).

6   **reapportionment:** Baker v. Carr, 360 U.S. 186, 266 (1962) (Frankfurter, J., dissenting).

6   **"enter":** Colegrove v. Green, 328 U.S. 549, 556 (1946).

7   **talent scout:** Snyder, *House of Truth*; Brad Snyder, "The Judicial Genealogy (and Mythology) of John Roberts: Clerkships from Gray to Brandeis to Friendly to Roberts," 71 Ohio St. L.J. 1149 (2010).

7　　**liberal establishment:** Geoffrey Kabaservice, *The Guardians* (2004); Kai Bird, *The Color of Truth* (1998); Kai Bird, *The Chairman* (1992); Isaacson & Thomas, *Wise Men*.

CHAPTER 1: MISS HOGAN

9　　**Miss Annie E. Hogan:** FFR, 4–5; John Mason Brown, "The Uniform of Justice," Saturday Review, 10/30/1954, at 45; The City Record, 7/29/1903, at 103; Annie E. Hogan Death Record, 7/9/1904, New York City Municipal Deaths, 1795–1949, Family History Library microfilm 13232056.

9　　**"daze":** FFR, 4–5.

9　　**origin story:** Biographers have repeated errors about FF's early life, errors that originated in a three-part *New Yorker* profile. Matthew Josephson, "Jurist-II," New Yorker, 12/7/1940, at 37. For example, FF arrived in America when he was eleven, not twelve, and did not start school at P.S. 25 until he was "nearly twelve." FF to Matthew Josephson, 7/22/1942, Brandeis Autograph Collection 334–442, Folders 378–79 (enclosing handwritten memoranda and identifying thirty-five errors in profile).

10　　**"There is hardly":** Stefan Zweig, *The World of Yesterday*, 12 (1943).

10　　**one of many:** Marsha L. Rozenblit, *The Jews of Vienna, 1867–1914*, at 13–45 (1983).

10　　**Emma:** Emilia "Emma" Winter, Birth Record, 3/10/1854, Uhersky-Ostroh Births 1849–1875, Image #22/150.

10　　**her father and grandfather:** Dr. Heinrich Flesch, "Geschichte Der Juden in Ung. Ostra.," at 4 in *Jews and Jewish Communities of Moravia in the Past and Present*, 576 (Hugo Gold, ed. 1929) (listing Emma's father Salomon in 1880–1888 and grandfather Löbl in 1860 as appointed chairman to deal with Jewish matters).

10　　**Leopold:** Leopold Frankfurter Passport Application, 3/1/1909, NARA, U.S. Passport Applications, M1490, Roll 78, #1351 (Pressburg birth on 1/26/1854).

10　　**Leopold's mother:** https://www.geni.com/people/Lotte-Frankfurter/6000000010422722495 (Lotte Frankfurter died on 2/16/1854).

10　　**Leopold's father:** Emanuel Frankfurter, Death Record, 5/31/1891, Index of the Jewish Records of Vienna and Lower Austria, No. 391181 (civil servant of Jewish community).

10　　**yeshiva:** Leonard Baker, *Brandeis and Frankfurter*, 41 (1984) (yeshiva); cf. Michael E. Parrish, *Felix Frankfurter and His Times*, 8 (1982) (rabbinical school).

10　　**traveling salesman:** Lehmann Vienna City Directory 305 (1880) (Leopold as handels agent, Emma as convenience store worker); Lehmann Vienna City Directory 373 (1887) (Leopold as handels agent).

10　　**Leopoldstadt:** Rozenblit, *Jews of Vienna*, at 76–77 & tbl. 4:1 (48.3 percent of Viennese Jews in 1880 lived in the Leopoldstadt).

10　　**Felix was born:** FF, Birth Record, 11/15/1882, Austria, Vienna, Jewish Registers of Births, Marriages, and Deaths, 1784–1911, Vol. 2–2, 1882, #4017, LDS Roll 152.

10　　**Ella:** Estelle "Stella" Frankfurter Int. with CEW, 11/28/1973, at 1, CEWP-MHS, Carton 26; Ella Frankfurter, Birth Record, 10/12/1892, Hungarian Births Database, LDS microfilm 642971, Vol. 21, Page 359, Line 2231.

10　　**miserable:** FF Int. with Max Freedman, LC audio files 1618219-3-3 & 16182190-3-17; Budapest School Reports, 1893–94, at 82, Radixindex School Reports, radixindex.com (listing his brother Otto).

10　　**two years:** FF to Adolph Lippe, 8/28/1941, FFLC, Box 123; FF to MML, 11/6/1941, Monte Lemann Papers.

10 **Salomon Frankfurter:** Evelyn Adunka, "Salomon Frankfurter (1856–1941)," in *Bibliotheken in der NS-Zeit*, 209 (2008); Evelyn Adunka, "Salomon Frankfurter," *Österreichiches Biographisches Lexikon* (ÖBL) Online Edition, Lfg. 5, 11/25/2016.

11 **bathtub:** Estelle "Stella" Frankfurter Int. with CEW, 11/28/1973, at 1.

11 **"oppressively":** FFR, 5.

11 **"his high":** FF to Hans W. L. Freudenthal, 11/17/1960, FFLC, Box 124.

11 *Gymnasium:* Rozenblit, *Jews of Vienna*, 99–125; Steven Beller, *Vienna and the Jews, 1867–1938*, at 49–55 (1989); Zweig, *The World of Yesterday*, 28–32. Searches of incomplete Vienna *Gymnasia* files have not produced a record for FF for the 1893–1894 school year.

11 **"deep":** FF to Adolph Lippe, 8/28/1941; FF Int. with Max Freedman, n.d., at 2–3, FFHLS, Pt. III, Reel 40, Pages 269–70.

11 **Emanuel:** Emanuel Frankfurter, Death Record, 5/31/1891, Index of the Jewish Records of Vienna and Lower Austria, Vol. E, # 3405.

11 **five dollars:** S.S. *Indiana*, 5/31/1893, Philadelphia Passenger Lists, 1883–1945, NARA, Roll T840, Roll 19, Line 22 (five dollars).

11 **"Children":** BG, 1/8/1939, at C4 (based on int. with Paul Frankfurter).

11 **320:** http://www.theshipslist.com/ships/descriptions/ShipsM.shtml.

11 **120:** NYTrib, 8/10/1894, at 12.

11 **steerage:** S.S. *Marsala*, 7/25/1894, Hamburg Passenger Lists, Staatsarchiv Hamburg, Vol. 373-7 I, VIII A 1 Band 088 A; Page 527; Microfilm No. K_1751; S.S. *Marsala*, 8/10/1894, New York Passenger Lists, 1820–1897, NARA Roll M237, Roll 60, Line 34.

11 **Dover:** NYT, 7/28/1894, at 9.

11 **Statue of Liberty:** FF, "The Morris Cohen Library," 5/3/1958, in *Of Law and Life and Other Things That Matter*, 107 (Phillip B. Kurland, ed. 1965).

11 **1:00 p.m.:** NYTrib, 8/10/1894, at 12.

11 **perfect:** NYT, 8/11/1894, at 11.

12 **99 East Seventh & "breathed":** FF, "The Cooper Union: Pacemaker," 10/6/1956, in *Of Law and Life and Other Things That Matter*, at 48.

12 **philosopher:** BG, 1/8/1939, at C4.

12 **peddler:** 1895–96 NY City Directory at 473 ("pedlar"); 1897–98 NY City Directory at 429 & 1899–1900 NY City Directory at 418 (drygoods); 1901–2 NY City Directory at 443 (agent); 1900 U.S. Census, T623_1114, E.D. 756, Page 5B, Line 82 (merchant). Leopold was not a furrier. FF to Josephson, 7/22/1942; *cf.* Josephson, "Jurist-II," New Yorker, 12/7/1940, at 37 (describing him as "retail fur merchant").

12 **whistling & dinner:** FF Int. with Freedman, n.d., at 5–6.

12 **pet & "Anybody":** FF Int. with Freedman, n.d., at 6, 8.

12 **"Hold":** FF, "The Best Advice I Ever Had," 8/1956 in *Of Law and Life and Other Things That Matter*, 38.

12 **"the greatest":** FFR, 8–9.

12 **reading:** BG, 1/8/1939, at C4.

12 **newspapers:** FF Int. with Freedman, n.d., at 9–10.

13 **red leather & forum series:** FFR at 4.

13 **"two-fifths":** FF, "The Cooper Union: Pacemaker," in *Of Law and Life and Other Things That Matter*, 42, 47–50.

13 **Hoboken:** FFR, 6–7; NYT, 9/24/1896, at 2.

13 **John Adams:** Program, Grammar School No. 25, 6/29/1897, FFLC, Box 234. *Cf.* FFR, 8 (recalling it was speech by William Pitt in the House of Lords).

13 **scholarships & Horace Mann:** FFR, 9–10; NYT, 6/9/1897, at 12.

13 **one of seven:** NYT, 6/24/1897, at 3.

14 **"the universal":** FF, "Experiment in Democracy," 11/1946, City College Alumnus, Vol. 42, No. 8, at 139, FFLC, Box 198.

14 **ugly:** FF, "The Morris Cohen Library," 5/3/1958, at 4, in *Of Law and Life and Other Things That Matter*, at 108.

14 **red:** FF, "Address at the Inauguration Dr. Harry N. Wright as Sixth President of City College," 9/30/1942, at 1, FFLC, Box 219.

14 **classical:** FFR, 11–12.

14 **Isador Goetz:** FFR Transcript, 5/1953, at 130–31, FFLC, Box 205.

14 **Morris Raphael Cohen:** FF, "The Morris Cohen Library," 5/3/1958, at 4, in *Of Law and Life and Other Things That Matter*, at 108–9; FF, "Morris R. Cohen," in *Of Law and Men*, 294–95 (Philip Elman, ed. 1956); NYT Book Review, 3/27/1949, at 1, 21.

14 **Lenox Library:** FFR, 12.

14 **read Hebrew:** Estelle "Stella" Frankfurter Int. with CEW, 11/28/1973, at 1.

14 **abandoned:** FFR, 289–90.

14 **craps:** FF Int. with Max Freedman, n.d., at 8.

14 **Third Avenue Elevated:** Louis S. Posner to FF, 1/14/1939, at 1, FFHLS, Pt. III, Reel 21, Page 648.

14 **bounced:** Nathaniel Phillips, "F.F.C.C.N.Y.," in *Felix Frankfurter: A Tribute*, 86 (Wallace Mendelson, ed. 1964).

14 **Clionia:** 1900 Microcosm, at 41, 44, CCNY Archives.

14 **"Resolved":** Program, "Sixty-First Semi-Annual Joint Debate Clionian and Phrenocosmian Literary Societies," 5/3/1901, FFHLS, Pt. III, Reel 39, Pages 682–5.

15 **"vehement":** College Mercury, 5/1/1901, at 160.

15 **"his stunning":** Phillips, "F.F.C.C.N.Y.," in *Felix Frankfurter: A Tribute*, 83.

15 **Accounts:** Milton S. Hoffman to FF, 1/9/1939, FFHLS, Pt. III, Reel 21, Page 644 (recalling Clionia lost & Supreme Court reversed); Downes v. Bidwell, 182 U.S. 244 (1901).

15 **second:** Merit Rolls, 1900–1901, at 10, CCNY Archives, Box 4.

15 **vice president & assistant editor:** Commencement Number, College Mercury, 6/1902 & Quips and Cranks, CCNY Archives, Box 9.4.3.

15 **third:** Merit Rolls, 1901–1902, at 1, CCNY Archives, Box 4 (3rd, demerits not listed).

15 **"The Perversion":** 1902 Fifteenth Annual Commencement program, 6/19/1902, at 2, CCNY, Box 117 & The College of the City of New York 54th Annual Register, 1902–1903, at 57 & NYT, 6/20/1902, at 5.

15 **$1200 & $1050:** FF Employment File, n.d., 11/25/1959, FFLC, Box 224; FFR, 14–15; City Record, 1/12/1903, at 259 (listing him as temporary clerk at $1200 as of 11/12/1903); City Record, 1/31/1905, Pt. 3, at 350 (clerk & $1050).

15 **druggists:** 1900 U.S. Census, Roll T623_1114, E.D. 756, Page 5B, Lines 84–85.

15 **bank clerk:** 1905 New York Census, A.D. 29, E.D. 18., Page 9, Line 33.

15 **"already":** FF to CCNY Board of Trustees, 1/1/1903, at 1–2, CCNY Archives, Box 281.

15–16 **"bad" & "blew":** FFR, 15. *Cf.* Estelle "Stella" Frankfurter Int. with CEW, 11/28/1973 (recalling doctor advised FF not to go to law school in New York City to preserve his health).

16   **Meyer Rosensohn:** *Id.* at 15–16; City Record, 1/31/1905, Pt. 3, at 349.

16   **Sam Rosensohn:** Harvard Law School Catalogue, 1903/1904, at 38.

16   **$150:** Harvard Law School Catalogue 1904/1905, at 11.

CHAPTER 2: A QUASI-RELIGIOUS FEELING

17   **1707 Cambridge Street:** 1904–1905 Harvard Law School Catalogue, at 34; Quinquennial Catalogue of the Law School of Harvard University, 1817–1919, "Alphabetical List," 89 (1920) (noting FF's October 5, 1903 start date).

17   **"That's the Archangel":** FFR, 17–18.

17   **"one of the most" & "virtuoso":** FFR, 18. The two-time All-American was Edward Bowditch, Jr. Harvard Law School Catalogue 1904–1905, at 31.

17   **Langdell & case method:** Bruce A. Kimball, *The Inception of Modern Professional Education: C. C. Langdell 1826–1906*, at 7–9, 311 (2009); Daniel R. Coquillette & Bruce A. Kimball, *On the Battlefield of Merit*, 344–435 (2015).

18   **"blind":** FF to JNF, 12/18/1933, at 1, Frank Papers, Ser. 2, Box 12.

18   **"a Mama's":** FFR, 17.

18   **every day:** FF Int. with Max Freedman, n.d., at 7.

18   **"You go":** FFR, 31–32.

18   **"optionals":** *Id.* at 18–19.

18   **"artist" & "model thinker":** FF, "Samuel Williston," 76 Harv. L. Rev. 1321, 1322–23 (1963).

18   **Ames & "the most versatile":** FFR, 18–22.

18   **"electric":** FF, "Joseph Henry Beale," 56 Harv. L. Rev. 701, 702 (1943).

18   **"shy":** FF, "Eugene Wambaugh," 54 Harv. L. Rev. 7, 8 (1940).

19   **two-week span:** Harvard Law School Scrapbook 8, 1903–1904 March–June, at 2233.

19   **297:** 1904–1905 Harvard Law School Catalogue, at 46.

19   **235:** 1905–1906 Harvard Law School Catalogue, at 47.

19   **"I have":** FFR, 19.

19   **returned:** FFR, 32; FF to Birns, 11/30/1959, FFLC, Box 224 (noting resignation date of September 1, 1904, from Tenement House Department); New York City Directory, 1905–1906, at 469 (listing FF as clerk at 931 Park Avenue).

19   **mid-August:** FFR, 35; FF, "The Profession of the Law," 4/30/1960, in *Of Law and Life and Other Things That Matter*, 169–70 (Philip B. Kurland, ed. 1965).

19   **"There was":** FFR, 27.

19   **80:** "First-Year Grades," FFHLS, Pt. III, Reel 40, Page 247.

19   **His torts:** Max Lowenthal, "Felix Long Ago," in *Felix Frankfurter: A Tribute*, 124 (Wallace Mendelson, ed. 1964).

19   **Harvard Law Review:** "Notes," 1 Harv. L. Rev. 36 (1887); Coquillette & Kimball, *On the Battlefield of Merit*, 574–91.

19   **third-year students:** "Editorial Board," 18 Harv. L. Rev. 527 (1905).

20   **Stanley King:** "Editorial Board," 19 Harv. L. Rev. 119 (1905).

20   **generosity:** Elihu Root, Jr., to MD, 11/22/1919, at 1–3, FFLC, Box 91.

20   **"too late":** FF, "Samuel Williston," 76 Harv. L. Rev. at 1322.

20   **heart disease:** Harvard Bulletin, Vol. IV, No. 19 (February 19, 1902): 1.

20   **"rule" & "very clear" & "beyond" & "combination":** James B. Thayer, "The Origin and

Scope of the American Doctrine of Constitutional Law," 7 Harv. L. Rev. 129, 150, 144, 151, 138 (1893).

20 **legislators:** Thayer, "The Origin and Scope," 156 & James B. Thayer, Letter to the Editor, "Constitutionality of Legislation: The Precise Question for a Court," The Nation, 4/10/1884, at 315.

20 **"too common" & "to dwarf" & "thought by" & "the good" & "The judiciary":** James Bradley Thayer, *John Marshall* 107, 109–10 (1901).

21 **"in the air":** FF to AMS Jr., 6/18/1963, at 2, FFLC, Box 101 & in R&FF, 25.

21 **Wambaugh:** FF, "Samuel Williston," 76 Harv. L. Rev. at 1322.

21 **"the most important" & "Because":** FFR, 300–1.

21 **"other motives":** Lochner v. New York, 198 U.S. 45, 64 (1905). *Compare* David E. Bernstein, *Rehabilitating Lochner* (2011) (explaining Peckham's opinion and attributing law to powerful bakers' union); Paul Kens, *Judicial Power and Reform Politics* (1990) (defending the law and bakers' union as protecting exploited workers).

22 **usually paid:** Paul Kens, "Review of Bernstein, David E., *Rehabilitating Lochner*," H-Law, H-Net Reviews, 6/2013, http://www.h-net.org/reviews/showrev.php?id=36949.

22 **several studies:** Lochner, 198 U.S. at 70–71 (Harlan, J., dissenting).

22 **highlighted:** NYT, 4/18/1895, at 1; CT, 4/18/1895, at 1; WP, 4/18/1895, at 11; 18 Harv. L. Rev. 618, 618–19 (1905).

22 **"The Fourteenth":** Lochner, 198 U.S. at 75–76 (Holmes, J., dissenting).

22 **Fogg:** This speech summarized prior lectures LDB gave on May 4 and 5, 1905, at the Harvard Ethical Society. LDB to AGB, 10/18/1912, *The Family Letters of Louis Brandeis*, 197 (Melvin I. Urofsky & David W. Levy, eds. 2002) (referring to Fogg Museum speech to law students); FF to LDB, 11/12/1936, at 1–2, FFLC, Box 29 (recalling speech in law student days); Melvin I. Urofsky, *Louis D. Brandeis*, 205 (2009) (placing FF's attendance at subsequent law student lecture at Fogg Museum).

22 **A German-speaking Jew:** Peter Scott Campbell, "Notes for a Lost Memoir of Louis D. Brandeis," Journal of Supreme Court History 43, no. 1 (2018): 28–46.

23 **Morris Raphael Cohen:** Morris Raphael Cohen, *A Dreamer's Journey*, 133–34, 176 (1949); Leonora Cohen Rosenfield, *Portrait of a Philosopher*, 40–42 (1962).

23 **Emory Buckner:** Martin Mayer, *Emory Buckner*, 7–21 (1968).

23 **Easter break:** FFR, 35.

23 **82 average:** "Second-Year Grades," FFHLS, Pt. III, Reel 40, Page 247.

24 *Review* **president:** "Editorial Board," 19 Harv. L. Rev. 119 (1905) (Roger Ernst as president).

24 **excluded Jews:** Jerold S. Auerbach, *Rabbis and Lawyers*, 150–51 (1990); Jerold S. Auerbach, *Unequal Justice*, 106–8, 121–23 (1976).

24 **"was made" & "Yes" & "the life" & "a good office":** FFR, 35–36.

24 **Dwight Morrow:** FF to LH, 10/19/1931, at 1, LHP, Box 104B, Folder 104-21.

24 **uncle Salomon:** FF to JB, 9/6/1941, JBP, Box 8, Folder 3.

24 **"You'll encounter" & "this is a good":** FFR, 37–38.

24 **third-year student:** "Third-Year Grades," FFHLS, Pt. III, Reel 40, Page 247.

24 **83 & first:** AWS to MML, 5/28/1946, Scott Papers, Box 11, Folder 11-8.

24–25 **"spoke into" & "like asking" & "Oh you" & "No, I really" & "Dear Frankfurter":** FFR, 23–24.

26   **Henry Stimson:** FF started working for Stimson on August 7 and could not have worked at Hornblower for more than a few weeks. HLS to William Henry Moody, 8/10/1906, at 5, HLSP, Reel 11, Vol. 1, Page 155 & NARA, Department of Justice, RG 60, Box 596 (referring to August 7 start date). *Cf.* FFR, 38–39; Samuel Spencer, Jr.'s, Notes of FF, GC Conversation—Summer 1947, at 3, FFHLS, Pt. III, Reel 15, Page 253 (placing phone call in September 1906 and two months at Hornblower).

26   **five-foot-five:** FF 1918 Passport Application, U.S Special Passport Applications 1916–1925, Vol. 3, at 352 (listing FF's height as 5'6"); FF 1920 Application, U.S. Application, Reel 1231, Page 582 (listing FF's height as 5'5").

26   **Boone & Crockett & eight miles:** HLS, "Previous Relations with Colonel Roosevelt," HLSD, Reel 1, Vol. 2, Page 12; Henry L. Stimson & McGeorge Bundy, *On Active Service in Peace and War*, xii–xxii, 3–4 (1948).

27   **White House interview:** Memorandum, 1/17/1909, HLSD, Reel 1, Vol. 1, Pages 1–10.

27   **he hired:** FFR, 38–40; Memoranda, 1/17/1909 & 8/15/1909, HLSD, Reel 1, Vol. 1, Pages 6–14; Diary entry, 11/8/1930, at 2, HLSD, Reel 2, Page 135 (recalling he hired FF and Winfred T. Denison even though they "were at no time and in no possible way party men, but who had become most valuable assistants"); FFR Transcript, 5/1953, at 138 (recalling Stimson did not ask him party affiliation).

27   **$22,000 budget:** HLS & MB, *On Active Service*, 5–7.

27   **He wrote:** HLS to Ames, 6/30/1906, at 1–3, HLSP, Reel 11, Vol. 1, at 126–28.

27   **"the most able":** HLS to Moody, 8/10/1906, at 6.

27   **$750:** FFR, 39; HLS to Moody, 8/10/1906, at 4–5.

27   **"clerks":** Root Jr. to MD, 11/22/1919, at 3–4.

28   **"it isn't" & "I suggest":** FFR, 39–40. *See* Samuel Spencer, Jr.'s, Notes of FF, GC Conversation—Summer 1947, at 3; FF, "The Profession of the Law," 4/30/1960, in *Of Law and Life and Other Things That Matter*, 160–61 (Philip B. Kurland, ed. 1965) (similar comments).

28   **his colleagues:** FFR, 40 (partner reactions).

28   **"His work":** HLS to Moody, 8/10/1906, at 5.

28   **"We have" & "a study":** FFR, 41–42.

28   **motion to quash:** NYT, 10/16/1906, at 4.

28–29 **$108,000 & removed it:** FFR Transcript 2/24/1954, at 13–14; New York Central R.R. v. United States, 212 U.S. 481, 486, 490 (1909).

28   **"People talked":** FFR, 41.

29   **Stimson's trust:** HLSD, 8/15/1909, at 12–14.

29   **only immigrant:** FFR, 43 HLS, Circular, n.d., "Assignment of Work to Take Effect Jan. 1, 1909," at 2–3, NARA Department of Justice, RG 60, Box 596; United States ex rel. Funaro v. Watchorn, 164 F. 152 (S.D.N.Y. 1908). At Ellis Island, he befriended a young interpreter for Italian immigrants, Fiorello La Guardia. FF, "Fiorello H. La Guardia," 9/20/1957, at 1, FFLC, Box 200.

29   **Emil Sonner:** FFR, 42–43.

29   **suicide:** Leavenworth Times, 12/17/1909, at 2.

29   **recruitment:** Samuel R. Spencer, Jr.'s, Notes of FF, GC Conversation—Summer 1947, at 3; Elting E. Morison, *Turmoil and Tradition*, 97 (1960) (based on 9/29/1954 int. with FF); HLSD, 8/15/1909, at 11 (hiring WTD, Dorr, FF, and Bird in July and August).

29   **office mate:** FFR, 4.

29   **Denison:** HLS to Moody, 8/10/1906, at 2.

29   **weekends:** HLS and MB, *On Active Service*, 7.

29   **E. H. Harriman:** FFR, 46–48; Harriman v. ICC, 211 U.S. 407 (1908), rev'g, 157 F. 432 (1908).

30   **search warrant:** FFR, 48–49.

30   **Morse:** HLS and MB, *On Active Service*, 10; Morse v. United States, 174 F. 539 (2d Cir. 1909).

30   **dummy loans:** NYT, 10/22/1908, at 6.

30   **"the excitement":** FFR, 44–45.

30   **Heinze:** NYT, 4/26/1910, at 20; NYT, 5/6/1910, at 1; NYT, 5/28/1910, at 8; BDE, 6/2/1910, at 4; United States v. Heinze, No. 2, 218 U.S. 547 (1910).

31   **"The Case":** Outlook, 5/9/1909, at 25–38. *See* HLS and MB, *On Active Service*, 10–11; Outlook, 8/6/1910, at 771–84.

31   **special prosecutors:** FFR, 50.

31   **U.S. attorney's office:** Wise to Attorney General George Wickersham, 12/18/1909, & Wickersham to Wise, 12/21/1909, & Wise to Wickersham, 12/23/1909, NARA, Department of Justice, RG 50, Box 600.

31   **subpoena:** NYT, 5/25/1910, at 3.

31   **books and papers:** Outlook, 8/6/1910, at 776.

31   **front-page news:** NYT, 1/15/1910, at 1.

31   **unsuccessfully appealed:** Heike v. United States, 217 U.S. 423 (1910).

31   **Court of Appeals:** FF to HLS, 6/7/1911, at 1, HLSP, Reel 25, Page 114; ERB to FF, 6/22/1911, at 1–2, FFLC, Box 30.

31   **Supreme Court:** HLS and MB, *On Active Service*, 11–14; Morison, *Turmoil and Tradition*, 107; Heike v. United States, 227 U.S. 131 (1913), aff'g, 192 F. 83 (2d Cir. 1911).

32   **governor of New York:** HLS, "Personal Recollections of the Convention and Campaign of 1910," at 1–8, HLSD, Reel 1, Vol. 2.

32   **5:40 p.m.:** NYTrib, 9/30/1910, at 1.

32   **half dozen:** NYSun, 9/10/1930, at 3.

32   **"closely associated":** NYT, 9/30/1910, at 4.

32   **many hats:** HLSP, Reel 20.

32   **"He has"** NYT, 9/29/1910, at 5.

33   **Denver:** TR, "The Nation and the States," 8/29/1910, Denver, Colorado, http://www.theodore-roosevelt.com/images/research/txtspeeches/691.pdf; United States v. E. C. Knight, 156 U.S. 1 (1895); Lochner v. New York, 198 U.S. 45 (1905).

33   **Osawatomie:** TR, "New Nationalism," Osawatomie, Kansas, 8/31/1910, http://www.theodore-roosevelt.com/images/research/speeches/trnationalismspeech.pdf.

33   **accused the judiciary:** John Milton Cooper, Jr., *The Warrior and the Priest*, 144–52 (1985); Edmund Morris, *Colonel Roosevelt*, 107–13 (2010); Victoria F. Nourse, "A Tale of Two Lochners," 97 Cal. L. Rev. 751, 778–85 (2009).

33   **moment of truth:** FFR, 51–52; Buffalo Evening News, 11/2/1910, at 1, 6 (TR's speeches).

34   **"would make":** HLS, "Personal Recollections of the Convention and Campaign of 1910," at 1.

34   **"Darn it":** HLS and MB, *On Active Service*, 26. *Cf.* FFR, 50 (similar quotation).

34   **Grand Music Hall:** NYTrib, 11/1/1910, at 1.

34   **"And if Tammany"** & **"If there":** *Id.*

34   five more cars: NYSun, 11/1/1910, at 4; NYH, 11/1/1910, at 6; NYW, 11/1/1910, at 4.
34   "the greatest" & "the chance to work" & "the chance for" & "stand": NYT, 11/1/1910, at 3.
35   "Isn't": Id.
35   upstate: NYSun, 11/9/1910, at 5.
35   dinner: NYT, 11/9/1910, at 5 (dinner).
35   watch: HLS to FF, 12/2/1910, at 1–2, FFLC, Box 103; FF to HLS, 12/8/1910, id.
35   he made sure: FF to HLS, 6/7/1911, HLSP, Reel 25.
35   "I feel": TR to FF, 12/2/1910, FFLC, Box 98.
36   Holmes's: FF to TR, 1/9/1911, at 1–2, TRP, Reel 96, Series 1, Images 443–44 (Holmes opinion).
36   "the most efficient": FF to TR, 1/14/1911, at 1–2, id., Images 772–73.
36   six-page outline: FF to TR assistant Frank Harper, 1/21/1911, at 1, id., Reel 97, Series 1, Image 422; Outline, at 1–6, id., Images 424–29.
36   few skeptics: FF to TR, 1/31/1911, id., at 1–3, Reel 96, Series 1, Images 112–13.
36   "I believe": TR to Israel Fischer, 6/30/1911, TRP, Reel 378, Series 3A, Vol. 22, Image 229 (original includes handwritten corrections by TR) (copy of original on file with author).
36   weekly meeting: TR Secretary to FF, 6/30/1911, id., Image 230; FF to TR, 7/4/1911 tel., id., Reel 109, Series 1, Image 111; FF to TR, 7/7/1911, id., Image 722.
36   steamship: NYT, 1/5/1911, at 1.
36   lumber: NYT, 5/20/1911, at 1.
36   magazine: NYT, 6/28/1911, at 6.
36   steel wire: NYT, 7/1/1911, at 3.

CHAPTER 4: THE HOUSE OF TRUTH

37   "There is": FF to HLS, 5/11/1911, at 2, HLSP, Reel 24, Page 406.
37   Justice Department: HLS to FF, 6/30/1911, at 1–3, FFLC, Box 103; HLS to FF, 7/1/1911, at 2, id.; FF to Wickersham, 7/2/1911 tel., HLSP, Reel 25; Wickersham to FF, 7/13/1911, at 1–2, FFLC, Box 111.
37   law officer: HLS to FF, 7/3/1911, FFLC, Box 103.
37   "junior": FFR, 56.
37   "Faithful": HLS to Lewis Stimson, 8/3/1911, at 6, HLSP, Reel 25, Page 611.
37   many meals: FF to ERB, 9/26/1911, at 3–5, FFLC, Box 30.
37   walked: FFR, 57–58.
38   "collects": HJL to OWH, 7/20/1925, 1 HLL at 766.
38   "I assume" & "faith in democracy" & "old laissez-faire" & "problems": FF to HLS, 9/9/1911, at 1–6, HLSP, Reel 26, Pages 189–94.
38   Supreme Court: United States v. E. C. Knight Co., 156 U.S. 1 (1895); Standard Oil Co. of New Jersey v. United States, 221 U.S. 1 (1911); United States v. American Tobacco Co., 221 U.S. 106 (1911).
39   longhand: HLSD, Reel 1, Vol. 2, Pages 54–58; HLS to WHT, 9/13/1911, at 1, HLSP, Reel 26, Page 292; HLS to Mabel Stimson, 9/21/1911, at 3, id., Page 473.
39   preconceived: DFF, 10/23/1911, at 107.
39   Louis Brandeis: Snyder, The House of Truth, 20–22 (2017).
39   "[p]erfectly": DFF, 10/20/1911, at 104.
39   "doesn't care" & "has no": DFF, 10/26/1911, at 112.
39   "patience" & "very big": DFF, 10/20/1911, at 104.

40 "how to deal": DFF, 10/22/1911, at 105.

40 Detroit: CT, 9/19/1911, at 1, 4.

40 pleaded: DFF, 10/23/1911, at 106; *id.*, 10/24/1911, at 108–9.

40 "I think": Speech at 24, WHTP, Reel 361, Series 6, CF42, at 10657.

40 circulated: DFF, 10/27/1911, at 112; *id.*, 10/28/1911, at 114; *id.*, 10/29/1911, at 114.

40 "I am very": Nagel to HLS, 10/31/1911, at 2, HLSP, Reel 26, Page 791.

40 permission: HLS to Lewis Stimson, 11/7/1911, at 1–3, HLSP, Reel 26, Pages 891–93; HLSD, Reel 1, Pages 57–58.

40 Panama: WHT to HLS, 11/2/1911, HLSP, Reel 26, Page 824.

41 "stillborn" & "I'd give": DFF, 11/3/1911, at 115–16 & *id.*, 11/6/1911, at 118. *See* Snyder, *House of Truth*, 13–16.

41 "left" & "amiable" & "vision": DFF, 11/3/1911, at 116.

41 Wambaugh: Joseph Beale to FF, 11/15/1911, MRCP, Box 5, Folder 12.

41 Pound: FF to Beale, 11/16/1911, at 2, *id.*; ERB to FF, circa 11/18/1911, FFLC, Box 110; RP to ERB, 11/20/1911, at 1–2, FFLC, Box 30; Arthur E. Sutherland, Jr., "One Man in His Time," 78 Harv. L. Rev. 7, 17 n.15 (1964) (FF on "Liberty of Contract" article and Pound's hiring).

41 "a conservative" & "failed" & "selfish": DFF, 10/27/1911, at 113.

42 "I have": OWH to HJL, 3/4/1920, 1 HLL, at 249. *Cf.* OWH to FF, 3/24/1914, H-FF Corr., at 19 ("a law should be called good if it reflects the will of the dominant forces of the community even if it will take us to hell").

42 "Dear Judge": JCG to OWH, 11/17/1911, NARA, Bureau of Insular Affairs, RG 350, Series 5A, Box 666, #12603.

43 second-floor study: "Residence of Justice Oliver Wendell Holmes, 1720 I Street," 14 photographs circa 1935, Lot 10304 (G), LC P&P; "Study of Justice and Mrs. Oliver Wendell Holmes' Washington, D.C. residence," 4/9/1905, Harvard Law School, olvwork392139.

43 talking: FFR, 58.

43 "I came": FF to JCG, 11/27/1911, NARA, Bureau of Insular Affairs, RG 350, Series 5A, Box 666, #12603.

43 For years: Snyder, *House of Truth*, 305–16.

44 "a foolish": OWH to HJL, 3/4/1920, 1 HLL, at 249.

44 relative obscurity: Snyder, *House of Truth*, 316–18.

44 customs: NYTrib, 1/30/1910, at 7.

44 Denison was listed: Snyder, *House of Truth*, 18–19.

44 "that damn": FFR, 108.

44 Baker: DFF, 11/21/1911, at 120–21.

45 Valentine: Snyder, *House of Truth*, 26–33.

45 Sophie: SFV Diary 1910 (misdated), 11/2/1911, RGVP, Carton 16, Folder 3; SFV to RGV, 11/3/1911, at 2, *id.*, Carton 7, Folder 54 (FF visit).

45 "very *realest*": FF to ERB, 12/26/1911, at 2, FFLC, Box 30 (emphasis in original).

45 Mayer: Mayer to HLS, 12/7/1911, at 1–3, HLSP, Reel 27, Pages 338–40; Lloyd Griscom to Root, 12/12/1911, at 1, *id.*, Page 410; CCB to HLS, 12/29/1912, at 1–2, *id.*, Pages 648–49; Augustus Hand to HLS, 1/2/1912, *id.*, Page 704; LH to HLS, 1/24/1912, at 1–3, *id.*, at Pages 1032–34; NYT, 1/23/1912, at 3.

45 insisted: FF to Herbert Brownell, 3/19/1957, at 2, FFLC, Box 30; FF to ERB, 2/6/1932, at 2, FFLC, Box 206; FFR, 279.

46 "The thing": FF to ERB, 1/6/1912, at 5, FFLC, Box 30.

46   **"We Progressives"** & **"to free"** & **"in the hands"** & **"responsible"**: TR, "A Charter of Democracy," 2/21/1912, Columbus, Ohio, in *The Works of Theodore Roosevelt*, Vol. 17, 120 (Hermann Hagedorn, ed. 1926).

46   **recall:** *id.* at 135–39, 143–47 (discussing Ives v. South Buffalo Ry. Co., 201 N.Y. 271, (1911)).

46   **on notice:** TR to HLS, 2/5/1912, at 3–4, HLSP, Reel 28, Page 190.

46   **"I may":** TNR, 10/1/1924, at 113.

46   **"My hat":** NYT, 2/22/1912, at 1.

47   **"prepossessions"** & **"textual":** FF to ERB, 3/4/1912, at 2–4, FFLC, Box 30.

47   **"keen"** & **"moral"** & **"more disciplined"** & **"his party's"** & **"the Republican Party":** *Id.* at 4–6.

47   **"Oh,":** FFR, 53–54.

48   **"carried out":** HLS, "The Progressive Character of President Taft's Administration," 3/5/1912, at 1, HLSP, Reel 130, Page 76.

48   **"great mistake":** HLS to Lewis Stimson, 2/26/1912, at 2–3, *id.*, Reel 28, Pages 490–91.

48   **poor leadership:** "Personal Reminiscences, 1911–1912," HLSD, Reel 1, Vol. 2, Pages 32–35.

48   **honest conversations:** FF to ERB, 3/4/1912, at 7–8; FF to HLS, 4/30/1912, at 1–3, HLSP, Reel 29, Pages 279–81; FFR, 54.

48   **religious garb:** RGV to Superintendents in Charge of Indian Schools, 1/27/1912, WHTP, Series 6, No. 515C, Reel 397, Page 56765; WHT to Walter L. Fisher, 2/3/1912, at 1–2, *id.* at Pages 56775–76; Snyder, *House of Truth*, 27.

48   **invited:** Snyder, *House of Truth*, 33.

48   **Christie:** Snyder, *House of Truth*, 34

48   **"friends":** LCC to FF, 2/25/1911, at 2–3, FFLC, Box 43.

48   **"an attractive":** DFF, 10/29/1911, at 114.

48   **Percy:** Snyder, *House of Truth*, 34–35.

49   **"much more of":** FFR, 105.

49   **"The days":** FF to ERB, 4/20/1912 at 7, FFLC, Box 30.

49   **Holmes:** RGV to SFV, 5/22/1912, at 2, RGVP, Carton 7, Folder 61.

49   **"the system"** & **"the majority":** OWH, "Natural Law," 32 Harv. L. Rev. 40, 40 (1918).

49   **naming:** OWH to NCG, 11/6/1919, at 2–3, OWHP, Reel 23, Page 684, Box 32, Folder 12 (attributing name to Denison).

49   **"How or why":** FFR, 106.

49   **"a Roosevelt":** FB, *A Casual Past*, 265–71 (1961).

49   **Biddle's boss:** OWH to FB, 7/17/1912, at 2, FBP-GU, Box 2, Folder 31; Snyder, *House of Truth*, 48–49.

50   **"if they could":** OWH to LE, 10/28/1912, H-E Letters, at 74.

50   **"the undisciplined":** FF to FH, 5/24/1912, H-FF Corr., at 7.

50   **"the movement":** Robert M. La Follette, "Introduction" (March 1912), in Gilbert E. Roe, *Our Judiciary Oligarchy*, v (1912).

50   **counterproductive:** LDB to George Rublee, 3/16/1912, 2 LLDB, at 568–69; LDB to Walter Pollak, 4/9/1912, *id.* at 577; LDB to Alfred Brandeis, 4/30/1912, *id.* at 611.

50   **"class hatred":** FF to ERB, 4/20/1912, at 3–4.

50   **made the rounds:** RGV to SFV, n.d. 1912, at 1, RGVP, Carton 7, Folder 56.

51   **"I don't see":** LCC to FF, 6/20/1912, at 1–3, FFLC, Box 43.

51   **"big bosses,"** & **"great crooked"** & **"good of mankind"** & **"We fight":** TR, "The Case against the Reactionaries," 6/17/1912, in *The Works of Theodore Roosevelt*, Vol. 17, 209, 231.

51 "Fine!": NYT, 5/29/1912, at 4.

51 early July: HLS to mother, 7/10/1912, at 3, HLSP, Reel 29, Page 945.

51 Brandeis advised: LDB to FF, 7/12/1912, HBHS, at 20.

51 "you would": TR to Paul A. Ewert, 7/5/1912, 7 Letters of TR at 572.

51 "here I am": FF to Sofy Buckner, 7/17/1912, at 2, FFLC, Box 30.

52 "more like": Herbert Knox Smith to RGV, 8/10/1912, RGVP, Carton 8, Folder 84.

52 "the difference": FFR, 85.

52 front page: NYT, 9/11/1912, at 1.

52 Privately: RGV to Robert P. Bass, 9/10/1912, at 1, RGVP, Carton 23, transcript R27.

52 "the high tide" & "deep blemishes" & "open-mindedness" & "very much": FF to SFV, 8/28/1912, at 1–5, RGVP, Carton 15, Folder 68.

52 "I find": FF to HLS, 9/10/1912, at 1, FFLC, Box 103.

52 "real work": HLS to FF, 9/19/1912, at 1–2, id.

53 promised: FF to HLS, 9/26/1912, id.

53 "If you haven't" & "I return": RGV to FF, 9/22/1912, RGVP, Carton 9, Folder 68.

53 "real job" & "with the Colonel": RGV to FF, 9/28/1912, at 1, id.

53 "[A]fter": FF to LH, 8/26/1912, at 2, LHP, Box 104A, Folder 104-1.

53 three-member commission: WHT to WTD, 8/21/1912, at 1, WHTP, Reel 361, Series 41J at 9930; WHT to WTD, 10/19/1912, id. at 9965; FF to WHT, 10/19/1912, id. at 9966.

53 "It takes": BaltSun, 10/15/1912, at 1.

54 "inquiries": FF to TR, 12/18/1912, TRP, Reel 161, Series 1, Image 824.

54 Panama Canal: "Panama Trip," HLSD, Reel 1, Vol. 2, Pages 119–20; WP, 11/13/1912, at 7.

54 review: FF and Capt. George H. Shelton, "Secretary Stimson's Administration of the War Department: A Review," HLSP, Reel 140, Page 590; BET, 3/12/1913, §2, at 2.

54 grateful: FF to HLS, 3/3/1913, FFLC, Box 103.

CHAPTER 5: TO A MAN, WE WANT FRANKFURTER

55 four-page memorandum: FF, Memorandum, 7/5/1913, FFR, 80–84.

55 "industrial counselor": Henry P. Kendall, "The First Industrial Counselor—Robert G. Valentine, 1871–1916," The Survey, 11/25/1916, at 189.

55 "We have discovered": RGV to FF, circa 12/1912, at 1–2, RGVP, Carton 9, Folder 69.

56 "Government": FF & RGV, "A Tentative Social Program," at 1, 8, RGVP, Carton 9, Folder 67 & FFLC, Box 216.

56 "worked out": RGV to SFV, 7/16/1912, at 2, RGVP, Carton 7, Folder 66.

56 "Dear Pardner": FF to RGV, circa 12/1912, at 1–2, RGVP, Carton 9, Folder 69.

56 prospectus: Office of Robert G. Valentine Counsellor of Industrial Relations, 1/3/1913, id., Carton 13, Folder 26.

56 dinner & Borglum: RGV to SFV, 1/14/1913, at 1, RGVP, Carton 7, Folder 75.

56 "going": FF to RGV, 1/7/1913, at 1, id., Carton 9, Folder 70.

56 "The silence": FF to RGV, 2/10/1913 tel., id.

57 "as the biggest": FF, "The Zeitgeist and the Judiciary," The Survey, 1/25/1913, at 542–43, FFLC, Box 194.

57 investigation & fired: Report, 2/15/1913, at 18, FFLC, Box 51; NYT, 3/4/1913, at 4.

57 Supreme Court: Porto Rico v. Rosaly, 227 U.S. 270 (1913); Tiaco v. Forbes, 228 U.S. 549, 558 (1913); WTD to SFV, 6/13/1913, at 2–3, RGVP, Box 15, Folder 58 (recalling Justice Joseph Rucker Lamar's praise for FF's argument in the Philippines case).

57   **going-away party:** WES, 3/28/1913, at 7.
57   **"I hope you"** & **"You mix":** FFR, 109. *Cf.* ERB to FF, 4/16/1914, at 1, FFLC, Box 30, (hearing it was Chief Justice White, not Lurton).
57   **"Felix keeps":** WTD to Emma Frankfurter, 10/26/1912, at 2, FFLC Box 51.
57   **"You are right":** LDB to AGB, 11/24/1913, FLLDB, at 224.
58   **children's party:** FF to RGV, 5/18/1913, at 4, RGVP, Carton 9, Folder 71.
58   **pie & monkey:** WTD to SFV, 5/20/1919, at 6–7, *id.*, Carton 15, Folder 64.
58   **"Truth":** FF to FH, circa 1913, OWHP, Reel 61, Page 440, Box 79, Folder 11.
58   **broached:** WTD to Edward Warren, 6/12/1913, FFLC, Box 51.
58   **"To a man":** Warren to Denison, 6/16/1913, *id.*
58   **"I would let":** FFR, 78.
58   **"jurisprudence"** & **"the great":** FF, Memorandum, 7/5/1913, in FFR, 81–82.
58   **"the Valentine"** & **"inscrutable"** & **"Southern-Democrat"** & **"party"** & **"first-class"** & **"citizen-lawyer"** & **"best five":** *Id.* at 83–84.
59   **"greatest faculty"** & **"at the center"** & **"side track":** HLS to FF, 6/28/1913, at 2–4, FFLC, Box 103.
59   **Frankfurter replied:** FF to HLS, 7/7/1913, at 3–5, *id.*; FF to LH, 6/28/1913, at 1, LHP, Box 104A, Folder 104-2.
59   **"have to adjust"** & **"be content":** FFR, 79.
59   **"What does":** LH to FF, 7/3/1913, at 2, LHP, Box 104A, Folder 104-2.
59   **five-year tryout:** FF to OWH, 7/4/1913, H-FF Corr., at 10–11.
59   **"more nourishment"** & **"academic life":** OWH to FF, 7/15/1913, *id.*, at 12–13.
60   **"saddened":** FF to RGV, 8/26/1913, at 1, RGVP, Carton 9, Folder 71.
60   **Phi Betta Kappa:** 1912 Smith College Yearbook, at 67.
60   **president:** CSM, 10/1/1910, at 13.
60   **Luina:** OWH to LH, 4/19/1918, OWHP, Reel 26, Page 477, Box 36, Folder 3; OWH to HJL, 1/15/1920, 1 HLL, at 234.
60   **5'7":** MD Passport Application, 5/3/1918, at 2, NARA, U.S. Passport Applications, M1490, Roll 511, Certificate #15869.
60   *The Reef:* FF to MD, 6/11/1913, FFLC, Box 5; FF to MD, 7/15/1913, at 1, *id.*; Liva Baker, *Felix Frankfurter* 40–41 (1969).
60   **angrily refused:** FFR, 79.
60   **Only one:** FFR, 86.
61   **accept the offer:** FF to Ezra Thayer, 7/30/1913, Harvard Law School Dean's Office, Box 1, Folder "Frankfurter, Felix."
61   **$1000:** LDB to Thayer, 11/4/1913, *id.*; Felix Warburg to Thayer, 11/17/1913, *id.*; Thayer to LH, 11/13/1913, *id.*; Thayer to OWH, 11/25/1913, *id.*; JWM to Thayer, 11/29/1913, *id.*
61   **Wyman:** FFR, 80; Cornell Daily Sun, 1/6/1914, at 3.
61   **Herbert Croly:** WL, "Notes for a Biography," TNR, 7/16/1930, at 250.
61   **"philosopher"** & **7500:** FF, "Herbert Croly and American Political Opinion," TNR, 7/16/1930, at 247.
61   **Roosevelt:** Herbert Croly, *The Promise of American Life,* 168–71 (1909).
61   **failed to find success:** FF, "Herbert Croly and American Political Opinion," at 247; David W. Levy, *Herbert Croly of* The New Republic, 3–95 (1985) (early life); *id.* at 132–61 (reception of *The Promise*).
61   **"It was":** HC to LH, circa late 1/1913, at 3, LHP, Box 102, Folder 102-20; LH to Croly, 1/30/1913, at 1, *id.* (agreeing).

62 **"Buddha"**: Mabel Dodge Luhan, *Movers and Shakers*, 89, 119 (1936) & Ronald Steel, *Walter Lippmann and the American Century*, 31 (1980).

62 **"radically progressive" & "weekly"**: NYT, 4/24/1914, at 11.

62 **proposed names**: WL, "Notes for a Biography," at 251. On history of magazine, *see* Charles Forcey, *The Crossroads of Liberalism* (1961); Levy, *Herbert Croly of* The New Republic; David Seideman, *The New Republic* (1986).

62 **"If I only"**: HC to LH, 12/21/1913, at 3, LHP, Box 102, Folder 102-21. *See* FF to HC, n.d., *id.*, Box 104A, Folder 104-2 (choosing Harvard over *New Republic*).

62 **Harvard Corporation & Board of Overseers**: HLS, "The New Professor at the Law School," Harvard Alumni Bulletin, 4/1/1914, at 431.

62–63 **"[T]he great changes" & "His industry"**: *Id.* at 432–33.

63 **"counsellors"**: "A Dinner *of* Introduction *and* Anticipation *given* at The Players *on the night of* April *the* Ninth, Nineteen hundred and fourteen *by the* Republic *to its* Counsellors Contributors *and* Friends," Invitation to Robert Valentine (on file with author).

63 **incorporators**: NYT, 4/30/1914, at 13.

63 **editorial board**: FF to Ezra Thayer, 8/28/1914, at 1, Harvard Law School Dean's Office Files, Box 1.

63 **contributor**: NYT, 11/7/1914, at 2.

63 **Colonel Roosevelt**: WL Diary, 7/4/1914, at 2–3, WLP, Reel 160; NYT, 5/28/1914, at 4; NYSun, 5/28/1914, at 5.

63 **"the ablest"**: ERB to FF, 4/16/1914, at 2.

63 **"That means"**: FF to TR, 7/8/1911, at 1, TRP, Reel 187, Series 1, Image 673.

64 **"the right behavior"**: TR to FF, 7/11/1914, *id.*, Reel 384, Series 3A, Image 44.

64 **November election**: TR to FF, 8/6/1914, *id.*, Image 119.

64 **resigned**: WP, 6/7/1914, at E2.

64 **"Three happy years"**: FF to RGV & SFV, n.d., at 1, RGVP, Carton 9, Folder 75.

64 **"Did you ever"**: WashTimes, 5/31/1914, at 10 & in RGVP, Carton 22, Folder 7 (with FF's handwritten comments: "Think of the opportunity of living *that* down.") (emphasis in original).

64 **South Station**: FFR Transcript, 6/27/1957, at 6, FFLC, Box 205.

64 **Few people**: FF to Alfred Mitchell-Innes, 11/7/1914, at 1, FFLC, Box 30.

CHAPTER 6: NOT BRANDEIS'S FIGHT, BUT OUR FIGHT

65 **Langdell Hall**: HCrim, 9/26/1907; https://hls.harvard.edu/library/about-the-library/history-of-the-harvard-law-school-library/.

65 **Frederick W. Taylor**: FFR Transcript, 6/27/1957, at 6.

65 **Rose Schneiderman**: FF to MRC, 7/23/1914, in Leonora Cohen Rosenfield, *Portrait of a Philosopher*, 243 (1962).

65 **Beverly Farms**: FF to ERB, circa 7/1914, FFLC, Box 30.

65 **Roosevelt & "all in books"**: FF to ERB, circa 8/1914, *id.*

65 **"scared"**: FFR, 86.

65 **In the fall**: Harvard Law School Catalog 1914–1915, at 6–8.

66 **"happy"**: FF to ERB, circa 7/1914 ("happy family").

66 **"wild"**: Thayer to RP, 8/24/1915, at 4, RPP, Pt. I, Reel 13, Page 875.

66 **"exhilarating"**: FF to MD, 10/4/1914, at 1, FFLC, Box 6.

66 **"those boys"**: FF to MD, 10/4/1914, at 1.

66　**socialized:** Recollection of Robert Porter Patterson by Chauncey Belknap, COH, 4/27/1960 (1961), at 12, & Belknap, COH, 4/29/1975, at 7.

66　**memorable group:** "Rank List," 1915, FFHLS, Pt. III, Reel 19, Page 646.

66　**"the ablest":** FF to Mrs. Ezra Thayer, 1/7/1916, "Third Year Men," at 1, Frankfurter SMC, HLSSC.

66　**regaled them:** Belknap Diary, 10/7/1915, in Todd. C. Pepper et al., "Clerking for God's Grandfather: Chauncey Belknap's Year with Justice Oliver Wendell Holmes Jr.," Journal of Supreme Court History 43 (2018): 257, 263.

66　**twelfth:** 1916 Grades, FFHLS, Pt. III, Reel 19, Page 636.

66　**never forgave:** Jordan A. Schwarz, *Liberal*, 14–15 (1987).

67　**"You Learn":** Francis T. P. Plimpton, "In Personam," at 9, 1924, Plimpton Papers, HLSSC, Box 1, Folder 1-3.

67　**student notes:** Charles P. Curtis Class Notes, HLSSC, Box 1, Folder 1 (criminal law 1915); John Raeburn Green Class Notes, HLS, Box 2 (public utilities 1915) & Box 3 (criminal law 1915).

67　**treating utilities:** FF, "The Utilities Bureau," Annals of the American Academy of Political and Social Science, 1/1915, at 293–94.

67　**"live" & "an inspiring":** The Independent, 3/22/1915, at 419. *See* ERB, Typescript, FFLC, Box 30 & FF to ERB, 3/29/1915, *id.* (ERB as ghostwriter of *Independent* article).

67　**casebook:** FF, "Prefatory Note," *A Selection of Cases under the Interstate Commerce Act,* iii (1915).

67　*New Republic:* TNR, 11/7/1914, at 3.

67　**2:00 a.m.:** WL COH, at 54 & WL, *Public Persons,* 100 (1976).

67　**875:** "A Review of the Growth and Prospects of the *New Republic,*" 8/1916, at 1, Straight Papers, Reel 5, Segment 4.

67　**defended Roosevelt's:** TNR, 11/14/1914, at 7.

67　**"a futile":** NYTM, 12/6/1914, at SM1.

68　**"blindly":** TNR, 12/12/1914, at 5.

68　**never spoke:** WL, COH, at 55 & WL, "Notes for a Biography," at 251.

68　**"three anemic":** Alvin Johnson, *Pioneer's Progress,* 245 (1952).

68　**"disinterested":** TNR, 6/5/1915, at 109.

68　**9000:** "A Review of the Growth and Prospects of the New Republic," 8/1916, at 1.

68　**"indifference" & "antiquated":** FF to TR, 10/11/1915, at 4, TRP, Reel 201, Series 1, Image 723. *See* Salt Lake Telegram, 8/17/1915 at 9; Salt Lake Tribune, 8/17/1915, at 12 (similar comments).

68　**blamed:** TR to FF, 10/18/1915, *id.,* Reel 359, Series 2, Image 310.

68–69　**"demand" & "We must" & "find" & "fresh":** FF, "The Law and the Law Schools," A.B.A. J. 1, no. 4 (October 1915): 536, 539–40.

69　*Coppage:* Coppage v. Kansas, 236 U.S. 1, 11 (1915).

69　**thirteen:** *Id.* at 47 n.2 (Day, J., dissenting).

69　**"equality":** *Id.* at 27 (Holmes, J., dissenting). *See* FF to OWH, 1/27/1915, H-FF Corr., at 25–26.

69　**Holmes raised:** Frank v. Mangum, 237 U.S. 309, 346–47, 349 (1915) (Holmes, J., dissenting); Brad Snyder, *The House of Truth,* 116–18 (2017).

69　**Brandeis:** LDB to RP, 11/27/1914, 3 LLDB at 373.

69　**urged:** TNR, 4/24/1915, at 290.

69 **Frank wrote:** Leo Frank to OWH, 7/10/1915, at 2, OWHP, Reel 31, Page 364, Box 43, Folder 2.

69 **"A man":** Memorandum of talk with FF, 8/10/1964, at 1, MDHP, Box 22, Folder 26.

70 **most prominent:** Steve Oney, *And the Dead Shall Rise*, 339–42, 513–28, 560–71 (2003).

70 **"a judge":** TNR, 1/30/1915, at 4.

70 **"we only":** FF, *A Selection of Cases under the Interstate Commerce Act*, i.

70 **"brilliant":** FF, "The Constitutional Opinions of Justice Holmes," 29 Harv. L. Rev. 683, 698 (1916).

70 **shocked:** Gus Karger to WHT, 1/29/1916, WHTP, Reel 162, Series 3.

70 **spellbinding:** William Hitz to FF, 12/17/1914, LDB-Louisville, Reel 119; Charles Warren to FF, 4/6/1939, FFLC, Box 127.

70 **"temperamentally":** NYT, 1/31/1916, at 18.

70 **overjoyed:** FF to KL, 1/27/1916, at 1, FFLC, Box 79; FF to LH, 1/30/1916, at 1–2, LHP, Box 104A, Folder 104-5; FF to WL, 2/2/1916, at 2, WLP, Reel 9, Box 10, Folder 419.

70–71 **"who are" & "one of the great" & "has offended" & "inevitable" & "believes" & "the spirit":** FF to Cosmos Club, 1/19/1915, at 1–2, FFLC, Box 26.

71 **"highest":** Wilson to Cosmos Club, 2/1/1915, 32 WWP, at 167.

71 **partisan:** FF to Editor of BET, 1/28/1916, FFLC, Box 26.

71 ***Boston Post*:** WP, 2/3/1916, at 5; FF to Norman Hapgood, 2/5/1916, FFLC, Box 128.

71 **Edward H. Warren:** LDB to Edward McClennen, 3/14/1916, FFLC, Box 128.

71–72 **"One public" & "pure" & "the concerns" & "nation-wide" & "the final" & "given" & "a mind" & "no doctrinaire":** TNR, 2/5/1916, at 4–6.

72 **February 17:** WL to FF, 2/18/1916, at 1, PPWL at 37 & WLP, Reel 9, Box 10, Folder 419.

72 **"the fight":** FF to WL, n.d. 1916, at 3, WLP, Reel 9, Box 10, Folder 419.

72 **"It is terribly":** FF to JWM, 1/31/1916, FFLC, Box 81.

72 **"The other night":** FF to WL, 3/20/1916, at 1, WLP, Reel 164, Box 1, Folder 29. *See* FF to KL, 2/16/1916, at 3, FFLC, Box 79 (similar comments).

72 **"half brother":** LDB to FF, 9/24/1925, HBHS, 212. *Cf.* LDB to MD, 11/3/1919, FFLC, Box 26 (describing them as "half son, half brother").

73 **"In good truth":** TNR, 3/4/1916, at 119.

73 **Samuel Warren:** William H. Dunbar to FF, 2/1/1916, FFLC, Box 128.

73 **"Somerset Club":** Chart, 3/2/1916, Straight Papers, Reel 5, Segment 3 & FFLC, Box 128.

73 **Willard Straight:** Croly to Straight, 3/2/1916, Straight Papers, Reel 5, Segment 3.

73 **"group" & "the most":** TNR, 3/11/1916, at 139.

73 **"the last":** TNR, 3/18/1916, at 165.

73 **"had collapsed":** TNR, 3/25/1916, at 202.

73 **home:** FF to OWH, 3/5/1916, H-FF Corr., at 46 (call home).

73 **pneumonia & Mount Hebron:** Leopold Frankfurter Death Certificate, 3/7/1916, FFLC, Box 18.

74 **$125:** Leopold Frankfurter Probate Record, Bronx County, NY, 4/8/1916, at 2.

74 **"Yes":** FF to ERB, 3/1916, FFLC, Box 30. *See* BG, 1/8/1939, at C4 (quoting brother Paul Frankfurter about their father: "He tried to make a living all his life. It was pathetic. He never did.").

74 **He was teaching:** Harvard Law School Catalog, 1915–1916, at 6–7.

74 **"inadequately" & "governed" & "common" & "cut" & "epoch making":** FF, "Hours of Labor and Realism in Constitutional Law," 29 Harv. L. Rev. 353, 365, 369–71 (1916).

75   **House of Truth:** Belknap Diary, 4/11/1916; FF to KL, 4/15/1916, at 3, FFLC, Box 79.

75   **letter:** BET, 5/10/1916, Pt. 2, at 2.

75   **Lowell:** FF to LH, 1/4/1916, at 1, LHP, Box 104A, Folder 104-5.

75   **Roscoe Pound:** RP to Sen. William E. Chilton, n.d., LDB Nomination Hearings, Vol. 2, at 251–52 (1916).

75   **Eliot:** Charles W. Eliot to Sen. Charles Culberson, 5/17/1916, *id.* at 241–42.

75   **Arthur Dehon Hill's:** FF to LH, circa 5/11/1916, at 1–2, LHP, Box 104A, Folder 104-6.

75   **"poor":** FF to LH, circa 4/25/1916, at 2, *id.*

75   **Fox:** FF to LH, circa 4/20/1916, at 2, *id.*

75   **"Brandeis":** FF to KL, 5/12/1916, at 1–2, FFLC, Box 79.

75   **lay low:** FF to WL, 5/4/1916, FFLC, Box 128.

75   **"character" & "exceptionally":** WW to Culberson, 5/5/1916, 36 WWP at 609–11.

75   **no longer:** FF to LH, circa 5/15/1916, at 1, LHP, Box 104A, Folder 104-6.

75   **party loyalty:** Alpheus Thomas Mason, *Brandeis*, 502–4 (1946); Melvin I. Urofsky, *Louis D. Brandeis*, 457–58 (2009); A. L. Todd, *Justice on Trial*, 230–31, 238–41 (1964); 53 Cong. Rec. 9032 (1916).

75   **"Felix's judgments":** RGV to Marie Christie, 6/12/1916, RGV, Carton 9, Folder 5.

75   **"The Brandeis" & "Mr. Brandeis's":** TNR, 6/10/1916, at 134.

76   **Shelton Hale:** OWH to FF, 1/29/1916, H-FF Corr., at 45; FF to MD, 4/29/1916, at 1–2, FFLC, Box 5.

76   **"The lad":** OWH to FF, 3/27/1917, H-FF Corr., at 70.

76   **tied for sixth:** "Rank List," 1916; FF to Mrs. Ezra Thayer, 1/7/1916, "Third Year Men," at 1; BP, 9/30/1916, at 7.

76   **"very helpful":** LDB to FF, 12/1/1916, 3 LLDB at 268.

76   **institutionalized:** FF to LH, 12/22/1914, LHP, Box 104A, Folder 104-3; Brad Snyder, "The Judicial Genealogy (and Mythology) of John Roberts," 71 Ohio St. L.J. 1149, 1162–66 (2010).

76   **"Everything":** "Justice Felix Frankfurter's Contribution to the BBC's Harold Laski Programme," British Broadcasting Corporation, 11/15/1961, at 1, FFLC, Box 207 & FF, *Of Law and Life and Other Things That Matter*, 218 (Philip B. Kurland, ed. 1965).

76   **"Oxford":** FF to MD, 6/26/1916, at 7–8, FFLC, Box 5.

76   **American tennis:** OWH to Frederick Pollock, 2/18/1917, 1 H-P Letters at 243; FF, Foreword, 1 HLL, at xv ("Good talkers are apt to embellish their tales and Laski's stories often gained in the telling.").

77   **raised money:** FF to KL, 1/27/1916, at 1–2, FFLC, Box 79; FF to LH, 1/22/1916, at 1–3, LHP, Box 104A, Folder 104-5.

77   **Theodore Roosevelt:** FF to ERB, 1/26/1916, FFLC, Box 30.

77   **"I am":** WL to FF, 1/17/1916, at 1, WLP, Reel 9, Box 10, Folder 419 & PPWL, 33–34.

77   **Hughes:** FF to TR, 6/28/1916, TRP, Reel 212, Series 1, Image 122.

77   **Adamson Act:** FF to TR, 9/8/1916, at 1–2, TRP, Reel 214, Series 1, Image 339; BH, 10/9/1916, in FFLC, Box 194.

78   **"Surely":** FF, "The Election of 1916," at 22, FFLC, Box 204.

78   **liked Hughes:** FF to MRC, 10/3/1916, in Rosenfield, *Portrait of a Philosopher*, 247–48.

78   **snubbed:** Merlo J. Pusey, *Charles Evans Hughes*, Vol. 1, 335–49 (1951).

78   **Around midnight:** SFV, 11/16/1916, at 3–5, RGVP, Box 2, Folder 8; Dr. Herman M. Adler to SFV, 11/16/1916, at 2, *id.*, Carton 15, Folder 20; NYH, 11/15/1916, at 5.

78   **"Poor":** FF to LDB, 11/15/1916 tel., LDB-Louisville, Reel 47.

78 **"With love":** FF, 11/14/16, RGVP, Carton 15, Folder 23.

78 **Roosevelt & pallbearers:** TR to SFV, 11/16/1916, RGVP, Carton 15, Folder 20; BET, 11/17/1916, at 1.

78 **"You will":** FF to OWH, 11/16/1916, H-FF Corr., at 60.

79 **250:** BG, 1/8/1917, at 9 (250 to 300).

79 **"We have" & "asked" & "not only" & "Surely":** Remarks of Felix Frankfurter in Presiding at the Memorial Meeting to Robert G. Valentine at Faneuil Hall, 1/7/1917, at 1–2, FFLC, Box 188 & RGVP, Box 2, Folder 15.

79 **"Valentine was":** FF, "Robert Grosvenor Valentine '96," Harvard Alumni Bulletin, Vol. 19, No. 12, 12/14/1916, at 228, 230. *See* FF, "Valentine, Robert Grosvenor," *Dictionary of American Biography*, Vol. 19, 142–43 (1936); Snyder, *House of Truth*, 147–57.

80 **Oregon's attorney general:** George M. Brown to James D. Maher, 10/3/1916, Bunting v. Oregon Clerk's Office File, NARA, RG 267, Box 4641, Appellate Case File 24346; Josephine Goldmark to Maher, 9/1/1916, *id.*; Maher to Goldmark, 9/6/1916, *id.*; Goldmark to Maher, 10/13/1916, *id.*; Maher to Goldmark, 10/14/1916, *id.*; Goldmark to Brown, Goldmark to Joseph N. Teal, 10/17/1916 tels., FFLC, Box 128; Brown to FF, 10/18/1916 tel., *id.*

80 **"take":** FF to White, 10/20/1916 tel., FFLC, Box 183.

80 **Worried:** FFR, 98–101.

80 **late January:** NYT, 10/25/1916, at 18; Bunting v. Oregon, No. 38, 1916 Term Supreme Court Docket Book, at 7, NARA, M216, Roll #15, Dockets of the Supreme Court of the United States, 1915–18, Original and Appellate.

80 **so soon:** FF to KL, 1/14/1917, at 3–4, FFLC, Box 80.

80 **Laski & Denison:** LDB to HJL, 4/3/1916, at 4 LLDB at 142; WTD to Mather, 9/8/1916, Stettler v. O'Hara Clerk's Office File, NARA, RG 267, Box 4618, Appellate Case File 24,248.

80 **$8 & $6:** Simpson Record, at 2–3, 10–11, Stettler v. O'Hara Clerk's Office File. *See* Stettler Record at 10–11; Stettler v. O'Hara, 139 P. 174, 745 (Or. 1914); Simpson v. O'Hara, 141 P. 158 (Or. 1914).

80 **$50:** Bunting v. Oregon, 243 U.S. 426, 434 (1917).

81 **Differences:** FF, "Hours of Labor and Realism in Constitutional Law," 29 Harv. L. Rev. at 367 (citing State v. Bunting, 71 Ore. 259, 271, 139 P. 731, 735 (1914)).

81 **"intently" & "a small":** "Notes from the Capital: Felix Frankfurter," The Nation, 3/15/1917, at 320.

81 **"the facts" & "snapped" & "How":** Wisconsin State Journal, 1/24/1917, at 12.

81 **practical effects:** Emporia Gazette, 2/9/1917, at 2.

81 **racist and anti-Semite:** PC, 3/27/1937, at 1 (protesting McReynolds's comment that "he had tried to protect 'the poorest darky in the Georgia backwoods as well as the man in the mansion on Wall Street'"); Robert L. Carter, "The Long Road to Equality," The Nation, 5/3/2004, at 28 (alleging McReynolds turned his back on Charles Hamilton Houston during a 1938 graduate school segregation argument); John Knox, *The Forgotten Memoir of John Knox*, 36–37 (Dennis J. Hutchinson & David J. Garrow, eds. 2002) (noting McReynolds's refusal to speak to Jewish justices Brandeis and Cardozo).

81 **landed:** EMH to FWB, 4/8/1936, FFLC, Box 127; EMH to WW, 7/15/1914, 30 WWP at 285.

81 **March 1913:** RGV to SFV, 3/26/1913, at 3, RGVP, Carton 7, Folder 76.

82 **"What you" & "May I":** FF Int. with JA, at 3–4, n.d., circa 1938, JSAP, Box 93, Folder 3.

Cf. Joseph Alsop and Robert Kintner, *Men Around the President*, 49 (1939) (similar quotation); FF to HLS, 4/16/13, FFLC, Box 103 ("What a horde of office seekers is wearing away the strength and time of men like McReynolds—who let them!").

82   **"Ten hours!" & "Your honor" & "Good":** FFR, 101–3. *See* FF to LH, circa 5/11/1916, at 3, LHP, Box 104A, Folder 104-6 (describing McReynolds as "dull").

82   **"Mr. Frankfurter's":** "Oregon May Be Right," The Independent, 2/5/1917, at 203.

82   **blue tie:** FF to SFV, 1/20/1917 tel., RGVP, Carton 15, Folder 72.

82   **April 9:** Bunting v. Oregon, 243 US. 426, 438–39 (1917); Stettler v. O'Hara, 243 U.S. 629 (1917) (per curiam).

83   **supported Wilson's:** FF to WL, 1/31/1917 (#9), at 1–2, WLP, Reel 9, Box 10, Folder 420; FF to KL, 2/5/1917, at 1, FFLC, Box 80; FF to WL, 2/1917, WLP, Reel 9, Box 10, Folder 420.

83   **disliked:** FF to LH, 1/24/1917, LHP, Box 104A, Folder 104-6.

83   **"could not":** FF to MD, 4/6/1917, at 3, FFLC, Box 5.

83   **labor committee:** Samuel Gompers to FF, 3/22/1917, FFLC, Box 59; FF to Gompers, 3/26/1917, *id.*

83   **the same mistake:** FF to Gompers, 4/3/1917, *id.*; FF to Gompers, 4/20/1917, *id.*; FF to MD, 4/1/1917, at 1–2, FFLC, Box 5.

CHAPTER 7: THESE DAYS WE ARE ALL SOLDIERS

84   **"to see":** FF to MD, 4/16/1917, at 2, FFLC, Box 6.

84   **permanent stay:** FFR, 114.

84   **"indefinitely":** NDB to ALL, 4/22/1917 tel., ALLOP, Box 85, Folder 1163. *See* FF to MD, 4/22/1917, at 3–4, FFLC, Box 6.

85   **Judge Advocate General's Corps:** Enoch Crowder to FF, 8/14/1916, FFLC, Box 50; Crowder to FF, 1/18/1917, *id.*

85   **Baker:** Douglas B. Craig, *Progressives at War*, 65–67 (2013); Daniel R. Beaver, *Newton D. Baker and the American War Effort*, 1–8, 37 (1966); Frederick Palmer, *Newton D. Baker*, Vol. 1, 6–11 (1931).

85   **a million men:** NYT, 4/6/1917, at 1.

85   **War Department job:** WL to FF, 4/1917, at 2–3, FFLC, Box 77; WL to NDB, 5/10/1917, at 1–2, NDBP, Reel 2, Pages 137–38.

85   **second-floor:** Ronald Steel, *Walter Lippmann and the American Century*, 120 (1980); Brad Snyder, *The House of Truth*, 170–73 (2017).

85   **"as of old":** FF to MD, 4/30/1917, at 4, FFLC, Box 5.

85   **"a truly":** FF to MD, 5/15/1917, *id.*

85   **"I'd rather":** FF to MD, 6/8/1917, *id.*

86   **Henry Morgenthau, Sr.:** Morgenthau to WW, 6/7/1917, 42 WWP at 462–63; FF to WL, 3/20/1916, at 2–3, WLP, Reel 164, Box 1, Folder 29.

86   **thanked:** WW to FF, 6/11/1917, 42 WWP at 475.

86   **"These days":** FF to WW, 6/12/1917, *id.* at 486.

86   **Lowell:** FF to ALL, 6/18/1917, ALLOP, Box 85, Folder 1163.

86   **public purpose:** NYHT, 6/20/1917, at 7.

86   **secret purpose:** Robert Lansing to WW, 5/17/1917, *Papers Relating to the Foreign Relations of the United States: The Lansing Papers*, Vol. 2, 1914–1920, at 17–19 (1940); Memorandum of Henry Morgenthau's Secret Mission, 6/10/1917, at 101–5, Unpublished Lansing Diary Blue Boxes, Box 2, 4/4/1916 to 12/30/1919, Reel 1.

86   **families pause:** Liva Baker, *Felix Frankfurter*, 40–41, 49–50 (1969) (based on 6/8/1968 int. with Marion's sister Helen).

86   **photograph:** FF to MD, 6/20/1917, at 1, 3, FFLC, Box 5; FF to MD, 6/21/1917, at 3, *id.*

86   **"as a talisman":** FF to MDF, 2/21/1933, at 2, FFLC, Box 14.

87   **Max Lowenthal:** Max Lowenthal, "Felix Long Ago," in *Felix Frankfurter: A Tribute*, 126–27 (Wallace Mendelson, ed. 1964); Snyder, *House of Truth*, 176, 219–20.

87   **casebook:** FF, "Prefatory Note," *A Selection of Cases under the Interstate Commerce Act*, iii (1915); Interstate Commerce Act Casebook handwritten drafts, MLP, Box 24, Folders 1–2.

87   **Zionist:** Lowenthal to FF, 10/22/1914, FFLC, Box 79.

87   **closed:** "ML – Dates in life of," n.d., at 1–2, 5, Lash Papers, Box 65, Folder 1.

87   **worst fears:** FFR, 146–48.

87   **Gibraltar:** William Yale, "Ambassador Henry Morgenthau's Special Mission of 1917," *World Politics* 1, no. 3 (Apr. 1949): 316–20; Chaim Weizmann to Sir Ronald Graham, 7/5/1917 & Weizmann to Graham, 7/6/1917, *The Letters and Papers of Chaim Weizmann*, Series A, Vol. 7, at 460–65 (Leonard Stein, ed. 1975).

87   **impressed:** FFR, 149.

87   **panicked:** Frank Polk to WW, 7/12/1917, 43 WWP at 159–60 & n.1 (containing telegram from FF and Henry Morgenthau, 7/8/1917).

88   **Brentano's:** FFR, 151–52. *See* Henry Morgenthau Sr. Diary, 7/13/1917, Henry Morgenthau Papers, Box 2, Reel 2.

88   **"fiasco":** EMHD, 7/14/1917, Series II, Vol. 5, at 213.

88   **"This morning":** Lansing to WW, 8/13/1917, 43 WWP at 442 (enclosing FF's memorandum).

88   **"the real":** FF to MD, 8/19/1917, at 2, FFLC, Box 5.

88   **thanked:** FF to LDB, 8/14/1917, FFLC, Box 29.

88   **"the sense":** FF to KL, 8/14/1917, at 2, FFLC, Box 80.

88   **"in a judicial":** FF to NDB, 9/18/1917, at 2, FFLC, Box 132.

88   **Judge Mack:** Harry Barnard, *The Forging of an American Jew*, 210–11 (1974); Jeremy K. Kessler, "The Administrative Origins of Modern Civil Liberties Law," 114 Colum. L. Rev. 1083, 1111–43 (2014).

88   **unpacked & opposed:** FF to MD, 10/1/1917, at 1, FFLC, Box 5.

88   **recommended:** NDB to WW, 9/1/1917, 44 WWP at 120; FF, Memorandum for the Secretary of War, 9/4/1917, *id.* at 161–64.

89   **incorrectly:** FF to EMH, 9/4/1917, at 2, EMHP, Box 45, Folder 1443.

89   **"a very":** NDB to WW, 9/7/1917, *id.* at 161.

89   **"'The Education'":** FF to WL, 10/3/1917, FFLC, Box 77.

89   **Globe:** FF to MD, 10/17/1917, at 1–3, 10, FFLC, Box 5 & FF to LDB, 10/20/1917, at 1–11, FFLC, Box 29.

89   **"the men" & "no security":** FF to MD, 10/9/1917, at 1–3, 10, FFLC, Box 5.

89   **Allied leaders:** FF to MD, 10/27/1917, at 5–6, FFLC, Box 5.

90   **Lewisohn & Percy:** FFR, 120–21.

90   **Stanley King:** FF to WL, 10/2/1917 tel., FFLC, Box 77; SK to FF, 10/4/1917 tel., *id.*; FF to WL, 10/22/1917, at 1, WLP, Reel 9, Box 10, Folder 420.

90   **Globe strike:** FF to SK, 10/25/1917, NARA, Labor Department, General Records, RG 174, Box 1.

90   **Clifton strike:** FF to MD, 10/30/1917, FFLC, Box 5; Basis of Settlement Clifton-Morenci-

Metcalf Strike, 10/31/1917, Presidential Mediation Commission, NARA, Labor Department, General Records, RG 174, Box 1.

90 **reasonable & peaceful:** President's Mediation Commission Session at Bisbee Arizona, 11/1–5/1917, at 18, 28, 62, 351–52, NARA, General Records, RG 174, Box 1. *See* Report on the Bisbee Deportations Made by the President's Mediation Commission, 11/6/1917, at 1–7 (Washington 1918); James W. Byrkit, *Forging the Copper Collar,* 144–244 (1982); Jonathan D. Rosenblum, "Felix Frankfurter and the Bisbee Deportation," Western Legal History 31, no. 2 (2021): 131–67.

90 **bed:** FFR, 136–37.

90 **Father O'Dwyer:** FFR, 117; FF to MD, 10/27/1917, at 8–9; FF to WL, 10/3/1917.

91 **"is not":** President's Mediation Commission Session at Bisbee Arizona, 11/6/1917, at 615–16.

91 **"wholly":** President's Mediation Commission, "Report on the Bisbee Deportations," 11/6/1917, at 7. *See* Philip Taft, "The Bisbee Deportation," Labor History 13, no. 1 (1972): 3–40.

91 **"I don't" & "the National":** FF to LDB, 11/7/1917, at 1, FFLC, Box 29.

91 **pipe bomb & tried:** Richard H. Frost, *The Mooney Case,* 80–102, 173–93 (1968).

91–92 **President Wilson & last name & contacted:** FFR, 130–31; FF to Max Thelan, 9/26/1917 tel., FFLC, Box 154; Thelan to FF, 9/29/1917 tel., *id.*

92 **deliberations & interviewed & "a bad":** FFR, 131–35.

92 **"[T]he feeling":** "Report on the Mooney Dynamiting Cases in San Francisco," 1/28/1918, Official Bulletin, at 15 in FFLC, Box 194. *See* Frost, *Mooney Case,* 164–72, 493–95.

92 **socialized & dinner coat:** FF to MD, 12/14/1917, at 3, FFLC, Box 5; FFR, 121–27.

93 **telephone company:** FF to SK, 11/22/1917 tel., NARA, Labor Department, General Records, RG 174, Box 1.

93 **Baker & Gompers:** FF to LDB, 12/14/1917, at 1–4, FFLC, Box 29.

93 **lumber & meat-packing:** FFR, 127–29; FF to John Walker, 3/10/1929, at 2–3, FFLC, Box 110.

93 **"Americans" & "to re-affirm":** TR's secretary to FF, 8/30/1917, FFLC, Box 98.

93 **"You know":** FF to TR, 8/31/1917 tel., at 1–2, *id.* & TRP, Reel 244, Series 1, Images 607–8.

93 **"the issue":** SFExam, 11/18/1917, at 1.

93 **"is in nowise":** FF to ERB, 11/20/1917 tel., at 1, FFLC, Box 31 & TRP, Series 1, Reel 252, Image 838.

94 **"an attitude" & "to any":** TR to FF, 12/19/1917, at 1, TRP, Reel 398, Series 3A, Image 214 & FFLC, Box 98.

94 **"Your report" & "the I.W.W.":** TR to FF, 12/19/1917, at 3–4.

94 **"the effective" & "in a thoroughgoing" & "a trained" & "Surely":** FF to TR, 1/7/1918, at 1–5, TRP, Reel 258, Series 1, Images 561–66 & FFLC, Box 98.

94 **"I cannot":** TR to FF, 1/18/1918, TRP, Reel 399, Series 3A, Image 165 & FFLC, Box 98.

95 **Alice Roosevelt Longworth:** FFR, 137–39; FF to William Hard, 4/14/1926, Hard Papers, Box 1, Folder 9.

95 *Boston Herald:* BH, 6/4 or 6/1919, FFLC, Box 154.

95 **James M. Beck:** TNR, 10/12/1921, at 189–90; TNR, 10/19/1921, at 218–19; TNR, 1/18/1922, at 212–14; TNR, 1/18/1922, at 215–20; TNR, 1/18/1922, at 221–22.

95 **pardoned:** Mooney v. Holohan, 294 U.S. 103 (1935); Frost, *Mooney Case,* 483–85.

95 **opposed Brandeis:** EMHD, 1/3/1913, 27 WWP at 23; EMHD, 1/17/1913, *id.* at 61; EMHD,

1/24/1913, *id.* at 71; EMHD, 2/13/1913, *id.* at 110; Charles E. Neu, *Colonel House*, 78–79, 82 (2015).

95   **out of the country:** EMHD, 1/28/1916, Series II, Vol. 4, at 37; Neu, *Colonel House*, 254–55.

95   **"a silent":** EMH to WW, 9/20/1917, 44 WWP at 226.

95   **damaged:** EMH to WW, 10/3/1917, *id.* at 298.

96   **Lippmann failed:** WL to FF, 12/28/1917, at 1–2, WLP, Reel 9, Box 10, Folder 420; WL to EMH, n.d. 1917, EMHP, Box 70, Folder 2324.

96   **meeting & not breathed:** FF, "Memorandum on Breach of 'Confidence,'" n.d., at 1, 3, FFLC, Box 67.

96   **reorganize:** FF to LDB, 12/14/1917, at 4–6.

96   **three jobs & "Necessary":** FF, Memorandum, 1/7/1918, at 3–7, FFLC, Box 189, & NDBP, Reel 4.

96   **preempt:** FF to NDB, 1/4/1918, NDBP, Reel 5.

96   **"freed":** FF, Memorandum, 1/7/1918, at 3–7, FFLC, Box 189, & NDBP, Reel 4.

96   **"Baker was rather":** EMHD, 1/9/1918, Series II, Vol. 6, at 11.

96   **Brandeis concurring:** LDB to EMH, 1/9/1918, at 1–2, FFLC, Box 26.

96   **overseas assignment:** NDB to FF, 1/27/1918, FFLC, Box 189; EMHD, 1/30/1918, Series II, Vol. 6, at 42; FF to MD, 1/30/1918 & 1/31/1918, Box 5.

96   **air raid & Lloyd George:** FF to MD, 2/29/1918, at 2-3, *id.*

96   **"a little bit":** FF to KL, 3/14/1918, at 2, FFLC, Box 80. *See* Journal entries, early 1918, FFLC, Box 189.

96   **"The ascendency":** FF to EMH, 3/24/1918, at 12, FFLC, Box 189.

97   **"the 'hot dog of war'" & "[t]his little Jew":** Walter Hines Page to Arthur W. Page, 2/24/1918, at 13–14, Walter Hines Page Papers, Box 989, #128.

97   **in person:** EMHD, 3/27/1918, Series II, Vol. 6, at 91.

97   **suffragist:** MD to FF, 9/6/1917, FFLC, Box 5.

97   **special assistant:** MD to Fosdick, 4/19/1918, NARA, Records of War Department and General and Special Staffs, RG 165, General Corr. 1917–21, NM 84, Entry 393, Box 51, at 25337.

97   **social worker:** Marion Denman Passport Application, 5/3/1918, at 1–2, NARA, U.S. Passport Applications, M1490, Roll 511, Certificate #15869.

97   **engagement:** Baker, *Felix Frankfurter*, 75–76 (based on int. with Helen Denman).

97   **"I want you":** MD to FF, 5/7/1918, at 2, FFLC, Box 5.

97   **stop publishing:** NYT, 5/10/1918, at 10.

97   **Britain:** NYT, 6/2/1918, at 16.

98   **wounded:** FF to KL, 8/9/1918, at 4, FFLC, Box 80.

98   **"This is":** FF to MD, 6/9/1918, at 2, FFLC, Box 5.

98   **National War Labor Board:** NYT, 2/28/1918, at 10; NYT, 3/6/1918, at 1.

98   **director general:** FF and SK to NDB, 4/30/1918, NDBP, Reel 5, Page 194; WW to Robert Woolley, 4/27/1918, 47 WWP at 449.

98   **praised:** NYTrib, 5/12/1918, at 8.

98   **"Uniting":** NYT, 5/26/1918, at SM2.

98   **Lippmann declared:** ERB to FF, 5/16/1918, at 1, FFLC, Box 31.

98   **"his chief":** TNR, 5/18/1918, at 71.

98   **"Since":** NYTrib, 5/15/1918, at 4.

99   **Roland Dagenhart:** Hammer v. Dagenhart, 247 U.S. 251, 271–74 (1918); Lowell Mellett,

"The Sequel to the Dagenhart Case," American Child 6, no. 1 (1/1924), at 3; Logan E. Sawyer III, "Creating *Hammer v. Dagenhart*," 21 Wm. & Mary Bill Rts. J. 67 (2012).

99   **"The national":** Hammer, 247 U.S. at 277–79, 281 (Holmes, J., dissenting).

99   **To assist:** FF to HJL, 7/25/1918, at 1, FFLC, Box 74.

100   **1906:** R&FF, 10–11.

100   **"friendly":** "Samuel Spencer Notes of FF, GC Conversation-Summer, 1947," at 3–4, FFHLS, Pt. III, Reel 15, Pages 256–57.

100   **same floor:** FFR Transcript, 7/23/1957, at 325, FFLC, Box 206.

100   **lasting impression:** HBE, "Felix," in *Felix Frankfurter: A Tribute,* 101 (Wallace Mendelson, ed. 1964).

100   **almost daily:** Freedman, R&FF, 12.

100   **"an interesting":** ER to Sara Delano Roosevelt, 10/1918, at 3, FDRL, Roosevelt Family Papers Donated by the Children, Eleanor Roosevelt 1903–1945 and Undated, Box 13. This letter is often incorrectly cited as 5/12/1918.

100   **Réquin:** FFR, 110–11; OWH to HJL, 5/8/1918, 1 HLL, at 153.

100   **Baruch:** FF to Baruch, 8/22/1918, NARA, WLPB Records, RG 1, Corr. of the Chairman and the Exec. Sec., May 1918–February 1919, Entry 2, Box 3.

100   **Lucy Mercer:** Joseph P. Lash, *Eleanor and Franklin,* 225–27 (1971); Joseph E. Persico, *Franklin & Lucy,* 215 (2008); David Michaelis, *Eleanor,* 155–56, 164–68 (2020).

100   **"You know":** Baker, *Felix Frankfurter,* 76 (based on int. with Helen Denman).

101   **begin to fail:** FF to KL, 8/9/1918, at 3–4.

101   **chest X-ray:** "Report of Roentgen Findings in the case of Miss Marion Denman," 7/25/1918, FFLC, Box 5; FF to MD, 8/13/1918, at 1, *id.*

101   **"wide":** Fosdick Memorandum, 11/9/1918, NARA, Records of War Department and General and Special Staffs, RG 165, General Corr. 1917–21, NM 84, Entry 393, Box 115, at 42194.

101   **history:** Fosdick to Frederick Keppel, 12/2/1918, *id.,* Box 130, at 45351; Memorandum to Major Foote, 7/12/1919, *id.,* Box 153, at 50545; *see id.,* Box 160, at 52181.

101   **eight-hour workday:** "Report of President's Mediation Commission to the President of the United States," 1/9/1918, at 21, FFLC, Box 191; "Report to War Labor Policies Board: Eight-Hour Law," 6/22/1918, at 1, 3–5, FFLC, Box 190.

101   **basic eight-hour day:** Meeting Minutes, War Labor Policies Board, 6/28/1918, at 1, FFLC, Box 191 (attaching "Report of Committee on Eight-hour laws").

101   **"Mr. Frankfurter" & "My only":** Executive Minutes, 5/11/1918, at 30, 45, NARA, National War Labor Board, RG 2, Box 1.

102   **Taft & Walsh:** WHT to WBW, 10/15/1918, at 1, FFLC, Box 190; Walsh to FF, 9/16/1918, *id.;* FF to WHT, 10/16/1918, FFLC, Box 191.

102   **"I did":** FF to MD, 10/15/1918, at 5, FFLC, Box 5.

102   **challenged:** Walsh to FF, 9/2/1918, FFLC, Box 190.

102   **Charles M. Schwab:** FF to H. F. Perkins, 7/1/1918, NARA, WLPB Records, RG 1, Corr. of Chairman and Exec. Sec., May 1918–February 1919, Entry 2, Box 12; FF to Elbert Gary, 7/9/1918, FFLC, Box 190.

102   **New York City:** Gary to FF, 7/19/1918, NARA, Records, Corr. Chairman and Exec. Sec., May 1918–February 1919, Entry 2, RG 1, Box 12.

102   **"to discuss":** FF to Gary, 7/19/1918, at 2, FFLC, Box 190.

102   **following up:** FF to Gary, 7/25/1918, *id.;* FF to Gary, 9/17/1918 tel., *id.;* FF to Gary, 9/19/1918, *id.;* FFR, 140.

102 **"a sham" & "a wage increase" & Henry Ford:** Gary Meeting Minutes, 9/20/1918, at 2–7, FFLC, Box 190. *See* FF to Gary, 9/20/1918, *id.*

102 **ten hours:** NYTrib, 9/25/1918, at 10.

103 **"Professor Frankfurter" & "Ah,":** FFR, 140–41.

103 **summarizing:** FF to Baruch, 9/25/1918 & FF to WBW, 9/25/1918 tel., NARA, WLPB Records, RG 1, Corr. of Chairman and Exec. Sec., May 1918–February 1919, Entry 2, Box 12.

103 **Five days:** NYTrib, 9/25/1918, at 10.

103 **"really big" & "its immediate":** FF to WBW, 9/25/1918 tel., at 1, FFLC, Box 5 (handwritten to MD).

103 **"honored":** FF, "The Conservation of the New Federal Standards," The Survey, 12/7/1918, at 291, FFLC, Box 194.

103 **took months:** Report re: "Regulations Governing Night Work of Women," 9/16/1918, FFLC, Box 190; Meeting Minutes, War Labor Policies Board, 11/15/1918, FFLC, Box 191.

104 **"I'm a warrior" & "He was a warrior":** TNR, 1/11/1919, at 291.

104 **peace talks:** FF to TR, 8/27/1918, TRP, Reel 294, Series 1, Image 139.

104 **"pessimistic" & "reactionary forces":** FF to WL, 1/13/1919, at 1, WLP, Reel 9, Box 10, Folder 420a.

104 **resigned:** FF to WBW, 2/8/1919, FFLC, Box 191.

CHAPTER 8: PERSONALIA IN PARIS

105 **informed:** FF to RP, 2/22/1919, at 1–2, FFLC, Box 6.

105 **"noble":** Jacob de Haas, *Louis D. Brandeis: A Biographical Sketch*, 52 (1929).

105 **"My approach":** Brandeis, "The Rebirth of the Jewish Nation," in *id.* at 163 & Jewish Advocate, 10/2/1914, at 6.

106 **lieutenants:** LDB to JWM, 3/19/1915, 3 LLDB at 487; Harry Barnard, *The Forging of an American Jew*, 172–98 (1974).

106 **Arthur Balfour:** Balfour to Lord Rothschild, 11/2/1917, 7 CWP at iv.

106 **"undivided":** Journal, 2/16–18/1918 & 2/22/1918, at 1, 4–5, FFLC, Box 189.

106 **pleaded:** CW to LDB, 11/26/1918, 9 CWP at 38; CW to LDB, 12/3/1918, *id.* at 52; CW to AA, 12/22/1918, *id.* at 80.

106 **funding:** "Zionism," at 7, LDBP-Brandeis U, Box 121; LDB to FF, 11/19/1916 & LDB to FF, 11/25/1916, HBHS, at 26–27; David W. Levy & Bruce Allen Murphy, "Preserving the Progressive Spirit in a Conservative Time," 78 Mich. L. Rev. 1252, 1261–63 (1980); Bruce Allen Murphy, *The Brandeis/Frankfurter Connection*, 40–45 (1982); Melvin I. Urofsky, *Louis D. Brandeis*, 502–5 (2009); David Luban, "The Twice-Told Tale of Mr. Fixit," 91 Yale L.J. 1678 (1982); David J. Danelski, "Review: Brandeis and Frankfurter," 96 Harv. L. Rev. 321 (1982); Robert Cover, "The Framing of Justice Brandeis," TNR, 5/5/1982, at 17–18.

107 **equal citizenship:** LDB to Louis Kirstein, 9/10/1915, 3 LLDB at 587.

107 **"I wish" & "we must":** FF to MD, 2/9/1919, at 1–2, FFLC, Box 6.

107 **flowers & notes & "as I":** MD to FF, circa 2/15/1919, at 1, FFLC, Box 6.

107 **obsessive:** FF to MD, 2/28/1919, at 3, *id.*

108 **"So much":** FF to MD, 3/10/1919, at 1, *id.*

108 **Rue de Rivoli:** FF to MD, 2/28/1919, at 3.

108 **"had a foothold":** Ella Winter, *And Not to Yield*, 50 (1963). Ella Winter may have been

in love with FF and, after she learned of his engagement to MDF, married journalist
Lincoln Steffens. Stella Frankfurter Int. with Joseph Lash, 11/4/1983, Lash Papers, Box
65, Folder 1; JLR Int. with Lash, 11/14/1983, *id.*, Box 68, Folder 2.

108 **Prince Faisal:** CW to Balfour, 7/17/1918, 8 CWP at 228–30; CW to AA, 10/4/1918, *id.* at
276; CW to AA, 12/12/1918, 9 CWP at 62–63; *id.* at 86–87.

108 **"quiet" & "fascinating" & "The Arab prince":** FF to LDB, 3/3/1919, at 3, FFLC, Box 6
(handwritten to Marion).

108 **"said all" & "said exactly":** *id.*

108 **exchange letters:** FF to Meyer Weisgal, 12/3/1929, at 1–2, CZA, Box A264, Folders 9 &
35; FF, Memorandum, n.d., at 1–2, FFLC, Box 162.

109 **"We feel" & "We are working":** Prince Faisal to FF, 3/[1]/1919, at 1, FFLC, Box 162. There
is some dispute as to the date of the first letter. The original Faisal-FF letter is dated
March 1; FF's copy is dated March 3.

109 **reply:** FF to Weisgal, 12/3/1929, at 1–2; FF, Memorandum, n.d., at 2; NYT, 3/5/1919, at 7.

109 **"We knew" & "For both" & "We each":** FF to Prince Faisal, 3/[5]/1919, FFLC, Box 162.
FF delayed delivering his response because of a bout with the flu. FF to Colonel Lawrence, 3/23/1919, *id.* The dates on the reply also differ. The original FF-Faisal letter is
dated March 5; FF's copy is dated March 23. Neil Caplan, "Faisal Ibn Husain and the
Zionists," International History Review 5, no. 4 (November 1983): 561–614.

109 **"Oriental" & "wise" & " 'a caravan' " & "That's":** FF to MD, 3/27/1919, at 1–2, FFLC, Box 6.

110 **"THE ARAB QUESTION":** FF to LDB, 3/3/1919, at 2–3.

110 **discovered:** Aaron Aaronsohn, "Agricultural and Botanical Explorations in Palestine,"
8/4/1910, Bulletin No. 180, Bureau of Plant Industry, U.S. Dept. of Agriculture (Washington, DC: GPO, 1910).

110 **Turkish atrocities:** Alexander Aaronsohn, *With the Turks in Palestine* (1916); Alexander
Aaronsohn, "Our Swords Are Red, O Sultan," Pt. 1, Atlantic Monthly (7/1916): 1–12 &
Pt. 2 (8/1916): 188–96.

110 **"confession" & NILI:** AA to JWM (Confession), 10/9/1916, at 1–2, FFLC, Box 162; Alex
Aaronsohn, "The 'NILI' or 'A' Organization," in *Agents of Empire*, 312–13 (Anthony Verrier, ed. 1995).

110 **exposed:** Shmuel Katz, *The Aaronsohn Saga*, 258 (2007); Patricia Goldstone, *Aaronsohn's Maps*, 201–13 (2007).

110 **Sarah:** AA Diary, 12/1/1917, NILI Archives, 46_3_10 September till December 1917 I
(translated from French) & *Agents of Empire*, at 295.

110 **"beyond":** FF to MD, 1/4/1918 (or 1/11/1918), at 3, FFLC, Box 5.

110 **"the wonderful":** OWH to FF, 10/11/1915, H-FF Corr., at 34.

110 **inspired:** LDB to Alfred Brandeis, 1/7/1912, 2 LLDB at 537.

110 **Roosevelt:** AA Journal, 3/15/1913, at 1–3, Bullitt Papers, Box 174.

110 **House of Truth:** AA, Addenda, 10/9/1916, at 1, NILI Archives, 21_1_56.

110 **travel companion:** AA Diary, 3/18/1918, NILI Archives, 48_3_3 March 1918 A (translated from French).

110 **intermediary:** AA to Alex, 11/26/1918, at 1–2, Bullitt Papers, Box 173.

111 **clashed:** AA Diary, 2/18/1919, *Agents of Empire*, 302; AA to JWM (AA's Confession),
10/9/1916, at 9.

111 **trust him:** FF to LDB, 3/23/1919, at 3, FFLC, Box 162.

111 **"He is *persona*":** FF to LDB, 3/3/1919, at 9 (emphasis in original).

111 **"the enfant" & greatly aided:** FF to LDB, 3/3/1919, at 9 (handwritten in margin). *See* AA Diary, 2/18/1919.

111 **House and Weizmann:** CW to AA, 1/19/1919, 9 CWP at 96.

111 **backpedaling:** Eustace Percy, *Some Memories*, 60, 73–74 (1958); FF to MD, 4/25/1919, FFLC, Box 7; FF to MD, 5/22/1919, at 1–2, *id.*

111 **"Why don't" & "Tell these" & "I can't":** FF to MD, 4/13/1919, at 1–2, *id.*

111 **Arab uprisings:** Alex Aaronsohn to AA & FF, 5/8/1919, NILI Archives, 29_4_24.

111 **"As a passionate":** FF to WW, 5/8/1919, at 1, FFLC, Box 162 & WWP, Series 5B, Reel 405.

111 **"how deeply":** WW to FF, 5/13/1919, *id.*

112 **"occasioned":** FF to WW, 5/14/1919, at 1, *id.*

112 **"I never":** WW to FF, 5/14/1919, *id.*

112 **"slowly" & "there will":** Henry Alsberg to FF, 5/12/1919, at 1, 3, FFLC, Box 162.

112 **vouched:** FF to EMH, 5/16/1919, *id.* & EMHP, Box 45, Folder 1435.

112 **negotiating directly:** FF to MD, 5/29/1919, FFLC, Box 7.

112 **skilled negotiator:** FF to MD, 4/17/1919, at 4, *id.*

112 **"No wonder":** FF to MD, 5/24/1919, at 1, 5, *id. See* TNR, 3/10/1920, at 64 & TNR, 4/13/1921, at 202, FFLC, Box 194 (criticizing WW for negotiating alone at Paris Peace Conference).

113 **Aaronsohn's behavior:** FF to LDB, 3/3/1919, at 9; FF to LDB, 3/23/1919, at 3.

113 **tears & "I must":** FF to MD, 5/17/1919, at 4, FFLC, Box 7.

113 **waited:** FF to Walter Gribbon, 5/13/1937, at 2, FFLC, Box 57.

113 **never found:** FF to David Fairchild, 5/16/1919 tel., FFLC, Box 162; CW to Julius Simon, Victor Jacobson, and Shmarya Levin, 5/17/1919, 9 CWP at 142; Goldstone, *Aaronsohn's Maps*, 252–56, 259; Katz, *The Aaronsohn Saga*, 340–41; ToL, 5/23/1919, at 14.

113 **"And now":** FF to MD, 5/17/1919, at 1.

113 **relieved:** MD to FF, 5/19/1919, at 1, FFLC, Box 7.

113 **"cold" & "I hear" & "great Romantic":** FF to MD, 6/10/1919, at 1, 3, *id.*, Box 8. *See* Manchester Guardian, 5/20/1919, at 6.

113 **"I sorrow":** LDB to FF, 5/20/1919 tel., FFLC, Box 162.

114 **disagreed:** FF to LDB, 5/21/1919 tel., FFLC, Box 162; LDB to FF, 6/5/1919, HBHS at 31.

114 **"I made" & "Your failure":** FF to MD, 6/6/1919, at 1–3, FFLC, Box 8 (emphasis in original).

114 **"vacation":** WP, 6/10/1919, at 4.

114 **waiting:** FF to MD, 6/20/1919, at 3, FFLC, Box 8.

114 **"at the very":** FF to MD, 6/21/1919, at 3, FFLC, Box 8.

114 **"a sound" & "a world" & "No statesman":** FF, "Memorandum re: Brandeis Interview with Balfour," 6/24/1919, *Documents on British Foreign Policy 1919–1939*, First Series, Vol. IV, 1919, at 1276 78 (1952).

114 **"their first" & "simply":** FF to MD, 6/25/1919, at 1–3, FFLC, Box 8.

115 **choose Palestine:** FF to MD, 6/19/1919, at 2, *id.*; FF to MD, 6/25/1919, at 5.

115 **disappointment:** FF to MD, 6/25/1919, at 1, 4–5.

115 **signed:** FF to MD, 6/29/1919, at 1, FFLC, Box 8.

115 **Alsberg phoned:** FF to MD, 6/13/1919, at 1, FFLC, Box 8.

115 **Hugh Gibson:** FF to MD, 6/30/1919, at 2, *id.*; FF to Hugh Gibson, 6/28/1919, *id.*

115 **Morgenthau & agreed:** Philip Kerr to Sir Percy Wyndham, 7/16/1919, *id.*; WL to FF, 7/28/1919, at 1, WLP, Reel 9, Box 10, Folder 420a.

115   **Nothing prepared:** FF to MD, 7/27/1919, at 3–4, FFLC, Box 8; FF to MD, 7/31/1919, at 4–5, *id.*; FF to MD, 8/2/1919, at 1–2, *id.*, Box 9.

115   **"systematic" & "live" & "to study":** FF to WL, 7/30/1919, at 1–2, WLP, Reel 9, Box 10, Folder 420a.

115   **"as if":** Steffens to Laura & Allen, 8/2/1919, *The Letters of Lincoln Steffens*, Vol. 1, at 478 (1938).

115   **"Aaronsohn was":** LDB to AGB, 7/10/1919, 4 LLDB, at 417–18.

116   **twenty-three & "Felix was":** LDB to AGB, 8/1/1919, *id.* at 419–20.

116   **"a different man" "was thrilled" & "talk Poland":** FF to MD, 8/4/1919, at 2, FFLC, Box 9.

116   **made the rounds:** FF to MD, 8/10/1919, at 1–2, *id.*

116   **warned Weizmann:** FF to MD, 8/16/1919, at 1–2, *id.*

116   **"Brandeis could":** CW to FF, 8/27/1919, 9 CWP at 205.

116   **"a common":** FF to CW, n.d., at 2, 1919, CZA, Box A264, Folder 34.

116   **Rotterdam:** FF to MD, 8/29/1919, FFLC, Box 9; FF to MD, n.d., *id.*

116   **"buried":** FF to MD, 8/14/1919, at 4–5, *id.*

CHAPTER 9: A DANGEROUS MAN

117   **"summons" & "Very likely":** RP to JWM, 3/1/1919, RPP, Reel 78, Page 554.

117   **"a general" & "Bolshevists":** RP to FF, 4/28/1919, at 1, FFHLS, Pt. III, Reel 17, Page 890.

117   **"if he had":** RP to FF, 5/17/1919, at 1–2, *id.* at Page 892.

117   **read & "It's a real":** FF to MD, 5/15/1919, at 3–4, FFLC, Box 7.

117   **first steamship:** RP to LDB, 5/24/1919, at 1–2, LDB-Louisville, Reel 48; FF to RP, 6/3/1919, at 1, RPP, Reel 7, Page 46.

117   **City Club:** FF to LDB, 6/6/1919 tel., LDB-Louisville, Reel 48; LDB to RP, 6/10/1919, RPP, Reel 3, Page 83.

117   **"Do nothing":** FF to MD, 6/21/1919, at 7, FFLC, Box 8.

117–118   **"Pound is" & "It's a":** *Id.* at 4–5, 7.

118   **"Don't worry":** FF to MD, 6/24/1919, at 7, FFLC, Box 8.

118   **predicted:** *Id.* at 6–7; FF to MD, 6/21/1919, at 6–7.

118   **"Old Boston":** LDB to AGB, 6/14/1919, 4 LLDB at 400.

118   **Frankfurter's enemies:** RP to FF, 4/28/1919, at 1.

118   **corrupted:** FF to MD, 6/21/1919, at 6–7.

118   **Perkins:** FF to TNP, 6/13/1918, TNP to FF, 7/1/1918, TNP to FF, 7/3/1918, RPP, Reel 7, Pages 28–30; TNP to FF, 2/12/1919 & FF to TNP, 4/14/1919, FFLC, Box 89.

118   **House of Truth:** FF to LH, 5/20/1920, at 5–6, LHP, Box 104A, Folder 104-9; FFR, 174–75.

119   **"dangerous men":** OWH to HJL, 4/4/1919, 1 HLL at 193.

119   **informed:** HJL to OWH, 4/20/1919, *id.* at 196; OWH to HJL, 5/1/1919, *id.* at 200.

119   **"a great":** HJL to OWH, 5/11/1919, 1, *id.* at 201.

119   **"clear" & "falsely":** Schenck v. United States, 249 U.S. 47, 52 (1919). *See* Frohwerk v. United States, 249 U.S. 204 (1919); Debs v. United States, 249 U.S. 211 (1919).

119   **regret:** OWH to HJL, 3/16/1919, 1 HLL at 190.

119   **encouraging:** OWH to Baroness Charlotte Moncheur, 4/9/1918, at 2, OWHP, Box 36, Folder 3, Reel 26, Page 476; OWH to HJL, 4/9/1918, 1 HLL at 148; OWH to HJL, 12/3/1918, *id.* at 176.

119   **facts:** OWH to HJL, 5/18/1919, *id.* at 204–5.

119   **"He is":** FF to MD, 6/21/1919, at 7.

120 **Grinnell:** OWH to HJL, 5/18/1919.

120 **"most people" & "would be":** RP to OWH, 5/29/1919, OWHP, Box 48, Folder 20–23, Reel 36, Page 736.

120 **"If the school":** OWH to HJL, 6/1/1919, 1 HLL at 210–11.

120 **"a very strong":** OWH to ALL, 6/2/1919, 1 HLL at 211 n.2 & ALLOP, Box 102, Folder 250.

120 **"very glad" & "somewhat" & "What you":** ALL to OWH, 6/10/1919, ALLOP, Box 102, Folder 250.

120 **"Think of Holmesy":** FF to MD, 6/21/1919, at 8.

120 **"Red Summer":** Cameron McWhirter, *Red Summer* (2011); Carl Sandburg, *The Chicago Race Riots*, 1 (1919).

120 **At 11:15 p.m.:** CT, 6/3/1919, at 1; WashTimes, 6/3/1919, at 2; WashHerald, 6/3/1919, at 1; NYT, 6/3/1919, at 1.

120 **Bureau of Investigation:** NYTrib, 6/13/1919, at 6; Kenneth D. Ackerman, *Young J. Edgar*, 6–7 (2007).

121 **"He and Mack" & "I rejoice":** RP to LDB, 10/31/1919, LDB-Louisville, Reel 48.

121 **chaired:** BG, 11/12/1919, at 5–6; FFR, 174–75.

121 **"no patience":** FF, Russian Meeting, 11/11/1919, FFLC, Box 89.

121 **"Why do" & "very unreasonable":** FFR, 175.

121 **"You know":** FF to TNP, 11/25/1919, at 1, FFLC, Box 89.

121 **"being" & "*the* best" & "inquisitioned" & "instructors" & "You see":** FF to ERB, 12/17/1919, FFLC, Box 31 (emphasis in original).

121 **cautioned:** OWH to FF, 12/4/1919, H-FF Corr., at 78; P.S., 12/5/1919, *id.* The activities of FF, RP, and HJL may have increased contributions because of the stand for academic freedom. Bruce A. Kimball & Daniel R. Coquillette, *The Intellectual Sword*, 101 (2020); Bruce A. Kimball, "The Disastrous First Fund-Raising Campaign in Legal Education," Journal of the Gilded Age and the Progressive Era 12, no. 4 (October 2013): 574–75.

122 **Jacob Abrams:** Abrams v. United States, 250 U.S. 616, 624 (1919).

122 **Three of Holmes's:** DA to AMB, 6/2/1960, DAP, Reel 2, Box 3, Folder 34 (recollecting conversation with OWH secretary Stanley Morrison).

122 **"poor" & "the best" & "immediate" & "to save":** Abrams, 250 U.S. at 627–28, 629–30 (Holmes J., dissenting).

122 **"And now":** FF to OWH, 11/12/1919, H-FF Corr., at 75.

122 **conservative friends:** John H. Wigmore, "Abrams v. U.S.: Freedom of Speech and Freedom of Thuggery in War-time and Peace-time," 14 Ill. L. Rev. 539, 550 (1920); OWH to FF, 11/30/1919, H-FF Corr., at 77 (Perkins).

122 **"dangerous":** OWH to NCG, 12/10/1919, OWHP, Box 36, Folder 5, Reel 26, Page 557.

122 **"said things":** OWH to Ellen Curtis, 12/7/1919, at 1, *id.* at Page 554.

122 **"jumped up" & "Dickie" & "Tell her":** Garson Kanin, "Trips to Felix," in *Felix Frankfurter: A Tribute*, 39–40 (Wallace Mendelson, ed. 1964).

122 **Mrs. Holmes:** MDH, *Justice Oliver Wendell Holmes: The Shaping Years, 1841–1870* at 200–201 & n. i (1957); FF to MD, 11/3/1919, FFLC, Box 9.

122 **"loving parents":** FF to MD, 11/4/1919, at 2, *id.*

123 **"very devoted":** FF to MD, 11/6/1919, at 3, *id.*

123 **twists and turns:** ERB to FF, 11/14/1919, FFLC, Box 31; FF to ERB, 12/1919, *id.*; LH to FF, 12/3/1919 at 1, FFLC, Box 63.

123 **"two cooing":** HJL to OWH, 1/14/1920, 1 HLL at 233.

123 **subway train:** NYH, 11/6/1919, at 1.

123 **could not stop thinking:** FF to MD, 11/7/1919, at 1–2, FFLC, Box 9.

123 **raided:** NYT, 11/9/1919, at 1, 3.

123 **Berkman & Goldman:** WP, 12/22/1919, at 1.

123 **ACLU:** RNB to FF, 2/13/1920, FFLC, Box 125 & ACLU Papers, Reel 16, Vol. 120, Page 166.

124 **"tactics":** FF to RNB, 2/18/1920, *id.*, Page 50. On the ACLU, *see* Laura Weinrib, *The Taming of Free Speech* (2016); Robert C. Cottrell, *Roger Nash Baldwin and the American Civil Liberties Union* (2001); Samuel Walker, *In Defense of American Liberties* (1990).

124 **1600 pages & pattern & "lack of":** Colyer v. Skeffington, 265 F. 17, 20–22, 30–49, 69–71, 79–80 (D. Mass. 1920). *See* FFR, 170–71.

124 **appealed:** Skeffington v. Katzeff, 277 F. 129 (1st Cir. 1922); BH, 12/29/1920 in FFLC, Box 159.

124 **"illegal acts":** National Popular Government League, *To the American People*, 4 (1920). *See* FFR, 173–74; David Williams, "The Bureau of Investigation and Its Critics, 1919–1921," *Journal of American History* 68, no. 3 (December 1981): 560–79; William Anthony Gengarelly, "Resistance Spokesmen: Opponents of the Red Scare, 1919–1921" (PhD diss., Boston University, 1972).

124 **explained:** "Correspondence between Attorney General Palmer and Professors Frankfurter and Chafee Regarding Aliens Held for Deportation," at 1, FFLC, Box 159.

124 **retraction:** AMP to FF, 6/4/1920 tel., *id.*

124 **under oath:** FF and ZC to AMP, 6/4/1920 tel., *id.*; NYT, 6/5/1920, at 27.

125 **chided:** BaltSun, 3/6/1921, at ED17.

125 **"earliest":** Memorandum from George Kelleher to Frank Burke, "Attention of J. E. Hoover, Esq.," 5/26/1920, at 1 (quoting 5/20/1920 tel.), Investigative Case Files of the Bureau of Investigation, 1908–1922, Old German File #120964, NARA, M1085, Roll 504.

125 **secret file:** Investigative Case Files of the Bureau of Investigation, 1908–1922, NARA, M1085, Rolls 504 & 831, Old German File #379228, Old German File #120964.

125 **travel:** Hoover to W. L. Hurley, 6/10/1920, Roll 504, OG 120964, at 76; Hurley to Hoover, 6/11/1920, *id.* at 87.

125 **"confirmed":** "Memorandum to Mr. Hoover In re Felix Frankfurter, Zachariah [sic] Chafee, Lawrence G. Brooks et al.," 6/15/1920, at 12, OG 379228, at 105; Sam Crockett, *Frankfurter's Red Record*, 1 (1961) (quoting letter from Hoover to Hurley, 2/23/1921, NARA, State Department File, 1910–29, 861.00/8795) (declaring Frankfurter and thirty-one others were "all known to be actors in this [Bolshevik] movement."); Hoover to Tolson, Mohr, & DeLoach, 9/25/1961, Frankfurter FBI File, 1-9-20 (disclaiming 2/23/1921 letter and blaming "an attorney in his division" for signing it on his behalf).

125 **"the most":** *Diaries of Drew Pearson, 1949–1959*, at 284 (Tyler Abell, ed. 1974). During the 1940s, Pearson worked with Hoover "to build up the FBI." Hoover, in turn, leaked to Pearson. Donald A. Ritchie, *The Columnist*, 40–41 (2021).

125 **Board of Overseers:** HJL to Upton Sinclair, 8/16/1922, at 1; Upton Sinclair Papers-IU, Box 4; Harvard Alumni Bulletin, 1/22/1920, Vol. 22, No. 17, at 399.

125 **final straw:** Harvard Lampoon, 1/16/1920, Vol. 78, No. 10; HJL to Lowell, 1/28/1920 & 4/19/1921, ALLOP, Box 141, Folder 46a; Brad Snyder, *The House of Truth*, 293–94 (2017).

125 **"no" & "poor":** RP to LDB, 4/24/1920, at 1–2, LDB-Louisville, Reel 48.

125 **fought:** JWM to RP, 4/20/1920, RPP, Reel 36, Page 898; JWM to RP, 4/26/1920, *id.*, Pages 895–96; JWM to RP, 6/12/1920, *id.*, Page 897.

125 **concerned:** OWH to RP, 4/27/1920, RPP, Reel 77, Page 535.

125 **not to worry:** FF to OWH, 5/15/1920, H-FF Corr., at 89–90.

125 **talk of the faculty:** RP to LDB, 5/15/1920, LDB-Louisville, Reel 48; Harvard Alumni Bulletin, 10/12/1920, Vol. 23, No. 2, at 37.

126 **charges:** RP to Henry Bates, 5/25/1921, at 1, Henry Bates Papers, Box 1 (indicating the charges against FF and RP "collapsed in about five minutes" because of fabricated evidence).

126 **"the very" & "the fit":** FF to WL, 5/24/1921, at 1, WLP, Reel 9, Box 10, Folder 422.

126 **finished second:** Student Grades, "Class of 1913," at 2, FFHLS, Pt. III, Reel 19, Page 632. On Chafee's trial, *see* Kimball & Coquillette, *Intellectual Sword*, 136–41; Donald L. Smith, *Zechariah Chafee, Jr.*, 36–57 (1986); Peter H. Irons, "'Fighting Fair,'" 94 Harv. L. Rev. 1205 (1981); Jerold S. Auerbach, "The Patrician as Libertarian," New England Quarterly (December 1969): 524–27.

126 **"avowed":** FF to WL, 5/24/1921, at 1, WLP, Reel 9, Box 10, Folder 422.

126 **voted to dismiss:** FF to LDB, 5/24/1921, at 2–3, FFLC, Box 29; FF, Handwritten Notes of 'trial' and on prosecution's briefs, FFLC, Box 142; FFR, 175–77.

126 **single vote:** Henry Aaron Yeomans, *Abbott Lawrence Lowell*, 323 (1948).

126 **corrections:** 35 Harv. L. Rev. 9, 10–14 (1921).

126 **"only" & "reaction's":** The Nation, 8/17/1921, at 163.

CHAPTER 10: THE POSSIBLE GAIN ISN'T WORTH THE COST

127 **"the morass" & "such soviet" & "With all" & "to decide":** El Paso Times, 2/15/1921, at 3 (syndicated column by Norman Hapgood).

128 **D.C. law:** Adkins to FF, 10/19/1920, Adkins Papers, Box 6, Folder 6–36; FF to Adkins, 10/21/1920, *id.*

128 **"the end":** FF to LH, 3/16/1921, at 3, LHP, Box 104A, Folder 104-9.

128 **Debs & "out":** FF to LH, 7/22/1920, at 1, *id.* FFR, 7/23/1957, at 328, FFLC, Box 206 (recalling protest vote for third-party candidate in 1920).

128 **accused:** Duplex Printing Press Co. v. Deering, 254 U.S. 443, 484 (1921) (Brandeis, J., dissenting).

128 **"its broad":** TNR, 1/26/1921, at 248.

129 **"established":** FF to LH, 1/4/1921, at 1, LHP, Box 104A, Folder 104-9.

129 **"Not so":** TNR, 2/23/1921, at 361. See Berger v. United States, 255 U.S. 22, 37 (1921) (Day, J., dissenting); *id.* at 42 (McReynolds, J., dissenting).

129 **"Mr. Justice Holmes":** TNR, 3/30/1921, at 124. See United States ex rel. Milwaukee Social Democratic Pub. Co. v. Burleson, 255 U.S. 407, 417 (1921) (Brandeis, J., dissenting); *id.* at 436 (Holmes, J., dissenting).

129 **Four justices:** Block v. Hirsh, 256 U.S. 135, 159, 162 (1921) (McKenna, J., dissenting).

129 **worried:** FF to LH, 4/1/1921, at 2, LHP, Box 104A, Folder 104-9.

130 **"the price":** *Id.* at 2–3.

130 **"leave":** FF to LH, 9/7/1921, at 2, *id.*, Folder 104-10.

130 **book:** FF to LH, 6/20/1921, at 2, *id.*, Folder 104-9.

130 **too soon:** Adkins to FF, 6/6/1921, Adkins Papers, Box 6, Folder 6-36.

130 **unusual situation:** Children's Hospital v. Adkins, 52 App. D.C. 109, 284 F. Supp. 613, 623–26 (1922) (Smyth, C.J. dissenting); Jeffrey Brandon Morris, *Calmly to Poise the Scales of Justice*, 73–75 (2001).

764   NOTES

130   **judicial nightmare:** FF to LH, 7/26/1921, at 1–2, LHP, Box 104A, Folder 104-10.

130   **"professionally":** LH to FF, 7/27/1921, at 2, *id.*

130   **claimed the credit:** FF to LH, 7/29/1921, at 1–3, *id.*

131   **"new school" & "Socialist":** TNR, 10/27/1920, at 208–9. *See* Robert C. Post, "Mr. Taft Becomes Chief Justice," 76 U. Cin. L. Rev. 761 (2008).

131   **"submissiveness" & "a good" & "judicial competence" & "contributed" & "the only":** TNR, 7/27/1921, at 230–31.

131   **learned:** Adkins to FF, 9/13/1921, Adkins Papers, Box 6, Folder 6–35.

131   **objected & so offended:** WashTimes, 11/5/1921, at 2.

132   **right to property & favoring:** Truax v. Corrigan, 257 U.S. 312, 328, 339–40 (1921).

132   **"informed":** TNR, 1/18/1922, at 191 (quoting TNR, 7/27/1921, at 230–31).

132   **"it does":** *id.* at 192 (quoting Truax, 257 U.S. at 330).

132   **"fraught" & "not the arbiter":** *id.* at 192–93.

132   **"'delusiveness exactness'":** *id.* at 193 (quoting Truax, 257 U.S. at 342 (Holmes, J., dissenting)).

132   **"in the most":** *id.* at 194.

132   **"I never" & "in favor of":** WHT to Elihu Root, 12/21/1922, at 1, Elihu Root Papers, Box 166, Folder 12.

133   **future cases:** United Mine Workers v. Coronado Coal Co., 259 U.S. 344, 391, 413 (1922); TNR, 8/16/1922, at 328–30; LDB to FF, 8/31/1922, HBHS, at 104.

133   **second attempt:** Bailey v. Drexel Furniture Co., 259 U.S. 20, 43–44 (1922); LDB to FF, 5/16/1922, HBHS, at 100-1.

133   **"We must":** TNR, 7/26/1922, at 248.

133   **"the actual":** Robert La Follette, 6/14/1922, at 2, 15, La Follette Family Papers, Box I:B226.

133   **Kelley:** Cincinnati Enquirer, 6/15/1922, at 1.

133   **not their means:** TNR, 7/26/1922, at 249–50; FF to SSW, 5/30/1922, at 1–5, FFLC, Box 157; FF to Alice Paul, 6/30/1921, *id.*, Box 153.

133   **criminal justice reform:** *Criminal Justice in Cleveland* (Roscoe Pound & Felix Frankfurter, eds. 1921); TNR, 10/19/1921, at 204–6.

134   **Brandeis explained:** LDB-FF Conversations, July 9 [1922], at 4, LDBHLS, Pt. II, Reel 33, Page 268.

134   **"beyond":** TNR, 1/25/1922, at 238 (quoting Truax v. Corrigan, 257 U.S. 312, 344 (1921) (Holmes, J., dissenting)).

134   **heavily influenced:** LDB-FF Conversations, 11/30/1922, LDBHLS, Pt. II, Reel 33, Page 277; Walter F. Murphy, "In His Own Image: Mr. Chief Justice Taft and Supreme Court Appointments," Supreme Court Review (1961): 159, 162–63.

134   **Clarke, resigned:** John Hessin Clarke to WW, 9/9/1922, 68 WWP at 130; Hoyt Landon Warner, *The Life of Mr. Justice Clarke,* 112–15 (1959); Carl Wittke, "Mr. Justice Clarke in Retirement," 1 Western Res. L. Rev. 28, 33–35 (1949).

134   **"a mediocre":** LDB-FF Conversations, 11/30/1922, LDBHLS, Pt. II, Reel 33, Page 278.

134   **William R. Day:** Jesse R. Bair, " 'The silent man,' " Journal of Supreme Court History, 40, no. 1 (2015): 38–54.

134   **Liberals:** David J. Danelski, *A Supreme Court Justice Is Appointed* (1964); David Schroeder, "More Than a Fraction" (PhD diss., Marquette University, 2009); John Paul Frank, "The Confirmation of Pierce Butler" (MA thesis, University of Wisconsin, 1940).

134 **"a reactionary":** TNR, 12/13/1922, at 66.

134 **squelched:** FF to Pierce Butler, Jr., 12/9/1922, FFLC, Box 38; Pierce Butler, Jr., to FF, 1/20/1923, *id.*; FF to Senator Knute Nelson, n.d., *id.*

134 **Taft vetoed:** WHT to Root, 12/21/1922, at 1–2.

135 **banning mining:** Pennsylvania Coal Co. v. Mahon, 260 U.S. 393 (1922).

135 **secretary:** LDB to FF, 1/3/1923, HBHS, at 132 (blaming Holmes's secretary Robert Benjamin).

135 **silence:** OWH to HJL, 1/13/1923, 1 HLL at 473; OWH to FF, 2/14/1923, H-FF Corr., at 150.

135 **"We live" & "the symbol" & "Behind":** TNR, 12/20/1922, at 84–85.

135 **"deeply moved":** OWH to FF, 12/22/1922, H-FF Corr., at 149–50.

135 **health improved:** LDB to FF, 12/28/1922, HBHS, at 130; LDB to FF, 1/3/1923, *id.* at 132.

135 **finally released:** Children's Hospital v. Adkins, 52 App. D.C. 109, 284 F. 613 (1922).

136 **$1000:** LDB to FF, 1/16/1923, HBHS, at 135–36 n.1 & "L.D.B. Cash," 1923, LDBP-Brandeis U, Box 120.

136 **enlisted:** DA to FF, 2/1/1923 & 2/2/1923, FFLC, Box 153.

136 **"an application" & "Let the end":** District of Columbia Minimum Wage Cases, Brief for Appellant, xviii (1923) (quoting McCulloch v. Maryland, 17 U.S. (4 Wheat.) 316, 421 (1819)).

136 **1000 pages:** District of Columbia Minimum Wage Cases, Brief for Appellant.

136 **"had one" & "took me":** FF to MDF, 3/12/1923, at 1–4, FFLC, Box 11.

137 **"freedom":** Adkins v. Children's Hospital, 261 U.S. 525, 546 (1923).

137 **"struck":** FFR, 103.

137 **Taft argued:** Adkins, 261 U.S. at 562, 564 (Taft, C.J., dissenting).

137 **worried:** WHT to Robert Taft, 4/16/1923, at 3–4, WHTP, Reel 252, Series 3.

137 **"The criterion" & "not for":** Adkins, 261 U.S. at 568–71 (Holmes, J., dissenting).

137 **"no one":** OWH to FF, 4/13/1923, H-FF Corr., 152.

138 **"[T]he possible" & "reasonable":** FF to LH, 4/11/1923, at 1, LHP, Box 104A, Folder 104-10.

138 **"at the rate":** FF to Florence Kelley, 10/19/1923, National Consumers' League Records, Reel 83, Page 385. *See* FF to Kelley, 10/25/1923, *id.* at Page 374; FF to Kelley, 7/29/1924, *id.* at Page 430 (opposing amendments).

138–139 **"Of course" & "The more":** FF to LH, 6/5/1923, at 1, LHP, Box 104A, Folder 104-10.

139 **"behaved":** FF to LH, 8/24/1923, at 1, *id.*, Folder 104-11.

139 **"to 'unreasonable' ":** FF to LH, 4/28/1924, at 2, *id.*

139 **"[N]o juryman" & "prevent":** Moore v. Dempsey, 261 U.S. 86, 89–91 (1923).

140 **released:** Scipio Jones to Walter White, 1/13/1925 tel., NAACP Records, Pt. I, Box D-44; Brad Snyder, *The House of Truth*, 277–78, 353–54 (2017); Grif Stockley, *Blood in Their Eyes* (2001); Ida B. Wells Barnett, *The Arkansas Race Riot* (1920).

140 **"Should" & "great exception" & "The Supreme Court":** FF, "Twenty Years of Mr. Justice Holmes' Constitutional Opinions," 36 Harv. L. Rev. 909, 915, 919, 932 (1923).

140 **"read":** "Honor to Justice Holmes," Time, 7/16/1923; TNR, 9/12/1923, at 62.

140 **continued enforcement:** FF to Adkins, 4/16/1923, FFLC, Box 153.

140 **"We have":** Stenographer's Report of Minimum Wage Conference Called by National Consumers' League, 4/20/1923, at 4–5, 12, National Consumers' League Records, Reel 82, Pages 691–92, 695.

140–141 **"The heart" & "I am":** *Id.* at 7, Page 693.

CHAPTER II: THE TRUE FUNCTION OF A "LIBERAL"

142   **Ford's anti-Semitism:** Norman Hapgood, "The Inside Story of Henry Ford's Jew-
       Mania," Hearst's International (June 1922): 14–18, 128; Victoria Saker Woeste, *Henry
       Ford's War on Jews and the Legal Battle Against Hate Speech* (2012).
143   **"unfortunate":** ALL to JWM, 3/14/1922, FFLC, Box 81.
143   **"his whole":** ALL to JWM, 3/20/1922, *id.*
143   **off the committee:** HCrim, 6/6/1922; NYTrib, 6/23/1922, at 1.
143   **"the quality":** ALL to JWM, 6/14/1922, FFLC, Box 81.
143   **"violent" & "extreme":** FF to ALL, 6/19/1922, FFLC, Box 126.
143   **defended:** ALL to FF, 6/20/1922, *id.*; FF to ALL, 6/21/1922, *id.*; ALL to FF, 6/24/1922,
       id.; FF to ALL, 6/29/1922, *id.*
143   **"pictures":** WL, *Public Opinion* 12 (1922).
143   **"rich and vulgar":** American Hebrew and Jewish Messenger, 4/14/1922, at 575.
143   **"most liberal" & "who all" & "Don't":** FF to WL, 5/25/1922, at 2–3, WLP, Reel 10, Box 10,
       Folder 423.
143   **flurry:** FF to WL, circa 6/22 & FF to WL, 6/8/1922, *id.*.
143   **privately:** WL to Arthur N. Holcolmbe, 6/14/1922, PPWL at 148; WL to Lawrence J.
       Henderson, 10/27/1922, *id.* at 148–49.
144   **"policy":** Committee Report, 4/9/1923, at 1, FFLC, Box 126. *See* Bruce A. Kimball &
       Daniel R. Coquillette, *The Intellectual Sword*, 178–81 (2020).
144   **fired:** FF to LH, 6/4/22, at 1–2, LHP, Box 104A, Folder 104-10; LH to FF, 6/8/1922, *id.*
144   **"an arrogant":** FF to LH, 6/7/1922, at 1–2, *id.*
144   **"sickens":** FF to WL, 1/29/1923, WLP, Reel 10, Box 10, Folder 424.
144   **"were a good":** TNR, 7/4/1923, at 147.
144   **At graduation:** BH, 6/21/1923, at 2, FFLC, Box 126.
144   **"the most":** FF to LH, 8/24/1923, at 3–4, LHP, Box 104A, Folder 104-11.
144   **op-ed:** NYW, 6/24/1923, Editorial Section, at 1.
144   **"a reporter's":** FF to WL, 6/30/1923, at 1–2, WLP, Reel 10, Box 10, Folder 424.
144   **Three months:** WL to FF, 11/8/1923, *id.*; WL to FF, 11/23/1923, FFLC, Box 126.
144   **"a journal" & "the factors":** FF to My dear New Republicans, 7/6/1923, at 1,
       FFLC, Box 126.
145   **drafted:** Alvin Johnson to FF, 7/17/1923, *id.*; TNR, 7/25/1923, at 221–22.
145   **"responsibility":** TNR, 9/5/1923, at 49.
145   **"the corrosive" & "wholly out" & "a ferment" & "apt":** FF to Dartmouth College Presi-
       dent Ernest Hopkins, 11/2/1923, at 6–7, FFLC, Box 126.
145   **"Having survived":** FF to WL, 8/6/1923, WLP, Reel 10, Box 10, Folder 424.
145   **corruption:** TNR, 4/30/1924, at 247–48; TNR, 5/21/1924, at 329–31.
146   **declined:** William H. Harbaugh, *Lawyer's Lawyer: The Life of John W. Davis* 191–92 &
       572 n.32 (1973); CCB to FF, 10/23/1924, at 1, FFLC, Box 163.
146   **"under retainer" & "He has":** TNR, 4/16/1924, at 193–94.
146   **Brandeis hoped:** LDB to FF, 4/16/1924, HBHS, at 165.
146   **angry:** The Nation, 7/30/1924, in FFLC, Box 194.
146–147 **opposed McAdoo:** FF to WL, 6/19/1924, WLP, Reel 10, Box 10, Folder 425.
147   **"disqualifying" & "cardinal":** FF to WL, 6/20/1924, at 1–2, *id.*
147   **"the most" & "one law":** La Follette, Introduction, vi, in Gilbert E. Roe, *Our Judicial
       Oligarchy* (1912).

147 **"You see"**: FF to WL, 7/18/1924, at 1–2, WLP, Reel 10, Box 10, Reel 425a & FFLC, Box 163. *See* FFR at 199; FF to WL, 7/11/1924, at 1, WLP, Reel 10, Box 10, Folder 425a.

147 **"before" & "that any" & "[t]he violent"**: NYW, 7/22/1924, at 6.

147 **furious**: FF to Editor of World, 7/22/1924, at 4, FFLC, Box 163; FF to WL, 7/25/1924 tel., WLP, Reel 10, Box 10, Folder 425.; FF to WL, 7/28/1924, FFLC, Box 163; WL to FF, 7/28/1924, *id.*; FF to WL, 7/30/1924, *id.*; FF to WL, 8/3/1924, *id.*

148 **replied**: NYW, 8/3/1924, at 2E; FF to Editor of the World, 8/3/1924, FFLC, Box 163.

148 **"the matter" & conceded**: WL to FF, 8/11/1924, *id.*

148 **"Really"**: FF to WL, 8/13/1924, *id.*

148 **"too liberal" & "things"**: TNR, 7/23/1924, at 225–26.

148 **"the constitutional" & "If"**: TNR, 8/6/1924, at 285–87.

149 **"sacred" & "knows" & "a mutilated" & "an independent" & "protecting" & "this doctrine" & "Mr. Davis"**: TNR, 10/1/1924, at 110–13.

149–150 **"put the fear" & "a temporary" & "The 'fear' "**: *Id.* at 113.

150 **numerous editorials**: Boston Traveler, 11/1/1924, at 6; BH, 10/4/1924; HCrim, 10/14/1924, at 1, 6 in FFLC, Box 163.

150 **persuade friends**: Raymond Fosdick to FF, 10/1/1924, FFLC, Box 163; FF to LH, 10/3/1924, *id.*; CCB to FF, 10/20/1924, *id.*; SSW to FF, 9/28/1924, *id.*

150 **" 'great inequality' " & "stand" & "the greatest" & "solid" & "educating" & "the claims" & "economic" & "all"**: TNR, 10/22/1924, at 200–201.

150 **predicted**: TNR, 10/29/1924, at 218–19.

150 **"a pretty"**: FF to LH, 10/3/1924 at 2, LHP, Box 104A, Folder 104-11.

151 **doctorate**: CHH, "Functional Study of the Requirements of Notice and Hearing in Governmental Action in the United States," 1923, Harvard Law School Library, Red Set. *See* Genna Rae McNeil, *Groundwork*, 46–56 (1983); Gilbert Ware, *William Hastie*, 28–34 (1984); Kimball & Coquillette, *Intellectual Sword*, 183–89.

151 **Sheldon**: FF to Donald Murray, 5/11/1950, FFLC, Box 67.

151 **teach**: FF to CHH, 1/3/1924, Houston Papers–Howard University, Box 163-9, Folder 9.

151 **doctoral thesis**: WHH, "Doctrine and Practice of Federal Receiverships in Federal Courts," 5/1/1930, WHHP, Pt. II, Reel 42, Page 959.

151 **promoted**: William LePre Houston to FF, 3/27/1942, *id.*, Box 163-2, Folder 9 (asking to recommend son for D.C. municipal judgeship); FF to FB, 5/4/1942, FFLC, Box 67 (recommending Houston for judgeship); FF to WHH, 2/8/1937, WHHP, Pt. II, Reel 42, Page 524 (congratulating him on federal judgeship in Virgin Islands).

151 **missionary & scholarship**: Donald A. Ritchie, *James M. Landis*, 6–28 (1980); Daily Princetonian, 5/9/1921, at 4.

151 **Before he set**: James M. Landis, "The Commerce Clause as a Restriction on State Taxation," 20 Mich. L. Rev. 50 (1921).

151 **struggled socially**: Erwin N. Griswold, "James McCauley Landis—1899–1964," 78 Harv. L. Rev. 313, 313 (1964); W. Barton Leach, "Landis: Roommate and Dean," Harvard Law Bulletin 19:4 (March 1968): 16–17.

152 **dazzled**: JML COH, at 32–33.

152 **Sears Prize & 81**: "List of Sears Prize Winners," at 1, Corcoran Papers, Box 135; "1924 Grades," FFHLS, Pt. III, Reel 19, Page 637.

152 **fourth year**: FF to MDF, 2/16/1925, at 1, FFLC, Box 13.

152 **nervous breakdown**: MDF to FF, 12/12/1923, at 3–4, FFLC, Box 11.

152 **$1500**: FF to LDB, 9/23/[1925], at 1, FFLC, Box 29; LDB to FF, 9/24/1925, HBHS, at 212.

152   **"Oh Fixi"**: MDF to FF, n.d., FFLC, Box 12.

152   **"not interested" & "going to bed"**: Mary Howe Int. with Lash, 9/3/1974, at 1, Lash
       Papers, Box 51, Folder 6. *But see* Vivian Pomeroy to MDF, 4/11/1945, at 1, Pomeroy
       Papers, Box 534/2 (recounting Mary Howe's speculation about OWH's sexless female
       relationships and deriding her "silly talk").

152   **"a deeply"**: William J. Mann, *Kate*, 572 (2006) (speculating based on FF's friendship
       with closeted gay playwright Garson Kanin and a conversation with an FF scholar).
       Other FF friends rumored to be gay included classics scholar Maurice Bowra, literary
       critic Edmund Wilson, and journalist Joseph Alsop.

152   **infertility**: Only one of FF's five siblings, younger brother Paul, had children. BG,
       1/8/1939, at C4 (based on interview with Paul Frankfurter).

153   **"F.F." & "He never"**: JML to Jean Smith, 6/30/1925, at 2, JML-LC, Box 8.

153   **great team**: FF & JML, "Power of Congress over Procedure in Criminal Contempts in
       Inferior Federal Courts," 37 Harv. L. Rev. 1010 (1924); FF & JML, "The Compact Clause
       of the Constitution—A Study in Interstate Adjustments," 34 Yale L.J. 685 (1925); FF
       & JML, "The Business of the Supreme Court of the United States: I," 38 Harv. L. Rev.
       1005 (1925).

153   **Brandeis's secretary**: JML, "Mr. Justice Brandeis: A Law Clerk's View," 46 Publica-
       tions of the American Jewish Historical Society, no. 30 (1957): 467, 468; JML to FF,
       11/1/1925, FFLC, Box 74; FF to Joseph Warren, 11/19/1925, *id.*

153   **77 average**: "List of Sears Prize Winners," at 1; "1925 Grades."

153   **co-authored**: FF and TGC, "Petty Federal Offenses and Constitutional Guaranty of
       Trial by Jury," 39 Harv. L. Rev. 917 (1926); FF to TGC, 2/7/1926, at 1, TGCP, Box 135.

153   **"that if he'd"**: TGC with Philip Kopper, "Rendezvous with Democracy," Intro D/30–
       D/34, TGCP, Box 586.

153   **only child**: HJF Ints. by Ellen Robinson Epstein & David Epstein, 7/1/1973, Pt. I, Side
       1, at 5–7, *in* Ellen Robinson Epstein & David Epstein, *Henry J. Friendly: An Oral His-
       tory* (1974); Sunday Morning Telegram (Elmira, NY), 9/20/1970, at 9A, HJFP, Box 235,
       Folder 95–3; Brad Snyder, "The Judicial Genealogy (and Mythology) of John Roberts,"
       71 Ohio St. L. Rev. 1149, 1166–68 (2010).

154   **Brattle Inn**: HJF to FF, 2/23/1957, FFLC, Box 56.

154   **tryout**: HJF, "Mr. Justice Frankfurter," 41 U. Va. L. Rev. 552, 552 (1965).

154   **Old French**: HJF OH, 7/4/1974, Pt. V, Side 1, at 5–6; Snyder, "The Judicial Genealogy
       (and Mythology) of John Roberts," 71 Ohio St. L. Rev. at 1168–71.

154   **Thomas Reed Powell**: FF to LH, 1/27/1926, at 1, LHP, Box 104B, Folder 104-12; Colum-
       bia Law School Catalogue 1926–1927, at 94.

154   **own pocket**: HJF OH, 7/4/1974, Pt. V, Side 1, at 3–4; Martin Mayer, *Emory Buckner*, 181
       (1968); Snyder, "The Judicial Genealogy (and Mythology) of John Roberts," 71 Ohio
       St. L. Rev. at 1171–72.

155   **"Given"**: LDB to HJL, 8/3/1925, at 3, YLS.

155   **Holmes**: TGC with Kopper, "Rendezvous with Democracy," Holmes D/2-1–Holmes
       D/2-40, TGCP, Box 586; TGC Int., 8/18/1979, at 2–3, 15, Monagan Papers, Box 1, Folder
       1–3; TGC Int. in Katie Louchheim, *The Making of the New Deal*, 21–25 (1983).

155   **"restless" & declined**: TGC to FF, n.d., at 1, OWHP, Reel 42, Page 13.

155   **not too disappointed**: FF to TGC, 2/7/1926, at 1.

155   **"make"**: LDB to FF, 10/28/1926, HBHS, at 257.

155   **working for Brandeis**: LDB to FF, 11/9/1926, *id.* at 261.

155 **diversity:** HJF to FF, 7/20/1927, FFLC, Box 26; HJF, "The Historic Basis of Diversity Jurisdiction," 41 Harv. L. Rev. 483 (1928); Snyder, "The Judicial Genealogy (and Mythology) of John Roberts," 71 Ohio St. L. Rev. at 1172–89.

155 **Thayer or Ames:** FF to LH, 11/27/1926, at 2–3, LHP, Box 104A, Folder 104-13.

155 **annoyed with Buckner:** FF to ERB, 11/30/1926, FFLC, Box 31; ERB to FF, 12/21/1926, *id.*; HJF OH, 7/4/1974, Pt. IV, Side 2, at 9; Snyder, "The Judicial Genealogy (and Mythology) of John Roberts," 71 Ohio St. L. Rev. at 1172.

156 **advising him:** FF to WL, 4/7/1924, at 1, WLP, Box 10, Folder 425, Reel 10, Page 40; HFS to FF, 4/15/1924, *id.*; Alpheus Thomas Mason, *Harlan Fiske Stone*, 148 (1956); HFS to FF, 1/19/1925, at 2, FFLC, Box 104.

156 **"liberal ideas":** FF to HFS, 1/22/1925, at 3–4, *id.*

156 **"If you call":** FF to LH, 11/10/1924, at 4, LHP, Box 104A, Folder 104-11.

156 **revised:** FF to LH, 3/10/1926, at 1–2, *id.*, Box 104B, Folder 104-12.

156–157 **"a 'revolutionary'" & "single revolutionary":** Gitlow v. New York, 268 U.S. 652, 658, 666, 669 (1925).

157 **"no present" & "incitement" & "[e]very" & "should be":** *Id.* at 672–73 (Holmes, J., dissenting).

157 **"the liberty":** Pierce v. Society of Sisters, 268 U.S. 510, 534–35 (1925).

157–158 **"gives" & "did immediate" & "vague" & "These words":** TNR, 6/17/1925, at 86.

158 **"to make" & "'good'" & "the real":** *Id.* at 86–87.

158 **Holmes graced:** Time, 3/15/1926; NYT, 3/7/1926, at E8 & SM1.

158 **"Wherever":** TNR, 3/17/1926, at 88.

158 **"veto" & "the costs" & "own judgment" & "How dubious":** TNR, 3/31/1926, at 158. *See* Schlesinger v. Wisconsin, 270 U.S. 230, 241 (1926) (Holmes, J., dissenting); Weaver v. Palmer Bros. Co., 270 U.S. 402, 415 (1926) (Holmes., J., dissenting).

159 **made no secret:** TNR, 11/4/1925, at 272; The Nation, 12/9/1925, at 652–53; JML to FF, 11/5/1925, at 1–3, FFLC, Box 74.

159 **robust democracy:** Whitney v. California, 274 U.S. 357, 372–74, 377, 379 (1927) (Brandeis, J., concurring).

CHAPTER 12: LET MR. LOWELL RESIGN

160 **armed:** 1 SV Trial Tr. at 75, 77.

160 **lied:** 2 SV Trial Tr. at 1726, 1731–32 (Vanzetti); *id.* at 1846, 1866, 1912 (Sacco).

160 **Salsedo:** FF, *The Case of Sacco and Vanzetti*, 5–6 (1927); TNR, 6/9/1926, at 76.

160 **Bridgewater:** G. Louis Joughin and Edmund M. Morgan, *The Legacy of Sacco and Vanzetti*, 48–49 (1948).

160 **Brandeis's:** EGE, "Mr. Justice Brandeis," The Survey, 11/1/1931, at 139.

160 **activist:** FFR, at 210; Springfield Sunday Union and Republican, 5/1/1932 & 5/8/1932, in FFHLS, Pt. III, Reel 33, Pages 354–57.

161 **noticed & vowed:** Springfield Sunday Union and Republican, 5/8/1932.

161 **not read the newspaper:** FFR, 208–10; FF to MDF, 7/13/1925, at 2, FFLC, Box 13; FF, "Newspapers and Criminal Justice," in *Criminal Justice in Cleveland*, 515–527 (Roscoe Pound & Felix Frankfurter, eds. 1921). Some have questioned FF's assertion that he had not paid attention to the trial. Moshik Temkin, *The Sacco-Vanzetti Affair*, 234–35 n.50 (2009); Robert H. Montgomery, "Felix Frankfurter and President Lowell in the Sacco-Vanzetti Case," at 11–17, Sacco-Vanzetti/Montgomery Papers, Box 8, Folder M7(15)

(observing that FF was in the country at the time of the murders, the New England Civil Liberties Committee had used his name to raise money for the legal defense fund as early as 1921, and FF had misdated the Proctor motion as 1925 when it was filed in 1923). FF made some minor factual errors in his reminiscences, yet at the time he insisted that he had not paid attention to the trial and did not become interested in the case until the Proctor motion in 1923. FF to Shattuck, 4/28/1927, at 1, FFHLS, Pt. III, Reel 34, Page 915; FF to JWM, 10/15/1927, at 1, *id.*, Page 944.

161 **"My opinion":** 1 SV Trial Tr. at 896.

161 **Thompson's motion:** BG, 11/2/1923, at 25; BG, 11/7/1923, at 13; TNR, 12/26/1923, at 117–18 (article by EGE).

161 **"repeatedly" & "When I" & "reprehensible" & "undermined":** FFR, 212–13.

162 **advised:** RNB to FF, 10/22/1924, ACLU Papers, Sub-Series 21, Vol. 260, Page 132; FF to RNB, 10/23/1924, *id.*; RNB to FF, 10/25/1924, *id.* at Page 135; RNB to EGF, 10/23/1924, *id.*, Vol. 261, Page 48; RNB, "Memorandum for Miss Flynn on Sacco-Vanzetti Case," 11/7/1924, *id.*, Page 49.

162 **In 1923:** RNB to EGF, 10/18/1924, ACLU Papers, Sub-Series 21, Vol. 261, Page 55.

162 **specifically requested:** WGT to SVDC, 11/20/1924, at 3, *id.*, at Pages 142–43.

163 **"I wish":** FF to HJL, 9/23/1926, at 1, FFLC, Box 74.

163 **Commonwealth Fund:** Max Farrand to FF, 9/17/1925 & Gates Application Form, FFLC, Box 131.

163 **clerk for Holmes:** SGates to W. G. Gates, 1/5/1927, at 1–6, Gates Family Papers; SGates to W. G. Gates, 12/25/1926, at 2–3, *id.*; TGC to FF, n.d., at 2, OWHP, Reel 42, Page 26.

163 **Gates drafted:** SGates to W. G. Gates, 5/30/1926, at 3–4, Gates Family Papers; FF to WL, 6/11/1926, WLP, Reel 10, Box 10, Folder 427a.

163 **read:** FF to WL, 6/8/1926, *id.*

163–164 **"bothering" & "Under":** TNR, 6/9/1926, at 75–76.

164 **"The prosecution" & "any Judge":** *Id.* at 76 (quoting Frank v. Mangum, 237 U.S. 309, 349 (1915) (Holmes J., dissenting)).

164 **"stand" & "you":** *Id.*

164 **"Damn them" & "The 2,000":** *Id.* at 76–77 (quoting Davis v. Boston Elevated Ry. Co., 235 Mass. 482, 497 (1920) (Rugg, C.J.)).

165 **Medeiros:** 5 SV Trial Tr. at 4359.

165 **getaway car:** *Id.* at 4632.

165 **not been involved:** *Id.* at 4641.

165 **find a job:** HBE, "Felix," at 3–12, 18–26, 28–30, in *Adventure of Living* (unpublished memoir), HBEP, Box 21, Folder 21-9; HBE, "Felix," *Felix Frankfurter: A Tribute*, 91–107.

165 **co-authored:** Reginald Heber Smith & HBE, "The Criminal Courts" in *Criminal Justice in Cleveland*, 227–372.

165 **asked Ehrmann:** EGE to Forrest Bailey, 5/17/1926, at 1–2, ACLU Papers, Sub-Series 21, Vol. 306, Page 321–22.

165 **Morelli gang:** HBE, *The Untried Case* (1933).

165 **$1500:** WGT to FF, 6/16/1926, at 1, FFHLS, Pt. III, Reel 36, Page 342; WGT to RNB, 10/29/1926, at 1, ACLU Papers, Sub-Series 21, Vol. 306, Page 309.

165 **advised:** Mary C. Crawford to RNB, 9/13/1926, at 1, *id.*, Vol. 306, Page 450; FF to RNB, 10/29/1926, *id.*, Vol. 306, Page 460.

165 **whole new:** EGE to Bailey, 5/29/1926, *id.*, Page 324.

165   **circumspect Lippmann:** FF to WL, 6/11/1926, at 1; FF to WL, 6/13/1926, WLP, Reel 10, Box 10, Folder 427a; WL to FF, 6/14/1926, *id.*

166   **Department of Justice:** NYW, 9/20/1926, at 6.

166   **changing the tone:** Crawford to RNB, 9/13/1926, at 1.

166   **hearing & knew:** NYT, 9/14/1927, at 13; FF to WL, 9/20/1926, WLP, Reel 10, Box 10, Folder 427a; FF to WL, 9/22/1926, *id.*; WL to FF, 9/23/1926, *id.*

166   **Thayer denied:** 5 SV Trial Tr., Defendant's Amended Bill of Exceptions for a Motion for a New Trial, 10/28/1926, at 4362.

166   **stifle calls:** Crawford to RNB, 9/13/1926, at 2 & FF to RNB, 9/13/1926, at 1–2, ACLU Papers, Sub-Series 21, Vol. 306, Pages 456–57.

166   **O'Brien:** ACLU to FF, 7/15/1926, *id.* at Page 455.

166   **"We Submit":** BH, 10/26/1926, reprinted in NYW, 5/3/1927, at 14; LDB to FF, 10/29/1926, HBHS at 258.

166   **"very difficult" & "pamphlet":** FF to MDF, 11/18/1926, at 1, FFLC, Box 14.

166   **"the more" & "an incredibly" & "absolutely":** FF to MDF, 11/17/1926, at 2, *id.* See SGates to W. G. Gates, 12/25/1926, at 3 (sixty-page manuscript with FF).

166   **promised:** FFR, 214.

166   **bankruptcy:** Memorandum, 10/25/1924 & Bankruptcy Petition, 10/1924, Dorothy Whitney Straight Elmhirst Papers, Reel 16.

166   **plummeted:** David W. Levy, *Herbert Croly of* The New Republic, 272, 288 (1985) (circulation at 14,500 in 1925).

167   **"quasi-Oriental":** Bruce Bliven, *Five Million Words Later*, 176–77 (1970).

167   **heard:** ES to FF, 12/23/1926, FFHLS, Pt. III, Reel 36, Page 300.

167   **$50,000:** ES, *The Happy Profession*, 156 (1946).

167   **"if it didn't":** FFR, 214–15.

167   **South America & London:** ES to JCM, 3/23/1927, at 1, Sedgwick Papers, Carton 4.

167   **offered:** ES to FF, 1/4/1927, at 1–2, FFHLS, Pt. III, Reel 36, Pages 329–30.

167   **decided to break:** ES to FF, 1/7/1927, at 1–2, *id.*, Pages 331–32; FFR, 214–15.

167   **circulation:** American Newspaper Annual and Directory (N. W. Ayer & Son), 1928, at 466 (132,348 for *Atlantic Monthly*) & 766 (25,000 for *New Republic*).

167   **two editors:** Bliven, *Five Million Words Later*, 183; Robert Morss Lovett, *All Our Years*, 183–85 (1948); Levy, *Herbert Croly of* The New Republic, 285–87.

167   **did not seem interested:** Edmund Wilson to AMS Jr., 1964, in Edmund Wilson, *Letters on Literature and Politics 1912–1972*, at 197 (1977).

167   **March 1927 issue:** FF, "The Portentous Case of Sacco and Vanzetti: A Comprehensive Analysis of a Trial of Grave Importance," Atlantic Monthly, 3/1927, 409–32.

167   **month later:** FF, *The Case of Sacco and Vanzetti* (1927).

167   **privately acknowledged:** FF, Inscription to W. G. Gates, *The Case of Sacco and Vanzetti* (1927), Gates Family Papers ("this little book, in the making of which Sylvester had a partner's share, unfortunately not revealed on the title page"); FF, Inscription to SGates, *The Case of Sacco and Vanzetti* (1954), *id.* ("But for your massive help this book may never have appeared, certainly not as effectively"); Int. with Oliver Gates, 5/8/2016 (recalling concerns with European co-author as inviting conspiracy theories about a Communist plot); Sacco-Vanzetti entry, Dictionary of American Biography, Vol. 8, 279–80 (1935) (authored by Gates).

167   **$125:** FF to Shattuck, 4/27/1927, at 2.

167   **"The Sacco-Vanzetti":** FF, "Prefatory Note," *The Case of Sacco and Vanzetti*, iii.

168   **to delay:** ES to FF, 1/4/1927, at 1; FF to John Maguire, 1/20/1927, at 1–3, FFHLS, Pt. III, Reel 33, Pages 535–37.

168   **to wait:** WGT to FF, 2/10/1927, at 1–2, FFHLS, Pt. III, Reel 24, at 561–62.

168   **offered & "scientific":** FF, Memorandum, 2/12/1927, at 1–2, *id.*, Pages 563–64.

168   **agreed:** WGT to FF, 12/21/1927, at 1, *id.*, Reel 25, Page 854; FF to John Moors, 12/19/1927, *id.*, Reel 33, Page 607.

168   **"The purpose":** JCM to ES, circa 3/23/1927, at 1, Sedgwick Papers, Carton 4.

168   **"hot-headed" & "upright":** ES to JCM, 3/23/1927, at 2, *id.*

168   **"estimate" & "unsympathetic" & "faith":** JCM to ES, 3/26/1927, at 1–2, *id.*, Carton 7.

168   **inconspicuous hotel:** FWB to FF, 6/28/1960, at 1–2, FFLC, Box 123; FWB, "Chum Felix," at 38–39, *id.*, Box 257.

169   **April 5:** 5 SV Trial Tr. at 4880; Commonwealth v. Sacco, 259 Mass. 128, 139–41 (Apr. 5, 1927).

169   **not in Massachusetts:** John M. Maguire, "Memorandum for Professor Frankfurter," 5/4/1927, at 1–2, FFHLS, Pt. III, Reel 33, Pages 538–39.

169   **courtroom:** NYW, 4/10/1927, at 1–2; BH, 4/10/1927, at 1, B12; BET, 4/9/1927, at 1, 15.

169   **"As I":** 5 SV Trial Tr. at 4896.

169   **"I am suffering":** *Id.* at 4904.

169   **cried & "by the passage":** 5 SV Trial Tr. at 4904–5.

169   **whisper:** BH, 4/10/1927, at 1.

169   **"moved":** NYW, 4/10/1927, at 2.

170   **defense counsel:** WGT to Stoughton Bell, 4/11/1927, RPP, Pt. I, Reel 74, Page 492; FF to Bell, 4/9/1927, *id.*, Page 491.

170   **Storey:** Maguire to RP, 6/11/1927, FFHLS, Pt. III, Reel 33, Page 540; FF to Maguire, 6/12/1927, at 1, *id.* at Page 541.

170   **endowment:** FF to RP, 4/6/1927, RPP, Pt. I, Reel 74, Page 487.

170   **1917 letter:** BET, 4/27/1927, at 2; BET, 4/29/1927, at 13.

170   **"timidity" & "fear" & changed:** FF to LDB, 4/22/[1927], at 1, FFLC, Box 29. *See* RP Diary Entry, 2/28/1927, RPP, Pt. II, Reel 40, Page 31 (describing complaints about FF's article as "very annoying").

170   **"one-sided":** RP to Spencer Montgomery, 5/12/1927, FFHLS, Pt. III, Reel 24, Page 663.

170   **not to confront:** FF to RP, 8/23/1927, at 1–2, RPP, Reel 74, Pages 509–10.

170   **never recovered:** HBE, "Felix," *Felix Frankfurter: A Tribute*, 99 (recalling publication as end of their friendship); RP to Wallace Mendelson, 3/26/1963, RPP, Pt. I, Reel 52, Page 574 (questioning FF's account of Sacco and Vanzetti's trial as a product of the Red Scare).

170   **conscientious objectors:** Jeremy K. Kessler, "The Administrative Origins of Modern Civil Liberties Law," 114 Colum. L. Rev. 1083, 1108–11, 1126–27 (2014).

170   **"the most":** Francis S. Philbrick to FF, 5/3/1927, FFHLS, Pt. III, Reel 25, Page 661.

170–171 **"dangerous" & "the character" & "playing" & "the facts":** "Memorandum as to Genesis of Wigmore Article on Sacco-Vanzetti Case," n.d., FFHLS, Pt. III, Reel 24, Page 642.

171   **"I have" & "Professor":** NYT, 4/11/1927, at 8. *See* Webster Thayer to Wigmore, 12/8/1927, Wigmore Papers, Box 47, Folder 26 (thanking).

171   **Bureau of Investigation:** Wigmore to Chief, Bureau of Investigation, 3/31/1927, *id.*

171   **"the plausible" & "errors" & "libel" & "approved":** BET, 4/25/1927, at 1, 12.

171   **Harvard Square & *Herald* & "be temperate":** FFR, 215–16.

171 **bill of exceptions:** FF to JWM, 10/6/1927, at 1, FFHLS, Pt. III, Reel 34, Page 925.

171 **"I say":** BH, 4/26/1927, at 1.

172 **"the plausible" & "the contra-canonical":** BET, 5/10/1927, Pt. 2, at 3.

172 **"I shall" & "serious charges" & "his original":** BET, 5/11/1927, Pt. 2, at 3.

172 **Thompson published:** BET, 5/23/1927, in FFLC, Box 246.

172 **"very fortunate" & "brought":** ERB to FF, 5/16/1927, FFLC, Box 31.

172 **"Wigmore is":** FFR, 217. *See* Michael Parrish notes on FF's 1927 Diary, 11/22/1927 (noting lunch with Norman Hapgood who discussed "in detail" his two-and-a-half-hour interview with ALL and that "Hapgood took notes of this interview which I shall try to incorporate in this diary") (on file with author). The 1927 diary has been stolen.

172 **He declared:** "Minutes of Meeting of Citizens' Committee of Sacco-Vanzetti Case," 4/7/1927, at 1–7, FFHLS, Pt. III, Reel 33, Pages 960–67.

172 **clemency petition:** WGT & HBE to Governor Fuller, 5/4/1927, 5 SV Trial Tr. at 4907.

172 **new information:** "Minutes of Meeting of Citizens' Committee of Sacco-Vanzetti Case," 4/7/1927, at 3–6.

173 **"those bastards" & "those damn" & "Just wait" & "that long-haired":** Vanzetti to Governor Fuller, 5/3/1927, 5 SV Trial Tr. at 4924, 4926, 4928.

173 **"Did you":** 5 SV Trial Tr. at 5065, 5418–19. *See* CEW to Francis Russell, 3/31/1986, Francis Russell Papers, Folder "1986 March 1–31" (CEW's father "found Thayer the most indiscreet judge he had ever known well.").

173 **petitions:** FF to Bailey, 4/15/1927, ACLU Papers, Vol. 326, Page 8.

173 **pleaded:** FF to WL, 5/9/1927, at 1, WLP, Reel 10, Box 10, Folder 428b.

173 **"partisan" & "fanning":** NYHT, 5/6/1927, in FFLC, Box 246.

173 *New York Times*: Lester Markel to FF, 5/26/1927, FFHLS, Pt. III, Reel 33, Page 612; Markel to FF, 6/8/1927, *id.* at Page 615; FF to Markel, 6/9/1927, *id.* at Page 616; FF. Memorandum, 6/17/1927, *id.* at Page 613.

173 **"The Prejudices" & Kirby's:** NYW, 5/6/1927, at 14.

173 **"One courageous":** FF to WL, 7/13/1927, at 6, WLP, Reel 10, Box 10, Folder 428b.

173–174 **"hostility" & "unquestionably" & "not very" & "only":** *Id.* at 4–5.

174 **small white house:** MDF to Mrs. Moors, FF Wiretap Transcript, 8/20/1927, at 3–4, FFHLS, Pt. III, Reel 38, Pages 505–6.

174 **"instances" & "lack":** FF to WL, 7/13/1927, at 5. *See* WGT to FF, 6/26/1928, at 1–3, FFHLS, Pt. III, Reel 25, Pages 897–99; WGT to FF, 3/31/1928, at 1–3, *id.*, at 1001–3 (unfairness of proceedings).

174 **perjury:** FF, "Memorandum Concerning Testimony of Albert Bosco and Felice Guadagni before Lowell Committee," at 1–3, *id.*, Reel 36, Pages 445–47.

174 **"I still":** FF to WL, 7/13/1927, at 5.

174 **"situation" & "hope" & "chance" & "that his children":** EGE to FF, 7/12/1927, at 1, 3, FFHLS, Pt. III, Reel 33, Pages 346, 348.

174 **"Thompson" & "After all":** FF to HBE, 7/14/1927, at 1–2, FFHLS, Pt. III, Reel 24, Pages 871–72.

174 **"shirt-sleeves":** BG, 8/4/1927, at 21.

175 **unsupported:** FF to Norton, FF Wiretap Transcript, 8/9/1927, at 2–3, FFHLS, Pt. III, Reel 38, Pages 395–96.

175 **"monstrous":** FF to WL, 8/4/1927 tel., 8:00 a.m., WLP, Reel 10, Box 10, Folder 428b.

175 **authorized:** Attorney General Arthur K. Reading to Commissioner of Public Safety Gen. Alfred F. Foote, 8/1/1927, FFHLS, Pt. III, Reel 38, Page 392. Reading also autho-

rized wiretapping room 301 at the Hotel Bellevue in Boston, the headquarters of the Sacco-Vanzetti Defense Committee. Reading to Foote, 8/8/1927, *id.* at Page 393. Only the FF transcripts survive; state officials released them fifty years later. NYT, 9/13/1977, at 16; NYT, 9/15/1977, at 46.

175   **"hard headed" & " 'officious' ":** FF to Mears, FF Wiretap Transcript, 8/16/1927, at 8, FFHLS, Pt. III, Reel 38, Page 471.

175   **tipped & "Moscow":** FFR Transcript, 7/16/1957, at 277–78, FFLC, Box 206. The friend was Frank Buxton.

175   **$413.73:** FF to GJ, 8/20/1927, FFHLS, Pt. III, Reel 24, Page 603.

175   **mumbling:** NYW, 9/12/1927, at 4, in FFLC, Box 249.

175   **The Paris-born:** Springfield Republican, 8/5/1927 & BH, 8/5/1927, at 1, 3, in FFLC, Box 247; BG, 8/5/1927, at 6; BG, 6/7/1919, at 9; William A. Truslow, *Arthur D. Hill,* 6–9, 14–16 (1996).

175   **letter of endorsement:** FF to OWH, 3/28/1916, H-FF Corr., at 50; OWH to RP, 3/29/1916, at 1–2, RPP, Reel 7, Pages 939–40.

176   **"brothers":** HBE, "Felix," *Felix Frankfurter: A Tribute,* 93.

176   **phoned:** ADH Office Journal, 8/1/1927, Arthur Dehon Hill Papers, Box 17.

176   **assisted Thompson:** BG, 3/17/1923, at 1, 5.

176   **Somerset Club:** ADH Office Journal, 8/3/1927 & 8/4/1927.

176   **frog pond:** "Arthur Dehon Hill, 1869–1947," at 4, FFLC, Box 67.

176   **$5000:** FF to ADH, 8/8/1927 & ADH to FF, 10/6/1927 & ADH to FF, 10/8/1927, at 1–2 & ADH to FF, 10/20/1927, FFLC, Box 67.

176   **"whatever":** FF to JWM, FF Wiretap Transcript, 8/21/1927, at 11, FFHLS, Pt. III, Reel 38, Page 542.

176   **refused to collect:** ADH Office Journal, 10/6/1927.

176   **duty:** ADH to FF, 10/20/1927; BG, 12/2/1947 at 14.

176   **"The point" & "rooted":** FF to ADH, 8/6/1927, at 1–2, FFHLS, Pt. III, Reel 33, Pages 418–19.

176   **agreed:** ADH to WGT, 8/9/1927, *id.,* at Page 394.

176   **filed motions:** 5 SV Trial Tr. at 5428–30.

176   **chief justice & Thayer & Sanderson:** ADH Office Journal, 8/6/1927; *id.,* 8/8/1927.

176   **Thayer denied:** BG, 8/9/1927, at 1; 5 SV Trial Tr. at 5433–61.

176   **Sanderson:** BET, 8/6/1927, at 1, 11, in FFLC, Box 247.

176   **to Boston:** MDF to WGT, 10:15 a.m., FF Wiretap Transcript, 8/10/1927, at 1, FFHLS, Pt. III, Reel 38, Page 400.

177   **Around 1:30 p.m.:** BET, 8/10/1927, at 1, in FFLC, Box 247. *Cf.* BP, 8/11/1927, at 12 (1:00 p.m.).

177   **Leo Frank's case & black sharecroppers:** Frank v. Mangum, 237 U.S. 309, 345 (1915) (Holmes. J., dissenting); Moore v. Dempsey, 261 U.S. 86, 89–90 (1923).

177   **knew this day:** OWH to Lewis Einstein, 5/19/1927, H-E Letters, at 268.

177   **privately praised:** OWH to FF, 3/18/1927, H-FF Corr., at 211.

177   **Old Boston:** OWH to HJL, 4/25/1927, 2 HLL at 938.

177–178 **"whether" & "most differences" & "prejudice":** OWH to HJL, 8/18/1927, *id.* at 971.

178   **"I know":** BH, 8/11/1927, at 1.

178   **Jitney Players:** MDF to Thelma Irving, FF Wiretap Transcript, 8/10/1927, at 3–4, FFHLS, Pt. III, Reel 38, Pages 402–3.

178   **"You know":** FF to Michael Musmanno, *id.* at 6, Pages 405.

178–179 **Sacco's wife & protesters & granted:** BP, 8/11/1927, at 1, 12; BG, 8/11/1927, at 10.

179 **"for me" & "To a considerable":** FF to WGT, 8/15/1927, at 1, FFHLS, Pt. III, Reel 33, Page 975. *See* FF to WGT, 8/22/1927, at 1, *id.*, Page 973 (staying in background).

179 **unwilling:** FF to JWM, FF Wiretap Transcript, 8/11/1927, at 1–2, FFHLS, Pt. III, Reel 38, Pages 406–7.

179 **reporter:** FF to GJ, FF Wiretap Transcript, 8/14/1927, at 5, *id.*, Page 441.

179 **"did a job":** FF to MDF, FF Wiretap Transcript, 8/18/1927, *id.*, Pages 493–94.

179 **"Doubt":** NYW, 8/19/1927, at 12–13.

179 **"They thought":** FF to MDF, FF Wiretap Transcript, 8/18/1927, FFHLS, Pt. III, Reel 38, Pages 493–94.

179 **Harvard alumni:** FF to JWM, FF Wiretap Transcript, 8/20/1927, at 23, *id.*, Page 525; FF to Paul Kellogg, FF Wiretap Transcript, 8/20/1927, at 7–8, *id.*, Pages 508–9.

179 **wrote the president:** Magruder to ALL, 8/16/1927, ALLPP, Box 83, Folder 2; JWM to ALL, 8/20/1927, *id.*; The New Republic Editors to ALL, 8/17/1927, *id.*

179 **advertisement:** NYT, 8/19/1927, at 11.

179 **Connecticut:** FF to MDF, 8/19/1927, at 1A, 1B, 2, FFHLS, Pt. III, Reel 38, Pages 497–99.

180 **picked apart:** NYT, 8/20/1927, at 14.

180 **petition:** "Emergent!" 8/17/1927, FFHLS, Pt. III, Reel 34, Page 816.

180 **"hostility":** Alice Hamilton to FF, 8/23/1927, at 1, *id.*, Reel 36, Page 729.

180 **was busy:** ADH Office Journal, 8/17/1927.

180 **Gardner Jackson:** GJ COH, at 182–84.

180 **"He is" & not giving up:** FF to GJ, FF Wiretap Transcript, 8/21/1927, at 14, FFHLS, Pt. III, Reel 38, Page 545.

180 **state Supreme Judicial Court & federal trial judge:** 5 SV Trial Tr., at 5499–503, 5527–31, 5534–35.

180 **stay:** Handwritten order, 7/14/1927, Bard v. Chilton, NARA, U.S. Supreme Court Appellate Case Files, File Nos. 33017–18, RG 267, Box 8356.

181 **"invaded" & "voidable" & "Far stronger":** OWH Handwritten Denial, 8/20/1927, at 1–3, OWHP, Box 69, Folder 10 & 5 S-V Trial Tr. at 5516–17.

181 **"more":** OWH to Einstein, 8/14/1927, H-E Letters, at 272. *See* Brad Snyder, *The House of Truth,* 442–76 (2017).

181 **Jackson pleaded:** GJ to FF, FF Wiretap Transcript, 8/20/1927, at 15–16, FFHLS, Pt. III, Reel 38, Pages 517–18.

181 **Brandeis's wife:** EGE to Fred Moore, 8/21/1921, at 1, SVDC-BPL, Box 13, Folder 10; EGE to Moore, 9/4/1921, *id.*; "Mrs. Brandeis Aids Sacco Defense Fund," Boston American, n.d., 1921, *id.*; Moore to EGE, 9/6/1921, *id.*

181 **$50:** Sacco-Vanzetti Defense Committee Financial Statement, at 22, FFHLS, Pt. III, Reel 36, Page 366.

181 **$3500 & $4500:** "L.D.B. Cash 1926," LDBP-Brandeis U, Box 120; "L.D.B. Cash 1927," *id. See* LDB to FF, 6/2/1927, HBHS, at 296.

181 **"You &":** LDB to FF, 8/5/1927, HBHS, at 306.

181 **"may feel himself":** Hill to FF, FF Wiretap Transcript, 8/20/1927, at 17, FFHLS, Pt. III, Reel 38 Page 519.

181 **"a statement" & "I read it" & "I haven't":** FF to W. S. Jackson, FF Wiretap Transcript, 8/21/1927, at 3, *id.*, Page 531.

182 **phoned:** FF to ADH, FF Wiretap Transcript, 8/21/1927, at 4, FFHLS, Pt. III, Reel 38, Page 532.

182   knickers: BH, 8/22/1927, at 1.

182   "I know": Louis Bernheimer to FF, FF Wiretap Transcript, 8/21/1927, noon, at 8, FFHLS, Pt. III, Reel 38, Page 539.

182   "personal relations": BH, 8/22/1927, at 1.

182   Stone: FF to ADH, FF Wiretap Transcript, 8/21/1927, at 17, FFHLS, Pt. III, Reel 38, Page 519.

182   "skillfully" & "a vain": FF to Sherman, FF Wiretap Transcript, 8/21/1927, noon, at 6, id., Page 534.

182   fishing boat: BP, 8/22/1927, at 4; BH, 8/22/1927, at 1.

182   denied: 5 S-V Trial Tr. at 5517; BG, 8/23/1927, at 9.

182   "Nothing": BP, 8/23/1927, at 12.

182   Taft & Coolidge: Musmanno to WHT, 8/21/1927 tels. (2) & n.d. tel., WHTP, Series 3, Reel 293; WHT to Musmanno, 8/22/1927, id., Reel 294; WHT to Henry Taft, 8/22/1927, at 2–3, id.; Michael A. Musmanno, After Twelve Years, 347–54 (1939).

182   third time: OWH to Einstein, 9/11/1927, H-E Letters, at 273; BH, 8/23/1927 at 7; BP, 8/23/1927, at 12.

183   "it is" & "Now don't": FF to GJ, FF Wiretap Transcript, 8/21/1927, at 15, FFHLS, Pt. III, Reel 38, Page 546.

183   11:00 a.m. train: FF to GJ, FF Wiretap Transcript, 8/22/1927, at 1, id., Page 551.

183   sympathetic friend: FF to Nathan Greene, 6/10/1941, at 1, FFHLS, Pt. III, Reel 10, Page 663. Greene was the friend.

183   "Sacco gone": Matthew Josephson, "Profiles: Jurist-II," New Yorker, 12/7/1940, at 46.

183   Marion did not: FF to Matthew Josephson, 7/22/1942, Note 24, Brandeis U., Autograph Collection 334–442, Folders 378–79 (FF's handwritten comments on Josephson's article and describing story of MDF's collapse as "Nonsense—she was deeply moved but 'collapsed' nonsense" and, in MDF's handwriting, describing Josephson's account as "a highly colored and inaccurate story of what happened").

183   depressed: MDF to FF, 10/12/1927, at 13–15, FFLC, Box 14.

183   Salmon: FF to Thomas Reed Powell, 9/4/1927, at 2, Powell Papers, Box A, Folder "A1b Correspondence to 1929: F.-L."

183   "very sensitive": GJ, COH, at 295–97. See Richard Polenberg, Introduction, The Letters of Sacco and Vanzetti, xxi–xxv (2007).

183   rest: FF to Sister, FF Wiretap Transcript, 8/29/1927, at 1, FFHLS, Pt. III, Reel 38, Page 556.

183   "To the end": LDB to FF, 8/24/1927, HBHS, at 306.

183   endowment campaign: Bruce A. Kimball and Daniel R. Coquillette, The Intellectual Sword, 207–8 (2020) (arguing the law school's failed fund-raising efforts from 1925 to 1927 had nothing to do with FF's involvement with the Sacco-Vanzetti case).

183   Rosenwald responded: Julius Rosenwald to President and Fellows of Harvard College, 12/24/1927, Rosenwald Papers, Box 17, Folder 19; ALL to JWM, 12/2/1927, id., Box 36, Folder 7; JWM to ALL, 12/4/1927, id., Rosenwald to JWM, 12/6/1927, id.

183   refuted: FF to JWM, 10/15/1927, at 1–3, FFHLS, Pt. III, Reel 34, Pages 944–47.

183   absolved & "nothing": "Memorandum of SV Discussion at Overseers' Meeting Sept. 27," at 1–5, id., Pages 893–98. See JWM to RP, 9/3/1927, at 1–2, id., Pages 852–53; RP to JWM, 9/16/1927, at 1–2, id., Page 872–73; JWM to RP, 9/28/1927, id., Page 898.

184   "Lawrence": FF to Richard, 9/4/1927, FFHLS, Pt. III, Reel 34, Page 855 & FFR, 202.

184   Lowell's report: FF to Powell, 9/4/1927, at 2.

184   **"When people":** FF to RP, 8/23/1927, at 2, FFHLS, Pt. III, Reel 34, Page 823.

184   **fifth:** "1923 Grades," FFHLS, Pt. III, Reel 19, Page 637.

184   **U.S. attorney's:** Nathan Margold Resume, circa fall 1930, at 1, NAACP Papers, Pt. 3, Ser. A, Reel 1, Page 470.

184   **Pound:** Thomas Reed Powell, Memorandum, n.d., at 6–7, Powell Papers, Box A, Folder A9.

184   **Frankfurter knew:** FF Diary Entry, 2/21/1928, at 1–11, FFHLS, Pt. III, Reel 17, Pages 677–88.

184   **"simply":** FF to WL, 4/28/1933, WLP, Reel 62, Box 72, Folder 817.

184   **Landis's promotion:** DFF, 6/14/1928 & 6/19/1928 & 6/25/1928 & 6/27/1928 & 6/28/1928, at 124–31; RP Diary Entries 6/25/1928 & 6/26/1928, RPP, Pt. II, Reel 40, Pages 279–80; FF to Powell, 8/9/1928, Powell Papers, Box A, Folder A9 (blaming Pound).

184   **book:** FF & JML, *The Business of the Supreme Court* (1927).

184   **nearly twenty-five:** Brad Snyder, "The Judicial Genealogy (and Mythology) of John Roberts," 71 Ohio St. L. Rev. at 1193–95 (2010) (Friendly passing on Harvard professorship); Kimball & Coquillette, *Intellectual Sword*, 173–75 (anti-Semitism in Harvard Law School faculty hiring); *id.* at 314–15 (hiring of PAF and Milton Katz in 1940); Jerold S. Auerbach, *Rabbis and Lawyers*, 155 (1990).

185   **"revolted":** GJ to FF, 10/7/1927, at 1–3, FFHLS, Pt. III, Reel 33, Pages 493–95.

185   **"an obstruction" & "removed":** Michael Parrish Notes on FF 1927 Diary, 10/4/1927.

185   **Lowell committee's investigation:** WGT to FF, 4/21/1928, at 1–3, FFHLS, Pt. III, Reel 25, Pages 875–77; FF to WGT, 4/24/1928, *id.*, Page 878; WGT to FF, 6/26/1928, at 1–3, *id.*, Pages 896–98; WGT to FF, 6/29/1928, at 1–2, *id.*, Pages 905–6.

185   **Rockefeller & Rosenwald:** Rosenwald to Bernard Flexner, 11/23/1927, Rosenwald Papers, Box 36, Folder 7; Flexner to Rosenwald, 1/28/1929, *id.*; CCB to Elihu Root, 3/27/1928, FFHLS, Pt. III, Reel 33, Page 217.

185   **"in every":** FF to EGE, FF Wiretap Transcript, 9/21/1927, at 3, FFHLS, Pt. III, Reel 38, Page 623.

185   **One day:** FF to JWM, 11/3/1927, at 1, *id.*, Reel 34, Page 963.

185   **defending & correcting:** FF, Editor's Note, 22 Ill. L. Rev. 461, 465–68 (1927); FF, Letter to Editor, A.B.A. J. 18, no .3 (March 1932): 208–9.

185   **fair trial:** Joughin and Morgan, *The Legacy of Sacco and Vanzetti*, 367–68.

185   **Historians:** *Compare* William Young and David E. Kaiser, *Postmortem* (1985) (concluding they were innocent) *with* Francis Russell, *Tragedy in Dedham* (1962) and Francis Russell, *Sacco and Vanzetti* (1986) and Francis Russell, "Why I Changed My Mind about the Sacco-Vanzetti Case," American Heritage, 6–7/1986 (concluding Sacco was guilty); Letters to Editor, New York Review of Books, 5/29/1986.

186   **nighttime guard:** TGC to FF, 9/13/1927, at 1–2, OWHP, Reel 42, Page 22–23.

186   **abusive letters:** TNR, 9/14/1927, at 83; FF to JWM, FF Wiretap Transcript, 9/6/1927, at 5, FFHLS, Reel 38, Page 582.

186   **heroes:** FF, "Mr. Justice Holmes and the Constitution," 41 Harv. L. Rev. 121, 127–28 (1927).

186   **peculiar animosity:** FF to WGT, 8/22/1927, at 2.

CHAPTER 13: THE MOST USEFUL LAWYER IN THE UNITED STATES

187   **marriage:** FDR to FF, 12/24/1919, FDRL, Assistant Secretary of Navy Files, Box 48.

187   **failed vice-presidential:** FF to FDR, 1/4/1921, FFLC, Box 97.

187   **polio:** "Samuel Spencer Jr.'s Notes of FF, GC Conversation – Summer, 1947," at 4, FFHLS, Pt. III, Reel 15, Page 256 & FFR Transcript, 7/23/1957, at 328, Box 206. *See* FDR to Dr. William Egleston, 10/11/1924, FDRL, Family, Business, and Personal Papers (describing polio in August 1921).

187   **radio audience:** FDR to WL, 8/6/1928, WLP, Reel 27, Box 29, Folder 1061.

187   **"Happy Warrior" & twenty-five:** NYHT, 6/28/1928, at 1, 11; NYT, 6/28/1928, at 1.

188   **"It is highly":** FF to WL, 6/16/1928, at 2, WLP, Reel 10, Box 10, Folder 429a.

188   **faulted:** Herbert Hoover, *American Individualism* (1922).

188   **"I think":** FF to WL, 6/16/1928, at 2, WLP, Reel 10, Box 10, Folder 429a.

188   **corruption & water power:** FF to WL, 7/1/1928, at 1–3, WLP, Reel 10, Box 10, Folder 429b.

188   **agreed & crash:** WL to FF, 7/3/1928, at 1–2, *id.*

188   **"should be able":** LDB to FF, 6/15/1928, FFLC, Box 27 & LLDB, 333.

189   **"more harm":** FDR to James Bonbright, 3/11/1930, *F.D.R.: His Personal Letters, 1928–45*, Vol. 3, at 109–10 (Elliott Roosevelt, ed. 1950). *See* WL to Belle Moskowitz, 6/25/1928, WLP, Reel 20, Box 21, Folder 845 (encouraging Prohibition in telegram).

189   **"If Tammany" & "the Harding":** FF to WL, 7/26/1927, at 1, WLP, Reel 10, Box 10, Folder 429b.

189   **gambling:** WAW to Helen Mahin, 12/18/1928, WAWP, Box C-138.

189   **"rose above" & "the blind":** FF to WAW, 8/1/1928, *id.*, Box C-137 & FFLC, Box 163.

189   **"the deeply":** FF to WL, 8/2/1928, at 1–2, WLP, Reel 10, Box 10, Folder 429b.

189   **"snobs" & "fair":** FF to WL, 9/12/1928, *id.*

189   **"The people":** FF to Samuel Williston, 10/18/1928, at 2, FFLC, Box 163.

190   *World* **editorial:** NYW, 9/26/1928, at 12; FF to WL, 9/28/1928, WLP, Reel 10, Box 10, Folder 429b.

190   **"On his":** FF to Belle Moskowitz, 8/11/1928, at 1, FFLC, Box 163.

190   **Magruder:** FF to WL, 10/2/1928, WLP, Reel 10, Box 10, Folder 429b; FF to Henry Moskowitz, 10/17/1928, FFLC, Box 163.

190   **water power:** FF to Joseph Proskauer, 8/15/1928, FFLC, Box 163; FF to WL, 8/15/1928, WLP, Reel 10, Box 10, Folder 429b.

190   **"the power":** TNR, 10/17/1928, at 240–43.

190   **"the most":** HC to FF, 10/18/1928, FFLC, Box 163.

190   **"process" & "master" & "indispensable" & "give" & "achieved" & "into":** TNR, 10/31/1928, at 293–95.

191   **nominated Roosevelt:** FF to WL, 10/2/1928.

191   **head table:** BG, 10/13/1928, at 4.

191   **"occasion" & "As a Jew":** FF to FDR, 10/9/1928, R&FF, 38.

191   **750,000:** BG, 10/25/1928, at 1, 23.

191   **editorials:** HCrim, 10/18/1928; Monmouth Democrat (Freehold, NJ), 9/27/1928, at 2.

191   **cheered:** BG, 11/5/1927, at 1, 7

191   **"the people" & "Governor Smith":** Opening Remarks of FF at Symphony Hall, 11/4/1927, at 1, FFLC, Box 163.

191   **might win:** FF to WL, 11/2/1928, WLP, Reel 10, Box 10, Folder 429b.

191   **stomach cancer:** Emma Frankfurter Death Certificate, 1/13/1928, FFLC, Box 18; FF to MRC, n.d., MRCP, Box 5, Folder 10.

191   **"great friends":** Freedman Int. with FF, n.d., at 6, 8, FFHLS, Pt. III, Reel 40, Pages 273, 275.

191   **"[t]here was":** FF to Belle Moskowitz, 11/8/1928, at 1, FFLC, Box 163.

192 **"Certainly":** FF to WL, 11/8/1928, at 1–2, WLP, Reel 10, Box 10, Folder 429b.

192 **"consolation" & "conception":** FF to FDR, 11/8/1928, R&FF, 39.

192 **"It's refreshing":** NYT, 1/18/1929, at 1.

192 **Smith's left:** NYT, 5/15/1929, at 26. *See* FF, Book Review, Atlantic Monthly, 11/1929, in FFLC, Box 196; FF to WL, 5/15/1929, WLP, Box 10a, Folder 430.

192 **"power":** BG, 5/15/1929, at 1, 11.

192 **public utilities:** FDR to FF, 7/5/1929, R&FF, 41; FF to FDR, 7/13/1929, *id.* at 41–42.

192 **criminal justice:** FF to FDR, 7/29/1929, *id.* at 42–43; FDR to FF, 8/5/1929, *id.* at 43.

192 **"clearly":** LDB to HJL, 11/29/1929, YLS.

192 **Wickersham Commission's:** MMLP; MLP, Box 4, Folder 2; James D. Calder, "Between Brain and State," 96 Marq. L. Rev. 1036, 1065 (2013); David Wigdor, *Roscoe Pound,* 247–48 (1974).

193 **scholarship:** FF & Nathan Greene, "The Use of the Injunction in American Labor Controversies," Pt. I, 44 L.Q. Rev. 164 (1928); FF & Nathan Greene, "The Use of the Injunction in American Labor Controversies," Pt. II, 44 L.Q. Rev. 353 (1928); FF & Nathan Greene, "The Use of the Injunction in American Labor Controversies," Pt. III, 45 L.Q. Rev. 19 (1929); FF & Nathan Greene, "Labor Injunctions and Federal Legislation," 42 Harv. L. Rev. 766 (1929); FF & Nathan Greene, "Legislation Affecting Labor Injunctions," 38 Yale L.J. 879 (1929); FF & Nathan Greene, *The Labor Injunction* (1930).

193 **drafting new legislation:** FFLC, Box 160.

193 **"politics" & "expertise":** FF, *The Public and Its Government,* 161 (1930).

194 **Joseph P. Cotton:** HLS to FF, 5/23/1929, HLSP, Reel 78; FFR, 218–28.

194 **first choice:** FF to WL, 4/2/1930, WLP, Reel 10, Box 10a, Folder 431.

194 **" 'the boys' ":** FF to WL, 2/5/1930, at 1, *id.*

194 **Cotton told:** FF to Merlo J. Pusey, 11/14/1956, FFLC, Box 147. Cotton died in 1931.

194 **discredited:** Hoover to CEH, 2/19/1937 & 2/25/1937, CEHP, Reel 5; Merlo J. Pusey, *Charles Evans Hughes,* Vol. 2, 650–53; PAF, "Charles Evans Hughes as Chief Justice," 81 Harv. L. Rev. 4, 5–8 (1967); Merlo J. Pusey, "The Nomination of Charles Evans Hughes as Chief Justice," 1982 Yearbook, Supreme Court Historical Society, 95–99.

194 **"if am right":** FF to WL, 2/5/1930, at 1.

194 **made it difficult:** FF to LH, 2/4/1930, at 2, LHP, Box 104B, Folder 104-17.

195 **"yielded" & "universal approval":** FF to WL, 2/5/1930, at 1. *See* NYW, 2/5/1930, at 10.

195 **"no petty":** NYW, 2/14/1930, at 10.

195 **"mere sniping":** FF to WL, 2/19/1930, WLP, Reel 10, Box 10a, Folder 431.

195 **Several senators:** 71 Cong. Rec. 3372–73 (1930) (Senator Norris) & *id.* at 3448–53 (Sen. Borah & Sen. Wheeler); Pusey, *Charles Evans Hughes,* Vol. 2, 654–62.

195 **52–26:** 71 Cong. Rec. 3591 (1930).

195 **"one of the healthiest" & "Charles":** FF to CCB, 2/19/1930, at 1–2, FFLC, Box 33.

195 **"Senate approval":** NYT, 3/22/1930, at 1.

195 **"just a":** FF to LH, 3/22/1930, at 1, LHP, Box 104B, Folder 104-18.

195 **"I think":** FF to WL, 4/1/1930, at 2, WLP, Reel 10, Box 10a, Folder 431.

196 **William Green:** FFLC, Box 59; UMW v. Red Jacket Consol. Coal & Coke Co., 18 F.2d 839 (4th Cir. 1927); Peter Graham Fish, "*Red Jacket* Revisited," Law and History Review 5 (1987): 51–104.

196 **"strengthen":** Parker Confirmation Hearings at 28.

196 **National Legal Committee:** FF to Walter White, 11/6/1929, FFLC, Box 111; Arthur Spingarn to FF, 11/12/1929, *id.*; White to FF, 11/12/1929, *id.*

196   **"the participation"**: Parker Confirmation Hearings at 74–75 (quoting Greensboro Daily News, 4/19/1920).

196   **White sent:** White Statement, 4/5/1930, FFLC, Box 111; White to FF, 4/23/1930 tel., *id.*

196   **"I know"**: FF to White, 4/24/1930, *id.*

196   **"the times"**: NYW, 4/15/1930, at 14.

196   **"threatens"**: FF to WL, 5/3/1930, at 1–2, WLP, Reel 10, Box 10a, Folder 431. *See* NYW, 5/6/1930, at 12.

196   **41–39:** 71 Cong. Rec. 8487 (1930).

197   **credited:** FF to WL, 5/8/1930, WLP, Reel 10, Box 10a, Folder 431.

197   **"In every"**: FF to LDB, 5/10/1930, at 1, FFLC, Box 29.

197   **"Who says"**: FF to OJR, 5/10/1930, OJRP, Box 1, Vol. 1.

197   **to educate:** FF to ML, 2/19/1930, at 1–2, FFLC, Box 183.

197   **"In theory"**: FF, "The United States Supreme Court Molding the Constitution," Current History, 5/1930, 240, in FFLC, Box 196. *See* FF, "The Place of the Supreme Court in Our Government," 5/13/1930, National League of Women Voters, *id.*; FF, "The Supreme Court and Public Opinion," Forum (June 1930): 329–34, *id.*

197   **Holmes's jurisprudence:** FF, *The Public and Its* Government, 76–77, 80 (1930).

197   **Hand believed:** LH to FF, 2/6/1930, at 3, LHP, Box 104B, Folder 104-17.

197   **unwritten rule & reading:** AH to FF, 12/13/1929, at 1-5, FFLC, Box 145; AH Int. in Katie Louchheim, ed., *The Making of the New Deal*, 25–26 (1983).

198   **"intended"**: Baldwin v. Missouri, 281 U.S. 586, 595 (1930) (Holmes, J., dissenting). *See* Farmers' Loan & Trust Co. v. Minnesota, 280 U.S. 204, 216 (1930) (Holmes, J., dissenting); Safe Deposit & Trust Co. v. Virginia, 280 U.S. 83, 96 (1929) (Holmes, J., dissenting).

198   **"ought"**: LDB to FF, 5/26/1930, HBHS at 429.

198   **"everything"**: FF to WL, 5/29/1930, WLP, Reel 10, Box 10a, Folder 431a.

198   **portrait:** OWH to Frederick Pollock, 6/9/1930, 2 H-P Letters at 268; OWH to FF, 5/29/1930, H-FF Corr., at 256; FF to LH, 6/6/1930, LHP, Box 104B, Folder 104-19.

198   **energetic:** FF to WL, 6/16/1930, WLP, Reel 10, Box 10a, Folder 431a.

198   **commencement:** OWH to HJL, 6/21/1930, 2 HLL at 1260; OWH to HJL, 6/26/1930, *id.* at 1263.

198   **"enchanted" & "a beautiful"**: OWH to Dear Friend, 8/7/1930, OWHP, Reel 27, Page 419, Box 36, Folder 28.

198   **"write on!"**: FF to OWH, 2/6/1931, H-FF Corr., at 261.

198   **published & edited:** FF, "The Early Writing of O.W. Holmes, Jr.," 44 Harv. L. Rev. 717 (1931); *Mr. Justice Holmes* (FF, ed. 1931).

198   **"writers"**: George W. Wickersham, Review of *Mr. Justice Holmes*, A.B.A. J. 17, no. 9 (September 1931): 613.

198   **"to the same"**: FF, Letter to the Editor, 9/8/1931, A.B.A. J., 17, no. 11 (November 1931): 776.

198–199 **"a Holmes" & "vanity"**: FF to AMS Sr., 3/20/1931, FFLC, Box 101.

199   **"Holmes is"**: FF to MDF, 3/7/1931, FFLC, Box 14.

199   **real liberal leader:** *Mr. Justice Brandeis* (FF, ed. 1932); New State Ice Co. v. Liebmann, 285 U.S. 262, 311 (1932) (Brandeis, J., dissenting) (states as laboratories); Myers v. United States, 272 U.S. 52, 240 (1926) (Brandeis, J., dissenting) (presidential power); Olmstead v. United States, 277 U.S. 438, 471 (1928) (Brandeis, J., dissenting) (wiretapping).

199 **"a moral":** FF, "Mr. Justice Brandeis and the Constitution," 45 Harv. L. Rev. 33, 105 (1931).

199 **states & avoiding:** *Id.* at 44–58, 79–87.

199 **"It is usually":** *Id.* at 87 (quoting Washington v. Dawson & Co., 264 U.S. 219, 235–39 (1924)).

199 **Arab uprisings:** LDB to FF, 9/20/1929, at HBHS, at 385–86; LDB to FF, 10/10/1929, *id.* at 393–94; LDB to FF, 10/29/1930, *id.* at 438–40.

199 **"Arab-Jewish":** FF, Letter to the editor, *Atlantic Monthly*, 10/1930, at 49–52, in FFLC, Box 196.

199 **speech & articles:** FF, "Revelation in Rooted Prejudice," New Palestine, 11/7/1930, at 127, 138, in, *id.*; NYHT, 12/14/1930, in, *id.*; FF, "The Palestine Situation Restated," Foreign Affairs, 4/1931, at 3–28, in *id.*

200 **"more far-reaching":** FF to WL, 6/22/1930, R&FF, 45.

200 **"I know":** FF to WL, 10/23/1930, *id.* at 52.

200 **accepted:** FF to FDR, 6/13/1931, R&FF, 55.

200 **reneged:** FF to FDR, 6/19/1931 tel., *id.* at 56.

200 **"on tap":** FF, *The Public and Its Government*, 161.

200 **"not the least":** FF to FDR, 6/19/1931 tel., *id.* at 56.

200 **"unprepared":** FF to WL, 1/14/1932, WLP, Reel 61, Box 72, Folder 816.

200 **not going well:** LDB to FF, 9/16/1931, HBHS, at 464; LDB to FF, 9/28/1931, *id.* at 466-67; LDB to FF, 10/5/1931, *id.* at 468; LDB to FF, 10/25/1931, *id.* at 469; LDB to FF, 12/27/1931, *id.* at 472.

200 **it was time:** LDB to FF, 1/10/1932, *id.* at 472; Chapman Rose Int. with Monagan, 9/17/1980, at 12, Monagan Papers, Box 1, Folder 1-14.

201 **"the gallantest":** FF to CCB, 1/20/1932, FFLC, Box 33.

201 **Borah:** SSW to FF, 1/19/1932, 1–4, SSWP, Box 108, Folder 19 & Andrew Kaufman Papers, Box 15, Folder 43.

201 **offer his resignation:** HFS to George Hellman, 11/30/1939, at 1, HFSP, Box 16.

201 **William D. Mitchell:** Van Devanter to Mrs. John W. Lacey, 1/11/1932, at 2–3, Van Devanter Papers, Box 16, Book 45.

201 **"another Parker":** FF to CCB, 1/20/1932.

201 **two critiques:** HFS to FF, 2/9/1932, FFLC, Box 105.

201 **"proves":** FF to HFS, 2/5/1932, *id.* *See* "Opinions of Judge Phillips," n.d., FFLC, Box 134.

202 **"dreadful":** FF to SSW, 2/8/1932, at 2, SSWP, Box 108, Folder 109.

202 **"nothing" & "an old-fashioned" & "strengthening":** FF to HLS, 2/9/1932, FFLC, Box 103.

202 **Cotton as under secretary:** HLS to FF, 5/23/1929, HLSP, Reel 78; FF to HLS, 5/25/1929, *id.*

202 **Bundy & Feis:** HLS to FF, 4/9/1931, HLSP, Reel 81; FF to HLS, 4/13/1931, *id.*; HLS to FF, 4/16/1931, *id.*; HLS to FF, 5/14/1931, *id.*; FF to HLS, 5/15/1931, *id.* & FFLC, Box 103.

202 **meeting:** HLSD, 1/16/1932, Vol. 20, Reel 4, Page 58.

202 **"*the* only" & "the geographic" & "would evaporate" & "what counts":** FF to HLS, 2/10/1932, at 1–2, FFLC, Box 103.

202 **"good candidates":** HLSD, 1/19/1932, at 3, Vol. 20, Reel 4, at Page 72.

202 **"safest bet":** HLSD, 1/22/1932, at 3, *id.* at Page 86.

202 **"first choice":** HLS to FF, 2/12/1932, FFLC, Box 103.

202 **Borah had not:** HLSD, 2/14/1932, at 3, Vol. 20, Reel 4, Page 171.

202 **"never":** FF to Hoover, 2/16/1932, FFLC, Box 67.

202 **"appointed Cardozo":** TNR, 2/24/1932, at 28. *See* Andrew L. Kaufman, *Cardozo*, 455–71

(1998); Andrew L. Kaufman, "Cardozo's Appointment to the Supreme Court," 1 Cardozo L. Rev. 23 (1979).

203   **Gerry Henderson:** Eugene Meyer COH, Vol. I, Pt. 3, at 371–72.

203   **three years:** FF to HJF, 4/30/1931, at 1–2, FFLC, Box 56; LDB to FF, 5/2/1931, HBHS, at 457.

203   **elected:** HJF to FF, 5/7/1931, *id.*; HJF to RP, 5/6/1931, *id.*

203   **turned it down:** HJF to FF, 2/16/1932, FFLC, Box 56; FF to HJF, 2/17/1932, *id.*; LDB to FF, 2/19/1932, HBHS, 477.

203   **"sinking ship":** HJF Int. by Lewis Paper, 12/27/1980, at 6, Paper Papers, Box 1, Folder 1–3; HJF to FF, 3/14/1959, HJFP, Box 191, Folder 191–13. *See* Brad Snyder, "The Judicial Genealogy (and Mythology) of John Roberts," 71 Ohio St. L.J. 1195–96 (2010).

203   **vouched:** Meyer to FF, 5/16/1932, TGCP, Box 198; FF to TGC, 6/16/1932, at 1, *id.*

203   **yearned:** TGC to FF, 11/18/1931, TGCP, Box 46.

204   **Sears Prize:** "List of Sears Prize Winners," at 1, TGCP, Box 135

204   **president:** PAF, "Henry M. Hart, Jr.: In Memoriam," 82 Harv. L. Rev. 1895, 1895–96 (1969).

204   **three installments:** FF & HMH, "Business of Supreme Court at October Term, 1932," 47 Harv. L. Rev. 245 (1933); FF & HMH, "Business of Supreme Court at October Term, 1933," 48 Harv. L. Rev. 260 (1934); FF & HMH, "Business of Supreme Court at October Term, 1934," 49 Harv. L. Rev. 68 (1935).

204   **high praise:** LDB to FF, 2/24/1931, HBHS, at 455; LDB to FF, 9/18/1931, *id.* at 465; LDB to FF, 1/21/1932, *id.* at 473.

204   **"interesting work":** PAF to HMH, 1/7/1932, at 2, HMHP, Box 3, Folder 3-4.

204   **academia & public service:** LDB to FF, 3/17/1933, HBHS, at 515; LDB to FF, 3/22/1933, *id.*

CHAPTER 14: FROM THE OUTSIDE

205   **"a highly" & "too eager" & "an excessively" & "is no tribune":** NYHT, 1/8/1932, at 19.

205   **"deep" & "sweet":** FF to SSW, 2/6/1932 at 1, FFLC Box 164.

205   **no problem:** FF to ES, 2/10/1932, at 1, *id.*

206   **"the most sought-after":** FF, "Extract from a letter to a Friend," 1/9/1932, at 1–2, *id.*

206   **"Baker, I am":** *Id.* at 2.

206   **"pontificate" & "lacks blood":** FF to ES, 2/10/1932, at 2.

206   **"apoplectic" & "lack of courage":** FF to CCB, 5/20/1932, FFLC, Box 33.

206   **"Out of":** FF to Proskauer, 2/22/1932 tel., FFLC, Box 164.

206–207 **"the logical":** NYHT, 2/12/1932, at 13.

207   **"limitations" & "general":** FF to Belle Moskowitz, 3/17/1932, at 1–2, FFLC, Box 164.

207   **dark-horse candidate:** NYHT, 4/28/1932, at 7; NYHT, 5/6/1932, at 19.

207   **fretted:** FF to CCB, 6/29/1932, FFLC, Box 118.

207   **at the convention:** Douglas B. Craig, *Progressives at War*, 315–22 (2013).

207   **Since January:** BG, 1/17/1932, at A2.

207   **several friends:** JWM to FF, 6/21/1932, extract, FFLC, Box 84; JWM to FF, 6/23/1932, *id.*

207   **faculty club:** FF to LH, 6/25/1932, at 1, LHP, Box 104B, Folder 104-23.

208   **"would cut off":** BG, 6/23/1932, at 1, 6.

208   **"I see":** NYT, 6/23/1932, at 23.

208   **"the greatest":** BG, 6/23/1932, at 1, 6.

208   **Anderson & Baker:** BG, 6/30/1932, at 32.

208 **law faculty:** BG, 7/2/1932, at 12.

208 **"the judicial temperament":** NYT, 6/26/1932, at E1.

208 **congratulatory letters:** FFLC, Boxes 118–19.

208 **decline:** LDB to FF, 6/23/1932, HBHS, 491; LDB to FF, 6/26/1932, *id.* at 492.

208 **to accept:** JWM to WGT, 6/27/1932, FFLC, Box 81.

208 **"[y]our" & "the long-term":** FF to Ely, 6/29/1932, at 1, FFLC, Box 53.

208 **hand-deliver:** "Memorandum of Conversation between Mr. Bradford, Governor Ely's Secretary, and Miss Cummings, Mr. Frankfurter's secretary," 6/29/1932, FFLC, Box 206. The letter was backdated by a day.

208 **in person:** FF, Memorandum, 7/2/1932, FFLC, Box 52.

208 **"that's where":** "Memorandum of telephone conversation between Felix Frankfurter and Governor Roosevelt," 7/2/1932, R&FF, 74. The conversation suggests it occurred after FDR landed in Chicago.

208 **reach out:** "Memorandum of Telephone conversation between Felix Frankfurter and Governor Roosevelt," 7/2/1932, R&FF, at 74–75.

209 **"I pledge":** NYT, 7/3/1932, at 8.

209 **apartment:** FF, "Memorandum of interview between Governor Ely and Felix Frankfurter," 7/6/1932, at 1–7, FFLC, Box 206.

209 **summarized & reconsidered:** FF, "Memorandum of conversation with Chapman Rose, secretary to Mr. Justice Holmes," 7/8/1932, *id. See* Chapman Rose to FF, 6/30/1932, at 2–4, FFLC, Box 98 (including FF note, 7/7/1932); Rose to FF, 7/8/1932, *id.*

209 **"never":** FF, "Memorandum of interview between Governor Ely and Frankfurter," 7/12/1932, at 1, FFLC, Box 206.

209 **"the greatest":** WOD to FF, 8/7/1932, FFLC, Box 119.

209 **"much more" & "one of":** FF to FDR, 7/22/1928, R&FF, 78.

209 **James:** FDR to FF, 7/14/1932, *id.* at 76–77.

209 **pressed:** FF to SIR, 7/11/1932, FFLC, Box 164; FF to Frances Perkins, 7/18/1932, *id.*

210 **"You see":** FF to Dewson, 7/18/1932, *id.*

210 **invited:** FDR to FF, 7/28/1928 tel., *id.*

210 **"astounding" & "one of":** FF to LDB, 8/7/1932, FFLC, Box 29.

210 **"You stimulate":** FDR to FF, 8/7/1932, at 1, R&FF, at 82.

210 **"the facts":** FF to FDR, 8/5/1932, R&FF, at 80.

210 **private line:** FDR to FF, 8/7/1932, *id.* at 82 & FFLC, Box 97 (handwritten note).

210 **"Warm":** FF to FDR, 9/2/1932 tel., R&FF, 85.

210 **"No one":** NYT, 9/7/1932, at 18.

210 **"very severe":** NYHT, 10/7/1932, at 21.

211 **"there is":** SSW to FF, 9/8/1932, at 1, FFLC, Box 164.

211 **"with an easy" & "courageous" & "a choice" & "an original":** FF to SSW, 9/14/1932, at 1–3, *id.*

211 **water-power:** Judson King, "Power Records of Hoover and Roosevelt," 9/9/1932, FFLC, Box 164; NYT, 9/12/1932, at 3.

211 **George W. Norris:** WP, 9/26/1932, at 1.

211 **suggested:** FF to SIR, 9/29/1932, FFLC, Box 164; SIR to FF, 10/4/1932, *id.*

211 **advised:** FF to FDR, 10/7/1932 tel. R&FF, 88; FF to FDR, 10/12/1932, *id.* at 88–89; FF to FDR, 10/12/1932, tel., *id.*; FF to FDR, 10/20/1932 tel., *id.* at 90; FDR to FF, 10/25/1932 tel., *id.* at 90–91.

212   **Albany:** NYT, 10/5/1932, at 17.

212   **Boston speech:** FF to Herbert Bayard Swope, 10/6/1932, FFLC, Box 164; Swope to FF, 10/7/1932, *id.*

212   **lunch:** FF to MDF, 10/2/1924, at 2–3, FFLC, Box 14.

212   **newspapers:** "Statement of Professor Felix Frankfurter," n.d., FFLC, Box 164.

212   **"storm" & "The best":** HCrim, 10/15/1932, at 1, 3 in FFLC, Box 197.

212   **"extreme" & "be put":** BG, 10/24/1932, at 12.

212   **"a little boy" & "smiles":** "Pledges of Hoover Not Fulfilled," n.d., FFLC, Box 164 (FF handwritten comments).

212   **advising Smith's aides:** FF to Belle Moskowitz, 10/14/1932, FFLC, Box 164.

212   **train:** FF to Smith, 10/24/1924, *id.*; FF to Swope, 10/26/1932 tel., *id.*

212   **special car:** BG, 10/27/1932, at 10.

212   **"unqualified" & "the salvation":** BG, 10/28/1932, at 1, 32, 33.

212   **"at his" & "the outpouring":** FF to WL, 10/28/1932, R&FF, 92.

213   **Groton School:** Springfield Republican, 10/31/1932, at 1.

213   **"As progressives":** BG, 10/31/1932, at 13.

213   **"Governor Roosevelt":** EGE, "Felix Frankfurter: Citizens, Teacher, Friend," Typescript, at 6–7 & Springfield Republican, 1/15/1933, EGEP, Reel 9.

213   **stops:** BP, 10/31/1932, at 1.

213   **hotel room & attack lines:** Raymond Moley, *After Seven Years*, 63–64 (1939). *See* FDR Speech, Boston Arena, 10/31/1931, FDRL, MSF, Series 1, Box 10, No. 582.

213   **15,000:** BG, 11/1/1932, at 1, 22.

213   **Roosevelt's request:** Freedman, R&FF, 93.

213   **"any awareness" & "well be":** FF, "Campaign Speech over W.B.J.," 11/5/1932, at 3, 5, FFLC, Box 197.

213   **"Your campaign":** FF to FDR, 11/7/1932 tel., R&FF, 93.

214   **"The end":** FF to FDR, 11/10/1932, *id.*

214   **Oxford:** NYT, 11/16/1932, at 19.

214   **attorney general:** BaltSun, 12/15/1932, at 1; NYT, 12/23/1932, at 8.

214   **difficult transition:** FF, Memorandum, 1/4/1933, R&FF, 101–3.

214   **unharmed:** NYT, 2/17/1933, at 1 (FDR's account); BaltSun, 2/16/1933, at 2 (reporter's account); NYHT, 2/16/1933, at 1; CT, 2/16/1933, at 1; NYT, 2/16/1933, at 1.

214   **Relieved:** FF to FDR, 2/19/1933, R&FF, 107–8.

214   **"You have":** FF to FDR, 2/23/1933, *id.* at 108.

214   **"godspeed":** FF to FDR, 3/1/1933, *id.* at 109.

214   **cloudy:** NYT, 3/5/1933, at 1; WP, 3/5/1933, at 1.

214   **"the only thing":** FDR, Inaugural Address, 3/4/1933, at 1, FDRL, MSF, Box 13, No. 610. *See* SIR, *Working with Roosevelt* 89–91 (1952) (describing the last-minute insertion of the "fear itself" paragraph into FDR's inaugural address).

214   **"I shall":** FDR to FF, 3/7/1933, R&FF, 109.

214   **"lose":** RCM Diary, 2/8/1933, RCMP, Box 1. *See* RCM Calendar, *id.* (showing meeting with Walsh with FF on 2/7–8/1933) & in Moley, *After Seven Years*, 146–47 (photo insert).

215   **"I am at a better" & "nose" & "fizz water" & "Young fellow":** "Memorandum by Frankfurter of a visit with Roosevelt on March 8, 1933, when the President asked Frankfurter to become Solicitor General," 3/15/1933, R&FF, 110.

215   **ambassador:** Donald Hiss Int. by Katie Louchheim, 11/14/1981, Tape I, Side I, Pages 7–10, in Louchheim Papers, Box 72, Folder 9 & "Recollection of Donald Hiss," in *The Making*

of the New Deal, 37 (Katie Louchheim, ed. 1983). *See* FFR, 242 (recalling the champagne had been produced by the wife of the justice's nephew Edward Holmes and that she said it was from the French embassy); Brad Snyder, *The House of Truth,* 561–64 (2017).

215 **"Frank" & "care[d]":** "Memorandum by Frankfurter of a visit with Roosevelt on March 8, 1933, when the President asked Frankfurter to become Solicitor General," 3/15/1933, R&FF, 111.

215 **"for all":** *Id.*

216 **"It is my" & "it just" & "of more":** *Id.* at 111–12.

216 **"I am" & "I can't":** *Id.* at 112.

216 **"a job" & "to think":** *Id.* at 112–13.

216 **5:30:** *Id.* at 113–14; FFR, 241–42.

216 **did not believe:** Donald Hiss Int. by Monagan, 10/13/1979, Pt. 2, at 45 & John S. Monagan, *The Grand Panjandrum,* 1–2 (1988).

216 **alpaca coat:** Donald Hiss Int. in Louchheim, ed., *The Making of the New Deal,* 37.

216–217 **Treasury Department & Thacher:** "Memorandum by Frankfurter of a visit with Roosevelt on March 8, 1933, when the President asked Frankfurter to become Solicitor General," 3/15/1933, R&FF, 113–14; FFR, 241–42.

217 **Brandeis & Thacher & "absurd" & "unwise":** "Memorandum by Frankfurter of a visit with Roosevelt on March 8, 1933, when the President asked Frankfurter to become Solicitor General," 3/15/1933, R&FF, 114.

217 **Marion:** *Id.*

217 **politics had consumed:** FF to MDF, 10/20/1932, at 1, FFLC, Box 14.

217 **"I would never":** MDF to FF, 7/24/1932, at 3–4, *id.*

217 **hospitalized:** LDB to FF, 9/29/1932, HBHS, at 500–501.

217 **"hard times":** FF to MDF, 2/15/1933, at 1, FFLC, Box 14.

217 **"a hectic":** FF to MDF, 12/17/1932, at 1, *id.*

217–218 **"how deeply" & "I can" & "I should":** FF to FDR, 3/14/1933, R&FF, 120.

218 **"You are":** FDR to FF, 4/5/1933, R&FF, 124. *See* FF to FDR, 4/14/1933, *id.* at 126 (treasuring the comment).

CHAPTER 15: THE HAPPY HOT DOGS

219 **clashed & made amends:** RCM to FF, 12/8/1930, FFLC, Box 84; RCM Diary, 1/29/1933, RCMP, Box 1; FF Reminisces Transcript 7/23/1957, at 331–32, FFLC, Box 206.

219 **"stark" & "eye to eye":** FF to AMS Jr., 6/18/1963, at 1–2, FFLC, Box 101. *See* Nelson L. Dawson, *Louis D. Brandeis, Felix Frankfurter, and the New Deal,* 21–23 (1980) (doubting Frankfurter's late-in-life protest).

219 **"bubbling":** RCM, *After Seven Years,* 179–80 (1939). *See* FF to CCB, 2/24/1933, at 1, CCBP, Box 4, Folder 4-11 (describing RCM as "not of a jealous disposition" and "an excellent influence"); FF to LDB, 2/8/1934?, at 2, FFLC, Box 29 (describing AAB & Tugwell as "greedy for power").

219 **new federal securities:** FDR, Message to Congress, 3/29/1933, *The Public Papers and Addresses of Franklin D. Roosevelt,* Vol. 2, 94 (1938).

219 **April 5:** DFF, 5/8/1933, at 138 (phone message—mistakenly referred to as Thursday 4/6).

220 **rooms for three:** FF to RCM, 4/5/1933 tel., RCMP, Box 68, Folder 6; RCM, *The First New Deal,* 312 (1966). *See* Michael E. Parrish, *Securities Regulation and the New Deal,* 62–65 (1970); Joel Seligman, *The Transformation of Wall Street,* 57–72 (1982).

220 **blue sky laws:** JML COH, 159–62; JML, "The Legislative History of the Securities Act," 28 G.W. L. Rev. 29, 33 (1959).

220 **In March:** FF to JML, 3/27/1933, at 1–2, FFLC, Box 182; Donald A. Ritchie, *James M. Landis*, 43–61 (1980).

220 **Muncie, Indiana:** BVC Int. by JA, 8/5/1938, at 1–2 JSAP, Box 93, Folder 3; Jerome Frank, "Ben Cohen," 11/7/1945, at 3–4, TGCP, Box 120; William Lasser, *Benjamin V. Cohen*, 7–24, 47–64 (2008).

220 **state minimum-wage:** FF to BVC, 11/5/1923, at 1, BVCP, Box 8.

220 **"two thin":** RCM, *After Seven Years*, 180–81. *See* JML, "The Legislative History of the Securities Act," 28 G.W. L. Rev. at 34–35; RCM Diary, 4/7/1933, RCMP, Box 1.

221 **6:30 p.m.:** FDR Day by Day, 4/9/1933.

221 **"Everyone" & "hopeful" & "I'm so":** FF to MDF, 4/8/1933, at 1–3, FFLC, Box 14.

221 **he testified:** DFF, 5/8/1933, at 139–40; JML COH, 161; JML, "The Legislative History of the Securities Act," 28 G.W. L. Rev. at 36.

221 **"watertight" & "Be assured":** FF to RCM, 4/12/1933 tel., RCMP, Box 68, Folder 6.

221 **peacemaker:** TGC, "Rendezvous with Democracy," Folio for Chapter 4-7-4-8.

221 **reassure Cohen:** FF to RCM, 4/12/1933, RCMP, Box 68, Folder 6; FF to RCM, 4/15/1933 tel., *id.*; FF to BVC, 4/14/1933 tel., FFLC, Box 182; FF to TGC, 4/17/1933, TGCP, Box 198.

221 **must specify:** FF to FDR, 4/14/1933 tel., FFLC, Box 182; FF to Rayburn, 4/14/1933 tel., *id.*

221 **"we are going":** Rayburn to FF, 4/18/1933, *id.*

221 **committee report:** FF to Rayburn, 4/24/1933, *id.*; FF to RCM, 4/27/1933 tel., *id.*

221 **"partly innocuous":** FF to RCM, 4/28/1933 tel., at 1, *id.*

221 **avoid unconstitutional:** FF to Rayburn, 5/1/1933, *id.*

221 **reminded:** FF to RCM, 5/10/1933 tel. *id.*

221 **relied on:** FF to Meyer, 5/10/1933 tel., *id.*

221 **encouraged:** FF to FDR, 5/10/1933 tel., *id.*

222 **thanked:** 77 Cong. Rec. 2916 (1933).

222 **"so readily":** BVC to JML, 5/5/1933, at 1, JMLP-LC, Box 6.

222 **"You are giving":** FF, Memorandum, 5/11/1933, at 1, JMLP-LC, Box 7.

222 **Pound:** JML, Memorandum, 5/10/1933, *id.*

222 **tipped off & informed Pound:** FF Diary Entry, 5/8/1933, DFF, at 138–39. Grenville Clark tipped off FF about ALL.

222 **"flexible" & "arbiters" & "ultimate":** FF, "Social Issues before the Supreme Court," Yale Review (Spring 1933): 476, 480, 487, 495 in FFLC, Box 197.

222 *Congressional Record:* 73 Cong. Rec. 1413–16 (1933).

222 **incorporated the ideas:** BG, 5/15/1933 at 18; LH & FF, "How Far Is a Judge Free in Rendering a Decision?" 5/14/1933, FFLC, Box 197.

222 **That morning:** FDR Day by Day, 5/27/1933.

222 **"some elementary":** FDR Statement, 5/27/1933, FFLC, Box 135 (FF's handwritten note on authorship).

223 **"a really":** FF to Bernard Flexner, 5/23/1933, at 1, Flexner Papers, Box 4.

223 **leadership:** FF to FDR, 5/23/1933 tel., R&FF, 133; FF to FDR, 5/24/1933, *id.* at 133–34.

223 **wondered & just fine:** Seligman to FF, 7/31/1933, at 2, FFLC, Box 135; FF to Seligman, 8/14/1933, *id.*

223 **questioned:** HLS to FF, 12/5/1933, FFLC, Box 135; FF to HLS, 12/19/1933, *id.*; HLS to FF, 1/26/1934, *id.*; FF to HLS, 2/20/1934, *id.*

223 **"on the principle" & "honestly" & "to take":** FF, "The Federal Securities Act II," Fortune 8 (August 1933): 111.

223 **"put people":** FDR, 5/17/1933, "A Recommendation to the Congress to Enact the National Industrial Recovery Act to Put People to Work," *The Public Papers and Addresses of Franklin D. Roosevelt*, Vol. 2, at 202–6.

223 **Unlike Brandeis:** FWB to Thomas Reed Powell, 9/5/1933, at 1, Powell Papers, Box A, Folder A3c.

223 **"this is":** FF, Memorandum, 5/30/1933, at 2, FFLC, Box 159.

223 **memorandum:** FF to Richberg, 5/30/1933 & FF to Perkins, 5/29/1933 & FF to Wagner, 5/30/1933, *id.*

223 **Wyzanski:** Richberg to FF, 6/1/1933, *id.*

223 **signed the NIRA:** FDR, Goal of the National Industrial Recovery Act, 6/16/1933, *The Public Papers and Addresses of Franklin D. Roosevelt*, Vol. 2, at 246–47.

223 **declined Johnson's offer:** WES, 5/30/1933, at A-2; FF to Alfred Cohn, 10/30/1935, R&FF, 288–89.

224 **"one-man":** Joseph P. Lash, "A Brahmin of the Law," DFF, 53.

224 **young lawyers:** FF to WL, 4/17/1933, R&FF, 128.

224 **"the most natural":** FFR, 249.

224 **often recommended:** FF to RCM, 3/29/1933, FFLC, Box 84; RCM to FF, 4/1/1933, *id.*; FF to RCM, 5/21/1933 tel., *id.*; RCM to FF, 6/19/1933, at 2, *id.*; FF to FDR, 5/19/1933, R&FF, 134; FF to Ernest Gruening, 6/21/1933, at 1–2, FFLC, Box 60.

224 **praised the hiring:** FF to FDR, 6/6/1933, R&FF, 138.

224 **"Politicians":** NYDN, 4/21/1933, at 27.

224 **"have":** Kiplinger Washington Letter, 6/24/1933, at 3.

224 **"[m]ore Jews":** Kiplinger Washington Letter, 7/1/1933, at 3.

225 **"dealt":** Kiplinger Washington Letter, 7/22/1933, at 4.

225 **"Jew Deal":** DFP, 4/2/1934, at 6.

225 **"Happy":** NYHT, 1/14/1934, at A2.

225 **"unbelievable" & "whitewash" & "fear" & "unless":** Unsigned to FF, 3/28/1933, FFLC, Box 81 & Ruth Mack Brunswick Papers, Box 1.

225 **Ruth Mack Brunswick:** FF to SSW, 3/28/1933, SSWP, Box 109, Folder 1; JWM to James McDonald, 5/2/1933 draft, FFLC, Box 188. *See* Harry Barnard, *The Forging of an American Jew*, 314 (1974); Paul Roazen, *Freud and His Followers*, 420–36 (1975); Lisa Appignanesi & John Forrester, *Freud's Women*, 373–76 (1992).

225 **important contacts:** Mark Brunswick to FF, 5/5/1933, FFLC, Box 188.

226 **"full discussion" & "started the train":** FF to Proskauer, 5/18/1933, at 1, FFLC, Box 137 (referring to April 7); FF to Hull, 5/23/1933, at 1, *id.* (referencing meeting); SSW to FF, 4/15/1933, at 1, SSWP, Box 109, Folder 1 (asking about meeting with "headquarters"). April 7 is plausible because of FF-RCM visit to White House that morning about the securities bill. More likely, it occurred during FF's April 9 private visit with FDR for an hour before dinner. FDR Day by Day, 4/9/1933.

226 **"alert" & "at the right":** FF to FDR, tel. n.d., at 1–2, FFLC, Box 137. The date is confirmed by Secretary of State Hull's response. Hull to FF, 5/6/1933, *id.* (confirming April 16 wire).

226 **"Time":** SSW to FF, 4/16/1938 day letter, SSWP, Box 109, Folder 1. *See* Melvin I. Urofsky, *A Voice that Spoke for Justice*, 260–75 (1982).

226   **"the President's" & "there isn't" & "traditional" & "the high":** FF to RCM, 4/24/1933,
      RCMP, Box 68, Folder 6 (enclosing 4/14/1933 memorandum to Perkins).
226   **Perkins assured:** Perkins to FF, 4/25/1933, *id.*
226   **University in Exile:** Alvin Johnson to FF, 5/2/1933, FFLC, Box 188; Johnson to FF,
      5/7/1933, *id.*; Johnson to FF, 5/12/1933, *id.*; Johnson to FF, 5/22/1933, *id.*
227   **fourteen German scholars:** NYT, 8/19/1933, at 1.
227   **ACLU petition:** NYT, 9/11/1933, at 10.
227   **"challenge":** FF to RCM, 6/13/1933, RCMP, Box 68, Folder 6.
227   **Hull wrote:** Hull to FF, 5/6/1933, at 1–2.
227   **twenty-five minutes:** FDR Day by Day, 5/7/1933.
227   **reviewed a draft:** FDR, "Fireside Chat #2 – 'Outlining the New Deal Program,'"
      5/7/1933, FDRL, MSF, No. 627; FF to FDR, 5/9/1933, R&FF, 130–31.
227   **"felt more":** LDB, "Confidential to S.S.W.," 5/11/1933, FFLC, Box 137.
228   **"To withhold" & "on a personal" & "sectarian" & "attached":** FF to Hull, 5/23/1933, at 1–2.
228   **blamed the inaction:** FF to Proskauer, 5/18/1933.
228   **"There are two":** SSW to FF, JWM, and LDB, Memorandum, 5/23/1933, at 2, SSWP, Box
      109, Folder 1.
228   **book burning:** NYHT, 5/12/1933, at 13.
228   **"the authentic":** NYHT, 5/19/1933, at 19.
228   **did not speak:** FF to WL, 11/28/1936, FFLC, Box 78 (quoting NYHT, 5/19/1933, at 19).
229   **"promptly" & "if he had":** FF to SSW, n.d., "Labor Day," at 1, SSWP, Box 189, Folder 30.
      The document was written after 1938 because it was on the justice's stationery.
229   **historians:** *Compare* Rebecca Erbelding, *Rescue Board* (2018) & Richard Breitman &
      Allan J. Lichtman, *FDR and the Jews* (2013) (arguing FDR did the best he could under
      the circumstances) *with* Rafael Medoff, *FDR and the Holocaust* (2013) & David S.
      Wyman, *The Abandonment of the Jews* (1984) (faulting Roosevelt).
229   **mine owners:** FF, Memorandum, 9/6/1933, R&FF, at 150–55; FDR Day by Day,
      9/6/1933.
229   **coal code:** FDR Day by Day, 9/14/1933; FDR Day by Day, 9/15/1933.
229   **wrote U.S. ambassadors:** FDR to Ambassador Robert Bingham (Britain), 10/2/1933,
      R&FF, 159–60; FDR to Ambassador Breckinridge Long (Italy), 10/2/1933, FFLC, Box
      97; FDR to Ambassador Hugh R. Wilson (Switzerland), 10/2/1933, *id.*
229   **keep tabs:** NYHT, 9/25/1933, at 15.
229   **lunchtime talk:** CEW to Augustus Hand, 9/15/1933, CEWP-MHS, Box 20.
229   **"secret":** WES, 9/20/1933, at A-2.
229   **"moved":** FF to TGC, 9/18/1933, TGCP, Box 638.
230   **promoting:** FF to Frances Perkins, 4/3/1933, FFLC, Box 150; FF to Perkins, 4/6/1933,
      id.; FF to Perkins, 4/11/1933 tel., *id.*
230   **"like having":** Perkins to FF, 4/25/1933, RCMP, Box 68, Folder 6.
230   **"unique":** FF to FDR, 9/26/1933 tel., R&FF, 157.
230   **invited Paul Freund:** TGC to PAF, 8/4/1933, TGCP, Box 198.
230   **letter of introduction:** FF to MLH, 9/24/1933, R&FF, 156.

CHAPTER 16: CHARMING EXILE

231   **friends:** Thomas Reed Powell to FF, 10/2/1933, at 3, FFLC, Box 117.
231   **photographers & 62-degree & 2:00 p.m.:** BG, 9/25/1933, at 1–2.

231 **wired the president & wrote Corcoran:** FF to FDR, 9/26/1933 tel.; FF to TGC, 9/26/1933, at 1–4, TGCP, Box 198.

231 **Oxford station & Eastman House & Lindsay:** FFR, 251–52.

231 **happiest:** FF to LDB, 10/5/1933, FFLC, Box 29.

232 **Oxford gowns & mortified:** FFR, 253–55; MDF to TGC, 1/10/1934, at 4, TGCP, Box 638.

232 **Gates:** FF to TGC, 10/7/1933, TGCP, Box 198.

232 **argued and bet:** SGates to IB, 6/23/1934, IBP, Box 103; A.J. Ayer, *Part of My Life*, 158 (1977); FFR, 261–62.

232 **New College & All Souls:** Michael Ignatieff, *Isaiah Berlin*, 59–68 (1998).

233 **"a++":** IB to A.J. Ayer, circa 1936, IBP, Box 105, #162 & in IB, *Letters 1928–1946*, at 180 (Henry Hardy, ed. 2004).

233 **"Bowra speaking":** FFR, 258–59.

233 **closeted:** Leslie Mitchell, *Maurice Bowra*, 120–48 (2009).

233 **poems:** Maurice Bowra, *New Bats in Old Belfries* (Henry Hardy & Jennifer Holmes, eds. 2005).

233 **"entirely":** C.M. Bowra, *Memories*, 318–19 (1966).

233 **tests:** FF to LDB, 11/7/1933, at 1, FFLC, Box 29.

233 **London doctor:** FF to LDB, 12/28/1933, at 1, *id.*

233 **"like nothing":** MDF to TGC, 1/10/1934, at 5.

233 **federalism & Blackwell's & economists:** FFR, 256–61, 263–65, 271.

233 **"wholly":** FF to JML, 1/10/1934, at 2, FFLC, Box 117.

233 **Mae West & *Three Little Pigs*:** FF to TGC, 12/28/1933, at 8, TGCP, Box 638.

233 **friends:** FF to FDR, 1/15/1934, R&FF, at 188–89.

233 **Keynes's & Rutherford's:** FF to LDB, 12/9/1933, at 1, FFLC, Box 29; FFR, 257–58.

233 **Inner Temple:** FF to LDB, 11/17/1933, at 2, FFLC, Box 29; FF to OWH, 11/23/1933, H-FF Corr., 275.

234 **ten to one:** Arthur Lehman Goodhart, "Legal Procedure and Democracy," Journal of the American Judicature Society 47, no. 3 (August 1963): 58.

234 **Derby & "Well":** FFR, 259–61.

234 **unsigned article:** "The Federal Securities Act," The Economist, 1/6/1934, at 4–6, FFLC, Box 197; FF to BVC, n.d., FFLC, Box 115; FF to BVC, 12/29/1933, at 2–3, TGCP, Box 638.

234 **Geoffrey Dawson:** FF to FDR, 1/29/1934, R&FF, 190–91; FDR to FF, 2/3/1934, *id.* at 192.

234 **BBC:** FF, "Transatlantic Misperceptions," The Listener, 2/21/1934, at 299–301, 332, FFLC, Box 197; ToL, 2/12/1934, at 8; FF to FDR, 3/19/1934, R&FF, 200.

234 **University of Manchester & Samuel Alexander:** Manchester Guardian, 3/10/1934, at 8; FF to LDB, 5/14/1934, FFLC, Box 29; FFR, 257.

234 **"not a lawyers'" & "a scheme" & "dynamic" & "fixed":** FF, "The Constitutional Aspects of President Roosevelt's Recovery Programme," 2/1/1934, at 3–4, 6, Record of the General Meeting of Chatham House, The Royal Institute of International Affairs, Chatham House Online Archives, RIIA/8/309.

234 **"could make":** FFR Transcript, 8/28/1957, at 361–62.

234 **"The Lord":** Freedman, R&FF, 13–14.

234 **"if the founders" & "drop dead":** FF, "The Constitutional Aspects of President Roosevelt's Recovery Programme," 2/1/1934, at 23.

234 **removed:** Freedman, R&FF, 13–14.

235 **"a member":** FF, "The Constitutional Aspects of President Roosevelt's Recovery Programme," 2/1/1934, at 19, 22.

235   "as masterly": HJL to OWH, 2/3/1934, 2 HLL at 1466.

235   "no visible": MDF to TGC, 1/10/1934, at 2–3.

235   Treasury Department: FF to TGC, 11/16/1933, TGCP, Box 638; FF to TGC 12/28/1933, at 2–3, id.; FF to TGC, 11/7/1933, id.

235   Acheson refused: FF to LDB, 11/17/1933, at 1, FFLC, Box 29; FF to FDR, 12/12/1933, R&FF, 176–77; FDR to FF, 12/22/1933, id. at 184; FF to DA, 12/24/1933, DAP, Reel 7, Folder 140; FF to DA, 2/5/1934, id.; DA to FF, 1/26/1934, FFLC, Box 115; DA to FF, circa 2/1934, id. See DA, Morning and Noon, 161–94 (1965); Robert Beisner, Dean Acheson, 11–12 (2006).

235   "to the wrong": FF to TGC, 1/8/1934, at 2, TGCP, Box 638 & FF to LDB, 1/7/1934, FFLC, Box 29.

235   Oxford economists: FF to FDR, 11/23/1933, R&FF, 167 (enclosing letter, id. at 168–73).

235   advance copy: FF to FDR, 12/16/1933, id. at 177–83 (enclosing John Maynard Keynes, "An Open Letter to President Roosevelt").

235–236 "Your letters" & "a practical": FDR to FF, 12/23/1933, id. at 183–84.

236   "the significance" & "The air" & "the forces" & "its people": FF to FDR, 10/17/1933, R&FF, 164.

236   James G. McDonald: FF to FDR, 11/23/1933, id. at 167–68 (enclosing McDonald to FF, 11/20/1933, id. at 173–74).

236   Austria's: FF to FDR, 2/20/1933 tel., id. at 194–95.

236   "the football": FF to FDR, 2/22/1934, id. at 195.

236   George Messersmith: FF to FDR, 3/22/1934, id. at 209.

236   "Palestine": FF, "Persecution of Jews in Germany," World Today, 4/1934, at 36–38, FFLC, Box 197.

236   $2000 gift: "L.D.B. Cash January 1–January 31, 1934," LDBP-Brandeis U, Box 121; FF to LDB, 5/14/1934, at 1.

236   "overwhelmed" & "Palestine": FF to LDB, 4/18/1934 [n.d.], at 2–3, FFLC, Box 29.

236   Aaronsohn: FF to OWH, 5/7/1934, H-FF Corr., 276.

236–237 "transcendent" & "Jewish Palestine" & "sizable growth": FF, "Notes on Visit to Palestine," 6/8/1934, at 2, FFLC, Box 197. See "Prof. Frankfurter's Itinerary in Palestine," & "Continuation of Prof. Frankfurter's Itinerary in Palestine," 4/1934, id.

237   kept tabs: FF to FDR, 2/14/1934, R&FF, 192–93; FF to TGC, 2/13/1934, at 1, TGCP, Box 638; FF to TGC, 3/6/1934, id.; FF to TGC, 3/14/1934, id.; FF to TGC, 4/24/1934, id.

237   called on Congress: FDR, "Another Step to Protect Investors and to Eliminate Destructive Speculation—Recommendation for the Securities Exchange Commission," 2/9/1934, The Public Papers and Addresses of Franklin D. Roosevelt, Vol. 3, at 90–93 (1938).

237   "extraordinary": FF to TGC, 5/7/1934, at 6, TGCP, Box 638.

237   "hot": WES, 2/27/1934, at A-2.

237   "succeeded": John Carter Franklin (aka The Unofficial Observer), The New Dealers, 322 (1934).

237   "Jew Deal": DFP, 4/2/1934, at 6.

237   "a little" & "10 to 18" & "the communistic": 78 Cong. Rec. 7085–88 (1934). See Katie Louchheim, "The Little Red House," Virginia Quarterly Review 56, no. 1 (Winter 1980): 119–34..

237   "Dear Horns" & "everything" & "remind": TGC to FF, 4/22/1934, at 1–3, TGCP, Box 638.

237   "Dear Little": FF to TGC and BVC, 5/15/1934, at 1–2, TGCP, Box 198.

238 **admiration:** TGC to FF, 5/11/1934, at 1–2, *id.*; BVC to FF, 5/11/1934, FFLC, Box 115.

238 **"general":** FF to TGC, 6/8/1934, at 1, TGC, Box 638.

238 **"the talk" & "the powerful":** FF to TGC, at 5/7/1934, at 1–4.

238 **"to keep":** FF to FDR, 5/23/1934, R&FF, 220.

238 **no hurry:** FF to LDB, 5/1/1934, at 1–3, FFLC, Box 29.

238 **Hawaii:** TGC & BVC to FF, 6/18/1934, *id.* at 223–25.

238 **June 30:** FF to FDR, 6/8/1934, R&FF, 222.

238 **"charming exile":** FF to TGC, 6/21/1934, at 2.

238 **Vivian Pomeroy:** BG, 7/9/1934, at 1, 17.

238 **"The New Deal":** BaltSun, 7/9/1934, at 7.

238 **Roosevelt requested:** FDR to FF, 6/11/1934, R&FF, 222.

CHAPTER 17: THE MOST INFLUENTIAL SINGLE
INDIVIDUAL IN THE UNITED STATES

239 **"What's" & "had come" & "there is":** MDF to TGC, n.d., at 2–4, TGCP, Box 638.

239 **NIRA & fair competition codes:** Schechter Poultry v. United States, 295 U.S. 495, 521–23 (1935); National Industrial Recovery Act, 48 Stat. 195 (June 16, 1933).

239 **Government lawyers & "Blue Eagle":** William E. Leuchtenburg, *Franklin D. Roosevelt and the New Deal,* 65–67 (1963); Peter H. Irons, *The New Deal Lawyers,* 28–30 (1982); Daniel R. Ernst, "Of Sheepdogs and Ventriloquists," 69 Buffalo L. Rev. 43 (2021).

240 **Minnesota law:** Home Building & Loan Ass'n v. Blaisdell, 290 U.S. 398 (1934).

240 **milk prices & "in the public":** Nebbia v. New York, 291 U.S. 502, 515, 530 (1934).

240 **Marion was struck:** FF to LDB, 8/31/[1934], at 1–2, FFLC, Box 29.

240 **American Liberty League:** Jared A. Goldstein, "The American Liberty League and the Rise of Constitutional Nationalism," 86 Temp. L. Rev. 287 (2014).

240 **"irrepressible":** FF to LDB, 8/31/[1934], at 1–2, FFLC, Box 29.

240 **pressing policy issues:** *Id.* at 2–4.

241 **Hutcheson & "best man":** *Id.* at 4–5.

241 **Moley:** FF to LDB, 7/24/1934, FFLC, Box 29.

241 **Corcoran & Cohen & Joseph Kennedy:** FF to TGC, n.d., at 1–5, TGC, Box 638; FF to LDB, 7/29/1934, FFLC, Box 29.

241 **Margold:** FF to LDB, 8/24/[1934], at 2, FFLC, Box 29.

241 **Wyzanski & Siegel & "the whole Jewish":** FF to LDB, 8/8/[1934], at 1–2, *id.*

241 **"put to him":** FF to LDB, 8/4/1934, *id.*

241 **"a government" & "expert":** NYTM, 9/30/1934, at 3–4.

242 **Pound had praised:** Paris Herald, 8/4/1934, FFLC, Box 90.

242 **accepted:** FF, "Memorandum of Conversation with Pound and President Conant regarding an invitation from Pound," 9/14/1934, at 1–3, *id.*

242 **"attend" & accused:** FF to RP, 9/14/1934, *id. See* RP to FF, 9/14/1934, *id.*; FF to RP, 9/15/1934, *id.*; RP Diary Entry, 9/17/1934, RPP, Pt. II, Reel 41, Page 509; JWM to RP, 9/18/1934, at 1–2, RPP, Pt. III, Reel 78, Pages 642–43; Bruce A. Kimball & Daniel R. Coquillette, *The Intellectual Sword,* 257–67 (2020); Peter Rees, "Nathan Roscoe Pound and the Nazis," 60 B.C. L. Rev. 1313 (2009).

242 **anti-Semitism:** FF to MRC, 6/6/1933, MRCP, Box 5, Folder 9.

242 **David Riesman:** RP to FF, 1/31/1934, FFLC, Box 118; FF to Magruder, 2/13/1934, *id.*; Magruder to FF, 2/24/1934, *id.*; Magruder to FF, 3/7/1934, at 1, *id.*; FF to RP, 4/23/1934,

id.; RP to FF, 5/4/1934, *id.*; RP to FF, 5/8/1934, *id.*; FF to RP, 5/14/1934, *id.*; FF to JWM, 5/16/1934, at 3–4, *id.*; RP to FF, 6/28/1934, FFLC, Box 90; FF, "Minutes of Conversation with R.P.," 9/21/1934, at 1, *id.*

242 **Willard Hurst:** Willard Hurst to Joseph H. Willits, 3/20/1957, at 2, Hurst Papers, Box 3, Folder 20 (describing Pound as "a great disappointment" and Harvard Law School as "an intellectually stodgy place" except for FF, Thomas Reed Powell, Henry Hart, and a few others); Kimball & Coquillette, *Intellectual Sword*, 272–76, 281–82.

243 **single lunch:** FDR Day By Day, 10/24/1934; *id.*, 10/25/1935.

243 **stayed overnight:** FDR Day by Day, 12/16/1934.

243 **missed:** FF to FDR, 1/4/1935 tel., R&FF, 249; FF to FDR, 1/6/1935, *id.* at 249–50.

243 **legislation & fascism:** FDR, State of the Union, 1/4/1935, FDRL, MSF, Box 20, No. 759.

243 **oil refiner & guidelines & factual findings:** Panama Refining Co. v. Ryan, 293 U.S. 388, 411–12, 430–33 (1935).

243 **"really" & "a good":** LDB-FF Conversations, "Gold Clause," at 1–2, LDBHLS, Pt. II, Reel 33, Pages 360–61. On Stephens's argument, CT, 12/11/1934, at 1, 14; WP, 12/11/1934, at 1, 11; NYHT, 12/12/1934, at 1, 6; CT, 12/12/1934, at 7; Daniel R. Ernst, *Tocqueville's Nightmare*, 57–59 (2014).

243 **exceeded:** FF to CEW, 1/22/1935, FFLC, Box 113.

244 **"truly A-1":** FF to TGC, n.d., at 5, TGCP, Box 638.

244 **"so completely":** LDB-FF Conversations, "Gold Clauses," at 1, LDBHLS, Pt. II, Reel 33, Page 362.

244 **refused to comply:** "FDR Proposed Statement re Gold Clause," 2/18/1935, FDRL, MSF, Box 21, No. 768 (with FDR handwritten notation); Henry Morgenthau, Jr., Diaries, 2/13/1935, Book 3, Pt. 2, Page 235, Morgenthau Papers (recounting 2/11/1935 conversation with FDR and referring to JPK's reaction); Sebastian Edwards, *American Default*, 167–69 (2018); Gerard N. Magliocca, "The Gold Clause Cases and Constitutional Necessity," 64 Fla. L. Rev. 1243, 1259–65 (2012).

244 **decisions:** Perry v. United States, 294 U.S. 330 (1935); Nortz v. United States, 294 U.S. 317 (1935); Norman v. Baltimore & Ohio R.R. Co., 294 U.S. 240 (1935).

244 **"The Constitution" & "This is":** NYDN, 2/19/1935, at 5.

244 **mocked the New Deal:** BG, 8/27/1934, at 4. *See* Barry Cushman, "The Secret Lives of the Four Horsemen," 83 Va. L. Rev. 559 (1997).

244 **"really impressive":** LDB to FF, 2/24/1935, HBHS, at 562.

244 **early 1935 meeting:** TGC Int. with Harry Hopkins, 4/3/1939, at 1, Hopkins Papers/Sherwood Collection, Box 299, Folder 6.

245 **"in surprisingly":** FF to LDB, 10/2/1934, FFLC, Box 29.

245 **final surprise:** FF to FDR, 1/24/1935, R&FF, 253; FDR to FF, 2/9/1935, *id.* at 255.

245 **immediately:** James Rowe to FF, 2/23/1935, FFLC, Box 145. *See* LDB to FF, 2/24/1935; FF to TGC, 2/26/1935, TGCP, Box 638.

245 **"ebbing":** FF to MDF, 3/1/1935, at 2, FFLC, Box 14.

245 **"Every":** FF to FB, 3/14/1935, FBP-GU, Box 9, Folder 69; FB to NYSun, 3/19/1935, *id.*

245 **"everybody" & "oh" & president & Cardozo & Stimson:** FF to MDF, 3/4/1935, at 1–4, FFLC, Box 14.

245 **bedside:** WES, 3/6/1935, at A-1, A-5.

245 **president's request:** FF to MDF, 3/4/1935, at 4.

245 **unforgettable dinner:** FF to MDF, 3/10/1935, at 2, FFLC, Box 14; FDR Day by Day, 3/7/1935.

245 **visited Brandeis:** LDB to FF, 3/12/1935, HBHS, at 563.

245 **"too stricken":** NYHT, 3/9/1935, at 10.

245–246 **Marion never:** EGE to AGB, 4/4/1935, at 3, EGEP, Reel 2, Folder 35.

246 **11:45 a.m.:** FDR Day by Day, 3/8/1935; Photograph, 3/8/1935, LC P&P, LC-H21-C-384.

246 **hat off & bugler:** Photograph, 3/8/1935, LC P&P, LC-H2-B-7174.

246 **rain & sleet & walked:** John Knox, "Some Correspondence with Holmes and Pollock," Chicago Bar Record, 3/1940, at 224, in John Knox Papers, Box 1, Folder 53; FDR Day by Day, 3/8/1935; Brad Snyder, *The House of Truth*, 574–77 (2017); G. Edward White, *Justice Oliver Wendell Holmes*, 471–75, 488 (1993); John S. Monagan, *The Grand Panjandrum*, 144–47 (1988).

246 **"And I":** FF to FDR, 3/7/1935, R&FF, 257 (emphasis in original).

246 **he published:** FF, *Mr. Justice Holmes and the Supreme Court* (1938).

246 **was proudest:** FF to Harris E. Starr, 3/19/1943, FFLC, Box 207; FF, "Sketch of the Life of Oliver Wendell Holmes," *Dictionary of American Biography*, Vol. XXI, Supp. 1 (1943), *id.*

246 **"the most influential" & "passionate":** FF, "Mr. Justice Holmes," 48 Harv. L. Rev. 1279, 1280 (1935)

246 **"eyes blaze":** FF to MDF, 3/25/1935, at 2, FFLC, Box 14.

246 **private conversation:** TGC Int. with Harry Hopkins, 4/3/1939, at 1, Hopkins Papers/ Sherwood Collection, Box 299, Folder 6 (placing it in early 1935); LDB-FF Conversations, "Gold Clause," at 1–2, LDBHLS, Pt. II, Reel 33, Pages 360–61; "Gold Clauses," at 1, *id.* at 362.

247 **dismissed the appeal:** NYT, 3/26/1935, at 1; United States v. Belcher, 294 U.S. 736 (Apr. 1, 1935).

247 **Richberg urged:** Richberg to FDR, 4/3/1935 tel., Richberg Papers LC, Box 45.

247 **Brooklyn butchers:** NYT, 4/5/1935, at 1; United States v. A.L.A. Schechter Poultry Corp., 76 F.2d 617 (2d Cir. 1935).

247 **Corcoran wired & Roosevelt's message:** FF, "Memorandum for the President," n.d., FFLC, Box 98; FF to LDB, 4/13/1935, FFLC, Box 29; TGC Int. with Harry Hopkins, 4/3/1939, at 1–2; R&FF, 259–60.

247 **weakness:** HID, 12/17/1934, HI, *The Secret Diary of Harold L. Ickes: The First Thousand Days, 1933–1936*, 247 (1953).

247 **recommending:** FF to HSC, 7/7/1935 tel., FFLC, Box 149; HMS to FF, 9/16/1933, at 1–2, *id.*

247 **Abe Feller:** Feller to FF, 2/2/1935, *id.*; FF to Feller, 2/23/1935, *id.*

247 **Harry Shulman:** HMS to FF, 2/19/1935, *id.*; FF to HMS, 2/21/1935, *id.*; HMS to FF, 4/15/1935, *id.*; FF to HMS, 4/24/1935, *id.*

247 **solicitor general:** SFR to FF, 3/18/1935, FFLC, Box 148; FF to LDB, 3/15/1935, FFLC, Box 29.

247 **Reed agreed:** FF to LDB, 4/4/1935, *id.*; PAF OH, 10/18/1982, at 00:58:28– :00:59:33, SFR OH.

248 **purge:** Daniel R. Ernst, "Mr. Try-It Goes to Washington," 87 Fordham L. Rev. 1 (2019).

248 **relayed:** FF to FDR, 4/22/1935, R&FF, 261–62 (enclosing DKN to FF, 4/22/1935).

248 **agreed to host:** FDR to FF, 5/2/1934 tel., *id.* at 269; FF to FDR, 5/3/1935, *id.* at 269–70.

248 **"to assert":** HID, 5/15/1935, HI, *Secret Diary of Harold L. Ickes: The First Thousand Days, 1933–1936*, at 363.

248 **big success:** FF to FDR, 5/16/1935, R&FF at 271.

248 **overnight guest:** FF to MDF, 5/14/1935, FFLC, Box 14; FDR Day by Day, 5/14/1935.

248 **"bad advice":** FF to LDB, 5/22/1935, at 2, FFLC, Box 29.

248   **Freund wrote:** FF to PAF, 5/3/1935, FFLC, Box 149.

248   **"stumbling":** FF to SFR, 5/4/1935, *id.*

248   **"made my":** SFR to FF, 5/7/1935, *id.*

248   **pension system:** Railroad Retirement Board v. Alton RR Co., 295 U.S. 330, 360 (1935); *id.* at 375 (Hughes, C.J., dissenting).

249   **"an ingrained" & "we'd be":** FF to LDB, 5/24/1935, at 1, FFLC, Box 29.

249   **"without precedent":** A.L.A. Schechter Poultry Corp. v. United States, 295 U.S. 495, 541 (1935).

249   **"running" & "the distinction":** *Id.* at 553–4 (Cardozo, J., concurring).

249   **just compensation:** Louisville Joint Stock Land Bank v. Radford, 295 U.S. 555, 601–2 (1935).

249   **"quasi-judicial":** Humphrey's Executor v. United States, 295 U.S. 602, 629 (1935).

249–250 **"visibly" & "You have" & "Make sure":** BVC, Memorandum, 5/27/1935, FFLC, Box 28 & BVCP, Box 20.

250   **boarded & 6:30 p.m.:** FF to FDR, 5/27/1935 tel., R&FF, 272; FDR Day by Day, 5/28/1935.

250   **"the Supreme Court vs.":** FF to FDR, 5/29/1935, R&FF, 272–73.

250   **he urged:** HSCD, 5/29/1935, HSCP, Reel 1; FF to LDB, 6/3/1935, at 1–2, FFLC, Box 29.

250   **prioritized & "false":** FF to FDR, 5/30/1935, R&FF, 273–75.

250   **Second New Deal:** Basil Rauch, *The History of the New Deal 1933–1938* (1944); Arthur M. Schlesinger, Jr., *The Age of Roosevelt: The Politics of Upheaval* (1960); Leuchtenburg, *Franklin D. Roosevelt and the New Deal*; David M. Kennedy, *Freedom from Fear* (1999).

250   **"horse":** FDR, Press Conference, 5/31/1935, at 7, 28, FDRL, Press Conference, Ser. 1, No. 209; NYT, 6/1/1935, at 1, 6.

251   **off guard:** FF to LDB, 6/3/1935, at 1.

251   **joined him:** FDR Day by Day, 5/30/1935.

251   **"a Jeffersonian":** John J. Burns to FF, 3/1/1935, FFLC, Box 28.

251   **admired:** FF to LDB, 6/3/1935, at 2–3.

251   **"heartbroken":** HID, 11/13/1935, HI, *Secret Diary of Harold L. Ickes: The First Thousand Days, 1933–1936*, at 467.

251   **nineteen nights:** FDR Day by Day, 6/6/1935; *id.*, 6/7/1935 (departed); *id.*, 6/13/1935 (overnight guest two days); *id.*, 6/15/1935 (departed); *id.*, 6/16/1935 (arrived); *id.*, 6/17/1935; *id.*, 6/18/1935; *id.*, 6/20/1935 (departed); *id.*, 7/6/1935; *id.*, 7/8/1935 (arrived); *id.*, 7/11/1935 (picnic in Laurel at Ambassador Breckenridge Long's); *id.*, 7/16/1935 (arrived); *id.*, 7/18/1935 (departed); *id.*, 7/22/1935 (arrived); *id.*, 7/24/1935 (departed); *id.*, 7/26/1935 (departed); *id*, 7/30/1935 (arrived); *id.*, 7/31/1935 (Sugarloaf Mountain picnic); *id.*, 8/2/1935 (departed); *id.*, 8/6/1935 (arrived); *id.*, 8/9/1935 (departed); *id.*, 8/13/1935 (arrived); *id.*, 8/24/1935 (dinner); *id.*, 8/25/1935 (*Sequoia* cruise); *id.*, 9/1/1935 (departed).

251   **"almost":** MDF to IB, 6/23/1935, at 6, IBP, Box 104, #88.

251   **"Well":** MDF to FF, 8/6/1935, at 5, FFLC, Box 15.

252   **"conferring":** WashHerald, 7/25/1935, in TGCP, Box 638.

252   **Critics:** CT, 7/24/1935, at 4 (Amos Pinchot's open letter to FF).

252   **"showing":** FF to LDB, 6/14/1935, at 1–2, FFLC, Box 29. *See* HSCD, 6/13/1935, HSCP, Reel 1.

252   **moral character:** MDF to FF, 7/7/1935, at 8–9, FFLC, Box 14.

252   **cleared his name:** FF to LDB, 7/17/1935, at 1–2, FFLC, Box 29.

252   **reinforced:** FF to MDF, 8/16/1935, at 2–5, FFLC, Box 15.

252   **"stratagems":** FF to MDF, 8/18/1935, at 2, *id.*

252 **"real fighting":** FF to MDF, 8/23/1935, at 2, *id.*

252 **guided & learned:** FF to MDF, 8/17/1935, at 3, FFLC, Box 15; FF to MDF, 8/18/1935, at 2–5, *id.*

252 **"John" & " 'conservative' ":** FF to MDF, 8/19/1935, at 3, *id. See* FF to MDF, 8/20/1935, at 1–4, *id.*; FF to MDF, 8/24/1935, at 1–4, *id.*

253 **"Cardinal" & "alive" & "got almost":** FF to MDF, 8/27/1935, at 1–2, *id.*

253 **"I'll see":** FF to MDF, 8/31–9/1/1935, at 3, FFLC, Box 15.

253 **Labor Day weekend:** FF to MDF, 8/31–9/1/1935, at 1–2.

253 **"on the theory" & "a sceptical" & "inside" & "great educational":** FF to MDF, 9/2/1935, at 2–4, FFLC, Box 15.

253–254 **"almost squalid" & "resigned":** FF to MDF, 9/2/1935, at 1–2, 4.

254 **Hyde Park:** *id.*; FDR Day by Day, 9/1/1935.

254 **"the heavily financed":** FF, "The Liberty League Supreme Court," Today, 9/1935, in R&FF, 285–87.

254 **Arthur Krock:** NYT, 5/28/1935, at 21; NYT, 5/29/1935, at 20; NYT, 7/29/1935, at 14; Krock, Private Memorandum, 3/11/1955, Krock Papers, Box 26 (refusing to speak to FF after episode).

254 **strategy of delay:** FF to FWB, circa 11/29/1935, at 1–6, FFLC, Box 38; FWB to FF, 12/18/1935, *id.* (FF's handwritten note).

254–255 **"The professor" & " 'boys' " & "the Hot Dog Pressure" & "diverted" "the original" & "sound money" "infest[ing] & "delousing":** General Hugh S. Johnson, "Think Fast, Captain!" Saturday Evening Post, 10/26/1935, at 7, 85–86 (emphasis in original).

255 **general counsel & heavy drinker:** FF to LDB, 9/17/1934, FFLC, Box 29; FF to Alfred Cohn, 10/30/1935, R&FF, 288–91.

255 **"man of the year":** Time, 1/1/1934; Jordan A. Schwarz, *The New Dealers*, 96–108 (1993).

255 **never spoke:** FF to LDB, 9/17/1934, FFLC, Box 29; FF to Alfred Cohn, 10/30/1935, R&FF, 288–91.

255 **tied for first:** 1919 Special Session, Grades, FFHLS, Pt. III, Reel 19, Page 636.

255 **declined an offer:** FF to MRC, 11/4/1935, MRCP, Box 5, Folder 8; Scott Donaldson, *Archibald MacLeish* (1992); William H. MacLeish, *Uphill with Archie* (2001).

256 **"the most" & "this silent" & "the IAGO" & "The actual" & "No one" & "packed" & "has done":** "The Young Men Come to Washington," 1/1936, Fortune, in R&FF, 303–10.

256 **"whitewashed":** FF, Memorandum, 1/29/1936, TGCP, Box 638.

256 **"well known":** AM to FF, 1/28/1936, *id.*

256 **"a few":** FF, Memorandum, 1/29/1936, TGCP, Box 638.

257 **reorganization & best lawyers:** FF to MDF, 8/21/1935, at 2–3, FFLC, Box 15.

257 **Hiss:** FF to LDB, 7/21/1935, FFLC, Box 29.

257 **Horsky:** Augustus Hand to FF, 8/22/1935, SFRP, FF Corr. Addendum, Folder 1.

257 **Wyzanski:** CEW to FF, 10/26/1935, FFLC, Box, 149; FF to CEW, 12/25/1935, *id.*, Box 113.

257 **"a superb" & "The Court":** FF to SFR, 11/27/1935, at 1, 3, SFRP, FF Corr. Addendum, Folder 1.

257 **fainted:** NYT, 12/11/1935, at 1, 9.

257 **"purely local":** United States v. Butler, 297 U.S. 1, 61, 64 (1936).

258 **"wisdom":** *Id.* at 78–79 (Stone, J., dissenting).

258 **"that Jesus":** FF to SFR, 1/10/1936, at 1, SFRP, FF Corr. Addendum, Folder 1.

258 **4:30 p.m.:** FDR Day to Day, 1/12/1936.

258 **draft message:** FF to FDR, 1/17/1936, R&FF, 312–13.

258   **"series"**: Ashwander v. Tennessee Valley Authority, 297 U.S. 288, 346–48 (1936) (Brandeis, J., concurring).

258   **"has lost" & "judgment" & "no respect"**: FF to MDF, 4/22/1936, at 2–4, FFLC, Box 15.

258   **"I wish"**: FF to MDF, 2/17/1937, at 3, *id.*

259   **"purely"**: Carter v. Carter Coal, 298 U.S. 238, 279–83, 304 (1936).

259   **"very fit" & Wheeler & reception**: FF to MDF, 5/20/1935, at 1–4, FFLC, Box 14. *See* HID, 5/22/1935, HI, *Secret Diary of Harold L. Ickes: The First Thousand Days, 1933–1936*, at 602; FDR Day by Day, 5/20/1936.

259   **New York minimum-wage law**: Morehead v. New York ex rel. Tipaldo, 298 U.S. 587, 592–93, 617 (1936).

259   **differentiated**: *Id.* at 619–27 (Hughes, C.J., dissenting).

259   *Adkins* **had been overruled**: *Id.* at 634–36 (Stone, J., dissenting). *See* FF to HFS, 6/5/1936, HFSP, Box 13.

259   **private lunch**: FDR Day by Day, 6/4/1936.

260   **"call"**: FF to FDR, 6/13/1936, R&FF, at 344–45.

260   **"principles" & "No Man's" & "the new" & "a dangerous"**: FF Draft, n.d., *id.* at 353–54.

260   **campaign**: HID, 5/22/1936, HI, *Secret Diary of Harold L. Ickes: The First Thousand Days, 1933–1936*, at 602.

260   **"This generation"**: FDR, 1936 Nomination Speech, 6/27/1936, at 11, FDRL, MSF, Box 26, File 879B.

260   **British press**: FF to FDR, 7/11/1936, R&FF, 345–46.

260   **"something"**: ALL to FDR, 2/20/1936, R&FF, 322. *See* FDR to FF, 2/24/1936, *id.* at 323.

261   **"a lesson"**: FF to FDR, 2/26/1936 tel., *id.*

261   **"Mr. Roosevelt" & "try"**: FF, Memorandum, n.d., *id.*

261   **"the impertinent"**: FF to FDR, 2/29/1936, *id.* at 324 (containing draft). *See* FF to FDR, 3/4/1936, *id.* at 324–25; FDR to ALL, 3/6/1936, *id.* at 325; ALL to FDR, 4/14/1936, *id.* at 326.

261   **"temper"**: FDR to FF, 4/16/1936, *id. See* FF to FDR, 4/19/1936, *id.*; FDR to FF, 4/29/1936, *id.* at 326–27; FDR to ALL, 4/29/1936, *id.* at 327.

261   **University of Heidelberg**: FF to GC, 3/3/1936, FFHLS, Pt. III, Reel 19, Page 817.

261   **drafted a preliminary**: Tercentenary Speech, 9/18/1936, R&FF, at 327–30. *See* FDRL, MSF, Box 27, No. 921.

261   **"members"**: R&FF, 330.

261   **Learned Hand showed**: LH to Lessing Rosenthal, 6/5/1936, *id.* at 331.

261   **"Now"**: BG, 9/19/1936, at 1, 6, 8. *See* FF to MLH, 9/18/1936 tel., R&FF, 355.

261–262   **"celebrated" & "wise sauciness" & "great triumph"**: FF to FDR, 9/19/1936 tel., R&FF, 356. *See* FDR to FF, 9/22/1936, *id.*; MDF to FDR, 9/27/1936, *id.*

262   **"tool" & "The most powerful"**: R&FF, 357–58 (enclosing FF to friend, 10/25/1936). *See* WAW to FF, 10/31/1936, *id.* at 359–60.

262   **"an old-fashioned" & "the conflict"**: FF to Arthur Hays Sulzberger, 10/1/1936, *id.* at 359.

262   **"you have"**: FF to FDR, Sunday before Election, *id.* at 361.

262   **Ben Cohen**: BVC to FF, 11/23/1936, BVCP, Box 7.

262   **"canvassing"**: FF to SFR, 12/14/1936, FFHLS, Pt. III, Reel 2, Page 765.

262   **put on hold**: BVC to FF, 1/6/1937, BVCP, Box 7 (containing FF's handwritten comments on amendments). *See* SFR to FF, 12/17/1936, FFHLS, Pt. III, Reel 2, Page 766 & FF to SFR, 12/28/1936, at 1–2, SFRP, FF Corr. Addenda, Folder 1 (commenting on a possible

amendment allowing Congress to overrule a Supreme Court decision by a two-thirds vote of both houses).

263   **"indispensable" & "petty"**: FF, *The Commerce Clause Under Marshall, Taney, and Waite*, unnumbered & 114 (1937).

263   **Thayer**: FF to FDR, n.d., R&FF, 367.

263   **"To F.D.R."**: *id.* at 366.

CHAPTER 18: AN AWFUL SHOCK

264   **"drenched" & "will be"**: FF to FDR, 1/21/1937, R&FF, 379–80.

264   **"one-third"**: FDR, Second Inaugural Address, 1/20/1937, at 4, 9, FDRL, MSF, Box 31, No. 1030.

264   **"Very confidentially"**: FDR to FF, 1/15/1937, R&FF, 376.

265   **"Are you trying"**: FF to FDR, 1/18/1937, *id.* at 378.

265   **Corcoran and Cohen**: TGC Int. with Harry Hopkins, 4/3/1939, at 2–3 (in dark until eve of announcement).

265   **after the election**: HSCD, 11/15/1936, at 2–3 & 12/23/1936 & 12/24/1936, HSCP, Reel 1.

265   **late January & Richberg & Rosenman**: HSCD, 1/30/1927, at 1–2 & 1/31/1927 & 2/2/1937 & 2/3/1937, at 1–2, & 2/4/1937, *id.*, Reel 2.

265   **revealing the bill & brainchild**: HSCD, 2/5/1937, at 1–3, *id.*; Raymond Clapper Diary, 1/20/1937, Clapper Papers, Box 8 (Richberg tipped off Clapper) & 2/8/1937, at 3, *id.* (Cummings took lead).

265   **"court-packing"**: FDR, "Message to Congress – Judicial Reorganization," 2/5/1937, FDRL, MSF, Box 31, No. 1033; Jeff Shesol, *Supreme Power* (2010); Barry Cushman, *Rethinking the New Deal Court* (1998); William E. Leuchtenburg, *The Supreme Court Reborn* (1995); Joseph Alsop & Turner Catledge, *The 168 Days* (1938).

265–266   **"And now" & "that means" & "it was clear" & "deep faith"**: FF to FDR, 2/7/1937, R&FF, 380–81.

266   **"There is"**: FF, "Supreme Court of the United States," *Encyclopedia of the Social Sciences*, Vol. 14, at 478 (1934).

266   **rejected calls**: MRC, "Fallacies about the Court," The Nation, 7/10/1935, at 39; FF to MRC, 6/10/1936, at 2, MRCP, Box 5, Folder 12; MRC to FF, 10/29/1936, at 1, *id.*, Folder 11.

266   **"I am" & "process" & "It is" & "unconstitutional" & "Do you"**: FDR to FF, 2/9/1937, R&FF, 381–82.

266   **"very difficult"**: FF to FDR, 2/15/1937, *id.* at 382–83.

266   **"oath"**: R&FF, 372 (revealing vow of silence yet private assistance to FDR to authorized biographer Max Freedman). *See* AMB to PAF, 1/28/1969, PAFP, Box 4, Folder 4-7 (arguing Freedman misunderstood "F.F.'s delicate position"); AMB Int. with Lash, 9/12/1974, at 3 (describing FF's "loyalty to Captain" as paramount and recalling FF's remark that FDR was not going to nominate a third Jew to the Court).

267   **Stevens & Hart & Rosenwald & Powell & Winship & Hill & "Damn this"**: FF to MDF, 2/13/1937, at 2–7, FFLC, Box 15.

267   **"strengthen" & "I have"**: FF to GC, 3/6/1937, at 2–3, FFLC, Box 34.

267   **"lawless"**: FF to CCB, 3/6/1937, *id.*

267   **"lived up"**: FF to CCB, 3/9/1937, at 1, *id.*

267　**New York lawyers:** FF to CCB, 3/13/1937, *id. See* CCB to FF, 3/14/1937, *id.*; FF to CCB, 3/16/1937, *id.*; GC to FF, 3/18/1937, at 2, *id.*; FF to GC, 3/19/1937, *id.*; FF to CCB, 4/3/1937, *id.*

268　**"cheap" & "I know":** MDF to FF, 2/14/1937, at 9–10, FFLC, Box 15.

268　**"have been more" & "I should have" & "My bottom":** FF to MDF, 2/1937, at 2–7, *id.*

268　**"We here":** FF to MDF, 2/17/1937, at 2–6, *id.*

268　**"the real":** FF to FDR, 2/18/1937, R&FF, 383–84.

268–269　**"has distorted" & "climax" & "personal economic" & "to protect" & "endure" & "to be adapted" & "embody a particular":** FF, Memorandum, *id.* at 384–87 (quoting *McCulloch* & *Lochner*).

269　**unpublished letter:** FDR to FF, 2/18/1937, R&FF, 387–89 (enclosing Stuart Chase, 2/15/1937, letter to *New York Times*).

269　**"take" & "the long" & "this major":** FF to FDR, 2/23/1937, *id.* at 389–90.

269　**"have ceased":** FF to MDF, 3/6/1937, at 4–5, FFLC, Box 15.

269　**"My formula":** FF to LH, 2/23/1937, *id.*, Box 64.

269　**nationally broadcast:** FDR, Democratic Victory Dinner, 3/4/1937, FDRL, MSF, Box 32, Folder 1040A.

269　**"[t]he country":** FF to FDR, 3/6/1937, at 1–4, TGCP, Box 210. This letter is not in their published correspondence.

270　**"Two" & "acting" & "has improperly" & "we must" & "an appeal" & "independent" & "new" & "pack" & "Justices":** FDR, Fireside Chat, 3/9/1937, at 4–5, 8, 10–11, 13, 15–16, FDRL, MSF, Box 32, No. 1041A.

270　**"false sanctity" & "relaxed":** FF to MDF, 3/11/1937, at 3–5, FFLC, Box 15.

270　**formidable adversary:** BKW, *Yankee from The West*, 294–318 (1962); Marc C. Johnson, *Political Hell-Raiser*, 182–214 (2019); ML, Memorandum re: BKW's Relationship with FDR, 10/24/1941, at 1–2, MLP, Box 5, Folder 51; FF to MDF, 3/11/1937, at 4–5; TGC, "Rendezvous with Democracy, Pack C/21–25, TGCP, Box 586.

271　**"crashed" & hallway:** TGC to Hopkins, 4/3/1939, at 3.

271　**"Tell your" & "I'm sorry":** TGC, "Rendezvous with Democracy," Pack C/14–17. *See* SIR, *Working with Roosevelt*, 156 (1952); Robert E. Sherwood, *Roosevelt and Hopkins*, 89–90 (1948) (based on 1939 Hopkins memorandum); MDF to FF, 2/11/1937, at 10, FFLC, Box 15.

271　**"Whom did":** LDB to FF, 2/5/1937, HBHS, at 593.

271　**He learned:** LDB to FF, 2/15/1937, FFLC, Box 28. Scholars believe FF destroyed many of his letters to LDB in the early 1940s. Introduction, HBHS, 10 & 13 n.21.

271　**Brandeis's wife:** Elizabeth Wheeler Colman, *Mrs. Wheeler Goes to Washington*, 165–66 (1989).

272　**"Well" & "The baby":** BKW, *Yankee from The West*, 328–29. On Hughes's role, *see* BKW, "My Years with Roosevelt," in *As We Saw the Thirties*, 203–5 (Rita James Simon, ed. 1967); Memorandum of Hughes's Conversation with Senator William H. King, 3/19/1927, CEHP, Reel 5; Memorandum of Hughes's Conversation with Senator Burton K. Wheeler, 3/19/1927, *id.*; CEH Autobiographical Notes, Chief Justice, 1930–1941, at 20–21, CEHP, Reel 140; Merlo J. Pusey, *Charles Evans Hughes*, Vol. 2, 755–56 (1951); CEH, *The Autobiographical Notes of Charles Evans Hughes*, 305 (David J. Danelski & Joseph S. Tulchin, eds. 1973); Marquis Childs, *Witness to Power*, 34–35 (1975); PAF, "Charles Evans Hughes as Chief Justice," 81 Harv. L. Rev. 4, 26–29 (1967); Richard D. Friedman, "Chief Justice Hughes' Letter on Court-Packing," Journal of Supreme Court

History 1 (1997): 76–86; Alsop & Catledge, *The 168 Days*, 124–27; Shesol, *Supreme Power*, 392–97.

272 **"fully abreast"**: CEH to BKW, 3/21/1937, at 1, BKWP-MSU, Box 8, Folder 16 & Hearings on S. 1392 before the Senate Comm. on the Judiciary, 75th Cong., 1st Sess., "A Bill to Reorganize the Judicial Branch of the Government," Pt. 3, 3/22-25/1937, at 487–92.

272 **"they are"**: BKW to PAF, 12/21/1962, BKWP-MSU, Box 1, Folder 1:6 & John L. Wheeler to Edward K. Wheeler, 12/9/1962, *id.* & PAF, "Charles Evans Hughes as Chief Justice," 81 Harv. L. Rev. at 27. *Cf.* ML, Memorandum, 7/15/1937, at 4, FFLC, Box 184 (quoting CEH as saying "that's the court").

272 **"phony" & disingenuous & "a characteristic" & "ridiculous" & "putting" & "the fear"**: FF, Memorandum, 3/21/1937, at 1–4, FFLC, Box 28 (handwritten notation by FF re: unsent). FF confirmed CEH's lie about his inability to reach the other justices. FF to HFS, 4/8/1937, HFSP, Box 13; HFS to FF, 4/8/1937, *id.*

273 **"freedom"**: West Coast Hotel v. Parrish, 300 U.S. 379, 389, 391, 400 (1937). *See* Helen J. Knowles, *Making Minimum Wage* (2021).

273 **"the switch"**: John Q. Barrett, "Attribution Time: Cal Tinney's Quip, 'A Switch in Time'll Save Nine,'" 73 Okla. L. Rev. 229 (2021).

273 **"Overruling"**: LDB to FF, 3/29/1937, HBHS, at 594.

273 **"one of life's" & "manner" & "confidence" & "a terrible" & "a shameless"**: FF to LDB, 3/31/1937, at 1–2, FFLC, Box 28.

274 **"a teacher" & "cynicism" & "Let Hughes" & "enduring" & "intervening" & "his disingenuous" & "Not even"**: *Id.* at 2–3. *See* FF to HFS, 3/30/1937, at 1–2, HFSP, Box 13 (similar comments); HFS to FF, 4/2/1937, *id.* (describing minimum-wage cases as "a sad chapter in our judicial history").

274 **"with" & "pretended" & "That Brandeis"**: FF to FDR, 3/30/1937, R&FF, 392.

274 **"I reserve"**: LDB to FF, 4/5/1937, HBHS, at 595.

274 **not to discuss**: R&FF, 396.

274 **came to regret**: FF to Thomas Reed Powell, 8/14/1946, at 4, Powell Papers, Box B, Folder B24 ("I now know from certain contemporaneous records about Roberts' two votes, on Minimum Wage. The facts would call for a much more complicated statement than his silence in the two cases naturally indicated."); FF, "Mr. Justice Roberts," 104 U. Pa. L. Rev. 311, 313–15 (1955) (quoting memorandum that OJR gave to FF on November 9, 1945). *See* Michael Ariens, "A Thrice-Told Tale, or Felix the Cat," 107 Harv. L. Rev. 620 (1994) (contending memorandum was a forgery); Richard D. Friedman, "A Reaffirmation: The Authenticity of the Roberts Memorandum, or Felix the Non-Forger," 142 U. Pa. L. Rev. 1985 (1994) (rebutting forgery claim).

275 **"close" & "not controlling"**: NLRB v. Jones & Laughlin Steel Corp., 301 U.S. 1, 38, 41, 43 (1937).

275 **"After today"**: FF to FDR, 4/12/1937 tel., R&FF, 397. *See id.* at 397–98 (distrusting Hughes's motives).

275 **"You are"**: FF to FDR, 4/5/1937, R&FF, 396–97 (FF handwritten note about 4/20 dinner from 5:00 p.m. to 9:50 p.m.).

275 **"flew" & "my long"**: FF to FDR, 4/21/1937, *id.* at 398. *See* FDR Day by Day, 4/20/1937 (FF 5:30 p.m. to 12:55 a.m.).

275 **"I have"**: FF to CCB, 4/29/1937, at 1, FFLC, Box 34. *See* FF to CCB, 7/22/1937, at 1, *id.*

276 **instrumental role**: Hughes Autobiographical Notes, Chief Justiceship, 1930–1941, at 16–18, CEHP, Reel 140; LDB to FF, 5/26/1937, HBHS, 597.

276 **halved the salaries:** Judge Glock, "Unpacking the Supreme Court," Journal of American History 106, no. 1 (June 2019): 47–71.

276 **first choice:** WP, 5/23/1937, at B1.

276 **Social Security Act:** Steward Machine Co. v. Davis, 301 U.S. 548 (1937).

276 **"pretty" & "political":** FF to HFS, 5/25/1937, at 2, HFSP, Box 13.

276 **"a needless":** Adverse Report, Reorganization of the Federal Judiciary, 6/14/1937, at 23.

276 **a compromise:** Joseph B. Keenan to HSC, 7/19/1937 2:30 p.m., HSCP, Box 199.

277 **last-ditch effort:** ML, Memorandum re: BKW's Relationship with FDR, 10/24/1941, at 1–2; ML, Memorandum, 8/3/1937, FFLC, Box 184.

277 **died with Robinson:** HSCD, 7/14/1937, HSCP, Reel 2; HSCD, 8/1/1937, at 1–2, id.

277 **"In the Court fight" & "unwise" & "candor":** FF to LDB, 7/15/1937, FFLC, Box 28 (includes handwritten note).

277 **"It will clarify":** FF to FDR, 8/9/1937, at 1–5, TGCP, Box 210. This letter also is not in the FF-FDR published correspondence.

277 **Cummings pared:** HSCD, 8/2/1937, at 1–3; "Memorandum in re Supreme Court," 8/3/1937, FDRL, PSF, Box 166; HSC to FDR, 8/9/1937, id., Box 165.

278 **Roosevelt conferred:** HSCD, 8/11/1937, at 1–3; Alsop and Catledge, *The 168 Days*, 296–307.

278 **Corcoran traveled:** Joseph P. Lash, *Dealers and Dreamers*, 311 & 485 n.43 (1988); SFR to FF, n.d., at 1, FFHLS, Pt. III, Reel 2, Page 792.

278 **"will certainly":** HSCD, 8/12/1937, at 1–5.

278 **white linen:** Birmingham News, 8/12/1937, at 2.

278 **The son:** Roger K. Newman, *Hugo Black*, 3–230 (1994); Steve Suitts, *Hugo Black of Alabama* (2005).

278 **Ku Klux Klan:** Newman, *Hugo Black*, 233–63; Suitts, *Hugo Black of Alabama*, 408–33.

279 **defended him:** FF to CCB, 8/16/1937, at 2, FFLC, Box 34.

279 **Borah & "character" & "'yes' man":** FF to CCB, 9/1/1937, at 2–3, id.

279 **outgrown & despised:** FF to CCB, circa 9/7/1937, at 1–2, id.

279 **Hutcheson:** FF to CCB, 9/9/1937, at 1, id.

279 **"more courage":** FF to CCB, 9/24/1937, id. See FF to CCB, 9/27/1937, id.; FF to CCB, 9/29/1937, at 1–2, id.; CCB to FF, 10/1/1937, at 2, id. (FF handwritten comments); R&FF, 409 (letters defending HLB).

279 **"acting" & "[s]omething" & "The President" & "realiz[ing]":** FF, "Notes for an Address on the State of the Union," 8/10/1937, R&FF, 404–6.

280 **inspired:** FF to FDR, 8/31/1937, at 1-2, FDRL, PSF, Box 135.

280 **"constant struggle" & "ultimately" & "a Constitution" & "it is" & "the modern" & "Whether" & "to find" & "the partisan" & "as Marshall":** FF Draft, Constitution Day Address, R&FF, 409–17.

281 **"The Constitution" & "great layman's" & "a charter" & "an unending":** FDR, "Constitution Day Address," 9/17/1937, at 8, 10–11, FDRL, MSF, Box 34, No. 1071.

281 **back:** FF to CCB, 9/1/1937, at 1; FF to MRC, 9/24/1937, MRCP, Box 5, Folder 9.

281 **"did not shoot" & "feels":** BVC to FF, 10/11/1937, at 6–7, FFLC, Box 28. See HID, 7/16/1938, HI, *The Secret Diary of Harold L. Ickes: The Inside Struggle: 1936–1939*, at 424 (1954) (TGC's anger at LDB for not resigning in favor of FF).

281 **backfired:** Richard L. Stokes to TGC, 10/4/1937, TGCP, Box 198; Stokes to FF, 10/6/1937, id.

281 **"Felix Frankfurter versus":** STLPD, 10/3/1937, at 69.

281   **"I am rather":** FF to TGC, n.d., at 1–2, TGCP, Box 198. *See* FF to Max Lerner, 10/7/1937, at 1, Lerner Papers, Series 1, Box 3, Folder 120 (Stokes interview and public silence).

282   **thrilled:** FF to Winifred Reed, 1/17/1938, SFRP, FF Corr. Addenda, Folder 2.

282   **Holmes speeches:** SFR to FF, 1/17/1938, FFHLS, Pt. III, Reel 2, Page 795; SFR to FF, 2/3/1937, *id.*, Page 796.

282   **first law clerk:** SFR to FF, 3/30/1938, *id.*, Page 815 (John Sapienza). *See* John D. Fassett, "The Buddha and the Bumblebee," Journal of Supreme Court History 28 (2003): 165–96.

282   **not-so-secret:** Sherwood, *Roosevelt and Hopkins*, 94 (recounting conversation with FDR in spring 1938 about replacing LDB with FF); HSCD, 12/18/1938, at 8, HSCP, Reel 2.

282   **mend fences:** FDR Day by Day, 1/26/1938.

282   **asked Hughes:** LDB-FF Conversations, 2/5/1939, LDBHLS, Pt. II, Reel 33, Page 369.

282   **"found":** Harry Barnard, *The Forging of an American Jew*, 318 (1974).

282   **$2000:** Letter to LDB, 12/21/1937, LDB-Brandeis U, Box 121.

CHAPTER 19: SORTA TOUGH AIN'T IT!

283   **cream stucco:** NYT, 7/12/1938, at 19.

283   **tall candle & roses:** NYHT, 7/12/1938, at 12A. Cardozo spent his final six months of life at the home of his good friend Judge Irving Lehman along with his law clerk JLR. Michael E. Parrish, *Citizen Rauh*, 40–42 (2010); Andrew L. Kaufman, *Cardozo*, 566–78 (1998); Richard Polenberg, *The World of Benjamin Cardozo*, 234–50 (1997); George S. Hellman, *Benjamin N. Cardozo*, 298–313 (1940).

283   **Twenty-Third Psalm:** NYHT, 7/12/1938, at 12A; Cardozo Funeral Notes, Kaufman Papers, Box 12.

283   **"a most" & "really" & "quite":** FF to Ella Frankfurter, 7/15/1938, FFLC, Box 256.

283   **Rauh & canopy & light rain:** NYT, 7/12/1938, at 19; NYHT, 7/12/1938, at 12A; Long Island Press, 7/12/1938, at 13.

284   **finished first:** WP, 2/28/1937, at B1; WP, 5/23/1937, at B1.

284   **"by all" & "Frankfurter would" & "the public" & "Well" & "I do" & "One":** Henry Morgenthau Jr. Diaries, 5/24/1937, Morgenthau Papers, Book 69, Reel 94, at 308.

284   **did not come:** Michael E. Parrish, *Felix Frankfurter and His Times*, 275 (1982) & Parrish, *Citizen Rauh*, 48 (arguing, on the basis of August 12, 1975, and August 17, 1985, interviews with JLR, that FF was not surprised by FDR's phone call because TGC and BVC had been keeping the Harvard law professor informed nightly by phone).

284   **pulled a fast:** HID, 1/15/1939, HI, *The Secret Diary of Harold L. Ickes: The Inside Struggle: 1936–1939*, at 559 (1954) (recalling FDR's description of FF's supporters as "a little bunch of conspirators" and HI's surmising that "until it was all over, the President did not realize that we had ganged up on him for Frankfurter"); R&FF, 481–82.

285   **William Allen White:** FDR to WAW, 10/13/1938, WAWP, Box C290. FDR's letter to WAW has not been featured in previous accounts of FF's nomination.

285   **"willingness" & "narrow":** HSCD, 7/6/1938, HSCP, Reel 2, at 96.

285   **"next":** CCB to HFS, 10/14/1938, at 2, HFSP, Box 7 (according to La Guardia). *See* Robert E. Sherwood, *Roosevelt and Hopkins*, 94 (1948) (in the spring of 1938, FDR told Hopkins he wanted to appoint FF to replace LDB, but that "the need was for a man west of the Mississippi since the entire area was then unrepresented on the Court").

285   **certain:** HSCD, 7/9/1938, HSCP, Reel 2, at 99–100.

285   **9:15:** FDR Day by Day, 7/5/1938.

285   **Frank Murphy:** FM to TGC, 11/10/1938, FMP, Roll 44, at 35.

285   **"Otherwise":** HID, 7/16/1938, HI, *Secret Diary of Harold L. Ickes: The Inside Struggle: 1936–1939*, at 423–24.

285   **Corcoran:** BVC to FF, 10/11/1937, at 6–7, FFLC, Box 28.

286   **"replied":** HID, 7/16/1938, HI, *Secret Diary of Harold L. Ickes: The Inside Struggle: 1936–1939*, at 424.

286   **"They call":** Time, 9/12/1938. *See* William Lasser, *Benjamin V. Cohen*, 199–201 (2002) (noting that BVC had less to do with the "purge" campaign and with domestic politics in late 1938 than TGC because of BVC's Zionist activities).

286   **overnight stay:** FDR Day by Day, 5/12/1938, & 5/13/1938.

286   **luncheon:** FF to FDR, 5/18/1938, R&FF, 457–58; HID, 5/15/1938, HI, *Secret Diary of Harold L. Ickes: The Inside Struggle: 1936–1939*, at 393.

286   **Georgetown set:** Gregg Herken, *The Georgetown Set* (2014); Robert W. Merry, *Taking on the World* (1996).

286   **court-packing fight:** Joseph Alsop & Turner Catledge, *The 168 Days* (1938).

286   **New Deal advisers:** Joseph Alsop & Robert Kintner, *Men Around the President* (1939).

286   **summer and fall:** JA to FF, 9/7/1938, JA to FF, 9/22/1938, JA to FF, 9/29/1938, JA to FF, 10/7/1938, JA to FF, 10/14/1938, JA to FF, 11/21/1938, JSAP, Box 32 (sending drafts); *id.*, Box 93, Folder 3 (FF and TGC interviews).

287   **"Mr. President" & "few" & "one-man" & "If" & "But":** BG, 7/18/1938, at 1–2. The Borah story regarding Cardozo may be overstated. He had met with Hoover on the eve of the nomination. Yet by that time, FF and other liberals had lobbied Hoover's secretary of state HLS and former attorney general HFS to advocate for Cardozo. Brad Snyder, *The House of Truth*, 535–40 (2017).

287   **"If there" & "if the President":** STLPD, 7/27/1938, in Norris Papers, Box 280. *See* Dilliard to Norris, 8/10/1938, *id.*

287   **Waupaca:** Richard Lowitt, *George W. Norris: The Persistence of a Progressive, 1913–1933*, at 541–42 (1971); Richard Lowitt, *George W. Norris: The Triumph of a Progressive, 1933–1940*, at 341 (1978).

288   **confirm Brandeis:** 53 Cong. Rec. 9032 (1916).

288   **court-packing bill:** WP, 3/13/1937, at 1 (asking for some remedy); NYTM, 5/30/1937, at 3, 25 (term limits); Lowitt, *George W. Norris: The Triumph of a Progressive, 1933–1940*; George W. Norris, *Fighting Liberal* (1945).

288   **"an opportunity" & "There is" & "the confidential" & "recently" & "Felix":** NYHT, 8/8/1938, at 2.

288–289 **"Dear" & "their great" & "He can" & "the best" & "to repudiate":** TGC to Norris, 8/6/1938, Norris Papers, Box 280.

289   **"letter":** Note, 8/1938, *id.*

289   **"The whole Times":** TGC to AM, 8/23/1938, TGCP, Box 205. *See* AM to TGC, 8/14/1938, *id.* (relaying conversation with *Times* editor Charles Merz about omission); NYT, 8/9/1938, at 3.

289   **"he would":** BaltSun, 8/9/1938, at 2.

289   **only handicap:** Wilkes-Barre Times Leader, 8/15/1938, at 13.

289   **"This Norris" & "an object" & "an idol":** Reading Times, 8/10/1938, at 6.

289   **Holmes's 1932 letter:** WES, 8/16/1938, at A-9.

289–290 **Senator Norris:** "Holmes's Opinion of Frankfurter," OWH to Governor James Ely, 1/15/1932, Norris Papers, Box 280.

290 **met with Roosevelt:** FDR Day by Day, 8/17/1938.

290 **Minton declared:** NYT, 8/19/1938, at 4.

290 **"Frankfurter's" & "the man" & "the movement" & "many Roman" & "it will":** WES, 8/16/1938, at A-9.

290 **"as good" & "former" & "favorably" & "geographical" & "racial" & "were not" & "they do not" & "has some" & "campaign" & "There's":** Minneapolis Star, 8/18/1938, at 12. *See* FF, "Mr. Justice Cardozo," A.B.A. J. 24, no. 8 (August 1938): 638–39.

291 **"White House" & "a ghost":** Charleston Gazette, 7/31/1938, at 6. *See* Drew Pearson & Robert S. Allen, *The Nine Old Men* (1936).

291 **American Bar Association convention:** Indiana Evening Gazette, 8/4/1938, at 6.

291 **"inside track" & "liberal":** Corpus Christi Times, 8/24/1938, at 4.

291 **10 to 1:** Nevada State Journal, 8/25/1938, at 4.

291 **"satisfied" & "The President" & "get word":** JAFD, 8/25/1938, at 2–3, 11, JAFP, Reel 4, Box 43. *See* Sacramento Bee, 8/30/1938, at 11 in FDRL, PSF, Box 56, Pt. 2 (political cartoon sent from JAF to HSC to FDR about lack of western representation on Supreme Court).

292 **"astonishing" & "a personal":** Alsop & Kintner, *Men Around the President*, 158.

292 **"made" & "go to" & "too old" & "doubted" & "I took":** HSCD, 9/8/1938, HSCP, Reel 2, at 121.

292 **Born in Nebraska:** Biographical Statement, at 1–2, HMSP, Box 1, Folder "Biographical Material"; Daniel R. Ernst, "Dicey's Disciple on the D.C. Circuit," 90 Geo. L.J. 787, 793–96 (2002); Daniel R. Ernst, "State, Party, and Harold M. Stephens," 14 W. Legal Hist. 123, 154–57 (2001).

292 **"C-Man":** FF to LH, 12/4/1939, at 1–2, FFLC, Box 64.

292 **humiliated:** LDB-FF Conversations, "Gold Clause," at 2, FFHLS, Pt. II, Reel 33, Page 360.

293 **law clerks:** HMS to FF, 6/22/1954, HMSP, Box 14; FF to HMS, 9/10/1935, *id.*; HMS to FF, 9/26/1935, *id.*; FF to HMS, 9/30/1935, *id.*; HMS to FF, 10/5/1935, *id.*

293 **"a toady":** FF to CCB, 1/3/1939, at 2, CCBP, Box 5, Folder 5-1.

293 **Stephens's surrogates:** HMSP, Box 91 (containing lists of contacts dated 2/16/1938).

293 **Cummings, like Farley:** HMS to HSC, 3/2/1939, *id.*; HSC to HMS, 3/7/1939, at 3, *id.*; FDR to HSC, 3/11/1939, *id.*, Box 94; HMS to HSC, 3/16/1939, *id.*; HMS to JAF, 3/21/1939, *id.*; JAF to HMS, 3/27/1939, *id.*

293 **"nothing" & "the appointment":** JAFD, 9/26/1938, at 4, JAFP, Reel 4, Box 43.

293 **Gallup poll:** NYHT, 9/19/1938, at 7.

293 **"definitely":** CT, 9/26/1938, at 12.

293 **Schwellenbach:** *id.*; FDR Day by Day, 9/28/1938.

293 **Albert Lee Stephens:** FDR Day by Day, 10/1/1938.

294 **"wealthy":** WES, 9/21/1938, at A-11. *See* Baltimore Evening Sun, 9/29/1938, at 13.

294 **Sulzberger:** HID, 9/18/1938, HI, *Secret Diary of Harold L. Ickes: The Inside Struggle: 1936–1939*, at 470–71.

294 **Nazi atrocities:** Deborah E. Lipstadt, *Beyond Belief* (1985); Susan E. Tifft & Alex S. Jones, *The Trust*, 215–19 (1999).

294 **bet:** Sulzberger, Memorandum, 5/27/1937, Sulzberger Papers, Box 256, Folder 5; Sulzberger to FF, 2/1/1938, *id.*; FF to Sulzberger, 2/2/1938, *id.*

294   **Billikopf:** JB to FF, 11/2/1938, at 1–2, FFLC, Box 183; JB to Sulzberger, 11/4/1938, *id.* At
       the time, Sulzberger denied talking to FDR directly yet later recollected he had. *Com-*
       pare Sulzberger to Harold I. Cammer, 1/23/1939, Sulzberger Papers, Box 256; Sulz-
       berger to FF, 1/5/1939, *id. with* Sulzberger to Orvil Dryfoos, 8/29/1962, *id.*; Sulzberger
       to Rabbi Jacob Weinstein, 3/16/1961, *id.*

294   **"our crowd":** Stephen Birmingham, *Our Crowd* (1967).

294   **Morgenthau Sr.:** JB to FF, 11/2/1938, at 1–2.

294   **Morgenthau, Jr.:** FDR Day by Day, 8/30/1938; *id.*, 8/31/1938.

294   **Corcoran:** FDR Day by Day, 9/1/1938; *id.*, 9/2/1938; *id.*, 9/3/1938; *id.*, 9/6/1938 (with
       Hopkins at Hyde Park).

294   **draft a letter:** TGC to AM, 9/26/1938, TGCP, Box 205.

294   **"would be":** Draft letter, at 1, *id.*

294   **"the rumors" & "got":** FF to JB, 11/15/1938, at 1, FFLC, Box 25.

294   **"one":** LDB to FF, 11/23/1938, HBHS, at 623.

294   **"there was" & "spoke":** HID, 12/3/1938, HIP, Reel 2, at 3065.

295   **"Never":** FF to GJ, 12/12/1938, GJP-FDRL, Box 29.

295   **"dragged" & "from":** NY Post, 3/18/1938, at 2; John Cooper Wiley to George S. Messer-
       smith, 3/18/1938 tel., NARA, State Department Files 1930–39, RG 59, Box 1685 (Salo-
       mon's daughter reported: 1:00 a.m. arrest & police prison in Elisabeth promenade);
       Jewish Exponent, 3/25/1938, at 1.

295   **collarless & prisoners:** NY Post, 1/24/1939, at 4 (Post photographer Ernest Klein-
       berg's account).

295   **friend in Vienna:** FF Int. with Max Freedman, n.d., at 2–3, FFHLS, Pt. III, Reel 40,
       Pages 269–70.

295   **Josef Redlich:** FFLC, Box 92; FF, "Josef Redlich," 50 Harv. L. Rev. 389 (1937).

295–296 **sparse & Rosenwald:** FF to Salomon Frankfurter, 12/28/1920, FFLC, Box 18; Salomon
       Frankfurter to FF, 10/20/1931, *id.*

296   **Nancy Astor:** FF Int. with Max Freedman, n.d., at 3–4, FFHLS, Pt. III, Reel 40,
       Pages 270–71.

296   **"promised" & "that unless":** Lady Astor to FF, May 1938, in R&FF, 473–74. *See* FF
       to Lady Astor, 6/2/1938, *id.* at 474–75; Astor to Westbrook Pegler, 8/30/1948, at 1–2,
       Pegler Papers, Box 35, Folder 5 (recalling her assistance to FF's uncle and her displea-
       sure that FF believed she was a Nazi sympathizer); Christopher Sykes, *Nancy,* 376–90
       (1972) (Astor's relationship with von Ribbentrop and assistance to FF).

296   **Feis & Messersmith & Wiley:** Feis to FF, 3/26/1938, at 1, FFLC, Box 54; Messersmith to
       FF, 3/30/1938, at 1, *id.*; FF to Messersmith, 3/17/1938, FFLC, Box 83; Rochester Demo-
       crat, 3/28/1938, at 1.

296   **Frankfurter's request:** Messersmith to Austria Legation, 3/13/1938 tel., NARA, State
       Department Files 1930–39, RG 59, Box 1685; Wiley to Messersmith, 3/18/1938 tel., *id.*

296   **"unknown":** Wiley to Messersmith, 3/19/1938 tel., *id.*

296   **"nervous":** Wiley to Messersmith, 3/22/1938, *id.*

296   **"good":** Wiley to Messersmith, 3/24/1938, *id.*

296   **astounded Roosevelt & seek favors:** FF to FDR, 10/24/1941 & FDR to FF, 10/27/1941,
       R&FF, 619–20. On Lady Astor story, *see* Liva Baker, *Felix Frankfurter,* 200–201, 353 n.17
       (1969); Leonard Baker, *Brandeis and Frankfurter,* 351–52 (1984); Parrish, *Felix Frank-*
       furter and His Times, 273, 321 n.1.

297   **distressed:** FF to FDR, 10/3/1938, R&FF, 461–63.

297 **draft wire:** BVC to MLH, 10/13/1938, *id.* at 463.

297 **fawning letters:** FF to FDR, 10/27/1938, *id.* at 463–64; FF to FDR, 11/25/1938, *id.* at 466.

297 **sponsored the publication:** Charles C. Burlingham et al., *The German Reich and Americans of German Origin*, vii (1938).

297 **"the President":** WES, 9/21/1938, at A-11.

297 **"Mr. Roosevelt":** The Nation, 10/8/1938, at 339.

297 **"extraneous":** Akron Beacon Journal, 9/8/1938, at 17.

298 **"to express":** JWM to FDR, 10/5/1938, WAWP, Box C287.

298 **"give" & "only reinforce":** Kellogg to FDR, 10/10/1938, at 4, *id. See* FDR to Kellogg, 10/15/1938, *id.*

298 **Calvin Coolidge:** William Allen White, *A Puritan in Babylon* (1938).

298 **"was":** Emporia Gazette, 1/6/1939, at 2.

298 **was determined:** WAW to FWB, 7/30/1938, WAWP, Box C285.

298 **"the Supreme Court":** Kellogg to WAW, 9/12/1938, at 2, *id.*, Box C287.

298 **"Isaiah" & "It was":** JB to Norris, 8/10/1938, at 1, Norris Papers, Box 280.

298 **"the big" & "their head":** WAW to Kellogg, 9/16/1938, at 1, WAWP, Box C287. *See* WAW to Kellogg, 10/15/1938, *id.*

299 **5:15 p.m.:** FDR Day by Day, 10/8/1938.

299 **"There's something":** FFR, 279–80.

299 **"I want" & "very definite":** FFR, 280–81.

299 **frowned:** Samuel R. Spencer, Jr., Notes of Int. FF GC Conversations, Summer 1947, at 8, FFHLS, Pt. III, Reel 15, Page 260.

299 **western judges:** FFR Transcript, 8/30/1957, at 386–89.

299 **countryside & "circles":** NYHT, 10/9/1938, at 33.

299 **"his old":** FFR, 281.

299 **"inside track":** CT, 10/9/1938, at 11.

299–300 **"representative" & "private" & "a problem" & "Sorta":** FDR to WAW, 10/13/1938.

300 **"best":** Indiana Evening Gazette, 7/27/1938, at 4.

300 **Murphy & Schwellenbach:** NYHT, 11/13/1938, at 23.

300 **"too radical":** WES, 11/19/1938, at A-11.

300 **"left wing" & "dark horse":** WP, 11/13/1938, at M8.

300 **reviewed & "did not":** HSCD, 11/18/1938, HSCP, Reel 2, at 190–1. *See* HSC to FDR, 11/30/1938, FDRL, PSF, Ser. 4, Box 56, Pt. 2.

300 **"could be" & "the right" & "the country" & "I know":** HSCD, 11/18/1938.

301 **"for I" & "well conceived" & "lucid":** FF to FDR, 11/17/1938 & Memorandum on Judge William Healy at 1 & Memorandum on Judge Albert Stephens at 2–3, FDRL, PSF, Ser. 5, Box 135.

301 **Not even:** NYT, 11/11/1938, at 1. *See* Martin Gilbert, *Kristallnacht* (2006); *The Night of Broken Glass* (Uta Gerhardt & Thomas Karlauf, eds. 2012).

301 **"Even if":** FF to HI, 11/29/1938, HI, *Secret Diary of Harold L. Ickes: The Inside Struggle: 1936–1939*, at 391–93; HID, 5/15/1938, *id.* at 396–99; FFLC, Box 69.

301 **helium:** HID, 5/15/1938; HI, *Secret Diary of Harold L. Ickes: The Inside Struggle: 1936-1939*, at 391 -93; HID, 5/15/1938, id. at 396 -99; NYT, 7/22/1938, at 9; NYT, 12/17/1938, at 8.

301–302 **"in the lead" & "since both":** HID, 11/19/1938; HI, *Secret Diary of Harold L. Ickes: The Inside Struggle: 1936 -1939*, at 505.

302 **"We who":** NYT, 10/2/1938, at 1.

302   **more complicated:** R&FF, 372.

302   **"up":** TGC, "Rendezvous with Democracy," Chapter X – Page 35, TGCP, Box 586.

302   **"pressure" & "make" & "incensed" & "the Corcoran-Cohen":** Binghamton Press, 12/2/1938, at 6.

302   **"the New Deal" & "like the" & "merely":** WES, 12/8/1938, at A-13.

302   **advised & revealed:** LDB to FF, 10/16/1938, HBHS, at 620; LDB to FF, 10/24/1938, *id.* at 621; LDB to FF, 11/23/1938, *id.* at 623.

302   **"will eventually" & "No":** FF to HJL, 5/25/1938, at 2, FFLC, Box 74. *Cf.* FF to "Boys," 5/17/[1938], at 2, TGCP, Box 198 ("I don't take any stock in the L.D.B. retirement talk – or should I").

302   **back trouble & memorial resolution:** RHJ to FF, 10/28/1938, RHJP, Box 81, Folder 6; FF to RHJ, 11/25/1938, *id.*

302   **his book:** FF, *Mr. Justice Holmes and the Supreme Court* (1938).

303   **battleship:** INB to TGC, 5/2/1963, INBP, Box 5; TGC to INB, 8/27/1936, *id.*; INB, *Storm over the* Constitution (1936).

303   **consultant to Ickes:** HID, 1/7/1939, Reel 3, at 3151 & HI, *Secret Diary of Harold L. Ickes: The Inside Struggle: 1936–1939*, at 550–51.

303   **Rutledge:** INB to FDR, 11/12/1938, INBP, Box 13.

303   **"because":** INB to Max Freedman, 1/22/1969, *id.*, Box 6.

303   **"pressure" & "closest" & "the western":** INB to Ralph Fuchs, 12/31/1938, at 1, *id.*, Box 7.

303   **kept Rutledge apprised:** INB to WBR, 11/12/1938, *id.*, Box 13; WBR to INB, 11/22/1938, *id.*; INB to WBR, 12/27/1938, at 1–2, *id.*; STLST, 9/6/1938, at 14; STLST, 10/4/1938, at 14.

303   **"Cummings":** INB to WBR, 1/14/1939, INBP, Box 13.

303   **"appeared":** BaltSun, 12/10/1938, at 1.

303   **Winchell:** Logansport Pharos-Tribune, 12/13/1938, at 5.

304   **"the matter" & "I thought" & "How did" & "I told" & "as a possibility":** HSCD, 12/18/1938, HSCP, Reel 2, at 248–49.

304   **"need not" & "Yes":** *Id.* at 249.

304   **Stephens's judicial opinions:** Parrish, *Citizen Rauh*, 48 (based on August 17, 1985, int. with JLR).

304   **lunch:** FDR Day by Day, 12/16/1938.

304   **"friends":** BG, 12/27/1938, at 1.

304   **"no longer" & "the inside":** NYHT, 12/27/1938, at 2.

304   **Schwellenbach:** TNR, 12/21/1938, at 200.

305   **"[l]argely":** Nevada State Journal, 12/30/1938, at 4.

305   **"pretended":** BG, 12/27/1938, at 1.

305   **lunch:** FDR Day by Day, 12/21/1938.

305   **"We discussed":** JAFD, 12/21/1938, at 2, JAFP, Reel 4, Box 43.

305   **private dinner:** FDR Day by Day, 12/28/1938.

305   **"having" & "In the first" & "belonged" & "not up" & "very much" & "had given" & "made":** JAFD, 12/28/1938, at 3–5, JAFP, Reel 4, Box 43. *Cf.* JAF, *Jim Farley's Story*, 161–62 (1948) (for revised comments & FDR quote that "Felix Frankfurter wants to go on in the worst way," which does not appear in the diary).

306   **"was qualified":** FFR, 282.

306   **should nominate Frankfurter:** WBR to INB, 11/22/1938, at 1–2, INBP, Box 13. See STLST, 12/28/1938, at 2; STLST, 12/29/1938, at 14; John M. Ferren, *Salt of the Earth*, 137–50, 157 (2004).

306 **2:00 p.m.**: FDR Day by Day, 12/29/1938.

306 **"was a legal" & "But will" & "If you" & "really" & "another"**: HID, 1/1/1939; HI, *Secret Diary of Harold L. Ickes: The Inside Struggle: 1936–1939*, at 539–40.

306 **"stupid" & "told her"**: HID, 1/1/1939, *id.* at 540.

306 **"the whole thing"**: HID, 1/7/1939, Reel 3, at 3151. *See* Kathryn Smith, *The Gatekeeper*, 124 (2016).

306 **nightly phone calls**: Parrish, *Felix Frankfurter and His Times*, 275 & Parrish, *Citizen Rauh*, 48 (based on August 12, 1975, int. & August 17, 1985, int. with JLR); JLR Int. with Lash, 6/10/1986, Lash Papers, Box 65, Folder 2.

307 **"so disgusted"**: HID, 1/1/1939, Reel 3, at 3126.

307 **three hours**: FDR Day by Day, 12/29/1938.

307 **"a chance"**: HID, 1/2/1939, Reel 3, at 3140–41.

307 **Hopkins and Jackson**: FDR Day by Day, 12/31/1938.

307 **"was on"**: RHJ, "Lunch at the White House on Saturday, Dec. 31, 1938," at 1, 3–4, RHJP, Box 81, Folder 3.

307 **"that all" & "notion" & "the President's" & "looked" & "the future" & "importance" & "leave me" & "said it" & "joined" & "agreed"**: RHJ, "Lunch at the White House on Saturday, Dec. 31, 1938," 4–5. *See* Eugene C. Gerhart, *America's Advocate*, 163–67 (1958); RHJ COH, 637, RHJP, Box 190, Folder 5; RHJ, *That Man* (John Q. Barrett, ed. 2003).

308 **"This appointment"**: HID, 1/2/1939. *See* Evatt to FDR, 11/11/1938, 1–3, FDRL, PSF, Ser. 4, Box 56, "Folder Homer Cummings 1938–44" Pt. 2 & Gerhart, *America's Advocate*, 157 (note from Australian High Court justice H. V. "Bert" Evatt arguing for FF's appointment).

308 **"The Frankfurter"**: RHJ, "Monday, January 2, 1939: Murphy Ceremony," at 1, RHJP, Box 81, Folder 3.

308 **"lingered"**: *Id.*

308 **"his influence" & "urge" & "told"**: *Id.* at 1–2. *See* Norris to FDR, 12/27/1938, at 2, RHJP, Box 81, Folder 3 (arguing it would be "a great mistake" if the president did not appoint RHJ as attorney general).

308 **4:30 p.m.**: FDR Day by Day, 1/2/1939.

308 **"strongly urged"**: HID, 1/7/1939. *See* HJL to Norris, 1/6/1939, Norris Papers, Box 280; Dilliard to Norris, 1/21/1939, *id.* (crediting Norris).

308 **"mildly ruffled"**: NYT, 1/4/1939, at 26.

309 **tea**: RHJ, "Monday, January 2, 1939: Murphy Ceremony," at 2; FDR Day by Day, 1/2/1939.

309 **Cardozo**: HFS to George Hellman, 11/30/1939, at 1, HFSP, Box 16.

309 **"get" & "will get" & "a man"**: HID, 1/7/1939, Reel 3, at 3152–53 & HI, *Secret Diary of Harold L. Ickes: The Inside Struggle: 1936–1939*, at 551–52.

309 **"felt"**: HID, 1/7/1938, HI, *Secret Diary of Harold L. Ickes: The Inside Struggle: 1936–1939*, at 552.

309 **Ickes & Murphy**: FDR Day by Day, 1/3/1939.

309 **"would go"**: HID, 1/7/1938, Reel 3, at 3153.

309 **"the most important"**: INB to Dilliard, 1/24/1939, INBP, Box 5.

309 **"a compromise" & "Stephens Expected"**: CT, 1/3/1939, at 2.

309 **"the orthodox" & "is out"**: BG, 1/3/1939, at 1, 11.

309 **"the inside"**: NYT, 1/3/1939, at 13.

310   **"confident" & "still":** NYHT, 1/4/1939, at 6A.

310   **"to the fore":** WP, 1/4/1939, at 1.

310   **"eminently":** HSCD, 1/4/1939, HSCP, Reel 2, at 4.

310   **"If":** Atlantic News-Telegraph, 1/11/1939, at 2 (Pearson & Allen).

310   **"There are":** HSCD, 1/4/1939, HSCP, Reel 2, at 4.

310   **12:45 p.m. & 2:00 p.m. & 4:15 p.m.:** FDR Day by Day, 1/4/1939. Alsop and Kintner may have known—because they dined at 7:30 p.m. with FDR, a half-hour after FDR's call to FF. *Id.*

310   **"Please" & "I told" & "Yes" & "You've" & "But wherever" & "insurmountable":** FFR, 282–84, 288.

310   **"moved":** FF to FDR, 1/4/1939, FDRL, PSF, Ser. 5, Box 135. *See* FF to CCB, 7/8/1942, at 1, FFLC, Box 35.

310   **"Marion":** FFR, 284.

310   **in the dark:** JAFD, 1/5/1939, JAFP, Reel 4, Box 43; JAF, *Jim Farley's Story*, 163.

311   **longhand:** FDR, 1/6/1936, LC P&P, LC-H22-D-5399.

311   **"I have done it":** WAW to Kellogg, 1/7/1939, FFLC, Box 227 (enclosing FDR to WAW, 1/5/1939 tel., 11:40 a.m.).

311   **newswires & shocked:** HSCD, 1/5/1939, HSCP, Reel 2, at 6 (noting he and FM learned of it from the "ticker"); JAFD, 1/5/1939; Atlantic News-Telegraph, 1/11/1939, at 2.

311   **blamed Corcoran:** HMS to HSC, 3/2/1939, at 2–3.

311   **"We were":** HID, 1/7/1939, HI, *Secret Diary of Harold L. Ickes: The Inside Struggle: 1936–1939*, at 552.

311   **"Even though":** Minneapolis Star, 1/6/1939, at 16.

CHAPTER 20: THE ODDEST COLLECTION OF PEOPLE

313   **"Says":** FF to FDR, 1/6/1939 tel., R&FF, 483–84.

313   **retired army colonel:** Testimony of Col. Latham R. Reed, 12/8/1938, Investigation of Un-American Propaganda Activities, Vol. 4, 75th Cong., 3rd Sess., at 2985–86; NYT, 12/9/1938, at 10.

313   **first modern:** Lori A. Ringhand, "Aliens on the Bench: Lessons in Identity, Race and Politics from the First 'Modern' Supreme Court Confirmation Hearing to Today," 2010 Mich. St. L. Rev. 795, 835.

314   **"this is" & "an office" & "duty":** FF Hearings at 1–2.

314   **"in person":** Neely to FF, 1/7/1939 tel., FFHLS, Pt. III, Reel 23, Page 740.

314   **if needed:** FF to Neely, 1/7/1939 tel., *id.* at 741. *See* DA to FF, 1/8/1939 tel., *id.* at Page 742; CCB to FF, 1/8/1939 tel., *id.*; FF to CCB, 1/8/1939 tel., at 1–2, CCBP, Box 5, Folder 5-1; WP, 1/8/1939, at 1.

314   **Tall and handsome:** DA, *Morning and Noon*, 161–94 (1965).

315   **"the oddest":** DA to Rublee, 1/17/1939, at 1–2, DAP, Reel 17, Box 27, Folder 340 & in *Among Friends* at 37 (David S. McLellan & David C. Acheson, eds. 1980). *See* DA, *Morning and Noon*, 201; Notes on Redd, Sullivan, & Cooper testimony, DAP, Reel 44, Folder 171.

315   **"an American" & "too old" & "Are you" & "Then why" & "interest in" & "corresponds":** FF Hearings at 3–7.

315   **loyalty oaths:** WES, 2/21/1937, at A-1.

315   **Dies & Red-hunting:** WES, 11/18/1938, at A-30; WES, 12/16/1938, at 12; WES, 6/15/1949, at B-1.

315 **gripped:** Sullivan photograph, 1/10/1939, LC P&P, LC-H22-D-5454.

315–316 **"Mr. Frankfurter's" & "a number" & "based":** FF Hearings at 9–10, 12, 21. *See* WES, 1/11/1939, at A-10.

316 **"proper" & "I think":** FF Hearings at 26.

316 **"lost":** Minneapolis Star, 1/11/1939, at 18.

316 **"cranks":** CT, 1/11/1939, at 4.

316 **"This pitiful":** Minneapolis Star, 1/11/1939, at 18.

316 **suburban Chicago:** Glen Jeansonne, *Women of the Far Right*, 10–28 (1996); Geoffrey S. Smith, *To Save a Nation* (1973); Stasia Von Zwisler, "Elizabeth Dilling and the Rose-Colored Spyglass, 1931–1942" (MA thesis, University of Wisconsin-Milwaukee, 1987).

316 **an entry:** Elizabeth Dilling, *The Red Network*, 282 (1934).

316 **"one of that clique":** Elizabeth Dilling, *The Roosevelt Red Record and Its Background*, 80–81 (1936).

316 **"as an American":** FF Hearings at 29–30.

316 **blue and gold:** Dilling photograph, 1/11/1939, LC P&P, LC-H22-D-5468; STLPD, 1/12/1939, at 11.

316 **"comely" & "fast" & "a high":** NYHT, 1/12/1939, at 10A.

317 **"that Felix Frankfurter" & "worked":** FF Hearings at 29–30.

317 **"prejudice" & "a communist":** FF Hearings at 30–33.

317 **"Communist supporter" & "socialistic" & " 'red' " & "The history":** FF Hearings at 33–34.

317 **"Frankfurter was":** FF Hearings at 35–36.

317–318 **"You classify" & "I didn't" & "one of the most" & "Brandeis" & "Do you want":** FF Hearings at 36, 45–47.

318 **high-pitched:** NYHT, 1/12/1939, at 10A.

318 **"picture" & "restless":** Life, 1/23/1939, at 16–17.

318 **"imbued" & "specialized" & "alien" & "communized":** FF Hearings at 66, 89, 90–91, 95–96, 100.

318 **"Pro-American" & movie:** NYT, 10/31/1938, at 10.

318 **picketing:** NYHT, 12/19/1938, at 5; NYT, 12/19/1938, at 24.

318 **"Down" & "Keep" & "Frankfurter is":** FF Hearings at 74, 93. Some of the picketers shouted "No Hot Dogs on the Supreme Court!"; "Americans in the Supreme Court!"; "We like chicken—not frankfurters!"; and "No Kosher Frankfurters!" "Memorandum on the Street Disturbances in New York City," n.d., American Jewish Committee file on Coughlin, ajcarchives.org, at 2–3. Seven months later, Zoll was indicted for trying to extort $7500 from the president of the radio station in exchange for ending the picketing. NYT, 7/2/1939, at 1.

319 **"because" & "You are" & "would stir" & "Some of" & "offensive" & "This appointment":** FF Hearings at 74–77.

319 **"caused":** WDN, 1/12/1939, at 26.

319 **"has not only" & rehashed:** FF Hearings at 78–86.

319 **produce proof:** FF Hearings at 87–88.

319 **obtained:** FFR, 286; SIR to DA, 1/13/1939, DAP, Reel 17, Box 26, Folder 331; DA, *Morning and Noon*, 202.

319 **consulting:** DA & Neely Photo, 1/11/1939, LC P&P, LC-H22-D-5467.

319 **"unsubstantiated" & "witnesses":** WP, 1/12/1939, at 10.

320 **Pat McCarran:** Michael J. Ybarra, *Washington Gone Crazy*, 211–12, 217–23 (2004).

320 **"is controlled" & "I just want" & asked Zoll & religious grounds:** FF Hearings at 41–42, 68, 76, 80–81, 99.

320   **executive session:** FF Hearings at 103.

320   **McCarran demanded:** Indiana Evening Gazette, 1/18/1939, at 4.

320   **"A long":** DA, *Morning and Noon*, 202–3.

320   **next morning's:** BG, 1/12/1939, at 1; NYT, 1/12/1939, at 1.

321   **Acheson's house:** NYHT, 1/12/1939, at 9.

321   **Madison Square:** FFR, 285.

321   **Caucus   Room:**   https://www.senate.gov/artandhistory/history/common/briefing/
       Caucus_Room.htm#4.

321   **hallway:** WES, 1/12/1939, at A-3.

321   **"S.R.O.":** Photograph, 1/12/1939, LC P&P, hec2009012506.

321   **shorter:** BaltSun, 1/12/1939, at 2; DA, *Morning and Noon*, 203.

321   **Prichard, Jr.:** Photograph, 1/12/1939, LC P&P, LC-H22-D-5475; EFP OH, 11/29/1982, at 9.

321   **hissed:** STLPD, 1/12/1939, at 11.

321   **subcommittee members:** NYHT, 1/12/1939, at 9; WES, 1/22/1939, at 8.

321   **"I suppose":** BaltSun, 1/13/1939, at 2.

321   **briefcase:** Photograph, 1/12/1939, LC P&P, LC-H22-D-5478.

322   **"just sat":** FFR, 285.

322   **"may become" & "the best" & "attitude" & "That is":** Hearings at 107–08.

322   **"a very":** Hearings at 108–10.

322   **nervous:** WES, 1/12/1939, at A-3; FWB notes of conversation with Boston Herald
       reporter Henry Ehrlich, 1/12/1939, at 1, FFHLS, Reel 23, Page 197.

322–323 **"the great" & "Of course" & Dilling's & "the nature":** FF Hearings at 110–13.

323   **November 1917 and January 1918 reports & Fickert & Greenway:** FF Hearings at 113–22.

323   **"I should like":** FF Hearings at 123.

323   **"doctor" & "a contagious" & "a plague":** FFR, 285.

323   **"There are" & "his associates" & "The record":** FF Hearings at 123–24.

324   **"what purports":** FF Hearings at 124–25. *See* FFR, 286.

324   **"very" & "Do you agree" & "Do you subscribe" & "Have you" & "just casually":** FF Hear-
       ings at 125–26.

324   **laughed:** STLPD, 1/12/1939, at 11.

324   **"What would" & "The doctrine" & "You see" & "Do you" & "I cannot":** FF Hearings
       at 125–26.

324   **"the time":** FFR, 285.

324   **"If it" & "Senator":** FF Hearings at 125–26.

325   **"broke into":** NYT, 1/13/1939, at 1. *See* FWB notes on conversation with Ehrlich,
       1/12/1939, at 1 ("brought down the house").

325   **"Is that" & "the ideology" & "You will":** FF Hearings at 126.

325   **"There is" & "to enlarge":** FF Hearings at 126–27 (citing FF, "Supreme Court, United
       States," in *Encyclopedia of the Social Sciences*, Vol. 14, 474, 478 (1934)).

325   **"refrained" & "the Court":** Memorandum, n.d., FFHLS, Pt. III, Reel 23, Page 729
       (marked "Not Used").

325   **"theories" & "I mean":** FF Hearings at 127.

326   **was worried:** DA, *Morning and Noon*, 207.

326   **"I am very" & "I infer" & "in a very hazy" & "Are you" & "I have" & "By that" & "I
       mean":** FF Hearings at 128. *See* FWB notes on conversation with Ehrlich, 1/12/1939,
       at 2 (describing moment as "very dramatic"); Marquis Childs, *Witness to Power*, 41–42
       (1975) (describing hearing and McCarran showdown).

326   **roared:** DA, *Morning and Noon*, 208.

326   **crowd & photographers:** FWB memorandum of Ehrlich conversation, 1/12/1939, at 1–2.

326   **Dilling . . . whispered & lurked:** STLPD, 1/12/1939, at 11; Photograph, 1/12/1939, LC P&P, LC-H22-D-5482.

326   **"called away":** Indiana Evening Gazette, 1/18/1939, at 4.

326   **"I think":** WP, 1/13/1939, at 1.

327   **"Tell me" & "crazy":** DA, *Morning and Noon*, 209–11.

327   **"The story":** *Id.* at 211–12. *See* FDR Day by Day, 1/12/1939 (not showing DA or FF).

328   **"sedentary":** DA, *Morning and Noon*, 212–15. *See* DA to FDR, 2/6/1939 & Memorandum, 2/7/1939, FDRL, PSF, Ser. 5, Box 91; FDR Day by Day, 2/6/1939.

328   **"road back":** DA, *Morning and Noon*, 195–227.

328   **Senator Wheeler:** BKW Statement, n.d. & ML to BKW, 1/13/1939, MLP, Box 14, Folder 6 & BKWP-MSU, Box 8, Folder 7.

328   **Senate Judiciary Committee:** 84 Cong. Rec. 351 (1939); WES, 1/16/1939, at A-1.

328   **"The question" & roll call vote:** 84 Cong. Rec. 409 (1939); WES, 1/17/1939, at A-1; BG, 1/17/1939, at 6.

328   **"Pardon" & "a storm":** BG, 1/18/1939, at 1, 6.

328   **dark green:** BG, 1/19/1939, at 1, 23. *See* Photograph, 1/19/1939, LC P&P, Unprocessed in PR 13 CN 1971:054.

329   **White House car:** WES, 1/19/1939, at A-4.

329   **Rosenman & Gellhorn & Dewson:** FDR Day by Day, 1/19/1939.

329   **other unofficial guests:** FF to FDR, 1/16/1939, R&FF, 485; NYT, 1/20/1939, at 2; WES, 1/20/1939, at B-3.

329   **"the centers":** WP, 1/20/1939, at 18.

329   **3624 Prospect Street:** WES, 1/28/1939, at A-2.

329   **Irving Dilliard:** STLPD, 1/29/1939, at 10A.

329   **new robe:** Thomas Waggaman to Powell, 1/9/1939, Powell Papers, Box A, Folder A7; FF to Powell, 2/27/1939, at 1, *id.*

329   **"one of":** NYT, 1/31/1939, at 26.

329   **Marion sat:** "Monday, Jan. 30, 1939," Waggaman Correspondence with FF, 1939–1944, Supreme Court Curator's Office.

329   **"too wobbly":** HLS to FF, 1/25/1939, at 3, FFHLS, Pt. III, Reel 21, Page 656.

329   **"so help":** WES, 1/30/1939, at A-1.

330   **bowed & listened:** NYT, 1/31/1939, at 26; NYHT, 1/31/1939, at 1A, 11; BaltSun, 1/31/1939, at 2; BG, 1/31/1939, at 5.

330   **5:45 p.m.:** FDR Day by Day, 1/30/1939.

330   **"In the mysterious":** FF to FDR, 1/30/1939, R&FF, 485.

330   **"the appointment" & "to make":** WDN, 1/6/1939, at 3.

330   **German newspaper:** B.Z. am Mittag, 1/6/1939, at 1.

330   **"America's president":** WDN, 1/6/1939, at 3.

330   **public rebuke:** FFR, 288.

330   **"The peoples":** Hitler, Reichstag Speech, 1/30/1939, https://www.ushmm.org/learn/timeline-of-events/1939-1941/hitler-speech-to-german-parliament. *See* Ian Kershaw, *Hitler: 1936–45 Nemesis*, 152–53, 349, 490 (2000) (prophecy of Jewish annihilation in the 1939 Reichstag speech).

330   **"a double barreled":** SSW to FDR, 1/5/1939 tel., SSWP, Box 68, Folder 6.

331   **"makes me":** The Nation, 1/21/1939, at 94.

331   **"feels":** HID, 1/22/1939, HI, *The Secret Diary of Harold L. Ickes: The Inside Struggle: 1936–1939*, at 563 (1954).

331   **"If we":** Borah to Fred Strobel, 1/23/1939, Borah Papers, Box 523.

331   **radio:** BDE, 1/6/1939, at 2.

331   **"rejoiced":** Lima (N.Y.) Record, 1/19/1939, at 2.

CHAPTER 21: THE BRANDEIS WAY

332   **February 5:** LDB-FF Conversations, 2/5/1939, at 1–2, LDBHLS, Pt. 2, Reel 33, at 369–70.

332   **fifth-floor:** 1939 Washington D.C. City Directory at 154 (2205 California Street Apt. 505).

332   **flu:** NYT, 1/10/1939, at 16 (revealing he had been ill with "grippe" for three days when he was forced to leave during the justices' conference on the afternoon of Saturday, January 7); Adrian Fisher Int. with Lewis Paper, 8/11/1980, at 4, Paper Papers, Box 1, Folder 1-3 (pneumonia), DA to Rublee, 1/17/1939, at 1 (serious illness).

332   **mild heart attack:** Lewis J. Paper, *Brandeis*, 395 (1983); Melvin I. Urofsky, *Louis D. Brandeis*, 748–49 (2009).

332   **"judgment" & Hughes:** LDB-FF Conversations, 2/5/1939, at 1–2. *See* LDB to Jennie Taussig Brandeis, 2/13/1939, FLLDB at 552 & Alpheus Thomas Mason, *Brandeis*, 634 (1946) (not ill health); HID, 2/4/1939, HI, *The Secret Diary of Harold L. Ickes: The Inside Struggle: 1936–1939*, at 572 (1954) (noting FF had seen LDB on "Sunday before coming out to dinner" and that LDB was "well").

332   *Erie:* Erie Railroad Co. v. Tompkins, 304 U.S. 64 (1938); FF to Max Lerner, 4/27/1938, Lerner Papers, Box 3, Folder 122; Edward A. Purcell, Jr., *Brandeis and the Progressive Constitution* (2000).

332   **"quantitatively" & "opinion":** LDB-FF Conversations, 2/5/1939, at 1–2.

332   **pre-conference meeting:** HFS to FF, n.d., with FF's handwritten notes, FFHLS, Pt. I, Reel 1, Page 199. *See* Fisher Int. with Louchheim, at 8–9, Louchheim Papers, Box 72, Folder 10 (recalling LDB did not want FF to come because caucus was for OJR).

332–333 **"this day" & "The country":** NYHT, 2/14/1939, at 1.

333   **"poignant" & "The work":** FF to LDB, 2/13/1939, at 1–2, FFLC, Box 29.

333   **"has always":** WES, 2/16/1939, at A-41.

333   **Zionist activities:** FF to JWM, 5/17/1939, at 2, FFLC, Box 81; Fisher Int. with Paper, 8/11/1980, at 4–5.

334   **little interest:** An exception was LDB's opinion declaring Ziang Sung Wan's murder confession to have been coerced by eleven days of police questioning while Wan was physically ill. Wan v. United States, 266 U.S. 1, 10–14 (1924). Three years later, however, LDB joined the Court's unanimous opinion reaffirming Mississippi's racially separate but equal school system. Gong Lum v. Rice, 275 U.S. 78 (1927).

334   **"What" & "Well":** JLR D.C. Circuit Historical Society Oral history by Bob Peck, at 15–16, 1/10/1992, JLRP, Box 298, Folder 13.

334   **worked day and night:** WP, 8/18/1983, A29 & Essay re: Cohen, Benjamin, 9/7/1983, JLRP, Box 286, Folder 8; JLR Int. with Louchheim, 1/4/1982, Louchheim Papers, Box 73, Folder 1. *See* Burco v. Whitworth, 81 F.2d 721 (4th Cir.), cert. denied, 297 U.S. 724 (1936); Michael E. Parrish, *Citizen Rauh*, 33–47 (2010); Joseph P. Lash, *Dealers and Dreamers*, 286–90 (1988); William Lasser, *Benjamin V. Cohen*, 142–46 (2002).

334   **like a son:** FF to JLR, 2/21/1938, JLRP, Box 286, Folder 12.

335   **gladly accepted:** FF to JLR, 1/18/1939 tel., *id.*

335 "You've": JLR HSTL OH by Niel M. Johnson, 6/21/1989, at 6.

335 official secretary: CSM, 2/2/1939, at 7 (hiring Elizabeth Thompson).

335 parade of journalists: FF to Marquis Childs, 3/28/1939, Childs Papers, Box 1 ("I know no better company than my friends who are journalists . . .").

335 "Felix's barbershop": Parrish, *Citizen Rauh*, 47–49.

335 tryout & dictated his opinions: Fisher Int. with Paper, 8/11/1980, at 1, 4; Fisher Int. with Louchheim, at 1, 5–6, 9. *See* FF, Note, 6/1/1938, in *Mr. Justice Holmes and the Supreme Court* (1938).

335 Rauh's wife, Olie: JLR Int. in Katie Louchheim, ed., *The Making of the New Deal*, 65 (1983); Parrish, *Citizen Rauh*, 48.

335 views: HID, 4/29/1939, Reel 3, at 3406; WP, 4/11/1939, at 12; BG, 4/30/1939, at D2.

336 "Felix": HID, 2/4/1939, Reel 3, at 3209.

336 White House dinner: FDR Day by Day, 2/5/1939.

336 "worse": Honolulu Star-Bulletin, 2/10/1939, at 4.

336 "helped": HID, 3/22/1939, HI, *Secret Diary of Harold L. Ickes: The Inside Struggle: 1936–1939*, at 601–2.

336 "under": Honolulu Star-Bulletin, 2/10/1939, at 4.

336 William Allen White: BG, 4/30/1939, at D2.

336 "enough" & "in a routine": Lilienthal Diary, 4/5/1939; David E. Lilienthal, *The Journals of David E. Lilienthal: The TVA Years, 1939–1945*, at 103 (1964).

336 "is dining": WP, 2/26/1939, at T3.

336 Gridiron: WES, 4/16/1939, at A-1, A-8; BG, 4/16/1939, at B12. Learned Hand's first name is Billings.

336 "He": FF to JWM, 5/17/1939, at 2.

336 Committee on Civil Service Improvement: NYHT, 2/1/1939, at 1; Daniel R. Ernst, "'In a Democracy We Should Distribute the Lawyers': The Campaign for a Federal Legal Service, 1933–1945," American Journal of Legal History 58, no. 1 (March 2018): 4–55.

337 McReynolds: BG, 2/10/1939, at 1.

337 "Dear C-i-C": FF to FDR, 3/8/1939, R&FF, 488.

337 "has been" & "impossible": FDR to FF, 3/14/1939, *id.* at 489 (enclosing memorandum).

337 "I recognize": FF to FDR, 3/14/1939, *id.*

337 March 25: FDR Day by Day, 3/25/1939.

337 "not words": FF to FDR, 4/15/1939, R&FF, 491–92. *See* NYT, 4/16/1939, at 1, 41.

338 inquired: FDR to FF, 5/3/1939, R&FF, 492.

338 "Archie" & "one of" & "He unites": FF to FDR, 5/11/1939, *id.* at 492–94.

338 prepared to decline: AM to FF, 5/15/1939 & AM to FDR, 5/28/1939 & AM to FDR, 6/1/1939, *Letters of Archibald MacLeish*, 299–303 (R. H. Winnick, ed. 1983).

338 "the Republic": AM to FF, 10/19/1945, *id.* at 334.

338 another lunch: Bernard A. Drabeck & Helen E. Ellis, eds., *Archibald MacLeish: Reflections*, 129–30 (1986); Scott Donaldson, *Archibald MacLeish*, 292–93 (1992); FDR Day by Day, 5/23/1939.

338 "Red": AtlConst, 6/20/1939, at 6. *See* 82 Cong. Rec. 6781, 8219, 8221 (1939) (AM as Communist fellow traveler); *id.* at 8221 (confirmed 63-8).

338 more than the Librarian: AM to FDR, 10/2/1939, FDRL, PSF, Box 141; FF to FDR, 11/21/1939, FFLC, Box 98.

338 two majority opinions: Hale v. Bimco Trading Co., 306 U.S. 375 (1939); Keifer & Keifer v. Reconstruction Finance Corp., 306 U.S. 381 (1939); WES, 2/27/1939, at A-3.

338 **"Ain't it"**: FF to Thomas Reed Powell, 2/27/1939, at 1, Powell Papers, Box A, Folder A7.

339 **not favorable**: Chicago Daily News, 3/28/1939, in FFHLS, Pt. III, Reel 10, Page 602; NYT, 3/29/1939, at 2; WES, 4/12/1939, at A-3; Asbury Park Press, 6/4/1939, at 18.

339 **"seductive cliché" & "touchstone"**: Graves v. New York, 306 U.S. 466, 489, 491 (1939) (Frankfurter, J., concurring).

339 **"linchpin"**: Texas v. Florida, 306 U.S. 398, 432–33 (1939) (Frankfurter, J.).

339 **"trivialize"**: O'Malley v. Woodrough, 307 U.S. 277, 282 (1939).

339 **"alembic"**: Texas v. Florida, 306 U.S. 398, 432–33 (1939) (Frankfurter, J.).

339 **bar**: Powell to CCB, 5/4/1939, Powell Papers, Box A, Folder A3c.

339 **limericks**: Powell to CCB, 6/21/1939, *id.*; FF, "Thomas Reed Powell," 69 Harv. L. Rev. 797, 799 (1956).

339 **alerted**: CCB to HFS, 6/2/1939, at 1, HFSP, Box 7; CCB to HFS, 8/4/1939, *id.*

339 **"Felix is luxuriating"**: HFS to CCB, 3/21/1939 at 1, *id.*

339 **alpaca coat**: CCB to HFS, 6/2/1939, at 1 (hearing story from former attorney general William Mitchell); JML COH at 89–90; Lash, "A Brahmin of Law: A Biographical Essay," DFF, at 66.

339 **"taut" & "To see"**: FF, "Chief Justices I Have Known," 39 Va. L. Rev. 883, 901–2 (1953). *See* FFR, 267–68.

339 **"political issues"**: Coleman v. Miller, 307 U.S. 433, 460 (1939) (Frankfurter, J., concurring).

340 **William O. Douglas**: David J. Danelski, "The Appointment of William O. Douglas to the Supreme Court," Journal of Supreme Court History 40, no. 1 (2015): 80–99; James F. Simon, *Independent Journey* (1980); Bruce Allen Murphy, *Wild Bill* (2003); David J. Danelski, "An Open Letter Concerning *Wild Bill*," 4/10/2003 (on file with author).

340 **"second only"**: HJL to FDR, 3/27/1939, R&FF, 490.

340 **joined Frankfurter's opinion**: Coleman, 307 U.S. at 456 (Black, J., concurring) (discussing political question doctrine).

CHAPTER 22: PREACHING THE TRUE DEMOCRATIC FAITH

341 **clear, 74 degree**: NYT, 6/15/1939, at 48.

341 **boarded**: NYT, 6/14/1939, at 30; NYHT, 6/15/1939, at 23.

341 **grim reminder**: FF to HFS, 8/16/1939, at 1–3, HFSP, Box 74.

341 **"nearly"**: R&FF, 496.

341 **"Felix"**: FDR to MLH, 6/6/1939, *id.* at 495 & FDRL, PSF, Box 135 (misdated in R&FF 6/3/1939).

341 **"peace"**: FDR, West Point Commencement Address, 6/12/1939, at 3, FDRL, MSF, Box 47, No. 1229.

341 **spoke**: FF to MLH, 6/13/1939 tel., FDRL, PSF, Box 135; Grace Tully to FF, 6/13/1939 tel., R&FF, 495.

342 **stayed with**: FF to Bowra, n.d., tel., FFLC, Box 161.

342 **"There is"**: MDF to IB, 7/13/1939, at 4–5, IBP, Box 107, Pages 115–16.

342 **nominated**: FF to Goodhart, 7/14/1939, at 1–2, Goodhart Papers, Ms. Eng. C. 2885, #18.

342 **"Happy"**: NYT, 6/22/1939, at 29. *See* ToL, 6/22/1939, at 10.

342 **"Don't"**: Bergen Evening Record, 7/5/1939, at 3.

342 **"grim"**: HJL to FDR, 8/19/1939, at 1, FFLC, Box 74.

342 **many hours**: FF to SGates, 7/1/1939, Gates Family Papers; FF, Inscription, *Mr. Justice*

Holmes and the Supreme Court, id. ("With warm memories of happy hours, in London & Oxford, June – July 1939").

342 **"not joyous" & "war atmosphere"**: FF to HFS, 8/16/1939, at 1–2.

342 **"in the menacing"**: ToL, 7/1/1939, at 16.

342 **"into"**: FF to HFS, 9/16/1939, at 1, HFSP, Box 74.

343 **"the one man"**: FF to HFS, 8/16/1939, at 2.

343 **a warning**: FF to FDR, 8/30/1939, at 2, R&FF, 497–98 (enclosing Quo Tai-chi to FF, 8/13/1939).

343 **isolationist**: David Nasaw, *The Patriarch*, 377–97 (2012).

343 **"come home"**: TNR, 6/21/1939, at 169.

343 **Joe Jr.**: JML to JPK, 7/17/1940, JPKP, Box 111 (informing him Joe Jr. finished with average of 72 in the top eighth of the 1L class).

343 **Jack**: JPK to JML, 8/6/1940, at 1, *id.* (indicating Jack would have started the coming year at Yale Law School because he did not want to compete with Joe Jr., but doctors told Jack to take a year off because of his bad health and stomach trouble).

343 **rejected**: Fredrik Logevall, *JFK*, xvii, 117–18, 122–23 (2020) (Jack's break from father's isolationism & Jack's dislike of Laski).

343 **three times**: FF to CCB, 8/7/1939, at 1–2, CCBP, Box 5, Folder 5-1 ("We saw him whom Joe Kennedy calls Neville . . . three times. He is a bewildered, ineffective, strangely obstinate, vain, old man. . . . Winston is the only public I saw who has the will & the energy to rule these days & for present circumstances.") (emphasis in original).

343 **"Aw, nuts"**: FF to CCB, 4/10/1941, at 1, *id.*, Folder 5-2.

343 **"Trying days"**: FF to JPK, 7/13/1939, JPKP, Box 106.

343 **Ziemer**: NYHT, 7/21/1939, at 13. *See* Gregor Ziemer, *Education for Death* (1941).

344 **"How ghastly" & "all"**: FF to HFS, 8/16/1939, at 3. *See* FF to HFS, 9/16/1939, at 2 ("our English visit left no doubt that war was coming").

344 **for good**: NYT, 7/20/1939, at 22; BDE, 7/20/1939, at 3; BG, 7/22/1939, at 2.

344 **Heath, Massachusetts**: FF to HFS, 8/16/1939, at 4; FF to HFS, 9/16/1939, at 5–6.

344 **two days**: MDF to IB, 9/13/1939, at 1, 10–12, IBP, Box 107, Pages 114, 117–18.

344 **"You at least"**: FF to FDR, 8/25/1939 tel., R&FF, 497.

344 **September 21**: FF to MLH, 8/30/1939, *id.*

344 **"glued" & "I reflect"**: FF to FDR, 8/30/1939, *id.*

344 **"will remain"**: FDR, Fireside Chat, 9/3/1939, at 7, FDRL, MSF, Box 47, No. 1240.

344 **speaking directly**: FF to FDR, 9/3/1939, R&FF, 499.

344 **"A so-called"**: FF to FDR, 9/13/1939, at 2, R&FF, 499–500.

344 **copied**: FDR Memorandum, 9/28/1939, *id.* at 500.

344 **repeal**: Message to Congress, 9/21/1939, at 1, FDRL, MSF, Box 48, No. 1243.

345 **"one of" & "we can" & "How can"**: NYHT, 9/22/1939, at 1. *See* BG, 9/22/1939, at 1, 31.

345 **"You know"**: FF to Goodhart, 9/12/1939, at 1, Goodhart Papers, Ms. Eng. C. 2885, at 19.

345 **"You would" & "everybody"**: MDF to IB, 9/13/1939, at 10–11.

345 **confirmation & swearing-in**: EFP OH, 11/29/1982, at 9; EFP Int. by Katie Louchheim, 3/27/1981, Pt. I, Page 2, Louchheim Papers, Box 72, Folder 10 & Katie Louchheim, ed., *The Making of the New Deal*, 68 (1983).

345 **Princeton lectures**: FF to Lally Weymouth, 11/5/1964, at 1, FFLC, Box 59; Daily Princetonian, 4/16/1935, at 1, 4; Daily Princetonian, 4/17/1935, at 1, 6; Daily Princetonian, 4/18/1935, at 1, 6.

345 **"Tiffany engraved"**: EFP OH, 11/15/1982, at 28, 32.

345 **Cardozo's law clerk:** FF to JLR, 8/19/1937, at 1, JLRP, Box 286 ("My man Prichard *has* made the Law Review, can you now make him your successor to Bennie J?! He would be a tonic for your sainted Justice.").

345 **research assistant & interacted:** EFP OH, 11/15/1982, at 28; EFP OH, 11/29/1982, at 3; HMH & EFP, "The Fansteel Case," 52 Harv. L. Rev. 1275 (1939); HMH, "The Business of the Supreme Court at the October Terms, 1937 and 1938," 53 Harv. L. Rev. 579 (1940); EFP to FF, 2/9/1939, at 1–2, FFHLS, Pt. III, Reel 21, Pages 577–78; Powell to EFP, 1/18/1940, Powell Papers, Box A12; Powell to Prichard, 2/19/1940, *id.*

346 **"When" & "I leave":** EFP OH, 11/24/1982, at 25 & EFP OH, 11/29/1982, at 6.

346 **"the 'future'":** LCJ, 6/7/1939, at 16. *See* Arthur Schlesinger, Jr., "'Prich': A New Deal Memoir," New York Review of Books, 3/28/1985; Tracy Campbell, *Short of the Glory* (1998).

346 **petitions & New Milford:** EFP OH, 11/24/1982, at 24; EFP OH, 11/29/1982, at 10, 15; FF to HFS, 8/16/1939, at 4.

346 **1511 Thirtieth Street:** MDF to IB, 9/13/1939, at 5; FF to HFS, 9/16/1940, at 6.

346 **Hockley & dinner parties & Katharine Meyer:** EFP OH, 11/15/1982, at 38–39; EFP OH, 11/29/1982, at 15–16; EFP Int. in Louchheim, *The Making of the New Deal*, 73; Katharine Graham, *Personal History*, 106–7 (1997); Schlesinger, Jr., "'Prich': A New Deal Memoir."

346 **Phil Graham:** Graham, *Personal History*, 117 (recalling outgoing review president Ed Huddleston introduced PG to FF); EFP OH, 11/24/1982, at 6–7 (recalling he introduced PG to FF). *See* George A. Smathers OH with Donald A. Ritchie, 8/1/1989, at 4–8; FF to Weymouth, 11/5/1964, at 1; Graham, *Personal History*, at 108–17; David Halberstam, *The Powers That Be* 158–72 (1979).

347 **promised:** FF to PG, 2/6/1939, FFLC, Box 59.

347 **co-editing:** *Law and Politics* (Archibald MacLeish & E.F. Prichard, Jr., eds. 1939).

347 **revise:** EFP OH, 11/29/1982, at 16–17.

347 **"Prich" & begged:** Schlesinger, Jr., "'Prich': A New Deal Memoir" & Schlesinger Jr. Reply to Mark Tushnet, 3/28/1985, New York Review of Books (based on recollections of Claytor and JLR).

347 **withdrew:** Oklahoma Packing Co. v. Oklahoma Gas & Elec. Co., 390 U.S. 4, 4 n.* (1940) (indicating opinion decided on December 4, 1939, and was withdrawn and replaced); Powell to EFP, 1/18/1940, at 1 ("Don't you think it would have been wise for you to have paged the Oklahoma Supreme Court volumes and advance sheets to date and not to assume that counsel from any place south of Mason and Dixon's line was competent to advise you sufficiently?"); FF Law Clerk Duties, Memorandum, n.d., at 5, FFHLS, Pt. III, Reel 9, Page 67 (reminding law clerks to check citations and referring to "the case of *Prichard v. Shepard*").

347 **under his wing:** HID, 12/3/1939, Reel 3, at 3956 (FF's concerns about FM's qualifications for the job).

347 **coerced:** Chambers v. Florida, 309 U.S. 227 (1940).

347 **Joe Vernon:** FF, Memorandum, circa 1/30/1941, FFHLS, Pt. I, Reel 2, Page 198 (recalling law clerk PG coming to his house at 11:00 p.m. and urging him to stay execution); Vernon v. Alabama, 313 U.S. 540 (April 7, 1941) (per curiam) (granting cert.); Vernon v. Alabama, 313 U.S. 547 (May 26, 1941) (per curiam) (reversing conviction). Vernon was retried, convicted, and executed. NJG, 11/18/1944, at A1.

347 **to Roosevelt:** FF to FDR, n.d., R&FF, 515–17.

348   **"when"**: HID, 12/3/1939, Reel 3, at 3956–57.

348   **robing room**: EFP Int. by Katie Louchheim, 3/27/1981, Pt. I, Pages 4–5; EFP OH, 11/29/1982, at 22–23. *See* Board of County Com'rs v. United States, 308 U.S. 343, 355 (1939) (Douglas, J., joining HLB's opinion).

348   **"Not even" & "difficulties" & "as a man"**: FF to FDR, R&FF, 511.

348   **"extraordinarily"**: FDR to FF, 1/9/1930, *id.* at 513.

348   **"the frankest"**: *Id.* at 511.

349   **"thought"**: MDF to IB, 6/8/1937, at 8–11, IBP, Box 105, Pages 222–27.

349   **did not trust**: IB to Marie and Mendel Berlin, early March 1939, IB, *Letters 1928–1946*, at 292 (Henry Hardy, ed. 2004) ("A. von Trott has been here. Honest he cannot be called. But with much charm."); Michael Ignatieff, *Isaiah Berlin*, 73–76 (1998).

349   **so badly & insulted Churchill & never said**: FF to AMS Jr., 6/11/1951, AMSP, NYPL, Box 432, Folder 7; FF to editor of Measure, 10/1/1951, *id.*, Box 45, Folder 3; Trott to FF, 1/9/1940, FFHLS, Pt. III, Reel 20, Box 191, Folder 6 & FDRL, PSF, Box 135 ("I cannot leave this country without at least sending you a brief note of farewell. I understand and respect the reasons why it has not at this time been possible to reestablish more than purely human contact.").

349   **they joked**: FDR to FF, 1/17/1940 & 1/24/1940, R&FF, 514–15; FF to FDR, 1/23/1940, FFHLS, Pt. III, Reel 20, Page 937 & FDRL, PSF, Box 135 (attaching letter from FF to MLH, 4/1/1940, and report from J. Edgar Hoover to General Watson, 2/19/1940, from FDR's Hoover's file 1-1940); Christopher Sykes, *Troubled Loyalty* 187-88, 302–4, 308, 320 (1968) (arguing FF alone not to blame).

350   **"almost" & "Capone" & "leadership"**: HID, 2/11/1940, HI, *The Secret Diary of Harold L. Ickes: The Lowering Clouds: 1939–1941*, at 128–29 (1955) & Reel 3, at 4147–48.

350   **William & Lillian**: Gregory L. Peterson et al., "Recollections of *West Virginia State Board of Education v. Barnette*," 81 St. John's L. Rev. 755 (2007); Shawn Francis Peters, *Judging Jehovah's Witnesses* (2000).

350   **a federal trial**: Minersville Sch. Dist. v. Gobitis, 108 F.2d 683 (3d Cir. 1939); Gobitis v. Minersville Sch. Dist., 24 F. Supp. 271 (E.D. Pa. 1938).

350   **pressed him**: FF to GC, 7/1/1937, GCP, Box 65, Folder 12.

351   **pleased & encouraged**: FF to GC, 8/23/1938, at 1–2, GCP, Box 78, Folder 126; GC to FF, 8/31/1938, at 1, *id.*; GC to FF, 11/14/1938, at 1–2, *id.*; FF to GC, 11/16/1938, at 1–2, *id.*

351   **"whole country"**: FF to GC, 12/31/1938, at 1, *id. See* GC to FF, 1/17/1939, *id.*; Hague v. Committee for Indust. Org., 307 U.S. 496 (1939); Donald W. Rogers, *Workers Against the City* (2020); Gerald T. Dunne, *Grenville Clark*, 97–109 (1986); Nancy Peterson Hill, *A Very Private Public Citizen*, 125–33 (2014).

351   **inquired**: GC to MML, 2/10/1939, GCP, Box 80, Folder 18.

351   **was opposed & agreed**: MML to GC, 2/18/1940, *id.*; MML to GC, 3/7/1940, *id.*; GC to MML, 3/11/1940, *id.*; MML to GC, 4/22/1940 tel., *id.*

351   **Footnote Four**: United States v. Carolene Prods. Co., 304 U.S. 144, 152 n.4 (1938).

351   **Not a single scholar**: Louis Lusky, *Our Nine Tribunes*, 126 (1993) ("in the entire four years between the Footnote's appearance and *Jones v. Opelika*, not one legal scholar had accepted the invitation that it extended for further analysis and discussion").

352   **"The philosophy"**: Brief of the Committee on the Bill of Rights of the American Bar Association as Friends of the Court, *Minersville Sch. Dist. v. Gobitis*, No. 690 (4/24/1940): 43.

352   **"To compel"**: NYHT, 4/29/1940, at 14. Counsel for the Gobitas children made this point in their brief. Respondent's Brief, *Minersville v. Gobitis*, at 3, 11.

352   **"Is it":** FF to FM, 4/25/1940, FMP, Roll 121, Page 22.

352–353 **"As I see" & " I come" & "profound" & "I don't":** "Observations of Chief Justice Hughes,"
at 2, FMP, Roll 121, Page 34. *See Gobitis* Conference Notes, 4/27/1940, at 1–2, WODP,
Box 49, Folder 15 (confirming CEH's quotes).

353   **Only Black:** *Gobitis* docket sheet, WODP, Box 38, Folder 7, Page 518.

353   **"because of":** PAF, "Charles Evans Hughes as Chief Justice," 81 Harv. L. Rev. 4,
41 (1967).

353   **psychological factors:** H.N. Hirsch, *The Enigma of Felix Frankfurter,* 148–53 (1981);
Richard Danzig, "How Questions Begot Answers in Felix Frankfurter's First Flag
Salute Opinion," Supreme Court Review (1977): 257; Richard Danzig, "Justice Frankfurter's Opinions in the Flag Salute Cases: Blending Logic and Psychologic in Constitutional Decisionmaking," 36 Stan. L. Rev. 675, 714 (1984).

354   **long-standing opposition:** FF to OWH, 4/18/1921, H-FF Corr., 108; FF to LH, 4/11/1923,
LHP, Box 104, Folder 104-10; FF to LH, 6/5/1923, *id.*; TNR, 10/1/1924, at 110–13; Meyer
v. Nebraska, 262 U.S. 390 (1923); Pierce v. Society of the Sisters, 268 U.S. 510 (1925);
TNR, 6/17/1925, at 86–87; TNR, 3/31/1926, at 158.

354–355 **Newton Cantwell:** Cantwell v. Connecticut, 310 U.S. 296 (1940).

355   **state and local laws:** Danzig, "How Questions Begot Answers," at 261–62 (observing FF
was guilty of "inflation" because the state had not passed a mandatory flag salute law;
the school board was one step removed from the state but for Fourteenth Amendment
purposes was treated as if it were the state).

355   **"grave" & "helped" & "every":** Minersville Sch. Dist. v. Gobitis, 310 U.S. 586, 591–
94 (1940).

355–356 **"inferior" & "it is" & "The ultimate" & "The flag":** *Id.* at 595–96.

356   **"the formative" & "a very":** *Id.* at 597–99. *See id.* at 597–98 ("courts possess no marked
and certainly no controlling competence").

356   **"the transgression" & "the remedial" & "to the legislature" & "To fight":** *Id.* at 599–600.

356–357 **"For by" & "make":** *Id.* at 601–3 (Stone, J., dissenting).

357   **conscientious:** Jeremy K. Kessler, "The Administrative Origins of Modern Civil Rights
Law," 114 Colum. L. Rev. 1083, 1111–43 (2014).

357   **"where" & "reasonable" & "there are":** Gobitis, 310 U.S. at 601–3 (Stone, J., dissenting).

357   **"politically" & "[t]he very" & "preclude" & "open" & "be subject" & "so momentous":**
Gobitis, 310 U.S. at 605–7 (Stone, J., dissenting).

357   **questioned Stone's liberalism:** Brad Snyder, *The House of Truth,* 463–65 (2017).

357–358 **"stirred" & "all my" & "[w]e are" & "I agree" & "time" & "a new":** FF to HFS, 5/27/1940,
at 1–4, FFHLS, Pt. I, Reel 1, Pages 753–56 & HFSP, Box 65. *See* Danzig, "Justice Frankfurter's Opinions," 36 Stan. L. Rev. at 686–90 (observing FF's *Gobitis* opinion read
more like the judicial deference in the text of *Carolene Products*).

358   **"a vehicle" & "foolish" & "to let":** FF to HFS, 5/27/1940, at 4–5.

358   **sent his May 27:** FF to FM, 5/27/1940, FMP, Roll 121, Pages 15–21 (enclosing FF to HFS,
5/27/1940).

358   **drafted:** FM Draft Dissent, n.d., *id.,* Pages 26–30. *See* J. Woodford Howard, *Mr. Justice
Murphy,* 250–51 & 533 n.62 (1968); Hirsch, *The Enigma of Felix Frankfurter,* 238 n.79.

358   **"This":** FM to FF, 6/3/1940, FFHLS, Pt. I, Reel 1, Page 869. *See* Sidney Fine, *Frank
Murphy: The Washington Years,* 182–87 (1984).

358   **"like you" & "Hugo":** Draft FF *Gobitis* Opinion, 6/3/1940, at 8, FFHLS Pt. I, Reel 1, Page
844 (FF's handwritten margin notes).

359   **"This is"** & **"done":** WOD to FF, n.d. & WOD to FF, n.d., FFHLS, Pt. I, Reel 1, Pages 865, 867.

359   **"You":** CEH to FF, n.d., *id.* at 852.

359   **"I have no":** OJR to FF, n.d., *id.* at 861.

359   **praised & surprised:** HFS to FF, n.d., *id.* at 858–59; HFS to Lusky, 6/5/1940, HFSP, Box 19.

359   **"a great":** HFS to HJL, 6/3/1940, *id.*

359   **reported:** DFF, 6/14/1943, at 255; FFR Transcript, 8/19/1944, at 26–27, FFLC, Box 205.

359   **"plunged"** & **"pulled"** & **"This is"** & **"Phil":** JLR, "An Unabashed Liberal Looks at a Half-Century of the Supreme Court," 69 N.C. L. Rev. 213, 221–22 (1990). *See* JLR Int. in Louchheim, *The Making of the New Deal*, 64; Parrish, *Citizen Rauh*, 59–60; JLR, "Felix Frankfurter: Civil Libertarian," 11 Harv. C.R.-C.L. L. Rev. 496, 503 (1976); JLR D.C. Circuit OH at 38–39; *id.* at 20.

359–360 **"the barbarians":** JLR Int. with Lash, n.d., Lash Papers, Box 65, Folder 2.

360   **"great large"** & **"Come along":** Graham, *Personal History*, 118, 121–22. *See* Halberstam, *The Powers That Be*, 173–74; WES, 6/6/1940, at B-3.

360   **"I want":** HJL to HFS, 7/10/1940, HFSP, Box 19.

360   **"when":** BVC to HFS, 6/11/1940, at 2, *id.*, Box 81.

360   **"Felix":** CCB to HFS, 2/28/1941, at 2, *id.*, Box 7. *See* CCB to FF, 6/4/1940, at 1, CCBP, Box 5, Folder 5-2 ("I think I should have voted with Stone.").

360   **"Since we":** TNR, 6/24/1940, at 843–44.

360   **"We don't":** The Nation, 6/15/1940, at 723, in HFSP, Box 81.

360   **"dead"** & **"a violation"** & **"a surrender":** STLPD, 6/4/1940, at 20 in *id.*

361   **"one of the most":** Lusky to HFS, 8/16/1940, at 1, *id.*

361   **Most of Frankfurter's:** ZC to GC, 6/5/1940, GCP, Box 78, Folder 11 (indicating "much criticism" of *Gobitis* in Cambridge); E. Merrick Dodd to FF, 6/4/1940, at 1, FFHLS, Pt. III, Reel 10, Page 576 (disagreeing with FF's opinion); ERB to FF, 6/8/1940, at 2, *id.*, Page 573 (agreeing with it).

361   **"sitting":** FF to Hamilton, 6/21/1940, at 1–2, *id.*, Pages 589–90.

361   **"Felix's":** John P. Frank, Book Review, 32 J. Legal Educ. 432, 442 (1982) (reviewing Bruce Allen Murphy, *The Brandeis/Frankfurter Connection* (1982)).

361   **"Battle of France"** & **"Due Process":** FF to Malcolm Sharp, 10/8/1941, FFHLS, Pt. III, Reel 10, Page 931.

361   **"what"** & **"The guns":** FFR Transcript, 11/26/1954, at 146–47, FFLC, Box 205.

361   **"angry vehemence":** FB, *In Great Authority*, 128–29. Biddle, who was present at the June 1 dinner, undoubtedly referred to that June 1 argument.

361   **"very emotional":** HID, 6/2/1939, Reel 3, at 4442–44 & HI, *Secret Diary of Harold L. Ickes: The Lowering Clouds: 1939–1941*, at 198 (describing previous night's stag dinner at AM's in honor of *PM* publisher Ralph Ingersoll including FF, RHJ, BVC, TGC, FB, and DA).

361–362 **"But you"** & **pro-British:** FB, *In Great Authority*, 128–29.

362   **"The latter":** HID, 6/15/1940, Reel 3, at 4446 & HI, *Secret Diary of Harold L. Ickes: The Lowering Clouds: 1939–1941*, at 199 (describing "a good deal of feeling" about the war between RHJ and FF). HI, who had left the dinner at 11:00 p.m., based his diary entry on BVC's account—which HI left out of his published diary.

362   **ideal public servant:** Snyder, *House of Truth*, 6–18, 74–75, 538–39; Elting E. Morison, *Turmoil and Tradition* (1960); HLS & MB, *On Active Service in Peace and War* (1948).

362   "ardently": HLSD, 5/8/1940, Reel 6, Vol. 29, Pages 45–50.

362   lunch: FDR Day by Day, 5/3/1940.

362   "disappointingly": HLSD, 5/8/1940, Reel 6, Vol. 29, Pages 45–50.

362   "He is": FF to FDR, 5/3/1940, at 1–2, R&FF, 521.

362   morning of May 25: FF to FDR, 5/26/1940, R&FF, 523; FDR Day by Day, 5/25/1940.

362–363 Clark & health & "goodbye": Samuel Spencer, Jr.'s, Notes of FF, GC Conversation –
       Summer 1947, at 7–8.

363   "very happy": FF to FDR, 6/4/1940, R&FF, 524. *See* FDR Day by Day, 6/3/1940.

363   "struck": Samuel Spencer, Jr.'s, Notes of FF, GC Conversation – Summer 1947, at 7–8.

363   "hard" & "the more" & "He has" & "Why" & "all": FF to FDR, 6/4/1940. *See* FDR to FF,
       6/5/1940, R&FF, 525–26.

363   "Ideas": FF to FDR, 6/5/1940, R&FF, 526–28 (attaching three-page reference letter
       about Patterson).

363   Patterson & Plattsburg: NYT, 5/23/1940, at 1, 13; NYT, 7/23/1940, at 1.

363   "available" & "regard": FF to FDR, 6/13/1940, R&FF, 529.

363   On June 19: HLSD, 6/25/1940, Reel 6, Vol. 29, Pages 55–56.

364   shocked official Washington: NYT, 6/21/1940, at 1.

364   "Simply": FF to FDR, 6/20/1940, R&FF, 530.

364   "You are": FF to HLS, 6/20/1940 tel., HLSP, Reel 103, Page 486.

364   small ceremony: FF to HLS, 6/27/1940, FFLC, Box 104; FF to FDR, 7/10/1940 tel.,
       R&FF, 538.

364   Patterson resigned: NYT, 7/12/1940, at 6; NYHT, 7/26/1940, at 1; NYT, 7/26/1940, at 1.

364   "I never": FF to HLS, 7/27/1940, HLSP, Reel 102, Page 185.

364   collaborated: DA, *Morning and Noon*, 222–27; NYT, 8/11/1940, at 58.

364   "thought" & "greatly": HLSD, 8/15/1940, Reel 6, Vol. 30, Pages 90–91. *See* RHJ, *That
       Man*, 81–103 (John Q. Barrett, ed. 2003) (recounting destroyer deal).

365   Moody & Brandeis & Taft & Stone: Robert B. McKay, "The Judiciary and Nonjudicial
       Activities," 37 Law & Contemp. Probs. 9, 32–33 (1970).

                   CHAPTER 23: UNCLE FELIX AND AUNT MARION

366   "Marion": FF to SGates, 6/22/1940 tel., Gates Family Papers.

366   cried: PGates to FF & MDF, 7/28/1940, at 1, FFLC, Box 57.

366   "There is" & twenty-four: SGates & PGates to FF, 6/25/1940 tel., at 1–2, *id.*

366   responded: FF to SGates & PGates, 6/25/1940 tel., Gates Family Papers.

366   so impressed & Oxford: FF to JMH, 4/10/1964, at 1, JMHP, Box 534; Brad Snyder, *The
       House of Truth*, 415–16, 419, 421 & 691 nn.20–21 (2017); FFR, 258, 262, 273.

367   Bowra & Pauline Murray: Maurice Bowra, "Sylvester and Pauline," *New Bats in Old
       Belfries*, 63 n.§ (Henry Hardy & Jennifer Holmes, eds. 2005).

367   "gratefully": SGates to FF, 7/4/1940 tel., FFLC, Box 57. *See* SGates to FF, 7/1/1940,
       at 2–3, *id.*

367   immediate passage: SGates to FF, 7/17/1940 tel., *id.*

367   "Delighted": FF to SGates, 7/18/1940 tel., Gates Family Papers.

367   *Duchess of Atholl*: BaltSun, 8/4/1940, at 10.

367   "All we": SGates to FF & MDF, 7/20/1940, at 10, FFLC, Box 57.

367   Cyril James: JB to FF, 7/19/1940, JBP, Box 8, Folder 3; FF to JB, 7/23/1940, *id.*

367   **9:00 p.m. & sleeper & Zavitz:** Edwin Zavitz to Cyril James, 7/23/1940, *id.*; JB to FF, 7/25/1940, *id.*; James to FF, 8/1/1940, FFLC, Box 57.

367–368 **telegram & 7:45 p.m.:** PGates to MDF, 8/13/1940, at 1, 3, FFLC, Box 57; MDF to PGates & SGates, 8/1/1940, at 1–5, Gates Family Papers.

368   **"It is":** MDF to PGates & SGates, 8/1/1940, at 6–7.

368   **office & bunker:** PGates to MDF, 10/6/1940, at 3–4, FFLC, Box 57.

368   **September 24:** FF to JB, 9/23/1940, JBP, Box 8, Folder 3; MDF to PGates and SGates, 8/30/1940, at 4.

368   **scholarships:** Kay Graham to FF, 8/15/1940, at 2, FFLC, Box 57; MDF to PGates & SGates, 10/2/1940, at 3, Gates Family Papers.

368   **breakfast:** MDF to PGates & SGates, 10/6/1940, at 2–3, *id.*

368   **"The children":** MDF to PGates and SGates, 10/2/1940, at 6.

368   **astonished:** FF to JB, 10/22/1940, JBP, Box 8, Folder 3; FF to JB, 11/28/1940, *id.*

369   **"Never":** FF to MML, 8/2/1940, at 3, MMLP.

369   **Lothian & Layton:** MDF to PGates & SGates,10/2/1940, at 8.

369   **"Do":** FF to HFS, 8/23/1940, at 1, HFSP, Box 74.

369   **Born in Riga:** Michael Ignatieff, *Isaiah Berlin*, 10–32 (1998).

369   **New York City and Washington, D.C.:** *Id.* at 97–108; HJL to FF, 6/10/1940, R&FF, 536–37; IB to Marie & Mendel Berlin, 9/16/1940, IB, *Letters 1928–1946*, at 315 (Henry Hardy, ed. 2004); *id.* at 309–13.

369   **Prich, Graham:** IB to Marie & Mendel Berlin, 10/26/1941, *id.* at 381; IB to Marie and Mendel Berlin, 7/31/1941, *id.* at 323 ("The Frankfurters could not be nicer to me, he does what he can, introduces, encourages etc.").

369   **"Mrs. Frankfurter":** IB to Mary Fisher, 7/30/1940, IB, *Letters 1928–1946*, at 319–20.

370   **"loses":** IB to Fisher, 8/21/1940, *id.* at 337. *See* IB to MDF, 8/23/1940, *id.* at 341–42; IB to MDF, 8/26/1940, *id.* at 343–45.

370   **impressed Marion:** MDF to Lady Mary Murray, 12/3/1940, at 3, Gates Family Papers.

370   *I Married* **& "beautiful" & "amazingly" & "Well":** MDF to PGates & SGates, 12/14/1940, at 1–3, 7, 9–10, *id.*

370   **"I don't":** FF to CCB, 4/10/1941, at 2, CCBP, Box 5, Folder 5-2.

370   **"high" & "a great" & "If I":** Alexander Woollcott to PGates, 12/15/1940, FFLC, Box 112 & in Samuel Hopkins Adams, *A. Woollcott, His Life and His World* 318–20 (1946).

370   **Jewish press & declined:** JTA, 12/10/1940, at 4; MDF to SGates & PGates, 12/13/1940, at 11.

370   **"Our three":** FF Holiday Card, circa 1940 (on file with author). *See* PGates to MDF, 12/30/1940, at 4, FFLC, Box 57.

370–371 **White House & hop:** White House invitation, 12/31/1940, Gates Family Papers; Oliver Gates Int. with author, 5/8–9/2016.

371   **encouraged:** FF to FDR, 6/26/1940, R&FF, 530–35 (enclosing memoranda from him and AM).

371   **Rosenman & "You have":** FF to FDR, 7/19/1940, *id.* at 538.

371   **"Terrible":** FF to FDR, 11/7/1940, *id.* at 550.

371   **"never":** R&FF, 552–53.

371   **"watered":** FF to FDR, 11/11/1940, *id.* at 553–60 (enclosing BG, 11/10/1940).

372   **William Hastie:** FF to WHH, 10/28/1940, WHHP, Pt. II, Reel 35, Page 791.

372   **no idea:** WHH to FF, 11/7/1940, *id.* at 792; Gilbert Ware, *William Hastie*, 95–109 (1984).

372   **"The negroes":** HLSD, 10/22/1940, at 2–3, Reel 6, Vol. 31, Pages 71–72.

372   **paid no attention:** Kai Bird, *The Chairman*, 49 (1992) (based on June 23, 1983, int. with JJM).

372   **Black Tom:** *Id.* at 78–95.

372   **"first class":** George Roberts to HLS, 7/12/1940, at 1–2, HLSP, Reel 102, Pages 114–15.

372   **part-time:** HLSD, 9/19/1940, at 2, Reel 6, Vol. 30, Page 179; NYT, 12/20/1940, at 18.

372   **corridors of power:** Jean Monnet, *Memoirs*, 153–54 (1978).

372   **"one of":** HLSD, 12/2/1940, at 2–3, Reel 6, Vol. 32, Pages 3–4.

372   **"has":** JJM to FF, 11/1/1941, FFLC, Box 81. *See* FF to Lord Halifax, 11/14/1941, FFLC, Box 85; Bird, *The Chairman*, 97.

373   **"New" & "a 'free'":** FF to FDR, 12/19/1940, R&FF, 566–68 (enclosing Monnet Memorandum, 12/18/1940).

373   **"Arsenal" & Frankfurter made:** R&FF, 573–74; Monnet, *Memoirs*, 160; FF to FDR, 12/25/1940, R&FF at 573 (enclosing notes for speech); Sixth Draft, Fireside Chat, 12/29/1940, at 20, FDRL, MSF, Box 58, No. 1351C (containing line for first time). *See* Robert E. Sherwood, *Roosevelt and Hopkins*, 226 (1948) (claiming Hopkins inserted phrase and attributing it to Monnet, William S. Knudsen, or newspaper editorial); SIR to FF, 7/16/1949, SIRP, Box 1 (FF handwritten: insisting line was Monnet's); SIR, *Working with Roosevelt*, 260–61 (1952) (indicating the phrase came from Monnet through FF and JJM).

373   **"they ever" & "a crime":** R&FF, 582.

373   **helped prepare:** HLSD, 1/26/1941, Reel 6, Vol. 32, Page 129.

373   **memorandum:** FF to FDR, 2/26/1941, R&FF, 582–85 (enclosing Memorandum 2/27/1941).

373   **Murrow:** FF to MLH, 4/15/1941, *id.* at 595 (enclosing Murrow to FF, 4/14/1941 tel.).

373   **White House visit:** HLSD, 12/18/1940, Reel 6, Vol. 32, Pages 40–41.

373   **Ireland:** Sherwood, *Roosevelt and Hopkins*, 230; Monnet, *Memoirs*, 164–67.

373   **"at length":** SIR, *Working with Roosevelt*, 269.

374   **Lend-Lease Bill:** HLSD, 2/16/1941, Reel 6, Vol. 33, Page 32.

374   **Ickes:** HID, 4/26/1941, HI, *The Secret Diary of Harold L. Ickes: The Lowering Clouds, 1939–1941*, at 485–86 (1955).

374   **"Supreme" & Pearson:** Minneapolis Star Journal, 2/28/1941, at 18.

374   **"Ten" & "army" & "U.S. Employment":** BaltSun, 4/6/1941, at 16.

374   **Holmes:** BaltSun, 3/4/1941, at 13.

374   **lukewarm:** FF to MLH, 2/4/1941, R&FF, 580–81 & FF, Memorandum, at 1, FDRL, PSF, Box 135.

374   **"add":** FF to CCB, 1/29/1941, at 1, CCBP, Box 5, Folder 5-2.

374   **"I Told":** WES, 2/5/1941, at 1.

375   **refused to work:** David Halberstam, *The Powers That Be*, 173 (1979) (interview with Kay Graham).

375   **switched:** FM to FF, 5/29/1941, FFHLS, Pt. I, Reel 4, Page 195 (FF handwritten).

375   **"You're" & "Black and Company":** FFR Transcript, 8/28/1957, at 8, FFLC, Box 206. *See* FF handwritten notes, n.d., Bridges v. California, FFHLS, Pt. I, Reel 4, Page 167; FF to AMB, 7/1963, at 1–2, FFHLS, Pt. III, Reel 33, at 51–52; FF to FM, 10/1946, at 4–5, Gressman Papers, Box 1, Folder 69 (informing him of LDB's "shock" over FM's vote in *Bridges* case). Scholars have questioned FF's invocation of LDB on *Gobitis* and *Bridges*. H.N. Hirsch, *The Enigma of Felix Frankfurter* 243 n.190 (1981) (based on conversation with anti-FF scholar Alpheus Thomas Mason). LDB, however, felt strongly about the autonomy of state courts and may have deferred to the California Supreme Court's decision.

375   "deep" & "among": FF to CCB, 6/4/1941, CCBP, Box 5, Folder 5-3.

375   great chief: FF, "'The Administrative Side' of Chief Justice Hughes," 63 Harv. L. Rev. 1 (1949).

375–376 "knew" & "I wish" & "the Nation's" & "candor": FF, Memorandum, "H.F.S. & C.J.'ship," 6/9/1941, at 1–2, FFHLS, Pt. III, Reel 4, Pages 472–73 & Alpheus Thomas Mason, *Harlan Fiske Stone*, 566–67 (1956). *See* FDR Day by Day, 6/5/1941 (CEH lunch); *Id.*, 6/9/1941 (FF lunch); FF to CCB, 6/12/1941, at 2, FFLC, Box 34 (handwritten p.s.: "Bob Jackson was perfectly handsome about it—for his 'build-up' was absurd."); FF to PAF, 9/24/1963, at 1, FFHLS, Pt. III, Reel 38, Page 353.

376   "delighted": FF to LH, 7/30/1941, at 2, LHP, Box 105A, Folder 105-8.

376   Henkin: HMH to FF, 3/8/1941, at 3, FFHLS, Pt. III, Reel 16, Page 574; FF to LH, 3/18/1941, FFLC, Box 64; LH to FF, 3/18/1941, *id.*; FF to Henkin, 4/30/1941, FFHLS, Pt. III, Reel 28, Page 807.

376   "not a brilliant": Norman I. Silber, *With All Deliberate Speed: The Life of Philip Elman*, 71 (2004); PE, Int. by Norman Silber, "The Solicitor General's Office, Justice Frankfurter, and Civil Rights Litigation, 1946–1960," 100 Harv. L. Rev. 817 (1987).

376   Stimson frequently: HLSD, 5/8/1941, Reel 6, Vol. 34, Page 18; HLSD, 5/25/1941, *id.*, Page 65; HLSD, 5/26/1941, *id.*, Page 73; HLSD, 5/27/1941, *id.*, Page 74; FF to FDR, 5/25/1941, R&FF, 600 (HLS's letter).

376–377 "I have" & "For": FF to FDR, 5/28/1941, *id.* at 601–2 & FDRL, PSF, Box 135 (enclosing BaltSun cartoon).

377   "ideal": FF to FDR, 6/15/1941, R&FF, 607–8 (enclosing memorandum); FF to FDR, 6/14/1941, *id.* at 607 (lunch).

377   "war" & "The Civil War" & "a country" & "expanded" & "more democratic": FF, 6/18/1941, "Democracy and False Shibboleths," Radcliffe Quarterly (August 1941): 7–9, FFLC, Box 198.

377   "covered": SGates to FF, 5/26/1941, at 4, FFLC, Box 57.

377   machine gunner: PGates to MDF, 5/27/1941, at 1–2, *id.*; SGates to FF, 6/1/1941, at 2, *id.*

377   photographs: FF to MLH, 5/21/1941, R&FF, 598.

377   "delighted": FDR to FF, 5/26/1941, *id.* & Gates Family Papers (FF handwritten note about 6/10 visit); FDR Day by Day, 6/10/1941.

377   "Uncle Felix": Beatrice Gates to MDF, 6/11/1941, at 4, FFLC, Box 57.

377   Draper & Maine: FF to CCB, 4/23/1941, at 2, CCBP, Box 5, Folder 5-2; MDF to PGates, n.d., at 3–7, Gates Family Papers.

377   "as there's": Nana to MDF, 7/7/1941, at 1, FFLC, Box 57.

377–378 sailing & boats & picture: Nana to MDF, 7/22/1941, at 1, *id.* (boats and picture); Nana to MDF, 8/11/1941, at 2, *id.*

378   Felix visited: FF to JB, 7/18/1941, JBP, Box 8, Folder 3; ER, My Day, 7/14/1941 & 7/15/1941 & 7/16/1941; MDF to SGates & PGates, 8/13/1941, at 3–4, Gates Family Papers.

378   Morgenthau, Jr. & "I might": MDF to Beatrice Gates, 7/20/1941, at 4–5, *id.*

378   national news: 87 Cong. Rec. App. A3284–85 (1941); NYHT, 6/19/1941, at 20; CSM, 6/18/1941, at 1.

378   sent a copy: FF to MLH, 6/25/1941, FDRL, PSF, Box 135 (enclosing speech in BG, 6/18/1941).

378   "we have": FF to FDR, 7/19/1941, R&FF, 610.

378   "a motley": NYT, 7/20/1941, at 23.

378   "If somebody": FDR to FF, 7/25/1941, R&FF, 611.

378 **Atlantic Charter:** Sherwood, *Roosevelt and Hopkins*, 349–65.

378 **"truth":** FF to FDR, 8/18/1941, R&FF, 612 (emphasis in original).

378 **3:30 p.m.:** FDR Day by Day, 9/26/1941.

379 **"In memory":** FF, Memorandum, 9/27/1941, at 1–2, FFLC, Box 98.

379 **Amberg:** FF to HLS, 10/3/1940, at 1–2, HLSP, Reel 102, Page 474–75; WP, 1/15/1941, at 14.

379 **Bundy:** HLSD, 4/6/1941, Reel 6, Vol. 33, Page 141.

379 **McCloy & Lovett:** HLSD, 4/22/1941, *id.*, Page 178.

379 **Acheson:** FF to DA, 2/17/1941, DAP, Reel 7, Box 11, Folder 142. *See* DA, *Present at the Creation*, 4–35 (1969); Robert L. Beisner, *Dean Acheson*, 13–27 (2006); Michael F. Hopkins, *Dean Acheson and the Obligations of Power* (2017).

379 **role model:** HLSD, 5/8/1941, at 4, *id.*, Vol. 34, Page 21.

379 **angling:** AABD, 10/24/1941, at 2, Reel 3; *id.*, 3/10/1942, at 3.

379 **"the Frankfurter boys":** AABD, 2/11/1941, at 2, Reel 2.

379 **"For a":** FF to FDR, 1/8/1941, R&FF, 577–78.

379 **"how much":** FDR to TGC, 1/20/1941, at 1, FDRL, PSF, Box 128.

379 **assistant secretary:** TGC, *Rendezvous with Democracy*, at Chapter X/Pages 35–36, TGCP, Box 586; BDE, 3/9/1941, at 12A.

380 **clean break:** AABD, 1/21/1941, at 3, Reel 2.

380 **defense contracts:** CT, 5/4/1941, at 22; CT, 9/20/1941, at 8.

380 **clear his name:** NYHT, 12/17/1941, at 19; NYT, 12/17/1941, at 20.

380 **Peggy Dowd & Irish neutrality:** TGC, *Rendezvous with Democracy*, at Credo/17–Credo/18, Chapter X/Pages 15–17, 31–38.

380 **Guthrie & hurt:** FF to TGC, 9/11/1940, TGCP, Box 198; FF to Corcoran, circa 1940, *id.*

380 **four other justices & Rowe:** TGC, *Rendezvous with Democracy*, at Chapter X/Pages 33–34; Memorandum from James Rowe to FDR, 6/25/1941, FDRL, PSF, Box 164 (endorsements from SFR, WOD, and HLB, but not FM and agreeing with FF); HID, 9/28/1941, Reel 4, Vol. 40, at 5916 (agreeing with FF but believing TGC "has had a very rotten deal at the hands of the administration").

380 **Pearson:** DFP, 9/29/1941, at 6.

380 **"stormed" & never:** TGC, *Rendezvous with Democracy*, at Chapter X/Pages 36–38. At a 1942 Union Station farewell for JLR, TGC saw FF and walked away. JLR Int. with Lash, 11/16/1983, at 1, Lash Papers, Box 65, Folder 2; JLR Int. with Lash, 4/13/1984, at 2, *id.*; Indianapolis Star, 6/13/1942, at 10.

380 **"I put":** JLR Int. in Katie Louchheim, ed., *The Making of the New Deal*, 67 (1983). *See* JLR Int. with Joseph Lash, 6/10/1986, Lash Papers, Box 65, Folder 2; EFP Int. in Louchheim, *Making of the New Deal*, 69–70; Bruce Allen Murphy, *The Brandeis/Frankfurter Connection*, 190–94 (1982) (based on ints. with BVC, TGC, and JLR).

380 **lackey & solicitor general:** JLR Int. with Lash, 11/16/1983, at 1–2, Lash Papers, Box 65, Folder 2; JLR Int. with Lash, 12/1983, at 1–2, *id.*; JLR Int. with Lash, 9/29/1982, at 1–2, *id.*, Box 68, Folder 2.

380 **"his self-indulgence":** IB to Marie & Mendel Berlin, 10/26/1941, IB, *Letters 1928–1946*, at 381–82.

380 **"most heartening":** LDB to FF, 8/24/1941, HBHS, 634.

380–381 **"Are the" & "I believe":** Lilienthal Diary, 10/2/1941, David E. Lilienthal, *The Journals of David E. Lilienthal: The TVA Years, 1939–1945*, 383 (1964).

381 **Rosensohn:** NYT, 5/12/1939, at 26.

381 **Abbott:** FF, "Grace Abbott: Social Inventor," The Child (August 1939): 49–50, in FFLC, Box 198.

381 **Lothian:** WP, 12/15/1940, at 1.

381 **Buckner:** NYT, 3/14/1941, at 20; FF to CCB, 3/11/1941, CCBP, Box 5, Folder 5-2.

381 **Christie:** FF to FDR, 4/8/1941, R&FF, 595; WES, 4/10/1941, at A-2.

381 **book collection & Gestapo & National Library:** Evelyn Adunka, "Salomon Frankfurter (1856–1941)," *Bibliotheken in der NS-Zeit*, 214–15 (Stefan Alker et al., eds. 2008); Evelyn Adunka, "Salomon Frankfurter," *Österreichiches Biographisches Lexikon (ÖBL)* Online Edition, Lfg. 5 (11/25/2016); Murray G. Hall & Christina Köstner, " . . . *allerlei für die Nationalbibliothek zu ergattern* . . . " *Eine österreichische Institution in der NS-Zeit* 268–69 (2006).

381 **requests & Lisa:** Evelyn Adunka, *Der Raub Der Bücher*, 212–13 (2002) (Elizabeth "Lisa" Frank estimated private library worth $50,000); Elfi Hartenstein, *Jüdische Frauen im New Yorker Exil*, 47 (1999) (Lisa joined brother in United States) (based on int. with Elizabeth "Lisa" Frank (née Frankfurter)); Ferdinand Baumgartner, "Habent sua fata bibliothecarii," Artibus atque modis (2011): 182–83; Elizabeth "Lisa" Frankfurter to JB, 12/2/1940, JBP, Box 8, Folder 3.

381 **"He is":** FF to JB, 8/21/1941, at 1–2, JBP, Box 8, Folder 3.

381 **"well":** FF to JB, 9/5/1941, *id.*

381 **Quaker contacts:** JB to FF, 9/9/1941, *id.*

381 **bronchitis:** Vienna obituary, n.d., Salomon Frankfurter Papers, Section 7, at 26. *See* NYT, 10/23/1941, at 23 (indicating Salomon planned on moving to United States); Hartenstein, *Jüdische Frauen im New Yorker Exil*, 47 (father rejected visa according to daughter Lisa).

381 **two years:** FF to Adolph Lippe, 10/28/1941, FFLC, Box 123; FF to MML, 11/6/1941, at 1, MMLP.

381 **"the true":** FF to HJL, 11/17/1941, at 1, FFLC, Box 75. *See* FF to FDR, 10/24/1941 & FDR to FF, 10/27/1941 & FF to FDR, 10/29/1941, R&FF, 619–20.

381–382 **"strange" & "he was not":** FF to Bernard Flexner, 10/28/1941, Flexner Papers, Box 4.

382 **coma:** Melvin I. Urofsky, *Louis D. Brandeis*, 753 (2009).

382 **"The morning":** FF to HJL, 11/17/1941, at 1.

382 **"extensive" & "If":** Milk Wagon Drivers v. Meadowmoor Dairies, 312 U.S. 287, 299 (1941).

382 **Greene:** Nathan Greene to FF, 6/9/1941, FFHLS, Pt. III, Reel 10, Page 662.

382 **"When Brandeis":** FF to Greene, 6/10/1941, at 2, *id.*, Page 664.

383 **tears:** Walter Brandeis Raushenbush Int. with author, 10/16/2019.

383 **hardest:** FF to Flexner, 10/28/1941. *See* FF to DA, 10/9/1941, DAP, Reel 7 Box 11, Folder 142.

383 **"His pursuit" & "found" & "My Sword":** "Remarks of Mr. Justice Frankfurter at the funeral services of Mr. Justice Brandeis," 10/7/1941, FFLC, Box 201 & Appendix to 87 Cong. Rec. A4762 (1941).

383 **article:** FR, "Felix Frankfurter, Conservative," Harper's magazine (October 1941): 449.

383 **"one":** FF to FWB, 7/29/1960, FFLC, Box 40. *See* FR to John M. Gaus, 2/18/1944, FRP, Box 10 ("I found him an amiable although not exciting teacher" & "At any rate, I used to like Felix, and he me.").

383 **Hand & fellowship:** FF to FR, 12/15/1930, FRP, Box 2; FF to FR, 12/24/1930, *id.*

383   **Pinchot:** FF to FR, 1/10/1931, *id.*; FF to FR, 3/27/1931, *id.*

383   **"intellectual":** FR, *Woe Unto You, Lawyers!* x (1939).

383   **criticizing:** FF to FR, 2/7/1940, FFLC, 97; FF to FR, 2/13/1940, FRP, Box 2.

384   **"stiletto":** FR to FF, 2/3/1940, FFLC, Box 97 (Helvering v. Hallock, 309 U.S. 106 (1940)).

384   **"I *still*":** FR to FF, 2/11/1940, at 2, *id.* (emphasis in original). *See* FR to FF, n.d., *id.*

384   **chambers:** FR to FF, 2/18/1941, MMLP, & Thomas Reed Powell Papers, Box B, Folder B24.

384   **baffled:** FF to JB, 10/2/1941, JBP, Box 8, Folder 3.

384   **Shulman:** FR, "Felix Frankfurter: Conservative," 459; FR to WOD, 3/7/1941, WODP, Box 367, Folder 6 (claiming *Journal* requested it, then rejected it at behest of "Felix's representative on the faculty"); FF to Shulman, 5/3/1941 & Shulman to FF, 5/11/1941, FRP, Box 5 (asking Shulman, who denied FR's account).

384   **"shocking":** FR to Gaus, 2/18/1944.

384   **mentioned:** Indiana Evening Gazette, 7/27/1938, at 4; Coshocton (Ohio) Tribune, 8/3/1938, at 4.

384   **critical:** Walton Hamilton, "Preview of a Justice," 48 Yale L.J. 819 (1939) (criticizing FF and *Law and Politics*); FR, "A Sprig of Rosemary for Hammy," 68 Yale L.J. 401 (1959); DA to AM, 5/25/1939, at 1, DAP, Reel 13, Box 21, Folder 268 (commenting on AM's draft introduction to *Law and Politics*, DA wrote that some of its words and phrases "I associate with the resentful, inferiority complex school of writing typified by Fred Rodell, Walter [sic] Hamilton, Drew Pearson, etc.").

384   **memorandum & critiques:** "Hammy" to FR, 5/31/1941, FRP, Box 3 (congratulating him on book review that separated "the satellite Murphy sharply from the planet Felix about which it was revolving? Keep it up until even the luminous body FF takes a new orbit."); "Hammy" to FR, 6/6/1941, at 1–2, *id.*, Box 1 (including Thurman Arnold's line that "the difference between FF and Sutherland—Sutherland wears his whiskers on the outside").

384   **"surprised":** FR, "Felix Frankfurter, Conservative," 457–59.

384   **Brahmin & polls:** *Id.* at 449–51.

384   **"Felix hasn't" & "a tragic" & "as the Court" & "as great":** *Id.* at 459.

384   **Yale-Harvard rivalry:** FF to CCB, 9/26/1941, at 1, CCBP, Box 5, Folder 5-3 ("Marion asked me what Rodell's animus is. . . . I can't for the life of me explain it except for the deep rooted, silly feeling against the H.L.S. that dominates so many of the Yale Law School people, plus also, the fundamental belief of so many of this crowd that law is merely a disguised way of translating sectarian political and economic desires into action"); FFR Transcript, 1/10/1955, at 28–29, FFLC, Box 205 (describing FR as "psychopathic. I think there's something the matter with him."); Andrew Yaphe, " 'Reputation, Reputation, Reputation,' " 36 J. Legal Prof. 441, 443 (2012) (attributing to "reproduction of hierarchy").

385   **"blind" & "pathetic" & "expressed":** JB to FR, 1/13/1942, at 1–2, MMLP.

385   **Roedelheim:** Frederick Bernays Wiener, Book Review, 51 Nw. U. L. Rev. 155, 160 & n.50 (1956) (reviewing FR, *Nine Men* (1955)); FR to FF, 5/29/1956, FFHLS, Pt. III, Reel 32, Page 94 (rejecting Wiener's insinuation that he was "referring to your Jewish ancestry" but to his Austrian heritage in a line in *Nine Men* about Frankfurter's "roots . . . thousands of miles to the East in a civilization long past its prime").

385   **numerous conversations:** HLSD, 9/11/1941, Reel 7, Vol. 35, Page 60; HLSD, 10/19/1941, *id.*, Page 141 & 10/21/1941, *id.*, at Page 146; HLSD, 11/6/1941, *id.*, Vol. 36, Page 55; JJMD, 8/15/1941, 9/12/1941, and 10/21/1941.

385 "extremely": HLSD, 12/1/1941, Reel 7, Vol. 35, Page 83.

385 leaked: BKW, *Yankee from the West*, 32–36 (1962); CT, 12/4/1941, at 1; JJMD, 12/4/1941; JJMD, 12/5/1941.

386 painful: MDF to PGates, 11/6/1941, at 2–4 & MDF to PGates, 1/31/1942, at 1–5, Gates Family Papers.

386 "Since": FF to MML, 11/6/1941, MMLP.

386 "wears": IB to Marie and Mendel Berlin, 10/26/1941, IB, *Letters 1928–1946*, at 382.

386 "I do not": MDF to Beatrice Gates, 7/20/1941, at 1–2.

CHAPTER 24: F.F.'S SOLILOQUY

387 Desvernine: JJMD, 12/7/1941.

387 "to find" & phoned: FF to FDR, 11/17/1941, R&FF, at 623.

387 2:05 p.m.: Cordell Hull, *The Memoirs of Cordell Hull*, Vol. 2, 1095–97 (1948).

388 "Hell no": FF OH, 2/20/1958, at 5, George C. Marshall Foundation, Notes 53N (based on conversation with HLS that day or the next day).

388 Acheson: FF to FDR, 12/7/1941, R&FF, 626.

388 Sandy Spring: DA, *Present at the Creation*, 34–35 (1969).

388 "pressing" & "headed" & "extremely": Memorandum, 12/13/1941, Remarks to the Cabinet, 12/7/1941, at 1–5, FDRL, MSF, No. 1399a.

388 "There": FF, "Franklin Delano Roosevelt, 1882–1945," Harvard Alumni Bulletin, April 28, 1945, Vol. 47, at 499–500, in *Of Law and Men*, 363 (Philip Elman, ed. 1956) (emphasis in original). *See* FF to CCB, 12/24/1941, at 1, CCBP, Box 5, Folder 5-3 ("Stimson is almost lyric about F.D.R's qualities as Commander-in-Chief.").

388 "the whole": FF to FDR, 12/7/1941, R&FF, 625.

388 "I said": FF OH, 2/20/1958, at 4, George C. Marshall Foundation.

388 packed & Marion: NYT, 12/9/1941, at 5; WES, 12/8/1941, at A-1; WP, 12/9/1941, at 12, 22.

389 "a date" & "unprovoked": FDR, Address to Congress, 12/8/1941, at 1, 3, MSF, FDRL, No. 1400-A.

389 at their home: FF to FDR, 12/9/1941 tel., R&FF, 626.

389 "calm": FF to FDR, 12/9/1941, at 1, FDRL, PSF, Box 135.

389 "about": Norman I. Silber, *With All Deliberate Speed*, 83 (2004).

389 "Your cable" & "seem": MDF to PGates and SGates, 12/10/1941, at 1–2, Gates Family Papers.

389 "toy": WES, 12/19/1941, at A-1, A-3.

389 photograph: WES, 12/20/1941, at A-4.

389 greens fees: FF OH, 2/20/1958, at 4, George C. Marshall Foundation; White v. Winchester Country Club, 315 U.S. 32 (1942) (argued Dec. 12, 1941)

390 Cox: JJMD, 12/9/1941.

390 next morning: JJMD, 12/10/1941.

390 Roberts: JJMD, 12/16/1941.

390 memorandum & "some" & "entirely": FF to FDR, 12/17/1941, R&FF, 628–32.

390 "best": JJMD, 12/30/1941.

390 "united": FFR, 8/28/1957, at 9, FFLC, Box 206.

390 "Black": *Id.* at 8.

391 "clear" & telegram & editorials: Bridges v. California, 314 U.S. 252, 261–63, 271–8 (1941).

391 "trial by" & "essential" & "the right" & "Free speech" & "impartial" & "a doctrinaire"

& "a collection" & "the Bill": Bridges v. California, 314 U.S. at 279–84 (Frankfurter, J., dissenting).

391   read a summary: HFS memo, 12/8/1941, FFHLS, Pt. I, Reel 4, Page 197; JFB, 12/8/1941, *id.* at 204.

391   "why" & "ready": FFR, 8/28/1957, at 7, 9.

392   "Hugo" & "Has": FF handwritten note, n.d., WOD join memo in *Gobitis*, FFHLS, Pt. I, Reel 1, Page 867. *See* DFF, 3/12/1943, at 209 (similar quotation).

392   Opelika, Alabama: Jones v. Opelika, 316 U.S. 584 (1942). *Id.* at 586–87 (City of Opelika law); *id.* at 588–92 (two other ordinances); *id.* at 600 (Stone, C.J., dissenting).

392   "wrongly decided" & "The First": *Id.* at 623–24 (Black, Douglas, Murphy, JJ., dissenting). WOD's handwritten and typewritten drafts of the joint dissent, WODP, Box 73, Folder 1 (indicating it was circulated May 29).

392   "never": FF note, n.d., Jones v. Opelika, FFHLS, Pt. I, Reel 4, Page 911 (indicating he received it on May 30).

393   applauded: STLPD, 6/12/1941, at 2D, in WODP, Box 73, Folder 1.

393   "For years": Newsweek, 6/29/1942, at 68, in HFSP, Box 80.

393   "the Axis": DFF, 1/30/1943 & 2/26/1943, at 176, 198. *See* Eugene Gressman Diary, 2/9/1944, Gressman Papers, Box 1, Folder 76 (referring to "the Axis").

393   Drew Pearson: Pearson accused DA of trying "to get me indicted for criticism of the Supreme Court (at the instance of Justice Frankfurter)." Drew Pearson, *Drew Pearson Diaries 1949–1959*, at 8 (Tyler Abell, ed. 1974).

393   "Justice Frankfurter" & "intimate terms" & "Almost": LCJ, 6/1/1942, at 4. In the fall of 1941, FF, CCB, and LH promoted CEW for a district judgeship. FF to CCB, 9/26/1941, at 2 & FF to CCB, 10/2/1941, at 1, CCBP, Box 5, Folder 5-3; FF to LH, 10/1/1941 & LH to FF, 10/3/1941, LHP, Box 105A, Folder 105-8; FB, *In Brief Authority* 201–2 (1962).

393-394 "the persecution" & "long" & "considers": LCJ, 6/1/1942, at 4. This was not the only time Pearson attributed "Jewish" motives to FF. During the late 1950s, he ascribed FF's promotion of HJF for a Second Circuit judgeship to the fact that HJF was Jewish, not that he was one of the most brilliant students in the history of Harvard Law School and one of Wall Street's finest lawyers. *Drew Pearson Diaries 1949–1959*, at 542.

394   "cooled" & "too indiscreet" & "greatest": LCJ, 6/1/1942, at 4.

394   "sheer joys": FF to SGates, 6/30/1942, at 2, Gates Family Papers.

394   thriving: MDF to PGates, 1/21/1942, at 1–8, *id.*; Venetia Murray Fifth Grade Report Card & Ann Murray Ninth Grade Report Card, *id.*

394   called the officers: HLSD, 6/30/1942, at 3, Reel 7, Vol. 39, at 135.

395   Pan American executive: JJMD, 6/30/1942.

395   "as good" & "We hate": FF to SGates, 6/30/1942, at 2–3.

395   "relieved" & "found" & "the children": FF to CCB, 7/8/1942, at 1–2, FFLC, Box 35. *See* FF to LH, 7/18/1942, at 1–2, LHP, Box 105A, Folder 105-9; FF to JB, 7/14/1942 & FF to JB, 8/8/1942, at 2, JBP, Box 8, Folder 3.

395   "seems" & "I hope" & "Oliver leaned": MDF to Beatrice Gates, 9/14/1942 at 2–3, Gates Family Papers.

396   "should be": HLSD, 6/29/1942, Reel 7, Vol. 39, Page 131.

396   the president: FDR to FB, 6/30/1942, at 1–2, FDRL, PSF Box 56 (wanting to try saboteurs by court martial and believing that the crimes were "more serious than any offense in criminal law" and "the death penalty is called for").

396   one of the prosecutors: HLSD, 7/1/1942, Reel 7, Vol. 39, Page 136.

396   media observers: *Id.*, 7/6/1942, *id.* at 144–45.

396   "not": *Id.*, 7/8/1942, *id.* at 151.

396   declined to see: FB to FDR, 7/6/1942, FDRL, PSF, Box 56; HLS to Marvin McIntyre, 7/7/1942, *id.*; FDR to FB, 7/8/1942, *id.*; FB to FDR, 7/9/1942, *id.*

396   flew to Philadelphia: FB, *In Brief Authority*, 337.

396   anticipated: HFS to BB, 7/23/1942, HFSP, Box 69.

397   banned officers: HLSD, 7/28/1942, Reel 7, Vol. 39, Page 213.

397   military uniform & disqualified: HLB Conference Notes, 7/29/1942, at 1, WODP, Box 77, Folder 25; FM Conference Notes, 7/29/1942, Gressman Papers, Box 1. Folder 63; J. Woodford Howard, *Mr. Justice Murphy*, 275–76, 300 (1968); Sidney Fine, *Frank Murphy: The Washington Years*, 218, 404 (1984).

397   Frankfurter's urging & "It was not": FF to FM, 8/14/1942, at 1–2, Gressman Papers, Box 1, Folder 68.

397   Stone's son: *id.* at 2; Alpheus Thomas Mason, *Harlan Fiske Stone*, 655, 863 n.21 (1956) (based on 6/22/42 letter from Lauson Stone).

397   Byrnes: FB to JFB, 1/10/1942 & FB to JFB, 1/14/1942, JFBP, Series 3, Box 6, Folder 6 [Folder 1230]; JFB, *All in One Lifetime*, 147–57 (1958).

397   "immediately": HLB Conference Notes, 7/29/1942, at 1.

397   former student: FF to Royall, 4/20/1942, FFLC, Box 99; FF Diary, 1/26/1943, DFF, 171; NYT, 8/1/1942, at 2; WP, 7/31/1942, at 5; FF to CCB, 9/1942, at 1–2, FFLC, Box 35.

398   "For heaven's": Minneapolis Star Journal, 8/4/1042, at 10. *See* NYT, 7/30/1942, at 4 (noting FF's active questioning).

398   one hour: Revised Rules of the Supreme Court of the United States, 306 U.S. 671, 709 (1939).

398   "sustain": NYHT, 7/31/1942, at 1.

398   trumped: *Id.* at 4.

398   not bound: NYT, 7/31/1941, at 4; BaltSun, 7/31/1941, at 1.

398   "final": WP, 7/31/1942, at 4.

398   "I won't": FB, *In Brief Authority*, 331. *See* FBD, 7/17/1942, at 1, FBP-FDRL, Box 1 (FDR refusing to obey court order to give up saboteurs).

398   "president will order": FM Conference Notes, 7/29/1942, at 1 (OJR, having spoken to FB, relayed the warning).

398   "lawfully": Ex Parte Quirin, 317 U.S. 1, 19 (July 31, 1942) (per curiam). *See* FF Conference Notes, 7/30/1941, FFHLS, Pt. III, Reel 43, Pages 485–89; HFS Draft, 7/31/1942, *id.* at Page 491.

398–399   "a bit" & "would have" & "for": HFS to FF, 8/2/1942, at 1–2, FFHLS, Pt. III, Reel 43, Pages 497–98.

399   praised: FF to HFS, 8/3/1942, at 1–4, HFSP, Box 69.

399   president announced: Speech, 8/8/1942, FDRL, MSF, Box 67, No. 1426A. In 1946, HST commuted the sentences of the two remaining men and deported them to Germany.

399   "legal": HFS to BB, 8/5/1942, at 2, HFSP, Box 69.

399   "advisory" & "some embarrassment": HFS, "Memorandum re: Saboteur Case," 9/25/1942, at 1–2, *id.*

399   "It seems": HFS to FF, 9/10/1942, at 3–4, FFHLS, Pt. III, Reel 43, Pages 511–12.

399   "fluid": FF to HFS, 9/5/1942, at 2–3, HFSP, Box 69.

399   tried to calm: FF to HFS, 9/14/1942, at 2–3, *id.*

399   Bennett Boskey: BB, Memorandum re: Articles of War, n.d., BB Law Clerks' Memo-

randa, Box 6, Folder 8 & in Ross E. Davies, "Some Clerical Contributions to *Ex Parte Quirin*," 19 Green Bag 2d 283, 315–22 App. E (2016).

399 **"make weights":** HFS to FF, 9/16/1942, at 1, HFSP, Box 69.

400 **"very happy":** FF to HFS, 9/27/1942, FFHLS, Pt. III, Reel 43, Page 558. *See* FF, Memorandum, 9/30/1942, at 1, *id.* at Page 561.

400 **national news:** NYHT, 10/1/1942, at 21; NYT, 10/1/1942, at 25.

400 **"We did" & "spiritual" & "a war" & "The difference" & "the special" & "self-destructive" & "The ideal":** FF, "Address by Associate Justice Felix Frankfurter at the Inauguration of Dr. Harry N. Wright," 9/30/1942, at 139–41, 144–48, FFLC, Box 198.

400 **suggested compromise:** FF, Memorandum for OJR, 10/14/1942, FFHLS, Pt. III, Reel 43, Page 566; FF, "Comments on Brothers Roberts' Suggestion," 10/16/1942, *id.* at 568.

400 **made revisions:** HFS, Memorandum, 10/17/1942, *id.* at 569; HFS, Memorandum, 10/17/1942, *id.* at 570.

400 **more changes:** OJR Memorandum, 10/20/1942, *id.* at 601.

400–401 **"unlawful" & "properly" & "The magnitude" & "had a right":** RHJ Memorandum, 10/19/1942, at 3–4, *id.* at 611–12.

401 **"And":** FF handwritten note, n.d. RHJ Memorandum, 10/19/1942, at 4, RHJP, Box 124. *See* Jack Goldsmith, "Justice Jackson's Unpublished Opinion in *Ex Parte Quirin*," 9 Green Bag 2d 223 (2006).

401 **avoid:** FF to HLB, n.d., at 3, HLBP, Box 269 (preferring the narrowest possible ground without deciding "any constitutional questions where every ground of 'jurisdiction' is precarious.").

401 **"damned" & "low-down" & "procedural" & "You've" & "foolish":** "F.F.'s Soliloquy," n.d., at 1–2, FFHLS, Pt. III, Reel 43, Pages 621–22 (noting circulated 10/23/1942).

401 **"Some" & "very" & "internecine" & "What in":** "F.F.'s Soliloquy" at 3, *id.* at Page 623. *See* G. Edward White, Felix Frankfurter's 'Soliloquy' in *Ex Parte Quirin*, 5 Green Bag 2d 423 (2002); Michal Belknap, "Frankfurter and the Nazi Saboteurs," 1982 Supreme Court Year Book: 66–71.

401 **exchanging notes:** Note, FFHLS, Pt. III, Reel 43, Page 624 (on bench on p.m. of 10/23/1942 after circulation of "Soliloquy").

401–402 **"How" & "Your Anatole":** RHJ Note, *id.* at 628. On FM's unhappiness, *see* FM, 10/23/1942, "F.F Soliloquy," FMP, Reel 127, Page 110 (handwritten note: "John—now do you believe me? FM").

402 **"Have I said":** OJR Note, FFHLS, Pt. III, Reel 43, Pages 629–32.

402 **"fullest" & "deepest":** FF Note, *id.* at 625.

402 **"A new":** RHJ Note, *id.* at 634.

402 **made revisions:** HFS, Memorandum, 10/24/1942, FFHLS, Pt. III, Reel 43, Page 643.

402 **"in time" & "the armed" & "admitted" & "others" & "foreclose":** Ex Parte Quirin, 317 U.S. 1, 25, 45, 47–48 (1942).

402–403 **"an incurable" & "applicability" & "now" & "Someday":** FF to HLB, 10/29/1942, HLBP, Box 269, Folder 18.

403 **"the opinion" & "disregarded":** Frederick Bernays Wiener to FF, 11/5/1942, at 1, FFHLS, Pt. III, Reel 42, Page 694.

403 **"the president's" & "sufficient" & "was palpably" & "were lawfully" & the same:** *Id.* at 8–10, *id.* at Page 701–3. *See* Paul R. Baier, *Written in Water* 142–43 (2020).

403 **"not a happy":** FF, Memorandum, 6/4/1953, at 8, FFHLS, Pt. I, Reel 70, Page 256. *See* Louis Fisher, *Nazi Saboteurs on Trial* (2003); Andrew Kent, "Judicial Review for Enemy

Fighters," 66 Vand. L. Rev. 150 (2013); David J. Barron & Martin S. Lederman, "The Commander in Chief at the Lowest Ebb: A Constitutional History," 121 Harv. L. Rev. 941, 1051–55 (2008); Louis Fisher, "Military Commissions: Problems of Authority and Practice," 24 B.U. Int'l L.J. 15 (2006); David J. Danelski, "The Saboteurs' Case," Journal of Supreme Court History 1 (1996): 61; Michal R. Belknap, "The Supreme Court Goes to War," 89 Mil. L. Rev. 59 (1980).

403 **unanimous opinion:** FF to CCB, 9/1942, at 2.

404 **laughed out:** JLR Int. with Louchheim, 5/11/1981, at 19, Louchheim Papers, Box 72, Folder 10.

404 **South Pacific:** Michael E. Parrish, *Citizen Rauh*, 67–68 (2010).

404 **Army Air Forces:** Fisher LBJL OH, 10/31/1968, at 1.

404 **army intelligence:** Katharine Graham, *Personal History*, 133–37, 141–46 (1997).

404 **drafted & Office of Economic Stabilization:** EFP OH, 3/3/1983, at 14; EFP to Louchheim, 8/20/1982, at 1, Louchheim Papers, Box 72, Folder 10.

404 **"They":** Newsweek, 8/16/1943, at 59.

404 **"a houseful":** FF to FDR, Thanksgiving Day 1942, R&FF, 677.

404 **"the most":** Graham, *Personal History*, 106.

404 **custodian:** Sheldon to MDF, n.d. & Sheldon to FF, 2/17/1942, FFLC, Box 99.

404 **so moving:** FF to FDR, 11/30/1942, *id.*

404 **funeral:** FF Diary, 3/16/1943, DFF, 217.

404–405 **"leader" & "Uncle Bill" & "died" & "exaggerated" & "There is no":** WES, 3/26/1943, at A-10 & WP, 3/23/1943, at 10. *See* FF to LH, 10/5/1943, at 1, LHP, Box 105A, Folder 105-10 (enclosing editorial as capturing what "Bill Sheldon meant to us—Marion as well as me").

405 **killed himself:** Oakland Tribune, 3/14/1943, at A-9; EFP OH, 11/15/1982, at 28–29. *Cf.* Sheldon, Princeton Alumni Weekly, 4/23/1943, at 6 (repeating story about disease in South Pacific).

CHAPTER 25: A GREAT ENEMY OF LIBERALISM

406 **"most congenial" & "the first":** FF to FDR, 9/30/1942, R&FF, 670–71. *See* FF to JFB, n.d., at 1–2, JFBP, Ser. 3, Box 1, Folder 10 [Folder 116]; FF to CCB, 10/9/1942, FFLC, Box 35.

406 **"assistant":** JFB, *All in One Lifetime*, 155–57 (1958); David Robertson, *Sly and Able*, 311–23 (1994).

406 **Learned Hand:** Gerald Gunther, *Learned Hand*, 553–70 (1994).

406 **Masses:** *Id.* at 151–61; Masses Publishing Co. v. Patten, 244 F. 535 (S.D.N.Y.), rev'd, 264 F. 24 (2d Cir. 1917); Gerald Gunther, "Learned Hand and the Origins of the Modern First Amendment Doctrine," 27 Stan. L. Rev. 719 (1975).

407 **Second Circuit:** Gunther, *Learned Hand*, 257–61.

407 **"Not":** FF Int. with Gunther, 9/15/1960, at 6, FFHLS, Pt. III, Reel 28, Page 708.

407 **"legal learning" & "outstanding":** "Frankfurter Memorandum on Learned Hand," at 1, R&FF, 674.

407 **five or six:** *Id.* at 671.

407 **"a chance":** FF to FDR, 9/30/1942, R&FF, 672.

407 **"on the score" & "the only" & "*the* one" & "Every other":** FF to FDR, 11/3/1942, *id.* (emphasis in original).

408 **"all more":** FF to FDR, 11/3/1942, R&FF, 673.

408   **early November:** *id.*; FDR Day by Day, 11/12/1942.

408   **Rutledge:** FF Int. with Gunther, 9/15/1960, at 7.

408   **"Jehovah's":** Busey v. District of Columbia, 129 F.2d 24, 38 (U.S. App. D.C. 1942) (Rutledge, J., dissenting) (vacated by 319 U.S. 579 (1943)).

408   **could not criticize:** INB to Max Freedman, 1/22/1969, INBP, Box 6; John M. Ferren, *Salt of the Earth*, 208–21 (2004).

408   **Burlingham:** CCB to FDR, 11/6/1942, at 1–2, FFLC, Box 35; CCB to HFS, 11/11/1942 tel., *id.*; HFS to CCB, 11/14/1942, *id.*; CCB to FDR, 11/18/1942, *id.*; George Whitney Martin, *CCB*, 3, 160–63, 501–4 (2005).

408   **Stone secretly:** FF Int. with Gunther, 9/15/1960, at 7.

408   **told the president:** FBD, 11/6/1942, at 2, FBP-FDRL, Box 1.

408   **cooled:** FB, *In Brief Authority*, 193–94 (1962).

408   **"The longer":** CCB to FF, 11/20/1942, FFLC, Box 35. *See* CCB to FF, 11/23/1942, at 1, *id.* (quoting FDR to CCB, 11/20/1942).

409   **"to prepare" & "He still":** FBD, 11/20/1942, at 3, FBP-FDRL, Box 1. FDR Day by Day, 11/20/1942 (cabinet meeting).

409   **"only truly" & "the only":** FF to FDR, 12/3/1942, R&FF, 673.

409   **announcement:** Draft Hand announcement, *id.*

409   **"private" & "sometimes":** FDR to FF, 12/4/1942, *id.* at 673–74. *See* FF to FDR, 12/7/1942, *id.* at 674; FBD, 12/31/1942, at 2, FBP-FDRL, Box 1 (wishing to proceed with FB's recommendation of WBR).

409   **learned from:** DFF, 1/11/1943, at 154.

409   **"I shall" & "Except":** LH to FF, 1/11/1943, FFLC, Box 64.

409   **"your regret" & "one" & "the pure":** FF to LH, 1/26/1943, LHP, Box 105A, Folder 105-10.

409   **"Felix raised":** LH to Henkin, 2/21/1943, *id.*, Box 73, Folder 6 & Constance Jordan, ed., *Reason and Imagination*, 235 (2013).

409   **"I don't":** LH to CCB, 1/15/1943, at 1–2, CCBP, Box 6, Folder 6-16.

410   **"pressured":** Pottstown (Pa.) Mercury, 2/25/1943, at 4 (blind item from columnist Dorothy Kilgallen claiming FF-FDR "feud" about the LH appointment). *See* Gressman Diary, 10/7/1943 ("FDR told FM that he had the hardest fight of his career to ward off FF [about LH] & to appoint Rutledge"); WOD, *Go East Young Man*, 331–32 (1974) (claiming in his exaggerated memoirs that FDR told him at a poker game that FF had "overplayed his hand"); FB, *In Brief Authority*, 193–94 (hearing similar rumors); Gunther, *Learned Hand*, 561–62 (characterizing rumors as "old Washington gossip" yet considering it a "probable reason").

410   **"the most foolish" & "the most liberal" & "might" & "the acclaim":** FF, Memorandum on Judge Learned Hand, R&FF, 675.

410   **wheat:** Wickard v. Filburn, 317 U.S. 111 (1942).

410   **"contentious":** DFF, 1/9/1943, at 152.

411   **"the Axis" & "in all":** *Id.*, 1/30/1943, at 176.

411   **"a jumping-off" & "how many" & "Well, I don't" & "Well" & "When":** DFF, 1/11/1943, at 155. *See* Gressman Diary, 10/3/1943 (noting FM's displeasure with WOD's "running for the presidency all the time"); Gressman Diary, 10/8/1943 (similar quote).

411   **"quest":** DFF, 1/18/1943, at 161.

411   **"fine":** *Id.*, 2/2/1943, *id.* 177–78.

411   **reassigned:** *Id.*, 2/3/1943, *id.* 178–81 (HLB told OJR who told FF).

411   **Democratic Party boss:** Pendergast v. United States, 317 U.S. 412 (1943).

411   **outraged:** DFF, 2/4/1943, at 181–82.

411   **"conspicuous":** Johnson v. United States, 318 U.S. 189, 202 (1943) (Frankfurter, J., concurring).

412   **to withdraw:** DFF, 2/6/1943, at 183–84; *id.*, 2/8/1943, *id.* 185.

412   **snapshot:** DFF, 141–261.

412   **speechwriters:** SIR, *Working with Roosevelt*, 207–8 (1952); FF to SIR, 12/20/1949, SIRP, Box 1 (heavily editing SIR's description of FF's speechwriting).

412–413 **dictated & instructed & edited & editing skills:** Norman I. Silber, *With All Deliberate Speed*, 80–87 (2004) (disputing characterization of interviews with PE in Bruce Allen Murphy, *The Brandeis/Frankfurter Connection*, 270–71 (1982)); FF Law Clerk Duties, Memorandum, n.d., at 6–7, FFHLS, Pt. III, Reel 9, Pages 68–69 (FF dictating opinions).

413   **collaboration:** Silber, *With All Deliberate Speed*, 103–4.

413   *Chenery I:* Securities & Exchange Comm'n v. Chenery, 318 U.S. 80, 87 (1943).

413   **button:** DFF, 2/21/1943, at 193.

413   **"quite gray":** Lilienthal Diary, 10/10/1942 & 11/26/1942, David E. Lilienthal, *The Journals of David Lilienthal: The TVA Years, 1939–1945*, at 549, 563 (1964).

413   **"thinner" & "a cricket":** IB to Marie and Mendel Berlin, 9/26/1943, IB, *Letters 1928–1946*, at 467 (Henry Hardy, ed. 2004).

413   **"do you":** Louis Henkin Int. with Lash, 9/11/1974, Lash Papers, Box 51, Folder 6.

413   **"stock":** DFF, 2/16/1943, at 190. The published version of the diary misspells FF's secretary's name as "Lee Waters." Eleanor "Lee" Watters worked for FF until her marriage in 1943 when her sister Katherine became FF's secretary. WES, 7/4/1943, at D-4; WP, 7/16/1949, at B3.

413   **"running":** CT, 3/15/1943, at 3.

414   **"radical":** 89 Cong. Rec. 2820 (1943).

414   **"I don't":** DFF, 5/12/1943, at 237–38.

414   **"Do you" & "none" & "every":** DFF, 1/30/1943, at 173–74.

414   **"expected" & "Rutledge":** *Id.*, 3/6/1943, at 205.

414   **"We talked":** DFF, 5/14/1943, at 239.

414   **"guidance" & "the matter":** *Id.*, 5/16/1943, at 242.

415   **"I have" & "It is" & "to decide":** DFF, 3/12/1943, at 209.

415   **"tired" & "tired" & "the way" & "have" & "strong":** DFF, 4/17/1943, at 227–28.

415   **"beautifully" & "meticulously":** DFF, 3/20/1943, at 221. *See id.*, 3/28/1943, at 224.

415   **months:** R&FF, 699.

415   **"democratic" & "no":** FF "The Permanence of Jefferson," 4/13/1943, at 2, 7–8, FFLC, Box 211 & FF, *Of Law and Men*, 230, 235 (Philip Elman, ed. 1956).

415   **enduring ideas:** Brad Snyder, "Frankfurter and Popular Constitutionalism," 47 U.C. Davis L. Rev. 343, 345 (2013).

416   **"no longer":** DFF, 5/19/1943, at 243.

416   **"I have":** *Id.*, 5/26/1943, at 245.

416   **Weizmann & Welles:** *Id.*, May 27, 1943, at 246.

416   **late June:** The exact date of the meeting is unknown; it was not in FF's 1943 Diary, which ends in mid-June, and FF left Washington in mid-July.

416   **Karski:** Timothy Snyder, "Biographical Essay of Jan Karski," in *Story of a Secret State*, xxv–xxxi (Georgetown University Press ed., 2014).

416   **"I do not" & "Felix" & "Mr. Ambassador":** Jan Karski, Int. with Claude Lanzmann,

October 1978, https://www.youtube.com/watch?v=7YVTfG_qE2Y; Claude Lanzmann, The Karski Report (2010), digital video, 49 min.

417   **white paper & camps & extinction:** JTA, 10/31/1939, at 1, 5; CCB to FF, 11/20/1939, at 1, CCBP, Box 5, Folder 5-1 (thanking him for white paper).

417   **Polish ministry's:** "The Mass Extermination of Jews in German Occupied Poland" (Dec. 10, 1942).

417   **met with Roosevelt:** FDR Day by Day, 7/28/1943.

417   **"When I":** Jan Karski, *Story of a Secret State*, 387–88 (1944).

417   **"idea man":** WES, 8/26/1943, at B-1.

417   **not recorded:** Grace Tully, *F.D.R.: My Boss*, 290 (1949) (FF, WOD, FM, and RHJ were "frequent 'off the record' White House callers").

417   **tea:** FDR Day by Day, 10/19/1943.

417   **"unanimous":** FF to FDR, 10/20/1943, R&FF, 705–6.

417   **"what" & "brains" & "the New Deal":** HLSD, 11/6/1943, Reel 8, Vol. 45, Page 28.

417   **phoned:** 10/6/1943 & 10/9/1943, JJMD; 1/25/1944 & 2/3/1944 & 2/21/1944 & 2/23/1944, JJMD.

417   **evenings:** HLSD, 11/28/1943, Reel 8, Vol. 45, Page 67; *id.*, 12/7/1943, *id.*, Page 96.

418   **"the steps":** HLSD, 2/20/1942, Reel 7, Vol. 37, Page 144.

418   **criticism:** Monroe E. Deutsch to FF, 3/24/1942 tel., NARA, RG 107, CWRIC 3077, Reel I:57; FF to McCloy, 04/2/1942, NARA, RG 107, CWRIC 1740; *Personal Justice Denied: Report of the Commission on Wartime Relocation and Internment of Civilians*, 113 (1982).

418   **"Then" & "Not so" & "military" & "will not":** 11 United States Law Week 3345–46 No. 44 (May 18, 1943).

418   **justices agreed:** FM Conference Notes, 5/15/1943, at 1–5 (mislabeled 5/16/1943, which was a Sunday), FMP, Reel 127, Hirabayashi, at 62–66.

418   **Douglas circulated:** Hirabayashi v. United States, 320 U.S. 81, 105–9 (1943) (Douglas, J., concurring).

419   **"[t]he most shocking" & "Well":** DFF, 6/5/1943, at 251.

419   **two-hour & "a thousand":** FF to HFS, 6/4/1943, at 1–2, HFSP, Box 68.

419   **"a thousand" & "hoax" & "it promised":** DFF, 6/5/1943, at 251.

419   **"impossible":** DFF, 6/6/1943, at 252.

419   **"ancestry":** DFF, 6/5/1943, at 252.

419   **"on the assumption":** FF to FM, 6/5/1943, FMP, Reel 127, Page 138.

419   **"I would" & "That's":** FM to FF & FF to FM, 6/5/1943, *id.*, Page 137.

419   **encouraged:** FF to FM, 6/5/1943, *id.*, Pages 139–40.

419   **"the great":** FF to FM, 6/10/1944, at 1–2, *id.*, Pages 143–44.

419   **relief:** FF to FM, n.d., *id.*, Page 136.

419   **"the first" & "based" & "two classes":** Hirabayashi, 320 U.S. at 111 (Murphy, J., concurring).

419   **"For":** FF Join Memo, n.d., HFSP, Box 68.

420   **revoked Schneiderman's citizenship:** United States v. Schneiderman, 33 F. Supp. 510 (N.D. Cal. 1940), aff'd by, 119 F.2d 500 (9th Cir. 1941).

420   **seven-member Court:** FM Conference Notes, 4/22/1942, FMP, Reel 125, Pages 402–4.

420   **"this case" & "As one" & "American citizenship" & "attached":** DFF, 3/13/1943, at 211–12 & Schneiderman Conference Discussion, 12/5/1942, at 4–5, FFHLS, Pt. I, Reel 7, Pages 913, 915.

420   **reargue:** Schneiderman Conference Discussion, 12/12/1942, at 1–3, FFHLS, Pt. I, Reel 7, Pages 922–24.

420   **Few newspapers:** NYT, 3/13/1943, at 15.

421   **"Is there"** & **"Is it"** & **"with blazing"** & **"The Hearst"** & **"I don't"** & **"Of course":** DFF, 3/12/1943, at 209.

421   **"reflects"** & **"deeply":** DFF, 5/31/1943, at 248–49. *See* Gressman Diary, 10/8/1943 (noting, based on conversations with FM, that WOD "has one eye on White House all the time" and mentioning WOD's *Schneiderman* concurrence).

421   **"skates"** & **Roberts suspected:** DFF, 6/1/1943, at 249 & Notes on the Schneiderman Case, 6/1/1943, at 1, FFHLS, Pt. I, Reel 7, Page 925.

421   **"shocked"** & **"skullduggery"** & **"it was":** DFF, 6/15–16/1943, at 257–59 & Notes on the Schneiderman Case, 6/15–16/1943, at 2–5, FFHLS, Pt. I, Reel 7, Pages 926–29.

421–422 **"If Law were":** FF Join Memo in *Schneiderman*, n.d., HFSP, Box 69. *See* FF to HFS, 6/21/1943, *id.*; Schneiderman v. United States, 320 U.S. 118 (1943); David Fontana, "A Case for the Twenty-First Century Constitutional Canon," 35 Conn. L. Rev. 35 (2002).

422   **"very"** & **"ashamed"** & **"inexcusable"** & **"did not":** DFF, 5/4/1943, at 234.

422   **"merely"** & **jeopardized:** Murdock v. Pennsylvania, 319 U.S. 105, 135, 140 (1943) (Frankfurter, J., dissenting). *See* Jones v Opelika, 319 U.S. 103 (1943) (per curiam); Martin v. Struthers, 319 U.S. 141, 152 (1943) (Frankfurter, J., dissenting).

422   **Kennebunk:** BG, 6/10/1940, at 1, 4. *See* Shawn Francis Peters, *Judging Jehovah's Witnesses*, 72–95 (2000) (discussing mob attacks in Texas, Maine, Illinois, Maryland, West Virginia, and elsewhere).

422   **"for the purposes":** West Virginia v. Barnette, 319 U.S. 624, 626 & n.1, 628 (1943).

422   **local custom:** Richard Danzig, "How Questions Begot Answers in Felix Frankfurter's First Flag Salute Opinion," Supreme Court Review (1977): 261–62; Richard Danzig, "Justice Frankfurter's Opinions in the Flag Salute Cases: Blending Logic and Psychologic in Constitutional Decisionmaking," 36 Stan. L. Rev. 675, 714–17 (1984).

422   **pipefitter:** NYT, 9/11/1988 at 1, 30; Walter Barnett, 1940 U.S. Census, Roll T627_4416, Page 24B, ED 20-119, Line 41 ("laborer" in "chemical factory").

422   **two daughters:** Gregory L. Peterson et al., "Recollections of *West Virginia State Board of Education v. Barnette*," 81 St. John's L. Rev. 755, 767–71 (2007) (recollection of Gathie Barnett Edmonds and Marie Barnett Snodgrass); David L. Hudson, Jr., "Woman in Barnette Reflects on Flag Salute Case," FreedomForum Institute, 4/29/2009, https://www.freedomforuminstitute.org/2009/04/29/woman-in-barnette-reflects-on-flag-salute-case/.

422   **other families:** Peters, *Judging Jehovah's Witnesses*, 245.

423   **"religious liberty"** & **"impaired":** Barnette v. West Virginia, 47 F. Supp. 251, 252–53 (S.D. W. Va. 1942).

423   **briefs in support:** Brief of the Committee on the Bill of Rights of the American Bar Association, 1942_WL_75727 & Brief for American Civil Liberties Union, 1943_WL_71854.

423   **assigned:** Peterson et al., "Recollections of *West Virginia State Board of Education v. Barnette*," 81 St. John's L. Rev. at 784 (recollection of BB).

423   **Having concurred and dissented:** Douglas v. Jeannette, 319 U.S. 157, 166 (1943) (Jackson, J., concurring in result and dissenting in *Murdock v. Douglas* and *Martin v. Struthers*); FF to RHJ, 4/9/1943, FFLC, Box 69 & FF to RHJ, 4/29/1943, *id.* (joining RHJ's concurrence in *Douglas v. Jeannette* and commenting on his opinion); John Q.

Barrett, "Justice Jackson in The Jehovah's Witnesses' Cases," 13 F.I.U. L. Rev. 827, 840–41, 844–50 (2019) (RHJ's opinion in *Douglas v. Jeannette* as dissent in *Murdock*).

423   **believed & had made:** RHJ, *The Struggle for Judicial Supremacy*, 284–85 & n.48 (1941) (noting *Gobitis* as exception to Court's protection of free speech); HID, 6/15/1940, HI, *The Secret Diary of Harold L. Ickes: The Lowering Clouds: 1939–1941*, at 211 (1955) (describing RHJ as "bitter" about *Gobitis* at previous day's cabinet meeting).

423   **"the individual's" & "public":** West Virginia v. Barnette, 319 U.S. 624, 634 (1943).

423   **"oversimplification":** *Id.* at 636.

424   **"The very" & "may not":** *Id.* at 638.

424   **"rich" and "If there is":** *Id.* at 642. *See* RHJP, Box 127, Folders 10–11.

424   **refused & anxious & drawer:** Silber, *With All Deliberate Speed*, 111–12.

424   **June 2 and 3:** DFF, 6/2/1943 & 6/3/1943, at 250.

424   **"the expression":** FF to RHJ, 6/4/1943, FFLC, Box 69.

424   **stayed home:** FF to FM, 6/10/1943, at 1, FMP, Reel 127, at 143.

424   **9:00 p.m. & food:** Silber, *With All Deliberate Speed*, 112–13 (recalling they stopped at 3:00 a.m.).

424   **2:00 a.m.:** DFF, 6/10/1943, at 253.

424   **"huge" & "rearranged":** Silber, *With All Deliberate Speed*, 114–15 (claiming FF "immediately" circulated it the next day to his colleagues after reading it only once).

424   **reading and editing:** DFF, 6/11/1943, at 253.

424   **next morning:** Handwritten note on RHJ Draft Opinion, 6/11/1943, at 1, RHJP, Box 127, Folder 10 (noting FF dissent circulated on morning of June 12).

424   **"One":** Barnette, 319 U.S. at 646–47 (Frankfurter, J., dissenting).

425   **"disinterestedness" & "Phil":** Silber, *With All Deliberate Speed*, 113–14.

425   **"as a" & "ought" & "duty" & "a Jew" & "to go" & "not mentioning" & "to keep":** DFF, 6/13/1943, at 253–54.

425   **"as" & "for" & "too" & "for months" & "what I":** DFF, 6/14/1943, at 254. *See* FF to FM, 6/14/1943, at 1–6, Gressman Papers, Box 1, Folder 68 (thanking FM for suggestion to delete opening sentence and explaining why he included it).

425   **Burlingham:** CCB to Powell, 9/13/1943, Powell Papers, Box A, Folder A26.

425–426 **"reasonable" & "good" & "judicial" & "comparable" & "free" & " 'it must' " & "responsibility":** Barnette, 319 U.S. at 647–49 (Frankfurter, J., dissenting) (quoting Missouri, Kan. & Tenn. Rwy. Co. v. May, 194 U.S. 267, 270 (1904)).

426   **had a choice & Cardozo's:** Barnette, 319 U.S. at 656–58 (Frankfurter, J., dissenting) (citing Pierce v. Society of Sisters, 268 U.S. 510 (1925) & Hamilton v. Regents, 293 U.S. 245, 266, 268 (1934) (Cardozo, J., concurring).

426   **five prior:** *Id.* at 664 (citing Leoles v. Landers, 302 U.S. 656 (1937) (per curiam) & Hering v. State Board of Education, 303 U.S. 624 (1938) (per curiam) & Gabrielli v. Knickerbocker, 306 U.S. 621 (1939) (per curiam) for lack of federal question & Johnson v. Deerfield, 306 U.S. 621 (1939) (per curiam) for summary opinion & Minersville v. Gobitis, 310 U.S. 586 (1940), which was reviewed only because a lower court injunction contradicted those rulings).

426   **"outstanding" & "to mention":** *Id.* at 664–65.

426   **"writhe" & "be changed" & "no such" & "without":** DFF, 6/14/1943, at 255.

426   **private docket books:** In *Leoles v. Landers* in December 1937 and *Hering v. Board of Education* in March 1938, HFS and LDB voted to postpone a decision on federal juris-

diction for an argument on the merits. LDB 1937 Term Docket Book, *Leoles v. Landers*, at 428 (HFS & LDB voting to postpone to merits); OJR 1937 Term Docket Book, *Leoles v. Landers*, at 382 (same); Butler 1937 Term Docket Book, *Leoles v. Landers*, at 409 (same); HFS 1937 Term Docket Book, *Leoles v. Landers*, at 380 (same); Butler 1937 Term Docket Book, *Hering v. Board of Education*, at 555 (HFS & LDB voting to dismiss); OJR 1937 Term Docket Book, *Hering v. Board of Education*, at 511 (same); HFS 1937 Term Docket Book, *Hering v. Board of Education*, at 513 (same). Cardozo voted with majority in *Leoles* and was absent in *Hering*.

In *Gabrielli v. Knickerbocker* in April 1939, the Court unanimously voted to dismiss for lack of a federal constitutional question. Butler 1938 Term Docket Book, *Gabrielli v. Knickerbocker*, at 544; Roberts 1938 Term Docket Book, *Gabrielli v. Knickerbocker*, at 489; HFS 1938 Term Docket Book, *Gabrielli v. Knickerbocker*, at 521. And in *Johnson v. Deerfield* in May 1939, the Court unanimously voted to deny on merits because of the three prior cases. Butler 1938 Term Docket Book, *Johnson v. Deerfield*, at 545; OJR 1938 Term Docket Book, *Johnson v. Deerfield*, at 490; HFS 1938 Term Docket Book, *Johnson v. Deerfield*, at 522. HFS joined both decisions, which is why FF accused his colleague of hypocrisy in *Gobitis* and *Barnette*.

Both HFS and HLB initially voted to "pass" in *Gobitis*—supporting HLB's claim that he suppressed his negative vote in that case but not in any of the prior ones. HFS 1939 Term Docket Book, *Minersville v. Gobitis*, at 521.

426–427 **"pressures" & "take" & "[t]hat which"**: Barnette, 319 U.S. at 665 (Frankfurter, J., dissenting).

427 **"admonition" & "judicial" & "We are" & "to dwarf" & "Of course" & "a great"**: *Id.* at 667, 669–671 (Frankfurter, J., dissenting) (quoting James Bradley Thayer, *John Marshall*, 104–10 (1901)).

427 **"perfect"**: Reed to FF, n.d., FFHLS, Pt. I, Reel 7, Page 809.

427 **"point[ing] strongly"**: TNR, 7/5/1943, at 18.

427 **apologized**: Powell to FF, 7/8/1943, FFHLS, Pt. III, Reel 10, Page 711; FF to Powell, 7/9/1943, *id.* at 710; Powell to FF, 7/17/1943, *id.* at 711. *But see* Powell to PAF, 7/26/1944, at 1, Powell Papers, Box B, Folder B25 (insisting FF "behaved rather badly" in response to his criticism).

427 **"I can't"**: Powell to CCB, 9/2/1943, at 1–2, Powell Papers, Box A, Folder A26.

428 **"one"**: FF to CEH, 6/15/1943, FFHLS, Pt. I, Paige Box 10, Reel 7, Pages 807.

428 **"as cogently" & "knocked" & "authority" & "to provide" & "appreciation" & "unless"**: CEH to FF, 6/17/1943, at 1–2, *id.* at 810–11.

428 **late afternoon visit**: FDR Day by Day, 6/27/1943.

428 **"They ought"**: R&FF, 699–700.

428 **"there seemed"**: Lash, "A Brahmin of the Law," DFF, 70 (citing Joseph Lash, *Eleanor Roosevelt*, 159 (1964)); FDR Day by Day, 8/6/1940 (Hyde Park overnight visit). It wasn't the day *Gobitis* was decided because ER was not at that tea. FDR Day by Day, 6/3/1940.

428 **"'stupid, unnecessary'"**: R&FF, 701.

428 **Max Stephan**: Stephan v. United States, 133 F.2d. 87 (6th Cir. 1943), *cert. denied*, 318 U.S. 781 (April 5, 1943); 49 F. Supp. 897 (E.D. Mich. May 6, 1943), denied by 319 U.S. 423 (June 1, 1943) (per curiam).

428 **voted not to hear**: DFF, 5/24/1943, at 244–45.

428–429 **"profoundly wise" & "evil"**: FF to FDR, 7/1/1943, R&FF, 703. DFP, 7/3/1943, at 6.

CHAPTER 26: RACE, REDEMPTION, AND ROOSEVELT

430   **for years:** Nixon v. Herndon, 273 U.S. 536 (1927); Nixon v. Condon, 286 U.S. 73 (1932); Grovey v. Townsend, 295 U.S. 45, 52–53 (1935) (managers of primary election not state officers).

431   **"This is":** PC, 11/20/1943, at 20.

431   **special counsel:** Mark V. Tushnet, *Making Civil Rights Law*, 99–108 (1994).

431   **Hastie had resigned:** ChiDef, 2/6/1943, at 1; WHH OH, Truman Library, at 16–23; Gilbert Ware, *William Hastie*, 124–41 (1984).

431   **first Supreme Court:** ChiDef, 11/20/1943, at 2.

431   **refused & insisted:** United States v. Classic, 313 U.S. 299, 315–21, 329 (1941); David M. Bixby, "The Roosevelt Court, Democratic Ideology, and Minority Rights: Another Look at *United States v. Classic*," 90 Yale L.J. 741, 792–812 (1981); FB, *In Brief Authority*, 159–60, 187–88 (1962).

431–432 **"The Fourteenth" & "There are":** FF to HFS, 5/21/1941, HFSP, Box 66 (second note handwritten).

432   **"destroys" & "redden[ed]":** BAA, 11/20/1943, at 9.

432   **November 13:** WBR 1943 Term Docket Book, *Smith v. Allwright*, No. 51, at 348; OJR 1943 Term Docket Book, *Smith v. Allwright*, No. 51, at 377 (noting he had "Passed" on November 13); WOD Conference Notes, 11/13/1943, WODP, Box 94, Folder 7.

432   **granted:** Motion of Texas Attorney General, Smith v. Allwright Clerk's Office File & Gerald Mann to Clerk's Office, 11/24/1943 tel. & Clerk to Mann, 12/13/1943, NARA, RG 267, Appellate Case Files 51–52 O.T. 1943, Box 3412; WOD 1943 Term Docket Book, *Smith v. Allwright*, WODP, Box 93, Folder 12 (granting Texas motion on Dec. 6) & SFR 1943 Term Docket Book, *Smith v. Allwright*, at 349, SFRP (same).

432   **"could whip":** ChiDef, 1/22/1944, at 1.

432   **"Texas" & "they must":** PhillyTrib, 1/22/1944, at 14. *See* Ware, *William Hastie*, 177–83.

432   **"without":** FF, "Memorandum on *Smith v. Allwright*," 4/10/1944, at 3, FFHLS, Pt. I, Reel 10, Page 165.

433   **"irrelevant":** "Supreme Court Memoranda, 1943–1944," FFHLS, Pt. I, Reel 10, Page 1055. *Cf.* FM Conference Notes, *Smith v. Allwright*, at 3, FMP, Reel 129, October Term 1943, at 63 (only notes of 1/15 conference, misinterpreting FF's view).

433   **"You are" & "accusations" & "Of course":** FF, "Memorandum on *Smith v. Allwright*," 4/10/1944, at 1–2.

433   **"the Court's decision":** RHJ to HFS, 1/17/1944, at 1, HFSP, Box 75.

433   **"we were" & "did not" & "political":** FF, "Memorandum on *Smith v. Allwright*," 4/10/1944, at 2–3.

433   **"personal":** Mercoid Corp. v. Mid-Continent Inv. Co., 320 U.S. 661, 673 (1944) (Black, J., opinion) (joined by Murphy, J.).

434   **"what is":** Federal Power Comm'n v. Hope Natural Gas Co., 320 U.S. 591, 619 (1944) (Black & Murphy, JJ., opinion).

434   **"tendency":** Mahnich v. Southern S. S. Co., 321 U.S. 96, 113 & n.9 (1944) (Roberts, J., dissenting) (joined by Frankfurter, J.).

434   **"a wholly":** Brown v. Gerdes, 321 U.S. 178, 191 (1944) (Frankfurter, J., concurring).

434   **"Frankfurter Views":** LAT, 1/5/1944, a 1. *See* Gressman Diary, 1/5/1944 & 1/15/1944 (FM concerned not with newspaper coverage but with discord on Court).

434   **"Frankfurter Adds":** NYT, 2/8/1944, at 1. *See* WP, 1/8/1944, at 8; WP, 2/12/1944, at 6.

434   "An Unstable": NYT, 2/4/1944, at 14.

434   "his third": STLST, 3/1/1944, at 14, FFHLS, Pt. III, Reel 11, Page 119.

434   "the Frankfurter" & "the Black": PE to Lerner, 2/9/1944, FFHLS, Pt. III, Reel 11, Page 138 (quoting PM, 2/9/1944).

434   rebutting: PE to PM editor, 2/29/1944, id., Page 140 (see PM, 3/5/1944, at 10).

434   challenging: DA to Elliston, 2/16/1944, at 1–3, id., Pages 146–48.

434   "The Justice's": IB to JA, 2/11/1944, IB, Letters 1928–1946, at 485 (Henry Hardy, ed. 2004).

434   "written": LH to FF, 2/6/1944, FFHLS, Pt. I, Reel 11, Page 256.

435   "member" & "growing": NYHT, 1/10/1944, at 16.

435   "the history": FF to CCB, 1/11/1944, at 1, FFLC, Box 35.

435   "the importance": CCB to FF, 1/13/1944, at 1, id.

435   "I have" & "They are": CCB to FF, 2/4/1944, at 1–2, id.

435   "as old" & "it is": FF to CCB, 2/8/1944, at 1, 4, id. See Lilienthal Diary, 2/13/1944, David E. Lilienthal, The Journals of David E. Lilienthal: The TVA Years, 1939–1945, at 624–25 (1964) (FF "very sensitive" about criticism).

435   "Is there": BVC to CCB, 1/28/1944, CCBP, Box 2, Folder 2-19.

435   multiplicity: BVC to FF, 1/19/1944, FFHLS, Pt. III, Reel 11, Pages 127–28.

435   "addressed": FF to BVC, 1/20/1944, id., Page 126. See FF to JFB, 3/17/1944, JFBP, Ser. 5, Box 5, Folders 5–6 [Folder 145] (suggesting BVC for vacancy on federal court of appeals in D.C.); JFB to FF, 3/24/1944, id. (agreeing).

436   "fundamentally": Phillips to FF, 8/19/1957, at 1, in FFR, 8/28/1957, FFLC, Box 206 (quoting FF). See Gressman Diary, 10/17/1943 & 10/23/1943 (recounting FM's displeasure with how HFS ran conference compared to CEH); PE to FF, 4/3/1944, FFHLS, Pt. III, Reel 11, Page 77 (HFS "owed it to his many admirers to explain why 'after long reflection' he realized that he voted the wrong way in Grovey v. Townsend").

436   "I did not" & "delicacy" & "a soldier": FF, "Memorandum on Smith v. Allwright," 4/10/1944, at 3.

436   "at length" & "the importance": Id.

436   "now": FM Conference Notes, Smith v. Allwright, at 3.

436   March 10: SFR Draft Majority Opinion, 3/10/1944, SFRP, Box 80, Folders 1 & 2 (handwritten note: circulated only to HFS and FF).

436   "had begged": FF, "Memorandum on Smith v. Allwright," 4/10/1944, at 3–4.

436–437 "You are" & "a square" & "disingenuousness" & "our inescapable" & "a deviation" & "For myself": FF to SFR, 3/15/1944, at 1–3, FFHLS, Pt. III, Reel 40, at Pages 216–18 & SFRP, Box 80, Folder 2.

437   "would not" & "the only": FF, "Memorandum on Smith v. Allwright," 4/10/1944, at 3–4.

437   "appeasement": FF to HFS, 3/17/1944, HFSP, Box 74.

437   "We are" & "as a dynamic" & "a different" & "the great" & "if in fact": FF Unpublished Concurrence in Smith v. Allwright, 4/10/1944, at 1–2, FFHLS, Pt. I, Reel 10, Pages 169–70.

438   "Something": FF to HFS, 3/17/1944, HFSP, Box 74.

438   joined: HFS to SFR, 3/16/1944, HFSP, Box 76.

438   "before" & "something": HFS to FF, 3/18/1944, FFHLS, Pt. I, Reel 11, Pages 461–62.

438   "We should": FF to HFS, 3/18/1944, HFSP, Box 74.

438   Mahnich: HFS to FF, 3/18/1944, FFHLS, Pt. I, Reel 11, Pages 461–62.

438   "[t]he evil": Mahnich v. Southern S.S. Co., 321 U.S. 96, 112 (1944) (Roberts, J., dissent-
       ing). *See* Gressman Diary, 2/2/44 (recounting publicity about OJR's *Mahnich* dissent).

438   "I wrote": FF to SFR, circa 3/17/1944, SFRP, Box 80, Folders 1 & 2.

438   "I congratulate": FF to SFR, 3/28/1944, *id.*

438   "had a difficult" & "seriously": Harlan B. Phillips, "Notes on Conversations with Mr.
       Justice Jackson," 12/1–4/1952, at 1, in FFR, 8/28/1957, FFLC, Box 206. *Cf.* FF to Phil-
       lips, 8/8/1957, at 1–2, *id.* (denying any friction between him and RHJ). FF had forgotten
       that he had written the *Smith v. Allwright* concurrence until reminded of it by Phillips,
       a Columbia University oral historian, in August 1957. *Id.* at 2–3. Phillips had initially
       seen the unpublished concurrence on May 1, 1953, when RHJ showed it to him. Phil-
       lips to FF, 8/19/1957, at 1–2, *id.* Phillips preserved the concurrence and understood its
       historical significance. He also contributed important corroborating memoranda and
       generated correspondence about the case with FF as part of the rough draft of FF's
       Reminisces in his Library of Congress Papers. FFR Transcript, 8/28/1957, FFLC, Box
       206. The concurrence has been overlooked by scholars.

438   "furious": Phillips, "The Texas White Primary Case," at 3, in FFR, 8/28/1957, FFLC,
       Box 206 (based on notes of 12/1–4/1952 conversations with RHJ).

438   "I think" & "could not swallow": FF, "Memorandum on *Smith v. Allwright*,"
       4/10/1944, at 4.

439   "circulated": FF Unpublished Concurrence in *Smith v. Allwright*, at 1, 4/10/1944 in FFR,
       8/28/1957, FFLC, Box 206 (FF handwritten note).

439   "Mr. Justice Frankfurter": Smith v. Allwright, 321 U.S. 649, 666 (1944) (Frankfurter,
       J., concurring in result).

439   "my Brethren act": FF, "Memorandum on *Smith v. Allwright*," 4/10/1944, at 4.

439   "separate": Plessy v. Ferguson, 163 U.S. 537 (1896); Gong Lum v. Rice, 275 U.S. 78 (1927).

439   Margold: Press Release, "Margold to Direct National Legal Campaign for Negro
       Rights," 11/9/1930, NAACP Papers, Pt. 3, Series A, Reel 1, Page 503; Margold Report,
       circa 1930, *id.*, Reel 44, Page 560.

439   Donald Murray: Pearson v. Murray, 182 A.590 (Md. 1936).

439   Lloyd Gaines: Missouri ex rel Gaines v. Canada, 305 U.S. 337 (1938).

440   railroad cars: Mitchell v. United States, 313 U.S. 80 (1941).

440   "the greatest": "The Reminisces of Thurgood Marshall" (Columbia Oral History
       Research Office, 1977), in *Thurgood Marshall: His Speeches, Writings, Arguments, Opin-
       ions and Reminisces*, 512 (Mark V. Tushnet, ed. 2001). *See* Charles L. Zelden, *The Battle
       for the Black Ballot* (2004); Darlene Clark Hine, *Black Victory* (1979); Michael J. Klar-
       man, "The White Primary Rulings: A Case Study in the Consequences of Supreme
       Court Decisionmaking," 29 Fla. St. U. L. Rev. 55 (2001).

440   "slavish" & "citizenship" & "equality" & "as a dynamic" & "post-war" & "frustrated" &
       "duty": FF, Unpublished Concurrence in *Smith v. Allwright*, 4/10/1944, at 1–2.

440   "I Am" & presented: WES, 5/22/1944, at A-7.

441   "the bold" & "Freedom" & "moral" & "the most significant": FF, "On Being an Ameri-
       can," *Survey Graphic*, 7/1944, at 309–10, in FFLC, Box 198.

441   "dedicated" & "the moral": FF, Tribute to Walter White, 5/25/1944, in FFLC, Box 198.

441   "a challenge": FF, Foreword, *Chaim Weizmann* (Meyer W. Weisgal, ed. 1944), in *id.*

441   "Just": FF to FDR, 12/20/1943, R&FF, 708.

441   "I realized": FDR to FF, 12/23/1943, *id.* at 709.

441   **"selfish" & "overconfidence":** FDR, Radio address re: State of Union, 1/11/1944, at 9, FDRL, MSF, Box 77, No. 1503.

441   **300 copies & "Don't":** R&FF, 716–17.

441   **happy:** FF to FDR, 1/30/1944, R&FF, 717.

441   **"long":** FF to FDR, 3/11/1944, *id.* at 718.

441   **"in the doghouse":** FDR to FF, 3/17/1944, PSF, FDRL, Box 136. *See* FDR Day by Day, 3/13/1944.

441   **"without pain":** FF to CCB, 4/24/1945, at 1, FFLC, Box 35.

442   **"All":** FDR to Bob Hannegan, 7/10/1944, FDRL, MSF, Box 79, No. 1523 (released on 7/11/1944).

442   **never forgot & fatigue:** R&FF, 722–23, 713–14.

442   **"with subterranean":** Hopkins to FF, 7/10/1944, CCBP, Box 5, Folder 5-5 (FF handwritten). *See* FF to CCB, n.d., at 1, *id.* (describing Wallace as a "good man").

442   **Roosevelt wrote:** FDR to Hannegan, n.d., R&FF, 722–23; OJR to FF, 7/16/1944, at 1, FFHLS, Pt. III, Reel 3, Page 163 ("And what do you say to the C-I-C's indication that W.O.D. would make an acceptable running-mate? Am I mad or do I dream?").

442   **retype:** Grace Tully, *F.D.R: My Boss,* 275–77 (1949). *See* Bruce Allen Murphy, *Wild Bill,* 605–08 (2003); Michael Janeway, *The Fall of the House of Roosevelt,* 51–52, 238 n.25 (2004).

442   **"finally" & "but the leaders" & "And instead":** FF to MDF, 9/14/1944, at 2–4, FFLC, Box 15. *See* FF to JFB, 9/14/1944, JFBP, Ser. 4, Box 20, Folder 1 [Folder 138(2)] (discussing conversation re: WOD).

442   **had considered:** John Q. Barrett, "Attorney General Robert H. Jackson and President Franklin D. Roosevelt," Journal of Supreme Court History 44, no. 1 (2019): 90, 104 (discussions with FDR in 1944 about vice presidency).

442   **"major":** FF to DA, 8/3/1944, at 1, DAP, Reel 7, Box 11, Folder 143.

442   **"very serious":** FF to JJM, 8/26/1944, JJMP, at 3–4, Box 1, Folder 59. *See* FF to CCB, 8/22/1944, at 1 (mislabeled 1940), CCBP, Box 5, Folder 5-2; OJR to FF, 8/30/1944, at 1, FFHLS, Pt. III, Reel 3, Page 167.

442   **operation:** Her surgeon was renowned Brookline gynecologist George van Siclen Smith. Alfred Cohn to George B. *[sic]* Smith, 8/8/1944, FFLC, Box 48; BG 4/3/1984, at 13.

442   **tea:** FDR Day by Day, 10/16/1944.

442–443   **gray & "sore" & "Jew" & "I was" & "Why, I don't" & "You see":** JPK, "Diary Notes on the 1944 Political Campaign," at 5, 7 JPKP, Box 101. FDR Day by Day, 10/26/1944; David Nasaw, *The Patriarch,* 574 (2012).

443   **running mate:** HST to HLS, 12/31/1946, at 1, HLSP, Reel 116, Page 694 ("until the time of President Roosevelt's death, I had no knowledge of the atomic bomb").

443   **"some distinguished":** FF, Memorandum for Lord Halifax, 4/18/1945, at 1–2. Oppenheimer Papers, Box 34, Folder 7.

443   **Lowen:** ER to FDR, 7/27/1943, FDRL, Selected Documents on the Topic of the Atomic Bomb, Box 1, Pt. 3.

443   **White House meeting:** FDR Day by Day, 7/28/1943.

443   **Eleanor continued & dismissed:** James Conant to Vannevar Bush, 7/31/1943, at 1–3, Bush Conant Files (S-1), NARA, RG 227, Microfilm #1392, Reel 1; Lowen to FDR, 10/29/1943, FDRL, PSF, Box 141; FDR to Conant, 11/8/1943, *id.*; Conant to FDR, 12/30/1943, *id.*; FDR Day by Day, 12/6/1943 (Lowen's overnight stay at White House

as ER's guest); Lowen to ER, 2/15/1944, FDRL, Atomic Bomb File, Box 1, Pt. 3; Bush to FDR, 3/7/1944, *id.*

443   **presumably & worried:** Bush to Conant, 9/22/1944, AEC Doc. No. 185, at 1–2, Bush Conant Files (S-I), NARA, RG 227, Microfilm 1392, Reel 4 (suggesting FF learned about the bomb from Lowen though he could not remember Lowen's name, describing Lowen as a disgruntled scientist who had met with the first lady and the president); Joseph P. Lash, *Eleanor and Franklin,* 704–7 (1971); James G. Hershberg, *James B. Conant,* 195–96 (1993).

443   **Oxford:** FF, Memorandum for Lord Halifax, 4/18/1945, at 1, Oppenheimer Papers, Box 34, Folder 7.

443   **April 1939:** FF, Memorandum re Frankfurter-Bohr Relationship, 5/6/1945, at 1, *id.*

443   **"hit it off" & tea:** FF, Memorandum for Lord Halifax, 4/18/1945, at 1.

444   **"cultural":** FF, Memorandum re Frankfurter-Bohr Relationship, 5/6/1945, at 1.

444   **"made a very" & "might be" & "He was":** FF, Memorandum for Lord Halifax, 4/18/1945, at 2–3.

444   **"it might" & "the possibility" & "worried":** *Id.* at 3.

444   **"disturbed":** Bush, "Memorandum of Conference," 9/22/1944, at 1, AEC Doc. No. 185. *See* Bush to Conant, 9/23/1944, at 1, AEC Doc. No. 186, Bush Conant Files (S-I), NARA, RG 227, Microfilm 1392, Reel 4 (expressing security concerns in light of Bohr and FF disclosures); Bush to Bundy, 4/25/1945, at 1, *id.* (discussing second Bohr visit and recalling Bohr-FF situation).

444   **"a formula":** FF, Memorandum for Lord Halifax, 4/18/1945, at 3, Oppenheimer Papers, Box 34, Folder 7.

444   **Churchill distrusted:** Bohr to Churchill, 5/22/1944, Oppenheimer Papers, Box 34, Folder 7; R&FF, 723–28; Martin Sherwin, *A World Destroyed,* 99–112, 122–25 (1975, repr. 1987 Vintage edition) (analyzing FF's meeting with FDR, describing Bohr's meeting with Churchill as a "disaster," and observing that Bohr and FF misjudged FDR's enthusiasm as "more apparent than real").

444   **passed along & urged:** FF to FDR, 7/10/1944, R&FF, 728 (enclosing Bohr memorandum, 7/3/1944, *id.* at 728–35).

444   **August 26:** FDR Day by Day, 8/26/1944.

444   **instructed:** FF, Memorandum for Lord Halifax, 4/18/1945, at 4.

444   **follow-up & "my Danish":** FF to FDR, 9/8/1944, R&FF, 735–36. *See* FF, Memorandum for Lord Halifax, 4/18/1945, at 4.

445   **secret agreement:** Aide de Memoire of Conversation between the President and the Prime Minister at Hyde Park, 9/18/1944, FDRL, Selected Documents on the Topic of the Atomic Bomb, Box 1, Pt. 3.

445   **listened:** HLSD, 6/14/1944, Reel 9, Vol. 47, Pages 114–15.

445   **postwar Germany:** JJMD, 9/21/1944.

445   **"snorted":** HLSD, 9/7/1944, Reel 9, Vol. 48, Pages 51–52.

445   **Second Quebec:** HLSD, 9/20/1944, Reel 9, Vol. 48, Page 93 (FF arguing the actions of FDR and Churchill "couldn't stand" re: lack of trials for Nazi war criminals).

445   **Morgenthau plan:** HLSD, 9/11/1944, Reel 9, Vol. 48, Page 67; JJMD, 9/12/1944.

445   **"And generally":** FF to JJM, 8/26/1944, at 2.

445–446   **Clyde Sarah & surgery & welder & girlfriend:** FBI Int. with Fred Korematsu, 6/4/1942, at 1–5, NARA, RG 60, Department of Justice Files, 146-42-7, Section 1, Box 1; Korematsu Trial Statement, District Court Case File, Supreme Court Clerk's Office File, Korematsu, 22 O.T. 1943, Box 3820; Peter Irons, *Justice at War*, 93–99 (1993).

446 **selected Endo:** Irons, *Justice at War*, 99–103.

446 **"a Jap's":** WP, 4/14/1943, at 1.

446 **"enemy race":** J.L. DeWitt, *Final Report: Japanese Evacuation from the West Coast*, 34 (1943).

446 **radio signaling & footnote:** Edward J. Ennis, Memorandum for the Solicitor General, 1/21/1944, Fahy Papers, Box 37, Folder 3; Hoover to Attorney General, 2/7/1944, *id.* (enclosing FBI report); Ennis, Memorandum for the Attorney General, 2/26/1944, *id.*; John L. Burling, Memorandum for the Solicitor General, 4/13/1944, *id.*

446 **displeasure & Fahy:** Burling to Wechsler, 9/9/1944, at 1–2, NARA, DOJ, RG 60, Violation of Curfew Litigation Case Files, 1942–1982, No. 146-42-7, Section 2, Box 7; Ennis to Wechsler, 9/11/1944, *id.*

446–447 **September 30 & Fisher & printer & McCloy & Wechsler:** Burling to Ennis, 10/2/1944, at 1–2, *id.*; Fisher to McCloy, 10/2/1944 & Transcript Fisher-Wechsler Telephone Conversation at 11:30 a.m., 10/2/1944, NARA, War Department Files, RG 107, Papers of John J. McCloy, Box 9, Folder I-M; Ennis to Wechsler, 9/30/1944, NARA, RG 21, United States v. Korematsu, 1981, Exhibit B; Irons, *Justice at War*, 284–92.

447 **final brief:** U.S. Government Supreme Court Brief, *Korematsu v. United States*, at 11 n.2 ("We have specifically recited in this brief the facts relating to the justification for the evacuation, of which we ask the Court to take judicial notice, and we rely upon the *Final Report* only to the extent that it relates to such facts.").

447 **"protective custody" & "mob violence":** Burling to Cooley, 4/21/1944, NARA, RG 60, Department of Justice, Violation of Curfew Litigation Case Files 1942–1986, Entry# A1-COR, File 146-42-7, Box 7; Irons, *Justice at War*, 297. Copies were supposedly sent to Ennis, Justice Department attorney Nanette Dembitz, and FF—though FF's copy has not been found.

447–448 **"military" & "Does your" "tryable" & "extraordinary" & "in their homes" & "temporary":** Notes of Col. Archibald King at *Korematsu* Argument, 10/11–12/1944, at 1–3, NARA, RG 153, Entry A1-60A, Stack 270, Row 2, Compartment 26, Box 6 & Irons, *Justice at War*, 314–16, 318; LAT, 10/12/1944, at 2. *See* Peter Irons, "Fancy Dancing in the Marble Palace," 3 Const. Comment. 35, 47–60 (1986) (questioning Fahy).

448 **tipped off:** Charles Horsky OH, D.C. Circuit Historical Society, at 45 (recalling John Burling told him about falsehoods in the DeWitt Report "on the QT").

448 **how long:** LAT, 10/13/1944, at 7 (FF and other justices questioned Fahy about confinement of loyal Japanese Americans).

448 **agreed with Stone & Congress had ratified & "absence":** RHJ Conferences Notes, *Korematsu v. United States*, at 2, RHJP, Box 132, Folder 7. *See* WOD Conference Notes, *Korematsu v. United States*, at 6, WODP, Box 113, Folder 18.

448 **no choice & drew the line & "without":** FM Conference Notes, *Korematsu v. United States*, at 1–2, FMP, Reel 131, O.T. 1943, at 17–18.

448 **"ready":** FF to HLB, 11/9/1944, FFHLS, Pt. III, Reel 1, Page 34.

448 **a paragraph:** FF Concurrence, 12/1/1944, RHJP, Box 132, Folder 7.

449 **more like a dissent:** FF Concurrence, 12/2/1944, *id.*; FF Memorandum to Conference, 12/2/1944, *id.* (adding "To find"). *See* Jacobus tenBroek, "Wartime Powers of the Military over Citizen Civilians within the County," 41 Calif. L. Rev. 167, 185 (1953) ("the real dissenter in the *Korematsu* case, on the war powers issue, was Justice Frankfurter").

449   **"the power" & "the war":** Korematsu v. United States, 323 U.S. 214, 224 (1944) (Frankfurter, J., concurring) (quoting Hughes).

449   **lacked the knowledge:** *Id.* at 245 (1944) (Jackson, J., dissenting).

449   **"To find":** *Id.* at 225 (Frankfurter, J., concurring).

449   **"constitutional restriction":** FF to RHJ, 10/27/1944, RHJP, Box 132, Folder 7.

449   **"concentration":** Korematsu, 323 U.S. at 226, 230 (Roberts, J., dissenting).

449   **"ugly":** *Id.* at 223.

449   **"this legalization":** *Id.* at 242 (Murphy, J., dissenting).

450   **"all legal" & "to the most":** *Id.* at 216.

451   **"an immigrant" & "it would" & "Now":** AtlConst, 3/13/1945, at 7. *See* AtlConst, 2/28/1945, at 7 (criticizing HLB and FF for *Korematsu* opinions).

451   **champagne & midnight:** FF to CCB, circa 11/1944, FFLC, Box 35; FF to FDR, 11/14/1944, R&FF, 737.

451   **"He has" & "a faraway look":** FF to CCB, 4/24/1945, at 1–2 (quoting Churchill's speech before Parliament, 4/17/1945).

451   **Alger Hiss:** BaltSun, 2/13/1945, at 1.

452   **"grave":** NYT, 3/1/1945, at 21.

452   **"a 'ghastly' sight":** FF to CCB, 4/24/1945, at 1–2.

452   **"Life":** FF to FDR, 3/14/1945, R&FF, 742.

452   **Hutchinson & Trohan & dossier:** FBI memo re: "Otto N. Frankfurter," n.d., FBI Official and Confidential Files, Reel 6, Page 150. FM, in frequent contact with J. Edgar Hoover, knew about the *Tribune* stories in advance of publication and about the impeachment campaign. Gressman Diary, 2/26/1944.

452   **Otto:** CT, 12/25/1942, at 3.

452   **bad check:** CT, 11/2/1948, at 14. The article neglected to mention that Otto admitted writing bad checks in 1909 while working as a traveling pharmaceuticals salesman in the Midwest. NYT, 3/8/1909, at 2.

452   **"'palace'" & "grand" & "held":** CT, 2/18/1945, at 12. *See* Walter Trohan, *Political Animals* (1975).

452–453 **"the Rasputins" & "back":** 79 Cong. Rec. App. 694 (February 19, 1945).

453   **"the acceptance":** 79 Cong. Rec. 1370 (February 22, 1945).

453   **Neely & "Jew baiter" & "criticized" & "If Justice":** 79 Cong Rec.-House 2226–30 (March 14, 1945). Pearson reported that Hoffman's quote about "between him and his conscience" initially read "between him and his God" but Representative Wilbur Mills, the presiding officer at the time, "ordered it expunged from the Record." WP, 3/20/1945, at 9.

453   **"high-strung":** HID, 3/10/1940, Reel 3, Vol. 31, at 4245.

453   **promoting Margold:** HID, 4/5/1940, *id.* at 4298 (reminding Attorney General RHJ about Margold for federal bench); HID, 9/28/1941, Reel 4, Vol. 40, at 5917 (lobbying Attorney General FB to put Margold on federal bench); HID, 4/11/1942, Reel 5, Vol. 42, at 6528 (lining up endorsements with BVC for Margold); HID, 4/19/1942, *id.* at 6545 (FF urged HI to lobby to make Margold chief judge of new court for District of Columbia); HID, 6/21/1942, *id.*, at 6731 (asking FF to speak to president about Margold); HID, 6/28/1942, *id.* at 6741-43 (discussing efforts to land Margold a judgeship despite his personality).

453   **municipal court:** HID, 7/5/1942, at 6772.

453   **continued:** HID, 1/13/1945, Reel 7, Vol. 58, at 9471–72 (TGC on trying to land Margold federal judgeship).

453 **Roosevelt nominated:** HID, 1/27/1945, *id.* at 9517 (FDR thought Margold would get confirmed but worried about McCarran's "doublecrosses").

454 **Biddle & Fahy & Ickes:** Hearings on Nathan Margold, Pt. 1, 2/27/1945, hrg-1945-sjs-0012.

454 **Washington lawyers:** Hearings on Nathan Margold, Pt. 6, 7/25/1945, hrg-1945-sjs-0038.

454 **not renominated:** HID, 5/6/1945, Reel 7, Vol. 59, at 9701–2 (HST did not like Margold).

454 **died:** WES, 12/16/1947 at A-2. *See* FF to Thomas Reed Powell, 12/25/1947, Powell Papers, Box B, Folder B-24 ("Poor Margold's death stirs in me all sorts of reflections in me on the ways of man to man . . .").

454 **Acheson as solicitor general:** FF to FDR, 3/17/1945, R&FF, 742–43.

454 **"What":** FDR to FB, 3/20/1945, *id.* at 744.

454 **Pearson:** WP, 3/23/1945, at 3; WP, 4/2/1945, at 7. *See* Donald A. Ritchie, *The Columnist*, 188 (2021) (describing FB as "one of Pearson's best sources in the cabinet").

454 **assured Acheson:** DA to David Acheson, 4/30/1945, *Among Friends*, 51 (David S. McLellan & David C. Acheson, eds. 1980).

454 **"fear[ed]" & "doomed" & "ghastly":** FF to CCB, 4/24/1945, at 1–2.

455 **Lyttleton & Llewellin:** FDR Day by Day, 3/29/1945.

455 **"simply" & "One cannot" & Wilson:** FF to CCB, 4/24/1945, at 1–2. *See* FF to HJL, 4/17/1945, at 1–2, FFLC, Box 75 ("There is one solace—that he went swiftly (it's been a process of a year and a half at least) and was saved Wilson's fate").

455 **"very pleasant":** HLSD, 4/13/1945, Reel 9, Vol. 51, at 31.

455 **"disorderly":** *Id.*, 4/12/1945, *id.*, at 28.

455 **especially Stimson:** JJMD, 4/13/1945.

455 **funeral train:** HLSD, 4/14/1945, Reel 9, Vol. 51, at 32; FDR Day by Day, 4/14/1945, Ushers Log, at 1; NYHT, 4/15/1945, at 1, 2.

455 **six white horses:** WES, 4/14/1945, at A-3.

455 **other justices:** RHJ, *That Man*, 166 (John Q. Barrett, ed. 2003) (with HLB and WOD).

455 **East Room & second row & 4:00 p.m.:** NYHT, 4/15/1945, at 1; NYT, 4/15/1945, at 3; FDR Day by Day, 4/14/1945, Ushers Log, at 2.

455 **forgot to stand:** Robert E. Sherwood, *Roosevelt and Hopkins*, 881 (1948).

455 **hot:** Lilienthal, *The Journals of David E. Lilienthal: The TVA Years, 1939–1945,* 4/14/1945, at 691–92.

455 **"beautifully":** FF to CCB, 4/24/1945, at 2.

455 **9:30 p.m.:** WES, 4/15/15, at A-6 (described them as "early arrivals").

456 **"The Secret Service":** NYT, 4/16/1945, at 2. *See* Robert Klara, *FDR's Funeral Train* (2010).

456 **Frances Watson:** FBI Wiretaps, 5/8/1945 9:35 p.m., FF and Prichard, at 5, The J. Edgar Hoover Official and Confidential File, Reel 1, Folder 2, Pt. 1.

456 **west side:** NYT, 4/16/1945, at 1, 3.

456 **eight West Point:** *id.* at 3; HLSD, 4/15/1945, Reel 9, Vol. 51, at 34–35; NYHT, 4/16/1945, at 1, 4.

456 **"I wish":** FF to CCB, 4/24/1945, at 2. *See* FF to FWB, circa 4/16/1945, FFLC, Box 39 ("flawless").

456 **"Franklin Roosevelt" & "friendliness" & *There* is" & "the utter":** FF, "Franklin Delano Roosevelt, 1882–1945," Harvard Alumni Bulletin, 4/28/1945, Vol. 47, at 499–500, FFLC, Box 198 & FF, *Of Law and Men*, 359–64 (Philip Elman, ed. 1956).

456 **"Roosevelt will":** *Id.*

457 **train home:** Henry Morgenthau Jr. Diary, 4/16/ 1945, at 4–8, Vol. 7, FDRL; RHJ, *That Man*, 167.

457   **no interest:** FF to CCB, 4/24/1945, at 4.

457   **"dimmed":** CT, 4/14/1945, at 1 & CSM, 4/14/1945, at 14.

457   **"spend" & "palace":** LAT, 4/15/1945, at 8.

457   **same personal relationship:** Marion (Ohio) Star, 4/17/1945, at 6; Palladium-Item (Richmond, Ind.), 4/22/1945, at 8 (Pegler).

457   **"Justice Felix Frankfurter":** Ft. Lauderdale Daily News, 4/18/1945, at 4. In October 1945, O'Donnell was forced to apologize for untrue comments in his October 3 column that high-ranking Jewish officials, including FF, were responsible for the removal of General George S. Patton. JTA, 10/21/1945, at 3.

457   **"may have" & "was so" & "he is":** FF to CCB, 4/24/1945, at 3. *See* FF to FWB, circa 4/16/1945 (HST's educability).

CHAPTER 27: THE REAL ARCHITECT OF THE VICTORY

458   **"on some":** HLSD, 5/1/1945, at 3, Vol. 51, at 87.

458   **"quite":** HLSD, 5/3/1945, Reel 9, Vol. 51, at 95–96. *See* FF, Memorandum, 4/26/1945, at 1, Oppenheimer Papers, Box 34, Folder 7 (containing handwritten note "The original of this I handed to Secretary Stimson in his office at the Pentagon on Thursday May 3, 1945—when I lunched with him & told him the details of my conversations with F.D.R. & Bohr on this."). HLS already had been briefed about FF's knowledge of S-1, but not how much he knew. Bush to Conant, 9/25/1944, at 3, Bush Conant Files, NARA, RG 227, Microfilm 1392, Reel 5, at 466 (briefing HLS on 9/22/1944 conversation with president and mentioning FF).

458   **no knowledge & declined to answer:** HST to HLS, 12/31/1946, at 1, HLSP, Reel 116, Page 694. *See* Elting E. Morison, *Turmoil and Tradition*, 616 (1960).

458   **first time & presented:** HLSD, 3/15/1945, Reel 9, Vol. 50, at 189–90; *id.*, 4/25/1945, at 1–2, *id.*, Vol. 51, at 68–69.

458–459 **"Within" & "a certain":** Memorandum discussed with the President, 4/25/1945, at 1–2, *id.* at 70–71.

459   **"was much":** HLSD, 5/3/1945.

459   **"The road":** FF to HLS, 5/8/1945, at 1–2, HLSP, Reel 112, Pages 643–44.

460   **"mismanaged" & "seems":** FBI Wiretaps, 5/8/1945, 9:35 p.m., EFP and FF, at 3–4, Technical Summaries Sent to White House, Vol. 1, The J. Edgar Hoover Official and Confidential File, Reel 1, Folder 2, Pt. 1. Tracy Campbell, *Short of the Glory*, 99–105 (1998).

460   **Davies:** Joseph E. Davies, *Mission to Moscow* (1941); Elizabeth Kimball MacLean, *Joseph E. Davies* (1992).

460   **"Pollyanna" & "He took":** Charles E. Bohlen, *Witness to History*, 44–45 (1973).

461   **invited him & Molotov:** Davies Diary, 4/23/1945 & 4/30/1945, Davies Papers, Box I-16.

461   **"get tough":** "Beginning of 'Get Tough Policy,'" *id.*

461   **"was worried" & "feared" & "'insulting'" & "much" & "'high'" "a 'one-two'" & "great" & "to avert":** "Sustaining Opinion From Justice Frankfurter," Journal, 5/13/1943, at 1–2 (typed version 11/7/1950), Davies Papers, Box I-16. *See* Original Diary Entry with handwritten edits, 5/13/1945, at 1, *id.* (containing specifics about the section of Adams's memoirs); *Memoirs of John Quincy Adams*, Vol. 2, Ch. VII ("The Mission to Russia") (Charles Francis Adams, ed. 1874). A problem with relying on Davies's diary entries is that he periodically revised and updated them for an unpublished book, *Missions for Peace*. Davies Papers, Boxes I:104–110. FF was referring to an April 23, 1945, meet-

ing before HST's meeting with Molotov. Diary Entry, 4/23/1945, *The Forrestal Diaries*, 49–51 (Walter Millis, ed. 1951); *The Diaries of Edward R. Stettinius, Jr., 1943–1946*, at 329 (Thomas M. Campbell & George C. Herring, eds. 1975) (describing April 23 meeting); *id.* at 318–19 (describing April 13 meeting about deteriorating Soviet relations and HST's remark that "we had been too easy with them"). FF's likely sources were DA, Herbert Feis, or JJM. JJMD, 4/23/1945–4/24/1945 (meetings with HLS and Forrestal).

461   **health & informed:** "Sustaining Opinion From Justice Frankfurter," Journal, 5/13/1943, at 2 (typed version 11/7/1950).

461   **"the rapid" & "in the best" & "out-tough" & "might":** Davies to HST, 5/13/1945, at 1–3, Davies Papers, Box I-16.

461   **"a great":** Davies Diary Entry, 5/13/1943, at 2, *id.* (original handwritten version).

461–462   **"greatly" & scotch:** Davies Diary Entry, 5/13/1943, at 3, 7 (original version with handwritten comments). Walter Isaacson & Evan Thomas, *The Wise Men*, 279–80 (1986).

462   **"heartened" & Churchill:** "Mr. Justice Frankfurter's Reaction," Davies Diary Entry, 5/18/1945, Davies Papers, Box I-16.

462   **garden & never sent:** Davies Diary Entry, 5/20/1945, *id.* MacLean, *Joseph E. Davies*, 133–49.

462   **"The reputation":** HLS to HST, 5/16/1945, at 2, HLSP, Reel 112, at 723.

462   **"new weapon" & "a Frankenstein" & "a project":** HLSD, 5/31/1945, at 1–2, Reel 9, Vol. 51, at 146–47. Alice Kimball Smith, "The Decision to Use the Atomic Bomb," *Bureau of Atomic Scientists* 14, no. 8 (October 1958): 297–98 (discussing disagreement between Under Secretary of the Navy Ralph Bard and scientist Arthur H. Compton about whether alternatives were discussed on May 31).

462   **"precision":** HLSD, 6/6/1945, at 4, Reel 9, Vol. 51, at 160.

462   **"straight" & "large" & "a number":** "Memorandum of Conversation with General Marshall and the Secretary of War, 5/29/1945, JJMD.

462   **"[t]hat there":** HLSD, 6/6/1945, at 3, Reel 9, Vol. 51, at 159.

462   **civilian casualties:** HLSD, 6/1/1945, *id.*, at 149.

463   **"the United States" & "bombed" & "laughed":** HLSD, 6/6/1945, at 4–5, *id.*, at 160–61.

463   **"made":** HLSD, 6/12/1945, *id.*, at 172.

463   **departing:** JJMD, 6/21/1945.

463   **"long talk" & "recent":** HLSD, 6/19/1945, at 2, Reel 9, Vol. 45, at 184.

463   **"the services":** FF to Davies, 6/28/1945, at 2, Davies Papers, Box II:42, Folder 4.

463   **"judgment" & "The situation":** Davies to FF, 7/4/1945, FFLC, Box 51.

463   **"to try":** HLSD, 7/2/1945, at 1–2, Reel 9, Vol. 52, at 1–2. *See* "Proposed Program for Japan," 7/2/1945, at 1–5, *id.* at 5–10.

463   **"working" & "pretty" & "intended":** HLSD, 7/3/1945, at 2, *id.* at 12.

463   **consented:** HLSD, 7/4/1945, *id.*, at 15.

463   **received word:** HLSD, 7/16/1945, Reel 9, Vol. 52, at 23.

464   **more detailed & "pepped":** HLSD, 7/21/1945, at 2, *id.* at 31.

464   **"a changed":** HLSD, 7/22/1945, at 2, *id.* at 33.

464   **disagreement:** HLSD, 7/24/1945, at 2–3, *id.* at 38–39.

464   **emperor provision:** HLSD, 8/10/1945, at 1, *id.* at 72.

464   **Kyoto:** HLSD, 7/24/1945, at 2–3, *id.* at 38–39.

464   **remove & governor-general:** HLS & MB, *On Active Service in Peace and War*, 157 (1948); Morison, *Turmoil and Tradition*, 633; MB, *Danger and Survival*, 68, 78–80 (1988); Leslie R. Groves, *Now It Can Be Told*, 272–76 (1962).

464   **"This is":** Davies to FF, 7/24/1945, FFLC, Box 51. MacLean, *Joseph E. Davies*, 152–76.

464   **marginalized:** HLSD, 7/23/1945, at 2, Reel 9, Vol. 52, at 35.

464   **"Reading" & "new":** FF to HLS, 8/7/1945, at 1–3, HLSP, Reel 113, Pages 159–61.

465   **"full" & "the first" & "the prompt":** FF to Davies, 8/7/1945, at 3–4, Davies Papers, Box
       II-42, Folder 5.

465   **blamed & "anti-emperor":** HLSD, 8/10/1945, at 1–3, Reel 9, Vol. 52, Pages 72–74.

465   **"the Emperor":** JJM to Fisher, 8/10/1945, JJMP, Box 1, Folder 56.

465   **"Everything":** FWB to FF, 8/6//1945, FFLC, Box 39 (FF handwritten).

465   **suggested:** FF to JJM, 9/10/1945, at 1–2, JJMP, Box 1, Folder 59.

465   **"The long":** FF to HLS, 8/16/1945, at 1–2, HLSP, Reel 113, Pages 252–53. *See* FF to PE,
       8/8/1945, at 4, PEP, Box 1, Folder 1-55 ("Now, truly, man's destiny is in his own hands.
       A new international morality is imperative."); FF to CCB, 8/18/1945, at 2, CCBP, Box
       5, Folder 5-6 ("Of course the atomic bomb should have been used—to put a stop to a
       much larger loss of life & more cruelly continuing war. But now mankind is truly up
       against it to devise an international life of sanity & live and—let-live.").

465   **"in his":** HLSD, 8/12–9/3/1945, at 3, Reel 9, Vol. 52, at 80 & HLSD, 9/4/1945, at 2, *id.* at
       90. *See* HLSD, 9/21/1945, at 3, *id.* at 165.

466   **"I consider":** HLS to HST, 9/11/1945, at 1–2, *id.* at 118–19 & Memorandum for the Pres-
       ident Re: Proposed Action for Control of Atomic Bomb, at 2, *id.* at 121.

466   **agreed:** HLSD, 9/12/1945, at 1–2, *id.* at 113–14.

466   **"the safest":** HLSD, 9/17/1945, at 2–3, *id.* at 136–37.

466   **"rather":** HLSD, 9/11/1945, at 3, *id.* at 122. HLS & MB, *On Active Service in Peace and
       War*, 634–55; Morison, *Turmoil and Tradition*, 637–40. On Bush and Conant's advocacy
       of sharing nuclear secrets, *see* Bush & Conant to Stimson, 9/30/1944, Bush Conant
       Files, NARA, RG 227, Microfilm 1392, Reel 4, at 107–13; Conant to Bush, 5/18/1945,
       AEC Doc. No. 209, *id.*, at 151–52; Bush to Bundy, 4/24/1945, at 1, *id.* at 130; Bush &
       Conant to Interim Committee; 7/18/1945, AEC Doc. No. 210, *id.*, at 214–15; Bush to
       HST, 9/25/1945, AEC Doc. No. 217, *id.*, Reel 1, at 1023–29; James G. Hershberg, *James
       B. Conant*, 197–98 (1993).

466   **wife & generals:** HLSD, 9/21/1945, at 4, Reel 9, Vol. 52, at 166; Mabel Stimson to MDF,
       10/18/1945, HLSP, Reel 114, Page 288; FFLC, Box 104 (containing photograph from
       magazine); HLS & MB, *On Active Service in Peace and War*, 668–69; Morison, *Turmoil
       and Tradition*, 641–43.

466   **"Marion":** FF to HLS, 9/21/1945 tel., HLSP, Reel 113, at 472.

466   **"over a million":** HLS, "The Decision to Use the Atomic Bomb," Harper's magazine,
       February 1947, 102. *See* HLS & MB, *On Active Service in Peace and War*, 612–33; MB,
       Danger and Survival, 92–93 (conceding consideration of alternatives lacked depth and
       blaming Roosevelt); Kai Bird, *The Color of Truth*, 90–98 (1998) (detailing problems with
       Harper's article and MB's later regrets); Kai Bird, *The Chairman*, 240–64 (1992); Hersh-
       berg, *James B. Conant*, 293–301. Harvard president James Conant, one of the scientists
       involved in the Manhattan Project, persuaded HLS and MB to omit much of the article
       justifying the decisions. Conant to MB, 11/30/1946, at 1–8, HLSP, Reel 116, at 497–504.

466–467 **harbored doubts & encouraged:** FF to HLS, 11/24/1946 tel., *id.*, at 481; HLS to FF,
       12/12/1946, *id.* at 584; FF to HLS, 12/16/1946 tel., *id.* at 612; FF to HLS, 12/16/1945, *id.*
       at 613; FF to HLS, 12/20/1946, *id.* at 636; FF to HLS, 1/6/1947, *id.* at 724.

467   **"five epic":** FF to HLS, 10/7/1945, at 4, HLSP, Reel 114, Page 108. HLS's diaries exposed
       his *Harper's* article to criticism and led revisionist historians to conclude that the

atomic bomb was used against Japan not because of military objectives but to gain the upper hand on the Soviet Union. Gar Alperovitz, *The Decision to Use the Atomic Bomb*, 141–54 (1995).

467   "on the job": Davies to FF, 8/25/1945, at 2, FFLC, Box 51.

467   "views": FF to Davies, 8/25/1945, at 2, Davies Papers, Box II-42, Folder 5.

467   "its statesmen" & "we must": FF to Davies, 9/1/1945, 2–4, *id.*

467   "because" & "explosive": Davies to FF, 9/15/1945, FFLC, Box 51.

467   "It irks": Davies to FF, 9/26/1945, at 1–2, *id.* ToL, 8/11/1945, at 5.

CHAPTER 28: FRANKFURTER AGAINST BLACK

468   **resignation letter:** OJR to HFS, 6/30/1945, HFSP, Box 76; OJR to HST, 6/30/1945, *id.*; HST to OJR, 7/5/1945, *id.*

468   **legal requirements:** 28 U.S.C. §§ 375 & 375 a (1940 ed.); Artemus Ward, *Deciding to Leave* (2003).

468   **"judicial executor":** OJR to FF, 10/12/1944, FFHLS, Pt. III, Reel 3, Page 172.

468   **stunned:** FF to HFS, 7/22/1945, at 2, HFSP, Box 75; OJR to FF, 7/16/1945, at 1, FFHLS, Pt. III, Reel 3, Page 189.

468   **minimum-wage laws:** FF to Thomas Reed Powell, 8/14/1946, at 4.

468–469 **Hughes & "rare":** OJR to FF, 7/16/1945, at 1–2.

469   **other justices:** HFS to FF, 8/13/1945, at 3–4, FFHLS, Pt. III, Reel 18, Pages 359–60.

469   **"profound" & "that" & "You" & informing:** HFS to FF, 8/18/1945, at 1–3, *id.*, Pages 363–65 & HFS to RHJ, 8/18/1945, at 1–3, RHJP, Box 119, Folder 8.

469   **"fidelity" & "outstanding" & "gross" & "the minimum" & "devotion":** FF to HFS, 8/20/1945, at 1–3, FFHLS, Pt. III, Reel 18, Pages 368–70.

469   **include the original:** FF to HFS, 8/25/1945, at 1, *id.*, Page 371; HFS to FF, 8/27/1945, at 1–4, *id.*, Pages 373–76.

469   **"fidelity" & "in the highest" & "My numerous":** FF to Brethren, 8/31/1945, FFHLS, Pt. III, Reel 18, Page 380.

469   **none too pleased:** FF to HFS, 8/31/1945, *id.*, Page 382 (enclosing letter); HFS to FF, 9/5/1945, at 1–4, *id.*, Pages 384–87.

470   **"To such":** FF to HFS, 9/7/1945, at 1–2, *id.*, Pages 389–90.

470   **"Black's":** FF to RHJ, 9/1/1945, at 1, RHJP, Box 119, Folder 8.

470   **"I am" & "You":** RHJ to HFS, 9/8/1945, at 1, *id.* & FFHLS, Pt. III, Reel 18, Page 391.

470   **"You may":** FF to RHJ, 9/12/1945, at 1, RHJP, Box 119, Folder 8.

470   **"or something":** HFS to FF, 9/18/1945, at 1–2, FFHLS, Pt. III, Reel 18, Pages 393–94.

470   **Chester Springs:** FF to secretary Katherine Watters, n.d., at 2, FFHLS, Pt. III, Reel 18, Page 325.

470   **no letter:** OJR to FF, 10/12/1944.

470   **enjoyed:** OJR to FF, 7/16/1945, at 1, 3–4.

470   **"the Saint" & "silly" & "John Marshall" & "hypocritical":** OJR to FF, 7/28/1945, at 1–2, FFHLS, Pt. III, Reel 18, Pages 187–88. *See* OJR to FF, 8/6/1945, at 1–2, *id.*, Pages 193–94.

471   **"unanimity" & "not 'washing'" & "to think":** FF, Memorandum, 9/27/1945, FFHLS, Pt. III, Reel 18, Page 349.

471   **"intellectual" & "helpless":** FF, Memorandum, 9/28/1945, *id.*, Page 350.

471   **sworn in:** FF, Memorandum, 10/1/1945, *id.*, Page 351.

471   **Parker:** OJR to FF, 7/16/1945, at 4; FF to HFS, 7/22/1945, at 2.

471   "low-C": FF to LH, 6/15/1953, at 2, LHP, Box 105C, Folder 105-19. Brad Snyder, "Taking
       Great Cases: Lessons from the *Rosenberg* Case," 63 Vand. L. Rev. 885, 897–98 (2010).

471   "I could" & "reading" & "at least a dozen" & "guilty" & "in" & " 'I am' " & "mumbled":
       FF, Memorandum, 10/1/1946. *See* 326 U.S. viii (10/1/1945), in FFHLS, Pt. III, Reel 18,
       Page 353 (reprinting HFS's speech).

471–472 "everybody" & "let": FF, Memorandum, 10/2/1945, at 1, FFHLS, Pt. III, Reel 18, Box 187,
       Folder 11.

472   "I will" & "acquiesced": *Id.* at 1–2.

472   "Why" & "Stanley" & "Reed" & "rudimentary" & "satisfied" & "with" & "And then":
       Id. at 2–3.

472   skewed account: FF to AMB, 12/6/1956, FFHLS, Pt. III, Reel 18, Page 362; FF to PBK
       12/6/1956, *id.*, Page 363; FF to Ernie Brown, 12/6/1956, *id.*, Page 261; Alpheus Thomas
       Mason, *Harlan Fiske Stone: Pillar of the Law,* 765–69 (1956).

473   Lord Wright & Folger: FF to Powell, 4/24/1946, Powell Papers, Box B, Folder B24.

473   happy: Mason, *Harlan Fiske Stone,* 803–6 & 873 n.14 (based on 4/7/1953 int. with FF).

473   repeated: HHBD, 4/22/1946, Reel 2; WBR to Luther Ely Smith, 4/23/1946, at 1–2,
       WBRP, Box 41, Folder 10.

473   1:45 p.m.: NYHT, 4/23/1945, at 1A.

473   "something": NYT, 4/24/1945, at 28.

473   pale & gray & voice: WP, 4/23/1945, at 1.

473   "The case": NYHT, 4/23/1945, at 1A.

473   "Almost": FF to Powell, 4/24/1946, at 1. *See* FF to LH, 4/28/1946, at 1, LHP, Box 105B,
       Folder 105-12 ("There have been physiological signs for the last two years that went
       unheeded.").

473   advised Roosevelt: FF, "H.F.S. & CJ'ship," 6/9/1941, at 1–2, FFHLS, Pt. III, Reel 4,
       Pages 472–73.

473   "He would": Wechsler to FF, 7/22/1946, at 5, *id.*, Page 462 (FF handwritten).

473   memorial essay: FF, "Harlan Fiske Stone (1872–1946)," *American Philosophical Society
       Year Book* 335–40 (1946), FFLC, Box 198. *See* FF to LH, 6/20/1946, LHP, Box 105B,
       Folder 105-12 (attaching page of article about HFS and identifying falsehoods); FF to
       LH, 6/27/1946, at 1–2, *id.*; FF to LH, 12/23/1946, at 1, *id.* ("As to my piece on Stone may
       God—who, I am told knoweth all—have mercy on my soul.").

474   "two liberal": Radio Script, 4/28/1946, at 4, Pearson Papers, G182 (1 of 3), Folder 3. *See*
       RHJ, "The Black Controversy," circa January 1947, RHJP, Box 26, Folder 2.

474   Hill: HST Appointment Calendar, 4/30/1946, HSTL (10:45 am).

474   "seem" & "Well" & "Yeah" & "It's": TGC to Ernest Cuneo, 4/28/1946, at 3, FBI Wire-
       taps, Reel 4, Folder 2, Part 7. TGC and Cuneo were frequent sources of Pearson's. Don-
       ald A. Ritchie, *The Columnist,* 53, 56 (2021).

474   USS *Williamsburg*: HST Appointment Calendar, 4/21–27/1946.

474   more confident: TGC to Cuneo, 4/28/1946, at 5.

474   Hughes: HST Appointment Calendar, 4/29/1946.

474   "Frankfurter's man": TGC to "Harvey," 4/29/1946, 8:15 p.m., FBI Wiretaps, Reel 4,
       Folder 2, Part 7.

474   "Frankfurter's present": TGC to Pearson, 5/5/1946, 10:15 a.m., at 1–2, *id.* & TGC to
       Henry Grunewald, 5/5/1946, 4:20 p.m., at 5–6, *id.*

474   later insisted: Eugene C. Gerhart, *America's Advocate,* 277–88 (1958) (quoting 5/29/1947
       memorandum by CEH biographer Merlo Pusey and annotated by CEH, but HST's sec-

retary insisted in a 4/29/1952 letter that CEH had recommended FMV); Merlo J. Pusey, *Charles Evans Hughes*, Vol. 2, 802 n.12 (1951).

475 **twice:** HST Appointment Calendar, 5/2/1946; *id.*, 5/21/1946.

475 **Rosenman:** SIR's May 1 meeting was not on HST's calendar, but they spoke by phone the previous day. HST Phone Records, 4/30/1946, White House Office Files, Telephone Records, Box 3.

475 **"then" & "went" & "the thing":** TGC to Pearson, 5/4/1946, 9:45 a.m., at 2, FBI Wiretaps, Reel 4, Folder 2, Part 7. *See* TGC to Winifred Reed, 4/30/1946, 10:40 p.m., at 3–4, *id.*; "Harvey" to TGC, 4/29/1946, 8:15 p.m., at 1, *id.* (SFR "is pluggin' strong for" WOD).

475 **"greatest" & "who could":** Radio Script, 5/5/1946, at 2, Pearson Papers, G182 (1 of 3), Folder 4.

475 **"the portal" & "surreptitiously":** WES, 5/16/1946, at A-15.

475 **"from inside":** RHJ to FF, 6/19/1946, FFHLS, Pt. III, Reel 2, Page 79. *See* HID, 5/19/1946, at 17–18, Reel 7 (WOD informed him that "Frankfurter put on a very real campaign for Jackson which failed only because of Black's refusal to along with it").

475 **newspapers:** WES, 1/4/1946, at 1, RHJP, Reel 6, Box 100.

475 **Nuremberg:** RHJ COH at 1475, RHJP, Box 191, Folder 2.

475 **from friends:** Frank Shea to RHJ, 5/17/1946, at 1, RHJP, Reel 6, Box 100.

476 **"high":** FF to RHJ, 6/12/1946, at 1, FFHLS, Pt. III, Reel 2, Page 77.

476 **miscast:** EFP to FF, 6/29/1946, at 2–3, FFLC, Box 91; EFP to FF, 8/23/1946, at 3, *id.*

476 **error:** RHJ, "The Black Controversy," circa January 1947, at 29 (explaining he consulted no one besides his son Bill and his secretary ED and conceding he had made a "capital blunder").

476 **Crampton Harris:** Roger K. Newman, *Hugo Black*, 102–3, 256–57 (1994).

476 **Black had represented:** Newman, *Hugo Black*, 652 n.1; Steve Suitts, *Hugo Black of Alabama* 121, 522 (2005).

476 **did not know:** RHJ, "The Black Controversy," at 33–34 (learning, after the controversy, about HLB's representation of the United Mine Workers from *Saturday Evening Post* journalist Harry Newman).

476 **changed his vote:** WOD *Jewell Ridge* 1944 Term Docket Book, WODP, Box 107, Page 496 & Note, RHJP, Box 26, Folder 2.

476 **"Stooge":** FF to RHJ, n.d., at 1–2, RHJP, Box 26, Folder 2 ("The point is that the Stooge was again used & then the Stooge did not perform as expected, so he was told what was expected from him (via his ghost) & then came the result of which the world now knows!").

477 **Jackson observed:** Jewell Ridge Coal Corp. v. Local No. 6167, 325 U.S. 161, 170 & 177–78 n.5 (1945) (Jackson. J., dissenting). *See* Tennessee Coal, Iron & R. Co. v. Muscoda Local No. 123, 321 U.S. 590 (1944).

477 **multi-paragraph:** Jewell Ridge Coal Corp., 325 U.S. at 897–98 (Jackson, J., concurring in denial of petition for hearing) (June 18, 1945).

477 **"'declaration'" & "would":** RHJ to HST, 6/7/1946, at 2–7, RHJP, Box 26, Folder 3.

477 **only justice:** FF to HLB, 6/9/1945, WODP, Box 108, Folder 16 (explaining his decision to join Jackson); RHJ Draft Concurrence, FFHLS, Pt. I, Reel 12, Page 223 (FF handwritten comments: noting that HFS was supposed to join them, got RHJ to shorten the opinion, yet, to FF's dismay, "finally walked out on it!"). In 1947, RHJ drafted an extended account, written in the third person, of his relationship with HLB. RHJ, "The Black Controversy." Eugene Gerhart interviewed RHJ and relied on the justice's memorandum. Gerhart,

America's Advocate, 235–77. *See* Newman, *Hugo Black*, 333–37, 341–48; Edwin M. Yoder, Jr., "Black v. Jackson" in *The Unmaking of a Whig*, 3–104 (1990); Dennis J. Hutchinson, "The Black-Jackson Feud," Supreme Court Review (1988): 203–43.

477 **"made good"**: RHJ to HST, 6/7/1946, at 2–7, RHJP, Box 26, Folder 3.

477 **"the quiet" & "at personal"**: WP, 6/14/1946, at 5.

477 **"The trouble"**: FF to LH, 6/27/1946, at 1.

478 **"Never"**: FF to FM, 6/10/1946, FFHLS, Pt. III, Reel 2, Page 649.

478 **"this" & "hope" & "I can't"**: FF to RHJ, 6/12/1946, at 1.

478 **"gave" & "had not" & "Black"**: RHJ to FF, 6/19/1946, at 1.

479 **sitting**: FF to FM, 1/6/1947, FFHLS, Pt. III, Reel 2, Page 654.

479 **scribbling**: *Id.* at Pages 658–67. FM's anger with FF had been building for several years. Gressman Diary, 10/3/1943 (describing FM's hatred for FF).

479 **"unmitigated"**: FF to FM, 1/6/1947.

479 **a boy**: AMS Jr., *A Life in the 20th Century*, at 37, 53, 115, 358, 376–379 (2000).

479 **"super-legislature"**: DFF, 10/20/1946, at 275–76.

479–480 **"judicial" & "The unspoken"**: AMS Jr., *A Life in the 20th Century*, at 420. *See* Richard Aldous, *Schlesinger* 110–13 (2017).

480 **"work" & "only" & after its publication**: FF to FM, 1/6/1947.

480 **"judicial activism" & "promoting" & "judicial self-restraint"**: AMS Jr., "The Supreme Court: 1947," Fortune (January 1947): 201–2.

480 **"surely" & "[t]he larger"**: *Id.* at 208.

480 **"bullying" & "highly" & "fond" & presidential**: *Id.* at 75.

480 **"strange" & "messianic" & "cocky" & "warm" & "satirical" & "self-righteous"**: *Id.* at 76.

480 **"ulterior" & "slow"**: *Id.* at 78.

481 **legal realism & Yale Law School & "a cover"**: *Id.* at 201–2, 208.

481 **Rodell and Janeway**: Janeway to FR, 1/23/1947, AMSP, NYPL, Box 432, Folder 7. Prior to publication, AMS Jr. showed the article to FR of Yale and Thomas Reed Powell of Harvard. AMS Jr. to *Fortune* managing editor Ralph "Del" Paine, Jr., 2/4/1947, at 1, *id.*

481 **"Yale thesis"**: JNF to *Fortune* publisher William D. Geer, 12/14/1946, at 1, *id. See* AMS Jr. to JNF, 1/18/1947, *id.*

481 **"naïve" & "unfair"**: JNF to AMS Jr., 1/22/1947, at 6, *id. See* HID, 1/4/1947, at 10, Reel 8 (TGC "insisted that Frankfurter had supplied the tone for the article. . . . The article makes Frankfurter the outstanding man on the Court and does its best to gloss over the shift from left to right that has taken place in Frankfurter's political outlook since he became a member of the Court.").

481 **dinner party**: AMS Jr., *A Life in the 20th Century*, 421–25.

481 **"could not" & "the profession" & "really"**: FF to AMS Jr., 3/19/1947, AMSP, NYPL, Box 432, Folder 7.

481 **"think"**: AMS Jr. to FF, 3/22/1947, *id.* (FF handwritten).

481 **"For A.M.S. Jr."**: FF to AMS Jr., n.d., note on FF, "Some Reflections on the Reading of Statutes," 47 Colum. L. Rev. 527 (1947), AMSP, JFKL, Box P-14.

481 **"of unusual"**: AMS Jr., "The Supreme Court: 1947," 73.

481 **federal government**: Barron v. Baltimore, 32 U.S. 243 (1833).

481 **Jacob Howard**: Congressional Globe, 39th Cong., 1st Sess. 2764–68 (May 23, 1866) (speech of Jacob M. Howard).

482 **useless**: Slaughter-House Cases, 83 U.S. 36 (1873).

482 **"implicit" & " 'fundamental' "**: Palko v. Connecticut, 302 U.S. 319, 325, 328 (1937).

482 **"Take"**: Francis v. Resweber, 329 U.S. 459, 481 n.2 (1947) (Burton, J., dissenting).

482 **"it was"**: Gilbert King, *The Execution of Willie Francis*, 71 (2008). *See* Arthur S. Miller & Jeffrey H. Bowman, *Death by Installments* (1988); Deborah W. Denno, "When Willie Francis Died: The 'Disturbing' Story Behind One of the Eighth Amendment's Most Enduring Standards of Risk," in *Death Penalty Stories*, 17–93 (John H. Blume & Jordan M. Steiker, eds. 2009); William M. Wiecek, "Felix Frankfurter, Incorporation, and the Willie Francis Case," Journal of Supreme Court History 26, no. 1 (2001): 53–66; Willie Francis, as told to Samuel Montgomery, *My Trip to the Chair* (1947), reprinted in *Demands of the Dead*, 33–44 (Katy Ryan, ed. 2012).

483 **June 4**: HLB, Memorandum to Conference, 6/4/1946, WBRP, Box 141, Folder 8.

483 **three votes**: WOD 1945 Term Docket Book, at 288, IFP No. 1302, WODP Box 122, Folder 4 & Note, n.d., WODP, Box 140, Folder 5.

483 **"abysmal"**: Atlanta Daily World, 11/24/1946, at 1.

483 **asked & debated**: BaltSun, 11/19/1946, at 2.

483 **voted 6–3**: WOD *Francis* Docket Book, WODP, Box 138, Folder 5; HHB *Francis* Docket Book, HHBP, Box 137, Folder 1.

484 **"not" & "technicalities" & "progressive"**: WOD *Francis* Conference Notes, WODP, Box 140, Folder 3. *See* FM *Francis* Conference Notes, FMP, Roll 136, Page 85 ("it is good illustration of 14th Amendment & due process. Cruel and unusual punishment is guided by Weems case—a progressive notion. I get to Holmes statement that certain things make me puke. I have to affirm.").

484 **admired**: FF to Matthew Nimetz, 11/20/1964, at 1, FFLC, Box 86.

484 **"with sympathy" & "made" & "extremely" & "I cannot" & "struggling" & "satisfaction" & "one"**: FF to HHB, 12/13/1946, at 1–2, HHBP, Box 150, Folder 4.

484 **"I am"**: FF to HHB, 12/31/1946, *id. See* HHB to FF, 12/26/1946, FFLC, Box 38.

484 **"contrary"**: FF, "Memorandum to Conference," 1/11/1947, FFHLS, Pt. I, Reel 16, Page 742.

485 **"The Fourteenth" & "very broad"**: Francis v. Resweber, 329 U.S. 459, 467–68 (1947) (Frankfurter, J., concurring).

485 **"it involves" & "great" & "this Court" & "my private" & " 'repugnant' " & "I cannot"**: *Id.* at 470–72 (quoting *Palko*, 302 U.S. at 323).

485 **the governor**: Louisiana Constitution of 1921, Art. V, §10.

485 **execute a child**: Mrs. Harold Evans to FF, 1/19/1947, at 2, FFHLS, Pt. III, Reel 11, Page 28.

485 **"You will"**: FF to Mrs. Harold Evans, 1/21/1947, *id.*, Page 45.

485–486 **"I have" & "heavily" & "humaneness" & "compassion"**: FF to MML, 2/3/1947, in Arthur S. Miller & Jeffrey H. Bowman, "Slow Dance on the Killing Ground," 32 DePaul L. Rev. 1, 74 App. L (1983) (reprinting original document) & in Miller and Bowman, *Death by Installments*, 125 26. *See* FF to MML, 4/22/1947, 32 DePaul L. Rev. at 37; Miller & Bowman, *Death by Installments*, 125–26. Miller and Bowman found the 2/3/1947 and 4/22/1947 letters to MML in Box 38 of FFLC in correspondence with HHB, but the letters are no longer there. Nor are they in HHBP. And the Francis folder for MMLP has been misplaced.

486 **"I realize" & "wrote"**: MML to James Simon, 4/16/1947, HHBP, Box 69, Folder 1. FF to Court, 4/23/1947, *id.* (enclosing MML's letter to Simon).

486 **"most admirable"**: LH to FF, 12/9/1947, at 2, LHP, Box 105B, Folder 105-13.

486–487 **Irish Home Rule & Rau & India's new constitution**: DFF, 11/19/1947, at 328; FF, "Remarks of Mr. Justice Frankfurter," 9/16/1958, at 7, FFHLS, Pt. III, Reel 32, Page 435.

487   **"One"**: FF to LH, 12/11/1947, at 2, LHP, Box 105B, Folder 105-13. *See* FF to LH, 11/4/1947, *id.*; LH to FF, 11/14/1947, *id.*; FF to LH, 11/21/1947, *id.*

487   **"Twining is"** & **"It is"**: HHB *Adamson* Notes, HHBP, Box 139, Folder 2. *See* FM *Adamson* Notes, at 4, FMP, Roll 136, at 25; WBR *Adamson* Notes, WBRP, Box 152, Folder 3; FF to SFR, 3/27/1947, FFHLS, Pt. III, Reel 2, Page 922.

487–488   **"the judicial"** & **"one"** & **"eccentric"** & **"alert"** & **"mindful"**: Adamson v. California, 332 U.S. 46, 59, 62 (1947) (Frankfurter, J., concurring).

488   **"in a 'sense'"** & **"the political"** & **"recognize"** & **"Remarks"** & **"uprooted"**: *Id.* at 63–64 ("Frankfurter, J., concurring) (quoting Eisner v. Macomber, 252 U.S. 189, 220 (1920) (Holmes, J., dissenting)).

488   **"certain"** & **"basic"** & **"those canons"** & **"standards"** & **"an alert"**: *Id.* at 65–68 (Frankfurter, J., concurring) (quoting Palko, 302 U.S. at 325).

489   **"civilized"** & **"fundamental"** & **"natural"** & **"I fear"**: *Id.* at 71–72, 89–90 (Black, J., dissenting).

CHAPTER 29: MY EYES HATH SEEN THE GLORY OF THE COMING OF THE LORD

490   **balconies**: Jewish Advocate, 12/6/1945, at 8.

490   **"A Jewish"** & **"a dreamer"**: "Remarks of Mr. Justice Frankfurter telephoned from Washington, D.C. to the dinner in honor of Dr. Chaim Weizmann, held at the Waldorf-Astoria on Tuesday, November 27th, 1945," at 2, 4, FFLC, Box 111 & Jewish Advocate, 12/27/1945, at 7.

491   **declined invitations**: FF to Abba Silver, 4/14/1943, FFLC, Box 102; FF to Abba Silver, 4/15/1943 tel., *id.*

491   **underplayed**: FF to Forrestal Diaries editor Walter Millis, 1/19/1953, at 5, FFLC, Box 136; DFF, 345–49.

491   **"There isn't"** & **"can"**: Eliahu Elath, *Zionism at the UN*, 292–93 (1976) (translated from Hebrew).

491   **social reformers**: LDB to DKN, 11/19/1932, DKNP, HSTL, Box 35; HJL to DKN, 1/17/1936, *id.*; Evans to DKN, 3/4/1936, *id.*

492   **rally progressives'**: FF to DKN, 8/21/1935 tel., DKNP, HSTL, Box 31.

492   **Harry Hopkins & special assistant**: Application for Service Credit, 1/15/1946, *id.*, Box 34; DKN to Edwin McKim, 5/28/1945, *id.*

492   **"palace"**: CT, 12/17/1943, at 5.

492   **"this Harvard"**: 89 Cong. Rec. 2818–20 (Pt. 2, April 1, 1943). *See* FF Diary, 5/12/1943, DFF, 237–38.

492   **Carlton Hotel**: ML OH, at 76, HSTL; Garrison Nelson, *John William McCormack*, 181–83 & 203 nn.33–36, 384–88 (2017); Abram L. Sachar, *The Redemption of the Unwanted*, 190–224 (1983); Garrison Nelson, "'A Mania for Anonymity': The Mysterious Presidential Aide, David K. Niles of Boston," New England Political Science Association presentation 4/26–28/2012; Alfred Steinberg, "Mr. Truman's Mystery Man," Saturday Evening Post, 12/24/1949, at 24, 69, 70; David A. Friedman, "Against the Experts: Harry S. Truman, David K. Niles, and the Birth of the State of Israel, 1945–1948" (Undergraduate thesis, Whitman College, 2011); David B. Sachar, "David K. Niles and United States Policy Toward Palestine" (Undergraduate thesis, Harvard University, 1959).

492   **"passion"**: BH, 5/9/1943, at 1, 26.

492   **homosexuality:** FBI memorandum, 2/28/1951, File No. 100-23256, DKN FBI file, File 4 Section 2 (on file with author) (memorializing Whittaker Chambers's accusations that during the 1930s DKN had "a homosexual affair" with Matthew Silverman, a New Deal lawyer and alleged member of a Communist cell, the Ware Group).

492   **Communist ties:** Numerous people contacted DKN seeking help for suspected Communists, which showed up in FBI files and the Venona files decrypting the transmissions of Soviet intelligence agencies. DKN FBI file, File 4, Sections 1–3 (on file with author); John Earl Haynes & Harvey Klehr, *Venona*, 284–85 (1999) (mentioning a person's appeal to DKN for transit visas and that an associate of DKN's may have been bribed). DKN, however, steadfastly denied that he was a Communist.

492   **"hostile":** Memorandum of Conversation between FDR and King Ibn Saud, 2/14/1945, at 2, HSTP, PSF, Box 161.

492   **State Department officials:** Secretary of State Edwin Stettinius, to HST, 4/18/1945, *id.*; Acting Secretary of State Joseph Grew to HST, 5/1/1946, *id.*; HST, *Memoirs: Years of Trial and Hope, 1946–1952*, at 132–42 (1955). *See* David Nasaw, *The Last Million* (2020) (documenting Europe's displaced persons after World War II).

493   **made lists:** SIR, Memorandum for the President, 11/19/1945, SIRP-HSTL, Box 4. SIR's list included two longtime friends of FF's, AM and Reinhold Niebuhr.

493   **Sacco-Vanzetti:** FWB, "Chum Felix Frankfurter," at 38, FFLC, Box 257; FWB to FF, 3/17/1927 & FWB to FF, 3/22/1927 & FWB to FF, 4/1927 & FWB to FF, 5/12/1927 & FWB to FF, 6/22/1927 & FWB to FF, 6/1927 & FWB to FF, 7/11/1927, FFHLS, Pt. III, Reel 33, Pages 221–28; FWB to FF, 10/19/1927, FFLC, Box 38.

493   **civic organizations:** BG, 9/7/1974, at 30.

493   **Byrnes's list:** JFB, Memorandum for the President, 11/21/1945, at 1, HSTP, PSF, Box 161; HST, Memorandum for Secretary of State, 11/27/1945, *id.*

493   **"I presume":** FWB to FF, 12/4/1945, FFLC, Box 39.

494   **meetings & prospects:** FWB to FF, 12/17/1945, FFLC, Box 39; FWB to FF, 12/18/1945, *id.*

494   **"At the end":** FWB, "Chum Felix Frankfurter," at 49.

494   **"so sickened" & "I am afraid" & "I hope":** FWB to FF, 2/15/1946, at 1–3, FFLC, Box 40.

494–495   **"Free" & "Only" & "My English" & "We can't" & "declaration":** FWB to FF, 2/24/1946, at 1–2, *id.* Richard Crossman, *Palestine Mission*, 87 (1947) (recalling FWB returned with conviction that Polish Jews "were determined to emigrate" to Palestine).

495   **"Not" & "devoured" & "vulgar" & "the principles" & "need" & "Due regard" & "Safeguarding" & "no statesman" & "the first":** FF to FWB, 3/13/1946, at 1-2, FFLC, Box 40.

495   **"Now":** FWB to FF, 4/4/1946, at 2, *id.*

495   **anti-Zionist:** FWB to FF, 7/23/1946, *id.*

495   **lobbying:** Hutcheson to Gentlemen of the Committee of Inquiry, 4/1/1946, *id.*; Bartley C. Crum, *Behind the Silken Curtain*, 270 (1947).

495–496   **"The miraculous":** FWB to FF, 4/4/1946, at 1.

496   **"and the":** FWB to FF, 4/2/1946, at 2. *See To the Gates of Jerusalem: The Diaries and Papers of James G. McDonald, 1945–1947* (Norman J.W. Goda et al., eds., 2014); Crossman, *Palestine Mission*; Crum, *Behind the Silken Curtain*.

496   **"perhaps" & "I have" & "heart" & "My regret" & "launched" & "prefer":** DKN to HST appointments secretary Matthew Connelly, 5/1/1946, HSTP, PSF, Box 161.

496   **"the further":** Statement by the President, 4/30/1946, DKNP, Box 29.

496   **Truman forwarded & Niles advised:** HST to DKN, n.d. & DKN to HST, 5/7/1946, HSTP, PDF, Box 161.

496   **Niles dismissed:** Taylor to HST, 5/15/1946, DKNP, Box 29.

497   **"May I":** DKN to HST, 5/27/1946, at 2, *id.*

497   **Niles drafted:** HST to Taylor, 5/27/1946, *id.*; Niles to Political Action Committee for Palestine, 5/31/1946, *id.*; *The Forrestal Diaries*, 7/26/1946, at 188–89 (Walter Millis, ed. 1951) (blaming Jewish propaganda for president's acceptance of report and 100,000 Jewish immigrants).

497   **"agitation" & "because":** NYT, 6/13/1946, at 1.

497   **"I think":** FF to FWB, 6/22/1946, at 2, FFLC, Box 40.

497   **Georgetown mansion:** JA to IB, 4/30/1946, at 1, IBP, Box 239 #20.

497   **publisher & married:** JA to IB, 1/17/1947, at 1–2, *id.* at #28 & #29.

497   **worried his friends & missed Berlin:** JA to IB, 5/29/1946, *id.* at #23.

497   **"Mrs. L":** JA to IB, 11/8/1947, *id.* #36.

497–498 **"in a" & "spoke" & "mild" & "no heart" & "denounced" & "true":** JA to IB, circa 1947, at 2, IBP, Box 239, #41. This undated letter may have been written in 1946. In August 1946, JA wrote a series of columns about Palestine, including one with a negative reference about HST almost getting "carried away" by Wallace, SIR, and the "ineffable" DKN. It is the only JA column from 1946 and 1947 that mentioned both Palestine and DKN, and it was written with several others from London. WP, 8/18/1946, at B5. *See* WP, 8/14/1946, at 7; WP, 8/16/1946, at 8.

498   **"revered" & "intimate" & "learned" & "their emotion":** DA, *Present at the Creation*, 169 (1969).

498   **Grady report:** NYT, 5/4/1946, at 5; NYT, 6/26/1946, at 1.

498   **Truman recalled:** Presidential Statement, 7/31/1946, DKNP, Box 29.

498   **Buxton assured:** FWB to FF, 8/9/1946, FFLC, Box 40.

499   **Acheson:** NYT, 8/10/1946, at 1.

499   **rebuked:** NYT, 8/24/1946, at 5.

499   **"had gone" & "had in it":** DA, *Present at the Creation*, 176. *See* James Reston, *Deadline*, 390–91 (1991) (overestimating DA's anti-Zionist influence on HST).

499   **"You spent":** FF to DA, 7/30/1946 tel., DAP, Reel 8, Box 11, Folder 144.

499   **"My dear":** FF to Lord Inverchapel, 8/7/1946, *id.* FF to DA, 8/8/1946, *id.*

499   **"You will":** FF to DA, 11/14/1946, *id.*

499   **refugees suffered:** FWB to FF, 7/15/1946, FFLC, Box 40 (enclosing Hutcheson to FWB, 7/12/1946).

499   **"be entirely":** FF to FWB, 7/17/1946, at 3, *id.*

499   **ignored & opposed:** Presidential Statement, 7/2/1946, DKNP, Box 29; *The Forrestal Diaries*, 12/3/1947, at 346–47 (recounting discussion with JFB who blamed DKN and SIR for decision to turn down Grady report).

499   **notified:** HST, *Memoirs: Years of Trial and Hope, 1946–1952*, at 152–53.

499   **"means":** FF to FWB, 7/17/1946, at 3, FFLC, Box 40.

499   **"insoluble":** HST, *Memoirs: Years of Trial and Hope, 1946–1952*, at 152–53.

499   **"Not in":** FWB to FF, 9/12/1946, at 1, FFLC, Box 40.

500   **initially agreed:** Acting Secretary of State Will Clayton to HST, 9/12/1946 & HST to Clayton, 9/14/1946, HSTP, PSF, Box 161.

500   **endorsed:** Presidential Statement, 10/4/1946, *id.*, Box 162.

500   **Pearson:** WP, 10/11/1946, at 12.

500   **"one" & "short":** Time, 10/14/1946, in DKNP, Box 29.

500   **gunned for:** ML OH, at 76–77.

500 **"Marshall has"** & **"the problem"**: FF to FWB, 1/23/1947, at 2, FFLC, Box 40. NYT, 1/10/1947, at 23 (Crum predicting that Marshall would be sympathetic to displaced persons).

500 **"I hope"**: CW to FF, 1/7/1947, at 1, FFLC, Box 111.

500 **blamed Truman**: HST, *Memoirs: Years of Trial and Hope, 1946–1952*, at 153–54. FF to CCB, 10/8/1948, at 1, CCBP, Box 5, Folder 5-8 (blaming Marshall's anti-Zionism on Bevin).

500–501 **"of long"** & **"shared"**: NYT, 2/27/1947, at 1.

501 **"I have tried"** & **"but this"** & **"in the name"**: CW to FF, 5/1/1947, at 1–3, FFLC, Box 111.

501 **political bickering**: FF to FWB, 6/3/1947, FFLC, Box 40.

501 **"joy"** & **"in full"**: CW to FF, 6/22/1947, *The Letters and Papers of Chaim Weizmann*, Vol. 22, at 351–52 (Barnet Litvinoff, ed. 1979).

501 **"The Jews"** & **"The Jews"**: HSTD, 7/21/1947, at 1–2, HSTL, PSF, Box 226.

502 **Niles-drafted**: Presidential Statement, 6/5/1947, DKNP, Box 29.

502 **John Hilldring**: DKN to HST, Memorandum for the President, 7/29/1947, at 1–2, DKNP, Box 29.

502 **medal of merit**: FF to DKN, 9/24/1947, at 1, *id.*, Box 32.

502 **"Mazel"**: FF to DKN, 10/13/1947, DKNP, Box 32.

502 **Philippines**: *The Forrestal Diaries*, 1/7/1948, at 357–58 (based on Forrestal's conversation with Henderson); Sachar, "David K. Niles and the United States Policy Toward Palestine," 72–73 & n.81 (based partially on 1/6/1959 int. with Ginsburg and BVC about FF and the Philippines).

502 **"untruth"** & **"I never"**: FF to Millis, 1/19/1953, at 5, in DFF, 348.

502 **"a far-sighted"**: FF to CW, 11/17/1947, CWP, No. 23-2787. *See* FF to CW, 11/22/1947, *id.*, No. 2-2788a.

502–503 **French ambassador**: CW to FF, 10/22/1947, FFLC, Box 111.

503 **Indian delegation**: CW to FF, 11/24/1947, *id.*

503 **Bonnet**: FF to CW, n.d., CWP, No. 31-2794A (enclosing Bonnet to FF, 12/1/1947); FF to CW, 12/3/1947 tel., *id.*, No. 26-2796. *See* Chaim Weizmann, *Trial and Error*, 452–57 (1949) (UNSCOP testimony and United Nations vote on November 29, 1947).

503 **stag lunch**: WES, 10/4/1947, at B-11.

503 **Philadelphia Orchestra**: WES, 10/21/1947, at B-3.

503 **buffet**: WES, 11/15/1947, at B-11.

503 **Luxembourg**: WES, 11/18/1947, at B-3.

503 **Forrestal & Lovett**: *The Forrestal Diaries*, 8/8/1947, at 303–4 & 9/4/1947, at 309–10 & 12/1/1947, at 346.

503 **"The memory"**: CW to FF, 11/24/1947. *See* FF to CW, 11/22/1947 (handwritten: "The memory of that lovely evening will long remain vivid."); Eliahu Elath, *The Struggle for Statehood*, Vol. 2A, 401–2 (1982).

503 **November 19**: Weizmann, *Trial and Error*, 458–59

503 **close contact**: FF to CW, 10/10/1947, CWP, No. 31-2775; FF to CW, 11/22/1947; CW to FF, 11/24/1947; FF to CW, 11/23/1947 tel., CWP, No. 10-2788A.

503 **"You came"**: FF to CW, 12/16/1947 tel., *id.*, No. 8-2800.

504 **"importuned"** & **"annoyed"**: *The Forrestal Diaries*, 12/13/1947, at 348–49.

504 **"wisdom"** & **"[t]he alternative"**: FF to Lovett, 11/29/1947 tel., FFLC, Box 78 & DFF, 348.

504 **"a little"**: FF to Millis, 1/19/1953, in DFF, 348.

504 **looming concern**: Forrestal Diary, 9/29/1947, *The Forrestal Diaries*, at 322 ("I asked the

President whether it would not be possible to lift the Jewish-Palestine question out of politics.").

504 **Marshall rebuffed:** Marshall to FF, 3/15/1948, IBP, Box 253; FF to Marshall, 3/10/1948, *id.*; Elath, *The Struggle for Statehood*, Vol. 2B, 576–77 (Marshall's rebuff of CW meeting).

504 **Eddie Jacobson:** HST Appointment Calendar, 3/18/1948 (noting CW 12:15 p.m. meeting "Requested from New York City from Edward Jacobson"); *id.*, 3/13/1948 (Jacobson 10:45 a.m. meeting); Eddie Jacobson, Chronology of events relating to Palestine and the recognition of Israel, 1945–1949, at 3, HSTL (noting on 3/13 he arranged CW meeting with HST and saw HST again 3/17 in NYC to discuss CW meeting); Eddie Jacobson to Josef Cohn, 4/1/1952, at 2–7, HSTL.

505 **"strip[]ed":** HST to Mary Jane Truman, 3/21/1948, at 2, HSTP, Personal and Family Papers, Box 20.

505 **"a liar":** HSTD, 3/20/1948.

505 **temporary:** Press Release, 3/25/1948, HST, PSF, Box 162; HST, *Memoirs: Years of Trial and Hope, 1946–1952*, at 160–64; CW, *Trial and Error*, 472–73.

505 **"Tragedy":** FF to CW, 3/26/1948, at 1–3, CWP, No. 2-2820.

505 **After the war:** "ML – dates in Life of," n.d., at 5–7, Lash Papers, Box 65, Folder 1; Personal History, MLP, Box 21, Folder 40.

505 **Wickersham Commission:** FF to ML, n.d., circa 9/1930, MLP, Box 22, Folder 9.

505 **1934 Securities Exchange Act & shied:** Telford Taylor COH, at 183–87; JLR Int. with Joseph Lash, 12/5/1984, at 1, Lash Papers, Box 65, Folder 2; Clark Clifford, *Counsel to the President*, 7 (1991) (recalling discussions with ML in Lafayette Park because ML believed J. Edgar Hoover had him under surveillance).

505 **Truman & Brandeis & monopolies & wiretapping:** ML OH, at 23–25; ML to Jonathan Daniels, 12/10/1949, at 1, MLP, Box 13, Folder 29; Daniels to ML, 11/18/1949, at 1, *id.*

505 **"You know":** Note, n.d., at 2, *id.*

505 **vice-presidential spot:** "A Few Notes on the July 1944 Democratic Convention," *id.*

506 **"Actions":** "Actions," 3/25/1948, Clifford Papers, Box 31.

506 **"shot":** Eben Ayres Diary, 3/25/1948, at 55, Ayres Papers, HSTL & in *Truman at the White House*, 250–51 (Robert H. Ferrell, ed. 1991).

506 **"see":** FF to CW, 4/6/1948, tel., CWP, 5-2823.

506 **"We want":** FF to CW, 4/14/1948, *id.*, 27-2824 (enclosing WP cartoon, 4/14/1948).

506 **"it seems":** FF to CW, 4/14/1948, *id.*, 15-2825A.

506 **"Keep":** FF to CW, 4/19/1948, *id.*

506 **five or six:** MLD, 5/11/1948, at 8–9, MLP, Box 8, Folder 62; ML to Clifford, 5/11/1948 & other memos, *id.*, Folder 63.

506 **Truman listened:** MLD, 5/12/1948 8:30 p.m.; Ayres Dairy, 5/12/1948, in *Truman in the White House*, at 257.

506–507 **next day & not scared & agreed:** MLD, 5/13/1948 11:00 a.m., at 1; MLD, 6/1/1948, at 2; Clifford, *Counsel to the President*, 3–25; Clifford, "Factors Influencing President Truman's Decision to Support Partition and Recognize the State of Israel," 38–42 in *The Palestine Question in American History* (Clark M. Clifford et al., eds. 1978). *Cf.* Lowenthal OH, at 76–78 (claiming he did not have much to do with Palestine).

507 **letter from Weizmann:** CW to HST, 5/13/1948, *The Letters and Papers of Chaim Weizmann*, Vol. 23, at 116 (1980).

507 **made up his mind:** Ayres Diary, 5/14/1948, at 100, Ayres Papers.

507 **nor oppose:** Forrestal Diary, 5/14/1948, *The Forrestal Diaries*, at 440.

507 **"Dave"**: Sachar, "David K. Niles and the United States Policy Toward Palestine," 1 & n.1 (based on May 1948 conversation between Abram I. Sachar in May 1948 and confirmed by HST to Abram Sachar, 3/10/1959).

507 **"jubilant"**: MLD, 5/14/1948, at 1.

507 **"It's been" & "There have"**: FF to DKN, 5/17/1948, at 1–3, DKNP, Box 32.

507 **pleaded & arranged**: MLD, 5/19/1948 7:45 p.m., at 1–2.

507 **navy & Waldorf**: MLD, 5/22/1948 9:15 p.m. at 1–3; MLD, 5/24/1948, at 2.

507 **State Department opposed**: Ayres Diary, 5/24/1948, *Truman in the White House*, at 258.

508 **"'My'"**: FF to CW, 5/16/1948, at 1, CWP, 3-2831.

508 **Blair House & quiet**: FF to CW, 5/29/1948, *id.*, 10-2839; MLD, 5/25/1948 11:20 a.m., at 2–3.

508 **"I always"**: NYT, 5/26/1948, at 4. CW, *Trial and Error*, 480–81.

508 **hands**: WP, 5/25/1948, at 1, 2.

508 **"At last"**: FF to CW, 5/29/1948.

508 **editorial**: MLD, 6/4/1948 10:40 a.m.

508 **General Hilldring**: MLD, 6/9/1948, at 3.

508 **McDonald**: Forrestal Diary, 6/23/1948, *The Forrestal Diaries*, at 440–41.

508 **Czechoslovakia**: MLD, 6/2/1948 11:45 a.m. at 4.

508 **praised**: FF to CW, 2/15/1949, CWP, 20-2886.

508 **"It has"**: FF to DKN, 5/15/1949, at 1–2, DKN, Box 32. *See* CW to DKN, 2/20/1949, DKN-Brandeis U, Box 8a (crediting DKN).

509 **seventy-fifth**: FF to CW, 11/20/1949, CWP, 12-2906A.

509 **"tower"**: HST to DKN, 5/17/1951, HSTP, PSF, Box 248, Folder 15.

509 **stomach cancer**: Blumgart to FF, 10/11/1952, FFHLS, Pt. III, Reel 39, Page 371.

509 **"the underprivileged" & dream**: HST Official Statement, 9/28/1952, HSTP, PSF, Box 632, #2238.

509 **retirement**: JA to IB, 1/17/1947, at 2, IBP, Box 239, #29; JA to IB, circa 1947, at 2, *id.* #41.

509 **health problems**: MDF to Blumgart, 8/22/1948, FFHLS, Pt. III, Reel 39, Page 238–42; FF to Blumgart, 8/24/1948, *id.*, Page 343–44 (MDF's neurological problems and visits to Boston doctors).

CHAPTER 30: I DON'T CARE WHAT COLOR A MAN HAS

510–511 **"color" & "The upshot" & "power" & "an explosive" & "the umpire" & "to keep" & "there was" & "might" & "of course" & "I asked" & "noble" & "this is" & "the very"**: DFF, 12/20/1947, at 334–36. *See* Ross E. Davies, "A Christmas Gift for the Supreme Court," 17 Green Bag 2d 311–54 (2014).

511 **December 16**: PAF to FF, 12/16/1947, at 1–3, FFHLS, Pt. III, Reel 9, Pages 9–11.

511 **finished first**: WTC enrolled at Harvard Law School in 1941, served in the military, then graduated magna cum laude in November 1946. Harvard Law Record, 6/11/1947, at 1. During the confusion about who was in what graduating class after the war, he was not awarded the Fay Diploma for finishing first in his class. PAF to Judge Herbert Goodrich, 1/31/1947, FFHLS, Pt. III, Reel 9, Page 6 (WTC as first in class of 75 with 76 average). Six decades later, the law school corrected the oversight. Harvard Law Today, 2/25/2009, https://today.law.harvard.edu/william-coleman-46-honored-in-the-u-s-senate/.

511 **broken protocol**: WTC to FF, 1/15/1948, FFHLS, Pt. III, Reel 9, Page 14; FF to WTC, 1/22/1948, *id.* at Page 15; PAF to FF, 1/28/1948, at 1–3, *id.* at Pages 19–21.

511   **dean:** FF to CCB, 5/8/1946, at 2–3, CCBP, Box 5, Folder 5-6.

511   **Beale Prize & "From":** PAF to Goodrich, 1/31/1947.

512   **"would welcome":** PAF to FF, 12/16/1947, at 1.

512   **"power" & "I don't":** FF to PAF, 12/18/1947, FFHLS, Pt. III, Reel 9, Page 13. In 1946, WTC also had written directly to HLB, but the justice had already filled his clerkship. WTC to HLB, 6/20/1946, HLBP, Box 442, Folder 2; HLB to WTC, 6/24/1946, *id.*

512   **didn't know & tried to help:** HMH to WTC, 1/22/1948, FFHLS, Pt. III, Reel 9, Page 17; PAF to FF, 12/16/1947, at 2–3.

512   **Boston firms:** WTC, *Counsel for the Situation,* 73–74 (2010).

512   **Hand & Magruder & Garrison:** PAF to FF, 1/28/1948, at 1–2.

512   **"willing":** HMH to WTC, 1/22/1948.

512   **accepted:** HMH to FF, 1/23/1948, *id.* at Page 18; FF to HMH, 2/11/1948, *id.* at Page 22 (FF handwritten: February 27 notified); WTC, *Counsel for the Situation,* 76–77 (recalling phone call from HMH but confusion about whether FF had hired him).

512   **"For":** WP, 4/27/1948, at 1.

512   **letters:** FFHLS, Pt. III, Reel 9, Pages 23–44.

513   **not deserving:** FF to Rep. John McCormack, 4/30/1948, *id.* at Page 29.

513   **"Tom" & "Mr. Justice":** PAF, "Felix Frankfurter: Reminisces & Reflections," 11/19/1982, at 12–13.

513   **Jackie Robinson:** WTC, *Counsel for the Situation,* 78–94; Todd C. Peppers, "William Thaddeus Coleman, Jr.," Journal of Supreme Court History 33, no. 3 (2008): 353–70 (making Robinson analogy).

513   **"third degree":** Lee v. Mississippi, 332 U.S. 742 (1948).

513   **"Murphy made":** DFF, 12/30/1947, at 337.

513–514   **"mild" & "should deal" & "third":** FF to FM, 1/3/1948, FFHLS, Pt. III, Reel 2, Page 652.

514   **Brandeis opinion:** Wan v. United States, 266 U.S. 1 (1924).

514   **"This satisfies":** FF's note joining FM's opinion, FMP, Roll 138, Lee file, Page 39. *See* FF handwritten comments on FM's recirculated draft, *id.* Pages 35–38. Lee was re-tried and sentenced to 20 years in prison; his conviction was affirmed on appeal. Lee v. State, 39 So.2d 868 (Miss. 1949), *cert. denied,* 338 U.S. 803 (1949).

514   **Sarah Elizabeth Ray:** Bob-Lo Excursion Co. v. Michigan, 333 U.S. 28, 30–31 (1948).

514   **At conference:** HHB, *Bob-Lo* Conference Notes, at 1, HHBP, Box 154, Folder 9; WOD, *Bob-Lo* Conference Notes, at 1, WODP, Box 161 Folder 4.

514   **"the very":** WBR, *Bob-Lo* Conference Notes, WBRP, Box 157, Folder 2.

515   **"led me" & "Forgive":** FF to WBR, 1/2/1948, WBRP, Box 157, Folder 2.

515   **"little sermon" & offensive language:** WBR to FF, 1/2/1948, at 1–2, *id.* (referring to Fisher v. United States, 328 U.S. 463, 477 (1946) (Frankfurter, J., dissenting)). David M. Siegel, "Felix Frankfurter, Charles Hamilton Houston and the 'N-Word,'" 7 S. Cal. Interdisc. L.J. 317 (1998).

515   **"My point is" & "this Court should":** FF to WBR, 1/2/1948, WBRP, Box 157, Folder 2.

515   **"Felix":** WBR to secretary Edna Lingreen, 1/5/1948, *id. See* WBR to FF, 1/2/1948, *id.* (typewritten copy of handwritten agreement to changes).

515   **"impose":** Bob-Lo Excursion Co. v. Michigan, 333 U.S. at 40.

515   **Ada Lois Sipuel:** Sipuel v. Board of Regents, 332 U.S. 631, 632 (1948) (per curiam); Ada Lois Sipuel Fisher, with Danney Goble, *A Matter of Black and White* (1996).

515   **Lloyd Gaines:** Missouri ex rel. Gaines v. Canada, 305 U.S. 337 (1938); James W. Endersby

& William T. Horner, *Lloyd Gaines and the Fight to End Segregation* (2016); Chad Garrison, "The Mystery of Lloyd Gaines," Riverfront Times, 4/4/2007.

515 **four possible options & "not in sympathy"**: HHB *Sipuel* Conference Notes, at 1, HHBP, Box 154, Folder 8. *See* WBR *Sipuel* Conference Notes, WBRP, Box 164, Folder 5.

516 **"legal education" & "in conformity"**: Sipuel, 332 U.S. at 632–33.

516 **"should avoid"**: FF, Memorandum, 2/13/1948, at 1, Fisher v. Hurst, No. 325 Misc., FFHLS, Pt. III, Reel 12, Page 880.

516 **Oklahoma courts**: Fisher v. Hurst, 333 U.S. 147 (1948) (per curiam).

516 **to hear & could not be equal**: *Id.* at 151 (Rutledge, J., dissenting). In June 1949, Ada Sipuel-Fisher was admitted to the University of Oklahoma Law School. CT, 6/19/1949, at 8.

516 **restrictive housing covenants**: WOD *Shelley* Conference Notes, WODP, Box 161, Folder 8; HHB *Shelley* Conference Notes, HHBP, Box 154, Folder 7; Shelley v. Kraemer, 334 U.S. 1 (1948); Jeffrey D. Gonda, *Unjust Deeds* (2015).

517 **"not for any"**: Hurd v. Hodge, 334 U.S. 24, 36 (1948) (Frankfurter, J., concurring).

517 **charmed**: Powell to FF, 1/22/1947, Richardson Papers, Box I:50 (FF handwritten comments).

518 **first choice**: Paul Bender Int. with author, 2/15/2017.

518 **"exclusionary rule"**: Wolf v. Colorado, 338 U.S. 25 (1949).

518 **Richardson's research**: Wolf v. Colorado file, FFHLS, Pt. I, Reel 36, Pages 897–988 & Reel 37, Pages 1–79; FF to Richardson, 10/1/1952, Richardson Papers, Box I:50; WTC, *Counsel for the Situation*, 82.

518 **limiting the scope**: Wolf docket book, FFHLS, Pt. I., Reel 37, Page 107; HHB *Wolf* Conference Notes, at 1–4, HHBP, Box 167, Folder 8; WOD *Wolf* Conference Notes, at 1–2, WODP, Box 177, Folder 1; WBR *Wolf* Conference Notes, 10/23/1948, at 1–2, WBRP, Box 173, Folder 1.

518 **chambers & Coleman's parents & red toy car**: WTC, *Counsel for the Situation*, 80, 82.

518–519 **Shakespeare & badminton & godfather**: *Id.* at 81, 87; WTC Int. with author, 10/16/2006.

519 **Mayflower Hotel**: WTC, *Counsel for the Situation*, 93; WTC Int. with author, 10/16/2006.

519 **"noticed"**: WTC Int. with Robert H. Jackson Center, 5/18/2005, https://www.youtube .com/watch?v=8K8cM3pYPp8.

519–520 **factual matter & "No one" & "the advantages" & "the exchange" & "the only" & "must be"**: WTC, "Memorandum for Mr. Justice Frankfurter on Sweatt v. Texas, No. 44, October Term, 1949, and McLaurin v. Oklahoma State Regents for Higher Education, No. 34, October Term, 1949," 8/5/1949, at 16–20, FFLC, Box 218. Al Sacks Int. with Michael Parrish, 7/15/1974, at 4 (discussing WTC's memorandum at FF's request at end of term).

520 **"rights"**: WTC, "Memorandum," at 21–22 (quoting Hurd v. Hodge, 334 U.S. 24, 36 (1948) (Frankfurter, J., concurring)).

520 **"When" & "classifications" & "segregation does" & "in the South" & "Segregation is"**: *Id.* at 22–24 (quoting 1 Vand. L. Rev. 403 (1948)). WTC clamed in his memoir that his June 1949 memorandum was about a South Carolina school segregation case brought by Thurgood Marshall, and that he and Richardson had urged Frankfurter to reject South Carolina Governor JFB's plea to remand the case for more factual finding. WTC, *Counsel for the Situation*, 83–84. There are a few problems with WTC's recollections. A South Carolina case about the lack of funding for a school bus for black children, *Pearson v. Clarendon County Board of Education*, was dismissed by the district court in March

1948 because of a lack of standing. This case was not appealed. Richard Kluger, *Simple Justice*, 15–18 (1976). Nor does it appear anywhere in FF's Supreme Court docket book and conference list during the 1948 term. The next South Carolina school segregation case, *Briggs v. Elliott*, did not begin until November 1949 after WTC's clerkship. JFB, moreover, did not become governor of South Carolina until January 16, 1951. WTC, therefore, must have been referring to his memo at the end of the 1948 term about *Sweatt* and *McLaurin*.

521   "imponderable" & "Restriction": FF Notes, n.d., at 1–2, FFHLS, Pt. I, Reel 40, Pages 1–2.

521   *Segregation in Washington*: Id. at Pages 12–62, Box 34, Folder 3 (*Segregation in Washington: A Report of The National Committee on Segregation in the Nation's Capital* (1948)).

521   life in the nation's capital: Constance McLaughlin Green, *Secret City* (1967); Brad Snyder, *Beyond the Shadow of the Senators*, 2–3 (2003).

521   "This is so": Goesaert v. Cleary, 335 U.S. 464, 465–66 (1948). *See* Dictated First Draft, 12/1/1948, FFHLS, Pt. I, Reel 32, Page 316.

521   Twenty-First Amendment: HLB to FF, 12/2/1948, *id.* at Page 328; FF to Richardson, n.d., *id.* at Page 356.

521   "By your": Dr. Alice E. Palmer to FF, 12/23/1948, *id.* at Page 365.

521   "Your enmity": Alma Booker to FF, *id.* at Page 366.

522   all-male Bartenders Union: DFP, 12/29/1948, in *id.* at Page 313.

522   all-male Court: HHB *Goesaert* Conference Notes, HHBP, Box 167, Folder 14; WOD *Goesaert* Conference Notes, WODP, Box 177, Folder 2.

522   "it is hard" & "We have": TCC *Sweatt* Notes, at 1–2, TCCP, Box A2.

522   framers & "This is no": *Id.* at 2.

522   "should not": HHB *Sweatt* Notes, at 4, HHBP, Box 182, Folder 1.

522   Holmes's speech & strength: WOD *Sweatt* Notes, at 2, WODP, Box 192, Folder 2.

522   "To have": TCC *Sweatt* Notes, at 2, TCCP, Box A2.

522   condemned: Cassell v. Texas, 339 U.S. 282, 290–91 (1950) (Frankfurter, J., concurring in the judgment).

522–523 "symbolic" & "A totally": FF, Memorandum for the Conference, 5/31/1950, at 2, FFHLS, Pt. I, Reel 39, Page 755.

523   take on segregation: FF to HHB, 5/26/1950, at 1–2, FFHLS, Pt. III, Reel 1, Pages 243–44 (asking him not to use *Henderson* to outlaw racial segregation).

523   "intangible" Sweatt v. Painter, 339 U.S. 629, 632–35 (1950). *See* Michael Klarman, *From Jim Crow to Civil Rights*, 206–12 (2004); William M. Wiecek, *The History of the Supreme Court of the United States, Volume XII: The Birth of the Modern Constitution: The United States Supreme Court, 1941–53*, at 681–93 (2006).

523   "the most rewarding" & Taney: WTC, *Counsel for the Situation*, 85–86, 91–92.

523   "absolute": WTC, "Mr. Justice Felix Frankfurter," 1978 U. Ill. L. F. 279, 296.

523   "without" & "judicial" & "I have" & "too many" & "a joy" & "What I": WTC, *Counsel for the Situation*, 91–92 (quoting letters from FF to WTC).

CHAPTER 31: THE FRANKFURTER CULT ON TRIAL

525   "wanted" & "In fact" & "Since": Katherine Watters, "Conversation between a man who called and identified himself as Westbrook Pegler and Katherine Watters, about 12:15 p.m., December 17, 1948—this summary was made shortly after the conversation took place," WBRP, Box 177, Folder 5. AH had testified before HUAC on the previous day. It

was almost certainly Pegler. He admitted he had tried to call WOD on the night of the Gridiron dinner six days earlier. In fact, Pegler had been introduced to FF that night at the Statler Hotel. Cincinnati Enquirer, 12/17/1948, at 8; Cumberland (Md.) Evening Times, 12/17/1948, at 4 (confirming Pegler's account).

526 **"invisible":** AtlConst, 10/4/1948, at 9. AtlConst, 10/5/1948, at 9; Indianapolis Star, 10/6/1948, at 16; Cincinnati Enquirer, 10/11/1948, at 3; Indianapolis Star, 10/12/1948, at 16; Indianapolis Star, 10/14/1948, at 18.

526 **do no wrong:** Murray Kempton, *Part of Our Time*, 29 (1955) (quoting Lee Pressman: "He gave you a sense of absolute command and absolute grace. I think Felix felt it more than anyone. He seemed to have a kind of awe of Alger.")

526 **"shabby":** *Id.* at 14, 17.

526 **William Marbury:** William L. Marbury, "The Hiss-Chambers Libel Suit," 41 Md. L. Rev. 75, 75–76 (1981).

526 **first-name basis:** AH, *Recollections of a Life*, 10–19 (1988); R. Bruce Craig, *The Apprenticeship of Alger Hiss*, ch. 1 (2013).

526 **unwritten rule:** AH to FF, 12/13/1929, at 1–2, FFLC, Box 145.

526 **"benign":** AH Int. in Katie Louchheim, ed., *The Making of the New Deal*, 25–26 (1983). *See* AH, *Recollections of a Life*, 35–37; AH Int. with John Monagan, 1/18/1980, Pt. 3, at 61–62, Monagan Papers, Box. 1, Folder 1; G. Edward White, *Alger Hiss's Looking-Glass Wars*, 17–24 (2004).

526 **"one" & "a man" & "a Godsend":** FF to JLO, 4/1/1930, FFLC, Box 87.

526 **accepted:** FF to JLO, 3/10/1938, *id.*; JLO to FF, 1938, 3/12/1938, *id.* FF also may have tried to get AH to take a job with ML on the Wickersham Commission. FF to ML, circa January 1930, at 1, MLP, Box 4, Folder 13 ("I'm more doubtful about Alger than I sounded over the phone.").

526 **social set & Donald Hiss:** Brad Snyder, *The House of Truth*, 532–33, 561–62 (2017).

527 **AAA & Frank & purge:** FF to JNF, 6/6/1933, Frank Papers, Box 12, Folder 84; Allen Weinstein, *Perjury*, 116–17, 134–37 (2nd ed. 1997); JNF COH, 178–79, 186–91; GJ COH at 472, 474–75, 619–21, 624–28.

527 **Ware Group:** Whittaker Chambers, *Witness*, 331–52 (1952); Sam Tanenhaus, *Whittaker Chambers*, 79–119 (1997).

527 **back off:** GJ to Richard Rovere 12/18/1946, at 5, Rovere Papers, Box 1. *See* DFP, 12/9/1948, at 6.

527 **special assistant:** FF to LDB, 7/21/1935, FFLC, Box 29; FF to SFR, 11/27/1935, at 1, 3, SFRP, FF Corr. Addendum, Folder 1.

527 **Berle:** Chambers, *Witness*, 463–71; Tanenhaus, *Whittaker Chambers*, 160–63; Weinstein, *Perjury*, 2nd ed., 55–59, 291–93.

527 **In 1946:** Kempton, *Part of Our Time*, 20–21 (contending, perhaps based on his interview with Pressman, that by 1946 FF believed that AH "was a very nice person but that somehow he had not quite come up to the promise of his youth.").

527 **relied on:** MLD, 5/11/1948, at 7, 9 & 5/14/1948 at 1 & 5/21/1948 3:30 p.m. & 6/5/1948 at 7–8, MLP, Box 8, Folder 6.

528 **phoned Hiss & farm in Connecticut & full time:** MLD, 8/7/1948, at 1, 7, *id.*, Folder 2; ML, "Talk with Senator Wheeler," 12/17/1948 3:40 p.m., at 2–3 & ML, "Talk with Senator Wheeler at 4:15 p.m.," at 3, 12/18/1948, *id.*, Box 24, Folder 30.

528 **On November 4:** MLD, 11/4/1948 11:00 a.m., at 1, MLP, Box 8, Folder 23.

528 **Rosenwald disagreed:** MLD, 11/6/1948, at 3, *id.*, Folder 29.

528 **"You are"**: ML, "Talk with Senator Wheeler at 4:15 p.m.," at 3, 12/18/1948.

529 **Richard Nixon**: Nixon Grand Jury Testimony, 12/13/1948, NARA, NY, RG 21, Box 3.

529 **"an honorable" & "Either"**: ML, "More Talk with Senator Wheeler, 12/17/1948 3:40 PT," at 2.

529 **"intrinsic"**: FF to CCB, 1/12/1949, at 1, CCBP, Box 5, Folder 5-8. *See* FF, Groton School Quarterly, 4/1949, in FFLC, Box 198.

530 **"a biased"**: Hearings before the Committee on Un-American Activities, House of Representatives, 80th Cong., 2d Sess. (1948) (8/30/1948) 1291–96 (testimony of Adolf A. Berle, Jr.). *See* AABD, 9/4/1939, *Navigating the Rapids, 1918–1971*, at 249–50 (Beatrice Bishop Berle & Travis Beal Jacobs, eds. 1973); Chambers, *Witness*, 463–71; Weinstein, *Perjury*, 2nd ed., 55–59, 291–93.

530 **"pathological" & "a boring"**: FF to Max Lerner, 3/20/1953, at 3, Lerner Papers, Box 3, Folder 136.

530 **vendetta & jealous of Acheson**: AABD, 4/19/1940, at 10, Reel 2; AABD, 2/11/1941, at 1, *id.*; AABD, 10/24/1941, at 2, *id.*, Reel 3; AABD, 11/18/1941, at 2–3, *id.*; AABD, 3/10/1942, at 3, *id.*; AABD, 3/28/1942, at 7, *id.*

530 **anti-Semite**: CCB to FF, 10/26/1942, at 1, FFLC, Box 35; DFF, 1/24/1943, at 168; Jordan A. Schwarz, *Liberal*, 194–203 (1987).

530–531 **"served" & "intimate" & "my friendship" & "gone" & "executive" & "associations" & "embarrassing" & "associations" & "complete" & "closed"**: Nomination of Dean G. Acheson to be Secretary of State, Hearing before the Committee on Foreign Relations, United States Senate, 81st Cong., 1st Sess. 6–8 (GPO: 1949) (January 13, 1949) (testimony of DA). DA extensively researched AAB's HUAC allegations and checked them against State Department personnel files. DAP, HSTL, Box 86, Folder 86-2; DA, *Present at the Creation*, 250–53 (1969).

531 **wired**: 95 Cong. Rec. 460 (1949).

531 **"An assertion"**: 95 Cong. Rec. 460 (1949).

531 **83–6**: *Id.* at 468.

531 **Frankfurter watched**: NYT, 1/22/1949, at 1.

531 **"Dear Dean"**: John Quincy Adams Photograph Inscribed by FF, 1/21/1950 (courtesy of Carol Bundy).

531 **"the whole"**: AtlConst, 6/28/1949, at 13.

531 **typewriter**: Weinstein, *Perjury*, 2nd ed., 344–56.

532 **Lloyd Paul Striker**: Fred Rodell, "Trial Lawyer," Life magazine, 5/26/47, at 107–8, 110, 113–14, 116.

532 **"Call" & "ordinary"**: Time, 7/4/1949, at 18.

532 **second-year & "indispensable" & "the reputation" & "good" & "I never" & "I would"**: AH First Trial Transcript, Testimony of FF, 6/22/1949, at 1571–72, 1575, in Conspiracy Trials in America 1919–1953, Reel 4. *See* G. Edward White, "The Alger Hiss Case: Justices Frankfurter & Reed as Character Witnesses," 4 Green Bag 2d 77–79 (2000).

532 **"wasn't" & "differences" & "did not" & "It didn't" & "fence" & "thought" & "highly" & "Yes"**: Testimony of FF, 6/22/1949, at 1576–77, 1579.

532 **Lee Pressman**: Kempton, *Part of Our Time*, 52–53 (describing Pressman as having "caught . . . the social gospel" from FF but that FF was "a shade uncomfortable" with Pressman).

533 **less effusive**: White, "The Alger Hiss Case," at 80.

533   "duty": NYT, 7/21/1949, at 7.

533   "appeared": FF to Blumgart, 10/27/1952, FFHLS, Pt. III, Reel 39, Page 372 (FF hand-written on NYT article).

533   "particularly" & "had": White, "The Alger Hiss Case," at 68, 71.

533   first-rate trial lawyer: FF to Stryker, 11/22/1950, FFLC, Box 106.

533   "I don't": AtlConst, 7/13/1949, at 11. *See* AtlConst, 7/12/1949, at 11; AtlConst, 7/18/1949, at 11; & AtlConst, 10/12/1949, at 13.

533   "unprecedented": U.S. News & World Report, 8/29/1952, at 37, in FFLC, Box 145.

533   "introduced" & "his conduct": FF to CCB, circa 7/1952, FFLC, Box 36.

533   numerous letters: Letters of criticism, FFLC, Box 145.

533   judicial ethics: Herbert E. White to FMV, 7/29/1949, FFHLS, Pt. III, Reel 4, Page 580.

533   "the past": FF to FMV, 8/6/1949, *id.* at 581.

533   "As for Alger": FF to HJL, 7/27/1949, at 2, FFLC, Box 75.

534   A critic: James Laughlin to FF, 8/8/1949, at 3, FFLC, Box 145.

534   federal prison & appeal: Tracy Campbell, *Short of the Glory*, 137–52 (1998) (indictment); *id.* at 153–70 (trial); *id.* at 171–79 (appeal); Arthur Schlesinger, Jr., "'Prich': A New Deal Memoir," New York Review of Books, 3/28/1985.

534   shook: PAF to FF, 4/5/1950, at 1–2, FFHLS, Pt. III, Reel 38, Pages 65–66 (FF handwrit-ten re: MDF's comment "are we to know nothing these days except bad news" before learning of denial of EFP's appeal).

534   "I take the line" & "for once": IB to Bowra, 5/14/1949, in IB, *Enlightening: Letters 1946–1960*, at 87–88 (Henry Hardy & Jennifer Holmes, eds. 2009).

534   "keep": FF to Cohn, 11/21/1949, at 1–2, FFLC, Box 48. Cohn drafted a letter to Murrow, but it is unclear whether he sent it. Cohn to FF, 11/23/1949, *id.*

534   "risk": AH, *Recollections of a Life*, 15–16.

534   "antagonized": A.J. Liebling, "The Wayward Press: Spotlight on the Jury," New Yorker, 7/23/1949, at 61–62, in FFLC, Box 145.

535   "forgery": NYT, 1/26/1950, at 1 & AH, *In the Court of Public Opinion*, 323 (1957).

535   vowed: MDF to IB, 1/10/1950, at 3, IBP, Box 122, Page 25.

535   "dreadful" & "a little": MDF to IB, 2/2/1950, 1–2, *id.* at Page 123.

535   "I do not": NYT, 1/26/1950, at 1 & DA, *Present at the Creation*, 360.

535   lengthy statement: NYT, 3/1/1950, at 1–2.

535   eternal admiration: MDF, 1/30/1954, FFHLS, Pt. III, Reel 31, Page 771.

535   urged & "To me": FF to CCB, 1/27/1950, CCBP, Box 5, Folder 5-9.

535   "The timid": FF to CCB, 6/22/1950, at 1, *id.*

535   "This is": FF to LH, 1/15/1950, at 1–2, LHP, Box 105B, Folder 105-15. HLS wrote a letter questioning the process of investigating in the State Department. NYT, 3/27/1950, at 22.

535   "I know": Edmund M. Morgan to FF, 1/31/1950, FFHLS, Pt. III, Reel 17, Page 750.

536   "wholly": FF to Morgan, 2/16/1950, *id.*, Page 751.

536   "much": American Communications Ass'n v. Douds, 339 U.S. 382, 419, 421 (1950) (Frankfurter, J., concurring).

536   membership & belief: HHB *Douds* Docket, HHBP, Box 180, Folder 13; HHB *Douds* Conference Notes, 10/17/1949, at 1–2, HHBP, Box 181, Folder 11.

536   "probing": American Communications Ass'n v. Douds, 339 U.S. 382, 419, 421 (1950) (Frankfurter, J., concurring).

536–537 "the tragic" & "The most" & "That isn't" & "victim": NYT, 10/13/1950, at 14.

537   **"becomes"**: WOD *Bailey* Conference Notes, 10/14/1950, at 3, WODP, Box 199, Folder 8.

537   **"This hearing"**: HHB *Bailey* Conference Notes, 10/14/1950, at 4, HHBP, Box 194, Folder 7.

537   **obvious constitutional issues**: FF, Memorandum, 11/22/1950, at 13–14, HHBP, Box 202, Folder 1.

537   **allowed to stand**: Bailey v. Richardson, 182 F.2d 46 (D.C. Cir. 1950), aff'd by equally divided court, 341 U.S. 918 (1951).

537   **Unable**: WOD *Joint Anti-Fascist* Conference Notes, 10/14/1950, WODP, Box 199, Folder 7 (FF passed); HHB *Joint Anti-Fascist* Conference Notes, 11/14/1950, at 2, HHBP, Box 194, Folder 7 (FF waited for *Bailey*).

538   **"The requirement"**: Joint Anti-Fascist Refugee Comm. v. McGrath, 341 U.S. 123, 162 (1951) (Frankfurter, J., concurring).

538   **"a democratic"**: *Id.* at 170.

538   **"to organize"**: Dennis v. United States, 341 U.S. 494, 517 (1951) (Frankfurter, J., concurring) (citing 18 U. S. C. § 10 (1940)).

538   **"whether"**: United States v. Dennis, 183 F.2d 201, 215 (2d Cir. 1950) (Hand, L.J.).

538   **"an unhappy" & "a highly" & blockaded Berlin & "We do"**: *Id.* at 212–13. LH's reformulation of clear and present danger was influenced by his *Carroll Towing* decision a few years earlier about allocating risk and the cost of accidents. United States v. Carroll Towing Co., 160 F.2d 482 (2d Cir. 1947); Irving Dilliard, "Introduction," *The Spirit of Liberty*, xvi–xvii (Irving Dilliard, ed. 1952) (criticizing LH's *Dennis* decision as a departure from OWH's clear and present danger test).

539   **"a compassionate" & "much" & "now" & "Peerless" & "this Old"**: LH to FF, 8/5/1950, LHP, Box 105B, Folder 105-15.

539   **Calkins**: HCrim, 5/1/1969.

539   **"fewer"**: WP, 12/5/1950, at 2.

539   **clear and present danger**: NYT, 12/5/1950, at 20; WES, 12/5/1950, at A-2.

539   **"didn't know" & did not vote**: HHB *Dennis* Conference Notes, 12/9/1950, at 1, HHBP, Box 195, Folder 7; HHB *Dennis* Docket, *id.*, Box 193, Folder 14.

539   **"The amazing"**: WOD *Dennis* Conference Notes, 12/9/1950, at 1–2, WODP, Box 206, Folder 25 ("The amazing" and notation that FF voted to affirm were in a dark blue ink as opposed to the light blue marker of the original conference notes).

539   **"farrago"**: FF to CCB, 7/2/1951, at 1, CCBP, Box 5, Folder 5-9. *See* Dennis, 341 U.S. at 510.

539   **"argumentative" & "with"**: FF to SFR, 3/14/1952, FFHLS, Pt. I, Reel 46, at Page 464. *See* FF to SFR, 2/12/1951, *id.* at Page 454; SFR to FF, 2/12/1951, *id.* at Page 455; FF to SFR, 2/13/1951, *id.* at 456; SFR to FF, 2/14/1951, *id.* at Page 457; FF to SFR, 2/17/1951, *id.* at 458; SFR to FF, 2/17/1951, *id.* at 459; FF to SFR, 2/20/1951, at 1–2, *id.* at Pages 460–61; SFR at FF, 3/13/1951, *id.* at Page 462; FF to SFR, 3/14/1951, *id.* at Page 463; SFR to FF, 3/15/1951, at 1–2, *id.* at Pages 464–65; FF to SFR, 3/15/1951, *id.* at Page 466; John D. Fassett, *New Deal Justice*, 500–501 (1994); John D. Fassett, "The Buddha and the Bumblebee: The Saga of Stanley Reed and Felix Frankfurter," Journal of Supreme Court History 28, no. 2 (2003): 187–88.

540   **"literal" & "rule"**: Calkins to FF, Memorandum, 4/27/1951, at 1, FFHLS, Pt. I, Reel 46, Page 583.

540   **"competing" & "No matter"**: Dennis, 341 U.S. at 525, 542–43 (Frankfurter, J., concurring) (quoting PAF, *On Understanding the Supreme Court* 27–28 (1949)).

540 **"We must"**: FF, Handwritten Notes, "Dennis," n.d., FFHLS, Pt. I, Reel 46, Page 189 (quoting McCulloch v. Maryland, 17 U.S. 316, 407 (1819)).

540 **"the single" & "greatest"**: FF, "John Marshall and the Judicial Function," 69 Harv. L. Rev. 217, 219 (1955).

540 **broad outline**: McCulloch, 17 U.S. at 407 ("only its great outlines should be marked") & *id.* at 415 (describing the Constitution as "intended to endure for ages to come, and consequently, to be adapted to the various *crises* of human affairs.") (emphasis in original).

540–541 **"government" & "The right"**: Dennis, 341 U.S. at 519–20 (Frankfurter, J., concurring) (quoting Cohens v. Virginia, 19 U.S. 264, 414 (1821)).

541 **alternative**: *Id.* at 521–24 (Frankfurter, J., concurring).

541 **"free" & "national" & "relevant" & "only" & "this Court's" & " 'an exercise' "**: *Id.* at 524–26 (quoting Burns Baking Co. v. Bryan, 264 U.S. 504, 534 (1924) (Brandeis, J., dissenting) (joined by Holmes, J.))

541 **"merely"**: *Id.* at 540.

541 **"there is"**: *Id.* at 542 (Frankfurter, J., concurring).

541 **HUAC testimony**: *Id.* at 547.

541 **Fuchs**: *Id.* at 548 n.13

541 **"a conspiracy" & "it would be"**: *Id.* at 546.

541 **"that the danger"**: *Id.* at 550.

541 **"Our duty"**: *Id.* at 552.

541 **Haley & Kennan**: *Id.* at 553–55 (Frankfurter, J., concurring).

542 **"The mark"**: *Id.* at 556.

542 **May 29**: FF memorandum to Conference, 5/29/1951 & FF memorandum re No. 337, 5/29/1951.

542 **in sections**: FF draft opinion, 6/1/1951, RHJP, Box 169, Folder 1.

542 **infuriated**: FF to CCB, circa 6/1951, FFLC, Box 36 (enclosing NYT, 6/5/1951).

542 **"from people" & "misconceptions"**: FF to CCB, 7/2/1951, at 1.

542 **"amending"**: STLPD, 6/5/1951 at 2C, in FFHLS, Pt. I, Reel 46, Page 27.

542 **dismissed**: FF to Dilliard, 6/8/1951, FFHLS, Pt. I, Reel 46, at Page 26; FF to CCB, 7/2/1951, at 1; The Nation, 6/15/1951, at 52–53.

542 **"very moving"**: Dilliard to FF, 6/6/1951, at 1, FFHLS, Pt. I, Reel 46, Page 24.

542 **"very persuasive"**: Niebuhr to FF, 6/20/1951, *id.* at Page 45. ZC to Bernard Freyd, 10/26/1951, at 2, ZCP, Reel 3, Page 385.

542 **peeved**: LH to FF, 6/8/1951, FFLC, Box 64.

542 **"the voice"**: FF to LH, 4/2/1952, LHP, Box 105C, Folder 105-17. See Michal R. Belknap, "Why *Dennis v. United States* is a Landmark Case," Journal of Supreme Court History 34 (2009): 289; William M. Wiecek, "The Legal Foundations of Domestic Anticommunism: The Background of *Dennis v. United States*," Supreme Court Review (2001): 375; Michal R. Belknap, "*Dennis v. United States*: Great Case or Cold War Relic?" Journal of Supreme Court History 18 (1993): 41.

542 **body of work**: AMB Int. with Lash, 9/12/1974, at 4, Lash Papers, Box 51, Folder 6 (arguing *Dennis* concurrence should be read in conjunction with *Sweezy* concurrence).

543 **"Bitter" & "does" & "accuser"**: Sacher v. United States, 343 U.S. 1, 23–24, 28 (1952) (Frankfurter, J., dissenting). See RHJ to FF, 11/23/1953, FFHLS, Pt. III, Reel 2, Page 270; FF to RHJ, 11/23/1953, *id.* at 271.

543 **"grayer"**: JA to IB, circa 1951, at 3, IBP, Box 239, Page 54.

543   **Laski:** FF, "Tribute to Harold Laski," Vol. XLVI, No. 1, Clare Market Review (Michelmas, 1950): 51–3 in FFLC, Box 199.

543   **Houston:** FF to Donald Murray, 5/11/1950, FFLC, Box 67.

543   **massive library:** FF to James Warburg, 9/25/1952, at 1, MLP, Box 14, Folder 9.

543   **attended Stimson's:** NYT, 10/24/1950, at 30.

543   **honorary pallbearer:** NYT, 11/14/1950, at 32.

543   **"have not":** JA to IB, circa 1951, at 3, IBP, Box 239, Page 54.

543   **"seems":** JA to IB, circa 1951, at 2, IBP, Box 239, Page 57.

544   **"the trouble":** FF to LH, 12/15/1950, at 2, LHP, Box 105B, Folder 105-15. *See* FF to CCB, 2/25/1952, at 1, FFLC, Box 36.

544   **"singularly":** WP, 4/28/1951, at 6.

544   **"condemn" & "exploiting":** FF to PG, 4/28/1951, Pt. III, Reel 16, Page 75.

544   **"to cross":** JA to IB, circa 1951, at 2–3, Pages 53–54.

544   **"shiver":** FF to CCB, 3/27/1952, at 2, FFLC, Box 36.

544   **"disgraceful":** FF to CCB, 9/9/1951, at 2, *id.*

544   **disqualifying:** FF *Prichard* Docket Book, FFHLS, Pt. I, Reel 44, Page 73.

544   **Trumbo & Lawson:** JA to IB, circa 1951, at 2–3, Pages 53–54.

544   **"Felix Frankfurter's":** CT, 12/23/1950, at 4.

544   **"Please":** EFP to PE, 1/9/1951, PEP, Box, Folder 2-30.

544   **"His experience":** FF to PE, circa 1/1951, *id.*, at 1–2.

545   **"Don't":** EFP to FF, 12/8/1951, at 2, FFLC, Box 91.

545   **sad:** IB to MDF, 1/3/1952, in IB, *Enlightening: Letters 1946–1960*, at 269; Campbell, *Short of the Glory*, 184–200; Schlesinger, Jr., "'Prich': A New Deal Memoir."

545   **"man" & "unswerving":** 95 Cong. Rec. 14150–51 (1950).

545   **answered questions:** "Hearings Regarding Communism in the United States Government—Part 2, Hearings before the Committee on Un-American Activities House of Representatives, 81st Cong, 2d Sess. (September 15, 1950): 2959–64 (government service); *id.* at 2965–67 (Crum); *id.* at 2968–69 (National Lawyers' Guild); *id.* at 2974–75, 2978–79 (International Juridical Association); *id.* at 2980–81 (radical lawyer).

545   **book:** ML, *The Federal Bureau of Investigation* (1950).

545   **admired:** FF to ML, 9/27/1952, at 2, FFLC, Box 78.

545   **"you sure":** JLR Int. by Lash, 12/5/1984, at 1, Lash Papers, Box 65, Folder 2.

545–546 **"utterly" & "One may":** 95 Cong. Rec. 15781 (1950).

546   **Remington's ex-wife:** BaltSun, 12/29/1950, at 1.

546   **"the second":** AtlConst, 1/5/1951, at 13.

546   **"a pushful" & "study-boys":** Cincinnati Enquirer, 1/2/1951, at 3. Remington was convicted of perjury, which was reversed on appeal, only to be convicted again. The second time, over LH's dissent, the conviction was affirmed. The Supreme Court fell one vote shy of agreeing to hear Remington's case; FF was one of three justices who voted to hear it. FF to LH, 3/3/1954, at 3, LHP, Box 105C, Folder 105-20. Eight months before his release, Remington was murdered in prison. Gary May, *Un-American Activities* (1994); Gerald Gunther, *Learned Hand*, 612–25 (1994).

546   **Frankfurter left:** FF Miscellaneous Docket Book 1950 Term, Hiss v. US Entry, FFHLS, Pt. I, Reel 54, Page 165.

546   **4–2:** Hiss v. US Docket entry, 1950 Term, HHBP, Box 193, Folder 16; Hiss v. US Docket Entry, WODP, Box 199, Folder 1.

546 **Douglas wrote:** WOD, *Go East, Young Man*, 378–79 (1974).

546 **grateful & never tried:** AH, *Recollections of a Life*, 16.

546 **Erwin Griswold:** MDH to FF, 5/14/1963, at 1, FFHLS, Pt. III, Reel 16, Page 885; FF to MDH, 5/16/1963, *id.*, Page 887; FF to PAF, 5/16/1963, at 2, *id.*, Reel 38, Page 334; EG to FF, 6/3/1963, *id.*, Reel 16, Page 530.

547 **bar license:** G. Edward White, "The Reinstatement of Alger Hiss's Law License," 8 Green Bag 2d 383 (2005).

547 **Venona project:** John Earl Haynes et al., *Spies* (2009); Kai Bird and Svetlana Chervonnaya, "The Mystery of Ales," American Scholar (Summer 2007): 20–35; John Ehrman, "The Mystery of 'ALES,'" Studies in Intelligence, 51, No. 4 (2007), https://www.cia.gov/static/2216f2c9852468f9e6d2fa8ca89034fd/once-again-alger-hiss.pdf.

CHAPTER 32: THE FIRST SOLID PIECE OF EVIDENCE THERE REALLY IS A GOD

548 ***Independence* & Key West:** Log of President Truman's Tenth Visit to Key West, Florida, 11/21/1951, at 22–23, Log 10, HSTL.

548 **declined:** HST, *Memoirs: Years of Trial and Hope, 1946–1952*, 489–90 (1955).

548 **shivers:** FF to CCB, 3/27/1952, at 2.

548 **high hopes:** FF to RHJ, 6/12/1946, at 1, FFHLS, Pt. III, Reel 2, Page 77.

549 **"decent" & "shallow":** FF to LH, 4/15/1952, at 2, LHP, Box 105C, Folder 105-17.

549 **"Tonight" & "These are":** Radio and Television Address to the American People on the Need for Government Operation of the Steel Mills, 4/8/1952, Public Papers, Harry S Truman 1945–1953.

549 **"not fit" & "could not":** *Id.* HST, *Memoirs: Years of Trial and Hope, 1946–1952*, at 471–78; Maeva Marcus, *Truman and the Steel Seizure Case* (1977).

549 **phoned:** Transcript of Proceedings before Judge Alexander Holtzoff, 4/9/1952, in Transcript of Record, Youngstown Sheet & Tube Co. et al. v. Sawyer, No. 744 & No. 745 (May 2, 1952) at 219.

550 **"the balance":** *Id.* at 266.

550 **disqualified:** Transcript of Proceedings before Judge Walter Bastian, 4/10/1952, *id.* at 268.

550 **"Our position":** Transcript of Proceedings before Judge David A. Pine, 4/24/1952, *id.* at 362.

550 **"unlimited" & "He has" & "I suppose" & unreviewable:** *Id.* at 371–72.

550 **"It is":** *Id.* at 380.

550 **District of Columbia Circuit:** *Id.* at 440–49. Youngstown Sheet & Tube Co. v. Sawyer, 103 F. Supp. 569 (D.D.C. 1952); Sawyer v. United States Steel Co. et al., 197 F. 2d 582 (D.C. Cir. 1952).

550–551 **"what will" & "deepest":** HHB *Youngstown* Conference Notes, 5/3/1952, at 2–4, HHBP, Box 211, Folder 1.

551 **deny certiorari & Only Burton:** HHBD, 5/3/1952, Reel 3; FF *Youngstown* Docket Book and Conference Notes, 5/3/1952, FFHLS, Pt. I, Reel 60, Page 19; Youngstown Sheet & Tube Co. v. Sawyer, 343 U.S. 937, 938 (1952) (Memorandum of Burton, J., joined by Frankfurter, J.).

551 **"the best":** FF to LH, 5/8/1952, at 1–2, LHP, Box 105C, Folder 105-17. *See* LH to FF, 5/6/1952, *id.*

551 **"Had you":** FF to CCB, 5/15/1952, at 1, CCBP, Box 5, Folder 5-11.

551   **300 people:** NYT, 5/13/1952, at 14; CT, 5/13/1952, at 1; BaltSun, 5/13/1952, at 1; Eugene
       (Ore.) Register-Guard, 5/15/1952, at 12.

551   **"folly" & "is sizzling":** FF to CCB, 5/15/1952, at 1, CCBP, Box 5, Folder 5-11.

551   **questioned candidate:** Brad Snyder, *The House of Truth*, 367–74 (2017).

552   **fifty-three minutes:** LCJ, 5/13/1952, at 14.

552   *Midwest Oil:* Youngstown Oral Argument Transcript at 893, in *Landmark Briefs and
       Arguments of the Supreme Court of the United States*, Vol. 48 (Philip B. Kurland & Ger-
       hard Casper, eds., 1975) (FF asking about United States v. Midwest Oil Co., 236 U.S,
       459 (1915)).

552   **Vinson:** *Id.* at 896–897.

552   **"Why does" & "This strange":** FF to RHJ, n.d., & FF to Jackson, n.d., RHJP, Box
       176, Folder 2.

552   **president's conduct:** *Youngstown* Oral Argument Transcript at 885–89.

552   **Article II:** *Id.* at 889–94.

552   **Baldridge's assertions:** *Id.* at 895.

552   **"In questions":** *Id.* at 900 (quoting Jefferson's Kentucky Resolution).

552   **unimpressed:** RHJ to FF, circa July 1952, at 2, FFHLS, Pt. III, Reel 2, Page 249 ("Noth-
       ing becomes Perlman's official life like his quitting of it.").

552   **striped pants:** NYT, 5/13/1952, at 1.

553   **"any legal":** *Youngstown* Oral Argument Transcript at 907–8, 937.

553   **"specifically":** *Id.* at 912.

553   **"tall" & "I point" & "Justice Frankfurter":** *Id.* at 916.

553   **presidential seizures:** *Id.* at 917–21, 928.

553   **Defense Production Act:** *Youngstown* Oral Argument Transcript at 957.

553   **"This is" & "police" & war-related & "But he":** *Id.* at 959–60.

553   **"absurd" & "an artist":** FF to CCB, 5/19/1952, at 1–2, CCBP, Box 5, Folder 5-11. *See*
       HHBD, 5/13/1952, Reel 3.

553   **Vinson:** FF *Youngstown* Conference Notes, at 1–2, 5/16/1952, FFHLS, Pt. I, Reel 59,
       Pages 423–24.

554   **"to supply" & "no doubt":** WOD *Youngstown* Conference Notes, 5/16/1952, at 2, WODP,
       Box 221, Folder 1.

554   **"a defiance" & "world":** WOD *Youngstown* Conference Notes at 4.

554   **"world":** HHB *Youngstown* Conference Notes, 5/16/1952, at 1–2, HHBP, Box
       211, Folder 1.

554   **"irrelevant":** RHJ *Youngstown* Conference Notes at 1, RHJP, Box 174, Folder 2 & WOD
       Youngstown Conference Notes at 2 & FF *Youngstown* Conference Notes at 3 & HHB
       Youngstown Conference Notes at 3.

554   **"The President":** RHJ *Youngstown* Conference Notes at 1.

554   **Reed, taking:** RHJ *Youngstown* Conference Notes at 2 & WOD *Youngstown* Conference
       Notes at 7 & FF *Youngstown* Conference Notes at 4 & HHB *Youngstown* Conference
       Notes at 4–6.

554   **all the justices:** WOD *Youngstown* Conference Notes at 8.

554   **contrast to Black:** RHJ *Youngstown* Conference Notes at 2; WOD *Youngstown* Confer-
       ence Notes at 9.

554   **Brandeis's *Myers*:** HHB *Youngstown* Conference Notes at 9 & WOD *Youngstown* Confer-
       ence Notes at 11.

554   **"a legislative":** HHB *Youngstown* Conference Notes at 10 & RHJ *Youngstown* Conference

Notes at 2 & WOD *Youngstown* Conference Notes at 11 & FF *Youngstown* Conference Notes at 5.

554   **"can throw"**: WOD *Youngstown* Conference Notes at 12.

554   **"little"**: RHJ *Youngstown* Conference Notes at 2.

554   **Burton read:** WOD *Youngstown* Conference Notes at 12–13 & RHJ *Youngstown* Conference Notes at 3 & FF *Youngstown* Conference Notes at 5–6.

554   **Clark & Minton:** WOD *Youngstown* Conference Notes at 13–16 & HHB *Youngstown* Conference Notes at 11–12 & RHJ *Youngstown* Conference Notes at 3 & FF *Youngstown* Conference Notes at 6.

555   **"stem" & "The Founders"**: Youngstown Sheet & Tube Co. v. Sawyer, 343 U.S. 579, 585, 589 (1952).

555   **congratulated & disclaimer:** FF to HLB, n.d., HLB Papers, Box 313, Folder 4.

555   **"complicated"**: Youngstown Sheet & Tube Co. v. Sawyer, 343 U.S. at 589 (Frankfurter, J.).

555   **wrote separately:** HLB opinion, 5/28/1952, HLB Papers, Box 313, Folder 4 (noting FF, WOD, RHJ, and HHB joined and HHB writing concurrence); Abram Chayes Int. with Michael Parrish, 7/16/1974, at 5–6 (recalling FF joined HLB's opinion over Chayes's objection and to ensure a five-justice majority opinion).

555   **"necessity" & "rigid"**: FF to CCB, 6/8/1952, at 2, CCBP, Box 5, Folder 5-11.

555   **"greatest" & "it is *a constitution*" & "to avoid"**: Youngstown, 343 U.S. at 596 (Frankfurter, J., concurring) (quoting McCulloch v. Maryland, 17 U.S. 316, 407 (1819)).

555   **not authorized:** *Id.* at 597–609.

555   **"comprehensively"**: *Id.* at 597.

555   **"[t]he Constitution" & "Deeply" & "a systematic" & "as a gloss"**: *Id.* at 610–11.

556   **history of presidential seizures:** Youngstown, 343 U.S. at 611–14 & App. I, *id.* at 615–28 (Frankfurter, J., concurring); Chayes Int. with Parrish, 7/16/1974, at 5 (recalling FF instructed clerks to prepare chart while case still in the district court).

556   **"not to promote" & "not to avoid" & "inevitable friction" & "not a pleasant" & "exceeded" & "that the President"**: Youngstown, 343 U.S. at 613–14 (quoting *Myers v. United States*, 272 U.S. 52, 293 (1926) (Brandeis, J., dissenting)).

556   **"at its maximum" & "a zone" & "at its lowest"**: Youngstown, 343 U.S. at 635–37 (Jackson, J., concurring).

556   **coal mines:** United States v. United Mine Workers of America, 330 U.S. 258, 261 (1947).

556   **concurring opinion:** Youngstown, 343 U.S. at 660 (Clark, J., concurring in the judgment).

556   **Clark credited:** TCC to FF, 5/31/1952, TCCP, Box B48.

557   **"an important"**: FF to TCC, 5/31/1952, *id.*

557   **upset.** Merle Miller quoted HST calling TCC "his biggest mistake" and "such a dumb son of a bitch." Merle Miller, *Plain Speaking*, 225–26 (1974). HST's comments about TCC are not on the log of the tapes in Miller's papers, only in Miller's typewritten notes. *See* Notes in Tom Clark file, Merle Miller Papers, Box 5 (noting HST's regret about nominating TCC with similar quotations). Scholars have cast serious doubt on Miller's quotations. *See* Alexander Wohl, *Father, Son, and Constitution*, 148–49 (2013); Alexander Wohl, "Writing biography in the age of Wikipedia," SCOTUSblog, 9/23/2013 9:35 a.m., https://www.scotusblog.com/2013/09/writing-biography-in-the-age-of-wikipedia-removing-a-shadow-from-the-life-of-justice-tom-clark/ (noting historian Robert H. Ferrell did not find HST's derogatory quotation about TCC on Mil-

ler's tapes); Robert H. Ferrell & Francis H. Heller, "Plain Faking?" American Heritage, 5–6/1995 (questioning veracity of Miller's book and accusing him of adding profanity into HST's quotations).

557 **Vinson read:** HHBD, 6/2/1952, Reel 3.

557 **international issues:** Youngstown, 343 U.S. at 668–69 (Vinson, C.J., dissenting).

557 **"duty":** *Id.* at 671–72.

557 **"the President's":** *Id.* at 679 (emphasis in original).

557 **"judicial":** *Id.* at 710.

557 **The drafter:** Handwritten drafts *Youngstown* dissent, Howard Trienens Papers, Box 2, Folders 19–21.

557 **"He felt":** Trienens Int. by Terry L. Birdwhistell, 2/28/1975, FMV OH Project 26:46.

557 **"off the record":** HST Appointment Calendar, 2/25/1952 (6:00 p.m. meeting); *id.,* 4/2/1952 (FMV at state dinner); *id.,* 4/8/1952 (FMV 1:00 p.m.); HHBD, 4/8/1952, Reel 3 (HST steak lunch at the Court, FF absent); HST Appointment Calendar, 4/14/1952 (FMV 1:00 p.m. stag luncheon for Swedish prime minister); *id.,* 5/2/1952 (FMV 1:00 p.m. stag luncheon for Nicaraguan president); *id.,* 6/20/1952 (5:00 p.m. FMV "off-the-record" meeting in president's study).

557 **"The only thing":** FF to PE, 7/10/1952, at 1, PEP, Box 2, Folder 45 & Silber, *With All Deliberate Speed,* 130–31 (2004).

557 **"I just":** RHJ to FF, 7/12/1952, at 1, FFHLS, Pt. III, Reel 2, Page 246. FMV's rival, Truman's secretary of the treasury, John Snyder, repeated the rumors to historians. Robert J. Donovan, *Tumultuous Years,* 386 (1982). FMV's biographers claim Snyder had an axe to grind, but HST's daughter Margaret also repeated the story. James E. St. Clair & Linda C. Gugin, *Chief Justice Fred M. Vinson of Kentucky,* 216–18 (2002). FF and RHJ's contemporaneous suspicions, coupled with FMV's frequent access to the president, support Snyder's story.

558 **"a bit":** WOD, *Go East Young Man,* 450 (1974).

558 **steak:** HHBD, 6/9/1952, Reel 3.

558 **"excellent":** FF to HLB, 7/16/1952, at 2, HLBP, Box 60.

558 **"I have little":** FF to PE, 7/10/1952, at 2 & Silber, *With All Deliberate Speed,* 131.

558 **"What is":** FF to TCC, 7/5/1952, at 8, TCCP, Box B48.

558 **short concurrence:** HHBD, 5/10/1952 & 5/21/1952 & 5/28/1952, Reel 3.

558 **related to Clark:** RHJ Appointment Calendar, 5/3/1952, RHJP, Box 207, Folder 1 (2:00 p.m. lunch with TCC after steel seizure cert grant); *id.,* 5/12/1952 (possible 1:00 p.m. lunch with TCC after steel seizure conference).

558 **helped Clark:** TCC to FF, 5/31/1952.

559 **"shocks" & "decencies":** Rochin v. California, 342 U.S. 165, 172–73 (1952).

559 **"accordion-like":** *Id.* at 177 (Black, J., concurring).

559 **"erosion":** *Id.* at 179 (Douglas, J., concurring).

559 **Hand questioned:** FF to LH, 1/17/1952, LHP, Box 105C, Folder 105-17 (troubled that LH read *Rochin* as interpreting the Due Process Clause as a "jural command"); FF to LH, 1/11/1952, at 1–2, *id.;* Chayes Int. with Parrish, 7/16/1974, at 6 (explaining *Rochin* as FF's "existential response to the kind of brutal, physical intrusion by the police").

559 **"Some tough":** RHJ to FF, 8/16/1952, at 4, FFHLS, Pt. III, Reel 2, Page 253.

559 **"became":** PE, "The Solicitor General's Office, Justice Frankfurter, and Civil Rights Litigation, 1946-1960: An Oral History," 100 Harv. L. Rev. 817, 839 (1987) & PE Int. by Silber 250 (1986) (Columbia Oral History Project, Interview 4).

559 **Justice Department & prosecutors & judges:** A. H. Belmont to D. M. Ladd, 3/16/1951, FBI File, Julius Rosenberg HQ Files, Vol. 17, #894; Ladd to FBI Dir., 4/3/1951, in The Kaufman Papers (National Committee to Reopen the Rosenberg Case, 1976); Roy M. Cohn & Sidney Zion, *The Autobiography of Roy Cohn*, 65–70 (1988).

559 **"worse":** United States v. Rosenberg, 195 F.2d 583, 605 n.28 (2d Cir. 1952). *See* Brad Snyder, "Taking Great Cases: Lessons from the *Rosenberg* Case," 63 Vand. L. Rev. 885 (2010); Ronald Radosh & Joyce Milton, *The Rosenberg File* (2nd ed. 1997); Michael E. Parrish, "Justice Douglas and the Rosenberg Case: A Rejoinder," 70 Cornell L. Rev. 1048 (1985); William Cohen, "Justice Douglas and the *Rosenberg* Case: Setting the Record Straight," 70 Cornell L. Rev. 211 (1984); Michael E. Parrish, "Cold War Justice: The Supreme Court and the Rosenbergs," American Historical Review 82, no. 4 (1977): 805.

560 **"a case" & Black & "strong" & "with startling":** FF, Memorandum: Re: Rosenberg v. United States, Nos. 111 and 687, October Term 1952, 6/4/1953, at 1–2, FFHLS, Pt. I, Reel 70, at 249–50. FF's memorandum and addendum dated June 19, 1953, are based on contemporaneous handwritten notes. *See id.* at 243–48, 311–12, 428. FF's law clerk, AMB, wrote the first draft on the basis of those notes and after heavy editing by FF submitted the final draft at the end of his clerkship. AMB to FF, 8/22/1953, at 4, FFHLS, Pt. III, Reel 31, Page 752.

560 **"heightened":** FF, Memorandum: Re: Rosenberg v. United States, 6/4/1953, at 2.

560 **clemency:** Rosenberg v. United States, 344 U.S. 889, 890 (1952) (Frankfurter, J.); Memorandum re: Rosenberg v. United States, 6/4/1953, at 3.

560 **"betrayed":** NYT, 2/12/1953, at 17.

560 **week of March 9:** NYT, 2/17/1953, at 1.

560 **Saypol & rejected:** United States v. Rosenberg, 108 F. Supp. 798 (S.D.N.Y. 1952).

560 **"wholly":** United States v. Rosenberg, 200 F.2d 666, 670 (2d Cir. 1952).

561 **"I charge" & "in the same":** FF, Memorandum: Re: Rosenberg v. United States, 6/4/1953, at 4. FF Docket Sheet, No. 687 Rosenberg v. United States, FFHLS, Pt. I, Reel 72, Page 990 ("WOD – *deny, without a word.*") (emphasis in original).

561 **"a real" & "I cannot":** FF, Memorandum: re: Rosenberg v. United States, 6/4/1953, at 5–6.

561 **"the Court's" & "moral" & "feeding":** FF, Memorandum for the Conference, at 1, 5/20/1953, FFHLS, Pt. I, Reel 70, Page 566.

561 **"wholly":** WOD, Memorandum to Conference, 5/22/1953, FFHLS, Pt. I, Reel 70, Page 568.

561 **"the end" & "to sleep":** FF, Memorandum to Conference, 5/22/1953, *id.*, Page 570.

561 **Burton in chambers:** HHB Diary Entry, 5/22/1953, HHBP, Reel 3.

561 **"puts" & "a cloud" & "heedless":** FF to HHB, 5/23/1953, at 1–2, FFHLS, Pt. 1, Reel 70, Pages 571–72.

562 **"Don't" & "the dirtiest":** FF, Memorandum: re: Rosenberg v. United States, 6/4/1953, at 6.

562 **"bluff":** FF, Memorandum: re: Rosenberg v. United States, 6/4/1953, at 9.

562 **"prejudicial" & "in an impossible" & "It was":** *Id.* at 7.

562 **"What he":** *Id.* at 8.

562 **Jackson withdrew:** Docket Sheet No. 687, WODP, Box 222 & Docket Sheet No. 687, HHBP, Box 222.

562 **"That S.O.B.'s":** FF, Memorandum: re: Rosenberg v. United States, 6/4/1953, at 9.

562 **visited Black:** AMB Int. with Kluger, at 1, 8/20/1971, BvBP, Box 1, Folder 4 & AMB Int. with Lash, 9/12/1974, at 5, Lash Papers, Box 51, Folder 6.

562   **shingles:** HLB to FMV, 5/19/1953, HLBP, Box 314.

562   **Josephine & children:** FF-HLB early 1950s Correspondence, HLBP, Box 60; Hugo Black, Jr., *My Father*, 229–30 (1975).

562   **"untrue" & "wholly":** FF, Memorandum: re: Rosenberg v. United States, 6/4/1953, at 9.

563   **console table:** Trial Transcript at 739 (direct examination of David Greenglass); Trial Transcript at 900–901 (cross examination of David Greenglass); Trial Transcript at 1013–14 (direct examination of Ruth Greenglass); Trial Transcript at 1564, 1689–90 (direct examination of Julius Rosenberg); Trial Transcript at 1791–1802 (cross examination of Julius Rosenberg); Trial Transcript at 1930–31, 1933–34A (direct examination of Ethel Rosenberg); Trial Transcript at 2025–27 (cross examination of Ethel Rosenberg); Trial Transcript at 2221–24 (defense counsel Emanuel Bloch's summation); Trial Transcript at 2298–99 (prosecutor Irving Saypol's summation).

563   **"was important":** Malcolm P. Sharp, *Was Justice Done?* 111 (1956).

563   **denied the motions:** *Id.* at 158–59; NYT, 6/9/1953, at 13; Radosh & Milton, *Rosenberg File*, at 360–66.

563   **"pre-trial":** Petition for Stay to Justice Jackson, at 4–5, June 12, 1953, NARA, RG 267, Box 607–687 O.T. 1952 4 of 5, Folder 687 O.T. 1952.

563   **recommended:** *Id.* at 1 (RHJ handwritten note).

563   **voted:** Rosenberg v. United States, 346 U.S. 273, 280–81 n.7 (1953); Rosenberg v. United States, 345 U.S. 989 (1953) & FFHLS, Pt. I, Reel 70, Page 573 & FF, "Addendum" 6/19/1953, at 1, *id.*, Page 584.

564   **"every time":** FF "Addendum" 6/19/1953, at 4.

564   **invited:** Marquis Childs, *Witness to Power*, 48–49 (1975); Marquis W. Childs COH, 11/6/1957, at 83–84; WP, 6/20/1953, at 9; STLPD, 6/19/1953, at 3B.

564   **"[You've] got" & "Oh! no!":** FF, "Addendum," 6/19/1953, at 1 & FF Handwritten Notes, FFHLS, Pt. I, Reel 70, at 243. *See* Mooney v. Holohan, 294 U.S. 103, 112 (1935) (per curiam) (declaring due process violation because of "a deliberate deception of court and jury by the presentation of testimony known to be perjured").

564   **Black and Frankfurter:** Rosenberg v. Denno, 346 U.S. 271, 271–72 (1953) (per curiam); Rosenberg v. United States, 345 U.S. 1003, 1003–1004 (June 15, 1953) (petition for rehearing denied) (FF refused to disclose vote, HLB said petition should be granted).

564   **two new lawyers:** FF, Addendum, 6/19/1953, at 2–4 & FF, Memorandum, 6/16/1953, at 1–3, FFHLS, Pt. I, Reel 70, Pages 305–7.

564   **with Vinson:** Transcript of Conversations between Justice William O. Douglas and Professor Walter Murphy, 4/5/1963, at 4, Tape 15 ; Mercedes Eichholz tel. int. with author, 4/2/2008.

564   **Sheraton:** In May 1953, Sheraton purchased the Wardman Park and renamed it the Sheraton Park. WP, 5/27/1953, at 25.

565   **"very":** HLB to WOD, 6/17/1953, WODP, Box 234.

565   **"Do" & "this was":** FF, "Addendum," 6/19/1953, at 5–6.

565   **chief justice's apartment:** Robert L. Stern, "The Rosenberg Case in Perspective—Its Present Significance," Journal of Supreme Court History 15 (1990): 79, 82–83. The Brownell-Vinson meeting is also memorialized in a fourth-hand account in an FBI memo that is based on what Assistant U.S. Attorney James B. Kilsheimer III told Judge Irving Kaufman, who told the FBI's New York supervisor Tom McAndrews that "last night on the recommendation of Justice Jackson, the Attorney General and Chief Justice Vinson met at 11:00 P.M. to determine whether to call the complete Court into

session . . ." Belmont to Ladd, 6/17/1953, FBI, Julius & Ethel Rosenberg Headquarters File, Vol. 32, Pt. 2, #1823. There is no evidence, however, that RHJ "arranged," much less attended, the Vinson-Brownell meeting. Stern did not recall RHJ's presence or involvement. Stern, "The Rosenberg Case," at 83.

565 **met again & conferred & spoke by phone:** Chief Justice's Log, May–Sept. 1953, 6/17/1953, FMVP, Box, 299, Folder 13 (meeting Brownell in chambers from 12:25 to 1:10 p.m., HHB, TCC & RHJ from 2:15 to 3:30 p.m. & 4:45 to 5:50 p.m., and phoning out-of-town justices). The first special term was in *Ex Parte Quirin*; the second was in denying the original writ of habeas corpus on June 15 in the *Rosenberg* case. *Rosenberg v. United States*, 346 U.S. 273, 281–82 (1953).

565 **phoned Frankfurter:** FF, "Addendum," 6/19/1953, at 6.

565 **porch:** JLR, "Felix Frankfurter: Civil Libertarian," 11 Harv. C.R.-C.L. 496, 514 (1976). *See* Parrish, "Cold War Justice," 835 n.84 (JLR int.).

565 **"unjudicious" & "haste" & "grandstand":** JLR, "An Unabashed Liberal Looks at a Half-Century of the Supreme Court," 69 N.C. L. Rev. 213, 225 (1990).

565 **Black objected:** Rosenberg v. United States, 346 U.S. 273, 296 (1953) (Black, J., dissenting); HLB to TCC, n.d., TCCP, Box A26, Folder 9 (arguing chief justice did not convene special term in *Quirin* on his own); WOD to FR, 6/25/1953, at 1, FRP, Box 1, Folder 827 (entire Court not polled).

565 **law clerk's:** Law Clerk Memorandum re: Application of Attorney General, at 1, n.d., FMVP, Box 284, Folder 6.

566 **blamed Clerk:** FMV's chief clerk James C. N. Paul tel. int. with author, 11/25/2008 (hearing story from FF's clerk AMB that FMV said, "Well, Willey said I could").

566 **twelve minutes:** CT, 6/19/1953, at 4.

566 **"in advance":** WOD to FR, 6/25/1953, at 2.

566 **"The fact is":** FMV draft, 7/3/1953, at 7, FFHLS, Pt. I, Reel 70, Page 413 (FF handwritten).

566 **"a race":** TCC *Rosenberg* Conference Notes, 6/18/1953, at 2–3, TCCP, Box A26, Folder 9. *See* HHB *Rosenberg* Conference Notes, 6/18/1953, at 1, HHBP, Box 238, Folder 4.

566 **"screaming":** William Oliver Int. by Terry L. Birdwhistell, 2/26/1975, at 00:29, FMV OH Project.

566 **"it is never":** TCC *Rosenberg* Conference Notes, 6/18/1953, at 6.

566 **voted:** HHB *Rosenberg* Conference Notes, 6/18/1953, at 7; Handwritten Notes and Docket Sheet, June 18, 1953, WODP, Box 222; Handwritten Notes, FFHLS, Pt. I, Reel 70, at 245–48.

566 **6:29 p.m.:** NYT, 6/19/1953, at 1; HHBD, 6/18/1953, Reel 3.

566 **Around 11:00 a.m.:** HHBD, 6/19/1953 (10:45 a.m.) & Chief Justice's Log, 6/19/1953 (11:00 a.m.).

566 **"in a low":** LAT, 6/20/1953, at 4.

566 **"emotion-filled" & "a high-pitched":** WP, 6/20/1953, at 1.

566 **"wholly":** Rosenberg v. United States, 346 U.S. 273, 297 (1953) (Black, J., dissenting).

567 **"complicated":** Rosenberg, 346 U.S. at 289.

567 **"I am" & "pathetic" & "But history":** Id. at 310 (Frankfurter, J., dissenting).

567 **praised:** LH to FF, 7/6/1953, at 1, FFHLS, Pt. III, Reel 27, Page 327 ("You were at your best in re Rosenberg; really, the only one of the Nine to be right."); PAF to FF, 9/3/1953, at 4, FFLC, Box 56; PE to FF, 6/25/1953, FFLC, Box 53; WTC to FF, 9/4/1953, at 1, FFHLS, Pt. I, Reel 70, Page 236; David Ginsburg to FF, 7/27/1953, id. at 285.

567 **"for the sake":** PE to FF, 7/15/1953, FFLC, Box 53.

567 **"This isn't":** PE Int. by Silber, at 251 & Silber, *With All Deliberate Speed*, 218.

567 **8:31 & moved them up:** NYT, 6/19/1953, at 45; NYT, 6/20/1953, at 1, 6.

567 **"leverage":** Posting of Sam Roberts to N.Y. Times City Room Blog, 6/26/2008, *Podcast: Spies & Secrecy*, http://cityroom.blogs.nytimes.com/2008/06/26/podcast-spies-and-secrecy/ (based on int. with Deputy Attorney General William P. Rogers).

568 **David admitted:** Sam Roberts, *The Brother* (2001); David Greenglass Grand Jury Transcript, 8/7/1950, at 9173, 9191 (on file with author) (not mentioning console table & denying having spoken to sister about atomic secrets); Ruth Greenglass Grand Jury Transcript, 8/3/1950 (on file with author) (not mentioning typewriter).

568 **ten days:** Radosh and Milton, *Rosenberg File*, 162–67, 197–98.

568 **spy ring:** Memorandum, Information about the Work of Camp-2, 1/8/1945, https://www.nsa.gov/news-features/declassified-documents/venona/dated/1945/assets/files/8jan_victor.pdf; Memorandum, Julius's recruitment of Ruth Greenglass, 9/21/1944, https://www.nsa.gov/news-features/declassified-documents/venona/dated/1944/assets/files/21sep_recruitment_by_rosenbergs.pdf.

568 **Ethel knew:** Memorandum, Ethel Rosenberg's knowledge of the conspiracy, 11/27/1944, in https://www.nsa.gov/news-features/declassified-documents/venona/dated/1944/assets/files/27nov_mrs_rosenberg.pdf; Steven T. Usdin, "The Rosenberg Ring Revealed," Journal of Cold War Studies 11, no. 3 (2009): 140–43; Anne Sebba, *Ethel Rosenberg*, 223–25, 257 (2021).

568 **"the most":** FF, Memorandum, 6/4/1953, at 1.

568 **did not believe & troubled:** FF to at CCB, 6/24/1953, at 1–3, FFLC, Box 37 (describing the case as "trying and unedifying," not Sacco-Vanzetti whom he was "reasonably sure" were "innocent," but troubled by allegations against Saypol); FF to Herbert Feis, at 2, 6/29/1953, Feis Papers, Box 34 ("not edifying" and "Men's devotion to law is not profoundly rooted"); FF to PE, 7/2/1953, at 2–3. PEP, Box 57, Folder 2 ("unedifying and the softest spoken were perhaps the blindest and thereby the most ruthless," but distinguishing case from Sacco-Vanzetti) & Silber, *With All Deliberate Speed*, 217; FF to JMH, 10/23/1956, at 2, FFHLS, Pt. III, Reel 1, Page 562 ("the manner in which the Court disposed of that case is one of the least edifying episodes in its modern history.").

568 **self-inflicted:** FF to HHB, 5/23/1953, at 2.

568 **"primitive":** FF to PE, 7/2/1953, at 3.

568 **Douglas's grandstanding:** Snyder, "Taking Great Cases," 63 Vand. L. Rev. at 907, 938–41 (accusing WOD of having a "hero complex" and questioning his "inconsistent" votes); Parrish, "Cold War Justice," at 826 (faulting WOD for inconsistent votes); *but see* Cohen, "Justice Douglas and the Rosenberg Case," 70 Cornell L. Rev. at 211, 228–36 (attacking "hostile witnesses" against WOD and defending his inconsistent votes).

569 **Only Burton:** FF to Max Lerner, 5/17/1952, at 2, Lerner Papers, Box 3, Folder 135 (holding HHB "in higher esteem on the score of judicial character" than any other justice); FF to LH, circa 6/15/1953, at 1, LHP, Box 105C, Folder 105-19 (agreeing about HHB's "stainless integrity").

569 **last justice:** Rosenberg v. United States, 346 U.S. 273, 277 n.* (1953) (opinion dated July 16).

569 **"pseudonymous":** FF to PE, 7/18/1953, at 2. Telephone Int. with FMV clerk James C. N. Paul, 11/25/2008 ("He didn't write any of his opinions. He didn't write anything" [referring to FMV's opinions and speeches]).

569 **"in high" & "I'm in" & "Phil":** Silber, *With All Deliberate Speed*, 219.

569 **"an act"**: AMB Int. with Lash, 9/10/1974, at 4. *See* John David Fassett et al., "Supreme Court Clerks' Recollections of *Brown v. Board of Education*," 78 St. John's L. Rev. 515, 531 (2004) (FF clerk Frank E.A. Sander recalling that the justice's line about believing in God occurred in chambers); Jerome Cohen Int. with Parrish, 7/2/1974, at 4 & Cohen Int. with Laura McCreery, 11/19/2004, at 11 (repeating his belief that FMV's death was "the only evidence I ever had of the existence of a divine being").

CHAPTER 33: THE WISE USE OF TIME

570 **In January**: Briggs v. Elliott, 342 U.S. 350 (1952) (per curiam). *See* Briggs v. Elliott, 98 F. Supp. 529 (E.D.S.C. June 23, 1951) (initial order to equalize schools but denying desegregation), 103 F. Supp. 920 (E.D.S.C. March 13, 1952) (detailing procedural history in South Carolina).

570 **"wholly"**: Briggs, 342 U.S. at 352 (Black and Douglas, JJ., dissenting).

570 **"You think"**: Newton Minow Int. with author, 1951 term law clerk to FMV, 9/20/2006.

570 **"embarrassed" & "grow up" & "In retrospect"**: Abner Mikva tel. int. with author, 1951 term clerk to SM, 9/24/2006. *See* CT, 4/23/1978, at H58.

570 **In June 1952**: FF 1951 Term Docket Book, *Briggs v. Elliott* No. 273, FFHLS, Pt. I, Reel 60, Page 423 (issuing per curiam remitting to district court); FF 1951 Term Docket Book, *Briggs* No. 816, *id.* at 971 (noting appeal June 3); FF 1951 Term Docket Book, *Brown v. Board of Education*, No. 436, *id.*, at Page 587 & WOD 1951 Term Docket entry, *Brown v. Board of Education*, No. 436, WODP, Box 1150 (noting HLB and WOD's desire to grant case); WOD 1952 Term Docket entry, *Brown v. Board of Education*, No. 8, *id.*

571 **"Only" & "kept" & "The outcome" & "deny[ing]" & "not a fixed" & "evolution" & "Law must"**: FF, Memorandum, 9/26/1952, at 1–2, EWP, Box 571, Folder 3 (FF handwritten note: "written during the summer of 1952 and revised in September 26, 1952 by F.F.").

572 **"a real"**: AMB Int. with Margie Scarf, 10/28/1974, at 9, AMBP, Box 13, Folder 8, quoted in Laura Kalman, *Yale Law School and the Sixties*, 52 (2005).

572 **passed over**: HMH to FF, 4/13/1950, at 2, FFHLS, Pt. III, Reel 16, Page 598 (passing over AMB because of Weaver Dunnan's friendship with Hugh Calkins and Gus Hand's lobbying for Dunnan).

572 **Chayes & Trautman**: AMB to FF, 4/16/1952, at 1–2, *id.*, Reel 31, Page 745–46; FF to AMB, 4/23/1952, at 1–2, *id.* at Page 747–48; Donald T. Trautman, "A Personal Word," 88 Harv. L. Rev. 695, 695 (1974).

572 **Irish poetry & middle names**: Abram Chayes, "Alexander M. Bickel, A Personal Remembrance," 88 Harv. L. Rev. 693, 693 (1974).

572 **"I am"**: HMH to FF, 4/12/1952, at 1, FFHLS, Pt. III, Reel 16, Page 608.

573 **cart**: AMB Int. with Kluger, 8/20/1971, at 2, BvBP, Box 1, Folder 4.

573 **"I am currently"**: AMB to FF, 8/8/1952, FFHLS, Pt. II, Reel 4, Page 330.

573 **raving**: FF to PE, 8/12/1952, at 2, PEP, Box 2, Folder 2-48.

573 **critical role**: FF to James H. Chadbourn, 11/24/1953, at 1–2, FFHLS, Pt. III, Reel 15, Pages 775–76; PE Int. with Kluger, 8/19/1971, at 1–2, 4, BvBP, Box 2, Folder 27; Norman I. Silber, *With All Deliberate Speed*, 199–201 (2004).

573 **"FF was talking"**: Silber, *With All Deliberate Speed*, 203. *See* PE Int. with Kluger, 8/19/1971, at 2.

574 **"orderly"**: Brief for the United States as Amicus Curiae, *Brown v. Board of Education* at 27 (12/3/1952).

574   "the Frankfurter Way": PE Int. with Kluger, 8/19/1971, at 4. *See* Richard Kluger, *Simple Justice*, 558–61 (1976).

574   "Phil": PE Int. with Kluger, 8/19/1971, at 4. *See* Silber, *With All Deliberate Speed*, 205.

574   judicial ethics: NYT, 3/24/1987, at A30; Randall Kennedy, "A Reply to Philip Elman," 100 Harv. L. Rev. 1938, 1944 (1987).

574   unrepentant: NYT, 4/1/1987, at A30; PE to Kennedy, 7/16/1990, PEP, Box 2, Folder 2-53; PE to PAF, 12/15/1952, *id.* (worrying about outcome of cases); PE to FF, 7/15/1953, at 1, FFLC, Box 53 (worrying about his "role" on brief in 1953).

574   "the one thing": Silber, *With All Deliberate Speed*, 202 & PE Int. by Silber, "The Solicitor General's Office, Justice Frankfurter, and Civil Rights Litigation, 1946–1960: An Oral History," 100 Harv. L. Rev. 817, 827 (1987). *See* PE Int. with Kluger, 8/19/1971, at 4; Kluger, *Simple Justice*, 558.

574   300 people & in line: NYHT, 12/10/1952, at 24; BAA, 12/20/1952, at 7; NYT, 12/10/1952, at 1.

574   "very sensitive" & "long-established" & "should be faced" & "should be overruled": Oral Argument, *Brown v. Board of Education*, 12/9/1952, in *Landmark Briefs and Arguments of the Supreme Court of the United States*, Vol. 49, *at* 289–90 (Philip B. Kurland & Gerhard Casper, eds. 1975).

574   "intended": *Id.* at 294.

574   "the social": *Id.* at 301. *See* Paul E. Wilson, *A Time to Lose* (1995).

575   Elman did not think: PE Int. with Kluger, 8/19/1971, at 4, 6; Kluger, *Simple Justice*, 560.

575   "distinctions": Oral Argument, *Briggs v. Elliott*, 12/9/1952, in *Landmark Briefs and Arguments*, Vol. 49, at 315.

575   natural law & "unreasonable" & "I follow": *Id.* at 316, 318.

575   "more complicated" & "I agree": *Id.* at 319.

575   "only thing" & "I think": *Id.* at 320–21.

575   "John W. Davis!": Marshall Int. with Harbaugh, 10/26/1966, at 8, BvBP, Box 4, Folder 65.

575   A southerner: Kluger, *Simple Justice*, 525–29; William Henry Harbaugh, *Lawyer's Lawyer* (1973).

576   "common" & "in the condition": Oral Argument, *Briggs v. Elliott*, 12/9/1952, in *Landmark Briefs and Arguments*, Vol. 49, at 331.

576   "conditions" & "a living" & "commerce" & "equal": *Id.* at 332–33.

576   "if conditions": *Id.* at 334.

576   black and white dolls: *Id.* at 335–36.

576   "Negroes" & "under": *Id.* at 339.

577   "the solution": *Id.* at 342.

577   "to avoid" & "a problem" & "the rights": *Id.* at 345–46.

577   power to enforce: Oral Argument, *Davis v. County School Board*, 12/10/1952, in *Landmark Briefs and Arguments*, Vol. 49, at 377–79, 386–87.

577   interracial marriage & "legislation": Oral Argument, *Bolling v. Sharpe*, 12/10/1952, *id.* at 406.

577   no vote: HHB Conference Notes, *Brown v. Board of Education*, 12/13/1952, at 7, HHBP, Box 251, Folder 10 & TCC Conference Notes, *Brown v. Board of Education*, 12/13/1952, at 5, TCCP, Box A27, Folder 4. Regarding the Court's conference discussions, I tend to start with HHB's notes because they are the most detailed, reliable, and unbiased. WOD's notes, in particular, tend to cast FF and RHJ in a negative light. After the 1952

term argument, WOD also divided his notes among the different state and D.C. cases instead of writing one set of notes as the other justices did. Even though I start with HHB's notes, I corroborate them with other justices' notes.

577   **"courage" & "wisdom"**: HHB Conference Notes, *Brown v. Board of Education*, 12/13/1952, at 1–2 (guessing he might affirm). *See* TCC Conference Notes, *Brown v. Board of Education*, 12/13/1952, at 1; WOD Conference Notes, *Bolling v. Sharpe*, 12/13/1952, at 1, WODP, Box 1150; RHJ Conference Notes, *Brown v. Board of Education*, 12/12/1952, at 1, RHJP, Box 184, Folder 5.

577–578   **"same" & "per se" & racial violence & front lines:** HHB Conference Notes, *Brown v. Board of Education*, 12/13/1952, at 2–3. *See* WOD Conference Notes, *Bolling v. Sharpe*, 12/13/1952, at 1; TCC Conference Notes, *Brown v. Board of Education*, 12/13/1952, at 2–3; RHJ Conference Notes, *Brown v. Board of Education*, 12/13/1952, at 1–2; FF Conference Notes, *Brown v. Board of Education*, 12/13/1952, at 1, FFHLS, Pt. I, Reel 74, Page 771.

578   **"different" & rights of states:** HHB Conference Notes, *Brown v. Board of Education*, 12/13/1952, at 3–4. *See* WOD Conference Notes, *Brown v. Board of Education*, 12/13/1952, at 2–3; TCC Conference Notes, *Brown v. Board of Education*, 12/13/1952, at 3–4; RHJ Conference Notes, *Brown v. Board of Education*, 12/13/1952, at 2.

578   **reargument & "most important" & District of Columbia's & "intolerable" & "physical things" & "what justifies":** HHB Conference Notes, *Brown v. Board of Education*, 12/13/1952, at 4–6.

578   **Coleman:** WOD Conference Notes, *Bolling v. Sharpe*, 12/13/1952, at 2.

578   **purpose of the Fourteenth Amendment:** WOD Conference Notes, *Brown v. Board of Education*, 12/13/1952, at 3–4 & TCC Conference Notes, *Brown v. Board of Education*, 12/13/1952, at 4–5 & RHJ Conference Notes, *Brown v. Board of Education*, 12/13/1952, at 2.

579   **"very simple":** TCC Conference Notes, *Brown v. Board of Education*, 12/13/1952, at 5.

579   **cannot classify:** RHJ Conference Notes, *Brown v. Board of Education*, 12/13/1952, at 2. *See* HHB Conference Notes, *Brown v. Board of Education*, 12/13/1952, at 6; FF Conference Notes, *Brown v. Board of Education*, 12/13/1952, at 1.

579   **words & "sociology" & "legal" & "would have" & "conscious" & library & "be a party":** HHB Conference Notes, *Brown v. Board of Education*, 12/13/1952, at 7–8. *See* RHJ to Charles Fairman, 3/13/1950, at 1–3, RHJP, Box 12, Folder 10 (describing his "doubts" about how to resolve issue of segregation in education and questions about legislative history of Fourteenth Amendment); RHJ to Fairman, 4/5/1950, *id.*; RHJ to Fairman, 3/13/1950 handwritten draft, *id.*; RHJ handwritten talking points, n.d., *id.*, Box 184, Folder 5 (discussing segregation in education).

579   **"bad" & Congress:** TCC Conference Notes, *Brown v. Board of Education*, 12/13/1952, at 5–6. *See* WOD Conference Notes, *Brown v. Board of Education*, 12/13/1952, at 4; WOD Conference Notes, *Bolling v. Sharpe*, 12/13/1952, at 2.

579   **"crossed" & black nurses & "time to comply":** WOD Conference Notes, *Brown v. Board of Education*, 12/13/1952, at 5–6. *See* TCC Conference Notes, *Brown v. Board of Education*, 12/13/1952, at 6; RHJ Conference Notes, *Brown v. Board of Education*, 12/13/1952, at 3.

579   **same result & Mexican American children:** HHB Conference Notes, *Brown v. Board of Education*, 12/13/1952, at 8.

579   **"led":** WOD Conference Notes, *Brown v. Board of Education*, 12/13/1952, at 5–6 & RHJ Conference Notes, *Brown v. Board of Education*, 12/13/1952, at 3.

579   **"whittled" & "invidious":** WOD Conference Notes, *Brown v. Board of Education*, 12/13/1952, at 7.

579 **"not reasonable" & "segregation":** HHB Conference Notes, *Brown v. Board of Education,* 12/13/1952, at 8–9. *See* TCC Notes, *Brown v. Board of Education,* 12/13/1952, at 6; RHJ Conference Notes, *Brown v. Board of Education,* 12/13/1952, at 3.

580 **delayed:** FF Docket Entry, *Terry v. Adams,* FFHLS, Pt. I, Reel 72, Page 355.

580 **black voters & wrote separately:** Terry v. Adams, 345 U.S. 461, 470 & 475–76 (1953) (Frankfurter, J.). *See* FF to HHB, 3/17/1953, FFHLS, Pt. I, Reel 70, Page 888 & FF to TCC, 3/17/1953, *id.* at 889 (proposing decree); FF to HHB, 3/18/1953, *id.* at 890 (wanting to join a judgment in favor of black voters depending on decree).

580 **Jackson voted:** RHJ Docket Entry, *Terry v. Adams,* RHJP, Box 179, Folder 9; Rehnquist certiorari memo, *Terry v. Adams, id.;* Rehnquist, "Re: Opinions of Black and FF in Terry v. Adams," *id.;* Jackson *Terry v. Adams,* dissent, 4/3/1953, *id.*

580 **Thompson's Restaurant:** District of Columbia v. John R. Thompson Co., 346 U.S. 100 (1953).

581 **"Why":** AMB Int. w Kluger, 8/20/1971, at 1. *See* Kluger, *Simple Justice,* 595; FF Docket Entry, *District of Columbia v. John R. Thompson Co.,* FFHLS, Pt. I, Reel 72, Page 920 (noting SFR voted to affirm); Joan Quigley, *Just Another Southern Town* (2016); Wendell E. Prichett, "A National Issue: Segregation in the District of Columbia and the Civil Rights Movement at Mid-Century," 93 Geo. L.J. 1321, 1331–32 (2005).

581 **Bickel drafted:** AMB Int. with Kluger, 8/20/1971, at 3.

581 **"disclose" & "in opposite":** FF, Memorandum to Conference Re: The Segregation Cases, 5/27/1953, at 1, FFHLS, Pt. II, Reel 4, Pages 242.

581 **The first three:** *Id.* at 1–3

582 **Byrnes:** NYHT, 12/7/1952, at 47.

582 **"[F]or me":** FF, "Memorandum to Conference Re: The Segregation Cases, 5/27/1953, at 1–3.

582 **Vinson liked:** FF, Conference Notes re: Questions, n.d., at 1–2, FFHLS, Pt. II, Reel 3, Pages 954–55.

582 **Black and Douglas:** *Id.;* HLB to FF, 6/5/1953, *id.,* Reel 4, Page 226. *See* TCC to FF, 6/5/1953, *id.* at 230; FF to TCC, 6/4/1953, *id.* at Page 210.

582 **"It can't":** FF Docket 1952 Term, *Davis v. County School Board,* FFHLS, Pt. I, Reel 72, Page 494 (FF handwritten).

582 **reminded Vinson:** FF to FMV, 6/8/1953, at 1–2, *id.,* Pt. II, Reel 4, Pages 237–38.

582 **"enjoyed":** AMB to FF, 8/22/1953, at 1, FFHLS, Pt. II, Reel 4, Page 211.

582–583 **"nowhere" & "In any event" & "all this":** *Id.* at 1–2.

583 **"I think":** *Id.* at 3.

583 **Without consulting:** FF to HLB, 8/5/1953, at 1–2, HLBP, Box 60.

584 **The Vinson Court:** Carlton F. W. Larson, "What if Fred Vinson Had Not Died of Heart Attack in 1953?" 45 Indiana L. Rev. 131 (2011) (arguing that FMV would have voted with the majority in *Brown* based on his past opinions on race and the federal government's support for plaintiffs); HHBD, 5/8/1954, Reel 4 (suggesting the vote would have been 6–3 under FMV with the chief justice among the three dissenters).

584 **Krock:** NYT, 9/18/1953, at 22.

584 **Childs:** WP, 9/29/1953, at 10.

584 **"a 'political'":** DDE to Swede Hazlett, 10/23/1954, at 2, Hazlett Papers, DDEL, Box 2.

584 **swear in:** NYT, 10/6/1953, at 1; Jim Newton, *Justice for All,* 254–56 (2006); Bernard Schwartz, *Super Chief* (1983).

584 **"equivalent":** Silber, *With All Deliberate Speed,* 209. *See id.* at 208–12; PE Int. with

Kluger, 8/19/1971, at 4–5; Supplemental Brief for the United States in Reargument, *Brown v. Board of Education*, 11/27/1953.

585 **"the unreliability" & "one" & "devote[d]" & "every" & "a fair" & "the legislative" & "the 39th"**: FF, Memorandum for the Conference, 12/3/1953, FFHLS, Pt. II, Reel 4, Page 58. The leading history was Horace E. Flack, *The Adoption of the Fourteenth Amendment* (1908).

585 **legislative history**: *Briggs v. Elliott* Oral Argument, 12/7/1953, in *Landmark Briefs and Arguments*, Vol. 49A, at 458–63.

585 **1871 Civil Rights Act**: *Id.* at 469.

585 **Necessary and Proper**: *Id.* at 488–89.

586 **"The argument"**: *Id.* at 521.

586 **"to find" & "as near" & "as is"**: *Id.* at 522–23.

586 **"informally"**: HHB *Brown v. Board* Conference Notes, 12/12/1953, at 1–2, HHBP, Box 251, Folder 10 & WOD *Brown v. Board* Conference Notes, 12/12/1953, WODP, Box 1150.

586 **"separate" & "proves" & "were intended"**: WOD *Brown v. Board* Conference Notes, 12/12/1953, at 1. *See* FF *Brown v. Board* Conference Notes, 12/12/1953, at 1, FFHLS, Reel 4, Page 451 & EW Handwritten notes, n.d., EWP, Box 571, Folder 3.

586 **"a dynamic" & "what was"**: HHB *Brown v. Board* Conference Notes, 12/12/1953, at 2. *See id.* at 3–4; WOD *Brown v. Board* Conference Notes, 12/12/1953, at 1–2; FF *Brown v. Board* Conference Notes, 12/12/1953, at 1.

586–587 **"The awful" & "was not" & "they looked" & Due Process Clause & "inconclusive" & "Gold Almighty" & "psychological changes"**: HHB *Brown v. Board* Conference Notes, 12/12/1953, at 4–5. *See* WOD *Brown v. Board* Conference Notes, 12/12/1953, at 3.

587 **circumspect**: HHB *Brown v. Board* Conference Notes, 12/12/1953, at 5–6 & WOD *Brown v. Board* Conference Notes, 12/12/1953, at 2–3 & SFR *Brown v. Board* Conference Notes, 12/12/1953, at 1, SFRP, Box 41.

587 **"go" & "a political" & "to justify"**: HHB *Brown v. Board* Conference Notes, 12/12/1953, at 6–7.

587 **"if we"**: WOD *Brown v. Board* Conference Notes, 12/12/1953, at 4. *See* FF *Brown v. Board* Conference Notes, 12/12/1953, at 2 & SFR *Brown v. Board* Conference Notes, 12/12/1953.

587 **"no choice"**: WOD *Brown v. Board* Conference Notes, 12/12/1953, at 4.

587 **Clark**: HHB *Brown v. Board* Conference Notes, 12/12/1953, at 7–9; WOD *Brown v. Board* Conference Notes, 12/12/1953, at 6.

587 **"weak reed"**: HHB *Brown v. Board* Conference Notes, 12/12/1953, at 9. *See* WOD *Brown v. Board* Conference Notes, 12/12/1953, at 7.

587 **Burton's chambers**: HHBD, 12/23/1953, Reel 3.

587 **"As is" & "under conditions"**: FF to Brethren, 1/15/1954, EWP, Box 571, Folder 3.

588 **"declaration" & "physical" & "social betterment" & "social deterioration" & "Not even" & "a fact-finding"**: FF, Memorandum at 1–2, *id.* (quoting Virginia v. West Virginia, 222 U.S. 17, 20 (1911)). FF had invoked "all deliberate speed" in two prior opinions. Addison v. Holly Hill Fruit Products, 322 U.S. 607, 619 (1944); Radio Station WOW v. Johnson, 326 U.S. 120, 132 (1945).

588 **"future"**: FF, Memorandum, at 3, EWP, Box 571, Folder 3.

588 **special masters & "raise"**: *Id.* at 4–5.

588 **"as little" & Black**: FF Conference Notes, 1/16/1954, at 1, FFHLS, Pt. II, Reel 4, Pages 447.

588 **"to adjust" & "generosity" & Jackson**: *Id.* at 2.

588   **Burton & Clark & "throwing":** *Id.* at 3.

588   **"simmer" & "praying" & "storm":** *Id.* at 4–5. *See* HHBD, 1/16/1954, Reel 4.

589   **eleven times:** EW Calendar, March–May 1954, EWP, Box 29, Folder 1.

589   **"May":** FF to EW, n.d., EWP, Box 353, Folder 2. The highball was likely Monday, March 29, when he saw FF at 4:00 p.m. EW Calendar, 3/29/1954. *See* AMB Int. with Lash, 9/12/1974, at 5 (recalling FF "endless talks" with EW on *Brown*); FF to LH, 4/10/1954, LHP, Box 105C, Folder 105-20 (describing EW as "a dedicated, whole-souled desire to do his job within those consideration that you and I deem relevant—and no other!").

589   **formal vote:** It is unclear when this formal vote took place or what the total was. In his memoirs, EW recalled that it was in February. EW, *The Memoirs of Earl Warren*, 285 (1977). The Court, however, was in recess for much of February and probably had not voted. WOD to HHB, 2/27/1954, at 1–2, HHBP, Box 314, Folder 9 (urging "expedition of the big cases" and looking forward to EW's confirmation). The vote was likely after EW's confirmation on March 1 and swearing-in on March 20 and could have been as late as the April 3, April 10, April 12, or April 24 conference. EW Calendar, 4/3/1954, 4/10/1954, 4/12/1954, 4/24/1954, EWP, Box 29, Folder 1. EW met with FF and HLB on April 8; FF on April 9 and 14; HHB on April 20; and RHJ in the hospital on April 22. EW Calendar, 4/8/1954 (FF and HLB), 4/9/1954 & 4/14/1954, (FF), 4/20/1954 (HHB), 4/22/1954, *id.* (RHJ).

589   **preliminary thoughts:** HHBD, 4/20/1954, Reel 4.

589   **yellow paper:** EW, Memorandum, n.d., EWP, Box 571, Folder 3.

589   **April 29 or 30:** Earl Pollock Int. by Laura McCreery, circa 2004, at 13–14, Regional Oral History Office, The Bancroft Library, University of California, Berkeley, 2013; John David Fassett et al., "Supreme Court Law Clerks' Recollections of *Brown v. Board of Education*," 78 St. John's L. Rev. 515, 549–51 (2004).

589   **On May 3:** Pollock to EW, 5/3/1954, EWP, Box 571, Folder 3; EP Draft Opinion, 5/4/1954, *id.*

589   **met privately & again:** EW Calendar, 5/1/1954, EWP, Box 29, Folder 1; EW Calendar, 5/3/1954, *id.*

589   **"jottings":** FF to EW, 5/4/1954, EWP, Box 573, Folder 1. HHB did not see the draft until the next day. HHBD, 5/5/54, Reel 4.

589   **"puts":** EW Original Handwritten Draft, at 8.

589   **"generates":** FF, Memorandum, 5/4/1954, at 1, EWP, Box 573, Folder 1. *See* Fassett et al., "Supreme Court Law Clerks' Recollections of *Brown v. Board of Education*," 78 St. John's L. Rev. at 556 & Pollock Int. by McCreery at 14 (regretting FF's change).

589   **hand-delivered:** Pollock Int. by McCreery at 14 & Pollock Int. by Kluger, 8/19/1974, BvBP, Box 5, Folder 102.

589   **"as a basis" & "were prepared":** EW to Court, 5/7/1954, EWP, Box 571, Folder 3.

589   **Burton responded:** HHB to EW, 5/8/1954, at 1, *id.*; HHBD, 5/8/1954, Reel 4.

590   **March 30:** ED Calendar, 3/29/1954, RHJP, Box 207, Folder 5; *id.*, 3/30/1954, *id.*; *id.*, 3/31/1954, *id.* ("very ill").

590   **April 20 and April 29:** ED Calendar, 4/20/1954, *id.* (FF); *id.*, 4/29/1954, *id.* (FF).

590   **showed to Warren:** EW. Note, n.d., RHJP, Box 184, Folder 8 ("RHJ working papers—various drafts of memo which was not circulated to members of the Court or used in any way except in conference with C.J. Warren at Doctors Hospital, where Justice Jackson was a patient until May 17, 1954."). It is unclear when RHJ shared his draft concurrence with EW; it could have been before his March 30 heart attack or in the hospital.

See ED Calendar, 4/22/1954, RHJP, Box 207, Folder 5 (EW visit); *id.*, 4/30/1954, *id.* (EW visit), the May 8 visit, or EW Calendar, 5/13/1954, EWP, Box 29, Folder 1 (EW visit).

FF may not have seen RHJ's draft concurrence until more than two years after the first *Brown* decision. ED note, n.d., RHJP, Box 184, Folder 5 (FF requested 3/15 draft concurrence on 6/27/1956). For RHJ's drafts, *see id.*, Folder 8; David M. O'Brien, *Justice Robert H. Jackson's Unpublished Opinion* in Brown v. Board (2018).

590 **"memorandum"**: Memorandum by Justice Jackson, 3/15/1954, at 1, 20–21, RHJP, Box 184, Folder 8.

590 **"begin"**: EBP, "Re: Nos. 1–4," n.d., at 1, RHP, Box 184, Folder 5 (emphasis in original).

590 **"I say" & "dealing"**: *Id.* at 3.

590 **"about to start"**: EBP, "Notes re: Segregation Decision," 12/15/1954, at 1, EBPP, Box 2, Folder 2.

590 **morning of May 8**: ED notation on record of opinions, Segregation Cases, RHJP, Box 184, Folder 4; ED note on EW, 5/7/1954 Memorandum, *id.*, Folder 5 ("Deliv'd by C.J. to RHJ at hospital"); EBP, "Notes re: Segregation Decision," 12/15/1954, at 1 (noting EW personally delivered). EW hand-delivered the draft to HHB that same morning. HHBD, 5/8/1954, Reel 4.

590 **"agreed" & paragraph & returned & "Today"**: EBP, "Notes re: Segregation Decision," 12/15/1954, at 1–2; Brown v. Board of Educ., 347 U.S. 483, 490 (1954).

590 **hallway**: EBP Int. with author, 9/18/2008.

591 **three times**: EW Calendar, 5/7/1954, EWP, Box 29, Folder 1; *id.*, 5/10/1954; *id.*, 5/12/1954.

591 **"deep"**: John D. Fassett, *New Deal Justice*, at x (1994).

591 **He thought**: *Id.* at 567; SFR to law clerk Robert L. Randall, 7/14/1953, at 1, Fassett Papers, Box 1, Folder 2; SFR to "Colleagues," 8/2/1953, *id.* (refusing to equate segregation with discrimination or else issue already decided).

591 **began to draft & Fassett faulted**: SFR Draft Dissent, n.d. at 2, *id.* (Fassett handwritten); Fassett et al., "Supreme Court Law Clerks' Recollections of *Brown v. Board of Education*," 78 St. John's L. Rev. (2004): 547–48; Fassett, "Mr. Justice Reed and *Brown v. Board of Education*," Supreme Court Historical Society Yearbook (1986): 57–59; Fassett, *New Deal Justice*, 570–71; Fassett Int. with Kluger, 9/19/1974, at 1, BvBP, Box 5, Folder 84.

591 **"krytocracy"**: Fassett, *New Deal Justice*, 567 & Fassett, "Mr. Justice Reed and *Brown v. Board of Education*," 55.

591 **Reed realized**: Another SFR clerk, George Mickum, quoted the chief justice saying: "Stan, you're all by yourself in this now. You've got to decide what's best for the country." Mickum Int. with Kluger, 10/20/1974, BvBP, Box 5, Folder 84. Fassett doubts his co-clerk Mickum would have been present during this conversation as SFR and EW spoke only in private. Fassett, *New Deal Justice*, 571–72; Fassett et al., "Supreme Court Law Clerks' Recollections of *Brown v. Board of Education*," 547.

591 **May 13 & Jackson**: EW Calendar, 5/13/1954, EWP, Box 29, Folder 1.

591 **two days earlier**: EW Calendar, 5/11/1954, *id.*

591 **aboard**: FF to MDF, 5/10/1954, BvBP, Box 2, Folder 2 (visiting RHJ in hospital); HHBD, 5/12/1954, Reel 4 (noting EW read him revised draft and "[i]t looks like a unanimous opinion.").

591 **"very" & "When"**: FF to EW, 5/13/1954, at 1–2, EWP, Box 571, Folder 3.

591 **avoid leaks**: HHBD, 5/15/1954, Reel 4.

591   **"An opinion"**: FF to EW, 5/15/1954, EWP, Box 571, Folder 3.

591   **checked out**: ED Calendar, 5/17/1954, RHJP, Box 207, Folder 5.

592   **postponed**: PC, 5/22/1954, at 14.

592   **minor opinions**: NJG, 5/29/1954, at 15.

592   **12:52**: NYHT, 5/19/1954, at 15.

592   **"unanimously"**: EW Reading Copy of *Brown v. Board of Education*, 5/17/1954, at 11, EWP, Box 571, Folder 3 (handwritten).

592   **gasped**: Fassett et al., "Supreme Court Law Clerks' Recollections of *Brown v. Board of Education*," 561–62 (Fassett claiming SFR smiled at Marshall and doubting story that SFR cried & EBP recalling crowd reaction when EW said "unanimously"); *Cf.* Mickum Int. with Kluger, 10/20/1974 (recalling SFR cried at announcement).

592   **"inconclusive"**: *Brown v. Board of Educ.*, 347 U.S. 483, 489 (1954).

592   **"In approaching"**: *Id.* at 492.

592   **studies & "To separate" & "in the field"**: *Id.* at 494–95 & n.11.

592   **"*This*"**: FF to EW, 5/17/1954, EWP, Box 571, Folder 3 (emphasis in original).

593   **"would have"**: FF to SFR, 5/20/1954, FFHLS, Pt. II, Reel 4, Page 405.

593   **"I am"**: *Id.*

593   **"was appreciated" & "the factors"**: SFR to FF, 5/21/954, *id.*, Pages 407–8.

593   **"difficult" & "part"**: WTC to FF, 5/20/1954, FFHLS, Pt. II, Reel 3, Page 940.

593   **"grand"**: Silber, *With All Deliberate Speed*, 207.

594   **"It is a long"**: FF to LH, 7/21/1954, at 1, FFLC, Box 65 (emphasis in original).

594   **"mainly"**: FF to PE, 7/21/1954, at 2, PEP, Box 2, Folder 2-70.

594   **"if the great"**: FF to LH, 7/21/1954, at 1–2.

594   **"the wise"**: FF to CCB (copied to GC), 4/15/1957, FFHLS, Pt. II, Reel 3, at 699. *See* FF to CCB, 5/28/1954, FFLC, Box 37 ("Of course personalities played their role. Time played perhaps the most important role in the Court's role. One does not have to be a soothsayer to know that the new Chief Justice is one person and his predecessor was another. On the other hand there are always people who like to reduce a complicated result to a simple single explanation."); FF to PAF, 6/12/1954, at 4, FFHLS, Pt. III, Reel 38, Page 121 ("Between you & me, if Black and Douglas had had their way, the *School* cases would have been a disaster!!!") (emphasis in original); WP, 3/19/1961, at E4, *id.*, Reel 32, Page 771 (FF handwritten reaction to conclusion that EW's judicial statesmanship led to unanimous result: "SURELY NOT. He had to be led like an agreeable child.").

594   **one of five justices**: WOD to File, 5/17/1954, at 1–2, WODP, Box 1149.

594   **"history"**: WOD *Brown v. Board* Conference Notes, 12/12/1953, at 3.

595   **"Today"**: WOD to FF, 5/29/1954, EWP, Box 353, Folder 2. *See* FF to Conference, 6/1/1954, *id.* (enclosing letter).

595   Michael Klarman's reliance on WOD's 1953 conference notes and May 17, 1954, memorandum undermines the credibility of his arguments about FF's willingness to affirm *Plessy*. Michael Klarman, *From Jim Crow to Civil Rights*, 297–304 (2004). Mark Tushnet does not rely on WOD's dubious accounts, yet interprets other evidence to claim that FF's indecisiveness, not FMV's lack of leadership, prevented the Court from achieving unanimity during the 1952 term. Mark Tushnet & Katya Lezin, "What Really Happened in *Brown v. Board of Education*," 91 Colum. L. Rev. 1867, 1872–75, 1883–85, 1918–21, 1929–30 (1991); Mark Tushnet, *Making Civil Rights Law*, 188 (1994) (describing FF's delay as based on his ambivalence "whether a legally satisfactory opinion overruling

Plessy could be written"). *See* Brad Snyder, "Frankfurter and Popular Constitutional-ism," 47 U.C. Davis L. Rev. 343, 397–400 (2013) (addressing Klarman's claims and reliance on WOD's accounts); *id.* at 400–403 (responding to Tushnet's claims about FF's indecisiveness).

595   "storm": FF Conference Notes, 1/16/1954, at 4.

CHAPTER 34: ALL DELIBERATE SPEED

596   "mischievous": FF, "A Puny Platonic Dialogue," 7/8/1954, at 3, FFHLS, Pt. III, Reel 38, Page 126.

596   Holmes & Brandeis & "less" & "serious" & "I am": FF to LH, 6/28/1954, at 4, LHP, Box 105C, Folder 105-20. *See* LH to FF, 7/11/1954, at 2–3, *id.*

597   streets of Cambridge: MML to FF, 5/15/1954, at 1, FFLC, Box 74.

597   first and fourth: Austin Scott to MML, 5/28/1946. Austin Scott Papers, Box 11, Folder 11-8.

597   political machine: FF to MML, 6/15/1954 at 1, MMLP; Stephen Lemann to Thomas Lemann, 1/30/1961, *id.*

597   solicitor general: FF to MML, 1/12/1953, *id. See* Thomas Lemann Int. with author, 9/29/2018; FF, "A Legal Triptych," 74 Harv. L. Rev. 433, 445–47 (1961); Thomas B. Lemann, "Monte M. Lemann," in *The Lemann Family of Louisiana*, 158–69 (Bernard Lemann, ed. 1965).

597   leading member: MML to FF, 6/10/1954, FFLC, Box 74 (enclosing letter from John H. Tucker of Louisiana State Law Institute).

597   "I've been": FF to MML, 6/23/1954, at 1–2, MMLP.

598   "While": MML to FF, 6/29/1954, *id.* & FFLC, Box 74.

598   "I suppose" & "that have" & "The Southern": FF to EW, 7/5/1954, at 1–2, FFHLS, Pt. III, Reel 4, Page 718–19 & EWP, Box 574, Folder 3.

598   "'chaotic'" & "throughout": FF to EW, 7/8/1954, at 1–3, EWP, Box 574, Folder 3.

598   "isolated": EW to FF, 9/27/1954, FFHLS, Pt. III, Reel 4, Page 728 (quoting JFB). *See* Greenville (S.C.) News, 9/25/1954, at 1.

599   "Jimmy saddens": FF to EW, Monday, n.d., at 1–2, EWP, Box 353, Folder 2.

599   received letters: MML to FF, 7/17/1954, at 1–2, MMLP. *See* NYT, 7/7/1954, at 34.

599   chief justice: FF to EW, 7/21/1954, EWP, Box 353, Folder 2.

599   "The Lemann": FF to MML, 8/9/1954, MMLP.

599   November elections: FF to EW, 7/21/1954.

599   "'we have'": EW to FF, 9/27/1954.

599   declined to attend: Norfolk Virginia Pilot, 9/26/1954, at 1, 3; Richmond Times-Dispatch, 9/26/1954, at 1, 4; Richmond News Leader, 9/25/1954, at 1, FFHLS, Pt. III, Reel 4, Pages 725–27.

599   "I am": FF to EW, Monday, n.d., at 2.

599   skipped: RHJ to FF, 8/23/1954, FFLC, Box 70.

600   tired & laid down: ED Calendar, 10/8/1954, RHJP, Box 207, Folder 6.

600   "He said": EBP. Int. with author, 9/18/2008. *Cf.* Noah Feldman, *Scorpions*, 403 & 479 n.77 (2010) (based on EBP Int., 1/29/2010) ("Justice Jackson is dead," FF told EBP. "We have a bit of a problem. He was in Elsie's house on Mass. Ave.").

600   walked in: EBP Int. with author, 7/20/2012.

600   **$1000 & papers:** RHJ, Last Will and Testament, 12/26/1952, at 1–2, RHJP, Box 241, Folder 3.

600   **11:45 a.m.:** ED Calendar, 10/9/1954, RHJP, Box 207, Folder 6.

600   **four and a half:** WP, 10/10/1954, at 1.

600   **J. Edgar Hoover:** Walter Trohan, *Political Animals*, 406 (1975); Feldman, *Scorpions*, 403–4 (insinuating, presumably based on his interview with EBP, that FF may have concocted the story about going to Sears and being near her apartment). The facts are not as far-fetched as they initially seem. Sears, located at 4500 Wisconsin Avenue, was 6.1 miles from RHJ's McLean home Hickory Hill via Chain Bridge Road and may have been one of the closer shopping areas at the time. ED's apartment at 4201 Massachusetts Avenue was 1.2 miles from Sears. Regardless of whether the story was true, his death in ED's apartment was an embarrassing fact in light of their long-rumored affair. There is no reason to doubt EBP's recollection that FF phoned him and said "we've got a problem."

600   **convened briefly:** WP, 10/12/1954, at 18.

600   **funeral & pallbearers:** WP, 10/13/1954, at 18; WES, 10/13/1954, at A-3.

600   **"All of Jamestown":** FF to CCB, 10/27/1954, at 1, CCBP, Box 5, Folder 5-13.

600   **"preference" & "He liked":** FF, Foreword, 55 Colum. L. Rev. 435, 436 (1955).

601   **turned:** Manchester Guardian, 10/11/1954, at 5.

601   **"nervous" & "not in good" & "somewhat":** WP, 10/14/1954, at 71.

601   **labored:** FF to AMB, 6/2/1955, at 2, FFHLS, Pt. III, Reel 31, Page 949.

601   **"Justice Jackson wrote" & "style sometimes" & "No man" & "temper" & "Deeper" & "Solicitor General" & Nuremberg:** FF, "Mr. Justice Jackson," 68 Harv. L. Rev. 937, 938–39 (1955).

601   **"the key":** FF to PE, 7/18/1953, at 1, PEP, Box 2, Folder 58.

601   **"the most satisfying":** RHJ COH at 1475, RHJP, Box 191, Folder 2.

601   **"had a profound" & "how ultimately" & "His voice":** FF, Foreword, 55 Colum. L. Rev. at 437.

602   **"the oasis":** FF to LH, 11/5/1954, at 1–2, LHP, Box 105C, Folder 105-20.

602   **"a self-righteous" & "largely vegetable" & "the most cynical":** *Id.* at 2.

602   **"a purity":** *Id.* at 2–3.

602–603 **"very friendly" & "gives":** *Id.* at 3.

603   **"the best":** *Id.* at 3–4.

603   **"would have":** *Id.* at 4. See FF to LH, 9/16/1955, at 1–2, LHP, Box 105C, Folder 105-21 (describing EW as upgrade over HFS and FMV because EW was "a straightforward, honorable character" who "behaves as the head of our Court should").

603   **team of six clerks:** Outline-Segregation Research Project, n.d., EBPP, Box 2.

603   **November 17:** "Segregation Research Report," 11/17/1955, FFHLS, Pt. II, Reel 4, Pages 592–676.

603   **"virtually":** Gordon B. Davidson et al., "Supreme Court Law Clerks' Recollections *of Brown v. Board of Education II*," 79 St. John's L. Rev. 823, 840 (2005).

603   **From the outset:** FF to CCB, 10/27/1954, at 2.

603   **John Marshall Harlan II:** 101 Cong. Rec. 3012 (1955); Tinsley E. Yarbrough, *John Marshall Harlan* (1992); Norman Dorsen, "John Marshall Harlan and the Warren Court," *The Warren Court in Historical and Political Perspective*, 109–22 (Mark Tushnet, ed. 1993).

604   **turned to other friends:** FF to LH, 10/15/1954, LHP, Box 105C, Folder 105-20.

604 **"outstanding":** LH to FF, 10/18/1954, *id. See* FF to CCB, 11/5/1954, at 1 (relaying endorsement to EW).

604 **"direct slur":** NYT, 2/9/1955, at 37.

604 **"Communist" & "one-worlder":** Brad Snyder, "How the Conservatives Canonized *Brown v. Board of Education*," 52 Rutgers L. Rev. 383, 401 (2000).

604 **Frankfurter wished:** FF to JMH, 1/3/1955, at 1–2, JMHP, Box 532.

604 **"should change" & "To lay" & "No sir":** Nomination of John Marshall Harlan: Hearings Before the Senate Comm. On the Judiciary, 84th Cong. 140 (1955).

604 **horned-rim:** Newsweek, 3/21/1955, at 29.

604 **71–11:** 101 Cong. Rec. 3036 (1955).

604 **well mannered & grandfather:** FF to CCB, 4/25/1955, at 1, CCBP, Box 5, Folder 5-14.

605 **"the 'liberals' " & "undeserved":** FF to CCB, 5/9/1955, at 2, *id. See* FF, "John Marshall and the Judicial Function, 69 Harv. L. Rev. 217, 230 (1955) (contrasting the *Plessy* line with the first Justice Harlan's opinion in *Cummings*).

605 **"John will carry" & "I miss":** FF to LH, 5/10/1955, at 1, LHP, Box 105C, Folder 105-20.

605 **"to uphold" and "obey":** DDE, press conference, 5/19/1954, https://www.presidency.ucsb.edu/documents/the-presidents-news-conference-454 & NYT, 5/20/1954, at 1.

605 **"moderate":** DDE to Hazlett, 10/23/1954, at 3, Hazlett Papers, DDEL, Box 2.

605 **"there" & "Let us" & "No" & "No":** *Brown II* Oral Argument, 4/12/1955, *Landmark Briefs and Arguments of the Supreme Court of the United States*, Vol. 49A, at 1168.

605 **"white parents":** *Id.* at 1185–86.

605 **"it is interesting":** *Id.* at 1196. *See* Davidson et al., "Supreme Court Law Clerks' Recollections of *Brown v. Board of Education II*," 79 St. John's L. Rev. at 866–67, 869–70 (SFR clerk Gordon Davidson recalling Virginia's argument and Marshall's response); *id.*, at 868–69, 872 (EW clerk Earl Pollock recalling how "angry" EW was at exchange).

605 **since February:** FF, "Attached are four possible decrees," 2/1955, FFLC, Box 219; FF, Memorandum on the Segregation Decree," 2/10/1955, *id.*

605–606 **" 'bare' " & "some" & "Platitude":** FF, "Memorandum on the Segregation Decree," 4/14/1954, at 1–3, *id.*

606 **"tentative" & "From what":** FF to EW, n.d., "Thursday," at 1–2, *id.*

606 **Warren & "should":** HHB *Brown II* Conference Notes, at 1–2, HHBP, Box 251, Folder 9. *See* FF *Brown II* Conference Notes, at 1, FFLC, Box 219; WOD *Brown II* Conference Notes, 4/16/1955, at 1–2, WODP, Box 1150.

606 **Black & "Nothing":** EW *Brown II* Conference Notes, at 2, EWP, Box 574, Folder 3. *See* FF *Brown II* Conference Notes, at 2; HHB *Brown II* Conference Notes, at 2.

606 **Reed & no mention:** HHB *Brown II* Conference Notes, at 3–4.

606 **Frankfurter & "by all" & "this is":** EW *Brown II* Conference Notes, at 3. *See* HHB *Brown II* Conference Notes, at 4–5; WOD *Brown II* Conference Notes, 4/16/1955, at 4 ("he now says he filibustered this problem under Vinson for fear that the case would be decided the other way Under Vinson!!").

606 **Douglas & no deadline & remedy:** EW *Brown II* Conference Notes, at 5.

606 **Burton:** FF *Brown II* Conference Notes, at 3 & EW *Brown II* Conference Notes, at 6.

607 **Clark & "careful" & Minton & "big" & Harlan & struck:** FF *Brown II* Conference Notes, at 3–4.

607 **"as simple" & "guideposts" & "maximum":** EW, *Brown II* "Memorandum," 4/28/1955, at 1, EWP, Box 574, Folder 3.

607   "**in good-faith**": FF comments on EW Draft, n.d., at 3, *id.*

607   "**with all**": FF Comments on EW Draft, 4/28/1955, at 3 (FF handwritten) (including citation to *Virginia v. West Virginia*). *See* "Decree # 2," n.d., at 2, FFLC, Box 219 (FF handwritten).

607   **English Chancery**: Virginia v. West Virginia, 222 U.S. 17, 20 (1911). OWH to Pollock, 3/7/1909, Mark DeWolfe Howe, ed., *Holmes-Pollock Letters*, Vol. 1 152 (1941); FF to PAF, 7/22/1958, FFHLS, Pt. III, Reel 38, Page 207; FF to AMB, 9/4/1958, *id.*, Reel 32, Page 410; NYHT, 9/26/1958, at 14 (reprinting letter from FF to Doyle Hennessy) (not finding it in English Chancery, but denying "The Hound of Heaven" as source).

607   "**And unperturbed**": Francis Thompson, "The Hound of Heaven" (1893).

607   **began drafting**: "Revised Statement (Prepared by Gerry Gunther)," 5/18/1954, EWP, Box 574, Folder 3; "Memo: C.J.'s Draft," 5/23/1954, *id.*

607   "**at the earliest**" & "**with all**": FF to EW, 5/24/1954, *id.*

607–608   "**I still strongly**" & **the nearest**" & "**I think**": FF to EW, 5/27/1955, *id.*

608   **Frankfurter's dismay**: FF to LH, 9/8/1957, LHP, Box 105D, Folder 105-23.

608   "**racial discrimination**": Brown v. Board of Educ. II, 349 U.S. 294, 298 (1955).

608   "**practical**" & "**public**" & "**personal**" & "**the courts**" & "**to take such**": *Id.* at 300–301. *See* EW reading copy, EWP, Box 574, Folder 3.

608   "**The harvest**": FF to EW, 5/31/1954, at 1–2, *id.*

608   **fall guy**: Richard Kluger, *Simple Justice*, 742–44 (1976) (portraying EW as having been duped by FF); Bernard Schwartz, *Super Chief*, 123–24 (1983) (claiming EW believed he had been "sold a bill of goods" by FF in *Brown II*); Mark Tushnet, *Making Civil Rights Law*, 229–31 (1994) (arguing HLB and WOD, not FF, were "right" in *Brown II* to call for immediate token integration of named plaintiffs); Michael Klarman, *From Jim Crow to Civil Rights*, 315–20 (2004) (contrasting FF's approach with HLB's); Lucas A. Powe, Jr., *The Warren Court and American Politics*, 55 (2000) (describing FF as "gradualism's most ardent supporter"); Michal R. Belknap, *The Supreme Court under Earl Warren, 1953–1969*, at 41 (2005) (arguing *Brown II* "failed miserably" because of "all deliberate speed"); Mark Tushnet with Katya Lezin, "What Really Happened in *Brown v. Board of Education*," 91 Colum. L. Rev. 1867, 1884 (1991) ("the failure of the nation to resolve its problems of race relations can be laid to some degree at Frankfurter's door. The gradualism he favored, it seems, evidently failed, in part because there were fewer 'good Southerners' than Frankfurter believed there were.").

609   **air conditioning & Marion's health**: FF to CCB, 10/26/1955, at 1–2, CCBP, Box 5, Folder 5-14; FF to PBK, 1/5/1955, PBKP, Box 14, Folder 1; FF to Wilmarth Lewis, 2/26/1955, at 1–2. FFHLS, Pt. III, Reel 29, Pages 662–63; FF to Lewis, 6/4/1955, at 1, *id.* at 668; FF to Lewis, 8/18/1955, at 2, *id.* at 670; FF to GC, 6/8/1955, at 1–2, *id.*, Reel 15, Pages 223–24; MDF to Bob [Szold], 9/14/1956, Gates Family Papers.

609   "**to turn**": MDF to IB, circa 1953, at 1, IBP, Box 136, Page 442.

609   "**so naïve**" & "**doubtful**": MDF to IB, circa 11/1953, at 1–2, *id.*, Page 299.

610   "**sensitiveness**": MDF to IB, circa 1953, at 2, *id.*, Page 445.

610   **Berlin's visits**: IB to "Dearest Mama," 12/21/1955, *Enlightening*, at 516 (Henry Hardy and Jennifer Holmes, eds. 2009) (seeing FF and bedridden MDF and observing "she *could* get up, but obviously doesn't *want* to: wants to remain alone in a room forever") (emphasis in original).

610   "**I see**": MDF to IB, circa 11/1953, at 1.

610   **Friends**: EFP to IB, 3/11/1953, at 1–2, IBP, Box 133, Page 538.

610   "the feeling" & "more": JA to IB, circa 1953, at 4–5, IBP, Box 239, Pages 68–69.

610   phone calls: MDF to IB, circa 1953, at 1, IBP, Box 136, Page 444.

610   "as happy": FF to CCB, 10/26/1955, at 2.

611   "the Court" & "institutional" & "the Court": FF to law clerks, 2/2/1955, at 1, FFHLS, Pt. III, Reel 7, Page 1.

611   Richardson's response: Richardson to FF, 2/18/1955, at 1–2, id., Pages 8–9; FF to Richardson, 2/23/1955, at 1, id. at Page 11. See id. at Pages 3–189 (clerks' responses).

611   immersed: FF to LH, 8/30/1955, at 2, LHP, Box 105C, Folder 105-21; FF to LH, 9/16/1955, at 2.

611   "hardheaded" & "deep" & "ambiguously" & "vitally": FF, "John Marshall and the Judicial Function," 69 Harv. L. Rev. 217, 222–23 (1955). See David S. Schwartz, The Spirit of the Constitution, 9–23, 229–30 (2019) (Marshall's "defensive" nationalism in McCulloch and the link between McCulloch's "capable Constitution" and Brown).

611   "Only" & "are precisely" & "inconclusive" & "not for" & "vagueness" & "make": FF, "John Marshall and the Judicial Function," 69 Harv. L. Rev. at 228–29.

612   "courts" & Ashwander & Dred Scott & the Sixteenth Amendment & West Coast Hotel: Id. at 234–35.

612   "an old-fashioned" & "the humane" & "the limited" & "the pervasiveness" & "release" & "If judges": Id. at 237–38.

612   Lamberth: Naim-Lamberth Marriage Record, 7/26/1952, NC Marriage Records, 1741–201l, RG 48; Klarman, From Jim Crow to Civil Rights, 321–23; Gregory Michael Dorr, "Principled Expediency: Eugenics, Naim v. Naim, and the Supreme Court," 42 Am. J. L. Hist. (April 1998): 119–59; Peter Wallenstein, "Race, Marriage, and the Law of Freedom: Alabama and Virginia 1860s–1960s," 70 Chi-Kent. L. Rev. 371 (1994).

613   "from enacting": Naim v. Naim, 87 S.E. 2d 749, 756 Va. (1955).

613   declined & Linnie Jackson: Jackson v. Alabama, No. 118 Misc., O.T. 1954, Cert petition, FFHLS, Pt. II, Reel 14, Pages 796–97; OT 1954 Conference List, 11/20/1954, id., at Page 914; Conference List, 11/13/1954, id., at Page 918 (originally considered); WOD Jackson Docket Book, O.T. 1954, WODP, Box 1155 (noting HLB, WOD, and EW voted to grant and FF and four others voted to deny); EW Jackson Docket Book, O.T. 1954, EWP, Box 368, Folder 4.

613   two years: Jet Magazine, 3/4/1954, at 15.

613   denied: 348 U.S. 888 (11/22/1954).

613   "big mistake": Norman I. Silber, With All Deliberate Speed, 245–46 (2004).

613   "So far" & "substantial": FF, "Memorandum Read to Conference on Naim v. Naim," 11/4/1955, at 1, FFLC, Box 219 (FF handwritten: read at conference on 11/4).

613–614 "a Court" & "deep" & "moral" & "the issue" & "moral" & "the enforcement" & "very seriously": Id. at 2–3. On FF's cautious approach to racial issues in state courts in 1955, see Williams v. Georgia, 349 U.S. 375, 376–91 (1955); Del Dickson, "State Court Defiance and the Limits of Supreme Court Authority," 103 Yale L.J. 1423 (1994).

614   Frankfurter and four: WOD Naim Docket Book, OT 1955, Box 1163 & EW Naim Docket Book O.T. 1955, Box 369, Folder 1 & HHB Naim Docket Book O.T. 1955, HHBP, Box 264, Folder 13.

614   "subsidiary": FF, "Memorandum Read to Conference on Naim v. Naim," at 3 (FF handwritten).

614   Burton raised: Law clerk William Norris to WOD, "Supplemental Memo, n.d., WODP, Box 1165.

614 **raised by Clark:** TCC, Handwritten Note, n.d., TCCP, Box A47, Folder 3.

614 **"the shortest":** FF to TCC, n.d., at 1, TCCP, Box A47, Folder 3.

614 **"inadequacy" & "the failure" & " 'in clean-cut' " & "for action":** Naim v. Naim, 350 U.S. 891, 891 (November 14, 1955) (mem.) (per curiam) (quoting Rescue Army v. Municipal Court, 331 U.S. 549, 584 (1947)).

614 **"The decree":** Naim v. Naim, 90 S.E. 2d 849, 850 (Va. 1956) (per curiam).

614 **"Did":** WP, 1/23/1956, at 16.

615 **"sought" & "deftly":** Richmond Times-Dispatch, 1/19/1956, at 12.

615 **held the case:** FF Conference Lists OT 1955, FFHLS, Pt. II, Reel 20, Page 616.

615 **voted five:** EW *Naim* Docket Book & WOD *Naim* Docket Book.

615 **"leaves":** Naim v. Naim, 350 U.S. 985, 985 (March 12, 1956) (mem.).

615 **University of Alabama:** Lucy v. Adams, 350 U.S. 1 (1955) (per curiam).

615 **beaches and bathhouses:** Mayor and City Council of Baltimore City v. Dawson, 350 U.S. 877 (1955) (per curiam).

615 **municipal golf:** Holmes v. City of Atlanta, 350 U.S. 879 (1955) (per curiam).

615 **Virgil Hawkins:** Florida ex rel. Hawkins v. Board of Control, 350 U.S. 413 (1956) (per curiam).

615 **refused to admit:** State ex rel. Hawkins v. Board of Control, 93 So. 2d 354, 360 (Fla. 1957). *See* Darryl Paulson & Paul Hawkes, "Desegregating the University of Florida Law School: Virgil Hawkins v. The Florida Board of Control," 12 Fla. St. U. L. Rev. 59 (1984).

616 **"Declaration":** 102 Cong. Rec. 4459–61 (1956).

616 **"The unwarranted" & "a clear" & "encroach[ed]" & "became" & "parents" & "undertook" & "which":** *Id.* at 4460.

616 **Thurmond:** *Id.* at 4461–62.

616 **Morse & Humphrey:** *Id.* at 4462–63. *See* Justin Driver, "Supremacies and the Southern Manifesto," 92 Tex. L. Rev. 1053 (2014).

617 **"uneducative":** FF to PAF, 4/19/1956, at 1, FFHLS, Pt. III, Reel 38, Page 158.

617 **moderate:** FF to AMB, 4/2/1956, at 2, *id.*, Reel 32, Page 83.

617 **impassioned:** FF to EG, 4/10/1956, at 1–4, FFHLS, Pt. III, Reel 16, Pages 358–61 (arguing Harvard should hire AMB); FF to EG, 4/13/1956, at 1–3, *id.*, at Pages 365–67; Al Sacks to FF, 4/10/1956, at 1–2, *id.*, Reel 18, Pages 376–77.

617 **"maturity":** EG to FF, 4/11/1956, at 1, *id.*, Reel 16, Page 362.

617 **sent Bickel:** FF to AMB, 12/1955, *id.*, Reel 32, Page 46.

617 **"had its":** AMB to FF, 1/10/1956, *id.*, Reel 14, Page 833.

617 **strongly encouraged:** FF to AMB, 8/23/1955, at 1–2, FFHLS, Pt. III, Reel 31, Pages 967–68.

617 **responded:** FF to AMB, 5/21/1956, *id.*, Reel 32, Page 89; FF to AMB, 5/28/1956, *id.* at Page 90; EW to FF, 5/26/1956, *id.* at Page 91; AMB, "Frankfurter's Former Clerk Disputes Byrnes's Statement," U.S. News & World Report, 6/15/1956, at 132 (responding to JFB, "The Supreme Court Must be Curbed," U.S. News & World Report, 5/13/1956, at 52).

617 **"by any" & "lawful means" & "deliberately" & "astonishingly":** TNR, 4/23/1956, at 11–13.

618 **"superb" & "deftly":** FF to AMB, 4/2/1956, at 1–2, FFHLS, Pt. III, Reel 32, Pages 82–83.

618 **casebook:** PAF et al., *Constitutional Law: Cases and Other Problems* (1954).

618 **editorship:** FF to PAF, 5/31/1956, FFHLS, Pt. III, Reel 32, Page 95.

618 **"proves" & "undoubtedly" & "the relatively":** CSM, 3/26/1956, at 18. *See* CSM, 3/27/1956, at 16.

618   "exquisitely": FF to PAF, 4/19/1956, at 1, FFHLS, Pt. III, Reel 38, Page 158.

618   commencement: PAF, "The Rule of Law," 1956 Wash. U. L. Q. 314 (1956).

618   "the kind": FF to PAF, 6/26/1956, at 1, FFHLS, Pt. III, Reel 38, Page 162.

618   "still" & "Sobeloff": AP Story, 7/15/1956, in FFHLS, Pt. III, Reel 32, Page 40. *See* BG, 7/15/1956, at 57.

619   "Good God!": AMB to FF, 7/15/1956, *id.*, Reel 14, Page 75.

CHAPTER 35: RED MONDAY

620   Paul Buck: BH, 6/15/1956, at 1.

620   "need": NYT, 6/15/1956, at 52.

620   chatted: BG, 6/15/1956, at 17.

620   "A brilliant": NYT, 6/15/1956, at 52.

621   "cannot escape": "Remarks of Felix Frankfurter at the Gravesite of Franklin D. Roosevelt, Hyde Park, NY," Memorial Day, 1956, at 1–2, FFLC, Box 200.

621   "100 per cent": FWB to MDF, 6/16/1956, at 2, FFLC, Box 40.

621   "cultivated": "Remarks of Felix Frankfurter at the Law School-Graduate School Alumni Day, Harvard Law School, Cambridge, MA," 6/13/1956, at 6, FFLC, Box 200.

621   dinner: Memorandum, 5/15/1956, FFHLS, Pt. III, Reel 29, Page 702; MML to CEW, 6/30/1956, MMLP.

621   "What": Remarks of AM, 6/14/1956, at 2, FFHLS, Pt. III, Reel 29, Page 706.

621   "poet": FF to Wilmarth Lewis, 6/26/1956, at 2, *id.*, at Page 712.

621   "the most" & "asks" & "it is" & "For": Remarks of PAF, 6/14/1956, at 1–2, *id.*, at Page 708–9.

621   enjoyed & 1:00 a.m.: FWB to MDF, 6/16/1956, at 1–2; Blumgart to FF, 6/20/1956, FFHLS, Pt. III, Reel 39, Page 380; MMLP to FF, 7/20/1956, at 2, MMLP ("I wish there could have been a tape recording of your remarks, which seemed to me to constitute a saga of your life.").

621   "rather" & "it gave": JA to IB, 7/12/1956, at 2–3, IBP, Box 239, #83–84. *See* FF Int. with JA, n.d., circa 1938, JSAP, Box 93, Folder 3.

622   Marion & rear garden: FF to LH, 8/21/1956, at 1–2, LHP, 105D, Folder 105-22; FF to MML, 9/17/1956, MMLP (FF handwritten).

622   "really very" & "the prospect" & "The Justice" & "fairly": JA to IB, circa 1956, at 2, IBP, Box 239, #98.

622   "good company": FF to CCB, 9/8/1956, at 2, CCBP, Box 5, Folder 5-15.

622   Dewey & Dulles & Brownell: NYT, 9/9/1956, at 56.

622   Parker & Vanderbilt: CT, 9/10/1956, at 22.

622   Ilastic: WP, 9/26/1956, at 51.

622   presidential election: FF to LH, 7/5/1956, at 2, LHP, Box 105C, Folder 105-21. FF to LH, 8/21/1956, at 1, *id.*, Box 105D, Folder 105-22; FF to CCB, Thanksgiving 1956, at 1, CCBP, Box 5, Folder 5-15.

622–623   "the difficulty" & "damn little" & "shining contrast": FF to LH, 9/5/1956, at 1–2, LHP, Box 105D, Folder 105-22.

623   found his man: Seth Stern and Stephen Wermiel, *Justice Brennan*, 71–95 (2010); MML to FF, 10/3/1956, MMLP (confessing he had never heard of WJB).

623   "a blend" & grades: PAF to FF, 10/9/1956, at 1, FFHLS, Pt. III, Reel 15, Page 916.

623   "that martinet" & "a very": FF to PAF, 10/4/1956, at 1, FFHLS, Pt. III, Reel 38, Page 169.

623   **"under-value" & "in Jackson's":** FF to PBK, 12/27/1956, PBKP, Box 14, Folder 3.

623   **"delighted":** FF to WJB, 10/25/1956, FFLC, Box 30.

623   **"very reassuring" & "geography" & "best":** PAF to FF, 10/30/1956, at 3, FFHLS, Pt. III, Reel 15, Page 924. *See* PAF to FF, 10/18/1956, at 1, *id.* at 920 (describing letter from New Jersey Supreme Court justice Nathan Jacobs to FF about WJB as "interesting and encouraging").

623   **"a 'friend' ":** WJB to FF, 10/3/1956, at 2, FFHLS, Pt. III, Reel 1, Page 124.

624   **great impression:** MML to FF, 11/19/1956, MMLP; FF to Harrison Tweed, 10/22/1956, FFLC, Box 108; Tweed to FF, 10/23/1956, at 1, *id.*; JLO to FF, 12/10/1956, FFLC, Box 87.

624   **"plot"** Stern & Wermiel, *Justice Brennan,* 103. *See* WJB Int. 31, at 8 with Stephen Wermiel (recalling FF's dinner guests "surely gave me a working over").

624   **Acheson:** NYTM, 10/5/1986, at 77–78.

624   **legal luminaries:** FF to MML, 10/18/1956, MMLP ("You can find out for yourself all you want to know. I can assure you now that you will find him a very agreeable person."); FF to LH, 10/25/1956, LHP, Box 105D, Folder 105-22; LH to FF, 10/29/1956, *id.*

624   **"a hard-working" & "a most agreeable":** FF to LH, 11/22/1956, at 1–2, LHP, Box 105D, Folder 105-22. *See* FF to MML, 10/10/1956, MMLP; FF to CCB, 10/3/1956, at 1, CCBP, Box 5, Folder 5-15.

624   **Brennan joined:** Fikes v. Alabama, 352 U.S. 191, 198 (1957) (Frankfurter, J., concurring); WJB to FF, 1/8/1957, FFHLS, Pt. II, Reel 21, Page 929.

625   **"Suffice":** FF to LH, 2/6/1957, at 2–3, LHP, Box 105D, Folder 105-22.

625   **geography & judicial experience:** FF to LH, 3/21/1957, *id.*; FF to CCB, 2/18/1957, at 1–2, CCBP, Box 5, Folder 5-16; FF to CCB, 2/21/1957, P.S., *id.*

625   **twenty-eight:** FF, "The Supreme Court in the Mirror of Justices," 105 U. Pa. L. Rev. 781, 783 (1957).

625   **"Greatness":** *Id.* at 784.

625   **Holmes & Cardozo:** *Id.* at 786.

625–626 **"One" & "functional" & "the confidence" & "ultimate":** *Id.* at 795–96.

626   **Stewart & Schaefer & "I read":** FF to LH, 3/21/1957. *See* FF to CCB, 2/18/1957, at 2; FF to CCB, 2/21//1957, P.S.

626   **pulled Brennan aside:** FF, 10/25/1956, Typewritten Note at bottom of WJB handwritten note, FFHLS, Pt. III, Reel 1, Page 127.

626   **Henry J. Friendly:** FF to Brownell, 1/14/1957 & FF to LH, 2/1/1957, at 1, LHP, Box 105D, Folder 105-22; Brad Snyder, "The Judicial Genealogy (and Mythology) of John Roberts: Clerkships from Gray to Brandeis to Friendly to Roberts," 71 Ohio St. L.J. 1149, 1199–1203 (2010).

627   **bus system & boycott:** Gayle v. Browder, 352 U.S. 903 (1956) (per curiam); Taylor Branch, *Parting the Waters,* 143–205 (1988); David J. Garrow, *Bearing the Cross,* 11–82 (1986).

627   **law graduates:** Konigsberg v. State Bar, 353 U.S. 252, 274 (1957) (Frankfurter, J., dissenting).

627   **"wholly":** Schware v. Board of Bar Examiners, 353 U.S. 232, 249 (1957) (Frankfurter, J., concurring).

627   **"splendid":** JMH to FF, 4/17/1957, FFHLS, Pt. II, Reel 25, Page 292.

627   **Red Monday:** Michal R. Belknap, *The Supreme Court under Earl Warren, 1953–1969,* at 51–79 (2005); Lucas A. Powe, Jr., *The Warren Court and American Politics,* 92–103 (2000); Arthur J. Sabin, *In Calmer Times* (1999).

628   **Before the term:** Jerome Cohen Int. with Michael Parrish, 7/2/1974, at 1 & Cohen Int.

with Laura McCreery, 11/19/2004, at 16–17 (recalling FF instructing him to "think" and write a memorandum about *Yates* in August 1956).

628 **five years & $10,000:** *Yates v. United States*, 354 U.S. 298, 302 (1957).

628 **"not prepared":** WOD *Yates* Conference Notes, 10/12/1956, at 5, WODP, Box 1177 & HHB *Yates* Conference Notes, 10/12/1956, at 4, HHBP, Box 280, Folder 1.

628 **sided:** WOD *Yates* Conference Notes, 11/2/1956, at 1, *id.*; HHB *Yates* Conference Notes, 11/2/1956, *id.*

628 **"organize":** *Yates*, 354 U.S. at 310.

628 **statute of limitations:** *Id.* at 312.

628 **jury instructions:** *Id.* at 312–27.

628 **acquittals & retrial:** *Id.* at 331, 333.

628 **John Service:** *Service v. Dulles*, 354 U.S. 363 (1957).

628 **Douglas insinuated:** Note, WOD *Service* Conference Notes, WODP, Box 1174 (handwritten note).

628 **voted with majority:** HHB *Watkins* Docket Books, O.T. 1956, HHBP, Box 279, Folder 2.

628 **John T. Watkins:** *Watkins v. United States*, 354 U.S. 178, 183–85 (1957).

628 **"not a First" & "save us":** FF to EW, 5/27/1957, at 2–3, EWP, Box 580, Folder 2.

629 **"hands off":** TNR, 5/21/1924, at 329–31.

629 **"is relevant":** FF to EW, 5/31/1957, at 3, EWP, Box 580, Folder 2. *See* FF to JMH, n.d., JMHP, Box 29.

629 **"weakness":** FF to LH, 6/30/1957, at 3, LHP, Box 105D, Folder 105-23.

629 **separate concurrence:** *Watkins*, 354 U.S. at 217 (Frankfurter, J., concurring).

629 **"rancor":** FF to LH, 6/30/1957, at 3, LHP, Box 105D, Folder 105-23.

629 **"unnecessary" & *New Republic* article:** *Watkins*, 354 U.S. at 218, 224–25 (Clark, J., dissenting).

629 **right to free speech:** *Sweezy v. New Hampshire*, 354 U.S. 234, 238–44 (1957).

629–630 **"wide" & "chief" & "privacy" & "our very":** FF to EW, 6/3/1957, at 1–2, EWP, Box 580, Folder 2

630 **separate concurrence:** *Sweezy v. New Hampshire*, 354 U.S. at 255 (Frankfurter, J., concurring in result).

630 **"to enforce":** FF to EW, 6/5/1957, at 1, EWP, Box 580, Folder 2.

630 **one of his best:** AMB Int. with Lash, 9/12/1974, at 4 (suggesting FF's *Sweezy* and *Dennis* opinions represented two sides of same coin).

630 **"the right" & "an overriding" & "an impersonal":** *Sweezy*, 234 U.S. at 266–67 (Frankfurter, J., concurring in result).

630 **closest friends:** FF to CCB, 7/5/1957, at 1–2, CCBP, Box 5, Folder 5-16 (describing EW's *Watkins* opinion as "water-logged" and indicating the chief justice's *Sweezy* opinion garnered only four votes); FF to LH, 6/30/1957, at 3 (describing EW's *Watkins* opinion as "mush and excessive & poor rhetoric").

631 **amendment:** 103 Cong. Rec. 10057 (1957).

631 **impeachment & Eastland & "The court":** NYT, 6/25/1957, at 15.

631 **introduced legislation:** 103 Cong. Rec. 10120 (1957).

631 **FBI to disclose:** *Jencks v. United States*, 353 U.S. 657, 658–66 (1957).

631 **voted with the majority:** HHB *Jencks* Conference Notes, 10/19/1956, at 1–2, HHBP, Box 280, Folder 5 (no FF vote); HHB *Jencks* Conference Notes, 3/22/1957, at 1, *id.* (FF votes to reverse and remand on jury instruction on "membership" and exclusion of defense counsel from discussion of FBI reports); WOD *Jencks* Conference Notes, 10/19/1956,

at 2–5, WODP, Box 1174; WOD *Jencks* Conference Notes, 11/2/1956, at 1–2, *id.*; WOD *Jencks* Conference Notes, 3/22/1957, at 1.

631   **detailed comments:** *Jencks* draft, 5/6/1957, at 1, WJBP, Box I:3, Folder 5.

631   **"I'm still" & Clark's dissent:** *Jencks* draft, 5/12/1957, at 1, *id.*

631   **"I remain":** *Jencks* draft, 5/21/1957, at 1, *id.*

631   **FBI reports & trial judge:** *Jencks,* 353 U.S. at 667, 669.

632   **"close":** *Id.* at 681 (Clark, J., dissenting).

632   **Eastland:** Pittsburgh Press, 6/5/1957, at 39.

632   **Nixon:** NYT 8/15/1957, at 14.

632   **Hoover:** NYT, 8/18/1957, at E10.

632   **certain:** NYT, 9/1/1957, at 1.

632   **Jencks Act:** Jencks Act, 18 U.S.C. 3500 (1957).

632   **"We can":** 103 Cong. Rec. 12809 (1957).

632   **"hot air" & "I firmly" & "the enslaved":** FF to WJB, 8/29/1957, at 1, WJBP, Box I:3, Folder 7. *See* WJB to FF, n.d., circa Summer 1957, at 1, FFHLS, Pt. III, Reel 1, Page 133.

633   **"you suggested":** WJB to FF, 8/31/1957, at 1, FFHLS, Pt. III, Reel 1, Page 135.

633   **"cheered" & "which I interpreted":** FF to WJB, Sunday, n.d., at 1–2, WJBP, Box I:3, Folder 7.

633   **"The past is":** FF to WJB, 9/4/1957, at 1–2, *id.*

633   **read the entire & Ervin's:** FF to WJB, Sunday, n.d., at 1. *See* FF to MML, 8/24/1957, at 2, MMLP; FF to MML, 9/26/1957, at 2, *id.* FF to CCB, 8/15/1957, CCBP, Box 5, Folder 5-16; FF to LH, circa July 1957, at 2, LHP, Box 105D, Folder 105-23; 103 Cong. Rec. 13113, 13144–48, 13159, 13277, 13318, 13429, 13453–55, 13471, 13737, 13850 (1957) (Ervin).

633   **credited him:** FF to FWB, 8/6/1957, at 1–2, FFLC, Box 40. *See* FF to AMB, 8/6/1957, FFHLS, Pt. III, Reel 32, Page 253 (referring to PAF and MDH); 103 Cong. Rec. 13306-7 (1957) (JFK reprinting MDH and PAF remarks).

633   **rode to Phil Graham's:** Katharine Graham, *Personal History,* 241 (1997); Robert A. Caro, *Master of the Senate,* 928 (2002); FF to JLR, 9/1/1957, at 1, JLRP, Box 286, Folder 14 (praising JLR's "contagious level-headedness").

634   **72–18:** 103 Cong. Rec. 13900 (1957).

634   **"I rejoice":** FF to WJB, Sunday, n.d., at 3.

CHAPTER 36: THE JUDICIAL RESPONSE TO LITTLE ROCK

635   **Elizabeth Eckford:** David Margolick, *Elizabeth and Hazel* (2011); David Margolick, "Through a Lens Darkly," Vanity Fair 9/2007; https://www.facinghistory.org/resource-library/audio/elizabeth-eckfords-words?backlink=https://www.facinghistory.org/resource-library/her-own-words-elizabeth-eckford.

635   **400 people & epithets:** NYT, 9/5/1957, at 1, 20. *See* Daisy Bates, *The Long Shadow of Little Rock,* 61–68 (1962, 1987); Elizabeth Jacoway, *Turn Away Thy Son,* 1–6 (2007); Tony A. Freyer, *Little Rock on Trial* (2007); Tony Freyer, *The Little Rock Crisis* (1984); Bernard Schwartz, *Super Chief,* 289–305 (1983); J.W. Peltason, *Fifty-Eight Lonely Men,* 161–92 (1961); Josh Blackman, "The Irrepressible Myths of *Cooper v. Aaron,*" 107 Geo. L.J. 1135 (2019); Tony A. Freyer, "*Cooper v. Aaron* (1958): A Hidden Story of Unanimity and Division," Journal of Supreme Court History 33, no. 1 (2008): 89; Dennis J. Hutchinson, "Unanimity and Desegregation: Decisionmaking in the Supreme Court, 1948-1958," 68 Geo. L.J. 1, 73–86 (1979).

635   **Orval Faubus:** NYT, 9/3/1957, at 1, 21; NYT, 9/4/1957, at 1, 37.

636   **"Of course":** FF to LH, 9/8/1957, LHP, Box 105D, Folder 105-23.

636   **"a natural-born":** FF to CCB, 9/12/1957, CCBP, Box 5, Folder 5-16.

636   **lukewarm:** DDE to Hazlett, 7/22/1957, at 4–6, Hazlett Papers, DDEL, Box 2 ("I think that no other single event has so disturbed the domestic scene in many years as did the Supreme Court's decision of 1954 in the school segregation case. . . . But I hold to the basic purpose. There must be respect for the Constitution—which means the Supreme Court's interpretation of the Constitution—or we shall have chaos.").

636   **"You cannot":** NYT, 9/16/1957, at 19.

636   **"The demands":** DDED, 9/13/1957, *The Eisenhower Diaries*, at 313 (Robert H. Ferrell, ed. 1981). *See* Arthur Krock, 4/7/1960, at 4–5, Krock Papers, Box 26 (int. with DDE refusing to endorse *Brown* and criticizing Court).

636   **met with Faubus:** DDED, 10/8/1957, *The Eisenhower Diaries*, at 347–48 (recollecting 9/14/1957 meeting).

636   **"disgraceful":** NYT, 9/24/1957, at 1.

637   **drove:** "Some Recollections By JWD," at 2, J. William Doolittle Collection of Materials Relating to Justice Felix Frankfurter (on file with author); Bill Doolittle Int. with author, 1/11/2018 & 12/6/2018.

637   **directly to chambers & letters:** WES, 11/15/1957, at A-2; FFLC, Box 122 (five folders of letters).

637   **11:00 a.m. & 5:00 p.m.:** HHBD, 11/15/1957, Reel 4.

637   **sixteen former clerks:** "Present 11/15/1957," FFLC, Box 122.

637   **"warm" & "Well, now":** FF to CCB, 11/27/1957, CCBP, Box 5, Folder 5-16.

637   **profiled:** BG, 11/10/1957, at A1, A14; WP, 11/15/1957, at A16; BG, 11/15/1957, at 44.

637   **"[h]ow could":** NYT, 11/17/1957, at E10.

637   **Felix Frankfurter Scholarship Fund:** WP, 11/23/1957, at B7 & photos, in FFLC, Box 182; HHBD, 11/22/1957, Reel 4; Benjamin F. Goldstein to FF, 12/18/1957, FFHLS, Pt. III, Reel 19, Page, 307.

637   **editors:** 67 Yale L.J., ii (1957) (dedication); Sir Owen Dixon, "Mr. Justice Frankfurter: A Tribute from Australia," *id.* at 179–86; PBK, "Mr. Justice Frankfurter, The Supreme Court and the Erie Doctrine in Diversity Cases," *id.* at 187–218; Ernest J. Brown, "The Open Economy: Justice Frankfurter and the Position of the Judiciary," *id.* at 219–39; Nathaniel L. Nathanson, "Mr. Justice Frankfurter and Administrative Law," *id.* at 240–65; Clyde W. Summers, "Frankfurter, Labor Law and the Judge's Function," *id.* at 266–303; Louis H. Pollak, "Mr. Justice Frankfurter: Judgment and the Fourteenth Amendment," *id.* at 304–323.

638   **"In fair":** TNR, 11/18/1957, at 7–9.

638   **"the World Series":** FF to CCB, 11/21/1957, at 1, CCBP, Box 5, Folder 5-16.

638   **Griswold & "the Law":** Howard Kalodner Int., 12/13/2018.

638   **To former students:** FF to Donald Trautman, 9/12/1956, FFHLS, Pt. III, Reel I, Page 201; FF to Reston, 10/16/1956, *id.* at 202; AL to FF, 1/11/1957, *id.* at 205; FF to PAF, 10/16/1956, *id.*, Reel 38, Page 172; FF to Sacks, 8/23/1956, *id.*, Reel 18, Page 379; FF to HMH, 9/27/1956, *id.*, Reel 8, Page 810; AL to FF, 2/27/1956, ALP, Box II:9 (thanking for lunch); FF to Chayes, 9/12/1956, *id.*; FF to AL, 9/22/1956, *id.*; FF to AL, 1/14/1957, *id.*

638   **"very few":** FF to Arthur Hays Sulzberger, 6/24/1957, *id. See* Lincoln Caplan, "Anthony Lewis: What He Learned at Harvard Law School," 79 Mo. L. Rev. 871 (2014) (quot-

ing AL's notes from PAF's and HMH's classes); AL, 106 Harv. L. Rev. 1, 16–18 (1992) (recalling PAF's class).

638–639 **"more thorough" & "more reflective" & "serious" & "the really"**: AL, "Meeting with FF – Friday, Aug. 9, 1957," at 1–2, ALP, Box II:9.

639 **"The Stars" & "judicial" & "the idea"**: NYTM, 11/10/1957, at 25.

639 **ability to frame & fair criminal procedures**: *Id*. at 25, 78. *See* McNabb v. United States, 318 U.S. 332, 347 (1943) (reversing conviction because of involuntary confessions and observing: "The history of liberty has largely been the history of observance of procedural safeguards."); Harris v. United States, 331 U.S. 145, 155 (1947) (Frankfurter, J., dissenting) (objecting to warrantless search of home); United States v. Rabinowitz, 339 U.S. 56, 68 (1950) (Frankfurter, J., dissenting) (objecting to scope of search incident to arrest).

639–640 **"electric" & "No one"**: NYTM, 11/10/1957, at 78–79.

640 **"exponent" & "a man" & "passionate" & "judicial" & "I regard"**: *Id*. at 79. FF to AL, 11/10/1957, at. 1–2, ALP, Box II:9 (thanking for profile).

640 **May 3 conference**: WOD Conference Notes, 5/3/1957, at 2–3, WODP, Box 1191.

640 **"The issues"**: FF, "Memorandum for the Conference," 6/7/1957, FFHLS, Pt. II, Reel 32, Page 501. *See* Patrick Weil, *The Sovereign Citizen*, 145–65 (2012).

641 **"Felix irritates" & forbade**: Jerome Cohen Int. with Michael Parrish, 7/2/1974, at 4 & Cohen Int. with Laura McCreery, 11/19/2004, at 4, 9–10 & Jerome Cohen Int., 12/14/2018. *See* FF, "To the Editor," circa 10/1/1961, FFHLS, Pt. III, Reel 32, Page 838 ("brainwashes").

641 **other clerk**: EW to FF, 7/14/1956, FFHLS, Pt. III, Reel 8, Page 901 (describing Cohen as "able young man" and claiming "no objections" to FF's hiring him); James F. Simon, *Eisenhower vs. Warren*, 237 (2018) (describing EW as "all-business" and "livid" about the FF clerkship) (based on 3/8/2016 int. with Cohen). Cohen was hired because HMH had forgotten to tell Aram J. Kevorkian he had been selected to clerk for FF; Kevorkian, who was stationed in La Rochelle, France, could not arrange for a discharge. FF to HMH, 6/25/1956, at 1–2, FFHLS, Pt. III, Reel 8, Page 895–96; FF to Kevorkian, 9/27/1956, at 1–2, *id*. Page 908–9.

641 **Cohen wrote**: Jerome Cohen, "Perez v. Brownell," 7/1957, FFHLS, Pt. II, Reel 32, Page 502.

641 **Warren no longer**: WOD *Perez & Trop & Nishikawa* Docket Book, O.T. 1957, Box 1184; HHB *Trop* Docket Book, O.T. 1957, Box 294, Folder 7.

641 **"These" & "tough" & "you are" & "this is" & "this Court"**: FF to JMH, 10/29/1957, FFHLS, Pt. II, Reel 32, Page 441.

641 **memoranda & drafts**: Memorandum, 11/1957, *Perez v. Brownell*, FFHLS, Pt. II, Reel 32, Page 519; Memorandum, *Nishikawa v. Dulles*, 10/1957, *id*., Page 243; Doolittle to Todd Peppers, Email, 6/17/2009 (recounting work on denationalization cases).

641 **"excellent"**: Whittaker to FF, 11/15/1957, FFHLS, Pt. II, Reel 32, Page 504.

642 **"a great"**: Whittaker to FF, 3/5/1958, at 1, *id*. at Page 598.

642 **"a shock"**: FF to Whittaker, 3/5/1958, at 4, *id*., Page 603.

642 **"The Chief" & "the overtones" & "But every"**: FF to WJB, 3/27/1958, at 1–3, FFHLS, Pt. II, Reel 32, Pages 259–61 (quoting *Nishikawa v. Dulles* draft); Nishikawa v. Dulles, 356 U.S. 129 (1958). *But see* Perez v. Brownell, 356 U.S. 44, 78 (1958) (Warren, C.J., dissenting) ("The power to denationalize is not within the letter or the spirit of the powers with which our Government was endowed.").

642 **"The importance"**: Perez, 356 U.S. at 57–60. *See* HHB Conference Notes, *Perez v. Brownell*, 10/29/1957, at 2, HHBP, Box 296, Folder 2 (FF observing that the Necessary and Proper Clause "applies to 'all other powers' ") (quoting Art. I, §8, Cl. 17).

643 **"All persons" & "basic"**: Perez v. Brownell, 356 U.S. at 64–66 (Warren, C.J., dissenting) (quoting Amend. XIV, §1, cl. 1).

643 **legislative supremacy**: *Id.* at 79 (Douglas, J., dissenting).

643 **"the dignity" & "the evolving"**: Trop v. Dulles, 356 U.S. 86, 100–1 (1958) (plurality opinion).

643 **"All power" & "clearly" & "judgment" & "the gravest" & "This is" & "it is"**: *Id.* at 119–20 (Frankfurter, J., dissenting) (quoting Blodgett v. Holden, 275 U.S. 142, 148 (1927) (Holmes, J., separate opinion)).

644 **"remarks"**: NYT, 4/3/1958, at 17.

644 **"adjectival" & "deep"**: FF to AL, 4/3/1958, ALP Box II-9 (quoting AL's article). *See* AL to FF, 4/9/1958, *id.* (responding that the philosophical "differences" sometimes result in "surface irritations").

644 **"nothing"**: NYT, 4/3/1958, at 17.

644 **"his opinion"**: Memo for Record, n.d., FFHLS, Pt. II, Reel 32, Page 912.

644 **"Does he"**: Note, *id. See* Weil, *Sovereign Citizen*, 147 (quoting EW clerk Dallin Oaks's journal on announcement).

644 **"a vigorous" & "more restrained"**: NYT, 4/3/1958, at 17.

644 **packed**: LH to FF, 2/10/1958, at 1, FFHLS, Pt. III, Reel 27, Page 561; Gerald Gunther, *Learned Hand*, 653 (1994).

644 **classrooms & radio**: FF to CCB, 2/14/1957, at 1, CCBP, Box 5, Folder 5-17; BG, 2/4/1958, at 19; BG, 2/5/1958, at 24.

644 **"the whole"**: Learned Hand, *The Bill of Rights*, 27–29 (1958).

645 **"a third" & "its own"**: *Id.* at 54–55.

645 **"For myself"**: *Id.* at 73.

645 **"central" & "you cannot" & "whether" & "square"**: FF to LH, 2/13/1958, at 1–2, LHP, Box 105D, Folder 105-23. *See* LH to FF, 2/22/1958, at 1–2, *id.* (agreeing he might have joined the majority); FF to JMH, circa 1958, at 1, JMHP, Box 533 ("While I regret that B felt he had to give his views on the Segregation Cases, I quite appreciate that he may have thought it would be lacking in candor not to do so.").

645 **miscegenation laws**: FF to LH, 9/8/1957, at 1, LHP, Box 105D, Folder 105-23 (asking about miscegenation laws); LH to FF, 9/13/1957, *id.*; FF to LH, 9/17/1957, at 1–3, *id.* (defending his ducking of miscegenation cases, observing the Fourteenth Amendment "makes no reference to color," and discussing AMB's law review article).

645 **"justified" & "inconclusive"**: LH to FF, 9/25/1957, *id.*; FF to LH, 9/27/1957, at 1–2, *id.* LH to FF, 10/10/1957, *id.*

645 **"the boys" & "for the love"**: FF to LH, 10/12/1957, at 2–3, *id. See* FF to LH, 2/13/1958, at 2 (insisting *Brown* does not necessarily mean overruling miscegenation laws); Constance Jordan, ed., *Reason and Imagination*, 374–82 (2013). LH's biographer Gerald Gunther blamed FF's "incessant hammering" for LH's change of heart about *Brown*. A former LH clerk whom FF had encouraged to write the biography, Gunther claimed that LH had been unaware of the Court's subsequent summary opinions desegregating municipal swimming pools, golf courses, buses, and other public accommodations. Gunther, *Learned Hand*, 666, 670. Whether he read those opinions or not, LH proved himself to be a less-than-astute interpreter of the Fourteenth Amendment's text and history in con-

cluding initially that they prohibited all racial classifications. Moreover, LH explained at the time that he added his discussion of *Brown* at the last minute "under the proper pressure of that Law Clerk to beat all Law-Clerks, Roland *[sic]* Dworkin, and one or two others who said 'You simply cannot duck that one,' I took up the pros and cons as best I could . . ." LH to FF, 2/22/1958, at 1. Months after the lectures, LH read AMB's article about the history of the Fourteenth Amendment and concluded that *Brown* was "unnecessary and bad law." LH to FF, 11/1/1958, at 2, Hand Papers, Box 105D, Folder 105-24.

645   **Hand announced:** NYT, 5/8/1958, at 15.

646   **"may well":** Manchester Guardian, 2/8/1958, at 5.

646   **"I'm afraid" & "These liberals":** FF to CCB, 2/14/1958, at 1–2.

646   **"Read Monday's batch":** FF to Arthur Sutherland, 4/1/1958, LHP, Box 105D, Folder 105-23 (FF handwritten to LH).

646   **"permanently" & "It upset":** JA to IB, 4/30/1958, at 2, IBP, Box 239, #108. *See* JA to IB, 3/20/1958, at 2, *Id.*, #103.

646   **content:** MDF to AMB, 8/5/1958, at 1–2, FFHLS, Pt. III, Reel 32, Pages 390–91; FF to LH, March 1958, LHP, Box 105D, Folder 105-23.

647   **Robert Carter:** Oral Argument of Robert Carter, 1/15/1958, at 00:33:01, https://www.oyez.org/cases/1957/91.

647   **"The less":** HHB Conference Notes, *NAACP v. Alabama*, at 3, HHBP, Box 296, Folder 12. *See* WOD Conference Notes, *NAACP v. Alabama*, at 2, WODP, Box 1186; TCC Conferences Notes, *NAACP v. Alabama*, at 1, TCCP, Box A60, Folder 5.

647   **$10,000 to $100,000:** NAACP v. Alabama ex rel. Patterson, 357 U.S. 449, 451–54 (1958).

647   **extensively edited:** FF to JMH, 4/23/1958, JMHP, Box 533; JMH to FF, 4/24/1958, *id.*; FF to JMH, 4/24/1958, *id.*; FF to JMH, 4/28/1958, *id.*; FF to JMH, n.d., *id.*

647   **"not inflexible" & "will be":** FF comments, *NAACP v. Alabama* draft, at 9, FFHLS, Pt. II, Reel 32, Page 60. *See* JMH to FF, 5/2/1957, *id.* at Page 70; FF to JMH, 5/23/1957, *id.* at Page 71.

647   **"a break":** FF to TCC, 6/25/1957, at 1, *id.* at Page 72.

647   **retaliated:** Bates, *Long Shadow of Little Rock*, 116–22 (recalling harassment and expulsion of Minnijean Brown).

647   **"the time":** Aaron v. Cooper, 163 F. Supp. 13, 30 (E.D. Ark. 1958).

647   **lunch:** HHBD, 6/23/1958, Reel 5 (EW, HLB, WOD, TCC, JMH, WJB, and Whittaker "discussed Little Rock").

647–648 **"stiff fight" & "tepid" & "Some plain":** FF to AMB, circa 8/20/1958, FFHLS, Pt. III, Reel 32, Page 403 (FF handwritten).

648   **"we'd be" & "professional" & "inexperience" & "shortsightedness":** FF to AMB, 8/29/1958, *id.* at Page 401.

648   **"We have":** Aaron v. Cooper, 357 U.S. 566, 567 (1958) (per curiam). *See* Draft, FFHLS, Pt. II, Reel 35, Page 906 & Drafts, *id.*, Reel 28, Pages 225–43.

648   **two California death row & Frankfurter dissented:** Caritativo v. California, 357 U.S 549, 550 (1958) (per curiam); *id.* at 552–60 (Frankfurter, J., dissenting). *See* FF to JMH, 6/26/1958, JMHP, Box 52.

648   **"it would":** NYT, 7/2/1958, at 19 (quoting Caritativo, 357 U.S. at 559 (Frankfurter, J., dissenting)).

648   **"said nothing":** Frankfurter written notation, Caritativo v. California, 1957 Term Doolittle Bound Volume, at 969. *See* HHBD, 6/30/1958, Reel 5; EW Calendar, 6/30/1958, EWP, Box 30, Folder 4 (5:00 p.m. visit to FF's chambers).

648 **"Neither" & "I merely"**: NYT, 7/2/1958, at 19 (quoting Caritativo, 357 U.S. at 559 (Frankfurter, J., dissenting)).

648 **"the final break"**: Schwartz, *Super Chief,* 254 (quoting unnamed justice, probably WJB). FF was quoted as referring to EW as "That Dumb Swede." The source, which claimed that FF and his former clerk PG had used the term, was an undated note in the files of an FF antagonist, syndicated columnist Drew Pearson. Jim Newton, *Justice for All,* 347 & 563 n.11 (2006) (relying on undated memorandum, quoting PG quoting FF, in Pearson's files). As Newton acknowledged, FF never used this phrase in his voluminous correspondence.

649 **"intellectually"**: FF to AMB, 8/2/1958, at 2–3, FFHLS, Pt. III, Reel 32, Pages 387–88.

649 **"I hope"**: JMH to FF, 7/15/1958, at 1–2, FFHLS, Pt. III, Reel 1, Page 591–92.

649 **August 18**: Aaron v. Cooper, 257 F.2d 33 (8th Cir. 1958).

649 **"wiser"**: FF to AMB, 8/18/1958, FFHLS, Pt. III, Reel 32, Page 392.

649 *Smith v. Allwright*: FF to AMB, circa 8/19/1958, *id.* at 397 ("Someday let me tell you the story of this.") (attaching *Smith v. Allwright* concurrence).

649 **special term**: NYT, 8/26/1958, at 1, 18.

649 **conferred**: Freyer, *Little Rock on Trial,* 151 & Freyer, *Little Rock Crisis,* 148 (Whittaker flew from Kansas City to Los Angeles to confer with EW and WJB) (based on WJB int.).

650 **European vacation**: Martin to Secretary of State, 8/26/1958 tel., HHBP, Box 307, Folder 16.

650 **Frankfurter and Black**: EW Calendar, 8/28/1958, EWP, Box 31, Folder 1.

650 **"The special"**: AMB to FF, 8/21/1958, FFHLS, Pt. III, Reel 32, Page 404 (FF handwritten).

650 **"for my"**: FF to Conference, 8/27/1958, FFHLS, Pt. II, Reel 36, Page 500.

650 **"Compliance"**: "Memorandum by Justice Frankfurter on Little Rock," 8/27/1958, at 4, *id.* at 504. *See* "The Little Rock Story," n.d., FFHLS, Pt. II, Reel 36, Pages 75–79; FF, "Facts pertinent to No. 1 misc. Aaron v. Cooper Prior to Proceedings before Judge Lemley," Drafts, n.d., *id.* at Pages 72–74; *id.* at Pages 80–90; Final draft, *id.* at Pages 160–64; FF Handwritten draft, n.d., *id.*, Pages 488–95; FF typewritten draft, 8/27/1958, *id.* at 496–99.

650 **"here" & "that these children"**: Cooper v. Aaron oral argument, 8/28/1958, Pt. I, 33:29, https://www.oyez.org/cases/1957/1_misc.

650 **"a surrender"**: *Id.,* 34:20.

650 **"a national"**: *Id.,* 1:38:08.

650–651 **"relieved" & "much wiser" & "Of course"**: FF to JMH, 9/2/1958, at 1, FFLC, Box 65. *See* HHBD, 8/29/1958, Reel 5 (lunch with EW, WJB, JMH, and HHB); Oral Argument, 8/28/1958, Pt. 2, 6:16, https://www.oyez.org/cases/1957/1_misc (EW to Butler: "But I have never heard such an argument made in the Court of Justice before and I've tried many a case over many a years. I never heard a lawyer say, that the statement of the Governor as to—to what was legal or illegal should control the action of any court.").

651 **"These are"**: FF to JMH, 9/2/1958, at 1–2. FF referred to the publisher of the *Atlanta Journal*; he probably meant to refer to McGill, the editor of the *Atlanta Constitution.*

651 **"courageous" & "was" & "a good" & "My own"**: FF to EW, 9/11/1958, at 1–2, EWP, Box 584, Folder 3 (quoting WP, 9/4/1958 in FFHLS, Pt. III, Reel 32, Page 428). *See* FF to AMB, 8/29/1958, P.S. ("We were lucky to have had a gentlemanly, *real* lawyer represent Little Rock.").

651 **"And may"**: Oral Argument, 9/11/1958, pt. 1, 03:09, https://www.oyez.org/cases/1957/1_misc.

651–652 **"blunt" & "prosecutorial" & "Butler" & "a snowball's" & "aim":** FF to AMB, 9/12/1958, at 2–3, FFHLS, Pt. III, Reel 32, Pages 418–19.

652 **the Court announced:** Opinion Announcement, 9/12/1958, https://www.oyez.org/cases/1957/1_misc; Cooper v. Aaron, 358 U.S. 1, 5 n.* (1958) (reprinting per curiam 9/12/1958).

652 **suspended:** NYT, 9/13/1958, at 1.

652 **"the extremely" & "very" & "harmful":** FF to AMB, 9/12/1958, at 1.

652 **cocky & sensitive:** FF to JMH, 9/12/1958, JMHP, Box 537.

652 **"the basic":** WJB First Draft, 9/17/1958, at 9, *id.*, Box 57.

653 **alternative opinion:** JMH Draft, 9/19/1958, at 22–23, FFHLS, Pt. II, Reel 36, Page 188–89 & JMHP, Box 57.

653 **same reference:** WJB Second Draft, 9/23/1958, at 13–14, JMHP, Box 57.

653 **inserting five pages:** JMH to WJB, 9/23/1958 & "Suggested Substitute of Pages 10–15 of W.J.B.'s Draft Beginning After the First New Paragraph on Page 10," *id.*

653 **"a patchwork" & "terrible":** WJB Third Draft, 9/24/1958, at 13, 18, *id.* (JMH handwritten). *See* Insert A & Insert B from HLB, n.d., WJBP, Box I-15, Folder 2.

653 **Brennan insisted:** JMH Conference Notes, *Cooper v. Aaron*, 9/23/1958, at 1, JMHP, Box 57. *See* Freyer, *"Cooper v. Aaron* (1958): A Hidden Story of Unanimity and Division," at 95–96.

653 **"I strongly":** WJB draft, 9/22/1958, at 15, FFHLS, Pt. II, Reel 36, Page 300 & WJBP, Box I-15, Folder 2 (FF handwritten).

653 **"You have":** WJB draft, 9/25/1958, at 1, *id.*, Folder 1 (FF handwritten). *See* Draft, n.d., *id.*, Box I-14, Folder 34.

653 **he announced:** HHBD, 9/26/1958, Reel 5.

653 **"bombshell" & Warren & Black & Harlan:** WOD, Memorandum re: Cooper v. Aaron, 10/8/1958, at 2, WODP, Box 1199. *See* EW, *The Memoirs of Earl Warren,* 298–99 (1977) ("caused quite a sensation"); FF to HLB, 5/7/1963, at 2, FFHLS, Pt. III, Reel 38, Page 329 (HLB's reaction). FF informed HLB that the concurrence was coming. FF to HLB, n.d., HLBP, Box 335, Folder 1 ("In what I propose to utter individually (wholly concurringly) in this case, which I outlined, in short hand, my own short hand scribble weeks ago, there is one word that I'm sure of you will approve. I don't want to tell you till you see it in context.").

653 **"with varying":** FF to LH, 11/4/1958, at 2, LHP, Box 105D, Folder 105-24.

653 **delay publication:** FF to CCB, 11/12/1958, at 1–3, CCBP, Box 5, Folder 5-17; FF to CCB, 11/20/1958, at 1, *id.*

653 **Frankfurter's suggestion:** JMH 9/19/1958 draft, at 1, FFHLS, Pt. II, Reel 36, Page 167; Freyer, *"Cooper v. Aaron* (1958): A Hidden Story of Unanimity and Division," at 96.

653 **Only Tom Clark:** TCC Draft dissent, n.d., TCCP, Box A73, Folder 2.

653 **Warren read:** HHBD, 9/29/1958, Reel 5; NYT, 9/30/1958 at 1, 20.

653 *Marbury* **& much-criticized:** Cooper v. Aaron, 358 U.S. 1, 18 (1958). *See* Larry D. Kramer, *The People Themselves,* 221 (2004) (describing it as "bluster and puff"); Barry Friedman, *The Will of the People,* 248 (2009) ("The Court was the Constitution, and the Constitution was the supreme law—at least so long as there was force backing it up."); Barry Friedman & Erin F. Delaney, "Becoming Supreme: The Federal Foundation of Judicial Supremacy," 111 Colum. L. Rev. 1137, 1174 (2011) (describing it as "the Court's strongest statement of supremacy to date"); Edwin Meese III, "The Law of the Constitution," 61 Tul. L. Rev. 979, 986 (1987) (declaring *Cooper* "arrive[d] at con-

clusions about its own power that would have shocked men like John Marshall and Joseph Story").

653 **draft concurrence:** *See* FF draft concurrence incorporating second memorandum, n.d., FFHLS, Pt. II, Reel 36, Pages 92–97; Concurrence cover page, 10/1958, *id.* at Page 144; FF concurrence "as revised by FF," 9/22/1958, *id.* at Pages 230–38; Draft, "7/22/1958 [sic] revised by FF," *id.* at Pages 239–46; Draft, n.d., *id.* at Pages 249–66; Draft, n.d., 10/1958, *id.* at Pages 267–74; Draft, n.d., 10/1958, *id.* at Pages 275–82; Final draft, 10/6/1958, *id.* at Pages 459–66.

654 **"Every Act":** Cooper, 358 U.S. at 23 (Frankfurter, J., concurring) (quoting United States v. United Mine Workers, 330 U.S. 258, 308 (1947) (Frankfurter, J., concurring)).

654 **"Particularly":** *Id.* at 24–25 (Frankfurter, J., concurring).

654 **"Southern":** FF to AMB, 9/4/1958, at 2, FFHLS, Pt. III, Reel 32, at 411.

654 **Brennan's behest:** FF Draft, 10/3/1958, at 1, JMHP, Box 57 (JMH handwritten: October 6 conference at WJB's "instance").

654 **Warren and Black:** WOD, Memorandum re: Cooper v. Aaron, 10/8/1958, at 2. *See* FF, Memorandum, 10/6/1958, FFLC, Box 220; HHBD, 10/6/1958, Reel 5.

654 **"must":** WJB & HLB Oct. 6 concurrence, *id.*

654 **"doubt[ed]" & "material":** JMH Concurring in Part and Dissenting in Part, 10/6/1958, *id.*

655 **directly to southern lawyers:** FF to CCB, 11/12/1958, at 1–3 & FF to CCB, 11/20/1958, at 1–2; Howard Kalodner Int. with author, 12/13/2018.

655 **A.F. House & Lemann:** FF to HLB, n.d., HLBP, Box 335, Folder 1 (enclosing 10/7/1958 letter from House); FF to Brethren, 11/10/1958, WJBP, Box I-15, Folder 2 (enclosing MML excerpt).

655 **several justices:** FF to CCB, 11/12/1958, at 2–3; FF to CCB, 11/20/1958, at 1.

655 **observers & Acheson & Cohen & Pound:** FFHLS, Pt. II, Reel 36, Pages 426–35, Pages 468–70; FFLC, Box 132; FWB to FF, 10/9/1958, at 1, FFLC, Box 40 (indicating he and MDH thought it superior to majority).

CHAPTER 37: A HEALTH SCARE

656 **premiere:** WP, 11/24/1958, at B5.

656 **"an athletic":** FF to LH, 12/1/1958, at 2, LHP, Box 105D, Folder 105-24 (not DA).

656 **photograph & Stewart & mild heart attack:** *id.*; FF Appointment Calendar, 11/22/1958, FFLC, Box 3; *id.*, 11/24/1958.

656 **ashen:** Max Freedman to PAF, 12/2/1958 tel., FFHLS, Pt. III, Reel 38, Page 221.

656 **four times:** FF Appointment Calendar, 11/7/1958 & 11/12/1958 & 11/17/1958 & 11/21/1958 (visits to Dr. Walter A. Bloedorn).

656 **"This onset":** FF to LH, 12/1/1958. at 2.

656 **three times:** Freedman to PAF, 12/2/1958 tel.

656 **"rest":** ED to PAF and Sacks, 11/28/1958, FFHLS, Pt. III, Reel 38, Page 218. *See* FF to PAF, 12/1/1958, *id.* at 219 (ED note); ED to Edmund M. Morgan, 12/3/1958, FFLC, Box 124.

657 **two tax cases:** FF to TCC, 12/4/1958, TCCP, Box 48.

657 **"take":** TCC to FF, 12/10/1958, *id.*

657 **"generous":** ED to TCC, 12/9/1958, *id.*

657 **"Please":** JFK to FF, 12/19/1958, FFLC, Box 71 (FF handwritten). *See id.*, Box 124 (six folders of get-well letters).

657 **"admirer":** James Rowe, Jr., to LBJ, 12/4/1958, LBJL, LBJA Famous Names, Box 4. The

drafter of the note was former FF student and LBJ aide James Rowe. *Id.* (Rowe handwritten: "If you do send it, I suggest you read a copy to [FF clerk Richard] Goodwin."); Draft, n.d., *id.* & LBJ to Rowe, 12/8/1958, Rowe Papers, FDRL, Box 90 (approving draft but changing dove hunting to quail hunting because of season).

657 **chrysanthemums:** ED to LBJ, 12/3/1958, at 1–2, LBJL, LBJA Famous Names, Box 4.

657 **"It is not":** LBJ to FF, 12/6/1958, at 1, *id.* & FFHLS, Pt. III, Reel 15, Page 951.

657 **"I have been" & "behave" & "keep" & "concessions" & "mental depression" & "This 'heart'":** LBJ to FF, 12/6/1958, at 1–2. *See* Adrian Fisher to FF, 12/19/1958, FFLC, Box 124 (indicating MDF showed him the letter).

657 **"heart-warming" & "store up":** FF to LBJ, 12/18/1959, at 1–2, LBJL, LBJA Famous Names, Box 4.

657 **"the Johnson":** FF to LBJ, 1/31/1959, *id.*

658 **Civil Rights Act of 1957:** Katharine Graham, *Personal History*, 238, 240 (1997).

658 **"wisdom" & "right":** FF to AMB, 1/28/1959, at 1, FFHLS, Pt. III, Reel 32, Page 478 (enclosing TNR, 2/2/1959, at 5–6, *id.* at 480).

658 **doctors & summoning:** Howard Kalodner Int. with author, 12/13/2018.

658 **reflected:** FF to Fisher, 1/25/1959, at 2, FFHLS, Pt. III, Reel 32, Page 477.

658 **"the Black":** FF to PAF, 1/1/1959, at 1, FFHLS, Pt. III, Reel 38, Page 226.

658 **stairlift:** Richard Goodwin to JLR, 12/18/1959, JLRP, Box 34, Folder 7; FF to Fisher, 1/25/1959, at 2.

658 **questioning lawyers:** NYHT, 1/13/1959, at 12; WP, 1/13/1959, at A2.

658 **"The Court":** WP, 1/14/1959, at A18.

658 **"His influence" & "his approach" & "his continued":** NYT, 2/1/1959, at E10.

658 **lobbying:** FF to AMB, 3/12/1959, at 2, FFHLS, Pt. III, Reel 32, Page 501; FF to CCB, 3/11/1959, at 2, CCBP, Box 5, Folder 5-17; FF to LH, 3/12/1959, LHP, Box 105-D, Folder 105-24; FF to LH, 3/24/1959, *id.*

659 **"From Clerk":** NYT, 3/11/1959, at 38.

659 **"all":** FF to LH, 8/19/1959, at 1, LHP, Box 105D, Folder 105-25. *See* FF to AMB, 4/1/1959, FFHLS, Pt. III, Reel 32, Page 504 (Dodd); LBJ Senate Daily Diary, 8/12/1959 (noting 12:30 FF request to see him); *id.*, 8/19/1959 (9:50 a.m. meeting with FF); *id.*, 9/11/1959 (6:30 p.m. meeting in Speaker's office with FF and DA).

659 **"great":** FF to LBJ, 9/9/1959, LBJL, LBJA Famous Names, Box 4.

659 **morning train & 3:30 p.m.:** FF Appointment Calendar, 4/10/1959, FFLC, Box 3.

659 **without notes:** FF to FWB, 4/20/1959, at 1–2, FFLC, Box 40.

659 **"lucky" & "the joy":** FF Remarks, 4/10/1959, at 3, FFHLS, Pt. III, Reel 32, Page 523. *See* LH to FF, 4/25/1959, LHP, Box 105D, Folder 105-25; FF to LH, 4/27/1959, at 2, *id.* ("lucky not to get on the Nine"); FF to CCB, 4/7/1959, CCBP, Box 5, Folder 5-17; PAF to FF, 4/13/1959, FFHLS, Pt. III, Reel 15, Page 961 (describing it as a "virtuoso performance"); NYT, 4/11/1959, at 1, 12.

659 **Alfonse Bartkus:** Bartkus v. Illinois, 359 U.S. 121, 121–22 (1959).

659–660 **Fairman's conclusion & appendix:** Bartkus, 359 U.S. at 124–25 & *id.* at 140–49 App.

660 **"implicit":** *Id.* at 127 (quoting Palko v. Connecticut, 302 U.S. 319, 324–25 1937)).

660 **"two-sovereignty":** *Id.* at 127–28, 134. *See* WJB Docket Book, *Bartkus v. Illinois*, WJBP, Box I:15, Folder 4; WOD Conference Notes, *Bartkus v. Illinois* 1957 Term, WODP, Box 1201 (FF arguing *Palko* controlled and only "limitation" was Fourteenth Amendment due process); WOD Conference Notes, at 1, *Bartkus v. Illinois* 1958 Term, *id.* (FF emphasizing belief in "our federalism").

660   **"double" & "one" & "If double":** Bartkus, 359 U.S. at 150–55 & n.1 (Black, J., dissenting).

660   **"actually":** Bartkus, 359 U.S. at 165–66 (Brennan, J., dissenting).

660   **not to publish:** FF to Al Sacks, 6/17/1959, FFHLS, Pt. III, Reel 18, Page 384 (expressing "regret" over not publishing supplemental memorandum in *Bartkus*); FF to AMB, 4/4/1959, *id.*, Reel 32, Page 505 (enclosing memorandum and remarking: "I give up the to do on double jeopardy.").

660   **circulated & responded:** "Memorandum of Justice Frankfurter in reply to the Dissenting Opinion circulated by Mr. Justice Brennan," 2/6/1959, WJBP, Box I:16, Folder 11 & FFHLS, Pt. II, Reel 36, Page 557; WJB, "Memorandum to the Conference," 2/6/1959, WJBP Box I:16, Folder 11 & FFHLS, Pt. II, Reel 36, Page 850.

660   **"hot":** WJB 1958 Term Case History, at v, WJBP, Box II:6.

660   **to narrow:** Abbate v. United States, 359 U.S. 187 (1959); FF to WJB, 2/6/1959, WJBP, Box I:17, Folder 8; FF to WJB, 2/9/1959, *id.*; FF notes on WJB draft, 2/20/1959, at 1 (FF handwritten note advising WJB not to publish concurrence to his own majority opinion).

660   **rejected the application & upheld:** Frank v. Maryland, 359 U.S. 360 (1959). *See* FF to WJB, 4/16/1959, at 1–2, WJBP, Box I:24, Folder 11; WJB to WOD, 4/23/1959, at 1–2, WODP, Box 1210; WOD Conference Notes, at 1, *Frank v. Maryland*, 3/6/1959, *id.*; FF to WJB, 5/19/1959, WJBP, Box I:24, Folder 11; FF to JMH, 5/19/1959, at 1–2, JMHP, Box 68 (EW and WJB switched from FF's majority to WOD's dissent). The dissent's position prevailed eight years later. Camara v. Municipal Court, 387 U.S. 523 (1967).

661   **Lloyd Barenblatt:** Barenblatt v. United States, 360 U.S. 109, 113–14 (1959).

661   **investigatory powers:** FF to JMH, 6/3/1939, at 1–2, JMHP, Box 61; JMH Draft, 2/10/1959, *id.* (FF handwritten: praising JMH's opinion for explaining Court's decisions in *Watkins* and *Sweezy* and affirming FF's decision to assign the case to him).

661   **North Dakota widow:** Dick v. New York Life Ins. Co., 359 U.S. 437, 447 (1959) (Frankfurter, J., dissenting). *See* AMB to FF, n.d., FFHLS, Pt. II, Reel 37, Page 195.

661   **"folksy" & "This is a case":** NYT, 5/19/1959, at 1. *See* NYHT, 5/19/1959, at 1.

661   **"It is disheartening":** NYHT, 5/20/1959, at 18.

662   **"They don't":** Kalodner Int. with author, 12/13/2018.

662   **selected:** FF to HMH, 6/25/1957, at 1, FFLC, Box 66 (ending his selection of clerks); Todd C. Peppers & Beth See Driver, "Half Clerk, Half Son, Justice Frankfurter and His Law Clerks," *In Chambers*, 141–60 (Todd C. Peppers & Artemus Ward, eds., 2012).

662   **"distinguished" & "most impressive" & "tops" & "equally" & "In terms" & "her qualities" & "extraordinary" & "I believe":** Sacks to FF, 11/30/1959, at 1–2, FFHLS, Pt. III, Reel 8, Pages 761–62. Sacks incorrectly told FF that Ginsburg was second in her Columbia class, not tied for first. *Id.* at 762.

662–663   **"problems" & "the doctors" & "a very personable" & "The very" & "an appraisal" & "As I":** *Id.* at 2.

663   **"Had" & "Mrs. Ginsberg [sic]" & "I am":** FF to Sacks, 12/7/1959, FFHLS, Pt. III, Reel 8, Page 763.

663   **"You can't" & "We both":** Paul Bender Int. with author, 2/15/2017.

663–664   **"I can't do" & "I work" & "the least" & "Well, I curse" & "He didn't" & "He was willing":** *Id. See* Peppers & Driver, "Half Clerk, Half Son," at 142 (quoting Bender).

664   **broke:** Sacks to FF, 11/30/1959, at 2.

664   **"He said" & "typical 1950s":** Ruth Bader Ginsburg Int. with author, 11/16/2016. *See* Peppers & Driver, "Half Clerk, Half Son," 141 & 157 n.6 (quoting 6/10/2011 letter from Ginsburg about not being surprised).

664   **liked women:** Margery Mendelson, 1/15/1964, "FF and His Impact on the Ladies, or Love is a Cheesecake," FFLC, Box 216.

664   **blind spots:** Goesaert v. Cleary, 335 U.S. 464 (1948); Hoyt v. Florida draft, 11/14/1961, at 1, 5, JMHP, Box 534 (FF handwritten: "You gave this more consideration than it deserved and so I agree" but questioning inclusion of JMH's stereotypes of women); *but see* United States v. Dege, 364 U.S. 51, 54 (1960) (recognizing "vast changes in the status of woman").

664   **Lucile Lomen:** David J. Danelski, "Lucile Lomen: The First Woman to Clerk at the Supreme Court," Journal of Supreme Court History 24, no. 1 (1999): 43–49.

665   **"high regard":** BG, 9/28/1959, at 1, 23.

665   **"the most effective" & "the training":** "Proceedings in Honor of Mr. Justice Frankfurter and Distinguished Alumni," 4/30/1960, at 8, FFLC, Box 200.

665   **"ever-continuing":** *Id.* at 10.

665   **"the outstanding" & "in the most provocative":** *Id.* at 25–26.

665   **"the scaredest":** *Id.* at 38. *See* FF to LH, 5/14/1960, at 1, LHP, Box 105D, Folder 105-25; BG, 5/1/1960, at 21.

666   **Phillips & Oral History Project:** American Heritage, 12/1954; Phillips to FF, 4/19/1953, FFLC, Box 89.

666   **correspondence:** Phillips to FF, 9/28/1953, at 1–3, *id.*; Phillips, "Memorandum in re Justice Frankfurter's Papers," n.d., at 1, *id.*

666   **book:** Reynal to FF, 10/25/1956, FFLC, Box 93; FF to Reynal, 10/29/1956, *id.*; FF to Reynal, 11/5/1956, *id.*

666   **not an autobiography & "just":** FF to Reynal, 1/17/1957, *id.*; Harlan B. Phillips, "Foreword," *Felix Frankfurter Reminisces*, ix (1960).

666   **answered Phillips's questions:** FF to FWB, 7/11/1960, at 1, FFLC, Box 40 ("Heavens I didn't tell Phillips all the happenings of my life. I prattled as his questions guided the trail.").

666   **"an appalling":** IB to AMS Jr., 9/29/1960, at 2, AMSP, NYPL, Box 12, Folder 5.

666   **"It has":** WES, 5/29/1960, at B-5.

667   **six printings:** NYT, 11/2/1960, at 37.

667   **all the royalties:** FF to Reynal, 7/14/1960, FFLC, Box 89 (discussing Phillips's financial situation); FF to Reynal, 7/17/1957, at 1–2, FFLC, Box 93; FWB to FF, 9/13/1960, FFLC, Box 40 (FF handwritten: "Not a penny in my pocket! All the royalties go to Phillips, to whom I had assigned all rights when agreeing to publication."); Reynal to FF, 7/27/1961, Box 93 (prevailing upon FF to accept $2500, half the paperback advance).

667   **scores of letters:** FFLC, Box 123–24.

667   **Maine & more reclusive:** FF to LH, 8/10/1959 or circa 6/1959, at 1, LHP, Box 105D, Folder 105-25.

667   **not improving:** DA to Jerry Cohen, 12/26/1960, DAP Papers, Reel 5.

667   **"hellish" & "burdensome" & "maintains":** PG to IB, 10/9/1960, at 1, IBP, Box 161, Page 37.

667   **Phil Graham & Johnson:** Graham, *Personal History*, 259–74; JLR OH, 12/23/1965, at 92–93, JFKL.

667   **"not my":** Richard N. Goodwin, *Remembering America*, 25 (1988). *See* PG to IB, 10/9/1960, at 2 & FF to PBK, 7/20/1960, at 2, PBKP, Box 15, Folder 6 (lukewarm views on JFK).

667–668 **hated Richard Nixon:** FF to AMB, circa end of 10/1960, FFHLS, Pt. III, Reel 32, Page 715.

668   **"a wiser":** FF to AMB, circa 11/1/1960, *id.* at 717. *See* WP, 10/27/1960, at A27.

668   "know": FF to FWB, 7/19/1960, at 1, FFLC, Box 40.

668   DuPont's training program: SGates to FF, circa 1959, at 1, 8, FFLC, Box 58; FF to American Embassy, 11/23/1959, *id.*

668   job interview & medical: Oliver Gates Int. with author, 5/8/2016.

668   weekends: Oliver Gates to FF & MDF, 6/4/1960, FFLC, Box 58.

668   Bickel: FF to AMB, circa 10/1960, FFHLS, Pt. III, Reel 32, Page 714; Liva Baker to AMB, 2/5/1969, FFHLS, Pt. III, Reel 33, Page 156 (based on int. with Oliver Gates); AMB to Baker, 2/13/1969, *id.* at 157; Email from Oliver Gates to author, 1/11/2019.

668   "betrayed" & "a *de facto*" & "'immaturity'" & "more people": FF to AMB, circa end of 10/1960.

668–669 "I dare" & "hubris" & "comeuppance" & "slid" & "my confidence": FF to AMB, 11/25/1960, at 1–2, FFHLS, Pt. III, Reel 32, Pages 727–28.

669   Ten former: In addition to PE, Chayes, and Goodwin, others included Adrian Fisher (deputy director, Arms Control and Disarmament Agency), PG (incorporator for Communications Satellite Corporation [COMSAT]), EBP (special assistant to attorney general), J. William Doolittle (solicitor general's office), Howard Kalodner (Labor Department), Paul Bender (solicitor general's office), and John French (counsel to FTC commissioner PE). *Cf.* William E. Nelson et al., "The Supreme Court Clerkship and the Polarization of the Court," 13 Green Bag 2d, 65 (Autumn 2009) (counting eight FF clerks in administration).

669   rumored: FF to EG, 11/29/1960, FFHLS, Pt. III, Reel 32, Page 730 (FF handwritten to Joey Bickel: "Can it be true that P.F. is ready & willing to be S.G.? I can't believe it!!").

669   "to set": PAF to FF, 12/5/1960, at 2, FFHLS, Pt. III, Reel 15, Page 983.

669   "to stay": PAF to FF, 12/5/1960, at 4.

669   Roosevelt and Kennedy: *Id.* at 3; FF to AMB, 12/22/1960, at 1–3, FFHLS, Pt. III, Reel 32, Page 740–42

669   Holmes Devise: Stanley N. Katz, "Official History: The Holmes Devise History of the Supreme Court," Proceedings of the American Philosophical Society, 141, no. 3 (1997): 297–304; CEW, "Paul Abraham Freund," 89 Harv. L. Rev. 1663, 1664 (1976).

670   "The soul-searching": PAF to FF, 12/9/1960, at 1, FFHLS, Pt. III, Reel 15, Page 986.

670   "I thought": Victory S. Navasky, *Kennedy Justice*, 284–5 (1971).

670   "as tho": FF to AMB, 12/12/1960, FFHLS, Pt. III, Reel 32, Page 734. *See* FF to Charles Merz, 12/7/1960, at 1–2, *id.* at Pages 735–36 (responding to NYT, 12/7/1960, at 42).

670   romantic fantasy: FF to AMB, 12/22/1960, at 1–3, *id.* at Pages 740–42.

670   "discordant": FF to AMB, 12/27/1960, *id.* at Page 743.

670   "obstinacies": FF to AMB, 1/7/1961, at 1–3, *id.* at Pages 745–47.

CHAPTER 38: THE POLITICAL THICKET

671   4:00 p.m.: Bernard Taper, *Gomillion versus Lightfoot*, 78 (1962).

671   Montgomery Bus Boycott: Gayle v. Browder, 352 U.S. 903 (1956) (per curiam), aff'g Browder v. Gayle, 142 F. Supp. 707 (M.D. Ala. 1956).

671   "the most": Fred D. Gray, *Bus Ride to Justice*, 119 (rev. ed. 2012).

671   "fascinated": Taper, *Gomillion*, 84.

671   map: Gray, *Bus Ride to Justice*, 3–5, 117–18.

671   28-sided & "sea dragon": Gomillion oral argument, 10/18/1960, at 07:08, 30:49, https://apps.oyez.org/player/#/warren7/oral_argument_audio/14354; *cf.* Gray, *Bus Ride to Justice*, 113 ("25-sided sea dragon").

672 **Frank Johnson & court of appeals:** Gomillion v. Lightfoot, 167 F. Supp. 405 (M.D. Ala. 1958), aff'd by 270 F.2d 594 (5th Cir. 1959).

672 **"political":** Colegrove v. Green, 328 U.S. 549, 556 (1946).

672 **"We are":** Colegrove, 328 U.S. at 552.

672 **dissented again:** South v. Peters, 339 U.S. 276 (1950) (per curiam); Hartsfield v. Sloan, 357 U.S. 916 (1958) (per curiam).

672 **"It is":** Gomillion oral argument, 10/18/1960, at :03:30, https://apps.oyez.org/player/#/ warren7/oral_argument_audio/14354.

672 **knew:** Gray, *Bus Ride to Justice*, 4–5.

673 **impressed:** FF to WTC, 1/2/1962, at 2, FFHLS, Pt. III, Reel 32, Page 864.

673 **"We take" & "is as gross":** Gomillion oral argument, 10/18/1960 at 19:03 & 22:19, https://apps.oyez.org/player/#/warren7/oral_argument_audio/14354.

673 **not asking:** Gomillion oral argument, 10/19/1960, at 06:24, https://apps.oyez.org/ player/#/warren7/oral_argument_audio/14535. *See* Robert L. Carter, *A Matter of Law*, 161–62 (2005).

673 **"in substance" & "class legislation":** Gomillion oral argument, 10/19/1960, at 36:16, 40:16, https://apps.oyez.org/player/#/warren7/oral_argument_audio/14535.

673 **"If the courts":** *Id.* at 1:30:05, *id.*

673 **"The abatement":** *Id.* at 1:30:49, *id.*

673–674 **"distinction" & "was done":** WJB *Gomillion* Conference Notes, at 1, WJBP, Box I:43, Folder 15.

674 **all cities & "simple" & "nothing" & "negroes":** WOD *Gomillion* Conference Notes, 10/21/1960, at 1–2, WODP, Box 1234.

674 **heavily edited:** FF, *Gomillion* memorandum, FFHLS, Pt. II, Reel 62, Pages 741–49 (FF handwritten).

674 **look in the South:** FF to AMB, 11/25/1960, at 2–3, FFHLS, Pt. III, Reel 32, Pages 728–29.

674 **cried:** Guido Calabresi Int. with author, 8/24/2018.

674 **hostile:** WOD *Gomillion* Conference Notes, 10/21/1960, at 1.

674 **"avoiding":** FF to HLB, 11/1/1960, FFHLS, Pt. II, Reel 62, Page 933.

674 **references to *Colegrove*:** FF handwritten note on draft opinion, 11/2/1960, at 1, *id.* at Page 871; FF to AMB, 11/25/1960, at 3.

675 **"crookery" & "shamelessness" & "the most unqualified":** FF to LH, 4/27/1959, at 1, LHP, Box 105D, Folder 105-25.

675 **canoe trip:** WOD Memorandum re: *Cooper v. Aaron*, 10/8/1958, at 1, WODP, Box 1199.

675 **anti-Semitic:** AMB Int. with Lash, 9/12/1974, at 5–6; FF, "To the Editor," circa 10/1/1961, FFHLS, Pt. III, Reel 32, Page 838 (writing AMB about "when Douglas told Justice Murphy, who had joined a dissent by Frankfurter, J. that the latter had expressed mischievous views to help out some of his New York Jewish financial friends").

675 **"used to say":** AMB Int. with Lash, 9/12/1974, at 5–6.

675 **private memoranda:** WOD Memorandum, 11/21/1960, WODP, Box 1234 (objecting to FF's "violent outbursts" at him and threatening to absent himself from the conference).

675 **threatened to publish:** WOD to FF, n.d., FFHLS, Pt. II, Reel 62, Page 941; FF to HLB, 11/9/1960, *id.* at 938; FF to EW, 11/10/1960, *id.* at 939.

675 **Fourteenth Amendment:** Gomillion, 339 U.S. at 349 (Whittaker, J., concurring).

675 **clear case:** FF to Whittaker, 11/4/1960, FFHLS, Pt. II, Reel 62, Page 936.

675 **"The decisive":** Gomillion v. Lightfoot, 364 U.S. 339, 346–47 (1960).

675 **"unreconstructed":** AL to FF, 11/15/1960, FFHLS, Pt. II, Reel 62, Page 643.

676   **to register:** Communist Party v. Subversive Activities Control Board, 367 U.S. 1 (1961).

676   **Brandeis's admonition:** Poe v. Ullman, 367 U.S. 497, 503 (1961) (quoting Ashwander v. Tennessee Valley Authority, 297 U.S. 288, 341, 346 (1936) (Brandeis, J., concurring)). *See* FF to AMB, 8/4/1961, at 1–2, FFHLS, Pt. III, Reel 32, Pages 810–11.

676   **lone dissenter:** Monroe v. Pape, 365 U.S. 167, 202 (1961) (Frankfurter, J., dissenting).

676   **53-page memorandum:** FF, Memorandum to Conference, 11/9/1960, FFHLS, Pt. II, Reel 67 at Page 939.

676   **historically narrow:** *Id.* at 942; Screws v. United States, 325 U.S. 91, 138, 140–42 (1945) (Roberts, Frankfurter, Jackson, JJ., dissenting).

676   **failed to persuade:** WJB *Monroe v. Pape* Conference Notes, WJBP, Box I:43, Folder 15; WOD *Monroe v. Pape* Conference Notes, 11/11/1960, WODP, Box 1246; FF, *Monroe v. Pape* Conference Notes, 11/11/1960, at 1–3, FFHLS, Pt. II, Reel 67, Pages 929–31 & Handwritten notes, n.d., *id.* at Page 936.

676   **Warren admitted & "firm":** JMH to FF, 9/11/1960, *id.* at 940.

676   **joined Harlan's dissent:** Mapp v. Ohio, 367 U.S. 643, 672 (1961) (Harlan, J., dissenting).

676   **"the worst tragedy":** Polly J. Price, "*Mapp v. Ohio*: A Law Clerk's Diary," Journal of Supreme Court History 35, no. 1 (March 2010): 63 (quoting WJB clerk Richard S. Arnold's diary from that term).

676   **bad feelings:** FF to Conference, 1/30/1962, at 1–2, FFHLS, Pt. III, Reel 32, Pages 945–46; WOD to Conference, 1/30/1962, *id.* at 947; FF to Conference, 1/31/1962, *id.* at 948; WOD to Conference, 1/31/1962, *id.* at 949.

676   **"If I told":** FF to AMB, 7/31/1961, at 2, FFHLS, Pt. III, Reel 32, Page 798.

677   **federal larceny:** Milanovich v. United States, 365 U.S. 551, 556 (1961) (Frankfurter, J., dissenting).

677   **"but of course":** NYT, 3/21/1961, at 1, 18.

677   **murder conviction:** Stewart v. United States, 366 U.S. 1, 11 (1961) (Frankfurter, J., dissenting).

677   **"lecture" & "degrading" & "I'll leave":** NYT, 4/25/1961, at 1, 27. *See* Time, 5/5/1961, at 19; FF to DA, n.d., DAP, Reel 8, Box 12, Folder 148 (referring it as "the case that gave rise to the Swede's Explosion" and noting that new U.S. Attorney David Acheson would have to decide whether to try Stewart a fourth time).

677   **"disgraceful" & "so sensitive":** FF, Memorandum, 4/25/1961, FFHLS, Pt. III, Reel 32, Page 780. *See* FF to AMB, 5/1/1961, *id.* at Page 781 ("inexcusable"); PBK to FF, 3/23/1961, PBKP, Box 15, Folder 7 (FF's handwritten comments referencing TCC and how "thin-skinned" EW is).

677   **delayed:** *Baker* Docket sheet, TCCP, Box 182; *Baker* Docket Sheet, WJBP, Box I:43, Folder 16; WJB Term History, OT 1961, at I, *id.*, Box I:6, Folder 4. The Court did not note probable jurisdiction until November 21, a week after the decision in *Gomillion*. WOD Docket Book, OT 1960, Box 1232.

677   **favored rural voters:** Brief for Appellants, *Baker v. Carr*, February 21, 1961, at 6–12; Baker v. Carr, 369 U.S. 186, 331–32 (1962) (Harlan, J., dissenting). *See* Gene S. Graham, *One Man, One Vote* (1972); Richard L. Hasen, *The Supreme Court and Election Law* (2003); J. Douglas Smith, *On Democracy's Doorstep* (2014).

677   **"rue":** WOD *Baker* Conference Notes, 4/20/1961, at 1, WODP, Box 1267.

678   **"a brilliant":** WJB Term History, OT 1961, at I–II.

678   **A week later:** WOD *Baker* Conference Notes, 4/28/1961, WODP, Box 1267.

678   **"extraordinary":** FF to Henkin, 1/23/1963, at 2, FFHLS, Pt. III, Reel 28, Page 947.

678　　**void-for-vagueness:** Anthony G. Amsterdam, Note, "The Void-For-Vagueness Doctrine in the Supreme Court," 109 U. Pa. L. Rev. 67 (1960).

678　　**"about your":** FF to Henkin, 11/25/1959, FFHLS, Pt. III, Reel 28, Page 916.

678　　**interviewed with Stewart:** FF to Henkin, 12/5/1959, at 1, *id.* at 915; Henkin to FF, circa 11/1959, FFLC, Box 66.

678　　**mesmerized:** Amsterdam COH at 20–22 (2010).

678　　**nonpaying position:** Email from Anthony Amsterdam to author, 7/8/2021.

679　　**"24-hour-a-day":** WJB Int. 14, at 3 by Stephen Wermiel, 5/1987.

679　　**attic:** Daniel Mayers Int. with author, 1/10/2017.

679　　**Amsterdam drafted:** FF, *Baker v. Carr* memorandum draft, FFLC, Box 221.

679　　**By July:** FF, *Baker v. Carr* memorandum draft, 7/1961, FFHLS, Pt. II, Reel 82, Pages 302–62.

679　　**After his clerkship:** Amsterdam COH at 25–28.

679　　**honorary degree:** FF, "F.F.'s Remarks at Luncheon After Receiving the Degree of Doctor of Law, Yale University Commencement," 6/12/1961, FFLC, Box 200.

679　　**"You are" & "fallen" & "all the time" & "your Court" & "popular" & "the impossibility":** LH to FF, 6/13/1961, at 1–3, FFHLS, Pt. III, Reel 27, Pages 659–61.

679　　**"This has been" & "because of" & "Oh liberty":** FF to LH, 6/15/1961, at 2, LHP, Box 105D, Folder 105-26.

679–680　**Maine & Frances Watson:** FF to AMB, 7/18/1961, at 1–2, FFHLS, Pt. III, Reel 32, Pages 794–95; FF to AMB, 7/24/1961, *id.* at Page 796; FF to Herrman Blumgart, 7/11/1961, at 2, *id.*, Reel 39, Page 397; FF to PBK, n.d., PBKP, Box 15, Folder 7.

680　　**heart attacks & St. Luke's:** Mary Darrell to FF, 8/9/1961, at 1, FFHLS, Pt. III, Reel 27, Page 662.

680　　**"B DIED":** Frances Hand to FF, 8/18/1961 tel., *id.* at Page 664.

680　　**"A truly":** FF Statement, 8/18/1961, *id.* at 671.

680　　**"lucky" & "would have been":** NYT, 8/20/1961, at 57. *See* FF, Dedication, Harvard Law School Yearbook 4 (1962), FFLC, Box 200.

680　　**"coup" & "a bevy":** Learned Hand, *The Bill of Rights*, 54–55, 73 (1958).

680　　**"saving" & "the great" & "too discursive" & "initial" & "a very" & "supreme":** LH COH at 99–101.

680　　**never endorsed:** FF to AMB, 9/1/1961, at 2, FFHLS, Pt. III, Reel 32, Page 817 ("As you know, I don't go the last stretch with L.H. on judicial review, but I go a long, long way & I do so because a *Mapp* result, reached for so indefensible . . . a consideration as it was . . .").

681　　**"neither side":** FF Memorandum to Conference, 10/10/1961, FFHLS, Pt. II, Reel 80, Page 388.

681　　**"the independence" & refrain:** JMH to PS & Whittaker, 10/11/1961, at 1–2, FFLC, Box 65.

681　　**praised:** FF to JMH, 10/11/1961, JMHP, Box 135.

681　　**"I should":** WJB Memorandum to Conference, 10/12/1962, at 2, WODP, Box 1267.

682　　**"a good" & "a weak":** WOD *Baker* Conference Notes, 10/13/1961, at 1, WODP, Box 1267.

682　　**"approximately fair"** FF *Baker* Conference Notes, 10/13/1961, at 1, FFHLS, Pt. II, Reel 82, Page 546. *Cf.* Colegrove v. Green, 328 U.S. 549, 572 (1946) (Black, J., dissenting) ("approximately equal").

682　　**"dangerous":** WJB *Baker* Conference Notes, 10/13/1961, at 1, WJBP, Box I:60, Folder 1.

682　　**white power & "with most":** WJB Term History OT 1961, at III.

682　　**"no constitutionally":** FF *Baker* Conference Notes, 10/13/1961, at 2, FFHLS, Pt. II, Reel 82, Page 547.

682 **"denial" & "getting into" & "the greatness" & "What does" & "an equal" & "very shaky" & "diametrically":** WOD *Baker* Conference Notes, 10/13/1961, at 3–5.

682 **allay:** FF to Whittaker, 10/6/1961, at 1–2, FFHLS, Pt. II, Reel 80, Pages 516–17.

682 **no political:** WOD *Baker* Conference Notes, 10/13/1961, at 6.

682 **heavy burden:** WJB Term History OT 1961, at III.

683 **"I assume" & "The whole" & "legally" & "in kind" & "Disallowing":** FF to PS, 10/13/1961, FFHLS, Pt. II, Reel 80, Page 518.

683 **Stewart's views & Brennan:** WJB Term History OT 1961, at III–IV; WJB to WOD, n.d., WJBP, Box I:65, Folder 1.

683 **"Five votes":** Nat Hentoff, "Profiles: The Constitutionalist," New Yorker, 3/12/1990, at 60. FF has been quoted by WJB as saying: "I always wanted my students to think for themselves, but Brennan goes too far." *Id.* at 48. *Cf.* "A Visit with Justice Brennan," *Look* magazine, 12/18/1962, at 127 (similar quote). FF apparently made the comment in August 1960 at a dinner in honor of Oxford University scholar Arthur Goodhart at Justice Harlan's house. It is unclear, however, whether WJB was actually there. *Compare* WJB Int. 31, at 8 with Stephen Wermiel (he was) with WJB Int. with Anthony Lewis, 5/13/1992 (he wasn't). Either way, FF was troubled by WJB's willingness to privilege finding five votes over following precedent.

683 **"black nights":** WJB Term History OT 1961, at IV.

684 **draft to Stewart:** WJB to PS, 1/22/1962, WJBP, Box I:63, Folder 2.

684 **"full discussion":** WJB to EW, HLB, WOD, 1/27/1962, *id.*

684 **Douglas wanted:** WOD to WJB, 1/29/1962, WODP, Box 1267.

684 **"looks":** WJB to HLB, 1/31/1962, *id.*

684 **The day after:** FF dissent, 2/1/1962, WODP, Box 1266; WJB *Baker* Docket Sheet, WJBP, Box I:63, Folder 2.

684 **Stewart joined:** PS to WJB, 2/1/1962, *id.*

684 **"unanswerable":** TCC to FF, 2/3/1962, FFHLS, Pt. II, Reel 80, Page 250.

684 **"a remarkably":** JMH to FF, 2/5/1962, *id.* at 389.

684 **open mind:** JMH to PS, 2/8/1962, *id.* at 391.

684 **privy:** WJB to Whittaker, 1/31/1962, WJBP, Box I:63, Folder 2.

684 **"much uncertainty":** Whittaker to FF, 2/14/1962, FFHLS, Pt. II, Reel 80, Page 251; Craig Alan Smith, *Failing Justice* (2005).

684 **switched:** TCC to FF, 3/7/1962, FFHLS, Pt. II, Reel 80, Page 704.

684 **"enjoin" & original:** WOD *Baker v. Carr* Concurring Opinion at 6, n.d., WODP, Box 1267 (FF handwritten & WOD handwritten).

685 **"a great day":** EW, note, n.d., WJBP, I:64, Folder 4.

685 **"the most":** EW, *The Memoirs of Earl Warren*, 306 (1977).

685 **"impos[ing]":** FF to JMH, 3/5/1962, at 1–2, JMHP, Box 534.

685 **political question & "case-by-case" & "ultimate" & "well developed" & "simply":** Baker v. Carr, 369 U.S. 186, 211, 226 (1962).

686 **African Americans & "denial" & "not a case":** *Id.* at 285–86, 267, 300 (Frankfurter, J., dissenting).

686 **"futility":** *Id.* at 267, 280–81 (Frankfurter, J., dissenting).

686 **criticized & "Talk" & "their private" & "provides":** *Id.* at 267, 300–302 (Frankfurter, J., dissenting).

686 **"one person":** Reynolds v. Sims, 377 U.S. 533, 558 (1964).

687 **"In a democratic":** Baker v. Carr, 369 U.S. 186, 270 (1962) (Frankfurter, J., dissenting).

687   **"recognized"**: *Id.* at 280–81 & n.10 (1962) (Frankfurter, J., dissenting) (citing AMB, Foreword: "The Passive Virtues," 75 Harv. L. Rev. 40, 45 et seq. (1961)).

687   **"legitimating it"**: AMB, "The Passive Virtues," 75 Harv. L. Rev. at 50.

687   ***"Plessy v. Ferguson's* Error"**: AMB, "The Durability of *Colegrove v. Green*," 72 Yale L.J. 39, 45 (1962).

688   **"legal process"**: HMH & Albert M. Sacks, *The Legal Process*, 145–52 (William N. Eskridge, Jr. & Philip P. Frickey, eds. 1994); William N. Eskridge, Jr. & Philip P. Frickey, "An Historical and Critical Introduction" in HMH & Sacks, *The Legal Process*, at cii, ciii; AMB and Harry H. Wellington, "Legislative Purpose and the Judicial Process: *The Lincoln Mills Case*," 71 Harv. L. Rev. 1 (1957); Herbert Wechsler, "Toward Neutral Principles of Constitutional Law," 73 Harv. L. Rev. 1 (1959); HMH, "The Supreme Court, 1958 Term—Foreword: The Time Chart of the Justices," 73 Harv. L. Rev. 84 (1959).

688   **"one of"**: Eskridge & Frickey, "An Historical and Critical Introduction," at civ n.234.

688   **"Felix Frankfurter"**: HMH & Herbert Wechsler, *The Federal Courts and the Federal System*, ix (1953). *See* FF to HMH & Wechsler, 10/3/1953, at 1–2, Wechsler Papers, Box 94, Pt. 6.

688   **" 'slick' " & "shockingly" & "to break" & "the impossible" & "that the attempt"**: AMB to FF, misdated ca. 8/18/1962, at 1, FFHLS, Pt. III, Reel 14, Page 562.

689   **"Am I right" & "I'm afraid"**: FF to AMB, 4/4/1962, at 1–2, FFHLS, Pt. III, Reel 32, Pages 964–65.

689   **"Rationality" & "the Supreme Court" & "grave" & "that legitimated"**: AMB, "The Durability of *Colegrove v. Green*," 72 Yale L.J. at 43, 45.

689–690   **"deviant" & "counter-majoritarian" & "undemocratic" & " 'vital' " & section on *Baker v. Carr***: AMB, *The Least Dangerous Branch*, 16–18, 26, 189–97 (1962) (quoting Eugene V. Rostow, "The Democratic Character of Judicial Review," 66 Harv. L. Rev. 193, 208 (1952)).

690   **"necessarily"**: AMB to FF, 10/22/1962, FFHLS, Pt. III, Reel 33, Page 7.

690   **health prevented**: FF to AMB, 11/14/1962, *id.*, Page 15.

690   **"chief" & "He finally"**: ED to AMB, 1/23/1963, *id.*, Page 24.

CHAPTER 39: FATHER TO THEM ALL

691   **"join"**: WP, 3/28/1962, at B10.

691   **bookshop**: HarCour, 3/27/1959, at 24A.

691   **"Robert Frost"**: Remarks of Mr. Justice Frankfurter, 3/26/1962, FFLC, Box 200 & FF, *Of Law and Life and Other Things That Matter*, 232 (Phillip B. Kurland, ed. 1965).

691   **speakers**: (1) Dean Erwin Griswold (FF student, colleague); (2) Elliot Richardson (law clerk); (3) Wayne G. Barnett (JMH clerk); (4) Judge John Dooling, Jr. (student); (5) Frederick Bernays Wiener (student); (6) Prof. Paul Freund (student); (7) Prof. Edmund M. Morgan (colleague). *See* Richard Posner to FF, 10/25/1961, FFLC, Box 142; FF to Posner, 10/30/1961, *id.*; Posner to FF, 3/13/1962, *id.*; FF to Posner, 3/15/1962, *id.*; FF to Wiener, 3/22/1962, PBKP, Box 16, Folder 1; PE to AMB, 3/19/1962, FFHLS, Pt. III, Reel 32, Page 958.

692   **looking forward**: FF to AMB, 4/4/1962, at 2, *id.*, Reel 32, Page 955.

692   **4:30 p.m. & Ward Just**: FF Calendar Sheets, 4/5/1962, FFLC, Box 4.

692   **mumbling & couch**: Garson Kanin, "Trips to Felix," in *Felix Frankfurter: A Tribute*, 46 (Wallace Mendelson, ed. 1964).

692 **"transient"** & **"cleared"** & **"a short"**: Report of Dr. George A. Kelser, 4/6/1962, FFLC, Box 124.

692 **second stroke:** DA to Robert Menzies, 4/10/1962, DAP, Reel 14.

692 **"improved":** Medical report, 4/19/1962, FFLC, Box 124.

692 **"in due":** Statement, 4/23/1962, *id.*

692 **"further":** Statement, 4/30/1962, *id.*

692 **"continues":** ED to PAF, 5/1/1962, FFHLS, Pt. III, Reel 38, Page 298.

692 **"gaining":** ED to PAF, 5/15/1962, *id.* at 299.

693 **Harlan:** FF to JMH, 4/30/1962, JMH, Box 534.

693 **possibility of a return:** DA to Menzies, 4/23/1962, at 1–2, DAP, Reel 14.

693 **"In short":** DA to Menzies, 4/10/1962.

693 **"a blue"** & **"I was"** & **"whether"** & **"He is not"** & **"had a good"** & **"felt"** & **"quite":** SNB to IB, 5/15/1962, at 1, IBP, Box 168, Page 229. *See* SNB to Ruth Gordon, 5/15/1962, Behrman Papers, Box 13, Folder 3; Kanin, "Trips to Felix," in *Felix Frankfurter: A Tribute*, 46–47.

693 **"a kaleidoscopic"** & **"the improvement":** Blumgart to MDF, 5/2/1962, FFLC, Box 124.

693 **Marion:** *Id.*

693 **"nearly":** FF to PBK, 2/6/1962, at 2, PBKP, Box 16, Folder 1. *See* FFHLS, Pt. III, Reel 23, Pages 982–1024.

693 **photograph:** Kanin, "Trips to Felix," in *Felix Frankfurter: A Tribute*, 47.

694 **every night** & **visit:** ED to Mrs. Gouverneur, 5/11/1962, FFLC, Box 124.

694 **"terribly":** MDF to Blumgart, 5/4/1962 (mistakenly labeled 1961), at 1–2, FFHLS, Pt. III, Reel 39, Pages 398–99.

694 **keep her away:** DA to JMH, 8/2/1962, DAP, Reel 10, Folder 193. *See* AMB Int. with Lash, 9/12/1974, at 2 (suggesting MDF was not fond of DA).

694 **"I adore":** IB to SNB, 5/28/1962, at 1, Behrman Papers, Box 3, Folder 1.

694 **July 7:** ED to Feis, 7/9/1962, Feis Papers, Box 34.

694 **struggled** & **low** & **left arm** & **left leg:** DA to Menzies, 8/14/1962, at 1, DAP, Reel 14 & in *Among Friends*, 233–34 (David S. McLellan & David C. Acheson, eds. 1980).

694 **hospital orderly:** ED to PAF, 7/17/1962, FFHLS, Pt. III, Reel 38, Page 300.

694 **nurse:** Bessie P. Dubin to JFB, 9/8/1962, at 3–4, JFBP, Ser. 8, Box 28, Folder 13 [Folder 1092(2)] (reporting on FF's "determined and courageous fight" to return to Court and her friendship with FF as his nurse).

694 **chaise lounge:** ED to JMH, 7/24/1962. *See* Kanin, "Trips to Felix," in *Felix Frankfurter: A Tribute*, 51.

694 **"The best"** & **"a great"** & **"the most":** MB to JFK, 3/30/1962, JFKPOF-088a-011-p.0008, JFKL (emphasis in original). *See* Sorensen to JFK, 3/29/1962, JFKPOF-088a-011-p.0016 & Clark Clifford OH, Pt. 3, 2/4/1975, at 46, JFKL (agreeing with MB).

694 **Bobby Kennedy:** *Robert Kennedy: In His Own Words*, 115 17 (Edwin O. Guthman & Jeffrey Shulman, eds. 1988).

695 **"just one":** Arthur Schlesinger, Jr., *Robert Kennedy and His Times*, 376–77 (1978).

695 **White over Freund:** FF to AMB, circa March or April 1962, FFHLS, Pt. III, Reel 32, Page 963.

695 **"I guess":** AMS Jr. Diary, 4/5/1962, in AMS Jr., *Journals, 1952–2000*, at 154 (2007). *See* Justin Feldman Int. with Joseph Lash, 6/10/1974, Lash Papers, Box 51, Folder 6 & Justin Feldman Int. with Donald Ritchie, 6/11/1975, at 2, JML-LC Papers, Box 203, Folder 8 (recounting FF-JML lunch where FF agrees to retire if JFK names JML as replacement).

695 **"What does":** FF OH, Pt. 2, 6/19/1964, at 51.

695   **sapped:** DA to JMH, 8/2/1962, at 1.

695   **"[T]he spirit":** DA to Menzies, 8/14/1962, at 2.

695   **refused to see & Harlan:** ED to AMB, 8/13/1962, Pt. III, Reel 32, Page 970.

695   **dreaded:** ED to AMB, 8/3/1962, FFHLS, *id.* at Page 967.

695   **"with confident":** FF to AMB, 8/16/1962, FFHLS, Pt. III, Reel 32, Page 972.

695   **handwritten letters:** FF to AMB, 11/5/1962, *id.*, Reel 33, Page 13.

695   **labored & editorial assistance:** DA to FF, 8/25/1965, FFLC, Box 121; JMH to DA, 8/24/1965, *id.*

695   **effective immediately:** FF to Conference, 8/28/1962, WJBP, Box II:110, Folder 9.

695–696   **"uncertainty" & "I am" & "reluctance" & "for the solicitude":** FF to JFK, 8/28/1962, JFKPOF-088a-011-p.0021, JFKL.

696   **"shared" & "been part" & "a very great" & "not to retire" & "our respectful":** JFK to FF, 8/28/1962, at 1–2, JFKPOF-088a-011-p.0019–20, JFKL.

696   **"very friendly" & "the fruitful":** FF to JFK, 8/29/1962, JFKPOF-088a-011-p.0022, *id.* *See* FF to AMB, 11/1/1962, FFHLS, Pt. III, Reel 33, Page 12 (describing JFK's response as "very fine").

696   **"deserved":** Schlesinger Jr., *Robert Kennedy and His Times*, 378–79 (quoting Robert Kennedy Memorandum, September 1962). *See* Clifford OH, Pt. 3, 2/4/1975, at 46; *Robert Kennedy: In His Own Words*, 117.

696   **"What have":** Drew Pearson Diary, 9/1/1962, in Drew Pearson, *Washington Merry-Go-Round, The Drew Pearson Diaries, 1960–1969*, at 141 (Peter Hannaford, ed. 2015).

696   **"wealth" & "his scholarly" & "his deep":** JFK Press Conference, 8/29/1962, JFKL.

696   **Bundy:** Newsweek, 9/10/1962, at 23.

697   **"at the same":** MB to FF, 9/19/1962, FFHLS, Pt. III, Reel 27, Page 788.

697   **"self-inflicted":** FF OH, Pt. 2, 6/19/1964, at 53–54 (quoting CEH).

697   **"I suggest":** FF to MB, 11/29/1962, Pt. III, Reel 27, Page 803. *See* PAF to AMB, 9/20/1962, at 2, AMBP, Box 3, Folder 57 (PAF handwritten: describing it as "the best of both worlds" to be mentioned for Supreme Court but able to stay "in the happy academic halls" at Cambridge).

697   **Friendly & Wyzanski:** FF to AMB, 3/18/1963, at 1, FFHLS, Pt. III, Reel 33, Pages 21.

697   **"the scholar":** FF to AMB, 11/14/1962, *id.*, Page 15.

697   **"a minor":** DA to Estelle Frankfurter, 10/26/1962, DAP, Reel 44, Folder 174.

697   **loaned the justice:** DA to PG and Kay Graham, 11/13/1962, *id.* (thanking them for "making the purchase of the apartment for Felix possible").

697   **"Justice Brandeis":** DA to Benjamin F. Goldstein, 11/14/1962, *id.*

698   **miffed:** Robert Miller to DA, 12/16/1963, *id.*, Folder 175.

698   **"only":** DA to Donald Hiss, 10/2/1962, at 2, *id.*, Folder 174.

698   **"cheerful" & "a man" & "infinitely" & "denounced" & "materialism" & "as delightful":** IB to Bowra, 10/27/1962, at 2, IBP, Box 246, Page 42.

698   **Isaac Stern:** ED to AMB, 10/25/1962, FFHLS, Pt. III, Reel 33, Page 9.

698   **Vienna Boys Choir:** FF Appointment Calendar 1963, 1/5/1963, FFLC, Box 3; DA to Goldstein, 2/26/1963, DAP, Reel 44, Folder 175.

698   ***Mona Lisa:*** WES, 2/12/1963, at 13.

698   **sapped him:** FF to AMB, 11/14/1962, FFHLS, Pt. III, Reel 33, Page 15.

698   **"gently":** DA to WTC, 1/14/1963, DAP, Reel 44, Folder 175 (quoting IB).

699   **sedatives & outbursts:** DA to WTC, 1/14/1963; Kanin to DA, 1/30/1963, DAP, Reel 44, Folder 175.

699 **"horror":** DA to AM, 10/24/1963, DAP, Reel 14.

699 **duty:** DA to Wilmarth Lewis, 4/12/1963, DAP, Reel 12.

699 **"I have" & "know":** WES, 4/22/1963, at 25. *See* Schlesinger Jr., *Robert Kennedy and His Times*, 379.

699 **"must be":** JLR to DA, 4/24/1963, at 1–2, DAP, Reel 44, Folder 175.

699 **one of the first justices:** HLB to FF, 4/6/1962, FFLC, Box 124.

699 **"We miss":** FF to AMB, 9/23/1962, FFHLS, Pt. III, Reel 33, Page 3. *See* PAF to HLB, 2/11/1963, PAFP, Box 4, Folder 4-15; HLB to PAF, 2/15/1963, *id.*; Engel v. Vitale, 370 U.S. 421 (1962).

699 **separation of church:** Everson v. Board of Educ., 330 U.S. 1, 28 (1947) (Frankfurter, J., joining Jackson & Rutledge, JJ., dissenting); Illinois ex rel. McCollum v. Board of Educ., 333 U.S. 203, 212 (1948) (Frankfurter, J.); DFF, 1948, at 339–43; Zorach v. Clauson, 343 U.S. 306, 320 (1952) (Frankfurter, J., dissenting).

699 **wrote Black:** FF to HLB, 5/7/1963, Pt. III, Reel 38, Page 328; FF to HLB, 5/8/1963, *id.* at 331.

699 **"should not":** ED note to file, 5/8/1963, FFHLS, Pt. III, Reel 38, Page 327.

699 **kept writing:** FF to HLB, 12/15/1964; HLB to FF, 12/22/1964, WODP, Box 323, Folder 1.

700 **kept visiting:** FF Appointment Calendar, 3/18/1963 & 11/6/1963, FFLC, Box 3; FF Calendar Sheets, 7/5/1963, 11/6/1963, 4/28/1964, 7/8/1964, 8/21/1964, 11/27/1964, *id.*, Box 4; Hugo Black Jr., *My Father*, 237 (1975).

700 **"These":** ED to PAF, 5/17/1963, FFHLS, Pt. III, Reel 38, Page 335 (ED handwritten).

700 **"I came":** Kanin, "Trips to Felix," in *Felix Frankfurter: A Tribute*, 57 & Henkin Int. with Lash, 9/11/1974, at 1 & PAF, "Felix Frankfurter: Reminisces and Reflections," 11/19/1982, at 12.

700 **crying:** PAF, "Felix Frankfurter: Reminisces and Reflections," 11/19/1982, at 12. *See* FF Calendar Sheets, 5/24/1963, FFLC, Box 4; Wilmarth Lewis Diary, 5/2/1963, Lewis Papers, Box 1, Folder 8; CEW Int. with PAF, 11/8/1973, CEWP-MHS, Carton 26.

700 **"I'm so":** FF to PAF, 5/24/1963, at 1, FFHLS, Pt. III, Reel 38, Page 336.

700 **"Every one":** FF to PAF and Henkin, 5/2/1963, *id.*, Page 326.

700 **to law:** FF to PAF, 5/16/1963, at 1, FFHLS, Pt. III, Reel 38, Page 333.

700 **"I wish":** FF to PBK, 7/20/1960, at 1, PBKP, Box 15, Folder 6.

700 **Bickel & Elman:** FF to ED, 7/19/1962, FFHLS, Pt. III, Reel 32, Page 971. *See* JLR to AMB, 5/26/1971, PAFP, Box 4, Folder 4-7; AMB to JLR, 7/2/1971, *id.* (PE declining to be FF biographer).

700 **embittered:** Mary Howe Int. with Lash, 9/3/1974, at 1–2.

701 **"While":** Arthur Schlesinger, Jr., "'Prich': A New Deal Memoir," New York Review of Books, 3/28/1985.

701 **countless:** BG, 4/28/1963, at 23 (thirteen former clerks in academy).

701 **possible Harvard lecture:** Amsterdam to JMH, 6/5/1963, JMHP, Box 534; ED to JMH, 6/28/1963, *id.* ED to JMH, 7/18/1963, *id.*

701 **June 17:** FF Calendar Sheet, 6/17/1963, FFLC, Box 4; JFK Daily Log, 6/17/1963, JFKL; FF OH Pt. 1, 6/10/1964, at 16–17.

701 **"Mr. Buttinsky":** FF OH Pt. 1, 6/10/1964, at 13 & FF OH, Pt. 2, 6/19/1965, at 40-41.

701 **"extremely pleasant":** FF to AMS Jr., 6/18/1963, at 1, FFLC, Box 101 & R&FF, 24–26. *See* FF to JFK, 6/19/1963, at 1, JFKPOF-029a-007, at 8.

701 **"a great":** Wilmarth Lewis to FF, 6/19/1963, at 1, FFLC, Box 77.

701 **"three Yale":** FF to JFK, 10/12/1963, JFKPOF-029a-007, at 6 & FFLC, Box 71.

701   **Medal of Freedom:** JFK to FF, 7/1/1963, at 1 tel., FFLC, Box 152; John W. Macy, Jr., to FF, 11/26/1963 tel., *id.*

702   **"My confident" & "qualities":** FF to LBJ, 11/29/1963, at 1–2, LBJL, Confidential File, Name File, Box 145 & FFLC, Box 70.

702   **suicide:** PE to FF, 8/22/1963, at 1, FFHLS, Pt. III, Reel 15, Page 784.

702   **mental illness:** Katharine Graham, *Personal History*, 305–11, 330–32 (1997).

702   **"devoted":** FF to LBJ, 11/29/1963, at 2.

702   **"one":** FF to LBJ, 11/29/1963, at 2.

702   **"I need":** LBJ to FF, 12/5/1963, LBJL, Confidential File, Name File, Box 145 & FFLC, Box 70.

703   **"Jurist":** Remarks of the President, 12/6/1963, WES, 12/6/1963, at A-6.

703   **nurse & rose:** NYT, 12/7/1963, at 1, 14.

703   **"a rather":** JJM to DA, 12/10/1963, DAP, Reel 13.

703   **"Whatever":** FF to LBJ, 12/7/1963, FFLC, Box 70.

703   **"the best" & "serious" & "The Secret Service":** LBJ to FF, 12/19/1963, *id.*

703   **"wise men":** Walter Isaacson & Evan Thomas, *The Wise Men* (1986).

703   **"father":** AMS Jr. to Doris Kearns Goodwin, 1/21/1988, AMSP, NYPL, Box 52, Folder 4.

703   **convicted:** FF to JMH, 10/16/1963, JMHP, Box 534 (reading minutes of JML's sentencing and concluding Judge Sylvester Ryan acted as "a compassionate human being"). *See* Donald A. Ritchie, *James M. Landis*, 189–202 (1980); Victor S. Navasky, *Kennedy Justice*, 378–91 (1971).

704   **"I loved":** Wallace Cohen Int. by Donald Ritchie, 9/18/1974, at 1, JML-LC, Box 203, Folder 8.

704   **3:45 p.m. & Seven minutes & charmed & 4:15 p.m.:** LBJ Daily Diary, 4/11/1964, LBJL; Reminder, 1/6/1964, LBJL, Presidential Papers, Confidential File, Name File, Box 145.

704   **book:** FF to Feis, 4/16/1964, FFLC, Box 54; FF to Feis, 5/2/1961, Feis Papers, Box 34.

704   **cook & elevator operator:** Marion Star, 4/13/1964, at 6.

704   **"allow me":** LBJ to FF, 4/14/1964, *id.*

704   **airplane:** FF to LBJ, 4/19/1964, LBJL, Presidential Papers, Confidential File, Name File, Box 145.

704   **Levi Eshkol:** FF to LBJ, 6/24/1964, at 1–2, FFLC, Box 70; LBJ to FF, 7/7/1964, LBJL, Presidential Papers, Confidential File, Name File, Box 145.

704   **pen:** LBJ to FF, 7/20/1964, *id.*

704   **Elman:** FF to Walter Jenkins, 8/28/1964, at 1–2, *id.*

705   **last letter:** FF to LBJ, 9/8/1964, at 1–3, FFLC, Box 70; FF to LBJ, 1/22/1964, *id.*

705   **"I am sure":** LBJ to FF, 1/28/1965, LBJL, Presidential Papers, Confidential File, Name File, Box 145.

EPILOGUE

706   **2:53 p.m.:** LBJ Diary, 2/24/1965.

706   **windy:** WP, 2/25/1965, at C4.

706   **hangdog:** UPI Photo, 2/24/1965.

706   **130:** FF Calendar Sheets, 2/24/1965, FFLC, Box 4 (130). *See* WES, 2/26/1965, at B5; WP, 2/25/1965, at C3; FF Appointment Calendar, 2/24/1965, FFLC, Box 3; ED to PAF, 2/10/1965, FFHLS, Pt. III, Reel 38, Page 386.

706 **tears & Florida:** Diary Entries, 2/23/1965 & 2/24/1965, HLB & E. Black, *Mr. Justice and Mrs. Black*, 101–2 (1986).

706 **flew:** SGates to MDF, 2/23/1965 tel., FFLC, Box 123; Oliver Gates Int. with Author, 5/8/2016.

706 **"small drink":** FF Appointment Calendar, 2/16/1965, FFLC, Box 3.

706 **antique glasses &** *"the* Quintet" **& old-fashioned & shook hands:** Max Isenbergh, "Reminisces of FF as a Friend," 51 Va. L. Rev. 564, 580 (1965).

706 **held Acheson's:** DA to AM, 3/5/1965, at 1–2, AMP, Box 1.

706 **4:30 p.m.:** WP, 2/23/1965, at A1.

707 **"I hope":** BG, 2/28/1965, at A2. *Cf.* Greenwood (Miss.) Commonwealth, 1/2/1977, at 14 (Beasley recalling the justice's last words as: "I have one regret, Tom. I can't take you with me.")

707 **Acheson arranged:** DA to AM, 3/5/1965, at 2.

707 **cremated & Isenbergh:** FF Appointment Calendar, 2/24/1965; FF Calendar Sheets, 2/24/1965; Isenbergh, "Reminisces of FF as a Friend," 51 Va. L. Rev. at 564.

707 **Handel:** Memorandum, n.d., DAP, Reel 44, Folder 176.

707 **barely audible:** Wiener to DA, 2/25/1965, DAP, Reel 22.

707 **"three great" & "an unabashed" & "iron" & "explosive" & "solicitous" & "For genius" & "Good" & "sacred" & "In the end" & "forbearance":** PAF Funeral Remarks, 2/24/1965, at 1–3, FFHLS, Pt. III, Reel 24, Pages 349–50.

707 **"My Sword"** *Id.* at 3. *See* PAF to JMH, 3/3/1965, at 1, JMHP, Box 537 (revealing FF wanted lines from *Pilgrim's Progress*).

708 **translated:** BG, 2/25/1965, at 19.

708 **Mozart:** Memorandum, n.d., DAP, Reel 44, Folder 176.

708 **"very":** DA to AM, 3/5/1965, at 2.

708 **condolences:** WP, 2/25/1965, at C3.

708 **"Poor Marion":** DA to EFP, 9/23/1965, DAP, Reel 16.

708 **brother & decline:** DA to CEW, 4/20/1965, at 2, CEWP-MHS, Carton 26; DA to SGates, 6/15/1965, Gates Family Papers; DA to Monnet, 1/4/1966, DAP, Reel 15.

708 **Elsie Douglas & "burst":** Donald Hiss to CEW, 11/2/1973, at 1, CEWP-MHS, Carton 26.

708 **raised money:** Fisher & Sacks to Rowe, 9/23/1974, at 1–2, Rowe Papers, FDRL, Box 90.

708 **two deep:** Stella Landis to MDF, 3/3/1965, FFLC, Box 123. *See* BG, 2/27/1965, at 2.

708 **"a great":** Harv. L. Rec., 3/11/1965, at 4 & Austin W. Scott et al., *Felix Frankfurter: Talks in Tribute*, 2/26/1965, at 7, FFHLS, Pt. III, Reel 24, Page 355.

709 **"a grand" & "Tell me":** Harv. L. Rec., 3/11/1965, at 5 & Scott et al., *Felix Frankfurter: Talks in Tribute*, at 9–10.

709 **most moving:** Stella Landis to MDF, 3/3/1965.

709 **"It always":** Harv. L. Rec., 3/11/1965, at 17 & Scott et al., *Felix Frankfurter: Talks in Tribute*, at 16.

709 **memorial resolution:** DA to EFP, 11/23/1965; "Proceedings of the Supreme Court of the United States in Memory of Mr. Justice Frankfurter," 382 U.S. xix (1965); WP, 10/26/1965, at A2.

709 **a dozen & read passages:** PAF to Donald Hiss, 11/30/1965, PAFP, Box 22, Folder 22-25.

709 **"The history":** McNabb v. United States, 318 U.S. 332, 347 (1943).

709 **February 1962:** FF Calendar Sheet, 2/24/1962, FFLC, Box 4.

710 **"That's":** Sir Howard Beale, "A Man for All Seasons," in *Felix Frankfurter: A Tribute*, 18–19 (Wallace Mendelson, ed. 1964).

710   **A 1977 exhibit:** "A Passionate Intensity: Felix Frankfurter Public Servant, Teacher, Jurist, Colleague" (Harvard Law School Library Manuscript Division, 1977).

710   **"neurotic" & "idealized":** H.N. Hirsch, *The Enigma of Felix Frankfurter*, 201, 205 (1981).

710   **Brandeis's funding:** Bruce Allen Murphy, *The Brandeis/Frankfurter Connection*, 40–45 (1982).

710   **centennial celebration:** PAF, "Felix Frankfurter: Reminisces & Reflections" & Harvard L. Rec., 11/19/1982, at 8 & Harv. L. Rec., 12/3/1982, at 2.

710   **begun to reassess:** Cass R. Sunstein, "Home-Run Hitters of the Supreme Court," Bloomberg View, 9/23/2014, https://www.bloomberg.com/opinion/articles/2014-04-01/home-run-hitters-of-the-supreme-court; Cass R. Sunstein, "Constitutional Personae," Supreme Court Review Vol. 2013 (2014): 433, 444; Samuel Moyn, "On Human Rights and Majority Politics: Felix Frankfurter's Democratic Theory," Vanderbilt Journal of Transnational Law 42 (2019): 1135, 1140–1156; Lael Weinberger, "Frankfurter, Abstention Doctrine, and the Development of Modern Federalism," 87 U. Chi. L. Rev 1737 (2020).

711   **loved America:** R&FF, 744 (Two days before his death, he told Max Freedman: "Let the people know how much I loved Roosevelt, how much I loved my country, and let them see how good a man Roosevelt really was.").

SELECTED BIBLIOGRAPHY

MANUSCRIPTS

Aaron Aaronsohn Papers, NILI Museum-Beit Aaronsohn, Tel Aviv, Israel

Dean Gooderham Acheson Papers, Manuscripts and Archives, Yale University Library, New Haven, CT

Joseph and Stewart Alsop Papers, Library of Congress, Washington, DC

American Civil Liberties Union Papers, Seeley G. Mudd Manuscript Library, Princeton University, Princeton, NJ

S. N. Behrman Papers, Manuscripts and Archives Division, The New York Public Library, New York, NY

Adolf A. Berle Papers, Franklin D. Roosevelt Presidential Library, Hyde Park, NY

Isaiah Berlin Papers, University of Oxford, Bodleian Libraries, Oxford, UK

Francis B. Biddle Papers, Franklin D. Roosevelt Presidential Library, Hyde Park, NY

Jacob Billikopf Papers, American Jewish Archives, Cincinnati, Ohio

Hugo LaFayette Black Papers, Library of Congress, Washington, DC

Louis D. Brandeis Papers, Brandeis University, Waltham, MA

Louis D. Brandeis Papers, University of Louisville, Louis D. Brandeis School of Law Library, Louisville, KY

Louis Dembitz Brandeis Papers, Harvard Law School Library, Historical & Special Collections, Cambridge, MA

Irving Brant Papers, Library of Congress, Washington, DC

William J. Brennan Papers, Library of Congress, Washington, DC

Brown v. Board of Education Collection, Manuscripts and Archives, Yale University Library, New Haven, CT

Charles Culp Burlingham Papers, Harvard Law School Library, Historical & Special Collections, Cambridge, MA

Harold H. Burton Papers, Library of Congress, Washington, DC

James F. Byrnes Papers, Clemson University Libraries Special Collections, Clemson, SC

Raymond Clapper Papers, Library of Congress, Washington, DC

Grenville Clark Papers, Dartmouth College, Rauner Special Collections Library, Hanover, NH

Tom C. Clark Papers, University of Texas Law School, Tarlton Law Library, Austin, TX

Clark Clifford Papers, Harry S Truman Library, Independence, MO

Benjamin V. Cohen Papers, Library of Congress, Washington, DC

Morris Raphael Cohen Papers, Hanna Holborn Gray Special Collections Research Center, University of Chicago Library, Chicago, IL

Thomas G. Corcoran Papers, Library of Congress, Washington, DC

Homer Stille Cummings Papers, Special Collections Department, University of Virginia Library, Charlottesville, VA

Joseph Edward Davies Papers, Library of Congress, Washington, DC

Winfred T. Denison Papers, Maine Historical Society, Portland, ME

William O. Douglas Papers, Library of Congress, Washington, DC

Herbert B. Ehrmann Papers, Harvard Law School Library, Historical & Special Collections, Cambridge, MA

Philip Elman Papers, Harvard Law School Library, Historical & Special Collections, Cambridge, MA

Elizabeth Glendower Evans Papers, Radcliffe Institute, Schlesinger Library, Harvard University, Cambridge, MA

Charles Fahy Papers, Franklin D. Roosevelt Presidential Library, Hyde Park, NY

Herbert Feis Papers, Library of Congress, Washington, DC

Felix Frankfurter Papers, Harvard Law School Library, Historical & Special Collections, Cambridge, MA

Felix Frankfurter Papers, Library of Congress, Washington, DC

Felix Frankfurter Small Manuscript Collection, Letter to Ethel Randolph Thayer, Harvard Law School, Historical & Special Collections, Cambridge, MA

Frankfurter Family Papers, Leo Baeck Institute, New York, NY

Salomon Frankfurter Collection, Leo Baeck Institute, New York, NY

Paul A. Freund Papers, Harvard Law School Library, Historical & Special Collections, Cambridge, MA

Henry J. Friendly Papers, Harvard Law School Library, Historical & Special Collections, Cambridge, MA

Arthur Goodhart Papers, University of Oxford, Bodleian Libraries, Oxford, UK

Ruth Gordon and Garson Kanin Papers, Library of Congress, Washington, DC

Eugene Gressman Papers, Bentley Historical Library, University of Michigan, Ann Arbor, MI

Learned Hand Papers, Harvard Law School Library, Historical & Special Collections, Cambridge, MA

John Marshall Harlan Papers, Department of Special Collections, Princeton University Library, Princeton, NJ

Henry Melvin Hart Papers, Harvard Law School Library, Historical & Special Collections, Cambridge, MA

Edward E. "Swede" Hazlett Papers, Dwight D. Eisenhower Library, Abilene, KS

Arthur Dehon Hill Papers, Portsmouth Athenaeum, Portsmouth, NH

Oliver Wendell Holmes Papers, Harvard Law School Library, Historical & Special Collections, Cambridge, MA

J. Edgar Hoover Official and Confidential File, Federal Bureau of Investigation Files, National Archives and Records Administration, College Park, MD

Harry Hopkins Papers, Franklin D. Roosevelt Presidential Library, Hyde Park, NY

Colonel Edward House Papers, Yale University Law School, New Haven, CT

Charles H. Houston Papers, Howard University, Washington, DC

William L. Houston Papers, Library of Congress, Washington, DC

Mark DeWolfe Howe Papers, Harvard Law School Library, Historical & Special Collections, Cambridge, MA

Charles Evans Hughes Papers, Library of Congress, Washington, DC

Harold L. Ickes Papers, Library of Congress, Washington, DC

Robert Houghwout Jackson Papers, Library of Congress, Washington, DC

Lyndon B. Johnson Papers, Lyndon B. Johnson Library, Austin, TX

Andrew Kaufman Papers, Harvard Law School Library, Historical & Special Collections, Cambridge, MA

John F. Kennedy Papers, John F. Kennedy Library, Boston, MA

Joseph P. Kennedy Sr. Papers, John F. Kennedy Library, Boston, MA

Philip B. Kurland Papers, Hanna Holborn Gray Special Collections Research Center, University of Chicago Library, Chicago, IL

Joseph P. Lash Papers, Franklin D. Roosevelt Presidential Library, Hyde Park, NY

James McCauley Landis Papers, Library of Congress, Washington, DC

Laski-Brandeis Papers, Yale Law School Library, New Haven, CT

Harold Laski Papers, Hull History Centre, Yorkshire, UK

Monte M. Lemann Papers, Louisiana Research Collection, Tulane University, New Orleans, LA

Max Lerner Papers, Yale University Library, New Haven, CT

Anthony Lewis Papers, Library of Congress, Washington, DC

Wilmarth Sheldon Lewis Papers, Lewis Walpole Library, Yale University, Farmington, CT

Walter Lippmann Papers, Manuscripts and Archives, Yale University Library, New Haven, CT

Katie Louchheim Papers, Library of Congress, Washington, DC

A. Lawrence Lowell Official Papers, Harvard University Library, Cambridge, MA

A. Lawrence Lowell Personal Papers, Harvard University Library, Cambridge, MA

Max Lowenthal Papers, University of Minnesota, Minneapolis, MN

Julian William Mack Papers, American Jewish Museum Archives, Cincinnati, OH

Archibald MacLeish Papers, Library of Congress, Washington, DC

John J. McCloy Papers, Amherst College Archives and Special Collections, Amherst, MA

Agnes Meyer Papers, Library of Congress, Washington, DC

John S. Monagan Papers, Harvard Law School Library, Historical & Special Collections, Cambridge, MA

Frank Murphy Papers, Bentley Historical Library, University of Michigan, Ann Arbor, MI

National Association for the Advancement of Colored People Collection, Library of Congress, Washington, DC

National Consumers' League Records, Library of Congress, Washington, DC

New York Times Company Records & Arthur Hays Sulzberger Papers, New York Public Library, Manuscripts and Archives Division, New York, NY

David K. Niles Papers, Harry S. Truman Library, Independence, MO

George W. Norris Papers, Library of Congress, Washington, DC

J. Robert Oppenheimer Papers, Library of Congress, Washington, DC

Walter Hines Page Papers, Houghton Library, Harvard University, Cambridge, MA

Lewis J. Paper Papers, Harvard Law School Library, Historical & Special Collections, Cambridge, MA

Drew Pearson Papers, Lyndon B. Johnson Library, Austin, TX

Roscoe Pound Papers, Harvard Law School Library, Historical & Special Collections, Cambridge, MA

Thomas Reed Powell Papers, Harvard Law School Library, Historical & Special Collections, Cambridge, MA

President's Mediation Commission Files, National Archives and Records Administration, College Park, MD

E. Barrett Prettyman, Jr., Papers, University of Virginia School of Law, Charlottesville, VA

Edward F. Prichard, Jr., Oral History Project, University of Kentucky, Lexington, KY

Joseph L. Rauh Papers, Library of Congress, Washington, DC

Stanley Forman Reed Papers, University of Kentucky, Lexington, KY

Elliot L. Richardson Papers, Library of Congress, Washington, DC

Donald R. Richberg Papers, Library of Congress, Washington, DC

Owen J. Roberts Papers, Library of Congress, Washington, DC

Fred Rodell Papers, Haverford College Quaker and Special Collections, Haverford, PA

Eleanor Roosevelt Papers, Franklin D. Roosevelt Presidential Library, Hyde Park, NY

Franklin D. Roosevelt Papers, Franklin D. Roosevelt Presidential Library, Hyde Park, NY

Theodore Roosevelt Papers, Library of Congress, Washington, DC

Samuel I. Rosenman Papers, Franklin D. Roosevelt Presidential Library, Hyde Park, NY

James Rowe Papers, Franklin D. Roosevelt Presidential Library, Hyde Park, NY

Wiley Rutledge, Jr., Papers, Library of Congress, Washington, DC

Sacco-Vanzetti Defense Committee Records, Boston Public Library, Boston, MA

Sacco-Vanzetti Papers, Harvard Law School Library, Historical & Special Collections, Cambridge, MA

Austin Wakeman Scott Papers, Harvard Law School Library, Historical & Special Collections, Cambridge, MA

Arthur M. Schlesinger, Jr., Papers, Manuscripts and Archives Division, New York Public Library, New York, NY

Arthur M. Schlesinger, Jr., Personal Papers, John F. Kennedy Library, Boston, MA

Ellery Sedgwick Papers, Massachusetts Historical Society, Boston, MA

Martin J. Sherwin Collection Related to J. Robert Oppenheimer, Library of Congress, Washington, DC

Potter Stewart Papers, Manuscripts and Archives, Yale University Library, New Haven, CT

Henry Lewis Stimson Papers, Manuscripts and Archives, Yale University Library, New Haven, CT

Harlan Fiske Stone Papers, Library of Congress, Washington, DC

Supreme Court Clerk's Office Files, National Archives and Record Administration, Washington, DC

Supreme Court Curator's Office Files, Supreme Court of the United States, Curator's Office, Washington, DC

Supreme Court Docket Books, Supreme Court of the United States, Curator's Office, Washington, DC

William H. Taft Papers, Library of Congress, Washington, DC

Harry S. Truman Papers, Harry S. Truman Library, Independence, MO

Robert G. Valentine Papers, Massachusetts Historical Society, Boston, MA

Willis Van Devanter Papers, Library of Congress, Washington, DC

Frederick Moore Vinson Papers, University of Kentucky, Lexington, KY

War Labor Policies Board Records, National Archives and Records Administration, College Park, MD

Earl Warren Papers, Library of Congress, Washington, DC

Edwin M. Watson and Frances N. Watson Papers, Special Collections, University of Virginia Library, Charlottesville, VA

The Weizmann Archive, Weizmann House, Rehovot, Israel

Burton K. Wheeler Papers, Montana Historical Society Research Center Archives, Helena, MT

Burton K. Wheeler Papers, Montana State University Library, Bozeman, MT

William Allen White Papers, Library of Congress, Washington, DC

Woodrow Wilson Papers, Library of Congress, Washington, DC

Stephen S. Wise Papers, Robert D. Farber University Archives & Special Collections, Brandeis University, Waltham, MA

Charles E. Wyzanski, Jr., Papers, Harvard Law School Library, Historical & Special Collections, Cambridge, MA

Charles E. Wyzanski, Jr., Papers, Massachusetts Historical Society, Boston, MA

ORAL HISTORIES

Columbia Oral Histories

Chauncey Belknap

Bruce Bliven

Harvey Bundy

Philip Elman

Jerome Frank

Felix Frankfurter

Learned Hand

Alger Hiss

Gardner Jackson

Robert H. Jackson

James M. Landis

Walter Lippmann

Thurgood Marshall

Eugene Meyer

John Lord O'Brian

Joseph L. Rauh, Jr.

George Rublee

Ordway Tead

Charles E. Wyzanski, Jr.

George C. Marshall Foundation Oral Histories

Felix Frankfurter

John F. Kennedy Library Oral Histories

Isaiah Berlin

McGeorge Bundy

Felix Frankfurter

Robert F. Kennedy

Lyndon B. Johnson Library Oral Histories

Adrian Fisher

Elliot Richardson

ON FILE WITH AUTHOR

Chauncey Belknap Diary 1914–1915

Dorothy Koval Collection (additional papers relating to Robert G. Valentine)

Frida Laski Oral History
Gates Family Papers
J. William Doolittle Collection of Materials Relating to Justice Felix Frankfurter
Max Freedman Interviews with Felix Frankfurter, Library of Congress audio files
Michael Parrish Notes on Felix Frankfurter Diaries & Papers & Interviews

INTERVIEWS WITH AUTHOR

David Acheson, December 10, 2017, Washington, DC
Mary Acheson Bundy, December 6, 2017, Boston, MA
Paul Bender, February 15, 2017, Phoenix, AZ
Guido Calabresi, August 24, 2018, New Haven, CT
Jerome Cohen, December 14, 2018, New York, NY
William T. Coleman, October 16, 2006, Washington, DC
J. William Doolittle, January 11, 2018, and December 6, 2018, Washington, DC
Mercedes Eichholz, April 2, 2008, telephone interview, Santa Barbara, CA
Oliver Gates, May 8, 2016, Pewsey, Wiltshire, UK
Ruth Bader Ginsburg, November 16, 2016, Washington, DC
Howard Kalodner, December 13, 2018, New York, NY
Andrew Kaufman, June 23, 2010, and December 7, 2017, Cambridge, MA
Thomas Lemann, September 29, 2018, New Orleans, LA
Daniel Mayers, January 10, 2017, Washington, DC
Vincent McKusick, August 22, 2006, telephone interview, Portland, ME
Abner Mikva, September 24, 2006, telephone interview, Chicago, IL
Sarah Homet Milam, December 20, 2018, Bethesda, MD
Newton Minow, September 20, 2006, Chicago, IL
James C. N. Paul, August 31, 2006, Trappe, MD
E. Barrett Prettyman, Jr., September 18, 2008, Washington, DC
Walter Brandeis Raushenbush, October 16, 2019, Washington, DC
Daniel Rezneck, January 2, 2018, Washington, DC
Elisabeth Sifton, December 13, 2018, New York, NY
Howard Trienens, September 20, 2006, Chicago, IL

BOOKS

Acheson, Dean. *Morning and Noon*. Boston: Houghton Mifflin, 1965.
———. *Present at the Creation: My Years in the State Department*. New York: Norton, 1969.
Alsop, Joseph, and Turner Catledge. *The 168 Days*. Garden City, NY: Doubleday, Doran, 1938.
Alsop, Joseph, and Robert Kintner. *Men Around the President*. New York: Doubleday, Doran, 1939.
Baker, Leonard. *Brandeis and Frankfurter: A Dual Biography*. New York: Harper and Row, 1984.
Baker, Liva. *Felix Frankfurter*. New York: Coward-McCann, 1969.
Barnard, Harry. *The Forging of an American Jew: The Life and Times of Judge Julian W. Mack*. New York: Herzl Press, 1974.
Beisner, Robert L. *Dean Acheson: A Life in the Cold War*. New York: Oxford University Press, 2006.
Berle, Adolf A., Jr. *Navigating the Rapids, 1918–1971: From the Papers of Adolf A. Berle*, edited by Beatrice Bishop Berle and Travis Beal Jacobs. New York: Harcourt, Brace, Jovanovich, 1973.

Berlin, Isaiah. *Letters 1928–1946*, edited by Henry Hardy. Cambridge, UK: Cambridge University Press, 2004.

———. *Enlightening: Letters 1946–1960*, edited by Henry Hardy and Jennifer Holmes. London: Random House UK, 2009.

Biddle, Francis. *A Casual Past*. New York: Doubleday, 1961.

———. *In Brief Authority*. New York: Doubleday, 1962.

Bird, Kai. *The Chairman: John J. McCloy: The Making of the American Establishment*. New York: Simon and Schuster, 1992.

———. *The Color of Truth: McGeorge Bundy and William Bundy: Brothers in Arms*. New York: Simon and Schuster, 1998.

Black, Hugo, Jr. *My Father: A Remembrance*. New York: Random House, 1975.

Black, Hugo L., and Elizabeth S. Black. *Mr. Justice and Mrs. Black: The Memoirs of Hugo L. Black and Elizabeth Black*. New York: Random House, 1986.

Blum, John Morton, ed. *Public Philosopher: Selected Letters of Walter Lippmann*. New York: Ticknor and Fields, 1985.

Bothwell, Robert. *Loring Christie: The Failure of Bureaucratic Imperialism*. New York: Garland, 1988.

Bowra, C. M. *Memories: 1898–1939*. Cambridge, MA: Harvard University Press, 1967.

Bowra, Maurice. *New Bats in Old Belfries*, edited by Hendy Hardy and Jennifer Holmes. Oxford: Robert Dugdale, 2005.

Campbell, Tracy. *Short of the Glory: The Fall and Redemption of Edward F. Prichard, Jr.* Lexington: University Press of Kentucky, 1998.

Cohen, Morris Raphael. *A Dreamer's Journey: The Autobiography of Morris Raphael Cohen*. Boston: Beacon Press, 1949.

Coleman, William T. *Counsel for the Situation: Shaping the Law to Realize America's Promise*. Washington, DC: Brookings Institution, 2010.

Cooper, John Milton, Jr. *The Warrior and the Priest: Woodrow Wilson and Theodore Roosevelt*. Cambridge, MA: Belknap Press of Harvard University Press, 1985.

———. *Woodrow Wilson: A Biography*. New York: Knopf, 2009.

Coquillette, Daniel R., and Bruce A. Kimball. *On the Battlefield of Merit: Harvard Law School, the First Century*. Cambridge, MA: Harvard University Press, 2015.

Craig, Douglas B. *Progressives at War: William G. McAdoo and Newton D. Baker, 1863–1941*. Baltimore: Johns Hopkins University Press, 2013.

Croly, Herbert. *The Promise of American Life*. New York: Macmillan, 1909.

Dawson, Nelson L. *Louis D. Brandeis, Felix Frankfurter, and the New Deal*. Hamden, CT: Archon, 1980.

de Haas, Jacob. *Louis D. Brandeis: A Biographical Sketch*. New York: Bloch, 1929.

Domnarski, William. *The Great Justices, 1941–1954: Black, Frankfurter, Douglas, and Jackson in Chambers*. Ann Arbor: University of Michigan Press, 2006.

Donaldson, Scott, in collaboration with R. H. Winnick. *Archibald MacLeish: An American Life*. Boston: Houghton Mifflin Harcourt, 1992.

Douglas, William O. *Go East Young Man: The Early Years*. New York: Random House, 1974.

———. *The Court Years, 1939–1975*. New York: Random House, 1980.

Dunne, Gerald T. *Grenville Clark: Public Citizen*. New York: Farrar, Straus and Giroux, 1986.

Ehrmann, Herbert B. *The Untried Case: The Sacco-Vanzetti Case and the Morelli Gang*. New York: Vanguard Press, 1933.

———. *The Case That Will Not Die: Commonwealth vs. Sacco and Vanzetti*. Boston: Little, Brown, 1969.

Elath, Eliahu. *The Struggle for Statehood: Washington 1945–48*. Vols 2A–2B. Tel Aviv: Am Oved, 1982 (Hebrew).

Ernst, Daniel R. *Tocqueville's Nightmare: The Administrative State Emerges in America, 1900–1940*. New York: Oxford University Press, 2014.

Farley, James. *Jim Farley's Story: The Roosevelt Years*. New York: McGraw-Hill, 1948.

Fassett, John D. *New Deal Justice: The Life of Stanley Reed of Kentucky*. New York: Vantage, 1994.

Feldman, Noah. *Scorpions: The Battles and Triumphs of FDR's Great Supreme Court Justices*. New York: Twelve, 2010.

Ferren, John M. *Salt of the Earth, Conscience of the Court: The Story of Justice Wiley Rutledge*. Chapel Hill: University of North Carolina Press, 2004.

Fine, Sidney. *Frank Murphy: The Washington Years*. Ann Arbor: University of Michigan Press, 1984.

Frankfurter, Felix. *The Case of Sacco and Vanzetti: A Critical Analysis for Lawyers and Laymen*. Boston: Little, Brown, 1927.

———. *Mr. Justice Holmes and the Constitution: A Review of His Twenty-Five Years on the Supreme Court*. Cambridge, MA: Dunster House Bookshop, 1927.

———. *The Public and Its Government*. New Haven, CT: Yale University Press, 1930.

———, ed. *Mr. Justice Holmes*. New York: Coward-McCann, 1931.

———. *The Commerce Clause under Marshall, Taney and Waite*. Chapel Hill: University of North Carolina Press, 1937.

———. *Mr. Justice Holmes and the Supreme Court*. Cambridge, MA: Harvard University Press, 1938.

———. *Law and Politics: Occasional Papers of Felix Frankfurter, 1913–1938*, edited by Archibald MacLeish and E. F. Prichard, Jr. New York: Harcourt, Brace, 1939.

———. *Of Law and Men*, edited by Philip Elman. New York: Harcourt, Brace, 1956.

Frankfurter, Felix, and Nathan Greene. *The Labor Injunction*. New York: Macmillan, 1930.

Frankfurter, Felix, and James M. Landis. *The Business of the Supreme Court: A Study in the Federal Judicial System*. New York: Macmillan, 1927.

Freedman, Max, ed. *Roosevelt and Frankfurter: Their Correspondence, 1928–1945*. Boston: Little, Brown, 1967.

Freyer, Tony A. *The Little Rock Crisis: A Constitutional Interpretation*. Westport, CT: Greenwood Press, 1984.

———. *Little Rock on Trial: Cooper v. Aaron and School Desegregation*. Lawrence: University Press of Kansas, 2007.

Frost, Richard H. *The Mooney Case*. Palo Alto, CA: Stanford University Press, 1968.

Gerhart, Eugene C. *America's Advocate: Robert H. Jackson*. Indianapolis: Bobbs Merrill, 1958.

Goodwin, Richard N. *Remembering America: A Voice from the Sixties*. Boston: Little, Brown, 1988.

Graham, Katharine. *Personal History*. New York: Knopf, 1997.

Gray, Fred D. *Bus Ride to Justice: Changing the System by the System: The Life and Works of Fred Gray*. Rev. ed. Montgomery: New South, 2012.

Gunther, Gerald. *Learned Hand: The Man and the Judge*. New York: Knopf, 1994.

Hagedorn, Hermann, ed. *The Works of Theodore Roosevelt: Social Justice and Popular Rule*. Vol. 17. National ed. New York: Charles Scribner's Sons, 1926.

Hand, Learned. *The Bill of Rights*. Cambridge, MA: Harvard University Press, 1958.

Harbaugh, William H. *Lawyer's Lawyer: The Life of John W. Davis*. New York: Oxford University Press, 1973.

Herken, Gregg. *The Georgetown Set: Friends and Rivals in Cold War Washington*. New York: Knopf, 2014.

Hershberg, James G. *James B. Conant: Harvard to Hiroshima and the Making of the Nuclear Age*. New York: Knopf, 1993.

Hirsch, H. N. *The Enigma of Felix Frankfurter*. New York: Basic Books, 1981.

Hiss, Alger. *In the Court of Public Opinion*. New York: Knopf, 1957.

———. *Recollections of a Life*. New York: Seaver Books, 1988.

Howard, J. Woodford. *Mr. Justice Murphy: A Political Biography*. Princeton, NJ: Princeton University Press, 1968.

Howe, Mark DeWolfe, ed. *Holmes-Pollock Letters: The Correspondence of Mr. Justice Holmes and Sir Frederick Pollock, 1874–1932*. 2 vols. Cambridge, MA: Harvard University Press, 1941.

———, ed. *Holmes-Laski Letters: The Correspondence of Mr. Justice Holmes and Harold J. Laski, 1916–1935*. Cambridge, MA: Harvard University Press, 1953.

———. *Justice Oliver Wendell Holmes: The Shaping Years, 1841–1870*. Cambridge, MA: Belknap Press of Harvard University Press, 1957.

———. *Justice Oliver Wendell Holmes: The Proving Years 1870–1882*. Cambridge, MA: Harvard University Press, 1963.

Hughes, Charles Evans. *The Autobiographical Notes of Charles Evans Hughes*, edited by David J. Danelski and Joseph S. Tulchin. Cambridge, MA: Harvard University Press, 1973.

Hull, N.E.H. *Roscoe Pound and Karl Llewellyn: Searching for an American Jurisprudence*. Chicago: University of Chicago Press, 1997.

Ickes, Harold L. *The Secret Diary of Harold L. Ickes: The First Thousand Days, 1933–1936*. New York, Simon and Schuster, 1953.

———. *The Secret Diary of Harold L. Ickes: The Inside Struggle: 1936–1939*. New York: Simon and Schuster, 1954.

———. *The Secret Diary of Harold L. Ickes: The Lowering Clouds: 1939–1941*. New York: Simon and Schuster, 1955.

Ignatieff, Michael. *Isaiah Berlin: A Life*. New York: Metropolitan Books, 1998.

Irons, Peter H. *Justice at War: The Story of the Japanese Internment Cases*. Berkeley: University of California Press, 1993.

———. *The New Deal Lawyers*. Princeton, NJ: Princeton University Press, 1993.

Issacson, Walter, and Evan Thomas. *The Wise Men: Six Friends and the World They Made: Acheson, Bohlen, Harriman, Kennan, Lovett, McCloy*. New York: Simon and Schuster, 1986.

Jackson, Robert H. *That Man: An Insider's Portrait of Franklin D. Roosevelt*, edited by John Q. Barrett. New York: Oxford University Press, 2003.

Jordan, Constance, ed. *Reason and Imagination: The Selected Correspondence of Learned Hand 1897–1961*. New York: Oxford University Press, 2013.

Kalman, Laura. *Legal Realism at Yale, 1927–1960*. Chapel Hill: University of North Carolina Press, 1986.

———. *The Strange Career of Legal Liberalism*. New Haven, CT: Yale University Press, 1998.

———. *Yale Law School and the Sixties: Revolt and Reverberations*. Chapel Hill: University of North Carolina Press, 2005.

Katz, Shmuel. *The Aaronsohn Saga*. Jerusalem: Gefen, 2007.

Kaufman, Andrew L. *Cardozo*. Cambridge, MA: Harvard University Press, 1998.

Kimball, Bruce A. *The Inception of Modern Professional Education: C. C. Langdell 1826–1906.* Chapel Hill: University of North Carolina Press, 2009.

———, and Daniel R. Coquillette. *The Intellectual Sword: Harvard Law School, The Second Century.* Cambridge, MA: Belknap Press of Harvard University Press, 2020.

Klarman, Michael. *From Jim Crow to Civil Rights: The Supreme Court and the Struggle for Racial Equality.* New York: Oxford University Press, 2004.

Kluger, Richard. *Simple Justice: The History of Brown v. Board of Education and Black America's Struggle for Equality.* New York: Knopf, 1976.

Kramnick, Isaac, and Barry Sheerman. *Harold Laski: A Life on the Left.* New York: Allen Lane/Penguin Press, 1993.

Kurland, Philip B., ed. *Of Law and Life and Other Things That Matter: Papers and Addresses of Felix Frankfurter, 1956–1963.* Cambridge, MA: Belknap Press of Harvard University Press, 1965.

———, ed. *Felix Frankfurter on the Supreme Court: Extrajudicial Essays on the Court and the Constitution.* Cambridge, MA: Belknap Press of Harvard University Press, 1970.

———, ed. *Mr. Justice Frankfurter and the Constitution.* Chicago: University of Chicago Press, 1971.

Lash, Joseph P. *Eleanor and Franklin: The Story of Their Relationship Based on Eleanor Roosevelt's Private Papers.* New York: Norton, 1971.

———, ed. *From the Diaries of Felix Frankfurter: With a Biographical Essay and Notes.* New York: Norton, 1975.

———. *Dealers and Dreamers: A New Look at the New Deal.* New York: Doubleday, 1988.

Lasser, William. *Benjamin V. Cohen: Architect of the New Deal.* New Haven, CT: Yale University Press, 2002.

Levy, David W. *Herbert Croly of The New Republic: The Life and Thought of an American Progressive.* Princeton, NJ: Princeton University Press, 1985.

Lilienthal, David E. *The Journals of David E. Lilienthal: The TVA Years, 1939–1945.* New York: Harper and Row, 1964.

Lippmann, Walter. *Public Opinion.* New York: Harcourt, Brace, 1922.

———. *Public Persons,* edited by Gilbert A. Harrison. New York: Liveright, 1976.

Logevall, Fredrik. *JFK: Coming of Age in the American Century, 1917–1956.* New York: Random House, 2020.

Louchheim, Katie, ed. *The Making of the New Deal: The Insiders Speak.* Cambridge, MA: Harvard University Press, 1983.

MacLeish, Archibald. *Letters of Archibald MacLeish,* edited by R. H. Winnick. Boston: Houghton Mifflin, 1983.

Marcus, Maeva. *Truman and the Steel Seizure Case: The Limits of Presidential Power.* New York: Columbia University Press, 1977.

Martin, George Whitney. *CCB: The Life and Century of Charles C. Burlingham, New York's First Citizen, 1858–1959.* New York: Hill and Wang, 2005.

Mason, Alpheus Thomas. *Brandeis: A Free Man's Life.* New York: Viking, 1946.

———. *Harlan Fiske Stone: Pillar of the Law.* New York: Viking, 1956.

Mayer, Martin. *Emory Buckner.* New York: Harper and Row, 1968.

McLellan, David S., and David C. Acheson, eds. *Among Friends: Personal Letters of Dean Acheson, 1893–1971.* New York: Dodd, Mead, 1980.

McNeil, Genna Rae. *Groundwork: Charles Hamilton Houston and the Struggle for Civil Rights.* Philadelphia: University of Pennsylvania Press, 1983.

Mendelson, Wallace. *Justices Black and Frankfurter: Conflict in the Court.* Chicago: University of Chicago Press, 1961.

———, ed. *Felix Frankfurter: The Judge.* New York: Reynal, 1964.

———, ed. *Felix Frankfurter: A Tribute.* New York: Reynal, 1964.

Mennel, Robert M., and Christine L. Compston, eds. *Holmes and Frankfurter: Their Correspondence, 1912–1934.* Hanover, NH: University Press of New England for University of New Hampshire, 1996.

Miller, Arthur S., and Jeffery H. Bowman. *Death by Installments: The Ordeal of Willie Francis.* Ann Arbor: University of Michigan Press, 1988.

Mitchell, Leslie. *Maurice Bowra: A Life.* New York: Oxford University Press, 2009.

Moley, Raymond. *After Seven Years.* New York: Harper, 1939.

———. *The First New Deal.* New York: Harcourt, Brace and World, 1966.

Monagan, John S. *The Grand Panjandrum: Mellow Years of Justice Holmes.* Lanham, MD: University Press of America, 1988.

Monnet, Jean. *Memoirs.* New York: Doubleday, 1978.

Morison, Elting E., ed. *The Letters of Theodore Roosevelt, The Square Deal: 1901–1903.* Cambridge, MA: Harvard University Press, 1951.

———. *Turmoil and Tradition: A Study of the Life and Times of Henry L. Stimson.* Boston: Houghton Mifflin, 1960.

Murphy, Bruce Allen. *The Brandeis/Frankfurter Connection: The Secret Political Activities of Two Supreme Court Justices.* New York: Oxford University Press, 1982.

———. *Wild Bill: The Legend and Life of William O. Douglas.* New York: Random House, 2003.

Nasaw, David. *The Patriarch: The Remarkable Life and Turbulent Times of Joseph P. Kennedy.* New York: Penguin Press, 2012.

Navasky, Victor S. *Kennedy Justice.* New York: Scribner, 1971.

Nelson, Garrison. *John William McCormack: A Political Biography.* New York: Bloomsbury Academic, 2017.

Neu, Charles E. *Colonel House: A Biography of Woodrow Wilson's Silent Partner.* New York: Oxford University Press, 2015.

Newman, Roger K. *Hugo Black: A Biography.* New York: Pantheon, 1994.

Newton, Jim. *Justice for All: Earl Warren and the Nation He Made.* New York: Riverhead, 2006.

Oney, Steve. *And the Dead Shall Rise: The Murder of Mary Phagan and the Lynching of Leo Frank.* New York: Pantheon, 2003.

Paper, Lewis J. *Brandeis.* Englewood Cliffs, NJ: Prentice Hall, 1983.

Parrish, Michael E. *Securities Regulation and the New Deal.* New Haven, CT: Yale University Press, 1970.

———. *Felix Frankfurter and His Times.* New York: Free Press, 1982.

———. *Citizen Rauh: An American Liberal's Life in Law and Politics.* Ann Arbor: University of Michigan Press, 2010.

Peabody, James Bishop, ed. *The Holmes-Einstein Letters: Correspondence of Mr. Justice Holmes and Lewis Einstein, 1903–1935.* New York: Macmillan, 1964.

Pearson, Drew. *Drew Pearson Diaries 1949–1959*, edited by Tyler Abell. New York: Holt Reinhart Winston, 1974.

———. *Washington Merry-Go-Round: The Drew Pearson Diaries, 1960–1969*, edited by Peter Hannaford. Lincoln, NE: Potomac Books, 2015.

Peppers, Todd C. *Courtiers of the Marble Palace: The Rise and Influence of the Supreme Court Law Clerk.* Stanford: Stanford University Press, 2006.

———, and Artemus Ward, eds. *In Chambers: Stories of Supreme Court Law Clerks and Their Justices*. Charlottesville: University of Virginia Press, 2012.

Percy, Eustace. *Some Memories*. London: Eyre and Spottiswoode, 1958.

Peters, Shawn Francis. *Judging Jehovah's Witnesses: Religious Persecution and the Dawn of the Rights Revolution*. Topeka: University Press of Kansas, 2000.

Phillips, Harlan B., ed. *Felix Frankfurter Reminisces*. New York: Reynal, 1960.

Purcell, Edward A., Jr. *Brandeis and the Progressive Constitution*. New Haven, CT: Yale University Press, 2000.

Pusey, Merlo J. *Charles Evans Hughes*. 2 vols. New York: Macmillan, 1951.

———. *Eugene Meyer*. New York: Knopf, 1974.

Radosh, Ronald, and Joyce Milton. *The Rosenberg File*, 2nd ed. New Haven, CT: Yale University Press, 1997.

Ritchie, Donald A. *James M. Landis: Dean of the Regulators*. Cambridge, MA: Harvard University Press, 1980.

———. *The Columnist: Leaks, Lies, and Libel in Drew Pearson's Washington*. New York: Oxford University Press, 2021.

Roberts, Sam. *The Brother: The Untold Story of the Rosenberg Case*. New York: Random House, 2001.

Roosevelt, Franklin D. *The Public Papers and Addresses of Franklin D. Roosevelt*. Vols. 1–4. New York: Random House, 1938.

Roosevelt, James, and Sidney Shalett. *Affectionately, F.D.R.: A Son's Story of a Lonely Man*. New York: Harcourt, Brace, 1959.

Rosenfield, Leonora Cohen. *Portrait of a Philosopher: Morris R. Cohen in Life and Letters*. New York: Harcourt, Brace and World, 1962.

Rosenman, Samuel I. *Working with Roosevelt*. New York: Harper, 1952.

Rozenblit, Marsha L. *The Jews of Vienna, 1867–1914: Assimilation and Identity*. Albany: State University of New York Press, 1983.

Sacco, Nicola, and Bartolomeo Vanzetti. *The Letters of Sacco and Vanzetti*, edited by Marion Denman Frankfurter and Gardner Jackson. New York: Viking, 1928.

Schlesinger, Arthur, Jr. *The Age of Roosevelt: The Crisis of the Old Order, 1919–1933*. Boston: Houghton Mifflin, 1957.

———. *The Age of Roosevelt: The Coming of the New Deal*. Boston: Houghton Mifflin, 1958.

———. *The Age of Roosevelt: The Politics of Upheaval*. Boston: Houghton Mifflin, 1960.

———. *Robert Kennedy and His Times*. Boston: Houghton Mifflin, 1978.

———. *A Life in the 20th Century: Innocent Beginnings, 1917–1950*. Boston: Houghton Mifflin, 2000.

———. *Journals, 1952–2000*. New York: Penguin Press, 2007.

Schwartz, Bernard. *Super Chief: Earl Warren and His Supreme Court*. New York: New York University Press, 1983.

Schwarz, Jordan A. *Liberal: Adolf A. Berle and the Vision of an American Era*. New York: Free Press, 1987.

———. *The New Dealers: Power Politics in the Age of Roosevelt*. New York: Knopf, 1993.

Scott, Austin W., et al. *Felix Frankfurter: Talks in Tribute*. Cambridge, MA: Harvard Law School, 1965.

Sedgwick, Ellery. *The Happy Profession*. Boston: Little, Brown, 1946.

Sherwin, Martin. *A World Destroyed: Hiroshima and the Origins of the Arms Race*. New York: Vintage, 1987.

Sherwood, Robert E. *Roosevelt and Hopkins: An Intimate History.* New York: Harper and Brothers, 1948.

Shesol, Jeff. *Supreme Power: Franklin Roosevelt vs. the Supreme Court.* New York: Norton, 2010.

Silber, Norman I. *With All Deliberate Speed: The Life of Philip Elman.* Ann Arbor: University of Michigan Press, 2004.

Simon, James F. *Independent Journey: The Life of William O. Douglas.* New York: Harper and Row, 1980.

———. *The Antagonists: Hugo Black, Felix Frankfurter and Civil Liberties in Modern America.* New York: Simon and Schuster, 1989.

———. *FDR and Chief Justice Hughes: The President, The Supreme Court, and the Epic Battle over the Supreme Court.* New York: Simon and Schuster, 2012.

———. *Eisenhower vs. Warren: The Battle for Civil Rights and Civil Liberties.* New York: Liveright, 2018.

Smith, Donald L. *Zechariah Chafee, Jr., Defender of Liberty and Law.* Cambridge, MA: Harvard University Press, 1986.

Snyder, Brad. *The House of Truth: A Washington Political Salon and the Foundations of American Liberalism.* New York: Oxford University Press, 2017.

Steel, Ronald. *Walter Lippmann and the American Century.* Boston: Little, Brown, 1980.

Stern, Seth, and Stephen Wermiel. *Justice Brennan: Liberal Champion.* Boston: Houghton Mifflin Harcourt, 2010.

Stimson, Henry L., and McGeorge Bundy. *On Active Service in Peace and War.* New York: Harper, 1948.

Strum, Philippa. *Louis D. Brandeis: Justice for the People.* Cambridge, MA: Harvard University Press, 1984.

Suitts, Steve. *Hugo Black of Alabama: How His Roots and Early Career Shaped the Great Champion of the Constitution.* Montgomery: New South, 2005.

Sutherland, Arthur E. *The Law at Harvard: A History of Ideas and Men, 1817–1967.* Cambridge, MA: Belknap Press, 1967.

Sykes, Christopher. *Troubled Loyalty: A Biography of Adam von Trott.* London: Collins, 1968.

Tanenhaus, Sam. *Whittaker Chambers: A Biography.* New York: Random House, 1997.

Thayer, James Bradley. *John Marshall.* Boston: Houghton Mifflin, 1901.

Thomas, Helen Shirley. *Felix Frankfurter: Scholar on the Bench.* Baltimore: John Hopkins Press, 1960.

Todd, A. L. *Justice on Trial: The Case of Louis D. Brandeis.* New York: McGraw-Hill, 1964.

Truman, Harry S. *Memoirs: Year of Decisions.* New York: Doubleday, 1955.

———. *Memoirs: Years of Trial and Hope, 1946–1952.* New York: Doubleday, 1955.

Truslow, William A. *Arthur D. Hill.* Boston: Hill and Barlow, 1996.

Tully, Grace. *F.D.R.: My Boss.* New York: C. Scribner's Sons, 1949.

Tushnet, Mark V. *Making Civil Rights Law: Thurgood Marshall and the Supreme Court, 1936–1961.* New York: Oxford University Press, 1994.

Urofsky, Melvin I. *Felix Frankfurter: Judicial Restraint and Individual Liberties.* Boston: Twayne, 1991.

———. *Louis D. Brandeis: A Life.* New York: Pantheon, 2009.

Urofsky, Melvin I., and David W. Levy, eds. *Letters of Louis D. Brandeis.* 5 vols. Albany: State University of New York Press, 1971–1978.

———, eds. *"Half Brother, Half Son": The Letters of Louis D. Brandeis to Felix Frankfurter.* Norman: University of Oklahoma Press, 1991.

————, eds. *The Family Letters of Louis D. Brandeis*. Norman: University of Oklahoma Press, 2002.

Verrier, Anthony, ed. *Agents of Empire: Anglo-Zionist Intelligence Operations, 1915–1919: Brigadier Walter Gribbon, Aaron Aaronsohn, and the NILI Ring*. London: Brassey's, 1995.

Ware, Gilbert. *William Hastie: Grace Under Pressure*. New York: Oxford University Press, 1984.

Weinstein, Allen. *Perjury: The Hiss-Chambers Case*, 2nd ed. New York: Knopf, 1997.

Weizmann, Chaim. *Trial and Error: The Autobiography of Chaim Weizmann*. New York: Harper and Brothers, 1949.

————. *The Letters and Papers of Chaim Weizmann*, edited by Barnet Litvinoff. Vols. 21–23, Series A. New Brunswick, NJ: Transaction Books, 1979 and 1980.

Wheeler, Burton, with Paul F. Healy. *Yankee from the West: The Candid, Turbulent Life Story of the Yankee-born U.S. Senator from Montana*. Garden City, NY: Doubleday, 1962.

White, G. Edward. *Justice Oliver Wendell Holmes: Law and the Inner Self*. New York: Oxford University Press, 1993.

————. *Alger Hiss's Looking-Glass Wars: The Covert Life of a Soviet Spy*. New York: Oxford University Press, 2004.

Wiecek, William. *The History of the Supreme Court of the United States, Volume XII: The Birth of the Modern Constitution: The United States Supreme Court, 1941–53*. Cambridge, UK: Cambridge University Press, 2006.

Wigdor, David. *Roscoe Pound: Philosopher of Law*. Westport, CT: Greenwood Press, 1974.

Winter, Ella. *And Not to Yield: An Autobiography*. New York: Harcourt, 1963.

Yeomans, Henry Aaron. *Abbott Lawrence Lowell, 1856–1943*. Cambridge, MA: Harvard University Press, 1948.

Yoder, Edwin, Jr. *The Unmaking of a Whig and Other Essays in Self-Definition*. Washington, DC: Georgetown University Press, 1990.

Zweig, Stefan. *The World of Yesterday: An Autobiography*. New York: Viking Press, 1943.

ARTICLES

Adunka, Evelyn. "Salomon Frankfurter (1856–1941)." In *Bibliotheken in der NS-Zeit*, edited by Stefan Alker et al. Göttingen: V&R Unipress, 2008: 209–220.

————. "Salomon Frankfurter." *Österreichiches Biographisches Lexikon (ÖBL)* Online Edition, Lfg. 5, 11/25/2016.

Barrett, John Q. "Justice Jackson in the Jehovah's Witnesses' Cases." *FIU Law Review* 13, no. 4 (Spring 2019): 827–52.

Chafee, Zechariah, Jr. "A Contemporary State Trial: The United States versus Jacob Abrams et al." *Harvard Law Review* 33, no. 6 (April 1920): 747–74.

————. "A Contemporary State Trial: The United States versus Jacob Abrams et al." *Harvard Law Review* 35, no. 1 (November 1921): 9–14.

————. "Harold Laski and the Harvard Law Review." *Harvard Law Review* 63, no. 8 (June 1950): 1398–1400.

Coleman, William T., Jr. "Mr. Justice Felix Frankfurter: Civil Libertarian as Lawyer and as Justice: Extent to Which Judicial Responsibilities Affected His Pre-Court Convictions." *University of Illinois Law Forum* no. 2 (1978): 279–300.

Danelski, David J. "The Appointment of William O. Douglas to the Supreme Court." *Journal of Supreme Court History* 40, no. 1 (March 2015): 80–98.

Danzig, Richard. "How Questions Begot Answers in Felix Frankfurter's First Flag Salute Opinion." *Supreme Court Review* (1977): 257–74.

———. "Justice Frankfurter's Opinions in the Flag Salute Cases: Blending Logic and Psychologic in Constitutional Decisionmaking." *Stanford Law Review* 36, no. 3 (February 1984): 675–724.

Davidson, Gordon B., et al. "Supreme Court Law Clerks' Recollections of *Brown v. Board of Education II*." *St. John's Law Review* 79, no. 4 (Fall 2005): 823–86.

Elman, Philip, Interviewed by Norman Silber. "The Solicitor General's Office, Justice Frankfurter, and Civil Rights Litigation, 1946–1960: An Oral History." *Harvard Law Review* 100, no. 4 (February 1987): 817–52.

Ernst, Daniel R. "Dicey's Disciple on the D.C. Circuit: Judge Harold Stephens and Administrative Law Reform, 1933–1940." *Georgetown Law Journal* 90, no. 3 (March 2002): 787–812.

———. "Ernst Freund, Felix Frankfurter, and the American Rechtsstaat: A Transatlantic Shipwreck, 1894–1932." *Studies in American Political Development* 23 (October 2009): 171–88.

Eskridge William N., Jr., and Philip P. Frickey. "An Historical and Critical Introduction." In Henry M. Hart, Jr., and Albert M. Sacks, *The Legal Process*, edited by William N. Eskridge, Jr., and Philip P. Frickey. Westbury, NY: Foundation Press, 1994.

Fassett, John D. "The Buddha and the Bumblebee: The Saga of Stanley Reed and Felix Frankfurter." *Journal of Supreme Court History* 28 (June 2003): 165–96.

———, et al. "Supreme Court Law Clerks' Recollections of *Brown v. Board of Education*." *St. John's Law Review* 78, no. 3 (Summer 2004): 515–68.

Frankfurter, Felix. "The Law and the Law Schools." *Reports of the American Bar Association* 1, no. 4 (October 1915): 532–40.

———. "Hours of Labor and Realism in Constitutional Law." *Harvard Law Review* 29, no. 4 (February 1916): 353–73.

———. "The Constitutional Opinions of Justice Holmes." *Harvard Law Review* 29, no. 6 (April 1916): 683–702.

———. "Twenty Years of Mr. Justice Holmes' Constitutional Opinions." *Harvard Law Review* 36, no. 8 (June 1923): 909–39.

———. "The Portentous Case of Sacco and Vanzetti: A Comprehensive Analysis of a Trial of Grave Importance." *Atlantic Monthly* (March 1927): 409–32.

———. "Mr. Justice Holmes and the Constitution: A Review of His Twenty-Five Years on the Supreme Court." *Harvard Law Review* 41, no. 2 (December 1927): 121–73.

———. "The Early Writings of O. W. Holmes, Jr." *Harvard Law Review* 44, no. 5 (March 1931): 717–827.

———. "Mr. Justice Brandeis and the Constitution." *Harvard Law Review* 45, no. 1 (November 1931): 33–111.

———. "Mr. Justice Holmes. 8 March 1841–6 March 1935." *Harvard Law Review* 48, no. 8 (June 1935): 1279–80.

———. "Valentine, Robert Grosvenor." In *Dictionary of American Biography*, Vol. 19, edited by Dumas Malone. New York: Charles Scribner's Sons, 1936: 142–43.

———. "Eugene Wambaugh." *Harvard Law Review* 54, no. 1 (November 1940): 7–9.

———. "Mr. Justice Brandeis." *Harvard Law Review* 55, no. 2 (December 1941): 181–83.

———. "Joseph Henry Beale." *Harvard Law Review* 56, no. 5 (March 1943): 701–3.

———. "Chief Justices I Have Known." *Virginia Law Review* 39, no. 7 (November 1953): 883–906.

———. "John Marshall and the Judicial Function." *Harvard Law Review* 69, no. 2 (December 1955): 217–38.

———. "Mr. Justice Roberts." *University of Pennsylvania Law Review* 104, no. 3 (December 1955): 311–17.

———. "Samuel Williston: An Inadequate Tribute to a Beloved Teacher." *Harvard Law Review* 76, no. 7 (May 1963): 1321–23.

Frankfurter, Felix, and Thomas G. Corcoran. "Petty Federal Offenses and Constitutional Guaranty of Trial by Jury." *Harvard Law Review* 39, no. 8 (June 1926): 917–1019.

Frankfurter, Felix, and James M. Landis. "The Compact Clause of the Constitution: A Study in Interstate Adjustments." *Yale Law Journal* 34, no. 7 (May 1925): 685–758.

Friedman, Richard D. "A Reaffirmation: The Authenticity of the Roberts Memorandum, or Felix the Non-Forger." *University of Pennsylvania Law Review* 142, no. 6 (June 1994): 1985–1996.

———. "Chief Justice Hughes' Letter on Court-Packing." *Journal of Supreme Court History* 1 (1997): 76–86.

Freund, Paul A. "Charles Evans Hughes as Chief Justice." *Harvard Law Review* 81, no. 1 (November 1967): 4–43.

Freyer, Tony A. "*Cooper v. Aaron* (1958): A Hidden Story of Unanimity and Division." *Journal of Supreme Court History* 33, no. 1 (2008): 89–109.

Hutchinson, Dennis J. "Unanimity and Desegregation: Decisionmaking in the Supreme Court, 1948–1958." *Georgetown Law Journal*. 68, no 1 (October 1979): 1–96.

———. "The Black-Jackson Feud." *Supreme Court Review* (1980): 203–44.

———. "Felix Frankfurter and the Business of the Supreme Court, O.T. 1946–O.T. 1961." *Supreme Court Review* (1980): 143–210.

Irons, Peter. " 'Fighting Fair': Zechariah Chafee, Jr., the Department of Justice, and the 'Trial at the Harvard Club.' " *Harvard Law Review* 94, no. 6 (April 1981): 1205–36.

Isenbergh, Max. "Reminisces of FF as a Friend." *Virginia Law Review* 51, no. 4 (May 1965): 564–81.

Josephson, Matthew. "Jurist-I." *New Yorker* (November 23, 1940): 24–32.

———. "Jurist-II." *New Yorker* (December 7, 1940): 36–46.

———. "Jurist-III." *New Yorker* (December 14, 1940): 32–42.

Kaufman, Andrew L. "Cardozo's Appointment to the Supreme Court." *Cardozo Law Review* 1, no. 1 (Spring 1979): 23–54.

Kessler, Jeremy K. "The Administrative Origins of Modern Civil Liberties Law." *Columbia Law Review* 114, no. 5 (June 2014): 1083–1166.

Kimball, Bruce A. "The Disastrous First Fund-Raising Campaign in Legal Education." *Journal of the Gilded Age and the Progressive Era* 12, no. 4 (October 2013): 535–78.

Kramnick, Isaac. "The Professor and the Police." *Harvard Alumni Magazine* (September–October 1989): 42–45.

Landis, James M. "Mr. Justice Brandeis and the Harvard Law School." *Harvard Law Review* 55, no. 2 (December 1941): 184–90.

Lash, Joseph P. "A Brahmin of the Law." In *From the Diaries of Felix Frankfurter: With a Biographical Essay and Notes*, edited by Joseph P. Lash. New York: Norton, 1974: 3–98.

Levinson, Sanford V. "The Democratic Faith of Felix Frankfurter." *Stanford Law Review* 25, no. 3 (February 1973): 430–48.

Levy, David W., and Bruce Allen Murphy. "Preserving the Progressive Spirit in a Conservative Time: The Joint Reform Efforts of Justice Brandeis and Professor Frankfurter, 1916–1933." *Michigan Law Review* 78, no. 8 (August 1980): 1252–304.

Louchheim, Katie. "The Little Red House." *Virginia Quarterly Review* 56, no. 1 (Winter 1980): 119–34.

MacLeish, Archibald. "Mr. Justice Frankfurter." *Life* (July 12, 1940): 34–36, 80–84.

Messinger, I. Scott. "Legitimating Liberalism: The New Deal Image-makers and Oliver Wendell Holmes, Jr." *Journal of Supreme Court History* 20, no. 1 (1995): 57–72.

———. "The Judge as Mentor: Oliver Wendell Holmes, Jr. and His Law Clerks." *Yale Journal of Law and the Humanities* 11, no. 1 (1999): 119–52.

Miller, Arthur S., and Jeffrey H. Bowman. "Slow Dance on the Killing Ground: The Willie Francis Case Revisited." *DePaul Law Review* 32 (Fall 1982): 1–76.

Murphy, Walter F. "In His Own Image: Mr. Chief Justice Taft and Supreme Court Appointments." *Supreme Court Review* (1961): 159–93.

Nelson, Garrison. "'A Mania for Anonymity': The Mysterious Presidential Aide, David K. Niles of Boston." New England Political Science Association presentation, April 26–28, 2012.

O'Connell, Jeffrey, and Nancy Dart. "The House of Truth: Home of the Young Frankfurter and Lippmann." *Catholic University Law Review* 35, no. 1 (1985): 79–96.

Parrish, Michael E. "The Supreme Court and the Rosenbergs." *American Historical Review* 82, no. 4 (October 1977): 805–42.

———. "Felix Frankfurter, the Progressive Tradition, and the Warren Court." In *The Warren Court in Historical and Political Perspective*, edited by Mark Tushnet. Charlottesville: University of Press of Virginia, 1993: 51–63.

Peppers, Todd. "William Thaddeus Coleman, Jr.: Breaking the Color Barrier at the U.S. Supreme Court." *Journal of Supreme Court History* 33, no. 3 (November 2008): 353–70.

Peterson, Gregory L., et al. "Recollections of *West Virginia State Board of Education v. Barnette*." *St. John's Law Review* 81, no. 4 (Fall 2007): 755–96.

Polenberg, Richard. "Introduction." In *The Letters of Sacco and Vanzetti*, edited by Marion Denman Frankfurter and Gardner Jackson. New York: Penguin Books, 2007.

Pusey, Merlo J. "The Nomination of Charles Evans Hughes as Chief Justice." *Supreme Court Historical Society Yearbook* (1982): 95–100.

Putney, Diane T. "Robert Grosvenor Valentine, 1909–12." In *The Commissioners of Indian Affairs*, edited by Robert N. Kvasnicka and Herman J. Viola. Lincoln: University of Nebraska Press, 1979: 233–42.

Rauh, Joseph L., Jr. "Felix Frankfurter: Civil Libertarian." *Harvard Civil Rights–Civil Liberties Law Review* 11, no. 3 (Summer 1976): 496–520.

———. "An Unabashed Liberal Looks at a Half-Century of the Supreme Court." *North Carolina Law Review* 69, no. 1 (November 1990): 213–50.

Ringhand, Lori. "Aliens on the Bench: Lessons in Identity, Race and Politics from the First 'Modern' Supreme Court Confirmation Hearing to Today." *Michigan State Law Review* (Fall 2010): 795–835.

Schlesinger, Arthur M., Jr. "The Supreme Court: 1947." *Fortune* 35 (January 1947): 73, 201–2, 208.

Snyder, Brad. "Taking Great Cases: Lessons from the *Rosenberg* Case." *Vanderbilt Law Review* 63, no. 4 (May 2010): 885–956.

———. "The Judicial Genealogy (and Mythology) of John Roberts: Clerkships from Gray to Brandeis to Friendly to Roberts." *Ohio State Law Journal* 71, no. 6 (2010): 1149–1244.

———. "The House That Built Holmes." *Law and History Review* 30, no. 3 (August 2012): 661–720.

———. "Frankfurter and Popular Constitutionalism." *UC Davis Law Review* 47, no. 1 (November 2013): 343–417.

Snyder, Brad, and John Q. Barrett. "Rehnquist's Missing Letter: A Former Law Clerk's 1955 Thoughts on Justice Jackson and *Brown*." *Boston College Law Review* 53, no. 2 (March 2012): 631–60.

Thayer, James B. "The Origin and Scope of the American Doctrine of Constitutional Law." *Harvard Law Review* 7, no. 3 (October 1893): 129–56.

Tushnet, Mark, with Katya Lezin. "What Really Happened in *Brown v. Board of Education*." *Columbia Law Review* 91, no. 8 (December 1991): 1867–1930.

Urofsky, Melvin I. "Attorney for the People: The 'Outrageous' Brandeis Nomination." *Supreme Court Historical Society Yearbook* (1979): 8–19.

———. "The Brandeis-Frankfurter Conversations." *Supreme Court Review* (1985): 299–340.

———. "Conflict among the Brethren: Felix Frankfurter, William O. Douglas and the Clash of Personalities and Philosophies on the United States Supreme Court." *Duke Law Journal* 1988, no. 1 (February 1988): 71–113.

———. "The Failure of Felix Frankfurter." *University of Richmond Law Review* 26, no. 1 (Fall 1991): 175–212.

———. "Wilson, Brandeis, and the Supreme Court Nomination." *Journal of Supreme Court History* 28, no. 2 (July 2003): 145–56.

White, G. Edward. "Felix Frankfurter, the Old Boy Network, and the New Deal: The Placement of Elite Lawyers in Public Service in the 1930s." *Arkansas Law Review* 39, no. 4 (1986): 631–68.

———. "The Alger Hiss Case: Justices Frankfurter & Reed as Character Witnesses." *Green Bag 2d* 4 (Autumn 2000): 63–83.

———. "Felix Frankfurter's 'Soliloquy' in *Ex Parte Quirin*." *Green Bag 2d* 5, no. 4 (Summer 2002): 423–38.

Williams, David. "The Bureau of Investigation and Its Critics, 1919–1921." *Journal of American History* 68, no. 3 (December 1981): 560–79.

Yale, William. "Henry Morgenthau's Special Mission of 1917." *World Politics* 1, no. 3 (April 1949): 308–20.

THESES AND DISSERTATIONS

Friedman, David A. "Against the Experts: Harry S. Truman, David K. Niles, and the birth of the State of Israel, 1945–1948." Undergraduate thesis, Whitman College, 2011.

Gengarelly, William Anthony. "Resistance Spokesmen: Opponents of the Red Scare, 1919–1921." PhD diss., Boston University, 1972.

Levinson, Sanford Victor. "Skepticism, Democracy, and Judicial Restraint: An Essay on the Thought of Oliver Wendell Holmes and Felix Frankfurter." PhD diss., Harvard University, 1969.

Niznik, Monica Lynne. "Thomas G. Corcoran: The Public Service of Franklin Roosevelt's 'Tommy The Cork.'" PhD diss., Notre Dame University, 1981.

Sachar, David B. "David K. Niles and the United States Policy Toward Palestine." Undergraduate thesis, Harvard University, 1959.

Scheuer, Michael Frank. "Loring Christie and the North Atlantic Community, 1913–41." PhD diss., University of Manitoba, 1986.

Wasniewski, Matthew A. "Walter Lippmann, Strategic Internationalism, the Cold War, and Vietnam, 1943–1967." PhD diss., University of Maryland, 2004.

ILLUSTRATION CREDITS

Harvard Law School Library, Historical & Special Collections/Clifford Berryman
Harvard Law School Library, Historical & Special Collections/Harris & Ewing
Harvard Law School Library, Historical & Special Collections/Felix Frankfurter Papers
Harvard Law School Library, Historical & Special Collections
Reprinted with permission of the DC Public Library, Star Collection ©Washington Post
Photograph by Art Seder, Courtesy of the Supreme Court Historical Society/Todd Peppers
George Tames/New York Times/Redux
Library of Congress, Manuscript Division, Robert Houghwout Jackson Papers
George Skadding/The LIFE Picture Collection via Getty Images
Reprinted with permission of the DC Public Library, Star Collection ©Washington Post
Harvard Law School Library, Historical & Special Collections
Franklin D. Roosevelt Library
New York Times/Redux/ Harvard Law School Library, Historical & Special Collections
Photograph by Verner Reed/The LIFE Picture Collection via Getty Images
Collection of the Supreme Court of the United States/photograph by Paul Bender
Collection of the Supreme Court of the United States/photograph by Paul Bender
Reprinted with permission of the DC Public Library, Star Collection ©Washington Post/
    Collection of the Supreme Court of the United States
Photograph by Cecil Stoughton/White House photographs/John F. Kennedy Presidential
    Library and Museum
Reprinted with permission of the DC Public Library, Star Collection ©Washington Post
UPI via Getty Images
Photograph by John F. Costelloe/Courtesy of Costelloe Family/Collection of the Supreme Court
    of the United States

INDEX